PIMLICO

86

EDITH WHARTON

Hermione Lee is also the author of an internationally acclaimed biography of Virginia Woolf, of books on Elizabeth Bowen and Willa Cather, of a collection of essays on life-writing, *Body Parts*, and of a short book on Biography. She is a well-known reviewer and broadcaster and chaired the Man-Booker Prize judges in 2006. From 1998-2008 she was the first woman Goldsmiths' Professor of English at Oxford University, and in 2008 she became President of Wolfson College, Oxford. She is a Fellow of the British Academy and of the Royal Society of Literature, and in 2003 was awarded a CBE for services to literature. She is publishing a new biography of Penelope Fitzgerald with Chatto & Windus in 2013.

Also by Hermione Lee

The Novels of Virginia Woolf
Elizabeth Bowen
Philip Roth
Willa Cather: A Life Saved Up
Virginia Woolf
Body Parts: Essays on Life-Writing
Biography: A Very Short Introduction

As editor

Stevie Smith: A Selection
The Hogarth Letters
The Mulberry Tree: Writings of Elizabeth Bowen
The Secret Self: Short Stories by Women (Vols 1 and II)
The Short Stories of Willa Cather
Virginia Woolf: A Room of One's Own and Three Guineas
To The Lighthouse
The Years
One Being III

EDITH WHARTON

HERMIONE LEE

PIMLICO

Published by Pimlico 2013

2 4 6 8 10 9 7 5 3 1

Copyright © Hermione Lee 2007

Hermione Lee has asserted her right under the Copyright, Designs
and Patents Act 1988 to be identified as the author of this work

First published in Great Britain in 2007 by
Chatto & Windus

First published in Great Britain in paperback in 2008 by Vintage

Pimlico
Random House, 20 Vauxhall Bridge Road,
London SW1V 2SA

www.vintage-books.co.uk

Addresses for companies within The Random House Group Limited can be found at:
www.randomhouse.co.uk/offices.htm

The Random House Group Limited Reg. No. 954009

A CIP catalogue record for this book
is available from the British Library

ISBN 9781845952013

The Random House Group Limited supports the Forest Stewardship Council®
(FSC®), the leading international forest-certification organisation. Our books carrying
the FSC label are printed on FSC®-certified paper. FSC is the only forest-certification
scheme supported by the leading environmental organisations, including Greenpeace.
Our paper procurement policy can be found at:
www.randomhouse.co.uk/environment

Printed and bound in Great Britain by Clays Ltd, St Ives PLC

For
John Barnard

Edith Wharton's passport photograph, 1927.
The details read: Height: 5'5"
     Hair: Chestnut
     Eyes: Brown
     Occupation: Author

Contents

PART THREE

List of Illustrations

PART I

I

An American in Paris

In Paris, in February 1848, a young American couple on their Grand Tour
of Europe found themselves, to their surprise, in the middle of a French
revolution. Up to then, the travels of George Frederic Jones and his wife
of three years, Lucretia Stevens Rhinelander Jones, with their one-year-old
son Frederic, had been undramatic. They had a lengthy European itinerary,
the usual thing for Americans of their class, backed by the substantial funds
of the Jones family, one of the leading, old-established New York clans.
Starting in England and Paris in April 1847, they had 'done' Brussels,
Amsterdam, Hanover, Berlin and Dresden, Prague, Linz, Salzburg and
Munich, Frankfurt, Cologne, Coblenz, Friburg, Geneva, Lake Como and
the major Italian cities. George Frederic, at twenty-seven an experienced
traveller (his father had taken him on his first European tour when he was
seventeen), was able to indulge all his appetites for architecture, scenery,
paintings, collectable objects, shopping, theatre, entertainment and seeing
life. 'Lu', though more limited by looking after little Frederic and by her
frequent illnesses and 'her tremendous headaches', was very definite about
what she liked and did not like on her first trip abroad: 'Lu rather disgusted
with the Catholic ceremonies'.[1]

George Frederic voiced his own prejudices confidently all over Europe.
'More disgusted than ever with London ... London prices are fearful ...
Decidedly disgusted with Milan.' In Amsterdam, 'the smell from the canal
in most parts of the city fearful ... Drove to the Jewish synagoage [sic]
... but as soon as the carriage stopped, we were surrounded by such an
infernal-looking set of scoundrels that we gave it up in disgust.' (But he
enjoyed the Breughels.) In a Berlin restaurant, 'the company mostly men,
all hard eating, hard drinking, loud talking and very little refinement
anywhere'. In the Dresden picture gallery, he was 'much pleased' with the
card players of Caravaggio, and a head of Christ by Guido. (Just the sort
of thing that the 'simpler majority' of nineteenth-century American tourists
always liked and bought copies of, Edith Wharton would remark).[2] In the

3

Prague Cabinet of Antiquities, 'the cameos were particularly beautiful, one, the apotheosis of Augustus, is said to have cost 12,000 ducats'. In Venice he was very pleased with the Palace of the Doges [the Palazzo Ducale]. In Florence he rated the Pitti Palace 'a much finer gallery than the other'.

But his heart belonged to Paris. When they first landed at Boulogne at the start of the trip, he wrote: 'Glad to be again in France'. Once they settled into their rooms on the Champs-Élysées, everything interested him: the Palais Royal, the Louvre, the riding at Franconi's, the flower market, a new ballet at the Académie Royale ('some pretty grouping but on the whole rather tedious'), the Hôtel des Invalides where they were building a chapel to contain the remains of Napoleon. Meanwhile Lu, as her daughter would note, was buying clothes, among them 'a white satin bonnet trimmed with white marabout and crystal drops . . . and a "capeline" of *gorge de pigeon* taffetas with a wreath of flowers in shiny brown kid, which was one of the triumphs of her Paris shopping'.[3]

After the long tour, back in Paris early in 1848, they were all set to resume their busy schedule of pleasurable activities. But on 22 February 1848, walking down from their hotel, the Windsor in the Rue de Rivoli, to the Place de la Concorde at 11 a.m. to see the results of the Reform Banquet, George Frederic found it had been put a stop to, and that an immense and very excited crowd had gathered. (Opposition parties, prevented from calling large-scale political meetings, had set up 'reform banquets' all over France, where speeches were made against the government and toasts to reform were drunk. The one scheduled in Paris was prevented by order of Louis-Philippe and his regime: that was the spark for the upheaval.) By 4 p.m., barricades were being built and troops were out 'in immense numbers'. 'Matters in a state of great uncertainty', George Frederic reported. On the 23rd, he heard of 'considerable fighting' and of the resignation of François Guizot, the chief minister, and his government. On the 24th, there was heavy fighting, and they could see much of the action from their window: 'The whole city in a complete state of insurrection'. The National Guard had joined the uprising. He 'took Lu out to see the state of things, but she was so much frightened that we could not go far'. On the way back they heard a great firing in the Place Vendôme and so 'had to beat a hasty and most undignified retreat through the side streets'. Louis-Philippe abdicated and fled with his wife across the Tuileries gardens, witnessed from their balcony by the Joneses. (Her mother, Wharton said, was more interested in what the queen was wearing than in the political crisis.) The people pillaged the palace, and a provisional government was declared. 'Immense enthusiasm for the Republic. The tricolor cocade [*sic*] universally worn.' By 28 February, order was restored, but George Frederic Jones 'had no confidence in the present state of things. Think the French entirely unsuited to a Republic.'

The next day, he (and Paris) were beginning to get back to normal: an evening show at the Palais Royal, followed by dinner at the Trois Frères; an Italian opera (where the Marseillaise was sung between the acts); a masked ball at the Grand Opera, very amusing; letter-writing, an outing to the vaudeville. But there was 'not so much refinement as before – everything too democratic and republican'. At the opera, he found 'a great change in the appearance of the audience – everyone very little dressed'. And it was more and more difficult to procure money through letters of credit. On 15 May there was a massive street demonstration in support of revolutionary governments in eastern Europe ('Another remarkable day in French history . . . deep-laid conspiracy to overthrow the government . . . great alarm . . . Paris looked like a besieged city'). But the Joneses were leaving for 'stupid and uninteresting' London – and then home to New York. 'Leave Paris with great regret, which, changed though it is since the Revolution, is more agreeable than any place I ever was in.'[4]

Nearly seventy years later, a lifetime away, Edith Wharton was in Paris at the outbreak of the European war of 1914, watching the behaviour of the people in the streets, gauging the political and social temperature, and coming to her own firm conclusions about this nation in wartime. As she watched the mobilisation of conscripts and volunteers, the throng of foot-passengers in the streets, the incessant comings and goings of civilians under martial law, the crowd's quiet responses to the first battle-news, and, gradually, the influx into the city of 'the great army of refugees', she was struck by the 'steadiness of spirit', the orderliness and 'unanimity of self-restraint' of Paris at war. The contrast with 1848 – or 1870 – was extreme: 'It seemed as though it had been unanimously, instinctively decided that the Paris of 1914 should in no respect resemble the Paris of 1870.' As war-conditions became the norm, she noted that the Parisians had started to shop again, to go to concerts and theatres and the cinema. But she noted too a consistent look on the faces of the French at war, grave, steady, and stoic.[5]

Wharton set to, and did what she could for France in wartime, including writing that account, 'The Look of Paris', mainly for the benefit of an American public as yet unsure about joining the battle. For the next four years she sacrificed much of her life as a writer and a private citizen to her work for war-victims and to proselytising for France. She became – it was not surprising to those who knew her – a high-powered administrator and benefactor. And though this was her period of greatest involvement with French public life, for which she was honoured with the Légion d'honneur in 1916, her attention and commitment to 'French ways and their meaning' continued. As an old lady, long since disgusted with post-war Paris, hardened in her political opposition to anything that smacked of 'Bolshevism', living in seclusion in her winter house on the Mediterranean, she listened intently in February 1934 to the news on the wireless of the bloody anti-government demonstrations in Paris. She feared for her property and for the future of her adopted country. 'I do find it rather depressing to sit alone in the evenings & wonder what's happening in Paris', she wrote from Hyères to her friend Bernard Berenson.[6]

Between these nineteenth- and twentieth-century American versions of Paris in crisis is the gap of a generation, of historical change, and of widely differing personal knowledge and experience. Edith Wharton turned her back on the genteel dilettantism of George Frederic and Lucretia Jones. She was a knowledgeable inhabitant and lover of France, not a tourist; a writer, not a leisured traveller keeping a diary. In this, as in many other ways, she broke with her parents' attitudes and customs, and created a different kind of life for herself. No wonder there is a much-repeated rumour that Edith Jones was not George Frederic's daughter at all. (Wharton's own fictions of illegitimacy, adoption, and hidden parentage fuel these intriguing stories.) In her accounts of her childhood, she seems a stranger in the house, a changeling child. That is how she described her parents' view of her in the unfinished, unpublished version of her autobiography, 'Life and I'. So different was she from what they wanted or expected that they 'were beginning to regard me with fear, like some pale predestined child who disappears at night to dance with "the little people"'. (One of her favourite poetic characters was the young woman who is spirited away to another world, and when she comes back cannot speak of it: 'For Kilmeny had been she ken'd not where, And Kilmeny had seen what she could not declare.'[7]) But Wharton grew up neither pale nor predestined. With prolonged, hardworking, deliberate ambition, she pushed out and away from her family's mental habits, social rules and ways of life – of which that 1840s Grand Tour is a perfect example – to construct her own personal and professional revolution.

All the same, George Frederic Jones's 1848 diary does provide a strong entry-point for the life-story of this European American. Wharton detached herself from her family, and defined herself against it, but in some ways she followed in a family pattern. Though she describes them as at bottom all provincial New Yorkers, they were forever Europe-bound. The Jones family lived in Italy and France, for financial reasons, between 1866 and 1872, and so set the course of Wharton's life: after those childhood years she would always think of herself as 'an exile in America'.[8] They went back to Europe for the sake of her father's health in 1881; father and daughter went sight-seeing together in Italy, with Ruskin in hand.[9] Her father died at Cannes in 1882. Her mother lived permanently in Paris from 1893 till her death in 1901. Her two much older brothers lived for many years – and died – in France. All the Joneses, not just Edith, were Americans settled in France; George Frederic's 'great regret' at leaving Paris set the tone.

There is a faint echo of George Frederic in Wharton's world-travels. She remembered his enthusiasms affectionately, though she would be at pains to distinguish her own responses from his. He had, she recalled, 'a vague enjoyment in "sight-seeing", unaccompanied by any artistic or intellectual curiosity, or any sense of the relation of things to each other'; all the same, he was 'delighted to take me about'.[10] Perhaps she was unfair to him, or unfair to the young man he had been years before her birth, with his avid, choosy pursuit of culture, his interest in the history and politics of the places he visited, his love of art and theatre, his quick prejudices. Wharton's travels were those of a connoisseur: highly informed, well organised, passionate. But they connect to her father's eager tourism. All her life, she was greedy for cultural adventures and experiences, in France, England, Italy, Spain, Germany, Greece, North Africa, and all round the Mediterranean. She acquired a profound knowledge of the places she went to. She prided herself on always getting off the beaten track. From her childhood years in Europe, she wrote and spoke and read three languages – French, German, and Italian – fluently. She hardly ever went anywhere without writing a book about it. Above all, she wrote of France, drawing on it for three non-fiction books (A *Motor-Flight Through France, French Ways and Their Meaning, Fighting France*), and for many of her novels and stories, most notably *Madame de Treymes, The Reef, The Custom of the Country, The Marne, A Son at the Front, The Children* and *The Gods Arrive*.

How French did she become? She spoke French immaculately and formally, though with a strong 'English' accent. Her letters and her diaries are full of French words and phrases, almost instinctively used. Much of her correspondence – and her conversation – was in French. She was divorced through the French courts, in order to avoid American publicity. She dealt with every aspect of French bureaucracy, law, and administration, particularly in wartime, with tremendous competence. She had numerous French friends, French publishers, and French readers. She could write fiction in French and closely supervised her French translators. After her Paris years, she bought and redesigned two French houses, and gardens, and became involved in her local communities. Whether she dreamed or thought in French we do not know. What we do know is that she remained an American citizen and continued, in spite of her almost thirty years of life in France, to write in English principally about American life and American character. When Wharton was awarded the Légion d'honneur she was described in France as *'une des personnalités les plus connues de la colonie américaine'*. When she died, and was buried at Versailles, her French obituaries noted that though she was a French settler and a cosmopolitan traveller, this did not prevent her from being *'Américaine jusqu'aux moelles'*. Yet: *'Elle était très attachée à notre pays qu'elle habitait. Elle le comprenait et le faisait comprendre.'* Two things at once, not to be separated: a great lover and interpreter of France, and an American to her marrow. And, above all, *'C'était une grande Européenne, citoyenne de l'univers'*.[11]

This, then, is the story of an American citizen in France. She was a European on a grand scale who left her old home and made new ones for herself, who was passionately interested in France, England and Italy, but who could never be done with the subject of America and Americans. Over and over again, in a spirit of complex contradiction, she returned to the customs of her country, and to versions of herself as the daughter of her family and her country. Between 1897 and 1937 Wharton published at least one book almost every year of her life. (She has, altogether, forty-eight titles to her name.) In almost every one of them there is a cultural comparison or conflict, a journey or a displacement, a sharp eye cast across national characteristics. At the end of her life (as is often the case with long-lived writers) she returned with ever more obsessive attention to where she came from. One of her last pieces of writing, published after her death in 1938, took her back home. It was a fragment of autobiography, a postscript to her memoir of 1934, *A Backward Glance*, called 'A Little Girl's New York'. She described this piece of writing as 'an old woman laying a handful of rue on the grave of an age which had finished in storm and destruction'. It began with her bringing back to her memory the uniform brownstone houses of the old Fifth Avenue, the double lines of horse-drawn carriages, and the tiny details of the social life that those carriages and houses represented. It is a nostalgic, critical retrospect on her American past, written in old age, in a French house, between two wars, by a woman who has travelled a long way, in place and time, from her first American home:

Everything that used to form the fabric of our daily life has been torn in shreds, trampled on, destroyed; and hundreds of little incidents, habits, traditions, which, when I began to record my past, seemed too insignificant to set down, have acquired the historical importance of fragments of dress and furniture dug up in a Babylonian tomb.[12]

2

Making Up

A little American girl, born into the middle of the Civil War, is growing up in the 1860s and 1870s in a well-established New York family. She is a late child, with much older brothers, so her childhood feels like an only childhood. She is taken to Europe when she is very young, and has a bad illness while she is there, which makes her more anxious and fearful than she was before it. She enjoys her early exposure to Paris, Rome, and Spain, and when the family gets back to New York, she finds it ugly and alien, and always feels like a stranger there. She is red-haired, awkward, shy, eager to please, in love with the sound of words and passionate about dogs. She is happier when she is running about, swimming and boating at the family's seaside home in Newport, or alone in her father's library, than when her mother dresses her up and takes her into society. She is devoted to her Irish nurse, affectionate with her father, less fond of her mother, and puts up with being teased by her brothers. She tells herself stories all the time. She is to have no formal education.

Edith Wharton wrote three autobiographical versions of her childhood. Two of them were published (*A Backward Glance*, and its shorter sequel, 'A Little Girl's New York') and one ('Life and I') was private, and much more uncensored. This was typical of her. When she was having a passionate secret affair in Paris in 1908, she kept two diaries covering the same period of time. One was a record of social engagements and the weather, with coded phrases in German referring to her meetings with her lover. The other, kept under lock and key, told the intense emotional story of the relationship, selectively, and shaping it like a novel. Wharton's life-story often feels like a cover story, with tremendously articulate activity on the surface, and secrets and silences below. This is partly due to the missing bits in the archive, missing because she – or someone else – deliberately made away with them. There is no remaining correspondence with her parents or her brothers, and hardly any of their own documents. There are only a few letters from the most important person in her life, Walter Berry: she destroyed most of his letters to her, and managed, also, to retrieve and make away with hers to him; only four of these slipped through the cull. There are very few of her many letters, some of them extremely personal, to Henry James: he burnt them. (But there are plenty from him to her.) There are only three painful letters from her to her husband, and few traces of him. There are no letters from her lover, Morton Fullerton, though hers to him came to light many years after her death (how she would have hated it). Her published autobiography is selective and evasive. Privacy is of great importance to her, and its violation is one of her subjects.

Reserve and concealment are everywhere in her fiction. Her characters often live double lives, and keep the most important fact about their past a secret not just for a few months or years (like George Darrow in *The Reef* or Justine Brent in *The Fruit of the Tree*), but for ever. Newland Archer in *The Age of Innocence* buries his love for Ellen Olenska in the tomb of his role as good citizen, husband and father; Kate Clephane in *The Mother's Recompense* will never be able to tell her daughter that she has married her mother's ex-lover; the real mother in 'The Old Maid', whose illegitimate daughter has been raised (and taken over) by her cousin, has to live with her secret and her jealousy; the woman in 'Atrophy' has to go on concealing her love-affair even at the threshold of her lover's death-bed. The heroine of Wharton's posthumously discovered fragment, 'Beatrice Palmato' – itself one of the most surprising secrets of her writing life – keeps her incestuous relationship with her father a deadly secret.

Many of these cover-ups have to do with children. The story Wharton tells of childhood is usually one of alienation or secrecy. There are foundling children, like Charity in *Summer*, whose guardian ominously becomes her husband, or (in a comic version of the theme) Jane in 'The Mission of Jane' who sabotages her adoptive parents' lives so that they can't wait to get rid of her. There are children passed from parent to parent through a series of divorces, like poor lonely Paul Marvell in *The Custom of the Country*, or the young Wheaters in *The Children*. There are children given up by their mothers, as in *The Mother's Recompense*, or whose true parentage has always been concealed for the sake of appearances, as in 'The Old Maid', or the great story that sustains its secret of parentage until the last sentence, 'Roman Fever'. In one of her most peculiar stories, 'The Young Gentlemen', a widowed father who has concealed all his life the secret of his two 'dwarf' twin sons kills himself when they are about to be exposed to public eyes. And there are children who have the sense that they might as well be deformed, since they feel like strangers in the family they are growing up in. Her first full-length novel, *The Valley of Decision*, set in eighteenth-century Italy, begins with the pathetic scene of the 'neglected and solitary' nine-year-old Odo Valsecca, the foster-child of peasant farmers (but in reality an aristocrat and future ruler) finding consolation for his 'ardent and sensitive' nature in the medieval frescos of the chapel, away from the rough house of the farm.

The foundling who is really a prince, or the child who does not belong to its family, is an old and powerful story. But it does seem to have particular force for Wharton. In two of her novels, *The Glimpses of the Moon* and *The Children*, she imagined a rowdy group of children protecting themselves against adult whims by banding together in a rough-and-tumble solidarity. But this pleasurable fantasy of childhood companionship was an unusual one for her. Most of her children are solitaries like Odo. Sometimes these single children will be unhealthily close to their mother, as in her early novel *Sanctuary*, where the over-vigilant mother uses her son to work out her own guilt, or in 'The Pelican', a story in which the mother goes on giving public lectures for the sake of her little boy long after he has grown up and she has become an embarrassment to him. More often, though, the mothers are neglectful or unsympathetic – and the fathers are nowhere. The sensitive, talented child who is constrained by the mother's narrower standards of correctness repeats all through Wharton's work. And the inadequate education of American girls is a recurring subject – as here in *The Fruit of the Tree*:

> Isn't she one of the most harrowing victims of the plan of bringing up our girls in the double bondage of expediency and unreality, corrupting their bodies with luxury and their brains with sentiment, and leaving them to reconcile the two as best they can, or lose their souls in the attempt?[1]

The word 'unreality' is insistent in Wharton. 'She's lived too long among unrealities', says the true mother in 'The Old Maid', considering her daughter's false upbringing. A sense of unreality at some point comes over all those characters, like Lily Bart, who have been educated into social ambitions that go against their more natural desires. The subject of education – especially for girls – suffuses Wharton's work. Material advantage versus sentimental romance: are there no other choices for women? What place does that leave for intellect, independence, natural passion, or professional ambitions? Wharton often uses a conflict between a mother and a daughter to argue that how we educate our children makes our society what it is. Typically, this subject is both of large-scale historical importance and, also, intensely personal.

In an unfinished, undated draft of a novel called 'Logic', Candida Lake is growing up with her widowed mother Mrs Lake in 'Sailport' (alias Newport). Mrs Lake comes across as a close version of Lucretia Jones and Candida of Edith Jones. Mrs Lake is unhappy with Candida, who seems to her unfeminine and much too intellectual. In one scene, the mother makes her daughter wear a pink frock to a party.

> 'I don't want to go', she said suddenly . . . Her mother looked at her despairingly. The girl's moods were as incomprehensible to her as the movements of some strange animal. Mrs Lake had always enjoyed what she was expected to enjoy; especially occasions demanding a pink frock.

For Candida, 'the pink frock assumed the sacredness of a sacrificial garment', and she makes a slow journey to the party as if going to the stake. She thinks the pink frock is 'peculiarly calculated to emphasise her lean height, the abruptness of her movements and the sallow tints of her long Italian looking face'. But she puts it on and, martyr-like, wears it as part of the price of 'being misunderstood'. Later, she will make a terrible marriage to an unfaithful husband: the link between the mother's standards and the daughter's fate is evident.

One of the childhood scenes in 'Logic' describes the daughter's secret reading. Candida is in the library reading 'the Portuguese sonnets. She was fifteen and Mrs Browning was her poet.' In 'her corner in the window seat' she overhears her mother telling a visitor that Candida is 'cold. So different from my other children . . . but she is perhaps the most intelligent.' But Candida knows that when she reads Mrs Browning 'she was a volcano'. The hidden daughter, reading for her life against her mother's ambitions and desires for her, is clearly a version of Edith Jones. 'Logic' was never finished or published, but it was one of many fictions and memoirs in which Wharton 'made up' versions of herself as a child and of the world she grew up in.[2]

The phrase 'making up' is hers, and she uses it to describe the most essential activity of her childhood. She does this in her memoirs, and in the draft of another unfinished novel, 'Literature', the story of a boy who becomes a writer. 'Making up' began for her when 'Pussy', as she was called, was four or five, and the family had just moved to Europe. She had begun inventing stories before then – from the moment she could remember, in fact – but now she 'found the necessary formula'. The 'formula' is described very precisely: it was ritualistic, solitary, and very physical. She had to have a book in her hands, preferably with lots of thick black type, and she would walk rapidly up and down in an 'ecstasy' of invention, turning the pages as if reading, regardless of whether the book was upside down or not, and improvising out loud, and very fast, an imaginary story. 'Making up' overlapped with learning to read: she would use the books partly to improvise with and partly to read from.

In her published memoir, A Backward Glance, Wharton describes this activity as ecstatic and compulsive, and sets it comically against her mother's demands for her to socialise with other children. 'Mother' (she would say, urgently) 'you must go and entertain that little girl for me. I've got to make up.' Her mother disapproved: she thought this habit 'deplorable'. Wharton describes her parents spying on their child's peculiar activity through half-closed doors, 'distressed' and 'alarmed' by her need for solitude in which to pursue her obsession, and trying to distract her with toys and playmates. (Though she notes, too, that her mother made some attempt to take down the stories she was 'reading aloud', but could not keep up, the words were coming so fast.) She links this ritualised, solitary procedure with a later phase, after the family's return from Europe (when she was ten or eleven) when she would 'steal away' to read for hours, lying on the rug in her father's library. The same words are used in the memoirs for this addiction to reading as for her earlier 'making up': 'secret ecstasy', 'enraptured sessions'.

In the unpublished version of her memoir, 'Life and I', she gives an even more physical account of her passion for story-telling, and her relief when released into it from social obligations, 'the rapture of finding myself again in my own rich world of dreams'. Her account of 'the ecstasy which transported my little body' is extremely erotic: there is evidently something masturbatory and orgasmic about these 'enraptured sessions', and the anxious spying parents treated them as dangerous and unhealthy. In 'Literature', Dicky Thaxter is described as being so 'excited' by 'the act' that he has to pace up and down, almost running, and becomes hot and feverish with the 'thrill and stimulus' of 'making up'. Like an emission or a discharge, the story he is inventing seems to 'curl up from the page like a silver mist'. This involuntary, compulsive initiation into the gratification of authorship was linked to her childhood passion for the sound of words, which she often talked about. In 'Literature', Dicky's enthralment to the music and power of words, which he tries to transcribe phonetically before he understands their meaning, is what first inspires his interest in books.

'Making up' took place in private, but it also connected to the outside world. As a child, she despised – even feared – fairy-stories. In Paris, the stories she was 'making up' were based – as they would be in future years – on the lives she imagined for 'the ladies and gentlemen who came to dine, whom I saw riding and driving in the Bois de Boulogne', even though they became somewhat mixed up with the stories of Greek gods and goddesses she was being told by a family friend. (Sitting on this old man's knee to hear about the Olympians is one of her most pleasurable childhood memories, tinged with a faintly creepy eroticism.) When her real reading began, and she started to write (a flurry of teenage novels, poems, verse dramas and epics) it was, similarly, the young 'gods and goddesses' of 1870s Newport who inspired her first novels. 'Making up' might be a solitary ecstasy, but it was firmly linked to the realities of the physical world, to her relationship with her parents, and to the social life which she escaped from in order to 'make up', but also used for her material.

Wharton tells the story of her childhood as a tremendously well-furnished, well-dressed and socially entangled narrative, solid with structures, objects, habits, money, food and clothes. But it is also a solitary story of a fragile secret self whose most passionate relations are with nature, animals, and the sound of words, and who suffers from inexplicable fears and anxieties. In *A Backward Glance*, published in 1934, when she was seventy-two, the private self is more withheld, and the narrative wanders around inside the mesh of history, family stories, and cultural environment. So we jump from her first memory of a walk with her father up 'the Fifth Avenue', to a visit at fifteen to the naval academy at Annapolis where she sees pictures of her great-grandfather, a Civil War hero, then to her maternal grandmother's prejudices, her parents' courtship, her memory of a 'black sheep' cousin, and so on. The pendant to *A Backward Glance*, 'A Little Girl's New York', is a vivid and more satirical description of the vanished world of her childhood, was published posthumously, and gives more away. But only in 'Life and I' (started some time before *A Backward Glance* in the 1920s, but left unfinished, and not published until 1990) does she expose the private feelings of what she calls in *A Backward Glance* 'the little girl who eventually became me'.[3] Yet the public and private memoirs, read together, make a novelist's version of the childhood of Edith Newbold Jones which insists on certain key ingredients: the thick enclosing texture of wealthy late-Victorian genteel America; the conservative manners and habits of her provincial tribe; the aesthetic shock of moving early between Europe and America; her sense of the incompatibility between her parents; and her acute feelings that her passions and needs were at odds with her upbringing.

What she does not do is to start with the birth of a girl on 24 January 1862 at 14 West 23rd Street, New York City, to George Frederic Jones and Lucretia Stevens Rhinelander Jones. These were rather old parents – aged forty-one and thirty-eight – for a presumably unexpected third child, whose much older brothers, Frederic Rhinelander Jones and Henry Edward Jones – Freddy and Harry – were then sixteen and twelve. Nor does she give the details of the baptism of 'Edith Newbold Jones' on 20 April 1862 – Easter Sunday – at Grace Church on Broadway and 11th Street (where all the best New Yorkers had their children baptised) with, in attendance, Lucretia's brother Frederick Rhinelander, her sister Mary and Mary's husband Thomas Newbold (from whom Edith got her middle name) and a maternal cousin we never hear of again, Caroline King. (The King cousins were neighbours of the Joneses in Newport, and Edith's cousins Freddy and Le Roy King would be her executors.) Nor, surprisingly, does she say anything about the war she was born into. Apart from her description of her parents' social life in the 1850s as typical of 'the young people who ruled New York society before the Civil War', or her explanation for their departure to Europe in 1866 as a result of 'the depreciation of American currency at the close of the Civil War',[4] she tells the story of her childhood as if there was no national crisis going on. Her family was not involved in it, though touched by its financial effects.

Wharton puts the emphasis, in her childhood landscape, on her tall handsome father, her beautifully dressed and usually disapproving mother, and her kind 'easy-going' nurse, Hannah Doyle, or 'Doyley'. This Irishwoman in her forties who had been Harry's nurse and Lucretia's sewing-woman (a standard part of a middle-class household) is remembered, always, as reassuring and protective. She was the first of a number of women in Wharton's life who – unlike her mother, it seems – took care of her and looked after her affairs. And the gift of her first small dog at the age of three was evidently as life-changing an event as her first publication, or her first car, would be.

The childhood story turns, most of all, on the family's move to Europe when she was four. She makes this into the crucial first moment: nothing is the same afterwards. It leads into a set of vivid, colourful childhood memories of Rome, of travels in Spain, of the beginnings of story-telling in Paris. But Europe is also the stage for a more disturbing event, which Wharton marks as a moment of profound change in her character. While the family was at a spa in the Black Forest, she had a severe attack of typhoid fever which nearly killed her, at the age of nine. She tells it as a dramatic story: if a passing doctor at the Spa – 'the physician of the Czar of Russia', she notes grandly – had not recommended plunging her in cold water, she would have died.[5] The return from Europe a year later is also told as a life-changing trauma. New York seemed to the ten-year-old, after six years in Europe, startlingly ugly and drab, and in spite of the pleasure of rural Newport of the 1870s, from this moment on she felt like an exile in America. She describes herself, in relation to her parents' lavishly described social life, as an attentively watching outsider. She is being shaped by very mixed educational processes – dancing-lessons, governesses, her mother's literary censorship and social rules, her father's teaching her to read, the rapid acquisition of languages abroad, the beginning of a career as auto-didact in her father's library. She creates a retrospective picture of herself as an alienated, solitary figure, a writer-in-the-making.

These formative stories are not told in her memoirs as consecutive factual narrative. Instead, she plunges us into the texture of the now-vanished world of her 1860s childhood. The first thing we see is the little girl's knee-high survey of a Fifth Avenue which is made to seem monotonous and confining, and at the same time an exotic lost civilisation, like Atlantis, or Troy. The Joneses' house was a standard brownstone residence just off Fifth Avenue and Madison Square Park, and opposite the grand new Fifth Avenue Hotel (thought ostentatious by old New Yorkers). It was an item in the homogenous New York building plan of the 1840s and 1850s, of three-, four- or five-storey houses, all with their Dutch 'stoop' of three or four steps going up to the front door, all with a parlour and dining room on the ground floor, all with their similar façades, and built in such 'desperate uniformity of style' that if you were not careful you might find yourself going to dinner at the wrong house. The overall effect of what Wharton in *The Age of Innocence* called 'the uniform hue [which] coated New York like a cold chocolate sauce' would come to be criticised as 'dingy' and 'funereal'. Its social boundaries were Washington Square to the south and Gramercy Park to the east, where the Joneses had their first marital home when it was 'just within the built-on limits of New York'. When Edith Jones was born at West 23rd Street in 1862, fashionable New York was just starting to spread uptown. George Augustus Sala, an English writer who visited New York first in 1863 and then in 1879, noted: 'When I came here first, Twenty-fifth Street was accounted as being sufficiently far "up town", and Fortieth Street was Ultima Thule. Beyond that the course of town lots planned out and projected, but structurally yet to come, was only marked by boulders of the living rock.' Newland Archer's father-in-law, Mr Welland, has his eye, in the early 1870s, on 'a newly built house in East Thirty-Ninth Street' for the couple, in a 'neighbourhood that was thought remote'. The staggering, competitive display of grandiose, post-war Gilded Age mansions further uptown was still to come.[6] But in the mid-1860s, New York society still felt stable, provincial, and regulated. For the little girl, it was a semi-rural, quiet, slow-paced small town, with fields and chickens and grazing animals on the edges of these rows of safely recognisable buildings. The Fifth Avenue brownstones gave way to a pasture for cows and to the huge Croton water reservoir between 40th and 42nd Streets (which looked like an Egyptian temple and gave a good view of the surrounding countryside, and which would make way for the New York Public Library in 1899). Up and down this thoroughfare would go the 'genteel landaus, broughams and victorias . . . at decent intervals and a decorous pace',[7] or the Sunday strollers in their best hats and bonnets, their pedigrees, family trees, marital alliances, dinner-tables and madeiras all intimately known to one another. The other New York of the 1860s, the tenement slums of the lower East Side, the shanty-towns of squatters on the far reaches of the West Side, land that was going to be developed (in one police precinct alone, the *Times* reported in 1865, '10,000 people were living in not fewer than 800 shanties or cabins, each one containing from one to six prolific families, along with their cows, goats, pigs, geese and chickens'), was as remote from West 23rd Street as the moon.

Wharton presents her childhood's urban landscape as a timid and conformist architectural environment. The tone was set, she notes, by the 'blind dread of innovation' in the city planners of the 1820s, who chose not to model the street-plan of New York on the French designs for Washington, 'because it was thought "undemocratic" for citizens of the new republic to own building-plots which were not all of exactly the same shape, size – and *value*!'. In 'The Old Maid' (1924), set in the 1850s, she derides these town-planners for their fear of being thought undemocratic by 'people they secretly looked down upon'. She identifies the architectural landscape of old New York with a state of mind. The streets are made to represent a society of emotional immaturity, unimaginativeness, conservatism and narrow educational or cultural opportunities: 'The little brownstone houses . . . marched Parkward in an orderly procession, like a young ladies' boarding school taking its daily exercise.'[8] The uniform façades are the embodiments of the psyche of the average New Yorker.

This was a way of life defined by its architecture, interior design, clothes, fixtures and fittings. Wharton always characterises families and societies through the decoration of houses. So she tells her family story in her memoirs, not through a chronological account of family trees, not through quoting letters or reporting conversations, but through the symbolic objects that struck her as a child. Her way of introducing us to the only notable figure among her colonial forebears (mostly prosperous 'merchants, bankers and lawyers' of mixed Dutch and English pedigrees) is to remember being shown, in Washington (with no explanation from her parents), John Trumbull's paintings of the War of Independence, with her maternal great-grandfather Ebenezer Stevens featuring in *The Surrender of Burgoyne* and *The Surrender of Cornwallis*. At the time she was a bored and uncomprehending young girl, but she came to like the sound of this Revolutionary war-hero for his energy and gallantry, for his 'love of luxury' and 'tireless commercial activities' – and for his passion for France.[9] Fort Stevens, one of the defences built in New York harbour in 1812, was named after him. After his military career, he made a fortune as an East India merchant, and built a country house on Long Island with the profits, which he named Mount Buonaparte after his hero. But when Napoleon became emperor, the republican Stevens, in disgust, renamed his house 'The Mount', a name his great-granddaughter would borrow. Wharton imagined that this vanished house must have been full of 'Empire furniture from Paris', since the one relic that came down to her was 'a pair of fine gilt andirons crowned with Napoleonic eagles'.[10]

The patriotic Trumbull paintings and the imported French andirons sum up that ancestor and what he meant to her. Similarly, the relics she most cherished from the other branch of her mother's family, the Rhinelanders, were two stories, one of a sable cloak and the other of a 'yellow coach with a fringed hammer-cloth'. General Stevens had two wives, the second, a 'Lucretia' whom Wharton refers to, intriguingly (could this be a hint of mixed race in the Stevens pedigree?), as 'dusky', once lost a sable cloak when driving out with General Washington. By this dusky Lucretia and by his first wife, the general, energetic in everything, had fourteen children. In the early years of the nineteenth century this brood married into some of the leading prosperous New York family tribes: Schermerhorns, Gallatins, Rhinelanders. One of them, Mary, Edith's grandmother, married a member of the wealthy Rhinelander family (who could trace their entrepreneurial Huguenot forebears back to the seventeenth century and to a history of lucrative and probably ruthless New York dealings in sugar, ships and tenement rentals). Mary Stevens Rhinelander acquired, with her marriage, a 'spirited' mother-in-law of French-Huguenot descent. Whenever Mary Rhinelander was driving along the road to the city from Long Island by the East River, her mother-in-law's yellow carriage with its fringe had to take precedence, throwing the dust back at her daughter-in-law. Mary Rhinelander's daughter would inherit that tyranny of precedence rule: roughly fifty years after the days of the yellow carriage, Lucretia Jones did not forgive her newly married daughter for letting an inexperienced coachman overtake her carriage on Ocean Drive in

Newport. That 'canary-coloured coach' – one of the symbolic objects from her family past – gets into Delia Ralston's tribal family history in 'The Old Maid'.

Mary Rhinelander, the grandmother who had had to give way to her mother-in-law, died in 1877 at nearly eighty (the Stevenses were a long-lived lot), when Edith Jones was fifteen; Edith had known and liked the old lady. She came to live with the Jones family in Paris one winter, and was remembered for a whole cluster of things that summed up 'the abstract type of an ancestress': lace cap and lappets, black silk dress, gold charms dangling from a 'massive watch chain', and, above all, 'a black japanned ear trumpet'. The ear-trumpet was what her granddaughter remembered best because, at the age of six or seven, she would shout poetry into it for hours on end – mainly Tennyson, which she liked for the rhythms. So does Dicky Thaxter in 'Literature', where Grandma Boole's ear-trumpet is more fancifully described as 'a big black horn such as a Bad Angel might have put to his lips to sound a blast against the walls of heaven' – and down it Dicky bellows the *Lays of Ancient Rome*, *Morte d'Arthur*, fragments of *Tamerlane*, Percy's *Reliques*, and Longfellow's 'Evangeline'.[11]

Grandmother Rhinelander had not benefited from the considerable wealth either of her father the general, or of the Rhinelander family. Her husband (known for his love of reading) left the business management of his own and her finances, when he died, to his older brother, who grew rich at the expense of his widowed sister-in-law and her four children. Wharton notes this with some sharpness in her memoir. It explained some of the attitudes of her mother, the eldest of those four impoverished children; and it anticipated her own brothers' preferential financial treatment. The object which for her summed up her mother's resentment at this shabby-genteel childhood, 'up the River' in the family home at 'Hell Gate', opposite Long Island Sound, was a pair of slippers. When Lucretia 'came out', 'she wore a home-made gown of white tarlatan, looped up with red and white camellias from the greenhouse, and her mother's old white satin slippers; and her feet being of a different shape from grandmamma's, she suffered martyrdom, and never ceased to resent the indignity inflicted on her'. In 'The Old Maid', those slippers have even more of a history. 'Charlotte . . . had not been used to pretty things . . . and [she] entered society in her mother's turned garments, and shod with satin sandals handed down from a defunct aunt who had "opened a ball" with General Washington.' No wonder that Lucretia, once married into the prosperous Jones family, was passionately fond of clothes, and infected her daughter with the excitement of the yearly arrival of the 'trunk from Paris' and a desire to grow up to be 'the best-dressed woman in New York'.[12]

In *A Backward Glance*, and before that in 'False Dawn', a story set in the 1840s, Wharton turns her parents' courtship into a romance of youthful idealism against parental opposition. She tells the tale, which she must often have heard in her childhood, of how her father, aged twenty – that would have been in 1841 – forbidden by his parents to visit the impoverished Miss Rhinelander of Hell Gate, rigged his bed-quilt up as a sail for his rowing-boat and stole across the waters of Long Island Sound to court his beloved. In fact, George Frederic's father Edward Renshaw Jones had died in 1839, leaving his son a substantial fortune. And the family opposition, such as it was, gave way quite soon. The couple were married, at twenty-two and nineteen, from the bride's house, a marriage imagined in 'The Old Maid', in the old house 'with its thin colonnaded verandah', its drawing rooms furnished 'with their frail slender settees, their Sheraton consoles and cabinets', and the bride 'in her high-waisted "India mull" embroidered with daisies, her flat satin sandals, her Brussels veil' standing under 'the bell of white roses in the hall'. (That 'India mull', a gauzy dress imported from India for great-grandmother Lucretia Stevens's wedding, was another item in the family trunk that appealed to Wharton's imagination.[13]) The couple honeymooned in Cuba (a fashionable destination then), moved into their Gramercy Park brownstone and became one of the prototypical families of that generation of Joneses. The fact that Lucretia Rhinelander was once thought a dubious choice by her husband's family presumably contributed to her own insistence on protocol and social exclusivity.

The Joneses were one of the largest, wealthiest and most socially prominent families of the inter-married network of mid-nineteenth-century New York. They were 'a patrician clan' who had made their money through real estate, and who 'for generations, in a most distinguished way, had done nothing whatever remarkable'.[14] They were distinguished for their money and their commitment to leisure and consumption, not for professional ambitions, military prowess or social responsibilities. When Wharton re-created her grandfather Jones's world as that of the Raycies in 'False Dawn', she draws it as parochial, self-approving, solid and absurdly conventional, and with the heartiest of appetites:

Oh, that supper-table! ... In the centre stood the Raycie *épergne* of pierced silver, holding aloft a bunch of June roses surrounded by dangling baskets of sugared almonds and striped peppermints; and grouped about this decorative 'motif' were Lowestoft platters heavy with piles of raspberries, strawberries and the first Delaware peaches. An outer flanking of heaped-up cookies, crullers, strawberry short-cake, piping hot corn-bread and deep golden butter in moist blocks still bedewed from the muslin swathings of the dairy, led the eye to the Virginia ham in front of Mr Raycie, and the twin dishes of scrambled eggs on toast and broiled blue-fish over which his wife presided.[15]

In this family of hide-bound, leisured guzzlers, there were few individuals who caught Wharton's imagination: there were no General Stevenses in the paternal family web of Joneses, Gallatins, Colfords and Schermerhorns, with their ugly flat Dutch voices. She passes over a potentially interesting uncle, George Frederic's older brother Edward, who died when she was seven, a doctor with a lifelong involvement in the administration and development of Columbia University. And she has rather little to say about the eccentric millionaire cousin, Joshua Jones, who changed her life, by leaving to her, among a number of bequests to relations he never met, $120,000 in 1888. (He features in histories of New York as a property developer who offered to sell a parcel of land in 1882 between 74th and 75th Streets for the building of the long-planned Episcopal cathedral of St John the Divine, but whose price was too exorbitant.[16]) The one member of her father's family who does appeal to her is her father's aunt by marriage, Mary Mason Jones, a huge ugly old lady, long widowed, who in the distant past was known to have broken her husband's will and got all his money. She and her sister Rebecca shocked all the other Joneses by building, on land they had inherited from their father John Mason, a founder of the Chemical Bank, two huge blocks, way uptown, above 57th Street – almost in the countryside – in 1871. The phrase 'keeping up with the Joneses' is supposed to have been coined in reference to these great-aunts of Edith Wharton. Mrs Mason Jones's block was a daring cream-coloured Parisian mansion, with unheard-of French windows, ground-floor bedrooms, ballroom, and sensual French decorations. Here she set her own social rules and continued to dominate the society she had outraged.[17] She is dramatised as Mrs Manson Mingott in 'The Old Maid' and in *The Age of Innocence*, where she is described as 'dauntless' and 'audacious', ruling and challenging her world with a 'kind of haughty effrontery'.

Mrs Mason Jones's audacity is symbolised by her French windows, and it was by their houses that Wharton characterised her Jones relations. As well as the pioneering Mason Jones Parisian mansion, she remembered her grandfather's house on the sound, which, in a print she owned, still had the old slaves' cabin next to it. Another Jones residence made a vivid, and unpleasant, impression. It belonged to a solitary, wealthy aunt, Elizabeth Schermerhorn Jones, who lived in lonely state in a huge house on the Hudson River, named after the nearby village of Rhinecliff. The very young Edith disliked visiting it and found it frightening and intolerably ugly. (The house, later named 'Wyndecliffe', still stands, deserted, its roof fallen in and its many doors and windows gaping empty, a spooky ruin hidden away in a wilderness of straggling trees, fences, and No Trespassing signs.) Wharton describes it in *A Backward Glance* as a hideous example of 'Hudson River Gothic', a red-brick Romanesque structure with tunnels and arched windows. It struck her as an embodiment of her aunt's 'granitic' temperament.[18]

Wharton takes pleasure in the forceful individualism of some of her ancestors – qualities she might well have recognised in herself. But what interests her most in her family's story is its typical quality, its tribal nature. Powerfully underlying her light-toned, anecdotal memoir is a lifetime's reading in science, philosophy and anthropology – and a lifetime of translating social history into fiction. One of her first and most determined exit strategies from her parents' society was her self-education as a cultural analyst, from the late 1870s onwards. She read herself out of 'old New York' via Herbert Spencer, Darwin, Nietzsche, Ernst Von Haeckel on evolution, T.H. Huxley, George Romanes, Max Weber, the anthropologists Paul Topinard and Edvard Westermarck, James Frazer's *The Golden Bough* and Thorstein Veblen. (Much later, in the 1920s, she read and came to know the ethnologist Bronislaw Malinowski.) Such early readings gave her a way of analysing the world she grew up in. She has been described as a 'novelist-ethnographer', trying to 'understand modern society through the lens of ethnographic estrangement', analysing it through reading the signs of 'tribal membership'.[19] In *The Age of Innocence* (1920) Newland Archer, who reads too many books on anthropology for his own good, takes part in the rituals of his tribe with a sense of alienation. The social structures he lives by seem unreal to him. In her memoirs, Wharton reconstructs herself as a child in a cultural system which, because it is defunct, can be summed up as an anthropologist might a Melanesian kinship system.[20] This makes in part for an aloof, satirical tone on those vanished, now unreal-seeming absurdities: but not entirely. There is nostalgia, respect, and regret, too, in her backward glance.

Part of the complexity of Wharton's approach to her parents' society is that her analysis, in some ways, reiterates their prejudices. She is describing a 'tribe' which sustains itself, and eventually weakens itself, by its insistence on exclusivity. It defines itself by what it is not. She understood very well, and wrote a great deal about, the anxiety produced by this commitment to exclusivity, and the fact that New York society, even while it tried to preserve itself, had what has been called 'uncertain and constantly changing boundaries'.[21] Her treatment of this 'old New York' society also defines through exclusion. What were they *not*, she asks. They were not, she insists, 'aristocracy'. To make this point, she cites her mother's distinction (given to Mrs Archer, who has all Lucretia's opinions, in *The Age of Innocence*) between the old New York families, Dutch or British in origin, with aristocratic forebears, like the Rutherfurds or the Van Rensselaers (families very well known to the Joneses), and the merchant/professional class to which she belonged. In her fiction she refers to 'New York gentility' or to 'the rich and respected citizens' of 'a ruling class'. But in her memoir she distinguishes her own 'middle class' from the grander families, and, equally, from the incomers with more money and no pedigree who were coming in to swamp them.

What did they call themselves? Mrs John King Van Rensselaer, lamenting the demise of the old New York society in *The Social Ladder* (1925), a book of breathtakingly unexamined snobbery, looks back longingly on a 'dignified, exclusive set of blood and breeding', on 'the Society of Birth' as opposed to 'the Society of Wealth'. Philip Hone, a prosperous businessman, the diarist of New York social life from the 1820s to the 1850s, talks complacently about taking part in social events with 'the most genteel people in town' or 'the better sort' or 'the élite'. Ward McAllister, writing on the need for the exclusive society of the Four Hundred which would keep out the new millionaires, said that 'we have to draw social boundaries [on the basis of] old connections, gentle breeding, perfection in all the requisite accomplishments of a gentleman, elegant leisure and an unstained private reputation'. Writers on Wharton speak of a 'clan', a 'little world', 'aristocracy', 'a patrician group', 'New York society', 'high society' or 'polite society', 'old money'. Some writers on the leisure class define them as the 'Knickerbocker' society, after the exclusive club which came to stand for the whole social group; some simply talk about 'the American upper class'. Louis Auchincloss, a descendant of and an expert on the social groupings that are Wharton's subject matter, uses the term *'haute bourgeoisie'*.[22]

So they were not aristocrats. They were not religious fanatics or ideologues, like the dim and distant Stevenses who settled in New England. New Yorkers were more 'easy-going'. (A historian of the Hudson Valley houses, H.D. Eberlein, writing in 1924, remarks – perhaps she read him – on the 'comfortable, easy-going mode of life' of the New York Dutch, as opposed to the 'austere, gloomy religionists of New England'.) They were not involved in politics or matters of state. They did not take on public responsibilities. They were not energetic and ruthless like the generation before them – 'What has become of the spirit of the pioneers and the revolutionaries?' she asked – or the entrepreneurs who came after them. Living mainly on inherited incomes, they were not falling over themselves to make more money. None of her father's friends was in business, and anyone in the retail trade was rigorously excluded. Writers, too, were out, as either they were not gentlemen, or they were Bohemian, or common. Jews, foreigners, crooks, and women with dubious reputations, were, one or two exceptions aside, completely beyond the pale.[23]

Instead of having puritan convictions about the Elect and the damned, her parents' generation were on a perpetual red alert for 'ill-breeding' and practised an elaborate policy of 'social ostracism'. This could have its good side too, Wharton argued. It did involve standards of 'probity', truthfulness and incorruptibility. She is kinder about this in A *Backward Glance* than she is with her earlier fictional family, the Ralstons, in 'The Old Maid'. Since the eighteenth century, the Ralstons had flourished by being prudent, solid, institutional and conservative. By the fourth generation they 'had nothing left in the way of convictions save an acute sense of honour in private and business matters'. They 'had done little to shape the destiny of their country . . . no Ralston had so far committed himself as to be great . . . it was safer to be satisfied with three per cent: they regarded heroism as a form of gambling. Yet by merely being so numerous and so similar they had come to have a weight in the community.' By the 1850s their character has become so 'congenital' that a wife of the tribe wonders whether 'were she to turn her own little boy loose in a wilderness, he would not create a small New York there, and be on all its boards of directors'.[24]

Her father was, indeed, a director – like Philip Hone and all the 'better sort'. He sat on charitable boards like the Bloomingdale Insane Asylum (up on Morningside Heights, until it made way for Columbia College buildings in 1888) and the Blind Asylum – for which Mrs Reggie Chivers organises the Martha Washington Ball in *The Age of Innocence*, while her husband is practising for the International Polo Match. But he did not have to work for a living. The second son of the family, he had a gentleman's education at Columbia College ('The Literature and Scientific Course'), avoided the draft, and inherited enough from his father's real-estate holdings in Manhattan and Brooklyn to live a life of leisure. But by contrast to William H. Vanderbilt – who inherited $90 million from his father in 1877, built his 'Triple Palace' in 1882 for $2 million, and had a fortune of

$200 million to be divided, with notorious acrimony, between his eight children – George Frederic Jones had a house in New York worth $20,000, and in 1861 built on Harrison Avenue, Newport, Rhode Island, a large Tudor-style country house called 'Pencraig', worth $60,000, with a smaller (ten-room) 'cottage' on the premises.[25] He could afford to run these two houses with a full staff of servants, to keep a good table, to travel and to entertain, and to send his son Freddy to Columbia College and his son Harry to Trinity Hall, Cambridge.

Even so, Wharton's dominant memory of her father was the sight of him bent over his desk in 'desperate calculations', in 'the vain effort to squeeze my mother's expenditure into his narrowing income'. She partly blames her parents for their problems: her father for 'bad management of his property', her mother for being a compulsive shopper with over-grandiose aspirations (witness an unfinished conservatory at West 23rd Street). But they were also caught up in economic circumstances beyond their control. The slump in property values after the Civil War affected a whole generation, and the Joneses were not the only couple of their class to lease out their houses to 'the profiteers of the day' in the late 1860s and to go to live in Europe in order to economise.[26] Their life-style in Europe, in good hotels and apartments, was hardly penurious, and their youngest child certainly felt no constraints. But after six years abroad, they came back to a rocky economy, the end of a boom. Investment was not keeping pace with inflation, 'money was tight, new construction had fallen off, and the stock market had the jitters'. The failure of the powerful banking house Jay Cooke & Co. sparked off the Wall Street panic of September 1873 and led to a 'crippling' decline, the 'Great Depression' of the 1870s, and the collapse of the real-estate economy.[27] (The failure of Julius Beaufort's bank in The Age of Innocence invokes the instability just under the surface of the 1870s.) Like many other affluent citizens of his generation, George Frederic Jones was never free of money anxieties after that, though he was not, by any stretch of the imagination, hard up. The return of immense prosperity to America in the opulent years of the 1880s (until the next economic collapse in 1893) came too late for him. Though the family was never less than comfortable, Edith Jones's 'coming out' was a rather muted affair, and it was not until after her father's death that a large family inheritance from the Rhinelanders made her mother securely wealthy again.

But if the Joneses were not Astors or Vanderbilts, they gave off a pretty well-upholstered air. Wharton describes the fixtures and fittings of her childhood as a collection of solid objects, strong colours, and thick textures. Huge pieces of furniture and acres of clutter and plush loom up out of her memory. In 'the full-blown specimen of Second Empire decoration' that was her family home, they were surrounded by 'monumental pieces of modern Dutch marquetry', yards of old lace, dark copies of minor Italian Masters. The vestibule was painted 'in Pompeian red frescoed with a frieze of lotus-leaves', the drawing room had 'tufted purple satin arm-chairs' and a table of 'Louis-Philippe *buhl*, with ornate brass heads at the angles'. (The banker Julius Beaufort, in *The Age of Innocence*, has a library furnished with 'Spanish leather . . . buhl and malachite'.) The 'huge oak mantelpiece sustained by vizored knights', matched at the corners of the vast writing-table in her father's study, was the product, she thought, of a vague idea that there was 'some obscure (perhaps Faustian) relation between the Middle Ages and culture'.[28]

In 'The Old Maid', she does the bric-à-brac of her mother's generation with a vengeance:

> The rosewood what-nots on each side of the folding doors . . . were adorned with tropical shells, feldspar vases, an alabaster model of the Leaning Tower of Pisa, a pair of obelisks made of scraps of porphyry and serpentine picked up by the young couple in the Roman Forum, a bust of Clytie in chalk-white biscuit de Sèvres, and four old-fashioned figures of the Seasons in Chelsea ware, that had to be left among the newer ornaments because they had belonged to great-grandmamma Ralston.[29]

That is an 1850s drawing room – though as she notes there, every drawing room keeps on some of the last generation's relics. By the time we get to May Archer in the early 1870s in *The Age of Innocence* the rosewood what-nots have turned into 'little plush tables densely covered with silver toys, porcelain animals, and efflorescent photograph frames'.[30]

The psychology of these homes is summed up in their curtains. Wharton likes to show her genteel families framed in their windows, protecting themselves from interference while spying on the world outside. The family in 'New Year's Day', one of the *Old New York* stories, who keep up the Dutch custom of exchanging visits and gifts on that day, cluster at their window on West 23rd Street all afternoon, a little tribe of voyeurs, to watch the comings and goings outside the Fifth Avenue Hotel opposite. The 'voluminous purple satin curtains festooned with buttercup yellow fringe' of her mother's drawing room, replicated in Mrs Welland's drawing room in *The Age of Innocence*, are analysed for their psychological implications in 'A Little Girl's New York':

Its tall windows were hung with three layers of curtains: sash-curtains through which no eye from the street could possibly penetrate; and next to these draperies of lace or embroidered tulle, richly beruffled, and looped back under the velvet or damask hangings which were drawn in the evening. This window garniture always seemed to me to symbolise the superimposed layers of undergarments worn by the ladies of the period – and even, alas, by the little girls.[31]

When Wharton published her recommendations for a new kind of domestic interior design, in her first book, *The Decoration of Houses* (a book which was as much a critique of her parents' tastes and lives as *The Age of Innocence* or *Old New York* would be), she had a great deal to say about curtains:

Who cannot call to mind the dreary drawing-room ... ? The windows in this kind of room are invariably supplied with two sets of muslin curtains, one hanging against the panes, the other fulfilling the supererogatory duty of hanging against the former; then come the heavy stuff curtains, so draped as to cut off the upper light of the windows by day, while it is impossible to drop them at night: curtains that have thus ceased to serve the purpose for which they exist.[32]

Whenever Wharton writes about the decoration of houses, she is writing about behaviour and beliefs. The activities of her parents' class match their furniture. Their pleasures, as she describes them, were settled and conventional. Abroad, there were the well-trodden paths of the cultural tourist, shopping, and the society of other Americans – but not of the natives. (A trip to Spain when she was only three or four seems to have been unusually daring.) At the country house in Newport, still in the '60s and '70s a quiet, genteel, pastoral retreat, there were outdoor pastimes like walking, riding, and archery contests. But the heavy-curtain principle held good here, too: the 'lovely archeresses' all wore thick veils, since physical beauty was held in such high esteem, and the preservation of a 'perfect complexion' was all-important. (In *The Age of Innocence*, the 'floating veils' of the lady archers provide Newland with a useful metaphor for the 'curtain' that cuts off his nice, beautiful wife from reality.) Later, the new game of lawn tennis superseded archery, and for Edith Jones and her young friends, there were fishing-parties, boat-races, and the endless, ritualistic round of drives and calls, in one's very best clothes from Paris, up and down Ocean Drive and Bellevue Avenue.[33]

In New York, her parents did what everyone did: a few charities, walks in the Park, endless 'calls', and outings to the newly fashionable Italian opera at the Academy of Music on 14th Street and Union Square, to see and be seen and to talk to their friends throughout the music. At the start of *The Age of Innocence*, this exclusive venue, in which all the boxes were taken by the old families, is already under threat from the 'new people' who want to build a bigger, grander, and less stuffy opera house.

Her parents' main social occupation was their dinner parties, where the leisurely intake of 'a prodigious amount of good food', vintage claret and the celebrated Jones Madeira would be rounded off at 10.30 p.m. with a cup of tea. Wharton waxes lyrical in her descriptions of the food at her parents' table, and never misses a fictional opportunity to describe what people eat. It's as if the lavish richness of these social meals makes up for the aridity of other aspects of their lives. And she celebrates the memory of her mother's black cooks, 'great artists', who poured out their cornu-copias of 'terrapin and canvas-back ducks . . . broiled Spanish mackerel, soft-shelled crabs with a mayonnaise of celery . . . peach-fed Virginia hams cooked in champagne . . . lima-beans in cream, corn soufflés and salads of oyster-crabs'. The exoticised African-American figures of Mary Johnson and Susan Minneman provide the labour on which the white society relies: otherwise they are as invisible in Wharton's story of her childhood as 'the poor' for whom her mother's sewing circle convenes.[34]

Wharton describes the 'amiable chat' at these dinners as limited to 'small parochial concerns': food, wine, property, sport, travel, and a little mild culture. Politics, religion, art and literature were avoided, or only touched on within the limits of acceptability. The war, too, presumably fell into the category of subjects to be avoided: she wrote two bitter stories, 'The Lamp of Psyche' and 'The Spark', on members of her father's generation who managed to get out of it. (George Frederic Jones did not register for the draft, though he was legally required to. Others of his class did register, but paid 'commutation fees' not to be called up, or sent substitutes.[35]) Open discussion of sexual matters was taboo. *A Backward Glance* is full of unmentionable episodes, scandalous black sheep who have dropped out of sight, instructions to look away, banned reading matter. Sexual and cultural censorship were intimately linked, under a rigid system of rules – which she always associated with her mother – about what would and would not do. She makes a comedy in her memoirs out of these rules, but they are also the source of pain, in her fictions and in her life.

Veils, curtains and layers of undergarments were meant to keep the family insulated against dangerous infections, and to protect, and infantilise, the young girl. But they also suggested to her exciting possibilities of a world elsewhere. The Joneses had a disreputable cousin, George Alfred (a financial con-man and adulterer whose malefactions came to light when Edith Jones was ten years old). Whenever he was mentioned, her mother would 'dart away' from his name, and when challenged about what he had done would only mutter, 'Some woman.' When the mistress of the notorious banker August Belmont was seen driving shamelessly down Fifth Avenue in her canary-coloured brougham (just like Fanny Ring, Beaufort's mistress in *The Age of Innocence*), Lucretia told her daughter to turn her head away and 'look out of the other window' – which she obediently did. (In an early, unfinished novel called 'Disintegration', the daughter of a runaway mother is forbidden by her Irish nurse Noony to look at her mother in public, or to ask questions about her. 'They all slammed the same door in her face, and such unanimity of opposition kept her curiosity glued to the crack.') The proscriptions gave the young Edith a tantalising hint of some 'perilous' region 'just beyond the world of copy-book axioms'. But when she asked her mother about her own developing sexuality, she was told 'It isn't nice to ask about such things', and felt an unpleasant sense of contamination and bafflement. Committing adultery, she thought as a child, having read the word without knowing its definition, meant 'having to pay a higher rate in travelling' – because she had seen a notice on a train or a boat reading 'Adults 50 cents, Children 25 cents'. Why would they have to pay more? Probably, she thought, as a punishment for their guilt. Under the system of censorship of her upbringing, strong ideas about paying for what you had done were developed.[36]

Sex, culture and the imagination were closely linked in the codes of prohibition Wharton is describing. 'Look out of the other window' was a generally applied rule. Lucretia's insistence on good manners, and her reverence for 'Usage', extended to her ideas about literature. Lucretia had had English tutors and governesses; Edith's brothers had 'an extremely cultivated English tutor'. Standards of 'scrupulous perfection' were applied to language as to social behaviour. There was as strong a fear of 'deterioration and corruption' arising from the misuse of English as from the sight of a courtesan's carriage in Fifth Avenue. One of Wharton's most painful childhood memories is of being mocked by her parents for using slang or malapropisms: 'I still tingle with the sting of their ridicule.' It was part of a general mockery she endured – for having red hair and big hands and feet, for not being pretty. When in *A Backward Glance* she describes her childhood house, when her brothers were home, as 'ringing with laughter', it may be that that laughter was not always kind.[37] Nevertheless, she carried that scorn of bad language and poor usage into her own fastidious adult life.

Wharton turns the family laughter, in her memoirs, on to her mother, especially on to the fierce system of literary censorship which Lucretia set up, in contrast with the free range which the reading daughter had in her father's library. No slangy American children's books were allowed – so, presumably, no Mark Twain, Bret Harte, or 'Uncle Remus'. Louisa May Alcott just got by, but Edith preferred *The Water Babies* or *Alice in Wonderland*. After she was found, as a very young girl, reading a risqué French play, her reading was carefully monitored for adult – or adulterous – content. Traces of that monitoring lingered on. In *A Backward Glance*, she says it was a play about what her mother's friends would call 'one of those women'; in 'Life and I' she calls it 'the story of a prostitute'.[38]

Though her mother read nothing but novels herself, these were banned for her daughter, a rule Lucretia had inherited, like her drawing-room furniture, from her own mother, who had 'forbidden her to read any of Scott's novels, except "Waverley", till after she was married'. So Edith, obediently, read everything else except novels until 'the day of my marriage'.[39] This kind of censorship spread far beyond the Jones household. Every late-Victorian American novelist was plagued by the 'young girl' standard: fiction had to be fit for virgins. Lucretia's total ban was simply a more extreme policy than that of most of the cultural monitors of the time. And Wharton treats this astounding fact about her childhood with rueful appreciation. She says that her mother did her a favour in forcing her to read the classics, philosophy, history, and poetry. At least Lucretia allowed her to read. The granddaughter of George Frederic Jones's sister, when caught by her mother with her nose in a book, was told that if she read too much she would be like 'weird cousin Edith'.

Wharton is scornful about the censoring of writers – not just of writing – in her parents' society. That her parents, though respectful of literature, 'stood in nervous dread of those who produced it', seemed to her one of the great absurdities of her environment. 'On the whole, my mother doubtless thought, it would be simpler if people one might be exposed to meeting would refrain from meddling with literature.' 'In the eyes of our provincial society authorship was still regarded as something between a black art and a form of manual labour.' (Mrs Archer, in *The Age of Innocence*, is extremely suspicious of 'people who wrote'.) It has been observed that Wharton exaggerated the intellectual barrenness of New York society after the Civil War: in reality it was not quite such a cultural desert as she makes out – there were a good many writers to be found among the upper classes. But what she remembered in her own home was a culture of provincialism, censoriousness and timidity. Walt Whitman, for whose work she developed a great passion, was thought to be particularly shocking. In the households Wharton remembered from her childhood, '*Leaves of Grass* was kept under lock and key, and brought out, like tobacco, only in the absence of "the ladies", to whom the name of Walt Whitman was unmentionable, if not utterly unknown'. In her New York fictions, she likes to slip those unacceptable writers into her critique of the society, like the Raycies' horror at the blasphemous atheist Mr Poe in 'False Dawn', or the influence of Whitman in 'The Spark' in *Old New York*. For Newland Archer, as for Edith Wharton, the alternative, a place where artists and writers mix freely in society, is, of course, Paris.

That genteel censoriousness persisted into the early years of Wharton's professional life; she plays it up in her memoir because it affected her career. When one of Wharton's early editors told her that in writing for publication one must avoid 'religion, love, politics, alcohol, or fairies', it must have been like hearing her mother's voice all over again.[40]

In the fifty years of writing that came between her childhood and her autobiographical version, one of her achievements was to write with hard, penetrating, analytical realism about a society 'wholly absorbed in barricading itself against the unpleasant'. In her reworkings of that world, she exposed everything it wanted to conceal, while conveying with a high level of precision its method of dealing in 'faint implications and pale delicacies'. Yet her published autobiography seems to suffer from some of the inhibitions she is satirising. Of the many things she did not choose to talk about – the failure of her marriage and her divorce, her most intimate relationships, the catastrophic family rifts that would divide her brother Frederic from the rest of the family, the financial battles that followed her mother's death, her estrangement from her brother Harry over sex and money – one of the most scandalous items was the question mark hanging over her own paternity. Persistent rumours circled around Lucretia's late third child. She was, perhaps, the daughter of an eminent elderly Scottish peer, the lawyer Lord Brougham, who was living in Cannes when the Joneses were there in the early '60s (and had red hair, and was an intellectual with an interest in science, like Edith). Or she was the result of an intramural affair between Lucretia and her sons' 'cultured' young English tutor, who was supposed to have then gone out West and been killed by Indians. These rumours, which kept surfacing in posthumous anecdotes about Edith relayed by friends and acquaintances, and which she is supposed to have heard about from her brother Harry after the war, are unprovable – though support could be derived from the many fictions she wrote about dubious or concealed parentage (including an unfinished fragment called 'Old Style', which has a husband who resents his wife for obliterating the memory of their dead son with her new child, a child who resembles the young English tutor they had for the older boy).[41] Whether she believed these rumours or not, she never puts them on record. The code of genteel censorship left its trace.

Wharton's stories of families and societies are always about resistance. The irruption of the illegitimate or misfit child, the disruptive newcomer, into the established community, produces an involuntary drawing-back, an attempt to expel the foreign body. But the irruption is necessary for any kind of new life. 'Atrophy', like 'unreality', is one of her key words (and the title of one of her most desolating stories). When Newland Archer and his mother visit those arbiters of society, the van der Luydens (fictional Van Rensselaers, representatives of the best old Dutch families going back to the first 'Patroon', governor of the seventeenth-century Dutch colony), Archer sees Mrs van der Luyden as 'having been rather gruesomely preserved in the airless atmosphere of a perfectly irreproachable existence, as bodies caught in glaciers keep for years a rosy life-in-death'. Hayley Delane, the prosperous banker of the 1860s story 'The Spark', whose mind had stopped taking in anything new ('snapped shut on what it possessed, like a replete crustacean never reached by another high tide'), is another of those moribund old New Yorkers. 'People all stopped living at one time or another, however many years longer they continued to be alive', comments the narrator of 'The Spark'. Atrophy gives her the horrors: and there were plenty of examples of it close to home. One of the Joneses' family stories was of an eccentric wealthy cousin who had lived in the same huge house for sixty years and 'then, in his last years, *sat on a marble shelf, and thought he was Napoleon*'. The grandest of Wharton's distant relatives was Caroline Schermerhorn, a first cousin of her father's, who became Mrs William B. Astor – *the* Mrs Astor, the queen of New York society, maintaining its moral standards and respectability against the influx of new money, supported by her social disciple and master of ceremonies Ward McAllister, who coined the term 'the Four Hundred' to describe the number of people who could fit into her ballroom. Mrs Astor became senile in her last years, before her death in 1908, and was reported to have gone on entertaining imaginary guests in her French Renaissance chateau on Fifth Avenue and 65th Street, long after society had by-passed her doors.[42]

To die without ever having questioned the habits of your generation, to be fixed, as in a story by Edgar Allan Poe, like a bust on a mantelpiece, in living death, seemed to her a horrible fate. She is at pains to describe herself, from her very earliest days, as 'making up' another story of her life than the one she had been given. By contrast, her description of her parents as individuals – rather than as prototypes of a society – does not allow them any unconventionality or capacity for change. Her father seems to have been too weak, her mother too conservative.

The handsome blue-eyed father whose hand she is holding in her first memory, whose chief rule of conduct was to be kind, whose appetite for travel took her on her exciting early journey to Spain while they were in Europe, and with whom, in the year before his death, she shared Ruskinian explorations of Italy, is presented in her autobiography as benign but ineffectual: worrying over the bills, taking second place to his wife. But he gave his daughter affection and he gave her her first serious form of education through his 'gentleman's library'. It was only a younger son's collection, and she implies that he had not read all that much of it himself. But by her teens she knew it by heart. Wharton, so careful and loving of her own books, often wondered what happened to all those old New York 'gentleman's libraries': scattered, sold? It is a mark of her attachment to her father and his books that so many of the titles she names in A Backward Glance as formative reading, remained in her library all her life: sets of Defoe, Milton, Carlyle, Lamartine, Hugo, Racine, Cowper, Thomas Moore, Lamb, Byron, Wordsworth, Ruskin, Washington Irving, all marked 'G.F. Jones'.

There are dark, sinister father-figures in Wharton's work, and her fascination with incest as a literary theme in fictions such as Summer, 'Beatrice Palmato' and The Mother's Recompense has led to speculation that Wharton may have been an abused child, who concealed or repressed a traumatic history. But a concealed secret remains a secret. No trace of evidence shows up in the tone she uses about George Frederic Jones. He seems more likely to have been the inspiration for the bafflement and disappointment, the sense of a missed chance in life, that she gave to characters like Newland Archer, Ralph Marvell, or Ethan Frome. She always wondered what 'stifled cravings' he had repressed; she thought of him as a lonely person, 'haunted by something always unexpressed and unattained'.[43] George Frederic Jones died young, at sixty-one, of an illness that began in exhaustion and nervous prostration and ended with a stroke, when Edith was twenty. She remembered all her life his expression on his death-bed. There was something he wanted to say to her, and he never managed it.

By contrast, how much she blames her mother. Wharton's version of Lucretia Jones is one of the most lethal acts of revenge ever taken by a writing daughter. The fictional materials were inexhaustible – Wharton was still 'doing' her in her seventies – and Lucretia remained unforgiven. It is almost impossible to get a sense of Lucretia separate from Wharton's account of her, apart from those glimpses of the strait-laced young wife on the Grand Tour, and a leather-bound commonplace book of 1836, with pressed flowers from journeys to England and Ireland, conventional poems beautifully copied out on lost love, childhood, and woman's inspiration ('Woman thou art a lovely thing / A bright and cherished thing'), and an anecdote of Napoleon's saying that 'the youth of France' needed 'mothers who shall know how to educate their children'.[44]

There is a benign version of Mrs Jones in a late and sentimental reminiscence by Wharton's childhood friend Emelyn Washburn, remembering, sixty years on, how Mrs Jones was delighted by the gift of a Christmas tree and 'went with us to choose the decorations', how she told Emelyn, when asked what Edith could read when the girls were together, 'Puss may read anything you think right', how it was Mr Jones, when he was ill and troubled by money worries, who 'would not allow her to economize in anything', and how 'devoted' her sons were to her.[45] But this whitewash job by an old lady (whom Edith had come to despise) pales beside the ferocious account of Lucretia in Wharton's memoirs. She takes every possible occasion to disparage her. Her mother is indolent, spendthrift, censorious, disapproving, superficial, 'incurably prosaic', 'exaggeratedly scrupulous', 'icy', 'dry', and 'ironic'. And Wharton can sound quite as dry and ironic herself when she talks about her mother, as when she attributes Lucretia's wariness of writers to 'the sort of diffidence which, thank heaven, no psychoanalyst had yet arisen to call a "complex"'.[46] If Lucretia Jones had known about psychoanalysts, that would have been just the tone she would have used about them.

There are suggestions that Lucretia might have had her daughter's interests at heart, in her attempts to take down the stories the child is rapidly 'making up', in her arranging for Edith's poems to be privately printed when she was sixteen, and in Wharton's discovering, when her mother died, that she had kept a number of her childhood letters. But the key story about Lucretia and her writer-daughter is not one of encouragement:

> My first attempt (at the age of eleven) was a novel, which began: 'Oh, how do you do, Mrs Brown?' said Mrs Tompkins. 'If only I had known you were going to call I should have tidied up the drawing-room.' Timorously I submitted this to my mother, and never shall I forget the sudden drop of my creative frenzy when she returned it with the icy comment: 'Drawing-rooms are always tidy.'[47]

Wharton says that this comically mortifying scene temporarily quashed her fictional ambitions and turned her to writing poetry. The story of her relationship with her mother is always like this: one of anxiety and guilt produced by disapproval. Because her mother laughed at her literary pretensions, her solecisms, and her looks, she became a 'painfully shy self-conscious child'. She longed for love and admiration, but found 'unsought demonstrations of affection' repugnant, and was called cold and inexpressive. She describes herself as always pulled between the side that wanted to be admired and sought after, to flirt, to wear nice clothes and to be a social success, and the solitary, secret, imaginative side, passionately taken up with nature, animals, and language.

Her very first memory, a pleasurable one, was of walking along Fifth Avenue holding her father's hand and wearing a new bonnet with a veil, when a little boy, a cousin, came up to her, lifted up her veil, and kissed her cheek. Her needs 'to love and to look pretty' were both satisfied at once, she says. But in one version she calls this 'vanity' – the kind of criticism her mother might have made of her. Another very early memory, of herself at five or six at dancing-class in Paris, raised a painful ethical dilemma, also associated with her mother. She told a little boy that the dancing-teacher's mother looked like an old goat, and then confessed what she had said to the teacher. This did not go down well. Immediately, the child thought that her mother would disapprove – of the embarrassing exposure, rather than of the original insult. Her anxiousness to please her mother was mixed up with a fixed idea of a punitive and vengeful God, a Being who had little in common with her parents' mild, conventional strain of Episcopalianism. Where Wharton derived her childhood Puritan ethics – other than from her New England forebears – is hard to say. She liked to refer occasionally to the curse of a Puritan ancestry, as when telling her publisher how 'useless & troublesome a possession a New England conscience is'. But she was, as she described herself in 'Life and I', a 'God-intoxicated' child. She was taught by her parents that it was wrong to tell lies, and she had 'worked out of my inner mind a rigid rule of absolute, unmitigated truth-telling, the least imperceptible deviation from which would inevitably be punished by the dark Power I knew as "God"'. This 'dark Power' was as absolute as the other authority of her childhood. 'For years afterward I was never free from the oppressive sense that I had two absolutely inscrutable beings to please – God and my mother.' But 'God's standard of truthfulness' seemed to her the opposite of her mother's insistence on 'the obligation to be polite'. 'Between these conflicting rules of conduct I suffered an untold anguish of perplexity, and suffered alone.' Ideas of punishment and shame weighed on her mind. One of the last things Wharton talked about, shortly before her death, was her childhood anxiety about 'naughtiness'. It seems that everything this child felt and did led to a dread of disapproval. And she could never be sure what reaction she would get. There was something baffling to her in her mother, 'a mysterious impenetrability, a locked room full of bats and darkness'.[48]

Though small boys and dancing-teachers and governesses are scattered through the memoirs, they are allowed only a passing influence on what is described essentially as a solitary childhood, for all its self-consciousness about society. In the year the family spent in Rome, from 1867 to '68, she made friends with Margaret and Arthur Terry, children of the American painter Luther Terry, who had got to know George Frederic on his 1848 tour. Luther Terry married a talented and impressive woman, Louisa Crawford, widow of the sculptor Thomas Crawford (by whom she had Francis Marion Crawford, who would write popular historical novels). Louisa's sister was Julia Ward Howe, famous for the Battle Hymn of the Republic. Louisa and Luther Terry's daughter, Margaret, known as 'Daisy', remembered Edith, as a child in Rome, with red-gold hair and 'a smart little sealskin coat'. They were the same age, and played together in the gardens of the Monte Pincio, the gardens above the Piazza del Populo, and spent hours at the windows of the Palazzo Odescalchi, where the Terrys were living, looking at the street-life of Rome. But Daisy never thought of 'Pussy Jones' as a real Roman, like her. When they met as teenagers in America they did not make much contact (Daisy retrospectively attributed that to Edith's shyness) but later, in Paris, they became close, lifelong friends. Daisy was a Catholic, and a talented musician. She went to America for the first time at the age of seventeen, with a strong Italian accent, and found it utterly alien. She married her cousin Winthrop Chanler, a sportsman, traveller, and distant relation of the Joneses, a year after Edith's marriage. One of their seven children was a godson of Theodore Roosevelt, and Edith was at the christening. The two women shared a great many friends, including Henry Adams and Minnie Jones, and Daisy Chanler would be a frequent travelling companion in later years.[49]

Wharton passes over that later friendship in her memoir. Daisy is mentioned as part of her vivid, idealised memories of mid-nineteenth-century Rome – the villas, the processions, the Campagna, the Spanish Steps, the fragments of Imperial Rome littering the ground around the Palace of the Caesars, the 'texture of weather-worn sun-gilt stone'. After Rome, on the exciting journey in Spain to the Alhambra and Seville and the Escorial, and in the months spent in Paris and in a spa in the Black Forest, no new friendships are mentioned. The most important figures in her life were her grandmother, her dog Foxy, and the imaginary characters of her own stories. Back in America, there was a playful friendship with the young sons of the distinguished astronomer Lewis Rutherfurd, who was the Joneses' neighbour at Newport. (His son Winthrop would be the lover of Consuelo Vanderbilt, one of Wharton's inspirations for *The Buccaneers*; his daughter Margaret, one of the lovely Newport 'archeresses', would marry Roosevelt's favourite ambassador, Henry White, whom Wharton would come to know well in Paris.) But more important to Edith's life than the Rutherfurd children was their governess. Anna Bahlmann was a young German girl who began, at nineteen, giving Edith Jones German lessons, although she did not think Goethe was suitable reading for her. She gradually became part of the Joneses' household, and then of the Whartons', staying as a companion and secretary till she fell ill in 1915. Of this forty years' service the memoir says nothing.

A *Backward Glance* is silent, too, about one of the most important women in Wharton's life, her sister-in-law, who came into her family when Edith was seven years old. Her brothers figure only distantly in her memoirs: they laugh at her, and they play games at Newport. Harry and his friends were closer to Edith after she 'came out': Teddy Wharton was part of this slightly older group of her brother's friends. Her main connection to her older brother was through his wife. Frederic Jones, who went to Columbia College like his father and set up as a bookbinder in New York, married Mary Cadwalader Rawle, a beautiful, dark, energetic young woman of a 'good' old Philadelphian family, in 1870. Two years later, they had a girl, Beatrix, known as Trix, who would grow up to become, in her own profession, as well known as her aunt. But this was not a happy family. Fred was unfaithful to 'Minnie' (as the family called her), and the breakdown of the marriage, twenty years on, would pull the Jones family apart. But Minnie made herself a life in New York (and at Reef Point in Bar Harbor, in Maine) that survived in spite of, and long after, her wretched marriage. Formidably active, practical and efficient, she threw herself into the cause of reforming New York hospitals. This was more than an upper-class lady playing at good works. Minnie Jones became famous in the city, not just for overseeing every detail of improvements to the City Hospital School of Nursing, but for her longer view of better facilities for the care of hospital patients, and higher status and respect for the nursing profession. In this, as in other aspects of her life, she sounds like Edith. She was a brilliant, forceful young woman confined in an unsuitable marriage and pushing against New York conventions like 'a high-bred, high-strung Arab horse, among an equally well-bred but quite different herd'. A young neighbour in New York remembered her in her red parlour at 21 East 11th Street, 'surrounded by books, magazines, and foreign literary reviews, [studying] the pages of French memoirs, looking up with those quick sympathetic eyes'. That quick sympathy, with her zest for life, her shrewdness about human character, her common sense and her wide interests, made her much sought-after. 'She was a prodigious stimulus to her friends, and what friends she had': among them Henry James, Henry Adams, and Theodore Roosevelt, all of whom Edith would inherit from her.[50]

Minnie Jones, twelve years older than Edith, immediately took to her. When she went to meet her new husband's family in Paris, she encountered 'his little sister . . . a clever child with a mane of red-gold hair, always scribbling stories on any paper that came handy . . . She became closer than a sister of my own blood.'[51] Minnie was the missing older sister, or the better mother. She continued, all her life, to be Edith's collaborator, dogs-body, confidante, correspondent and admirer; in turn, she was the recipient of Edith's support and financial help. In the interests of privacy, Minnie went unmentioned in *A Backward Glance*. Another adolescent female friend is even more dismissively treated. Emelyn Washburn was six years older than Edith, the only daughter of the Rector of Calvary Church, a serious intellectual with a beautiful voice. He was a powerful influence on the teenage Wharton, whose 'religious preoccupations were increasing', mixed up with an adolescent 'passion' for the Reverend Washburn. Emelyn was an intense, literary young woman who shared Edith's passions for Dante and Anglo-Saxon and Goethe. Like her, Emelyn had the run of her father's library, only this was a more advanced collection. They used to sit on the roof of the library and read Dante together. If Edith was half in love with the scholarly, mellifluous Reverend Washburn (the sound of his voice spurring her on to some experiments in writing sermons), then Emelyn was half in love with her. Unforgivingly, Wharton calls Emelyn's affection a mark of 'degeneracy' in her unpublished memoir. In the published version, she does not even name her. A lifetime of responding to Emelyn Washburn's needs, a sad and demanding old lady who had wasted her talents, soured the memory of their childhood friendship. Emelyn was 'a brilliantly educated woman, a remarkable linguist with a really learned mind': Edith had no patience with her for not having done more with her life.[52] But Emelyn provided her with an important stage in her education, and testimony to that fact remained in Edith's library: a copy of Longfellow's translation of Dante's *Divine Comedy*, a gift from E.W.W. to E.N. Jones, and an inscribed copy of Goethe's works, dated May 1876.

Wharton left these women friends out of her autobiography, partly because she preferred not to talk about her personal friendships, but also because she shapes her life-story as one of solitude, self-education, and self-creation. Especially after her typhoid, her parents believed that any formal education which required 'committing to memory and preparing lessons in advance' was too much of a strain for her. So she had 'French, German, music and drawing' (she remembered reading the Bible in German, as a child), but no Greek and Latin, no 'cultured' tutor such as her brothers had, and no training in concentration. She called it 'an intellectual desert'. Emelyn Washburn recalled that 'as a child [Edith] did not know how to study and did nothing thoroughly'.[53] But Emelyn was, in fact, the uncomprehending witness of an extraordinary process of self-development: compulsive, passionate, and determined, Edith made herself, unstoppably, into a reader and as a writer. Daisy Chanler used to say that Edith Wharton and Teddy Roosevelt were both 'self-made men. She was pleased with the saying and repeated it to me.'[54]

But self-creation process was attended by confusion and anxiety. Wharton remembers herself as a troubled child, for all the normal robust pleasure she took in outdoor games and sports, playing with puppies and flirting with little boys. After her typhoid attack, she became nervous, 'haunted by formless horrors' and subject to 'states of chronic fear'. There is much more about this in the unpublished memoir: *A Backward Glance* only tells us about her earliest childhood fears of nursery stories like 'Red Riding Hood' and her 'terror' of ugly places. But 'Life and I' is eloquent about her nervous symptoms: fear of the dark, fear of some nameless menace dogging her footsteps, making it agony for her to wait on the doorstep of her house in case 'It' caught her before she got in, fear of ghost-stories.[55] This lasted well into her twenties: she would be so disturbed if there were ghost-stories in the house with her at night that she had to get rid of them, or burn them. She says nothing in her memoir about how useful such fears were to her for the writing of her own terrifying ghost-stories.

Later, she developed a 'morbid preoccupation' with the suffering of animals, a sense that she was closer to them than she was to human beings. All her life, she would feel it acutely when her beloved dogs fell ill or died. There is a sense of loneliness in all this, constantly underlying the busy network of social relations and obligations. Emelyn describes her as having few friends who were contemporaries, of seeming to veer suddenly between ages ('sometimes she looked like a little, most lovable child – and again she seemed years older'), and of being 'a nervous child, always wanting to do something with her hands'. Wharton looked back on this nervous fidgeting child as having been in a condition of 'complete mental isolation', 'morbid, self-scrutinising and unhappy', alone with her intense passion for words, her secret feelings for nature and animals. Above all, she spent her childhood with a constant 'sense of bewilderment', looking for answers that did not come.[56]

This childhood story is shaped by the memoir-writing novelist as a series of key events, starting points that made her into a writer. She gives us a set of beginnings: the first kiss, the first pet, the first intense arousal of aesthetic responses in Europe, the illness that led to her morbid fears, the first story-telling, the shock of re-entry to America at ten, when everything struck her as mean, squalid and ugly, and her feelings of alienation and exile began. (This experience of 'bitter disappointment' in her native country, which she tells as an intensely personal one, was a very common reaction in Americans returning from long visits to Europe.[57]) In all these key moments, there is a conflict between defining herself as a stranger to her environment, an alien changeling, and as a product of it. And when she started to write, that conflict provoked and energised her.

It took so long for Wharton to become a professional writer – in her late thirties, after years of illness, lack of confidence and marital confinement – that the explosion of juvenile writings has an almost poignant air to it: she looks like a natural unstoppable writer, yet she would be slow to refind that enormous confidence and energy. In her childhood, writing seems to emerge almost imperceptibly from 'making up' and reading: devouring Elizabethan plays and French drama, Ruskin and Anglo-Saxon poetry and German folklore, Goethe, Keats and Shelley, Browning and Tennyson, history and philosophy. Her sensual passion for the sound – and the rhythm – of words was fed by this great range of early reading, by the dramatic effect of the Reverend Washburn's Bible-speaking, and by the voices she heard at the theatre. The vocal, histrionic side of Wharton's early literary life was very important: from the start she had a fabulous ear and a powerful sense of drama.

Like all well-brought-up children Edith was taken regularly to Wallack's theatre on Broadway and 13th Street, as much of an institution as the Academy of Music, where 'everyone' went on the first night to see Lester Wallack's regular stars: the old English actress Madame Ponisi, the young leads Ada Dyas and Henry Montague, the comic actor Harry Beckett. Wharton saw them often, and gave them a scene for Newland Archer to watch, with tears in his eyes, in *The Age of Innocence*: the silent parting of the lovers in Dion Boucicault's *The Shaughraun*, which ran at Wallack's from 1874 to '75, and which she saw at the age of thirteen, with her parents. (Minnie Jones, who often acted as Edith's fact-checker, reminded her of these dates, and remembered the production well.[58]) There were visiting

English and European companies, too. The English actor George Rignold had a great triumph as Henry V at Booth's Theatre, two seasons running, in 1875 and '76. And she vividly remembered a German company giving Goethe's *Iphigenie auf Tauris* (a copy of which Emelyn gave to Edith in 1876). She was allowed to go to Barnum's famous three-ring circus, too, but the adult theatre was as exciting to her as any circus or pantomime. The excitement was above all the sound of the words. But it was also the sense of Europe: the sound of English blank verse, the German styles of acting.

At the age of about ten, after the return to the States, she started to pour out blank verse dramas, sermons, lyric poems and stories, begging for the brown wrapping paper that parcels came in, spreading them out on the floor and writing all over them in 'long parallel columns'.[59] This wrapping-paper story suggests that the activity was not given much status or approval by her parents. But, in fact, they seem to have taken a proud interest early on, and 'E.N.J.' gets into print with these juvenile writings remarkably quickly. At thirteen or fourteen, her works were being passed round family and friends: a solemn elegy on the death of a child, an Easter carol, a jokey ballad about a thwarted Spanish knight ('Don Luis Havapayne') who dies of 'baffled love' and of eating sugared plums. Her first published work was a translation from a German poet, Heinrich Brugsch, done with the assistance of (and published, in a new 'Saturday' magazine, under the name of) the Reverend Washburn, for which she got her first fifty dollars.[60]

She had written enough by the age of sixteen for one of her parents to have a volume of *Verses* privately printed at Newport late in 1878. Emelyn Washburn remembered this as done by her father. In her memoir, Wharton gives her mother the credit; but on her death-bed, she said it was her father's doing. She wrote in her copy: 'Who wrote these verses and this volume owns / Her unpoetic name is Edith Jones.'[61] Wharton would look back on these verses as completely unoriginal. 'Daisies', for example, confirms this judgement ('Daisies, does he love me? / Daisies, tell me true! – / Loves me ... does not love me ... / This will never do!'). The only one she liked was 'Opportunity', which bleakly tells how opportunity comes unnoticed and unknown, walking beside us in 'the narrow present'. And even at this stage, her life's theme of the missed chance is found in 'Some Woman to Some Man' (which should have been printed 'with acknowledgements to Browning and Meredith'):

> We might have loved each other after all,
> Have lived and learned together! Yet I doubt it;

> ... Who knows indeed? We choose our path, and then
> Stand looking back, and sighing at our choice ...
> ... We've but one life to live, and fifty ways
> To live it in, – and little time to choose,
> The one in fifty that will suit us best, –
> And so, the end is, that we part, and say,
> 'We might have loved each other after all!'

Two years later, her brother Harry negotiated the publication of a few more poems, via an editor he knew, who sent them to Longfellow, who was kind about them and passed them on to William Dean Howells, who published them in the *Atlantic Monthly* in 1880. These were highly respectable literary connections for an eighteen-year-old poet to have made, and there was some pride in seeing 'Areopagus', 'Patience', 'Wants', 'The Parting Day' and 'A Failure' among the serialisation of a Howells novel, *The Undiscovered Country*, stories and poems by lady writers such as Lucy Lee Pleasant and Louise Chandler Moulton, and essays on 'Literary and Philological Mammals' and 'Prisons and Penitentiaries'. Edith Jones's poems were about failed love, the endurance of loss, and the necessity of obedience to higher laws (forged by nature, not God). Like many teenage poems, they were extremely gloomy: one poem on women's desires begins with a call for happiness, love and friendship; when all these fail, women ask for 'duty, work to do / Some end to gain beyond the pale of self, some height to journey to', and, at the very end, all they ask for is 'rest'.

The most interesting – and morbid – of these early works came out under a pseudonym in a magazine called the *New York World* in 1879. In 'Life and I', she laughs at herself for having been so anxious about correct prosody that she sent a note to the editor saying that the uneven rhythm of the poem was intentional: an early example of Wharton's letting her publishers know her mind. She makes less of the poem's subject, written in response to a newspaper account of a twelve-year-old boy in a Philadelphia reformatory who was put in solitary confinement, and killed himself. The poem imagines the child's loneliness and vulnerability and the vanishing of 'his mother's face', criticises extreme punishment meted out for 'some little childish sin', and ends with a stern Blakean note of reprimand ('In a Christian town it happened / In a home for children built') and a dutiful hope that God will have room for all unwanted children.[62]

But Edith Jones's writing was not all so dark. Her farcical pastiche of 1871, 'Ye Romantic Ballad of ye Portuguese Plums, the fruit of that forbidden tree', set the jaunty tone for her first (surviving) fiction, a novel called *Fast and Loose*, written for Emelyn between 1876 and 1877. This highly literary concoction, under the pen-name of the continental-sounding male author 'David Olivieri', bursting at the seams with quotations and allusions and veering cheerfully between every imaginable genre – comedy of manners, pathetic tragedy, high romance, social satire – is a sad story of a coquettish eighteen-year-old English girl Georgina, who forsakes her poor young lover Guy for the rich, lascivious, elderly Lord Breton, and pays the price. She ends up not only with a wretched marriage (there's a nice cruel scene where she refuses to play chess with the old man) and the hollow 'social whirl' that surrounds 'those who are haunted by a life's mistake', but also a tragic death-bed scene of reunion and forgiveness, in Nice, milked for ultimate pathos in a chapter called 'Too Late': 'The clock ticked steadily; the afternoon sunshine waned, & the sand in an hour-glass trickled its last grains through to mark the ended hour.' The rejected lover finds an angelic helpmate called Madeline (blonde, loves flowers, encourages his painting). Their courtship, staged in an idyllic Roman spring, is contrasted with the artificial hot-house atmosphere surrounding Lady Breton. There is a promising but undeveloped side-plot of a picturesque Italian model. Though Guy marries Madeline, 'his heart is under the violets on Georgie's grave'.[63]

Fast and Loose moves along with great gusto, enjoying its own literariness, and, above all, its display of European travels and English culture. The Roman scenes are particularly heartfelt. The most interesting part of it is a batch of fake notices which Edith Jones added on to the end of the novel, from the *Saturday Review*, the *Pall Mall Gazette*, and the *Nation*, which reproach David Olivieri for sentimentalism and 'unaesthetic morality'. His readers expected 'racy trash', only to find a weak, spiritless narrative of dull, virtuous nonentities: for all the world like the work of 'a sick-sentimental school-girl'.[64] There is a sharp, knowing professionalism in her invention of these pastiche reviews. And making self-censorship into her main literary crime was very shrewd of her. Edith Jones was already aware that 'making up' must involve cutting free. Like the title of her first novel, she is both 'fast and loose', held in her world and a watchful stranger to it. She will always be dealing with – and drawing her energies from – that tension.

3
Pussy Jones

The story of a natural writer, energetically reading and writing herself into independent adulthood, now takes another turn. *Fast and Loose* was finished when Edith Jones was fifteen; *Verses* was printed when she was sixteen; 'Only a Child' came out the following year; the five poems in the *Atlantic Monthly* when she was eighteen. And then something happened. It would be nine years before a few more poems appeared, between 1889 and 1891, in *Scribner's Magazine*. She would publish her first story there, 'Mrs Manstey's View', when she was twenty-nine. It was another seven years before her first book publication, and eight years before her first volume of stories, marking the true beginning, at the age of thirty-seven, of her thereafter unstoppable professional career. The huge creativity of this exceptional young girl was somehow halted; it took 'Pussy' Jones a painfully long time to turn into the writer Edith Wharton.

Women writers were often held up like this, especially in the nineteenth and early twentieth centuries. They had years of domestic business to live through, or serious obstacles and pressures, internal and external, before they could see their way clear. (George Eliot, Willa Cather, and Virginia Woolf are three obvious examples.) Wharton's early story is part of a larger plot in the way it reflected her society's expectations for women of a certain class and type – expectations which would be one of her main subjects. As with many such delayed careers, the period of obstruction is the one that yields the richest materials, to which the writer returns in work after work. It is the fallow periods, Elizabeth Bowen quotes Proust as saying, 'that most often fructify into art'.[1] It was, eventually, greatly to Wharton's benefit that she had to perform, for years, not as a young writer, but as a young debutante, socialite, and wife, in a period of dramatic social change. Whatever her private frustrations, she missed nothing of what was going on around her, and would use everything.

*

Though Wharton describes the society of her youth as demure and provincial, it was in upheaval. Her greatest books would pinpoint the moment at which the complacent habits of a small group are destabilised by the action of larger forces. Wharton's version of the dramatic economic developments of the 'Gilded Age' was a personal and local one. She came at it through the lives of individuals, especially women, in the social group she knew. She was not an American realist like Upton Sinclair or Frank Norris. She did not 'do', head-on and large-scale, the building of the great monopolies in oil, steel, and meat-packing, the mighty expansion of the railroads, the settlement of the West, the great surge in technological inventions (the telephone, the car, the electric light), the expansion of the communications industry, the massive increases in post-war industrial productivity between 1870 and 1910, the more than doubling of the population, the gathering waves of immigration, the phenomenal rise in incomes at the top (and the savage decline at the bottom), the titanic power of the bankers and financiers, the huge building programmes in the cities.[2] Nor, like the social historians and 'naturalists' of her time, William Dean Howells or Robert Grant, Sinclair Lewis or Theodore Dreiser, did she turn her characters into case studies of these social conditions. But the hard facts of post-war economics are there in her books, pressing in on and changing the lives of her wealthy, insulated East Coast society. In her novels of the American bourgeoisie between the 1870s and the 1900s, whatever the vantage point – the figure alienated from his time and looking back at it over thirty years; the new arrival taking a closed world by storm; the woman who, ring-fenced inside her society, clings on and slips down inside it – the dense texture of habits and customs always seems solid and entrenched, and at the same time fluctuating and threatened.

This treatment of a shifting society is partly fuelled by nostalgia. Like many of her generation, especially those alienated from America, Wharton was an astounded observer of the disappearance of the social organisation which in her youth had looked so permanent. (The most eloquent, dismayed version of this is Henry James's *The American Scene*, in 1907.) But she did not just want to resurrect a vanished past in her writing. There is also a powerful need to understand what was happening to her country, and, by implication, to make sense of her own history. None of those great novels, *The Age of Innocence, The Custom of the Country, The House of Mirth*, is autobiographical. But all dramatise a struggle against confinement and reach toward – not always successfully – the possibility of tearing down barriers. *Tearing down*, or *tearing up*, was one of the key phrases for the period those novels describe. (James had a futuristic passage in 1907 on how 'tearing down' could turn into 'tearing up' if the fashion for skyscrapers became a fashion 'for building from the earth's surface downwards'; Wharton's expatriate friend Matilda Gay, reluctantly returning to New York in 1908, remarked that 'the perpetual tearing up of the city, and the noise and the smoke, now that the omnibuses have been replaced by autobuses, is enough to drive one mad'.[3]) Wharton's first published story, 'Mrs Manstey's View', of 1891, is about the beginnings of the tearing-down and building-up of old New York. With the building of the rapid transit system, the laying-out of Central Park (completed in 1876), the replacement of gas with electricity in the 1880s, the perpetual push of fashion and wealth uptown, and the building of the lavish urban palaces for the great fortunes of the time, the layout of the city – and the rules regulating its social movements – were in dramatic flux. The city's population doubled between 1850 and 1880; by 1890 it was one and a half million (as opposed to 500,000 in 1850). Wharton's twenties saw the period of sustained prosperity, between 1880 and 1893, when America (as in one often-quoted comment of 1883) was 'just beginning to be astonishing . . . It has begun to reinvent everything, and especially the house.'[4]

W.H. Vanderbilt spent $2 million of the $90 million he had inherited from his father on his New York 'palace'; his son George Washington Vanderbilt spent 3 million on Biltmore, his gargantuan French chateau in 150,000 acres of North Carolina. (Henry James described it to Edith Wharton as a 'strange, colossal, heart-breaking house', surrounded by what he called 'a vast niggery wilderness' – making it sound like the inspiration for Scott Fitzgerald's 'A Diamond as Big as the Ritz'. Wharton, however, rather enjoyed it, especially the gardens designed by Frederick Law Olmsted.) J.P. Morgan spent lavishly on a life-style to go with his new houses at 219 Madison Avenue in New York and on the Hudson: not only on collecting books, pictures, art objects and furniture, but on entertaining, philanthropic bequests, and luxuries:

> He had a saddle of Newport lamb delivered to 219 twice a week by a Rhode Island butcher, cases of whiskey sent up from Kentucky, and bottles of brandied fruit and tins of cream biscuits awaiting him at the White Star dock every time he sailed. His suits were custom-tailored in London . . . One afternoon in the eighties, he spent 275,000 Francs ($55,000) on jewelry at Tiffany's.[5]

The prosperity of the 1880s and 1890s also created large numbers of second order millionaires, whose fortunes ranged from $5 million to $15 million. The money was being made from railroads, steel, clothing, cloth mills, oil, meat packing, banking, real estate, publishing, and law. And it was being spent so as to show, in a great burst of competitively conspicuous consumption. But this vast display was also accompanied by a debate about the responsibilities of money. By the 1880s, American fascination with the ostentation of the post-war big spenders was beginning to turn sour, and a campaign of criticism and attacks on 'the Trusts' for rapaciousness and exploitation began in the muck-raking journals. Much was made of philanthropic and civic objectives in the spending of great wealth. (The relationship between capitalism and philanthropy was one of the subjects of Wharton's third long novel, *The Fruit of the Tree*.) First in the building and decorating of the private house, and then in the constructing of public institutions like the Metropolitan Museum of Art, the American Museum of Natural History, and 'universities, schools, galleries, libraries, orchestras and opera houses', the new rich were changing the face of the city, as the old had never thought to do. The leisure class who, like Wharton's parents, did nothing but 'hunting, sailing, traveling, drinking, racing horses and yachts' were being displaced by entrepreneurs with no pedigrees, but with the means and vision for an 'American Renaissance' of commerce and culture. 'Wealthy New Yorkers set out in expansive, nationalist mood to turn their metropolis into one of the cultural capitals of the world.' Certainly they were driven by a spirit of competitiveness; the urban palaces of the '80s and '90s were built to exhibit the owner's wealth and the fruits of his world travels. Such exhibitionism would be analysed and satirised in Thorstein Veblen's *Theory of the Leisure Class* and in the novels of Edith Wharton. Her claim, in a letter about *The House of Mirth*, that she was presenting a group which had 'fewer responsibilities attach[ed] to money than in any other societies', was to be echoed by critics of the unbridled spending and grotesque self-indulgence of the *fin-de-siècle* American leisure class, who accuse that society of being 'basically flawed in that it had no real relation to society in the larger sense of the word'. But the millionaires – or some of them – were also aware of their duties as civic benefactors. They contributed to a great upsurge in the decorative arts, seeing it as their role to enrich the city with the best possible demonstrations of American architecture and design. 'After 1880, fine architecture became a public responsibility of the rich.' In 1884, an article in the *American Architecture and Building News* said: 'A man's house, which used to be his castle, is now his museum.'[6]

In *The House of Mirth*, Wharton has her man about town, Ned Van Alstyne, give us a guided tour of the new buildings on Fifth Avenue, 'that versatile thoroughfare':

'That Greiner house, now – a typical rung in the social ladder! The man who built it came from a *milieu* where all the dishes are put on the table at once. His façade is a complete architectural meal; if he had omitted a style his friends might have thought the money had given out. Not a bad purchase for Rosedale, though: attracts attention, and awes the Western sight-seer . . .'

'And the Wellington Brys'? Rather clever of its kind, don't you think?'

. . . 'That's the next stage: the desire to imply that one has been to Europe, and has a standard. I'm sure Mrs Bry thinks her house a copy of the *Trianon*; in America every marble house with gilt furniture is thought to be a copy of the *Trianon*. What a clever chap that architect is, though – how he takes his client's measure! He has put the whole of Mrs Bry in his use of the composite order. Now for the Trenors, you remember, he chose the Corinthian: exuberant, but based on the best precedent. The Trenor house is one of his best things – doesn't look like a banqueting-hall turned inside out.'[7]

This knowing guide pins down the competitiveness, the crude mixing of architectural styles, the awed imitation of European models and the rapid turnover of fashion, that had characterised wealthy New York for about twenty years. William H. Vanderbilt's 'Triple Palace' was 'a great hodge-podge of styles'; Alexander and Cornelia Stewarts' gigantic 1869 'Marble House' on Fifth Avenue and 34th Street was a mixture of French, Greek and Renaissance, with fifty-five rooms of 'stupendous opulence', wall-to-wall Carrara marble, and a picture gallery. Inside these vast mansions there were acres of parquetry and marble floors, wood carvings in mahogany or walnut or stained-oak, brass, sconces and chandeliers, plush and velvet hangings, bric-à-brac from all over the world.[8]

The architectural competition on Fifth Avenue was echoed in the summer houses of the New York millionaires in Newport, Rhode Island. Just as the quiet brownstone landscape of Wharton's childhood was over-taken by the building boom of the '80s, so the rural seaside retreat she remembered from the 1860s was transformed into a bristling array of 'Gilded Age' 'cottages', vying with each other for prominence along Bellevue Avenue. 'The Breakers', Cornelius Vanderbilt II's four-storey Italianate palace, with seventy rooms, finished in 1895 at a cost of 200 million dollars, had a music room shipped from Paris, and a two-storey-high dining room, every inch of it bloated with chandeliers and gilding and shafts of red marble and velvet hangings. Upstairs, the bedrooms were designed in an elegant neo-classical style by Edith's friend Ogden Codman. 'The Elms', built between

1899 and 1901, was a massive pale-brown imitation eighteenth-century French chateau with grandiose marble staircases, an indoor winter garden, a Louis XV ballroom, a Venetian dining room and a 'chinoiserie' breakfast room, and, outside, great flights of steps and vast formal gardens dotted with fountains, urns, and mighty statues of the labours of Hercules. William K. Vanderbilt's Newport 'Marble House', built in 1892, was based on the Petit Trianon, with a marble-and-gold ballroom and bronze sculptures, a gothic hall, and a rose-marble dining room. In 1883, the amazing Alva Vanderbilt, wife of William K., gave a ball for five hundred there at which her daughter Consuelo became (extremely unhappily) engaged to the Duke of Marlborough. There were footmen in Louis XIV dress, hummingbirds and butterflies around the floral fountain in the hall, three orchestras, four hundred birds served at one dinner course, and other conspicuous trifles. A vast array of service and transportation industries catered for this summer colony: steamships from Manhattan to Fall River, coach-makers, couture shops on Bellevue Avenue, local employment agencies for staff. All the pastimes of the rich – golf and yacht clubs, the reading room and the casino, steeple-chasing, tennis, polo, the coaching parade, the automobile races – created a community dependent for its economy on the summer visitors.[9]

Henry James, musing on old and new America in *The American Scene*, invoked the vanished sweetness of the 'pure' Newport time, of unspoilt little 'lonely, sandy coves' and 'shallow Arcadian summer-haunted valleys'. He looked aghast at the evidence of national 'waste' in the rows of gigantic palaces and 'densely arranged villas', 'monuments of pecuniary power' – beginning, at the turn of the century, to turn into 'white elephants'. That repining tone is echoed by Mrs Van Rensselaer, who speaks of Newport as 'the summer capital of American society', but one whose 'charm and tranquillity' have been replaced by 'tinsel and plaster'. But Wharton is more sardonic about the ghosts of the vanished past. 'Old' Newport, as portrayed in *The Age of Innocence*, is picturesque and simple, done in bright clear lines ('The small bright lawn stretched away smoothly to the big bright sea'), but it is not romanticised. Its holiday pursuits have the air, to the alienated spectator, of 'children playing in a graveyard', and the habits of its regular inhabitants seem 'a chain of tyrannical trifles binding one hour to the next'. All her Newport stories and scenes have to do with social jostling, like 'The Introducers' (1905), in which a couple who work as social mentors to incomers with vast fortunes but no savoir-faire, make a satirical commentary on the snobbery and aspirations they are profiting from: 'Oh, the usual things – reminding Mrs Bixby not to speak of her husband as *Mr Bixby*, not to send in her cards when people are at home, not to let the butler say "fine claret" in a sticky whisper in people's ears, not to speak of town as "the city", and not to let Mr Bixby tell what things cost.'[10]

The social shifts that were happening throughout Wharton's twenties were still going on when she started to write about them in her late thirties, at the turn of the century. With a sharp-eyed glee, she unpicks them all for us: the dinners and the clubs, the balls and the outings, the country weekends, the hotels and the streets, the calls and the drives. But this material is never presented merely descriptively; it is always under analysis. How does a rich New Yorker behave on a weekend in a large country house? Who gets invited, who sits next to whom, who goes to church, who plays bridge? How would a weekend on the Hudson differ from one in Newport or on Long Island? When did lawn tennis supersede archery as the fashionable Newport sport? Which other resorts rivalled Newport for summer destinations – Bar Harbor in Maine, camping in the Adirondacks, Saratoga for the races, a 'cottage' in Lenox, the elite suburban enclave of Tuxedo Park just north of Manhattan?[11] Why would no one except an eccentric dream of giving a party in Newport on Cup Race Day? Why did every house on Fifth Avenue get an airing and a cleaning on 15 October? Which clubs and sports – like polo – were right for a gentleman? Where did 'everyone' go on the Riviera? When did it stop being fashionable to patronise the Horse Show? What were the right pictures to collect and when? What were you supposed to serve at dinner, what were the guests supposed to talk about, and when did they leave? How should a young hostess furnish her drawing room in 1870 – in 1880 – in 1890? These are a few of the questions about 'the great social machine'[12] which Wharton's fictions ask and answer, tracing fashions and customs minutely over a thirty-year period. If you were a time-traveller, you could use her books as an unerring etiquette manual, and you would not go wrong.

This paraphernalia of social customs is always seen as under threat or in transition. What Wharton observed, and what she grew up inside, was a highly regulated society fighting a rearguard action against changes which it was, at the same time, assimilating. The more threatened the old upper class was by the influx of new money and new names in the 1880s and 1890s, the more it tried to protect and perpetuate itself through strict, formulaic codes of the acceptable: codes based on a whole cluster of unexamined assumptions about how money is made, who should have it, and how it should be spent. (Mrs Astor, on the first marriage of William H. Vanderbilt's daughter Emily, to the rug-maker William Douglas Sloane, is supposed to have said: 'Just because we walk on their carpets doesn't mean we must dine at their tables.') But within those rigid, snobbish structures, a good deal of accommodation was in fact going on to the infiltration of 'new money', so the society was at once giving an appearance of 'highly ritualised' 'rigidity and exclusivity', and was gradually giving way to inevitable changes.[13] The social guardians or mentors, who are frequent characters in Wharton's fiction, are always destroyed by what they have trained or let in. They are bound to be displaced, in the continuous process of 'tearing up' that is Wharton's subject.

The ritual structure of social custom, which enclosed her in her youth, is marked in every move her characters make (as in the first paragraph of *The House of Mirth*, where for Lily Bart to be at Grand Central Station on a Monday in September with nowhere to go is at once noted as unusual and ambiguous). That formalism intensifies as the rules are challenged. A close study of the Newport summer season notes that 'by the mid-1890s social life in Newport had become so formal that its original attractions as a watering place where one could relax ... had been marred ... by the expectations of society hostesses'.[14] Yet although other resorts came into favour, in Newport, as in all the other centres for the leisure classes, regimented patterns of behaviour were maintained for a long time against deviations and challenges.

'Leisure' was a supervised, timetabled, and self-conscious process. If you did not go to Newport or Bar Harbor for the summer or Florida in the winter, you went abroad: to Europe. Grace Wilson, who married Cornelius Vanderbilt, might spend April in Paris for the shopping, take a Mediterranean cruise, visit Bad Nauheim for the 'cure', go to London for the season in June, then grouse shooting in Scotland, a short stay at Deauville, Paris in the early autumn for the couturiers, and back to New York for the winter season. New Yorkers 'moved like migratory birds, in flocks and at certain times of the year'. In the city, 'the annual social calendar developed over the years into a finely detailed schedule of events'. Every day had its regimented rituals: Wall Street or the clubs for the men; shopping, luncheons, teas, 'calls' and card-leaving (a time-consuming and elaborate system, not immediately displaced by the invention of the telephone in the 1890s) for the women. The evenings were for private dinners, dances, opera and theatre. But by the 1880s and 1890s all this was beginning to change, as public dining in restaurants and hotels increasingly became the fashion, and anxieties about publicity, display, and vulgarity took hold.[15]

Who set these standards and drew up these timetables? American metropolitan high society has always been fixated on social leaders, their power, their rise and fall. Elaine Showalter compares the billionaire western incomer Elmer Moffatt, in *The Custom of the Country*, to Donald Trump. But the social rules were set by women, by the 'old' New York hostesses, who had, for a time, extraordinary powers of veto. They were the self-created aristocrats of the metropolis, in imitation of a European court or a Roman dynasty. Mrs Astor and Mrs Hamilton Fish were two of the rulers of their world, even though they came eventually to stand for 'dull respectability'. The annual Astor ball, in January, held in Mrs Astor's gigantic ballroom, was always said to be the 'climax' of the season. Her dinners in town, her picnics and pageants in Newport, were the invitations everyone wanted. With her right-hand man and *cavaliere servante*, the snobbish Ward McAllister, she set up a screening system to keep the right people in and the wrong ones – new money, tradesmen, Jews, divorcees and the like – out. Ward McAllister, 'that incredible fop', helped her set up the 'Patriarchs', from 1872 onwards, as custodians of invitations to the subscription balls, held every year in Delmonico's or the racier Sherry's, or the Waldorf Astoria. (The 'Ladies Assemblies' were a similar organisation, 'presided over by a committee of ladies'. Wharton has her incomers in *The Buccaneers* mortified by their exclusion from the Assembly Ball, the nearest thing to 'being invited to the Court in England', and resorting to outrageous strategies in order to get in.) The Patriarchs, wrote Mrs Van Rensselaer, fondly, were trying 'to keep birth and lineage as the primary requisites for social distinction'; but such attempts were 'destined to fail'.[16]

Ward McAllister, besotted with the idea of belonging to and preserving the 'crème-de-la-crème of New York society', laid down the law in his smug memoirs on every detail of fashionable social life, from how to give a successful cotillion dinner, a private ball at Delmonico's, a fancy-dress dance or a Newport picnic, to the keeping-out of 'objectionable elements', the honouring of dinner invitations ('once accepted ... a sacred obligation'), and the 'proper way of introducing a young girl into New York society': 'You can launch them into the social sea, but can they float?'[17] The decorator Elsie de Wolfe remembered in her debutante years in the 1880s how Ward McAllister was the monitor of the carefully guarded gates of society, and 'blue-pencilled the list of eligibles'.

Ward McAllister's list of 'the Four Hundred' was not the only document of the time intended to 'establish the border separating the aristocrat from the parvenu'. The New York Social Register, produced by the 'Social Register Association', first appeared in 1887, containing the full names and address of members of prominent families grouped together, and the marriage, death and European arrival and departure of each person as it may occur. The name of Married Maidens who have married into families of other cities appear among the Married Maidens of their former city with their present married name and the city of their residence in italics.

Fewer than two thousand families were deemed fit to have their details included. This was the American upper class's attempt to define itself just at the point when the definitions were coming undone.[18]

The listings also give, in shorthand, the person's graduating class, college, and club, among these pre-eminently K for Knickerbocker; also Daughters of the American Revolution, Turf and Field, Yale and Harvard Graduates, the Racquet, the Union, the Downtown, and, eventually, the Automobile Association of America. Families resident abroad are listed under 'Dilatory Domiciles'. In 1893, for example, among the Aldriches and Auchinclosses, the Belmonts and Bigelows, the Coolidges and Calhouns and Cuttings, the Danas, the Fields, the Fishes and Griswolds, the Hamiltons and Harrimans, the Jameses and Jewetts, the Loomises and Macys and Peabodys, the Scribners and Sedgwicks, the Tylers and Vanderbilts and Washburns and the hundreds of Vans (Cortlandt, Rensselaer, Winckle, Wyck), are listed a good many Joneses (Mr and Mrs Frederic Jones at 21 East 11th, Mrs George Frederic Jones at 28 West 25th), and 'Mr and Mrs Edward R. Wharton (Edith Jones): Knickerbocker, Racquet, Harvard '73'. In 1903, Mr and Mrs Edward Wharton are 'abroad', as are Mrs Cadwalader Jones (Mary C. Rawle) and Miss Beatrix Cadwalader: 'abroad Lusi. [i.e. the *Lusitania*] July 16th'. In 1914, the year after her divorce, 'Edith Jones (Mrs Edward Wharton)' still appears under Married Maidens; in 1915, Mr and Mrs Edward Wharton are still listed as a couple. Only in 1919, six years after she finally left America, is Mrs Edward Wharton listed on her own, under Dilatory Domiciles, at 53 Rue de Varenne, and Edward Wharton and his sister Nancy are listed under 58 East 72nd Street. So tenacious was the grip of the system she grew up in, so slow and indirect in its acknowledgement of divorce, so loath to give up on its Married Maidens.

But though this record tried to give an air of permanence to New York elite society, the very existence of the register betrayed anxieties about contamination, anxieties played out on a grand scale over the question of invitations. Every book on New York society rehearses the famous story of the social stratagem Alva Vanderbilt played on Mrs Astor (a story of social rivalry much played up by the press, by now the arbiters of New York social life). When invitations went out for her great costume ball of 26 March 1883, to mark the opening of William K. Vanderbilt's chateau on 52nd Street, Mrs Astor's daughter very much wanted to go. Mrs Vanderbilt let it be known that she could not invite Miss Astor unless Mrs Astor would acknowledge her existence; and so the call was made. The Vanderbilt ball was indeed very grand, but it sounds modest compared with the most famous, or infamous, ball of the next decade, the Bradley Martin costume ball at the Waldorf Astoria hotel in February 1897. The Bradley Martins (just like the Wellington Blys in *The House of Mirth*) had pressed in on New York society by giving ever more ostentatious parties. Now, at a time of national depression, they transformed the Waldorf Astoria ballroom into the Palace of Versailles and invited their guests to wear Louis XV costumes. (Still, one came as Pocahontas, another as an Algonquin chief.) Mrs Bradley Martin, wearing Marie Antoinette's ruby necklace, sat on a throne to receive her seven hundred guests. The financier August Belmont arrived in a suit of gold-inlaid armour valued at $10,000; the reputed cost of the evening's entertainment was $369,000. The affair was thoroughly execrated in the national press, and shortly thereafter the Bradley Martins went to live in England.[19]

But by the time of that ball, the regime of the Patriarchs and the Assemblies had been overthrown. Ward McAllister had become 'quaint and outmoded' and died in 1895. Mrs Astor was thought dull and old-fashioned and was soon to sink into senility. A different kind of party had become popular, the sort given by Mrs Stuyvesant Fish, with private theatricals, chorus girls, a jazz-band and mocking take-offs of the first families and – worst of all – 'intellectuals'. By 1890, Louis Auchincloss says, 'society had had its fill of playing the stately game of Windsor Castle with Mrs Astor as Queen Victoria; it was ready for Harry Lehr and Mamie Fish and parties with elephants and chimpanzees'. The press said that Mrs Fish and her camp major-domo, Harry Lehr (who had defected from Mrs Astor's service), 'held up American society to ridicule'. But 'American society' was no longer definable.[20]

The battles for social dominance also took place in the cultural realm. *The Age of Innocence*, set in the early 1870s, anticipates the supplanting of the old Academy of Music, founded in 1854, with its eighteen carefully guarded boxes for the 'aristocracy', by the new Metropolitan Opera House on 39th Street, with its three tiers of thirty-six boxes each, funded by the powerful new rich (including Morgan, the Vanderbilts, Jay Gould, William Rockefeller, William Whitney, and the Californian millionaires, Mills and Huntington). Two years after the Metropolitan opened in 1883, the Academy closed its doors.[21]

New money was pouring into such great new projects, like the Metropolitan Museum of Art (also used as a setting in *The Age of Innocence*) and the New York Public Library. Yet, at the same time, there was a strong will to maintain the gentility of 'brownstone culture',[22] of the elite institutions like the highly conservative Century Association, the Astor Library (established through John Jacob Astor's legacy in the 1850s), the Union League Club, and the New York Historical Society. And similar battles would be fought, as Edith Wharton became a professional writer, between genteel realist writers and hard-hitting 'naturalists', between middlebrow and popular magazines, between high art and best-sellers.

What was at the heart of the resistance to social change? Snobbery, self-interest, conservatism, fear of the alien, complacency, and lack of imagination, all played their part. Racial and sexual protectionism was deeply ingrained in the resistance to the new. The rising rate of divorce was one of the press's (and Wharton's) hottest subjects. The ambivalent relation of Jewish financiers to the establishment can be seen in the contrast between a short-lived 'American Society for the Suppression of the Jews' in the 1870s, demanding that they be 'excluded from all first class society', and the meteoric rise of the millionaire Jewish financier August Belmont. (Wharton made good use of this in the characters of Simon Rosedale in *The House of Mirth* and Julius Beaufort in *The Age of Innocence*.) Mixed with anxieties about sexual and racial purity was a new dismay at the idea of life lived in the 'glare' (a much-used word) of publicity.[23] Polite notes in the Social Register and society pages on who was abroad, who was getting married, and who was giving a dinner, shifted, in the course of the 1880s, to lavish coverage in magazines such as *Town Topics* of private affairs, divorces and scandals. The presence of crowds and reporters at society weddings and gala opera nights, the fashion for dining out in restaurants and living in big hotels, the opening of tea-rooms, gave rise to a debate in the 1890s about the 'right to privacy' which went into much of Wharton's work, especially *The Custom of the Country*.

Most of Wharton's class and type looked back with melancholy nostalgia on the old ways. But Wharton herself would write, with unquenchable fascination, not simply about the lost past or the torn-up city or the dispossessed elite, but about the jostle of social forces. Her New York novels are all shaped by plots of social ostracism and infiltrations. Julius Beaufort's rapacious moves onto 1870s New York in *The Age of Innocence*; the rise of the Wellington Brys, the Gormers and Simon Rosedale in *The House of Mirth*; Undine Spragg's conquest of old New York and her buccaneering partnership with Elmer Moffatt, in *The Custom of the Country*: these are only the most dramatic examples. Although the shrinking dismay of 'old New York' is vividly reimagined in these novels, Wharton is not on the side of the establishment she comes from. Like her governess-heroine in *The Buccaneers*, 'she felt that she had cast in her lot once for all with the usurpers and the adventurers ... her sympathies were with the social as well as the political outcasts'.[24]

These social wars acutely affected Edith Jones at her point of entry into adult sexual life. The year she published her poem about a child who commits suicide in prison, 1879, was also the year she 'came out'. This happened a year earlier than was customary, when she was seventeen, perhaps because of her father's now severe ill-health, and because her parents were worried about her becoming too shy and intellectual – and therefore unmarriageable. It was not an extravagant coming-out. Most girls in the late 1870s had a reception at home for their coming-out, or their parents hired the ballroom of Delmonico's fashionable restaurant (on 26th Street between Fifth and Madison, where it had recently, in 1876, moved up from its old home on Fifth Avenue and 14th Street. Stuffy old New Yorkers would still be talking about the 'uptown' Delmonico's, well into the next century.) But Edith Jones was taken to a dance at 85 Fifth Avenue, given by a wealthy hostess, Anna Morton, second wife of the financier and congressman Levi P. Morton, a close associate of J.P. Morgan. This would have been in December, the 'right' month for debutantes to come out. She bared her shoulders and put her hair up for the first time, wore a pale green brocade dress with a white muslin skirt and carried a bouquet of lilies of the valley – and suffered 'an agony of shyness', mitigated only by dancing with a much older friend of the family (a pointer towards her marriage six years later). After that, her social calendar would involve the highly select Assembly Balls, with quadrilles and square dances and cotillions and 'succulent' suppers, outings to the Academy of Music, and the strictly followed daily social rounds. She was still reading avidly in any time she had to herself. But from the end of 1879, as she records bleakly in 'Life and I', her literary activity was 'checked'.[25]

Her social life in the early 1880s, in Newport and New York, was structured by her family, particularly by her younger brother Harry. When Edith was twelve, his fiancée was drowned on a transatlantic crossing, along with a sister and a niece of Lucretia's. But he had now surrounded himself with a jolly tennis-playing, bathing, yachting, lunching, dancing, flirting crowd. All this could be good fun for her. Harry was well disposed to his younger sister. He had already helped her to get her poems published; now he brought her into a coterie mostly of young marrieds, who took her up because of her brother's popularity. Only decades later, when she came to write *The Children*, about a mature man's attraction to a young girl, did she realise that among these friends of her brother's, 'men 15 or 20 years older than I was', there might have been some who were sexually attracted to a girl in her late teens. This girl was now on the marriage market, and this was the group from which her husband would be drawn; he had been an acquaintance of the Joneses since she was eleven. Frederic and Minnie Jones, too, were established at Pencraig Cottage in Newport, across the road from their mother's family house, with 'Trix', their only child, born in 1872. Edith's intimacy with Minnie must have taken root now, though she does not mention this in her memoir, nor another Newport connection, Matilda Travers. The strong-willed and sharp-minded Matilda, seven years older than Edith, who married the painter Walter Gay in 1889 and spent her whole adult life in France, had a similar upbringing in comfortable houses in New York and Newport, and lived through the same 'Newport gaieties' as Edith, which she did not enjoy. But they would not become close friends until much later. The only person Wharton singles out in her memoirs among the great throng of the Anglo-American upper classes in those Newport summers was the young and brilliant diplomat Cecil Spring-Rice, because he told interesting stories which brightened up a dull afternoon. Her keen memory of this young man, who played no part in her later life, suggests the general lack of intellectual stimulation in her set.[26]

The year Pussy Jones came out, the Jones family spent part of the summer at Newport and part at the less formal resort of Bar Harbor, on Mount Desert, many miles north of New York, off the coast of Maine, where Frederic and Minnie Jones were setting up a 'cottage', Reef Point. (Here their daughter Beatrix would learn her trade, and she would eventually turn it into a legendary American garden and horticultural centre.) Mount Desert's wild, remote beauty had been a magnet for American painters since the 1850s, attracted by its northern light, its wonderful sunsets, and romantic, hilly, wooded scenery. From the 1880s onwards it was becoming a summer resort, a freer, more natural and adventurous alternative to Newport. ('Lake and ocean, mountain and forest, extend their arms lovingly toward those who seek happiness in the realms of Nature . . . No fashionable element can destroy their beauty or dim their charms', read the 1890 *Bar Harbor Guide*.) Painters were still coming – John La Farge, whose wife became a friend of Edith's, was a guest of Minnie Jones's in the mid-1890s. But hotels and summer residences were springing up, as Morgans and Vanderbilts moved in. The resort was famous for its flirtations and liaisons, for opportunities provided by unchaperoned canoeing and walking. In 1894, Francis Marion Crawford (who knew the Jones family) wrote a 'Bar Harbor Tale' of summer romances there, called *Love in Idleness*, with a strong-minded dashing young heroine very like Trix Jones, and eloquent descriptions of the island and the village-harbour 'which has grown to be the centre of civilization since the whole place has become fashionable'.

> Earth, sky, and water are of the north – hard, bright, and cold . . . The village . . . lies by the water's edge, facing the islands which enclose the natural harbour. It was and is a fishing village . . . In the midst of it, vast wooden hotels, four times as high as the houses nearest to them, have sprung up to lodge fashion in six-storied discomfort . . . But behind and above all are the wooded hills.[27]

This was the setting of Edith's early romances. During the summer of 1880, there was a flirtation, or a courtship – something serious enough to be noticed – between Pussy Jones and a young man three years older than she was (so not part of her brothers' set), Henry Leyden Stevens – Harry, as he was known. (Almost all these young Americans gave each other pet names or short names. Edith was 'Lily', and sometimes 'John', as well as Puss or Pussy.) All that is known about Harry Stevens is that he had been ill with TB and had spent some time in Oxford and Switzerland, but was now a sporty, attractive type, due to inherit an extremely large fortune. His family was well known to the Joneses, and not approved of. His father, Paran Stevens, had been one of the most aggressive self-made businessmen in New York, known as 'the Napoleon of Hotels'. He ran the Fifth Avenue Hotel, whose gaudy goings-on were in the Jones family's eye, across the street, all through Edith's childhood. After that great success story, he built the 'Stevens House' on 27th Street and turned it into the 'Victoria Hotel', the very latest kind, with luxury apartments and steam elevators. His hobby was breeding racehorses. He died in 1872, and his widow, a grocer's daughter from Lowell, Massachusetts, 'forced herself' (Emelyn Washburn remembered) 'into New York society by way of Newport'. Her trump card was her daughter's marriage to an English aristocrat, one of many often ill-fated unions between wealthy, pretty American girls and English titles which would make the plot of *The Buccaneers*, seventy years later. Mrs Stevens's shocking introduction of Sunday night soirées attracted numerous gentlemen followers. She went to the famous Vanderbilt ball dressed as Queen Elizabeth, and entertained Oscar Wilde on his visit to New York in 1882. But the Joneses were not impressed. Mrs Mary Mason Jones, Edith's formidable great-aunt, refused to have her in her house, and it would be one of Mrs Stevens's triumphs that after Mary Mason Jones's death she bought that house.[28]

In the autumn of 1880, the doctors advised George Frederic Jones to return to Europe: a remedy frequently recommended for American nervous exhaustion. Right in the middle of her debutante season and her courtship, Edith resumed what was much more to her taste, the comfortable itinerant life of Americans abroad. They went to England, and she paid enthralling visits to the National Gallery. They went to a spa in Germany where she had a flirtation with someone else's fiancé. They went to Italy, where she and her father pursued Ruskinian itineraries in Florence and Venice. And they settled for the winter in Cannes, where she made friends with a bevy of upper-class Anglo-French *'jeunes filles en fleurs'*. (Some of these well-brought-up young ladies would return twenty years later, married into French titled families, as part of her Parisian social scenery on the Faubourg St-Germain.) Harry Stevens followed the Joneses to Europe: he was there in Venice, and in Cannes, where George Frederic died of a stroke, aged only sixty-one. Edith was twenty. (News of the Reverend Washburn's death came to her at the same time.) How much did the young man's sympathy and kindness, at such a moment, intensify this friendship? Emelyn Washburn thought he was 'desperately in love'.[29]

The life of the family changed. The widow and her daughter went back to America. Lucretia inherited an annuity (of $600) and a lump sum (of $30,000) for a new home, and soon after came into a substantial legacy from a relative. Edith, too, inherited money from her father, but she did not see much of it, even when she turned twenty-one. A legacy of $20,000 and an equal share of the estate with her brothers – in total about $600,000 in real-estate holdings – was held in trust, by the brothers. She was entitled to live off the interest from these holdings, which came to about $10,000 a year.[30] Lucretia rented out West 23rd Street and bought a new house at 28 West 25th, which she 'did up'. Though the brothers were in the picture, Edith was thrown together with her mother after her father's death. She draws a veil over this period.

The courtship resumed: the summer after her father's death was spent at Newport, and the engagement between Edith Jones and Henry Leyden Stevens was announced in *Town Topics*, on 19 August 1882, with a wedding set for October. In October, however, the engagement was as publicly broken off, with a piece of tattle in *Town Topics* about Miss Jones being too much of 'an ambitious authoress' for Mr Stevens: 'The only reason for the breaking of the engagement . . . is an alleged preponderance of intellectuality on the part of the intended bride.' 'Mrs Stevens is at the bottom of it all', a

Rhinelander relative noted. She may have wanted to hang on to her son's millions, which he was due to inherit either on his marriage or at twenty-five. Or she may have been getting her own back on the sniffy Joneses. Observers could not deduce much from Edith's behaviour. It was officially given out that *she* had broken off the engagement, and she and Lucretia went back to Paris for the autumn. 'She didn't appear particularly sad', a fifteen-year-old Rhinelander cousin said. Her vulnerability to the public eye was noted, however, by her escort at the Patriarchs Ball in January 1883, who felt her trembling nervousness under disapproving scrutiny. But there is no record of any emotion when Harry Stevens died of TB in 1885. (Had she married him, Edith Stevens might, at twenty-three, have been an immensely wealthy young widow, free to do what she wanted.)

Wharton is dismissive and cool about any early love-interest in her memoirs, though in her description of the flirtation at the German spa she does give a sense of a girl testing out her sexual powers. But she says that she did not fall in love until she was twenty-one, and that the 'suitors' who turned up in Cannes from New York were not interesting to her. The only clue to her feelings, apart from some relish in the use of Mrs Paran Stevens as the basis for the social-climbing Mrs Lemuel Struthers, 'the Shoe Polish Queen', in *The Age of Innocence* and 'New Year's Day', and a note to herself, over thirty years later, to use her for the acquisitive and vulgar mothers in *The Buccaneers*, was a comic poem.[31] She wrote this at around the same time as a solemn elegy for the Reverend Washburn, full of hopes that 'the cloud of human strife' should not have followed him to his 'new sphere of being'. 'Intense Love's Utterance', dated 13 September 1881, has a quite different tone. It is a wry squib (dedicated 'To – whom?') of a devoted lover's proposal to his 'heart's Lady', which interrupts its wooing with the fear that he cannot afford to provide her with 'High art' and all the furnishings that go with it:

> How far could a poor fellow's income
> Extend in your dadoes and friezes,
> Your Chippendale table, your ceiling
> From a study of Paul Veronese's . . .
> You are used to a Crown Derby tea-set,
> And your tea pot is always Queen Anne, dear.
> Could you bear to pour out from Britannia
> Into plain white and gilt – if you can, dear?

The poem ends with a knowing, modern dig at Pater's new theory of life lived as a succession of 'fleeting pulsations': better high art, the suitor says, renouncing her, than love, which is 'a thing out of date'. There is no clue in this to Edith's true feelings for Harry Stevens. But it shows how precisely she recognises the materialism and snobbery that hemmed her in. There was no free, private zone for her where she could try out new relationships outside the circuit of family expectations and the tight jostling for social and financial status. Her feelings at nineteen, twenty, twenty-one, have to be deduced: there is hardly any first-hand evidence. But the public exposure of her first, failed 'affair' coincided with her father's ill-health and early death, and it is hard not to read mortification into these events, nor to see them as partial explanations for her marriage a few years later.

She needed all her youthful sharpness and irony. She had lost a benevolent and encouraging ally. 'I often think of Papa', she wrote, tellingly, to a family friend in 1905 when *The House of Mirth* came out, 'and wish he could have been here to encourage me with my work.' She was living with a mother who was unsympathetic to her, she had been publicly humiliated in her first sexual relationship, and she was not writing anything of substance yet. Sara Norton, the sensitive and intelligent daughter of Charles Eliot Norton, soon to become one of Edith's closest women friends, thought that this period after her father's death was crucial and formative: she became more sceptical now, 'loosening the bond' with the Church.[32] Her moving away from her dark childhood religious preoccupations, and from conventional church-going practices, was part of the process of growing up, and of separating herself, after her father's death – if only internally at this stage – from the family. The process was speeded up by the reading she was doing in the 1890s on evolution, ethics and anthropology. The Commonplace Book she began to keep in the late 1890s habitually mixed up Pascal and Marcus Aurelius, Herbert Spencer and Schopenhauer, and quoted at length from the French philosopher Jean-Marie Guyau on the slow evolution of beliefs and the opposition between religion and philosophy. In a 1902 essay on George Eliot, Wharton would show particular interest in the morality Eliot evolved after moving away from her early 'theological' preoccupations towards agnosticism. Wharton who, like George Eliot, would in her novels be profoundly interested in ethics and morality, moved away from her childhood fear of a punitive God, and from her family's bland, conservative Christianity, to an undeclared position of sceptical agnosticism, which she maintained for many years until, much later in her life, she became increasingly attracted to Catholicism. There are no consolatory beliefs for most of her fictional characters, and no sense of rewards in eternity for any of them. The practising Christians in her novels and stories are mostly sentimentalists or grotesques. But there is, at the same time, a powerful sense that conduct matters, that people are answerable for their actions, and that they may not always be in control of their own destinies.

Scepticism and intelligence were necessary weapons in the close relationship she began in the summer of 1883, a relationship much more important than that with poor Harry Stevens, and which would dominate much of her life – though that was not how it looked that summer. A year after George Frederic's death and the failed engagement, Lucretia took Edith back to Bar Harbor. Was this a husband-hunting expedition? Over a period of a few weeks in the summer of 1883, Edith went walking and cycling and canoeing with a new acquaintance, Walter Van Rensselaer Berry. In her memoir, she describes these few weeks as 'a fleeting hint of what the communion of kindred intelligences might be'.[33] Then he left, and Teddy Wharton immediately loomed into view. About thirteen years later, Edith Wharton and Walter Berry became intimate friends, by which time she had been married for over ten years and was at last starting to write professionally. Walter arrived at precisely the point when she needed literary encouragement and advice: and, for good or ill, this is what he gave her and how they consolidated their intimacy.

Much has been made of their false start in 1883, when Edith Jones was twenty-one and Walter Berry was twenty-four. In the picturesque, unchaperoned environment of Mount Desert, she found herself able to talk about what interested her to a young man with an air of distinction, who belonged to her social circle but was also well read and intellectually challenging. He stood out in several ways from the general run of upper-class young men with excellent pedigrees and an establishment career ahead of them, who liked golf, high society, and pretty women. Literally stood out: he was remarkable-looking, very tall and thin, very debonair and elegant, with striking blue eyes and good bone structure. He cultivated a fine moustache from early in his life. His thinness was the result of severe illness: he had had malaria in his childhood, and was perpetually plagued with poor health.

The romantic view of this encounter would be that she fell in love with him for life. The more realistic possibility is that the conversation they had that summer was a pleasurable and exciting opening of a door to intellectual intimacy, a glimpse of the sort of relationship she would most enjoy with the men in her life, but not a *coup de foudre*.

It is hard to judge, because the mystery that settled around Wharton and Berry has everything to do with the survival of evidence. Who keeps and who publishes the love-letters of the famous writer-to-be was one of Wharton's favourite subjects, as in her first short novel, *The Touchstone* (written with much advice from Walter Berry). She knew very well that how her story would be told depended on what would survive and who owned it. When Walter Berry died in 1927, she immediately retrieved and destroyed her correspondence to him, and she also destroyed most of the hundreds of letters he must have written to her over twenty-eight years. Unknown to her, four letters she wrote to Berry between 1905 and 1908 did survive – friendly, intimate, but not passionate – tucked away in the papers of one of Berry's lady friends, Alice Garrett. Wharton did keep the letters he wrote to her between 1899 and 1904, and one letter, and a telegram, of 1923. The telegram, sent from Berry to Wharton two days before the letter arrived, read: 'THE LETTER IS REALLY THERE DON'T LOSE IT DEAR.'[34] 'The letter' was clearly written in response to some expression of memory or regret on her part – marking, probably, the forty years since they met:

> Dearest – The real dream – mine – was in the canoe and in the night, afterwards, – for I lay awake wondering and wondering, – and then, when morning came, wondering how I could have wondered, – I, a $less lawyer (not even that, yet) with just about enough cash for the canoe and for Rodick's [the big Bar Harbor hotel] bill – And then, later, in the little cottage at Newport, I wondered why I hadn't – for it would all have been good, – and then the slices of years slid by.
>
> Well, my dear, I've never 'wondered' about anyone else, and there wouldn't be much of me if you were cut out of it. Forty years of it is yours, dear. W.[35]

The lost dream; the missed chance, and the 'long run' of disappointment and compromise that follows it; the by-passing of the one true intimacy; the stifled lifelong longing: these are Wharton's subjects, and Walter may have inspired them. But we cannot assume from this one tender (if self-preserving) note from an old friend in his mid-sixties, or from her fiction, that Edith Wharton spent the years of her marriage, and the rest of her life, wishing she had been married to Walter Berry. What she felt about him changed over the years. And much of what she felt is hidden from us. It would also be rash to assume that if she *had* married Walter Berry it would have been a story of happiness and fulfilment. He was the pre-eminent example of the kind of man whom she found – and who found her – interesting and magnetic. This was not a type who would necessarily make a good husband – as is suggested by an unsympathetic fictional version, Anna Leath's late husband Fraser Leath, in *The Reef*:

In such an atmosphere as his an eager young woman, curious as to all the manifestations of life, yet instinctively desiring that they should come to her in terms of beauty and fine feeling, must surely find the largest scope for self-expression. Study, travel, the contact of the world, the comradeship of a polished and enlightened mind, would combine to enrich her days and form her character; and it was only in the rare moments when Mr. Leath's symmetrical blond mask bent over hers, and his kiss dropped on her like a cold smooth pebble, that she questioned the completeness of the joys he offered.[36]

All Wharton's friends, from the 1900s onwards, had to share her with Berry. Ogden Codman described him as her tame cat. Many of them, especially the Berensons and her French friends, assumed they were lovers. A number of her friends disliked him and thought he was a baleful influence on her. Edmund Wilson, reviewing Percy Lubbock's spiteful memoir of Wharton, summed him up as 'dry, empty-hearted and worldly, a pretentious and unlikeable snob'. Others (and he had an astounding range of friends, from Roosevelt and James to Proust and Harry Crosby) admired his kindness, his sociability, his eye for the ladies and his ear for what was going on. Bring him with you when you visit, James often said to Wharton, he's such good company, 'he ought to exist for bringability'. All who visited him took pleasure in his amazing collection of books and paintings and fabulous objets d'art, especially his oriental pieces. Those who praised, rather than disliking, his fastidious taste, connoisseurship and erudition thought of him as a piece of 'exquisite porcelain'. He was aloof, guarded, 'alert', 'melancholy' (James's words), clever, observant, witty, intolerant, gallant, cynical, hedonistic, self-pleasing, and rational. His tone comes through in remarks quoted by those who admired him: 'It is easy to see superficial resemblances between things. It takes a first-rate mind to perceive the differences underneath.' 'It doesn't do you any good to read if you don't apply what you read to your work.' In his much-marked copy of La Rochefoucauld, which Edith inherited after his death, he marked a passage wondering whether a great love could ever, for him, pass from '*l'esprit au coeur*' – from the mind to the heart.[37] The young man Edith met in 1883 became a carefully constructed public figure with highly selective preferences and a well-worked-out plan for life's enjoyment. He was a complex character who could have afforded to live a life of leisure – after the settling of his mother's estate in 1913 he came into a vast inheritance – but who worked hard all his life in international – particularly Franco-American – legal relations, and became 'the first American citizen in Paris'. It is hard

to dig under that polished, worldly surface for any evidence of the Walter
Berry, aspiring young lawyer, who went canoeing with Pussy Jones in Bar
Harbor. He had impeccable social credentials, and prided himself on
knowing those who knew 'your front row in the 400'. The Van
Rensselaer/Berry tribe were distant relatives of Lucretia's. Walter and his
sister Natalie were the children of Nathaniel Berry and Catharine Van
Rensselaer, whose father was General Stephen Van Rensselaer of Albany.
These Albany grandees, with vast acres, could trace their ancestry back to
the Revolutionary War, and beyond that to the original Dutch 'Patroon'.
Berry complained that if 'those idiotic V.R.s' had settled in Manhattan
rather than Albany, he would have been much richer. Until he came into
his inheritance, he had to work for a living. But he had the privileges of
his class. He was born in Paris, grew up in Albany, went to St Mark's
School, Harvard and Columbia, trained as a lawyer and set up a firm in
Washington in 1882. He specialised in international law, very successfully.
He represented the French and Italian embassies in the States, and worked
closely with other diplomats (he speaks of getting a case of wine in thanks
from the Swiss foreign ministry) and with Senate legislation. He was
appointed judge of the International Tribune in Cairo in 1908, resigned
two years later and went to live in Paris, where, from 1917 to 1922, he was
president of the American Chamber of Commerce, promoting American
business interests in France. Though he knew everyone who counted in
Paris, was widely known and respected there, and rarely went back to the
States, it is said that he always described himself as being 'from Washington,
temporarily resident in Paris'.[38]

Reading back from the letters Berry wrote to Wharton in his early forties
to find the young man in his twenties is a risky procedure, though some
interests might have been in place from early on, like the passion for golf,
and for playing the stock market (on which he and Teddy Wharton
exchanged tips in the 1900s). The 1899–1904 letters to Edith (and the references to 'poor poor Walter' in James's letters to her) are also full of his
nervous crises, his symptoms, his exhaustion and 'raggedness', his attempts
at a cure in the Adirondacks, his bad 'lung-turns', his recommendation of
a medicine called 'Tropon' for 'plumping up' after weight loss. It was a point
of sympathy between them when Edith was ill and depressed. But it could,
in a marriage, have become a tiresome and insistent theme. And there is a
dark streak showing up in his remark to her in 1900 that he felt, like Peter
Quint in James's *The Turn of the Screw*, 'a white feeling of damnation'.[39] He
developed a jocular boastful tone with Edith, too, about his fondness for
decorative ladies (whom he referred to as 'fairies'), and even if he did not

make a point of this in their first summer together, his preferences must soon have been apparent to her. His 'man about town' act – as when he speaks of enjoying the Country Club races at Brookline, or of an evening at the Metropolitan Club in Washington in August with a cheery gang of eight chaps 'most of them finding a certain joie de vivre in the fact that their *légitimes* are not in town'[40] – would have taken shape in his twenties. His politics seem to have been right-wing and imperialist. During the Senate's debate on Puerto Rico in 1900 (ceded by Spain to the USA after the war in 1898), Berry eagerly awaited a result which would maintain the island as a territory of the USA, thereby – he hoped – allowing a great deal of money to be made in free trade. He opposed the anti-imperialist movement for self-government for Puerto Rico by leaders like William Jennings Bryan and Andrew Carnegie, and, in November 1900, was 'gloating over the passing of Bryan and the consequent booming of stocks'.

The surviving letters between them, and everything Wharton said about Berry, make clear what interested her in him: his rational scepticism, his cultural range, and his discriminating and fervent interest in literature. He would be the first person to encourage and criticise her writing, and one of the first with whom she shared her reading enthusiasms – which at the turn of the century were for Stevenson's letters, or *The Turn of the Screw*, or Whitman's poetry. He gave her an intellectual example which speeded her on her move away from everything the Reverend Washburn and Calvary Church had stood for. When he reappeared in her life in the late 1890s as literary adviser and devoted friend, and, later, opener of doors at the start of the Paris years, he took up the role that she liked her men-friends to play. Berry was not her only mentor. Before she became an established and famous novelist, she looked for such guides. Even when she had become more secure, she liked relationships where admiration played a part – as with James and Berenson – though she would tussle with them for dominance. The figure of the cultural mentor to a naive acolyte comes into her fiction: Benedetto Alfieri awakening Odo Valsecca to classical art in *The Valley of Decision*,[41] or Halo Spear inducting the raw, eager Vance Weston into poetry in *Hudson River Bracketed*.

When Walter Berry disappeared, Edith Jones got married. The timing makes this look like a substitution, and so it may have been. But the intellectual replacement for Walter appeared a couple of years later, just after her marriage. This was Egerton Winthrop, who would play a louder part in Wharton's life-story if the letters between them had not been done away with. It is evident that they corresponded voluminously and intimately for over thirty years.[42] He was the third wheel of the Wharton marriage for many years, and one of her most important intellectual advisers. He was also a person about whom she had mixed feelings.

Egerton Winthrop, as his name tells us, was in what Berry would describe as the 'front row in the 400'. He had a very grand pedigree, going back to Governor Peter Stuyvesant of New York and John Winthrop, the seventeenth-century governor of the Massachusetts Bay Colony. He was born in 1839 and was entrenched in New York and Newport high society. He had known the Jones family for ever, and when in 1921 Wharton started to write the novellas which became *Old New York*, she derived much of her family information from 'left-over reminiscences picked up from Mamma, grandmamma, and Egerton'. He was a lawyer and sat on various bank boards, but spent most of his life in leisure pursuits. Walter told Edith, in January 1902, that he envied people who 'can go and do just what they do want ... There's Egerton who'll turn up smiling, ready for anything.'[43] Winthrop married and went to Paris for the duration of the Civil War (an avoidance strategy made use of in 'The Lamp of Psyche'). After his wife's death in 1872 he stayed on in Paris until the mid-1880s, and then returned to America to put his sons through Harvard.

It is not, however, as a family man that Winthrop comes across, and it is not surprising that one of Wharton's biographers refers to him inadvertently as a 'bachelor'. He sounds more like one of the bisexual or homosexual men-friends with whom Wharton had some of her most satisfactory relationships. His life's main work was the exercise of good taste. He had a House Beautiful at 23 East 23rd Street, designed by Richard Morris Hunt, with a famous Louis XVI drawing room. Every article of furniture was imported from France, including the papier-mâché ornamentations. Here, and in Newport (where Ogden Codman designed his house), he devoted himself to 'the perfection of his dinners', to going everywhere and knowing everything. Wharton told their mutual friend Daisy Chanler, in 1903, that she had been amused by a letter from Winthrop saying that Newport was very quiet and 'he goes nowhere. Have you ever noticed that, while excluded people know they are excluded, gay people are always under the illusion that they "go nowhere"?'[44]

In her memoirs, Wharton praised Winthrop's style in interior decoration – 'his house was the first in New York in which an educated taste had replaced stuffy upholstery and rubbishy "ornaments" with objects of real beauty in a simply designed setting'. He was a deceptive character, his personal shyness sitting oddly with his social appetites. Lamenting his death, in 1916, to Sara Norton, she said that 'most people thought Egerton the slave of convention', but that he was honest, tender, and sincere. Something of Winthrop's tone comes through in remarks quoted in Wharton's letters: a joke about a bishop who said, of the French language: 'What a jargon! I never read worse', or a snooty generalisation about the stupidity of the servant class. Louis Auchincloss said that Winthrop was the prototype for all the 'sterile, polished parasites of perfect manners and little heart' in her novels. In *A Backward Glance* she presents him as a 'type' of New York gentleman, lamenting that a person of such intelligence should have wasted his life in trivia: no public service, no ambition, just a life of 'dilettantish leisure'. In her fiction he was used (with a touch of Ward McAllister thrown in) for the social regulator and busybody Sillerton Jackson in *The Age of Innocence* and *Old New York*, or for Ned Van Alstyne in *The House of Mirth* who 'prides himself on his summing up of social aspects' and who, in mourning, wears 'a coat that made affliction dapper'.

When Edith Wharton got to know Winthrop he was forty-six and she was twenty-three. He was in a position to be her adviser, even if the social advice he gave her, to make her mark as a New York hostess, was not to her taste. But he was more use to her in another way. In her memoir, she notes that Winthrop encouraged her reading in French literature and in the evolutionary sciences. It was because of Winthrop, she says, that she read Darwin, Huxley, Spencer, Haeckel, and others. In her library, her copy of Huxley's complete works is dated 1894–1900; Spencer's *The Principle of Ethics* is an edition of 1897, Romanes's *Animal Intelligence* is 1895, Haeckel's *The History of Creation* is 1893, and Westermarck's *The Origin and Development of the Moral Ideas* is 1906. (It was around this time that Berry, too, was recommending James Frazer's *The Golden Bough* and the work of the anthropologist Paul Topinard and the anatomist George Cuvier.) She took this reading very seriously. One surviving communication from Winthrop to Wharton shows how 'my new friend directed and systematized my reading, and filled some of the worse gaps in my education'.[45]

Darwinism, etc. Suggestions.
Read slowly, marking important parts in the margins with pencil. Re-read marked parts after finishing a chapter, and *all* back marked parts before beginning a new chapter.
    If a passage is not understood after two readings, mark an X in the margin, and wait till book is finished before trying again.
    Try to think over, at night, what has been read that day.
    Learn *each definition* of as many scientific words & terms as possible

and write them in the book, as indicated. Most people's idea of what a word means is 'à peu près'!

Also write in it the most important things that strike you. When the book is half full you wouldn't change it for the best book written!

Learn a few definitions, like that of evolution for instance 'by heart', – while your hair is being done!

If you haven't a good dictionary at your elbow, let me know and I'll send you one.

In the book, put definitions of words on one page and terms and quotations on the other.

Don't forget that this sort of thing will make you able to do everything better – from grasping the absolute to playing with [Illegible].

In her markings, for instance, in the preface to Huxley's *Discourses Biological and Geological* (1897), or to the first volume of her Haeckel, one can see her taking these lessons to heart. A passage in the Huxley preface on the taxing task of 'making difficult subjects intelligible' is underlined, as if as a comment to herself. She marks Haeckel's account of the value of the 'theory of the . . . animal descent of the human race', which he calls the doctrine of Filiation, or Transmutation: 'that of a gradual development of all (even the most perfect) organisms out of a single, or out of a few, quite simple, and quite imperfect original beings, which come into existence, not by supernatural creation, but by spontaneous generation'. She marks a passage on two kinds of transmission, of inherited and of acquired characteristics. 'Individuals can transmit, not only those qualities which they themselves have inherited from their ancestors, but also the peculiar, individual qualities which they have acquired during their own life.' And she marks passages on adaptation and parasitic modes of life, and on the lack of free will: 'Every physiologist who scientifically investigates the activity of the will . . . must of necessity arrive at the conviction that *the will is never free*, but is always determined by external or internal influences.' Her third volume of stories, of 1904, is called *The Descent of Man*. With Winthrop's help, she was acquiring information and arguments which would inspire her devastating fictional analysis of the very society of which he was a parasitic and highly adapted species.[46]

Egerton Winthrop was closely involved in Edith Wharton's life for a long time after these reading lessons. He travelled with her and her husband to Italy in the 1880s and 1890s, and persuaded Teddy to let Edith have some time away in London. He was a frequent house-guest at The Mount. He was one of her visitors in Paris during her affair in 1908, and he witnessed the last phase of the Wharton marriage. After that she saw less of him, but they wrote constantly, and she was devastated by his death in 1916. It was one of Wharton's characteristics to keep the people she liked in her life. Though she broke away from her roots, and though she is often described as restless and questing, she was deeply committed to conserving her friendships: witness her lifelong working relations with women such as Minnie Jones and Anna Bahlmann, or the lasting friendships with people she got to know in the 1890s and 1900s like Daisy Chanler, Ogden Codman, Sara Norton, and Egerton.

She kept her servants, too. Catherine Gross came to work for Edith Wharton on 10 October 1884 (they always marked this anniversary). Ten years older than Edith, she had had a tough past. She grew up in Brumath, a small town near Strasbourg in the Alsace, and had an illegitimate child when she was seventeen. The son became a farmer in Algeria; the story was that when 'Gross' or 'Grossie' (as Edith called her) went to visit him, he told her he was ashamed of her life as a servant, and she resolved never to see him again. Whatever anguish underlay this story is not known. Photographs show a solid, stolid, resolute-looking figure, inviting somewhat condescending descriptions by Wharton's biographers: 'buxom, round-faced, placidly competent'; 'more like a bulging rubber ball than ever'; 'rosy-cheeked and smiling'. Bernard Berenson reported, in 1931, an inaccurate-sounding story about Gross coming for a job when Edith was eight years old. She met Lucretia, decided she did not want to work for her, but then, on seeing Edith, changed her mind, because (she told Edith many years later) 'I saw that you knew exactly what you wanted.'[47] The dates do not fit, but the anecdote does suggest the quality of the relationship. Gross, like Doyley, and like other women in Edith Wharton's life, perhaps provided some substitute mothering, but this was also an efficient working relationship in which the housekeeper was given a great deal of responsibility, and remained unswervingly loyal to her mistress. She remained until her illness and death, at eighty-one, in 1933.

The faithful female servant who, even after death, tries to protect her mistress against her brutish, drunken, tyrannical husband, is the subject of one of Wharton's finest ghost-stories, 'The Lady's Maid's Bell'. But abuse and aggression would not have seemed likely behaviour from Teddy Wharton when he first began to be of interest to Edith Jones. Plenty of Wharton's later friends were on hand to assert that 'she never loved him'.[48] And, as a brittle Newport heroine, married to the wrong man, says in Wharton's story 'The Twilight of the God': 'The fact is, a girl's motives in marrying are like a passport – apt to get mislaid. One is so seldom asked for either.' But in 1884 Teddy Wharton did not seem a poor choice for an 'Unmarried Maiden' well into her twenties.

He was not a new arrival like Harry Stevens or Walter Berry, but a regular member of her older brothers' sporty, animal-loving, unintellectual Newport and New York set. Though he did not have the grand historical pedigree of an Egerton Winthrop, his father, William Craig Wharton, came of a large respectable Virginian family, and his mother, Nancy Willing Spring, born in Amherst, was of Boston and Philadelphia stock. Edward Robbins Wharton was their youngest child, born in 1850. His older brother William became a successful lawyer and politician. Edward also had two older sisters; one died young, and the other, Nancy, known as Nannie, never married and ended up living with and looking after him. She was, for some years, a great trial to her sister-in-law. The family lived on 127 Beacon Street in Boston, a very good address.

Wharton had some pointed things to say about Boston society in her memoirs. 'It was not until I went to Boston on my marriage that I found myself in a community of wealthy and sedentary people seemingly too lacking in intellectual curiosity to have any desire to see the world.' In this circle, 'indignant protests' greeted any deviation from the norm – such as not living in Boston. A joke she liked to make was that in Boston she was a failure because she was thought 'too fashionable to be intelligent', in New York because she was 'too intelligent to be fashionable'. One thing she appreciated about Teddy was that he had no desire to go on living in his home town: perhaps he wanted to put some distance between himself and his mother. All the references to her, particularly around the time of Teddy's illness, suggest a staid, oppressive and disapproving presence. And there are a number of 'narrow and inexorable' mothers-in-law in the fiction, like Kate Clephane's in *The Mother's Recompense*, a 'formidable chieftain' of her tribe, who keeps up a vendetta against the errant wife long after her son's death, or Anna Leath's in *The Reef*, as fussy and conventional as her son about 'the momentous minutiae of drawing-room conduct'.[49]

In the years of Teddy's illness and her own old age, Mrs Nancy Wharton would refuse to accept the reality of her son's condition. This could have had to do with her own marriage. William Craig Wharton suffered from 'melancholia' and was, periodically (and from around the time of the Wharton–Jones marriage, permanently) an inmate of Boston's insane asylum, McLean. Six years after his younger son's marriage to Edith Jones, in 1891, William Wharton committed suicide. The doctors assured the Wharton family that the condition was not heritable. And, in his thirties, Teddy

> *Mrs George Frederic Jones*
>
> *requests the honour of your presence*
>
> *at the marriage of her daughter to*
>
> *Mr Edward R. Wharton*
>
> *at Trinity Chapel*
>
> *on Wednesday April twenty-ninth*
>
> *at twelve o'clock.*

seemed nothing like his father; it was not until 1902 that an acute and ruthless observer, Ogden Codman, was the first to notice a connection between Teddy's 'queer' traits and the 'strange and irritable' behaviour for which old Mr Wharton had to be 'locked up'.[50] But at the time of the courtship, Teddy Wharton was a jolly chap, a big, handsome, fit, moustachioed sportsman, 'full of fun', as one of his nephews described him. Lucretia (according to Emelyn Washburn) thought he was 'like sunshine in the house'. In the early days, Edith would assert, he was 'the kindest of companions'; to the end of her life she would insist on his early kindness and good nature. He liked fast travel (cars would be a passion), dogs and horses, fishing, shooting, wine. He had been a not very successful Harvard student and was a member of the Knickerbocker Club. He was utterly unliterary, but had the kind of books an American gentleman ought to have: Emerson, Bret Harte's *Poetical Works*, records of men of action like Captain Mahan's *From Sail to Steam: Recollections of a Naval Life*. He had no job, and was not especially well-off. He was dependent on his mother for an allowance of $2,000 a year, and did not come into his inheritance until he was sixty.[51]

The family liked him; probably there was pressure, five years after 'coming out', for Edith to marry; probably she wanted to get away from her mother (though she did not, for a time, get very far). She may have been reacting to her disappointment with Walter Berry. But we have no record, no sense of her choice, no courtship letters. Teddy took her to the Patriarchs Ball in January 1884 and a year later the engagement was announced. The wedding took place very soon after – no time for any change of mind – in Trinity Chapel on West 25th Street, across the road from Lucretia's house, on 29 April 1885. The invitations referred to Edith, not by name, but as the daughter of Mrs George Frederic Jones. The rector who married them thought of the new bride as a pious type: 'I am sure you read your Bible now as you did when a young girl', he wrote to her when *The House of Mirth* was published.[52] She was given away by her uncle and godfather, Fred Rhinelander. Newport and New York family friends were in attendance; Teddy's best man was a Lowell, from Boston. There were no bridesmaids and no honeymoon. They went straight to Pencraig Cottage, the smaller house across the road from the Jones house in Newport, which, just as she had done for Frederic and Minnie, Lucretia gave them to live in. And then, what?

The New York society wedding at Grace Church, in *The Age of Innocence*, takes place in a spectacular blur of unreality, as the groom watches his own wedding 'rite' with a feeling of estrangement, as though it were a first night at the opera. To feel utterly alienated from the standard rituals of behaviour in which one is also participating, is the fate of most of Wharton's thinking characters. She gives this state of mind to a young New York bride in 'The Old Maid':

Yes – and afterward? . . .

Afterward: why, of course, there was the startled puzzled surrender to the incomprehensible exigencies of the young man to whom one had at most yielded a rosy cheek in return for an engagement ring; there was the large double-bed; the terror of seeing him shaving calmly the next morning, in his shirt-sleeves, through the dressing-room door; the evasions, insinuations, resigned smiles and Bible texts of one's Mamma; the reminder of the phrase 'to obey' in the glittering blur of the Marriage Service; a week or a month of flushed distress, confusion, embarrassed pleasure; then the growth of habit, the insidious lulling of the matter-of-course, the dreamless double slumbers in the big white bed, the early morning discussions and consultations through that dressing-room door which had once seemed to open into a fiery pit scorching the brow of innocence.

And then, the babies; the babies who were supposed to 'make up for everything', and didn't.[53]

This is not a description of Wharton's own marriage night, but of the tradition of sexual censorship and hypocrisy that led to it, of being brought up to think it 'not nice' to ask about sex. The undated, unpublished 'Beatrice Palmato' fragment gives another version of the 'startled puzzled surrender' and the 'terror' of the virgin's first sexual experience. Mr Palmato has to wait until after the 'dull misery' and 'rough advances' of his daughter's first time with her new husband, before he can take advantage of it.[54] The woman's experience in 'The Old Maid' is more likely to be a reconstruction of her mother's wedding night, judging from the lamentable story – also unpublished in her lifetime – that Wharton tells of her attempt to get some advice from Lucretia before her marriage.

> A few days before my marriage, I was seized with such a dread of the whole dark mystery, that I summoned up courage to appeal to my mother, & begged her, with a heart beating to suffocation, to tell me 'what being married was like'. Her handsome face at once took on the look of icy disapproval which I most dreaded. 'I never heard such a ridiculous question!' she said impatiently; & I felt at once how vulgar she thought me.
>
> But in the extremity of my need I persisted. 'I'm afraid, Mamma – I want to know what will happen to me!'
>
> The coldness of her expression deepened to disgust. She was silent for a dreadful moment; then she said with an effort: 'You've seen enough pictures & statues in your life. Haven't you noticed that men are – made differently from women?'
>
> 'Yes,' I faltered blankly.
>
> 'Well, then –?'
>
> I was silent, from sheer inability to follow, & she brought out sharply: 'Then for heaven's sake don't ask me any more silly questions. You can't be as stupid as you pretend!'
>
> The dreadful moment was over, & the only result was that I had been convicted of stupidity for not knowing what I had been expressly forbidden to ask about, or even to think of![55]

This vivid retrospective illustration of a system of 'training' which, Wharton says, 'did more than anything else to falsify & misdirect my whole life' (though she also says that she was able at last to escape that training) was written about fifty years after the event it describes. It is usually cited as a factual record of an event in Wharton's life, *circa* April 1885, not as a masterfully shaped piece of fictionalisation. But something like this happened; and there can be no doubt that Wharton blamed her mother for her marriage. Among the many unpublished, unfinished manuscripts she left behind, there are three frightening pages of an untitled story in which a mother and daughter are talking, in horror, about the daughter's intolerable marriage to a man who 'does' something unspeakable (Drinks? Drugs? Sexual violence?). The mother blames herself for having encouraged the match because 'the other mothers were envious': 'I shall never forgive myself – never!' The story ends as the daughter is about to answer the mother's question, 'What does he do?'[56]

What Teddy Wharton 'did' sexually is not known to us; the answer may be, not much. Writing about her sexual ignorance in 'Life and I', she says that she remained in this state 'till I had been married for several weeks'. This has led to such assertions as 'the marriage was not consummated for three weeks, and always thereafter the physical relationship between the pair . . . was agonized' or 'There is no question that the sexual side of the marriage was a disaster'. Nosy Ogden Codman had it down, by 1901, as a *mariage blanc.*[57] Everything, indeed, suggests 'a disaster': her frequent illness and depression in the years following her marriage, their separate rooms, their childlessness, their growing estrangement, and, in her writing, her interest in the subject of sexual privation and wretched marriages. But there is much darkness and silence here, out of which we can glimpse someone struggling to make the best of what has happened to her.

4

Italian Backgrounds

Edith Wharton was married at twenty-three, in 1885. She published her first, co-authored book at thirty-five, in 1897. In those twelve years, she constructed a life, as a married woman of her class, which was as interesting as she could make it; and she began to feel her way as a writer, publishing poems, stories and articles from the late 1880s onwards. This period of her life, though active and busy, is more obscure to us than her later years as a famous novelist, which teem with anecdotes, correspondence, and the record of her writings. By contrast, there are not so many glimpses of or stories about the young Mrs Edith Wharton. The best known is her first meeting with Henry James, at a dinner in Paris in 1887. Hoping to impress, she wore her newest Doucet dress ('a tea-rose pink, embroidered with iridescent beads') but was too shy to speak to him. 'I was probably not more than twenty-five, those were the principles in which I had been brought up.' He ignored her, and she was mortified. We do not know whether this shy, silent twenty-five-year-old was already writing the stories that would lead, within twenty years, to the career which made her Henry James's friend and equal, out-performing him in sales and popularity. She would look back on a 'Pelion and Ossa of slowly accumulating manuscripts, plays, novels and dramas' from this period, but it is not clear exactly when they began to accumulate. Some of the first stories she sent for publication in the early '90s or which were in her first collection of 1899 were painful marital tales – 'The Fullness of Life', 'A Journey', 'The Lamp of Psyche' – but it cannot be proved that she started writing those as early as the 1880s, turning to fiction 'to ease the tensions of her married life'.[1]

One of the obscurities of her marriage to Teddy centres on her health. There is no account of her suffering from asthma as a child, but after her marriage she developed a cluster of related bronchial troubles: asthma, hay fever, frequent heavy colds and 'flu, bronchitis and lung-congestion (she smoked, too). She also suffered from exhaustion, persistent nausea, and anaemia. Asthma is often linked to psychosomatic symptoms and to exceptional talents. Wharton said of her hero, Proust, a famous literary asthmatic, that there was 'a narrow margin between the man's genius and his physical disabilities'. Another of her heroes, and friends, Theodore Roosevelt, overcame childhood asthma through a determined commitment to the strenuous life. It is tempting to associate breathing difficulties with a sense of personal suffocation, and it has been asserted that 'whenever she was forced to share a bed with Teddy, she suffered attacks of asthma'.[2] Wharton had real enough bronchial symptoms to feel that the sea-air of Newport was bad for her, and to take a regular cure at the Italian spa, Salsomaggiore, from 1903 onwards. But she also identified her own symptoms as 'neurasthenic'. This was the version she gave, retrospectively, to Sara Norton, in 1908:

> For *twelve* years I seldom knew what it was to be, for more than an hour or two of the twenty-four, without an intense feeling of nausea, & such unutterable fatigue that when I got up I was always more tired than when I lay down. This form of neurasthenia consumed the best years of my youth, & left, in some sort, an irreparable shade on my life. Mais quoi! I worked through it, & came out on the other side.

She told Bernard Berenson in 1912 that she suffered from 'unget-at-able nausea for twelve years', a kind of 'seasickness' which was cured when she moved from Newport to Lenox.[3] Photographs from these years show her thin, tense-looking, and 'hollow-eyed'. In letters of late 1898 and early 1899 Wharton speaks of having been 'seriously ill' or having suffered from 'almost continuous ill-health and mental lassitude'.[4]

Biographers have read Wharton's illnesses in her twenties and thirties as a psychosomatic reaction to her marriage, and have deduced a series of breakdowns between 1895 and 1898. R.W.B. Lewis argued that she was 'very ill' in 1895 with a nervous collapse, and that in 1898 she was struck with 'paralysing depression and nervous exhaustion'. Because she spent time in Philadelphia that winter, followed by a quiet period in Washington, he claims that she underwent a cure with the famous Philadelphia nerve-doctor, Weir Mitchell, whose methods of treatment – confinement, rest, fattening up, isolation, separation from family, suspension of all work – were used on many women with mental or physical problems in the late nineteenth and early twentieth centuries, including Charlotte Perkins Gilman and Virginia Woolf. Shari Benstock, in her biography, notes that Mitchell was not in Philadelphia that winter, and that though Wharton may have been having a rest cure, she was staying at a hotel, not at his sanatorium (so was perhaps an 'outpatient' at the Mitchell clinic, being treated by another doctor called McClellan). And, far from being 'paralysed', she was engaged in plenty of activities in 1898 and 1899. But it is Lewis's version which is followed in most chronologies of Wharton's life, like this one: 'Suffers mental and physical breakdown in August 1898. Goes to Philadelphia in October to take the "rest cure" invented by Dr S Weir Mitchell.'[5] The romantic, dramatic version of Wharton's life before she succeeded as a novelist is that her unhappy and childless marriage drove her to neurasthenia and depression, that her initial attempts to write exacerbated this tension, leading to a breakdown in her thirties, but that she succeeded at last in writing her way out of her illness, and then never looked back.[6] Wharton gives credibility to this escape narrative by the dramatic rhetoric of breakthrough and self-creation she uses in her memoir:

At last [with the publication of *The Greater Inclination*, her first book of stories] I had groped my way through to my vocation, and thereafter I never questioned that story-telling was my job . . . I felt like some homeless waif who, after trying for years to take out naturalization papers, and being rejected by every country, has finally acquired a nationality. The Land of Letters was henceforth to be my country, and I gloried in my new citizenship. The publishing of *The Greater Inclination* broke the chains which had held me so long in a kind of torpor. For nearly twelve years I had tried to adjust myself to the life I had led since my marriage; but now I was overmastered by the longing to meet people who shared my interests.[7]

But this heroic retrospective narrative of depression giving way to achievement is too simple. It is not only that the evidence for the Weir Mitchell cure is inconclusive, or that her illnesses seem to have been 'real' enough, leading in later years, as asthma often does, to recurrent heart problems and congestive heart failure. It is also that she was leading a complicated, active, energetic life, all through the period in which she was *also* unwell, unhappy, and depressed. References to her intermittent ill-health, tiredness, and 'breakdowns' – to being 'buried fathoms deep in inertia, which is really tiredness' – go on into her forties. She wrote to Sally Norton, in January 1902: 'Don't I know that feeling you describe, when one longs to go to a hospital & *have something cut out*, & come out minus an organ, but alive & active & like other people, instead of dragging on with this bloodless existence!' And in March 1902: 'I have not for a long time had such a bad break-down . . . The Dr said I only needed a few days of rest, but at the end of eight I feel as lifeless, as inert, as unable to cope with life as I did at the beginning.'[8] Yet, at the same time, she was leading a life full of travel, house- and garden-making, new friendships, reading, and – increasingly – writing. There are three energetic strands in her twenties and thirties which are not stories of illness. One is the making of American houses, one is her entry into the literary market-place, and one is her taking possession of Italy.

The Whartons set up house under her mother's eye. They lived in Pencraig Cottage, in Newport, from 1885 until 1893, when they bought a house called 'Land's End', on the other side of Newport from her mother's house, for $80,000.[9] Between 1893 and 1900 she 'did up' and decorated the house, with the help of the designer Ogden Codman, and gardened and entertained at Land's End. In the seven years they spent at Newport, especially at Pencraig Cottage, they were often there from June to December, staying on after the summer people had left, 'alone with the utter aloneness of Newport Rhode Island in December', as she once wrote to Ogden Codman. Daisy Chanler describes what this felt like:

> By October the gay birds had all flown away and in November the avenues were leafless and deserted; then Newport resembled nothing so much as an unused ball-room carefully put away for the season, the curtains folded in piles, the furniture and chandeliers all swathed in brown holland. The great houses were closed and boarded up for the winter; the garden ornaments – shrubs, fountains, and marbles – boxed up and otherwise protected against the cold. What had ever led us to imagine it would be pleasant to live there the year round?[10]

In the first years of their marriage the couple had no New York home. When they went to New York, they stayed in Lucretia's house on 25th Street, except for the winter of 1888, when they rented a small house on Madison Avenue. In December 1889 they found a property on Park Avenue, a tellingly long way from 25th Street, on Lenox Hill, on the corner of 78th Street. First they rented it out, then they expanded and redesigned it (with Codman on hand, again) and in 1897 they moved into what was by then 884 Park Avenue, which they kept as a winter home for about ten years. (Their households were taken care of by Catherine Gross and by Teddy Wharton's man-servant Alfred White, who was hired as a young man in 1884 and would stay on with Edith for the rest of his life.) But Edith made sure that Newport and New York, which would have satisfied Teddy, were only half their life. Every year, between 1886 and 1897, they spent several months in Europe, mostly in Italy, but with frequent visits to

Paris and to England. Most of these journeys were made between February and June, but in 1896 they spent eight months abroad.

These were gregarious years, in which she made new and important close friendships. They were also years of upheaval in the Wharton and Jones families. Edith was left a substantial legacy in 1888, which financed their travels and their house-purchases. But her sister-in-law was less fortunate. Minnie Jones discovered her husband's infidelity in 1887, was separated from him in 1891 and divorced in 1896, with a very disadvantageous settlement. Her daughter Beatrix began her career as a landscape gardener in 1895, but she and her mother suffered badly from Frederic's actions. Lucretia sided with Frederic, Harry and Edith with Minnie: it was an irrevocable and unpleasant family rift. Both the brothers left America to live in France; Lucretia followed them to Paris in 1897, and fell ill there. Teddy's mother also moved, from Boston to Lenox, after her husband's suicide.

In its early years the Wharton marriage had its good moments. One piece of writing has survived, a record of one of the most enjoyable experiences of her mid-twenties. She told Bernard Berenson in 1925 that she 'kept a very meticulous diary of the cruise that Teddy and I made about thirty years ago'. This diary (which disappeared for years until it was chanced upon in the public library at Hyères in 1991) fills out the brief account she gives in *A Backward Glance* of the Mediterranean cruise of 1888, which she calls 'the greatest step forward in my making'. Planning an Aegean cruise in 1926, she set out to make it a match for this unforgettable journey of her youth.[11]

Against opposition from both sides of the family, the Whartons decided to spend their 'whole income for the year' – about $10,000 – on the cruise, of which the hire of the yacht was $4,000. They went with a wealthy New York friend, James Van Alen, who knew how to set about chartering a yacht from England, and who had experience of some wild travels in Greece. For a week or so they were also joined by the American consul in Greece in the *Vanadis*, a steam yacht (as she proudly described it in her diary) of '333 tons, with a length of 167 feet'. They had a deck-house sitting room, two comfortable bedrooms each with a 'large bath-tub', a room for Van Alen, a room for the maid and one for the valet and a separate room for the servants to eat in. There were sixteen crew including two cooks and two stewards. She liked the crew, but found the captain 'surly and inefficient'.[12]

It was an ambitious and carefully planned journey. They boarded the yacht on 17 February after a cold foggy stay in Paris, a train journey to Marseilles, and a steamer to Algiers. From Algiers they went to Tunis,

Malta, Sicily (with trips to Taormina and Monreale), Corfu, the island of Zante, a number of the Cycladic islands, and Rhodes. Then up the Turkish coast to Chios, Smyrna and Mitylene, across the Aegean to Mount Athos, down between the coast of Greece and Euboea to Marathon and Athens, and westwards to Cephalonia and Ithaca. Then up the Dalmatian coast, with a trip inland to 'unconquered Montenegro', north to Ragusa (Dubrovnik), Spalato (Split) and Zadar (Zara), and last across the Adriatic to Ancona, where they left the yacht on 7 May, and took the train to Rimini.

The American minister's appearance sets the social tone for the trip. Wharton would always travel in style, and this was no exception. Bank directors were ready at various ports to deal with letters of credit and money. When they went to inspect the Festival of the Annunciation on the island of Tinos, they arrived with the American consul and an introduction from the governor of the Cyclades, and made their entrance 'preceded by the Mayor and a soldier to clear the way'. At Mitylene they went ashore in the governor's boat, flags flying. At Corfu they were entertained by the consul's wife, 'who showed us her large collection of Dalmatian buckles, Albanian peasant ornaments, embroidered dresses from Cyprus, and silver yataghans and pistols'. After a wild journey to Cettinje, in Montenegro, they had lunch with the English chargé d'affaires, the Hon. Walter Baring, in his 'wretched little house': 'Cettinje cannot be a very pleasant round in the diplomatic ladder'.

Doors opened to these privileged American sight-seers, who stopped now and then to do a little shopping, or retreated to the yacht when tourism became tiring. Wharton had some of the standard views of her time, as when she speaks of 'a long bridge and causeway, built, of course, like every other good road in the Ionian islands, under the English administration'. Turks usually feature as 'barbarians', or in 'a crowd of Turks, Jews and infidels'; the inhabitants of one island are 'a sullen, ill-favoured lot'. She was fussy, as she always would be, about the hotels. But like all travellers to remote parts, she wanted everything to be picturesque and was disappointed when the sights turned out to be westernised or commercial. True to her reading in Ruskin, she disapproved of restoration.

This was no ordinary American tourist, though, but a 'passionate pilgrim' (in Henry James's phrase), bursting with historical information and literary expectations. She may have been fussy and grand, but she was game for anything, and always very proud of getting far off 'the beaten track', of riding on mules and donkeys, of climbing for eight hours in a horse-drawn carriage up into the wild country of Montenegro, of rescuing a drowning fisherman, or of stoically enduring swelling seas: 'we bounced about so much that our Greek friends were rather unnerved.' She wanted to see everything and she looked with curiosity, judgement, and an intense susceptibility to the beauties of colour, landscape, sea and sky. She had done her homework, and was able to transcribe in her diary the bloody history of the Balkans ('After the subjugation of Servia by the Turks in the fourteenth century, Montenegro asserted itself as an independent state') or the origins of the monasteries on Mount Athos. She always imagined herself into the past, as at Marathon, where she thought of the battle on the plain and the 'dead Greeks' buried beneath the beach. Her imagination was especially fired by the history of the Knights of St John – founded by Italian merchants in the eleventh century in Jerusalem, growing from pilgrim-hospitallers to a military order, driven by the Turks to Cyprus and then to Rhodes, and then retreating, under the Grand Master L'Isle Adam, to Malta. In Rhodes she looked for every architectural trace of the 'Knights in their crowning days of strength', and fantasised about their feelings of exile: 'No wonder that the heart of L'Isle Adam yearned over Rhodes, and that he hesitated and temporized long before abandoning all hopes of its recovery and accepting instead the desolate rock of Malta.' In Malta she found, of all the relics of the order, 'saddest and most interesting of all, the silver trumpet which sounded the retreat from Rhodes'. You can see her beginning to make a novel out of it, one of her narratives of cultural conflict, high ideals dwindling into decadence, failure and longing – like the plot of her Italian novel, *The Valley of Decision*, fourteen years on.

Her aesthetic judgements were choosy and definite. Unlike the guidebooks, she found the cathedral at Monreale too bright, and preferred the Benedictine cloister next door. She quarrelled with a description of a church at Lindos as Byzantine, and found the Golden Gate of the palace at Spalato 'over-praised'. So she went on her way, noting, comparing, and refusing any ready-made opinions. At the same time she was thinking hard about the lives of the inhabitants, even if she was sometimes caricaturing or dismissive. Women's lives – and their clothes – especially interested her: the Jewesses in their silk dresses and gold-embroidered jackets in Algeria, the gorgeously dressed peasant-women with enormous silver shoe-buckles in Corfu, the 'silent and interested' women of the Greek consul's household on Patmos. Priests, monks and hermits also fascinated her (and would continue to do so). She was so frustrated at not being allowed onto Mount Athos that she had the launch from the yacht go 'as near to the forbidden shores' as it could, only to be waved away by wild-looking hermits.[13] Hens, she noted caustically, were not allowed on the island, so eggs had to be brought in. 'As we blew our whistle in passing a hermit appeared on each balcony with the promptitude of cuckoos in Swiss clocks when the hour strikes.' But she was allured by the idea of a way of life that had gone on 'unaffected by modern inventions' for centuries.

Wharton's appetite for scenery was insatiable. She wrote with particular eloquence about gardens: for instance, of the Duc d'Aumale's palace at Palermo:

> On we rambled between hedges of China roses, laurustinus and cytisus, with the golden and pale yellow fruit hanging in masses over our heads, and the ground everywhere carpeted with blossoming yellow oxalis, coming now upon a stone seat under an olive-tree, now coming upon a fountain smothered in ivy and adiantum ... now wandering through shrubberies of oleander, salvia and geranium; but always finding ourselves again under the interminable shade of the orange and lemon groves ...

She said nothing about her relations with her fellow-travellers. But in one of those descriptions, of the enchanting spring hillsides of Ithaca, she made a point of noting that 'we' – she and Teddy, presumably – waited alone for their companions in a grove of olive trees, with bees humming over their heads and the air full of sweetness. It is tempting to imagine from the language used that, for this moment at least, the couple shared some feelings of pleasure and enchantment.

But it is hard to imagine Wharton sharing her literary allusions with Teddy. Europe came at her through her reading, not just of guide-books, and travel narratives like Kinglake's popular 1844 account of the East, *Eothen*, but of Homer and Shelley, Pindar and Macaulay. She took her marked-up copy of Andrew Lang's translation of the *Odyssey* on this cruise, as she would again in 1926.[14] On her first sight of Sicily, from the coast, Wharton saw what seemed to her 'the very goatherds of Theocritus'. She expected her sights to live up to their literary billing: 'The Girgenti of which we have talked and dreamed, the *splendour-loving Acragas* of Pindar, the *topaz-bastioned city* of Symonds – was this Girgenti?' Above all, she was influenced by Goethe, whom she had been reading and marking up since she was fifteen. Her cruise diary had an epigram from *Faust* – his expression of longing for a magic cloak that would carry him into unknown lands. The 'wanderlust' that Goethe gives his romantic heroes, particularly Wilhelm Meister (whose 'apprenticeship' and 'travels' Wharton knew well), inspired this travel-book, as it does all her later travel writings. *Wilhelm Meister* gave her one of her favourite sayings (which she used as one of the epigrams for A *Backward Glance*), 'Kein Genuss ist vorübergehend': 'No pleasure is transitory.'[15]

Wharton was always inspired by Goethe's northern longing for the South. The final destination of the *Vanadis* was Italy, and some of the most eloquent writing in the cruise diary was about Sicily. Twenty years later, she wrote a book on her Italian experiences, *Italian Backgrounds*, which reworked long passages from this diary, especially the descriptions of the country around Syracuse, in this 'clear smiling land where only the spring seemed to have written its tale'.[16] She reused her descriptions from the cruise diary of Sicilian 'gardens of fantastic beauty' – the paths shaded by orange and lemon trees, the dark cypresses. That was the Italy Goethe longed for, the Italy invoked in the plaintive song of Mignon, the androgynous waif of *Wilhelm Meister* who yearns for the country she comes from and never finds again. Back in Rome as an old lady, in 1932, rereading Goethe, nearly fifty years after the cruise of the *Vanadis*, Wharton thinks again of Mignon's song, '*Kennst du das Land*': '*Kennst du das Land, wo die Zitronen blühn . . . Dahin, dahin, möcht Ich mit Dir, O mein Geliebter, gehn!*': 'Do you know the land where the lemons blossom? / The golden oranges gleam among dark leaves, / a gentle wind blows from the blue sky, / the myrtle grows quietly, the laurels tall. / Do you really know it? / Thither, thither / I long to go with you, O my beloved.'[17] 'Do you know the land?' Mignon repeats to Wilhelm after she has sung the song. 'It must be Italy,' he replies.

As for many nineteenth-century lovers of Italy, Goethe's *Italian Journey* (written between 1786 and 1788), as well as *Wilhelm Meister*, was, for Wharton, one of the inspirations for Italian travels. She marked up her copy, referred to it on the *Vanadis* cruise, and took detailed notes from it in her work-books for *The Valley of Decision*. Goethe gave her a model for reading European culture. 'It is impossible to understand the present without knowing the past', he wrote. Wharton often said, of historical facts, especially while writing *The Valley of Decision*, that 'they are no use to me unless I can live into them'.[18] But in order to 'live into' the past, the novelist must be as informed and objective as the historian or archaeologist. Goethe often said that his aim was to 'stick to the objective and concrete', to suppress his 'imagination and emotions in order to preserve [his] faculty for clear and unbiased observation'. There is no point in looking – no point in travelling – unless you can train yourself to understand what you are seeing. And this requires immersion: 'The impressions of a mere tourist are bound to be false', says Goethe in Rome. 'Only in Rome can one educate oneself for Rome.'[19]

Wharton too was determined to be more than an amateur tourist. Her 'travel-fever'[20] was not born of mere restlessness or indulgence. She dedicated herself to the study of European culture through twenty years of reading and travelling. When she reviewed an American guide to Italian cities in 1901, she said that the only useful thing the 'average writer' on Italy could do was to light on 'some unnoticed place, some unrecorded phase of art'. In *Italian Backgrounds*, she reiterated: 'One of the rarest and most delicate pleasures of the continental tourist is to circumvent the compiler of his guide-book.'[21] So began an essay which told, with relish, of her discovery in 1894 that some little-known terracotta figures at the monastery of San Vivaldo (in a remote part of Tuscany) which had been thought to be minor seventeenth-century work, were probably earlier, perhaps late fifteenth-century, a reattribution confirmed by an 'expert' museum-curator in Florence. This discovery set the tone for her writings on Italy; she was transforming herself from eager tourist to cultural expert. Amateurish 'impressions' and raw emotions were not enough. The yearning that fills '*Kennst du das Land*' had to be backed up by years of acquired connoisseurship. Yet responsiveness was vital too. For all Goethe's insistence on objectivity, his *Italian Journey* is loaded with deep romantic emotion, as when in Venice, listening to the gondoliers singing Tasso and Ariosto to each other across the canals by moonlight. In her books on Italy, Wharton does not talk about her feelings, but they pour through her technical descriptions and historical scenes. Italy was a rite of passage for her, an awakener of powerful emotions, and, it may be, a compensation for a frustrated, barren married life.[22]

Wharton's acquisition of Italy through German romanticism and a wide range of European literature was not unusual – it followed the path of many cultured American travellers, some of whom she knew. But she was particularly responsive and well equipped. She had German, Italian and French (and she did not acquire her Goethe through Carlyle's translations, as many of her contemporaries did). This woman who never went to school or university was still educating herself through an ambitious and strenuous programme of reading. From about 1885 to 1905, when the last of her Italian books appeared, she immersed herself in Italian history, art, architecture and literature. Because she wrote only one novel set in Italy, and because the main subjects of her life's work were America and France, this Italian involvement has been rather underplayed in Wharton's life-story. But it dominated her life for twenty years, and was renewed by her later friendship with Berenson. In her seventies, she returned to Rome, the city of her childhood, and set one of her last and greatest stories there, 'Roman Fever', a story about memory and the past, bringing her Italian interest full circle. She wrote to Ogden Codman during her Italian travels in 1895:

'The older I grow, the more I feel that I would rather live in Italy than anywhere. The very air is full of architecture ... Everything else seems coarse or banal beside it ... What an unerring sentiment for form! ... It breaks my heart every time I have to leave it.' To a great extent Italy made her a writer, and provided the space for her to grow up and out of the confines of her class and sex. Among Wharton's favourite quotations – lines which she cherished like talismans – was an image from Wilhelm Meister's account of *Hamlet*. It is of an 'oak tree planted in a precious pot which should only have held delicate flowers; the roots spread out, the vessel is shattered'.[23] It was partly through her journeys to Italy that Wharton spread her roots and burst through the vessel that was meant to hold her.

The Whartons travelled extensively in Europe, and, like their cruise, these travels were done in style, with servants in tow, and a network of contacts to call on. (When these came in useful, like the American ambassador in Rome offering the use of his motor-car, or the Florentine aristocracy opening doors to little-known villas, they were welcomed; but there could be far too much 'Roman tea-drinking' for her taste.) Good hotels were booked ahead: the letters mention the Hotel Royal in San Remo, the Bristol in Rome, the Cavour in Milan. Edith complained bitterly when out-of-the-way inns were dirty or dingy. One of Egerton Winthrop's roles, as their travelling companion, was to calm her down when she 'grumbled a little more than usual'.[24]

The way Edith managed her travels can be deduced from her sister-in-law Minnie Jones's practical tips in *European Travel for Women* (1900). After her divorce in 1896, Minnie and Beatrix frequently travelled to Europe together, especially in the mid-1890s, when they met up with the Whartons in Italy. Minnie's efficient travelling habits would have been very like Edith's. Her book list for Italy is very similar, and so are her attitudes: 'Remember, when you go to a strange country, that its inhabitants have not sent for you ... It is scarcely worth while to go to Europe for the purpose of proclaiming all the time that America is in every way better; if that is your opinion you may show it by going home and never leaving it again.' She tells her readers everything they could possibly need to know: how to avoid getting ill in Italy ('Don't get overheated and then chilled . .. don't eat overripe fruit'), how to exchange letters of credit at foreign banks, how to deal with luggage, porters, trains, omnibuses, touts and timetables. She is particularly helpful on how to cross the Atlantic comfortably: 'Get to know the cabin and bath stewardess ... Interview the deck steward and tell him to put your chair in a sheltered position every morning.'

She knows how to keep fellow travellers at bay: 'A pushing person, encouraged perhaps because you had nothing better to do, may become an intolerable nuisance after you land.' She advises on sensible clothes: 'A proper hat for the sea is one that fits the head closely ... and has a slight brim to protect the eyes from the glare.' 'Wear very simple underclothes while travelling, as they will receive very hard usage from the washerwomen.' She tells you how to identify your luggage easily to Continental porters who may not be able to read, by using colour-coded ribbons for trunks and keys. She knows exactly how and what to pack. There must be a stout leather valise for books, a canvas cover for rugs and shawls, a bag in which 'each little bottle or box, button-hook or nail-file ... has its leather cubby-hole or strap in which it is always to live'. Hand-luggage essentials should include a paper cutter ('not so fine that it would be heartbreaking to lose it'), a fan, a thick gauze veil for dust, a small bottle of brandy, a tin box with a Yale lock for money, slippers, extra buttons, an inkstand and a blotting-book. A medicine chest should have quinine, laxative, and seasickness granules. A rubber hot-water bottle with a separate flannel coat, and a folding waste-paper basket for use on the ship, come in handy. And a portable rubber bath-tub is 'very little trouble'. At the back, useful phrases, in four languages, give the tone of an intrepid lady traveller of Wharton's family, class, and opinions: 'If you treat your horse well, I will give you a good tip.' 'To discourage beggars: Go away!'[25]

Like her sister-in-law, Wharton was a fussy but ruthless tourist. For a woman who was so often ill, she showed phenomenal energy: Europe made her feel better. (It was Alice James, Henry's sister, who described Europe as 'the great American sedative'. For Edith it was more of a tonic.) Most of her Italian travelling was done in the days before the motor-car. Their trip in the American ambassador's car in 1903, from Rome to the Villa Caprarola and back in a day, a hundred-mile round-trip, was her first, and converted her immediately, with amazed exhilaration – and in spite of an attack of laryngitis from the dust – to 'motor-flights'.[26]

In the pre-motor days, though, she prided herself on her stamina, as on their 'toilsome expedition' one spring, in a heavy carriage drawn by tired horses, 'from Florence to Urbino and the Adriatic, by way of San Marino, San Leo, Loreto, Ancona, Pesaro and Rimini'; or their long trek by train, funicular car, and donkey-and-cart, from Florence up to the heights of Vallombrosa, one ravishing spring day in March. Her account of getting to the Tuscan shrine in 1894 makes much of their arduous journey to the little-known San Vivaldo, on a four-hour drive in 'an archaic little carriage' across 'an unknown world', the mountains from San Gimignano towards

Volterra. In 1896, when they spent most of the year in Europe, they discovered the pleasures of bicycling on empty Italian country roads. That
year, their journeys in northern Italy included Venice, where they saw an
exhibition of Wharton's favourite painter, Tiepolo. In the summer of 1899,
travelling with Paul and Minnie Bourget, the Whartons went in arduous
pursuit of an 'interesting church with sculptures' at Cerveno, a remote hill-
village, high above the road that went from Edolo, at the foot of the Alps,
down to Lake Iseo. They reached Cerveno by cart and on foot, to find a
'Via Crucis' of chapels with terracotta figures of the Passion lining the route
up to a church with elaborate wood-carvings: their reward for a very long
detour. (And this was only a few months after she had been 'resting' in
Philadelphia and Washington.) These long travels always had an end in
view: a shrine, a church, a monastery, a historical site, a ruin: the less well-
known the better. There was also a great deal of shopping. She wrote to
Codman in June 1896: 'I never before realised the absurd cheapness of 18th
century furniture in Italy, & there is so much of it left . . . Late Louis XVI
commode, white & gold, very much ornamented, marble top, 125 lire!! 6
Louis XVI armchairs, 100 lire!!!'[27]

Gradually, over years of travel and reading, Wharton came to feel in
possession of Italy. She wrote three books on the country (as well as poems
and stories with Italian themes): a historical novel that came out in 1902;
then, because of its success, a book on Italian villas and gardens that the
editor of *Century Magazine*, Richard Gilder, asked her to write; and lastly
a book of travel-essays that had been published as magazine articles during
the 1890s and 1900s.

She worked hard on the research for the villas all through 1903, covering
the ground assiduously. Letters to Sara Norton, in the spring of 1903, give
a glimpse of her itinerary. After a stay in Rome, they went to Viterbo,
Montefiascone, Orvieto, 'the delicious villas near Siena', and then to
Florence. 'I am doing far too much,' (she wrote to Sally on 23 March 1903)
'as I know a few people living in the villas outside Florence, and the temptation to go and take tea on a terrace at Fiesole or at San Miniato, interferes
with my real work, which is hunting up and photographing old villas.'[28]
Her path crossed with a great many Anglo-American lovers of Italy – the
archaeologist William Buckler and his wife; Mary Crawshay, an impressive
Englishwoman living in Rome, who would remain a friend; the brilliant
Bayard Cutting and his young Irish wife Sybil, a future thorn in Edith's
flesh. There was a disastrous first meeting with the Berensons at the Villa
La Doccia in March 1903 ('We disliked her intensely', Mary Berenson
noted; it would take several years for the friendship to be made).[29] In Rome,

one of her favourite venues was the Countess Pasolini's. Maria Pasolini, a friend of Daisy Chanler, whom Edith found cultured and intelligent (unlike some of the other Italians she was meeting), was the sister-in-law of the Countess Angelica Rasponi. The Countess Rasponi had inherited the Villa Font'allerta, near Florence, in 1876, from her father, Count Pasolini, who had been a leader of the 'Young Italy' party and the main mover behind the union of Venice and Italy in 1866. Their neighbour Janet Ross described the Villa Font'allerta enthusiastically in her *Florentine Villas* of 1901. A more sceptical view of this Anglo-Tuscan society would be provided a few years later by the young Virginia Stephen, travelling in Italy in 1909, and meeting Janet Ross ('brusque & imperious'), the Berensons and other local notables. Virginia Stephen, aged twenty-seven, drew a swift and disrespect-ful portrait in her diary of the Countess Rasponi, whom Edith Wharton so much admired:

> The Countess is an Anglo Italian celebrity – a stout, decisive woman, broad, almost squat featured; her cheek dark red, & scarred by a dogs bite; her eye prominent – altogether her appearance is vigorous, im-perious, & subtle too at the same time. She watches & springs, but calculations go on forever within the brain.[30]

As well as mixing in Florentine and Roman society, villa-hunting and travelling, Edith also took the 'cure' at Salsomaggiore, the grand, ugly spa town in the hot plains of Emilio Romagna, just west of Parma. Suffering from bursts of asthma and exhaustion in the middle of all her activity, she went to 'Salso' (which she described as looking like the 'backyards of Jersey City, as seen from the train') for the first time in April 1903. It was then, she said, 'beginning to be the fashionable cure for throats & noses. It is a desperate-looking hole, planted in the middle of bare volcanic hills, just high enough to prevent one from seeing the real Apennines beyond. There are no walks, & worse than no drives . . . penitential.' But: 'I have been taking the inhalations strenuously for 12 days & the immediate effect is wonderful.'[31] She returned there whenever she felt the need, in later years because of high blood pressure and circulation problems, overweight and 'dry congestion' in the head. She stayed at Cesar Ritz's Grand Hôtel des Thermes (with '*tutte le comodità moderna*' including '*luce elettrice*', '*ascen-sore*', '*un superbo parco*' and '*disinfezione delle camere*'). 'Mrs Edith Warthon' would feature in *Il Gazzetino di Salsomaggiore* and the *Gazzettino Balneare* (Salso had enough society to support two local papers), among the other arrivals and departures under 'Il Mondo a Salsomaggiore'. There were wealthy health-seekers from Italy, Russia, Egypt, France, England, the USA

– among them (in the list for 1912), Princesse Dorothy Radziwill of Rome, Princesse de Lyar of Paris, Mme Charles Hunter of London, Mr André Ponomaroff of St Petersburg, Mr and Mrs Allen Curtiss of Boston, Mrs Bruce Geddes of Scotland, M. Edouard Hermann of Paris, and the Marquise de Ripon Lady de Gray of England. The Grand Hotel advertised itself as *'preferito dalla grande società internazionale'* – or as Edith would describe it to Morton Fullerton in 1911, it was full of 'shrieking squalling Princesses, Duchesses & prostitutes'.

This upper-class, international crowd moved in leisurely, sickly fashion all day long from the monumental grandeur of the hotel, to the marble halls, caryatids, stucco and oriental decor of the vast Egyptian-style 'Terme Berzieri', to the tea-rooms and couture-shops and concerts provided by the little town. Every day, they had doctors' consultations and took inhalations, massages, baths and exercises for arthritis, sciatica, neuralgia, asthma, stomach disorders, weight problems and nervous conditions. Edith was sent on walks on the dusty roads around the spa, and drank in 'salt steam' inhalations, improving (as she put it) her 'snuffatoires'.[32]

When her villa essays began to be serialised, in November 1903, it occurred to her that her travel-essays might also make a timely book: 'for there is such a great rush to Italy every autumn now on the Mediterranean steamers, & people so often ask me where these articles can be found'. She discussed with her editor, William Brownell, what her title should be. He turned down her suggestion of 'Italian Impressions'. 'It isn't cathedral enough', he told her. She suggested 'Italian Backgrounds', to mean that 'the most interesting Italy is the one in the background, behind the official guide-book Italy'.[33] *Italian Backgrounds* was the last of her three Italian books to be published, but it took shape during those adventurous journeys of the 1890s. It included her essay on her discovery in the Tuscan shrine, published in *Scribner's Magazine* in 1895 – her first piece of non-fictional prose writing. An 1899 journey from Switzerland into northern Italy was written up as two separate essays, published in June 1900 and August 1902. Essays on Parma, and on the pilgrimage shrines of the Italian Alps, were also published in 1902, and another essay on Milan was published in February 1903. For the book, she added three more essays, one on hermits, one on 'March in Italy' (Syracuse, Orvieto and Vallombrosa) and one called 'Italian Backgrounds' (Rome and Venice) to match the book's now-agreed title. She planned to use her own photographs, but an illustrator, E.C. Peixotto, was brought in. The book was done by the summer of 1904, but, to avoid too much overlap with *Italian Villas and Their Gardens* (published in November 1904 after its magazine serialisation was over), *Italian*

Backgrounds did not come out until April 1905 – only six months before *The House of Mirth*. So it has the look of a mature book of her forties, but in fact was compiled over ten years and was a fusing-together of twenty years of looking, learning and loving.

In *Italian Backgrounds*, Wharton makes a point of distinguishing her knowledgeable travels from those of the usual American tourists, 'Americans going "right through", with their city and state writ large upon their luggage'. By contrast, she delights in the out-of-the-way shrine, the artist not praised by Ruskin, the kind of town (like Tirano) which 'holds in reserve for the observant eye a treasure of quiet impressions', or the kind of landscape (like Lake Orta, west of Lake Maggiore) which 'has a secret charm . . . that makes it seem the special property of each traveller who chances to discover it'. She often talks about travelling and looking as a kind of reading in brackets, or in the margins: 'It is in the intervals between such systematized study of the past, in the parentheses of travel, that one obtains those more inti-mate glimpses.' 'Italy, to her real lovers, is like a great illuminated book, with here and there a glorious full-page picture, and between these, page after page of delicately-pencilled margins.' Reading in the margins means looking over the shoulder of the central figures in the famous pictures or frescos (as, best of all, in Carpaccio) to the landscapes behind them, 'to catch a glimpse of the life around which the painting originated'. In some of the poems she wrote about Italy, like a poem on the landscape behind the Mona Lisa, she says nothing about the main figure at all.[34] In the Italian countryside, she often feels as if she has entered into the backgrounds, or margins, of such paintings. An early start through the Tuscan landscape near San Gimignano has the fresh brightness of a Botticelli. 'We seemed to be driving through the landscape of a missal.'[35]

In the backgrounds of the great paintings, she looks for the representa-tion of ordinary lives. In her travels, it is always the lives of nameless people which arouse her imagination, whether these are the poor mountain folk who line the shrine of the Black Virgin at Oropa with votive offerings, 'so that the whole church is lined with heart-beats', or the patients she imag-ines sunning themselves in the courtyard of the magnificent Ospedale Maggiore in Milan, or the hedonistic citizens of eighteenth-century Venice. In the religious buildings of Italy, she tries to get a sense of the 'way in which in Italy, nature, art and religion continue to enrich the humblest lives'. She is fascinated (as at Mount Athos) by hermits and 'desert saints' and their representation in Italian art. She vividly imagines the solitary lives of such men, in touch with 'the terror and the poetry' of the wilderness – and wrote one of her strangest Italian stories on this theme in 1906, 'The Hermit and the Wild Woman'. This side of Wharton's writing seems remote from the characters in her fiction who are engrossed in worldly, materialistic society. Yet they, like their author, are often attracted by the idea of solitude. The hermits and solitaries appeal to her as an antidote to the modern world; and because they suggest a link or transition between the old heathen gods and Christianity. 'The gods know when their time has come', she says, sadly. In mythological fourteenth-century paintings such as those of Piero di Cosimo, with their 'half-human, half-sylvan creatures', 'one has the impression of that intermediate world, the twilight world of the conquered, Christianised, yet still lingering Gods'. It is typical of her to be so interested in the evolution of beliefs and in periods of cultural transition.[36]

In this country she has made her own, she speaks out very firmly about her likes and dislikes. She lavishes her eloquence on her special preferences, some of them little-known or not at all in fashion: the friezes in the baptistery at Parma, with their 'great vehemence of gesture and expression', or the baroque architecture of Rome, expressing 'the *bravura* spirit of Bernini and Borromini'. Among many such individualistic enthusiasms, there is a dazzling account of the exquisite Portinari Chapel of Sant'Eustorgio in Milan, which she likes because of its perfect match between architectural design and decorations, and its ravishing colours:

> From the cupola, with its scales of pale red and blue, overlapping each other like the breast-plumage of a pigeon, and terminating in a terra-cotta frieze of dancing angels, who swing between them great bells of fruit and flowers, the eye is led by insensible gradations of tint to Foppa's frescoes in the spandrels – iridescent saints and angels in a setting of pale classical architecture – and thence to another frieze of terra-cotta seraphs with rosy-red wings against a background of turquoise-green; this lower frieze resting in turn on pilasters of pale green adorned with white stucco *rilievi* of little bell-ringing angels.[37]

So much did Wharton make Italy her own 'special property' that she came to feel that she was more worthy of Italy than the Italians:

> I think sometimes that it is almost a pity to enjoy Italy as much as I do, because the acuteness of my sensations makes them rather exhausting; but when I see the stupid Italians I have met here, completely insensitive to their surroundings, & ignorant of the treasures of art & history among which they have grown up, I begin to think it is better to be an American, & bring to it all a mind & eye unblunted by custom.[38]

This was not an unusual boast for a cultured American traveller. Wharton's reaction to Italy was her own, but it was also influenced by a nineteenth-century tradition of Europhilia. One of the leading figures in this tradition was the American academic and art-historian Charles Eliot Norton, the most venerable and learned of several mentors who introduced her to Italy and Italian culture. Norton had spent much of his early life in Italy. Giotto, Dante and Ruskin were his idols. He was Harvard's first professor of art history from 1875 to 1898, and his influential lectures on Italy followed his friend and mentor Ruskin in rejecting everything after the late medieval period. When Edith came to know him he was one of the grand old men of American culture. He lived in a beautiful, bookish New England house, in Ashfield, in the Deerfield Valley, a sheltered landscape in north-west New England. Widowed young, he had brought up six children, rather strictly, with the help of his sister Grace. Of the two daughters he had pressed into loving service, and who never married or left the parental home – highly intelligent women who both suffered from depression and illness – Sara, or 'Sally', was Edith's good friend from the 1900s. Sally's self-sacrifice, her life's dedication to her distinguished father, which went on after his death, as such lives of service often do, in her editing of his letters, lay beneath Wharton's story 'The Angel at the Grave' (1901), written well before Norton's death in 1908. Like other stories set in a New England academic context ('The Pretext', 'The Descent of Man') the story, of male intellectual tyranny and female self-obliteration, suggests that Wharton cast as satirical an eye on Boston high-mindedness as she did on the hermits of Mount Athos.

But her personal relation to Norton was one of quasi-filial reverence and intellectual obligation, as in the respectful sonnet she wrote in his honour when he was eighty. When she mentioned to Sally in 1901 that she needed books for *The Valley of Decision* about the 'état d'âme' (a Nortonish phrase) of Italians in the 1790s, he sent her some otherwise unobtainable history books. Returning these, she wrote nicely: 'They have given me so much companionship these last months that to send them back to you is like parting with old friends.' When *The Valley* came out, Sally copied to Edith a letter Charles Norton had written to a friend, praising the novel as a 'work of genius' for its scholarship, but adding that 'It is too thoughtful and too fine a book to be popular'. Norton embodied the tradition of 'genteel' American culture which felt alienated from modern America's 'aggressive materialism'. He wrote to his friend William Dean Howells in 1902: 'I feel like an exile in my own country.'[39] The tone is echoed in Wharton's much-quoted statement to

Sally Norton the following year, 1903, on her return from Italy and England:

> My first few weeks in America are always miserable, because the tastes I am cursed with are all of a kind that cannot be gratified here, & I am not enough in sympathy with our 'gros public' to make up for the lack on the aesthetic side. One's friends are delightful; but *we* are none of us Americans, we don't think or feel as the Americans do, we are the wretched exotics produced in a European glass-house, the most déplacé and useless class on earth! All of which outburst is due to my first sight of American streets, my first hearing of American voices, & the wild, dishevelled backwoods look of everything when one first comes home! You see in my heart of hearts, a heart never unbosomed, I feel in America as you say you do in England – out of sympathy with everything.[40]

The reader of this 'outburst' would have been reminded of her father's own sense of internal exile and chronic longing for Europe – a state of mind he shared with many cultured, alienated Americans. Wharton would have continued to speak in that voice if she had never left America. But she had something tougher than genteel longing and fine feeling. It is revealing that Norton found *The House of Mirth* too risqué and worldly for his taste. Nevertheless, his erudition and taste helped to shape Wharton's approach to Italy and to art.[41]

She had two other remarkable 'introducers' to Italy, Paul Bourget and Vernon Lee. Paul Bourget was the first novelist she came to know well. They met when Bourget was visiting America in 1893, collecting impressions for his book *Outre-Mer* (which began life as a series of articles for the *New York Herald*). Wharton was a young hostess in Newport which Bourget, she said, thought of as an overseas 'Deauville'. In her 1936 reminiscence of this meeting, she remembered their mutual eagerness: hers to meet her first 'great French writer', his to see at first hand the 'worldliness' of this American resort where she and Teddy spent their summers and which by then she was finding 'frivolous and monotonous'.[42] Bourget's *Outre-Mer: Impressions of America* (1895) would be a strong influence on Wharton when she started to make her own cross-cultural comparisons between America and France. But they first made friends not because of her interest in France but because of their shared passion for Italy. It was the Venetian furniture and the books on Italy that made Bourget's eyes light up when he visited Land's End. The two writers, one in his early forties, much travelled, already well known as a 'psychological' novelist, a brilliant opinionated talker, the other in her early thirties, not yet published, confined in her role as a married hostess, but full of informed interest in the country they were both in love with, rapidly talked themselves into friendship, with an affable Teddy and a delicate, quiet, sensitive Minnie Bourget in attendance. Both these spouses would fall victim to mental illness; the Wharton marriage would break apart, the Bourget marriage would become grimly reclusive and morbid. But in the 1890s this four-way relationship worked well. Minnie Bourget, née David, had the kind of international European background which greatly appealed to Wharton. Her father's family were Belgian Catholics from Antwerp; her mother, Emma Meticke, came from a Trieste family of Jewish bankers, operating in Italy and Austria. Minnie moved to Paris from Antwerp when she was twelve, and the family also had a house in northern Italy. Paul Bourget had been going to Italy for years when he met Wharton, and had just published *Sensations d'Italie*, in 1892. The book described a journey made in the autumn of 1890, but (as Wharton would in *Italian Backgrounds*) Bourget conflated into it many years of travel. After their meeting in 1893 they travelled to Italy together several times, and their journey together in 1899 was one of the main sources of material for *Italian Backgrounds*.

Retrospectively, Wharton was dismissive about the amateurish impressionism of some of the 'agreeable volumes of the cultured dilettante type' like *Sensations d'Italie*, which had, in their time, 'opened the eyes and stimulated the imagination of countless intelligent travellers' before they were superseded by more professional, specialised writings. But Bourget's knowledge and tastes did influence her response to the country. She looked back with affection on the journeys the four of them made to see 'beautiful forgotten things in unknown corners', ending the day in an inn, talking about what they had seen over 'spaghetti and chianti'. She often referred to *Sensations d'Italie*, respectfully in *Italian Backgrounds*, or as a private joke with their mutual friends. 'I haven't had time to send you my "sensations d'Ashfield"', she wrote to Sally after a visit to the Nortons in August 1901. 'Send me your "sensations de Rome"', she ordered Daisy Chanler in the spring of 1903.[43]

Bourget's impressions were based, like Goethe's, on an overwhelming passion for the country (when he first started going to Italy in the 1870s he was 'almost ill, so much was I intoxicated by the passion for art and beauty'), an immersion in the same historians and poets that Wharton was reading and a desire, like hers, to 'work the miracle of resurrection' bringing history alive. His reading of Italy was coloured with an intense melancholy, a pessimistic, reactionary sense of the inevitable failure of all '*risorgimentos*' (which she echoed in *The Valley of Decision*) and an elegiac feeling – very much of its time – for classical ruins. At the temple of Hera Lacinia of Cotrone in Calabria, where only one pillar remains out of the original forty-four, reached, in order to garner his 'sensations', after a long and arduous boat-journey, Bourget meditates on 'time which never ceases to pass, to increase and to decrease eternally, the sea with its everlasting shuddering and sighing, and the human ideal which ceaselessly protests against the inexplicable decay which all its best work suffers', and is struck by his boatman's comment: '*E col tempo anche questa caderà*', said he ('In time this one will fall also').⁴⁴ Presumably there was quite a lot of this over the spaghetti and chianti, and that tone of elegy gets into Wharton's Italian work. She too was concerned – and not only in Italy – with the ephemerality of highly evolved civilisations.

Wharton met through Bourget the third of her Italian mentors, the only one of the three to have gone enviably native. 'Vernon Lee', the extraordinary Englishwoman Violet Paget, was only six years older than Edith, and provided her first close encounter with a professional woman writer. Wharton made few friendships with other women writers, and Vernon Lee, brilliant, loquacious, difficult, eccentric and mannish (she wore 'the style preferred by intellectual lesbians – a man's shirt, foulard and velvet jacket over a long skirt'),⁴⁵ was not to be a lifelong friend. But, just when Wharton needed it, she was a perfect guide to Italy and an inspiring intellectual example.

Wharton often told Vernon Lee what an important guide she was to her, that when she was twenty 'your *Eighteenth century studies* were letting me into that wonder world of Italy which I had loved since my childhood without having the key to it'. Vernon Lee's *Studies of the Eighteenth Century in Italy* (1880) gave vivid evocations of the hitherto neglected musical, literary and theatrical life of the period. In Vernon Lee's 'aesthetic essays' *Belcaro* (1880), which Wharton called one of her 'best-loved companions of the road' in Italy, she would have recognised glimpses of a childhood in Rome very much like her own. 'The Child in the Vatican' remembers – as Wharton did – playing in the ruins, picking up pieces of ancient porphyry, watching the religious processions, and imbibing – in the classical term Lee made her own – the 'genius loci', the spirit of the place. Like Wharton, Vernon Lee had an itinerant European childhood. Hers was with a domineering mother, an absentee father, and a permanently ill, demanding and gifted half-brother, Eugene Lee-Hamilton, whom one Wharton biographer calls 'a neurasthenic paralytic'. Edith was as much intrigued by the frail, poetic Lee-Hamilton as by his sister. He visited her at The Mount in 1906 and she was delighted when he compared *The Valley of Decision* to

Stendhal. When he died, she wrote an effusive tribute to him, comparing his poems to Leopardi's.[46] The family settled in Florence in the 1880s, where they met the Bourgets, and then moved outside the city in 1889 to the Villa Il Palmerino, where Vernon Lee lived for most of her life. The simple, rambling house stood on the road winding up from Florence, over-shadowed by a tall umbrella pine, backing onto fields, vineyards and woods, and surrounded by olives and cypresses.

Violet Paget was much quicker and more assertive than Edith Wharton in her jump into literary fame. She took the name Vernon Lee in her teens, as she was sure that 'no one reads a woman's writing on art, history or aesthetics with anything but unmitigated contempt'. The *Studies of the Eighteenth Century in Italy* was her first book, published when she was twenty-four. It made her into a young literary success in late-Victorian England, where she got to know Henry James, Maurice Baring, Ethel Smyth, Mrs Humphry Ward, William Morris and Leslie Stephen. She followed her early success with a Germanic, quasi-incestuous romance, *Ottilie*, clearly based on her relationship with Eugene, and a decadent novel, *Miss Brown* (1885), deeply embarrassing to Henry James, to whom it was dedicated, for what he called its 'intellectual rowdyism'. Then there was a succession of essays on places, art and aesthetics, and of plays and romances set in Italy.

She quarrelled with everybody (notably, in 1897, with her neighbour Berenson, who accused her of plagiarism; they did not make up until 1920, by which time Wharton was firmly in the Berenson camp). In the years when Wharton came to know her, between 1894 and 1906, there were tumultuous fallings-out not only with her fellow Anglo-American Florentines, but with Eugene (who made a miraculous recovery in 1896, and even got married, much to his half-sister's horror) and with her companion Kit Anstruther-Thomson, who, like others of Vernon Lee's women friends, gave her up in despair to go and look after some other woman's needs. Everyone, even people who liked her, made rude jokes about her. Max Beerbohm, who caricatured her, called her a 'dreadful little bore and busybody'. Nicky Mariano, Berenson's companion, used to see her in the 1920s on the tram from Settignano to Florence, mannishly dressed, and marvelled at her face of 'almost baroque ugliness and high intelli-gence'.[47] Wharton was so amused by Henry James's spoken description of Vernon Lee that she noted it down:

> The long lean face of a starved horse, large and intelligent eyes not wholly devoid of obliquity, a flabby pendulous nose covered with cuta-neous scabs, an underhung jaw revealing a dental display of a really

deplorable character, and on her head, my dear boy, from nine to thirteen hairs.[48]

But everyone who met her said how wonderful it was to be shown Italy by Vernon Lee, and that passionate inwardness with the country is found in her books. She loved to lure the reader into a historical moment through evocations and personalities, and then let the figures of the past linger like ghosts. In her essay on 'Old Italian Gardens' of 1897, in the middle of a hard-headed account of the phases of fashion in Italian garden-design, she breaks into a fantasy about how these gardens are haunted by 'the ladies and cavaliers of long ago' and by 'the ghost of certain moments of their existence, certain rustlings, and shimmerings of their personality . . . which have permeated their old haunts', and invokes Verlaine's poem 'Clair de Lune' (a favourite of Wharton's, too), as set to music by Fauré, to sum up the haunted magic of the gardens: '*Votre âme est un paysage choisi / Que vont charmant masques et bergamasques / Jouant du luth . . . Et leur chanson se mêle au clair de lune . . .*'[49]

Wharton occasionally allows herself such flights of fancy in *Italian Villas and their Gardens*, which she dedicated to Vernon Lee ('Who, better than anyone else, has understood and interpreted the garden-magic of Italy'), as when the 'mysterious silence' and neglect of the gardens of the Florentine Villa Campi makes her think of 'a haunted grove in which the statues seem like sylvan gods fallen asleep in their native shade'. In *Italian Backgrounds*, Wharton also quotes 'Clair de Lune', and says that, under the spell of the poem's '*masques et bergamasques*', she was so allured by the idea of the 'Bergamasque Alps' that in 1899 she dragged her travelling companions for miles in pursuit of them, though in the end 'the most imperturbable member of the party' (Teddy, as he was then) noted that, interesting though their journey had been, they had never actually reached them.[50]

Vernon Lee gave Wharton a model for a way of invoking the past, an authoritative woman's voice confidently taking on the male terrain of travel and aesthetics, and a deep knowledge of and passion for Italy, especially its eighteenth-century history. When Vernon Lee reviewed *The Valley of Decision* in 1903, in Italian, greeting it with generous enthusiasm as 'a wonderful account of historical truth', she would have seen her own influence at work in the novel.[51] (This essay was to be an introduction for an Italian translation of the novel which never materialised.) She was equally influential, ten years later, on the young writer Geoffrey Scott, a protégé of the Berensons, who would become a close friend of Wharton's, and whose book *The Architecture of Humanism* (1914) helped to revive a taste for the Italian baroque. It was written with Vernon Lee in mind, and with much advice and encouragement from Wharton, by then an acknowledged Italian expert: 'Her opinion is the most useful I can get', Scott said.[52]

Wharton had to outgrow Vernon Lee, as she did her other 'introducers'. She made a point of telling her editor at *Scribner's Magazine* that her discovery about the terracotta figures at San Vivaldo was news even to 'Miss Paget, who has lived so long in Italy and devoted so much time to the study of Tuscan art'. When Vernon Lee's unperformed 'romance in five acts', *Ariadne in Mantua*, came out in 1903, Wharton told her it was 'exquisite' but lacking in 'movement and clash of emotions'. In later years, when in bossy letters Vernon Lee would tell her that she should write about Proust with less 'piety', or that *Hudson River Bracketed* contained too much 'cult chat', Wharton received these criticisms ironically: 'for a damsel of over seventy (a good deal) this is symptomatic, isn't it?' By then Vernon Lee was a sad figure, suffering from failing health and deafness, and the two women were not close. But Wharton still wrote to her kindly, sympathising with her affliction and assuring her of her achievements:

> I was very much grieved by what you told me of the increase in your deafness. I cannot tell you how I feel for you in this great privation, and how distressed I am when I am with you that my voice should be so powerless to reach you. I am particularly unfortunate in this respect for my voice has no carrying power, and I feel I can be of so little use or companionship to my friends who cannot hear. And yet we did manage to have a talk that last day at Il Palmerino, and it seemed to me that we were as much together as we used to be in the old days when the physical barrier did not exist.

> If you *don't* know the great figure you've been, in letters & friendship, to me & many others I cd name it's time you learnt it, & I'm proud to be your informant! So there —[53]

Wharton earned her special relationship with Italy through wide reading as much as through people. In her memoir, she says it would be impossible to list 'even a fraction' of the books she was reading in the 1870s and 1880s – it would turn her autobiography into 'a library catalogue'. But she also says that omitting even one of her books is like omitting 'the name of a human friend'.[54] Instead of love-affairs, or children, or an absorbing marriage, the romance and excitement of Wharton's life were, for many years, her Italian reading, travelling and writing.

Behind her reading for Italy lay her formative interests in philosophy and science. Nietzsche, Darwin, Herbert Spencer, and William Hamilton's

History of Philosophy developed her thinking about the power of the will, humanity's perpetual argument between faith and rationality, and the relation of the individual to processes of biological and cultural evolution. She liked to think on a large scale and she liked specialist information. She did not just read Dante, she read a study of the *Paradiso*, and books on Dante and thirteenth-century Catholic philosophy. She did not want just to have a 'misty haunting sense of the beauty of old buildings', and so lapped up James Fergusson's *History of Architecture*, one of the few books available in the 1880s, she says, which gave her the precise historical information she needed. (John Addington Symonds in his *Sketches in Italy and Greece* [1879], another of her background books, made use of Fergusson too.) Fergusson linked to her reading in Darwin and Spencer by giving her an evolutionary model for European history. Like Goethe, she wanted to study cultural developments in Italian history. For this she read Jacob Burckhardt's *The Civilization of the Renaissance in Italy*, which brought to life the rule of the tyrants during the wars between the Guelfs and the Ghibellines, or the *commedia dell'arte*, or the Renaissance investment in fame, wit and individualism. She read Cornelius Gurlitt's book on the Italian baroque, and John Addington Symonds's *The Renaissance in Italy*, which described (under headings like 'The Age of the Despots', or 'The Revival of Learning') how the 'intellectually barren and inert' medieval age was displaced by new energies and freedom. Symonds, writing in the 1870s, drew explicitly on 'Darwinian speculation': he saw 'the history of civilization' as a process of evolution, like 'the biography of man'. He contrasted the vigour and confidence of the Renaissance with modern neuroses: 'Ennui and the fatigue that springs from skepticism, the despair of thwarted effort, were unknown.'[55]

That was a strong Victorian theme, also voiced by Matthew Arnold, or Robert Browning in his dazzling, psychologically fascinating portrayals of the Italian Renaissance in all its glamour, violence and amorality, in poems like 'My Last Duchess', 'Fra Lippo Lippi', or 'The Bishop Orders his Tomb at Saint Praxed's Church'. Many other poets influenced her feelings about Italy – Dante, Goethe, Verlaine, and the great romantic pessimist, Leopardi, to whose home in the remote town of Recanati she would one day make a pilgrimage.[56] But Browning was a huge influence on her, and her Italian books are full of him. In her account of Venice in *Italian Backgrounds* she draws on his 'A Toccata of Galuppi's', with its elegiac, wistful *memento mori* of eighteenth-century Venice and its 'dear dead women, with such hair, too –': 'What of soul was left, I wonder, when the kissing had to stop?' It is one of her favourite poems, and she often quotes it, not just when she is writing about Italy.

As well as the poets, her library had Alfieri's romantic tragedies, the librettist Da Ponte's 'Venetian love-adventures', the works of Machiavelli, Castiglione's *Book of the Courtier*, Casanova's eventful *Mémoires*, and the plays and poems of D'Annunzio (though he was not a favourite of hers). She was addicted to memoirs and travel journals. She enjoyed Dr Burney's eighteenth-century diaries, or John Evelyn's gossip, or the letters of the French magistrate Charles de Brosses, a highly cultured visitor to Italy in the 1730s. De Brosses's delightful accounts of taking a boat up the Brenta canal – with some good wine – to visit the 'beautiful houses of the noble Venetians', or the parade of human curiosities he found in Venice, provided colour for *The Valley of Decision*.[57] She liked Arthur Young's traveller's reports, always noticing terrible roads, poor food and eccentric character-types, and parodied them, very well, in the novel. She marked up in her books the comments on Italy which caught her interest, like Browning's description of Rome in a letter to Elizabeth Barrett in September 1845, or, in her copy of James's letters, his outburst to his brother William from Rome, on 30 October 1869: 'At last – for the first time – I live!'

It was 'the patient accumulation of detail' that most attracted her. One 'delightful book, half romance, half autobiography', of 1807, the *Confessions* of a romantic young man from the Veneto, Ippolito Nievo (who fought with Garibaldi, was always hopelessly in love, and died at twenty-nine) gave Wharton a vivid sense, much as a 'Dutch genre painter' might have done, of the lives of the provincial nobility in the beautiful little northern towns she loved, like Mantua and Sabbioneta. She enjoyed, too, (as Vernon Lee did) the *Useless Memoirs* (1797) of the Venetian playwright Carlo Gozzi, conservative, patriotic and belligerent, full of vivid pictures of Venetian life and gossip about his feud with the great Goldoni, over whether the *commedia dell'arte* had had its day, and should be superseded by a more natural comedy. Gozzi's and Goldoni's eighteenth-century Italy was especially attractive to her. She attributed her interest in the period not, initially, to her reading of Vernon Lee, but to an encounter with a chair. This took place in the house of the painter Julian Story, who was painting her portrait, unsatisfactorily, in Paris in 1886. (He was a friend of Teddy's and the son of William Wetmore Story, whose life Henry James wrote.) Story told her that the chair she was admiring in his studio for its simple elegance was 'eighteenth-century Venetian' – a period, he said, neglected by art-critics and historians alike. This, she would say – as usual dramatising a crucial moment of change in her memoir – all at once gave 'a new turn' to her imagination.[58] She could see that the Italian Renaissance was too crowded a field for her to get a foothold in. As on her journeys to obscure destinations, she was eager to make a cultural space for herself. In choosing eighteenth-century Italy she turned her back on her father's generation's dedication to Ruskin, who had no interest in the Italian baroque or anything after it.

She liked the realism and the sense of ordinary lives she could get from eighteenth-century Italian culture. In *Italian Backgrounds*, Wharton compared Goldoni's plays, with their 'quietly humorous observation', to the paintings of Pietro Longhi, who opened little windows on to 'Venetian domestic life'. She lists Longhi's subject matter affectionately – breakfast scenes, dancing lessons, marionette-shows – and praises him, as she does Goldoni, for simplicity and naturalness, for pictures that are like 'actual transcripts from life'. Wharton (as John Addington Symonds did, in a passage she noted) compares Longhi's paintings with Goldoni's 'kindly glance and absence of gravity or depth'.[59] She was developing her thoughts, in her Italian readings, about how fiction could balance realism with the excitement of romantic drama.

All the books she read on Italy would at some point exclaim on the theatricality of Italian life and on the charm, vulgarity and immorality of the old *commedia dell'arte*, whose characters had lingered on in the carnivals of Rome and Venice. Goethe gave Wilhelm Meister his own childhood passion for his Italian puppet theatre, and Wilhelm Meister's life in Italy with the travelling players influenced *The Valley of Decision*. (Wharton would recall it again when she visited George Sand's house at Nohant in 1907 and saw her marionette theatre.) Wharton took copious notes (from Symonds and others) about the history and performance of the *commedia dell'arte*, in her research for her novel. She noted that the term 'masks' referred to the leather masks the actors wore, but also to the fixed character-types, like Pantalone, Pulcinella and Colombina, who were drawn from the different regions of Italy, and who entranced her.[60]

It was the spectacular, theatrical, illusory quality of Italy that most aroused her. From her childhood in Rome, she had been fascinated by the colourful rituals, the music, the costume-drama, 'the flowery bombardment of the Carnival procession watched with shrieks of infant ecstasy'. She loves to write about the carnival, the popular songs and the travelling players, like the Columbine and Scaramouche of 'the old popular theatre' bounding on stage in *The Valley of Decision* with their inexhaustible 'flow of jest and repartee', or the Puritan American boy out of Hawthorne, bamboozled by masqueraders in her story of 1760s Venice, 'A Venetian Night's Entertainment' (1903). *Italian Backgrounds* is eloquent about the Farnese Theatre in Parma ('an immediate evocation of the strolling theatrical life of the seventeenth and eighteenth centuries'), or her pursuit of the Bergamasque Alps for their association with 'the jolly figures of Harlequin and Brighella'.[61] But there is something melancholy, too, about these spectacles. *Italian Backgrounds* ends (with a sad little echo of Browning) by describing the mannequins dressed in eighteenth-century costume in the Museo Correr in Venice, like defunct characters from an old play, representing what is 'essentially a world of *appearances*'.

> There they stand, poor dolls of destiny, discarded playthings of the gods, in attitudes of puzzled wonder, as if arrested in their revels by the stroke of the dread Corsican magician – for it was not Death, but Napoleon, who 'stepped tacitly and took them' from the plots and pleasures, the sunshine and music of the canals, to that pale world of oblivion where only now and then some dreamer curious of the day of little things revisits their melancholy ghosts.[62]

She is haunted, too, by the old folk-songs of regional Italy. (She had a copy of the 1856 *Canti Popolari Toscani* in her library, signed 'Edith Jones, 1878', and would quote one of the unhappy love-songs in her love-diary for 1908.) In *The Valley of Decision*, the life-story of the actress who plays Columbine breaks off for a plaintive song of the Abruzzi: 'Flower of the thyme! / She draws me as your fragrance draws the bees, / She draws me as the cold moon draws the seas, / And summer winter-time.'[63]

Her own poems of Italy are loaded with romantic longing and a powerful sense of the past. The first poem she ever published professionally was 'The Last Giustiniani', in *Scribner's Magazine* in October 1889. It is an eighteenth-century Venetian story of a monk who has to go back into the world and marry, because he is the last of his family line. Henry James used (and modernised) the plot in his catastrophically unsuccessful play of 1895, *Guy Domville*. In James's play, the hero comes out reluctantly into the world; in Wharton's poem, though torn away from his worship of the Virgin and his hours working on his missal, laying in 'the gold-leaf slowly' in the silence of his cell, he is brought into 'a new-found world', moved and changed by the sensual beauty of his wife. Other Italian poems, written between 1889 and 1902, much influenced by Morris, Browning and Swinburne, are absorbed by the 'spirit of place' and the power of art.[64] A poetry notebook of unpublished fragments from the 1890s suggests how much Italy aroused romantic, sensual yearnings in her. One fragment, marked 'Italy, March 1892', a poem of unrequited love, ends: 'What will it matter, when all are dead / That we died apart, with one word unsaid?' On the opposite page is a song for 'Spring, Italy, March 1892', 'Avowal'. Whether the poem (which owes something to Browning's story of love's missed chance, 'The Statue and the Bust') has a particular person in mind, or comes out of a more generalised sense of thwarted yearning, or is an exercise in a literary style, is impossible to know.

> If only I might say with all my soul
> What all my senses in your presence say;
> 'Come, let us live our life & have our way,
> Reject the half, & boldly take the whole,
> Believe the world was made for our control,
> And put all scruples with all doubts away.'
> Yea, had I strength to take a sword & slay
> The lives that lie between us, till we sole
> Stood face to face in love's high solitude –
> Well, & what then? This only, that between
> Us & our memory's revengeful brood,
> Gorged with the life-blood of the should-have-been,
> And flocking fast to seize us for their food,
> One moment of full life might intervene.[65]

Wharton wrote several Italian stories between 1899 and 1906, sometimes using the country as a background for her American expatriates' frustrations. In two of her best early stories, both published in 1899, 'The Muse's Tragedy' takes Iseo and Venice as its settings for a story of a woman's sacrifice of her life to a poet's art, and 'Souls Belated' puts its unhappy adulterers in a train going from Bologna to the northern lakes and in a 'fashionable Anglo-American hotel on the water's brink'. Other Italian stories written around the time of *The Valley of Decision* have an American observer witnessing a colourful historical Italian drama, like the eighteenth-century Venetian masquerade in 'A Venetian Night's Entertainment' (1903), or stories of 1840s revolutionary heroism and treachery in 'The Confessional' (1901) and 'The Letter' (1904).

Her three strongest historical Italian stories show her fascination with the dark, violent side of Italian drama and colour. 'The Duchess at Prayer' (1900) (invoking Browning's 'My Last Duchess') tells of a repressive, jealous marriage in a vividly evoked eighteenth-century villa, which ends cruelly, with the entombing alive of the duchess's lover.[66] There is the same kind of cruelty in a more 'modern' story, with echoes of Hawthorne and James, 'The House of the Dead Hand' (1904), in which the sinister Dr Lombard keeps his daughter imprisoned in his Sienese house, as the custodian of a priceless Leonardo. 'Might not the accumulated influences of such a house modify the lives within it in a manner unguessed by the inmates of a suburban villa with sanitary plumbing and a telephone?' asks the American narrator.[67]

Wharton's strangest Italian story, 'The Hermit and the Wild Woman' (1906), is set in medieval Italy and imitates the naive style of *The Golden Legend or Lives of the Saints*, which she mentions affectionately in *Italian Backgrounds*. ('Englished by William Caxton in 1483', all seven volumes, in a 1900 Dent edition, were in her library.) The hermit, an aesthete turned ascetic, disappointed in his pilgrimage to the self-mortifying 'Saint of the Rock', finds companionship with a 'wild woman' who has run away from a convent. She is identified with water, sensuality, fruitfulness, and the wild creatures of the forest; only at her death does it become apparent that it is she who is the saint.

There is darkness and sadness in these stories, as well as vivid drama. Italy was a theatre for Wharton, in which she saw acted out the survival of the ancient and the classical. As for many nineteenth-century admirers of the country, that drama of survival was also a melancholy one. She is fascinated by the driving-out of the old gods by Christianity, or of the old unwritten *commedia dell'arte* by the new realism, because these shifts point to a perpetual battle between tradition and change, and that is always her subject.

The Valley of Decision, her first long novel, is about that kind of conflict at the end of the eighteenth century in Italy. She wanted it to be historically authentic and serious, but also entertaining, vivid and saleable. She read a great many novels about Italy, which gave her strong ideas about her own ambitions for the book. Her big American models were Hawthorne's *The Marble Faun* (1860), and the novel it influenced, Henry James's *Roderick Hudson* (1875). Hawthorne's haunting romance treats the powerful impact of the classical, European world on the Puritan imagination. His Americans do not feel at home in Italy. In their dark moods, they think of priest-ridden, Catholic, nineteenth-century Rome as a place of 'ancient depravity'. A surreal, hedonistic carnival ends the book, like a 'feverish dream'. Hawthorne's New England girl longs for home: 'How she pined under this crumbly magnificence, as if it were all piled upon her human heart!'[68] (Like George Eliot's Dorothea Casaubon or James's Isabel Archer in Rome, she is oppressed by the sense of the past pressing down on her.) *Roderick Hudson* (which Wharton read with care, marking up the 'Preface' in her copy) is also intently attuned to the 'sinister charm' of Rome and its 'immemorial, complex, accumulated splendour'. The American characters are pulled between wanting Italy as the place in which to become an artist, and hating the 'dreadful' break with their past: 'It's a wretched business', says Roderick's friend Rowland Mallet, 'this virtual quarrel of ours with our own country.'[69]

Wharton's main fictional model (and challenge) was Stendhal's *The Charterhouse of Parma* (1839), 'one of the greatest of French novels', she thought. (She acknowledged it as an influence in the 'blurb' she wrote for *The Valley*, and gave her hero a name which echoed Stendhal's hero.[70]) She admired the dense historical context that underpins the story of Fabrizio Valserra del Dongo's Napoleonic fortunes in love, battle and court politics. She liked Stendhal's great woman adventuress, the Duchessa Sanseverina, and was moved by the novel's ultimate turn from worldly life to monastic retreat.

What always interested her about novels set in Italy was the extent to which the novelists had felt their way into the historical facts. She wanted to avoid the kind of colourful pot-boilers that Daisy Chanler's stepbrother, Francis Marion Crawford, churned out on Italian themes – *A Roman Siege* (1892), *The Heart of Rome* (1903), *Marietta: A Maid of Venice* (1901) – though she liked his dramatisation of the story of Paolo and Francesca. She was fascinated by George Sand, but she disliked her novel *Consuelo*, set in eighteenth-century Venice, because she thought her 'totally lacking in . . . the historic imagination'. She preferred 'that enchanting hybrid', *John Inglesant* (1881) – then much read, now almost forgotten. J.H. Stonehouse's novel is set in the 1650s and has a sensitive young man, very like Odo in *The Valley of Decision*, caught between worldly ambition and the spiritual life, with vivid descriptions of Italy's colourful and strange theatricality: 'as the night came on there seemed to him to be in the world nothing but play within play, scene within scene.'[71]

With all these models and with so much knowledge of Italy, this was the first big challenge she set herself as a novelist. It was to be in two volumes, and her work-notes show how thick with detail it was to be, like *The Charterhouse of Parma*. There are notes on everything – the 'masks' of the *commedia dell'arte*, the corruption of the clergy and the behaviour of servants, the craze for the opera, the favourite scents and toilet waters of the 'dear dead women' of eighteenth-century Venice ('jonquil, portugal, flower de luce, jasmine, bergamot, musk', etc.), the fact that 'thousands of caged nightingales sing at night in Venice'.[72] She was not going to miss anything or get anything wrong. In her eagerness to show her expertise and her historical knowledge, she sometimes forgot – as she said in a review of a minor English novelist's version of eighteenth-century Italy – that 'art is limited, is a compromise, a perpetual process of rejection and elision'.[73]

The novel, dedicated to the Bourgets 'in remembrance of Italian days together', tells the story of Odo Valsecca, the son of Piedmontese nobility, born in 1752. As a child, unhappily fostered out to a peasant family, he draws consolation from some faded Giotto-like frescoes of St Francis on the walls of the farmhouse chapel. From these primitive beginnings, she takes him through a series of set-piece awakenings which show-case her own self-taught enthusiasms. Odo becomes the ruler of one of the small northern duchies ('Pianura', a cross between Parma and Mantua) in the time of Austrian control of Italy. The story spans about twenty years, from 1774 to 1793, when the infiltration of new liberal philosophies sweeping across the Alps from France was beginning to threaten established beliefs. Influenced by a succession of mentors, Odo tries to put new ways of thinking into practice in his kingdom, but his troubled rule ends in catastrophe. So does his love-story. Apart from a mild flutter for a travelling actress, his heart belongs to the daughter of a radical philosopher, Fulvia Vivaldi, a self-righteous revolutionary thinker. Their relationship has moments of high romance, like an escape from a Venetian nunnery which ends in a stormy crossing of Lake Garda by night. But for political reasons he has to marry an Austrian duchess, a brittle, glamorous figure (rather like Stendhal's Duchessa Sanseverina) whose love for him he never realises. (In one scene, which anticipates the marriage between Ralph and Undine in *The Custom of the Country*, Odo tries to get the duchess to take an interest in politics: 'The lifelong habit of referring every question to a personal standpoint made it difficult for her to follow a general argument, and she leaned back with the resigned eyelids of piety under the pulpit.'[74]) Fulvia eventually becomes his mistress, and tries to direct his politics, but her unpopularity speeds his downfall.

Odo sees how 'the social conditions of the country' need improving, and is moved by the excitement and sensuality of the new thinking. There is a touching scene when he is reading Rousseau's *La Nouvelle Héloïse* while riding through the spring landscape outside Turin, just before his first sight of Fulvia: 'What he wanted now were books which appealed not to his reason but to his emotions ... Here at last was an answer to the blind impulses agrope in Odo's breast.' But he is always being brought up against the limits of revolutionary sentiment, the difference between 'theoretical visions of liberty and their practical application'. In eighteenth-century Italy (as in nineteenth-century New York), 'nowhere among the better classes was there any desire to attack existing institutions'. He is always having to compromise and retreat, and suffers from attacks of 'fatal lethargy'. There are times when he sees the value of endless struggle:

> For generations, for centuries man had fought on; crying for liberty, dreaming it was won, waking to find himself the slave of the new forces he had generated, burning and being burnt for the same beliefs under different guises ... And as the vision of this inveterate conflict rose before him, Odo saw that the beauty, the power, the immortality, dwelt not in the idea but in the struggle for it.

But more often he sees life as 'an incomplete and shabby business, a patchwork of torn and ravelled effort'.[75]

Because *The Valley of Decision* is so heavy with historical research, it takes a little effort to see how profoundly autobiographical the story is. Odo acts out Wharton's acute feelings about the painful difficulty of personal evolution. Beneath all the homework, her hero's self-doubt shows the tension of these years of marriage, travel, house-making, writing and illness, a tension between immense energy and aspirations, and a clogging sense of being held down.

Wharton thought, early in 1902, of writing a sequel to *The Valley of Decision* called *The New Day*. It would be set in 1835, after the death of Odo and the fall of Napoleon. His widow now dominates the life of the court, and is busy redesigning the palace according to the new fashions, 'replacing the formal gardens by an English park, with a swannery and a Temple of friend-ship adorned by the chisel of Canova'. There was to be a romance with a young count – and so on. Fortunately Walter Berry cut this short with a strong warning against sequels. 'I am dead against it ... Please *don't*. That N.Y. novel ought to come next.' In this, he anticipated Henry James, who, a few months later, in his first, long, polite letter to Mrs Wharton in response to *The Valley of Decision*, praised it, in careful terms, as 'so accomplished, pondered, saturated, so exquisitely studied & so brilliant & interesting from a literary point of view', but urged her next towards 'the *American Subject*'.[76] It was a letter that marked the beginning of a great friendship, and pointed towards her greatest work.

Walter Berry was her literary adviser throughout the writing of *The Valley*, in 1900 and 1901. (His letters about the novel were the only ones she kept.) They had an ongoing debate about 'culture-essay' versus 'heart-interest' (his terms). The novel should neither be a dry parade of knowledge, nor just a love-story. Berry wrote to her in November 1901 that 'you have *got* to put in a lot of po[litical] econ[omy] now, if the book is to amount to anything. I'm beginning to believe you want to make Odo & Fulvia do love-struck right down to finis, so as to crowd into the Six Best Selling Books.' Whatever she thought of Walter advising her to play down the love-interest, she did what he advised. When it was published he praised her for not having written a 'heart-interest-historical-When-Valley-Was-in-Flower-Book' (a reference to a best-selling historical romance of 1898, Charles Major's *When Knighthood Was in Flower*).[77] Wharton's persistent anxieties about combining the rival goals of high art and popularity were evident in this big, serious novel, which could easily have been just a colourful best-selling romance. It was a decisive moment – as decisive as any of Odo Valsecca's political choices – in the making of her career and her reputation.

The Valley of Decision, out in February 1902, was a success, had a rapid second printing, and sold about 25,000 copies in six months. The two Italian books that followed it rode on the back of that success. *Italian Villas and Their Gardens* involved negotiations with her publishers which show what a firm sense Wharton had by now of the kind of writing on Italy she wanted to be known for. *Italian Villas and Their Gardens* was commissioned for the *Century Magazine* as a vehicle for illustrations by the immensely popular American artist Maxfield Parrish, whose dream-like pictures of castles and magic landscapes illustrated children's books like Kenneth Grahame's *Dream Days*.[78] But in Wharton's arguments in 1903 with the magazine's editors, Richard Gilder and Robert Underwood Johnson, during the transition from magazine articles to book, she did not see herself taking second place to this famous illustrator, whose 'fairy-tale' paintings of the villas she thought sentimental, evocative of 'moonlight and nightingales', not of her serious technical and historical analysis. (She and Parrish did not visit the villas together, and he was always falling behind on their deadlines.) She was dismayed to hear, when she sent Gilder her first article, that he thought it too 'dry' for the illustrations, and had something more popular in mind. 'I regret very much not having written exactly the kind of article that you & Mr Johnson were hoping for', she wrote haughtily to Gilder in August 1903. 'I have written a new introduction which I trust is more in the key you want, & I shall do my best to amplify and simplify the articles ... though architecture and desultory chat are not easy to amalgamate.' She was not impressed by being asked to write as though for a 'young lady from the West'. She told Vernon Lee: 'I am going to do the long deferred articles on Italian villa-gardens; not from the admiring-ejaculatory, but, as much as possible, from the historical &

architectural stand-point; & I shall want all the help & advice you are willing to give me.'[79]

While the book was being produced, she argued with the publisher over everything. The rules of English spelling must be respected. 'In the magazine I suppose one must submit to being Websterized; but I can't stand the thought of being made to say clew & theater permanently ... In a book about beautiful gardens, there ought not to be any vulgar orthography!' The proof-reader's corrections exasperated her: '[they] are not of the slightest use to me ... I am a very careful proof-reader, & do not need to have my attention called to details of spelling & punctuation, as they seldom escape me.' She had immersed herself in ground-plans, guide-books, architectural treatises, diaries and travellers' accounts, from the fifteenth to the nineteenth centuries, in four languages, and she was bitterly disappointed that the publishers would not let her use as illustrations the historical garden-plans she had laboured to track down. (Rightly so, as reviewers complained at their absence.) And she wanted more money ($2,000 for six articles instead of $1,500) since she was writing 'with some sort of system & comprehensiveness on a subject which, hitherto, has been treated in English only in the most amateurish fashion' and 'it is *sure* to have a popular success'. ('I receive $500 for a short story, which is much less hard work.'[80]) The same kind of professional perfectionism that had already gone into her book on American house-design, her planning for her Italianate house in Massachusetts and her research for her Italian novel, were brought to bear on *Italian Villas and Their Gardens*.

Though she told Gilder that the introduction would be 'more in the key you want', it was not a simplifying account of her subject, but a severe and practical exhortation to her American readership to look at Italian villa-gardens with their history and function in mind. The point of her book was to explain, not to bask in 'vague admiration' of, the enchantment of Italian gardens by studying 'the garden in relation to the house, and both in relation to the landscape'. Her analysis is always trying to 'go deeper', to excavate the 'underlying design'. How is it, she asked, that the garden and the landscape seemed to 'form part of the same composition'? How did 'nature and art' become 'fused' in this way? The answer could only be found by looking at the history and the techniques of these compositions of the 'landscape-architects' from the sixteenth to the eighteenth centuries, and working out the ingredients that made up their 'deeper harmony of design'. It was not just the use of materials (water, stonework, foliage), it was the 'grouping of the parts', the care taken with transitions and contrasts and 'the relation of the whole composition to the scene about it', that had to be judged. Above all, each Italian villa-garden needed to be appreciated for its 'essential convenience and liveableness'. Design was always at the service of utility. 'The old Italian garden was meant to be lived in.'[81]

This is the voice of an authority. Wharton's study of over seventy-five villas – Florentine, Sienese, Genoese, Lombard, in and near Rome, and in the Veneto, some famous, some obscure and hard of access – was a pioneering achievement, and an astonishing one for a self-educated 'amateur'. It is still much cited by writers on garden-history. The Anglo-Florentine writer, aesthete and socialite Harold Acton, an acquaintance of Wharton's through the Berensons from the 1920s, often referred to her admiringly in his own book on Tuscan villas. (He knew his subject intimately, having inherited La Pietra from his father, Arthur Acton, who had created 'an English Edwardian interpretation of a Florentine garden'.[82]) Of the Villa Vicobello, near Siena, for instance, which Wharton commends for 'discretion and sureness of taste', Acton says (in 1973): 'Her description of it in 1904 cannot be bettered.' Garden-historians have returned to Wharton's book for its importance in the resurgence of interest in her time in the 'classic Italian gardens'. One authority calls it 'the book which led to dozens in its wake and spearheaded the revival of an interest in Italian principles in the style of landscape'. The American critic Van Wyck Brooks, who describes Wharton, misleadingly, as a 'collector', like Isabella Stewart Gardner and Pierpont Morgan, says that her book became 'a working manual for landscape gardeners and architectural students'.[83]

Wharton's book was all the more impressive because there was so little for her to go on. Apart from Vernon Lee, when she started there were as few writers in English interested in researching the history of these gardens as there were specialists in eighteenth-century Italian culture. In her bibliography, Wharton cites mainly French, German and Italian sources. She omits her most significant competitors, though, of whom she must have been aware. One of these was Janet Ross, Vernon Lee's neighbour (and frequent antagonist) at Poggio Gherardo, across the hill from I Tatti. She was one of the most knowledgeable of the Anglo-Florentine chatelaines, and published a stream of lively and informative books on Tuscan gardening, cooking and architecture, starting with *Florentine Villas* in 1901 and *Leaves From a Tuscan Kitchen* in 1903. *Florentine Villas* had more historical than architectural information, but was beautifully illustrated with reproductions of etchings by Zocchi, dating from 1744, which Wharton cites in her book. Another competitor was the American writer and garden-designer Charles Platt, who published *Italian Gardens* in 1894, the first book in English to introduce Italian villa-gardens to an American readership. Platt had a network of American links to Wharton – he was a close friend, for instance, of Maxfield Parrish. They agreed on many things, from large issues like the importance of 'harmony of design' to detailed points about particular gardens: the absence of 'magic' in the Boboli Gardens in Florence, or the grotesque sculptures in the water-theatre at the Villa Aldobrandini above Frascati, which Platt thought 'bad' and Wharton 'pompous'.[84]

Italian Villas coincided with the other major book of the period on this subject, *The Gardens of Italy* (1905), a lavish two-volume production dedicated to the King of Italy, with gorgeous photographs by Charles Latham and a sprightly text by Evelyn March Phillips, entirely lacking in architectural analysis and doing exactly the sort of thing Wharton did not want to do. Where Phillips rhapsodises, on the gardens of the Villa Medici in Rome, about going into 'a deep, dark ilex wood, a haunt for fauns and dryads', Wharton has a technical analysis of what makes them so magical ('it is worth the student's while to try and analyze the elements of which the sensation is composed'), noting the contrast and relationship between the ilex walk, the flower-garden in front of the house, and the view: 'This is one of the first of the gardens which Gurlitt defines as gardens to look out from, in contradistinction to the earlier sort, the gardens to look into.'[85]

Wharton, Ross, Platt and Latham were at the head of the fashion for such books – mostly by English writers – which in turn influenced the restoration of old gardens in Italy and the planning of new ones in America. After Wharton came Sir George Sitwell's *The Making of Gardens* (1909), Harold Eberlein's *Villas of Florence and Tuscany* (1922) and Inigo Triggs's immensely grand *The Art of Garden Design in Italy*. Triggs notes in his preface, written in January 1906, that a great many books had been published on this topic in the last few years, in particular 'a very interesting series of papers, recently contributed to the *Century Magazine* by Edith Wharton, [which] contain much valuable criticism'.[86]

Wharton's criticism was directed against the nineteenth-century fashion for Anglicisation and restoration. She is wonderfully scathing about what she calls 'senseless change'. In Tuscany and Lombardy in particular, 'the enthusiasm for English gardens' had swept in 'like a tidal wave, obliterating terraces and grottoes, substituting winding paths for pleached alleys, and transforming level box-parterres into rolling lawns which turn as brown as door-mats under the scorching Lombard sun'. 'Almost everywhere the old garden-magic has been driven out by a fury of modern horticulture. The pleached alleys have made way for lawns dotted with palms and bananas, the box-parterres have been replaced by star-shaped beds of begonias and cinerarias, and the groves of laurel and myrtle by thickets of pampas-grass and bamboo.' The 'spirit of improvement' has also involved, to her disgust, the scrubbing of fountains and statues 'to preternatural whiteness' and the repainting of grottoes, destroying 'that exquisite *patina* by means of which the climate of Italy effects the gradual blending of nature and architecture'.[87]

Gardens are made, and gardens change: they are not natural, or static. Wharton knew this very well; she was utterly realistic and unsentimental about them. (One of her terms of abuse for the nineteenth-century English garden is 'sentimental'.) She thought the argument for 'sincerity' produced by the followers of Repton and Capability Brown, who shuddered at the 'frank artifice' of the Italian garden-style, ridiculous. One kind of garden was as mannered or artificial as the other: each should be judged, 'not by any ethical standard of "sincerity", but on its own aesthetic merits'.[88] Her passion for the old Italian garden did not arise from an elegiac feeling for the vestiges of the past or the slow workings of time (though she responded strongly to villas with mysterious haunted glades or wild romantic woods) but from a conviction that, from the Renaissance to the eighteenth century, a style of gardening had developed that was organic, harmonious and serviceable. Hence her preference for box-parterres over flower-gardens. By '*thinking away*' the flowers, she says, one can get at 'the deeper harmony of design'. This, for instance, is her ideal, at the Villa Muti, 'in the Roman countryside on the hill above Frascati':

> On the right, divided from the court by a low wall surmounted by vases, lies the most beautiful box-garden in Italy, laid out in an elaborate geometrical design, and enclosed on three sides by high clipped walls of box and laurel, and on the fourth by a retaining-wall which sustains an upper garden. Nothing can surpass the hushed and tranquil beauty of the scene. There are no flowers or bright colours – only the contrasted tints of box and ilex and laurel, and the vivid green of the moss spreading over damp paths and ancient stonework.[89]

All the other books of the time on Italian gardens make similar points, but Wharton's personal tastes and feelings come through strongly. This is another version of her fiction's preoccupation with evolution and adaptation. She likes to discern the traces of a medieval garden hidden inside a Renaissance setting, or to work out how architectural lines have been adapted to a particular site, such as a steep hillside or a narrow ledge of rock.[90]

Italian Villas and Their Gardens shares with *The Valley of Decision* her passion for the theatrical. She takes huge pleasure in dramatic structures:

layers of terraces, flights of steps, groups of statues, contrasts between dark shady walks and sudden vistas, surprising perspectives or revelations. Sensational water-effects bring out her best writing: the 'tragic grandeur' of the Villa d'Este at Tivoli with its 'omnipresent rush of water' ('drawn up the hillside at incalculable cost and labour'), or the cascades and beautiful fountain-architecture at the Villa Torlonia at Frascati (equally admired, and painted in 1907, by Vernon Lee's great friend John Singer Sargent),[91] or the amazing torrent of water pouring through the centre of the Villa Pliniana on Lake Como, echoing the mountain torrent on the cliff behind:

> The old house is saturated with the freshness and drenched with the flying spray of the caged torrent. The bare vaulted rooms reverberate with it, the stone floors are green with its dampness, the air quivers with its cool incessant rush. The contrast of this dusky dripping *loggia* . . . with the blazing blue waters of the lake . . . is one of the most wonderful effects in *sensation* that the Italian villa-art has ever devised.[92]

What she loves about that torrent is that it fits perfectly into its landscape. Grand theatrical gestures must be harmonious, like the famous sculptures on the upper terrace of the great Villa Caprarola, whose 'audacity' has 'a quality of inevitableness' about it. She does not like grandiosity or monumentality for its own sake. She finds Palladio, on the whole, too stately, cold and formal. Grotesque grotto-ornamentation is not much to her taste ('humour is the quality which soonest loses its savour') and she resists the heavier, more elaborate aspects of the baroque. As for later imitations, she has nothing but scorn for the 'ridiculous' Villa Pallavicini near Genoa, 'a brummagem creation of the early nineteenth century' and a lure for 'throngs of unsuspecting tourists'. Wharton's sure judgements can be harsh, like her revulsion at the 'dismal' manufacturing suburbs around Genoa, where the villa-hunter has to persevere through 'squalid tenements' and 'waste ground heaped with melancholy refuse', or her preference for grounds laid out at the back 'secured to the private use of the inmates, instead of being laid open by a public approach to the house'.[93]

But that preference for privacy is part of her tender feelings for these places. She loves the little secret gardens, or the tiny points of detail, like (in the small grounds of the Villa of the Knights of Malta, her old heroes) the 'green tunnel' framing a Roman prospect, where 'by a touch peculiarly Italian, the keyhole of the gate has been so placed as to take it in'. She adores the little open-air theatre of the Villa de'Gori (La Pallazino), near Vicobello in the Sienese countryside, surrounded by ilex hedges, with rows of cypresses running up to the back of the stage. 'No mere description of its plan can convey the charm of this exquisite little theatre, approached through the mysterious dusk of the long pleached alley, and lying in sunshine and silence under its roof of blue sky, in its walls of unchanging verdure.' She likes woodland temples, marble dolphins, miniature garden-houses, *trompe-l'oeil*. She has fun with stucco (an acquired taste), for instance, in the palace of the Isola Bella, that fairy-tale seventeenth-century 'pyramid of flower-laden terraces' on Lake Maggiore. Its lower rooms, ornamented with 'delicatedly tinted stucco', pebble-work and shells, gave her ideas for her own house-design:

> These low vaulted rooms, with marble floors, grotto-like walls, and foun-tains dripping into fluted conchs, are like a poet's notion of some twilight refuge from summer heats ... As examples of the decoration of a garden-house in a hot climate, these rooms are unmatched in Italy, and their treatment offers appropriate suggestions to the modern garden-architect in search of effects of coolness.[94]

As so often, fancifulness is balanced here by practicality. Emotion must be controlled, just as 'audacity' must be 'harmonious' and, where possible, simple. One slightly anomalous garden chosen for the book was the sixteenth-century Botanical Garden at Padua – not a villa-garden, but one she likes for its practical functionality, which she describes in appropriately plain language, as well organised and serviceable as its subject matter: 'In the garden itself the beds for "simples" are enclosed in low iron railings, within which they are again subdivided by stone edgings, each subdivision containing a different species of plant.' The opposite of that are the passages where she conjures up visions of Renaissance courtiers or eighteenth-century Venetians. But even at her most Vernon Lee-ish, where, at Caprarola, for example, she imagines the soldiers outside and the ladies and cavaliers in the rose-arbours 'discussing a Greek manuscript or a Roman bronze',[95] the point is to show that the sixteenth-century architecture is in transition from fortified castle to pleasure-house.

The mixture of analysis and emotion is perfectly combined in Wharton's treatment of the early seventeenth-century Villa Gamberaia, 'overlooking the village of Settignano and the wide-spread valley of the Arno', every connoisseur's favourite Florentine villa. Wharton thought it 'the most perfect example of the art of producing a great effect on a small scale'. She saw it after it had been taken over (in a neglected state) by the reclusive Princess Ghyka and her companion Mary Blood. These two eccentric and dedicated ladies set to work to create an elaborate, box-hedged water-parterre and a dazzling flower-garden with rose-arches, backed by yew hedges, on the south side of the house. Wharton refers, warily, to the remodelling of 'the old fishpond' as being 'unrelated in style to the surroundings'. Otherwise, the Gamberaia enthrals her, and she describes it eloquently and judiciously. The villa is a substantial, typically Tuscan house, with projecting eaves, and an unusual pair of flying arcades at each end (from one of which a little spiral staircase connects the principal bedroom with the water-garden below). On the west side of the house, there is a grassy terrace with a low stone wall decorated with urns and 'solemn-looking stone dogs', overlooking the farmland above Settignano. On the east side a very long bowling-green or alley runs, for 630 feet, in between the side of the house and a high retaining wall set with statues and geraniums. At one end the bowling-green ends in a dark semicircular grotto with a fountain and baroque statues overshadowed by giant cypress trees. At the other end, it reaches a balustrade looking out over the Arno valley and the hills beyond. A gate in the retaining wall opens into a narrow, secret 'cabinet' garden with playful rococo statues and shells and stones set into the walls, and another fountain. A little flight of steps leads up to a lemon garden with its '*limonaia*' (or '*stanzone*', as Wharton correctly calls it) where 'the lemon and orange trees, the camellias and other semi-tender shrubs are stored in winter'. On either side of the cabinet garden and lemon terrace are dark ilex woods or '*boschetti*'. Wharton's commentary on this magical and complicated place expresses all the qualities of her Italian writing: accurate informed observation, pleasure in the relation of parts, and a feeling for 'utility' (a term derived from her grounding in architectural theory). Her emotions are banked down, but they play through the passage's coherence, like a fountain in its stone basin:

> The Gamberaia . . . combines in an astonishingly small space, yet without the least sense of overcrowding, almost every typical excellence of the old Italian garden: free circulation of sunlight and air about the house; abundance of water; easy access to dense shade; sheltered walks with different points of view; variety of effect produced by the skilful use of different levels; and, finally, breadth and simplicity of composition . . . Here, also, may be noted . . . the value of subdivision of spaces. Whereas the modern gardener's one idea of producing an effect of space is to annihilate his boundaries . . . the old garden-architect proceeded on the opposite principle, arguing that, as the garden is but the prolongation of the house, and as a house containing a single huge room would be less interesting and less serviceable than one divided . . . so a garden which is merely one huge outdoor room is also less interesting and less

serviceable than one which has its logical divisions. Utility was doubt-less not the only consideration . . . Aesthetic impressions were considered . . . But the real value of the old Italian garden-plan is that logic and beauty meet in it, as they should in all sound architectural work.[96]

Could such 'logic and beauty' – of design, architecture, garden-planning – be adapted to America?

5

The Decoration of Houses

Mary Cadwalader Jones and her daughter Beatrix (equipped, no doubt, with gauze veils, rubber bath-tubs, and sensible underwear), were also looking at Italian villas in 1894 and 1895. They were a redoubtable pair. Minnie – formidably energetic and organised, and now independent – was travelling for pleasure, and as a distraction from her impending divorce; 'Trix' was travelling with intent. She was by now an elegant, reserved and determined young woman in her early twenties. Like Edith Wharton, her head was full of writers on garden-design, and like her she was looking analytically at these Italian gardens. (She makes careful descriptions of parterres, terraces, and water-structures, is quick to note beauties arising from simplicity and 'refinement', and has harsh words for inappropriate designs, like an English garden at the Vatican 'which is of course, a maze of tortuous paths leading nowhere'.[1]) Ten years younger than Edith, she was at the start of her career (which her aunt would help to advance) and was thinking just as hard about the ways in which European and English styles might be adapted to American landscapes. Trix Jones became Beatrix Farrand in 1913, and was by then one of America's leading women landscape gardeners. Like Wharton, she was part of, and contributed to, changes in American style and taste.

In the years when Wharton was travelling in Italy and turning herself into a professional writer, she was also constructing American homes, and, in her co-authored, first book, *The Decoration of Houses*, a theory of American design. Starting with Pencraig Cottage, moving on to Land's End and the house in Park Avenue, and, from 1901, with the building and designing of The Mount, she created the kind of habitat she wanted. By her early forties, she had made herself into one of America's best-known writers, and an influential cultural figure. But these were also years of illness and depression, when she was up against obstructions she could not overcome: in some respects she was a very unhappy woman. Because of these personal strains, her ambitions for an American way of life turned into an insoluble conflict.

Wharton was an extraordinary exception to any rules. But (like her talented and equally strong-minded niece) she was not working or thinking in isolation. The links between her Italian writings, her interest in the decoration of houses, and the harsh, witty analysis of her society she was starting to make in her stories and novels, were part of a complex cultural argument about America at the turn of the century. One of the key topics in this argument was the morality of taste, something that interested her very much.

Conspicuous consumption, the wholesale importing of European arte-facts and styles, the rapid appearance and disappearance of gigantic, opulent and (as she put it) 'dubiously eclectic'[2] private houses – everything that Wharton witnessed, and wrote about, in the New York and Newport of her youth – gave rise to a strenuous debate among architects and designers about ethics and aesthetics. Edith Wharton and Beatrix Farrand both took part. The pioneering American landscape theorist Andrew Jackson Downing (whose magnificently illustrated *Treatise on the Theory and Practice of Landscape Gardening, Adapted to North America, With a View to the Improvement of Country Residences*, was one of the prize possessions of Wharton's library, in its 1859 [sixth] edition, closely read and marked) placed great emphasis on the house as 'a focus for moral and spiritual values', and on the social purpose of landscape gardening.[3] Downing influenced some of the outstanding American house and landscape designers, including Beatrix Farrand. One of these was Charles Sprague Sargent, the Harvard Professor of Horticulture (and cousin of the painter), who created a beau-tiful estate at Brookline, Massachussetts, and with whom Beatrix worked at the Arnold Arboretum in Boston, that romantic, intelligently structured wilderness for ordinary citizens to roam in. Another was Charles Eliot, pres-ident of Harvard and a supporter of horticulture and the environmental sciences. A third was Sargent's great collaborator, Frederick Law Olmsted, the designer of (among many other American landscapes) Central Park, the grounds of the US Capitol, and the vast Vanderbilt estate at Biltmore, where Edith and Beatrix were both admiring visitors at different times. ('This divine landscape', Edith called it.) Olmsted passionately believed in the Ruskinian ethic of 'service' through art, and of landscaping's prime object being to 'affect the emotions' (as he confided to his friend, Edith's mentor Charles Eliot Norton, in 1881). Olmsted agreed with Ruskin that a man's house should 'make all that is true, beautiful and good in his own character, tastes, pursuits, and history manifest in it'.[4]

Olmsted and Sargent both encouraged indigenous, natural-looking land-scaping. Both disapproved of elaborate artifice and the craven imitation of

European gardens. Beatrix Farrand took up Olmsted's principle of 'designs that are in keeping with the natural scenery and topography; respect for, and full utilization of, the genius of the place'. A different view was taken by Charles Platt, who was fanatical about Italian gardens and villa-architecture, and wanted to introduce them into American landscapes. The proof of his point was Faulkner Farm, in Brookline, 'a Renaissance villa garden in Massachussetts' based on the Villa Gamberaia, and built between 1897 and 1898 – just when *The Decoration of Houses* came out. Its formal Italianate gardens were conceived as a series of apartments extending from the house, complete with temples, walled terrace with statues, flower-garden and pavilion. Wharton's gardens at Land's End (worked on between 1893 and 1898) and at The Mount (worked on between 1902 and 1908) also imported Italianate features to American landscapes. Like Platt, she thought American gardens should use foreign designs for inspiration, but should not follow them slavishly.[5]

A similar debate between formal, European-style gardening and pictur-esque 'natural' beauty was going on in England. The leading 'picturesque' proponents were William Robinson and Gertrude Jekyll, with their passions for structuring drifts of colour and creating woodlands within gardens, and their immense applied knowledge of plants; while Reginald Blomfield, in *The Formal Garden in England* (1892), argued for gardens designed in the formal seventeenth-century style, with walled 'rooms' and straight lines and statuary.[6] When Beatrix went to England in 1895 – just after touring Italian villas with the Whartons – she encountered both Robinson and the anti-social Miss Jekyll, as brusque with the admiring Trix in 1895 as she would be years later with Wharton:

> I put one timid question to Miss Jekyll, who answered curtly, and turned her back on me to point out a hybrid iris to an eminent statesman who knew neither what a hybrid nor an iris was; and for the rest of the visit she gave me no chance of exchanging a word with her.[7]

These gardening mentors were all in Wharton's library. She had an early edition of Blomfield's book, and sent him a dedicated copy of *The Decoration of Houses* in 1897 'in gratitude for the pleasure and instruction that we have derived from his books'.[8] She bought Jekyll's *Lilies for English Gardens* and *Roses for English Gardens* as they came out, in 1901 and 1902, at the start of her work on The Mount, and later, in 1921, her *Colour Schemes for the Flower Garden*. She had already acquired Robinson's *The Wild Garden* in 1888; and she had a 1901 edition of his *The English Flower Garden and Home Grounds*. These garden-writers were influential, too, on a great friend of her later years, the English gardener Lawrence Johnston, from whom Wharton took a great deal of advice when she came to create two French gardens for herself after the war.

Beatrix Jones and Wharton would often have talked about landscaping styles and principles. Beatrix took a 'middle way' between the formalists and the naturalists in her achievements at Reef Point and Dumbarton Oaks, and on the Princeton and Yale campuses. With her talent for fitting a garden into its landscape, her imaginative use of colour and her interest in harmony between house and grounds, she developed 'exquisite combinations of European classicism and American naturalism'.[9] Her principles were summed up in an article called 'The Garden as a Picture', published in the same issue of *Scribner's Magazine* (July 1907) in which Wharton's third long novel *The Fruit of the Tree* was being serialised. Beatrix invoked 'the great Italian garden artists' in her piece, with illustrations from the Villa Castello, but also stressed the need for adaptation: 'A model seen in Rome is now often repeated in an alien American garden, merely because it looked well in the place for which it was intended.' Though she is eloquent about the challenge of making a 'natural' garden as opposed to a 'formal' garden, and about the need for a successful garden to be 'in scale with its surroundings as well as appropriate to them', she insists that 'it cannot be too often repeated that a garden is an absolutely artificial thing'.[10]

Beatrix uses a moral language for the rules of landscape gardening. Choices are 'good' or 'bad'; gardeners must notice, care, learn, and distinguish. The same kind of moral rhetoric coloured the arguments of the time over architectural styles. A little set of satirical fables Wharton was writing in 1894 or '95, 'The Valley of Childish Things', has an architect at the gate of heaven, whose crowning work is a 'magnificent temple', but who knows his buildings are really 'pretty bad'. 'When he came before the judgement angel he was not asked how many sins he had committed, but how many houses he had built.' He is given the choice of being shown up or having his false reputation maintained, and naturally chooses the latter. That Wharton should be yoking bad architecture and the afterlife together, in the mid-1890s, points to the current anxieties about the ethics of style. As the vast European-style palaces went up and came down, and rich men commanded into being instant landscapes complete with mature trees, commentators were asking whether it was possible to legislate for a national taste, and whether a recognisably American architecture could be nurtured. In Newport, there was a lively phase of American vernacular in the 1880s, with some imaginative Queen Anne and Colonial revival houses, and some innovative 'shingle style' designs, like McKim, Mead & White's enchanting

1883 house for the cotton trader Isaac Bell. But by the late 1880s and 1890s, in Newport and wherever else the rich were building, house-styles were mostly 'antiquarian and reactionary' – Beaux-Arts or Colonial pastiche, Gothic or Renaissance giganticism – like The Breakers, Cornelius Vanderbilt's Renaissance palace (which Wharton called a 'Thermopylae of bad taste'). By 1905, *Town and Country* magazine could report on 'a Virginia House in New Jersey, a Cape Dutch House in Santa Barbara, a French farmhouse in Connecticut, a Tudor House on Lake St Clair, an Anglo-French House in Texas, and a version of Groombridge Place, Kent on Long Island'.[11]

One famously grandiose example was the Boston Venetian *palazzo*, Fenway Court, which the wealthy collector Isabella Stewart Gardner ('Mrs Jack') had been creating (complete with a Dutch Room for the Rembrandts) as a dazzling show-house for her treasures since the late 1890s. Wharton was a critical guest at its gala opening on New Year's Eve, 1903 – long before her friendship with Mrs Jack's adviser and supplier, Bernard Berenson. A much-repeated tale of their mutual animosity has it that Mrs Wharton remarked that the food at the gala was fit for a provincial French railway station, and that Mrs Jack, bidding her farewell, reassured her that she would not be invited to this station restaurant again.[12]

Wharton's thinking about American taste was anticipated by another influential, pioneering upper-class American woman, Mariana Griswold Van Rensselaer. She belonged to Wharton's social group: a distant relation of Walter Berry's by her marriage to Schuyler van Rensselaer, a close friend of Minnie Jones and of one of Wharton's publishers, Richard Gilder (who had a farm-house at Tyringham, near The Mount, where Van Rensselaer was often a guest). Like Olmsted, Van Rensselaer wanted architecture to be 'moral'. She preferred 'natural' to 'formal' gardens. She criticised the extremes of self-assertion in contemporary architecture and landscaping, like the 'love of display united to a lack of public spirit, which should certainly not characterize a refined community', or the exaggerated individualism of some rich people's country homes: 'Some of them have taken upon themselves far too self-asserting, far too independently dignified an air; forgetting that . . . their relation to their neighbors . . . should not have been ignored.' She argued for 'simplicity', 'fitness', and 'homogeneity'. She believed that an American style could evolve, gradually, out of working with tradition, and this could be done by everybody, not just by Vanderbilts: 'Architectural decoration is within the reach of every man who builds himself a home.' She was not a stickler for 'sincerity': 'Stucco is not intrinsically immoral.' As long as decoration and artifice were appropriate, there was room for them. So, describing the fancifully elaborate decorations of the Richard Morris Hunt house for W.K. Vanderbilt on 52nd Street and Fifth Avenue, she comments:

> It [the exterior decoration] is so skilfully applied and so charmingly executed; it is so *architectural* in spite of its delicacy, that we have not the heart to wish it altered. Indeed, I think we may greatly rejoice in this sumptuous accumulation of beauty; for, while it is necessary that the virtues and possibilities of simplicity should be preached, it is well to be reminded . . . that the richest elaboration need not be ostentatious, much less vulgar . . . [13]

Wharton was equally interested in the ethics of style, whether in the production values of her books, in her house and garden designs, in her appreciation of Europe, or in her theorising of interior decoration. In all these areas, she had mentors or collaborators – editors, literary advisers, travelling companions. One of the most energising of these was the architect Ogden Codman. She called him 'Coddy', and in her memoir she labelled him, a little drily, as the 'clever young Boston architect'. From the early 1890s, for about ten years, this was an inspiring professional relationship for her. It was an energetic partnership; it was also competitive and quarrelsome, and frequently degenerated into a comedy of accusations and grudges. Codman was a well-brought-up Bostonian with excellent connections, devoted to his powerful mother, a combination of aesthete, scholarly preservationist, and ambitious practitioner. A family member called him 'gifted, intelligent, scholarly, ambitious, at once obstinate, caustic, but never boring'. He was sexually ambivalent – people were surprised by his mid-life marriage to a wealthy older woman (a happy but short marriage, since she died only a few years later – the marriage, and the death, going equally unacknowledged by Edith, who once told Bernard Berenson that 'Mrs Coddy' was 'something more than "difficile". If she would stick to her Profile & her Frocks & her Housewifery she would be adorable. But her Art Pose is such that she is the only woman I have ever known who has tempted me to personal violence.'). Coddy could be 'difficile' too, and he knew it: 'I can be fairly disagreeable, at least I flatter myself I can', he wrote to his mother, his regular correspondent. He was 'grand and fussy', a 'gentleman decorator' who considered himself the equal of his clients, and drove some of them, including the Whartons, to despair with his high-handed business methods and frequent absences. [14]

Immensely snobbish ('I always decide against poverty when I see very good bric-a-brac'), he had a double attitude towards his rich clients. He was delighted to profit from their grandiose plans for immense mansions at Newport or refurbished brownstones in New York ('Imagine Paines, Cuttings, Coolidges, Millers, Winthrops, Whartons – all owing money!') but extremely critical of their tastes: 'I did not think much of the collection of architectural types our multi-millionaires assembled [at Newport], utterly neglecting to follow the example set them in colonial times when a number of charming and appropriate houses were built.'[15] His attitude to The Breakers, where, thanks to Wharton's recommending him, he made his name, was typical. Like her, he criticised the vulgarity and over-opulence of the house as a whole, but dedicated himself with the utmost skill and meticulousness to his commission for decorating the French and Italian eighteenth-century-style bedrooms. The results, light, elegant, and airy, are immaculate. He disparaged his clients while he adored the work. His passion was for preservation (especially of America's eighteenth-century houses) as much as for decoration. Very knowledgeable (his work at The Breakers financed the growth of his historical and architectural library), he was also fabulously gifted, with an unerring eye for colour and structure. Evidence of his talent was widespread: at Newport, in the 'eighteenth-century' rooms at The Breakers, and in his ravishingly delicate, green-silk-walled Louis XV reception room at Château-sur-Mer, so out of line with the pompous grandiosity of the rest of the house as to seem like an ironic comment on it. Elsewhere, he did an elegant house on Long Island called Hautbois, modelled on The Mount, for Wharton's great friends Eunice and Walter Maynard. And he designed some chic, stylish New York interiors for his admirer, the designer, actress, and idiosyncratic leader of fashion Elsie de Wolfe (disliked by Wharton). Like Wharton, Codman had a passion for Italy (some of her most enthusiastic travel letters were written to him), for French architecture, and for eighteenth-century art and design; like her he placed a serious value on style; like her he wanted to improve American taste. Like her, he eventually left America for France.

For a few years in the early 1890s, 'Coddy' saw the Whartons all the time. Like Egerton Winthrop, he was a third wheel to the marriage. She was Mrs Pussy; she and Ogden were Mr and Mrs PussCod. Edith once said to him: 'I really think I shall have to end by marrying you Coddy. I feel as if it will be my fate!' He replied: 'You'll have to marry someone very rich first'; but 'she did not seem to quite like it'. He was her adviser and collaborator for her first house. There had not been much scope for radical new design at Pencraig Cottage, her mother's smaller house across Harrison Avenue (a quiet, sheltered street) from the Jones mansion, Pencraig, which, like West 25th Street, had all the Victorian features that *The Decoration of*

Houses would criticise. Still, in that modest frame house (modest, that is, by Newport standards: it stood on a lot of 324,652 square feet – as opposed to The Breakers's 573,519 acres – and had three floors with five rooms on each, the top floor for the servants), Wharton did make some changes. She laid out a new garden, skilfully managing an awkward strip of land. And she changed the tone of the house – shocking her mother-in-law, she remembered, by getting rid of the thick muslin curtains. A photograph of the drawing room looks gay and attractive, with simple white chairs, pretty rugs, and light-coloured curtains – though still with more drapes and knick-knacks than *The Decoration of Houses* would allow.[16]

In the early '90s, the purchase of a house in New York and of Land's End was made possible by the legacy Wharton received from a reclusive millionaire cousin, Joshua Jones. It gave her the first opportunity to shape her own environment. Land's End was much bigger than Pencraig Cottage, well away from her mother's house. It was on Ledge Road, which runs from Ocean Drive, down to the promontory called Coggeshall Ledge, and was round the corner from the exclusive Bailey's Beach. Instead of the quiet, tree-lined, almost suburban gentility of the Jones domain on Harrison Avenue, there was the big house sticking out crudely on its own, its nearest neighbour Mrs Gardner Brewer's 'Finisterre', and, opposite, two large lots owned by the Baker and Aldrich families. At the end of the road, there were the low cliffs, and the waves beating, and the seabirds, and the bright, flat, northern light over the Atlantic, and nothing else, endlessly.[17] For about five years, in between Italian journeys, this house was one of her main interests, until illness and unhappiness at Newport drove her away, at last, to Lenox.

Land's End cost $80,000: an extremely expensive house. (In 1898 she also took out a $50,000 mortgage on it.[18]) Wharton called it, retrospectively, an 'incurably' 'ugly wooden house with half an acre of rock and illimitable miles of Atlantic Ocean'. It had large mansard roofs, big chimneys, and an over-decorated interior. She and Codman redesigned it, inside and out. They made a formal Italianate garden with a circular courtyard, high hedges and an elaborate eighteenth-century-style trellis, his first ('a screen with panels linked by columns and a trellis niche'), of which the twenty-one-year-old Beatrix Jones made a pretty water-colour sketch. As at Faulkner Farm, there were clipped lawns, straight paths, a pergola, a terrace, and statuary. Inside, though there were some features (like the damask wall-coverings in the dining-room) of the sort which *The Decoration of Houses* would criticise, elegance and airiness were the aim, created by light colours, restrained decoration, French fabrics (Codman usually imported from France all the fabrics and furniture for his clients' houses) and Wharton's own imports, the eighteenth-century Italian furniture which caught Paul Bourget's eye on his first visit in 1893.

The spacious entrance hall and curving stairs, with wrought-iron and wooden balustrades, sofa and French wall clock, were as dignified and spare as their book would recommend. (This is now all that remains of the Wharton–Codman era at Land's End.) The drawing room had books and fine mirrors and busts against the wallpaper and an oriental carpet. The comfortable library had bookcases built in on either side of the marble fireplace, decorated plaster-work and Louis XVI panelling, and a medallion of a Roman emperor over the fireplace. The boudoir had pretty toile fabric with bird and leaf designs. But 'Wharton & Codman''s best stroke was their glassed-in verandah (the panels brought from Italy), with handsome cane furniture and a wonderful view of the garden and the ocean. The plan had been for Wharton to bring back a ceiling for this room from Italy; failing that, Codman designed an Adamesque 'tent' ceiling with coloured sky and clouds. It was not installed: but this was a room with high ambitions.[19]

Codman was also working, in the same years, on 'a little shanty in Park Avenue', number 884, on the corner of 79th Street – the smallest house in New York, the Whartons called it. They bought this brownstone for $19,670 in 1891, but rented it out (for $1,300 a year) until 1896, when Wharton started to 'do it up', in exactly the same period she and Codman were writing their book. Letters came from Aix-les-Bains about the plumbing. Codman enjoyed the work:

> Mrs Wharton's house will be a great success . . . The things are so pretty. Just what I have always wanted to do myself. I never saw any one learn so quickly as she has, she gets very different things from what she did when I first knew her – I think we have both learned much and each has taught the other.[20]

In 1898 the Whartons bought the house next door, 882 Park Avenue, which they used to house their staff (Alfred White, Catherine Gross, and the maids). In 1899, they had plans drawn up to convert the two houses into one, but these came to nothing. The house was their New York base until about 1905. After that it was hardly in use, and was sold in 1910, by which time Wharton had come to hate New York as much as Newport.

The little rooms at 884 were formally decorated, on the kind of 'appropriate' scale that *The Decoration of Houses* would recommend. As at Land's End, fine prints, classical ornaments, and eighteenth-century Italian furniture were used. The parlour had striped wallpaper and matching chair fabrics, the dining room an elaborate mirror, a marble fireplace, elegant upright chairs, and a colourful wallpaper design of trees and flowers, echoing the 'arabesque' eighteenth-century fantasies praised in *The Decoration of Houses*. Some friends found the Codman style of the New York house a little precious: Henry James, in 1905, described it as a 'bonbonnière of the last daintiness naturally'. Elsie de Wolfe told a satirical story about the house and its mistress, on what may well have been her only visit there:

> I noticed but eight chairs in her dining room. I remarked about this to her, as it was then the custom to give large and formal dinners. 'Yes, Miss de Wolfe', she replied, 'there are but eight people in the whole of New York whom I care to have dine with me.'[21]

Another barbed reminiscence was provided by Sybil Cutting, who had married a New York friend of Wharton's, Bayard Cutting, but would later fall out with her. She said, many years later, that Mrs Wharton had been chilly and daunting when the younger, newly married woman called on her at the Park Avenue house, designed with 'a minute and studied perfection'. But just as Sybil was leaving, abashed, Ogden Codman turned up, and she heard Edith calling out to him, in a quite different, 'warm, kind, eager voice': 'What do you think, Ogden – could one in a little house like this allow a Chippendale clock in the hall?'[22]

'Wharton & Codman''s practical collaboration led to a literary partnership. *The Decoration of Houses* is the product of two remarkably like-minded thinkers, though it is not clear quite how the writing-collaboration worked. Both gave their own accounts retrospectively, Codman claiming that the book had been mostly his work and that 'Edith had simply polished up his sentences', Wharton looking back ironically on a literary partnership that joined forces enthusiastically, 'only to discover that neither of us knew how to write!' This allowed her to attribute their eventual success to the intervention of Walter Berry (now back on the scene), who gave the 'lump' of a manuscript one look, laughed, and said: 'Come, let's see what can be done.' Others would play a part too. The distinguished architect Charles McKim gave advice and encouragement. The English publisher Macmillan's rejected the manuscript, it seems because Codman mishandled things ('Before we embark on any other experiments with the book', Wharton wrote severely to him in May 1897, 'I am going to make it a condition that you leave the transaction entirely to me'). But William Crary Brownell at Scribner's, who had been taking Wharton's poems and stories since 1889, accepted it, with Daniel Berkeley Updike as the printer and designer. Both of them were at once inundated with commands and suggestions. Wharton was the guiding force for the whole project, as Codman's letters of the time make clear: 'Mrs Wharton is a great help, & is very much interested. She takes my notes & puts them into literary form, & adds a good deal out of her own head.'[23]

Two pieces of hers in the *Newport Daily News* in 1896 and 1897 set the tone for *The Decoration of Houses*. The first was a letter protesting against the prevailing misuse of the term 'Colonial', the demolition of many old Newport houses, and misplaced 'originality' in modern architecture: 'The desire to do differently for the sake of doing differently is puerile.' The second was a report of a speech she had made to the 'School Committee of the City of Newport', for which she was doing some volunteer work, giving prizes for essays about cruelty to animals, and donating pictures and plaster busts to be put up in schoolrooms, 'not only on artistic grounds but on moral grounds as well'. 'Beautiful pictures and statues may influence conduct as well as taste.'[24] The argument was developed in a whole chapter on schoolrooms in the book.

That socially responsible tone coloured *The Decoration of Houses*. But what did morality have to do with door-knobs and dados? Both authors believed passionately that 'interior decoration should be considered a branch of architecture'. 'The interior of a house is as much part of its organic structure as the outside.' Even if a house was being redone, rather than built from scratch, that ought to be the essential principle. Wharton and Codman had been putting this into practice at Land's End, where he was both architectural renovator and decorator: 'a somewhat new departure', she noted, 'since the architects of that day looked down on house-decoration as a branch of dress-making, and left the field to the upholsterers, who crammed every room with curtains, lambrequins, jardinières of artificial plants, wobbly velvet-covered tables littered with silver gew-gaws, and festoons of laces on mantelpieces and dressing-tables'. There is a perfect example of this Pencraig-style upholstery in May Newland's 1870s interior decoration in *The Age of Innocence*:

Mrs Newland Archer's drawing-room was generally thought a great success. A gilt bamboo jardinière, in which the primulas and cinerarias were punctually renewed, blocked the access to the bay window (where the old-fashioned would have preferred a bronze reduction of the Venus of Milo); the sofas and arm-chairs of pale brocade were cleverly grouped about little plush tables densely covered with silver toys, porcelain animals and efflorescent photograph frames; and tall rose-shaded lamps shot up like tropical flowers among the palms.[25]

'Wharton & Codman' wanted to convince the American public that interior decoration should be 'simple and architectural'. 'Structure conditions ornament, not ornament structure.' *The Decoration of Houses* loathed mid-nineteenth-century clutter: too many knick-knacks; pictures hung over flowered wallpaper; 'portières', or 'superfluous draperies' covering door-openings ('yards of plush or damask, with the addition of silk cord, tassels, gimp and fringe'); frightful fire-screens and elaborate hooped and ruffled muslin window-curtains ('Lingerie effects do not combine well with architecture').[26] But they were also setting themselves against the eclectic tastes of newly rich millionaires (some of whom, of course, were Codman's clients) who thought they ought to have a 'Colonial' verandah, a Louis XV bedroom, Queen Anne furniture, a chinoiserie dining room and a Renaissance ballroom. No: 'uniformity of style' did not have to be 'servile', 'formal', or 'pretentious'. 'Each room should speak with but one voice.' The terms that run through the book are appropriateness, harmony, organic proportions, simplicity, common sense. The approach was rational: 'A building . . . must have a reason for being as it is and must be as it is for that reason.' One of Wharton's suggested titles for the book was 'Rooms & Their Reasons, or Logic in House Decoration'.[27] They minded about the misuse of rooms, where common sense had been sacrificed to fashion or pretension. Some 'old' features of house-decoration, they said (sounding like Odo Valsecca, or like the narrative voice of *The Age of Innocence*) 'are merely survivals of earlier social conditions, and have been preserved in obedience to that instinct that makes people cling to so many customs the meaning of which is lost'.

> Everyone is unconsciously tyrannized over by the wants of others . . . The unsatisfactory relations of some people with their rooms are often to be explained in this way. They have still in their blood the traditional uses to which these rooms were put . . . It is only an unconscious extension of the conscious habit which old-fashioned people have of clinging to their parents' way of living.[28]

But 'to go to the opposite extreme and discard things because they are old-fashioned is equally unreasonable'. As in her thinking on fiction, Wharton maintained that 'originality in art' is 'never a wilful rejection of what have been accepted as the necessary laws of various forms of art'. Codman recommended the study of 'the best models' – thoroughly un-Ruskinian models of classical symmetry, proportion, and balance. Their illustrations were a Renaissance doorway in the ducal palace at Mantua, or a Louis XV '*lit de repos*', or the eighteenth-century bathroom in the Pitti Palace in Florence, or the library of Louis XVI at Versailles. They did allow for synthesising different historical models, but not (as she argued again in *Italian Villas and their Gardens*) for having a house full of random bits and pieces of Italian stuff.[29]

A great deal was being written at the time about 'honesty' in architecture and design: a typical turn-of-the-century title was *The Honest House*.[30] One of the central issues in *The Decoration of Houses* (as in the discussion of authenticity in gardens) was 'sincerity'. The authors often argue that tactics which might be judged 'insincere' – such as painted or woven imitations of pilasters or mouldings in wall-decorations like frescos or tapestries – had virtue:

> As in imaginative literature the author may present to his reader as possible anything that he has the talent to make the reader accept, so in decorative art the artist is justified in presenting to the eye whatever his skill can devise to satisfy its requirements; nor is there any insincerity in this proceeding.[31]

There was nothing wrong with artifice, they maintained, as in the use of frescos, or stucco. Concealed doors could be useful where there was limited wall-space or a badly planned room; painted or decorated ceilings presented no difficulties for Renaissance architects untroubled by 'the fear of insincerity'. What was essential, though, was simplicity. Why should comfort in the American drawing room be 'sacrificed to a vague feeling that no drawing-room is worthy of the name unless it is uninhabitable'? This made for as sad a room in a grand house as 'the shut-up "best parlor" of a New England farm-house', to be found in *Ethan Frome* and in the front parlor in the New England story 'Bewitched', with its black stove, rickety beadwork table, and deathly air, 'at once close and bitterly cold'.[32]

Wharton was particularly eloquent about the need for a well-designed library. There should be 'plain shelves filled with good editions in good bindings', not 'ornate bookcases lined with tawdry books'. The bookcases should be set into the walls as 'an organic part of the wall-decoration'. There should be large, substantial writing-tables, and any ornaments (the fewer the better) should be chosen to 'harmonize with the spirit of the room'. The recommendations drew on Renaissance models, and also on examples from English eighteenth-century aristocratic precedents, from which developed the 'gentleman's library' which Wharton was now beginning to make her own

– in *The Decoration of Houses*, in her own homes, and in her fiction.[33] In her first novella, *The Touchstone* (1900), published three years after *The Decoration of Houses*, she describes the rooms of one of her favourite 'types', a wealthy, leisured New York collector:

> The apartment which Flamel described as his studio showed, as its one claim to the designation, a perennially empty easel, the rest of its space being filled with the evidences of a comprehensive dilettanteism. Against this background, which seemed the visible expression of its owner's intellectual tolerance, rows of fine books detached themselves with a prominence showing them to be Flamel's chief care.
>
> Glennard glanced with the eye of untrained curiosity at the lines of warm-toned morocco, while his host busied himself with the uncorking of Apollinaris.
>
> 'You've got a splendid lot of books,' he said.
>
> 'They're fairly decent,' the other assented, in the curt tone of the collector who will not talk of his passion for fear of talking of nothing else; then, as Glennard, his hands in his pockets, began to stroll perfunctorily down the long line of bookcases – 'Some men,' Flamel irresistibly added, 'think of books merely as tools, others as tooling. I'm between the two; there are days when I use them as scenery; other days when I want them as society; so that, as you see, my library represents a makeshift compromise between looks and brains, and the collectors look down on me almost as much as the students.'[34]

Wharton's novels and stories are full of book-lined studies and discriminating collectors. Private libraries are the place where friendships are made or started. In *The Decoration of Houses*, books spread themselves. 'Those who really care for books are seldom content to restrict them to the library, for nothing adds more to the charm of a drawing-room than a well-designed bookcase: an expanse of beautiful bindings is as decorative as a fine tapestry.' And in her fiction, the drawing room is often a bookish space, dominated by the character and taste of a woman. It is associated with flowers, pictures, comfort, hospitality, and human sympathy. Lizzie Hazeldean in 'New Year's Day' has contrived an 'enchanting' atmosphere, created by a woman who can somehow see to it that 'the flowers grow differently in their vases, the lamps and easy-chairs have found a cleverer way of coming together, and the books on the table are the very ones one is longing to get hold of'. This was what Edith Wharton would make for herself.[35]

Her preferences make themselves felt, too, in the book's insistence on the need for privacy, described as 'one of the first requisites of civilized life'.

The authors hate 'the indifference to privacy which has sprung up in modern times' and which was reflected in the new fashion for halls with open stair-cases, sheets of plate-glass between rooms, or rooms without doors. Open planning was not to their taste. Wharton's design of her own house, at The Mount, as an exclusive and private domain, is anticipated. 'Whatever the uses of a room, they are seriously interfered with if it be not preserved as a small world by itself.' Bedrooms should be designed as suites, 'preceded by an antechamber separating the suite from the main corridor of the house', and preferably with a separate door into the bathroom for the servants to use without disturbing the inhabitants of the bedroom, 'for greater privacy'. As for the entrance to the house, 'it should be borne in mind . . . that, while the main purpose of a door is to admit, its secondary purpose is to exclude'. The vestibule should be cut off from the inner hall or staircase by a glass door. All this was done at The Mount.[36]

Privacy, of course, is something you have to be able to afford. Class assumptions run unquestioned through *The Decoration of Houses*. These are houses for those rich enough to model their style on Versailles or Audley End, to have ballrooms, suites of bedrooms, private libraries, tapestries and statues, eighteenth-century furniture, marble floors and carved ceilings (many of these features imported wholesale from Europe), large teams of live-in servants, and architects and decorators commissioned to do the work. But, though its assumptions are remote from most readers of the book today, the idea was that good taste and good practice among the rich would have a trickle-down effect into less grandiose, ordinary houses. 'When the rich man demands good architecture his neighbors will get it too.' 'The book is not written for millionaires alone', Wharton told Brownell, their editor at Scribner's. There is a good deal of criticism of stupid expenditure on flashy, worthless things: 'The one-dollar china pug is less harmful than an expensive onyx lamp-stand with moulded bronze mountings dipped in liquid gilding.' Like Van Rensselaer, the authors wanted their advice to be taken by every kind of home-builder, and they often apply their principles to small houses without large means. 'When a room is to be furnished and decorated at the smallest possible cost', 'willow armchairs', 'solid tables', 'plain bookcases' and 'a cheerful drugget on the floor' are better than pseudo-Georgian or pseudo-Empire 'parlor suites'. 'A room treated in this way, with a uniform color on the wall, and plenty of lamps and books, is sure to be comfortable and can never be vulgar.' 'What must be done cheaply should be done simply.'[37] If this reads condescendingly, it was meant helpfully.

It is hard to take *The Decoration of Houses* quite seriously now. It has such high-handed prejudices; for instance, against the vulgar effects of 'the general use of gas and electricity in the living-rooms of modern houses'. It is so sure of being right: 'One need only look at the ceilings in the average modern house to see what a thing of horror plaster may become in the hands of an untrained "designer".' It is so snooty: 'No one should venture to buy works of art who cannot at least draw such obvious distinctions as those between old and new Saxe, between an old Italian and a modern French bronze, or between Chinese peach-bloom porcelain of the Khang-hi period and the Japanese imitations to be found in every "Oriental emporium".' But the book is not just about decor; it is about how best to live your life:

> If art is really a factor in civilization, it seems obvious that the feeling for beauty needs as careful cultivation as the other civic virtues . . . The habit of regarding 'art' as a thing apart from life is fatal to the development of taste . . . No greater service can be rendered to children than in teaching them to know the best and to want it.[38]

The Decoration of Houses sold well, was reprinted, and had a marked influence on house-design in America. Wharton even considered doing a sequel, and wrote proudly in 1903 to Richard Gilder at *The Century Magazine*: 'The Decoration of Houses, which began as a "popular" book, and was rather looked down on by the profession, is now having a steady sale among architects, here and in England as well.' (Batsford, who published the book in England, knew nothing about its authors; their flyer described this 'very interesting volume' as being by 'an American Lady Artist, and an Architect'.) It has been noted that the book 'killed off once and for all rooms in different styles in the same house', that it influenced a number of good early-twentieth-century American houses and was put onto the teaching agenda for architects at the Parsons School of Design. It certainly had an effect on Elsie de Wolfe, whose interior decoration schemes for her clients, and whose own houses in New York and France, put into practice a more daring, modern version of Codman's style (she went in for black and white floors, leopard skins, stripes, chintz, and *trompe l'oeil* effects, and she adored trellis-work) and whose popular manual *The House in Good Taste* (1913) was a more easy-going – and more feminist – sequel to *The Decoration of Houses*. She does not mention Wharton; her heroine was 'Mrs Jack' at Fenway Court. But their ideas overlapped: get rid of the clutter, keep it simple, do not overheat your houses, do not be 'swamped' by your furniture, and remember, you will be judged by your decor:

We endow with refinement and charm the person who welcomes us in a delightful room, where the colours blend and the proportions are as perfect as in a picture ... A woman's environment will speak for her life, whether she likes it or not.[39]

The Mount, the only American house Wharton created herself, would certainly 'speak for her life'. By the end of the 1890s she was finding Newport intolerable. She went through some dark months in Philadelphia and Washington under doctor's orders, being looked after as much by Walter Berry (now an attorney in Washington) as by Teddy. Whether or not she had a 'breakdown', she was very ill and depressed. Family matters were unpleasant. When Minnie and Frederic divorced in 1896 on the grounds of his adultery with Elsie West, with whom he had been living for some years in Paris and whom he later married, Lucretia took his side, against her daughter, who sided with Minnie. Lucretia went to live in Paris in 1897 or 1898 and remained very close to her eldest son. By 1899 she was terminally ill in Paris: there is no knowing how much this affected her daughter. Wharton wrote depressed letters to Codman from Washington: 'both life & diet [here] are becoming wearisome ...' 'Teddy & I are bored perfectly stiff.' Walter argued that the climate of Newport was to blame for the state of her health. He urged her in November 1899 not to go back there: 'Think what it means to have a relapse!' (Teddy thought so too: 'I believe this place does not agree with her', he wrote to Codman from Newport, 'we have been here too long.') Yet in 1899 and 1900, stories and novels and Italian essays were pouring out of her (her first volume of stories, *The Greater Inclination*, was published in 1899), she was travelling all over Europe with the Bourgets, and there were sightings of her full of energy and life. Christmas lunch in 1899 at 884 Park Avenue with Daniel Berkeley Updike, Minnie and Beatrix, saw 'Edith in sparkling form'.[40]

Much of that energy came from the revitalising idea of leaving Newport and buying land in Lenox. She made her first visit to the Berkshires that autumn (to visit Teddy's mother at her house, Pine Acre) and again in 1900, when, instead of going to Newport, the Whartons rented a house in Lenox for the summer, The Poplars, near the lake where The Mount would be built. That summer, Wharton wrote effusively to Coddy: 'I am in love with the place – climate, scenery, life, & all – & when I have built a villa on one of the estates I have picked out, & have planted my gardens & laid out paths through my bosco, I doubt if I ever leave here – [except] to go to Italy.' (Note 'I': in the planning of The Mount, as at Land's End, she was definitely the one in charge. It was done with her money, and according to her decisions.) Walter wrote congratulating her on the good effects of Lenox: 'I don't see that you need a jolly at all [their private word for a 'jollying-up', or encouraging, letter] . . . Run-abouting and riding are putting you in good shape, the littry is booming . . . How I wish I were la-bas . . . with you.'[41]

In the autumn the Whartons closed up Land's End for the last time (it was sold in 1903 for $122,500, a profit of $42,500 on the original price), and in February 1901, after some weeks of negotiation, they agreed to buy 113 acres of farmland, overlooking Laurel Lake, from Georgiana Sargent (a distant relation of the painter). On 29 June 1901 the purchase of 'Laurel Lake Farm' was completed. The purchase followed swiftly on the death of Lucretia Jones. She had been in a coma for some time, and she died in Paris on 1 June, aged seventy-six. One should be thankful, her daughter wrote to Sally Norton: 'She had been hopelessly ill for fourteen months, paralysed and unconscious for nearly a year.'[42] Teddy, not Edith, went to the funeral. Lucretia left a highly unsatisfactory and divisive will behind her. She gave cash bequests to both sons: $95,000 and some real estate (including the house on West 23rd Street) to her favourite, Frederic, $50,000 to Harry. Wharton was left a trust fund equivalent to about $92,000. But (just as with her father's legacy in 1881) she could only draw on the income, which came from rentals of Jones property in New York. She could not draw on the capital in her lifetime, and if she died without issue, the trust-fund (according to the laws of the time on female inheritance) would revert to Frederic, the eldest son. It was a humiliating position. Edith and Teddy felt (in legal parlance) that it was 'an attempt on the part of her brother Frederic to do her a grave injustice, and secure an unfair amount of his mother's fortune for himself'.[43] Acting together, Edith and Harry claimed that 'undue influence' had been exerted, and threatened to take Frederic to law. Edith crossed the Atlantic in July 1901 to deal with these matters: a 'tiresome business', she told Sally Norton.[44] Under pressure, Frederic resigned as a trustee and Teddy took over (not, as it turned out, a helpful substitution). The old trust was dissolved. But, due to legal incompetence, she would never get her full share of the inheritance, and the bitter fall-out of this affair would run on into old age – and after her death. Meanwhile, the three legacies she had (from her mother, her father, and from Joshua Jones) gave her about $22,000 annually.[45] Very soon, this would be bolstered by a growing writer's income.

The purchase of land in Lenox and the building of a large house was an expensive business. (Codman, who was initially the architect for The Mount, and then the interior decorator, reported that the Whartons were slow in paying their bills.) Edith would add 15 acres to the 113 she had bought. The land cost $40,600. Part of this cost was met by the sale of Land's End. Between 1901 and 1902 the cost of building and decorating the house (never mind the landscaping and the gardening) would be about $87,000. As with all building works, it came to more than they had expected: the estimate for building the house had been $41,000; in the end it cost $57,619. The architect took 10 per cent. Codman's bill was $2,116 in 1902 and $1,402 in 1903. The elaborate stable block came to about $20,000, the lodge-house to $5,300. In February 1902 Edith took out a $50,000 mortgage on The Mount, co-signed by Teddy. (In 1911, the house would be sold for $180,000, a profit, after all their expenses had been counted, of about $15,000.) These large sums, however, should be set against the building costs of some of the millionaires' 'cottages' in Lenox, which, at their highest, ranged from anywhere between $240,000 to $1 million.[46]

Once Wharton's energies were focused on the building of the house, everything rushed ahead. Inevitably there were problems, the first of which was a tremendous falling-out with Ogden Codman. Wharton had been putting him in the way of jobs through her social contacts and advising him (rather well) about how to treat his clients – for instance, to drop his charges: 'Human nature, take it all and all, is pretty much the same all over, & though when you make a general reputation you will find suckers who will pay any price because you are "the Fashion", you would not have found such in the beginning . . . I say, be content to make very little money now in order to make a great deal more later.' 'I don't want you to get into the way of shirking small jobs for big ones. If you only *would* believe me when I tell you it's bad policy!' She teased him about his over-demanding way with accounts, replying in kind: 'Now that my time has become so valuable I am obliged to charge for it, & as it has taken me two weeks to answer your letter, the charge will be $200. Please remit by next post.' But when she and Teddy became his clients, things did not go well. Codman did not like to be bossed: he wanted (as he wrote to his mother while working on The Mount) to have the Whartons eating out of his hand.[47]

And clearly he could not bear Teddy. Codman's letters are some of the most revealing evidence of Teddy's behaviour, long before the marriage fell apart. He was quick to see what the relationship was like, writing from France: 'Teddy Wharton has all the silliest of the regular Boston ideas which she has tried to weed out. He is always so sure a man ought to live in his own country.' Teddy's notes to Codman have a clumsily jovial, overbearing air. 'You are at times a demon & have lots of really bad qualities, but I forgave all your baseness of character when I saw the [wood]work in Puss's boudoir, which is more than half up. It is perfectly delightful to look at & does your taste credit.' 'Oh come off & don't be such an ass, you make me so tired.' When hostilities flared up over The Mount, Codman wrote venomous letters home about Teddy's stupidity, aggression, and weirdness ('There are times when I fully realise what an idiot Teddy is') and how impossible the Whartons were to work for (though he was evidently just as difficult himself). 'They are nearly enough to drive me crazy when they are clients . . . The idea of my asserting myself & becoming quite independent seems never to have occurred to them as a possibility.' They 'wear me to a shadow with their nonsense'.[48]

After the Whartons found another architect, Edith wrote a careful, appeasing letter to Coddy, saying that their old friendship was more important to her than their professional relationship. 'Now that you need not be on your guard against me as a client, perhaps I shall be all the more useful as a friend.' Codman began to rewrite the feud: 'It was entirely Teddy who has such a big head & thought he owned the earth.' Naturally, he was extremely critical of the final results of the architecture of The Mount, especially its semicircular courtyard ('an utter failure'). He thought they had moved in before it was ready and that it looked 'forlorn'. Their trouble was that they always thought 'they knew all they knew, & all I knew too. *Now they realize they don't.*'[49] His criticisms went beyond their behaviour as clients or the design of their house: Codman was one of the first people to see, as early as 1902, that Teddy was a deeply unstable person.

> Teddy Wharton seems to be losing his mind which makes it very hard for his wife. You know they had to shut old Mr Wharton up about seven years before he died as he got so strange and irritable . . . Well he has been queer for a long time getting slowly worse. I noticed it the day he came into my office two years ago . . . Part of the time he sat with his arms on the table and held his head in his hands. He looks very old and broken and has lost most of the hair on his head.
>
> He brought up a lot of strange accusations such as that I had written letters no gentleman would write to his wife . . . no one wants to quarrel with a maniac . . . after telling me that of course I was losing all my business because he had found me so hard to get on with he departed slamming the door . . . He has always been very strange about paying his bills . . . I am sure Mrs Wharton is much troubled and worried about him. I suppose she wants to put off shutting him up as long as she can, as he will probably never get any better.[50]

Codman's replacement, Francis Hoppin, of the firm of Hoppin & Koen, was a brilliantly talented architectural draughtsman and designer out of the Beaux-Arts school of architecture, an ex-employee of the firm of McKim, Mead & White, who were designing some of America's grandest houses, and a firm believer in classical style.[51] Walter Berry, who took Edith's side, of course – 'I never heard anything so disgusting as that about Coddy' – was amused by the shock-ripples the quarrel caused among Codman's other clients, such as the Wetmores (for whom Codman had designed, in 1897, his Louis XV green salon at Château-sur-Mer): 'I sat next Mrs Wetmore last night at a banquet. She said she had heard you were building a palazzo at Lenox and supposed of course that Coddy was doing it. When I said no, it's Hoppin, she nearly had a congestion.'[52] Building began in the summer of 1901 and went on all through that year and the next. (In the spring of 1902, Codman was forgiven and rehired as decorator.) The Whartons moved into the house in September, with Teddy in a very poor state of health. (Codman reported that Teddy had gone into Hoppin's office so enraged that he 'foamed at the mouth'.) At the start of 1903 they went to Italy for three months, leaving gardeners and decorators at work, but when they got back to Lenox in May they found that a drought had set back the garden plans terribly. That was their first long summer at The Mount. For the next five years – the years in which Wharton became a famous writer – they spent their summers and autumns there. It was her place for house-improvements, gardening, walking, entertaining, driving – and writing. By 1908, the marriage was in crisis, her feelings about America unhappier than ever, and her attention and desires fixed on France. She spent the next two years entirely away from Lenox, and, after a last terrible summer there in 1911, The Mount was sold, amid desperate quarrels and confusion. But for those six years, 1903 to 1908, it was her pride and pleasure.

Why did Edith choose Lenox? Proximity to the Wharton family – Teddy's conservative old mother Nancy, his neurotic sister Nannie, and his dull brother Billy, who paid visits from Groton with his equally dull wife – was not an incentive for her, though it would have been for Teddy. The widowed Mrs Nancy Wharton lived in the middle of the town, in 'Pine Acre', exactly the sort of heavily furnished, gabled, mid-nineteenth-century house, full of corner fireplaces, nooks and beams, which Edith had come to dislike. She and Teddy stayed there while The Mount was being built. Mr Wharton's suicide was kept quiet in Lenox, and the Wharton mother and sister were pillars of the community. When Mrs Nancy Wharton died in 1909, at eighty-nine, all the shops in Lenox closed for the funeral – which Edith did not attend. The lot which Mrs Wharton had bought in the graveyard of the Church-on-the-Hill, where she, Nannie, and Teddy, were buried one by one, was a lot with four graves: one place remained unclaimed.[53]

There were no close friends near by, but plenty of acquaintances. Teddy Wharton's doctor, Francis Kinnicutt, lived in Lenox, Richard Gilder of the *Century* was at Tyringham, the editor of *Vanity Fair*, Frank Crowninshield, was at Stockbridge. The attraction was a community of wealthy property owners from New York, living in grand houses, in a 'summer colony' quieter than Newport; a much better climate; and land to build their own houses on. To make the journey from Newport to Lenox was to move from a harsh, flat, grotesquely overbuilt resort, up into the ravishingly grand and tender landscape of Western Massachusetts – the Berkshire hills and the Housatonic valley. Yet, though this move brought a refreshing change of views and a definite break with the past, it was not a radical change of life-style. The Mount was not an experimental house, and Lenox was a predictable location for a woman of her class and upbringing. But it gave her that magnificent landscape, and strong literary associations.

Writers had been coming to the Berkshires, the 'Lake District' of New England, attracted by the rural serenity, the fall colours, and the simple little towns, for many years. (They go on living there and describing it to this day: see, for instance, the eloquent evocation of Tanglewood, just outside Lenox, in Philip Roth's *The Human Stain*.) In the 1840s and 1850s, Longfellow and Oliver Wendell Holmes were in Pittsfield; Hawthorne was at the 'Little Red House' on the edge of Lenox, writing *Tanglewood Tales* and *The House of the Seven Gables*; Melville was writing *Moby-Dick* and *Piazza Tales* at Arrowhead, his farm near Pittsfield. The famous first meeting between these two took place during a thunderstorm, in August 1850, on a walk with Holmes up Monument Mountain, one of the great romantic natural features near Lenox, where (wrote William Cullen Bryant, another local writer) 'the lovely and the wild mingled in harmony on Nature's face'. Hawthorne was one of Wharton's heroes; Melville she enjoyed as she did George Borrow, as a romantic, adventurous story-teller. In this she was very much of her time. By the 1870s, hundreds of pilgrims came to visit Hawthorne's house, but Melville was still counted as a minor figure. An amateurish guide to Lenox of 1902 by the Reverend DeWitt Mallary calls Melville the author of 'sea-tales, popular in their day, and still very much appreciated as first-rank stories of their kind'. Another literary predecessor in Lenox was the popular woman novelist Catherine Sedgwick, born in Stockbridge, author of *A New England Tale* (1822), *Hope Leslie* (1827) and many other moralistic best-sellers, with independent views on

Calvinism, marriage, and women's education. DeWitt Mallary gushed, 'Lenox had its real live authoress moving along the quiet village streets'. She had a literary salon, with visitors like Anna Jameson, Harriet Martineau and the actress Fanny Kemble, who fell in love with the Berkshires. Sedgwick was one possible model for Wharton, as an ambitious American woman novelist, and she was seen by some as her successor: 'Lately another woman distinguished in letters, Mrs Edith Wharton, has become enamoured of the Berkshire County, and is ... creating here a country seat, beautifully located near Laurel Lake ... This section of the town is full of literary associations.'[54]

Fanny Kemble called Lenox, surrounded by wooded hills, with its two little lakes, Stockbridge Bowl and Laurel Lake, 'the most picturesque scenery I have ever seen ... A landscape that combines every variety of beauty.'[55] 'It is a ravishing land', Henry James would echo, memorably describing the countryside around Lenox in its autumn colours as a 'bath of beauty'. The grand landmarks, Monument Mountain and Mount Everett to the south, Becket Mountain to the south-east, Greylock (or Saddleback) to the north ('Greylock with all his hills about him, like Charlemagne among his peers', as Melville wrote, fifty years before), the woods, the river valley, the lakes and ponds, the little isolated villages, the clear northern air, all pulled at the heart.[56]

But there was a bleak side to this landscape too. The grimness of the remote, inaccessible New England farms and of the 'mountain' people's lives in desolate little hill villages, particularly in winter, and the hard times of the industrial workers in the region, stirred Wharton's imagination quite as much as the life of the wealthy 'cottagers'. There were violent contrasts in this environment: between the opulence of Lenox or Stockbridge, and the deprivation of the rural poor, between the romance of the landscape and the industries being developed on the back of local resources. Lenox Dale, just outside the town, was an industrial centre. The Lenox Iron Works were founded in 1848. Clocks, carriages, china and muskets were made in Pittsfield. The Crane Paper Mills in Dalton, the industrial town on the banks of the Housatonic, were a nineteenth-century success story, succeeded by the Jones paper-making factory at Lee, near Lenox. Further north, in Adams and North Adams, there were cotton and wool mills and shoe factories. Technological progress – the building of railway lines and tunnels in the 1850s and, from the 1880s onwards, trolley-cars, motors, and an electrical company making alternating-current transformers, were changing the landscape.[57] This aspect of the Berkshires would feed into Wharton's shocking New England novellas, *Ethan Frome* and *Summer*, and would inspire her most politically concerned novel, written at The Mount, *The Fruit of the Tree* (1907), which sets 'the great glare of leisure' of the wealthy houses against the needs of the mill-workers.

As that novel makes clear, manufacturing industries, rural poverty, and the 'gilded' Lenox summer colony, were profoundly connected. The new railways had brought in the vacationers; their palaces were being built from local marble; many local people worked in service in the big houses, as a preferable alternative to the mills or the electric plant. The building of the summer colony, starting in the 1880s, completely transformed the 'little Calvinist settlement' that had been Lenox. It was a self-confident small town, always in competition with its neighbour, Stockbridge, proud of its revolutionary history and its religious associations (Jonathan Edwards, the great eighteenth-century Puritan divine, was a local figure, the minister Henry Ward Beecher had a farm at Lenox, and there was a Shaker community at nearby Hancock). It had a well-known academy, a school for girls, a grand old inn, the Curtis Hotel, the beautiful Church-on-the-Hill, in white wooden 'Berkshire Colonial' style, and its own court house, which became a library with about 14,000 books. (Wharton gave it some assistance.) But during the nineteenth century it was utterly changed. In 1800, its population was 104; in 1902, it was 3,000. Twenty-six big houses were built in the 1880s, forty-two more by 1902. In 1883, the total valuation of Lenox was \$1,599,711; in 1900 it was \$3,750,004.[58]

The millionaire 'cottages', competitively built to outshine each other, of 'Harrimans, Stuyvesants, Aspinwalls, Crockers, Adamses, Biddles, Vanderbilts, and Sloanes', started to go up in the 1880s. The most ostentatious was Shadowbrook, built at the cost of half a million dollars in 1893 by Anson Phelps Stokes (banker, investor, manufacturer) on 783 acres, the largest private country house in America (until Biltmore). It looked like an English Gothic cottage gigantically blown up, with red-tiled roofs and half-timbered gables. Boastful stories were told of its awesome capacities for hospitality; when the son of the house said he was bringing some of his Yale classmates for the weekend, his mother reputedly telegrammed: 'Many guests here; have only room for fifty.' Even more expensive was Bellefontaine, built in 1897 for Giraud Foster for \$1 million, designed by Carrère and Hastings, made of white marble, and surrounded by hundreds of imported statues. Elm Court, an enormous New England-style house, endlessly being added to, was built between 1886 and 1900, at a cost of about \$240,000, for the carpet manufacturer William Douglas Sloane, whose fortune was enhanced by his marriage to Emily Vanderbilt, the 'queen of Lenox'. J.P. Morgan's sister lived at Ventfort Hall, a brown-brick Victorian

Gothic pile. The 'electrical magnate' George Westinghouse set his vast red-and-white villa, Erskine Park, in acres of lawns and marble bridges and lakes and fountains. He also had a power-plant in his grounds which allowed him to install a frieze of 1,500 electric light bulbs in his house (this was very novel) and which generated enough power to light the streets of Lenox. As a result of the Westinghouse power-plant – which luckily had new gas-engines and an extra dynamo added on just as The Mount was being built – Edith was able to put into practice her enthusiasm for all the latest conveniences. 'Everything is pushing up new shoots', she wrote to Sally Norton in June 1902, 'not only cabbages & strawberries, but electric lights & plumbing.' She may have complained about too much electricity in the drawing room in *The Decoration of Houses*, but she liked her own house to be up-to-date.[59]

The rich came to Lenox for its scenery and its literary associations and because the other rich were doing it. Henry James called it 'the workable, the expensively workable, American form of country life'. In 1886, a guide-book called *The Book of the Berkshires* promised incomers a bracing climate, no cholera, industries like the paper-mills discreetly hidden away (so 'in no wise offensive'), good roads and services, New York papers available by midday, archery, golf, gymkhanas, horse-races, and a gentlemen's club. You could go to Saratoga or Newport for the horses and the sea in early to midsummer, and then on to the Berkshires for the leaves, before the New York winter season began. Lenox was 'an inland Newport where blue mountains were the equivalent of sand and rolling surf'. But it was preferable to Newport because less formal and showy: 'One didn't need as many gowns at Lenox.' The local paper, *Lenox Life*, wrote proudly in 1901: 'The better classes of New York society, and people of more conservative tastes prefer life in the Berkshires to life at Newport.' The kind of house that was required here, as Mariana Van Rensselaer described it in 'American Country Dwellings' in 1886, was one that would fit into a closely grouped colony and not be too 'self-asserting'. The model here, even more than at Newport, was the 'English country house ideal'.[60]

That was just the kind of house Wharton built. She fitted into the tone of the community, though she did not feel like a Stokes or a Vanderbilt. The Mount (named after her assertive great-grandfather's house) was not an ostentatious house, by their standards. The plans that Hoppin & Koen drew up had to be modified: Codman gleefully reported that Hoppin was going to have to change brick into stucco over wood for the fabric of the building, and some of the most ambitious first thoughts for the house – a five-windowed gallery (cut down to three), blasting through rocks to build a ground-floor grotto, elaborate ironwork gates – had to be abandoned. An extension for the servants' wing, planned in 1907, was not built, and a second garden had to wait until the income generated by the success of *The House of Mirth* in 1905. Still, it was by no means a modest house. It had thirty-five rooms, and a hundred windows (some were blind windows, made to balance real ones). It was built high into the side of a hill, with rocks below it and a wide vista beyond. It commanded its landscape. DeWitt Mallary described its view, in 1902: 'The little Laurel Lake forms part of the picture, with the long white chalk-line made by the Lee village church spire against the mountains; everywhere the rim of mountains; everywhere at night the brilliantly illuminated mansions thickly sown.'[61] Edith, who would take to star-gazing from the terrace, summed up the beauty of the setting, in her last year at The Mount, to Bernard Berenson:

> This place of ours is really beautiful . . . the stillness, the greenness, the exuberance of my flowers, the perfume of my hemlock woods, & above all the moonlight nights on my big terrace, overlooking the lake . . .[62]

Henry James would famously, and rather wickedly, describe it to their mutual friend Howard Sturgis as 'a delicate French château mirrored in a Massachusetts pond'. Since then, it has been called 'an Italian garden and a European house in Massachusetts'.[63] The Mount drew on a great mixture of styles and sources, but Hoppin, Wharton, and Codman between them worked these into a building of dignity and style. The H-shaped layout, with a double Palladian staircase and dominating cupola as the central features, were taken directly from the grand seventeenth-century Belton House in Lincolnshire, England. The Mount was done in white stucco instead of grey stone, and it was much smaller than Belton House, but its 'classical pedigree' was obvious. The model, though, was as much Italian as English. The long balustraded terrace that dominated the first floor of the house, with the grand staircases leading down into the garden (extending the house into the landscape in a way that Beatrix would have appreciated), was an Italian feature. So was the grotto-like entrance hall, complete with dripping water effects on the stuccoed walls, a fountain, and a statue of Pan. So too was the magnificent long gallery on the *piano nobile*, running parallel with the terrace, with vaulted ceiling, terrazzo floors, statues, and Italian furnishings, and with all the main rooms opening off it. But the plan of having the main rooms on the first floor 'enfilade', as a connecting row – dining room, drawing room, library, den – so that they opened onto both the gallery and the terrace and so that each room could be entered without going through from one to the other, was a French design. It was certainly a novel feature in an American country house of the time.

The house was international in other ways too. Beatrix, who worked on the approach to the house and on the kitchen-gardens, designed a long drive lined with sugar-maple trees, curving off through woods to the house, that was very French in feeling. The gardens Edith would design drew on all her Italian experience. Yet they were set above an English-style meadow and in front of an 'American suburban lawn'. The regularity of the house, with its emphatically symmetrical features, was 'typical of the American design of the period'. The green shutters on all the windows and the big striped awning over the centre of the terrace had an American Colonial flavour. This was an American Renaissance house drawn from 'French, Italian, and English sources'.[64]

The house was built for work, leisure, and selected visitors, not for show or large-scale entertaining. For all its lordly air, it is a functional house, planned for comfort and convenience. Outside – as with many of the big houses in the Berkshires – as well as the large kitchen garden and a big greenhouse, there was a working farm, on the model of an English landed estate. This had come with the land, but was actively kept up, partly to provide themselves and their guests with fresh vegetables, milk, eggs, and meat, partly to keep Teddy busy. There was an ice-house, a hen-house, a piggery, a wagon-shed, and a farmhouse. They also built a fine 'Georgian' stable-block, all white stucco, with a cupola to match the house. It had room for up to fourteen horses (Edith had horses at various times called Frank, Countess, and Fatty), and a carriage-room (later a garage) with the coachman's living-quarters above.[65]

In the house, as *The Decoration of Houses* recommended, privacy, convenience and proportion were the ideals. The principles of the book were put into practice from the drive into the semicircular courtyard and the grotto-like entrance hall. Instead of your walking straight on into the main rooms, or finding the main stairs directly in front of you, a glass door on the right cut off the staircase, which was enclosed 'in a subsidiary space off the vestibule' (as a house-planner might put it). Only by invitation were you allowed through the glass door, up the stairs, and into the inner regions of the house, the splendid gallery, the spacious and elegant living rooms with their high windows. The dramatic surprise of the terrace and its views could not be guessed at from the entrance courtyard. Throughout, the structure emphasised seclusion and 'distinctly articulated spaces'. On the second floor, where the long hall had doors opening off to the Whartons' separate (but adjoining) bedrooms and to the three guest-rooms, Edith had a suite, a bedroom, bathroom, and boudoir, which could be closed off from the rest of the house and where she could write in peace. The bedroom was painted pale yellow and had windows on the north and east side, with lovely variegated views and good light. The bathroom had a separate door for the servants to go in and out of without coming through the bedroom, as recommended in *The Decoration of Houses*. These rooms were above the library and the den, to ensure quiet.[66]

Codman's interior decoration showed scrupulous attention to detail. The rooms had character; they were meant for particular use by particular individuals, and did not have that 'diffused vagueness of separation . . . between place of passage and place of privacy' which James, writing on modern American houses in 1907, found 'a provocation to despair'.[67] The dining room had fruit and flower plaster-work in the manner of Grinling Gibbons carvings, with large Italian painted panels of still lifes set into the walls, to go with the dining-room furniture – eighteenth-century Italian, from Land's End. Teddy's den was formally decorated, suitably for the 'man's' room, with elegant rectangular panelling. Edith's boudoir (which she also called her sitting room) was more ornate, with eight little paintings of flowers set into the walls, elaborate fruit and flower plaster-work, parquet floors, and a fireback (as in some of the other rooms) with an allegorical motif. There were light patterned fabric curtains with matching fabric on the sofa and chairs, flower-vases, a French clock, photographs, a fire-screen, an elegant desk: not a cluttered room, but a charming and usable one. The library was supremely well done. It opened on all sides (to the terrace through French windows, to the gallery, to the drawing room next door, and (through a concealed door) to the den. Yet it had a feeling of warmth and enclosure, from the oak bookshelves built into the walls on three sides of the room, the green marble fireplace (often in use), its cast-iron fireback decorated with one of the Labours of Hercules (with the Nemean lion), the plaster-work decoration on the ceiling, the large oriental carpet, the tapestries, the solid, centrally positioned desk, the comfortable seating – *lit de repos*, cane-back writing chair, armchairs round the hearth – and the cunningly placed lampshades and flower-vases. The books provided the main furnishings, bound in blue, red, or brown morocco gilt, the effect 'warm, harmonious, subdued' and orderly.[68]

Wharton paid attention to every detail, as in this letter to Codman about the tapestries:

> The change of tapestries you suggest would not do as the two tapestries of which you have sketches are alike in colouring and composition,

whereas the one I intend to put in the library is absolutely different. I don't care to have the chimney in the drawing room moved, but surely, as the tapestries match so perfectly in the essentials – i.e. colour and composition – the fact that one is narrower than the other need not matter, since you can put an extra narrow panel on each side of the smaller tapestry. I am dreadfully sorry that the bust can't be recessed over the drawing room chimney. Could it be done by making a small chimney-breast? Of course they did have them in Louis XIV houses.[69]

That sort of attention to detail shows up everywhere: in the heart-shaped hooks for the guest-rooms (perhaps acquired from the Shakers, who made hooks just like these at their community in nearby Hancock?) and in the mother-of-pearl buttons for the servants' bells. These bell-pushes in the bedrooms were standard features, but they tell us a great deal about the life of the house. Bells for the servants were in every bedroom; the servants' hall still has the indicator box to say which bell was ringing: 'Mrs Wharton's bedroom, Mrs Wharton's boudoir, Mrs Wharton's bath, Mr Wharton's bedroom, Mr Wharton's bath, Mr Wharton's dressing room, East Guest Room, East Guest Room bath, West Guest Room bath, Small Guest Room'.[70]

The occupants of these rooms depended on the servants for every amenity. All the stories and novels that came out of Wharton's New England life make clear how conscious she was of that fact. Her novel *The Fruit of the Tree* is largely about worker–employer relations. Her two New England novellas have to do with lives in service. Her most alarming ghost-stories, both set in houses like The Mount, 'All Souls'' and 'The Lady's Maid's Bell', make sinister use of the mutual dependency of mistress and servants. As in the latter story, Wharton's maid was the only one of the in-house servants to have a bedroom on the same floor as the main bedrooms, connected to the second-floor hall and with easy access to her mistress's suite. There would have been seven or eight other members of house-staff: housekeeper and butler, Gross and Alfred White; the cook (or chef); Anna Bahlmann, Edith's secretary; a housemaid, a footman, a laundress and a scullery maid. Their service wing, at the south end of the house, and stretching under the terrace, had the kitchen, servants' dining room, scullery, laundry room, trunk room, wine cellar, butler's pantry, housekeeper's room, linen closet, and sewing room. The servants' bedrooms were in the attic. The house was heated by a coal-fired furnace (keeping warm was problematic, and the servants' rooms were probably very cold: but they were hardly ever there in the winter, except between December

1905 and February 1906). It was typical of Edith's investment in mod cons that the servants' wing had a hydraulic elevator, for moving luggage. There was a separate servants' entrance, and separate stairs. An Irish woman, Rosie, who worked at the house during and after the Whartons' ownership, was said never to have used the main stairs – yet she spoke of the house with warmth and proprietary feeling. Wharton was kind and conscientious with her servants, and they were loyal to her.[71] Working outside the house, there was a coachman, a groom, and a number of local men who were taken on as seasonal labourers. The most important of the outdoor staff were the chauffeur and the head gardener. Charles Cook, the chauffeur, from nearby Lee, would see the Whartons through all their early automobile adventures from 1904 onwards, and would eventually transfer himself with impressive adaptability, from the country roads of New England to driving in Paris and all over France.

In her memoir, Wharton recalled 'a big kitchen-garden with a grape pergola, a little farm, & a flower-garden outspread below the wide terrace overlooking the lake'. These gardens evolved gradually and with some difficulties. The Massachusetts climate of bitter winters and raging hot summers was a challenge. Beatrix's big kitchen garden was laid out right away, and a start was made on a shrubbery and a rock garden near the house (full of ferns), and a series of terraced lawns descending to the flower garden, with views of the meadows, lake and woods – an 'outdoor room' connecting the house to the landscape, as in an Italian villa. But they came back from Italy in the spring of 1903 to find that their first head-gardener had failed them – drink was thought to be the problem – and that a New England drought had retarded everything. He was replaced by Thomas Reynolds ('my devoted and admirable head gardener'), who lived in The Mount's two-storey Georgian gate-house, next to the greenhouse, and stayed with the Whartons until 1911. In spite of the setbacks, the first formal garden was coming into shape, with advice from Beatrix, and from an old Mount Desert friend of hers, George Dorr, a gardener and conservationist, founder of the Acadia National Park, who also had a house in the Berkshires. Wharton wrote him enthusiastic letters about the wild-flower garden she planned below the formal garden, about borders for paths and new varieties of phlox (one of her favourite flowers).[72]

This first garden, made between 1901 and 1904, was a symmetrical enclosed space with flower-beds, gravel walks, grass panels, topiary, trellis-work (from Land's End), and a central, oblong pond with a fountain, carved with dolphins, bordered by a hedge of white petunias. The colours and the smells were intense: mainly pinks, blues, purples, whites and reds.

She grew annuals and hardy herbaceous perennials: sweet peas, poppies, dianthus, penstemons, lilies, hollyhocks, and carnations (all of which won prizes in the Lenox Horticultural Society Flower Show in August 1904, as did her gladioli and antirrhinums in 1906). In June 1905, she described to Sally Norton the garden blooming with 'ten varieties of phlox, some very gorgeous' (by August the count had risen to thirty-two),

> snapdragons, lilac and crimson stocks, penstemons, annual pinks in every shade of rose, salmon, cherry and crimson – Hunnemannia [the poppy-like perennial], the lovely white physostegia [known as the 'obedient plant', this was the 'summer snow' variety, with close-set flowers and spikes], the white petunias . . . the intense blue Delphinium chinense [or 'grandiflorum' – perhaps the hardy, deep blue 'blue butterfly' variety], the purple and white platycodons [known as the 'balloon flower': lanterns when closed, stars when open] . . . hollyhocks of every shade from pale rose to dark red.

'Really,' she concluded, 'it looks, for a fleeting moment, like a garden in some civilized climate.'[73]

Over the next two years she worked on a second garden, to be paid for by *The House of Mirth*, south-east of the house, connected to the first by a straight path walled with linden trees and hemlock hedges. This was a sunken garden enclosed by stone walls with niches for statues at either end, and a central round pond with another fountain. It took its inspiration, in part, from the Villa Gamberaia. The completed effect was admiringly written up in 1911 by a visiting lady garden-critic.

> The house itself, adapted from an English model that drew from the Italian, dominates a hilltop, and is attained by sweeping drives and surrounded by down-dropping lawns shaded by fine trees. On one side there is a rock garden of great beauty and the shrubbery, curving like an approaching wave, edges the lawns nobly. But it is the double sunken gardens, set down into the hill, that are the distinction of the place. Each has its central fountain, surrounded by geometrically shaped beds and separated by narrow gravel paths and planted with brilliant flowers of contrasted hues. At their lower edge stand marble walls in the Italian style, with openings that permit exquisite glimpses of the view, and, at the same time, form a lovely background for a few of the taller flowers and some choice rose-trees. Looking down upon the two gardens, separated from each other by the terraced lawns, as you stand on the broad veranda of the villa, the glory of their colouring actually vibrates

in the sunlight; yet framed as they are in spacious green, they do not clash with the distant prospect.[74]

A less enthusiastic version was given by Beatrix Farrand's biographer, Jane Brown. According to her, the American ambassador to Britain, Joseph Choate, who lived in a McKim, Mead 'cottage', Naumkeag in Stockbridge (which itself had a magnificent garden plunging down a deep slope, with linden and arbor-vitae walks, formal parterres and rose-gardens)

> stepped onto her terrace and remarked: 'Ah, Mrs Wharton, when I look about me I don't know if I'm in England or in Italy.' He undoubtedly meant that if he were in England the grass would lap the terrace walls, offering serpentine vistas through the trees to the distant lake; but if he were in Italy he would expect elaborate, falling terraces at his feet, with beds of bright flowers, plopping fountains, gambolling stone cherubs ... The Mount owns a mixture that is neither: the enclosed, formal gardens floated in the middle distance, to the right and left of the view, as if stretched on a rack. They teeter at the end of a seesaw, which is the Lime Walk that tentatively connects them across the line of sight to the lake.[75]

Wharton herself felt pleased with her achievement, and with the serene effect of the Berkshires: 'There is lots of time here,' she wrote to Daisy Chanler even before they moved into the house, in the summer of 1902, '& one can sit under a tree with a beautiful view in one's eyes, talk & read & let things settle down with one, undisturbed.' When she was away, in New York or in Europe, she missed that quiet and solitude. In the summer and autumn months, she poured her energies into the house and gardens, and created a satisfying life for herself.

Her pet dogs were an integral part of that life, and eventually there would be a small graveyard for them in the grounds of The Mount, up on a sheltered mound. Since she was a child she had never been without dogs, and they feature in many of her photographs – Pekingese, Skye terriers, Pomeranians, poodles, and Papillons – sitting on laps or shoulders or being carried on horseback. She felt intensely, even uncannily, close to them, and grieved when they died. In the 1890s there had been Mouton and Sprite, a poodle and a Peke. In 1902 her lap-dog Mimi, whom she had had for eight years, died. At The Mount, there were Toto (who died in 1904), Miza, who was put to sleep in 1906, and Jules, a Skye terrier, who died in 1907, to her great sorrow. At this time she and Teddy were involved in the New York Society for the Prevention of Cruelty to Animals, a badly run organisation, in her view, which debated the rights and wrongs of euthanasia for dogs (her own were mercifully chloroformed when they were terminally ill) and ran a campaign, in which Wharton was active, to put drinking bowls in the streets for New York dogs. After Miza and Jules, the household pair of lap-dogs, both white Papillons with black patches on ears, eyes and nose, were Mitou and Nicette. In later life, in France, Wharton kept only Pekingese, Choumal, Tooty, and last of all her precious Linky. These spoilt, fastidious, shy and obstinate creatures, for whom she had special coats made by a dog-knitter, were close to her heart in a way that non-dog-lovers can hardly understand. To come back after a long absence and have the dogs 'turn somersaults for joy' was to feel at home. When she described the outbreak of war in France, one of the details she noted was that all the women seeing off their men had brought their dogs with them, who, 'snugly lodged in the bend of an elbow . . . looked out on the scene with the quiet awareness of the Paris dog'. In old age she often spoke about her almost mystical sense of communication with her dogs, and she judged her new friends partly by whether they shared this enthusiasm.[76]

While Teddy looked after the farm and the business management of the house, rode, fished, hunted, and, later, drove, she made her contribution to the community, proudly sending in her flowers for prizes and joining the Village Improvement Committee. In 1902 she went onto the Associate Board of Managers (with four other local ladies) of the Lenox Library, and helped to organise the cataloguing of the library, corresponding with the cataloguer, Miss Phelps, throughout the summer, and giving her a signed copy of *The Valley of Decision* in November 1902, in thanks for her work. Between 1902 and 1910, Wharton gave the Lenox Library an annual contribution of between $30 and $40, as well as new carpets and books: and it gave her the opening scene of *Summer*. In 1907, she furnished a clubroom for the French-speaking residents of Lenox Dale, and had her chef provide 'a delicious luncheon'.[77]

She was on civil but not intimate terms with her neighbours. The large Cram family at Highwood (the site of the future Tanglewood Music Festival) were close friends of Teddy's mother. The matriarch of the family also had a household in France, with connections to the Wharton servants: Gross was the sister-in-law of the Crams' butler. The daughters of the family, Henrietta and the beautiful red-headed Ethel Cram, a good pianist, became quite close friends in the Lenox years. (Another Cram sister, Lily, was an eccentric spinster who cried a lot, tore up handkerchiefs, raised birds in her smelly bedroom, and communicated with the rest of the family by notes – as curious a grotesque as any in Wharton's New England stories.) Ethel

Cram had a terrible accident in July 1905. The horse drawing her pony-cart, coming away from the Lenox Library, took fright at one of the town's motor-cars; she was thrown out and kicked, and her skull was fractured. She lingered unconscious, and died two months later. Painful letters on her condition passed between Edith and Sally Norton. The death would haunt her, and she put it straight into *The Fruit of the Tree*. But when she took a consolatory poem round to the Crams' house, she was rebuffed by Mrs Cram, who thought it 'cheeky'. Henrietta wept, 'and there was a terrible scene'. Old Mrs Cram always thought Edith treated her husband 'abominably': she sided with Mrs Wharton and Nannie.[78]

Stories of Edith's chilly relations with the nouveau-riche cottagers may be apocryphal – but there are rather a lot of them. Codman, who said that 'Poor Pussy is of course very unpopular . . . she has always rather gone out of her way to be rude to people', was delighted to hear, even before the move to Lenox, that she was in trouble with Mrs Sloane, Emily Vanderbilt, for a story published in *Lippincott's* in October 1900, 'The Line of Least Resistance', set in Newport, about a weak-willed rich husband unable to take a stand against his wife's infidelity – thought to be based on Emily Vanderbilt's brother-in-law. This would not be the last time that Wharton was accused of taking her plots too closely from life. According to Codman, 'the Whartons *wrote and apologized* for it'. But he was not a reliable witness – and the Sloanes did come to the Whartons' house-warming. Edith's appointment diary for 1905 contains at least one high-society item – 'Dinner with Mrs Astor to meet Prince Louis of Battenburg' – but this was an exception; on the whole she seems not to have socialised with the millionaires. If she did, they had to watch out. To one wealthy lady who was showing off her house, saying, 'And this I call my Louis Quinze room', Edith is supposed to have replied, 'staring about through her lorgnette, "*Why*, my dear?"' And, of another local couple (sounding in these anecdotes rather like Lady Bracknell), she remarked: 'The Xs tell me they have decided to have books in their library.' James's friend Howard Sturgis in 1904, reporting to Edith on a chance meeting with her Lenox neighbour Mrs Westinghouse at the opera in New York, made the kind of joke she clearly appreciated: 'She seemed to be under the impression that Mozart was an Italian.' The philistine millionaires of Lenox were her subject matter rather than her friends. Among neighbours and distant acquaintances, she was developing a reputation for superiority. One lady, Helen Aldis Lathrop, meeting her in 1906, was 'rather more pleased with Mrs Wharton than I expected to be for I thought she would seem very conceited from what people who don't like her had described . . . but she seemed easily enough pleased . . . She has fine eyes and refinement, but not good-featured otherwise.'[79]

The friends who knew her better than that, and whom she entertained at The Mount, were imported. They visited in small groups, stayed for several days, and fell into a schedule devised by the hostess (often described, with a mixture of admiration and ironical acceptance) which allowed for work, outdoor life, and talk. (There was a good table and a good cellar at The Mount, too, though Edith did not drink wine herself.) She wrote in bed and did the business of house-management in the morning. Guests might receive little notes on their breakfast-trays outlining the day's plans. Everyone met at lunchtime, or set out for a picnic. The afternoons were given over to walks, gardening, excursions to local beauty spots like Tyringham Cobble or (from 1904) drives further afield into the New England countryside, and evenings to conversation and readings in the library or the drawing room, on summer nights sitting on the terrace, star-gazing and talking. (They might discuss, for instance, Bielschowsky's life of Goethe or Wilhelm Ostwald's *Individuality and Immortality*, both in her diary's reading-list for 1906.[80])

In spite of the blusteringly genial and often oppressive presence of Teddy, she was forging new relationships with leading American intellectual, cultural and political figures, alongside her expanding European contacts and affiliations. She spent as much of her time as possible with people who shared her interests. Some of them – editors, publishers, fellow writers, academics – came to her through her work. Her friendships were settling and deepening. Walter was often at The Mount. She came to know Howard Sturgis and Henry James. She became closer to her musical and religious childhood friend Daisy Chanler, dedicated to her family and to her well-connected, sporting husband Winthrop. She had a fondness for the quiet, clever, chronically unwell Bayard Cutting, a person of 'ceaseless intellectual curiosity', private secretary to Joseph Choate, just married to Lady Sybil Cuffe, who found Mrs Wharton so 'chilling'. Eunice Ives, who grew up in Lenox and married the publisher Walter Maynard in 1903, became, like her husband, a close and dear friend. She liked Robert Minturn, one of those cultured, apolitical men of leisure who dominated the New York of her youth, and the Boston lawyer and writer Robert Grant, whose novel of a ruthless fortune-seeking divorcée, *Unleavened Bread* (1900) she admired very much (and would keep in mind). Grant, and another Boston lawyer, Bill Richardson, were two of the few people she would still count among her American friends in the mid-1920s. She also came to know, while at The Mount, the director of the Metropolitan Museum in New York, Edward

Robinson, an expert on classical art, funny and dry, the first of many art-historians, collectors and curators in her life.[81]

This network of distinguished Americans was closely interconnected. Edward Robinson was introduced to her by the Nortons, and, once at The Mount, the friendship with that eminent family in Ashfield – particularly with Sally Norton – became very important to her. Visits and letters and exchanges of books were continuous. Walter introduced her in Washington to 'Bay' Lodge, the son of the Massachusetts senator Henry Cabot Lodge; Lodge Senior was a close friend of the President, Theodore Roosevelt, and Wharton met Roosevelt through the Chanlers. Moving inside this mesh of acquaintances and friendships, Edith was selective and class-bound, but also open to new possibilities. She had an ability to cut across generations, never restricting herself to friends of a certain age. She was as interested in Charles Eliot Norton as she was in Sally. The two gifted young men in her circle who both died young, Bayard Cutting (sixteen years younger than she, who died in 1910) and 'Bay' Lodge (who died at thirty-six, in 1909) were as close to her as Egerton Winthrop had been or as Henry James would become.

George Cabot Lodge, always called 'Bay', was a dazzlingly precocious young man with an impeccable pedigree and a passionate love and talent for poetry. His interests were wide, his talk was exciting. Edith adored him (and was fond too of his young wife Bessy). She saw him as full of poten-tial, though she had reservations about his poetry. She went devotedly to Harvard in June 1906 to hear him read his 'Phi Beta' poem, saying she wanted 'to see my dear Bay as Laureate'. But she confided to Sally that she thought he lacked a 'real sense of visible beauty'. When she came to write an elegiac review of his posthumously published poems, *The Soul's Inheritance*, she balanced her warm feelings for his enthusiasm, charm, and seriousness, with her reservations ('his was not the lyric muse').[82] Her friend-ship with Bessy continued long after 'Bay''s death. When the older Lodges meanly tried to prevent the young widow with three children from marrying a French Catholic, Edith took Bessy's side. From the later vantage point of Paris in wartime, the Lodges came to stand for all the qualities of old Boston that she disliked, and often satirised in her stories – dry austerity, conser-vatism, hypocrisy.

'Bay' Lodge and his family were part of the cultured and powerful American community to which she belonged while she was at The Mount. A joke she told to Bay in the summer of 1904, about sitting at dinner next to a dim English aristocrat who thought that G.O. Trevelyan's history of the American Revolution was a first-hand account by an 'army man', was passed on delightedly in a letter from Roosevelt to a friend. When her tribute to Bay was published, Roosevelt wrote to Henry Cabot Lodge: 'I like Mrs Wharton's appreciation of him.'[83] Roosevelt had grown up in the same kind of New York as Edith Jones (his descriptions, in his autobiography, of the furnishings and decor of his childhood home are very like hers). She was very distantly related to his second wife. But they first talked at length when she went back to Newport from Lenox, in August 1902 (tennis week at Newport, and dazzling weather) for the christening of Daisy Chanler's son Theodore, godson to Roosevelt. Elected Vice-President in 1900, on the strength of his great popular acclaim for joining the Rough Riders and fighting in the war with Spain in 1898, Roosevelt had become President in September 1901, after the assassination of McKinley. 'I do delight in him', Edith wrote to Sally, '& the two hours I spent in his society at the Chanler christening gave me great satisfaction.'

The week after the christening, giving speeches in New England, Roosevelt was involved in a serious accident in Pittsfield. His carriage – an open landau drawn by four horses – was smashed into by a trolley-car and overturned, and his Secret Service guard was killed. Roosevelt was thrown out and, though injured, leaped to his feet, saying: 'I am not hurt.' (Another version of this story has him bellowing: 'This is a damnable outrage!') Edith was among the 'hushed assemblage' who saw him speak at Lenox after the accident, 'all bleeding and swollen'. She was tremendously impressed: he was her hero ever after and she put him into *The Age of Innocence* as an exemplary public man.[84] In 1905 she and Teddy lunched at the White House for Roosevelt's second inauguration, where (according to her memoir) he greeted her with cries of joy as the only person in the room who would understand him if he quoted *The Hunting of the Snark*. In June, they went to hear him make a speech at Williams College, where he was getting an honorary doctorate. She noted in her diary that the speech was 'halting, grimacing, and inappropriate'. However, she and the President again talked happily about books, including *The Valley of Decision*. Roosevelt was a widely read man with strong literary enthusiasms. 'Books are almost as individual as friends', he wrote in his autobiography, sounding very like Edith Wharton. He shared, for example, her pleasure in Grant's *Unleavened Bread*, which he called 'the strongest study of American life that has been written for many years'. 'American life' was the key phrase here. Writers had to play their part in the life of the nation and to appreciate the kind of language he used to Wharton, writing to her about the death of his son in the war in 1918: 'His death is heart-breaking, but it would have been far worse if he had lived at the cost of the slightest failure to perform his duty.'[85]

Roosevelt was extremely hostile to the writer who was becoming one of the most important people in her life, Henry James. James told Edith in January 1905 that he found Roosevelt 'a wonderful little machine . . . It functions astoundingly & is quite exciting to see.' But Roosevelt thought James was a traitor to his country, a 'poodle', who wrote about decadent un-American characters and lived an un-American life. 'Thank Heavens . . . he is now an avowedly British novelist . . . a very despicable creature . . . a miserable little snob . . . it makes one blush to think that he was once an American.'[86]

Wharton was making her own way between these ideas of being an American. She was a kind of patriot, though a critical and alienated one. She minded painfully about America's attitude to Europe in the war years; and she minded very much when James took British citizenship in 1915. She was in her forties when she was at The Mount, quite late in life to think of changing one's country. She had been publishing for a decade. There must have been times when she imagined herself staying there for ever – a Catherine Sedgwick of the twentieth century, a leading female literary lion, growing old in New England, with part of her year always spent in Europe, and with connections and contacts in every area of civilised intellectual American life. Her letters to Sally Norton in the early 1900s show her veering between the pleasure of her life at The Mount, and the powerful lure of Europe. Her frequent comparisons of climate and land-scape seem to stand, more deeply, for cultural comparisons. Returning to The Mount from Europe in 1903 impressed on her the 'wild, dishevelled, backwoods look of everything when one first comes home'. Writing about Italian gardens, that summer at Lenox, was a consolation to her for the rough, bare quality of the unfinished garden at The Mount. Visiting Cambridge, in England, in the spring of 1904, she exclaimed (as so many American writers had before her) on 'how much we miss in not having such accumulated beauties to feed on now & then at home! I enjoy them so keenly that the contrast makes me miserable, & I think it almost a pity for an American who loves the country ever to come to England.' 'The country' is ambiguous: it looks as if it means England, but it could mean America. By 1906, as the desire for Europe intensified – by now for France more than for Italy – these comparisons got harsher. 'The American land-scape has no foreground, & the American mind no background.' Returning from France to Lenox in June 1907, she wrote: 'The place looks well in its dry, spare, reluctant New England way . . . the landscape & the life lack juice!' She had transferred the adjective 'reluctant' from herself to the American scene. Rushing back to France that December, she was 'sunk in the usual demoralising happiness which this atmosphere produces in me. Dieu que c'est beau after six months of eye-starving!'[87] By now, images of starvation on one side of the ocean and demoralising happiness on the other were codes for a more intimate conflict.

'It was only at The Mount that I was really happy', she wrote years later, looking back on her American life.[88] But in later summers there, from 1908 to 1910, it was the setting for passionate longing, despair and frustration. The novels she wrote there, *The House of Mirth* (1905) and *The Fruit of the Tree* (1907), and the novellas and stories she set in New England, *Ethan Frome* (1911) and *Summer* (1917), 'The Pretext' and 'The Lady's Maid's Bell', 'Bewitched' and 'All Souls'', were full of bitter thwartings and failures. But as those writings show, this was also a place that would haunt her for ever, and a landscape that she would rewrite over and over. And it was here that she turned herself into a great writer, with the same kind of determination and pragmatic ambition that she had brought to the building of the house. Walter wrote to her at the end of 1904: 'I suppose the House of Mirth is being shingled and having its interior decoration attended to. May none of its chimneys smoke!'

6

The Republic of Letters

The House of Mirth made Edith Wharton, at the age of forty-three, a best-selling author and a household name. Serialised in *Scribner's Magazine* from January to November 1905 and published in October 1905, it sold 30,000 copies in its first three weeks of publication (the most rapid sales of any Scribner novel up till then) and 140,000 copies in its first year. Alongside macho realist epics like Frank Norris's *The Pit* or Upton Sinclair's *The Jungle*, it was one of the biggest 'serious' best-sellers of the turn of the century. By the time it was published it seemed there was nothing Wharton could not do. Novels, novellas, stories, plays, poems, books on Italy and on house-decoration: by 1905 it is hard to believe that she had ever had an uncertain or unproductive phase. In the six years between publishing her first book of stories, *The Greater Inclination* (1899), and *The House of Mirth*, she had, as she put it so dramatically in *A Backward Glance*, 'broke[n] through the chains which had held me so long in a kind of torpor'. A language of rebirth and excitement ('the incredible had happened!' – 'my recognition as a writer had transformed my life') fills this part of her autobiography: 'At last I had groped my way through to my vocation . . . The Land of Letters was henceforth to be my country, and I gloried in my new citizenship.'[1] A new land, a new century, a new life: she makes it sound like a sudden transformation. In fact (as she also says, in between these ecstatic bursts) this was a gradual process.

In *A Backward Glance*, she looked back with painful amusement on the tentative beginnings of her literary career. She describes herself as a naive, genteel New York lady. Mrs Wharton sent a few poems (on Italian and artistic themes) to *Scribner's Magazine* and to a few other reputable periodicals for all the family. They were 'copied out . . . in my fairest hand and enclosed . . . in an envelope with my visiting card'. Faint traces of that amateurish approach remain in some of her early letters to William Crary Brownell, senior editor at Scribner's: 'I am new at proofs'; 'Pray make allowances for my inexperience and tell me what to do'.[2]

Mrs Edward Wharton's first acceptance letters arrived in the winter of 1888, followed by her first cheque in July 1889 ($20 for her poem, 'The Last Giustiniani').[3] She remembered rushing up and down the stairs of their Madison Avenue rented house, not knowing how else to work off her excitement, and setting off, keen and hopeful, to Scribner's publishing house at 743–5 Broadway, to make friends with Brownell and with Edward Burlingame, the editor of *Scribner's Magazine*. (Scribner's stayed on Broadway until 1894, when it moved to 153–7 Fifth Avenue, a fine building designed by Ernest Flagg. In 1913 it moved much higher up Fifth Avenue, to 597–9, a building which is now a cosmetics shop, but still has the legend 'Charles Scribner's Sons' on the side of the wall.) Burlingame started to publish her stories as well as her poems: the first, in July 1891, was 'Mrs Manstey's View', which in 1893 appeared in Scribner's *Stories of New York*, bound in very dark red cloth with a gilt-edged title: stories by Anne Eliot, Bliss Perry, George Hibbard, John Wood, and (last) Edith Wharton, with a few delicate black-and-white illustrations and a note saying that this was supposed to be 'an example of book-making as dainty and perfect as possible'. This was her first book publication – and the bleakness of the story belied its lady-like setting.

Through the 1890s there were a few more sightings of Mrs Wharton in *Scribner's* and *Century* – nine poems (mainly inspired by Italy), six more stories, an essay on Tuscan shrines. Because of their interest in her, Scribner's rather reluctantly took over *The Decoration of Houses* from Macmillan.[4] *The Greater Inclination*, her first book of stories, was published in 1899. And then she was off. With astounding speed, there followed a novella, *The Touchstone* (1900), a second volume of stories, *Crucial Instances* (1901), the two-volume *Valley of Decision* (1902), a translation of a German play, a short novel, *Sanctuary* (1903), another book of stories, *The Descent of Man* (1904), two books on Italy, and *The House of Mirth*. (All were published by Scribner's except *Italian Villas*, which Century had serialised and so published in book form; from *The Descent of Man* onwards, until the mid-1920s, all her English editions were published by Macmillan.) Yet for all this activity, there were also doubts and hesitations.

The first five stories she published in periodicals in the 1890s were not included in *The Greater Inclination*. These were 'Mrs Manstey's View', a story of sad urban confinement and poverty; 'The Fullness of Life', a painful, revealing fable of a woman on her death-bed who has to choose, for the afterlife, between her husband's 'creaking boots' and her high-minded soul-partner (she is doomed to choose the boots); 'That Good May Come', about a New York poet who sells his talent and loses his 'moral footing' for the

sake of his poor little sister; 'The Lamp of Psyche', the marital disillusionment of a woman who finds that her Parisianised husband did not fight in
the Civil War; and 'The Valley of Childish Things', her group of ironical
fables about American infantilism and wastefulness.

Burlingame sent a good many polite rejection letters in the early days.
He thought 'The Valley of Childish Things' too esoteric (it was published
in *Century* magazine), and 'Twilight of the God', a disillusioning Newport
encounter between ex-lovers, too obscure. His most misguided rejection
was of her long, grim story 'Bunner Sisters'. Wharton tried this on him
twice, in 1892 and 1893: 'Though I am not a good judge of what I write,
it seems to me, after several careful readings, up to the average of my writings.' But 'Bunner Sisters' would not be published until 1916, in her wartime
volume, *Xingu*. Even then Charles Scribner did not want to publish it as
a separate novella because it was 'just a little small for the best results in
separate form'.[5] So this subdued, realist masterpiece of thwarted lives never
gained the status it would have had if it had come out as a separate novella,
like *Ethan Frome*.

Some early stories were left out of *The Greater Inclination* because of her
anxieties about self-exposure. 'The Fullness of Life' (published in *Scribner's
Magazine* in 1893) gave too much away about her isolation and frustration,
even if couched in metaphorical terms, like her much-quoted comparison
of a woman's life to 'a great house full of rooms':

> 'There is the hall, through which everyone passes in going in and out;
> the drawing room, where one received formal visits; the sitting-room,
> where the members of the family come and go as they list; but beyond
> that, far beyond, are other rooms, the handles of whose doors perhaps
> are never turned; no one knows the way to them, no one knows whither
> they lead; and in the innermost room, the holy of holies, the soul sits
> alone and waits for a footstep that never comes.'
>
> 'And your husband . . . never got beyond the family sitting-room?'
>
> 'Never,' she returned impatiently; 'and the worst of it was that he was
> quite content to remain there.'[6]

Burlingame kept asking her to revise this story, but she set it aside. Within
a few years of their magazine publications, she looked back on some of
these early stories as 'the excesses of youth'. 'They were all written "at the
top of my voice",' she said in 1898, '& "The Fullness of Life" is one long
shriek.'[7]

Anxieties, illness and distractions held up that first volume for a long
time. The letter she wrote to Burlingame after he suggested publishing it,

in 1894, is poignant and revealing: 'I seem to have fallen into a period of groping, & perhaps, after publishing the volume, I might see better what direction I ought to take and acquire more assurance (the quality I feel I most lack) . . . I am very ambitious to do better . . . I have lost confidence in myself at present . . .' There are many other such moments in the early letters. 'I have no confidence in my powers of self-criticism so soon after finishing a story', she wrote in February 1898. In the end, only two of the stories in *The Greater Inclination* ('The Pelican' and 'The Muse's Tragedy') had come out already in magazines; the others in the volume were written in a concentrated burst, at Land's End, in the summer of 1898. When the book came out, she described them as child-patients she had been nursing: 'The poor little stories have been reclaimed, as it were, inch by inch, from almost continuous ill-health & mental lassitude.'[8]

Walter encouraged her with examples of other great authors who had suffered from lack of confidence, like George Eliot feeling unsure about *Middlemarch*. When she burst out to him, in the throes of *The Valley of Decision*, that 'with all my trying I can't *write* yet . . . there isn't a single sentence in the book with natural magic in it – not an inevitable phrase', he quoted Flaubert on *Madame Bovary* to her: '*Je n'y vois rien que du noir . . . ça me semble petit. Rien qui enlève et brille de loin*'; and added: 'Ha, ha!' But it took a long time for her to gain assurance. 'I am growing nervous about my book title', she wrote to Brownell in December 1900 about her second book of stories, *Crucial Instances*: someone had told her it was 'presumptuous'. Fears of writing too little were superseded by fears of writing too much and too quickly. Brownell replied reassuringly: 'I wonder how you got the "feeling" that I, for one, had begun to think you were writing too much. I have never noted the slightest empirical evidence of that. And as to "publishing too hurriedly", I thought the lapse of a year between books long enough.' Even after *The House of Mirth*, she told Burlingame that 'I am always afraid of *over-psychologizing*, & this [in *The Fruit of the Tree*] has perhaps led me to the opposite extreme'.[9] It took time for her confidence and authority as a novelist to assert itself.

But from the moment she started to publish, the idea of a life without writing became horrifying to her. A poem called 'Finis', scribbled on the back of one of her 1890s Italian poems, is ostensibly a fantasy of a life without reading; but the word 'writing' could lurk before the word 'books' in the last line.

> The postman's ring, the doctor's call,
> The damage done by the plumbers' men,

The rise in wages, the mercury's fall,
Knitting-needles and crochet-hooks,
An afternoon nap in a nice warm shawl,
And now and then, as a special treat,
A funeral passing down the street.
That's the way the future looks
When I've grown tired of books.[10]

The Greater Inclination was a success. It sold about 3,000 by the end of the
year (very good for a volume of stories, Brownell told her) at $1.50, of
which Wharton took 10 per cent. The contract was witnessed (as many of
her contracts would be) by Walter Berry. The largely respectful reviews, in
America and England (where Scribner's had sent 500 copies to John Lane)
established two standard responses to her work, both of which would come
to irritate her. One was to call her a female Henry James, the other was to
call her a cold fish – accuse her of 'lack of sympathy' and 'cool detachment'. Still, 'I don't mind being called "cynical" & "depressing" by the
sentimentalists', she wrote – coolly – to her friend Barrett Wendell. In spite
of such reservations, her success seemed miraculous to her. Were there really
people going into shops and asking for a book by Edith Wharton? – and
'the clerk, without bursting into incredulous laughter, would produce it,
and be paid for it, and the purchaser would walk home with it and read it,
and talk of it, and pass it on to other people to read!'[11]

With the same formidable drive that propelled her Italian researches
and her house-making, she now hurled herself into life as a professional
author. She had already been extremely assertive about *The Decoration of
Houses*, negotiating strenuously between Codman, Scribner's, and the
designer she insisted on having, Coddy's friend Daniel Berkeley Updike,
who owned the Boston Merrymount Press. At every stage, she took
control. The decorations were too small, she told Brownell, and furthermore there should be fifty-six, not thirty-two plates. The title-page was
no good: 'I daresay I have already gone beyond the limits prescribed to
a new author in the expression of opinion; but, since you send me the
title page, I shall consider myself justified in criticizing it. To anyone who
cares for old Italics, such lettering seems very inadequate.' The right
reviewers had to be lined up (these included Walter, who fulsomely praised
the book he had helped to write, in the pages of the *Bookman*). She would
smooth the book's path in England by sending it to all the right architects and critics.[12]

She was determined and choosy, and she had a high-handed manner –

not unlike her mother's – when she felt she was not being treated properly. 'Gentlemen, Am I not to receive any copies of my book?' she wrote in March 1899 to Scribner's, a week after *The Greater Inclination* had come out. A stinging letter went out in April about their promotion – the sort of letter Scribner's was always getting from its authors. ('You can almost hear the sigh with which Charles Scribner took up his pen to reply,' wrote the firm's historian, Roger Burlingame.) 'I don't think I have been fairly treated as regards the advertising of *The Greater Inclination*', she wrote: 'Certainly in these days of energetic & emphatic advertising, Mr Scribner's methods do not tempt one to offer him one's wares a second time.'[13]

'Energetic & emphatic' could be a self-description. And she already had a strong enough sense of herself as a hot property to threaten to leave. With every book that followed there would be the same exacting forthrightness. Did she like the cover for *The Valley of Decision*? 'Words fail to express how completely I *don't* like it.' Her fierce negotiations with Richard Gilder over *Italian Villas and Their Gardens* were typical. She had longrunning arguments about whether her books should be illustrated, which came to a head with *The House of Mirth*, where she lamented that she 'sank to the depth of letting the illustrations be put in the book – & oh, I wish I hadn't now!' (In her own copy, she ran a line through the list of the illustrations and cut them all out of the book.) She had no timidity, from the start, about criticising books sent to her by more established writers. A firm letter to Robert Grant in 1904 told him exactly what she disliked about his novel *The Undercurrent*,[14] criticising the loss of 'forward movement' towards the end and the over-prominence of a minor character, which she said made her 'rather cross'.

> It's something like this – Every piece of fiction is an anecdote that exemplifies something, *an instance*. The lives of your characters are bound to touch at all points other lives irrelevant to the special anecdote you are telling about them, & part of the process of art is to discard these irrelevances, however interesting they are in themselves.[15]

She always hated the business of author-photographs: 'The last "impression" I saw looked like a combination of a South Dakota divorcée & a magnetic healer.' She found choosing titles for her story-collections difficult, and usually wanted something the publishers found too obscure. Trying out alternatives for *The Greater Inclination* she noted: 'I fear that "Middle Clay" would be classified as a manual of geology by the librarian who put Mill on Liberty & Mill on the Floss in the same category.' She hoped (she told Burlingame in 1898) that she was not 'uncertain, coy & hard to please'. Still: 'I always like to make my business arrangements as definite as possible' and 'I always care very much for the make-up of my books'. After one of her moments of anxiety, Brownell wrote to her with feeling: 'We have no idea of vagueness & vacillation in connection with you.' 'When are you going to "sag" just a little, I wonder', he wrote with awe and affection in 1901. 'You seem to tauten up every time. I hope the strings won't snap. They won't in *my* day, anyhow, probably.'[16]

William Crary Brownell was a literary editor of immense dedication. His 'Letter Book', covering many years, contained copies of hundreds of long, hand-written, meticulous letters to his authors. This gentlemanly politesse sums up the generation of high-minded bookmen who started Wharton's career and adjudicated on her early work. Their paternalistic assumptions about her as a 'lady' writer, expected to 'defer to their expertise' and to reach only a small, elite audience, were energetically challenged by Wharton from the start, in her determined arguments with them over every aspect of book-publishing.[17] She would leave them, outlive them, and eclipse them. By the time she stopped writing – that is, when she died – that 1890s world of letters had the look of a faded daguerreotype. The genteel censoriousness of Charles Scribner, known in the trade as an 'old Dodo', who would not publish George Moore's *Esther Waters* in 1894 because of its 'plainspokenness', or of Richard Gilder at the *Century*, who refused to put the thrilling but dangerous Whitman in his family magazine, or of Frederick Macmillan, her English publisher, who turned down H.G. Wells's 'new woman' novel, *Ann Veronica*, in 1909, on grounds of indecency, took Wharton back to the attitudes of her parents' generation. From the old New York institutions like the Century Association, these gentlemen 'continued' (as she put it, severely, in her memoir) 'to turn a contemptuous shoulder on society'. They would come under threat from new methods in publishing and new readers of fiction, in just the way that Old New York was threatened by new money and social changes.[18] The sort of courteous, unassertive, elegantly hand-written letter Frederick Macmillan would write to Mrs Wharton about 'Madame de Treymes' was, by 1907, beginning to look very old-fashioned:

> I find it a charming little story which certainly ought not to remain buried in the back numbers of a magazine. I fear that we shall not be able to do very much with it, but if you agree, we shall be happy to bring it out immediately as a little half crown volume . . . Even if it does not bring you in a great deal in royalties, it will serve to keep your name as a novelist before the English public. I am very grateful to you for refusing to listen to the offers of other publishers. It will be our aim to see that you do not lose anything by remaining in our hands.[19]

And the determined Mrs Wharton made sure that she did not. Once Macmillan started to publish her in England (after a false start with John Murray and *A Gift from the Grave*, his poor title for *The Touchstone*), the firm received streams of letters from her about the need for extensive advertising and larger advances, fierce complaints about misprints and punctuation, paper quality and late royalties, and rueful acceptance that her readership in England would never be as large as in America. (She pitched *The Custom of the Country* to them, in the hopes of attracting more attention, as the story of a young woman who 'has her eyes on London when the story ends'.) She never relaxed her vigilance with them, for instance, about their bindings of her books, which she always found too elaborate: 'May I ask you for *The Reef* to go back to a simpler binding style without the florid blind tooling & in fact as little decoration as possible & a cloth of a good dark red or blue? . . . I don't see why fiction should necessarily be more decorated than other forms of literature.'[20]

She asserted her authorial convictions from very early on. But when she began, these gentlemen of the publishing trade were her mentors. William Crary Brownell stood (as she told Daisy Chanler when he died in 1928) for everything that was in opposition to 'Main Street': 'And Main Street remained to the end utterly unaware of him.' She wrote a tribute comparing him to Matthew Arnold for his firm sense of a cultural 'centre', his impartiality and discernment, and for 'the eagerest open-mindedness . . . combined with an unwavering perception of final values'. His passion for French culture greatly influenced the way she approached France. And she liked his moral, high-toned critical writing – as in this piece on George Eliot, published in the same 1900 volume of *Scribner's Magazine* as her story 'The Duchess at Prayer':

> Her philosophy is of an ethical cogency and stimulant veracity that makes her fiction one of the notablest contributions ever made to the criticism of life . . . No other novelist gives one such a poignant . . . sense that life is immensely serious.[21]

Personally, she found him 'shy and crepuscular'. The fastidious tone of his letters reflects that character. It would be better, he thought, not to republish 'The Line of Least Resistance' if it had caused personal offence. *The Decoration of Houses* would hardly make 'a popular success . . . Its effect is distinctly, we should say, to an intelligent and educated rather than to the most numerous public.' Anything that might please that fiction-reading public (which was getting more numerous by the minute) risked lowering standards. In September 1899 he remarked that if *The Greater Inclination* 'had done very much better one might have wondered if it were really as good as it seemed'. Wharton sent him a clipping in 1901 (presumably about *The Touchstone*) meant to amuse him: 'Though beautifully written, the book will not fail to please.' With the sales of *The House of Mirth*, she could afford to tease the firm of Scribner's about this attitude: 'I am especially glad to find . . . that you think its large circulation is a sign of awakening taste in our fellow-countrymen – at least 100,000 of them.'[22]

Brownell was not completely unworldly: when Wharton was becoming a name to reckon with, after *The Valley*, he suggested she write a regular monthly article in the magazine about 'books and general impressions . . . People would look forward to what "Edith Wharton's Department" might contain. The rate of honorarium (delicious phrase – "*rate of honorarium!*") for it would be, say, $2^{1}/_{2}$ cents per word.' Though he knew he needed to reach big audiences and could do so through Wharton, his tone about them is always disdainful. 'As for "popularity" of the grosser kind . . . you don't seriously mean that you want that.' 'How can characters seem "real" to people who never "moved" in the circles to which they belong.'[23]

Edward Burlingame, who edited the magazine, was a more forthcoming and sociable fellow than Brownell; she remembered him as 'a man of real cultivation' and 'a good linguist'. It was he who moved her career along in its early stages, bearing with the slow evolution of the first collection of stories, helping her with the next two, *Crucial Instances* and *The Descent of Man* (which she dedicated to him), and bumping up her pace on *The House of Mirth* by starting serialisation (in January 1905) before she had finished the novel. His cultural attitudes were similar to Brownell's; she never forgot his warning to her not to become a 'magazine bore'.[24]

Richard Gilder, her editor at the *Century*, a handsome upper-class Philadelphian, a poet and an artist, had, like Brownell, 'an infinite capacity for taking pains'. He dealt personally with an impressive stable of authors, including Stevenson and Twain, and he moved in all the same circles as Wharton. In the stormy 1890s literary debates, in which 'naturalism' and 'realism' came to blows with 'romance', and authors and critics made rival claims to the truest kind of American literature (Jamesian Europeanised refinement or everyday provincial American life; epic, determinist fictions of railroads and meat-plants, or domestic psychological dramas of the ordinary man), Gilder made a plea for the 'ideal', as opposed to 'reality'. He knew that his magazine needed to 'buttonhole a couple of million readers', but he felt intensely that 'the vulgarization of everything in life and letters and politics and religion, all this sickens the soul'. Whether it was the sight of a millionaire's enormous, flashy steam-yacht (the *Hermione*) berthed at Newport, or an author who felt it necessary to 'stir up a violent stench in the language', all coarse effects dismayed him.[25]

Of the gentlemen of letters who played such an influential role in her early professional life, the most original and idiosyncratic was the printer, Daniel Berkeley Updike. Berkeley (as he was known) was a close friend of Codman's (and of another mutual acquaintance, the clever socialite Eliot Gregory, who wrote gossip columns called 'The Idler' and seemed, true to his pen-name, to do absolutely nothing all his life – even less than Egerton – except be charming and clubbable). For a short time, Pussy, Coddy, and Upsy made the kind of triangle she always enjoyed with her sexually ambivalent or homosexual friends. He could be on call as an escort (as when she asked the grand old Boston literary lady Annie Fields, in the summer of 1902, if she could bring Berkeley Updike as a substitute for Teddy). And he was the recipient of all Codman's bitchy complaints about working for the Whartons. Berkeley is going to Lenox, Codman wrote to his mother in July 1901, and 'he will have some amusing tales of the W's'. Berkeley was always trying to keep the peace between Codman and 'the W's', reminding him (at the height of the rows over The Mount) that 'at heart you like them'.[26]

As with Codman, her friendship with Berkeley Updike was rooted in a practical working relationship and admiration for his talents. A Rhode Islander with impeccable pedigree and connections, Updike was a printer and book-designer of genius, 'America's scholar-printer'. At the Merrymount Press, which he founded in 1893, he worked for many years in a rewarding partnership with an Italian immigrant printer, John Bianchi. Influenced, but not confined, by the Arts and Crafts movement, Updike's aim was 'to make work better than was currently thought worthwhile'. His products (which covered a huge range, from bookplates and diplomas to fine editions and musical scores) were scrupulously and imaginatively done; the work was always delicate and unostentatious. A religious man (his greatest

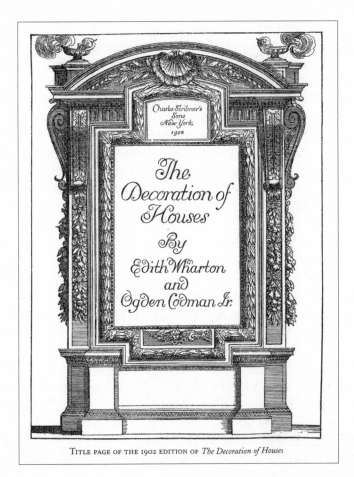

TITLE PAGE OF THE 1902 EDITION OF *The Decoration of Houses*

work was the Merrymount Press Book of Common Prayer of 1928), his attitudes to his work echoed those of Gilder or Brownell: 'Today's restless and
complex life may be reflected in our work ... tasteless exaggeration ...
may be traced to certain evil qualities in American life.' 'Tradition is not
a formula. It is the tribute which every true artist pays to the great men
who have gone before him ... Adequate craftsmanship – like great art –
should convey a sense of order, security, and peace, not of restless excitement.'[27] Wharton, who knew him socially, demanded that Scribner's use
him for *The Decoration of Houses* (he had worked for them before) and he
produced a grand, elegant and beautiful book. After that he designed six
more of her covers (*The Greater Inclination, The Touchstone, Crucial Instances,
The Valley of Decision, Sanctuary, Madame de Treymes*), and, much later, *The
Book of the Homeless*. Updike was a melancholy, perfectionist character,
whose dedication to his work did not bring him great happiness: 'I have
not seen life in the round', he wrote sadly to Edith a little before her death
in 1937. But he was a good friend, writing with warm sympathy and understanding when she was divorced. She used his work as her standard for
good looks and attention to detail: 'I feel like a new edition, revised &
corrected, in Berkeley's best type.'[28]

Dressed up by Berkeley in gilt-edged, olive-green or reddish-brown covers,
decorated with delicate curlicues and Italianate arabesques, the design
framed in a box, as if a curtain were about to go up on a play in an elegant
theatre, Wharton came before the public in high-toned fashion, every inch
a lady. And in the magazines in which she made her name, with poems,
stories, travel-articles and serialisations, she stepped on stage in a middlebrow, decorous context. Her bitter, ruthless stories of the 1890s and early
1900s, of marital unhappiness and emotional betrayal, jump out from this
setting with extraordinary force and freshness. Wharton's fiction kept
company with some of the big names of the time – Stevenson, Meredith,
Barrie, Harold Frederic, Howells, Roosevelt, and Kipling (whose story
'Wireless' appeared in the same edition as 'The Lady's Maid's Bell'), and
with hundreds of now-forgotten names, too. Men wrote on 'American Big-
Game Hunting', 'Personal Recollections of Gettysburg', ocean steamers, the
Canadian Mounties, 'Torpedo Boats in the War with Spain', and the New
York Rapid Transit System. Women (like Josephine Preston Peabody,
Martha Gilbert Dickinson and Theodosia Pickering Garrison) wrote love-
poems and nature-poems, touching domestic stories, and essays on
'Collecting Old China in New England' or 'The Woman's Paris'. 'A Little
Brother of the Books', by Josephine Dodge Daskam, in the same issue as
'The Lady's Maid's Bell', told of the death by typhoid of a little crippled

boy who loved reading. A poem on motherhood by E.C. Martin ('If mothers by their failings were condemned / Oh what an orphaned planet this would be!'), with tear-jerking illustrations, came out in the same issue as Wharton's cynical satire on an exploitative and superficial mother, 'The Last Asset'. In the same issue as 'The Lamp of Psyche', Wharton's early story of marital disillusion, there was a polemical piece by Robert Grant (whose fiction Wharton admired) on the position of women: 'It seems to me imperative to go back to the original poetic conception of woman as the wife and mother, the . . . self-abnegating companion of man . . . The eternal feminine is what we prize in woman, and wherever she deflects from this there does her power wane and her usefulness become impaired.'

Gender-roles were a burning topic when Wharton began to publish; so were the changing conditions of the literary market-place. William Dean Howells wrote in 1893 on 'The Man of Letters as a Man of Business', commenting on how easy it was nowadays to make a living from serial publication in magazines, which meant that 'in the US the fate of a book is in the hands of the women'. The 'Points of View' column in *Scribner's* for 1900 lamented the use of an author's name for product-promotions ('He beheld his name attached to the Cigar That Made Milwaukee Famous'), or the proliferation of books:

> When 'An Empty Life', by Sagamore Mullins, sells 150,000, he groans, because he knows there is nothing between the covers of that book that is really worth attention, and he wishes that the 150,000 buyers were getting something better worth their money and their time.[29]

Wharton's self-creation through the 1890s and 1900s as a woman writer who could not be categorised under 'feminine' or 'sentimental', and a highly cultured author who could also appeal to a big audience, was a remarkable one. The toughness of her stories was at odds with the context she published in, and with her illustrators, who softened and prettified her sharp edges. Maxfield Parrish's gorgeous Italian Renaissance illustrations for 'The Duchess at Prayer' (which led on to his work for *Italian Villas*) glamorised its chilling story of murderous domestic tyranny. The romantic pictures by Walter Appleton Clark for *Sanctuary* (fashionable ladies in attitudes of tortured anxiety) made it look more like a society drama than a claustrophobic study in maternal possessiveness.

The modernity and ruthlessness of *The House of Mirth* is astounding, in the context of its first magazine appearance. As noted earlier, it came out in monthly parts, from January to October 1905 (and like a Victorian novelist such as Dickens or Thackeray, she had not finished writing the novel when serialisation began). It sat next to items like 'The Dogs of War' by Lieut. Charles Norton Barney, 'Flowers of May', colour drawings by Sarah Stilwell, 'Herculaneum and its Treasures of Art' by Russell Sturgis, 'Italian Recollections: More Letters of a Diplomat's Wife' by Mary King Waddington, and poems ('Amid the Orchards', 'The Awakening') by Mary Findlater, Hildegarde Hawthorne, and Lucy Leffingwell Cable. The full-page illustrations she so hated (by A.B. Wenzell), tied to dramatic moments in the text, show elongated, glamorous figures, mostly in evening-dress, frozen in stiff dramatic poses, like the cast of a conventional Edwardian play.

But times were changing. The 1890s saw the start not only of Wharton's publishing career, but of dramatic shifts in publishing. Book-selling was now big business, and by the early 1900s the 'Commercialisation of Literature' had become a major point of controversy. There was an increasing emphasis on the author and book as product, an exploitation of personality to sell books, and an insistence that the writer should be accessible and provide entertainment. By the 1910s and 1920s, with a huge fiction boom before the war and a 'tidal wave' of book-publishing after it, books were being promoted to bigger and bigger audiences, via billboards, streetcars, sandwich-men, newspapers' book pages, electric signs, advertising campaigns on radio, books sections in department stores, jacket covers, blurbs and personal testimonials. By the 1930s, the ways of selling books to the public which we take for granted – including agents, bidding wars, author-interviews, and book-tours – were in place.[30]

For some literary writers, this increasingly commercialised market-place provoked a fearful resistance or disdainfully elitist withdrawal. But Edith Wharton's reaction was tougher and more complicated. Like many writers of her generation, she had mixed feelings about her own exposure.[31] By upbringing, class and temperament she was a cultural elitist, who believed in the highest standards. In the 1900s, her letters are full of attacks on American culture and literary declines. With Matthew Arnold's *Culture and Anarchy* in mind, she told Bliss Perry, the editor of the *Atlantic Monthly*, in 1905, that she admired him for 'maintaining the tradition of what a good magazine should be, in the face of our howling mob of critics & readers; & I hope the Atlantic will long continue to nurse its little flame of sweetness & light in the chaotic darkness of American "literary" conditions'. Come and visit her, she urged, '& let us despair together of The Republic of Letters'.[32] Writing to Sally Norton, she repeatedly returned to the theme of American vulgarity and bad taste: 'Did you see . . . that the heirs of some recently deceased "multi" were building a memorial to him, in the shape of a sky-scraper office building? – Truth is still far ahead of fiction!' The introduction of business courses at Harvard plunged her into 'such a depth of pessimism' that she wanted to break into 'Biblical curses . . . Alas, alas!'[33] Many of her stories of the 1890s and 1900s dealt with the conflict for the artist or author between privacy and publicity, high standards and popularity. This was a subject of profound anxiety for many other writers of the time, in England as well as America, among them James, Willa Cather, and May Sinclair.

The discussion about the writer's role always had to do with maintaining integrity, and that involved questions of privacy. From early on, Wharton was as concerned with decorum in her professional life as she was with good taste in house-decoration. When her biography was attached to her books, either in advertising copy or in reviews, she got very jumpy. Walter wrote to her at the end of 1899, evidently in response to a letter she had sent him about the publicity for The Greater Inclination: 'Tell me, did Scrib really get off that thing in the clipping about your position being "fully as good as," etc. C'est pantagruelique! Oh, why couldn't I be there to see the reporters waiting on the midnight doorstep . . .' Scribner's asked for her agreement to use some personal copy in the advertising for The Valley, and she returned a list of (very discreet) facts 'likely to appeal to Wanamaker's clientèle'. (This was Philadelphia's biggest department-store.) 'You notice that I have not struck out the Times's flattering allusions to my wealth & my first hand intercourse with fashion!' She joked to Sally about 'that undefinable Wanamaker Touch that seems essential to the booming of fiction nowadays'. She was pleased to hear from Minnie Bourget, in July 1902, that in Florence people were talking of nothing but The Valley of Decision; but, she added hastily, she did not want this quoted in advertising: 'I have never used a private letter in this way, & I think I'd rather not.' When James wrote a long letter to her about the novel, she forwarded it to Brownell, but warned him: 'You will see there is a personal note in it, so don't circulate it please, beyond Mr Scribner & Mr Burlingame.' Her position was complicated. She was elitist and fastidious, but she was not a genteel, highbrow novelist. She told Sally in 1902 that she did not want a novelist to be 'intellectual', but 'vivid, simple, dramatic, & the rest'. She was not reduced (like some of the highbrows of her time) to inertia and reclusiveness by the standards of American culture. And she was eager for money and fame.[34]

She was delighted to receive from Sally a copy of a 'flaming advertisement' for The Valley of Decision, and to hear that 'the Department Stores say they cannot keep up with the demand for the book'. Walter's letters reflected similar mixed feelings. On the one hand he derided crude advertising or advised her not to write 'down' to her audience 'so as to crowd into the Six Best Selling Books'. On the other hand, sending her praise of *The Touchstone*, he told her that 'if this sort of thing keeps up, you'll never be able to inscribe "To the Happy Few"' at the front of the novels. He was always encouraging her to ask for more from her publishers. In January 1900: 'Don't forget to strike for more each time.' By way of encouragement for her negotiations on her first book of stories, he sent her an apt quotation from Kipling:

> There once was a writer who wrote:
> 'Dear Sir: In reply to your note
>   Of yesterday's date
>   I am sorry to state
> It's no good at the prices you quote.'

High standards could go with high sales and big rewards, Walter believed. So did she. The proof came in 1905. She wrote to Charles Scribner on 11 November: 'It is a very beautiful thought that 80,000 people should want to read "The House of Mirth" & if the number should ascend to 100,000 I fear my pleasure would exceed the bounds of decency.'[35]

Could you be very good, and very popular? And if you were popular, rich and famous, would that inevitably corrupt you and spoil your talent? Wharton started an autobiographical novel in 1913 or 1914 called 'Literature', which she worked on intermittently for many years, but never finished. It was interrupted by the war, and then hung fire. Eventually, it became *Hudson River Bracketed*. Like that late novel and its sequel, *The Gods Arrive*, 'Literature' is about the making of a (male) American writer, whose childhood feelings about books are very close to her own. (It is also, painfully, about marriage.[36]) A sort of *Pilgrim's Progress* of the literary world, it was meant to deal with all the possible routes for a young writer entering the market-place – abortive attempts at play-writing, opposition from jealous critics, deviations into reviewing and magazine editing, writer's block, the aftermath of success, posthumous glory. It would have a poet enthusiastically reviewing a rival's book and citing all the weakest things (purposely) as an example of the poet 'at his best'. There would be spoof advertisements for fiction (like the fake notices for *Fast and Loose*): 'This novel plumbs the depth of human emotions'. There was to be a popular novelist whose 'art consisted in making the easy passages of his work so conspicuous that the hard ones – the ones he couldn't do – were over-looked'. A Jewish critic, Levick ('a genius without creative faculty') would give worldly, dry Flaubertian advice (not unlike Walter Berry's) on what it took to be a good novelist:

> It's no use to 'get up' experience . . . If it's in your nature to go about the streets with a monkey and a hand organ . . . or to live with the cannibals, go and do it – but if what you really crave is house-life in a sanitary suburb, do *that* – a good novel's just as likely to come out of one as the other.

The notes for 'Literature' show the same mixed feelings about the market-place as her letters. At one point she uses the French word '*cabotin*' to describe 'the author who works incessantly to create his own popularity . . . & is then, *quite sincerely*, the dupe of the illusion of celebrity he has himself created'. The word '*cabotin*' would come back in a 1932 story called 'A Glimpse', in which two artists, glimpsed by the narrator, may, he fears, turn out to be 'mere tawdry cabotins'. '*Cabotin*' originally meant travelling actor or hack performer; 'cabotinage' (in use in America from 1894) was 'playing to the gallery', or 'showing off'. Wharton is attracted by the romance of the travelling actor, as in *The Valley of Decision*, but she is also horrified by the idea of self-promotion. Early in 1908, she turned down a suggestion that an essay she was writing on the poetry of Whitman and Anna de Noailles should be read out loud, at the Théâtre des Arts in Paris: 'It savoured a little of self-advertising.'[37] *Cabotins* sell themselves: self-advertisement is, literally, to 'sell the self'.

'Literature' was to be about a writer whose career was littered with false starts and mistakes. Wharton's own writing life was, after 1899, so high-voltage, so prolific and efficient, that it is startling to find it crowded, too, with unfinished novels, plans for unpublished stories, poems that stayed in manuscript form, and abandoned sequels to several of her novels. She often worked on two books at once, one of which would succeed and the other not, and she had several long-running projects which eventually turned into something different, or were given up. In the early days, she would switch unpredictably between different projects. 'I never do write what I say I am going to', she wrote only half-apologetically to Scribner in 1905. She did not always know whether what she was doing was any good, especially with her poetry. 'There are degrees in prose & in poetry – below a certain point – well, it simply isn't poetry; & I am not sure I've ever reached the poetry line.'[38]

When Wharton talked in old age about her writing methods, she said (as many novelists do), that her characters 'arrived', 'coming seemingly from nowhere', complete with their names. They 'then began to speak within me with their own voices'. It sounds from this as though she subscribes to the idea of the writer as a kind of unconscious medium, through which the narrative flows onto the page. But she also says, firmly, that her characters never 'walk away with the subject': she knows 'from the first exactly what is going to happen to every one of them'. So she describes a double operation (which parallels the mixture of cool analysis and deep emotion in her fiction). The process of writing 'takes place in some secret region on the sheer edge of consciousness' but 'is always illuminated by the full light of my critical attention'.

That double process can be traced in her archives. Most of her novels and stories, whether finished or unfinished, can be tracked from first thoughts to reviews. First there are the notebooks and 'donnée' books, with plot suggestions, character lists, story outlines, and single aphorisms and epigrams waiting to find a good home. Then there are the résumés or 'scenarios' of the plots sent to the publishers, usually much as in the final version. Often the manuscripts of the novels are prefaced by chapter summaries in the present tense. The manuscripts have all gone through a similar process of evolution. Before the typing stage, they are written in black ink on blue paper, with many crossings-out and corrections. Where these are so numerous as to have become illegible, strips of paper are pasted over the original sheet of paper with the new versions (themselves, often, corrected). Some sheets will have three or four strips laid over them, and sometimes the original page has been cut up and stuck on again at the bottom, so that bits of the original text show through the strips or continue below them. What can read as a smooth, easy passage of prose, with a feeling of complete inevitability and confidence in the phrasing, has often gone through several such cut-and-paste jobs. Once the typing stage was reached, Jeanne Fridérich, Wharton's last secretary, said that she sometimes had to retype the same pages more than ten times. (Wharton once said of her revision processes that she was 'engaged in the wholesale slaughter of adjectives'.) But, Mme Fridérich added, these were not fundamental alterations ('*corrections de fond*'): '*elle avait ses livres même avant de les écrire*'.

In the conversation between Ellen Olenska and Newland Archer in the carriage in *The Age of Innocence*, for instance, the manuscript develops like this:

1. 'Is it your idea, then, that I should be your'
2. 'Is it your idea, then, that we should go off together'

3. 'Is it your idea, then, that I should be your mistress'
4. 'Is it your idea, then, that I should live with you as your mistress since I can't be your wife?' she asked abruptly.

(This, but without 'abruptly', was the final printed version.)

In the scene at the end of *The House of Mirth* when Lily slips out of consciousness, imagining that she is holding Nettie Struther's baby, the manuscript changes read:

1. She settled herself into a position
2. She settled herself into an easier position, pressing the little
3. into an easier position, hollowing her arm to receive the little head, and holding her breath lest a sound should disturb the child's sleep
4. should disturb the sleeping child

The final version is: 'She settled herself into an easier position, hollowing her arm to pillow the round downy head, and holding her breath lest a sound should disturb the sleeping child.'

In *The Reef*, Anna's desire to say goodbye to Darrow at Givré in the place where they were first reunited, is rewritten thus:

> Anna wanted, before he left, to return to the place where they had sat on their first afternoon together. She was deeply sensitive to the appeal of inanimate things, the look of rooms and of landscapes, the colour and texture of whatever, in emotional moments, wove itself into her dreams, and she wanted to hear Darrow's voice, and to feel his eyes on her, in the spot where, for the first time, bliss had flowed into her heart.

> Her sensitiveness to the appeal of inanimate things, to the colour and texture of whatever wove itself into her emotion, made her wish to hear Darrow's voice, and to feel his eyes on her, in the spot where bliss had first flowed into her heart.

(The printed version is slightly changed, again.)[39]

In all such key scenes, Wharton knew exactly what she wanted the scene to do and what the atmosphere should be like, but the detail is fine-tuned. Even the unfinished fragments that fill her archive (like the 'Beatrice Palmato' draft, written in pencil) are heavily corrected. And even after the success of *The House of Mirth* (which had been taking tentative shape in her notebooks since 1900 under the title 'A Moment's Ornament'), there were still plenty of such false starts. The ghosts of undated and abandoned projects lie thick in her archives, including 'Beatrice Palmato', 'The

Associates', an unfinished novel of Franco-American marital relations, and two historical novels, one set in Morocco ('The Sapphire Way'), and one in eighteenth-century Hyères, 'The Happy Isles'. Some false starts (like 'Logic' or 'Literature') were abandoned because too self-exposing. Some were saved up. A discarded title for *The Age of Innocence*, 'Old New York', would be used four years later for a collection of novellas. An unfinished murder-mystery play, 'Kate Spain', based on the Lizzie Borden case, was turned into a story called 'Confession'. An aborted wartime novel called 'Efficiency' eventually became *The Marne*. But some promising stories were simply abandoned, testimony to her superabundance of energy and inspiration, but also to self-doubt.

Wharton's *'salon des refusés'* is full of tantalisingly interesting characters and situations: the missionary's discontented daughter in Morocco who hates her new stepmother ('The Desert's Edge'); the old English woman with a shocking secret past, giving German lessons in a dull new England town ('Finishing Governess'); the shy married professor falling in love with a perfectly sympathetic friend, who gives him 'mental elbow room' ('Latmus'); the quietly snobbish Mr Grayson (in 'Tradition') keeping his family in 'self-complacent' seclusion in a small French town: '"Father doesn't much like America, does he? Or Americans either. I mean new Americans, the kind that didn't arrive in time to sign the Declaration."' One promising undeveloped story was 'The Great Miss Netherby', in which a sophisticated, expatriate house-decorator with a magical Mediterranean garden full of irises (and more than a touch of Edith Wharton about her) ironically inducts her American niece from Organ City (not as naive as she looks) into European worldliness – here, the pleasures of a comfortable bedroom:

> Miss Netherby smiled. 'You expected the usual sleeping-car shelf – the kind of thing that house-decorators consider *jeune fille*? I always thought Carpaccio's St Ursula must have inspired the first *wagon-lits* designer. But why shouldn't a virgin want to stretch and turn over now and then? I like a bed like a swimming-pool myself.'
>
> 'I'm sure I shall too – . . .' her guest acquiesced.
>
> 'Do you [ever] read in bed?' Miss Netherby pursued. 'Because here's the switch. But no, of course you don't.'
>
> 'Well, I hadn't thought of it,' Penelope confessed brightly.
>
> 'You just sleep and sleep, you fortunate child?'
>
> 'Well, what's a bed for?'
>
> 'Ah – what indeed,' murmured her aunt.[40]

One early casualty was a scandalous novel of contemporary American manners, to be called 'Disintegration'. (The title sounds gloomily *fin-de-siècle*.) She told Sally in May 1902 that she had 'planned' it before she began *The Valley*, and that spring Walter was urging her not to do an Italian sequel: 'That N.Y. novel ought to come next.' (So when James wrote in August advising her to 'DO NEW YORK', she was already at it.) She seems to have worked on it for several months in 1902, and then set it aside for 'A Moment's Ornament', which developed by fits and starts through 1903 and 1904 (alongside stories and Italian articles) into *The House of Mirth*. But a sizeable chunk of 'Disintegration' got written.[41] It was the story of a neglected young New York girl, Valeria Clephane, whose glamorous, 'improper' mother has run away with another man, leaving her to be looked after by her Irish nurse (clearly based on Doyley) and her self-disgusted, ineffectual father, Henry Clephane. Val – like Henry James's Maisie, but in what promises to be a very un-Jamesian novel – knows everything that is going on but cannot talk about it. The story of the Clephanes' divorce, and the errant wife's re-entry into New York and Long Island society as Mrs Tillotson Wing, is seen through the eyes of a cynical family friend, George Severance. A chorus of New York gossips have their say: 'One can't stay shocked for ever – it's such a strain on the moral muscles . . . besides, next to cutting a divorced woman there's nothing so interesting as taking her up again.' The tone is harsh, funny, and dark. Henry Clephane is thinking of writing a novel, and has a big speech about it:

'It's to be a study of the new privileged class – a study of the effects of wealth without responsibility. Talk of the socialist peril! That's not where the danger lies. The inherent vice of democracy is the creation of a powerful class of which it can make no use – a kind of Frankenstein monster, an engine of social disintegration. Taine saw it long ago – I'm only preaching from his text. But he merely pointed out the danger: he didn't study its results. The place to study them is here and now – here in this huge breeding-place of inequalities that we call a republic, where class-distinctions, instead of growing out of the inherent needs of the social organism, are arbitrarily established by a force that works against it! Think of the mass of evidence our society supplies! No laborious researches – no years wasted on the trail of a connecting link. All the species are here, spread out under the immense lens of our social publicity. Why, I'm the finest kind of an example myself: I can take down my own symptoms and note the progress of the disease in my own case.'[42]

This is a blueprint for *The House of Mirth*, though the plot of 'Disintegration' is different. Its names and subject matter would be used, as was her habit, in a much later book, *The Mother's Recompense* (1925).

Clephane's big speech perfectly illustrates one side of Wharton's writing, in the work of her early forties which made her name: disillusioned, caustic, unflinching, philosophical, worldly-wise. (The other side, entering deeply and subtly into passionate anguish and heartbreak, is glimpsed in the characters of Val and her mother.) The draft of 'Disintegration' is full of the sharp one-liners which were her hall-mark: 'She wore the most expensive gowns with a penitential air, as though she were under a vow of wealth.' Wharton's 'Donnée Book' for 1900 (one of a lifelong, intermittent series of writer's notebooks) had page after page of these brittle, wicked, stagy epigrams. ('Donnée', meaning germ or idea or situation for a story, was a term regularly used by Walter and Edith in their letters, long before she came to know James, who had made the word very much his own.) Some of these phrases were saved up for future use: 'Gryce was good-looking in a didactic way' eventually went into *The House of Mirth*; 'Mrs Plinth's opinions were as hard to move as her drawing room furniture' would be kept, slightly rearranged, for 'Xingu'; 'She's the kind of woman who runs cheap excursions to celebrities' came in handy in 'The Muse's Tragedy'. This was practice, like playing scales. 'Mr Roby had so evidently been a mere parenthesis in his wife's existence . . . They were as inseparable as those bores of one's childhood, the Picts and Scots . . . They would have been happily divorced years ago if it hadn't been for the poodle.' Some of these epigrams have a personal ring to them: 'Her manner *is* cold – at first. She doesn't light the fire till after the visitor has been shown in.' 'She had harvested that crop of middle joy that is rooted in young despair.' 'I foresee the day when I shall be as lonely as an Etruscan museum' (reused in 'Copy'). After 'A dim woman cloistered in ill-health', Wharton wrote: '(Myself! E.W.)'[43]

As in 'Copy', a story written as dialogue, she liked to turn these epigrams to theatrical use. One of the stories in *The Greater Inclination*, 'The Twilight of the God', took the form of a play – a Wildean, nineties drawing room comedy of disillusion, in which the characters say things like: 'I hope you like being surprised. To my mind it's an overrated pleasure.' Some distaste for this manner is built into the story: the lover reproaches his ex-mistress for being 'too pat' with her epigrams: 'How much I preferred your hesitations.' In another story in *The Greater Inclination*, 'The Portrait', a painter, famous for the unforgiving realism of his portraits, says of a crooked financier: 'His sentiments, good or bad, were as detachable as his cuffs.'[44]

Detachable epigrams are the material for theatre as much as for fiction.

Like Dick Thaxter in 'Literature', Wharton was experimenting as a drama-tist as well as a novelist in the early 1900s. Her fascination with the theatre would stay with her, and profoundly affected the way she wrote fiction. It was the theatricality of Italy she wanted for *The Valley of Decision*; it was New York society as an illusory stage-show, with Lily Bart performing, watched, framed, at the centre, which structured *The House of Mirth*. She would work closely with the playwright Clyde Fitch on his adaptation of the novel for the stage, in 1906 (which, as she expected, was a flop: too tragic for an American audience), and kept an interested eye on later drama-tisations of her work, especially *Ethan Frome*.

Her fascination with the stage went back to her childhood, and there are traces in her archive of youthful verse dramas on high themes (Esther, Lucrezia Borgia, a Christian prince and a pagan Sybil, 'The Banished God', set on the slopes of Helicon). But when she started thinking about writing for the contemporary stage, she planned witty prose comedies of manners, not verse epics. She and Walter shared an interest in the theatre; he told her what he had been seeing, and liked the idea of her making her name as a dramatist and going to lots of plays with him. 'Wouldn't it be fun knocking about the theatres together!' (The romance of the theatre would play more of a part in her affair with Morton Fullerton.) Walter gave her his opinions on a Barrie play – 'can't be anything but rotten' – or on some 'mawkish, treacly, pure-heart-interest' play he has just sat through. What would please an 'average audience' was the big question. She was trying to write a play called 'The Tightrope' early in 1900, and he thought she should call it 'a comedy of Distemperament'. Would it have a big enough 'situ-ation', he wondered. She should 'work up some good society gags to put in here and there'. Or what about an eighteenth-century drama? 'People love the costume of 100 years or so ago.' The following year, 1901, she was writing 'The Man of Genius', a Shavian comedy set in Hampstead, about a novelist whose secretary understands him better than his wife. 'Believe me', he writes to a fan who wants to meet him, 'if a man's books are worth anything it is because he has put the best of himself into them. What's left is only good for the waste-paper basket.'[45]

'The Man of Genius' was not produced, though there had been a private performance, *Lenox Life* reported in July 1901, of 'two little plays' by Mrs Wharton (whose stories 'are very popular especially among society people'), at the home of George Gould, in Lakewood, New Jersey. Another, very different kind of theatrical experiment was her version of the Abbé Prévost's novel *Manon Lescaut*. The love-story of the doomed, faithless society girl and the weak, childishly romantic Chevalier des Grieux appealed to her:

she owned two copies of the novel, and her version of it was intense, clearly structured, and carefully historical. Walter thought it 'simple' and good. In England in the spring of 1900, she tried to get it put on professionally through the theatrical agent Elizabeth Marbury; Walter hoped that 'muffins and tarts' would be the celebratory outcome. Again, in February 1901, it looked as if a production might happen in New York. Elizabeth Marbury was acting as agent, Charles Frohmann was the producer, and Julia Marlowe was supposed to play Manon (though in *A Backward Glance* Wharton said that she originally adapted it for Marie Tempest). One of Walter's letters suggests that Julia Marlowe left the production because Manon drowned at the end, and she 'made objection to jumping in a tub of cold water'. Elizabeth Marbury's friend, the actress and house-decorator Elsie de Wolfe (never a favourite of Edith's), was to take over the lead: but this too went badly, and the production was cancelled. 'Now's the time to drop the stage', Walter wrote consolingly 'and go at it [fiction-writing] hard.'[46]

But her theatrical interest continued. In May 1902 she wrote an enthusiastic review of the American actress Minnie Fiske's performance as Tess in an adaptation of Hardy's novel at the Manhattan Theater (she also saw her as Nora in *A Doll's House*): she said it was unconventional and unsentimental, and brought 'an unwonted thrill of reality' to the American theatre.[47] And she had her own small theatrical success in 1902, with a translation (done with the help of Anna Bahlmann) of a popular nineteenth-century German play by Hermann Sudermann. This seems an unlikely enterprise for her, though she had done a little translating for Scribner (three Italian stories, by d'Annunzio, among others, for a Scribner volume of 1898, *Stories by Foreign Authors*).[48] It was not her idea, but came out of an approach from Mrs Patrick Campbell, in America with her company. Edith disliked her English acting, 'like an elephant walking on the keyboard of a piano' – she preferred the French style. But she agreed to do the job, perhaps flattered by the approach – she was not, after all, a big name yet – and the play was put on in New York in October 1902, before touring, and playing in London in 1903. Wharton remembered the production as a flop, but the translation sold extremely well for many years, always 'an unintelligible phenomenon' to her. She is caustic in her memoir about Mrs Campbell's demands, and about the mistranslation that was forced upon her of the German title, *Es Lebe das Leben*, as 'The Joy of Living' – she wanted the 'bitterly ironic' 'Long Live Life'. It is hard to see what appealed to her in 'a tragedy based on the German "point of honour" in duelling', full of 'long German speeches' likely to be 'a severe strain' on English and American audiences – apart from the chance of launching herself into the theatre.⁴⁹ Perhaps the play's ironic treatment of German divorce laws had some interest for her, in this story about a middle-aged politician's wife with a weak heart, whose past (in the shape of her husband's political rival) catches up with her, and leads to a dread of exposure and scandal. But the real fascination evidently lay in the character of Berta, the 'woman who pays', whose speeches about her past love-affair leap out of the rest of the translation. She becomes an Edith Wharton character:

'I never gave you up. I never ceased to long for you, passionately, fever-ishly, day and night . . . all the while I was playing the cool, quiet friend.'

'We've grown old, you and I. There's a layer of ashes on our hearts . . . who knows what we were like before the fire went out. Not a trace is left to tell . . . The words are forgotten, the letters are destroyed, the emotions have faded. Here we sit like two ghosts on our own graves.'

For a moment, a powerful voice cuts through the ridiculous plot and the theatrical conventions, and Berta matters to us. 'I am not conscious of sinning', she says in her own defence. 'I did the best that was in me to do. I simply refused to be crushed by your social laws. I asserted my right to live; my right to self-preservation. Perhaps it was another way of suicide.'⁵⁰

Manon and Berta: these tragic theatrical heroines point towards Lily Bart. Wharton's writing – plays, poems, stories, novels – in the prolific years leading up to *The House of Mirth*, is absorbed in issues of freedom and choice, as much for writers as for women. She had been reading and writing and thinking about fiction since she was a child. And she developed, very rapidly, a forceful and distinctive style for her subjects. She did not cut her teeth as a literary journalist (like Willa Cather or Virginia Woolf), and she was not a natural or especially confident literary critic. But she had clear views on 'the writing of fiction', formed through 'pondering' deeply on the 'principles of her craft'. These views were very like her views on house-design. 'Your seeing a certain amount of architecture in it rejoices me above everything', she wrote to Brownell in response to his praise of *The House of Mirth*: she had thought it too 'loosely built'. Novels, like houses, should have a firm outline, a sound structure, and a quality of inevitableness. Wharton insisted on this when she wrote about her own work: 'My last page is always latent in my first.' A work of art must make you feel that 'it could not have been otherwise'. These qualities had to be produced through 'a perpetual process of rejection and elision'. No extraneous material and no redundant commentary; 'the objective attitude' was what she believed in. Her models were 'the greatest French fiction', in which the design was 'most organic, most inherent in the soul of the subject'. The language she favoured was the very best and purest English – against which she played, brilliantly, the slang and colloquialisms of her talkative characters.[51]

All this may sound clinical, but she wanted depth of feeling and spontaneity in fiction too, and believed there was something mysterious about artistic inspiration. Form alone was not enough. She wanted fiction to be robust, realist and far-reaching, as well as perfectly formed. It should have a sane and experienced relationship to the world. A 'novelist of manners', she said in 1902, writing critically of George Eliot, 'needs a clear eye and a normal range of vision to keep his picture in perspective'. Writing about *The House of Mirth* (admittedly to the rector of her old church in New York, which may have made her more solemn than usual), she thanked him for understanding her motives, unlike the critics who had called it 'unpleasant': 'No novel worth anything can be anything but a novel "with a purpose", & if anyone who cared for the moral issue did not see in my work that *I* care for it, I should have no one to blame but myself.' Beyond that, there had to be something larger than a statement of social conditions or a view of manners, something that could not be defined – as in the work of Tolstoy, which she thought created a kind of 'luminous zone' stretching out beyond its borders.[52]

Because her early publishing years before *The House of Mirth* were dominated by the historical drama of *The Valley* rather than the grim realities of 'Bunner Sisters', and because she made her name as an analyst of upperclass moneyed Americans in Newport and New York, Wharton's strong strand of compassionate realism – more Dreiser than James – has tended to be undervalued. 'Mrs Manstey's View' (written in 1890, published in 1891) imagined the life of an impoverished widow, whose view from her boarding-house window – her only pleasure – is to be obstructed by her landlady's new extension to the building. The tender attention Mrs Manstey gives to the drab backyards – from the magnolia next door to the distant smoke of a factory chimney – is a fine example of, in Robert Frost's words, 'what to make of a diminished thing'. In 'Friends' (written in 1894, published in 1900), a woman gives up her job as a teacher in an industrial New England town because she thinks she is going to be married. But, abandoned by her lover, she returns to find her post has been given to an even needier – but much less intelligent – friend. Her inner struggle between resentment and generosity is very well done. By the end she feels she is in touch 'with the common troubles of her kind'.

People have to get up and go to work and struggle to make a living – a

more frequent theme in Wharton than she is given credit for. In one of
the stories in *The Greater Inclination*, 'A Cup of Cold Water' (1899), a
young man who has got into debt and swindled his firm in order to marry
the girl he loves, falls through the surface of society (as Lily Bart will) and
spends a night in a grim New York hotel, listening to the wretched story
of the woman next door – a small-town adulteress – whom he has stopped
from killing herself. In the morning, as he goes to face up to his own situation, he sees the city going to work: 'that obscure renewal of humble duties
was more moving than the spectacle of an army with banners'. He quotes
to himself one of Wharton's favourite lines from *Hamlet*: 'For every man
hath business and desire.'[53]

'Bunner Sisters' is the most poignant and cruel of these early stories of
America's underclass. It is a story of two sisters making ends meet with
their shabby-genteel shop (rather like Hepzibah's shop in Hawthorne's *The
House of the Seven Gables*) in a run-down corner of New York. They are a
fretful and fussy pair, the older one, Ann Eliza, self-abnegating and anxious,
the younger, Evelina, spoilt and dissatisfied. A German clock-mender, Mr
Ramy, a creepy sensualist, courts them both. When Ann Eliza, who has
always indulged her younger sister's discontent, begins to fall in love with
Mr Ramy, the narrator tells us: 'She had at last recognised her right to set
up some lost opportunities of her own.' But he marries the younger, takes
her away, turns out to be a drug-addict, and abandons her. The older sister
is bereft; the younger at last comes home to die, having lost her baby, and
Ann Eliza is left on her own. This awful story is told with painstaking,
Balzacian exactness and a sombre interest – at times faintly condescending,
but always precise and scrupulous – in these compressed lives, whether it's
the district, the neighbours, the sisters' habits, an outing to Central Park
on a Sunday, or a ferry-crossing to Hoboken to visit Mr Ramy's friend, the
German washerwoman Mrs Hochmüller. This is a haunting piece of
American urban pastoral, unlike anything else in Wharton:

> When dinner was over Mrs Hochmüller invited her guests to step out of
> the kitchen-door, and they found themselves in a green enclosure, half
> garden, half orchard. Grey hens followed by golden broods clucked under
> the twisted apple-boughs, a cat dozed on the edge of an old well, and from
> tree to tree ran the network of clothes-line that denoted Mrs Hochmüller's
> calling. Beyond the apple trees stood a yellow summer-house festooned
> with scarlet runners; and below it, on the farther side of a rough fence,
> the land dipped down, holding a bit of woodland in its hollow. It was all
> strangely sweet and still on that hot Sunday afternoon . . .

But there is nothing sweet about the banal, realistic dialogue between the sisters.

> 'Don't you talk like that, Evelina! I guess you're on'y tired out – and disheartened.'
> 'Yes, I'm disheartened,' Evelina murmured.
> A few months earlier Ann Eliza would have met the confession with a word of pious admonition; now she accepted it in silence.
> 'Maybe you'll brighten up when your cough gets better,' she suggested.
> 'Yes – or my cough'll get better when I brighten up,' Evelina retorted with a touch of her old tartness.
> 'Does your cough keep on hurting you jest as much?'
> 'I don't see's there's much difference.'[54]

No moralising or sentiment is allowed for, and the obvious opportunity for softness – the love of the older for the younger sister – is implacably undermined. A sympathetic upper-class New York woman, who has troubles of her own, makes occasional visits to the Bunner sisters' shop, but we never find out her story, or even her name. It may be a Hitchcockian appearance by the author, but she never speaks as herself. She often uses an observant, dispassionate man as her narrator. And there is no autobiographical 'I' in any of her fiction – unlike her poems, where her emotions pour off the page.

Wharton established her tone rapidly in the short works of the 1890s and the 1900s that surround *The Valley* and 'Disintegration' ('early' work seems a misnomer, for a writer in her middle years with such a long period of self-education and apprenticeship behind her). Powerful, deep feelings – like Ann Eliza's sense of her 'lost opportunities' – run through narrow, constricting channels, pinned down in an unflinching language. As she said to Burlingame in 1898 about *The Greater Inclination*, 'each of the stories is really a study in motives'.[55] She is interested in the negotiation between the desires of individuals, and the pressures of convention, and she is fascinated by equivocation. 'Life is made up of compromises', says an embittered mother to her son's idealistic girlfriend, in 'The Quicksand' (1902). Ideals are not much use: 'How little, as the years go on, theories, ideas, abstract conceptions of life, weigh against the actual, against the particular way in which life presents itself to us – to women especially.'[56] Her stories are full of characters who have cut back their aspirations. 'If you make up your mind not to be happy, there's no reason why you shouldn't have a fairly good time', says an elderly philosophical character in 'The Last Asset' (1904). That tone of desolating stoic realism is typical – not that her characters are necessarily stoical themselves. All kinds of anguish, shame, cruelty, self-deception and ridiculous behaviour are on show – nowhere more than in the stories of marriage.

> Her husband's personality seemed to be closing gradually in on her, obscuring the sky and cutting off the air, till she felt herself shut up among the decaying bodies of her starved hopes. A sense of having been decoyed by some world-old conspiracy into this bondage of body and soul filled her with despair. If marriage was the slow lifelong acquittal of a debt contracted in ignorance, then marriage was a crime against human nature.[57]

In this story, 'The Reckoning' (1902), Julia has run away from her boring husband and agreed to set up a rational, modern relationship with her new lover, free to be broken off at any moment. Her new partner gives public talks about his 'creed' of a 'new morality' in fashionable New York studios. But when he decides to leave her for a younger devotee, Julia is thrown back, in agony and confusion, on the old 'instinct of passionate dependency and possessorship'. The liberating theories have not worked, and her life seems strange and alien to her: 'Her room? Her house? She could almost hear the walls laugh back at her.' She goes to ask her ex-husband's forgiveness, and wanders out – a woman alone on the streets – 'into the darkness'.

The escape that proves to be no escape at all is a favourite theme of Wharton's (in 1905 she told Brownell that 'The Reckoning' was the story 'most widely known & identified with my name'),[58] and it is usually the woman who suffers. 'The woman who pays', as familiar a figure in the plays and novels of the 1890s as 'the new woman', is often at the centre of Wharton's work. From Lily Bart to Halo Vance (with one outrageous exception) it is the women in Wharton who have to conceal their feelings, suffer betrayal and social punishment, compromise their lives and lose what they love. The politics of sexual injustice and inequality are very strongly felt, though she would have been appalled to be called a feminist.

In 'Souls Belated' (1899), Lydia, a woman who has left her husband and run away with her lover, wants, like Julia in 'The Reckoning', to establish new terms for a sexual relationship. A devastating satire on her husband's conservative family, clearly drawn from the Joneses and the Whartons ('Mrs Tillotson senior dreaded ideas as much as a draught in her back'), fuels her desire for her new 'voluntary fellowship' not 'to be transformed into bondage'. But at their fashionable Italian hotel on the Lakes, she spends her whole time trying to keep up conventional appearances, and is aghast when her bluff is called by a vulgar adulteress who is also waiting for her divorce. Lydia and her lover, perpetually exposed to each other's emotions, come to realise that the benefit of marriage is 'to keep people away from each other'.[59]

Some of these painful stories of relationships end in compromise; some in violence, torture and death. Wharton uses high-coloured, dramatic genres which would appeal to the magazine market (ghost-stories, historical costume-drama) so that she can force these personal situations to sensational extremes. In 'The Lady's Maid's Bell' (1902), a magnificent ghost-story, Hartley is hired to replace the dead maid (the last in a succession of maids) of Mrs Brympton, an invalid lady living in a large house on the Hudson, whose children have died, whose husband is often away, and whose only companion is her friend Mr Ranford: 'He would read aloud to Mrs Brympton by the hour, in the big dark library where she sat in the winter afternoons.' The husband turns out, by contrast, to be a bullying, tyrannical, jealous boor, 'coarse, loud, and pleasure-loving'. Hartley becomes aware, with nervous horror, of the presence in the house of the lady's dead maid, who is warning her to protect her mistress: but she cannot prevent the sinister tragedy from running its course. The beauty of the story is in the unsettling detail of the ringing bell, the empty corridor where someone has just passed, the feeling of unutterable things having taken place in the cold silent house, and the stifled, evasive suggestion of the husband's sexual brutality. We never quite know what 'dreadful things' have happened here: but we see the conspiracy between the women – the mistress, the maid, the ghost – tragically defeated.

Wharton's imagination (like that of many other American writers, from Poe and Hawthorne to James) enjoys playing with images of the living dead or of being buried alive. She does it as *Grand-Guignol* in an Italian story like 'The House of the Dead Hand' (written 1898, published 1904), and as New England comedy in one of her best early stories, 'The Angel at the Grave' (1901). Here, Pauline Anson has passed up all opportunities for a life of her own, in her dedication to the memory, and the House, of her literary grandfather, only to find that no one remembers or values him, and that the 'Life' she has dedicated her own life to writing has no market:

'It has been a long time for the public to wait,' [Miss Anson] solemnly assented.

The publisher smiled. 'They haven't waited,' he said.

She looked at him strangely. 'Haven't waited?'

'No – they've gone off; taken another train. Literature's like a big railway-station now, you know: there's a train starting every minute. People are not going to hang round the waiting-room . . .'

Miss Anson is rescued from desolation by a bright young man who comes in quest of her grandfather's one scientific discovery – he may have identified 'the missing link' – which is going, after all, to make his name. Wharton, unusually, allows for a consolatory comic ending here, but it does not lessen the poignancy of Miss Anson's immured life, her own personal evolution balked by patriarchal force.

In many of these stories, there is a feeling of being stuck inside a dilemma from which there is no exit. This is the mood of *Sanctuary*, serialised and published in 1903, the first short novel she wrote after *The Valley*, an odd, troubled, creaky piece of work (she called it 'Sank') about a possessive mother, Kate Peyton, whose marriage to a weak corrupt husband is a self-sacrificing compromise. She is trying to save her son from the same moral degeneration as his father. As in a play by Ibsen or Shaw, the mother battles to maintain integrity once she has realised that 'the fair surface of life was honeycombed by a vast system of moral sewage'. Meanwhile her husband's mother, as usual with Wharton's mothers-in-law, is capable of enveloping any scandalous situation in 'a mist of expediency'. The story's energy comes from Kate's neurotic inability – something like Lucretia Jones with her son Frederic – to let go of her son's life: 'Her soul rejected the thought that his future could ever escape from her.' She is his 'sanctuary', however much he might want to escape her: the benign-sounding title turns out to be darkly ironic.[60]

Story after story at this time deals with professional integrity, the betrayal of the artist's true self, or the loss of privacy in the literary market-place, told in a quizzical, jaunty, cool tone. In 'Copy: A Dialogue' (1900), two famous writers, once lovers, agree to burn each other's letters rather than publish them, 'to keep the excursionists out'. Literary fame has destroyed them. 'I died years ago', says the woman novelist, Mrs Dale. 'What you see before you is a figment of the reporter's brain – a monster manufactured out of newspaper paragraphs, with ink in its veins. A keen sense of copyright is *my* nearest approach to an emotion.'[61] In 'The Descent of Man' (1904), a science professor who sets out, as a joke, to write a popular book of 'pseudo-science', hits the jackpot, is inundated with interviews, advertising and product sponsorship, and never gets back to his real work. (She chose this as the title of her 1904 volume 'because I like that story rather particularly'.) The best of these is a ridiculous but painful story called 'The Pelican' (1898). The coolly observant narrator witnesses the career of a very pretty widow called Mrs Amyot, who embarks on a career of public lecturing to look after her son. Her mother was 'the female Milton of America', Irene Astarte Pratt. He hears her lecturing on Greek art and on Goethe, displaying 'the art of transposing second-hand ideas into first-hand emotions' – ideal for her audience of ladies. She becomes a fashionable 'lecturing-machine', but ten years on is found working a dim southern circuit, to tiny audiences, still pathetically claiming that she has an infant son to support. The son turns out to be an embarrassed bearded adult, mortified by his mother's continuing exposure of him. The dispassionate narrator and the outraged son both view the woman who began her public career out of need and has continued it out of addiction as a pathetic figure of fun.[62]

These subjects – the woman who pays, the threat to privacy, the commercialisation of literature – are masterfully handled in 'The Muse's Tragedy' (1899)[63] and in her first published novella, *The Touchstone* (serialised and published in 1900, in between *The Greater Inclination* and *Crucial Instances*). The two belong together: they are both about a woman's un-requited love, the publishing of private letters, and the cost of literary fame.

In 'The Muse's Tragedy', a young writer, Lewis Danyers, who has been much influenced by the great American poet Vincent Rendle, hears the story of Rendle's 'muse', Mrs Anerton, the 'Silvia' of Rendle's *Sonnets to Silvia* and the 'Mrs A' of his *Life and Letters*. He becomes fascinated by the woman who inspired and edited the poet's work, and who was 'the custodian of Rendle's inner self, the door, as it were, to the sanctuary'. But Mrs Anerton tells Danyers, eventually, that she was Rendle's friend and patron, but never his muse or his lover. As for the suggestive gaps in his published letters:

> Those letters I myself prepared for publication; that is to say, I copied them out for the editor, and every now and then I put in a line of asterisks to make it appear that something had been left out. You understand? The asterisks were a sham – *there was nothing to leave out.*

She renounces Danyers because she is afraid that, deep down, he is only interested in her because he wants to write the biography, or to turn her, 'after a decent interval, into a pretty little essay with a margin'.[64]

In *The Touchstone*, Stephen Glennard makes a great deal of money – enough to set up a dear little home with the new wife he adores – from the sale of letters written to him by Margaret Aubyn, a famous woman novelist, now dead, who had loved him unrequitedly years ago. (Her best-known novel is called *Pomegranate Seed*. Many years later, Wharton wrote her own story called 'Pomegranate Seed', in which, as in *The Touchstone*, a woman comes back from the dead to haunt the man she loved.[65]) The letters are published, and are displayed and discussed everywhere. (This massive publicity is described with a mixture of excitement and revulsion.) Glennard is full of self-disgust at what he has done, seeing the private letters in print like 'wounded animals in the open'. But he is 'saved' by the forgiveness of his long-suffering wife, who understands that, through his remorse, he has at last become the person worthy of the love of the dead novelist. As well as being a powerful story about exposure and commercialisation, it is, like 'The Muse's Tragedy' – and many more of her fictions – a story of a man who has failed to love a remarkable woman:

> To have been loved by the most brilliant woman of her day, and to have been incapable of loving her, seemed to him, in looking back, derisive evidence of his limitations; and his remorseful tenderness for her memory was complicated with a sense of irritation against her for having given him once for all the measure of his emotional capacity.[66]

The woman who has not been loved enough, who cannot find an escape route from her emotional dilemma, who is enclosed in the social role that has been constructed for her: all this pointed towards Lily Bart. But, unlike the women novelists Margaret Aubyn – or Edith Wharton – Lily has no lasting fame, no power to be heard, and no one to read her right.

7

Obligations

Edith Wharton's personal obligations were tangled in with the writing of *The House of Mirth*, and the novel shaped itself against a mixture of pressures and distractions. The two big successes of her fortieth year, *The Valley of Decision*'s appearance in February 1902 and the move into The Mount in September, were followed by difficult times. Teddy Wharton was unwell in the summer of 1902, and again, only much worse, in summer 1903. He seemed to be having 'a sort of nervous collapse': he was edgy, difficult, worrying about money, hyperactive, volatile, and suffering from headaches and insomnia. Wharton wrote troubled letters to Sally Norton in August 1903; the least worry, she said, seemed to 'take a monstrous shape to his poor imagination'. But she was a long way from attributing his behaviour to any kind of mental problem.[1] In September, he was in a state of disintegration. There had been phases of ill-health before in the eighteen years of their marriage, but nothing like this. Wharton was herself anxious and unwell, though, in comparison with the dark periods in Washington and Philadelphia a few years back, she was fitter than her husband. This was the first moment when something seemed to be very wrong with Teddy; and it coincided with his wife's first assured professional success.

When they sailed to Europe in the winter of 1903 they were both exhausted. She was suffering from 'nervous indigestion & bad headaches . . . influenza & laryngitis'.[2] But Europe had its usual tonic effect, and in 1904 they did not seem to be leading the life of invalids. Teddy bought his first car in January 1904, and their journeys of exploration began, in England, France, and New England. She was constructing *The House of Mirth*, by fits and starts, breaking off 'Disintegration' sometime in 1902, starting and abandoning 'A Moment's Ornament' in 1903, and finally settling down to write the novel in the summer of 1904. Meanwhile *Sanctuary*, *Italian Villas*, poems, and the stories called *The Descent of Man* came out. Anna Bahlmann, now in her fifties, was finding her secretarial duties intensifying, as Wharton's work accelerated. Wharton's European interests were developing, too. While her Italian articles were being published as books in 1904 and 1905, Wharton's attention was turning from Italy to France. In the winter of 1904 they went to Hyères to see the Bourgets. It was the first time that the Riviera delighted her, and its brightness and shimmer and flowery blueness would pour into *The House of Mirth*.

At The Mount, her social patterns were established, as her friends – Henry James and Howard Sturgis, Walter Berry, the Winthrops, the Lodges and the Chanlers – gathered for summer and autumn visits. In October 1904, she was writing *The House of Mirth* in the mornings, while, along the corridor, James was working on his essays for *The American Scene*. Afternoons were for trips in the new Pope-Hartford car, Charles Cook at the wheel. In the evenings, with the guests gathered round the fire and the little dogs in their baskets, there would be talk and readings: James reciting Whitman, for instance, in his memorably sonorous and rolling tones. Outside this charmed literary circle was the rest of America (as Wharton wrote to Sally Norton in August 1904): 'A whole nation developing without the sense of beauty, and eating bananas for breakfast'.[3] Were these her readers, too?

Reading books is not an advantageous thing to do in *The House of Mirth*. The only serious reader in the book is Lawrence Selden, and his pleasant bachelor library and nicely bound first editions of La Bruyère are no help to him managing his ambivalent feelings for Lily. They only cultivate the epicureanism and self-conscious detachment which make him step back from her, time after time, until it is too late. For everyone else, literature is either decorative or useless. Ned Silverton, a young man who once planned to write epics, but who gets more spoilt and decadent through the novel's year-and-a-half stretch (from September 1900 to April 1902), uses his literary talents to seduce rich married ladies, reading Theocritus (in Sicily) or Verlaine to Bertha Dorset, on her husband's enormous yacht. Lily's much-divorced friend Carry Fisher dabbles in bohemianism, building a studio onto the back of her house and inviting the fashionable portrait-painter, that lounge-lizard Paul Morpeth, to her soirées of singers and actors and 'plantation music' – but no writers. Most of Lily's 'friends' have never read a book in their lives. The library at Bellomont, the Trenors' magnificent house on the Hudson, is for assignations, not reading.

Simon Rosedale, the Jewish financier forcing his way up the social ladder, has a vague memory of 'a girl in some history book who wanted gold shields, or something, and the fellows threw 'em at her, and she was crushed under 'em: they killed her'. He is citing a story Wharton had read in her 1874 edition of Plutarch's *Lives*, translated by Dryden, in which the virgin Tarpeia betrays her city, Rome, to the Sabine warriors, for love of their golden bracelets, and is crushed to death by the bracelets and their shields. Lily, too, is a virgin who is going to be crushed to death by the weight of gold: but she has read no classical 'history books' where she might find such warnings.[4] She had a father who 'read poetry' in 'a score or two of dingy volumes' – 'dingy' being her dissatisfied mother's word for everything Lily does not want to be. But his stifled poetic nature did Hudson Bart no good at all: he ended up a bankrupt, reading nothing but creditors' bills. Lily's own teenage reading in sentimental fiction and her poetic susceptibility to beauty are worse than useless. They just encourage finer feelings and more romantic fantasies than her income allows.

Lily likes to think of herself as a reader, and one of the things that attracts her to Selden is that he makes her into a better one. When she scans her world through his 'retina', she finds she can 'classify' the people in it more sharply, and 'review' them as if they were second-rate literature, like 'Carry Fisher, with her ... general air of embodying a "spicy paragraph"'.[5] She envies Selden his library; she prides herself on her 'broadminded recognition of literature', and always carries 'an Omar Khayyám in her travelling-bag'; and her responses to hearing Theocritus read on the coast of Sicily confirm 'her belief in her intellectual superiority'.[6] But she has no real literary interests. We see her cutting the pages of a novel on the train going to Bellomont, but she never reads it: she is too busy seducing Percy Gryce. The only book which sticks in her mind is a copy of the *Eumenides* she once happened to pick up in someone's house, which teaches her about the implacable, vengeful Furies. Wharton often applied Aeschylus's Furies to her own life. But, unlike Wharton, when Lily is pursued by the Furies, the idea of solace through reading never occurs to her. On the last day of her life, she takes refuge in a little restaurant on 59th Street. It is full of women eating a quick lunch in the middle of their working day.

> But the sallow preoccupied women, with their bags and note-books and rolls of music, were all engrossed in their own affairs, and even those who sat by themselves were busy running over proof-sheets or devouring magazines between their hurried gulps of tea. Lily alone was stranded in a great waste of dis-occupation.[7]

Those 'sallow women' could be proof-reading the latest novel by Edith Wharton for Scribner's. Outside that world of work and writing, Lily feels a sense of 'profound loneliness'.

Yet *The House of Mirth* is full of things to read. The plot revolves around

letters, notes, bills, accounts, telegrams, newspaper scandal sheets, a will
(by which Lily is disinherited) and a cheque. Money is the marked paper
that matters most to people – there is even a scene, after an evening's
gambling, when the hostess 'left the table clutching such a heap of bills
that she had been unable to shake hands with her guests when they bade
her good-night'. Trying to distinguish herself from that kind of greedy materialism, Lily sets herself up to be 'read' romantically, by having a seal on
her letters which reads 'Beyond!' under the image of a flying ship. But she
cannot get much beyond the standard readings of her society. In the novel's
first scenes, she is using her encounter with Selden in his library to get
some 'tips' on 'Americana', in order to interest the millionaire she plans
to marry, Percy Gryce, whose only distinction is as a collector. And she is
paying her way at Bellomont by helping Judy Trenor with the 'chaos of
letters, bills and other domestic documents' which stream through the life
of a big hostess. During her last farewell scene with Selden in his room,
she burns the packet of love-letters to him from his ex-mistress Bertha
Dorset, which Lily has had possession of for months, but has failed to use
for her own advantage. She spends her last hours 'sorting her papers and
writing' at the little desk in the 'dingy' boarding-house to which she has
sunk. She clears her debt to Gus Trenor, the man who pretended to invest
her money for her, expecting to get her sexual favours in payment. Her last
act, before she takes the overdose of chloral which kills her, is to write a
cheque.

The stock-market has to be studied by the husbands, the gambling tables
and the cards at bridge require concentration from the wives. House-styles,
fashions, jewellery, wedding-gifts, menus and entertainments are read as
signs of status. Characters as far apart as the watchfully discriminating
Selden, disdainfully measuring the distance between Lily and the company
she keeps, or little Dabham, the gossip columnist of the 'Riviera Notes',
with his eyes out like 'tentacles' to catch whatever scandal is in the wind,
or Aunt Peniston, nosily registering every detail of 'festivities in which she
had not taken part', are all engaged in the same process of social surveillance. Some make a parasitic living (like Lily, for a time) training the
owners of new money, the tyro millionaires, to spend it with the proper
airs. These social 'introducers' draw their profit 'from facilitating social
contacts', and from providing (as Lily does briefly for the vulgar Mrs Hatch)
'the right turn to her correspondence, the right "look" to her hats, the right
succession to the items of her menus'.[8]

No one is so closely read as Lily, and no one is so hard to read: 'The
worst of it was, that in interpreting Miss Bart's state of mind, so many

alternative readings were possible.' She is always on view, and is always the subject of 'speculation'. Whenever Selden has a scene without Lily, someone is talking to him about her. She is always being gossiped about, whether by her disapproving aunt, or by the men who fancy her, or by the women who are trying to help or obstruct her. And she wants to be on view. Selden tells her that 'it's part of your cleverness to be able to produce premeditated effects extemporaneously'. She does not want to be alone in a picturesque natural setting; she wants someone to come and admire her in it: 'The combination of a handsome girl and a romantic scene struck her as too good to be wasted.' Wharton fills this book with the language of spectacle, drawn from the visual arts and the theatre, from house-decoration and architecture. Lily is variously seen as, or presents herself as, a framed painting, a performance, a collector's item, an actress, a model, a clothes-horse, a statue, a dryad, or a jewel.[9]

These images all come together in the episode of the '*tableaux vivants*', probably the best-known scene in all of Wharton's work, apart from the sled-ride in *Ethan Frome*. It takes place at the huge New York ball put on by the Wellington Brys, ambitious *arrivistes* who are (successfully) spending their way into social acceptability. They are using Lily, and Lily is using them, for mutually advantageous opportunities of display. She stage-manages their spectacle for them (the painter Morpeth is impressed by her 'vivid plastic sense'), a succession of lavishly costumed scenes on a stage with elaborate backdrops and lighting, in which society figures impersonate the subjects of famous paintings. The audience pride themselves on their sophistication in recognising the allusions and, at the same time, can admire members of their own set on show. But for the more discriminating, like Lawrence Selden, the living waxworks give 'magic glimpses of the boundary world between fact and imagination'.[10] So Lily appears as a romantic, magical illusion, and also as an artificial display. Her fine taste and brilliant control of 'effects' are seen at their best in her decision to choose, not a sophisticated or exotic figure like Tiepolo's Cleopatra, but Reynolds's portrait of 'Mrs Lloyd', an eighteenth-century English blonde beauty dressed in transparent, flowing draperies, posed in a rural setting. Deliberately contrasting herself with the more lavish, fancy tableaux that precede her, she relies on her own beauty, grace, and 'buoyancy' to give a 'natural' effect in this completely artificial scenario.

The result is sensational, but the readings are mixed. Selden and his cousin Gerty Farish, who is equally devoted to Selden and to Lily, see her, in this guise, as rare and distinguished, tragically at odds with her environment, 'the real Lily', 'the Lily we know'. The coarser men in the room see her as a provocative erotic display, as if she has appeared naked in front of them, showing off her 'points'. They make titillated, nudging comments on her performance: 'I never knew till tonight what an outline Lily has'; 'When a girl's as good-looking as that she'd better marry; then no questions are asked.'[11]

Lily's 'effects' always produce mixed readings. People want her as a collector's item, but in different ways: Percy Gryce, skilled only in 'the art of accumulation', would have added her to his warehouse; Simon Rosedale imagines her as the perfect chatelaine to show off his wealth; Gus Trenor wants her as a sexual prize for payments rendered; Lawrence Selden views her as a rare piece in a debased setting. Lily also has double feelings about her own performances. To create effects, to be a public show, is also to make oneself vulnerable, to be cheapened by exposure and to forfeit privacy and integrity. She knows how to market herself. She knows people want freshness and novelty, and that she must not get stale. She knows that the price of keeping up with society, for an orphaned, single woman of twenty-nine (her age at the start of the novel), is to be attractive but beyond reproach, charming but discreet, perfectly presented and always entertaining. She has to have *sprezzatura*, buoyancy without apparent effort. She knows she must sell herself in order to succeed: and success, in this world, means a rich marriage.

But she is always losing her opportunities, because she cannot quite turn herself into a commodity. In order to be an object for consumption, she would have to sacrifice what makes her special: her romantic impulses, her good taste, her desire for freedom and privacy. The plot of *The House of Mirth* is moved along by Lily's repeated missing of chances, as she slips down through the social strata into excommunication, isolation, and poverty. She gets so far with her seduction of Percy Gryce, then backs off out of sheer boredom. (Other examples from her past are cited which illustrate the same pattern of behaviour.) She buys her enemy Bertha Dorset's incriminating adulterous letters but fails to profit from them, when, by exposing Bertha, she could bring about her downfall and divorce, and marry George Dorset, who adores her, and is immensely rich; instead, she is out-manoeuvred by the ruthless Bertha, and publicly humiliated. She cannot overcome her 'repugnance' and accept Simon Rosedale's offer of marriage, for all his huge wealth. She will not stay with her aunt in order to make sure that she inherits her money. She does not bother to clear herself from accusations that she has been conspiring to marry off a wealthy young patrician to a vulgar divorcée, Mrs Hatch. Yet she is too much of a 'coward' (as she says of herself) to throw caution to the winds and commit herself –

supposing he were capable of commitment – to a life of romantic poverty with Selden, and too self-absorbed to get involved in charity work with the philanthropic Gerty Farish. Over and over again, she withdraws 'from an ambiguous situation in time to save her self-respect, but too late for public vindication'.[12] Her timing is terrible, and she is inconsistent: 'impulse' is always getting in the way of strategy.

Lily acts out a parallel – but much less successful – version of her author's professional career. She has the same ambivalence about self-marketing as Wharton does. If Lily were a novel, would she be a best-seller? Her desire to be marketable and to keep her integrity is like Wharton's eagerness for her novel to be a popular success and a responsible work of distinction. She said in a letter of 1905 that she did not just want it to be a superficial study of trivial people, and that her solution was to invest in the 'tragic implication' of a society with no 'inherited obligations' by concentrating on 'what its frivolity destroys'.[13] The language of the novel is versatile and agile, like its heroine. It hovers between harsh, bright realism and poetic romance. And it uses a severe terminology to investigate the human behaviour it puts on show.

The first thing we hear about Lily Bart is that she 'always aroused speculation'. She is caught inside the language of the money-market. Lily knows all about the social transactions her friend Carry Fisher, 'adept at creating artificial demands in relation to an actual supply', is so good at. She knows she has to 'pay her way' socially. But whenever real money is mentioned, she averts her eyes squeamishly and 'glosses over the transaction'. Simon Rosedale states his case more bluntly than Lily can stand: 'If I want a thing I'm willing to pay . . . I've got the money . . . and what I want is the woman.' The 'repugnant' Jew is the only person in the novel who makes explicit the interdependence of financial transactions and social relationships (or, as he puts it, of Wall Street and Fifth Avenue). 'Getting into things is a mighty useful accomplishment in business, and I've simply extended it to my private affairs'.[14]

There is something crushing (like those Sabine warriors with their shields) about the way Wharton traps Lily inside the novel's metaphors. Lily is trying unsuccessfully to 'play the game in her own way' – and she is also losing at cards. She never gets the chance to give 'her version of the case' or to 'gain a hearing' – and the law has a practical application too, in the delays over Aunt Peniston's will which are so injurious to Lily, and in the possibilities of blackmail and divorce which hang over the plot. Selden, the lawyer, is always making a case against Lily.[15]

Caught inside these terms, Lily seems to be wriggling about, trying to use 'adaptability' (another key term here for survival in the social jungle) and 'buoyancy' to keep her afloat. The language of the market, the law-case, and the gambling-table, is mixed with a more abstract vocabulary. 'Freedom' is Lily's greatest desire and 'success' her greatest necessity, but she is confused in her definitions – as in a long conversation with Selden at Bellomont. Is success to 'get as much as one can out of life', or, as Selden argues, the freedom to 'keep a kind of republic of the spirit', beyond 'all material accidents'? Selden mixes up 'freedom' and 'success' in his argument. So does Rosedale (who is always pitched against Selden in the novel) when he argues that freedom and success are, identically, to be so rich as not to have to think about money: 'to be able to take the earth for granted if she wanted to'.[16]

These terms are like dice, they keep coming up differently. Could success feel like failure, could failure ever be a kind of success? Wharton likes applying the word 'expediency' to Lily (as in 'each concession to ex-pediency had hardened the surface a little more'[17]), a perfect example of the narrow line between social success and moral failure. She makes a great deal of the interplay between 'opportunity' and 'obligation'. Lily has been trained by her mother to believe in the 'magnitude of her opportunities'. She believes that 'money' and 'society' should be thought of as 'opportunities' which can be transformed by the most discriminating user. But though she is alive to the opportunities her beauty and charm create, she is always passing them up: as Carry Fisher says to Selden, commenting wrily on Lily's 'discarded opportunities': 'Sometimes I think it's because, at heart, she despises the things she's trying for.'[18] With opportunities come 'obligations'. Lily has quite a strong sense of obligations but a horror of finding them unbearable. The last page of the novel is crammed with references to lost opportunities and burdensome obligations, and a terrible sense of waste.

The House of Mirth is a highly theatrical performance with a brilliant surface. Wharton puts into it everything she has been teaching herself in nearly thirty years of writing, since her juvenile satire Fast and Loose. The story takes place on a social stage, with crowd scenes and drawing-room dialogue and dramatic emotional duets – featuring attempts at rape and blackmail, as well as heart-tugging renunciations and farewells. The staginess ('I was punished enough at the time – is there to be no respite for me?') is itself the subject of dry comment. 'Don't talk stage-rot', says boorish Trenor to Lily. 'That sounds like stage-talk, don't it?' Rosedale comments on the blackmail plot.[19] Like an Oscar Wilde play, The House of Mirth shifts between intense personal drama and dazzling comedy.

Wharton's 'donnée' book of epigrams is put to use again here for cool one-liners: 'For always getting what she wants in the long run, commend me to a nasty woman.' 'Mr and Mrs Wetherall's circle was so large that God was included in their visiting-list.' Ned Van Alstyne, the old dandy who appears at funerals 'in a coat that made affliction dapper', prides himself on being able to place everyone by their menus, their interior decoration, and the architectural style of their houses. So does this novel, which pinpoints every ingredient in this shifting, acquisitive and self-displaying milieu: like the millionaire 'simple country wedding' on the Hudson, or the autumn opera-season, as seen by George Dorset: 'Well, here we are, in for another six months of caterwauling . . . It isn't so bad on Italian nights – then . . . there's time to digest. But when they give Wagner we have to rush dinner, and I pay up for it.' Sometimes 'the social stage' seems unreal, like the Brys' rapidly 'improvised' pleasure-hall, where 'one had to touch the marble columns to learn they were not of cardboard, to set oneself in one of the damask-and-gold arm-chairs to be sure it was not painted against the wall', or the carnival brightness of Monte Carlo, where the rich Americans (who have taken over the South of France and turned it into Manhattan) come in and out from yachts and trains and restaurants and casinos like performers in a costume play.[20]

But the descriptions are never just decoration. The 'slippery surface' is viewed in all its permutations, but Wharton keeps cutting down through it to show the workings of the machine. This is the study of the 'new privileged class' that Clephane wanted to write in 'Disintegration'. Under the economic and social analysis is an anthropological account of the social tribe as an example of evolutionary processes – where Lily is 'a water-plant in the flux of tides', or Selden looks, 'in a land of amorphous types', as if he belongs to 'a more specialised race'. Steeped in Darwin, Spencer and Lamarck, as well as Thorstein Veblen, Wharton demonstrates how 'the power of money' determines 'social credit' and morality, how the old money is complicit with and infected by the influx of the new, how consumption is increasingly linked to display and publicity, and how the role of women is created by, and dependent on, the financial imperatives of this society.[21]

Lily lives her thirty years at a point of transition, when the fixed, 'inherited obligations' for young women are beginning to shift. But for a virgin in the marriage-market, the rules are still implacable. As an orphaned single woman with no inheritance, whose father died bankrupt and who has no mother to promote her interests, Lily is always having to make sure of 'social sanction', and to look for protection. As a married woman, or that growing cohort of the population, a divorcée, she would have much more freedom to manoeuvre (for instance in borrowing money). A married woman was protected by her husband, whom society 'decreed ... should be the only judge of her conduct'.²² Her role was to spend the money on Fifth Avenue that he made in Wall Street.

The character who is most explicit and clear-eyed about the social machine is the Jew, Simon Rosedale. He is steadily going up as Lily is going down, and is one of the few people to benefit from 'a bad autumn in Wall Street'. Wharton's language about money and social status is always at its toughest when she brings him on. He gives the most forceful exposé of the system, because he is pragmatic and in control. The anti-Semitic colouring of this character is pronounced. He never comes on without our being alerted to his 'repugnant' glossiness or his 'plump jewelled fingers'. To excuse this by observing that, as the novel progresses, Rosedale gets more kindly and humane, is not much of an excuse. But what Wharton does give him, interestingly at odds with her racial stereotyping, is honesty. He speaks coarsely, but without pretences: 'As a girl gets older, and things keep moving along, why, before she knows it, the things she wants are liable to move past her and not come back.' When Lily faces facts, she sounds like Rosedale: 'And when a girl looks old to herself, how does she look to other people?'²³

Lily's own bursts of critical disdain for her society are not exactly analytical; they are more like movements of spontaneous revulsion from what wraps her round. These grow in intensity as she slips down the social scale, from the complacent elegance of the Trenors at Bellomont, to the 'social Coney Island' of the down-market Gormers, to Norma Hatch's vulgar decadence in her 'fashionable New York hotel', a 'limbo' of 'stifling inertia':

> Through this atmosphere of torrid splendour moved wan beings as richly upholstered as the furniture, beings without definite pursuits or permanent relations, who drifted on a languid tide of curiosity from restaurant to concert-hall, from palm-garden to music-room, from 'art exhibit' to dress-maker's opening.²⁴

At this point, Lily feels as if she has gone 'behind the social tapestry, on the side where the threads were knotted and the loose ends hung'. One stage further down, and we see her employed by 'Mme Regina's renowned millinery establishment' – not as a model in the showroom, which would have been a horrible travesty of her appearance as a '*tableau vivant*' – but sewing spangles onto hat-frames for the women who used to be her friends. 'Lack of early training' makes her incompetent at this (or any) labour. It is a lesson to her, we see, for thinking earlier in her career that the worst thing that could happen to her would be to have to 'dismiss her maid and learn to mend her own clothes', or for treating the charwoman who sells her Bertha's letters with revulsion, as a vile creature beneath contempt. (That woman, Mrs Haffen – aggressive, frightened, desperate – is one of the most powerful small parts in the novel. For a second Wharton lifts the lid on what her life might be like, and then closes the door on her.) Lily's humiliation in front of Mme Regina and the other milliners is a harsh, punitive masterpiece. She sees the 'social system' now, not from behind, but – as Mrs Haffen does – from underneath.[25] The next stage looks like destitution, from which Lily is momentarily rescued (in the novel's most piously moralistic moment) by Nettie, a working girl she has once been kind to, who was 'a fallen woman' but is now a happy wife and mother. The possibility that Lily might end up on the streets of New York, a *demi-mondaine* like Zola's Nana, rather than taking an overdose of chloral, is not explicit; but, by association with Nettie Struther, whom Lily once thought of as heading for the 'social refuse-heap', it is made clear that the system Lily has worked her way down inevitably entails prostitution for women.

This conclusion – in tune with the boldest 'naturalist' social writing of its period, Zola or Ibsen, Hardy or Dreiser – is what the novel has been driving at. Lily describes herself, finally, to Selden, as 'just a screw or a cog in the great machine called life',[26] but she is also a cog in the machine of Wharton's grimly moral plan. Given that we often hear how adaptable and intelligent Lily is, she is made incompetent and lacking in resources (idiotic about the stock exchange, easily taken in, easily shocked, incapable of any profession) so that Wharton can use her as a case-study for the damaging wastefulness of this society and its exploitation of women.

When *The House of Mirth* had its big success, part of its fame came from local scandal. As the novel came out in serial parts in *Scribner's* between January and November 1905, New Yorkers began to gossip about its closeness to their world. Like Lily Bart, horrified at the thought of exposure, Wharton was appalled when Scribner's put an ad on the wrapper of *The House of Mirth* when the book was published in October, reading 'For the first time the veil has been lifted from New York society'. She insisted they should remove the ad. 'The House of Scribner is at the moment the House of Mourning', Brownell wrote apologetically, assuring her they had got rid of the offending wrappers and their 'somewhat exotic spirit of enterprise'. She could be sure, he added, that Scribner's appreciated what the *New York Times* review had called the 'Aeschylean and Shakespearean' quality of the novel. 'At the same time, like Shakespeare, if not like Aeschylus, it has its sociological side – and that is of "value" too, isn't it?'[27] She was anxiously defensive about the accusation that she had '"stripped" New York society' in the novel.[28] But the big sales were undoubtedly enhanced by the fact that 'the publisher kept the papers well supplied with material about her life as a figure in New York society'.[29] Through the autumn, there was a heated debate in the pages of the *New York Times Saturday Review of Books* on whether the novel 'Held New York Society Up To Scorn' (as the *New York Times* review was headed) or made a moral reading of its material. Though the novel's success delighted her, and gave her the confidence to raise her price for *The Fruit of the Tree*, she wanted it to be read as a serious work, not as a juicy scandal-sheet.

The scandal it caused would come to seem absurd. Reviewers threw up their hands in horror at its shocking heroine, a member of their world, who 'rouged, smoked, ran into debt, borrowed money, gambled, and – crowning horror! – went home with a bachelor friend to take tea in his flat'.[30] Looking back on this from 1936, Wharton was amused to remember that the 'tame and blameless Lily Bart' caused such an outrage. Lily, pathetically, calls herself 'a bad girl', but she is not, after all, so very bad. She never has sex (in fact she recoils in fear at any direct sexual approach), she does not blackmail anyone, she is no good at tricking people, she pays her debt, and her overdose is probably an accident. But her author treats her, at times, very harshly. She is weak, greedy, proud, idle, snobbish, narcissistic, self-deceiving and artificial. We keep hearing from Selden how a 'hard glaze' is forming over her 'delicacies and susceptibilities'. Sometimes the narrator calls her, haughtily, 'Miss Bart' – as in 'Miss Bart had a fatalistic sense of being drawn from one wrong turning to another' – and presents her as a perfect representative of 'this crowded selfish world of pleasure':[31]

> She had reason to think that she had made herself equally necessary to her host and hostess; and if only she had seen any perfectly irreproach-able means of drawing a financial profit from the situation, there would have been no cloud on her horizon.[32]

But at other times she is a victim of Fate, pursued by the Furies, or the helpless product of her early training, 'so evidently a victim of the civiliza-tion which had produced her, that the links of her bracelet seemed like manacles chaining her to her fate'. We are often told that 'she can't help it – she was brought up with those ideas', that 'every dawning tendency' had shaped her for this life.[33] She is formed by her father's business failures and her mother's discontented investment in beauty and charm as a means to financial advancement. One of the strongest scenes in the book is the father's announcement of his bankruptcy, and some of its most subtle touches are Lily's resemblances to her dead parents.

And she is also a grand tragic heroine, fit to take centre stage with Manon or Emma Bovary, Gwendolen Harleth or Tess of the D'Urbervilles, Anna Karenina or Isabel Archer. As her fate darkens, she becomes grander: 'She had risen, and stood before him in a kind of clouded majesty, like some deposed princess moving tranquilly to exile.'[34] Breaking through the 'hard glaze' of the novel's social critique, a deep language of feeling (often in images of tides and floods) keeps pouring in. The scenes where Lily is alone and terrified at night, or exposes her emotions to Selden, or goes to his cousin Gerty for refuge, or, at the very end, takes comfort from holding Nettie Struther's baby, which seems to her to be lying in her arms as she dies, have an emotional expressiveness, in strange contrast to the novel's ruthless anti-sentimentalism. To make Lily into an autobiographical heroine would be to miss the point – it is exactly because Edith Wharton is not like Lily that she can write this novel. But some unstoppable personal feeling does keep rushing in, in Lily's agonising sense of solitude, her resentment of her mother, her childlessness and childishness, and the 'passion of her soul' for someone who does not have the capacity to return it.[35] Her troubled sense of being 'a stranger to herself', two split selves, a real one and a false one, makes her last farewell to Selden painfully touching:

> She paused again, trying to transmit to her voice the steadiness of her recovered smile. 'There is someone I must say good-bye to. Oh, not *you* – we are sure to see each other again – but the Lily Bart you knew. I have kept her with me all this time, but now we are going to part, and I have brought her back to you – I am going to leave her here. When I go out presently she will not go with me. I shall like to think that she has stayed with you – and she'll be no trouble, she'll take up no room.'
> She went towards him, and put out her hand, still smiling. 'Will you let her stay with you?' she asked.[36]

There is no home for Lily's best self, and having no home – spiritual or actual – is an essential part of her problem. But there is an alternative possibility – it is one of her missed opportunities – of making oneself 'at home' in the world. This is not Selden's precious and indulgent 'republic of the spirit', but the more workaday example provided by Gerty Farish, whose 'opportunities' *are* her 'obligations'. Gerty develops (like Rosedale), as the serialisation of the novel proceeded, from a caricature – a sentimental social-worker – to a more complicated figure. Gerty's attraction to and repulsion from Lily, culminating in the scene where Lily spends the night in her arms (with a superbly handled, embarrassed morning after) is one of the most surprising ingredients in a novel where women, on the whole, are cruel to each other. Gerty wants to detach 'the real Lily' from high society and to involve her in philanthropy, and the one gesture Lily makes in this direction, her visit to the Working Girls' Club, where she dispenses charm and glamour and a few dollars, like a 1900s Princess Diana, earns her her last respite in grateful Nettie Struther's kitchen. But the idea that if Lily was rich she would do something like 'founding a hospital' is a cruel joke on Selden's part. Like her mother, Lily has no 'other-regarding sentiments': she finds it impossible, even in her troubles, to 'de-centralise' her life. Gerty, by contrast, is capable of sublimating 'the wasted personal emotion' of her life 'into the general current of human understanding'. This does not make her into a rival heroine, but it does point towards other possibilities, hardly allowed into this novel. In the last pages, these are sombrely underlined, in a passage on the power of traditions, of a rooted past and inherited loyalties – everything Lily does not have: 'the power of broadening and deepening the individual existence, of attaching it by mysterious links of kinship to all the mighty sum of human striving'.[37]

Did *The House of Mirth*, Wharton's 'breakthrough book', and still the most famous of her novels, add to the 'mighty sum of human striving'? The personal passion that courses through it has to do, in part, with the responsibilities of authorship. Was it enough to glitter and entertain and rake in the money? In November 1905, at exactly the moment when *The House of Mirth* was making her more money than she had ever earned before – over $20,000, enough for the second garden at The Mount[38] – she wrote a story, in a week, called 'In Trust'. Paul Ambrose plans to bring 'aesthetic redemption' to America through his large inheritance, by building an Academy of Arts for the nation. But for all his idealism he is mean and indecisive, 'afraid to spend money', and is forever putting off the project. After his death, his materialistic widow marries one of Paul's old friends, Ned, who intends to resuscitate the great scheme. But she makes sure that all their energy and wealth go into their domestic expenditure: he is a 'capitalist' and she is a 'hostess'. They spend Ambrose's money on themselves, becoming more and more 'resplendent'. Ned struggles ineffectually against this, hating to see Paul's 'dreams turned into horses and carpets and clothes', but the 'obligation' is betrayed. This story was the bridge between *The House of Mirth* and *The Fruit of the Tree*, published two years later. Though the first of these has had such acclaim and fame, and the other is now hardly read, they are closely linked. *The Fruit of the Tree* met Gerty Farish's challenge to Lily Bart's existence, and turned *The House of Mirth* upside-down. This time, the American novelist takes on the responsibility of approaching American society not through 'opportunities', but through 'obligations'.

On the day she finished 'In Trust', Wharton immediately began to write 'Justine Brent', a title which suggested that the heroine was going to be, like Lily Bart, the focus of the new novel. Unlike the stop-go beginnings of *The House of Mirth*, the writing of this novel was borne along on the huge wave of confidence which her success gave her. She started it at the end of a pleasurable summer in Lenox. Teddy's health was improved; there had been satisfying visits and drives; The Mount was working well. She thought, at Thanksgiving, that they should be giving thanks 'for the best summer of our lives'.[39] The diary she kept at this time was filled with two sets of figures, often entered on the same day. They were the sales figures for *The House of Mirth* ('11 November: 20,000 more of H *of* M printing' . . . '5 December: H *of* M 3rd best-selling book in US in November') and the word-count for the new novel ('25 November: Written about 20,000 words of Justine Brent' . . . '7 December: Written about 30,000 words of Justine').[40] In the spring of 1906 she took a break from it, and they went to England and France, for her first plunge, via the Bourgets, into Paris society, and for two 'motor-flights'. Coming back to Lenox in June, she was 'dying to get back' to the novel.[41] She took it up again on 19 June 1906, and went on with it all summer, apart from writing up the 'Motor-Flight' articles, and travelling to Detroit and New York for two first nights of the play of *The House of Mirth*. (The first went well, apart from the Detroit hotel, which she described in her diary as 'vile hole opposite station'. The subsequent visit to Niagara passed without comment. The opening in New York was a flop: 'Not a success. Badly acted.'[42]) By November she had written 110,000 words and had a contract with Scribner's and Macmillan. She was the author of a best-seller, and correspondingly firm in her demands. (We have no evidence of Walter Berry's advice now, but he would certainly have backed her.) Complaints about Selden having been a 'weak' hero – or too 'absent', as James told her[43] – could now be countered:

> [This is] life in New York & in a manufacturing town, with the House of Mirth in the middle of the block, but a good many other houses adjoining. As for the hero, he is going to be a *very* strong man, so strong that I believe he will break all records. Perhaps in consideration of his strength you will think it not unreasonable to start in with a 20% royalty? If you were to refuse, he is so violent that I don't know whether I can answer for the consequences![44]

In December she was writing the last chapters at 'white heat' to meet the serialisation deadline.[45] The new novel – now called *The Fruit of the Tree* – started its serialisation early in 1907, while she was in Paris. It was published in book form in October 1907, after the usual arguments about illustrations: 'I herewith promise that my next novel is going to be so good that it won't need any illustrations to make it sell!'[46] The month it came out was a moment of dramatic personal change in her life. From that time on, though the process of extrication was long-drawn-out and complicated, her face was set against America and towards France. With Europe pulling at her so hard, she was intensely conscious of what *The Fruit of the Tree* was resisting. When the Boston historian William Roscoe Thayer sent her his book on Venice in 1905, she replied: 'I have been steeped in ideas so alien to all that romance & glory – the beginnings of a new novel, with the scene laid in an American factory town.'[47] Like *The Valley of Decision*, this novel too would analyse a particular historical moment in a society through a male character who has to make decisions about responsibility, and who is forced into a position of compromise. *The Fruit of the Tree's* subject is contemporary America, and much of its material, as with *The House of Mirth*, was drawn from her own social experience. But it also required researching, just as eighteenth-century Italy had. It was set, not in high society New York, but in the factory town of Westmore, and its adjacent residential town of Hanaford, about a four-hour train journey north from New York City, on the route to the Adirondacks. The novel switches between Westmore and Hanaford, and New York and Long Island, where the mill-owning family have their leisure homes, well away from the industry that finances them.

The moment Wharton started writing the novel, she went on a guided visit to the Plunkett cotton mills in North Adams, north of Lenox, and took notes. The factory was noisy, the tour was brief, and some technical mistakes were noted when the novel was serialised.[48] It would be easy to make a joke of this, and to accuse Wharton of a dilettantish and superficial relation to her subject. But she was thinking hard (as she would again for *Ethan Frome* and *Summer*) about the poverty and harsh conditions around Lenox in communities like Lenox Dale, North Adams, and Pittsfield. Her visit for Christmas 1905 to the gargantuan splendours of Biltmore, where presents for 350 workers on the estate were handed out in the banqueting hall by Ethel and George Vanderbilt, would have intensified her sense of the economic contrasts she was dealing with.[49]

She made use of some specific local materials. In the winter of 1905 to 1906 she was involved in New York with the work of the Society for the

Prevention of Cruelty to Animals, an organisation which was 'in such a bad way that its own members have had to lead the attack against it'.[50] The frustrations of committee work (anticipating her formidable activities in wartime) came in useful for Amherst's thwarted dealings with the conservative functionaries – lawyer, doctor, manager – of the mills. Also, she made use (not for the last time) of two terrible accidents in Lenox, within a year of each other. In March 1904 a sledding accident in the middle of the town killed one young girl and badly injured two others. And in July 1905, her good friend Ethel Cram had her fatal accident, lingering on for months until by some mercy she died in September. Better, Wharton wrote to Sally, to 'let life ebb out quietly in such cases'. The issue of euthanasia interested her. She thought that people, like dogs, had the right to be put down in extreme circumstances.[51] Wharton, too, had a minor accident in the new car, on the way back from Ashfield, in August 1906, in the middle of writing the novel. '!!!!!', she wrote rather proudly to Sally. '7 miles from your door we were in a ditch!'[52] A romantic night-time sled-ride takes place in *The Fruit of the Tree* without disaster: she would save that for *Ethan Frome*. But the ride is followed by a catastrophe which borrows, ruthlessly, from her friend Ethel's horrible slow death.

Paralysis in America: that was what she most feared. The characters in *The Fruit of the Tree* struggle against passivity, torpor, 'baneful lethargy'. One of her suggested titles for this novel was 'Atropos' – the name of the goddess who cuts short the thread of life. And the word that haunts the novel is 'atrophy' (also the title of a much later story). The physical paralysis of one of the main characters is a metaphor for the state Wharton most feared – the sapping of all her energies, being stuck in her tracks. In her marked-up copy of the Stoic philosopher Epictetus (one of the authors in her hero's library), she underlines: 'On the occasion of every accident that befalls you, remember to turn to yourself and inquire what power you have for turning it to use.'

The theme of social obligation that lurked on the edge of *The House of Mirth* now took centre-stage. This was a repositioning ploy, a clear decision to show that she was capable of writing a novel of 'issues'. She would never use quite this strategy again: in *The Custom of the Country* or *The Age of Innocence*, social obligations are meshed in more indirectly with the characters' personal choices. The result here is sometimes over-conscientious and laborious. But it points revealingly to her interior struggle, now very acute, about whether the American novelist had an obligation to use native subject matter, and to stay put. Would exile mean the loss of responsibility, even, the loss of a subject? She argued it out with Sally, who agreed with her that it was hard to 'love' this country.

> The trouble is, that when one has ever so slight a play of 'other-regarding activities' – the restless desire to better things about one – one would feel, I am sure, if one lived in another country, the alien's inability to take part, help on, assert one's self for good. Don't you think so? The social action on the community wd be impossible.[53]

John Amherst, her strong hero, who is dedicated to 'other-regarding activities', is the assistant manager at the Westmore textile mills. He is a pragmatic idealist, not a social revolutionary, who understands the necessity of 'compromises and adjustments', and wants to improve conditions for the mill-workers through benign, paternalistic methods. But he comes up against the cold profit-motive of the managers. He marries a beautiful, rich young widow Bessy Westmore, who owns the mills, but cannot turn her personal sympathy for one injured mill-worker into any kind of general interest in social reform. (Their relationship is like Odo's and the Duchess's in *The Valley of Decision*.) Helpless, untrained and ignorant – the childish American wife is Wharton's frequent target – Bessy withdraws into a spoilt life of leisure. Amherst finds a much more sympathetic presence in a young nurse at the mills, Justine Brent, who is competent, idealistic, and independent. When Bessy is injured in a riding accident, Justine witnesses her excruciating suffering, artificially prolonged by the triple edict of science, religion, and social convention, and administers a fatal, merciful dose of morphine. She conceals this act from Amherst. They marry, but their happiness seems dangerous, a temptation to the jealous gods. ('The Chariot of the Gods' was one of the novel's working titles.) Justine is blackmailed by a jealous doctor (a weak, melodramatic character) who knows her secret. When the truth comes out, Amherst cannot forgive her. Public scandal is averted, and the couple eventually construct a diminished life together, in which personal emotions take second place to their work for the community. This is the bitter, but not inedible, fruit of the tree of knowledge.

The novel was respectfully reviewed, with reservations. But Scribner's did not benefit from having paid out a bigger advance. The novel was a financial flop, its career partly sabotaged by the financial crisis on Wall Street in the autumn of 1907. Wharton's earnings in 1907 came to a third of what they had been (about $43,000) in 1906. The novel's three main issues – the need for welfare reform in industry, the inadequacies of American marriage, and the argument for euthanasia – have as much difficulty co-habiting as Bessy and John Amherst do. Justine is inconsistent, shifting from level-headed professional woman to frightened, dependent wife, and committing an action too drastic (as the novel's critics were quick to observe) for any trained nurse, however unconventional. Wharton was not at her best with working people, 'a dull-eyed stunted throng', and her serious consideration of their conditions ('how it was possible to put any sense of moral beauty into lives bounded forever by the low horizon of the factory') is condescending.[54] James claimed to like it but thought it had too much 'George Eliotizing'.[55] He was right: her determination to write a big, generalising novel (which had to do with her irritation at being compared with *him* so often) put her too much in debt to that nineteenth-century English model.

But *The Fruit of the Tree*, for all its awkwardness, is an ambitious, courageous, and tough piece of work. The change of title from a woman's name to a metaphor for experience shows that she did not want to be confined to one woman's story. She was concerned not to be type-cast as a woman novelist. A letter of 1907 to Robert Grant, whose conservative satires on American life she admired, wrestled with ideas of writing 'like a man' or 'like a woman':

> I conceive my subjects like a man – that is, rather more architectonically & dramatically than most women – & then execute them like a woman; or rather, I sacrifice, to my desire for construction & breadth, the small incidental effects that women have always excelled in.[56]

This conflict was also one of the subjects of the novel. Under the social 'issues' runs one of her main questions as a writer: can you draw general laws from particular cases, and act on them? Amherst is exasperated by Bessy because her feeling for an individual case does not open her mind to the general situation. Justine and Amherst both want to understand the deep structures of human behaviour and social arrangements, just as Wharton wanted her novels to do. But, in the end, their aspirations to clear-headedness and principled action are compromised. Like many other Wharton characters, they discover that 'life is not a matter of abstract principles, but a succession of pitiful compromises with fate, of concessions to old tradition, old beliefs, old charities and frailties'. The 'idealist' cannot cut a straight path through the 'tangled and deep-rooted growth' of human relations.[57] When Justine confesses to Amherst her mercy-killing of his first wife, she argues that her act was inspired by some lines she had read, copied into his volume of Bacon's *Essays*, in his collection of books of 'stoic wisdom' (Bacon, Seneca, Epictetus): 'We perish because we follow other men's examples ...'[58] But, faced with this philosophical justification for a shocking, morally ambivalent action, the free-thinking Amherst recoils in disgust.

The words 'sentimentality' and 'sympathy' run all through *The Fruit of the Tree*. 'Sentimentality' is almost always used pejoratively. Bessy is a creature of sentiment – she reads sentimental novels, she has a sentimental fancy about John Amherst. Justine fiercely resists being 'a wretched sentimentalist'. Her response to Wyant's emotional proposal is, 'I dislike sentimentality!' Yet she has a passionate 'sympathy' for her patients, and what she admires in John Amherst is his mixture of 'independence of judgment' and 'strong human sympathy'.[59] Amherst's social philosophy is based on the idea of a sympathetic bond between workers and employers (rather than on union organisation). 'Only through sympathy with its personal, human side could a solution be reached.'[60] Their marriage is tuned (at first) to 'the utmost pitch of sympathy'. This emphasis draws together the otherwise divergent strands of the plot – labour relations, marital incompatibility, and the relation of medical science to human needs. All three require sympathy, not sentiment, for their solution. But 'definitions are ambiguous', Amherst says at one point. Sympathy requires some sentiment, just as a novel of social issues also requires strong feeling. This was the challenge, for Wharton, at this moment in her literary career: to try and write a novel that would fulfil the obligations of the American novelist towards the social material that lay all around, *and* create sympathy for her characters, *and* avoid being branded as a sentimental, over-emotional woman novelist. You can see her working full out, with immense determination, to tackle these challenges in *The Fruit of the Tree*, the last novel she wrote in America.

8

The Legend

In March 1910, Edith Wharton published a story called 'The Legend', about a writer of genius so misunderstood by his public that he has disappeared and become a kind of ghost of himself. Everyone thinks that the American poet-philosopher John 'Pellerin' (French for 'pilgrim') had died twenty-five years ago. Since then, he has been posthumously taken up at a 'screamingly' loud pitch by disciples and discussion groups, and become the subject of legend and of conjectural biographies in which 'whole chapters ... were constructed in the conditional mood and made up of hypothetical detail'. But a young drama critic called Arthur Bernald has some friends who have picked up a strange, vagrant sixty-year-old, John Winterman, who has a benign, 'mysteriously fertilising' effect on those he meets. Bernald is magnetised, like a lover, by the 'large hovering sense of manifold latent meanings' in the older man's presence, and gets from his conversation 'a sense of lightness and liberation, as if the hard walls of individuality had melted'. He is not like anyone else: 'His observer had never known anyone so alive to human contacts and yet so secure from them.' His ideas seem extraordinarily like – Pellerin's.

And of course he *is* Pellerin. The older man explains that he vanished from 'an inattentive world' because nobody had taken any notice of his 'poor still-born books'. Finding at last, from the other side of the world, that he had become a cult, he has come back to find out what people were saying about him. But the famous expert on Pellerinism (a heavily satirised charlatan), when presented with Winterman's work, dismisses it as a poor imitation of Pellerin; and when Bernald takes Winterman to the Pellerin evening at the 'Uplift Club', he sees the great man, across the crowded room, send him a baffling look: 'What were Pellerin's eyes saying to him? What orders, what confidences, what indefinable apprehension did their long look impart?' He never knows the answer, because Winterman/Pellerin, after meeting his devotees, vanishes once more, and is never seen again. He left a message to say he was going home. 'Well, then, I suppose', said Bernald, 'he went home.'[1]

In its oblique way, the story invokes Henry James, and Edith Wharton's relationship with him. They had consolidated a tentative friendship a few years before, in 1904, when James went back to America after a twenty-one-year absence. The book he wrote out of that return (which he began while staying at The Mount) was *The American Scene*, but he thought of calling it 'The Return of the Novelist'. Wharton witnessed that return, and read, too, his terrifying story of self-haunting, 'The Jolly Corner', which came out of it. She observed James's intense disappointment at the financial and critical failure of the New York Edition of his works, which he had been labouring on since 1905, and which appeared between 1907 and 1910 to resounding indifference. James wrote many letters of gloom and distress about this failure, some of them to her: 'I blush to say that I have got at last rather demoralized – in the sense of feeling blighted beyond all my power to throw it off . . .'[2] In March 1910, just when 'The Legend' was published, she was horrified, on a visit to London, to find him in the grip of a paralysing depression. She wrote with great agitation to their mutual friend Morton Fullerton:

> I, who have always seen him so serene, so completely the master of his wonderful emotional instrument – who thought of him when I described the man in 'The Legend' as so sensitive to human contacts & yet so *secure* from them; I could hardly believe it was the same James who cried out to me in his fear, his despair, his craving for the 'cessation of consciousness', & all his unspeakable loneliness & need of comfort, & inability to be comforted![3]

After his death, she would say that she found a 'deep central loneliness' in him. She summed him up as 'a solitary who could not live alone', and a writer who 'could never wholly overcome the longing, not to be bought by the many but at least to be understood by the few'. She recognised 'a deep craving for recognition' in James. The word 'recognition' rings like a bell through her reminiscences of him: he must have secretly dreamed, she thought, of being a 'best-seller'; 'he certainly suffered all his life – and more and more as time went on – from lack of recognition'.[4] All this is movingly written into 'The Legend'.

But this was a complicated friendship, and 'The Legend' may also have been, in part, a response to an unkind comic story James had published in 1909, called 'The Velvet Glove'. This described a very different relationship between two writers, an established playwright called Berridge, and an ambitious lady writer whose pen-name is 'Amy Evans' and who in real life is a glamorous Europeanised – or European – princess. The playwright has glimpsed her in an intriguing intimacy with a handsome young lord in a train going from Cremona to Mantua. Now she makes a bee-line for him across a crowded Paris salon: 'They had found their eyes meeting, in deep communion, all across the great peopled room; meeting and wanting to meet . . .' Amy Evans has written a novel called *The Top of the Tree* (James's working title for this story) and she wants Berridge to write a 'lovely, friendly, irresistible, log-rolling Preface' to her next book, *The Velvet Glove*. As the princess, alias Amy Evans, captures him for a night-drive across Paris on 'a wondrous bland April night', and makes her wishes plain to him, his revulsion at the vulgarity of what he is being asked to do is painfully at odds with the romantic enchantment of the night-drive through the glimmering city, and the seductive female presence whose request he conclusively rejects: 'Nothing would induce me to say a word in print about you. I'm in fact not sure I shall ever mention you in any manner at all as long as I ever live.'[5]

'The whole thing reeks of you', James told Wharton. He had been thinking of the story since the occasion in 1907 when he had written to ask her if she had really told the editor of a 'personality paper' to ask him to praise *The Fruit of the Tree*. No, she replied at once, it was all a mistake, the editor was lying. James had thought as much; but perhaps, he added, awaiting his copy of *The Fruit of the Tree*, he *might* write something about her after he had read it. (It sounds as if he means to make mincemeat of me, Wharton commented to Charles Scribner, who published them both.) But then James read the novel, and an elaborate letter followed, explaining that now might not, after all, be the right moment for him to write about her – with a carefully moderated critique of the novel's structure and its 'George Eliotizing'. Wharton chose to read 'The Velvet Glove' as a tribute to their shared experience of Paris; she mentioned it in letters to friends without any trace of rancour or anxiety, as 'a delightful story'. In her reminiscences she made a point of attributing its plot to a quite different source, while claiming that its inspiration had been one of their Parisian drives together. She did not comment on the mockery in the figure of the rich, pushy lady writer at the top of her tree, nor he on the figure in *her* story of the writer so misunderstood that he has become a ghostly legend.[6]

This friendship has itself become the stuff of literary legend. For many readers and admirers of Edith Wharton, her relationship with Henry James is the main story of her life. To this day it is still rare for a book or an essay or a talk on Wharton not to mention James. Any conversation about

Wharton will be likely to invoke one of the famous, funny stories of their relationship – like the one about the car and the wheel-barrow, here told by Percy Lubbock, but found again in every life of Wharton:

> She mentioned once that the car in which they were riding had been bought with the proceeds of her last novel. 'With the proceeds of my last novel,' said Henry meditatively, 'I purchased a small go-cart, or hand-barrow, on which my guests' luggage is wheeled from the station to my house. It needs a coat of paint. With the proceeds of my next novel I shall have it painted.'[7]

Or the one (which she tells herself) about Henry James asking the way, from their car, at night, at great length and with immense elaboration, of 'an ancient doddering man', for directions to the King's Road in Windsor. His peroration concludes:

> 'In short, my good man, what I want to put to you in a word is this: supposing we have already (as I have reason to think we have) driven past the turn down to the railway station (which, in that case, by the way, should probably not have been on our left hand, but on our right), where are we now in relation to . . .'
>
> 'Oh, please,' I interrupted, feeling myself utterly unable to sit through another parenthesis, 'do ask him where the King's Road is.'
>
> 'Ah –? The King's Road? Just so! Quite right! Can you, as a matter of fact, my good man, tell us where, in relation to our present position, the King's Road exactly *is*?'
>
> 'Ye're in it,' said the aged face at the window.[8]

The retelling of these good stories (which are as revealing about their differences, as people and as writers, as about their affinities) goes alongside the version of Wharton – which has proved extremely hard to shift – as a female Henry James, a more superficial and middlebrow imitator of the Master, using the same kind of plots, characters, and society, but with less depth and subtlety. From the moment she started publishing fiction in the late 1890s, Wharton was compared by reviewers, critics, biographers and academics to James. This has not worked the other way. There are rather few accounts of James's work which suggest that *she* might have influenced *him*: that *Italian Backgrounds*, for instance, had an effect on *Italian Hours*, or that their exchanges on George Sand fed into his long essay on Sand in *Notes on Novelists*, or that her activities and her letters in wartime, and her call for contributions to her war-charities book, spurred him on in the writing of his war-pieces, like 'The Long Wards'. But her appearance in his writings – usually as a satirised figure – is often commented on. James's biographer Leon Edel (who talked to Wharton about her friendship with James) saw 'something deeply mocking and hostile' in James's treatment of her in 'The Velvet Glove'. In a 1909 story, 'Crapy Cornelia', a rich New York lady, Mrs Worthingham, is criticised for the 'rabid modern note' of her excessively luxurious life-style. The narrator prefers her dowdy, old-fashioned friend Cornelia, with whom he can exchange ironical reminiscences of their 'old' New York of thirty years ago, in 'those spacious, sociable Arcadian days' before skyscrapers.[9] But if Wharton is in this story, she is in it as *both* women: a rich New York hostess, and also a nostalgic celebrator of old values.

. Wharton's presence is certainly felt in *The American Scene*'s treatment of wealth, and in James's unfinished novel *The Ivory Tower*, started in 1913, set in Newport and Lenox, with a 'big social woman', Mrs Bradham, at the centre, in 'her great characteristic house'. But Wharton gets into James's late work, not just as a rich hostess, but also as a woman caught in a prolonged unhappy marriage and a drama of agonising adultery. In 'A Round of Visits' (1910), Mark Monteith, returning to New York after a long absence, is the confidant of the tragi-comic Florence Ash, who is divorcing from her hopeless husband, 'a pure pearl of a donkey', after a long struggle: 'He knew already, without the telling, that intimate domestic tension must lately, within these walls, have reached a climax and that he could serve supremely – oh, how he was going to serve! – as the most sympathetic of all pairs of ears.' In *The Sense of the Past*, the novel James was working on when he died, the grand, much-travelled Aurora Coyne, almost 'insolently' dazzling with her life of 'departures, absences, returns', has had a baffling marriage to a 'damaged' character, and 'an encounter, an adventure, an agitation, that . . . leaving behind it a wound or horror', has made her return to America, never to go back to Europe: her adventure has 'poisoned for her a continent'.[10] James used bits of Wharton's life in these late writings, in ways which suggest her importance to him and his ambivalence about her.

What is moving and engrossing about the friendship of these two great writers with twenty years between them is how sharpness, exasperation, even bafflement, coexisted with deep tenderness and – to use their kind of word – 'devotion'. But 'devotion', on Wharton's side, went (as 'The Legend' shows) with a definite desire not to be thought of as his disciple. By the time Wharton was at 'the top of her tree' with *The House of Mirth*, she was sick of always being compared to Henry James. Reading the reviews of *The Descent of Man* in 1904, she complained to Brownell: 'The continued cry that I am an echo of Mr James (whose books of the last ten years I can't read, much as I delight in the man)' made her feel 'rather hopeless'. Brownell replied: 'I sympathize with you about the James business. Do you remember the paper that called you "a masculine H.J."? Of course it is unpleasant not to have one's uniquity recognised, but sometimes you seem to come out of the mix better than he does, I notice.'[11]

The Fruit of the Tree deliberately tried to break free of the 'Jamesian' tag. And there would be nothing Jamesian about *Ethan Frome* or *The Custom of the Country*, *Summer* or *The Marne*. But the comparisons persisted, and still persist. And Wharton and James did share subjects and attitudes, character-types and social themes. As all writers do who are friends, they spent years exchanging literary allusions and jokes, thoughts on their reading, and gossip about authors; and they occasionally exchanged plots, too. In January 1908, James gave Wharton a 'donnée', a true story about a young Englishman (Jack Pollock) who uses a flirtation with a married American lady as a cover for breaking off an engagement at home. 'I give you all my *rights* in it', James wrote to her, after they had talked over this story. 'I applaud to the echo the fructification of [it] in your rich intelligence.' Wharton fructified, and turned the gift into a sad, cruel New England story of betrayal and humiliations, 'The Pretext' (1908). As a little signal of gratitude to James, the woman's name in the story is 'Ransom' – the surname of a main character in James's New England novel, *The Bostonians*.[12]

In 1909, Wharton told James the story of the 'Praslin murder', a nineteenth-century Parisian scandal in which a French governess is the cause of the Duc de Choiseul's stabbing his wife to death. The duc, Charles Praslin, kills himself, but the governess gets away to a new life as Mrs Deluzy-Field, wife of an American minister and a New York hostess. James replied that he remembered the 'closed & blighted' Hôtel Praslin from his childhood in Paris, and had met Mrs Deluzy-Field in New York. Wharton planned a novel called *The Keys of Heaven*, which was never finished; in the fragments that remain, the French governess, married to a New England minister, compares American puritan innocence with her dark, tragic European past, like James's baroness in *The Europeans*.[13] It is a story which would have suited either of them.

These exchanges of plot suggest how close their interests could be. And there are places where she deliberately writes with him in mind, or sees how she can follow on from what he has done. She paid him close attention. Her library shows his lifelong literary importance to her. There are books of his from the 1880s, signed 'Edith Jones'. There are marked-up copies of his *Partial Portraits* and his New York Edition (of which she had three sets). There is a gift from him of the volume of stories called *Terminations*, marking the Whartons' first visit to James, with the dedication: 'To Edith Wharton, in memory of Whit. Saturday 1904, Henry James, Lamb House, Rye'. There are copies of his work in her library which once belonged to Morton Fullerton, and there is a gift of *The Golden Bowl*, dedicated 'To Edith Wharton – in sympathy – Henry James November 1904'. And there is a dedication from James at the front of a book of comic poems of 1906 by Harry Graham called *Misrepresentative Women* (these include Lady Godiva, Mrs Grundy and Mrs Christopher Columbus): 'To a much misrepresented Woman from the largest of her admirers, November 1906'.

Wharton was reading James long before she met him, and when he began to write to her and give her literary advice, it was an important moment in her life. She was already launched on 'Disintegration' when, in his long letter about *The Valley of Decision* in 1902, he told her to 'DO NEW YORK'. But she was pleased enough by his letter to circulate it to close friends like Walter Berry and Sally Norton. He influenced her, too, in her gradual move between 1907 and 1912 towards France, with his deep knowledge of French culture. Her French journeys were made under James's influence, even before they started travelling in France together. In her 1920 copy of James's *Letters*, she marks many passages about his relation to Europe, such as a remark in a letter to William Dean Howells of 1876, saying he is turning into 'an old and very contented Parisian'. In turning herself into a Parisian, she was keenly aware that she was following in his footsteps.

It was as she was entering French life that she deliberately tried out a Jamesian model, to see what she could do with it. Her novella of Franco-American relations, *Madame de Treymes*, came out in *Scribner's Magazine* in August 1906. No one who had read James's *The American* (1876–7) could miss the parallels with the optimistic, dogged American suitor trying to wrest the woman he loves out of the grip of an old French family, setting the claims of individual freedom against the bonds of tradition and precedence. *Madame de Treymes* acts out Wharton's argument with herself about leaving America and moving to Europe ('Why did you never come back?' the Parisianised American heroine is asked), an argument which replays James's decision, made thirty years before, at the time of *The American*. But where James does Newman's doomed attempt to wrest Mme de Cintré from her sinister old French family as Gothic comedy, Wharton uses her characters' poignant situation for a clear-eyed, ironical cultural comparison.

Where Wharton does use James as a literary model, it is more often to write against him than to write under him. *The Reef*, always called her most 'Jamesian' novel (though he thought it was like Racine), is explicit and bold about sexual treachery and humiliation, where James – as in *The Golden Bowl* – is indirect and teasing. Even when her stories make use of one of James's strategies – an all-male group as a frame-narrative for a ghost-story, or a to-and-fro of conversations around a central deception – this can produce a critique, not an imitation, of James. 'The Dilettante', first published in December 1903 and then in *The Descent of Man* (1904), deals with a chilling character who has mastered 'a science of evasion' in his relationships, and who is accused of having 'sifted and sorted' his old mistress 'to suit his taste'. 'The Eyes', first published in June 1910, and then in *Tales of Men and Ghosts*, tells – to an all-male audience – of the implicitly homosexual Culwin, whose 'carefully guarded hours had been devoted to the cultivation of a fine intelligence and a few judiciously chosen habits', who has his coterie and his neophytes ('he liked 'em juicy'), cruelly refuses commitment or kindness to those who fall in love with him, and is haunted by a pair of eyes 'with an expression of vicious security'. Wilde's *Dorian Gray* and Edgar Allan Poe haunt this story too, and Wharton had other examples of self-pleasing, uncommitted bachelors to draw on, from Egerton Winthrop to Walter Berry. But James's self-protectiveness, and the evasiveness and artifice she disliked in his late work, play their part here.[14]

Yet Wharton's exasperation at being seen as James's imitator is understandable. She often deliberately does the opposite of what he might have done with a similar subject. In later years, after his death, she would pay him a kind of tribute in *The Age of Innocence*. But her earlier allusions to him were more like gestures of independence. She parodied one of his titles, changing *The Tragic Muse* into 'The Muse's Tragedy'. 'The Touchstone' turned *The Aspern Papers* on its head (it is a woman poet, not a man, whose privacy is exposed through the publication of her letters, and the 'publishing scoundrel' is redeemed by marriage, not, as in James, threatened by it). 'So many eminent critics have declared that you imitate H.J.', Walter Berry wrote, perceptively, of 'The Touchstone', 'that it would be good fun to show them the difference when you *do*.'[15] *The House of Mirth* rewrote *The Portrait of a Lady*, asking what a woman with as much beauty, ambition and desire for free choice as Isabel Archer would do if she did not go to Europe and did not have a fortune. *The Fruit of the Tree* has a climax which points up their difference. Towards the end of the novel, Amherst, after months of separation, seeks out Justine for a reconciliation. They are haunted by the memory of the dead Bessy.

She looked at him again. 'But what is really changed?'

'Everything – everything! Not changed, I mean – just gone back.'

'To where . . . we were . . . before?' she whispered; and he whispered back: 'To where we were before.'[16]

Unmistakably, the ending of *The Wings of the Dove* – James's first present to Wharton, in 1902 – is echoed – echoed but altered.

'I'll marry you, mind you, in an hour.'

'As we were?'

'As we were.'

But she turned to the door, and her headshake was now the end. 'We shall never be again as we were!'[17]

Wharton told Sally Norton she thought *The Wings of the Dove* was 'unpleasant', and she turned down a request from Scribner to review it. *The Sacred Fount* made her want to 'weep over the ruins of such a talent'. She hated *The Golden Bowl,* and she wished James had gone on writing in the earlier manner of *The Portrait of a Lady* or *English Hours.* After her first long conversation with James, she reported to Brownell that 'he talks, thank heaven, more lucidly than he writes'. As they grew closer, these brusque notes fall away, though she is still referring, in January 1911, to James's 'unhappy' play (*The Saloon*, adapted from his story 'Owen Wingrave'), which she had thought from the first 'doomed to certain disaster. Alas!' She even wrote a parody of him, 'An Open or Shut Question', part of the fond caricatures she exchanged with their 'inner circle'. She copied it out for one of them in September 1911, calling it 'this wicked old opus'. It was headed 'Advance Sheets of Mr Henry James's New Novel'.[18]

. . . It was not that, as Mrs Byas said, one couldn't always buy a new umbrella.

From the visibly permissible assumption of the conjecturer's solvency one might, it was clear, predicate without risk of tenable refutation, his congenital capacity for the spontaneous gratification of even more considerable exigencies. Figuratively & literally, Mr Valentine Grope would, one instantly surmised, be always able to buy a new umbrella; but then, as he, with a not wholly unapt delimitation of her axiom, permitted himself to point out to his admirable friend, it would always be a *new* umbrella.

'There, my good woman, is the rub.'

> She glanced at him with a sense of the after all never wholly evitable hindrances to complete communion.

And so it goes on, but of course the new umbrella never gets bought. This was for private entertainment; she was no keener to write about him in public than he was about her. James did finally mention her in print in one of his last essays, on the younger generation of new writers, published in the *Times Literary Supplement* in the spring of 1914. He praises her – in that abstracted, evasive late manner of his – for encouraging 'her expression to flower into some sharp image or figure of her thought when that will make the thought more finely touch us', and congratulates *The Custom of the Country* for its 'particular fine asperity': 'we move in an air purged at a stroke of the old sentimental and romantic values'; it is a manifestation of 'the masculine conclusion' crowning 'the feminine observation'. She responded with an essay, which he enjoyed, on the superiority of literary criticism in France compared to England or America. She said nothing about his or her work, but took, as her ideals for the novel, Balzac and Tolstoy. (One of her criticisms of James was that he was not sufficiently 'Balzacian' to take on the big American subject.[19])

She did not write about him publicly until she reviewed Percy Lubbock's selected edition of James's letters in 1920 (in the making of which she had been closely involved). She gave a tender account of their friendship, which she would quarry for her reminiscences, fourteen years later, in *A Backward Glance*.[20] But she also said, severely, why she did not like his late work, in its insistence that all the narrative must be composed around a central consciousness, and that the tale 'must be treated as a stellar system, with all its episodes revolving like "the army of unalterable law" round a central *Reason Why*'. In his late years, she complained, 'this formula ... became an inexorable convention'. Even in a devoted tribute, she could not resist a candid note of criticism.

The story of the friendship began on her side, as she would often recall, with veneration and shyness: the young New York married lady, putting on her best dress at a dinner in Paris in 1887 to meet the Master, and being ignored. Once she started publishing, however, they were bound to meet. There was every reason for them to get to know each other. They shared a common old New York and Newport background, and their paths had been criss-crossing in Italy and France for a long time before they met. They had the same publishers, and were writing for the same magazines, sometimes in the same issues. James had known well, for many years,

Minnie Jones, and the Bourgets (whom he and Wharton would much enjoy dissecting), Vernon Lee, and the Roman-American set of Wharton's childhood (Daisy Chanler's parents the Luther Terrys, Francis Marion Crawford). He knew Henry Adams, and Charles Eliot Norton was a dear friend. Norton's sister Grace was as close to Henry James as Sally Norton was to Wharton. (Of Sally, he wrote: 'The eldest of the girls is much the prettiest, & they go declining, whereby they are known in College as Paradiso, Purgatorio, & Inferno.' Sally was the eldest.) He knew the Ralph Curtises (the dilettante painter and his wife, living in Venice) and Florence La Farge, the clever architect's wife, and the wealthy, eccentric ex-Bostonian Howard Sturgis. James's great passion of the 1900s, the sculptor Hendrik Andersen, met Wharton in Rome in 1903 and described her as 'the woman who has written some very interesting books ... seems very fond of meeting titled people and has a very cunning little dog ... I don't think her literary success is turning her head'.[21]

Before that 'literary success', the first phase of their relationship was that of the younger and older writer in 'The Legend'. She made the first move, sending James her first book of stories, *The Greater Inclination*, in 1899; he wrote caustically to Minnie Bourget that Mrs Wharton had sent him 'the fruits of her literary toils'. She followed this up in October 1900 with 'The Line of Least Resistance', about a weak millionaire who is dissuaded from divorcing his unfaithful wife (the story which caused her so much trouble with the Vanderbilt-Sloanes in Lenox). He praised its 'admirable sharpness & neatness'; but found it a little *hard*. 'That's because you're so young, &, with it, so clever. Youth *is* hard – & your needle-point, later on, will muffle itself in a little blur of silk.' He 'eggs her on' – as he would repeatedly – 'in your study of the American life that surrounds you. Let yourself go in it & *at* it – it's an untouched field, really.' It was as if, from the first, he was encouraging her to do what he could not. 'Do send me what you write', he concluded, and promised to reciprocate. It was a generous first letter, if itself rather sharp and hard. Wharton sent it straight on to Walter, who called it a 'cryptograph': 'Won't it be fun, later, to watch your needle-point muffle itself in a little blur of silk!' James took the same tone in a letter to Minnie Jones two years later, thanking her for sending him her sister-in-law's *Crucial Instances* and *The Touchstone*, and praising Wharton's 'diabolical little cleverness'. But he was generous too: when he liked something, he added, he always wanted to 'write it over in my own way', and he had that impulse here. It was to Minnie, again, that James wrote after his first dinner with the Whartons – or the first when he took any notice of her – in London, in December 1903. 'She was *really* 'conversable', he thought; though when the Whartons came to Rye in a hired car in May 1904 and spent twenty-four hours at Lamb House, he found her 'a little dry'. However, the stage was now set for 'a free & easy postal relation' between them, and for James's visit to The Mount in the autumn of 1904. Here, the roles of mentor and apprentice rapidly transformed into those of guest and host.[22]

Wharton mocked, as she always would, his fussy arrangements for his visit, and James mocked, as he always would, the 'almost too impeccable taste' and luxury of her house and her hospitality. 'Every comfort prevails, and you needn't bring supplementary apples or candies in your dressing bag', he reassured Howard Sturgis, whom he had insisted on having as his only fellow guest. He was taking notes on American wealth, after his long absence. 'Everyone is oppressively rich and COSSU [luxurious]', he wrote to his English confidante Jessie Allan, with whom he was always much more relaxed and chatty than with Wharton. 'A million a year seems to be the usual income.' Still, his hostess's lavish arrangements for his comfort delighted him, and he fell in love with their drives through 'these really admirable little Massachusetts mountains, lakes, and woods'. This first visit to The Mount, in a golden autumn – writing next door to each other, motoring through the Berkshires, visiting the millionaire neighbours, attending to the little dogs (in whom James took a fond interest), reading aloud in the evenings, with Wharton and Howard Sturgis listening enraptured as James, in the Swinburnian manner of his generation, rolled out Whitman or Emily Brontë – all this set the tone for his future visits. After he left The Mount, he wrote copiously to Wharton about his American travels.[23]

The attempt to transfer their new intimacy to Park Avenue, at Christmas-time, did not go so well, though he read her the lecture on Balzac he was taking round the States. James complained to Howard Sturgis that the little house was claustrophobic, and that 'Teddy was more sandwiched between' them than at Lenox. He said quite different things about staying there to Wharton than he did to Minnie Jones, his 'alternative' New York hostess: 'I think I rather *did* make the point at Suite 884 (at the last) that I *couldn't* come back there.' He made elaborate secret arrangements with Minnie to prevent his having to go back to the Whartons, and Minnie teasingly called him Célimare, the '*bien-aimé*': a character in a French farce wanted by all the women. (James loved the names other people gave him, as well as the nicknames he gave them: for the Bourgets he was always 'ce cher Jems'.) James and the Whartons made an impressive sight to the unacquainted: a young bookseller at Scribner's bookshop remembered seeing them in the shop, James 'overhauled by Mrs Wharton under full sail' and the three 'moving down the avenue, James on one arm, Teddy on the other', and 'in this formation, sticks flashing, skirt whipping, with a somewhat spirited mien, the august spectacle receded'.[24]

James was back at The Mount at the end of June 1905, just before his return to England. The weather was fine, and they drove to Ashfield to visit the Nortons, on back roads, through out-of-the-way villages, past Becket Mountain. It was the beginning of their motoring-jokes. During James's October visit to The Mount, Teddy Wharton had bought his first car, a large showy Pope-Hartford. In the summer of 1905, Teddy was involved in a row with the local car-dealer, trying to trade in the Pope-Hartford for an even showier Pope-Toledo, but the new car never arrived ('I want my money', Teddy wrote threateningly), and they were instead driving an 'indefatigable' but unidentified motor. It amused James, and Wharton, to call the cars after characters in George Sand's circle of lovers and friends, one of their enduring fascinations. 'I know of no such link of true interchange as a community of interest in dear old George', James would write to her in 1912, thanking her for sending him the *Life* of Sand by Wladimir Karénine (with Sand's descriptions of her 'amours' to a friend of Chopin's marked by Wharton for James's attention). Reviewing the book in 1914, James suggests that Sand's 'art of life' disproves the 'homely adage' that 'we may not both eat our cake and have it'. They never got tired of discussing dear old George's sensational sex-life, and James loved calling the cars George, or 'Alfred' (de Musset), or Pagello/Pagellino, after the Italian doctor who was briefly George Sand's lover. By November 1906 he was calling Wharton's car her 'Vehicle of Passion'; later, it would become 'Hortense', after Hortense Allart, the French woman of letters with as colourful a love-life as her friend George Sand.[25]

They both found it intensely pleasurable, driving together through the New England countryside that hot summer, talking away as they went through the little villages and up the hills, chauffeured by Cook, 'prince of Pagellists', protected by hats and veils and rugs. After the eighty-mile trip from Ashfield to Lenox in June ('via Goshen, Williamsburg, Florence, Northampton, East and South Hampton, Westfield and Becket Mountain') Wharton told the Nortons that James had called their drive 'a bath of beauty'. James described it ecstatically to his brother William: 'I greatly enjoyed the whole Lenox countryside, seeing it as I did by the aid of the Whartons' big strong commodious new motor, which has fairly converted me to the sense of all the thing may do for one and one may get from it . . . if I were rich I shouldn't hesitate to take up with it.'[26]

It was their most relaxed, happy American time. Wharton was poised for her great success with *The House of Mirth*, James was looking forward to finalising his American impressions and embarking on the great project of his revised editions. The letters he wrote to her that autumn from England, though still addressed to Mrs Wharton, mark a definite shift in their intimacy. On 8 November 1905, for instance, he starts, charmingly and typically, with his excuse for not having written more: so many letters aren't *fair*, 'and I have wanted immensely, where you are concerned, to *be* fair'. He has been waiting till the final instalment of *The House of Mirth* came out to praise it, and he does, generously, but (as usual) with a sting in the tail: 'It is better written than composed.' To make that kinder, he at once goes on: 'I wish we could talk of it in a motor-car.' But he cannot stop himself pursuing the 'deadly difficulty' of what she has taken on, the '*roman de moeurs* in America'. Lily is 'big and true', but Selden is 'too *absent*'. But she knows that already, he adds. (How would this have felt to her? Half crushing, half flattering?) Then he jumps on to some new French novels, with a sharp account of Bourget's latest. Then, news of friends that he knows will touch her closely. He has seen Minnie and Trix, who is not looking so well. Trix ought to adopt his current fad, the Fletcher regime (which James swore by for years and which involved chewing your food to a pulp before swallowing: an irresistible analogy for the late prose-style Wharton herself found so indigestible). He is to visit Mrs Humphry Ward, whom (unlike Mrs Wharton) he finds almost impossible to read, and whose love of fame they both caricatured. He asks for news of dear Walter Berry, whom he always pointedly mentions. Then, his own work; he is writing up his 'Sensations' of America, and confides in her: 'Though I *shall* rejoice when it is over, I meanwhile quite like doing it.' He reverts, lyrically, to their drives, their 'flights' and 'swoops' in the Pagello (and has she read the latest 'lurid' account of George Sand and her daughter?). A melancholy memory of their parting from Norton at Ashfield (it would be the last time James saw him) leads him on to sympathy for the shocking news of Ethel Cram's accident. He urges her, not for the last time, to 'come out with Pagello' and buy a country house in England. In his next letter, he thanks her for the photograph she has sent him, the now well-known publicity portrait of 1905, of Wharton dressed up in furs and foaming lace, reading a piece of paper. You must be reading your press-cuttings, James teased her, 'so that you look thoroughly in possession of your genius, fame and fortune'.[27]

Their next trip was not so successful. The Whartons were in Paris in March 1906 and they were planning a trip to England to make some Easter visits. 'Do make them, so that we can talk about them', James urged her. They swept him up in the middle of a West Country excursion, meeting at Wells on 1 May, after much arranging and rearranging on his part. But the new Pagello (a second-hand 15 h.p. Panhard, bought by Teddy in April) was playing up, and the weather was terrible. Wharton and James went by train to Gloucester and then in pouring rain to Ross-on-Wye, Monmouth and Malvern. It was too wet to see Tintern Abbey, and James went back to London, 'discouraged', as Wharton noted. (He was also, she observed, in a state of acute anxiety about his brother, because of the San Francisco earthquake.) Once he had left, she added pointedly, in her diary, 'the sun came out'. She caught up with him a few days later in London – they went to see a new Sargent painting together, and to Windsor to see Howard Sturgis. Then the Wharton caravan moved on to France, for their first, successful French 'motor-flight'. Wharton boasted to her friend Eunice Maynard:

> We have not only 'scoured the plain' like 'swift Camilla' but climbed mountains and descended precipices, without being sick or sorry for a moment . . . We raced around England for a fortnight, and then . . . came back to the continent, and starting at Boulogne, rushed thro' Normandy and Touraine down to this beautiful, wonderful Auvergne, one of the most enchanting motor-grounds one can imagine – if only the rain did not pursue us! . . . We go up everything at a gallop!'[28]

James was filled with envy at their visit to George Sand's house, where he had never been: 'I said to myself suddenly: "They're on their way to Nohant, d—n them! They're going there – they *are* there! . . . So you owe me the *récit* . . . How you must have *smelt* them all!"' Meanwhile he was writing caustically to Minnie Jones:

> They had, the W's, I thought, a rather frustrated, fragmentary, merely – motory time . . . Poor Célimare, always moralising on everything, only rather thanked goodness, as he observed, and during a few days here a little participated in it, that such fantastic wealth and freedom were not *his* portion – such incoherence, such a nightmare of perpetually renewable choice and decision, such a luxury of bloated alternatives, do they seem to burden life withal! However, I had some very charming and enjoyable, even if half weather-blighted hours with our friends.[29]

The Whartons rented George Vanderbilt's Paris apartment at 58 Rue de Varenne at the end of 1906. James was excited and apprehensive for them. It will be very interesting, he wrote to Minnie, to see what this 'pilgrimage' opens up, even if it only illustrates further 'the wild, almost incoherent restlessness of wealth'. To Paul Bourget, at this point Wharton's closest French friend, he described her as *obéissant aux lois de la pendule et du cheque-book*', and attributed the decision entirely to her, not to Teddy. (To a mutual friend in Paris he called her 'the great and glorious pendulum', 'oscillating' between countries; I was 'the pendulum-woman', she said proudly in *A Backward Glance*.) To her, however, he wrote: 'I applaud the free sweep of your "line of life" with all my heart.' As usual this came with a literary warning. Much as he had admired *Madame de Treymes* in the August *Scribner's*, she should not go in too much for the French or the Franco-American subject, James mused (writing to her from the Reform Club); she would do better to make the 'real field of your extension *here*'. With typical mischievousness, having just read the most Parisian of her books so far, he preferred the idea of her, just then, as a novelist of England.[30]

James was happy to accept the Whartons' lavish hospitality at the Rue de Varenne, and to travel with them. This visit of his, in the spring of 1907, was the longest time they spent together *à trois*. They had two weeks in Paris in March, with a great deal of Franco-American company at the Rue de Varenne – Morton Fullerton was among the visitors – which James greatly enjoyed. As at The Mount, he also liked cohabiting with the little dogs, Jules, Mitou and Nicette, those choosy, fussy characters, settling into Parisian life like their mistress. On 20 March they set out on a long 'motor-flight' through France, returning on 12 April, and then they had almost another month together in Paris. James finally left them on 11 May, for Italy and Hendrik. His role as pleased and grateful guest, his close-up view of the marriage, the intimacy involved in travelling together, and their mutual passion for and knowledge of France, deepened and complicated their friendship.

The long, rapid journey through France was ambitious, luxurious and absorbing. The latest Vehicle of Passion was a Panhard-Levassor, which Teddy had had closed in from the elements and fitted with an electric light.[31] All three adored its newfangled opulence, which James now more than ever turned into a metaphor for Wharton herself, her summonses to him her 'silver-sounding toot', her 'life-style', 'the wondrous cushioned *general* Car of your so wondrously india-rubber-tyred & deep-cushioned fortune'.[32] His account of their travels – and their cost to him – to his gossipy friend Jessie Allan, is a typical mixture of gratification and resentment (often felt by Wharton's guests).

> France seen in this intimate and penetrating way (for that's how we
> *are* seeing it!) is of a captivating charm . . . and my companions . . .
> are full of kindness, sympathy, curiosity and all the right elements of
> amenity and convenience – to say nothing of travelling arrangements
> (with servants sent on ahead by train everywhere to have our rooms
> ready and our 'things out'), which makes the whole thing an expen-
> sive fairy-tale. (As I pay my own hotel bills, of course, the mere being
> attached to such a party makes my charges particularly handsome –
> a proof again of the old story that it's one's rich friends who cost
> one!) But I blush for such sordid details in the face of my high
> entertainment.[33]

It was a big journey, of over two thousand miles, to make in three weeks. Even with empty roads and all hotels pre-arranged, they must have licked up the miles and done some pretty brisk sight-seeing. It was a far cry from the leisurely meandering and inconvenient train-journeys of James's six weeks' *A Little Tour in France* of twenty-five years before, which he published in 1884. And, though Wharton's itinerary retraced some of his steps, perhaps deliberately, she also wanted to see, and to take him to, places he had not written about. (After their journey James returned to his book and revised it.) They took a huge loop through France, starting from Paris, via Chartres, Blois, and – of course – Nohant, to Poitiers. George Sand's modest, dignified, rural, bourgeois house at Nohant (which Wharton was revisiting and introducing him to), where so many great men came to stay, set in amenable French countryside and closely surrounded by the church and the village houses, had a profound effect on them both. They were as one in their passionate interest, but it expressed itself in rather different ways. James was fascinated to be at the scene of the crime, the very place where, as he would write to her later, George Sand and her crew had 'pigged so thrillingly together'. Wharton's possibly apocryphal memory of the visit had him gazing up at the windows and wondering '"in which of those rooms . . . did George Sand sleep? . . . Though in which, indeed –" with a twinkle – "in which indeed, my dear, did she *not?*"' Her imagination was more inflamed by the marionette theatre, with its two hundred figures, and by the amazing fact that the woman who showed them round 'remembered, as a child, sewing the little dresses which George Sand had cut out!' She described the little theatre, with its 'wistful rows' of *commedia dell'arte* puppets (just as in

Wilhelm Meister) in *A Motor-Flight*. These were the kind of details she loved, that 'for a moment brought Nohant within touch'.[34]

At Chauvigny, they all sent a postcard to Charles Eliot Norton, thinking of his passion for late medieval art, from the 'wonderful little old church in Poitou', Saint-Pierre. Wharton particularly liked it for its haunting Romanesque carvings, the 'mysterious baleful creatures' reaching back 'to a dim and fearful world'. At Poitiers, Henry James decided to buy a hat. She remembered that

> almost insuperable difficulties attended its selection. It was not until he had announced his despair of ever making the hatter understand 'that what I wanted was a hat like everybody else's', and I had rather impatiently suggested his asking for a head-covering '*pour l'homme moyen sensuel*', that the joke broke through his indecisions, and to a rich accompaniment of chuckles the hat was bought.[35]

Teddy, perhaps, was left out of the joke.

From Poitiers, they raced down to Angoulême and Bordeaux, and then on to that extremely civilised, 'dapper' south-western town, Pau, 'like a comfortable little spa', as Wharton put it. From the terrace, 'that astonishing balcony hung above the great amphitheatre of south-western France', the distant Pyrenees had 'a disconcerting look of irrelevance, of disproportion, of being subjected to a kind of indignity of inspection, like caged carnivores in a zoo'. She may have practised this image on her travelling-companion, as they gazed out. James had never been to the south-west, and she particularly enjoyed showing it to him, especially as Teddy came down in Pau with a timely attack of flu. James and Wharton spent three days making excursions on their own together, including Lourdes, which they agreed on as 'loathsome' but fascinating. Then, on through the south-west – the mysterious, ancient, remote church of St-Bertrand-de-Comminges, Toulouse, Carcassonne, the Pont du Gard. Then, along the coast to Aix and Hyères, which she found ravishingly beautiful and enchanting. She would return. And then up the Rhône, via Avignon and Orange, and an important stop to admire Mme de Sévigné's princely home at the Château de Grignan (which James, travelling by train on his earlier journey, had not seen). Wharton at once began to turn her into a character in a novel, vividly imagining her, exiled so far away from Paris for the sake of her daughter, and consoling herself by 'deliciously ridiculing the pretensions of Aix society'. Then on into the magnificent countryside of Burgundy – Bourg-en-Bresse, with the church of Brou, Dijon, Vézelay, Avallon – with 'almost a sense of suffocation from the excess of suggestions received', Wharton told Charles Norton – and then back to Paris via Sens and Fontainebleau.[36]

Her pilgrimage through France covered a more conventional tourist's itinerary than her Italian adventures, but she found it quite as rewarding. They wrote with equal enthusiasm about the trip. Mr James is 'unfailingly delightful, wise & kind', she told Norton; and to Sally, 'Never was there a more admirable travelling companion, more ready to enjoy & unready to find fault – never bored, never disappointed, & never (*need* I say?) missing any of the little fine touches of sensation that enrich the moments of the really good traveller.' James wrote ecstatically to Howard Sturgis: 'My three weeks of really *seeing* this large incomparable France in our friends' chariot of fire has been almost the time of my life.'[37]

Her essays on their travels were published in the *Atlantic Monthly* early in 1908. It was a continuation of accounts, serialised in 1906 and 1907, of her earlier motor-flight 'from Rouen to Fontainebleau'. The last of the 1908 articles covered a shorter journey in north-eastern France, made in May 1907 with Teddy, soon after James had left them. The book which came out of these three French journeys, published in September 1908, *A Motor-Flight Through France*, does not mention James or his *Little Tour*. But their mutual interests, their companionship, their differences of opinion about what they saw, and the literary and historical knowledge they pooled on their journeys, all make their way into her narrative.[38] This brilliant and masterful little travel-book, in which Edith Wharton, a relative newcomer to France, claims it as her territory, is both full of James and free of him.

In his introduction to a 1995 edition of *A Motor-Flight*, the novelist Julian Barnes compares Henry James's more leisurely view of France ('a highly sophisticated man taking his sensibility, like some great dog, for a walk') with Wharton's more 'modern' tourism: 'a hastier flurry of sense impressions, a quicker mental satiety'. He notes, particularly, the difference in their response to the Pont du Gard (she finds it a sublime reminder of 'the tremendous tread of the Roman legions', James sees 'a certain stupidity' in its largeness) and to the church at Brou, which James admires and Wharton dislikes extremely, finding it, with its 'chaos of overdone ornament', 'a kind of superlative "Albert Memorial" in which regardlessness of cost has frankly predominated over aesthetic considerations'. Sometimes they are entirely in sympathy, most of all in their disapproval of restoration (to which they both allow Carcassonne as an exception). But at times Wharton seems deliberately to set herself against James's tastes. The differences between the two books are most marked at Poitiers and at Dijon. Both prefer, at Poitiers, the Romanesque church of Notre-Dame-la-Grande to the cathedral. But Wharton is, typically, fascinated by the exuberant Gothic detail of the carvings, which James, in his more generalised musings on 'the touching look that resides in everything supremely old', 'the waves of time' that have 'worn its edges to a kind of patient dulness', completely overlooks. No vague patina of time for her: 'There is, in especial, one small bat, with outspread web-like wings, so exquisitely fitted into its allotted space, and with such delicacy of obser-vation shown in the modelling of its little half-human face, that it remains in the memory as having the permanence of something classical, outside of dates and styles.' At Dijon, the younger James was disappointed, and found the famous tombs of Philippe-le-Hardi and Jean-sans-Peur 'of limited interest'; he much preferred his stroll in the 'little old Parc, a charming public garden', where he lingered for a good while on a bench, thinking over his enjoyment of France. Wharton makes a great point (perhaps they argued over it) of calling Dijon 'the astonishing town which seems to sum up in itself almost every phase of French art and history', and the tombs – so much better than Brou! – confirm her idea, which is worked at all through A *Motor-Flight*, that 'a touch of free artistic emotion will break through the strongest armour of stock formulas'.[39]

However much James had enjoyed himself, he did not want to do it again. When, after a summer and autumn at The Mount, Wharton sent her 'silver-sounding toot' in his direction, trying to get him back to Paris for Christmas 1907, he refused with elaborate excuses. He was beginning, now, to dramatise the contrast between their two lives in a way that would become familiar to her. She is the 'majestic' traveller displaying an 'almost insolent maîtrise [mastery] of life', dancing her 'complex minuet' on the Aubusson carpet, 'the dear old Crimson Carpet' at 58 Rue de Varenne, which James liked to use to sum up her 'glorious scenes' with 'Paris at your feet'. Meanwhile he was the 'unvarnished', reclusive, 'affectionate old superstitious Islander', resolved 'never, never, never' to 'cross the Channel again', hiding 'in the dim, if snug, care of my permanent *retraite*'. He wrote to an English friend that he could not '*ever* again attempt, for more than a fleeting hour, to lead other people's [lives]'. He knew he was sacrificing a front-row view of the 'phenomena' of Wharton's life, but (absorbed in the revision of his work for the New York Edition) he had his own life to get on with, 'very, very quietly'.[40]

A letter to her in Paris at the start of 1908 shows how they have moved on from host and guest to mutual confidantes and professional peers. What is 'admirably' and 'ideally' established between them, he says, is that they can take some 'reasons' and 'causes' for granted. But he also wants to make it clear to her what a labour his edition is, and how he feels it is 'going forth into a soundless void', and how important her praise of his Preface to *The Portrait of a Lady* has been: half-jokingly, he says he has 'blubbered' 'long & loud' over it. Excuses proliferate for not coming to see her, but this is not an artificial letter: he gives her a detailed account of the two plays he is 'pegging away' at: 'I loathe the theatre, but the drama torment-ingly speaks to me.' They were close friends now, and in the course of this year his letters to her – and, by inference, hers to him – become ever more intimate. In the difficulties and sorrows that lay ahead for both of them, they would do what they could for each other.

9

Friends in England

Soon after she read Henry James's letter of October 1908, Wharton was on a ship from America to England, after an unhappy summer at The Mount. She travelled with Walter Berry, on his way to a diplomatic post at Cairo, who annoyed her by flirting with all the ladies on board. That autumn, she consoled herself for her unsatisfactory relationships – her dismal, impossible husband, her slippery old friend, her treacherous lover – by plunging into English high society. James witnessed this triumphal progress with admiration: the 'Lady of Lenox' is having the 'Time of her Life', he told Walter in Cairo. She had a great deal to show off. *The Fruit of the Tree* had come out the previous autumn, there were new stories that year in *Scribner's* and a new collection, *The Hermit and the Wild Woman*, published in September; *A Motor-Flight Through France* came out as a book in October.[1] She was the famous, best-selling, well-connected American novelist, to whom doors opened.

For the next five years, from this autumn until the outbreak of war, England, and the possibility of an English life, became very attractive and interesting to her. Since 1906, Paris had been her second home, but only intermittently: she did not settle there until 1911. Life in England was, in these pre-war years, as much a habit for her as France would soon become. As her marriage slowly and excruciatingly unravelled, she was gradually deciding where to make her future home. James encouraged her in the idea of an English life. He loved the phenomenon of Wharton on her Parisian stage, but he fancied her too as a grand English hostess, living in some splendid old house in, say, Gloucestershire – perhaps not *too* close to Rye – a rival to Mrs Humphry Ward or Mary Hunter. And it could have been so. She did not know England the way she knew Italy, or was coming to know France, but she had been an enthusiast for English culture, landscape, gardens, literature and houses since she was very young. One of the purest moments of pleasure she remembered from youth (from 1880, the year the Joneses went back to Europe for her father's health) was in the National

Gallery. And some of her most excited tourist's letters of the 1890s were written to Ogden Codman from England, enthusing about the sights of Oxford (Christ Church, New College chapel) or the grandeurs of Wilton House and its Italianate gardens.[2] In 1903, back in Lenox after spring in Europe, she wrote to Sally: 'In England I like it *all* – institutions, traditions, mannerisms, conservatisms, everything but the women's clothes, & then having to go to church every Sunday.'[3] Many years later, she told her friend Elisina Tyler: 'That country & I were made for each other – but for the winter climate!'[4] From 1908 onwards, she visited England for several weeks in almost every year of her life, and in 1913 and 1914 she hovered on the edge of deciding to make a life for herself there, like Henry James.

There were two main models on offer for an English life. One was that of the aristocratic, land-owning, Liberal or Tory hostess, with her big houses in London and in the country, for networking, lionising, politics, hunting, and adultery. James had had rich pickings from that world for his novels for over thirty years. The other interconnected world was that of writers, artists, and their friends, mainly establishment figures in the arts, with their clubs and their dinners, their well-established social rounds and their country houses. James opened some of these doors for her, as Bourget did in Paris. They made a number of trips to magical English settings – to the haunting Tudor house of Brede (where once poor Stephen Crane had lived; she never met him), to Bodiam Castle, to Gloucester. She would never forget the day, in November 1908, that James insisted on taking her to Box Hill to visit George Meredith. Wharton was extremely reluctant to be introduced, and wanted to stay in the car – she hated 'human sight-seeing'. James bullied her into the house to meet the deaf and immobilised Meredith, in a small room that seemed full of people, including Meredith's daughter (Howard Sturgis's sister-in-law) and a nurse eating her supper. Wharton's embarrassment and discomfort changed to delight to find that Meredith was in the middle of reading her *Motor-Flight*. But she could not respond to his courtly, generous questions about it because he could not hear anything she said, and she stepped back to let 'the great bright tide of monologue' flow on in James's direction. Watching the 'nobly confronted profiles of the two old friends', 'I felt I was in great company, and was glad'.[5]

The shyness that held her back in the tiny house at Box Hill, where her relationship with James seemed, for a moment, to drop back to its earliest phase of being Master and disciple, did not affect her in the stately homes of England. Here she walked in expecting a welcome. She often found the company dull and parochial – but she liked this aristocratic English world as theatre and amusement. Percy Lubbock gives his picture of Wharton arriving at an English house-party where she knew the people well:

> I can see her still, rustling forward with her quick step, hitching her scarf round her shoulders, advancing into the midst of the vast hall and the scattered company with a smile of embracing familiarity, with flying looks and side-glances of understanding – with an air of amused and confident anticipation.[6]

A number of her hostesses were expatriate Americans with links to her childhood, like Adèle Grant from New York, now Lady Essex, with an Elizabethan house, Cassiobury, near Watford, full (to Wharton's delight) of Grinling Gibbons carvings. One of the (unhappily married) hostesses famous for large-scale, fashionable parties, the Duchess of Manchester, had been the Southern belle, Consuelo Yznaga, whom Wharton had known in New York and Newport. Wharton would use her story, decades later, in *The Buccaneers*.[7] The Astors, at their vast Thames-side estate at Cliveden, where Wharton visited in 1908 and took James in 1912, were also part of her old New York world: William Waldorf Astor had married the Virginian heiress Nancy Langhorne, who was on the way to becoming a notable hostess.[8]

Some of the aristocratic English ladies she met were known just for their charm, money, and social influence. The beautiful Lady Bective, for example, became a running joke in the Sturgis circle for adorability: Howard Sturgis turned 'bective' into a synonym for charming, with 'abective' or without charm – 'like you, dear Edith' – as its opposite.[9] The Ranee of Sarawak, née Margaret de Windt, unhappily married to the colonial governor Charles Brooke, the 'White Rajah of Sarawak', held court at Ascot; she was an old friend of James's, and had been Morton Fullerton's mistress nearly twenty years before, though Wharton may not have known that when she took tea with her. Some of them wrote a little, like the historian Lady Bughclere and the Duchess of Sutherland, who published a few novels, and Wharton was surprised to find this socially acceptable, as it had not been in her slice of upper-class New York.[10] Some were known for their cultural patronage. Gladys, Marchioness of Ripon, at Coombe Court in Surrey, was a famous patron of the arts, particularly for her support – was it more than financial? – of Nijinsky and the Russian ballet. James wrote nudgingly to Wharton that she should be as benevolent to Fullerton as Gladys was to Nijinsky: 'DO be so far as possible his Lady Ripon.' At her house, Wharton particularly relished meeting the charming, brilliant and flirtatious Harry Cust, editor of the *Pall Mall Gazette*. But she found

Lady Ripon herself 'amiable but not interesting'.[11] These sets overlapped a good deal, and at first Wharton seems to have skimmed across the surface of the complex social network. But she preferred to make lasting friendships, and three of these upper-class English hostesses, all about her own age, became particular friends.

One of these, Lady St Helier (or Lady Jeune) had an insatiable appetite for society, and seems an unlikely friend for the more reserved Edith Wharton. But they took to each other, and Wharton stayed at her house in London, at 52 Portland Place, and at her country house near Newbury. Susan Mary Mackenzie had been through two husbands by the time they met. Her first was a colonel in the Coldstream Guards (their daughter, Dorothy Allhusen, became friendly with Wharton in the 1930s). Her second, Francis Henry Jeune, Baron St Helier, had recently died. Her grand-niece Clementine Hozier married Winston Churchill in 1908; they were all part of the Liberal Asquith set. She was an avid hostess, and took it as praise if her guests said to her, on leaving her parties, where there had been as usual a great crush in the entrance-hall: 'Good-bye, dear Lady Jeune; your party has been such a success, nobody thought they could ever get upstairs.'[12] Wharton had some reservations about her social style: 'She was a born "entertainer" according to the traditional London idea, which regarded . . . the act of fighting one's way through a struggling crowd of celebrities as the finest expression of social intercourse. I have always hated "general society", and Lady St Helier could conceive of no society that was not general.'[13]

Portland Place was one doorway for Wharton into Edwardian society; another was Stanway, the fine old house, near Winchcombe in Gloucestershire, where Mary Elcho held court. Lady Elcho, née Wyndham, had married into the Scottish Charteris family, the Earls of Wemyss; her husband was a fiercely Tory MP, who became the tenth earl in 1914. She was the long-term mistress (or at least the intimate companion) of Arthur Balfour, Conservative Prime Minister from 1902 to 1905; her husband found consolation elsewhere, but they entertained amicably together. Her beautiful and talented daughter, Cynthia, married the Liberal Prime Minister Herbert Asquith's son Beb in 1910 (to her father's disgust); the family tree involved Tennants, Glenconners and Waughs. James knew them well. His first meeting with Balfour in the late 1880s, at a time when Balfour was a notoriously inhumane and repressive chief secretary for Ireland, elicited one of James's coolest accounts of the 'sports & brutalities' of the 'dense & brutal clan', 'the stupid thousands of "society"' of upper-class England, in which Balfour stood out like 'a prodigy of amiable heartlessness'.[14] Lady

Elcho was variously described as 'a lovely and captivating creature' and, by Mrs Humphry Ward, as 'strong and very simple, with a natural charm working through a very reserved and often harsh manner'.[15] She endured dreadful losses in the war – two of her sons, Yvo and Ego, were killed. Her daughter Cynthia recorded her mother's reaction to Yvo's death, in a diary entry which gives the tone of their class: 'She was wonderful, quite calm after the first moment of horror. About five minutes afterwards she said something so sweet and natural, just what one feels when one is dazed: "What a bore!"' In old age Lady Wemyss was vague and vacant, and Wharton became rather impatient with her. But they had a long and affable, though not intimate, correspondence. Not until 1934, having known her for nearly thirty years, did Wharton shift from 'Dearest Lady Wemyss' to 'Dearest Mary', and asked her to 'drop the Wharton in writing to me. I'd so much rather just be Edith.'

She returned to Stanway all through her life. It was (in Cynthia Asquith's words) 'built of time-tinged golden Cotswold stone. Approached through the arch of the beautiful Inigo Jones gatehouse, the west front of the house with its four wide sixteenth-century gables, numerous mullioned windows, and one huge oriel . . . closely overlooks the village church.' Lawns rose behind it to a stone pyramid. Inside, the house was shabby, draughty, and always full of family. Violet Bonham-Carter, Cynthia's sister-in-law, described it as 'icy and comfortless, but very attractive with stone floors and rush carpets, *most* beautiful windows of discoloured glass and a stage wind always whistling'. For Wharton, it stood for everything she most loved about English traditions and English country-house architecture.[16]

Among these grand Edwardian hostesses, the woman who comes most colourfully into focus, and who provided probably the closest model for a life Wharton might have imagined for herself in England, was Mary Hunter, a close friend of Henry James. Wharton first met her at her Italian spa, Salsomaggiore, where Mrs Hunter's name often figured in the lists of visitors alongside Lady Ripon and Mrs Wharton. Five years older than Wharton, as Mary Smyth (sister of the feminist composer and intimate friend of Virginia Woolf, Ethel Smyth) she had married a Northumbrian coal-miner's son, Charlie Hunter, who made a fortune from coal and screws, and was a Tory MP. Mary was famous for saying: 'I consider it my *sacred duty* to spend every penny I can of Charlie's money.' From 1909 onwards, they rented a large and beautiful house in Essex, Hill Hall, at Theydon Mount, on the edge of Epping Forest. They had a Yorkshire house, too, called Wemmergill. Mary entertained on a grand scale before and during the war, filling the house with artists, writers, and musicians. She and

Charlie Hunter divorced in 1913 and he died in 1916. She was John Singer Sargent's intimate friend, some even thought mistress. His paintings of her and her daughters hung in the house, and he found congenial company at Hill Hall: Percy Grainger, Monet, Sickert, the Italian sculptor Antonio Mancini, Jacques-Émile Blanche, and Rodin, whose bust of Mary Hunter is in the Tate Gallery. In 1914, visiting Hill Hall, James reported to Wharton – it was the sort of joke they liked – that Rodin 'had a sordid and *inavouable* little wife, an incubus proceeding from an antediluvian error'.[17]

James described Hill Hall to Isabella Gardner as 'a very vast and beautiful William-and-Mary (and older) house of a very interesting and delightful character . . . and though, in the midst of Epping Forest, it is but at ninety minutes' motor-ride from London, it's as sequestered and woodlanded as if it were much deeper in the country'.[18] The architect Philip Tilden, who knew the house well, called it 'a place of peace'. Hard to imagine, he said, that 'the worst end of London' was only sixteen miles away. The late-sixteenth-century house was architecturally fascinating: it had a French-style inner courtyard, a splendid eighteenth-century east front with giant columns and a grand pediment; and, spreading away from a long stone terrace at the rear of the house, a broad swathe of grounds, landscaped by Humphry Repton, looking over towards the church spire of the village in one direction and the trees of Epping Forest in the other, with London in the far distance. There were peacocks on the green lawns, fish-ponds and cedar-trees.

Mary Hunter was generous and hospitable, but accounts of her behaviour also suggest wilfulness and extravagance. She was a model, in some ways, of how *not* to behave as a chatelaine. Wharton found her a generous if ramshackle hostess. She described the social life at Hill Hall as quite the opposite of the Parisian *salons* she knew, 'with friends tumbling in unexpectedly from everywhere, extra seats being hastily crowded into the long dining-room, fresh provisions hurried to the already groaning tea-table, spare rooms prepared, messages telephoned, people passing in and out with a sort of smiling fatalism, no questions asked, no explanations expected, just a continuous surge of easy good-humoured life through the big house'. Mary could be mischievous and perverse: she took grapes to her sister Ethel when Ethel was on hunger-strike with the other suffragettes in Holloway prison in 1912. 'To dangle a bunch of grapes before her sister's eyes was both improper and senseless . . . "Never mind – I did it", Mary Hunter apologized.' Locally, she is said to have been unpopular in the village and punitive against poachers. She was prosecuted for hoarding food in wartime and managed to 'feed her guests on dressed crab throughout the war years'.[19]

Her alterations to the house, with the help of the architect Reginald Blomfield, were also criticised as reckless. Still, her interior decoration was spectacularly good, and Wharton, on her many visits there, would have been intensely responsive to this. The magazine *Country Life* ran a series of articles on Hill Hall in 1917, praising the dining room's panelled walls and ceiling taken from a Venetian house, the beautiful large cupboards lifted from Italian sacristies, and the fine Italian guest-beds. Jacques-Émile Blanche remembered sleeping in a bed on 'a raised platform, enclosed by a partition with leaded panes of glass ... hidden behind loosely falling Florentine damask draperies, which made the room look like sepulchres on Good Friday in Catholic churches'.[20] The wallpapers – mid-Victorian and Chinese – were particularly good. And there was a fine and well-stocked library. Hill Hall's most exciting secret was not discovered until the 1930s: a series of sixteenth-century wall-paintings copied from Italian models, one roomful illustrating the story of Cupid and Psyche, another some violent Old Testament scenes.[21] Wharton may have slept in a guest-room with Cupid and Psyche plastered over on the walls.

The original Hill Hall formal gardens had been swept away by Capability Brown-style landscaping. *Country Life* noted 'masses of lavender bushes against the house, but no flowers', and 'great overgrown box-trees' in terra-cotta jars all along the terrace. But Mary Hunter had no interest in gardening, and 'used to walk away if women talked of flower-beds'.[22] There was, though, a flower-loving visitor to Hill Hall, the remarkable English woman gardener, Ellen Willmott, whose famous gardens at Warley Place were not far away. 'Miss Willmott' was scathing about Mary's horticultural inadequacies: 'Now' (she was said to have remarked) 'if Mary could have planted the beds with dressed crab and red cabbage, with large patches of cheese straws ... !'[23] Gertrude Jekyll called Miss Willmott 'the greatest of living women gardeners'. As well as the famous Warley gardens, she created gardens in Italy and – as Wharton would – in the south of France, near Aix. She was a self-taught genius, who started her own printing-press for her seed catalogues, spent all her money on collecting rare plants from abroad, and insisted on naming every new species after herself. In old age she was temperamental and eccentric. Wharton would vividly describe to Beatrix Farrand a visit to Warley in October 1923, which, like Hill Hall, was by then undergoing a post-war decline:

I managed to see Miss Wilmot's [*sic*] garden (& the lady herself!) while I was at Hill. Mrs Hunter took me over with two or three people that

Miss Wilmot knew (or knew about), so she paid not the slightest attention to *me*, & I was glad she didn't, as I felt half asleep, & couldn't
remember the name of a single plant! However, it all interested me *afterward* – you know how one sometimes wakes out of these trances, & finds
that one has mopped up something with one's spongy brain? The little
enclosed gardens must have been lovely when they were less jungly, but
the wild garden that happens suddenly in the lawn in front of the house
I thought appalling. The plants, of course, were most interesting, & all
in glowing health – & considering she has reduced her staff almost to
the vanishing point it's a marvel to see such vigour of vegetation. I wish
I could go back there some day with a clear brain, & a notebook.[24]

In wartime, Mary Hunter turned Hill Hall into a hospital for wounded
soldiers. After the war, her finances failed, and though she bought the
house, having been renting it, in 1923, she struggled to keep it up, and
had to sell in 1925. Onlookers were not entirely sympathetic: 'Mary Hunter
was being reduced to opulence', one said.[25] But her last years were difficult
(Ethel Smyth's letters to Virginia Woolf in the early 1930s are full of Mary's
troubles) and Wharton was among those who gave her some financial help
before her death in 1933.[26] Mary Hunter was an important figure for
Wharton, and she also played a part in Wharton's relationship with James.
Whenever Wharton visited England, delicate negotiations would go on
between the three of them. James liked the comforts of Hill Hall and
thought Mary Hunter stylish and gallant, but he also found her, like
Wharton, an insistent hostess: she could be 'rather a menace'.[27] Percy
Grainger noted how 'submissive' James was to Mrs Hunter – as in this letter,
of 12 May 1910:

If your motor will kindly meet us at the station I think the rest will be
very simple. I take the liberty to bring with me my tiny servant – he is
24 years old but extremely diminutive and utterly modest and self-
effacing. He can easily sit small by the chauffeur, and our small luggage
can go on the top . . . We throw ourselves thus on all your indulgence.[28]

James took a more demanding tone in making arrangements with
Wharton:

I have your telegram & am sorry, but would the 5th or the 7th do you
any good? – by which I mean enable you to do *me* any . . . I shld. be
able to manage *them* – but not, I fear, anything else. (I think by the way
you *did* say the 7th, alas, is taken. I might strain a point for the 8th –
with your company for my guerdon).[29]

But he flatters them both – here, to Mary: 'I owe you renewed, intensely emphasised thanks for all your beautiful offices of friendship . . . Everything you do is *en princesse*.'[30] Combining his two princesses was often a compli-cated business, and his letters dance an elaborate minuet between them: 'Howard' (he wrote to Wharton in November 1911) 'is *impossible* to me for Saturday–Monday, because I have promised, up to me eyes, to go to Mary Hunter, at Hill, for that occasion, & because she intensely wants me to induce you to come . . . It will be very pleasant, with a good many people, I infer – & I am absolutely booked for it.'[31] Sometimes he praises Mrs Hunter to Wharton ('with whom you will really always find, I think, a good rela-tion immensely easy & pleasant');[32] sometimes they exchange views on how poor Mary's judgement can be ('she makes, ever, such large & earnest & expensive preparations for being tremendously wrong'),[33] and sometimes they agree that Hill could be Hell: 'I accept the high philosophy of your view of the abysmal Hill.'[34] At the same time he enlists Mary Hunter in an intensifying battle to keep Wharton at bay, as here, in July 1912:

My dear Mary . . . If you haven't (as you won't have had time to) already written to Edith Wharton on the matter of her coming to England next month, will you very kindly stay your hand a little as regard marked emphasis or pressure in urging her to do so, and even bear lightly in case you should happen to have the air a little of speaking in a friendly and sympathetic way (so natural to you!) for me too. It isn't a bit that I shan't be absolutely delighted to see her if she comes of her own impulse and movement, but one will be a little in a false position (and it's as if you would be a little so too *for* me), if one puts out a very persuasive hand to draw her over. The reason of which is simply *this*: that if she does come she will come wound up for an extensive *motor-tour* of these islands, in which she will look to me, (very graciously and generously look) to accompany her. Now it happens that . . . very much continuous and sustained and long-drawn-out motoring . . . is the worst thing in the world for my health. If I could see her without that formidable question coming up it would be *admirable*! – but in fact it *always* comes up . . . I haven't said Do, *do* come and we will tour over England, Scotland and Wales . . . I think that what my little plea really amounts to is that you should most kindly not appear to throw *me* at all into the scales of persua-sion. That is all that is asked of you by your so precautionary and devoted old HENRY JAMES.[35]

When Wharton reminisced about Mary Hunter's relationship with James, she said, a little sharply: 'she could not resist baiting her hospitable hook with a name like James's'.[36] Probably there was some jealousy; probably she was aware that James sometimes played them off against each other.

The literary lionising which gave Wharton her entrée into English society was also what she found least attractive about it. As she said of her meeting with Meredith, she disliked 'human sight-seeing'. Still, it intrigued her to go to J.M. Barrie's first nights, or to sit next to the historian George M. Trevelyan, or Thomas Hardy (shy and uncommunicative), or the theatre critic William Archer, or Max Beerbohm, whom she relished. The writers she met could not be called bohemians: Rhoda Broughton, H.G. Wells, Alfred Austin the poet laureate; the melancholy and solemn Alice Meynell (whose husband, Wharton thought, treated her with amazing deference); Mrs Humphry Ward, magisterially hospitable at 'Stocks', her country house at Tring, which Wharton would come to know very well; Edmund Gosse, who took her to lunch at the House of Lords. Wharton's letters to Gosse showed her at her most formal:

> Dear Mr Gosse, If by chance you are disengaged on Thursday next would you lunch with me at 1.30ish in this squalid little hotel, where the food is not too bad, though not, alas, as good as it is reputed to be? It would be a great pleasure to see you again before I leave at the end of the week, & if you will come I will try to find one or two sympathetic people. Yours very sincerely, Edith Wharton. Perhaps you would be kind enough to have your answer telephoned.[37]

This was her tone with her English acquaintances, a largely conservative group. Good manners were expected. The overbearing and scandalous Irishman George Moore, to be found at all the big houses, was, according to Wharton, a 'monstrous, incredible, and repulsive ... bounder'. 'I had to annihilate him', she was pleased to report.[38] The younger generation were not much in evidence: it seems characteristic that Wharton turned down an evening with the novelist May Sinclair in order to meet the Duchess of Sutherland. All her friends, including James and Mrs Ward, were against the striking miners in 1910, and were anti-suffrage. Ethel Smyth was regarded as a liability. James wrote to Wharton in 1912 about 'the window-smashing women': 'Mary Hunter's sister, Ethel Smythe [*sic*] has just been condemned to two months' hard labour ... M.H.'s depressed & *obsessed* sense of her cold, her inanition ... & her isolation is somehow aggravated by her thinking she really quite deserves it.'[39]

In her retrospective accounts of pre-war English society, Wharton is at her blandest and grandest. (She is evasive, too, making it seem as if she and 'her husband' were making a stately progress around the aristocracy, whereas in her 1908 'season' Teddy was absent, thrashing around in America.) Anecdotes of various 'friendly tables', 'big dinners', 'charming little manors' and 'week-end parties' abound. At the time, too, in her letters to Sally, she is clearly boasting: 'Next week I am going up to Lady St Helier's where a long stream of engagements awaits me'; 'Today we have a lot of people, rather amusing, at luncheon'.[40] But under its warm varnish of nostalgia, A Backward Glance can also be sharp about the parochialism and philistinism of English society. In general, she found the people in 'the big politico-worldly society' 'rather narrowly confined to their own particular topics', with 'general conversation as rigorously excluded as general ideas': unlike in Paris. The American woman who has married into the Faubourg St-Germain warns Undine Spragg, in The Custom of the Country, that she will have to keep up with the conversation at Paris dinners: 'You're as handsome as ever, but people here don't go on looking at each other forever as they do in London.'[41] England in Wharton's fiction figured as an alien though very beautiful old landscape (coloured by her reading of Jane Eyre and Kipling, Trollope and Wilkie Collins, The Turn of the Screw and The Golden Bowl), in the shape of haunted houses inimical to American visitors ('Afterward', 'Mr Jones'), or farcical displays of upper-class behaviour. Over thirty years after her entry into English ruling-class society, Wharton embarked, with the energy and high spirits of a much younger writer, on a devastating satire on its stupidity, prejudice, and complacency. Yet even at her most satirical, from the juvenile Fast and Loose to the late, unfinished Buccaneers, a deep surge of romantic, historical feeling always comes through for 'the great rich garden'[42] of England.

Wharton felt most at home in England, not in the big houses, but with a small group of male friends whose centre of attraction was Henry James, and whose social refuge was Howard Sturgis's house. She was forever driving between Lamb House in Rye and Queen's Acre in Windsor (always known as Qu'Acre, and variously spelt Qu'acre, Quacre, and Quaker). She remembered both places with deep affection. Though she was condescending about James's 'anxious frugality' at Lamb House ('the dreary pudding or pie of which a quarter or half had been consumed at dinner reappeared on the table the next day with its ravages unrepaired'), she liked her welcome there:

> There he stood on the doorstep, the white-panelled hall with its old prints and crowded book-cases forming a background to his heavy loosely-clothed figure. Arms outstretched, lips and eyes twinkling, he came down

to the car, uttering cries of mock amazement and mock humility at the undeserved honour of my visit. The arrival at Lamb House was an almost ritual performance, from those first ejaculations to the large hug and the two solemn kisses executed in the middle of the hall rug.[43]

She felt the same confidence of a welcome at Qu'Acre. The homosexual or bisexual circle of men who paid homage to James in his last decade were among her closest friends. Wharton took several kinds of comfort from this group, which made up to her for her marriage, for the unreliability of her male intimates, Berry and Fullerton, for the rather formal friendships in her French life – and for the unsatisfactoriness of her family life in childhood. They all loved reading aloud, swapping quotations and favourite authors, going to exhibitions, seeing new and old plays, visiting stately houses, gardens, and historical sites, exchanging knowledge and enthusiasms. Taste and connoisseurship often slid into preciousness in this group: they liked to think of themselves as a little band keeping up standards in a vulgar world. But they all had a passionate, discriminating interest in what was 'best' in culture, and wanted to talk about it.

None of these men was a sexual challenge to her, though she could be flirtatious, wifely and imperious with them all. They were all emotionally involved with James, and found her, too, compelling, even attractive. They gave her admiration, attention, affection and gossip. She knew they teased and caricatured her and rolled their eyes about her, but she (mostly) liked their affectionate, mischievous private codes and nicknames. The letters between them all made much of one another's foibles; they loved it when one of the group acted up especially extravagantly to the character constructed for him or her. But they worried and fretted over each other too, and tried to take care of each other.

This was the only family where Wharton felt secure. But it must be added that this group of friends surrounding James was a snobbish group of minor talents, imitating the Master's manner without his genius. Their attitudes would affect Wharton's posthumous reputation, which was fixed by them, for many decades, as the 'piece of work' they all enjoyed admiring and resenting, the Master's domineering friend, and his inferior. Gaillard Lapsley, in his notes towards the memoir he never wrote, referred to 'her master Henry James'. In Percy Lubbock's book on Wharton, she appears (her friend Kenneth Clark noted in 1947) as a 'polished American Duchess'. But inside her 'inner circle', as Clark said, she took off her 'formidable armour': 'she laughed, told scandalous stories, read poetry and talked about the art of writing.'[44]

She would certainly have taken her armour off with Howard Sturgis, the mother-hen of the group. Qu'Acre, which he had bought in the 1890s, when he was in his forties, a chintzy, cosy, Victorian house designed by Champneys, on the edge of Windsor Great Park, near Eton (where Sturgis had been to school) was the group's main meeting point for years. It had a very good cook, and was much more comfortable and roomy than Lamb House. (James was always comparing his inferior premises and provisions, 'the lean yield of my tenth of an acre & no cow!') Sturgis had inherited a fortune from his Boston banking family, and he needed friends to spend it on. He had emerged only in middle age, 'as lost and helpless as a child', as Wharton observed, from a suffocating relationship with his beautiful and domineering mother. Though a big handsome man, he was frail and sedentary, and liked to be looked after. An addicted host, he would sit at the centre of his friends embroidering, pouring tea and gossiping, sometimes 'drawing broad pictures in his talk with penetrating strokes, with liberality and ribaldry', sometimes sitting and stitching 'demurely, never missing any flicker of thought in those around him', while they all – as James put it – feasted on him 'like a richly sugared cake'.[45] Wharton found him affectionate and endearing, but also contradictory: an 'odd blending of the whimsical and the shrewd . . . at once tender and malicious, indulgent and penetrating'. He lived for years with his Eton tutor, and then with William Haynes-Smith, known as the Babe. 'Howdie' financed the Babe, who inherited Qu'Acre, and in return he was the minder, and presumably at some point the lover. Sturgis's friends found him taxingly unintellectual: 'While Howdie read The Golden Bowl, the Babe studied form in the Pink 'Un.' But Sturgis too played dumb around Wharton and James: 'Now please remember', he would cry out, 'that I've read nothing, and know nothing, and am not in the least quick or clever or cultivated.'[46]

In fact he had written three novels, all mildly homoerotic and autobiographical. Wharton's copy of one of them, All That Was Possible, was dedicated, in 1903, to 'Mrs Edward Wharton, from a humble recruit to the profession she adorns'. She thought well of his third novel, Belchamber (1904), and recognised Sturgis in the character of 'Sainty', the sensitive inheritor of a stately home, who prefers needlework to hunting, and is 'feminine and maternal', 'a kind of old granny'. Like the hero of her first published poem, 'The Last of the Giustiniani', or Odo Valsecca, Sainty is too delicate and introspective for his inherited role; he cringes before the 'barbarism' of his tribe, the English landed aristocracy. The scene of his unfortunate wedding, which seems to take place through a 'mist' of unreality, gave Wharton an idea for Newland Archer's wedding in The Age of

Innocence, and Sainty's ambitious and unfaithful wife Cissy lent something to Undine Spragg. Wharton tried unsuccessfully to get Scribner's to publish *Belchamber*, and when it did eventually come out she wrote an essay on it which praised the ruthless Cissy 'as an extreme expression of a selfish nature's unwillingness to pay for what it has got'.[47]

James and Wharton had known Sturgis, separately, for many years, through his Boston family, and James had become very close to him in the late '90s. 'I *could* have lived with you', James told him in the 'yearning' style he favoured for his dearest men-friends. Arthur Benson, the Eton-and-Cambridge man of letters who was one of the links in the group, noted in his diary the love between Sturgis and the Babe, and between Henry James and Hugh Walpole, but was prim about James's physical expressiveness with his friends: '[James] lived in an atmosphere of hugging.' This was not Gordon Square: there was no Lytton Strachey here to talk about semen and buggery (as the young Bloomsbury Group were doing at the very time Wharton was making herself at home at Qu'Acre and Lamb House). Homosexual desires, in this upper-class Anglo-American, euphemistic older generation, were unvoiced or concealed. Until the late 1920s, there is no evidence of Wharton's speaking explicitly about homosexuality. But she liked the atmosphere of Qu'Acre, brimming with innuendo and anecdotes.

Hugging and yearning went along with satire and malice. Sturgis was cut to the quick when James criticised *Belchamber* savagely, though he was well known for tearing his dearest friends' books apart. Wharton, much more robust than Sturgis, often felt James's withering lash. She wrily recalled his issuing his verdict on an 'admirable' story of hers which, he could not resist adding, was 'conventionally treated'; or congratulating her for having, in 'Les Metteurs en Scène' (her French translation of her story 'The Introducers'), 'picked up every old worn-out literary phrase that's been lying around the streets of Paris for the last twenty years'. Wharton had her own reservations about James's work, and was resistant to, even amused by, these flashes of criticism. But Sturgis was devastated and never wrote another word (except an unpublished story about a younger writer crushed by a famous novelist).[48] James could be equally ruthless about Sturgis's domestic habits, as in a letter to Wharton of 1909 on 'the congestions of Quacre, the spell of Berlin wool, or the repleteness *before* (even) dinner, or the wallowing of Misery [Sturgis's dog] on the Sofa'.[49] This was part of an interminable flow of caricature that went round the group, reaching a climax of flurry and outrage when Wharton was at her most demanding. James's caricatures of Sturgis to Wharton are as nothing compared to his accounts to Sturgis of *her* behaviour – sometimes almost by the same post. A letter to Wharton asking her to drive him over to Windsor is followed by a letter to Howard saying that Wharton is insisting on taking him there:

> Our famous and invincible Firebird [they had all been to see Stravinsky's ballet, danced by Diaghilev's company] announces herself to me as flashing down here on Friday A.M. and culling me, as she passes, to present me as a limp field-flower that evening at Qu'acre. I needn't tell you that I can only, for the occasion, be all predestined limpness, and where the devastating angel catches me up there I shall yield to my fate – and where she produces me again there (since it's to be at Qu'acre) you will yield to yours.[50]

Everyone else picked up the tone. So Sturgis would write to Gaillard Lapsley, in imitation of James:

> The Firebird perched here for a brief fortnight; having announced that she had a long unoccupied Summer to dispose of & meant to bestow most of it on Henry and me. She came to the end of all either of us could be or do for her in about ten days. Picked us over, left us pros-trate, and was gone again to France in the twinkling of a motor . . .[51]

Gaillard Lapsley was one of the friends (like Morton Fullerton and Percy Lubbock) whom she met through James. His very name sounds like a Henry James character's. Gaillard (pronounced 'Gillyard') was born in 1871. Nearly ten years younger than Wharton and thirty years younger than James, he was to them a youthful version of the cultured New England expatriate, and he was also part of the Cambridge network which linked Arthur Benson, Sturgis, Lubbock and James. A thoroughly Anglicised Rhode Islander, he had been educated at Harvard and Cambridge, taught at Stanford as a medieval historian and took a Fellowship at Trinity College, Cambridge, in 1904. (In retirement, he went back to the States.) He published sparingly and drily, mainly on constitutional history – The County Palatine of Durham in 1900, An Essay on the Origins of the House of Commons in 1925 – and edited some essay-volumes, one on the historian F.W. Maitland, and one on The America of Today in 1918. He and Wharton were friends for over thirty years, and she made him her literary executor. By the 1930s Lapsley was a deeply conservative Cambridge historian, living for decades in the same comfortable college rooms, protective and guarded about the famous writers he had known. As her executor, he made sure Wharton's archive stayed under wraps for many decades. This makes it hard to imagine him as the witty young man who attracted James in the 1900s. 'What a beautiful, charming, & interesting being!' James exclaimed to Wharton – even if there was perhaps something a little 'carton-pierre', *papier-mâché*, about his magnificent looks. James wrote Lapsley some flirtatious letters, here sympathising with an illness: 'In fact, dearest Gaillard ... I *like* to keep you a little before me in the passive, the recumbent, the luxurious and ministered-to posture ... Lie as *flat* as you can ...'[52] Wharton met him in 1904. He remembered her then as

> slim, smartly dressed in pale blue with some kind of rose coloured trimming on the bodice, extremely décolleté, her hair parted in the middle, curling slightly at either side and fastened in a small chignon on the nape of her neck ... a few good jewels ... a rather shabby thumbstall on her right hand which she had injured or lamed in writing ... Her face was already worn and looked tired in repose, which it seldom was ... [with a] metallic radiance.[53]

By 1908 she was writing to him affectionately about his plans and his health, and with increasing frankness about the situation with Teddy, her work and her feelings. We do not have his letters to her, but they were clearly sympathetic and attentive. He managed to stay friends with both Wharton and Percy Lubbock after they fell out, and to put up with Walter Berry, whom he disliked. He and Wharton shared a passion for Housman, whom Lapsley knew, and for early Proust. As fellow expatriates, they enjoyed swapping ridiculous American headlines and clippings on her favourite topics ('felony, adultery, robbery, murder') which confirmed what they both agreed, after the war, was the 'chaos là-bas' of modern American life.[54]

One of Lapsley's closest friends was the writer Percy Lubbock. In the Qu'Acre days, Percy – young, eager, literary, and oozing with adulation and respect – was a favourite with James, and then with Wharton. Lubbock would become a Jamesian authority on 'the craft of fiction', a sporadic novelist and essayist, a writer of little sketches of people and places, and the guardian of the posthumous lives of Benson, James and Wharton; also, more surprisingly, a married man and Anglo-Florentine villa-dweller. As a young man, he belonged to Benson's Eton–Cambridge world – Benson appointed him librarian of the Pepys Library at Magdalene College. He was in his late twenties when Wharton met him at Qu'Acre, a sensitive, susceptible young plant, full of 'quivering young life', as James put it fondly to Wharton, forever falling in love with hopeless youths. His lanky Englishness was part of the attraction for the Anglo-Americans. His own sense of the value of Englishness comes through clearly in his 1920s sketch of the Shropshire rector's-daughter-turned-novelist, Mary Cholmondeley: 'She belonged, she never ceased to belong, to her stock, her county, her England

– an England of the English, far beyond earshot of the many strange accents in our hearing today.'[55] James coyly described 'dear blest' Percy's pen as his 'fine young wand', and Percy was, always, utterly devoted to James. But he did write a novel in 1925 called *The Region Cloud*, about a great artist as 'a powerful vampire, who needed young admirers to feed his incredible egotism'.[56]

At the start, he was 'rather terrified' of Wharton: 'What a woman', he wrote to Lapsley; she 'paralysed me by seeming to expect that I was going to be clever and intelligent all in a minute'. He fell in at once with the prevailing Qu'Acre tone about 'the Angel' and her domineering ways ('Edith actually *dares*, bless her heart, to lecture me about the moral danger of changing plans one has made – This from *her* – I ask you!')[57] but for a time he was her closest protégé, travelling-companion and guest. His thank-you letters were almost self-caricaturing in their obsequiousness: 'Dear & great & dear lady, I wish I could tell you, & I know I can't tell you, just what it was to me to have those days with you . . . It very seldom happens to me, in this country (except indeed at Trinity) to be with anyone who understands what I am doing or trying to do . . .'[58] And he confided his troubles, personal and literary, to her, as if he was trying to turn into Henry James:

> The torture of the wish to be making something, building up some piece of real true work, just about touches the verge of the unendurable at these moments . . . I . . . only burst out a little to you, which is natural, you understand how the burden of weariness drops on the spirit sometimes so *very* like an extinguisher – yet without putting it out really . . .[59]

Presumably she lent a sympathetic ear; but none of her letters to him survive.

Lubbock had been at Cambridge with a wealthy English boy called John Hugh Smith, who was the youngest, the newest arrival, and Wharton's most unqualified admirer, in the group. She met him at Stanway, and immediately after that at Qu'Acre, in 1908. He was twenty-seven, and had a career in banking. They embarked on a friendly, even flirtatious correspondence, in which 'Mr Smith', who rapidly became 'Mr John' and 'My dear John Hugh', copied out Yeats's poem to Maud Gonne ('When you are old and grey') for her, and worried that such a 'brilliant' person as she was, being so 'exceptionally kind' to him, made him self-conscious, especially under the glittering eyes of Sturgis and James. '*Was* I – or were *you* – all the complicated things you say?' she replied nicely, and directly. 'It seems to me so much simpler! I'm afraid I always go with outstretched hands towards any opportunity for a free & frank exchange of ideas.' Her letters to this new friend were intimate, even needy: exchanging views on Flaubert and Stendhal, telling him what to read, urging him to work harder, confiding in him about her difficulties with Teddy, and calling on him for sympathy and understanding:

I wish I were the unclouded luminary you imagine, describing serene curves through the seventh heaven; but I am, as you see, a shabby, close-to-the-ground, and frequently eclipsed planet, and just now I'm exceptionally dim, and need to have the 'optical glass' of sympathy fixed on me to be at all visible . . .[60]

She took to him, and he to her. James wrote nudgingly about whether it would be safe for her to talk about her new admirer in front of his nephew – and gave him this warning: 'Ah, my dear young man, you have made friends with Edith Wharton. I congratulate you; you may find her difficult, but you will never find her stupid, and you will never find her mean.'[61] John Hugh Smith's youthful crush on her graduated into a steady, undemanding, lifelong friendship. In later life, he became the most reactionary and old-fashioned member of her regular circle.

Some letters survive between Wharton and John Hugh Smith, and many more between her and Lapsley, which bear witness to the affectionate, confiding, steady tone of these long friendships. No correspondence remains, though, with Robert Douglas Norton, an Englishman who was one of Wharton's closest lifelong companions, often to be spotted in later photographs of picnics in France or on the terrace at Hyères. Wharton met him at Lady Elcho's at the same time as she met Hugh Smith, and twenty-five years later they were back at Stanway together, shedding a tear over the old visitors' book. In that quarter of a century, Norton, who clearly had private means, moved from working at the Foreign Office and in the City, acting as a private secretary to Lord Salisbury, and attached to the British Embassy in Paris (where, it was said, '*il a pris le goût de la culture et de la société française*'). After James's death, he moved into Lamb House. In his fifties, he gave up other occupations to pursue his passion for water-colours. His landscapes and scenes from his travels (in Greece, in Provence, in Morocco, on an Aegean cruise with Wharton in 1926) were praised for their delicacy and subtlety. One reviewer wrote that 'whether he is painting the Parthenon in luminous violet shadows against golden yellow highlights, or the depth of blue sea along orange-cragged St Tropez, or the mellowed stone face of an old gate in Aix-en-Provence, he never loses the sense or feeling of his liquid medium'.

Norton's personal relationship with Edith Wharton is somewhat mysterious. He was four years younger than she and outlived her by nine years.
Some of her aristocratic friends thought she was in love with him: 'Beau
Norts' was tall, dark and handsome, seemed to have been entirely at
Wharton's service for months on end after she moved to France, and went
with her on many of her travels when Walter was unavailable. But if their
devoted intimacy remains obscure, their closeness of opinions and constant
interchange of ideas is evident from Norton's book on art, *Painting in East
and West* (1913), and from their joint anthology of poetry, published after
her death. Norton's comparison of eastern and western traditions in painting
(reviewed in *The Nation* as a 'grave and thoughtful study') spoke eloquently,
in the tradition of Ruskin, about the spiritual and visionary qualities in all
great art, and our 'desire, even an anxiety' for something to transcend a
material and mechanistic universe, in a utilitarian age. His writing is lush,
Paterian, neo-pagan, aesthetic:

> To the artist it is given to hear voices and see visions withheld from
> other men; his world is peopled, like Hellas of old, with the living imper-
> sonations of godlike beauty. For him the Oread still haunts the mountains,
> and by the flowery margent of secluded streams the Naiads sport at dawn
> ... Where'er his path lie, it is beset, as by some enchantment, with
> never-failing visions of beauty. Even in squalid cities, amid the unsightly
> erections and mechanical devices of modern industry, they do not fail
> him.

Though her writing is never as flowery as this, she shared his interest in the
artist's innate feeling for beauty. Norton insists on the 'principle underlying
all Art' as 'the subordination of detail to general effect'. In *The Writing of
Fiction* (1925) she too would insist on 'the first assumption' in the art of
fiction as 'the need of selection' from all the available details: this is 'the
first step towards coherent expression'. They share quotations as well as
opinions. *Painting in East and West* is full of allusions to the writers Wharton
also admired. One of Norton's quotations about the artist's apprenticeship
is from the Goncourt brothers' *Journal*; the same quotation (from 1 February
1866) is underlined by Wharton in her copy of the *Journal*: '*Apprendre à voir
est le plus long apprentissage de tous les Arts.*' Another is from Shakespeare's
Sonnet 15 ('When I consider everything that grows'): 'the huge stage presen-
teth nought but shows / Whereon the stars in secret influence comment'.
This sonnet is the first in their choices from Shakespeare in *Eternal Passion
in English Poetry*. Norton ends his book on art with a long quotation about
beauty from Plato's *Phaedrus*, on the need for men to understand 'that the

beauty of the inward is more honourable than the beauty of the outward form'. Wharton's 'Commonplace Book', the collection of quotations she kept, intermittently, all her life, contains long extracts from the *Phaedrus*, including Socrates's prayer: 'Beloved Pan, and all ye other gods who haunt this place, give me beauty in the inward soul; and may the outward and the inward be one.' The same passage is underlined in her copy of Plato's *Dialogues*. These overlaps, in lieu of any more personal evidence, show what a close, long, companionable interchange these two friends shared. But at the time she first got to know the 'inner circle', the prospect of such settled habits of life and calm friendships would have seemed remote.[62]

In 1909, James and his friends were watching the 'Angel of Devastation' with alarm, but also with exhilaration. Exhausting as the Firebird was, the show she provided was also 'beautiful & interesting & damnable'. Howard Sturgis invented a menagerie of bird-life for James's amusement – who at once passed it on to Wharton. She was 'The Editha Steelpennata, called by the French l'Oiseau de feu: it is perpetually on the wing ... it lays a large egg & sometimes two every morning. Its true home however is the Empyrean where it soars & floats ... Once it gets its claws into a victim it seldom lets go till life is extinct.' Howard was the Quacker goose ('in the process of becoming extinct ... quite useless for breeding purposes') and James was the 'fat Hen or Ryebird', who 'lays a quantity of beautiful grass-green eggs, much prized by epicures for their exquisite & delicate flavour'. To the 'Bird of Paradise' herself, Sturgis wrote excitedly: 'Run your race. Fly your flight. Live your romances. Drain your cup of pleasure to the dregs.'[63]

But joking was beyond Henry James at the start of 1910. As Wharton settled into her new, long-term Paris home, James was in the grip of profound depression. Everything he had been labouring over – his plays, the great New York Edition – seemed to have failed. He could not eat or work. His brother and sister-in-law came to look after him, but William James was very ill himself. Wharton was appalled by James's condition, and asked his new secretary, Theodora Bosanquet, to send her bulletins; it was the beginning of a useful connection. She did what she could, encouraging Fullerton to write an appreciation of the New York Edition, whose neglect she took to be the main cause of James's collapse.

James went away with William and Alice James to Switzerland, and then to America. Though he slowly recovered, it was a tragic journey: William died in August. James wrote to Wharton from Boston that he was 'living here more & more *into* the difference in the world & the whole aspect of life [made] by the extinction of his so cherished & dominant presence'.[64] There was a profound note of tenderness in his letters to her at this time. In spite of his frequent exasperation, their mutual troubles were pulling them close: 'I cling to you, dearest Edith, through thick & thin, & believe that we shall find ourselves in some secure port together yet.' 'The great thing is that we always tumble together – more & more never apart; & for that . . . we may trust ourselves & each other to the end of time.' She kept these words, and copied them into her memoir many years later.[65]

That tenderness and intimacy continued, though in the years leading up to the war – some of the most difficult years of Wharton's life – it was often strained. The prospect of having Wharton living in England, which began to take shape in 1913, filled him with interest but apprehension. She very nearly bought a house near Hill Hall called Coopersale, which would have allowed her to combine the roles of Mary Hunter and Ellen Willmott, since it was not only a very substantial house, made for enter-taining on a large scale, but also had grounds of breathtaking possibilities. A mile or so away from Hill Hall and just outside Epping, the house stood off a country road which ran up a hill towards the tiny Coopersale village and church, with hilly woods and farmland all around and wide views towards Hill Hall and beyond to London. It was a large, three-storey, L-shaped, eighteenth-century villa, with a handsome red-tiled roof and a clock-tower, and a large lake below it. It must have had at least thirty rooms, quite as big as The Mount. Inside, there were fine wooden doors with panelling, stone floors, wooden beams, a splendid wooden staircase, and much stucco and panelling in the upstairs rooms. There were some unusual features, too: a pair of eighteenth-century painted Negro figures, 'blackamoors', on the staircase landing; some African heads and figures on the stucco frieze of one of the bedrooms (clearly one of the family had had some trading connection with Africa), a 'witch's bottle' set in the wall by the big brick chimney in the kitchen, to protect the house, and a room with a beautiful painted doorway. Henry James, in one of several letters in the autumn of 1913 encouraging her to buy the house, spoke of its 'broad acres' and its 'painted chamber'.[66]

And it was the 'broad acres' that would have been the main attraction. Coopersale had been an enormous estate of over 400 acres, owned by an inter-married Essex clan, the Archer-Houblon family, since the seventeenth century (one of whom was the founder of the Bank of England), who had built the house on their land and used it mainly as a dower house. A succes-sion of lonely widows, spinsters and estranged wives had lived there. At least one of these single ladies knew how to have a good time: in 1895 the lake had frozen over, and the chatelaine of the day, Miss Harriet Archer-Houblon, hung fairy lights and Chinese lanterns round the lake, invited skaters to come and held an ice carnival with fireworks.

When Wharton found it, the house had been unoccupied since 1898. The contents were auctioned in 1908 and in 1912 the estate was divided and put up for sale in lots, with the house and 116 acres as one. (This included a working farm, outbuildings and stables.) The sale catalogue, which Wharton would have read, gave a brief account of the grounds, noting that 'The Pleasure Grounds and Gardens are inexpensive to maintain . . . and include Shrubberies, Lawns, Shady Walks, exceptionally good walled-in Flower and Kitchen Garden with Round Pond, Potting and Tool Sheds, Vinery, Green House, Forcing Pits, etc.' Behind this brief account lay a garden-history which would have been of immense interest to this prospective buyer. The Essex garden designer Adam Holt was hired to improve the grounds of Coopersale in 1738. His design involved a sloping parterre in front of the house, a kitchen-garden, ponds, a bowling green, walks and avenues. Later additions included a serpentine walk round the lake, and a little Italianate garden.

This was a place for entertaining and gardening on no less grand a scale than at The Mount – or Hill Hall. But because the house had stood empty for so long, it needed an enormous amount of work; Wharton described it as 'dilapidated'. This was a big undertaking, and it was not cheap. Wharton offered £6,000, and it seems from one of James's letters that she had to raise this by £500. But the prohibitive consideration was not the immediate cost of the sale but the amount of work that would need to be done to the house and the grounds, and the very high British income tax levied on foreign residents.[67]

Excited letters went between the friends: James, Mary Hunter, Minnie Jones, Howard, Wharton herself, and her newer friends the Berensons, for about six months, while she decided whether or not to take what she was beginning to call 'my Epping house'. Was she going to 'Cooperbuy', as Sturgis put it? James was extremely keen on the idea. Think how good it would be 'for your work', he urged her: it would give her 'a more *settled* current of production, especially flowing between big thick green English banks . . . what a protective virtue & salutary strength I conceive that you may look to Coopersale to fling about you'. Joking about Qu'acre as a benign version of the House of Usher, he hoped that 'the House of Coopersale' would rise 'with all its cracks bouché & its dark tarns tidied'. To Minnie Jones, James said that he thought Coopersale was 'slowly closing round her', and added that he *'liked'* the thought of 'Edith being so near'. In a long letter to Mary Hunter, he imagined having Edith Wharton as a neighbour:

> It's delightful to me to hear of Edith W's seeming really caught up by Coopersale. If she *is* really captured I shall envy you the near view (from your commanding position,) of the operations there – they will certainly be so interesting, so brilliant. You don't know her till you have seen her as builder and restorer, designer, decorator, gardener. I only say to myself a little 'But *after* –?' However, I think the charm of the place itself answers a good deal that question ... She will be to you anything but a *banal* or negative neighbour.[68]

But – as James put it in his next letter to Mary about this 'romantic possibility' – 'She will do as she will do'.[69] Wharton changed her mind, and let Coopersale go. And James waited to see what would happen next.

Their friendship had settled into a drama, or a game, in which they had their appointed roles to play; but it was also a battle for control. And who was in charge? When Wharton took him for a grand country-house visit and insisted on sending him home with her chauffeur when he was taken ill, she was the masterful one. But when James caricatured her and his anxieties about her visits, he was fixing her as a character: he was the master. It is almost always she who writes first (is it the person who writes, or the person who replies, who is more in control?). Most of his letters are in response to hers: 'I'm horribly in arrears with you & it hideously looks as if I hadn't deeply revelled & rioted in your beauti-ful German letter'; 'I am now sufficiently *raffermi* to follow up ... my appreciation of the exquisite ingenuity & the truly divine subtlety of your letter'; 'You are very interesting this morning in spite of being rather tragic'.[70] Those tantalising absences, her vanished letters, are part of the battle for control, too: he burns her words, she keeps his: who wins?

Between 1911 and 1913, Wharton was involved in a series of plots on James's behalf. All were motivated by generosity on her part, but also by a desire to make her mark on his life. They had mixed results. First, she tried to get him the Nobel Prize for Literature, which had never gone to an American. Letters flew (she was excellent at this kind of plotting) all through the early months of 1911 between Wharton, Barrett Wendell, William Dean Howells, Edmund Gosse, and some eminent American historians, to gather support for 'a big appeal to present to the mysterious Swedish committee'. James did not know about it. (Wharton would know about her friends' attempts to do the same thing for her in 1927, but did not have high expectations for herself, partly because of what had happened with James.) In November 1911, she was 'aghast & pale' to find the prize had gone to the popular Belgian playwright, Maurice Maeterlinck. If the Nobel Prize committee was looking for best-sellers, she wrote bitterly to Edmund Gosse, 'it is evident that several hundred candidates will have precedence over ours, & that unless dear Henry James can get a few hints from Mr Barrie or the Bensons, our struggle will be vain'. She clearly wanted the honour for James mainly for financial reasons: 'He is undoubtedly worried about his future, & this material anxiety is not helping him to get well.'[71]

Her next plot, at the end of 1911, also had a generous motive. She commissioned Sargent to do a charcoal drawing of James, and he sat for it in January and February 1912. This was not the first time she had been involved with a portrait of James; his visit to Paris in 1908 had been dominated by the sittings she had arranged for him with the fashionable portraitist Jacques-Émile Blanche. When James left Paris, he had seen a full-face portrait which made him look 'very big & fat & uncanny & "brainy" & awful'; but when it was shown in London in November he found that Blanche had transformed it, from photographs he had taken, into a magisterial profile which James – and Wharton – both liked. The Sargent drawing was not initially a success – 'he finds me difficult, perverse, obscure' – and had to be redone. But James, though a willing sitter, was reluctant to fall in with her plan that she give him the picture. Hold on, he told her (as he often wanted to tell her): 'Wait, in short, *wait*, WAIT!'[72]

James could not prevent her next act of generosity, which was a closely kept secret between her and their publishers. On 27 September 1912 Charles Scribner wrote to Henry James offering him an advance of $8,000 for 'an important American novel' – an extraordinary advance for a novelist whose recent royalty statements had been so poor, who was nearly seventy, and not in good health. 'It seems strange to me', James wrote, perceptively, to his agent James Pinker. Scribner reassured him that there was no catch, and he accepted the deal: the first half of the advance was paid in March 1913. It seemed to him like a rather frightening 'fairy-tale of fortune'.[73] What he did not realise (or if he did he never said a word to anyone) was that Wharton had arranged with Scribner (with whom her own relations were now rather turbulent) to have the money paid out of her own royalties, and to keep it a secret. She was convinced that the main source of James's depression at the start of 1910 was his sense of professional failure and his low income, and ever since her distressing visit to him then she had been trying to think of ways of improving his situation. This one succeeded admirably, and the secret was kept. 'I feel rather mean & caddish', Scribner wrote to her: 'Please never give me away.'[74] Her act has come to symbolise everything good about her friendship with James. Yet it is ironic that the 'big American novel' for which he accepted the advance was the unfinished *Ivory Tower*, which cast a cold eye on Wharton's wealthy American world. Ironic, too, that her next, and last, attempt to help him financially, which coincided almost exactly with the payment of the secret advance, was a disaster.

This plot was supposed to be a secret too. James's seventieth birthday was on 15 April 1913. His English friends planned to give him a 'golden bowl', and to have his portrait painted by Sargent. About three hundred subscriptions were raised, none of more than £5, to buy him a silver Charles II porringer and dish and to commission Sargent. James knew about the plans, and refused to receive the portrait as a gift. Sargent would have to be paid (in fact he passed his fee on to a young sculptor who did a bust of James) and James would be the custodian, only, of the portrait, which he willed to the National Portrait Gallery. (Sargent's eloquent full-face picture of James duly took shape later in the year; in December, James sat next to it for three days in Sargent's studio while their friends flocked to see it; a year later it was knifed by a suffragette in the Portrait Gallery.) Wharton felt that James's American friends 'would always regret not having made a "geste" of the same kind'. A parallel scheme could be set up, with the difference that James would spend the money on whatever he chose, perhaps 'some handsome old piece of furniture'. With advice from Walter and Gaillard, she circulated a proposal in March, to raise $5,000 from James's American friends 'for the purchase of a gift, the choice of which would be left to him'. The letter was marked 'private and confidential', but William Dean Howells told James's sister-in-law Alice, who told her sons, who told James, by which time the proposal had come to sound like the raising of an annuity for his impoverished old age.

James was filled with 'unmitigated horror' and immediately cabled his nephew Bill to have the scheme put a stop to, following it up with an outraged letter: 'A more reckless & indiscreet undertaking, with no ghost of a preliminary leave asked, no hint of a sounding taken, I cannot possibly conceive – & am still rubbing my eyes for incredulity.' The idea of a 'crude raked-together *offrand* of a lump of money' raised from a large number of people, not all of them his intimate friends, was 'simply intolerable' to him. If only they had offered him 'a modest piece of plate or suchlike', that would have been acceptable.

The letter he wrote to Wharton about this has not survived: it must have been one of the very few she did not keep. Whatever James wrote to her, she was tremendously upset. 'My trip has been completely poisoned by

Henry's letter,' she wrote to Gaillard. 'There was nothing on earth I valued as much as his affection – I can never get over this.' She had to write to all the subscribers, cancelling or returning their donations. Publicly, she insisted that 'unfriendly misrepresentation' had prevailed. To closer friends she was beside herself about the breach of trust by Howells and the 'ultra-righteous' tone taken by Mrs James (who would hold Wharton at arm's length again, during and after James's death; the New England widow did not approve of the Parisian divorcée). James was as upset as she was about their breach: 'The sad part of the matter is that I fear I have incurred the grave reprobation & almost resentment of the friend [who launched the attempt] . . . really one of the best friends I have in the world.' He told Lubbock in mid-April that he was sorry about the quarrel. Lubbock told Lapsley: 'I asked if they weren't straight again now – he said "Not *yet* – but we shall be."'[75]

Wharton has been much blamed for this farrago: it is a good example of how her character fell into the hands of James's devotees. Edel reproaches her for having been 'guilty of a failure in empathy – and in strategy'; Fred Kaplan says she 'blundered into a project that might have damaged their relationship'. Her own view, for which there seems to be just as much evidence – that she had no intention of raising a sum of money to help him out, that James was misinformed and over-reacted, and came to 'regret' this 'very much' – has not prevailed. After his birthday, James circulated a formal letter of thanks to all his English friends for their gifts, with a list of names. As a way of healing the rift, he added to the list the names of some of his closest American friends. Wharton would have been cut to the quick had she not been included. It was a roll-call of all the friendships she shared with James: Berry and Fullerton, Bourget and Du Bos, Sturgis, Lubbock, and Lapsley, Norton and Hugh Smith, Mary Elcho and Mary Hunter and Lady St Helier, Walter and Matilda Gay, Edmund Gosse, Frederick Macmillan, John Sargent. Among the many English names appeared that of Virginia Woolf: one of the rare links between these two great women writers of different generations and nationalities, who neither knew nor admired each other.[76]

In spite of the public gesture, a three months' silence followed between James and Wharton. She broke it, and he responded with a charming, explanatory, appeasing letter, signing off: 'Yours, dearest Edith, with constant affection always'. They had made it up. But though he praised *The Custom of the Country*, which was running in *Scribner's Magazine* during 1913, he could not resist identifying her with its rapacious and restless heroine. 'Don't wholly & Undine-like abandon your waiting, wondering, refuge-in-literature-taking, & always fundamentally infatuated old compagnon de route.'[77]

War broke out, and everything was changed. Wharton abandoned her English plans and plunged into the work that had to be done in France. She saw James twice, briefly, before she left, in August and September 1914; it was their last good time together. But their letters, in the last year of their friendship, took on new energy. Ill, and confined to England, he was beside himself with anguish, 'sick horror' and rage at 'this crash of our civilization', 'the utter extinction of everything'. He did what he could, and followed every turn of the war with intensity and passion, criticising anyone who seemed insufficiently 'fanatic' or involved, and telling her of 'the fantastic force, the prodigious passion, with which my affections are engaged . . . & my soul is in the whole connection one huge sore ache'.[78] She and the 'inner circle' were impressed by 'this martial truculent Henry'. But this was as nothing beside his admiration for what she was doing in Paris. All the things he found exasperating about her now became 'gallant & magnificent'. He wrote not just to her but to others about 'Edith the transcendent'. He kept her war letters and showed them to his friends: 'The sense they give me of your heroic tension & valour is something I can't express.' The same old jokes persisted about her incredible energy and his abject passivity (when he wanted to show her how active he was being in her support he signed off 'Yours all bustlingly'), but transformed from caricature into veneration: 'You're magnificent & I am thrilled, & can't sufficiently rejoice in you & be proud of you.'[79]

By September 1915 James was very ill – angina attacks, stomach pains, weakness, breathing difficulties, depression – and in what would be his last letter to Wharton, on 22 September, he spoke of 'having the most damnable difficulties'. These were terrible last months for him, and Wharton would always feel that his horror and grief at the war exacerbated his illness. Theodora Bosanquet (as promised in the crisis of 1910) began to send Wharton health bulletins. At the beginning of October, Wharton came over from France to see him, staying at Bucklands Hotel in Brook Street. They met for dinner at Robert Norton's house on the evening of 3 October, but she found him not the 'Henry' she knew. Bosanquet called to give her a fuller report, and noted in her diary that Wharton, in an over-heated hotel room, was wearing 'a very elegant pink negligée . . . a cap of écru lace trimmed with fur', with manicured hands and 'good arms' emerging from 'very beautiful frills of sleeves'. She had 'good eyes and a strong mouth', but Bosanquet 'wasn't as much charmed as I ought to be'. A week later,

James was burning his papers and letters – not for the first, but for the last time – including, presumably, many from Wharton. On 2 December, he had a stroke. She heard from Gaillard that he was reported to have said 'So here it is at last, the distinguished thing!', as he was falling. Thereafter he was paralysed and incoherent; Bosanquet told Wharton: 'He was speaking about you on Thursday – his last conscious day.' He continued to dictate – passages in which he appeared to think he was Napoleon, and one in which he seemed to be going on a trip with Edith Wharton: 'We squeeze together into some motor-car or other and we so talk and talk that what comes of it . . .' Even after he ceased dictating, his hand still 'moved across his bedcover as if he were writing'.[80]

Regular reports came from Bosanquet. Wharton said goodbye to him in her heart, writing to Gaillard (and citing another of their mutual heroes, Housman): 'Yes – all my "blue distances" will be shut out for ever when he goes. His friendship has been the pride & honour of my life.' But there was still help to be offered. In 1913, she had paid towards James's nursing;[81] now she wanted to offer whatever help she could, though Bosanquet was being frozen out by the arrival of James's family. Wharton felt for Bosanquet, and even before James's death was offering her a new post as her secretary, though there were three 'difficult conditions':

1. Living in Paris, where you wd. probably be lonely at times.
2. Speaking & writing French easily – do you?
3. Having to begin work at 9 a.m. – & having to do queer odds & ends of things for me – a muddle of charity, shopping & literature.

James would have enjoyed the terms of this offer, which Bosanquet turned down, pretending she knew no French – 'too alarming a prospect'.

James died on 28 February 1916, and heart-broken letters went between the friends, as from Wharton to Lapsley: 'Let us keep together all the closer now, we few who had him at his best.'[82] Have him at his best she may have done, but a good deal had remained unknown and unspoken. There were things – to do with each other's work, with sex, with their deepest feelings about each other – that they very probably never talked about, and the last of these was James's final act of war-time solidarity with his country of adoption. When he took British citizenship on 26 July 1915, he said nothing about it in the letter he wrote to her that very day, and she did not write to congratulate him. 'I dare say my American friends *will* be shocked at my step', he wrote to Sargent, and Wharton was one of them. She thought it was 'a mistake . . . rather puerile, and altogether unlike him'. Years later she regretted not having written to him about it.[83]

But it brought up, acutely, at the very end of their friendship, the issue of nationality and expatriation that dominated so much of their conversation. They had disagreed in the past about Americanness: Wharton's admiration for Roosevelt was not shared by James; and Roosevelt thought James the worst kind of spoilt 'bolter' from America. James made his choice for Europe and for England long before Wharton, and watched her making hers with sympathy and fascination. He was always telling her that she suffered from not having 'a Country of your Own (comme moi pour exemple! [sic])'. When he first read her he wanted her to be the American Balzac of her time that he could not be. Later, he liked to imagine her as an English Mrs Wharton, making the same choice that he had, and turning her cool eye on English manners and habits: 'The real field of your extension is here.' He was sad that she decided not to settle in England in 1914. But he understood why. Just at the moment he was becoming a British citizen, she was being a heroine in France. And it was as a French heroine that he most enjoyed her.[84]

Though their meetings were mostly in England, with Anglo-American friends, their longest journey together was their discovery – his rediscovery – of France. The only letters he kept of hers were about France. Their literary exchanges were extremely Francophile – she claimed in A Backward Glance that she had introduced him to Proust – and their French literary chat slid easily and often into suggestive gossip. French literature, and the sex-lives of French writers like George Sand, Alfred de Musset and Hortense Allart, was their cover – as in their motor-car jokes – for erotic innuendo.

James cast Wharton as the star of a French play. He wrote to her as if they were both half-French, or playing at being French, shifting in and out of a distinguished brand of Franglais, their letters laced with French jokes and codes and word-play. Thinking of the heroine of a romantic play of the 1890s by Rostand, La Princesse Lointaine, he hailed her once, when she came back from her travels to Paris, as his 'Dear Princesse Rapprochée'. He loved to greet her, and to wish her good-bye, in her adopted language: 'goodbye and à bientôt j'espère'.[85] 'Goodbye, dear grande viveuse. Keep rising above (you do it so splendidly); yet drop some day again even to your faithfully-fondest old Henry James.'

PART II

10

Mme Warthon

One of the few letters from Edith Wharton which Henry James kept, written in September 1912 from 'Château de Barante, Dorat, Puy de Dôme', gave a vivid account of what they liked to call French 'Shatter-Life'. She was visiting the grandson of Prosper de Barante, who had been 'the friend, lover, cousin, correspondent . . . of nearly everyone in the de Staël–Récamier group'. To her great excitement, her host, who had a magnificent library and manuscript collection, had shown her letters from Madame de Staël, the author of *Corinne* (a novel based on the love-affair between de Barante and de Staël), and from other writers in this brilliant early-nineteenth-century circle, including Madame Récamier, Chateaubriand and Benjamin Constant (author of *Adolphe*, and another of Madame de Staël's lovers). She had also seen letters of Rousseau's and of the novelist Prosper Mérimée's. Before arriving at the chateau she had paid a (dreary) visit to the Bourgets, and called on the French ambassador Jusserand, who had a '*maison familiale*' in the Lyonnais. She was going on to the eastern Pyrenees, and then back to Paris. The letter ('very beautiful & wonderful, very splendid & *interesting*', James thought) is supremely in charge of its French materials. No wonder James congratulated her, in his reply, on her 'leading the great life in your great way'.[1]

Her French adventure began in Paris in 1906. She knew it of old, of course: settling there was a Jones family tradition. Lucretia died there in 1901, and both Wharton's brothers settled there.[2] Though Wharton did not have an address in Paris until 1907, she had been writing about the city for years. The first time she used Paris in her fiction was in 1893, in 'The Lamp of Psyche', in which a New Englander, adoringly married to a Parisianised dilettante, discovers he is a coward who avoided the Civil War. Paris, here, is the stage for all the pleasures the rich, discriminating expatriate can ask for: 'Delia thought tenderly of the mellow bindings, the deep-piled rugs, the pictures, bronzes, and tapestries; of the "first nights" at the Français, the eagerly discussed *conférences* on art or literature, the dreaming hours in galleries and museums, and all the delicate enjoyments of the life to which she was returning.'[3]

Wharton's American Parisians always fall on one or other side of a divide. They respond to the city's aesthetic lesson, like Vance Weston in her late novel *The Gods Arrive*, who senses through the beauty of Paris 'the fine vibrations of intelligence',[4] or they exploit it as a luxurious resource. Those who use Paris only for conspicuous consumption are those who frequent the 'Nouveau Luxe', Wharton's fictional version of the Ritz, which stood for everything she disliked about vulgar, nouveau-riche Americans in Paris. The 'Nouveau Luxe' comes into many of her fictions, always to show up a superficial, ostentatious life-style. Its perfect customer is Undine Spragg in *The Custom of the Country* (1913), who plunges avidly into pre-war Paris, hearing the city's 'immense orchestral murmur' only as the accompaniment to her appetite for gorgeous things, for social advancement, for variety and pleasure. Paris symbolises for her 'the glare and movement of her life', all done here as a rush of insatiable, unfocused activity:

> Every moment of her days was packed with excitement and exhilaration. Everything amused her: the long hours of bargaining and debate with dress-makers and jewellers, the crowded lunches at fashionable restaurants, the perfunctory dash through a picture-show or the lingering visit to the last new milliner; the afternoon motor-rush to some leafy suburb, where tea and music and sunset were hastily absorbed on a crowded terrace above the Seine; the whirl home through the Bois to dress for dinner and start again on the round of evening diversions; the dinner at the Nouveau Luxe or the Café de Paris, and the little play at the Capucines or the Variétés, followed, because the night was 'too lovely', and it was a shame to waste it, by a breathless flight back to the Bois, with supper in one of its lamp-hung restaurants, or, if the weather forbade, a tumultuous progress through the midnight haunts where 'ladies' were not supposed to show themselves, and might consequently taste the thrill of being occasionally taken for their opposites.[5]

Undine and her circle, anticipating Dick Diver's motley crew of hedonists, twenty years on, in Fitzgerald's *Tender is the Night*, impose a commercial imperialism onto the native culture. The idea of a self-engrossed American tribe exploiting, but not participating in, the civilisation which is hosting it, comes back in her novels of wartime France, *The Marne* and *A Son at the Front*, where the American community takes centre-stage, and in her post-war novels about Vance Weston, where Paris, with its 'fine vibrations of intelligence', is the setting for an American writer's aesthetic education.

Wharton mocks the parochialism of her Americans in Paris, like the lady do-gooders bent on 'teaching France efficiency' in *The Marne* ('We must carry America right into the heart of France'), or the international 'loafers' in *A Son at the Front* 'enclosed together, all of them, in an unreal luminous sphere, mercifully screened against the reality'. This type recurs: the Boykins, in *Madame de Treymes*, 'had created about them a kind of phantom America . . . a little world sparsely peopled by compatriots in the same attitude of chronic opposition to a society chronically unaware of them'.[6] Wharton's more interesting Americans are changed by being in France. But she hardly ever shifts the vantage-point to look at how the French characters have their lives altered by the influx of the Americans.

Her French readers came to think of her as an American who loved France and whose novels brilliantly explained America to the French. The critic Edmond Jaloux, in his 1925 book of essays on foreign writers, *Figures Étrangères* (dedicated to Walter Berry, '*grand explorateur des paysages littéraires*'), writing on *Au Temps de l'innocence*, noted that it would give French readers '*une idée plus juste, mais qui les étonnera, de certains Américains*'.[7] But when she wrote non-fiction books about France – *A Motor-Flight Through France*, *Fighting France*, *French Ways and their Meaning*, all serialised in American magazines – she thought of herself as providing an education about France for Americans. In all these books, Wharton presents herself as 'an outsider familiar with both races'.[8] Paris is at the centre of these non-fiction books. Though *A Motor Flight* ranges widely through France, Paris is its point of departure and return:

> These miraculous escapes from the toils of a great city give one a clearer impression of the breadth with which it is planned, and of the civic order and elegance pervading its whole system . . . To start on a bright spring morning from the Place du Palais Bourbon, and follow the tide of traffic along the quays of the left bank, passing the splendid masses of the Louvre and Notre Dame, the Conciergerie and the Sainte Chapelle . . . and cross the Seine at the Pont d'Austerlitz, getting a long glimpse down its silver reaches till they divide to envelop the Cité . . . to follow this route at the leisurely pace necessitated by the dense flow of traffic, is to get a memorable idea of the large way in which Paris deals with some of her municipal problems.[9]

In her writings on France, her emphasis is always on 'continuity'. France is 'grown-up'; America, by contrast, is infantile. (It is the same in *The Custom of the Country*.) French civilisation is 'so much older, richer, more elaborate and firmly crystallised' than that of America. And the typical qualities produced by that old civilisation are 'taste, reverence, continuity and intellectual honesty'. In *French Ways and their Meaning*, Wharton applauds the strict French observances of protocol, the 'ritual view of politeness', distinguishing firmly (if not always convincingly) between traditionalism and snobbishness. The French, as a nation, she says, have 'moral taste'. This idealisation of French culture suggests some indulgence (especially in wartime) towards her adopted country. A French translator of *Les Moeurs Françaises* picks out four crucial terms in her praise of France: '*adulte*'; '*le goût*', '*le panache*' and '*l'honnêteté intellectuelle*'.[10] (How different from her characterisation of English society!) But Wharton has a sharp eye, too, for the French bourgeois investment in thrift and industry, caution and bureaucracy. She admires French marriages, not matters of passion but associations for the benefit of the family and the economy, where the wife is her husband's business partner. Wharton prefers the relationship between the sexes in France, where there is outspokenness about sex, gaiety and hedonism, and where women have a strong influence over the men, but in company are expected to listen rather than to talk. (Presumably she did not apply this principle at her own dinner-table.)

Her admiration for France's cultural traditions, as found in French cooking, conversation, hospitality, marriage, architecture, gardening, agriculture, is a feature of her literary criticism, too. When she writes about French literature she always puts the emphasis on what has been evolved and deliberated. In the markings she made in her copy of Valéry's *Variété* (1924) she underlines a passage on Leonardo where Valéry says that the really great man is not original. '*Il ne rejette pas l'ancien, parce qu'il est ancien.*' Writing about standards of criticism, in her 1915 article in the *Times Literary Supplement* responding to James's essay on new writers, Wharton puts French criticism above that of America or England, because of the 'rich deposit' of its critical traditions. In *The Writing of Fiction* (which is full of French literature), describing the need for 'long patience' and 'thinking through' even in the simplest of short stories, she uses this analogy: 'A well-known French confectioner in New York was once asked why his chocolate, good as it was, was not equal to that made in Paris. He replied: "Because, on account of the expense, we cannot *work it over* as many times as the French confectioner can."'[11]

Her reading of France and of Frenchness belongs to a long American literary habit of comparison and cross-fertilisation. No American writing is free of it, whether it is rejecting Europe or Europeanising itself. (Both these things were happening during Wharton's writing lifetime, which overlapped with Mark Twain as well as Gertrude Stein.) Writers she knew, like

Henry James, William Dean Howells and Henry Adams, all played important parts, like her, in this American cultural debate. And she was well read in the two-way cultural traffic between France and America. (Her library contains, for instance, a marked-up 1850 edition, her father's copy, of de Tocqueville's *De La Démocratie en Amérique*).[12] Her own comparisons between the two cultures belong in a literary context of which she was keenly aware.

Her first French friend, Paul Bourget, wrote his transatlantic analysis, *Outre-Mer* (1894), after his visit to Mrs Wharton in Newport in 1893. (Looking back on *Outre-Mer* in 1936, she felt that Bourget's emphasis on North America as the 'land of dollars' had been exaggerated: in her circle, she maintained, fortunes were small and nobody talked about business. And, rereading his account of the 'rapidity and tumult' of his journey across 1890s America, she thought that it would now seem like 'a slow walk through a peaceful and sleepy Arcadia'.) Bourget caricatured certain recognisable American types in *Outre-Mer*, among them what he called '*la garçonnière intellectuelle*', the intellectual tomboy. This is the American girl who collects information; there is nothing she has not read, but she cannot discriminate. She only acquires information '*pour remplir ses tiroirs*', to fill her drawers. She is 'a thinking machine'. Opinions have varied as to whether this was based on the thirty-year-old Wharton – rather old for a tomboy, and too discriminating for this type. (If Bourget was caricaturing her here, he came to think of her later as a '*femme du monde*' with a serious work-ethic and a 'literary conscience'.) Whether or not she featured in *Outre-Mer*, the book was one model for the transatlantic analyses she would make herself. Like Raymond de Chelles in *The Custom of the Country*, Bourget found many aspects of America horrifying: he was shocked by its 'incoherence and its haste', the brutality of its street-life, its lack of proportion and taste, its competitiveness and abuse of energy. But he found the aspirations of a new democracy a hopeful lesson for the old world.[13]

Other French commentators gave apocalyptic views of modern America as a ghastly example of democracy, consumption and mechanisation run riot – though they praised American optimism, energy and individualism. The critic André Chevrillon wrote an essay in 1907 (responding to H.G. Wells's *The Future in America*) called 'L'Avenir aux États-Unis', describing the French traveller who, arriving in the terrifying incoherence of New York, is appalled by the skyscrapers, the huge numbers of immigrants, the brusque manners ('*chacun pour soi*') and the publicising of private lives. He is homesick for Paris – its noble bridges, the Tuileries, Richelieu's dome, the medieval spires and old grey houses: '*Quel décor, quelles harmonies, quelle beauté!'* The contrast is echoed years later in Georges Duhamel's *Scènes de la Vie Future* (1930), where American jazz, cinema, mechanisation, publicity, lack of solitude, and conformity seem the '*triomphe de la sottise barbare*', and France is warned: '*Regardez, gens d'Europe, regardez le nouvel empire!*' Wharton's acquaintance André Tardieu, journalist and politician, was similarly critical in *France and America* (1927), though he did justice to America's support for France in the war, mentioning Wharton. Tardieu contrasted American Protestantism with French classicism and Catholicism, American materialism with French self-cultivation, American love of liberty with French insistence on precedence and national unity. The contrast is between a nation in a hurry and a nation made up of 'ideals' and 'emotions' 'handed down from antiquity'. Wharton shared these French writers' views of the 'chaos là-bas' of post-war America.[14]

Chevrillon often mentions William Crary Brownell, one of the Francophile Americans whose accounts of France influenced Wharton's *French Ways and their Meaning*. For Brownell, in *French Traits* (1888), France was characterised above all by 'the social instinct'. The 'true centre' of the moral self was 'outside oneself'; the individual was constrained by 'institutions of public life'. 'While Paris made people into Parisians, he feared that New York simply absorbed people, resulting in a "noisy diversity".' In 1908, Wharton hoped to co-translate some chapters of *French Traits*, to be published with an appreciation of Brownell by Chevrillon, but to her disappointment, he 'chucked' the project. After Brownell's death in 1928, Wharton's tribute noted his admiration for French 'equipoise' and 'temperance'.[15]

Brownell's interest in the 'social instinct' in France was echoed in *The France of Today* (1907) by the Harvard academic Barrett Wendell, who was a visiting Professor of English at the Sorbonne in 1904. Wharton had known him a little since the late 1890s, and was anxious to have his support, as a representative of high-minded Boston, at the time of her divorce. When he died in 1921, she wrote to Berenson that he represented 'the last of the traditions we care for'. *The France of Today*, which was in her library, commented on the formality of French society, and its paradoxical history of revolutionary political turbulence and social conservatism. Wharton, similarly, wrote in *French Ways and their Meaning* 'that there is nothing like a Revolution for making people conservative'. Wendell found the French a 'reticent people'. 'After many a pleasant hour with them . . . you may find yourself surprised, on reflection, that you have not really got to know these friends any better than before.'[16] And Wharton may have felt this too.

These transatlantic cultural analyses of France were part of a long tradition. It sometimes seems as if every American who could write and who
spent more than five minutes in Paris produced a book on it. *French Ways
and their Meaning* might sit on a bookshelf of 'Americans in Paris' alongside such guides as Sisley Huddleston's *France and the French* (1925), *In and
About Paris* (1927), or *Bohemian Literary and Social Life in Paris* (1928), with
tips on the difficulties of dropping in on a French family, and accounts of
the Faubourg, with its 'sadly decayed' French aristocracy still constituting
'its own exclusive court'. There were many introductions to Paris for middle-
class visiting Anglo-American ladies, like *A Woman's Paris* (Anon., 1900),
which gave tips on hotel and apartment prices ($12,000 a year maximum
for an apartment), shopping for food ('Let the cook do everything'), French
meals (for dinner, soup, fish, an entrée and a joint, game or chicken or
salad, pudding or an ice, coffee and fruit), the inadequate heating of French
apartments, the need for endless tipping, suitable dress for outings (hats for
the theatre; for the opera, 'full evening toilette, *décolleté*, with no hat'), the
fashionable places to eat out ('At present people dress expressly for the
Ritz') and the difficulty of getting 'a slippery foothold within the excluding
portals' of the Faubourg.[17]

'Mme Warthon', as the French sometimes spelt her name, was no innocent
abroad or naive tourist. Among the childhood memories of 1860s Paris she
recalled in *A Backward Glance* was a dramatic image of a beautiful lady with
a little boy, riding in an open carriage down the Champs-Élysées (where the
Jones family were living) with 'a glittering escort of officers'. This woman
was the Empress Eugénie with her son the Prince Imperial, and 'the next
year' (1870, the year of the Franco-Prussian war) 'she and her procession
had vanished in the crimson hurricane'. With her memory of the empress,
Wharton is laying claim to a long, deep, inward knowledge of French history,
and suggesting too a nostalgia for the pre-republican days of Empire.[18]

But her conservative Francophilia was not a simple matter. Long before
she started living in France, she had to take sides (like everyone else with
an interest in France at the time) on the Dreyfus case. When the Jewish
captain Alfred Dreyfus was convicted as a spy in 1894 and deported to life-
imprisonment on Devil's Island, Wharton was in Newport, struggling with
illness and depression and trying to write stories. Over the next few years,
'*l'Affaire*', France's great crisis of the 1890s, gained momentum. Zola
published his defence of Dreyfus, *J'Accuse*, in January 1898. To the accompaniment of public riots and passionate disagreements amongst the educated
elite of France, Dreyfus was court-martialled again in August 1899. He was

again found guilty, by a divided court, and sentenced, this time to ten years rather than life, a sentence not quashed until 1906. (Morton Fullerton covered both trials for the Paris office of the London *Times*.) That summer, Edith and Teddy Wharton were staying in the Swiss Alps near the Bourgets. Minnie Bourget, who was Jewish, would not discuss '*l'Affaire*', and Teddy's views are not known. But Bourget and Wharton disagreed strongly. The anti-Semitic expressions she sometimes voiced, her social conservatism and her later attraction to Catholicism, might lead one to expect her to be an anti-Dreyfusard, like the monarchist and reactionary Bourget. Not so. She brought to the argument the kind of optimistic American individualism that she so often described in her fiction in conflict with French authoritarianism and traditionalism. Bourget and Wharton acted out the essence of the Dreyfus row in that Swiss resort, in between mountain walks and discussions of French literature. The split, which affected so many people so painfully, was not only between anti-Semites and their opponents, or between left and right, or between monarchists and republicans (though the clearing of Dreyfus's name led to a more left-leaning Third Republic during the years Wharton lived in Paris, and more suspicion of 'clerico-monarchist plots'). It was an argument over the maintaining of authority and order on the one hand, and justice for the individual on the other. Wharton noted that Bourget argued, above all, for 'the political duty to defend the army, by whatever means possible'. For her, the end could not justify the means. Returning to their debate in the year Dreyfus was finally pardoned by a civilian court, the first year of Clemenceau's premiership, she wrote to Bayard Cutting, from The Mount: 'Here is Dreyfus waiting to be talked about. I should have liked to be in France last week. One can't help hoping much from a nation that can turn about & make amends so openly & overwhelmingly as that. No – my glimpses, through Bourget, of reactionary French opinion, make me admire Clemenceau all the more.'[19]

The Dreyfus affair exposed the deep rift in French society during what would come, nostalgically, to be called '*la belle époque*', the years of peace between the Franco-Prussian war and 1914. It was a stable society, and, from the 1900s, an economically flourishing one, but it was deeply divided between an old backward-looking inheritance and a more modern spirit in the arts, politics and business. Wharton saw something of both worlds, but the Paris she made her own was – in spite of their disagreements – very much that of the Bourgets and the 'Faubourg'. Though she was in and out of Paris all through the 1890s, we do not associate her with the best-known features of the 'fin-de-siècle': decadent café society, *flâneurs*, night-clubs, Montparnasse, *la vie bohème*, the Moulin Rouge. She was scornful of the big popular event in Paris in 1900, the 'Universal Exhibition'. The Whartons were there in June that year, staying with the Bourgets, visiting Wharton's dying mother, and working with Minnie Bourget on a translation of her story, 'The Muse's Tragedy'. The exhibition had taken over the city. They would have seen the new Eiffel Tower (built in 1889) blazing with illuminations, and the balloon which was filming Paris for a photorama show. They would have walked along the Seine towards the twenty-foot-high female figure in the latest Paquin outfit, towering above the main gate of the exhibition, to look at the glittering, garish display of all the new scientific and industrial discoveries: colour-photography, wireless telegraphy, motor-cars, the Palace of Electricity with its enormous statue, the colonial pavilions representing forty nations (including an imitation gold-mine from California), and the displays of civil engineering and navigation, metallurgy and armaments. (Perhaps she visited the Alma Pavilion where the sculptor Rodin, soon to be her neighbour in the Rue de Varenne, was having a great success.) The exhibition was 'designed for the masses'; over 48 million people visited. Wharton wrote to Brownell that it was all 'very tawdry and dusty', and that Paris was 'a beer-garden of German tourists'. She would get an enthusiastic account from Walter Berry four years later about the great exhibition at St Louis: 'there's such a fine pell-mell of energy about the whole thing.' But the Universal Exhibition was too vulgar for her taste.[20]

The Whartons were staying with the Bourgets, in the Rue Barbet de Jouy, in the Faubourg Saint-Germain, that summer, for two reasons: her brother Harry had just given up his apartment at 146 Avenue des Champs-Élysées, where they would otherwise have been staying, and the hotels were all full. It would take a few more years for her to feel the need for a permanent base in Paris. Teddy represented her at Lucretia's funeral in Paris in 1901, and in 1902 the Whartons were busy moving into The Mount. Their travels in 1903 were mainly in Italy. But with the purchase of their first car at the start of 1904, and the accident of poor weather in Italy, they turned their faces towards France, motoring from January to April along the Riviera and westward to Pau and to Spain. In the spring of 1905 her asthma was plaguing her and she crossed (without Teddy and with Gross) for April and May in Salso and Paris. And in March 1906, fresh from the triumph of *The House of Mirth*, she set out (she told Sally) 'for the kind of mental refreshment that I can get only là bas. Oh, the curse of having been brought up there, & having it ineradically [sic] in one's blood!' Bourget opened the doors of the Faubourg to her, and her French adventure began. They stayed in the Hôtel Dominici and then with Harry, now at number

3 Place des États-Unis, and then they made the motor-flight that took in Rouen, Nantes, Tours and Nohant. By now it was apparent to her that the best way of being in Paris for any length of time was to have an apartment. In 1906 arrangements were made to rent 58 Rue de Varenne from the George Vanderbilts; they stayed there in the winters of 1907 and 1908. After that tenancy ended, Wharton stayed in her brother's apartment in the Place des États-Unis, then in the Hôtel Crillon, that very luxurious establishment on the Place de la Concorde, and finally, for a rent of about $75 a month, moved into an apartment which Harry found for her at 53 Rue de Varenne, where she would live until the end of 1919.[21]

That the Whartons rented their first apartment in the Faubourg from the millionaire Vanderbilts – old acquaintances from New York and Newport days, and more recently their hosts at Biltmore – suggests their place in the world of wealthy Americans in Paris in the 1900s. Paris was, in certain districts, just a high-class American town, Newport-by-the-Seine. There was a ready-made social life for her, with at least one exceptional American intellectual at its centre. Wharton was never close to Henry Adams, but she enjoyed his wit and style. By the time she arrived, he was a well-known Parisian figure in his seventies, a regular at the salons of the Faubourg. She and James agreed that he had a 'capacity to be very well taken care of'. He described, in 1910, 'our little American family group here', naming the American ambassador Robert Bacon, the Walter Gays, his intimate friend Elizabeth Cameron, Sturgis Bigelow, the Harry Whites, Walter Berry and Edith Wharton. Adams noted: 'We are rather sufficient to ourselves.' Of these American friends, Walter Berry went everywhere and opened many doors to her. The diplomat Henry White, the American ambassador to France between 1907 and 1909, had married her childhood friend from Newport, Margaret Rutherfurd. Sturgis Bigelow, a doctor turned lecturer on Buddhism, was a friend of Henry Adams, Bay Lodge and James, and gave Wharton some sound medical advice about Teddy. By the time Wharton moved into number 53, Lizzie Cameron had become a friend, and would be one of her staunchest co-workers during the war.[22]

She was very good friends with her contemporaries, the Roman Catholic painter Walter Gay and his wife Matilda. Matilda's father, William Travers, a Wall Street financier, had known the Joneses well, and she had had exactly the same kind of New York and Newport childhood as Wharton; she too felt like a European exile in America. She married Walter Gay, whom she met in Paris, when she was thirty-three. When Wharton was moving into 53 Rue de Varenne in January 1910, the Gays were moving from their previous Paris house into 11 Rue de l'Université, round the corner. They divided their time between Paris and an enchanting eighteenth-century house near Fontainebleau, set in a three-hundred-acre walled park, the Château de Bréau. They did up this beautiful home immaculately, filling it with good paintings and elegant furniture. Wharton loved this house; it inspired the Château Givré, in *The Reef*; and it influenced her decoration of one of her own French houses, the Pavillon Colombe. Walter Gay, a minor American Vuillard, made delicate, intimate paintings of the Château de Bréau and, later, of the Pavillon. His paintings of his friends' houses eloquently evoke the decorous domestic pleasures of Wharton's French life. And the Gays' friends (with exceptions like Elsie de Wolfe) were her friends: Egerton Winthrop, Henry Adams and Henry James, Daisy Chanler, Mildred Bliss, the George Vanderbilts, Morton Fullerton, Charles Du Bos, Marie de Vogüé and Rosa de Fitzjames. The Gays were close to the painter Ralph Curtis and his wealthy wife. When Wharton published 'The Verdict' in *Scribner's* in June 1908, the Curtises recognised themselves: 'It's all about me, and Ralph, and our house, where Teddy made us a visit, and his wife has put down his whole account of it even to the furniture of the bedrooms, and described me as a rich widow without any mind, who has let my artist husband give up his career', wrote Lisa Curtis furiously to Henry Adams. The Gays tried not to take sides.[23]

Mostly, Matilda Gay and Edith Wharton saw eye to eye. Matilda thought her an 'intelligent, brilliant woman', and their Franco-American ideas were remarkably close. (Matilda's were voiced in the diary she kept for many years.) They both preferred the Hôtel Crillon to the Ritz, thought men made better talkers at dinner-parties, believed in Dreyfus's innocence, disliked modern art, ran their houses with great efficiency, and adored eighteenth-century furniture, antique-collecting, motor-flights through France, and dogs. They agreed on 'the deteriorating effect on Americans resultant from a long residence in Paris ... they never seem to assimilate the intelligent side of French life'. The same things amused them, like a story about Lord and Lady Craven, who said: 'The Walter Gays are very rich, and yet he goes on painting all the same. Why the devil does he do it?' Matilda was not entirely uncritical. Visiting Wharton in 1909 at the Hôtel Crillon, she found her 'smoking cigarettes, surrounded by her little literary court, exchanging *mots* with them – a *mondaine bohémienne*'. She thought 53 Rue de Varenne was 'large and comfortable, but ugly and without personality'. She found her a 'nervous, rather fussy hostess', her humour rather forced ('a sort of malady of laughter'), much better as a guest or on her own ('How I love to get Edith in *tête-à-tête*'). She preferred her poetry to her novels. But she was immensely sympathetic to her during the break-up with Teddy, and was one of her most active and committed supporters in the war years. The last letter Wharton wrote, a few days before her death, was to Matilda Gay.

The Vanderbilt apartment, then, came with an American expatriate social life. But it also belonged to the ancient society of the Faubourg. The American hero of *Madame de Treymes* is surprised to see the old family name of the sombre 'Hôtel' he is visiting 'emblazoned in black marble over its still more monumental gateway'.[24] Now Wharton was going to live in one of those 'monumental drawing rooms', behind one of those great gateways.

The street-names of the Faubourg, once fields on the Left Bank of the Seine, speak their ancient history: the Rue de Varenne was once 'Garenne', a warren of wild rabbits; the Rue Vaneau, at right angles to it, comes from '*vanneau*', a lapwing, and the Rue de Belle Chasse, off the Boulevard Saint-Germain side of the Rue de Varenne, speaks for itself. Those royal hunting-grounds and rich monastic lands around the Abbey of Saint-Germain-des-Prés were built on by the aristocratic families – Montmorency, Broglie, Matignon, Maillé – in the late seventeenth and early eighteenth centuries; the district came to be known as the 'noble' faubourg. The '*hôtels particuliers*', the magnificent town-houses of the aristocracy, competed with each other for grandeur and size – much as the palaces of Fifth Avenue did in Edith Wharton's youth. Most of the *hôtels* were built to the same pattern, though they varied immensely within it, of an ornate exterior façade and great carriage-entrance on to the street, leading to a paved inner courtyard – the *cour d'honneur* – with a magnificent house at the rear of the courtyard, often with flights of steps and pillars and huge rows of balconied windows, highest on the *piano nobile*, the first floor with its 'grand salon'. Most had an extensive formal garden stretching behind the house. Even now, an aerial view of the streets between Les Invalides to the west, the Boulevard Raspail to the east, the Seine to the north and the Rue de Sèvres to the south, shows vast stretches of private gardens (most of them belonging to embassies or ministries), occupying far more space than anywhere else in Paris.

Wharton's long, narrow, sombre street, running from the Boulevard des Invalides to – and just across – the Boulevard Raspail, its forbidding, grandiose house-fronts at once advertising and concealing the splendours within, was packed tight with ancient families. Number 47 is the Hôtel de Boisgelin, built in 1732, whose original owner fled in 1790 and which was owned by the Rochefoucauld-Doudeauville family after 1860. Its first-floor 'grand salon' was a model of its time, with its chandeliers, Louis XIV furniture, giant carpets, clocks, vases, and elegantly panelled walls and doors. Number 56 is the Hôtel de Gouffier de Thoix, built in 1760 for the sister of Charles II's favourite, the Duchess of Portsmouth. The outer doorway has an extravagantly decorated porch, with a shell-shape medallion of foliage and garlands featuring Mars, a *cour d'honneur* framed with iron chains, and a house with a majestic frontage and a fabulously decorated interior, the 'grand salon' carved with wooden clouds and birds and cupids. (The quality of one's '*boiseries*' was a matter of great attention.) Number 57, one of the largest and most beautiful houses in Paris – fourteen great windows long, with enormous gardens behind, stretching all the way back to the next street – is the Hôtel de Matignon, built between 1723 and 1725, lived in by Talleyrand from 1808 to 1811, in Wharton's time the Austrian ambassador's residence, and now the Prime Minister's house. Number 77, at the Invalides end of the street, is the vast Hôtel de Biron, built between 1728 and 1731 (unusually, without a *cour d'honneur*) and inhabited, at different times, by the widow of Louis XIV's and Mme de Montespan's son, the Duc de Biron (who created the magnificent gardens), a papal legate, a Russian ambassador, and a convent of aristocratic girls (who wrecked the decorations). In Wharton's time, the garden was a wilderness and the house was tenanted; among the lodgers were Rilke, Cocteau, Isadora Duncan and Rodin. After the sculptor's death (and after Wharton had left Paris) it became the Musée Rodin.

Number 58, almost opposite the Hôtel Matignon, was the Hôtel d'Auroy, or d'Ourouer, built in 1730. It has a particularly ornate and imposing air to it: the frontage had an ornamental balcony over the '*portail*', and above the balcony a statue-niche with rounded pediment; inside, an immensely grand curving marble staircase led up from the entrance hall to the high windows and long sweep of the Vanderbilts' first-floor, opulently furnished apartment.[25] The furniture, the architecture, and the life-style all went together, as Wharton made clear in a delighted letter of January 1907 to Sally Norton. Wharton's description to Sally of the 'beautiful apartment, with charming old furniture, old Chinese porcelains and fine bronzes, against an harmonious background of *real* old boiseries (the hotel was built in 1750), in the heart of the most delightful part of Paris', led straight on to a satisfied account of her social engagements and Parisian occupations.

Three years later, by now a familiar figure in the Faubourg, she settled into Number 53, across the road, next door to the ancient Hôtel d'Angennes of 1699, belonging to the de Lévis-Mirepoix family, who would become her friends. She moved in January 1910, in the middle of the worst floods Paris had ever known. The Seine burst its banks, the Invalides became a great lake, and the Gare d'Orléans was like a swimming-pool. The inhabitants of the 7th Arrondissement got about in boats and lowered baskets down from their windows for food. Fortunately, Wharton's apartment (this time unfurnished) was on the second floor. Number 53 was a substantial but unexciting five-storey building. Unlike Number 58, it was not one of the original eighteenth-century houses of the Faubourg. It was built in 1884, one of the first Paris buildings to be constructed with steel girders. The solidity of its façade was relieved by ornamental balconies, pointed window-surrounds, shutters and patterns of horizontal stripes between the windows. A vast wooden doorway, with a mighty door-handle and decorative wooden fruit and flower carvings, led from the street along a narrow paved alley into a small paved courtyard, the 'courette', with stables (later garages) at the back. All along the left-hand side of the courtyard were the gates for the carriages, and on the right there were the doorways to the 'cave' (each apartment had its own basement-cellar, for wine or storage – and for the rats), and to the narrow, winding, wooden servants' staircase, with access to every floor. The occupants and their guests, however, would go in the front entrance, just inside the huge doorway. Big glass doors let them into a rather gloomy, black-and-white Second Empire-style entrance-hall, with a blue urn on a pedestal, and on the right the windows into the concierge's front room, where she could see who was coming in and out. A wide red-carpeted staircase, with gas-lights (later electricity) modelled as giant flambeaux, at every turning, led up to the landings, each with three tall wooden doors. The effect was dark, formal, and intensely private.

Wharton's second-floor apartment was the grandest in the building. (Teddy, she told John Hugh Smith in April 1909, would not have to keep his boots in the drawing room.) Like all the apartments, it had diagonally patterned wooden parquet floors throughout, Napoleon III fireplaces, and double windows against the cold. Her floor, with very high ceilings, had a long, imposing, narrow entrance-hall, from which the main rooms led off, in the *enfilade* structure she had used at The Mount: library, drawing room or salon, dining room and bedroom, could be entered either through the large doors from the entrance-hall or through the doors leading from one room to the other. The wood-panelled walls and ceiling dadoes were decorated with elaborate swags and cherub-motifs in Louis XVI style. Each fireplace had a grand mirror above it, set into the wall. The main rooms looked over the back of the house; curved and gilded handles opened the long windows onto a little balcony overlooking the courtyard. The wooden panelling gave the rooms a dark feeling, but light poured in from the south-facing rear windows. To the right of the long suite of main rooms, there were two further rows of rooms leading off in a T-shape, one set, a guest-suite, to the front of the house, and one set to the back, which included a kitchen, a pantry, a laundry-room, and rooms for Gross and the maid. Heating was pumped up to all the floors, but there were no fitted bathrooms until the 1950s. Out of the front windows, the house faced the Hôtel Gallifet. From the back windows, you could see gardens stretching far behind. On the left of Number 53, a curved entrance archway led from the street to the 'Cité de Varenne', a narrow little mews street of a few very elegant houses with a garden at the end, and beyond that was the garden of the Church of the 'Missions Étrangères'. Looking out to the right you could glimpse the vast gardens of the Hôtel Matignon. It would have felt like living in a country park, not a city: the Rue de Varenne is extremely quiet.

All the houses in the Faubourg were family properties, passed down or let out to descendants and relations. Number 53 was built and owned by a family called de Paul. The rules were strict, grounded on long tradition and precedent. Even in the 1950s you could not hang your washing out, shake your carpets out of the windows or make any loud noises – this included speaking in a high voice or working with a hammer. Animals were only tolerated on condition they brought no trouble to any of the other occupants (so the lapdogs would have had to be very well behaved). Sub-letting was allowed, but only to people of 'good lives and morals'.[26]

Gradually, between 1907 and 1911, living in the Rue de Varenne took the place of living at The Mount. Having created a European style for the decoration of houses in America, Wharton had moved into the authentic version of what she had so long admired. Number 53 was not much older than The Mount. It too carried an eighteenth-century decorative style forward into the late nineteenth century. It had the same qualities of stylishness and privacy. She had constructed her fantasy European house in America, and now she had come home to the real thing. And outside it lay, not 'a Massachusetts pond', but the noble Faubourg. The enormous distance between New England and Paris would be summed up when Wharton sat down in the Rue de Varenne to write, in French, as an exercise in improving her style, the first draft of *Ethan Frome*.

A good deal of the writing she did in the Rue de Varenne, like *Ethan Frome*, would be set in America. But in her Paris years she switched her subject increasingly to Franco-American relations, to the celebration and analysis of French 'ways', and to a series of novels and stories in which Americans negotiate a life for themselves in France, usually unsuccessfully.

Wharton herself was as far as possible from the kind of American woman in Paris she put into *The Reef*, the 'bohemian' Mrs Farlow from New England, sending off to the magazines her 'Inner Glimpses' of 'a Salon of the Faubourg St-Germain', or a 'Cross-Section of Montmartre'. Her own 'Inner Glimpses' of the Faubourg were written before she settled in there. *Madame de Treymes* (1907) takes its basic story from James's *The American* – the honourable American who wants to marry the widowed daughter of an ancient French family, and is thwarted by its corrupt, secret plotting. Wharton thickens the plot, in her perfectly structured and painful novella, by having the beloved be the American daughter-in-law of the old Catholic French family, abandoned by her husband: Fanny Frisbee of West 33rd Street become Madame de Malrive of the Faubourg. And the heroine is not Fanny, but the family's married daughter, Christiane de Treymes, subtle, manipulative, charming and vulnerable – Wharton's best French character – who both attracts and repels the Puritanical American hero, whom she blackmails and deceives. He is balked by the family's implacable opposition to divorce and second marriage, and their use as a bargaining counter of Fanny's child, who would automatically be returned to the father, however immoral, in the case of a divorce. (Wharton is arguing with Bourget's novel *Un Divorce* [1904], which held that divorce is 'destructive of family life, subversive of religion, the source of anarchy and revolution'.) Different types of Americans in Paris are displayed, to whom 'French ways' are baffling, even horrifying. The novella replays her argument with Bourget over the Dreyfus case: an argument between free choice and the force of tradition which she never quite resolves. John Durham's 'free individualism' is shocked by the 'dark feudal survival' of ancient family rules. He realises that Fanny has been absorbed by 'the tremendous strength of the organisation'. On their side, the inhabitants of the Faubourg regard their American visitors 'with the unblinking attention of a civilized spectator observing an encampment of aborigines'. Under this dark satire hangs the question the American lover asks of Fanny de Malrive: 'Why did you never come back?'[27]

Wharton will continue to use the American woman married into a French family as a test-case for cultural adaptation. She does it in *The Reef*, with Anna Leath's conservative mother-in-law, who completely identifies with the 'habits and prejudices' of the French family she has married into, and she does it in *The Custom of the Country*, with Undine's disastrous marriage to a French count, Raymond de Chelles. She planned to develop the theme, too, in one of her unfinished post-war projects, to be called 'The Associates'. An American girl, Tony Trevis, who thinks she knows everything about the French, is to marry into an old Faubourg family with as dark a side to it as the Malrives in *Madame de Treymes*, and as traditionalist as the de Chelles in *Custom*. Tony's sensitive French husband, Jean Dalbray, was to be a more forgiving partner than Raymond de Chelles: in the end the 'associates' were to become 'allies'. The plot summary ends: 'And Tony has learned something about the French.'[28]

But most of Wharton's fictional Americans are rebuffed by the Faubourg; their motives for staying are always questioned, and they never feel quite at home. The formalities and protocols which baffle her fictional Americans in France shaped her life there too: she does not seem to have become, ever, very intimate with the Faubourg set, and made only a few close French friends.

The eighteenth-century owners of the Faubourg houses were described, retrospectively, in a 1926 guide to '*Les Vieux Hôtels de Paris*', as bringing 'the art of conversation and polite manners to perfection' in their salons, where '*le bel usage*' and the 'classical spirit' infused the most civilised society in the world, '*la société la plus civilisée qui soit au monde*'. Proust described this perfect civilisation rather differently in the last volume of *À la recherche du temps perdu* (finished in 1922): 'The Faubourg Saint-Germain was like some senile dowager now, who replies only with timid smiles to the insolent servants who invade her drawing rooms, drink her orangeade, present their mistresses to her.' Wharton was amused by an exclusive society which was always complaining that '*tout le monde* had long since come in, that all the old social conventions were tottering or already demolished, and that the Faubourg had become as promiscuous as the Fair of Neuilly'.[29]

The French Revolution did not destroy the aristocracy, 'but' (in Roger Shattuck's words) 'set up beside it another, the Napoleonic'. The nobility was not a dying class in the nineteenth century – successive bills in parliament failed to abolish titles. Monarchism persisted, though the death in 1883 of the Comte de Chambord, Charles X's grandson, put an end to the last hope of the old Legitimist families. Long after the Third Republic had bedded down and the threat of royalism had faded away, it was still fashionable in some circles: you could still find an anti-republican aristocrat like Elizabeth de Clermont-Tonnerre, at the end of the nineteenth century, refusing to wear a necklace of red, white and blue pearls because it would be like wearing the tricolour.[30]

But by the time Wharton settled in the Faubourg, the old aristocracy had a marginal and unproductive role. Though it continued to think of itself as an exclusive and influential class, it was by now 'the least important [social] group' in the Third Republic. The main story of upper-class life in nineteenth-century France was the amalgamation of the nobility and the middle classes. Large numbers of wealthy bourgeoisie (industrialists, financiers) were absorbed into the nobility. Some of the noble families could trace their family trees back to the *ancien régime*, but some were bourgeois 'notables' who had appropriated a 'de' or a title. By the 1890s, the *haute bourgeoisie* had fused with the upper class, become increasingly divorced from the *petite bourgeoisie*, and taken on the customs and manners of their aristocratic predecessors.[31]

Like New York of the 1880s and 1890s, the Faubourg was not a static society – for all the forbidding and monolithic look of their grand doorways. The pre-war 'gratin' (upper-crust) was a complicated, shifting, eclectic mixture. Even in the confident and suave retrospect of *A Backward Glance* Wharton speaks of having had to 'get her bearings' in Paris. You needed to immerse yourself rapidly in the texture of the Faubourg to establish whether your hosts were Dreyfusard or anti-Dreyfusard, Legitimists, Bonapartists, Orléanists, or the newer brand of right-wing authoritarians who would have given support in the late 1880s to General Boulanger. The old conservatives detested the neo-royalists, with their 'aggressive nationalism, racialism', and 'anti-parliamentarism'. The traditionalist defenders of the Catholic Church opposed the anti-clerical movement and the drive to separate Church and State. Arguments were raging in the 1900s, too, between those who advocated regionalism and decentralised government, and those who supported a centralised regime. Wharton's French society was conservative and anti-socialist, but it also included some moderate republicans, middle-class lawyers and politicians, and liberal, secular writers and artists. Careful attention was required, in order not to be like 'the American woman' at the Guermantes' final party in *À la recherche*, 'for whom dinner-parties and fashionable entertainments were a sort of Berlitz school. She had the names and she repeated them, without having first learnt their precise value and significance.'[32]

Wharton entered the Faubourg in the 1900s, when Proust was starting to keep the notebooks that would, from 1910 onwards, turn into *À la recherche*. She read each volume as it came out, between 1913 and 1927. Though she never met Proust, her social world touched his at many points. Proust's history of Faubourg society between the 1870s and the 1920s, in all its snobbery and self-deception, its 'silliness . . . aggravated by malice', its jealousies and rivalries, its jokes and 'panache', its philistinism and its adulation of artists, its erotic secrets and perversions, fascinated her. She read and reread it, with great attentiveness, marking up several of her volumes. How well she knew her Proust comes out in a letter of June 1930 to Gaillard Lapsley, when she is reading À *la recherche* yet again: 'I have come across an absolutely forgotten episodic Balbec figure: the Comte de Crécy, a friend of the Cambremers . . . He appears and disappears. Is he destined to turn up later, as having been Odette's one-time husband? . . . or is he another broken thread, like Mlle de Stermaria and the femme de chambre of Mme Putbus?' She was squeamish about the sex. Her *Sodome et Gomorrhe* volume is unmarked (her reaction to it was 'Alas!'). What she called Proust's 'voyeurism', in his 'unedifying' or 'squalid' scenes, she would tell Berenson, belonged to 'pathology', not art. As the later volumes appeared – until she got to the last one – she lamented Proust's falling-off: Walter called *Albertine disparue* 'Proust Disparu', 'and he's nearly right', she told John Hugh Smith.[33]

Wharton's markings of Proust, in her volumes of À *la recherche* (as well as in her copies of his books of essays and stories, *Les plaisirs et les jours* and *Pastiches et mélanges*) show her responding to his thoughts on obsessive love, on the need for solitude, particularly for the artist, and on the passage of time. How impossible it is to understand what happens in love (during his relationship with Gilberte); how it is better to be alone than with friends; how we have two impulses, the social and solitary; how some streets in Paris are thick with memories of past love; how popular art is a dangerous and ridiculous idea; how the artist is not free to choose since the work of art pre-exists him, and so the real book does not have to be invented but already exists, and 'the function and task of the writer are those of a trans-lator': all these thoughts interest her. She marks, too, some of his most famous epigrams about time: 'The time which we have at our disposal every day is elastic; the passions that we feel expand it, those that we inspire contract it; and habit fills up what remains'; '. . . the true paradises are the paradises that we have lost'. In *Pastiches et mélanges*, she marks the passages in 'Journées de Lecture' about the function of the artist being to lift the veil of inertia which leaves us incurious before the universe ('*incurieux devant l'univers*').[34]

But she marks passages of social and psychological detail too, like the description of the troupe of young girls at Balbec (which she will remember for *The Buccaneers*). She draws an appreciative marginal line by the monstrous appearance of M. de Charlus in *The Captive* (one of the most vindictive examples of what Edmund White calls Proust's 'ugly picture . . . of homosexuals'), in which Charlus's attempts to disguise his homo-sexuality 'had the effect of bringing to the surface of his face precisely what the Baron sought to conceal, a debauched life betrayed by moral degener-ation'.[35] She has some rare exclamation marks ('!!!!') beside the passage ironically describing how men like Saint-Loup develop tender sympathy for their mistresses' ailments – 'those little ailments which he himself has never felt, which compose for him an occult world in whose reality she has taught him to believe' – and she enjoys comic passages such as the Duc de Guermantes' peculiar use of words like 'drolatic', or the salon talk about Victor Hugo. One marked passage – in which the narrator, at the opera to see Berma giving an act of *Phèdre*, observes the occupants of the Princesse de Guermantes' box – shows her keen eye for the way Proust's social comedy turns itself into a minute anthropomorphic study of specimens, as she does in *The Age of Innocence*:

> The Marquis de Palancy, his face bent downwards at the end of his long neck, his round bulging eye glued to the glass of his monocle, moved slowly around in the transparent shade and appeared no more to see the public in the stalls than a fish that drifts past, unconscious of the press of curious gazers, behind the glass wall of an aquarium. Now and again he paused, venerable, wheezing, moss-grown, and the audience could not have told whether he was in pain, asleep, swimming, about to spawn, or merely taking breath.[36]

Wharton typically admires Proust as a 'renovator', not an 'innovator': 'The more one reads of Proust', she says in *The Writing of Fiction*, 'the more one sees that his strength is the strength of tradition. All his newest and most arresting effects have been arrived at through the old way of selec-tion and design.' When she revisits him in an essay of 1934, she places him at the end of 'the long and magnificent line of nineteenth-century novelists', rather than as a modernist opening 'a new era'. It is his 'duality of vision', at once microscopic and vast, at once controlling and freeing, that fascinates her. He can 'lose himself in each episode' and 'all the while keep his hand on the main threads of the design'. She is in awe of the 'amazing virtuosity' which snatches us from the hawthorns at Combray to the 'slow tortures' of Swann's love for Odette and to the Balzacian human comedy of the Faubourg:

> This changing but never confusing throng is composed of most of the notable types of a society which still keeps its aristocratic framework: the old nobility of the 'Faubourg' with their satellites; rich and culti-vated Jews ... celebrated painters, novelists, actresses, diplomatists, lawyers, doctors, Academicians; men of fashion and vice, *déclassées* Grand

Duchesses, intriguing vulgarians, dowdy great ladies, and all the other figures composing the most various, curious, and restless of modern societies.[37]

The two great novelists moved edge-on, unknown to each other, through that society. Their literary connections are tantalisingly close. When their mutual friend, the literary count Robert d'Humières, who was working on a translation of *The Custom of the Country*, was killed in action in 1916, it was suggested that Proust might finish the translation. André Gide, who knew both Proust and Wharton, offered to act as the intermediary. But nothing came of this. Many years later, she was asked to finish the translation of *Time Regained*, after the death of Scott-Moncrieff. She was flattered to be asked – and said she might have done it if she had been forty or fifty years younger.[38]

In *A Backward Glance* she says that she deliberately went out of her way not to meet Proust even though he was the 'friend of some of my most intimate friends' (notably Walter Berry). The reason she gives is not prudishness. Proust, who had defended himself in 1897 in a duel (with another homosexual writer) against imputations that he was gay, and who disguised or attacked homosexuality in his writing, was very anxious that his sexuality should not be common knowledge. So Wharton might not have known he was homosexual. Even if she did, she was used to the sexually ambivalent or homosexual friends of James, and would surely not have been shocked by flamboyant characters like Robert de Montesquiou (Proust's Baron de Charlus) or by knowing that men she had met or knew (Lucien Daudet, Robert de Flers, Reynaldo Hahn, Robert d'Humières, André Gide, Jean Cocteau) were Proust's intimate friends or lovers. No, her reason for not wanting to meet Proust was that he was a snob. She had been told that 'the only people who really interested him were Dukes and Duchesses, and that the only place where one could hope to find him was at the Ritz'; and this was enough to put her off.[39]

Was Edith Wharton, then, not a snob? A descendant of the de Noailles family is said to have described her as '*très snob*'. And her account in *A Backward Glance* of the Faubourg of 'twenty-five years ago', its *douceur de vivre*, its idiosyncratic hostesses and 'distinguished and cultivated' French gentlemen, is certainly not without snobbery, if that means taking pleasure in exclusivity. If it means showing off, social climbing, and name-dropping, then 'snobbery' does not quite fit her. (She once said to her friend Charles Du Bos, who disliked salon society, that knowing upper-class socialites made one immune to snobbery.) Wharton lists her friendships with the aristocracy proudly, but she is just as proud of the writers and Academicians she knew. She makes much of her pleasure in the less formal, livelier 'table-end' of the Faubourg dinner-party, where the young Turks and up-and-coming talents were seated, with 'great rushes of talk and laughter'. Unlike Proust, who climbed avidly and rapidly into the Faubourg from the middle classes, and never quite shook off his sense of its glamour, she took the French aristocracy, as she did the British upper classes, in her stride, and was not eager to court society for its own sake. Janet Flanner, another brilliant American expatriate in Paris, gave a malicious portrait of 'Dearest Edith', 'too formal even for the *faubourg*'. As one duchess complained, '*On est trop organisé chez elle.*'[40]

Wharton's satirical but indulgent attitude to the old aristocracy is seen in her long friendship with her Rue de Varenne neighbours, the de Lévis-Mirepoix family (who also had a house near Hyères). The daughter of the family, Philomène de Lévis-Mirepoix, the future Comtesse Jules de Divonne, became one of Wharton's closest women-friends. But her mother seemed to Wharton a bizarre relic of a long-passed era. The *duchesse* was clearly a hoot, and there are some funny 1920s descriptions of her in letters to Wharton's fellow-Proustian Gaillard Lapsley:

> The other day she suddenly decided to go '*en pèlerinage*' to Lisieux for the translation of the bones of a recently deceased Carmelite nun '*qui sera* probablement *beatifiée*'. She added that she wished to pray to her '*parce que c'est une des Sultanes du ciel*'. She went, and there was no translation and no pilgrimage, but she came back perfectly delighted, and now spends her whole time at the cinema. She always writes to me on packs of visiting cards too.

She reports on the *duchesse*'s plunging into white china plates of 'petits fours' with 'more than her former cannibalism', and on her wearing 'an ermine stole *with tails* which she bought at Toulon for 185 Francs'. When the *duchesse* finally died in 1931, Wharton sent Gaillard the 'sublimely complete' family notice. Those who invited the recipient to join in mourning 'Henriette Catherine Marie de Chabannes la Palice, Duchesse Douairière de Lévis-Mirepoix et de San Fernando Luis', included le Duc de Lévis-Mirepoix, Chevalier de la Légion d'honneur, Croix de Guerre; le Comte de Chabannes la Palice, le Marquis et la Marquise de Chabannes la Palice, le Comte et la Comtesse de Sanderval, le Comte Jehan de Durat, le Comte Amédée de Lur-Saluces, le Comte Jean de Neufbourg, Mademoiselle Genevieve de Saint-Phalle en Religion R.M. Marie Agnès de l'Ordre de Saint Benoît, la Princesse de Merode Westerloo, née Princesse de Croy, le Comte Guillaume de la Roche Aymon, la Marquise d'Havrincourt, and numerous other family members. It reads like a parody of the party at the end of *Time Regained*.[41]

The inhabitants of the Faubourg who mattered to Wharton most were the intellectuals, the conversationalists, and the artists. Many of these were Proust's friends – Jacques-Émile Blanche, the Abbé Mugnier, Jean Cocteau, Anna de Noailles – and also his enemies, like the anti-Semitic, conservative Byzantinist Gustave Schlumberger. Of these connections between Wharton and Proust, the closest was Walter Berry. Proust knew him well in the last six years of his life, wrote him some affectionate letters, admired his tennis-playing – Proust told Jacques-Émile Blanche that Berry played tennis 'as if he were twenty years old' – and dedicated *Pastiches et mélanges* to him in 1919. (Wharton owned a much-marked-up first edition.) Walter had acted for many years as a lawyer for the French Embassy in Washington, followed by a brief spell as one of the judges on the International Tribunal in Francophile Cairo.[42] Ill-health cut short his time there, and in 1910 he settled permanently in Paris, in a beautiful seventeenth-century apartment in the Faubourg, just round the corner from the Rue de Varenne. He was known everywhere in Paris society. Tall, silver-haired, fastidious and charming, a wit, a literary connoisseur, a collector, a lady's man, always dapper in his 'morning coat of Edwardian cut, striped trousers and highly polished shoes', he was '*l'Américain des romans d'Henry James*'. Sayings about him went round the town: that 'when he saw a Duchess, he saw two hundred years of Duchesses'; that 'unlike some gentlemen callers who left their hostess with a baby, Berry left them with a book'. One saw him everywhere. He was present, for instance, on an unfortunate evening in 1919 when Jean Cocteau had invited Proust to listen to his new poem, and Proust arrived very late, with Walter and another friend, and Cocteau came rushing out, exclaiming that they had ruined his reading, and would have to leave. The 'society priest' Abbé Mugnier described a dinner in 1915 in Berry's apartment at the Rue Saint-Guillaume with Wharton, Bakst, Mme Astor, and Alice Garrett, a well-connected diplomat's wife, a friend of Wharton's and an intimate, perhaps a mistress, of Walter's. There were red roses on the table; the apartment ('that of an amateur, a dilettante') was full of books, open everywhere, even on the floor. Walter's charming rooms and beautiful things were often remarked on: they provided the perfect setting for a bachelor life.[43]

Gossip about Walter and Edith was general in their Franco-American circles; many people took it for granted that they were lovers. Paul Morand noted in 1917 that Berry could not console himself for the departure of Mrs Garrett, but that Mrs Wharton 'a remis la main sur son bien' (had got her property back). The wildly unreliable Caresse Crosby, wife of Berry's narcissistic and bohemian nephew, Harry Crosby, called Edith and 'Cousin Walter' 'such closely harnessed friends that one spoke of them, in those international circles, as a team'. After the war, when Edith left Paris, Walter took over the lease of number 53, and used sometimes to ask Caresse to 'play the part of hostess at his table'; she noted that Edith, used to this role, was jealous of her.[44]

Walter Berry was rich: after long difficulties over his inheritance, which lasted until 1913, he inherited his mother's 'hundreds of thousands', as James noted enviously.[45] But though he could have been a man of leisure like Egerton Winthrop, he did not spend all his time collecting books, chasing 'ces dames', and lounging around at Number 53. He was one of those characters who give the impression of doing no work at all, while carrying a responsible and complex job. The American Chamber of Commerce, his employer, was established in 1894. It had a social and cultural role, with its library of 20,000 books, and its annual banquets on the Fourth of July and on Benjamin Franklin's birthday, but its solid work (at the Rue Scribe and then at the Rue Taitbout, in the heart of the financial district) was to deal with trading rights between America and France, to represent and promote the American business community in Paris, and 'to further the development of commerce between the USA and France'. Berry was chairman of its Publications and Press Committee, and then, from 1917 to 1922, its president. It was in the war years that the Chamber did some of its most important work, founding a special committee for the protection of American property, helping and acting as bankers for Americans in France, and consolidating relations with the heads of the French government, who were regular guests of honour at the banquets. By the end of the war, he had become 'the most well-known American in Paris'.[46]

For all his political conservatism, Walter Berry, with his eclectic artistic, literary, and sexual tastes, was almost a bohemian companion, compared with Wharton's dominant mentor in her early days in Paris, Paul Bourget. Her friendship with the Bourgets was over ten years old by the time she settled there. She and the 'Minnie Pauls' were very close neighbours in Paris (the Rue Barbet de Jouy is at right angles to the Rue de Varenne) and, after the war, in Hyères. In the pre-war days she found him 'bustling and full of gaiety', friendly, curious, talkative, and generous, not the fossilised old man he would become. She thought of him respectfully as an 'older brother', though she and James had running jokes about the Minnie Pauls' hypochondria and rigid ways, and in later years, when Minnie (whose shy delicacy appealed to Wharton very much) descended into mental illness, and Bourget cut himself off from his friends, she found being with them desolating. As novelists, they were worlds apart. Wharton was never Bourget's 'disciple', and has long since eclipsed him – nobody reads his seventy-three volumes now, except as examples of the conservatism of his time. She made a point of saying, when he died, that 'she never much liked' his fiction. His novels, she thought, were like moral sermons. Still, she may have enjoyed his sketch of her in 'L'Indicatrice' (1905) as a rich American lady in Paris who looks like a Velásquez princess – Bourget's pet term for her. And she learnt from the stern, pessimistic psychological analyses in his novels; *Un Divorce* left its mark not only on *Madame de Treymes* but also on *The Reef*, with its relentless series of inquisitions about secrets, sex and morality. *Le Disciple* (1889), one of his most influential novels, created a monstrous figure of a mechanistic, rational philosopher (based on Taine, whom Bourget had once venerated) with no religious or moral beliefs. The philosopher's disciple, who suffers from the modern condition of '*dédoublement*' – a self split between the one who feels and the one who looks on impassively – is influenced by his mentor to commit murder. The novel marked Bourget's own conversion from positivism to a highly moral Catholicism (part of a wave of late nineteenth-century conversions of intellectuals, including Claudel, Huysmans, Francis Jammes, Jacques Maritain, and Charles Péguy). 'I have two soutanes, Monsieur Bourget,' said the ever-witty Abbé Mugnier, 'do you want one of them?' His Catholicism went with a whole package of reactionary opinions. He opposed universal suffrage ('the shameful enslavement of intelligence by numbers'), feminism, and divorce; he was a royalist, an élitist, and a linguistic purist, and never ceased to lament (in a volume of *Essais de Psychologie Contemporaine* which Wharton admired) '*le triomphe de la barbarie qui menace d'envahir aujourd'hui la langue*'.[47]

Bourget made a late (and successful) debut as a playwright in 1908, and she went more than once to see the stage-version – close to the bone for her – of *Un Divorce* at the Vaudeville Theatre. The only story she wrote in French, also in 1908, 'Les Metteurs en Scène', borrowed its metaphor from the theatre to describe a cynical pair of Franco-American social stage-managers who arrange other people's advantageous marriages, at the expense of their own happiness. And Bourget was Wharton's '*metteur en scène*' for her first appearances on the Faubourg stage, at the famous salon of her near neighbour, Rosa de Fitzjames. Rosa, so unhappy married to the brutal and unfaithful Count Robert de Fitzjames that she was known as Rosa Malheur, was widowed when Wharton met her. She was a Viennese Jew in her mid-forties, a small dark woman who played the piano well, walked with a limp and had 'a rather stiff manner and staccato voice'. Wharton called her 'my dear mondaine'. Her salon, beautifully decorated with eighteenth-century furniture and fine Old Masters (Walter Gay painted it more than once) was in the Rue de Grenelle; later, she moved to less seductive quarters in the Rue de Constantine. Rosa was affable, insecure, depressive, tactless, awkward in other people's houses, but a brilliant hostess. She had a talent for bringing together people from different professions and making them enjoy themselves. Elizabeth de Gramont (whose recollections provide a useful window onto the *'belle époque'*) described a mixture of Austrians and 'reactionary French fashionables' at Rosa's salon; she was known for inviting 'the leading figures in Europe', even if her guests came to talk to each other rather than to her, and even if one of them said snidely of her Tuesday dinners: *'Elle a voulu avoir un salon, elle n'a eu qu'une salle à manger.'* 'Schlum' was spiteful about the count's licentiousness and the countess's legendary gaffes – but that was because she was Jewish. Henry James referred to 'Rosa's rich oriental note'.[48]

In *A Backward Glance*, Wharton's acquaintances in pre-war Paris (many of whom she met at Rosa de Fitzjames's salon) figure as walk-on parts in a long-since closed theatre. There were the girls she had known as *'jeunes filles en fleurs'*, over twenty years before at Cannes, in the 1880s, part of the Anglo-French-American 'gratin', whose international marriages she would use in *The Custom of the Country* and *The Buccaneers*. One of these, Jane de Polignac, became the Countess d'Oillamson – 'delightful, admirable creature', Wharton calls her, making her sound like an eighteenth-century heroine – who translated several of Wharton's stories into French. Another was Marie de Contades, who married Comte Arthur de Vogüé, descendant of a line of literary aristocrats. They lived in a great house at Commarin, near Dijon, which, Wharton noted approvingly, 'passed untouched through the Revolution' (and whose Gobelin tapestries may have inspired the Comte de Chelles's family heirlooms in *Custom*). Their apartment in the Rue de Varenne was described by Gustave Schlumberger as *'un véritable musée de la France d'autre-fois'*, and when Arthur de Vogüé died, he lamented 'the disappearance of this superb type of the nobility of ancient France'. These, with the d'Haussonvilles and the de Lévis-Mirepoix family, were Wharton's closest contacts with the old aristocracy. And she took a strong flavour of 'ancient France' from the courtly old bibliophile Auguste Laugel, a devoted Orléanist and follower of the Duc d'Aumale, whose library at Chantilly

Laugel had helped to create. She liked hearing the history of this perfect old French gentleman – his life as a civil engineer, his days in America during the Civil War, his poetic grief over his wife's death – and was rewarded for her attention by the priceless gift of a first edition of Racine's *Phèdre*.[49]

Wharton was proud of the mix of professions in her Paris circle. There were playwrights and poets in her cast list: Paul Hervieu, for instance, a psychological novelist who was an early influence on Proust, is briefly characterised as 'gaunt, caustic, and somewhat melancholy'; Robert de Flers as 'rotund, witty and cordial'. De Flers, a gifted writer of opera libretti and light comedies, a theatre director, an editor of *Le Figaro*, an Academician and an ambassador, was a close friend of Proust, and a great charmer. One of the fastest talkers in Rosa's salon was the French-Corsican poet Abel Bonnard, who specialised in 'whimsical and half-melancholy gaiety'. Bonnard was famous in the Faubourg for his eloquence, the only person allowed to break the usual 'conversational time-allowance' of five minutes. (In one salon, the hostess rang a bell if anyone infringed the rule of general, shared conversation.[50]) Less welcome in Rosa's salon – because, as Wharton put it, 'her dazzling talk was always intolerant of the slightest interruption' – was the fabulously loquacious, intense and romantic poet Anna de Noailles. This original and talented personality, part-Greek, part-Rumanian, had been married very young to the Comte de Noailles, and was the mistress (and sexual slave) of the right-wing nationalist Maurice Barrès. (She was also a Dreyfusard – and fervently patriotic in wartime.) She was the intimate friend and sparring-partner of Cocteau, friend, model and inspiration for almost every major writer and artist of her time (including Proust, Gide, Blanche and Vuillard), a glutton for admiration and a rapid consumer of books: there are many descriptions of her receiving company in bed, and of her staggering monologues, summed up by Cocteau as 'The Countess is talking ... the Countess is talking ... the Countess is talking'. Gide, describing in 1910 her 'amazing volubility', her jet-black hair, her floating scarves and her artificial gestures, said that it was hard 'not to succumb to the charm of this extraordinary poetess with the boiling brains and the cold blood'.

Wharton found her 'very brilliant and witty' when Bourget brought her to tea in April 1906, and admired de Noailles's work. Her library contained marked copies of de Noailles's *Le Coeur Innombrable*, *L'Ombre des Jours*, and *Les Vivants et les Morts*. She marked some of her most febrile, pulsating love-poems: '*Tout ce qui vit dit oui / Tout ce qui vit dit: Prends, goûte, possède, espère*'. When she read *Les Éblouissements*, in 1907, she was struck by their 'white-heat' intensity, and by their 'deep-down, utterly un-French resemblance to Whitman's feelings about nature'. She told Brownell that she might write a comparison of the two poets, but it came to nothing. De Noailles contributed to her wartime anthology, *The Book of the Homeless*, and wrote Wharton a wartime letter paying tribute to her as a *'grand écrivain'* and *'amie de la France'*. Her admirers vied to compliment and charm her. One particularly smooth piece of flattery came from Morton Fullerton, in 1907, saying that on the monument that would one day be erected in her honour, in the middle of some vast Shakespearian forest, the saying would be engraved: 'À *la Comtesse de Noailles, La Nature Reconnaissante*'. Speaking of her affinity for nature, the Abbé Mugnier remarked that she went one better than St Francis: 'To the melon she says, "You are my brother", to the raspberry, "You are my sister."'[51]

Wharton would have been amused. Like all her friends in Paris, she revered the Abbé Mugnier, the Benedictine priest who seems to have been the close friend of everyone from Colette and Proust and Marthe Bibesco (who wrote a book about him) to Gide and Walter Berry. 'Confessor to the Paris Literati', the Abbé was famous for converting Huysmans to Catholicism, and for combining a hidden life as a chaplain of a convent with a passion for literature (especially Goethe and Chateaubriand), and a place in every literary salon. His 'wise and kindly sayings' (Wharton's phrase) and his capacity for producing 'a host of paradoxes' were celebrated. Elizabeth de Gramont described his 'black gown, his bird-like profile, and his smoke-coloured crest', his 'rugged handshake' and his quiet chuckle, as being always welcome. He was much in demand for last rites, officiating at Proust's death-bed and at the mass for Walter Berry. It was as if the Faubourg needed its symbol of devotion, but had to have it in witty and elegant form. However, as is often the way with renowned wits, memories of his *bons mots* read rather flatly. Paul Morand recorded his gently refusing a risqué invitation from some ladies to go with them to the Folies-Bergères, saying that he had to take confession instead: '*Ce sont mes Folies-Brebis.*' The Abbé was well aware of the peculiarities of his role as the Little Brother of the Rich. I have to be a chameleon, he wrote in his journal for June 1908: '*Je suis l'abbé Pluriel.*' Still, he had his own strong opinions – he was vehemently pro-Dreyfus and anti-war – as well as being a sharp and sympathetic observer. In his old age, he went blind, and Wharton was kind to him.[52]

Every memoir of pre-war Paris mentions the Abbé, but his name is obscure now, like many of the others cited in *A Backward Glance*. The 'well-known' poet and novelist Jean-Louis Vaudoyer, for example, was also an art-critic, a friend of Proust, and one of the many lovers of the brilliant and beautiful Marie de Heredia, wife of the neo-classical poet Henri de Régnier. The de Régniers were glamorous acquaintances: Wharton admired his poems, *Le Miroir des Heures*, his 'quiet epigrams', and Marie's 'subtle and exquisite charm', but (typically) says nothing about – or did not know about – the peculiarities of their marriage. Marie, the daughter of the Cuban-French poet, had been in love with the decadent writer Pierre Louÿs (who married her sister), was married off to de Régnier for financial reasons, and was consistently unfaithful to him.[53]

A *Backward Glance* gives a largely sanitised account of its stream of minor characters. Here is the strange-looking, garishly dressed, pithily intelligent Neapolitan novelist Matilde Serao, very popular in her day, whose novels Wharton owned, but said nothing about. (James called them 'loud, loquacious, abundant, natural, happy'.) Here is the charming and friendly historian, the Marquis Pierre de Ségur, who inscribed his books to Mme Wharton with '*Respectueux et admiratif hommage*'. Here is the Anglophile translator and critic André Chevrillon, nephew of Taine, editor of the *Revue de Paris* and friend of the Bourgets, whom Wharton thought 'the foremost critic in France' and 'a man of the finest *quality* all through'. His sister, Madeleine Taillandier, and her daughter, were two of Wharton's few lasting women-friends from these circles. They were both writers, and they co-translated *The Age of Innocence*. Another was Jeanne de Margerie, sister of the poet Edmond Rostand, wife of a French diplomat in Washington, a warm, quiet, likeable woman whom Wharton got to know at the end of the war. Rumour linked her name with Berry's, but Wharton spoke of her affectionately.[54] There was also a rival hostess to Rosa, the Comtesse Charlotte de Cossé-Brissac, the perpetual companion (and presumably mistress) of Gustave Schlumberger, and a great friend of Berenson's; but there is no evidence of a friendship here. In 1936, Wharton told Berenson she had staggered home exhausted after sitting with Mme de Cossé and another elderly Faubourg friend, while 'genealogies poured from their lips uninterruptedly for two hours'.[55]

Then there was the clever band of journalists, essayists, sociologists, and political commentators, forceful and talented French intellectuals who seem to have treated 'Mme Warthon' with respect. They included the young leader-writer and future politician, André Tardieu; the up-and-coming journalist André Chaumeix; René Doumic, the editor of the *Revue des Deux Mondes*, Academician and historian of French literature; and Etienne Grosclaude, described by Wharton as 'the well-known journalist and wit', who (after the war had turned *salonniers* into soldiers and wits into elegists) put together a five-volume *Anthologie des écrivains morts à la guerre*.[56]

One of Grosclaude's anthologised authors was a remarkable character, Jean Du Breuil de Saint-Germain, whom Wharton came to know better than just as a dinner-party conversationalist. She and Rosa de Fitzjames took a short but memorable trip to Spain with him in April 1912. At close quarters, she found him rather suffocating, and lacking in 'vibrations'; but she was on his side when he fell in love with her old friend Bessy Lodge, the widow of Bay Lodge, a relationship opposed by the Cabot Lodges back in Boston, for which Wharton came to dislike them. Poor Bessy, struggling to bring up her children alone, given this chance of happiness, was ready to convert to Catholicism; but Du Breuil's death (he was killed in action at Arras) put an end to all that. Wharton published a tribute to him in the *Revue Hebdomadaire*, praising his extraordinary range of interests, his life of action (as a soldier with the French volunteers in the Boer War, as an explorer in Central and South America), his passionate advocacy of women's rights (which she said, rather surprisingly, had a strong influence on her), his 'moral ardour', 'disdain for popularity', and 'thirst for justice'.[57]

Du Breuil was killed in the same year as Wharton's friend the Vicomte Robert d'Humières, Anglophile poet, playwright, translator and author of books on the English empire and contemporary England. She did not like his fiction ('drivelling' was the word she used for one novel, to Morton Fullerton), but found him and his wife very charming, and she and James agreed that they had a 'bonne grâce & a wit & a Parisianism' about them which was very pleasing. It was another invisible link to Proust (who used him as a model for his character Saint-Loup) that they both relished d'Humières's nobility and haughty good looks. Perhaps she was not aware of his double life in Proust's homosexual circle. Proust's most flamboyant and scurrilous friend de Montesquiou remarked: 'If you leave your son with Robert d'Humières, make sure you leave the light on.'[58]

D'Humières and Du Breuil, like thousands of other Frenchmen killed in the war, had no chance to become grand old men. But Wharton also knew plenty of Academicians and members of the French Institut, distinguished historians, archaeologists and linguists. As well as the ubiquitous 'Schlum', whose works on Byzantine history she kept in her library, there was the Baron Ernest Seillière, a specialist on German Romanticism, author of books on Rousseau, Flaubert, and Barbey d'Aurevilly, all inscribed to Mme Wharton with '*hommage très respectueux et fidèle souvenir*'; Alexandre de Laborde, 'learned bibliophile and authority on illuminated manuscripts' (who was also the maestro of Rosa's salon); and Victor Bérard, the director of the École des Hautes Études, an indefatigable Greek scholar, whom she described, appealingly, as 'a big handsome man, with a brain bursting with intellectual enthusiasms and rash hypotheses'. Bérard was one of the guests, with Jules Jusserand, Tardieu, Chevrillon, d'Haussonville – and Morton Fullerton – whom Wharton invited to take tea at the Rue de Varenne with Roosevelt, in April 1910.

Of these eminent scholars, one of the most impressive was the ex-Jesuit priest Henri Bremond, whose books on saints and Catholic writers she read, and whose eleven-volume study of religious sentiment in France she thought 'a great book'. Bremond was known after the war, also, for his dispute with the critic Paul Souday, over whether poetry could be pure sound, without meaning; he cited Valéry in support of his argument for '*la poésie pure*'. Bourget called Bremond 'a modernist, a philosopher, a theologian, but anti-Protestant and anti-Liberal'. Schlumberger, who met him at Mme Wharton's in 1922, described him as an 'impetuous' character with a 'beautiful head' and a warm sympathetic voice. They discussed the victory of Fascism in Italy – which everyone was talking about at the end of 1922.[59]

Such political conversations would have been habitual. And the politics of her French circles were overwhelmingly conservative. She would have detested the thuggery of Action Française, the fascistic, violently nationalistic movement founded in 1898 and dedicated 'to saving France from such un-French elements as the Protestants, the Freemasons, and the Jews'. She showed no signs of interest in its leader, Charles Maurras, apart from one disparaging remark about him in a letter to Fullerton. Her aristocratic friends would, on the whole, have been completely out of sympathy with his aggressive neo-royalists. But some of the people she knew and read in the 1900s were very far to the right – though 'the right' in early twentieth-century France was an extremely mixed entity. Bourget's Catholic, reactionary authoritarianism edged him quite close to Maurras, and Bourget was one of the founding members of Action Française. He spoke at their dinner the summer the Whartons were staying with him, in 1900. The quixotic Jean Du Breuil published in the pages of the magazine *L'Action Française*, in 1902, an article on Gordon of Khartoum, which Wharton admired. (But many intellectuals read the magazine's high-quality articles without sharing its politics.) Wharton read Anna de Noailles's lover Maurice Barrès (greatly admired by Bourget), with his 'cult of the self' against the barbarians and the bourgeoisie, and his detestation of parliamentary democracy. During the war, he contributed to her *Book of the Homeless*. All of Berry's copies of Barrès's works (*Sous l'oeil des barbares*, *Scènes et doctrines du nationalisme*, etc.) were in her library. She owned a couple of books by Léon Daudet (the most venomous and extreme of Action Française's journalists), and told Berenson in 1915 that she found Daudet's *Fantômes et vivants* 'poisonously amusing'. Abel Bonnard would contribute in the 1920s to *Le Nouveau Siècle*, the voice of the extreme right-wing 'Faisceau' movement; during the Second World War he became the Vichy government's Minister for Education and Culture, and was an anti-Semitic, fascist collaborator. André Tardieu became increasingly authoritarian in the course of his parliamentary career.

These are scattered examples, drawn from an eclectic group of thinkers. If there was one broad factor that linked Wharton to all these French right-wingers, it was the way she read history. Like many French intellectuals of her time, she was very interested in the work of Hippolyte Taine, whom she called 'one of the formative influences of my youth', and many of whose books she had in her library. Taine's historical pessimism, his anti-romanticism, his scientific positivism and his determinist accounts of human behaviour, were extremely important for Bourget, Barrès, Maurras – and Wharton. One of Wharton's favourite historians, also much influenced by Taine, was Jacques Bainville, whose 1920s *Histoire de France* she thought 'a masterpiece'. Bainville, anti-Jacobin and anti-republican, argued that the French character is essentially conservative, always battling against anarchist tendencies. He was a member of Action Française, shared many of Maurras's views, and in the 1920s became a strong supporter of Mussolini. Bainville, with a number of the other writers and historians in Wharton's circle, was a signatory to a post-war manifesto in the *Figaro* calling for an 'Intelligence Party', in a chauvinist polemic which described France as 'the guardian of all civilisation' (Proust opposed it). Among the signatories were Bourget, Daniel Halévy (a writer Wharton greatly admired), Edmond Jaloux (who wrote about her, and was a friend of Berry's), Maurras, Schlumberger, and Vaudoyer.[60] It would be dangerous, though, to over-dramatise Wharton's right-wing links. After the war, she expressed fleeting admiration for Mussolini's efficiency. She was resolutely anti-unions and anti-socialist. In wartime, she was a devoted supporter of General Lyautey and of the French empire, and expressed passionately anti-Boche sentiments. But she was not – as her novels show – a rigid or insensitive reactionary.

In *A Backward Glance*, Wharton listed a good handful of politicians, ambassadors and diplomats among her friends. Jules Cambon, whom she had known as the French ambassador in Washington before his move to Berlin, would help her with her travels to the Front in wartime (as well as supporting her nomination for the Nobel Prize for Literature in 1927). Maurice Paléologue, the last French ambassador to tsarist Russia, inscribed his books, on Talleyrand and Chateaubriand and on the tsars, to her, '*en hommage d'admiration pour son noble talent, en témoignage de respectueuse amitié*' from '*son fervent admirateur, fidèlement dévoué*'. She often met, socially, the diary-keeping diplomat Paul Morand, and the 'indefatigably brilliant' Charles de Chambrun. She does not mention the Comte de Chambrun's marriage to one of her most 'stimulating and vivid' Paris acquaintants, the Princesse Lucien Murat, nor that the princesse had been the lover of the playwright and gambler Henry Bernstein, whom Wharton met at Jacques-Émile Blanche's house, but this connection may have escaped her. Not that her Paris would have been gossip-free. As well as the busy diplomats and lawyers, there were plenty of leisured gentlemen with time on their hands. One of her favourite French companions seems to have been best known – like her old friend Egerton Winthrop, still much in evidence in her early Paris years – for doing nothing at all. Alfred de St André, not mentioned in *A Backward Glance*, was everybody's pet Parisian, good company, a gourmet, knowledgeable about the city, endlessly available for trips and visits and dinners. He could be tiresome (one post-war visit consisted of his going on relentlessly about why he disliked the telephone) but, like many such apparently leisured Frenchmen, he sprang into action in wartime.[61]

Wharton made a closer, and more useful, friendship with the remarkable Léon Bélugou, a widely travelled mining engineer, journalist, teacher, and well-known figure in Parisian high society. (It took many years for the extent of her intimacy with Bélugou to be revealed: not until his widow died in 1989 were their letters published.) He travelled to Indo-China, Japan and Russia, was an expert on Stendhal, devotee of Nietzsche, and friend of Valéry and Proust, and published some conservative essays on educational theory. Bélugou was a good friend of Morton Fullerton's; he got to know Wharton in 1908 and became one of her more intimate Parisian friends, through the war and into the 1920s. He found for her an invaluable lawyer, his friend André Boccon-Gibod – '*l'excellent Boc*', she called him – who would deal with her divorce. He translated one of Wharton's stories, 'The Letters', as 'Le Bilan', in the *Revue des Deux Mondes*, and she was delighted: '*Je suis ravie . . . C'est mieux qu'une adaptation, c'est ma nouvelle même*' ('I am absolutely delighted . . . It's better than an adaptation, it's my story itself . . .'). It amused him that she often asked him round '*à prendre une tasse de thé*' ('*prendre le thé*' was one of the few French idioms she never picked up), to meet Henry James or to have some literary chat – '*bouquiner*', as they put it, to talk about old books. She called him '*Cher Ami*' or '*Bien cher ami*'; he called her '*Chère Madame*' but might sign off, half-jokingly and half-formally, '*Milles aimables et respectueux compliments et Vive Dostoievski!*' They had running literary jokes about *Bouvard et Pecuchet*, or

Charlie Du Bos, or Bourget's view of Stendhal. They exchanged their latest reading; in 1912 she told him how much she was enjoying Sainte-Beuve's book on Chateaubriand: '*Ah, quel bon travail, à trois dimensions – pas comme les pauvres placages que l'on vous offre maintenant comme des chefs-d'oeuvres!*' ('Ah, what good, three-dimensional work, not like the pathetic superficialities which are presented these days as masterpieces'.) She told him about her musical enthusiasms, Berlioz's *Requiem* (a new discovery for her in 1912, splendidly 'savage', she thought) and a marvellous performance in 1914 of Bach's St Matthew Passion ('*la plus noble, la plus grande, la plus émouvante que l'on puisse imaginer*'). They exchanged sympathetic messages about moods of depression: '*Si je la connais, votre accidie? Mais je crois en détenir le record en ce moment!*' ('Do I not understand your lethargic melancholy? I think I hold the record for it these days!') He brought her presents from his travels, like a 'charming old God of longevity from Tokio' in September 1911. And they had one subject of consuming interest to her, their mutual friendship with Fullerton.

After the war, Bélugou's marriage to a much younger woman, an actress, Germaine Gien, seems to have estranged them somewhat (she wrote impatiently to Berenson in 1915 that 'Bélugou [was] as dear as ever, but much preoccupied by a tardy grande passion which doesn't agree with him – the object being 25 years old, & apparently silly & unsatisfactory'). But she was kind (as she often was to children) to their daughter Lucienne, and gave her a silver dog-whistle with a coral mouthpiece and 'Edith' engraved on it, which she had had since childhood. And he continued to be her 'beloved Bélugou', one of her faithful 'Bs': Bélugou, Berry, Berenson, Bourget, Du Bos, Blanche.[62]

The portrait-painter Jacques-Émile Blanche was a long-lasting friend, but not someone safe to confide in, like Bélugou. He opened the door to a society of artists as well as writers, and he was very talented. Influenced by Degas, a friend of Sickert and Beardsley, Blanche was one of the outstanding portraitists of his time. His subjects included Mallarmé, Gide, Cocteau, Stravinsky, Joyce, Bergson, Hardy, and Virginia Woolf – but not, alas, Edith Wharton. His strangely moribund and glittering-eyed portrait of the young Marcel Proust, and his impressive, sensitive profile of James (commissioned by Wharton), show his remarkable flair. James joked about his being 'agreeable and ravishing to sit to by reason of his extraordinary conversational powers; by which he systematically holds his sitters wreathed in smiles and with a look of infatuation on their faces – which makes them thus very brilliant to paint'. He was much in demand 'with all the billionaires', James added, and Blanche was a great frequenter of stately homes and a dedicated Anglophile (he was often at Hill Hall).

Not everyone found him as charming as James did. Blanche's father, Dr Esprit Blanche, and his grandfather were both 'alienists' (mind-doctors, who included Gérard de Nerval and Maupassant among their patients), but Blanche, notoriously spiteful and quarrelsome, seems not to have inherited their sensitivity. His great friend Cocteau called him '*le vipère sans queue*'; Schlumberger said he was 'caustic and vain', and Gide said there was something 'facile and light' about him that caused him 'indescribable discomfort'. Matilda Gay found him as 'cold and slimy' as a fish, 'and quite as slippery as though he lived in the water'. Those who liked him, as Wharton did, had to make the best of his defects. Proust decided that his malice was 'a protective neurosis'. James and Wharton invented puns on his name for his spiteful stories – his little 'blanchailles', his 'blanchissage'. He was malicious about them too, of course, in his gossipy memoirs, recalling how often James wanted to get rid of Wharton as a guest, and how she 'constantly went to see him, and stayed on'.

In spite of the malice, friends flocked to Blanche's two houses, with their magnificent collections of Impressionist paintings. One was in the beautiful semi-rural Parisian suburb of Passy (an enclave of châteaux, rest-homes and writers' houses) where Wharton took James to have his portrait painted in 1908. The other was his old Norman farmhouse at Offranville, near Dieppe, in a setting described by Wharton as 'a garden bursting with flowers' and 'a beautiful orchard' behind. (Blanche once said to Gide: 'I don't know how you can live on a street.') This was where she met Cocteau, and where she became a frequent visitor. George Moore, who knew Blanche well from Hill Hall, described Offranville as 'full of paintings of famous people all painted by Blanche, and books all dedicated to Blanche'.[63]

Wharton's most brilliant French literary acquaintances were Cocteau, Gide, and Valéry. She did not get to know André Gide until the first year of the war, though he lived round the corner, in the Rue Vaneau. Gide was only a few years younger than Wharton; when war broke out, he was in his mid-forties, and an immensely controversial and influential figure, since the publication of *Les Nourritures terrestres* (*The Fruits of the Earth*) in 1897, *L'Immoraliste* in 1902 and *La Porte étroite* in 1909. He became an editor of the *Nouvelle Revue Française* in 1908. Gide worked for the Foyer Franco-Belge in aid of refugees from Belgium and northern France from August 1914, for six months, during which time he came to know 'Mme Warthon' quite well. He contributed to her wartime anthology *The Book of the Homeless*. He sent her a copy of *L'Immoraliste* in 1917 and she said (writing to thank him in her impeccable French) that its atmosphere would be an inspiration during her trip to Morocco. In conversation with Mugnier, Berenson and Saint-André, she said she found the author of L'Immoraliste 'timide'. Much later, there was a suggestion that she might write prefaces to his book on Conrad or to Dorothy Bussy's translation of La Porte étroite. She relished his literary essays, Prétextes. Les Faux-monnayeurs (1925) may have influenced the literary world of The Gods Arrive. Whether or not Wharton knew about Gide's complicated, bisexual relationships and his homosexual circle, she adopted a slightly patronising tone in wartime about his being 'a mass of quivering "susceptibilities" . . . luckily he is so charming that one ends by not minding'. Gide's references to her in his journals are respectful, but not warm.[64]

Gide's hostile rivalry with the young Cocteau was beginning to take shape at the time Wharton met the dazzling young man, at Blanche's house, in 1912. She was tremendously struck by this 'passionately imaginative youth' and his 'young enthusiasm', which, over the years, she thought faded away. She had similarly mixed feelings about Paul Valéry, whom she met after the war. She liked him, but not his work, which she thought too 'cold' and 'meticulous'. Valéry cannot have known this, since he inscribed a copy of his Variété to her, effusively trusting that she would appreciate in it the very qualities which, in fact, she most disliked: 'Quoi que votre art, Miss Wharton [sic], soit de créer des êtres qui vivent, je sais que vous ne haïssez pas les figures abstraites et les personnages appauvris qui ne se rencontrent que dans les cerveaux. C'est pourquoi je me permets de mettre à vos pieds ce petit volume où ne manque point la sécheresse.' ['Even though your art, Miss Wharton [sic], is to create beings who live, I know that you don't dislike the abstract figures and the attenuated characters which are only met with in the brain. That's why I allow myself to place at your feet this little volume, which lacks nothing in dryness.'][65]

This dedication of Valéry's, in a volume pencilled with her markings, points to the heart of Wharton's French life: literature. If she and Teddy had just been wealthy, well-connected friends of the Vanderbilts, she would not have made this astounding range of cultural contacts. Doors opened to her because of the impact of the translation of The House of Mirth. And in this literary success her close working companion was Charles Du Bos, who lived and breathed literature, whom everyone made fun of, with whom Wharton was often exasperated, but who, with his wife and daughter, remained a friend for life.

Du Bos was in his twenties, and Wharton was forty-four, when the Bourgets introduced him to her in 1906 as the best possible translator for her novel. At that time the Whartons were staying in the Hotel Dominici, and Du Bos would go there to talk about Lily Bart, 'with whom he was a little in love' – and perhaps with her author, too. His translation appeared in the *Revue de Paris* from 1906 to 1907 as *La Demeure de Liesse*, published by Plon as *Chez Les Heureux du Monde* (1908). Matilda Gay told him that 'the French public would surely misunderstand both the characters and the *donnée* ... He said that he wanted to introduce Mrs Wharton's talent to the small minority in France who could understand her. I suggested that this was probably composed of himself and two other people.' But she was wrong. Wharton boasted to Brownell that her novel was having 'a wild, fantastic, unprecedented success, the like of which the Revue has not had in years ... it is rather unusual for a foreign author to be so rapidly and generally *répandu* [widespread]'. Du Bos continued to help. He found her the French teacher, in January 1911, who encouraged her to write the exercise that became *Ethan Frome*. They worked together on the French translation (which she thought 'singularly bad') of *Ethan, Sous la Neige*, for the *Revue des Deux Mondes* in 1912. Du Bos translated *The Reef* in 1922, when he planned a study of Wharton in his *Approximations*, which he never wrote.

Du Bos was always half-nervous of, half-devoted to, Wharton. She often cut him short: 'every topic was too swiftly shelved ... a certain impatience made her averse to concentrating'. (But he was known for 'talking like a printed book'.) Still, they carried on a literary conversation for many years. In 1912 they are discussing the perfection of Schopenhauer's style; in 1931, they are dining with Herbert Read and trying to remember whether Coleridge or Wordsworth said 'Every great and original writer ... must himself create the taste by which he is to be relished' (it was Coleridge). Du Bos refers in his journals to discussions with her about James, to whom she had introduced him, or the Goncourts, or the novels of George Eliot. They sent each other books (she gave him a Paul Claudel in 1913, and Sidney Colvin's life of Keats in 1917). He enjoyed her capacity for 'placing' writers, if he sometimes found her 'mental equipoise' forbidding. He liked her epigrams, and reapplied a remark she made about a character in Proust having the calm that comes from an 'impregnable bank account' to her own life.

Charlie, as his friends called him, was addicted to literature in English. He revered some of his French contemporaries, such as Anna de Noailles, Maurice Barrès, Bourget and Gide (with whom he had a painful quarrel), but his deepest passions were for Byron, Keats, Shelley and Pater. He was Anglo-French, with bright blue eyes, a thin red nose, long moustaches and a 'very French head' (Mario Praz's phrase). His pockets were always spilling over with pencils and papers. He was pernickety, vain, snobbish, naive, pompous and affectionate, a late convert to Catholicism, a self-conscious sensualist who could spend all day raving about the pleasures of getting his hair shampooed, a fusspot who had to have everything in his house 'just so', and an incompetent who (according to Gide) did not know how to refill his fountain-pen and had to go to a shop to get it done. Uxoriously married to the likeable Zézette (though with an intense interest, according to the Abbé Mugnier, in the increasing number of pederasts in their society), he entertained lavishly on a rather small income, first at the Rue de la Tour in Passy, and later on the Île-Saint-Louis. Mario Praz described his house as 'a cross between a doll's house and a church decorated for a festival'; Vaudoyer said it was like a grand Venetian painting, with aromas of the very best tea and cigars accompanying the endless talk on art, books, and music.

Du Bos became a well-known literary figure, solemn to the point of absurdity. He played an influential part in the culture, as a critic and translator (including of Joyce's *Dubliners*), and as the founder, in 1922, of Plon-Nourrit's *Collection des Auteurs Étrangers* – the first of its kind – in which *The Age of Innocence* and *The Reef* appeared, and which became *Feux Croisés* in 1927. He was also one of the key members of the '*entretiens*', or colloquies, set up every summer at Pontigny, in Burgundy, by Paul Desjardins and a group of writers including Gide, Valéry, Schlumberger, Mauriac, and André Maurois, to debate cultural subjects, with immense seriousness. Wharton sympathised with his shyness and his puritanism, but there was only one moment in their friendship when he felt she spoke completely openly to him. It was on a trip in 1912 to Montfort l'Amaury (a place that mattered to her), when she suddenly spoke about the 'miserable poverty of any love that lies outside of marriage'.[66]

It is through Du Bos that we see Edith Wharton most vividly as a naturalised woman of letters in France. When she first began her Paris life, she flung herself into all kinds of social engagements: trips to the theatre and the opera (everyone was theatre-mad then, and it was said that 'the whole of Paris was a vast gossipy green room'), musical parties, *conférences* (lecture-series on topics such as Shakespeare or Racine), art shows at the Petit Palais or exhibitions of theatrical portraits at the Louvre, drives in the Bois de Boulogne, embassy dinners, tea-parties, restaurant lunches and dinners, even a drive to see one of the new air-ships (which failed to take off).

But Wharton was no Undine Spragg. Paris high society impinged on her to an extent: she knew about the *Bottin Mondain* (the elite telephone subscribers' list, launched in 1903, in which hostesses listed their regular reception days); she knew how to shop in the Rue de Rivoli or at the great Left Bank emporium Au Bon Marché (mentioned in *Madame de Treymes*); she owned one of the new cars that, like the Metro and the autobus, were starting to transform the city; she was aware of the big parties and fancy-dress balls (at the most fashionable of which, even in staid Rue de Varenne, there was beginning to be jazz and dancing). But she was not interested in fashion, though we do catch a glimpse of her at her corset-maker's, via a conversation between Henry James and Marie Belloc Lowndes in 1913: 'He said that when she was lately at her staymaker's the latter said to her: "*Cela n'est pas tout à fait cela.*" Mrs Wharton replied: "But I feel very comfortable." The other observed, "*Oui, et ces corsets donnent à Madame de jolies hanches, mais ce ne sont pas les hanches de cette année.*"' And she was always very precise in her instructions to her dress-makers; a letter from her secretary in 1923 to Madame Denise, in the Place Vendôme, requires '*une robe noire avec des manches en crêpe Georgette, et une garniture égayant un peu le haut du corsage* [a trimming to brighten up the top of the blouse]. *Elle aime le corsage croisé ou bien tombant droit et formant un tablier devant, avec une ceinture qui part de chaque côté du tablier pour nouer derrière.*'[67]

But we see her, most of all, as an integrated, knowing participant in the literary world. We hear Cocteau having a 'sharp run-in' with Anna de Noailles at Wharton's apartment, coming to near-blows about Claudel, in 1916. We hear Bourget asking Gide, at his house in Costebelle in November 1915, while Wharton was out of the room, about whether his 'immoralist' was a practising pederast, and launching on his distinction between sadists and masochists (Bourget loved talking about sex). When she came back in, the subject was changed. ('It would have amused me to have Mrs Wharton's opinion, if she had one', Gide noted.) A moment later, he and Wharton were catching each other's eye incredulously, as Bourget waxed tearful over a second-rate book. We see her at dinner at the Crillon, with Schlum, the Bourgets, and Jaloux and his wife, in November 1922, talking about the overthrow of Lloyd George in the British elections, about the recently dead Proust, and about Charles Du Bos, always a target for friendly jokes. In April 1915 – when literary conversations would have been consoling – she was giving supper to her two *abbés*, Bremond and Mugnier, and Walter Berry, and telling them about James's life of the sculptor William Wetmore Story, a masterpiece done without any documents. James, she said, was like Péguy, only even more complicated. (A surprising comparison, perhaps for the Abbé Mugnier's benefit.) The name of Charles Péguy, the mystic, Catholic nationalist, came up again at the Restaurant Lucas in

February 1918, where Wharton was lunching with Mugnier, Berenson, Saint-André, Gide, and Princesse Murat. They discussed Claudel and Péguy and went on to a Picasso exhibition. At another wartime dinner, the diplomat Paul Morand met her at Marie Scheikevitch's, with Philomène, Walter, Grosclaude, and others. Morand noted an awkward moment when Berry snubbed the usually irrepressible Grosclaude. There was mockery of a second-rate journalist on the *Figaro*, Joseph Reinach, of whom one general had said, 'Joseph, stop writing or I'll stop winning.' Someone quoted Victor Hugo, someone repeated a gaffe of Rosa's, someone told a joke about a dog-owner who says to his visitor, 'Don't worry, you know the proverb, "Who barks does not bite." The visitor replies: "I know the proverb, you know the proverb, but does the dog know the proverb?"' Then Morand went off to visit the bedridden Proust. Wharton's contributions to this Parisian chatter went unrecorded.[68]

Nor did she contribute – though she certainly listened – on the one occasion, in 1923, when she attended one of the '*entretiens*' at Pontigny, with Walter, when the (post-war and patriotic) subject for discussion was 'Y *a-t-il dans la poésie d'un peuple un trésor réservé?*' ('Is there a private or incommunicable treasure, or value, in the poetry of a people, or nation?') There were discussions on translation and the untranslatable, and on whether national poets have a totemic value for their people; Charlie asked whether an 'uncultured' person could have a better taste for the poetry of his own country than a cultured foreigner. As well as the regulars (Gide, Desjardins, Maurois, Du Bos) the participants included Lytton Strachey, Hope Mirrlees, and Jane Harrison – probably Wharton's only encounter with these three English writers. She was not much impressed with the visit, and reported back to Berenson and the Abbé Mugnier that everyone was terribly silent – Gide had not been allowed to invite Valéry because it was thought he would talk too much. Berenson remarked (in the Abbé's view, justly), '*Je n'aime pas la célébralité collective.*'[69]

In all these glimpses of Edith Wharton in France, we see a person completely 'au fait' and in the swim. Most people said of her that she remained, essentially, an American exile. Blanche said: 'She loved Europe, she loved and knew France, England, Italy, better than any native – yet remained an American of the old fashion.' Her French friends lightly mocked her for speaking an antiquated French, learnt through her childhood reading – Bourget called it 'the purest Louis Quatorze'. There is a revealing sentence in a story from her early years in Paris, 'The Verdict': 'Don't you know, how in talking a foreign language, even fluently, one says half the time, not what one wants to, but what one can?' Yet she seems

completely in control of her life in a foreign language in her French correspondence – with Bélugou, with the Du Boses, with Gide, with the editors
at Plon-Nourrit, with Doumic at the *Revue des Deux Mondes*, Marcel Prévost
at the *Revue de France*, or Chaumeix at the *Revue de Paris*. Though she
used a secretary for her business correspondence, a great tide of complex
missives about money and legal matters, war-work, property, house moves,
book orders, arrangements with tradesmen, furniture, wine, travel, servants,
plants and gardens, went streaming out from her various addresses
throughout her life in France. There was nothing she could not deal with
and nothing that got past her. As she became a respected fixture on the
Plon list – with *Sous la Neige*, *Un Fils au Front*, *Au Temps de l'Innocence*,
Plein d'Été, *Vieux New York*, *Leurs Enfants* – she seemed almost to have
become a French novelist.

She usually worked with her French translators (who were often friends,
like Charlie or Minnie Bourget, Mme Taillandier or Louis Gillet), but she
could have done her own if she had chosen to. She revised their work carefully. Where possible she preferred to have two translators collaborating on
each book, one for '*le gros travail*' (the main work) and one for '*la mise au
point*' (the fine-tuning), '*pour la simple raison qu'il est extrémément difficile de
traduire de l'anglais en français, et que la personne qui fait la première version
a toujours tendance à serrer le texte de trop près. Il faut donc que quelqu'un
d'autre relise ce texte pour lui donner un tour plus français.*' ('The first translator always has a tendency to stick too close to the text, and so someone
else needs to go over it to give it more of a French turn of phrase.') As
well as writing her one story in French, 'Les Metteurs en Scène' (which
gave the title to the French collection of her stories published by Plon-
Nourrit in 1909) she translated her story 'Atrophy', published in English
in 1927 and in 1929 in the conservative magazine edited by René Doumic,
the *Revue des Deux Mondes*. One short extract (on a favourite theme) shows
that her version is more of an elegant rewriting than a literal translation:

What nonsense to pretend that nowadays, even in the big cities, in the
world's greatest social centres, the severe old-fashioned standards had
given place to tolerance, laxity and ease! You took up the morning paper,
and you read of girl bandits, movie-star divorces, 'hold-ups' at balls,
murder and suicide and elopement, and a general welter of disjointed
disconnected impulses and appetites; then you turned your eyes onto
your own daily life, and found yourself as cribbed and cabined, as beset
by vigilant family eyes, observant friends, all sorts of embodied standards,
as any white-muslin novel heroine of the 'sixties!

Que de lamentations on entendait au sein de la tribu sur le 'glissement moral'! Était-on bien juste, même à ne considérer que les grandes villes, les larges cercles sociaux? Les belles moeurs d'autrefois cédaient, disaient-on, à la tolérance, au relâchement, au sans-gêne. Que voyait-on le matin en dépliant le journal? Scandaleux réçits! Des jeunes filles cambriolant le revolver au poing, des divorces à la vapeur, des irruptions de bandits en plein bal, des assassin- ats, des enlèvements, l'invasion désordonnée des violences et des appétits. Oui, tout cela se lisait dans les journaux; mais en fait une Norah Frenway, consid- érant le champ de son existence, pouvait, comme tant d'autres, s'y trouver aussi parfaitement palissadée, clôturée et surveillée par la famille et la société aux aguets que la plus sage demoiselle des sages romans que lisait sa grand- mère.[70]

She sounds there like an impeccable French writer; and that mastery of style came from an enormous and wide-ranging knowledge of French liter- ature. It is no surprise to find her attracted to, and often citing, the great French rationalists and realists: Stendhal, Balzac, Alphonse Daudet, Flaubert, Maupassant, the Goncourts, Michelet, Joubert. But she also felt a profound attraction to the poems of Mallarmé, to the romantic disillu- sionment of Alfred de Vigny (her copy of *Journal d'un Poète* underlines such dark sayings as '*La vérité sur la vie, c'est le désespoir*'), as well as to the intense, sensitive poetry of her friends Anna de Noailles and Henri de Régnier. She enjoyed the most ghoulish and morbid of Baudelaire's *Fleurs du Mal*, in which she marks, in her 1896 edition, '*Sépulture d'un Poète Maudit*', '*Le Flacon*' ('The Scent-Bottle'), in which the lover is plunged by memory into the spectral corpse of an old, rancid love, and '*Une Charogne*' ('Carrion'), a lover's horrible encounter with a rotting corpse covered in flies and maggots, which his loved one will come to resemble.

In music, too, she had wide-ranging tastes. She went (with the d'Humières) to hear Proust's friend Reynaldo Hahn (an admirer of Saint- Saëns and Fauré) give a concert of his work, which she found 'exquisite', and she heard Yvette Guilbert, the popular, earthy chanteuse, in her white dress and black gloves and red lipstick immortalised by Toulouse-Lautrec, sing at a private house. (Guilbert was staging 'Yvette's Thursdays', concert- lectures on '*La Femme dans la Chanson*'.) She shared musical tastes with Charlie, who was delighted, in March 1914, to hear a piano recital at her apartment of Franck, Debussy's 'La Cathédrale Engloutie', and Ravel's 'Pavane pour une Infante défunte'. She was ravished by the dancing of Isadora Duncan, 'the dance I had always dreamed of, a flowing of move- ment into movement'. And like all Paris, she was in love with the wild colour and sensuality of the Russian ballet – 'our last vision of beauty before the war', as she remembered it.[71] Though she became less open to artistic experiments in the 1920s, and though she was never a part of the bohemian, decadent side of the gay, pre-war city, she had her adventures there, too. Paris meant romance, excitement and beauty to her, as well as order and tradition.

I I

L'Âme Close

Edith Wharton was forty-five in 1907 when, after a luxurious Atlantic crossing with two dogs and six servants (Gross, White, Charles Cook and the maids, who were all going to take French lessons) she and Teddy settled into 58 Rue de Varenne. Teddy thought the life suited her very well: 'I never knew her better in ten years.' Though French literary society was not for him ('I am no good on Puss's high plane of thought') he seemed pleased with the apartment and the car, 'all done over as new for Paris'. Edith was looking handsome and fine, in her dark furs and silks, her laces and pearls and elegant hats, her long, strong serious face with its large dark eyes and strongly arched eyebrows and ironical smile softened by a great sweep of dark-reddish hair pinned up in a large loose bun. She was not beautiful – her nose was too long, her chin too heavy and square, her build too stocky and her smile too tight, and her expression still showed something of that nervous apprehensive reserve that made her looks, in her twenties, so painfully tense. But intelligence and alertness, quick feeling and humour gleamed out of her face. In her day-clothes she looked rich, poised and impressive; and in décolleté evening dress, glinting with the choker of pearls, the long pendants, the bracelets and pearl-drop earrings she liked, you could see that her bare arms were rounded and shapely, her breasts were large, her neck long and graceful. She was not tall, but she carried herself well. She often writes about the erotic appeal of a self-possessed, distinctive-looking, grown-up woman. Selden is always wanting to penetrate the spontaneous womanly nature under Lily Bart's artifice; in *Madame de Treymes*, the American lover is moved when Fanny de Malrive, 'the kind of woman who always presents herself to the mind's eye as completely equipped, as made up of exquisitely cared for and finely related details', has forgotten, in the heat of the moment, to draw on her gloves. The idea of undressing and undoing the 'completely equipped' Mrs Wharton – rich married lady, mature woman, successful novelist – and exposing the concealed, thwarted, passionate self hidden under the gloves and furs, could have been very intriguing to a certain kind of curious, adventurous sensualist.[1]

Among the throng of people she met at Rosa's salon early in 1907 was Morton Fullerton, a thoroughly Frenchified forty-two-year-old American journalist, who had been working as a correspondent in the Paris office of the London *Times* since 1891, as well as writing articles for other papers, and book reviews for the *TLS*, and even trying his hand at a few sonnets. He wrote and spoke fluent French, and had a wide range of contacts in Parisian literary, journalistic and publishing circles. Léon Bélugou was his particular friend; they had known each other well since about 1902. Among Edith's American friends, he knew the Nortons from his Harvard days, and had been an intimate friend of Henry's since about 1890. Morton, though not tall, was a very attractive man, always stylish in immaculate shirts and suits (his wardrobe contained a great number of 'plastrons', detachable dress-shirt-fronts), sporting elegant cravats, shiny shoes and a cane. He had engaging manners, and 'a serious, eager, handsome face', with smooth dark hair, intense blue eyes, a flamboyant dark brown moustache and a sensual mouth. And he was interesting, a wide reader, an informed observer of French society and politics, who had written on subjects as various as Dreyfus, George Meredith, Cairo, patriotism and democracy, rural France, and French policy in Morocco. He had a piece on the new Prime Minister, Georges Clemenceau (whom he knew) in the February 1907 issue of the *National Review*, and had been writing articles on the Rhône valley in the *Revue de Paris* in 1905.[2]

Early in 1908, looking back on the beginning of the relationship, Edith found the perfect quotation (from Emerson's essay 'Character'): 'The moment my eye fell on him I was content.'[3] This may have been a retrospective literary shaping of something that started more imperceptibly. Initially, in the spring of 1907, he was simply a charming new acquaintance who could also be of professional use. Edith immediately asked him to help with placing the translation of *The House of Mirth*, which Charlie started work on in March 1907: would it be better to sell it for serialisation to *Le Temps* or to the *Revue de Paris*? Would he come and help her with her French proof-correcting, at which she was no good at all? Would he come and dine? – 'There will be no one else, and we can talk shop peacefully.' In the weeks before the 'motor-flight' in March with Teddy and Henry, and during Henry's long luxurious stay at the Rue de Varenne in April and May 1907, Morton was much in evidence. She mentioned him in a letter to Sally in April 1907. Morton was impressed with her, too, describing her in a letter to his mother as distinguished by *savoir-faire* and

'admirable intelligence'. Invitations went out to Mr Fullerton to come and
have tea with Mr James. By the time *Madame de Treymes* came out in March
1907, the tone had become playful (as it did, quickly, with younger friends
she warmed to, like John Hugh Smith or Percy Lubbock): she was delighted
he liked it but reproached him for his 'regrettable lack of critical integrity'.
On the way to America in June, she thanked him graciously for his
'persistent action' on behalf of *The House of Mirth*, safely placed in the
Revue de Paris, told him she was 'find-able' at The Mount if he was in
America, and said that she was eager to discuss the writings of Émile Faguet.
In her copy of Faguet's *L'Anticléricalisme*, she had marked several passages
on French character, including a page on how the French are preoccupied
with general ideas; if you hear Frenchmen talking in public, it is never
about practical matters, but only about political generalisations, or women.
This was the sort of thing she could not talk to Teddy about, and wanted
to discuss with Fullerton.

She was not sure if he would respond to her invitation; there was something unaccountable about him. 'Your friend Fullerton', she told Sally, 'is
very intelligent, but slightly mysterious, I think.' James warned her – and
it was a warning she should have noted – that, though he had told Fullerton
to get in touch with her in America, she should not count on him – 'He's
so incalculable' (not like 'your plain unvarnished & devoted Henry James').
When he did get in touch, to her great delight, asking to visit Lenox in
October, she teased him by repeating what James had said: 'You won't see
Fullerton.' James, with Walter Berry, Gaillard Lapsley and others, had also
been at The Mount that summer; James was the reason (or the one given
to Edith) that Fullerton could get to Lenox, as he was giving a lecture on
James at Bryn Mawr College; Edith was looking forward to reading it. James
was the patron of the relationship from the first.[4]

It was only a two-day visit, from 21 to 22 October 1907. Edith's old
friend Eliot Gregory was staying too. She and Morton had a friendly but
robust argument about his piece on James; she thought it was too 'emphatic',
but he would not 'abate one jot'. Edith took her guests out in the car (Teddy
did not go, as he and his sister were worried about his mother's bronchitis
– 'I think without reason', Edith told Sally.) The first snow of the season
had fallen the night before Morton arrived, and the roads were slushy. They
stopped so that Cook could fit chains to the wheels. Edith and Morton sat
on a wet bank in the woods, smoking, and found a shrub of witch-hazel in
bloom. Morton was dropped off at Westfield on his way home to his parents'
house in Brockton, Massachusetts. Eliot and Edith went on to the delightful
village of Farmington. In a burst of pleasure, she described the journey

exhilaratedly to Sally as 'a dazzling run across blue mountains, through arches and long vistas of gold & amber. I never saw such a pure clear revel of colour . . . I like these "motor-flights" in this season, & they make me feel so well.' She wrote to Sally's father, thanking him for his note about *The Fruit of the Tree*, and saying they had just had 'a tantalizing one-night visit' from Mr Fullerton 'that made me want to see much more of him'.[5]

A few days later, Morton sent her a thank-you letter. With the note there was a sprig of witch-hazel. This was all it took, at this moment in her life, to plunge her into deep emotion. It was as if she was waiting to be in love, and had recognised her opportunity. In her writing room at The Mount, looking out over the golden autumnal New England landscape, she at once started a journal, which she called 'The Life Apart: L'Âme Close'. The French phrase (which could be translated as 'the shut-in, or closed-down soul, or spirit') was taken from a poem by Pierre Ronsard, which she wrote out in full in the appointments diary she would keep alongside this secret diary: '*Une tristesse dans l'âme close / Me nourrit, et non autre chose.*' She would not have started this 'long-abandoned book', she wrote (sounding as if there might have been cause, long ago, for such a journal) if he had not enclosed the 'wych-hazel' without comment, 'thus telling me (as I choose to think!) that you knew what was in my mind when I found it blooming . . .' It made her feel that she had, 'after so long!', found 'someone to talk to'. 'For I had no one but myself to talk to, and it is absurd to write down what one says to one's self, but now I shall have the illusion that I am talking to you, & that – as when I picked the wych-hazel – something of what I say will somehow reach you . . .' She goes on to note the symbolism of the early snow-storm and the late-flowering 'old woman's flower'. (The yellow flowers of the witch-hazel, arriving in late autumn on bare twigs, are famed for their medicinal uses.) It is an elaborate literary contrivance: a letter to a recipient whose emotions she is inventing, written to create the illusion that she is not just talking to herself. At the same time she sent him an awkward little comic postcard, and mentioned his name as often as she could in her letters to Sally (who learnt that the Whartons had decided to leave for Europe earlier than planned) and in exchanges with James, to whom Morton had given a full report of his visit to The Mount. Morton was back in Paris by mid-November, and, over a month after his visit (this was the start of a recurring pattern of silences and delays), he wrote to her. 'Your letter from Paris . . .', she noted only, in the journal.[6]

The Mount was shut up, and the Whartons sailed for Europe on 5 December 1907, arriving on the 18th. A rapturous letter, ostensibly in praise of Paris, went back to Sally: 'I am sunk in the usual demoralizing happiness which this atmosphere produces in me. Dieu que c'est beau after six months of eye-starving! The tranquil majesty of the architectural lines, the wonderful blurred winter lights, the long lines of lamps garlanding the avenues & the quays – je l'ai dans mon sang!' In tandem with Edith's euphoria, Teddy fell ill, dropping into symptoms of rheumatism, 'nervous depression' and 'neurasthenia'. He became (as she described him impatiently to Sally) 'a very dolorous object'. Clearly, he disliked Paris and everything that was going on there as much as she loved it. And from now on, he settled into poor health, though it would be a long time before his symptoms began to be correctly understood.

Edith, however, was in fine fettle. Invitations at once flew out to Morton, to tea, to dinner, to lunch, to bring friends round, to come and read his essay on James, to take her to the Chamber of Deputies to hear the great socialist orator Jean Jaurès talking about Morocco. She asked Morton to escort her to the brilliant company of Sicilian actors who were giving D'Annunzio's passionate tragedy, La Figlia di Torio, at the Marigny Theatre, in Sicilian dialect (Teddy did not want to go as he 'objected to the language'). Their performance was 'd'une saveur et d'une puissance qui font sensation', it was noted. The 'sensation' for Edith was intense: 'Unforgettable hours', she wrote in her diary that night, 13 January.

Her notes were flirtatious from the first. 'Cher Monsieur, ami et Vice President du Henry James Club', one began, inviting him to do something 'mad & bad', like going to hear an American professor talk on 'Tamerlane' in a series of lectures at the Sorbonne on Elizabethan dramatists. She wore a black dress, and hoped that Morton would like it. The lecture was rather disappointing, and she came away 'amazed at the small amount of wisdom with which the young idea is fed'. The one on Othello was better.[7]

Her own dismally unheroic version of Othello went off to Cannes on 12 February for a few days to stay with the Curtises (providing Edith with the material for 'The Verdict'). On a cold grey wintry Saturday, 15 February 1908, Edith and Morton drove to the little suburban village of Herblay, high above 'a double sweep of the Seine', in quest of their – and Henry James's – latest literary heroine, Hortense Allart. They decided that 'she had lived in a little house just opposite the church'. (James envied them their trip to Herblay as he had envied her an earlier literary pilgrimage: 'Fancy there being a second & intenser Nohant!') All three of them were reading Léon Séché's two-volume life and letters of this daring nineteenth-century lady of letters, who made a fine presiding genius for Edith's affair. She described Allart to Sally as 'an extraordinary woman ... a George Sand without hypocrisy'. Allart wrote frankly erotic novels and passionate love-letters to her distinguished literary lovers (who included Chateaubriand, Bulwer Lytton, and Sainte-Beuve). She left her aristocratic husband, was a friend of George Sand's and a believer in sexual equality: *'Que veut donc la femme? Que demand-t-elle? Elle veut n'être pas livrée à l'homme comme un esclave noir.'* In Hortense's village, the *'âme close'* allowed itself to open up again. In the dramatic scene Edith created for herself afterwards in her secret diary, she sat in a shadowy corner of the little twelfth-century church while Morton talked to the curé, and a veiled figure 'stole up & looked at me a moment'. You might expect this fictional creation to have been the ghost of Hortense Allart. Or 'Was its name Happiness? I dared not lift the veil . . .'

Two evenings later, Edith and Morton sat together in the library at number 58, in the lamplight, while he read an essay by Chevrillon on Meredith and she told herself how intelligent he was. She imagined a life in which 'such evenings might be a dear, accepted habit'. Then he said something that spoilt it and broke the 'fragile glass cup'. She wrote, as if to him, in her diary: 'You hurt me – you disillusioned me – & when you left me I was more deeply yours.' Whatever he did or said – a too obvious sexual approach? a cynical remark? – pain and misunderstanding set in almost on the day that love was declared. Immediately, there was a check: Teddy came back gloomily from Cannes, and the 'happy day' that she and Morton were planning that Saturday to Montfort l'Amaury in the Île-de-France, had to be put off. She had been longing to spend the day with him, to talk 'à coeur ouvert, saying for once what I feel, and *all that I feel,* as other women do'. It was a beautiful day, 'soft & sunny, with spring in the air'; but it was 'some other woman's day, not mine'. Instead she sat indoors and wrote a poem about their lost day, and a sonnet called 'L'Âme Close'. It was a melancholy, ghostly dramatisation of love coming too late, a Baudelairean fantasy of a sad, decayed, shut-up house with one light high inside, a candle held by a 'lover's ghost' for one person: 'Yet enter not, lest, as it flits ahead / You see the hand that carries it is dead.' This began a burst of poetry-writing that kept pace with, and dramatised, the whole affair.[8]

But, for all its fears and doubts, *'l'âme close'* was allowed to have its spring awakening. (*Spring Awakening,* Wedekind's decadent, shocking play about forbidden love, had its Paris premiere, translated by Robert d'Humières, later in 1908.) After a few more miserable weeks in Paris, in mid-March Teddy gave up on Europe for that year. He left for Hot Springs, Arkansas, to take 'the cure', relieved to learn, she told Sally, that 'the terrible sensations in his head which used to depress him so much, are due to gout & nothing else'. She was free for the rest of the spring. Still, there were considerable complications. On 13 April, she had to move out of number 58 into her brother's house in the Place des États Unis. On 24 April, Henry James arrived for a very social two-week stay. After that the time ran very fast to her departure date: on 23 May, she had to leave Paris for Lenox. But in those few months of spring 1908, in the thick of high society, the beginning of serious marital difficulties, James's demanding visit, and a house-move, Edith, at forty-six, embarked on a passionate love-affair.[9]

When, a few years later, she came to write *The Reef*, she gave to the twenty-four-year-old Sophy Viner a version of her own excitement and pleasure. Taken to the Paris theatre for the first time, it is as though 'everything she was seeing, hearing, imagining, rushed in to fill the void of all she had always been denied'. The breathless questions which the naive Sophy asks her double-dealing lover – 'Is it true? Is it really true? Is it really going to happen *to me*?' – echo what Edith was asking, in her Paris spring. She felt like a much younger woman. As in her letters to Sally, where 'Paris' stands in for 'love', her pleasure in the city was inextricably mixed in with her feelings about Morton. This was a Parisian affair which would not have worked in the same way in New York or Lenox. Colouring it all – as for Sophy – were the plays of the Paris season that year. She was going to the theatre several times a week: to *Cavalleria Rusticana*, to Racine's *Andromaque* at the Comédie Française, where, it was noted, Segond-Weber gave a performance of savage power as the jealous Hermione; to Sophocles's *Electra* with Mme Silvain 'finer than ever', she thought; to the now-forgotten French plays of the day (Robert de Flers' *L'Amour Veille* [*Love Watches*], *Il Ne Faut Jurer De Rien*); to Bourget's eagerly awaited *Un Divorce*; to a bad play by Brieux, *Simone*, seen again with an improved ending; to a ridiculous adaptation of Sherlock Holmes; to *Le Roi*, again by Proust's friend de Flers, at the Variétés ('perfect rubbish'); to a translation of Shaw's *Candide* at the Théâtre des Arts, which the Parisians thought the same as Ibsen ('very curious effect to see Shaw's play in French, interpreted by French actors'). (*The Wild Duck* was also playing that season, as were *Ubu Roi*, *La Dame aux Camélias*, and *Peter Pan*.)

The Reef evokes, as dramatically as a Toulouse-Lautrec or a Sickert, what it felt like to go to the theatre in Paris: the dinner before the show, the dark recesses of the box or *baignoire*, the hushed attention for the great actors, the red velvet sofas of the foyer and the 'crowd surging up and down in a glare of lights and gilding', the congested café where you smoked and drank orangeade, the lavish illustrated programmes, the looks and glances as society took stock of who was there, the visits from box to box, the finery of the women, the tedium of hot afternoons at classic matinées that had been staged a hundred times in exactly the same way. At some of Edith's outings to these dramas of love, fate, and adultery, 'He *was near us . . . He was there*.' Two evenings particularly moved her. At the fashionable Renaissance theatre, Henry Bataille's *La Femme Nue*, a serious moral drama, was playing, with the wonderful Lucien Guitry in the lead role. She went with the Bourgets, and Morton slipped into their box – 'that little dim baignoire (number 13, I shall always remember!)' – for one act. Like Darrow watching Sophy's profile in their box, Morton watched her. She felt (she told herself) 'that indescribable current of communication flowering between myself & someone else . . . & said to myself: "This must be what happy women feel . . ."' In May, a few days before her departure, they went to see Albert Samain's *Polyphème* at the Théâtre Français. It was a verse drama which rewrote the Acis and Galatea story, with the suffering, lovelorn giant (Guitry again), who blinds himself, as the main character. After she had left Paris, she replayed the evening in her mind's eye with 'aching distinctness'. 'I don't suppose you know, since it is more of my sex than yours, the quiet ecstasy I feel in sitting next to you in a public place, looking now & then at the way the hair grows on your forehead, at the line of your profile turned to the stage . . . while every drop of blood in my body whispered "Mine – mine – mine!"' So, at the theatre, she staged her own intense private drama.[10]

In the theatre of the Paris streets and salons, they had their assignations and intimate dialogues. 'We are behind the scenes together . . . *on the hither side!*' Morton told her. Their paths crossed in their little cosmopolitan village. 'We met each other by chance in the street . . .' 'Just as we were leaving the house, he arrived to hand me a letter. He drove with us to the *Revue de Paris*. How peaceful, how happy I am when he is near.' 'We saw each other [sic] Place des Invalides.' They snatched at every opportunity for intimacy. On a Saturday in early March, before Teddy left Paris, they all went out to the suburban village of St Cloud, with its great park and woods, for a lunch with André Chevrillon, Robert d'Humières, and others. Harry Jones came to fetch Teddy for a drive; Edith and Morton went back alone in the car, in the snow – a 'dear half-hour . . . the flakes froze on the windows, shutting us in, shutting everything else out . . .'. She got back in time for tea with some countesses. They found out-of-the-way restaurants to meet in, 'at the end of the earth (*rive gauche*) where there is bad food & no chance of meeting acquaintances' – just as her lovers in Paris would do in *The Glimpses of the Moon*. As the weather improved ('Crocuses in bloom, radiant sunlight'), they escaped for a drive in the Bois de Boulogne. They drove out to St

Cloud and 'wandered in the wood'. One day they spent as tourists in Paris: they met at the Louvre, then walked to the ancient church of Saint-Germain-l'Auxerrois, then went by car to Les Arènes de Lutèce, the Roman arena overlooking the Seine, then to the Gothic and Renaissance church of Saint-Étienne-Du-Mont. Then they strolled in the Luxembourg Gardens, where (like so many Parisian lovers) they liked to walk and sit on warm days. A few days before she was due to leave, they went to the Tuileries and sat on a quiet seat under a tree, on a terrace above the Seine. He said: 'My love! My darling!', and she looked at the people 'walking up & down before us, not knowing – not knowing *that it was not worth their while to be alive*'. These stolen moments were graded for happiness: 'How happy I was! . . . Never had we been happier . . . Blissful hours.'[11]

It was never easy, even when Teddy was away. Sometimes the weather was their enemy; sometimes she had a 'grippe' and had to stay in. (The number of times that she mentions a bad cold or an attack of fatigue suggests that this adventure was taking its toll.) Once, they made plans to go to Versailles and dine, but 'the weather was doubtful, you were likely to be detained late at your work, & I was afraid of appearing eager to go when you were less so'. So they missed a chance, as he wrote in his note to her the next day, when 'we might have been happy together'. They planned one Saturday to go and see the great church of Saint-Denis, in the northern outskirts of Paris, by train ('some of the slums might be disagreeable in a motor, & it might be better to go more democratically'). But it rained, so they 'stayed at home & chatted' instead. Sometimes they missed each other by inches: 'I saw you disappearing down the rue de V, as I returned from an inevitable "course" [errand] at a quarter to 3 – Quelle ironie! You were too far to be signalled . . .'[12]

With Teddy in the house, meetings could be sombre. Occasionally, to keep up appearances, Morton dropped in to see them both. 'He came: two sad hours.' She had to work round the servants (though possibly the faithful Gross, as in 'The Lady's Maid's Bell', was in the know): 'Don't wait for me outside [the station], but let me come in & *find you* – À cause de Cook!' When she moved to Harry's apartment, she became more anxious about surveillance: 'Something gave me the impression the other day that we were watched in this house . . . commented on.' They developed discreet strategies for getting together in public: 'Can you not go away from the Du Bos's with me? I shall be alone. Manage to leave just after me, & I'll wait, & take you where you like.' There was one fine place for symbolically charged assignations: 'Meet you at the Louvre at one o'clock, in the shadow of Jean Gougon's "Diana".'[13]

Little notes and *pneumatiques* ('petits bleus') were crucial to these arrangements, and ran between the Rue de Varenne and Morton's office at the Rue de la Chaussée d'Antin or his apartment on the Rue Fabert every day, several times a day (the frequency of postal deliveries in Paris was as important a factor in this affair as Edith's motor-car or her absent husband). His 'little word' soon began to arrive 'almost every morning' with her breakfast tray, effusive, criss-crossed pencil notes he had written in the corner café on the way home from seeing her. None of these survives, but her replies to them do. Every word was hoarded and cherished. 'If you knew how I *love* it!' A deluge of messages were sent back, tender, anxious, imperious: 'Suis-je assez exigeante?' '3rd note in a week! Rassurez vous, cela n'est pas mon habitude.' 'I have just come home, & find your note saying you have not had a word from me! And I wrote you a *long* letter this morning . . . Who is reading it?'[14] These exciting messages gave them their chance (more secure than the telephone) to snatch at meetings: 'Send me a petit bleu in reply as quickly as you can . . . mi scrivi, caro, mi scrivi . . . !' 'I will blue you . . .' The rapid switches between endearments and arrangements, train timetables and passion, were typical of her. 'Here are some possibilities by motor . . . Start at 11 *sharpissimo* & get to Les Andelys [at about 1.30] . . . [Or] There's a train for Amiens at 12, one for Chartres at 12.50 – All I can see or feel about it is the divine possibility of being with you, away & alone, for one long golden day, at last – anywhere!' Even at her most abandoned she could not help checking her watch. It was partly temperamental. But it was also because the time was being eaten up: 'An absolutely perfect day . . . I still see you, meeting me at the station when I drove up at 11.20 . . . We were together from then till 9.15 in the evening. The sense of peace those long hours gave! And yet how they rushed & swept us with them!' 'The time is short – & life is so short!'[15]

After Herblay, in February, they managed a wander around Montmartre at the end of March (in between a Walter Gay show at the Georges Petit gallery, and a musical evening at the embassy). They saw 'the cathedral, the view from the terrace, the old church' – the Église Saint-Pierre, one of the oldest churches in Paris, newly rubbing shoulders with the Sacré-Coeur. But the next whole 'day' was not until 4 April. In bright sunshine and showers, they went by car – with Cook, presumably, discreetly at the wheel – to the picturesque old town of Montfort l'Amaury, forty kilometres from Paris. They left at 9.50 (*sharpissimo*) and were there by 12.10. They saw the Église Saint-Pierre, with its dazzling Renaissance stained-glass windows of scenes of the deposition, of Abraham and Isaac and the temptations and the presentation of the Virgin, all in colourful sixteenth-century dress. They walked – five minutes – up the hill to the ruined chateau, last vestige of the power of the counts of Montfort, with its sweeping views over the forest of Rambouillet. They had lunch in the Hôtel des Voyageurs (still there today, but sadly dilapidated), which had a shady terrace-courtyard at the rear. After lunch they went to see the town's curiosity, which Edith noted as 'old burying ground enclosed in arcaded cloister with wagon vault roof of wood'. This early seventeenth-century cemetery is an intensely quiet, reflective spot, with its monitory inscription: 'Vous qui ici passez / Priez Dieu pour les Trépassés / Ce que êtes, ils ont été; / Ce que sont, un jour serez.' On the way back something struck her about the impossibility of the relationship: 'I *knew* that day coming back from Montfort.' They were back in Paris by 4.10, in time for a tea-party Morton had promised to go to.[16]

Two Saturdays later, they had another happy day at Provins, this time in cold grey weather. Again they went by car, a journey of about three hours to the east. Provins, the old capital of the counts of Champagne and Brie, famous for its fairs, had once been the third greatest city in France. It is still a sight to rival Carcassonne, a medieval city inside its ring of walls. Edith called it 'an exquisite, compact, rich old town'. They saw all the right things: the eleventh-century church of Saint-Ayoul, with its magnificent but dilapidated carved portal; the church of Sainte-Croix, an architectural jumble with a beautiful sixteenth-century doorway; the Church of Saint-Quiriace, ugly outside, breathtakingly vast and light inside; the Tour de César (or 'Grosse Tour' as she called it), a mighty octagonal dungeon and look-out on a hill in the middle of the town. They lunched at the Hôtel de la Boule d'Or, and very likely they talked about the town's romantic associations with Héloïse and Abelard: he was Provins' most celebrated teacher-priest in the twelfth century, remembered for ever for his tragic love-affair.[17]

During Henry James's visit, the timetable was more difficult, and a complicated play was performed. Edith's notes to Morton pick their way through arrangements: '. . . Unless you & Henry want to disappear & dine together? . . . Away from my too permanent presence?' 'You could come back with me for an early cup of tea with the cher Maître, on his return from the Blanche sitting?' 'If we go to Versailles by train, ne le dites pas à H.J. – Je lui dirai que j'ai été invité à dîner avec des amis.' 'H.J. sits to Blanche *after luncheon*. If a 7.30 dinner hurries you, come to lunch today instead, or we'll go to the other Salon when J goes to his portrait . . . Telephone when you get this.'[18] James was in a delicate – indeed Jamesian – situation here. He had been a close friend and confidant of Morton Fullerton's since the 1890s.

It was James who sent Fullerton to Edith Wharton's door in 1907. But it is not clear what Fullerton told James about Wharton, or whether James told her what Fullerton had confided in him; or what she said to James about her affair. He was discreetly in attendance during this Paris visit in the spring of 1908 (describing to mutual friends his stay with the Whartons as a 'gilded bondage' or 'gorgeous vortex'),[19] accompanying the secret lovers on their outings, and observing the increasingly difficult state of the Wharton marriage.

On 1 May, Edith took Henry to Herblay, in fine weather. What they talked about is not recorded, but from then on Edith's car became, suggestively, 'Hortense'. The next day, one of the precious Saturdays, the plan was for Beauvais, a longer trip to the north. She knew that Morton was anxious about sharing their 'day' with Henry, but she noted in her diary that she had insisted: Henry wanted him to come very much, and 'If you don't, *who will have my Saturday?*' '*I begged* (against my usual habit!) & you yielded.' The day was beautiful, and she described their drive romantically, in the diary, 'across the windings of the Seine & Oise, through the grey old towns piled up above their rivers, through the melting spring landscape, all tender green & snowy-fruit-blossom, against black slopes of fir – till a last climb brought us out above the shimmering plain, with Beauvais's choir rising "like a white Albi" on its ledge . . .' She had already written up Beauvais Cathedral in *A Motor-Flight* (the second instalment of which was just out in the *Atlantic*, and must have been a subject of conversation), and she would use it again in *In Morocco*. The 'great mad broken dream' of the vast choir, the unfinished cathedral without a nave, 'the Kubla Khan of architecture . . . arrested, broken off, by the intrusion of the Person from Porlock . . . like a great hymn interrupted . . . [one of] the fragmentary glories of great art', spoke powerfully to her imagination. It was an evocative setting for a love-affair that would itself be arrested and fragmentary.

Her description in her diary of the day at Beauvais throbs with the desire to relive it, to keep the moment and not let it go: the easy-going lunch in the courtyard of the Hôtel d'Angleterre, with dogs and children and canaries, coffee and cigarettes; the stroll up through the fair in the central square to the cathedral, the mystic impression of the soaring interior, the quiet moment outside sitting on the steps in the sunshine ('*Dear, are you happy?*' he asked, to her intense delight), while Henry tactfully left them alone. (The situation might have seemed to him uncannily like the French encounter between Lambert Strether and the secret lovers in *The Ambassadors*.) She was struck by Morton's description of the choir seeming to 'cosmically spin through space' and the next day, 3 May, she looked up and copied out for him in a letter the passage in Dante it had reminded her of.

But happiness made her sad. 'Now I am asking to be happy all the rest of my life.' She wanted more; she wanted to go away with him to the country and spend the whole night together. She said to herself in the diary: '*I will go with him once before we separate.*' 'Why not?' 'It would hurt no one, it would give me my first, last, draught of life . . . And, as you told me the other day – *& as I needed no telling!* – what I have given already is far, far more.' It seems from this as if, so far, the affair had gone only as far as romantic embraces, long looks and intimate words. The timing of their first love-making – concealed even in her secret diary – is as obscured as she would have wanted it to be.[20]

The minute she had seen Henry off at the Gare du Nord on 9 May, they left for Montmorency, just to the north-west of Paris, on the edge of the Forest of Montmorency, where the chestnut-trees were in bloom. This was a pilgrimage to Rousseau country: it was where he wrote *Émile* and *La Nouvelle Héloïse* (of which Edith had a 1781, seven-volume edition). They looked at the church, the Collégiale Saint-Martin, with its fine windows, the Musée de Rousseau (which had been his house) and the now-vanished 'Hermitage' (Mme d'Épinay's garden-retreat, built for her beloved 'bear'). They had lunch at 'La Châtagneraie' – the waiter was nice to them – and heard a cuckoo call. Did they take a room in the hotel for the afternoon? She brought a chestnut leaf home, in memory of the day, and put no details in her diary.[21]

A week later, their day out to Senlis – that fascinating, historically layered city fifty kilometres from Paris – started with a mistake. They met at the Gare du Nord at 11.20, but stayed on the train one stop too far (the other passengers were very kind) and went on to Creil. So they had lunch there and saw the 'old crooked church', Saint-Médard. Then they got the train to Chantilly and took a car to Senlis – a short triangular deviation. They went to the cathedral, one of the great complicated religious buildings of northern France, with its fine spire, the doorway with the touching Assumption of the Virgin, the flying buttresses and vaulting. They saw the little Romanesque church of Saint-Pierre, and the ruined twelfth-century chapel of Saint-Frambourg (now a garage). But best of all was their wander through the old streets into the quiet, haunting gardens built into the ancient Roman ramparts. They 'sat for a long time on terrace above wall, looking out over W. front of Cathedral'. As they sat, she began to think up a poem. They had dinner in the Hôtel du Grand Cerf (two stars), where a 'Sneezing Man in the dining room' drove them out to eat under the lilac arbour in the courtyard. They caught the 7.45 train and were back in Paris by 9.15. On the train, they watched the full moon rise, and at one stop, heard a thrush singing on the edge of a wood: 'a moment of divine, deep calm . . . I knew then, dearest dear, all that I had never known before, the interfusion of spirit & sense, the double nearness, the mingled communion of touch & thought . . . One such hour ought to irradiate a whole life.' The next day she wrote out her poem – too private ever to publish – in which the cathedral spire and the Roman ramparts, the train journey, the moon and the singing thrush all merged together into an image of time being held at bay:

> In some divine transcendent hush
> Where light & darkness melt & cease,
> Staying the awful cosmic rush
> To give two hearts an hour of peace.

In the act of writing this down, she was struck by the contradiction between this transcendent ecstasy and 'a creature as exacting, scrutinizing, analytical as I am'. She was deliberately holding at bay not just the passage of time but her own ironic, critical powers.[22]

Two days later, they had their last outing. They caught a steam-boat from the Place de la Concorde, and then went up by cable-car (from 'Bellevue-Funiculaire') to the terrasse at Meudon (once part of the chateau of Louis XV's mistress, Mme de Pompadour) with its immense panorama of Paris and the Valley of the Seine. 'Back by boat 5.' Perhaps they spent the whole day looking at the view of Paris, and sampling Meudon's other attractions – the Observatory, the Orangerie, the forest, the museum, the aerostation. Or perhaps, again, they took a hotel room for the afternoon.[23]

Edith's 'happy days' would be turned into a litany of names which she needed to keep repeating, in her diary on the ship going back to America, in the letters she immediately started sending back to Morton, even in a letter to Sally: 'I made some beautiful excursions, to Provins, Montfort l'Amaury, Montmorency, & back to exquisite Senlis – & then Paris itself was so radiant! I hated to leave it.'[24] Those erotic cultural outings to destinations charged with the histories of legendary lovers (Hortense Allart, Rousseau, Abelard, Mme de Pompadour) and handy for Parisian adulterers wanting a picturesque destination within an easy one-day car or train journey, were in a landscape from now on central to Wharton's life. During the war, her sanatoriums for TB patients were at Montmorency and nearby Groslay. Senlis would be one of the key defence posts holding back the enemy from Paris. After the war, when houses which had been in the battle-zone were abandoned and going cheap, and she took her opportunity to acquire the Pavillon Colombe at Saint-Brice, she moved into the district, on the edge of the Montmorency forest, just north-west of Paris, which had been the scene of her 'happy days' with Morton. So, over ten years after those enchanted outings, she came to know the area in a quite different, everyday way. When she took her visitors on local excursions in the 1920s and 1930s, they went to some of the very places she and Morton had visited in secret.

But that spring, these places were charged up with romantic intensity and with a feeling that her life had changed. Several times in the diary she wrote: 'La vita nuova'. That literary annotation was part of the pleasure. Wharton dramatised her love-affair and watched herself having it. The affair had everything to do with writing; you imagine bedrooms full of papers: Morton's letters to her, glimpsed between the lines of hers to him; letters to him from past lovers, so troublesome to him now; Edith's love-letters, which she enjoyed writing perhaps as much as she enjoyed their meetings, but which she later wanted to claim back; letters she wrote to friends in which she always mentioned his name. The double narrative of her two diaries was a novelist's strategy. The engagement diary, in which meetings with Morton were coded in German ('Z' for *zusammen*, 'together'), in French and Italian phrases and in quotes from Petrarch or Dante, was meant to be the 'cover story', but the secret life kept leaking into the records of lunches and outings, in little outbursts: 'How happy I was . . .' 'Oh God – Oh God –' . . . 'blissful hours . . .' Meanwhile in the secret – but not entirely explicit – diary she was dwelling on her happiness, drawing general laws about sexual relations from the affair, brooding over misunderstandings and anticipating the end: 'In the empty future years I may say, going there alone, "We were here together once."' She made up romantic phrases, with deep feeling – and with professional care: 'I should like to be to you, friend of my heart, like a touch of wings brushing by you in the darkness, or like the scent of an invisible garden, that one passes on an unknown road at night . . .' Poems, stories, novels, are waiting to have this material poured into them.[25]

Like a Wharton heroine, the voice of the diary is bitterly regretful of lost chances and apprehensive of the future: 'I shan't see you, I shan't hear your voice, I shan't wake up to think: "In so many hours we shall meet".' It is unnerved by the force of her emotions: 'I who dominated life, stood aside from it so, how I am humbled, absorbed, without a shred of will or identity left!' . . . 'Oh my free, proud, secure soul, where are you? *What were you*, to escape me like this?' This was not an entirely pleasurable surrender.[26]

The see-saw between abandonment and self-consciousness, need and pride (familiar to readers of her fiction) colours the early love-letters. She takes a writer's pleasure in the new role of mistress. She acts girlish, delighted he has given her new dress the compliment of 'a little word', or pretending to need manly assistance: 'I never *could* find my way about a station.' She tells him her dreams: 'I woke just now from a dream of hunting through a confused house, full of topsy-turvy furniture & half-packed trunks (triste présage!) for a letter that hadn't come.' She blazes out with desire and determination: 'No, I won't give up, no, I won't believe it's the end, no, I am going to fight for my life – I know it now!' 'I am mad about you dear heart and sick at the thought of our parting'. She shows him her work, trustingly, delighted that in his reaction to 'The Verdict' he spots 'the one phrase that I care about', or touched that he thinks a poem she has given him worth sending to *The Fortnightly*. She advises him about his problems: from the start this is an important part of the relationship. 'Nothing could be more disastrous to a heart & mind like yours than to accept the small change of life in place of one of its big rewards ... Don't smile at this letter. I don't know many people who are worth having it written to them.'[27]

Her own sense of worth is not always as strong, and she is rashly open with him about her mixed emotions. She trusts him to be 'lenient' about her 'contradictions'. She wants him to forgive her for something she said 'yesterday': 'I can't explain ...' She tells him when she is feeling 'suicidally depressed'. She knows that she is one of a procession, and that there will be 'a woman who succeeds me in your heart'. In one remarkably self-revealing letter, she dramatises the difference between 'the way you've spent your emotional life, while I've – bien malgré moi – hoarded mine'. She longs to unpack treasures which 'have come to me in magic ships from enchanted islands', but fears that they will seem to him like 'the old familiar red calico & beads of the clever trader'; so all too often, she packs them back in her box. But what is she to do with herself, 'if you can't come into the room without my feeling all over me a ripple of flame, & if, wherever you touch me, a heart beats under your touch, & if, when you hold me, & I don't speak, it's because all the words in me seem to have become throbbing pulses, & all my thoughts are a great golden blur ...'.[28]

So she turns herself into the heroine of a French erotic novel. (Some of her love-letters sound very like Hortense Allart's.) She switches freely between English and French, lavishing him with endearments in both languages (dear, my dearest, cher, cher ami, mon aimé, 'my own correspondent', and often – most intimately – nothing at all). Sometimes she describes herself, suggestively, as a '*femme du monde*', if not '*la plus jolie fille du monde*'. She often signs off '*toujours votre amie*', and the like. Sometimes she switches languages within one sentence: '*Je me demande souvent, cher, si je ne suis pas bien sotte* to think that you ever want to see me!' Her letters often sound like speeches from a French play: '*Qu'il fait bon d'être souffrante, mon Coeur, puisque cela me procure la joie de te voir plus souvent!*' '*Oh, je t'implore, envoie moi un mot de temps en temps. Tu me parais si loin!*' Sometimes French seems to be the only possible language for what she wants to say: '*Si tu veux que nous nous aimions encore, aimons nous. J'aurais toujours le temps d'être triste après —*'[29]

Long before such bilingual complaints had begun, in the first passionate weeks, there are signs that Morton was flaunting his greater sexual experience in the face of his older, married, emotionally thwarted mistress (itself a perfect plot for a cynical French novel). On their first night out at the theatre together, to the Sicilian players, in a scene when the heroine kisses her lover farewell '*& then she can't let him go*', Morton turned to her laughing and said: 'That's something you don't know anything about.' But he must have seen, she thought, that she was worried about becoming too clinging, about not being 'younger & prettier', about becoming a burden; all the while he was reproaching her for 'always drawing away', for being 'inexpressive' or 'unwilling'. She came to feel that her inability to take, and give, complete happiness, was her fault: 'I have been too sad, for too long, & something in my nature – some lack, I suppose – has left me starving for what other women seem at least once in their life to know.' 'Before', she wrote retrospectively, and sadly, to him, 'I had no personal life: since then you have given me all possible joy.' But being like other women was a mixed blessing. She had also felt 'the pang . . . of what heart-broken women feel'. There were days when she felt 'calm', 'exalted' and mystically close to him: 'I never wonder what you are doing when you are not with me.' And there were 'tormented days' 'when in your absence I long, I ache for you, I feel that what I want is to be in your arms, to be held fast there – "like other women!" And then comes the terrible realisation of the fugitiveness of it all . . .'[30] Gradually, the pain of feeling that it could not last, that it had come too late for her, was compounded by a suspicion that the person she had opened herself up to was not a person she could depend on. Who *was* this 'cher ami'?

William Morton Fullerton, though remembered now only as Edith's unreliable lover, had a highly respectable puritan pedigree. Born in 1865, he was of solid New England stock. His father, Bradford, was a minister turned insurance man, his mother Julia a minister's daughter. Their letters to him are all made up of grave reproachfulness: why hasn't he written, is he smoking too much, is he getting stout, how could he get married without telling them, how could he fall into the clutches of a scheming woman? As well as Morton, they had another son, Robert, and a much younger adopted daughter Katherine. 'Will' Fullerton went to Harvard in the 1880s and studied art history under Charles Eliot Norton. Berenson and the great American philosopher Santayana (a repressed homosexual, who wrote him some bawdy letters) were contemporaries. Fullerton wanted a fellowship at Harvard, but to his lasting disappointment, did not get one. He travelled to Egypt and Europe, and met George Meredith, who became a hero of his. (Morton's egotistical and evasive life-story, reads, indeed, rather like a Meredith novel.) Attractive, smooth and intelligent, he made himself welcome in bisexual, upper-class Edwardian London circles. He had an affair with the sculptor Lord Ronald Gower, who was the model for Wilde's decadent Lord Henry in *The Picture of Dorian Gray*, and who wrote Morton some incriminating letters, and one with the Canadian poet Bliss Carman, who wrote affectionately of 'the beautiful Fullerton'. He shared rooms in London with the theatre designer Percy Anderson. He knew Verlaine, Symons, and Oscar Wilde, who, while living in Paris, after his prison-sentence, asked him for a loan in 1899. Morton turned him down pompously, and Wilde mocked him for it. He had a passionate intrigue in the 1890s with the Ranee of Sarawak, Lady Margaret Brooke, an exotic fixture on the Edwardian English artistic and literary scene, to whom James had introduced him. She wrote him reams of wild, self-consciously anarchic love-letters, which he unfortunately did not burn, bitterly complaining (as all Morton's correspondents did, sooner or later) about his evasiveness:

Not for one moment of these centuries of thinking since you left have you been out of my vision, and I want you now so much, so much . . . *Why* did you not leave one word for me . . . We are both supremely self-reliant and intolerant of any laws that others make for us. We must create our own worlds. This may be sublimely, Satanically immoral, audaciously Promethean; but it is the way we are bound to live and be . . .

There were also an 1890s liaison with Blanche Roosevelt, a popular novelist from the Midwest married to an Italian marquis, and a flirtatious friendship with the much older playwright, composer, world-traveller and Victorian dandy Hamilton Aidé, who often wrote teasingly to his 'Dearest Boy': 'I am now so accustomed to your silence that it was almost a shock to see your handwriting.' Henry James found Fullerton extremely alluring when he met him in the early '90s. But, as usual, Fullerton played hard to get. Yearning letters pursued him: 'My life is arranged – if arranged it can be called – on the lines of constantly missing you.' 'I want in fact more of you . . . You are dazzling . . . you are beautiful; you are more than tactful, you are tenderly, magically *tactile*. But you're not kind. There it is. You *are* not kind.' James looked back wistfully years later on 'something – ah, so tender! – in me that was only quite yearningly ready for you'. In one of his last letters to Wharton, James agreed that Fullerton was the most inscrutable of men – 'he will never pose long enough for the Camera of Identification'.[31]

In 1891, Fullerton took a job as a copy-editor on the London *Times*, and in 1892 he moved to its Paris office, working as an assistant to the chief Paris correspondent, Henri Blowitz. When Blowitz retired in 1902, Fullerton wanted, but did not get, his job (though he liked to give the impression, back home in Brockton, that he was a senior figure on the paper). He had some difficulties working under the editor Moberly Bell, who resented his publishing in other journals, and he resigned in 1910 to become a free-lance writer, after much agonising – all these problems shared with an intensely sympathetic Edith. After the war, he became the editor of the American news-page of *Le Figaro* ('Le Figaro aux Etats-Unis') and then a contributor to *Le Journal des débats*. He was a well-known figure in Paris, though his reputation could not compare with Walter Berry's. His writing became increasingly anti-democratic and reactionary. *Problems of Power* (1913) which Edith helped him with, was a survey of international poli-tics from 1866 to 1912, which argued that 'economics and finance' – multinational companies, banks, the migration of workers to richer nations – were determining political decision-making, and that strong authority, in government and the military, was needed over 'the populace or the mob'. It was full of sentences like: 'Equality is an absurd and a dangerous lie'. *Hesitations: The American Crisis and the War* (1916), which described France as 'the knight-errant of Humanity' and criticised America's reluctance to join the war, in terms Edith would have approved, described the USA as having lost its racial purity, 'selling her birthright for a mess of pottage, in which "Irish stew", "mulligatawny soup", "corn bread", "sauerkraut" and "lager beer" are staple ingredients'. Marion Mainwaring, Fullerton's bio-grapher, suggests that during the occupation of France in the Second World War, he may have been a collaborator.[32]

In one of his 1890s letters to Aidé, Fullerton cited Congreve's play *The Double Dealer*. To find him referring to that title is almost too good to be true, since in his private affairs, Fullerton was an exceptionally secretive 'double dealer'. In 1903, in Portugal, reporting on Edward VII's visit there, he married an opera singer called Camille Chabert, or Chabbert (stage name, Ixo) who had a daughter, not Fullerton's. He divorced her the following year. He was involved with (at least) three other women. One was Adèle Moutot, a minor actress in vaudeville and musical comedy (stage name, Mme Mirecourt) who had lived with him since 1893, at 40 bis Rue Fabert, to whom he returned after his marriage, and in whose house he was living while his affair with Edith was going on. In 1907, Mme Moutot, or Mirecourt, was blackmailing him with compromising papers of his in her possession, which could (presumably) expose his homosexual past, and his affair with Lady Brooke. He paid her off, with help and support from Henry – and Edith – in 1909. During his involvement with Edith, he had a brief affair with an American woman married to a French count, Francesca d'Aulby, who in 1910 was involved with her husband in a breach of confidence case over the sale of some fake Old Masters – a sensational trial which also involved adulterous love-letters. After his affair with Edith was over, Morton took up with Hélène Pouget, an artist's model from a Protestant family near Nîmes, who became, for forty years, from 1912 until he died in 1952, his lover, cook-housekeeper, and common-law wife. When Fullerton was dying, his ex-wife Camille went to Mme Pouget's house and took two trunks of his papers away at gunpoint: two old ladies in their seventies, at war over the love-letters of their eighty-seven-year-old Don Juan: what a story for Wharton that would have been.[33]

So, when Morton Fullerton met Edith Wharton in 1907, he had a potentially scandalous homosexual past, a French wife whom he had divorced with startling rapidity, a blackmailing mistress, in whose house he was still living (for convenience, not as a lover), and a frustrated career. Just after his visit to The Mount, he had confided some of these problems to James, who brimmed with sympathy ('you stir my tenderness even to anguish' . . . 'I howl and gnash my teeth over you'), and assured him that the attempts of 'a mad, vindictive & obscure old woman' to blacken his name would only rebound on her.[34]

But that was not all. Morton was also involved in an intense, quasi-incestuous relationship with his 'sister', Katherine Fullerton, in 1907 a highly intelligent and emotional young woman of twenty-eight, who had been brought up by Fullerton's parents (her father, Bradford Fullerton's half-brother, went missing, her mother died when she was a baby) and who, though she knew she was adopted, had since childhood felt strong emotions for her much older cousin. 'I . . . cling unflinchingly to the relationship of brother and sister that makes some affection from you to me almost a conventional necessity . . . Your loving sister – who would give anything in the world to serve you in whatever way she might', she wrote to him in 1899. A student at Radcliffe, and a lecturer in English Literature at Bryn Mawr from 1901 to 1910, she would from her thirties onwards write poems, novels, and literary criticism (including, in the early 1920s, ironically enough, a short critical study of Edith Wharton). She had been writing passionate and needy letters to Morton since her teens; by 1907, she was saying: 'Whether I marry you or not, I am yours to the deepest heart of me.' She knew about his marriage, and would hear about his blackmailing mistress. In October 1907, a day or two before his visit to The Mount, Morton asked Katherine to marry him. The Fullerton parents first opposed it (understandably) and then agreed. At the very time that Edith was starting her secret diary to Morton, Katherine was writing to him: 'Ah, my own, my own! You know that I'm quite simply desperately in love with you.' By 1908, while Morton was with Edith in Paris, Katherine was writing anxious and heartbroken letters to her absentee fiancé.

Katherine's story continued to keep pace with Edith's. She went to Paris early in 1909 to see Morton, but it seems that she did not know that Mrs Wharton was his mistress, any more than Edith knew that there was anything between Morton and his 'sister'. The ironies multiplied. Katherine sent Mrs Wharton a poem she had written about Dante and Beatrice (illicit love versus domestic happiness), and Wharton wrote back kindly, praising the poem, and suggesting that Katherine should spend a day at the Rue de Varenne, perhaps to go and see Isadora Duncan dancing: 'we might persuade Mr Fullerton to break away from his work long enough to go with us.' They all went out together, with another friend, a young oceanographer called Carl Snyder. Morton accidentally dropped one of Edith's notes in the car. She wrote to him afterwards about the incident, warning him to be more careful: 'Snyder picked it up, examined it curiously, & then, *at random*, handed it to me, instead of to your sister.' After Katherine's visit, Morton told Edith he was worried about his sister's religious bent. She told him not to be concerned: 'I hadn't talked with her an hour before it seemed to me the inevitable solution, or outcome.' Solution to what, she does not say.[35]

After her visit to Paris, Morton left Katherine hanging. She pursued him through 1909 and early 1910 with bitter reproaches, which reached him at the same time – perhaps by the same post – as Edith's ever more hurt and bewildered love-letters. 'I do not think any human being has the right to hurt another like this', Katherine wrote. 'How can you not have written to me . . . you must free me, must give me peace, must speak some word . . . Has any woman ever paid so much . . .' That summer Katherine gave him up at last, and made a safe marriage to a Princeton Chaucer scholar,

Gordon Gerould. (Professor Gerould's son, asked many years later about Morton Fullerton, summed him up as a 'con man'.) For all Edith's apparent unawareness, she struck an odd note in her letter to Morton about his sister's marriage. He had told her he felt 'very very unhappy'. Why? Edith asked. 'I know you wished your sister to marry. Do tell me what you mean, for I am anxious, & feel that you must have omitted something from your note which you meant to tell me.' But it seems he never did tell her what he had 'omitted'. A year later, *Scribner's Magazine* for summer 1911 contained the first instalment of *Ethan Frome*, an article by Fullerton, 'America Revisited', and Katherine Fullerton Gerould's story, 'The Wine of Violence', about an Italian actor, 'a frightful bounder' whose wife hates him so much that she plots to have him accused of murder. Edith told Morton she thought it 'remarkable'.[36]

'Frightful bounder' though he seems to have been, there was something about Morton Fullerton which made women give themselves completely away. When she was packing up to leave Paris in May 1908, Edith dramatised every moment of the departure – laying out the clothes she had worn with him, preparing herself for the last wave, the last smile, the last 'adieu' on the train to Le Havre, while her young cousin Le Roy King 'all unconscious, was lingering between us to the last' (it is like a scene from *Brief Encounter*), shaping the end of the affair into phrases and images: 'It is over, my Heart, all over . . . Et on n'en meurt pas, hélas!' 'How the wych-hazel has kept its promise.' In a spectacularly trusting gesture, she gave him 'L'Âme Close' to read the night before she left. He returned it to her on the train, with comments (which she tore out), and she went on writing in it, on the week-long transatlantic crossing.

Words poured out of her on board ship: letters, diary, a poem about the memory of sleeping together, a savagely painful story of adultery, 'The Choice', a chapter of her abandoned 'great American novel', *The Custom of the Country* (in which American divorce is discussed). She kept the Paris mood going by reading Paul Mariéton's story of George Sand and Alfred de Musset's love-affair. (Sand's fictional version of that affair, *Elle et Lui*, gave Henry James one of his suggestive nicknames for Edith and Morton. Her copy of de Musset's *Comédies et Proverbes* was given by Lord Ronald Gower to Morton Fullerton in Paris in 1891, with the inscription 'Amico amicis'.) She also channelled her emotions into some strenuous reading about evolution – two new books, Kellogg's *Darwinism Today*, and Robert Lock on heredity. She marked passages in Kellogg on natural selection and adaptation – on 'protective resemblance' among insects, and on the way that extreme or exceptional variants perish: 'It is quite as dangerous to be conspicuously above a certain standard of organic excellence as it is to be conspicuously below the standard. It is the *type* that nature favours.' Then the ship sailed into a symbolic New York fog, and Teddy came to meet his exceptional variant of a wife. She noted grimly in her diary that when, in the train from New York to Lenox, she showed him a passage in Lock that interested her, he said: 'Does that sort of thing really amuse you?' 'I heard the key turn in my prison-lock.' She realised immediately that what had been just about bearable, 'all those years' with no comparison, had all at once become insufferable. She had 'stood it' by creating 'a world of her own'. 'But since I have known what it was to have someone enter into that world & live there with me, the natural solitude I come back to has become terrible . . .' It is one of the most telling moments in Edith's life-story, as dramatic as her account of the conversation with her mother before her wedding-night, or the scene on the bank with the witch-hazel. But it does not, of course, allow for Teddy's point of view. Perhaps, after three months apart spent in ill-health and depression, he did not especially want to discuss *Recent Progress in the Study of Variation, Heredity and Evolution.*[37]

Back at The Mount, she wrote long, tender, poignant letters, stopped herself jumping on the next ship back to Paris, and waited for Morton's replies. 'Hold me long & close in your thoughts. I shall take up so little room, & it's only there that I'm happy!' A couple of notes came back. And then, nothing. He fell completely silent. What was he feeling? How could this happen? She felt entombed, suffocated. She imagined him comparing her to the unhappily married heroine of *La Princesse de Clèves*, the drama-tisation of the novel by Mme de Lafayette which he was seeing in Paris, without her: 'Mme de Clèves has never really lived.' 'Shut down in her black box again, she struggles with tragic futility, to push the lid back a little & breathe.' She told Sally she literally could not breathe; she had hay-fever, it was oppressively hot, there was 'a want of air': 'I can think of no place where I would like to be so much as on the deck of an ocean-steamer – turned eastward!'[38] Life went on: she read Nietzsche; *Custom* ground to a halt, as did 'L'Âme Close'; she wrote some love-poems. Friends came to The Mount – including Walter, and Carl Snyder, whom she made a point of telling Morton she could talk to. Anguished, baffled, dignified letters pursued him: 'Anything on earth wd be better . . . than to sit here and wonder: *What was I to him, then?*' 'This incomprehensible silence, the sense of your utter indifference to everything that concerns me, has stunned me.' 'Is it really to my dear friend – *to Henry's friend* – to "dearest Morton" – that I have written this?'[39]

A few weeks later she was writing about her situation to Henry James, himself depressed and discouraged in his work, who replied with one of his most tender and sympathetic letters. This was the advice she got, dated 13 October 1908:

I am deeply distressed at the situation you describe & as to which my power to suggest or enlighten now quite miserably fails me. I move in darkness; I rack my brain; I gnash my teeth; I don't pretend to understand or to imagine. And yet incredibly to you doubtless – I am still moved to say 'Don't conclude!' Some light will *still* absolutely come to you – I believe – though I can't pretend to say what it conceivably may be. Anything is more credible – conceivable – than a mere inhuman *plan* . . . Only sit tight yourself *&* *go through the movements of life*. That keeps up our connection with life – I mean of the immediate & apparent life, behind which, all the while, the deeper & darker & the unapparent, in which things *really* happen to us, learns, under that hygiene, to stay in its place . . . Live it all through, every inch of it – out of it something valuable will come – but live it ever so quietly; & – *je maintiens mon dire* – waitingly!⁴⁰

It is about himself as much as about her, and it is typical of him to advise quietude, passivity, and waiting, as a way of surviving and overcoming terrible difficulties. This was hard advice to give to a person who hated, above all things, to feel passive or inert, who desperately wanted to be able to make a plan, to take action and be in control.

But what had she told him? James would make a final bonfire of the many letters written to him, in the garden of Lamb House, in 1915, including most of Edith Wharton's letters. We can deduce the contents of these in part from what he says to her; in part from what she was saying at the time to other correspondents. Charles Eliot Norton was dying at last, and she wrote to Sally, in the same week that she wrote to James, telling her never to reproach herself for not having done enough for her father. But as for Sally's own life: 'Alas, I should like to get up on the house-top & cry to all who come after us: "Take your own life, every one of you!"' Take it and make the best use of it, don't waste it on others: she was surely thinking about herself as well as Sally.⁴¹ The stories and poems she was writing at this time give her away, too: 'The Pretext', the story of the unhappily married woman who gets one chance of love, which turns out to have been a false one; 'The Choice', in which the adulterous woman wants her lover to kill her husband (but it is the husband who survives); impassioned poems like 'Life' and 'The Mortal Lease', about taking hold of love. These are powerful clues. All the same, the two letters to Henry James written in October 1908, of the utmost importance for Edith Wharton's life, are lost, and cannot be invented.

Fullerton's silence continued. *The Hermit and the Wild Woman* and *A Motor-Flight* were published. Wharton went to England, and saw enormous numbers of people. She flirted with a new young friend, John Hugh Smith. In December, before her return to Paris, she wrote formally to Mr Fullerton, asking for her letters to be returned. He replied, at the very end of the year: 'The letters survive, and everything survives.' A year later, writing to 'My Dearest & Ever Dearest' on New Year's Eve, she remembered that reply, and 'all the ghosts of the old kisses'.[42] And the affair began again, in Paris, at the start of 1909. But everything was different: she had lost confidence.

Teddy was with her in Paris, in a very poor state. He was having dental problems, which 'did not help his nerves'. It was beginning to be impossible to control their life or to make plans. The lovers had a difficult reunion in February; Edith wrote to apologise for having been 'stupid, disappointing, altogether "impossible"'. Morton annotated this letter 'February 23: After!!!!' A few weeks later she told him: 'the tiresome woman is buried, once for all, I promise, & only the novelist survives!' If this meant that, after the 'long isolation' of the summer, she was sexually ill at ease with him, then she had a defensive strategy ready. She started to argue for a change in the relationship. 'Think of me, Dear, in the old way . . . if you come & dine, let it be with the old friend of last year . . .' 'The situation has changed, & I, who like to *walk up* to things, recognize it, & am ready to accept it – only it must be nettement!' But Morton did not like to *walk up* to things. As she once told him, he could never be described as '*un coeur simple*'. The difficult game of mixing secret meetings with social engagements and domestic pressures continued.[43]

From the spring of 1909 – possibly earlier – their secret game was opened up to the complicit understanding of Fullerton's great friend Léon Bélugou, whom he had introduced to Edith and Henry the previous May. In March 1909, Edith wrote Bélugou a charming letter, asking him to come to see her and discuss their mutual interest in Plato's influence on Nietzsche. 'Mr Fullerton', she wrote, 'who never lets an occasion go by without telling me how low he rates "women of letters", did not think to reassure me by revealing that you take a rather more lenient view of the species . . . But as the two of you have discussed me [*puisque vous avez causé ensemble de moi*], I hope he has told you . . . how I meet with a frank friendship those whose minds and ideas I relish.' Bélugou wrote a carefully worded reply: 'I had in fact noticed something but the something was too close to my wishes not to have sown doubts about my clear-sightedness.' ['*J'avais bien en effet remarqué quelque chose mais ce quelque chose répondait trop à mon désir pour ne pas m'inspirer des doutes sur ma clairvoyance*']. He accepted her invitation with pleasure, concluding: 'Fullerton is wicked to the point of sinfulness; I nevertheless forgive him almost everything, and today I feel even more indulgent towards him, since without him I would not have received your letter which has given me such joy.'

Thereafter, their friendly correspondence never failed to mention Fullerton, joking about his unreliability and exchanging news on his professional life or his state of mind. So, Edith to Bélugou, in April 1909: 'Mr Fullerton writes to me that he will certainly come [on Thursday]; there is therefore every reason to suppose that we won't have the pleasure of seeing him.' Bélugou to Edith, May 1909: 'I dreamt that Fullerton might spend one of his last evenings at my home with the two best friends he has in Paris.' Later, in September 1910, Edith to Bélugou: 'Like you, I have often advised him to acquire a permanent Mrs Fullerton. Let's hope he doesn't follow our advice!' And in November 1911, Bélugou to Edith: 'He is diabolical; one always falls into his traps and he always manages things so that one is forced to thank him.'[44]

But even if Bélugou was in the know, the double life still had to be sustained. The Whartons had visitors, friends who were welcome but who created obstacles. 'Will the hatefulness of things never leave us an hour to ourselves? . . . With S.N. [Sally Norton] here it's very hard! . . . Things are desperate here, & I miss you, I miss you!' Her new young friend John Hugh Smith came to stay in February, but 'it's intolerable to be dragging myself about with this cheerful boy when I can only think of one thing . . . let me know if there is a chance of seeing you *tomorrow*, so that I can arrange with John Hugh – I mean, escape from him!' From the start, she had been worried (understandably, given the incident in the car with Katherine Fullerton and Carl Snyder) about what might happen to her letters, imagining them falling into 'indifferent hands' or under 'derisive eyes', and ending up 'in an autograph album'. She often asked him to destroy them: 'I beg instant cremation for this.'[45]

The Whartons moved from number 58 to the Crillon in March 1909, and, after she and Teddy had tried a motor-flight to the south – a wretched failure – Teddy went back to the States. But arrangements were still problematic. Wistful invitations went out to resume the 'happy days': 'And should you like to motor out somewhere near Paris for luncheon? The days are so few . . .' Morton was now making difficulties about 'their' day: 'Oh, I want them *all*, the Saturdays!' 'Oh, how I *wish* you'd give up your Saturday dinner!' '*Pas libre, n'est-ce pas?*', she anticipated his reply almost mockingly (alluding, in this note, to something that had happened in the lift at the *Times* office: had she made a scene at his workplace?). When she did not hear from him she 'doubted & despaired of everything'. 'Give me up!' she ordered him sadly. 'Find somebody gay & fortunate instead . . .'[46] When he proposed a plan of going away together, she backed off and expressed 'reluctance', wondered if he was playing with her ('& I'm so proud!'), and minded being told to think about it: 'me whose curse it has always been to do so too much & too long!' She felt driven back 'into my numb dumb former self, the self that never believed in its chance of having any warm personal life, like other, luckier people'. She dreaded that 'numbness', as she wrote to the 'cheerful boy' John Hugh Smith (in whom she was now confiding about the misery of her marriage, but not about her affair): 'To have as few numb tracts in one's consciousness as possible – that seems to me, so far, the most desirable thing in life, even though the Furies do dance in hobnailed shoes on the sensitive tracts at a rate that sometimes makes one wish for any form of anaesthesia.'[47]

In this more sombre second year of the affair, Morton's own shadowy problems were coming into focus. There were things she knew nothing about (including the family secret that his brother had contracted syphilis).[48] She did not know how dangerous it would have been for Katherine to be handed that letter by Snyder; she did not seem to know, as James did, the details of Morton's scandalous youth. She may not have known he was bisexual, though the fact that she kept that de Musset book with the affectionate inscription to him from Lord Ronald Gower may suggest otherwise. She may not have known that he had once been married. She thought that the tiredness and preoccupation of which Morton often complained were largely caused by difficulties at work. But he did tell her about his situation with Mme Mirecourt. By the summer of 1909, when they were spending time with James in England, Morton's predicament had become a subject for discussion. That he had now confided in her – at least, up to a point – reconfirmed her tenderness and sense of usefulness to him.

She recommended to Frederick Macmillan, her own and James's English publisher, that 'Mr Morton Fullerton' should be asked to write a book on Paris. 'I know no-one half as well qualified to do the work charmingly as well as thoughtfully', and it would delight all 'lovers of Paris'. She asked James to ask Macmillan if they would pay Morton an advance of £100 on his behalf; Morton would think the money came from Macmillan, and

Macmillan that it came from James; but it would come, of course, from Edith. James joined in the plot enthusiastically, only hoping 'that the sum he [Morton] has to pay to the accursed woman isn't really a very considerable one', and that 'the incubus' would give him back his papers. Morton received the money, but he never wrote the book on Paris (in spite of frequent urgings from his two guardian angels). However, later that summer, he did pay off his 'incubus', and moved out of the Rue Fabert to the Hôtel Vouillemont (not far from the Crillon). Mme Mirecourt still had possessions of his, and Edith went on trying to help: 'Don't commit the folly of risking any unnecessary danger in contact with an irresponsible person . . . Is there no man you can consult?' She may have tried to pass another loan to him via James, but this one seems not to have been accepted.

James, who was playing a subtle and ambiguous part, said that they were Morton's joint guardians: 'We must keep him & surround him & help him to make up for all the dismal waste of power.'[49] He always mentioned Morton with concern in his elaborately suggestive letters, or linked them together teasingly. He was often with them, and was an intimate friend of both. He certainly guessed what was going on; and the fact that Bélugou knew about the affair makes it all the more probable that James knew too. But it is also possible that their triangular game was played out with Jamesian discretion and indirection. Since he burnt almost all his letters from Edith and any from Fullerton, we cannot know quite what he knew, or what was said.

Certainly he was a model of tact when they met that summer of 1909 in London. Teddy was in Canada, being diagnosed as a neurasthenic; Morton was on his way to the States for a brief family visit; Edith was going to spend her summer in England. The lovers had crossed a stormy Channel on 3 June and spent a 'seasick' night at the Metropole Hotel in Folkestone. (A letter to Bélugou, discreetly informative, told him that '*notre ami Fullerton m'a fait le plaisir de m'accompagner*'.) They met Henry James for dinner on 4 June at the Charing Cross Hotel; Edith and Morton spent the night there in Suite 92 (two bedrooms and a salon). Morton left early the next morning (James saw him off at Waterloo for the train to Southampton – really, he might as well have spent the night with them!). Morton sent a bunch of roses back to the hotel, where, as he left the room, Edith had picked up her pen and started to write.[50] What she was probably writing was 'Terminus', a long, passionate poem about the night they had just spent together, which would become one of her most famous pieces of unpublished erotic writing. It provided strong evidence that when Fullerton, many decades later, smugly attested to her powerful sexual appetite, he could, for once, be trusted.

Edith spent the few weeks of the summer mainly at Rye and Windsor, and driving a reluctant Henry around. She wanted to see Morton as soon as he returned, but his elusiveness made arrangements tricky as usual: 'I know so little of what you wish to do that it is difficult to make suggestions since you may have quite other plans.' He stayed at the Charing Cross Hotel again when he got back from the States: she hoped he was not in Suite 92. They met again at Rye: Edith came down for dinner and there he was, 'standing by the hearth in the drawing room talking to Henry', with his back to her. They spent a few days touring with Henry in 'Hortense', and then crossed together to Paris, after a storm delayed them in Folkestone. She told John Hugh Smith she had travelled alone with Henry James and described herself as the 'Hermitess of the Crillon'; she told Morton that she had been 'completely happy' since their reunion. She was making arrangements to take possession of the new apartment she had found at number 53; Morton was still dealing with Mme Mirecourt. In Lenox, Teddy's mother died; in Paris, Walter Berry came through, unwell (she told Morton, playing them off against each other, that she would need to spend time with her 'Egyptian Judge'). She began an interesting new friendship with Bernard Berenson. The move to number 53 in the January floods would be an excitement. But, by the autumn and winter of 1909, her chance of personal happiness seemed to be fading away. Just at the time she started to turn her desolating American story of paralysis and thwarted passion, *Ethan Frome*, from French into English, she moved into the most painful phase of her love-affair, and the most harassing and nightmarish last two years of her marriage.[51]

Regrets and resentments began to dominate the correspondence. She was getting very anxious about her letters, and wanted her old ones back: 'My love of order makes me resent the way in which inanimate things survive their uses!' An intriguing letter of 1910 implies that Morton was thinking of using Henry James as the 'custodian' for his papers, but with James so ill that was now out of the question. If any of 'those old letters in which I used to "unpack my soul" to you' still survived, she would rather 'immolate them on a beautiful pyre of bright flames' than have them fall into other hands. When her divorce was looming, her 'documents' were becoming an increasing cause for alarm, and she had 'very special reasons' for wanting them safely back. But Morton never did return them.[52]

Again, more urgently, she argued for a transition. She could not be 'natural' with him, she could not work out what he wanted, she was terrified of 'seeming to expect more than you can give'. She did not want to be a burden; she was ready to be his 'good comrade' again 'when the transition comes', but she was afraid of losing her will, her '*volonté*', when she was in his arms. They should have a pact: 'You shall give the signal, & one day simply call me "mon ami" instead of "mon amie".' So, characteristically, she offered to give up her '*volonté*', but wanted to exercise control. She was angry with him. If he would not agree to 'an easy transition' into friendship, then he should not keep letting her down: 'The one thing I can't bear is the thought that I represent to you *the woman who has to be lied to.*'

What you wish, apparently, is to take of my life the inmost & uttermost that a woman – a woman like me – can give, for an hour, now and then, when it suits you; & when the hour is over, to leave me out of your mind & out of your life as a man leaves the companion who has afforded him a transient distraction. I think I am worth more than that, or worth, perhaps I had better say, something quite different ... I know that a relation like ours has its inevitable stages ... I know you haven't time to come, often haven't time to write; but I know also that sometimes you have a moment, & that when one loves one never fails to use such a moment.[53]

At the end of 1909, her crisis with Teddy was reaching a climax. He 'confessed' to her that, while he was in America and she was in France, he had been speculating recklessly with her money and being unfaithful to her. 'He has put my affairs into rather serious (temporary) confusion', she wrote with some restraint to Morton in December 1909, saying that she found Teddy 'piteous'.[54] 'Morton must have devotedly rallied', James wrote, misguidedly. She got away with Anna Bahlmann for a few days to Germany, and treated Morton to a dazzling description of Augsburg ('all German romanticism is here'), punctuated by a cry of regret: 'Oh, if we could have gone up & down the earth together, just once!' She still loved him, and he was still – sometimes – behaving like a lover, sending her as a Christmas present a lavish edition of Joseph Bédier's *Tristan and Iseut*, with romantic coloured pictures of the doomed lovers, and a line of her love-poetry inscribed on the flyleaf. She responded with a sentimental note sent on New Year's Eve; on the day of the move to the new apartment she said she wanted him to be '*the first*' there. Her marriage was intolerable, and she was in 'a state of exasperated sensitiveness'. She wondered why she did not just 'lie howling'; but was still consoled by 'the source of light & laughter & renewal' 'you've set free in me'. Such moments of consolation grew fewer. James's shocking depression, early in 1910, and her visit to him at the same time that she was dealing with Teddy, darkened everything. She reported to Morton the 'excruciating' details – though there were a few consolations to be had in London, like the sight of a 'divine little Bonnington' ('surely he was the Keats of painting'), a comically suggestive night with Sturgis's 'Babe' at the Palace Theatre, with semi-naked dancing ladies, an Italian *Othello* in the company of Robert Norton, and some Turner watercolours.[55]

But back in Paris in the new apartment with an unstable Teddy and his obtuse sister, Edith was being driven to despair. She sent daily reports to Morton, as from a war-zone. In the spring of 1910, the Whartons went to Lausanne for Teddy to consult a specialist. Rest-cure and isolation were recommended – but that was what Edith needed, too. She could not work, she could not concentrate, she was exhausted: 'Oh, be kind, Dear, be sorry for me.' In Paris that summer, she told him how impossible Teddy's family were being ('The responsibility rests with his wife – we merely reserve the right to criticize').[56] But Morton was impossible too.

> I don't understand. If I could lean on *some feeling* in you – a good & loyal friendship, if there's nothing else! – then I could go on, bear things, write, & arrange my life . . . I don't know what you want, or what I am! You write to me like a lover, you treat me like a casual acquaintance! . . . I have borne all these inconsistencies & incoherences as long as I could, because I love you so much . . . My life was better before I knew you.

And so it went on: 'When one is a lonely-hearted & remembering creature, as I am, it is a misfortune to love too late, & as completely as I have loved you. Everything else grows so ghostly afterward.' 'You have made me very unhappy . . .' He said hurtful things to her: 'I thought I had grown a carapace, but some of the things you said the other day went through it.' Making love with him was becoming humiliating: 'Sometimes I feel that I *can't* go on like this . . . being left to feel that I have been like a "course" served & cleared away!' She felt split inside: the double life was taking its toll. 'Don't take my cry just now, "When are you coming to see me?" as anything but the instinctive, irrepressible voice of the deepest *me*. The reasonable reflective surface-me knows that you are busy & burdened & worried . . .' 'It's not my real self saying all this – only a temporary devil that a little peace & happiness wd soon exorcise.'[57]

Gradually, if bumpily, the transition she half-wanted and half-dreaded did take place, and 'amie' turned into 'ami'. She tried to help Morton with his problems at work, repeatedly encouraging him to leave the *Times*; his habitual treadmill there, she felt, had allowed him to 'let himself drift' with 'no definite goal'. Do not be like the lovers in Browning's poem 'The Statue and the Bust', she urged him (it was a personal message as well as a professional one) who wasted their whole lives deciding whether to run off with each other. She offered him another loan to get free, which he accepted, and urged him – graciously, and realistically – not to be anxious about repaying it, calling it 'a small service'. We do not know how much it was or whether he ever repaid it, but it did allow him to resign from his job in the summer of 1910.[58]

Edith tried to help him in his new career as a freelance journalist, advising him to take any writing jobs that came his way while looking around for 'a big offer for a foreign correspondence'. 'You have the immense "pull" of an extremely adaptable intelligence, varied gifts, & a charming personality.' But he did not always respond generously to her encouragement. One of her most frustrated efforts to advance his career – even before he had left the *Times* – was her attempt to draw him to Roosevelt's attention in the spring of 1910. The ex-President made a point of seeing Mrs Wharton on his trip to Paris – where he gave a controversial speech at the Sorbonne on 'Citizenship in a Republic', excoriating cynics and socialists and men of 'lettered leisure' who held attitudes of 'sneering disbelief'. Two days after his speech, she invited a distinguished company (of men only) to tea to meet 'Theodore the First', including Morton ('Come you *must*'). (Teddy made a brief appearance, too.) Fullerton talked to Roosevelt for ten minutes and told him 'the Parisians wouldn't have allowed any one else' to say to them what he had. The next day, she met Roosevelt at the Opéra, and he encouraged her to bring the interesting Mr Fullerton to the embassy reception the following night. Edith eagerly made her plans, but Morton refused to go; he felt the 'Embassy crush' would stop him speaking coherently and undo the impression he had made at the tea. Instead, he sent a long letter to Roosevelt via Edith, explaining how the French admired him as a 'teacher and a leader'. She passed the letter on, but was furious with him ('she thought me a fool', Fullerton noted), and her next letters were injured and glacial: 'My personal inconvenience, which was of the slightest, was nothing compared to my regret at having been importunate in trying to help you.' It was typical of his hurtful unreliability: 'If you tell me that at present we are not to see each other, I shall understand . . . The *not understanding* is the one unendurable & needless thing.'[59]

She kept on encouraging him, though. Perhaps he could write a book about his old friend Meredith, who died in 1909. He could send her some essays on Meredith, and she could look for 'some centre about which to group them, & some spaces to be filled. I want so much to help you! – Perhaps I could.' In the summer of 1910 she suggested to Burlingame that Fullerton should be hired to write 'a monthly article on European politics'. She helped him again financially by selling to the book-dealer Galignani's an expensive book Morton had given her, and sending him £100. She had done this, she explained, because she hated to see him slaving over endless commissions. One of these was an introduction to a new edition of *Gil Blas*, Le Sage's classic picaresque novel, an introduction which she might have felt cast an ironic light on its author. (The edition was in her library.) Fullerton wrote on Le Sage's treatment of 'caddishness', and said that Gil Blas was 'too agreeable a fellow for us to dream of parting company with him merely because of his escapades'.[60]

She went on urging him to write the non-existent book on Paris, encouraging him in March 1911 to send chapters of it to *Scribner's*, and not to let a projected book of 'French articles' get in the way, 'like the seductive irresistible *Autre* that breaks up so many legitimate ménages'. (Erotic and professional messages were inextricable as usual.) In the summer of 1911, she helped him with a translation of Bourget's anti-democratic play, *Le Tribun*, and tried to get it accepted by an English theatre-manager; but it was a waste of time for both of them. Jacques-Émile Blanche, dining with James on what James called 'a copious little dish of blanchailles', told James that Wharton had 'written in a love-scene' to Bourget's play. James told her that he 'yearned' to see this only slightly less than 'the passion with which he yearned for Morton'.

When Morton did at last write another book in 1913, *Problems of Power*, she commented very severely on the manuscript. She had a clearer view of his talents by now. 'If you would burn all your notes you'd do a better book.' 'The last paragraph of your introduction ... strikes me as very ponderous & rather High-School-Science (do forgive this rudeness!)' 'Drop 30 per cent of your Latinisms ("engendering a divergency" & so on), mow down every old cliché, uproot all the dragging circumlocutions, compress, diversify, clarify, vivify, & you'll make a book that will be read & talked of not only by the experts but by the big "intelligent public" you want to reach.' He knew he was lucky to get her literary advice, and inscribed the copy he gave her: 'To Edith Wharton, but for whom this book would never have been written'.[61]

In the 'problems of power' within their relationship, she was by far the stronger figure professionally – much richer, more successful, and an incomparably better writer. But he could still make her subservient to him emotionally. Her attempts to turn herself into his good friend were often entangled with feelings of grief, resentment and longing. Sometimes she wants to keep hold of him even while she is officially setting him free – as in this dignified letter of renunciation, fit for the heroine of a Wharton novel, of June 1910:

> Dear, there was never a moment, from the very first, when I did not foresee such a thought on your part as the one we talked of today; there was never a moment, even when we were nearest, that I did not feel it was latent in your mind. And still I took what you gave me, & was glad, & was not afraid.
>
> You are as free as you were before we ever met. If you ever doubted this, doubt it no more.
>
> And now let us think of your future –[62]

Her own future, at this point, seemed very dark. Locked in her crisis with Teddy, she wrote to Morton: 'Think of having had the chance of . . . *a life of my own*, in which I could write & think; & now *this*! . . . The only thing that keeps me from despairing is the hope that I may still, in some way, be of use to you.' She even asked him for his advice, as she was also asking Henry James and Walter Berry, back from Cairo, and lodging temporarily in the guest-suite at Number 53 (an arrangement which would be the cause of some gossip). Walter, close up to the horrors of the marriage, advised a separation. Morton gave no advice, but asked for his freedom.[63] As the marriage unravelled, he remained conspicuously uninvolved. After all, what was in it for him? His manageable, on-off affair with his distinguished, rich, passionate older mistress was turning into a dangerous proposition, an imbroglio with a well-known author whose marriage to a crazy husband was disintegrating amid scandal and chaos, with a divorce case clearly looming. Morton had quite enough scandalous liaisons in his life, and he backed off from this one. By the autumn of 1910, when they met in the Hotel Belmont in New York, at dinner with Henry James and Walter Berry, to see Teddy off on his 'world cruise', the affair was over. Edith was now signing herself 'Yr EW'. She was getting support from Walter, once again, and from her new friendship with Berenson. These two close male friends may never have known about the affair. If they did, there is no evidence of their thoughts about the mysterious Mr Fullerton, who now stepped back out of the close circle of Edith's world.

Between 1911 and 1913, Wharton struggled towards her divorce and managed, in the middle of tormenting and suspenseful personal circumstances (including the sale of The Mount, a break with her publishers, quarrels with her brother and with Henry James) to publish *Ethan Frome*, to work on *The Reef* and *The Custom of the Country*, and to produce some brilliant short stories. Her letters to Morton were now reminiscent, affectionate, and much less intense. There were business-like exchanges over the ill-fated project of the Bourget play, her new contract with Appleton (with which he was helping her),[64] and Scribner's dismay at her impending departure. She told him what she was reading: a life of Wagner, a French translation of Whitman. She told him about her work – noting that the prelude of *Ethan* had been the hardest part to do, or sending him a chapter of *Custom*, when she was struggling with it, with the words 'Either I can do it or I can't'. She boasted about the success of her story 'The Long Run' in the *Atlantic Monthly*, and of the serialisation of *Custom*: 'Undine is making the press ring'. She encouraged and criticised his writing. She used him for small services, asking him to forward her letters from Paris while she was staying at I Tatti with the Berensons. She was irritated because he would not take away some books he had left with her at the Rue de Varenne. She told him her troubles: the crises with Teddy, the death of her little dog Mitou in December 1911, a terrible meeting with her brother, probably in November 1912. She made a point of mentioning Walter and Berenson, and of referring to his own new friends – 'your petite amie', for instance, early in 1911. When she went on her travels with other people – to Spain with Rosa and Jean Du Breuil in the spring of 1912, to Germany with Berenson in August 1913, to Algeria with a group of friends in April 1914 – she would say flirtatiously that she only really wanted to be there with him. Vividly describing her adventures in Algeria, she ended drily: 'Is this the kind of letter you like to get from me? It would do very well in a memoir, wouldn't it? Only I don't know how to sign it –'[65] Her tone was wistful and resigned. Sitting on the terrace in a heat-wave at The Mount, the last summer she spent there, in July 1911 (and trying unsuccessfully to persuade him to join Henry James there on a visit) she thought of the cuckoo calling with 'the note of Montmorency', in a faint echo of the letter she had written to him three summers before, when she had heard the cuckoo-call, 'the very voice of Montmorency'. But that past self, she now felt, was 'dust'. If Morton wrote lovingly to her now, it was to '*notre vieille amie Mme d'Autrefois*'.[66]

There was only one point when a surge of the old feeling returned, and that was during the writing of *The Reef*. As she finished her novel of sexual jealousy, betrayal and humiliation, written fast between the summers of 1911 and of 1912, she called Morton in to help. She wanted to read the last chapters to him. So the ex-lover was summoned to give literary advice about the novel whose emotions he had inspired. (His advice has not survived, but she told him it was 'much improving' the novel as she revised it.) The scene she wanted his opinion on, which she was writing at Salso in June 1912, was 'the chapter in which . . . the truth begins to come out'. Unusually – and unfairly – she assured him that Walter had never read a word of this novel: 'He takes not the slightest interest in my literature.' No, it was Morton she needed now, just once more: 'I should like to turn myself into a writing-machine & give my remaining years of soundness & strength entirely to my work. (Only, when "The Reef" is finished, & the last pages sent . . . je voudrais bien, une dernière fois, t'embrasser!)'[67]

After this, they drifted apart. She congratulated him when he was made a chevalier of the Légion d'honneur in August 1913 (for his help 'in the general cause of Franco-American relations'), but his silence had begun to 'leave her numb'. 'Nothing I say reaches you.' In wartime, as she sprang into action, he was useless to her. By now she had his measure. She agreed with James that Morton's greatest accomplishment was 'that exquisite art in him of not bringing it off'. 'Morton has quite completely abandoned me', she told James. 'He will turn up again when I can be of use to him. Enfin!' Her secretary wrote one or two notes for her, still trying to get him to take his books out of her apartment. The few letters that she wrote to him between 1914 and 1916 told him she was too busy to see him (a nice twist). After the war, silence fell between them for many years, until an ironical, affectionate, desultory correspondence was resumed in her old age. In her memoir, she makes no mention of him.[68]

One of the humiliating things Fullerton said to Wharton – she reminded him – was that she would 'write better for this experience of loving'.[69] There was some truth in it. Powerful novels and stories emerged from this period, and certainly the love-affair turned her into more of a poet. *Artemis to Actaeon*, which was published in the middle of the affair, in April 1909, was her second and most interesting collection of poems (the first was her juvenile *Verses*, the last would be *Twelve Poems*, collecting up her wartime and post-war pieces). Some of *Artemis* was written well before her love-affair, like the title-poem, a meditation by the goddess who gives her lover the gift of drinking 'fate's utmost at a draught', instead of dwindling into immortality (like Tennyson's Tithonus), or the Browning-esque monologue 'Vesalius in Zante'. But most were love-poems.

In 'Survival' (the manuscript dated 'December 14th 1908') the lover imagines that after they have passed away, merged into 'life's divine renewal', whenever there is a radiant evening or a beautiful page, 'May it not be that you and I are there?' In 'All Souls' – a title she would use again – the lovers are ghosts in a graveyard, surrounded by 'phantom hearts'. Love's survival is also the theme of a sonnet sequence called 'The Mortal Lease' (the phrase is from a sonnet in Meredith's *Modern Love*, a favourite of hers). Wharton's lovers know that their emotions are produced by a primitive 'elemental law', but are also transcendent and infinite. The speaker is torn between her lover's hedonistic belief in living for the 'rounded moment' and her own sense of 'the cold surges of infinity'. She feels herself to be a reincarnation of all past lovers, re-enacting their conflicts between sensuality and spirituality. If she fails to grasp 'all that the insatiate heart of man can wring / From life's long vintage' she will be tortured by having missed her chance, but will have kept her conviction that there is something more than sensual appetite. She has always heard the god's footfall behind the everyday noises of humanity, 'the touch of silent fingers on my latch'. In the last sonnet she accepts that some hearts are made to live for the moment, 'but other hearts a long long road doth span', trampled by 'weary armies' and just occasionally by 'a sacred caravan . . . beneath the stars'.

This romantic language is a far cry from the tough realism of her fiction. It insists on love as something more than a love-affair, and couches her private experience – partly as a way of dressing it up for publication – in sublime, even sacred, terms. In 'Life', an impassioned reworking of Dante's journey with Beatrice in the *Commedia*, the speaker, a reed-flute, is being played on by Life's 'wild music', until the flute (or human poet) becomes 'god-like'.[70] The flute is 'stabbed . . . / With yearnings for new music and new pain', until she reaches her climax with the music of Love, that 'sucked my soul / Forth in a new song from my throbbing throat'. The poem throbs with pangs, tremors and kisses, bursting veins and penetrating fingers, suckings, pantings and leaping flanks, in a wild narrative of sexual climax dressed up as neo-pagan allegory.

The poems which came out in magazines after *Artemis to Actaeon* continued with these tactics of cloaking a secret love-story in poetic tropes. 'Summer Afternoon', published in *Scribner's* in March 1911, invokes a visit to Bodiam Castle when for one 'transcendent' moment the lovers are transformed: 'Suddenly / We took the hues of beauty, and became, / Each to the other, all that each had sought.' The inference, even with all the exalted lyricism – is that such moments did not happen very often.

'Ogrin the Hermit', a long narrative poem published in the *Atlantic Monthly* in December 1909, is the best example of the self-conscious literariness of Wharton's affair. It was inspired by Joseph Bédier's 1900 retelling of the legend of Tristan and Iseut (or Iseult). She had marked some of its most intense passages in her copy: '*Qu'importe la mort! Tu m'appelles, tu me veux, je viens!' 'Ni vous sans moi, ni moi sans vous.'* Her blank-verse version of the story is told from the point of view of the hermit with whom the lovers take refuge (as though Henry James were telling the story of Morton and Edith). There is an argument between the hermit's asceticism and Iseult's claim (as in Wharton's other love-poems) that there is more to love than momentary hedonism. 'Upon each other's hearts / They shall surprise the heart-beat of the world / And feel a sense of life in things inert.' The Hermit is attuned by Iseult's presence (Tristan barely gets a walk-on part) to 'such music of the heart as lovers hear / When close as lips lean, lean the thoughts between'. He is converted to the worship of the God of Love, whose intensity human beings have to escape from, 'dropping back to earth' and 'the dim shelter of familiar sounds'. Iseult will go back to her husband. (Wharton, fascinated by the hermits in their caves in early Italian paintings, also has an ascetic converted by a passionate woman in her story 'The Hermit and the Wild Woman'. She identifies as much with her hermits as with her female characters.) 'Ogrin' was written for Morton. In the copy she wrote out for him, she wrote: 'Per Te, Sempre Per Te'. In the edition he gave her of Bédier's book, he transcribed her line, 'such music of the heart as lovers hear'. She asked him if he was 'glad' to know that 'Ogrin' was written 'for you, and *by you*'. The poem was a public performance, and a secret message.[71]

But for every publishable love-lyric, there was another which was too erotic, too painful, or too self-revealing to be read by anyone but Morton. Some of these – 'Senlis', 'L'Âme Close', 'Herblay' – were part of the secret diary, where her emotions kept overflowing into poetry. A poem of parting ('When I am gone, recall my hair'), written on the transatlantic crossing in May 1908, described the transformation of her body by his contact, 'so warm and close in your possessing'. Some poems, like 'Bodiam Castle' and 'Survival', were messages to him in her letters – and she often complained that he did not respond to them. In the spring of 1910, when her love-letters were at their most bitter, she wrote him out a sonnet in which the woman offers her body and soul as bread and wine, as in the communion, and then asks the lover, his 'thirst appeased', to remember her, if only dimly – 'as one inland feels the sea'. Fullerton annotated this: 'EW after her visit chez moi, 15 April'. Two days later, in a letter making arrangements for Roosevelt's visit, she asked, in French, why he had crushed her sonnet with his silence.[72]

Many of these private unpublished poems were dark and painful. They often expressed an unreal sense of being split into two. One she did publish, in the *Atlantic Monthly* for December 1910, 'The Comrade', described a double life with a familiar, a 'sister', winged, free, and 'elfin', who has had to be tamed by 'the dull forms / Of human usage', but who has brought the speaker a sense of 'the heart of wonder in familiar things', and consolation in the wasteland of loneliness that follows love. This was a publishable allegory of the split self; but a more disturbing, less consolatory version stayed in manuscript. 'The Heavenly Powers' is a story of an unpleasant haunting, in a different tone from Wharton's usual lyric style:

> There is someone staying in the house – a demure brown figure –
> You'd never notice her – well it is she who collects my jokes for me,
> Gossip, news, the latest thing in art or books . . .
> She says very little? Yes – but every night she comes, & puts
> her thin white lips to my heart, & sucks till morning.

'Restoration', equally ghoulish, tells of a lover who dismisses his mistress as 'not young enough', but challenges Love to transform her for the duration of a kiss. Love lays on 'his old pigments', and paints her as one who has suffered from his attentions: 'dusted her eyes / With gloom of sleepless midnights', etc. The lover looks and is horrified: 'Good god, she's old!' '"Ah, that's my *patina*", Love grinned.'[73]

A series of short poems under the title 'Ex Tenebrae' or 'The Black Harp' are the darkest of all, and conjure up the mood of *Ethan Frome*. 'Jures-moi . . .' advises the lover to 'swear his faith' not by a moment of ecstasy but 'by the body of this death – / The change in you and me'. He should swear by the day 'When our sullen footsteps dragged apart / Just the length of habit's chain'. Would they 'love each other still', under those conditions? 'White Death' dreams of lying on the bitter ground, covered with icy snowflakes that turn her mouth to stone: 'It was your kisses I had felt.' Other fragments persist with the themes of disillusion and loss: 'No more at your step my heart will spring from my breast . . . No more my lips, trembling / Prepare the shy jest / For your sneer to prick it . . .' 'I have had your love and I have seen it go.' In an unpublished poem of July 1909 called 'The Room', the furniture all speaks of the lover's visit ('You pillows of my bed, / Where he stooped, where he laid his head'). But since he left her, the room is 'straiter now than a tomb'.[74]

'The Room' frankly dramatises a night of love. So does 'Terminus', a poem of extraordinary candour and (like her love-letters and love-diary) great literary self-consciousness. Whether or not composed in a post-coital rush sitting up in bed in the Charing Cross Hotel, as Fullerton would like us to think, it is a bold, agitatedly sexy poem. It is not as graphic as 'Beatrice Palmato', but Wharton could write with a powerful erotic charge, even when she did not spell out the sexual act. The thundering, rhythmic pulse of 'Terminus' – part train-shunting, part love-making, part metric experimentation – tells us everything we need to know about the 'secret night'. After its excited, fervent beginning ('Wonderful was the long secret night you gave me, my Lover / Palm to palm, breast to breast in the gloom') there is a scene, like a Sickert painting, of the lovers looking at each other in the mirror in the red lamplight of the hotel room while he undresses her. Then the poem turns to the atmosphere of the hotel room, its 'dull impersonal furniture', its much-used bed 'with its soot-sodden chintz' and 'the grime of its brasses'. This grimy realism – more like something out of Gissing or Zola than the usual rhapsodic scenery of her love-poems – allows her to identify with all the other bodies that have passed through the room in 'fagged' exhaustion or passionate ecstasy. She wants to feel herself part of 'the human unceasing current', and she expresses a post-Darwinian, determinist view of human beings as 'automata' 'whirled down the ways of the world like dust-eddies swept through a street'. She does not quite say that spending the night with her lover in a railway-hotel makes her feel like a prostitute, but she does want to identify with the women before her who may also have lain awake all night listening to the orgasmic 'night-long shudder of traffic' and 'the farewell shriek of the trains'. Like them, she has to face the 'terminus': the ending of the night and the journey onwards under 'the hand of implacable fate', he to the 'wide flare of cities' (he was sailing to New York), she to a 'dull town' on 'a low-skied marsh' (she was going to Rye). The vision of their journeys shifts into a ghost story, like the poem 'All Souls', with her train and its passengers and all who come to stare at it turned into ghosts: 'and scarcely the difference is felt'. She turns to escape such thoughts and to drink 'oblivion' from 'the sleeping lips at her side', as many others may have done in that room before her.

'Terminus' speaks of Wharton's deepest feelings, but it is also a literary exercise. Fullerton noted that Goethe's long-lined 'Roman Elegies' inspired it. And it drew too on Whitman, and Tennyson's 'Maud', and Swinburne's 'Hymn to Proserpine'. It was clearly meant to be read out loud, like the favourite poems she liked to copy out in her Commonplace Book.[75] 'Terminus' was a bold experiment; some of Wharton's other love-poems, like 'Ogrin the Hermit', with its plush Edwardian archaisms, look dated alongside the ruthlessly spare and modern *Ethan Frome*. But even in the most rapturous and transcendent verses there is a dark, downward pull. The high moment passes, the lovers fail to understand each other. After *Artemis to Actaeon* was published, she added a coda to 'The Mortal Lease', called

'The Coming of the God', or 'Colophon to the Mortal Lease', and sent it to Fullerton. It describes their love-making like the coming of a great god from far off: 'So beat by beat / My body hears the coming of the feet / Innumerable of surging ecstasies'. In the stillness that follows, gazing into her lover's eyes 'to read where we have been', the speaker realises that she cannot share her vision: 'Ah, close your eyes. They see not what I saw . . .' Annotating his copy, with a shrewd idea that he might one day be asked about the affair, Fullerton wrote: 'I saw not what she saw, & that's the tragedy of it.'[76]

It would be a travesty to suggest that all the stories of failed love, sexual treachery and claustrophobic marriages Wharton published in this period issued from her relationship with Morton Fullerton. These themes were already her speciality. The qualities that make Wharton a great writer – her mixture of harshly detached, meticulously perceptive, disabused realism, with a language of poignant feeling and deep passion, and her setting of the most confined of private lives in a thick, complex network of social forces – were the product of years of observation, reading, practice and refinement, not of a love-affair. And the chronology and publication of her work in the 'Fullerton' years is complicated, making it difficult to link it to particular events in her life. She had four novels on the go at once in the years between 1907 and 1912, when she was changing publishers; she kept interrupting herself, and did not publish a full-length novel in those years. Yet this messy, difficult time in her private and professional life saw some of her finest work. It was an especially rich and prolific period for short stories. She published three collections between 1908 and 1913 (*The Hermit and the Wild Woman* in 1908, her French collection *Les Metteurs en Scène*, in 1909, and *Tales of Men and Ghosts* in 1910). Some powerful stories – 'The Choice', 'Autres Temps . . .', 'The Long Run' – were published in magazines but not collected until the volume called *Xingu* came out in 1916.

The stories of this period show an impressive versatility. She turned her hand to lurid melodrama in 'The Bolted Door', about a neurotic failed play-wright, whose sense 'of his own personality clung to him like some thick viscous substance', so bent on suicide that he confesses to an elaborate crime in order to be executed. She did family tensions in 'His Father's Son', with a son so snobbish and so ashamed of his real father, a manufacturer, that he invents (a frequent American plot) an imaginary, romantic father for himself. She did satires on obsessive collectors, losses of professional integrity, artistic compromise and literary fame and envy, in 'The Daunt

Diana', 'In Trust', 'The Debt', 'Full Circle', 'The Pot-Boiler' and 'The Verdict'. She did corruption in American politics and business ('The Best Man', 'The Blond Beast') and she did a memorable haunted English house in 'Afterward'.

One of her most polished performances was 'Xingu', in which a New England women's intellectual lunch club and its star visitor, the rude and gloomy lady novelist 'Osric Dane', author of 'The Wings of Death', are thrown into shame and confusion by the charming, well-travelled, frivolous Miss Roby's mischievous invention of the deep subject of 'Xingu'. Xingu has many branches, an obscure source, and passages difficult to wade through. It turns out to be not a religion, a book, or a philosophy – as they variously pretend to think it is – but a river in Brazil. Yet even in this funny squib there is a painful autobiographical trace. Writing to Morton in October 1910, in a state of great fatigue, Wharton said: 'I look more like the Lady President of a New England Culture Club than like – Pleasure at the Prow!'

One coldly brilliant story, 'The Last Asset', of rich Americans marrying into the prim and proper French aristocracy, looks harshly impersonal. Greedy, exploitative Mrs Newell, sliding down the social scale, is desperately in search of her long-discarded husband in Paris to give the proper tone to her meekly innocent daughter Hermione's wedding to a young French count. The cynical, philosophical old husband ('If you make up your mind not to be happy there's no reason why you shouldn't have a fairly good time'), the moral, tender-hearted young male narrator, and an unpleasantly caricatured Jewish 'Baron Schenkelderff', Mrs Newell's 'glossy and ancient' source of income, add spice to the farcical social plot. In the last sentence, when the narrator contemplates the daughter's marriage as a happy romance surprisingly emerging out of the mother's schemings, there is the phrase 'life's indefatigable renewals'. It is a surprising echo of 'life's divine renewal', in her romantic love-poem to Morton of 1908, 'Survival'. Even in the most hard-edged of stories, there is a trace of her secret life.[77]

Some of the more passionate stories of this period are very revealing. Wharton wrote 'The Choice' on board ship going back to America in May 1908, and it was published in *Century Magazine* that autumn. (Could Teddy have read it?) It is set in a Lenox-style country community and features a boastful, drunken, boring, and financially incompetent husband, always besotted with the latest thing – canoes, motor-cars, motor-launches. He is probably her closest fictional version of Teddy (he is even speculating with his wife's fortune, as her trustee). His elegant, reserved wife is having an affair with the family lawyer, and they meet at night in the boat-house, where, in a long, powerful, remarkably uncensored speech, she tells him what she feels about her husband:

> Day by day, hour by hour, I wish him dead. When he goes out I pray for something to happen; when he comes back I say to myself: 'Are you here again?' When I hear of people being killed in accidents, I think: 'Why wasn't he there?' When I read the death-notices in the paper I say: 'So-and-so was just his age.' When I see him taking such care of his health and his diet – as he does, you know, except when he gets reckless and begins to drink too much – when I see him exercising and resting, and eating only certain things, and weighing himself, and feeling his muscles, and boasting that he hasn't gained a pound, I think of the men who die from overwork, or who throw their lives away for some great object, and I say to myself: 'What can kill a man who thinks only of himself?' And night after night I keep myself from going to sleep for fear I may dream that he's dead.

As if punishing herself for voicing these thoughts so openly, Wharton contrives a boat-house accident in which both men risk drowning: but it is the husband whom the wife calls out for, and the lover who is killed. She told Richard Gilder at the *Century* that it was not a very 'Christmassy' story.[78]

In 'The Pretext', Mrs Ransom, the middle-aged wife of a pompous New England professor in a small university town ('the kind of place where husbands and wives gradually grew to resemble each other') falls deeply in love with a charming young visiting Englishman, only to find out – from a comically insulting visit by his high-handed aristocratic aunt – that she has been used as a 'pretext' so that he can break off his engagement at home. The secret feelings she had cherished – 'as much outside the sphere of her marriage as some transaction in a star' – turn out to have been, probably (we are never quite sure), a deception. Wharton's own feeling of being too old for love, of returning to a 'phantasmal', lonely life after the end of the affair, are cruelly caricatured in the pale, provincial, self-denying figure of Mrs Ransom.[79]

In 'The Letters', her own humiliations are used for a risible liaison between a simple little governess in Paris and her older, married lover, a dilettantish painter, selfish and lazy, who 'let the loose ends of life hang as they would', and who mocks her for her inexperience in love. After his wife's death, he goes to America, leaving her in Paris, and she writes him many love-letters, to which he soon stops replying. Wharton turns her own lacerating experience – even the very phrases in her own passionate love-letters – into a cool satire on Lizzie's pathetic self-deception:

> She marvelled afterward at the reasons she had found for Deering's silence: there were moments when she almost argued herself into thinking it more natural than his continuing to write. There was only one reason which her intelligence rejected; and that was the possibility that he had forgotten her, that the whole episode had faded from his mind like a breath from a mirror. From that she resolutely averted her thoughts, conscious that if she suffered herself to contemplate it, the motive power of life would fail, and she would no longer understand why she rose in the morning and lay down at night . . . In a last short letter she explicitly freed him from whatever sentimental obligation its predecessors might have seemed to impose . . . And she ended, gracefully, with a plea for the continuance of the friendly regard which she had 'always understood' to be the basis of their sympathy . . . But . . . the letter, like those it sought to excuse, remained unanswered.[80]

After she has come into a fortune and her lover has opportunely reappeared, and married her, she discovers all her letters to him, still unopened. But instead of rejecting him, she accepts that real love has to be 'fashioned' out of 'mean mixed substances'. It takes a strong power of detachment to turn one's most painful humiliations into comedy in this way – or to offer as a love-gift a tale of cruelty and selfishness. Wharton told Fullerton that one of her most sinister and ghoulish stories, 'The Eyes', about the baleful aesthete Culwin, was '*à vous*'.[81]

In the two finest stories of this period, 'Autres Temps . . .' and 'The Long Run', she reworks her emotions with complete control. The stories are objective, socially observant, and perfectly structured, while harrowingly personal: at once everything, and nothing, to do with her own life. 'Autres Temps . . .' (which would be reworked for *The Mother's Recompense*) imagines a woman out of 'old New York', with a scandalous divorce and love-affair in her past for which she was shamed and ostracised, who has lived quietly in Italy for eighteen years, going back to America because her daughter is, in her turn, being divorced and remarrying. Mrs Lidcote returns in trepidation to the 'huge menacing mass' of New York (on a ship called the *Utopia*). 'Her own poor miserable past' seems 'like the afflicted relative suddenly breaking away from nurses and keepers and publicly parading the horror and misery she had, all the long years, so patiently screened and secluded'. She finds, to her amazement, that everything has changed for Leila's generation. 'There's no old New York left, it seems.' Divorce is easy, remarriage is no scandal, everyone stays friends, society is amorphous and shifting. She is told, firmly, that 'every woman had a right to happiness and that self-expression was the highest duty'. 'It's as if an angel had gone about lifting gravestones', she muses. But – in the brilliantly engineered scene of her visit to her daughter's new home, where she realises that she is being kept away from the company in case she imperils her new son-in-law's chance of a good diplomatic posting – it becomes apparent that nothing has changed for *her*. She is still the woman who sinned and paid, like 'a guilty woman in a play'. She is trapped inside her own past, even in this new, modern America. 'Finis was scrawled all over her.' There is nothing so hard to destroy as 'traditions that have lost their meaning'. Even the faithful friend who has waited years to offer her his love and support is shut up with her inside the 'tight little round of habit and association' they live by. This magnificent story imagines what it might be like for Wharton if she went back to live in New York. (It is also, typically, a profoundly ambivalent account of a mother–daughter relationship.) What speak loudest, under the surface of the masterly social satire, are the powerful images of being entombed, alone, without a second chance and with no escape: 'We're all imprisoned, of course – all of us middling people, who don't carry our freedom in our brains. But we've accommodated ourselves to our different cells, and if we're moved suddenly into new ones we're likely to find a stone wall where we thought there was thin air, and to knock ourselves senseless against it. I saw a man do that once.'[82] Wharton builds into this grim passage, by inference, the consolation she has (unlike most of her 'middling' characters) for her own troubles: she carries her freedom in her brain.

'The Long Run', written alongside *The Reef* early in 1912, after 'Autres Temps . . .' and *Ethan Frome*, looks ahead to *The Age of Innocence*, and asks what happens to people if they do not take their chance of love. It revisits her feelings about her affair as if they were a lifetime ago. Like *Ethan Frome*, it is told through flashback, by a narrator who, returning to New York after twelve years away, finds his old friend Halston Merrick, once a 'vivid and promising figure in young American life', sunk into dull conventionality. Another old acquaintance, Paulina Trant, once 'rare' and distinctive, now looks 'worn down. Soft but blurred, like the figures in that tapestry behind her.' Merrick and Paulina had once almost been lovers: he had been drawn to her 'as the moon-track seems to draw a boat across the water . . .' 'With her one had the sense that . . . the magic ship would always carry one further.' (Gautier's cycle of love-poems, *Nuits d'Été*, with its promised journey to the Happy Isles, magically set to music by Berlioz, may have been in Wharton's mind: she owned his poems.) But, like most of Wharton's lovers, Merrick is not bold enough for the journey. When Paulina offers her life to him, he is aghast (as she knew he would be) at the thought of the scandal. '"No, there's one other way," she exclaimed; "and that is, *not* to do it! To abstain and refrain; and then see what we become, or what we don't become, in the long run, and to draw our inferences."'[83] Like the lovers in Browning's poem 'The Statue and the Bust' (and like Newland Archer and Ellen Olenska in *The Age of Innocence*), these lovers do not take ship for the 'Happy Isles'. He retreats into 'a rage of conformity', she marries some other perfectly decent, boring fellow after her husband's death, and they continue to meet in society – for the rest of their lives.

'Autres Temps . . .' and 'The Long Run' are both retrospective New York stories about the baleful effects of social regulation; they are the link stories between *The House of Mirth* and *The Age of Innocence*. They are both, also, about being buried alive, living on as ghosts, and in that sense they are closer to *Ethan Frome* than they look. *Ethan* belongs with the story of Wharton's marriage and divorce. But the novel she was writing when *Ethan* came out in 1911 was the book that came most closely out of her love-affair. When Morton sent her one of the reviews of *Ethan Frome* from New York in October 1911, she responded: 'They don't know why it's good; but they are right: it *is* . . . Vous verrez que je ferai encore mieux!' Her next novel was meant for him.[84]

Henry James would call *The Reef* Racinian, her critics would call it Jamesian, and objected to its hothouse atmosphere and its gloomy unpleasantness. She called it theatrical, and wondered later why no one could see there was a play in it. *The Reef* was an extraordinarily candid expression of private feelings about her own desires and sexual knowledge, immaculately disguised by the novel's formal control and careful, dramatic design. Like *Ethan*, *The Reef* is one of her most autobiographical novels, looking not at all like autobiography. This painful and emotionally intricate novel is a study of, and an exercise in, disguise and evasion. The book behaves like both its central women characters: it is as guarded as Anna Leath and as openly emotional as Sophy Viner. It looks at once like a formal dance or a dissection in a laboratory, but it has a furnace blazing under it. Everything that is well managed and tactfully controlled comes under pressure, and threatens to break apart. 'The truth had come to light by the force of its irresistible pressure; and the perception gave her a startled sense of hidden powers, of a chaos of attractions and repulsions far beneath the ordered surfaces of intercourse.'[85]

Wharton poured her feelings about Fullerton, by now consigned to the past, into all the different characters in the novel. It looks as if Anna Leath, the elegant widowed New Yorker, survivor of her imprisoning marriage, living quietly in her chateau in France, holding back nervously from a full commitment to her suitor, would be Wharton's natural alter ego, and that Sophy Viner, the eager ingénue, with her slipshod unprotected upbringing, her naive inexperience and theatrical ambitions, would be likely to be an object of pathos and mild satire. The urbane, epicurean and attractive diplomat George Darrow's casual fling with Sophy in Paris would not seem to be much of threat to his main object of desire. It occurs, initially, as a brief sidetrack from his settled, if obstacle-ridden, pursuit of Anna, secluded in the beautiful autumnal French rural setting of Givré, with her fussy, antique mother-in-law, her charming little girl and her devoted, if temperamental, stepson. Anna is set to be the tragic romantic heroine, Sophy the light soubrette. The artificial, coincidental plot brings the two women's lives together. Anna hires Sophy, knowing nothing about her, as her daughter's governess, and her stepson Owen falls in love with the girl, so that when Darrow at last arrives in Givré, months after his passing affair with Sophy, he finds her, to his horrified surprise, already involved with Anna's family. At this point the reader might expect all the weight of sympathy to go towards Anna, especially since the narrative is constructed, on unusually Jamesian lines, entirely through two consciousnesses, Darrow's and Anna's. But the contrasts in this relentlessly disillusioning novel are complicated and surprising.

Wharton gives her own upbringing, with lethal precision, to Anna Leath, née Summers. The 'well regulated well fed Summers world' of her West 55th Street childhood, where 'the unusual was regarded as either immoral or ill-bred, and people with emotions were not visited', vividly recalls the Joneses. Anna is an alert and intelligent girl, aware of a world of passion and 'hidden beauty' in literature and nature, who is 'conquered' by the conditions, and grows up feeling a 'veil' between 'herself and life'. Her early attraction to Darrow is short-circuited by her virginal shyness and by his eye for a more adventurous (and sillier) kind of girl. Instead she marries a cosmopolitan aesthete, Fraser Leath, whose little subversive touches, which seem at first to mark him out from standard New York gentility, turn out to cloak a fanatic observer of forms who 'exacted a rigid conformity to his rules of non-conformity'. (James's Gilbert Osmond comes to mind.) If Anna is to be the tragic heroine, Fraser Leath is 'like the anarchist with a gardenia in his button-hole who figures in the higher melodrama'. Wharton gives him a lonely, shrouded first wife, a radical (but equally ineffectual) son, and a mother whose archaic sitting room embodies 'the forces of order and tradition', a combination of Catholic French landowning proprieties and of genteel old New York habits of mind. Wharton names her Lucretia, as a grim private joke. James wondered why these 'non-French people' had 'to have their story out there': it made him feel even more that Wharton needed, as a fiction-writer, 'a Country of your Own'. But these characters need to be displaced. Whether they live in hotel rooms or an old French chateau, they are all trying to find an emotional home.[86]

Wharton gives Anna her own feelings of never having experienced what other women have had. When she renews her relationship with Darrow, as a still-young widow, she speaks the romantic language of Wharton's love-letters and poems to Fullerton. Her imagination is 'spinning luminous webs of feeling', she is filled with a 'bliss' that 'wound itself into every fold of her being'. Kissed by him, she sits 'as if folded in wings'. 'She felt like a slave, and a goddess, and a girl in her teens . . .' Of course none of this can last. There is really no such thing as an ideal platonic conception of Love. Anna has been sexually jealous of Darrow long before she falls in love with him again; Darrow's idea of her – a knowing and rapacious one, even if couched in romantic terms – is that he could turn her from a lady into a woman: 'he would have put warmth in her veins and light in her eyes: would have made her a woman through and through'.[87]

Anna is carefully moved on from romantic bliss, to her first awareness that there is something between Darrow and Sophy Viner, to (in spite of his denials and evasions) a full, horrified realisation of their affair and its implications not only for herself but for her stepson. The plot is worked very hard, as in the kind of French melodrama Sophy might have enjoyed. There are carefully staged parallels between Anna and Sophy (two train journeys, two walks in the rain under umbrellas, and so on). There are letters which do not arrive in time and letters which are never sent. There is the eye-stretching coincidence of Sophy's being hired by Anna as her governess, and some unlikely bits of hidden information, like Anna's not telling Darrow the name of the girl Owen wants to marry. But these some-times strained manoeuvres create an atmosphere in which four people, living close together, are tangled in concealments, secrets and betrayals.

Wharton squeezes every ounce of pain out of Anna's humiliating sexual betrayal. Her most painful recriminations are against herself: 'There it lay before her, her sole romance, in all its paltry poverty, the cheapest of cheap adventures, the most pitiful of sentimental blunders.' But the novel does not just settle for self-lacerating disillusion. It pushes on into the dark places of sexual dependency. Anna, instead of sending Darrow away, goes to bed with him, and then experiences a 'new instinct of subserviency', 'a sort of suspicious tyrannical tenderness'. Nowhere did Wharton write better about the humiliating bondage of desire. It is all very well for Darrow to argue, in his role as experienced seducer, that Anna was 'made to feel everything'. In fact the rending of the veil which had hung between 'herself and life' is unpleasant, as well as necessary. It creates a self-estranging split between her 'body and soul', acted out in a typically formal, and cruel, metaphor:

> She recalled having read somewhere that in ancient Rome the slaves were not allowed to wear a distinctive dress lest they should recognize each other and learn their numbers and their power. So, in herself, she discerned for the first time instincts and desires, which, mute and unmarked, had gone to and fro in the dim passages of her mind, and now hailed each other with a cry of mutiny.[88]

Anna's agonising self-discovery is so powerful that it risks overwhelming the rest of the novel. But *The Reef* is a delicately balanced operation. Its settings are ambiguous. Givré looks harmonious and enchanting (like a Walter Gay painting of Le Bréau). Anna used to resent it, during her marriage, as 'the very symbol of narrowness and monotony', but has come to terms with it as 'the place where one had one's duties, one's habits and one's books'. (So Wharton imagines George Sand being changed by her quiet life at Nohant.[89]) But it is also a lonely, melancholy house, where the first Mrs Leath seemed to Anna, from her portrait, always 'to be waiting for visitors who never came',[90] and where, as the plot thickens around the characters, there is a gathering feeling of edgy, queer unreality. Givré turns out to be a haunted house rather than a safe haven. The novel's rival location, Paris, is contradictory too, switching between being dazzlingly romantic and shoddily claustrophobic.

And the balancing-act between the characters is complex. Sophy has to be part of a seedy, mondaine world and also (like Mattie in *Ethan Frome*) fresh and unspoilt. She speaks knowingly about sexual exploitation in the world of her much-divorced sister Laura (offstage until the very end), the louche Jimmy Brance and the coarse Mrs Murrett, and there is a suggestion that she has been sexually abused by at least one of her employers; but she is innocent and natural as well as bohemian. Her boyishness is emphasised, and she is intensely impressionable, 'an extraordinary conductor of sensation'. To start with, we share Darrow's demeaning view of her, as risibly naive and too stupid to write a letter. But she grows extraordinarily in stature and dignity, even while the narration keeps her at arm's length. Wharton gives Sophy her own bitter retrospect on an opportunist lover ('I wonder what your feeling for me was? . . . Is it like taking a drink when you're thirsty?') and her own feelings of erotic surrender ('I used to feel as if all of me was in the palm of your hand . . .'). Sophy's 'ardour' and passion give her a surprising tragic grandeur and mystery; and then, like Lily Bart, she is swept back down and out of sight.[91]

The internal landscape we do close in on is Darrow's, and a very murky one it is. In a dazzling act of fictional revenge, and with a kind of cool intimacy, Wharton exposes from the inside the double standards and appetites of a sexual diplomat. She does his sensual aestheticism knowingly – his critical judgements on the 'feminine types' he has encountered in a variety of 'flagrant adventures', his pleasure in looking at Sophy ('her lips were just far enough apart for the reflection of the upper one to deepen the colour of the other'), his intense alertness to their physical effect on each other ('he perceived that every drop of her blood must be alive to his nearness'). The half-deliberate, half-passive way he drifts into their affair on a rainy day in the Hotel Terminus (a sharp in-joke for Fullerton), his recoil from her closeness when he has tired of the adventure, the almost involuntary reigniting of his sexual interest in her at Givré, at exactly the moment he is trying to clear her out of his life, his obliviousness to her deep feeling for him, and his preference for Anna's fine sensations and high tone, are all done from his point of view. No moralising comment is required: 'As soon as he had kissed her he felt that she would never bore him again . . . The mere fact of not having to listen to her any longer added immensely to her charm.'[92]

Darrow's dilettantish diplomatic career – he has taken a posting to South America in order to write about it, and intends 'to resign from the service of my country' for a life (with Anna, as he hopes) of travel and writing – is not explicitly parallelled with his sexual life. But there are enough references to his 'tactics' and 'urbanity' to make the analogy between sex and diplomacy clear: 'The idea that his tact was a kind of professional expertness filled her with repugnance.' But Darrow is also intelligent, self-critical, and ardent. We have to feel he is worth falling in love with, and his judgements on the world often sound as if we are meant to agree: 'What rubbish we talk about intentions!' 'Life's just a perpetual piecing together of broken bits.'[93]

No simple judgement is passed against Darrow; the sexual politics of *The Reef* are far from straightforwardly feminist. Right and wrong are equivocally handled. And as usual in Wharton, the novel is not just a love-story. There is a wider argument going on about protection and freedom. The characters are arranged on a register of shockability, with Fraser Leath's mother at the top and Sophy's slatternly sister at the bottom. Sliding in between these points is a complicated idea of conventionality. Clearly Madame de Chanterelle's archaic, snobbish anti-modernism is as absurd and suffocating as her dead son's ritual obeisance to ancient customs. But her grandson's 'crude revolutionary dogmatizing' is seen as insubstantial – and does not prevent Owen Leath (an undeveloped study in neurosis) from being shocked by sexual truths. Anna is described by her mother-in-law as dangerously 'modern' ('I believe that's what it's called when you read unsettling books and admire hideous pictures'). She is in sympathy with the young and wants to be open to new experience. But Anna's 'modernity' has its limits: 'Much as she wished to think herself exempt from old-fashioned prejudice, she suddenly became aware that she did not like her daughter's governess to have a powdered face.' Though she takes Darrow as her lover, she has a powerful resistance to the idea of free love or feminism, 'the stuff that awful women rave about on platforms'. By contrast, Sophy's boast to Darrow of being 'awfully modern' seems to him (and to us) 'helplessly backward'. And Darrow's own sexual freedoms coexist with his old-fashioned, uninvestigated double standards.[94]

The sexually loaded word 'know' rings through the book. Anna, trustingly confiding in Darrow, says, 'I want you to know me as I am'; 'I know . . . of course I *know* . . . but there are things a woman feels . . . when what she knows doesn't make any difference.' He echoes her: 'I know – I know' . . . 'You know?' 'That this is no light thing between us.' Owen's speeches are all preoccupied with knowing: wanting 'everyone to know' about him and Sophy, wanting to know what Darrow knows. When the secret starts to break, the verb 'to know' becomes a weapon; and when the full truth is out, knowing becomes the subject: Anna is 'tormented by the desire to know more'; she is most tormented by feeling 'I shall never know what that girl has known'. She wants to know 'everything'.[95]

The novel ends, shockingly and inconclusively, with a harshly comic slice of realism. Anna, in Paris, goes in search of Sophy, who has run away from Owen and Givré. She wants to tell her that she has given Darrow up. But Sophy has vanished, and in her place is the louche sister we have heard about, who storms into the last pages of the book in a scene of magnificent coarseness and sexual decadence. In a tobacco-scented, disordered hotel-room, with what look like a Jewish money-lender and a gigolo in attendance, lies a large, blonde, semi-naked woman, whose bedroom is littered with little dogs and chocolates. That we are left with this apparition (an ending much disliked by *The Reef*'s critics) gives a bitter twist to the debate over knowledge. Laura's bedroom in the Hotel Chicago is as far as we can possibly get from the romance of the Château Givré. Laura is like a horrible parody of Sophy, her lover Jimmy of Darrow. This is where sexual knowingness at its coarsest can land you.

The faint hope that there might be a space for happiness, somewhere between overprotected romantic illusion, and dingy, disabused realities, struggles in the novel with an overwhelming sense of futility. Darrow is all too aware of his own 'huge fatuity' and of the 'futility' of his regrets. The 'reef' of the title, never fully explained, is of course the affair: 'It seemed such a slight thing – all on the surface – and I've gone aground on it because it *was* on the surface.'[96] (The *Titanic* met her fate while Wharton was writing this novel.) But they are all foundering, too, on the probability that futility is the condition of life. Sophy loses her happiness, and so does Owen; Anna struggles to hang on to hers, but it looks doomed. No one has anywhere to escape to.

In all the writings of these years of passion, sorrow, and disappointment – *Ethan Frome*, 'Autres Temps . . .', 'The Long Run', 'Afterward', 'The Pretext', 'The Choice', *The Reef* – there is a move out towards an imagined place of escape, freedom, and true relationships, and a move backwards, a return or a fixing, in some form of paralysis, thwarting or disillusion. As the lovers will recognise in *The Age of Innocence*, there is no other world, no escape, no exit point to the Happy Isles. There is only what you make of the life you have; and within it there comes, just occasionally, a moment of light – like the spring bursting into the room for the lovers in Wagner's opera *Die Walküre* (a scene she often refers to), or like an Italian coastal landscape of unimaginable beauty.[97] You recognise it when you see it – it is '*like being happy*'.

12

La Demanderesse

Given that she was married to Edward Wharton for twenty-eight years, from the ages of twenty-three to fifty-one, there is remarkably little trace of Teddy in Wharton's archive. There are photographs, of course (Teddy with the little dogs, Teddy on horseback, Teddy in plus-fours, Teddy and the motor-cars). There are financial statements about the purchases of property and the building of The Mount. There are a very few letters from her to him, but none from him to her: they were destroyed before she died, at her request, by Elisina Tyler. She does not mention him in her published accounts of her travels in Italy and France. There are a few traces of him in her library: his copy of Captain Mahan's *From Sail to Steam* (1907), a book of his about Charles Dickens and his friends, and his *Poetical Works* of Bret Harte (1870), of whom Teddy was particularly fond (when he died in 1928, after years of invalidism, he left 'all my editions of Bret Harte' to his nurse). There is one novel of Wharton's with Teddy's name in it, *The Fruit of the Tree*, and there is a complete Shakespeare, given to him on his wedding-day with 'faithful love' by his favourite aunt, Sarah Perkins Cleveland.[1]

Teddy's tone in early years – assertive, jocular, clumsy – is heard in a scatter of letters by or about him. A letter to his aunt of 1884, the year before his marriage, shows a jolly young man – a decent, average Bostonian type – joking about his 'Avunculus' 'whose charming manners have always been my model since I knew what manners were', chatting about a trip along the Hudson River ('I think it will be good fun, quite the life of a well-to-do tramp'), making affectionate jokes about his mother's 'suspicion of wordlyness' ('My spelling is weak') and his sister's stoutness, and comparing Emerson with Lowell. The darker side starts to come out in Ogden Codman's highly coloured picture of Teddy's outbursts in their rows over The Mount between 1900 and 1902. A business letter of 1905 about getting payment due for an exchange on a motor-car shows Teddy's hectoring side: 'I want my money, & I don't think Morse's note worth anything & it would be only another bother. He has no desire to pay unless pressed, & he must be pressed.'² A more benign, if boastful, note is struck in a letter to Sally Norton which seems to have slipped through the cull, perhaps because it shows Teddy in the best possible light. It is written in February 1907, just when Wharton was first getting to know Fullerton. Teddy's unsophisticated tone about France, his evident prefer- ence for American country life, his relish for his wife's worldliness (as opposed to her intellect) and his judgement of Henry James, suggest the kind of contrast Wharton would have been drawing between them. The letter shows, too, how their roles were to switch. At this point, Teddy was still looking after *her*.

> Just as poor Puss was beginning to have a very good time, down came the grippe, a very bad attack, & she has been in bed for over a week with a high fever & the beginning of an abscess in one of her ears, luckily the Doctors were able to treat it, so that it absorbed, but she has suffered a lot & is much pulled down. I shall motor her off to the South, as soon as she is well enough. Its' [sic] hard luck, as I never knew her better in ten years. Our experiment of taking out six servants, two dogs, our Motor & chauffer [sic], Cook, has worked perfectly ... I have a closed body for the old motor & I have had it all done over as new for Puss, with electric light inside, & every known accessorie [sic] for comfort. You know I am no good on Puss's high plain [sic] of thought, but you will agree that no lady of talent is as well turned out as she is, but she is a wonderful person, did it ever occur to you, that she has a nice, to me pleasant, wordly [sic] side ... When you next visit us [at The Mount] you will find I am, on a small scale, a farmer. Our new buildings are almost finished. I fear my cows, sheep, duck & hens will all die of old age, as I shall never want to kill them ... We are most comfortable [at 58 Rue de Varenne], & as all the servants are taking French lessons, I feel the cause of education is being advanced, which contents me greatly ... James is coming to stop with us ... One has to like him to read his last [*The Golden Bowl*] & the Public don't, its size in all ways is against it. Cut out 1/4 & it would have been good.³

Wharton's own correspondence is full of evidence about their marriage. There are many letters to friends, of increasing frankness, over a period of about six years, about him and their situation. There are letters to her of advice and sympathy. There are plenty of letters *about* the Whartons, written with varying degrees of horror, concern, and gleefulness, by Codman, Henry James, the Berensons, and others. There are doctors' letters and letters from relatives, and there is one pathetic attempt at a legal document written by Teddy, in a bad state, in May 1911.

In Wharton's fiction, there are plenty of husbands who are not on their wives' 'plain of thought', incarcerating marriages, claustrophobic partnerships, and squalid or ridiculous divorces. All through her writing from the 1890s to the 1930s, marital bondage, attempts to escape it, divorce and the illusions of freedom are some of her main subjects. It is very hard to find a happy marriage in Wharton's fiction; in fact marriage in her books comes to stand for what is wrong with American life. One of her great strengths as a writer is her ability to generalise from her own condition. She never wrote about her own situation for public consumption, except in one much-revised, highly circumspect paragraph in A Backward Glance about her husband's illness. But she used her own experience ruthlessly as fictional material.

The biographical tribunal on the Whartons' marriage lays out the following case. She was married, quite young, in accordance with the conventions of her tribe and under her mother's surveillance, to a friend of the family who seemed a perfectly reasonable (though not wealthy) match. She had already been emotionally attracted to at least one other man, but she was sexually naive and uninformed. The marriage was a sexual disaster from the first, and her misery and frustration expressed themselves as illness (notably, asthma) and depression. Though they took pleasure in travelling and motoring, and though they were re-energised by the building of The Mount, she grew out of Teddy very quickly, and sidestepped the narrow confines of the marriage through reading, friendships, and, above all, writing. By the time they started spending time in France, coinciding with her breakthrough to fame, she was bored to death with him and embarrassed by him, and had left him, intellectually and emotionally, far behind. None of this was disclosed directly, at the time, but the evidence is to be found in her fiction, in some of her poems, in the secret writings that accompanied her affair, in bitter comments made during the breakdown of the marriage, in many retrospective remarks, and in the testimonies of those who knew them.

The consensus about Teddy is that he was happy enough to look after her when she was ill, to run her affairs, to help with family matters (such as the funeral of her mother in Paris and the sorting-out of the will) and to benefit from her income. He enjoyed their motor-flights and house-building and shared her passion for the little dogs. He liked best to be in Boston, New York, Newport or Lenox. He was very close to his mother and sister, respected Lenox ladies whom Wharton found increasingly tiresome. He did not read much, he was not interested in ideas, and his conversational and writing skills were as primitive as those of many sports-loving, outdoor American gentlemen of leisure. After the first year in the Rue de Varenne, he did not enjoy Paris; he could not speak French, took no part in the social life that Wharton discovered there, and may well have felt humiliatingly out of place in that environment. Her decision to spend most of her time there went entirely counter to his needs and wishes. Possibly he felt patronised by her close male friends, Berry, Bourget, James and his circle. (Louis Auchincloss, in a short story called 'The Arbiter' (1976), reinvented the story of the Whartons' divorce from Teddy's point of view. 'Bob Guest' knows that his wife finds his philis-tinism unbearable, he cannot bear the condescension of her 'new friends', and is all too aware of his own deficiencies: 'But the real truth is that she was a genius and I was already a drunk.'[4]) The husband in 'The Choice' (1908) has long been the bane of his wife's life because of his drunkenness. But there is no firm evidence as to when Teddy's drinking began. It is not clear whether or not he knew she was having an affair in Paris, or when his own infidelities started. The most punitive case that could be made against her is that Teddy's mental instability was intensi-fied because she did not love him and was unfaithful to him. But it may also be that he was jealous of her professional success and resented her financial domination in the marriage.

Teddy's mental illness – which shows the classic symptoms of bipolar disorder, or manic depression – may have been an inheritance from his father, who (Ogden Codman often said) showed the same behaviour patterns, was 'put away', and killed himself. We cannot be sure when the condition first began to show itself. Manic depression can be triggered by stress or by traumatic events, is often accompanied by a variety of acute physical symptoms and by compulsive drinking, and can lead to suicide attempts. 'Really if he cannot die, it would seem as if he might as well follow his father's example and kill himself!' wrote Codman with cruel glee to his mother in 1910.[5] Wharton could have feared that her husband might do just that, and that was why she took so long to divorce him, afraid of destroying a dangerously unstable person.

Wharton's biographers have agreed that her upbringing and tempera-ment prevented her from contemplating divorce except as a shameful last resort. Percy Lubbock, in a sanitised version of events, played down any scandalous implications, said very little about Teddy, and insisted that there had been no bitterness, only courage, forbearance and generosity on her side in the process of the separation and divorce. R.W.B. Lewis points to the many examples of satire on American divorce in her work, maintaining that divorce 'was profoundly abhorrent to her', going against the grain of a character 'shaped by the conventions and pieties of a much older and narrower New York'. He describes her as 'exceedingly apprehensive about the figure she would cut as a divorced woman in the social circles back home'. Louis Auchincloss, similarly, speaks of 'the agony of her ... decision to divorce ... Divorce was not admitted in the New York of her childhood, and this New York had molded her conscience. Edith was nothing if not dutiful.' A letter of 1902 to Richard Gilder, the editor of *Century* magazine, shows her position clearly at that time. In his May 1902 editorial column, 'Topics of the Time', Gilder had an item on 'The Holy Estate of Matrimony', airing his dismay at the 'contagion' of divorce in America. He cited a paragraph from *The Valley of Decision* which argued that in the late eighteenth century there was a reaction towards a 'reverence for the marriage tie'. Gilder hoped for a similar reaction in contemporary America, adding: 'No agency is likely to be more effective than the literature produced by men and women who are true to an art solidly based upon the eternal verities ... celebrating the ... virtues of self-control, forbearance, devotion and honor.' Wharton responded to this enthusiastically, and thanked him for citing the *Valley*: 'The divorce question is one which I feel so strongly about that I am particularly glad to have contributed, even so indirectly, to "the side of the angels."' She referred him to 'The Reckoning', forthcoming in *Harper's*, her story of an advanced couple who believe in open marriage and divorce simply as a 'readjustment of personal relations' ('The new adultery was unfaithfulness to self'), until the husband falls in love with a younger woman, and the wife finds herself reverting to 'the old instinct of passionate dependency and possessorship'.[6]

This was her attitude to the public problem of divorce in America. And in her private life, she hated the thought of scandal. She kept up a front – for example, she never told Sally Norton (whom she saw, for all her sympathetic intelligence, as a shockable Bostonian) about her affair with Fullerton. She minded what people thought of her, and felt the need to protect herself, anxiously trying to avoid exposure. Her family history was scarred by the painful feud over Frederic's divorce and by its after-effects – financial and emotional – on Minnie and Beatrix; her brother Harry, too, was in a relationship she disapproved of. It took her a very long time to understand what was wrong with Teddy; for years she tried to keep the marriage going.

But Wharton's gallantly protective male biographers have established a version of her divorce which turns her too much into a long-suffering victim of her environment, rather than someone who could see, grimly, what she needed to do, but who could only struggle towards it, like a person wading slowly through mud in a nightmare. Like the version of Wharton's early married life which describes a sick person passively enduring years of depression, rather than someone of immense energies, with bursts of activity periodically interrupted by illness, the figure of the ladylike 'reluctant divorcee' does not do justice to her toughness and resolve. Once Teddy had become impossible to live with, divorce would have looked like a desirable option. There is good evidence that it came to seem to her – *in her case* – a reasonable and practical thing to do, and not a cause of moral anguish. She considered that she had a right to free herself, though she did not do it without great pain.

In the dark years when she was moving towards the end of her marriage, there is agony, reluctance and horror in her voice. On the other hand, the tone she takes about bad marriage and divorce can be remarkably firm and pragmatic. A dry, robust letter to John Hugh Smith, written early in 1909, when her affair was in its painful second year and Teddy was seriously unwell, takes him and Percy Lubbock to task for criticising a French play (*Olive Latimer*, by Rudolf Besier) about an unhappily married woman.

> As I cast my eye backward over literature, I seemed to remember a few other neurotic women who were discontented with their husbands and relations – one Clytemnestra, e.g., and Phaedra, and Iseult, and Anna Karenina, and Pia Tolomei, and Francesca da Rimini – who still live in the imagination, and will, I fancy, outlast Shaw – not to mention Barrie! And I wonder, among all the tangles of this mortal coil, which one contains tighter knots to undo, and consequently suggests more tugging, and pain, and diversified elements of misery, than the marriage tie – and which, consequently, is more 'made to the hand' of the psychologist and the dramatist?[7]

The reference to Shaw anticipates some revealing markings in Wharton's copy of his play *Getting Married*, in the *Doctor's Dilemma* volume of plays of 1911 (her last year of living with Teddy). Wharton marks all the passages in Shaw's polemical preface about the absurdity of 'indissoluble marriage' and the good reasons for easy, cheap, private divorce on demand:

> In Sweden, one of the most highly civilized countries in the world, a marriage is dissolved if both parties wish it, without any question of conduct ... The majority of married couples never get to know one another at all: they only get accustomed to sharing the same house! ...

Imagine being married to a liar, a borrower, a mischief-maker, a teaser or tormentor of children and animals, or even simply a bore! . . . The sole and sufficient reason why people should be granted a divorce is that they want one . . . There is no magic in marriage. If there were, married couples would never desire to separate. But they do. And when they do, it is simple slavery to compel them to remain together . . . Grant divorce at the request of either party, whether the other consents or not; and admit no other ground than the request, which should be made without stating any reasons.[8]

Wharton is as clear-headed as Shaw about marriage and divorce. She picks up in her fiction – most of all in *The Custom of the Country* – on the anxious turn-of-the-century debate in America about the proliferation of 'migratory divorces' and 'rotary marriages', owing to the libertarian laws in the American West (where, if you came from a state with more conservative divorce laws like New York, you could get a divorce in, say, Utah, or Nevada, after a startlingly short period of residence). Divorce figures in the States doubled between 1880 and 1900, and by 1920 had more than doubled again. These issues were picked up in the 'problem novels' of the time, notably by Wharton's friend Robert Grant, Boston lawyer and writer and college friend of Teddy's, who campaigned for uniform divorce laws. His novels, which Wharton admired, had Undine-Spragg-like heroines climbing up via adultery and divorce. Grant said that the plot of *The Orchid* (1905) was given to him by Wharton who told him the case (she would use it herself again in *Custom*) of 'a New York woman [who] as one of the terms of divorce from her husband had sold her baby to him for two million dollars'. Such cases made headlines repeatedly in the *New York Times* at the time of Wharton's divorce and the writing of *Custom*: 'Evil of Divorce Shown in Figures . . . 3,700,000 Persons Divorced in This Country in Forty Years . . . In the year 1912 over 100,000 Divorces Granted in this Country.' The paper was full of high-profile examples, as here in the autumn of 1912: 'Mrs Auchincloss To Ask A Divorce: Reluctantly Forced to it, she says, because of her Broker Husband's Desertion . . . Left Her and Went to Europe Without a Word of Farewell, Ex-Social Leader Declares.' 'Mrs Adre Gets Divorce: Husband Admits That He Spent All His Income on Himself.' 'Mrs Plant Gets Decree: Asks for no Alimony from Millionaire Shoe Manufacturer.'[9]

Wharton persistently satirises this American vogue in her fiction: 'Next to cutting a divorced woman there's nothing so interesting as taking her up again . . . And just think how soon our scruples will be obsolete! Before long the divorced will outnumber us, and then it may be the fashion to cut anyone who hasn't been to South Dakota.' She analyses the conditions and causes of American marital anomalies ('our legislation favours divorce – our social customs don't'), has some acid fun with short-term marriages ('Mr Roby had so evidently been a mere parenthesis in his wife's existence'), and – as in a note for a story, dated the same year as her divorce – often casts a baleful eye on the whole institution of marriage:

> 'Did you know that John and Susan committed suicide together on Tuesday?'
> 'What? No? – How?'
> 'They got married.'[10]

In some of these caustic epigrams, there is no great distance between her tone and that of the magazine she so abhorred, *Town Topics*, which frequently commented on the fact that 'divorce is now regarded as an everyday occurrence in the walks of fashion', and in the 1900s was full of jokes about migratory divorces and serial marriages. ('In Reno. *First Divorce*: They say Mrs Much Wed has disposed of her New York residence and will settle in Reno. *Second Divorce*: Well, I don't blame her. It's such a tiresome trip between marriages.') The magazine's coverage of fashionable marriages, in the month of Wharton's divorce, showed what she would have been exposed to if she had not divorced in Paris:

> The die is cast. Martha Jordan has left her husband's bed and board and declares she will never return. Public sympathy is with Eldridge Jordan ... Martha's discontent has been growing for a year or more, and her name has been linked with that of a young New Yorker for a good twelve-month.

> It is rumoured that the Rye colony has another divorce sensation under way which involves a prominent woman in society and an inconspicuous professional man – an affair that has been gossiped about for years. The woman is said to be in Reno.[11]

Wharton kept her privacy (just) and maintained a cool tone, in public, about her case. As her divorce was going through, warning Morton not to talk about it to any reporters, she said: 'It's a tiresome moment to traverse – but no more.'[12] But that tone of calm objectivity was hard-won.

Teddy Wharton had already had some kind of 'nervous collapse' in the summer of 1903, when the Whartons came back to Lenox from their travels in Italy (she was writing *Sanctuary* and *Italian Villas*), that summer of intense heat when America seemed horrible to her after Europe. It was not until the winter, when they crossed the Atlantic again for their first long French tour, that his health and spirits had improved. He was being looked after by Dr Francis Parker Kinnicutt, who had a house in Lenox and was very much part of their social world (it was said of him that his patients used to send a private railway car for his use when they needed a consultation). He was the head of the Presbyterian Hospital in New York and had a pioneering interest in mental illness. He was described as a person of 'gentleness, tact and sympathy' with 'a sweetness of character almost feminine'. Teddy would try out a number of doctors, but Kinnicutt was his constant adviser, and a friend.[13]

In the next three or four years, between 1904 and 1907, though Teddy spent quite a lot of time away from home, fishing in Canada, for instance, he seems to have been in good health. But in the spring of 1907, after settling into 58 Rue de Varenne, and during the motor-flight with James, he began to have some unpleasant symptoms again. In March, he complained of gout and 'facial neuralgia' – and he certainly did complain, as Wharton noted to Eunice Maynard: 'He isn't the best and most angelic of invalids, and I've been actively engaged in trying to make him forget his woes by the charms of my conversation and companionship.' It is an early example of her self-presentation – here still in playful tones – as the forbearing partner of a pathetic invalid. By the end of a year, for her, of exciting new Paris society, a deepening intimacy with James, the publication of *Madame de Treymes* and *The Fruit of the Tree*, and the visit to Lenox of her new friend Fullerton, Teddy had become very unwell. Back in Paris in December, while she was full of excitement at seeing Fullerton and immersed in Parisian life, he had fallen into a 'nervous depression'. A letter to Brownell, mainly about her work (proofs of *A Motor-Flight* had arrived) and her interesting conversations with Mr Fullerton, refers to Teddy's state as though it is an irritating disruption: 'My husband has been very poorly again for the last six weeks – much as he was four years ago – & this has upset my working plans, & seems likely to unsettle things for some time to come.' She was right.[14]

What did she think this illness was? By March 1908, when she was very keen to get rid of him to be free to spend time with Morton, she was calling it (to the dying Charles Eliot Norton, to Sally, to James and to Edward Burlingame) 'neurasthenia', brought on by 'gout in the head'. She also used the phrase 'nervous breakdown'. Kinnicutt recommended the spa at Hot Springs, Arkansas – where rich Americans went for their gout, to take the waters and breathe the high, dry south-western air – and she eagerly agreed that 'the baths & the out-door life' would be 'the best thing in the world for him'. So Wharton and the doctors were diagnosing in Teddy the same condition she had been told she was suffering from in her twenties and thirties, which she looked back on in a letter to Sally at this time and described as a combination of nausea and 'unutterable fatigue' that had gone on for twelve years. But she does not draw an analogy in this letter between her past illness and Teddy's present condition, nor does she ever say that she knows how he feels. Teddy's condition never seemed to strike her as being anything like hers (and, writing to Brownell ten years later, she refused to apply the term 'neurasthenic' to her own past illness).[15]

The treatment of mental illness in the nineteenth and early twentieth centuries in America – as in England – was dominated by ideas of 'nerves'. Pre-psychoanalytical terminology for mental states which could run from anxiety to full-blown mania or suicidal depression, were described as 'nervous' conditions: nervous breakdown, nervous exhaustion, neurasthenia, neuralgia. 'Neurasthenia' might be used to explain a wide range of physical symptoms – 'nervous' headaches, toothache, insomnia, eating disorders, sickness, lethargy – which were sometimes read as causes, sometimes as effects. If 'neurasthenia' was diagnosed as resulting from an ailment such as gout then the ailment itself could be treated by a doctor, or a 'cure', or a regime at a spa. By the end of the century, treatments for the condition of neurasthenia based on, or resembling, the Weir Mitchell programme of rest, isolation from family, feeding up and fresh air, were popular (and Edith may herself have tried some such programme in Philadelphia in 1899). But if 'mania' or mental illness was suggested, then a different language, and different solutions, came into play. (The diagnosis of 'neurasthenia' was sometimes used to avoid the stigma of mania or 'mental deficiency', for which a patient could be incarcerated, like Teddy's suicidal father.) Since the eighteenth century, programmes of 'moral management' had come to dominate the treatment of the insane. The mentally ill were encouraged to exercise 'self-control' through a system of rewards and punishment. The concept of self-control became deeply embedded in attitudes to mental illness, playing into the states of guilt and self-blame which form part of the syndrome of manic depression.[16] The turning-point in Edith's attitude to Teddy came when she was firmly told, by a celebrated 'nerve' doctor, that his illness was not neurasthenia, but 'an affection of the brain'.

In the summer of 1908, at The Mount, while she was waiting wretchedly for the letters from Morton which did not come, Teddy was better; as soon as they went back to Paris, early in 1909, he was ill again. By now, the second year of Teddy's poor health and the second year of her affair, 'nerves' and other symptoms had become inextricable. He was very depressed, and he also had very bad toothache. They tried a ten-day motor-flight to the South of France, with no success. They talked of his going back to the States, but he could not make up his mind. Her tone to Sally is a mixture of pity and exasperation; she was trying to 'manage' something that was becoming unmanageable:

> We are still anchored here by poor Teddy's dentistry, which is very painful, & does not help his nerves. He now says he won't go away, but that is part of his nervous condition . . . When he is in this state it is very difficult to make plans, & the only thing to do is to give him a sudden jerk at the opportune moment . . . I think Teddy is a little better than when I last wrote; or at least I think so today![17]

The Paris dentist came up with a diagnosis of 'Rigg's disease', and she clutched at this – still thinking in terms of a nervous ailment linked to physical symptoms – as a hopeful explanation for 'the incessant pain in his head, & consequent nervous depression'. He was indecisive and anxious about 'business', though in April 1909 he did sail back to the States to be with his family. (She stayed in Paris with Morton.) At first, reports were no better, though his anxieties about business proved groundless – '(naturally!)', she noted bitterly to Sally. She started now to complain about the attitude of the Whartons: 'The family seems annoyed with me for having sent him – they behaved exactly in the same way when he was ill before.' Even with Teddy gone, she felt unable to control her own life: 'My own plans are – that I have none. I live from hand to mouth.'[18]

Teddy went fishing in Canada, and some slightly better reports came from Dr Kinnicutt. The pain in his face and feet had improved. He was having serum treatment for gum disease. But his mother, to whom he was very close, was dying; and more ominous signs were showing up. In Lenox and Boston, Teddy was attracting attention; people were talking. Kinnicutt thought him in an over-excited state, and for the first time talked of his 'local irritations' directly affecting 'the deeper evil' – presumably he meant mental illness. Old Mrs Wharton died, after a long illness, at eighty-nine, in August. Nannie Wharton reported to Edith that Ted was '*perfectly* well and *perfectly* normal'; in fact, as her sister-in-law would discover in the autumn, the reverse was the case.[19]

James thought that the death of Teddy's mother might 'do Teddy good' and take him out of himself. Instead it seems to have triggered a phase of extravagant, manic, and reckless behaviour. In the summer of 1909, while

Edith (rather than attending Mrs Wharton's funeral at Lenox) was meeting Morton and James in England, and spending her night of love at the Charing Cross Hotel, she was in the dark about what was going on in America. It was the last phase of the marriage in which she could tell herself that the situation could be controlled. What she did not yet know was that rumours were now going round New York that the Whartons were separating and that the 'other man' in the case was Walter. The rumour had probably emanated from the gossipy Jacques-Émile Blanche, whom she had unwisely confided in about Teddy on a visit to Offranville; Rosa de Fitzjames warned Morton, in a note which suggests that she had at least some inkling of their affair, not to let Edith know about this 'calumny'. And Teddy's behaviour had also become a subject of scandal. At exactly the time when she was trying to preserve the secrecy of her own double life, she was being exposed to the kind of gossip she most abhorred. She felt surrounded by watchers and talkers.[20]

Dr Kinnicutt wrote that he was very anxious about Teddy and thought it would be better for him to keep up his interest in The Mount ('at present it is the one place in the world which he is most fond of') and predicting a 'swing of the pendulum' if Teddy returned to Paris. So it proved. Teddy made his dreaded return to Paris in October with his sister, and they all stayed in the Hôtel Crillon for weeks (in between apartments). Brother and sister changed their minds endlessly about what to do and where to go. The combination was more than Edith could stand: 'After numerous plans, and variations of plans, and modifications of the variations, and deviations from the modifications', Teddy and Nannie left for Pau (where the Whartons had motored together, with Henry, in happier days). Edith thought Teddy over-excited, especially about 'business'. By now she was no longer explaining his states to herself or to anyone else as neuralgia or gout or toothache, and she was exasperated and unsympathetic: 'The whole thing is complicated by Nannie's incredible blindness and stupidity and determination not to recognise ANY nervous disorder . . . I can make no plans, but only live from hand to mouth.' She escaped to Germany for a few days with Anna Bahlmann. When Teddy came back from Pau, she saw at once (she wrote immediately to Morton) that he was '*much worse*'.[21] Then the floodgates opened. On 8 December 1909, Teddy blurted out a pathetic, confused, and scandalous story.

It was one of the conventional and constricting features of her marriage that she was not in full control of the management of her inherited income. The income from Edith's trust funds – from rents on the real estate which she and her two brothers had inherited, but which she was prevented, by

the terms of both parents' wills, from administering herself – was managed
for her, first by her two brothers, and then by Teddy and Harry Jones. When
Lucretia died, leaving Frederic an unfair share of control over Edith's third
of the inheritance, it was Teddy and Harry who persuaded Frederic to waive
his rights. Teddy was also in charge of the business side of running The
Mount. His own income was between $2,000 and $10,000 a year; when
his mother died, he had at last, aged fifty-nine, come into his own inheritance. Teddy now told Edith that he had spent the summer speculating
with $50,000 of her money, had lost a good deal of it, and had bought an
apartment in Boston and set up a mistress in it. And there was some story
about renting rooms out to chorus girls.[22] Edith wrote with extraordinary
restraint to Morton:

> He has put my affairs into rather serious (temporary) confusion, and is
> of course brooding over this, & trying to work it out in his poor confused
> head. I am so sorry for him! His state is piteous, & I feel – Oh, irony –
> that if I had been less 'delicate', less desirous of letting him feel that he
> was completely trusted, things might not have turned out so. Mais quelle
> folie! As if the disease would not have found another outlet . . .[23]

To Nannie, she wrote a more severe letter, asking her what she knew.
Nannie replied that she was very shocked by what she had learnt, and that
she knew Teddy had been speculating, but did not know it was with Edith's
money. 'You have much to forgive dear Pussy.' Teddy had been in a terrible
state, but perhaps he would be better now that Edith knew 'how things
are'. He had told Nannie that Puss had been 'noble' to him. Perhaps it
could all be hushed up. Henry James, told about these 'startling revelations', was appalled: 'Is he absolutely *bien malade* . . . or is he only
unexpectedly selfish & perverse?' He told Sturgis and Lapsley about the
'quasi-demented excess' and 'sinister' financial misbehaviour of the
'unspeakable Teddy'. (All the same, why did an '*intellectuelle* – and an Angel
– require such a big pecuniary base'?) There could now be nothing but
inconvenience in having in her life, he told her, 'a personage so helplessly
out of gear in your existence at all'.[24]

But in this crisis – after which things could only get worse – she did not
take the opportunity to separate and start divorce proceedings. That she
was still involved with Morton may have played a part in her long-suffering
reaction to Teddy's abject confession. She sent him back to Boston to try
to sort things out (he would have to pay back what he had spent of her
money out of the inheritance from his mother) and put Dr Kinnicutt, her
cousin Herman Edgar, and her brother-in-law Billy Wharton on Teddy-

watch. She set in train the sale of their Park Avenue house. But – unwisely as it turned out – she did not insist on Teddy's resigning the co-trusteeship of her inherited finances, though she gave virtual control of these to Herman Edgar (a lawyer and real-estate broker) and to her brother Harry, and would repeatedly tell Teddy, from this point onwards, that the condition of their continuing to live together would have to be that he had nothing to do 'with the control of my money, whether income or capital'.[25]

Dr Kinnicutt by now thought that Teddy should be in a sanatorium, but Billy Wharton reported to the doctor that his brother would not be persuaded. He wanted to go back to Edith in Paris. She offered to send White to fetch him, or even to go herself, though she was in the middle of moving into 53 Rue de Varenne. In a letter to Brownell, she assured him that the sale of the New York house did not mean that 'the last links with America are cut', but that her husband was having 'a bad nervous breakdown' and the doctors had advised no more winters in New York. Kinnicutt, meanwhile, was checking Teddy's story, which was turning out to have a large element of delusional exaggeration about it. The chorus girls were a fantasy, though he had been living with an unidentified woman in her early thirties in a small flat in Mountfort Street in a smart area of Boston, which had cost $16,000 or $17,000 of Edith's money. It would be best to be at The Mount with him, Dr Kinnicutt repeated, and failing that she should not travel with Teddy without 'an intelligent, strong, & helpful physician'. But this, she told Sally, would only 'exasperate' Teddy. The Paris floods which surrounded her as she moved into her new apartment could well have seemed like a metaphor for her life.[26]

In Boston and Lenox, Teddy presented a pitiful spectacle. Ogden Codman reported that he had

> been terribly strange here and nearly driven the poor Willy Whartons mad too. He is so restless, and cannot stay anywhere long nor does he know what he is doing much of the time. His chief delusion is that he has lost all her money and nothing is left. He sits in the corner of the room and weeps with his face to the wall. This is his usual state, but he has intermissions of thinking he has made a vast fortune, and going about with a *wad* of banknotes giving them away right and left.

He came back to Paris at the end of February 1910, debts repaid, but immensely subdued and depressed. Edith wrote to her lover: 'Yes, I feel the bitterest resentment, & I am utterly unreconciled, & I had to "hold myself" yesterday to keep from putting my head down beside you & crying my eyes out . . .' To John Hugh Smith she wrote: 'Teddy's condition is very serious

... he cannot be left alone a moment, and my days are terrible. He is quite "lucid", but has acute melancholia. I don't know a much worse combination ...' The lucidity was short-lived: 'More "confusion in the head", that is his chief complaint now', she told Morton a few days later. She went to England to see James in his depression, a most distressing meeting. Teddy was brought over to Folkestone by Alfred White, his long-suffering and faithful butler. She was going to shuttle between her two invalids, but James was too low to see them, and they went back to Paris. Nannie Wharton arrived, no help at all. 'Things here growing rapidly and terribly worse', she told Morton.[27]

It seemed impossible to know what to do next. A number of doctors were consulted, two Paris 'nerve' specialists, Dr Dupré and Dr Isch Wall (who thought Teddy was rapidly getting worse), and Sturgis Bigelow, who had trained as a doctor before devoting himself to Buddhism. Bigelow was helpful to Edith, taking Teddy for drives. After an evening spent with the Whartons, he gave his opinion that it was not just Teddy's 'melancholy and exhilaration' that was the trouble, but 'that his mind itself – his consciousness and reasoning powers – are not connected nor consecutive'. This lack of coherence was increasing: 'these changes ... now occur in the time it takes to get from one room to the next.' He noted that Teddy's relations were still treating him 'as if he were a reasonable being like the rest of the world'.[28] Partly wanting to give her version to people who might be hearing the Whartons' view, partly in a state of desperation that made her drop her guard, Edith wrote two candid letters, in early April 1910, to Brownell and to Robert Grant. The letter to Brownell, lamenting James's state of mind, said that Teddy was no better and she could not see what to do about it. The letter to Robert Grant described her situation with bitter eloquence. This full account, with a rare criticism of Teddy's character, may have been easier to write to a person she respected, and whose good opinion she was anxious to keep, but who was not an intimate friend.

> I have been through a dreadful year, made very much worse by the Whartons' persistently assuring me all last summer that Teddy was perfectly well, & that the New York & Paris doctors had been entirely wrong in their diagnosis. When they finally changed their view, it was impossible to induce Teddy to take any kind of treatment at home, & his one idea was to return here ... Billy has no control over him & Dr Kinnicutt, in NY, not knowing what else to do, let him come. For two or three weeks he was perfectly content, though very depressed & listless. Now the restless phase has come on again, & his one idea is to

leave – he knows not for what quarter of the globe. It is all very difficult, & the more so as I cannot count on Nannie Wharton, who is here,
& whose views change every moment. Teddy wanted to try a rest cure
for two or three weeks, & when I spoke of it to the Dr he approved
highly. [A nursing home at Neuilly was suggested, with electric baths,
massages, hydrotherapy, and outings in the car.] . . . When it was proposed
to Nannie she became violently excited, said she was absolutely opposed
to it, and – what is really unpardonable – told Teddy so, & excited him
so much that it is now useless to refer to the subject . . . Teddy has always
been extremely self-willed, & has done, all his life, exactly what he
chose; & it is hopeless to try to direct him now . . . I can only watch,
passively, shelter Teddy as much as I can from worry, & from curiosity
& comment . . . & be prepared for the fact that any day he may yield
to some impulse like those which wrought such havoc in his life last
summer.[29]

Teddy was not well enough to go out, though he made himself present-
able 'out of politeness' for the important occasion at the Rue de Varenne
when Roosevelt came to tea, at the end of April. But when no one was
there except Edith and Nannie, he was very difficult. 'Today', she wrote to
Morton, 'there was a scene which made even ma belle soeur say that "something must be done".' But mostly, as she told him despairingly,

> the Whartons adroitly refuse to recognise the strain I am under, & the
> impossibility, for a person with nerves strung like mine, to go on leading
> indefinitely the life I am now leading. They say: 'The responsibility rests
> with his wife – we merely reserve the right to criticize.' *He* has only one
> thought – to be with me all day, every day. If I try to escape, he will
> follow . . . The Drs all tell me that as yet compulsory seclusion is im-
> possible . . . And if you knew, if you *knew*, what the days are, what the
> hours are, what our talks are, interminable repetitions of the same weary
> round of inanities & puerilities; & all with the knowledge that . . . what
> is killing me is doing him no good!

Walter wanted her to ask for a separation; what did Morton advise? No
advice was forthcoming.[30]

Perhaps one more nerve doctor, and a change of scene, would help.
Everyone in Paris with a case of nerves had heard of the celebrated Swiss
specialist in *'psychasthéniques'* or *'psychonévroses'*, Dr Roger Vittoz: he had
so many successes at his clinic at Verrières that the *rapide* which went there
from Paris was known as the 'train Vittoz'. In 1904 he had moved to

Lausanne, where he continued to develop his treatment of neurasthenia through hypnosis and 'brain control'. Edith, Teddy and Nannie set out for Lake Leman, only to be disappointed. Sitting in the gloomy splendour of the 'huge awful' Beau-Rivage-Palace Hotel at Ouchy-Lausanne, Edith wrote a long, wretched account to Morton:

> Teddy saw Dr Vittoz this morning, & the latter said to me immediately: 'But this is not a case for me; I am a neurologist, & this is not neurasthenia, but an affection of the brain'. He understood perfectly, however, that the Paris doctor knew this, & had sent Teddy here because they knew that, in his present state, some kind of rest-cure was absolutely necessary, & could be given only in the établissements where nervous diseases are treated ... He tells me that the Drs will certainly recommend isolation ... The experiment [of driving here] was a complete failure, & Teddy says so himself. Vittoz also told me that he was too ill to travel. So there seems nothing left but to try to dispose him toward trying a sanatorium.[31]

Making lighter of this to her new friend Berenson, she wrote: 'It appears that my poor husband hasn't the special form of neurasthenia that the Lake Leman "neurologues" deal with (oh, the Molière play that I could write on "specialists"!).' All the same, Vittoz's judgement clinched her view (not shared by her in-laws) that Teddy was mentally ill and that there could be no solution to it, only a series of expedients. (It is a curious coincidence of literary history that ten years later Dr Vittoz would be treating T.S. Eliot, who stayed in Lausanne – 'this decayed hole among the mountains' – writing *The Waste Land*.) The Whartons, rather like two lost souls from that poem, stayed on for a few days, wondering 'What shall we do now? What shall we ever do?' There was a possible 'hydrotherapic' cure to be had at Divonne, at the French end of Lake Leman. They went down the lake to Vevey, where Nannie's attitude became, finally, intolerable to Edith. She wrote to her sister-in-law a few months later that 'after your treatment of me at Vevey' there was no point 'exposing herself' any more to having 'my conduct criticized and my word doubted as they have been by you for the past year' – it was 'trying & unprofitable', and she would not see her any more. She was beginning to harden her position.[32]

The Swiss sanatorium Teddy finally settled on was the Kuranstalt Bellevue Clinic at Kreuzlingen, on Lake Constance, where he would follow the Weir Mitchell treatment of isolation, douches, massages, hydro- and electrotherapy, and light work in the garden. Alfred White took him off there by train in

June. Edith took a little refreshing journey to Dijon, back to Lake Leman and into Italy, and then returned to Paris. At last it was possible to write. She did some work on her next book of stories, *Tales of Men and Ghosts*. And she took out the story set in rural Massachusetts which she had begun as a French exercise. In the dark days of her marital crisis – and as a relief from it – she wrote *Ethan Frome*.

Ethan Frome comes as a great shock, and not just because of the violent switch from her usual upper-class, sophisticated, international territory to the remote hills and poor farmers' lives of nineteenth-century New England. But Wharton had been interested in American deprivation for a long time – as in 'Bunner Sisters', which would at last be published, in *Xingu*, in 1916. What is startling, after the eloquence of Lily or Mme de Treymes or Mrs Lidcote, is its quietness. James 'exceedingly admired' it, and had good reason to praise its control and its '*kept-downness*': he knew what a flood of emotion had been channelled into this highly controlled, spare, short masterpiece.[33] *Ethan Frome* is a story of silence and speech-lessness, numbness and dumbness. Voices and feelings are all 'snowed under'. (The first French translation, overseen by Charles Du Bos and Wharton, was aptly titled *Sous la neige*.) The characters live inside 'dumb melancholy', 'secretive silence', broken by sudden outbursts of long-kept-down emotion, and tailing off into dreary, low-key, ineffectual whining. It is the place – remote, closed-in, unbearably lonely – that does it. Even a 'grave and in-articulate' nature like Ethan's has shown an appetite for 'friendly human intercourse', but at 'Starkfield' 'the silence had deepened about him year by year'; and people become the products of their envi-ronment. The gravestones by the farm gate seem more articulate than the living ('We never got away – how should you?' they say). Their deep quiet, in the end, may be preferable to any words.[34]

Ethan was a frustrated figure long before the crash which dooms him to a slow lifetime of silent misery and endurance. The first sighting of him, a ruined giant, is of someone who seems to be dragged back persistently by 'the jerk of a chain', and that has been his story. As one neighbour puts it: 'You've had an awful mean time, Ethan Frome.' This grim-faced, poverty-stricken farmer once had potential and aspirations. A sensitive young man with intellectual curiosity, he had an appetite for information and travel, and interests in physics, astronomy, and geology. He is tender with his horses, a kind, honourable man with a sense of duty. (His boxroom 'study', with its home-made bookshelves, its engraving of Abraham Lincoln and its calendar with 'Thoughts from the Poets', suggests his qualities.) But he

was confined to hard labour on the remote farm because of his father's accident and breakdown and his mother's illness; he cannot escape 'the long
misery of his baffled past, of his youth of failure, hardship and vain effort'.
Ethan's disabled father is an almost invisible figure in the story, but his
mother's life, just touched in, is the saddest thing of all. A woman who
once kept her home 'spruce' and shining, watched her husband go 'soft in
the brain', the farm and sawmill run down, and the road by the farmhouse
go quiet after the railway took the traffic away: 'And mother never could
get it through her head what had happened, and it preyed on her right
along till she died.' In illness and solitude she became more and more silent:

> Sometimes, in the long winter evenings, when in desperation her son
> asked her why she didn't 'say something', she would lift a finger and
> answer: 'Because I'm listening'; and on stormy nights, when the loud
> wind was about the house, she would complain, if he spoke to her:
> 'They're talking so loud out there that I can't hear you.'[35]

That haunted silence is echoed in the wretched marriage Ethan makes to
the older cousin, Zenobia ('Zeena'), who comes to look after his mother
and who, after her death, seems a preferable alternative to utter loneliness.
('He had often thought since that it would not have happened if his mother
had died in spring instead of winter.') Over seven years, Zeena Frome turns
from an efficient manager into a joyless hypochondriac, and she too falls
silent, because – as she spoke 'only to complain' – Ethan has developed a
habit of never listening or replying. Under her 'taciturnity', 'suspicions and
resentments' fester.

Into this hostile household, summed up by the word 'exanimate', Mattie
Silver, Zeena's orphaned twenty-year-old cousin (everything in these
villages is a family matter) arrives to help keep house. Mattie is ardent,
sensual, innocent and fragile (it is one of the novella's triumphs that she
is touching and plausible, too) and Ethan falls deeply and silently in love
with her. In the one year she spends with the Fromes, the tender inarticulate relationship that grows up between them is marked by the rhythms of
rural life, as in a novel by Hardy or Gaskell: the village dance, church
picnics, walks home in the starry night. Ethan fantasises a life with Mattie.
Like the wife in 'The Choice' (and, undoubtedly, like Wharton) he finds
himself longing for his lawful spouse to die; but such visions of release are
instantly replaced by that of 'his wife lying in their bedroom asleep, her
mouth slightly open, her false teeth in a tumbler by the bed'. The climax
comes on the night that Zeena leaves them in the house (she has gone to
plot Mattie's replacement with a 'hired girl') and they spend the quiet

evening as if they were husband and wife, yet without touching each other. This sweet 'illusion of long-established intimacy' is disrupted when Zeena's special red-glass pickle-dish, which Mattie has got down from its secret place to 'make the supper-table pretty', is broken by the cat, Zeena's baleful familiar. So deep and sure is the tone of the book that this little, homely accident seems as great a tragedy to us as to the characters. Zeena returns, discovers the breakage, and bitterly laments her loss:

> 'You waited till my back was turned, and took the thing I set most store by of anything I've got . . . You're a bad girl, Mattie Silver . . . I was warned of it when I took you, and I tried to keep my things where you couldn't get at 'em – and now you've took from me the one I cared for most of all –'

It is one of the places in the novel where the pressure of feeling bursts through the silence. And though all our sympathies go to Ethan and Mattie, Zeena's own suffering – sick, lonely, unloved, betrayed – rushes onto the page.[36]

Zeena's 'inexorable' will, and the force of circumstances, means that there is no way out for the unconsummated lovers: Mattie must go and Ethan must stay. Their passion finally breaks through their shyness in intense, pared-down, simple utterances, words 'like fragments torn from' the heart, in which Wharton's deepest feelings are translated into a language that fits this story:

> 'Oh, what good'll writing do? I want to put my hand out and touch you. I want to do for you and care for you. I want to be there when you're sick and when you're lonesome.'

> 'Ethan, where'll I go if I leave you? I don't know how to get along alone. You said so yourself just now. Nobody but you was ever good to me. And there'll be that strange girl in the house . . . and she'll sleep in my bed, where I used to lay nights and listen to hear you come up the stairs . . .'

Urged by Mattie (Ethan's role throughout is to be at the service of his women), they take what they mean to be a fatal sled-ride, told with the utmost intensity and urgency. Because of the lyric beauty of these last speeches and scenes, the coda to *Ethan Frome*, one of the most quietly horrifying moments in all fiction, is cruelly effective. We find Ethan, twenty-eight years on, incarcerated with Zeena and the crippled Mattie, who has survived the crash and who, 'cranky', whining and withered, has become a second Zeena, while Zeena herself – this is all done with brilliant, ruthless speed – has thrived on the other woman's dependency, and become again the grimly efficient manager of the household. One of the village witnesses to this human incarceration says: 'the way they are now, I don't see's there's much difference between the Fromes up at the farm and the Fromes down in the graveyard; 'cept that down there they're all quiet, and the women have got to hold their tongues.'[37]

If this story came straight at us, with its grim twist saved up to the end, it would have been powerful enough. But, as in a number of Wharton's short stories, we come at it through a frame narrator, an incomer from another world, who sets up the 'flashback' into Ethan's story, signalled by several lines of dots (which she was very fussy about with the publishers).[38] He acts as the bridge between the reticence of Starkfield, and the eloquent piece of literature we are reading.

Wharton's acknowledged models for *Ethan Frome* (which, as it gradually became her most popular book, she commented on more than she usually did) were Emily Brontë's *Wuthering Heights* and – for their use of competing narrative versions – Browning's *The Ring and the Book* and Balzac's story 'La Grande Bretèche'. Ethan and Mattie owe something, too, to Hardy's Jude and Tess, and she had recently been reading Conrad and Nietzsche, who is behind Ethan's lost 'will to power' through his inertia and passive dutifulness. George Sand's rural love-story, written out of the countryside around Nohant, *La Mare au Diable*, also gives something to *Ethan Frome*: Wharton draws on the simplicity and tenderness with which Sand takes her widowed villager and young girl on their night-time journey through the forest, but she refuses Sand's benign optimism. The other, acknowledged, debt was to Hawthorne, always important for Wharton, but never more so than here. Ethan's name comes from Hawthorne's guilt-ridden, isolated hero Ethan Brand, and Zenobia's from the doomed feminist heroine of his satire on a New England utopia, *The Blithedale Romance*. Hawthorne uses a cynical observer in that novel, Coverdale, who is not as detached as he would like to be. Wharton's nameless narrator, like Brontë's Mr Lockwood or Hawthorne's Coverdale, seems to belong to another world – he is a man of progress, bringing electricity and communication with the outside world to Starkfield. But after a winter there he begins to understand the isolation and hardship of the natives.

The strategy allows Wharton to be both outside of, and inward with, her subject. (She would be extremely irritated by critics who accused her of remoteness from, or condescension towards, this material.) The narrator is like a biographer. He collects the evidence, listens to the different versions, and makes up his own story of the past from what he can gather.

The characters' imprisonment in their private tragedy pulls against the narrator-biographer's tendency to turn them into a case history of New England life. Wharton would repeatedly say that she wanted to present a truer picture – here, and in *Summer* – of the 'snow-bound villages of Western Massachusetts', with their grim facts of 'insanity, incest and slow mental and moral starvation', than she had ever found in the 'rose-coloured' versions of earlier New England writers, Mary Wilkins and Sarah Orne Jewett. (Unfair to Jewett, some think.) Her story had its factual origins: the terrible sledding-accident in Lenox in 1904 (she knew one of the injured survivors from her involvement with the Lenox library) and the lingering, fatal paralysis of her friend Ethel Cram, after her accident in Lenox in 1905. And it provides, by inference, a sociological commentary: on the transactions between local farmers and builders, on the effects of the railway, on attitudes to debt and the status of doctors, on the inadequate education of girls, on levels of rural – and urban – unemployment. Occasionally her narrator uses a phrase which opens up the distance between 'us' and 'them': 'the hard compulsions of the poor', 'a community rich in pathological instances'. As so often, she uses a unique, pitiful story for a generalised, determinist account of environmental pressures. And she maintains a perfectly controlled balance between realism and romance.[39]

All the bare, harsh matter of life in Starkfield – dogged conversations about money and work, details of journeys, luggage, buildings, medicines, farming, the omnipresent but useless church, the ingrown, watchful community, the practical difficulties created by the weather – are mixed with suppressed romantic emotions which are passionately invested in nature. What to the narrator seems a blank and desolate wilderness becomes, when we see it through Ethan's and Mattie's eyes, a landscape full of detail and beauty. Henry James rightly praised the novella's 'kept-downness', and the emotions that are so 'kept down' come through in a passionate sensual language straight out of Keats (one of her favourite poets). Ethan's awareness of 'huge cloudy meanings behind the daily face of things' calls up 'Huge cloudy symbols of a high romance' in Keats's anguished farewell to life and love, 'When I have fears that I may cease to be'. The wintry romance of Keats's 'The Eve of St Agnes' is touched in everywhere. The snow beats 'like hail against the loose-hinged windows', as, in Keats's poem, the 'frost-wind' blows the 'quick pattering' of the 'flaw-blown sleet' 'against the window-panes'. The warm little feast in the kitchen is a homely version of Porphyro's sensual banquet; the 'lustrous fleck' on Mattie's lip in the lamp-light is like the 'lustrous' light of Madeline and Porphyro's encounter, lit by moonlight. Mattie's erotic trance ('She looked up at him languidly, as though her lids were weighted with sleep and it cost her an effort to raise them') is like Madeline's tranced sleep; Ethan's 'ache' of cold weariness echoes Keats's sculptured knights in armour aching in their 'icy hoods and mails'. These lovers make a doomed attempt, like Keats's lovers, to flee away for ever into the storm; but the story, like the poem, ends with the crippled paralysis of an old 'beldame', who dies 'palsy-twitch'd, with meagre face deform'. In both there is the sense of its all having happened 'ages long ago'.[40]

The 'high romance' in *Ethan Frome* speaks through nature:

> Slowly the rim of the rainy vapours caught fire and burnt away, and a pure moon swung into the blue. Ethan, rising on his elbow, watched the landscape whiten and shape itself under the sculpture of the moon . . . He looked out at the slopes bathed in lustre, the silver-edged darkness of the woods, the spectral purple of the hills against the sky, and it seemed as though all the beauty of the night had been poured out to mock his wretchedness . . .

Wharton told Berenson at the time, and said years later, that it 'amused' her to do 'Starkfield, Massachusetts' and 'Shadd's Fall' in the Rue de Varenne, and that it gave her 'the greatest joy and the fullest ease' to write this story.[41] She knew that distance can create closeness, and that transforming painful materials can produce creative joy. *Ethan Frome* was an anguished elegy to love, and a description of being incarcerated in a terrible marriage. It was also her farewell to New England, written a long way away from it, and published as she would be leaving it for ever.

The respite Edith had in the summer months of 1910 to write *Ethan Frome* was a short one. Soon enough, Teddy was writing from the spa on Lake Constance, complaining of isolation, pains in his limbs, and boredom – there was no golf! – and threatening to come home. A sympathetic doctor at the clinic told her it should not be difficult to keep him there, but White, who stayed with Teddy in Switzerland, sounded more anxious. Dr Isch Wall, in Paris, who took Edith's side, wrote to Teddy warning him not to come back, as his wife was very '*faible*' and '*fatiguée*', and needed a complete rest: 'I think it necessary to isolate her from her family.' So the role of nervous patient was swapped between them.[42]

Edith wrote a long letter to her 'Dear Old Man'. (There would not be many more letters that started with this, evidently her habitual endearment for him.) She reproached him for not giving the treatment at the sanatorium 'a fair trial':

Apparently you can't put up with a few weeks of dulness & solitude, & I don't know that I can find any new reasons for urging you to give the cure a little longer trial . . . We went over this ground so many times during the winter & spring that you have heard all my answers . . . But I will remind you once more that you had the choice of doing what you wanted at every turn as you have always had it, ever since we have been married.

He had chosen the clinic himself, and had promised to try and keep his worries and complaints to himself and 'to control yourself a little'. She knows how hard it is to struggle against anything 'in the nature of a nervous break-down'; but he must see 'how impossible it is to help you if you won't make any effort yourself'. She cannot see what arrangements they can come to now, given that he has told her he does not want to be 'a passenger for the rest of your days', in charge neither of her 'money affairs' nor 'household matters'. He is still feeling terrible about having lost money. As a short-term measure, she invents a scheme of distraction, a trip to the Rockies and to California. She reminds him that he has often said he wanted to do this. He could go fishing – she could buy him an open car ('I am so flush now', she noted, perhaps not tactfully) – he might be able to find someone to go with him. Think about it, she concluded, '& don't see *the objections*, but the good side of the plan'. The letter is signed (as to most of her friends) 'Affly yours, E.W.'. It was one of several which she had copied by Anna Bahlmann and which was annotated along the bottom: 'Copy of a letter from Mrs Edward Wharton to Mr Edward Wharton. Paris, July 6–8, 1910'. She was marshalling the evidence for her side of the story.

Teddy wrote at once to agree; she set him up with a travelling-companion, a Bostonian writer and social worker called Johnson Morton, who would take on the role, for a fee. Then Teddy wrote again to say it was all impossible, and he was going to another Swiss spa, at Thun. 'Dear Old Man . . . Why "impossible"?' she asked. 'If you don't do something of this kind, what do you propose to do? . . . You know you are not in fit condition to come back & live with me . . . Each time that you have been with me, I have tried to do everything to make you contented, & each time it has been a failure – *& it will be till you are cured*.' She reiterates the travel-plan, and ends: 'Write to me when you receive this, & let me hear that you're ready to start soon.' Again, the letter is copied and dated. Sooner or later – she knows now – she is going to find a way out, and will need to present herself in a strong position. Her letters – weary, exasperated, trying to be patient, leaning heavily on the medical language of 'self-control', are being stored up as evidence. They would be kept in a dossier, and many years later, she would file them, with some other personal materials, in an envelope labelled 'For my biographer'.[43]

Though Fullerton was a broken reed, she had support at hand. Walter, who resigned his Cairo post in June 1910, took up temporary residence at the Rue de Varenne. (She read *Ethan* every day to him that summer.) Sturgis Bigelow, who took another look at Teddy when he did come back to Paris in August, told her that in his view it was an act of almost 'criminal neglect' of Teddy's brother Billy not to have put Teddy in confinement the year before: '*he ought to be put under restraint, & the sooner the better.*' She left Teddy with White in Paris and went travelling in England with Walter and Henry (much to his dismay). Henry was still very unwell, and so was his brother. They crossed the Atlantic in August and William died soon after they reached his farm in New Hampshire. James stayed on in America, dreading his return to Lamb House, which had turned from a refuge into a prison in his imagination (he never lived there permanently again). Mutual condolences passed between the bereaved brother and 'the poor dear goaded wanderer', who by early September was trying another disastrous motor-flight with Teddy, to a converted Carthusian monastery in the Haute-Savoie, near Mont Blanc, and across the border to Baveno on Lake Maggiore. But it was no good, she wrote to Morton. She was exhausted, with a cold and hay-fever, and Teddy was 'terribly depressed'. These beautiful and romantic places were 'all in vain'. At Baveno she felt desperate: 'really at times *the lake invites me.*' And Teddy only said: 'Yes, I am doing what I want. But it doesn't make any difference.'[44]

This dismal journey, their last attempt to travel together in Europe, made Teddy agree to the idea of a long trip away. Her Californian idea gradually turned into a round-the-world voyage, and they booked their passage to America so that Edith could see him off from New York. (No, she replied to a question from Fullerton, she was not setting out round the world: 'You are dreaming. How could you think I meant to go with Teddy. It is the one thing that all the Drs forbid.') Johnny Morton, however, was not perhaps the best choice of travelling-companion for Teddy. Over ten years later, when Edith heard of Johnny Morton's death, she wrote a sad letter about him. For all his 'good humour, his good spirits, & the fun & gaiety he put into all our lives', he led 'a frustrated, wasted life', and his friends could never 'lift' him 'out of the wretched muddle in which his youth & middle age were spent'. It sounds as if he and Teddy were two of a kind. And he was not discreet. Over drinks at the Ritz in Paris, he was regaling a group

of her acquaintances – Ogden, Elsie de Wolfe, Berenson – with gory details
about the Whartons. Ogden told his mother:

> [He] is supposed to have been imported by Mrs Wharton, to act as a
> sort of inexpensive keeper to Teddy . . . He had a lot to say about Teddy's
> condition which interested us all immensely, but which coming from
> him and under the circumstances seemed to me of unutterable bad taste
> and confirmed my low opinion of Johnson Morton, who is . . . certainly
> not a gentleman . . . Teddy seems to be in a very bad way and quite crazy
> – but still not bad enough to be shut up . . . She has been very selfish
> no doubt but one cannot help feeling that her punishment has been
> awful – tied to a crazy person, who is only just sane enough not to be
> locked up, but too crazy to be out – whose state of nervous breakdown
> is most dismal. She no sooner gets him settled in one place than he
> wants to go somewhere else, and is constantly in tears complaining either
> that he is spoiling her life or that he is being shamefully neglected.

Ogden ended this vigorous account with the recommendation that Teddy
should kill himself, like his father.[45]

The unhappy couple took up residence in September at the Belmont
Hotel, on the corner of Park Avenue and 42nd Street, in a New York which
Edith had not stayed in for about four years, and which she found monstrous.
Her friends – Morton, Walter, Henry – converged. Teddy left on his tour,
and that evening the friends dined together at the Belmont. It was not the
kind of gay, ebullient dinner she would remember 'the inner circle' having
in London with 'the laughing, chaffing, jubilant yet malicious James'.
Fullerton had just resigned from his job, and had had an emotional shock,
his sister's marriage. Walter Berry had also just resigned, because of ill-
health, as judge of the International Tribunal at Cairo, and was poised
between Washington and Paris, about to leave America. Her relation to
both these men was ambiguous and in flux; she was under extreme strain
about Teddy, and was 'still anxious' about James. He had come into New
York for a few days from Cambridge to see them all, but was still having
'depressing little relapses'. He wrote to Sturgis the next morning, describing
his feelings about William's death, Teddy's condition, Edith's state of mind:
'in moral (that is nervous & intimately personal) . . . *rags*, but as sublime
& unsurpassable as ever'. The Belmont Hotel was extremely luxurious –
'prodigious & unutterable' – and the dining room like 'the quarters of the
Gonzagas at Mantua'. In these lavish surroundings, the four American
friends, who had never before and would never again, all meet in America,
had their evening together, on 17 October 1910. There they sit: large, sad,

talkative Henry James; Morton Fullerton, short, edgy, charming, with his fine eyes and his big moustache; Walter Berry, tall and silver-haired and elegant; Edith Wharton, pale with exhaustion but in control, well turned-out, and greatly relieved to be rid of Teddy and to be with these three people; all of them riding on a current of secrets and knowledge and intimate personal histories; all of them immaculately well-behaved. They were seen by the wealthy Irish-American art-patron John Quinn, who happened to be dining at the Belmont that night, and noted Henry James, 'massive, slow-moving, awe-inspiring, at dinner with two gentlemen and a lady'.[46]

Henry James knew by now that Wharton was leaving America and that Europe was 'the only Habitat that is possible for her'.[47] The next day, she left for Paris, where (she told Sally) she went 'all to bits with nerves & indigestion'. Berenson wrote to his wife: 'She has been through hell over her husband, & looks a wreck.' Work was the thing: *Tales of Men and Ghosts* was coming out; she could concentrate on finishing *Ethan* and writing *Custom*. At first, reports from the world-travellers were good. Barrett Wendell, her Harvard professor friend (who had been a tutor of Fullerton's), happened also to be on his travels and encountered them in India. In a letter to Fullerton he said that Teddy seemed his old self, making rude remarks about 'the obsessive Indian consumption of whiskey and soda', enjoying the Taj Mahal, and with less 'rigidity of face'. But Teddy's own letters to Edith were 'a continuous ebb & flow of nervousness & agitation'.

She had five months off, in Paris, with what she described to Berenson as 'la bande' or 'the Bs': Berry (who moved out of number 53 into his own apartment in April 1911), Blanche, Bourget, Du Bos, Bélugou, and Berenson himself. She was building up this support group, along with Henry James's inner circle, and a few close women-friends. She was rallying her supporters, and this dependence on a select, loyal group would set the pattern of her future life.[48]

Teddy landed at Marseilles and was back in Paris on 4 April 1911. 'He is no better', she told Berenson, 'and I am much bothered about the future.' Concerned letters went between the friends of Henry: 'O dear O dear, how melancholy it is about the Angel', Percy Lubbock wrote to Gaillard Lapsley, 'Howard had a sad little postcard from her the other day, after Teddy's return.' She went to Salso, where it was hot and dusty. She had her usual affliction of serious hay-fever (a residue of the asthma of her youth), with the additional anxiety of high blood-pressure. She worked on *Custom*, in-between taking the cures and walking alone along the flat hot roads for her health (and weight, which she was gaining). Teddy left Paris in early May, and, once back in Boston, wrote an extraordinary letter to Herman Edgar, who was acting as agent for Edith's trust funds. Now Teddy wrote, with a mixture of pathos and aggression, that he wanted a full list of 'Puss's individual things', and that he should be consulted before any stocks were sold. 'I don't like to be a Trustee and know nothing about the property . . . for 25 years I looked after Puss's affairs and I did well until I went to pieces 2 years ago – I still take a great interest in them and I don't want to give it all up, I want to feel still that I know about them and can be of some use to her.' Herman Edgar told Edith that Teddy was trying to 'resume the management' of her affairs, and Edith, horrified, told Morton that 'this is the result of my "too-niceness" in not insisting on Teddy's resigning the Trusteeship when he lost all that money two years ago'. Her letter to her husband began, this time, 'Dear Teddy' and ended 'Yrs. E.W.'. It insisted, again, firmly, that since the fiasco of 1909 it was impossible for him to have control over her income, and demanded that he resign his trusteeship and give up the management of any of her household affairs. 'I must protect myself from this recurrence of the wearing & unprofitable discussions about money which have made the chief subject of our talks whenever we have been together lately.' She copied and dated the letter.[49]

Her position, which looked so clear on paper, was deeply contradictory and confused. She was about to set out for a summer at The Mount, and in a way was trying to settle back into her habitual routines there. Henry was in America, and so was Morton – though he managed to avoid visiting The Mount, however much she urged him. She wanted to socialise as usual, even though she described herself to Berenson as 'The Hermit of Western Massachusetts'.[50] Invitations went out to Walter, to John Hugh Smith, and to Gaillard Lapsley. She planned to go over to Ashfield to see Sally and Lily Norton. She tried to work on 'the Big Novel', *Custom*, set it aside, and started work on *The Reef*. 'Autres Temps . . .' and the serialisation of *Ethan Frome* were coming out in the magazines, and *Ethan* would be published in book form in September.

But it was impossible to treat this as an ordinary summer in America. Before she sailed, she had got to the point of thinking that she ought to sell The Mount. She had spoken to Herman Edgar about it, and asked him to 'put it' to Teddy, who seemed to agree at first, and then immediately raised some 'trifling obstacle' which put off the first possible purchaser. Teddy's confusions seemed like a distorted version of her own mixed feelings. Coming back to The Mount in the summer of 1911 after three years away, in a heatwave, she was delighted by how lovingly the gardens had been kept up, and felt proud of what she had achieved there. All the same it was a rather dull garden, she told Sally: no 'lovely flowering shrubs or creepers' would grow there, her clematis had died, and 'everything is uniform green'. She did not feel there was anything to compensate, in this 'grim New England country', for 'the complete mental starvation'. Yet in August she was writing teasingly to John Hugh Smith, who was making his first trip to the States, that she was glad he 'left America feeling it is a problem not to be solved in three weeks', and that Henry was wrong to dismiss the country so 'lightly', even if it wasn't 'exactly a propitious "ambience" for the arts'. She did love the 'sylvan sweetnesses' of The Mount, 'above all the moonlight [sic] nights on my big terrace, overlooking the lake'. These continuing debates over American materials for gardening and literature pointed to the central quandary of her life now, as she was nearing fifty. If she gave up The Mount, she would probably leave America for ever.[51]

It was difficult to think clearly in the turbulence. When she arrived on 2 July, Teddy had gone fishing with his brother. But, though alone, she was not tranquil. She told Morton: 'I am ... going through the worst moral struggle of my life. Teddy at present is violently opposed to selling the Mount ... Oh, if I were free – free – *free!* Isn't it awful to have a chain snaffled around one's neck for all time, without knowing it?' She told Gaillard that she had had a very good offer for The Mount, but that Teddy was very angry about it and she did not think she could proceed with it while he was away. It would have been better if the offer had come later in the summer, by which time, she wrote, prophetically, 'it would probably have been demonstrated that I could not live here with him'. Henry came for his visit on 8 July; Lapsley and John Hugh Smith joined them for a few days. On the 13th, Teddy arrived at The Mount. There was, immediately, a terrible scene of 'violent & unjustified abuse', witnessed by an aghast Henry James. Her immediate reaction was to insist that they should sell The Mount, and to tell Teddy she was going to leave him; he begged her not to. She agreed, on condition 'such scenes were not repeated'. Henry, who fled The Mount the next day, reported to Lapsley on 'the violent & scenic' Teddy, who was not, however, as 'awful' as 'the pleading, suffering, clinging, helpless Teddy'. He told Edith that she had no choice now: 'Deeper & deeper your dilemma, I know', he wrote. '2 things surely emerge clear: 1st that it's vital to get rid of the absolutely unworkable burdens & complications of the Mount; & 2d that with the recurrence of scenes of violence you must insist on saving your life by a separate existence ... These scenes are by the nature of the case recurrent.' She had to leave Teddy now, he told Minnie Jones, or he would destroy her.[52]

Teddy tried to behave better – in fact, she told Morton on the 19th, it was 'grotesque' to think that he was being a 'normal, reasonable, amiable person' just because he was 'terrified to death by the thought that I meant to leave him'. But the scenes of accusation inevitably started to recur, interspersed with abject demands for forgiveness. She tried to reach terms. She agreed to continue to spend the summers with him at The Mount, and even that he should go on managing the place, for which she would deposit a monthly sum in his bank. She would let him come and stay with her in Paris in the spring. In return, he would have to resign as her trustee, and to 'remain on pleasant terms' with her. On 22 July he accepted her conditions and promised to control his nerves and his temper. She wrote to Billy Wharton, summing up their agreement. Later that evening Teddy came to her room and she showed him the letter. And it all started again. 'You . . . accused me of seeking to humiliate & wound you . . . abusing me for my treatment of you over the last few years, & saying that . . . you preferred an immediate break.' It was enough. She wrote to Lapsley, who was due to return to The Mount, not to come – 'things took a sudden twist yesterday'. She wrote to Billy, telling him what had happened, and saying that she could no longer put up with Teddy's charges of 'cruelty, meanness, & vindictiveness'. She had tried to do everything she could, but she was exhausted. She wrote a formal letter to Teddy and had it sent to his room, giving him her account of what had happened, and telling him that she agreed with him there was no point going on. 'I now think it is best . . . that we should live apart.' Herman Edgar would deposit $500 a month in his account. And then she left, to stay with her old friend Egerton Winthrop in Newport for a few days. Walter was there, and both men supported her decision.[53] But it was not over yet, not by a long way. Edith told Morton that she had given Teddy 'notice' – 'with what result of shrieking & recriminations I leave you to guess'. Two weeks of 'pressure & entreaties' followed, from Teddy and from his brother, who put it to her that part of Teddy's troubles were caused by the 'realisation' that he and Edith were not so happy together as they used to be, and were becoming more and more 'estranged'. She denied it – not entirely candidly. But she agreed to 'give another trial' to the marriage. She came back to Newport (dropping in on Morton's family on the way), and found Teddy making a great effort. Life at The Mount resumed.[54]

Just then, a very good offer came through for the house. They were able to talk about it 'quietly & impartially', and decided that they ought to sell. She was now saying to her friends that it was too expensive for them to keep up. She told Sally about the offer: 'I have had a terrible two years', she wrote to her. The summer ended in disarray. Teddy went to yet another spa, at French Lick, Indiana. Before he left, she signed a document empowering him to rent or sell The Mount; at the same time, she asked him to promise not to do so until she had reached Paris and could confer with him. She left the house they had built together, and sailed for Europe on 7 September 1911. When she landed, she received a cable telling her that The Mount – that 'gorgeous millstone', as Henry was now calling it – was sold. Teddy 'declined the responsibility of it', she told Minnie bitterly, after she had given it back to him. She was 'much too tired to care greatly one way or the other'. To other friends she described it as 'an awful wrench' and a 'great regret'. She could not bring herself to sign the sale agreement for several weeks. But she put it behind her. She went to Salso and to Italy with Walter. Henry James was invited, but could not be persuaded to join them. 'The idea of going forth again on new & distant & expensive adventures fills me with – let me frankly say – absolute terror & dismay', he told her. And to Walter, by the same post: 'I really am entirely unable to start for any such glorious frolic.' Instead, he received a series of rhyming missives from northern and central Italy from the travellers, probably among the most cultured holiday postcards ever sent:

> Climbing hills & fording torrents / Here we are at last in Florence / Or rather perching on the piano / Nobile, at Settignano / Doing picture galleries? No, sir! / Motoring to Vallombrosa / Pienza, Siena, tutte quante, / High above the Dome of Dante; / Then (compelled by the busy lawyer), / Back to France by a scorciatoia.[55]

They stayed at I Tatti with the Berensons, and later that autumn she went to London, socialised, attended Beethoven concerts (her latest passion), and immersed herself in *The Reef.* Meanwhile Teddy was 'telling everyone that I "insisted" on selling The Mount, & thus have deprived him in his old age of a home & of his one hope of getting well'. And, though the house was sold, nothing was resolved.[56]

Her dilemma was made worse because it was not private. All through the summer, *Town Topics* was nudgingly referring to the Whartons' problems. On 3 August she was reported as giving Lenox 'a wide berth': 'She has lately been at Newport while her husband has been spending his time in and near Boston.' On the 10th, a long paragraph about Walter Berry ('recently recruited to Newport society', though usually in Paris) linked them together: 'Mr Berry . . . will be a guest of the Whartons at Lenox. Edith Wharton and Walter Berry are the most devoted of friends. She has sketched him in more than one of her novels, and the hero of *The House of Mirth* is said to be an accurate picture of him.' At the end of the month

'Mrs Edith Wharton's' plans to sell The Mount were reported on, with *Town Topics*'s own version of the reasons for the sale:

> It was not so many years ago that *The House of Mirth* appeared. Before that day Mrs Wharton and her husband had been fêted by the rich in their country homes, and catching the spirit the Whartons built a place near the George Westinghouse estate . . . Then followed the publication of *The House of Mirth* and its intimate portraits of persons in society. Lenox residents damned the book . . . There followed a social blight. Fewer and fewer became the cards left at The Mount, and finally the Whartons quit the game and went abroad. It is now said that they will make their permanent residence on the other side.

But a week later, *Town Topics*'s reporter noted that the sale was off:

> Mrs Edith Wharton has availed herself of a woman's constitutional prerogative, and the transfer of her property . . . will not take place. The high intellectual temperament of the literary lady is said to have ended negotiations, which were as good as settled, by a gentleman's agreement between the husbands of the ladies involved in the sale . . .[57]

Ethan Frome was published in September 1911; and she was still as immured in her 'dilemma' as her grim hero. The doctors in Indiana reported that Teddy had a 'psychosis' and that the prognosis was unfavourable; Dr Kinnicutt thought a sanatorium was the only answer. Teddy was threatening to come to Paris for Christmas, and Edith herself felt extremely unwell, with mysterious attacks of vertigo which were very unpleasant, she told Sally: 'Whenever I see anything drop I feel as if I were going to drop too.' They turned out to be caused by anaemia, not by 'an affliction of the inner ear'. (This cluster of health problems – breathing difficulties, dizziness, anaemia, and the high blood-pressure which would cause her increasing problems in old age – were clearly connected to stress and exhaustion.) And her oldest dog, Mitou, died – 'poor dear little world-worn Mitou', Henry lamented. She consoled herself with writing and reading. She went to England in November and December and visited her friends at Qu'Acre and Hill Hall. And she felt, more than ever, a need of good friends, as she wrote to Bélugou from London: '*Quel soulagement pour moi d'avoir un ami sûr et discret, sur qui je peux compter dans une situation aussi pénible!*' ['What a comfort to me to have a friend who is reliable and discreet, whom I can count on in such a painful situation!']

In early February 1912, Teddy turned up in Paris again, as bad as ever. Walter, now – unlike Morton – dedicated to helping her through this, in his own cool and ironical way, moved back into the guest-suite at Number 53. (*Town Topics* noted that 'since Edith Wharton went to live on the other side, [Walter Berry] finds it convenient to pass most of his time there. Not that there is any sentiment between Mrs Wharton and Walter Berry, they are merely very old and devoted friends, and, since there is no one to say them nay, see as much of each other as possible.') Henry sent his own kind of encouraging messages, which may or may not have seemed helpful: 'these phenomena essentially contain the germ of their own rapid evanescence . . .'; 'let everything *liquefy* . . .' But he told Howard that 'it sounds rather bad'.[58]

Teddy made a last, incoherent attempt to find common ground, though Edith's account (to Morton) suggests that he knew it was hopeless:

> This morning has been *terrible*. 'Learning French' has become an obsession (*why?* That is so strange!), & we have been having a 'lesson', & he has been crying, & saying over & over again: 'My mind is going, & the Drs don't see it.' It seems to me that he is failing *very* fast mentally. It is too terrible! . . . Oh, when I think of *ten years* of it! . . .

She told Berenson that Teddy 'won't budge without me . . . he *never* goes out, never, literally, unless I take him. He is well physically, but . . . I'm beginning to feel the dead weight of it.'[59] Work was impossible and plans were impossible. She told Bélugou that she had never been so depressed by her attempt to work (on *The Reef*): '*Tout ce que j'ai déjà écrit est bête, médiocre, terne et sans intérêt. Je n'ai jamais été dans un état plus complet de découragement littéraire.*' ['Everything I have written is stupid, mediocre, dull and without interest. I have never been in a more complete state of literary discouragement.'] After a few weeks of this she went away, leaving Teddy with White and Nannie, who was in Paris again. She took a trip to Spain (Saragossa, Madrid) with Rosa and Jean Du Breuil, and returned to Paris as slowly as she could, calling once more at Nohant on the way back. Ah, said Henry longingly, 'I seem to get the side wind of great adventures, past, present & to come, from you . . . You're ready for anything prodigious . . . It is the grande vie, don't deny that . . .' With his unerring acuteness, he was saluting her future freedom. Although the marriage was by no means over, Teddy left Paris on 5 May 1912, and never went back to the Rue de Varenne. As it turned out, this was the end of their life together.

Her friends watched in horror and fascination. This was not an easy time to be a close friend of Edith Wharton's. And it was at this point that James's most exaggerated caricatures of her develop, as she hurtled (it seemed to him) from place to place, ruthlessly sweeping up anyone she had a claim on, never at rest, spending money grandiosely, and compulsively making and changing rapid plans. It is this caricature that has come to dominate accounts of their relationship, partly because it was enthusiastically imitated by the 'inner circle', and partly because it is so irresistible and powerful in its comic malice. Now the 'golden eagle' and the 'barnyard fowl', the 'so high-flying Kite' who left him 'more dead than alive', leading the 'Grande Vie' with her 'Maenad motion' while he cowers like 'a mere aged British pauper in a work house', became, even more grotesquely, the Eagle and the Worm.[60]

The Eagle lands 'with a great flap of her iridescent wings' and in a ten-day visit does 'exactly 4,000 separate & mutually inconsistent things'. Depending on whether he was writing to Wharton or to her more-or-less devoted friends, the images shift from awe-struck to horror-struck; but the position he adopts is always that of an abject cowering figure trying 'to plunge my head under the bed-clothes & burrow there', lying down flat 'where I can best blubber into the Carpet' while she sweeps over on her 'immense & epic & terrible' voyages. He is stretched out, 'a faithful old veteran slave, upon the door-mat of your palace of adventure', while she steps over his 'prostrate form'. She is the Buccaneer, she is Ulysses, whose 'great globe-rushes & vast gyrations' make him 'crouch in terror'. 'How I wouldn't *be* her – for all her possessions.' Yet she is still fascinating: 'I'm so glad', he wrote to Mary Hunter, 'you will have seen – in Paris – our complicated – our *most* complicated – friend.'[61]

Wharton partly enjoyed and played up to the caricatures ('I led him a juggernaut 60-à-l'heure existence', she boasted to John Hugh Smith), but also resisted them: 'I feel less & less like the lurid exotic flamboyant volatile he persists in calling me', she wrote to Lapsley.[62] The climax came in the summer of 1912, when her arrival is marked by a letter to Sturgis headed 'Lamb House, Rye, Reign of Terror, ce vingt juillet, 1912'. James was settled into Lamb House for the summer, and his faithful housekeeper, Mrs Paddington, was away, leaving him unprotected against the Eagle, who was 'about to swoop & to catch me up in her irresistible talons'.[63] He did not escape the Angel, however: she spent late July and early August driving James between Lamb House, Cliveden, Qu'Acre and Ascot. On their second trip to Cliveden, James collapsed with an angina attack, and she sent him home in the car to Rye. He wrote in his diary: 'Had admirable car and dear Cook lent me by Edith for most beautiful and merciful return, by myself, across country, back to Rye . . . Went straight to bed.' He wrote a complaining letter to Howard on 'a lady who consumes worlds as you & I (*don't* even) consume apples . . . She uses up everything & everyone.' He told Mary Hunter about his 'ignoble collapse' at Cliveden, and said that his 'sorry case' had been 'little helped' by Wharton's behaviour. To Minnie, he confided that Edith was 'not without a hand' in his ill-health. And to Wharton, who was full of concern, he reproachfully attributed his attack to conditions of 'excitement & tension' and to 'the whole time-scheme & social chaos'.[64] This sounds more like resentment than friendship, and after this summer there would be no more motor-trips and few visits – and her arrivals would throw him into frenzies of anxiety. ('What terrifies me now . . . is the whole question of catching & meeting & proceeding with the least tension (or emotion!) along docks, railway-platforms, ups or downs of any kind where being *due* at some moment plays a part.')

Her own 'ups and downs' seemed ceaseless in the summer of 1912. There were months of rapid travel: to Salso in June ('fiction in the morning & friction in the pomeriggio', she noted to Berenson, who liked this kind of joke) and around Italy, as the sale of The Mount went through, with Walter. Walter was suffering from toothache and not enjoying some alarming incidents with the car in the Appennines and a near-fatal crash outside Modena, which Edith took in her stride. In July she was in England, and then in Vevey for a quiet few days writing *The Reef*. She went to Offranville, to Pouges-les-Eaux ('a vile place') to see the mouldering Bourgets; to the Château de Barante (vividly described to Henry) and on to the Pyrenees. In September she was in Avignon, Portofino, La Spezia and I Tatti again, with the Berensons. It was one of the most restless periods of her life, the beginning of two years of constant movement. But in these hectic travels, she was pulled back constantly by bad news of Teddy and by the need to resolve the situation once and for all.[65]

In July she heard that Teddy had had all his teeth out; she hoped that 'the relief from constant nagging pain' would improve his condition. Even now, she was still trying to think of bearable ways of living with him, and wrote suggesting that she should rent a house in New York in the winter. Perhaps they could even buy a smaller place in the country, in America, where she could write quietly and he could 'keep chickens'. It seemed a far-fetched plan, though it suggested at least a vestige of longing for America. To Gaillard she asked not to be told anything about The Mount, 'for there's a great ache there still'. Teddy cabled back frantically – 'Don't come – entirely disapprove plan' – and sent a twenty-page letter full of bitter reproaches for 'worrying' him. By September, after her travels in France, she told Sally firmly that 'the most earnest self-searching will *not* discover in me the least regret for having left America'.

But now Teddy's letters were beginning to sound too exhilarated, too jubilant. In November 1912, when Edith was back in Paris, he arrived in England, accompanied by 'shattering accounts' of his behaviour. He was once more, she told Gaillard, just as the doctors had predicted, 'in a full crisis of megalomania', which would be followed, inevitably, by 'another attack of acute depression'. He did not want Edith to join him. (And Dr Kinnicutt was advising her now that she should never live with him again.) He had 'met several "delightful people" on the steamer and was going to stay with them' and had 'brought over a high-powered motor and a chauffeur'. For the next few months, while Edith was in Paris, Teddy, her 'distracted and more than ever distracting friend', as Henry James put it, was 'much on the loose', dashing between London, Paris and Monte Carlo, turning up on people's doorsteps (though not Edith's), spending money (his own inheritance and the allowance she was paying him), drinking heavily, sending off bizarre letters, and generally striking everyone as 'half-crazed'. James described a letter from him as showing him to be 'just noisily and topsyturvily, and alas vulgarly, to say nothing of ruinously in the financial sense, off his poor little head'. The awful comedy of Teddy's performance is like a grotesque parody of her own restlessness.

Her friend Matilda Gay was particularly sympathetic. She recorded in her diary one 'long and painful visit' to Edith at the Rue de Varenne, where 'this poor distracted woman' talked of having 'to face the awful problem of saving a more than half-crazed husband from his own folly and danger. Her agony of mind and suspense were hard to witness.' Both Sally and Matilda, her closest women friends at this time, had heard a great deal about the problems with Teddy (even if they had been told nothing about Morton). Matilda had recorded an earlier conversation in which Edith 'became very confidential over her tragic domestic situation'. Matilda commented to herself: 'It makes one's heart ache, the hopelessness of her husband's malady, which can only be remedied by the Great Physician. And, to his misfortune and hers, his physical health is perfect.' Now, in December 1912, Teddy suddenly appeared at the gates of Le Bréau. 'He was dressed like a roaring blade of twenty; he talks incessantly about himself, his health, his clothes, and his purchases, and is as mad as a March hare. He told us that he had left Edith for good – it must be an enormous relief to her.' Matilda saw Henry James in London and told him the story; he relayed a vivid account of it to Minnie. 'He is truly as elatedly, and swaggeringly and extravagantly, mad as he can be . . . one of the first things he did was to say: "Have you seen my gold garters?" and then to whisk up his trousers and show them in effect his stockings held up with circles of massive gold!' The Gays also told him that he was 'showing, facially, strong marks of "la debauche"'. And his eyes, they said, had 'a terribly distressing and insane' look.[66]

Things were 'chaotic' for her; at times she felt, she told Mary Berenson, only half joking, that 'a little child could lead me – to suicide!' Word was going round in Boston and New York, and among the Americans they knew in England, France and Italy, about Teddy's 'exploits' and Teddy's version of the separation; the Berensons heard at I Tatti that Edith's situation was 'very well known & has been for years'. Codman spread the news:

> Teddy Wharton seems to have been acting strangely and I fancy soon they will have to lock him up after all – I hear he writes everybody the most awful letters accusing her of improper relations with Walter Berry and several others. – She never struck me as having much 'temperament' but I don't pretend to be a judge of such things.[67]

Just as her novel of American divorce, *The Custom of the Country*, started its serialisation in *Scribner's Magazine* in January 1913, she began to draw up the battle-lines for her own, now inevitable, divorce. But the Furies – as she would put it – were out in force. Her situation was made more painful, at this moment, by an ugly quarrel with her brother Harry. Though any correspondence with him was obliterated from her archive, they seem to have had an affable relationship at least up to 1908, when she was staying at his house in Paris. Harry, now in his sixties, had been living for some time with a woman called Anna Tekla, known as the Countess Tekla, who had a daughter. Edith now discovered that there was what she called a 'smouldering "rancune"' on Harry's side because Edith had never asked to meet 'the woman he lives with' ('How could I when he never even spoke to me of her?'). This story re-enacted the Jones family's split over Frederic's divorce from Minnie and his remarriage in 1896. Harry had, at that time, protected the financial interests of the women in his family, Minnie, Beatrix and Edith, against which Frederic was acting in favour of his new wife. Now, Harry's mistress (whom he would marry in 1920) was alienating him, in his turn, from his family, so that he would favour her financially. (There is no first-hand evidence about the wicked Countess Tekla, who sounds like a character out of a bad novel: Codman described her as Harry Jones's 'ancient harlot'.) It was particularly hard that this family quarrel should have burst out now, and that the wretched family history of the Joneses was coming back to haunt her just as the Wharton family were at their most hostile. (Frederic, who had been living in Paris for years, had also returned unhappily into her life the year before: he had suffered a serious stroke, and she and Harry, though both long estranged from him, had provided some assistance.) Her bitter memory of Frederic's maltreatment of Minnie, her loyalty to Minnie and Trix, and Teddy's similarly unreliable behaviour, may have made her act haughtily towards Harry and create resentment. But it is unpleasant to hear (from Codman, of course) that Teddy and *his* 'harlot', and Harry and the countess, were to be seen dining in Paris restaurants together and 'all making faces at Puss'.[68]

There was 'a party on "poor Ted's" side' in all this. But Edith was rallying her defences and making sure that she had the support she needed. She had kept all the necessary correspondence, and was warily throwing out other papers and letters of the last four years 'against the coming break up', she told Morton pointedly. Her cousin Herman Edgar came to France at the start of February and set about 'looking after' her 'interests'. He followed Teddy's trail to Monte Carlo, where, she told Mary Berenson, he found Teddy 'leading a life he wouldn't describe to me except in gestures of disgust, & I couldn't have listened to if he had'. She hoped that 'something may soon be decently, silently, & soberly arranged'. More evidence of past infidelities would surface: in April she told Lapsley: 'I find that Teddy has registered all his various temporary brides as "Mrs Wharton" in the hotels they frequented – rather a gratuitous last touch of ill-breeding.' (Another, much later, version of this story came from Daisy Chanler to Louis Auchincloss: she told him that, checking in at a strange hotel when travelling with Edith, 'as they were signing the register, Edith noted the prior entry of a "Mr and Mrs" Edward R. Wharton, and observed with a slight smile and shrug, "Evidently I *have* been here before."')[69]

In Paris, Edith was being helped by Bélugou and his friend the lawyer André Boccon-Gibod. In America, she was getting support from Daisy Chanler's husband Winslow, and from her cousin Tom Newbold. (His mother, Lucretia's sister Mary, had been at Edith's christening. Although she was now extricating herself from the last legacy of her relationship with her mother, she was also, more than at any other time in her adult life, drawing on old family connections.) As with any separation or divorce, both sides were putting their own spin on the case. The Wharton side, spearheaded by Billy and Nannie, was out in force in Boston, talking against her. Their line (as she told Minnie) was that 'Teddy is a homeless martyr, victimised by my frivolous tastes for an effete society'. But this was a deliberate ploy 'to relieve his family of any responsibility. They *know* his real condition, and the impossibility of living with him.'[70]

It was very important to her to have allies in Boston and New York. She particularly welcomed letters of support from people there who had known her and Teddy for years, such as Egerton Winthrop, Robert Grant,

Barrett Wendell, Daniel Updike, and Eunice Maynard. Replying to their letters of sympathy, she made a point of setting her own version of events against Teddy's. For example, she thanks Barrett Wendell for understanding her position: 'I do sometimes feel a great soreness and indignation at the way in which the Whartons have treated me. Bless you, my dear for your unfailing sympathy and for your affectionate words.'[71]

Right to the bitter end of the marriage, there was suspense, uncertainty, and confusion. Edith sat out most of March in Paris, racing to finish *Custom*, and waiting for Teddy to be pinned down so that divorce papers could be served on him. At last, on 23 March, she wrote to Gaillard: 'It's all settled! ... but ... the decree can't be pronounced till the courts sit again next week ... now at last [I] know how tired I am! ... The delay, of course, was due simply to the impossibility of "locating" T. – He suddenly arrived three days ago, & the citation was served, & everything settled, in 24 hours.' At exactly the same time, she was having her misunderstanding with James about his birthday present, and getting his outraged letter. It upset her very much.[72] On 28 March, she left Paris for Italy with Walter. On 15 April, Henry James had his seventieth birthday. On 16 April 1913, 'La dame Wharton''s divorce was granted, in her absence, by the Tribunal de Grande Instance de Paris. She was represented by André Boccon-Gibod. Though Wharton was an American citizen, she was being divorced, as '*la deman-deresse*' (the plaintiff), under French law. The statement of the case read as follows:

> *Le sieur Wharton a entretenu à Boston en mil neuf cent huit et mil neuf cent neuf des relations adultères ... Récemment malgré le pardon accordé par la dame Wharton qui avait consenti à reprendre à Paris la vie commune le sieur Wharton s'est affiché tant à Londres qu'à Monte Carlo avec différentes femmes et a eu avec elles des relations d'un caractère gravement injurieux pour la demanderesse.*[73]

The divorce was granted, and '*le sieur Wharton*' was to pay all expenses. (The rumour that Ogden Codman later put around, that Edith was paying Teddy alimony, sounds far-fetched.)

Wharton divorced in Paris to avoid publicity, since reporters were not allowed access to the court proceedings or reports. She managed to keep her divorce out of the *New York Times* and *Town Topics* (which was busy reporting, in the very same week, on some notable divorce cases amongst the English aristocracy: 'all efforts to keep what is likely to prove a rather sensational case out of the courts have completely failed'). She stated her situation very plainly – and without explicitly noting the irony of the situation – to Morton, who had been approached by reporters: 'You did *absolutely right* in telling the reporters you knew nothing of my divorce . . . I obtained it on the grounds of adultery in Boston, London & France, with documents à l'appui, duly recorded by the court . . . The public can't get at the register of the French courts.'[74]

In order to divorce in France, she had had to prove Teddy's adultery, which was not hard to do. (She would have had to do this in New York, too.) But it is worth noting the phrase *'gravement injurieux'*, a legal term of great importance in early twentieth-century French divorce proceedings. Divorce in France had only been back on the statute book since 1884 (it was abolished in 1816) and could only be granted by 'matrimonial fault', not by mutual consent. (Even that was strongly opposed by the Jesuit priests.) There had been later amendments. In 1886 couples were allowed to be represented by lawyers, rather than appearing in court. In 1904 it was made possible for the adulterers to marry their lovers after the divorce. And in June 1906 divorce became obligatory after three years of separation. But there were still no grounds outside 'matrimonial fault': that is, divorce could not be granted in France on the grounds of mental illness, or mutual consent, or incompatibility. It could be granted, from 1906 onwards, on the grounds of adultery, physical violence, cruelty, *'condemnation afflictive et infamante'* ('grievous and ignominious' sentences such as life imprisonment), or *'injures graves'*. The last term, which came to dominate divorce proceedings until mutual consent was introduced in 1975, became extremely flexible, in-definite, and widely used, covering any kind of moral cruelty – and it often subsumed 'mental illness'. Increasing numbers of couples were taking advantage of the more flexible grounds, though divorce proceedings were often very slow. In 1895 there were 6,751 divorces in France; by 1910 there were 14,261. In the period of Wharton's divorce, six out of ten French divorces were 'demanded' by women. That the court proceedings cited the 'gravely injurious' nature of Teddy's behaviour suggested that Boccon-Gibod had taken care to make the most of the available grounds: Teddy was not only an adulterer; he had also inflicted *'injures graves'*.[75]

'Teddy is now definitely & legally put away', Henry James reported to Howard Sturgis. According to Codman, he was going around saying 'it is "Damn bad form of Puss to divorce him" but that he is "damned well rid of her"'. ('I wonder what she will do next', Codman added thoughtfully.) A year later, while Edith was at I Tatti, she heard he was having an even more serious breakdown; it made her feel extremely sad.

She still had one more legal battle to fight, which was over the use of her name. Teddy's lawyers fought her over her 'right of dower' (whether she had legal claim on anything that Teddy owned); she agreed to surrender any such right, but in return wanted to keep 'her full right' to the name of Wharton – since it was her professional name – in order to avoid 'news-paper talk'. She added, bitterly, describing this last conflict of interests to a sympathetic Robert Grant, that, in the course of the divorce, 'Teddy has always done the kind of thing I should have thought him least capable of, and that would have filled him, in the old days, with the greatest disgust and contempt'. Her legal name was, thereafter, 'Edith Newbold Wharton', and her form of address would be 'Mrs Wharton'. She was, ever afterwards, extremely fussy about this, and never failed to pick people up who wrote to her as 'Mrs Edward Wharton'.

'I have had a trying year', Edith wrote, with some understatement, to Sally Norton. At the end of that year, Edith's niece Beatrix Jones got married. She wrote her a letter, almost a year after her divorce. It read:

Fasten with all your might on the inestimable treasure of your liking for each other and your understanding of each other – build your life on its secure foundations, and let everything you do and think be a part of it. And if you have a boy or girl to prolong the joy, so much the better. Be sure it's worth while. And times come when one would give anything in the world for a reason like that for living on.[76]

13

Getting What You Want

Edith Wharton, at fifty-one, had none of the 'secure foundations' she recommended to her niece, nor, for that matter, any of the securities that might be expected to underpin such a well-financed, successful, efficiently organised life. Her father had died over thirty years before her divorce. She never mentioned her mother, dead these twelve years. She was a middle-aged orphan, alienated now from all the Jones family except for Minnie and Trix. She had no husband, no lover, and no children. She had lost her American home. She had chosen to be an expatriate, and would shortly (though like many of her contemporaries she did not see this coming) be thrown into the catastrophic disruption and trauma of the war in Europe. Because of the stress and tension of the last few years, she was not in good physical shape: she looked older, her blood-pressure was high, she had put on weight. Her youth was gone, just as she told Morton it would go: sometimes she felt like 'Madame d' Autrefois'.

All the same, in the 'trying year' of 1913, she seems a far from pitiful figure. She was writing her greatest book, *The Custom of the Country*. She was in powerful charge of her professional life, and was in the process of acquiring a new publisher. She had a distinguished international reputation – even if her critics did find her last publications more gloomy and unpleasant than ever. Her energies poured into writing and travel, and, more than ever, into friendships: in particular, into one new relationship. Bernard Berenson, the most intimate new friend of her late forties and fifties, was susceptible to women and fell in love easily and often. He did not fall in love with Edith Wharton, nor she with him. But at exactly the time when she was most in need of support, she and Berenson selected each other for that rare achievement, a close, platonic, mid-life heterosexual friendship between equally successful and well-known contemporaries, which would last till death.

They were meant to know each other, though they had got off to a bad start. When the Berensons were introduced to 'Mrs Wharton', at the villa of a mutual friend, in 1903, while she was doing her homework on Italian houses and gardens, they both disliked her 'intensely', and found her snobbish and 'venomous'. This was the impression Berenson often made, too. Henry Adams (who provided the venue for Berenson's and Wharton's second meeting) described him as 'oilily sneering' at someone's paintings, and 'eviscerating the world with a Satanic sneer'. When Lord Ronald Gower, one of Morton's London lovers, called on the young art critic at Fiesole in 1895, he found him 'rather too positive in his judgements about early Italian art'. There is obvious anti-Semitism in these upper-class gentry finding Berenson oily and over-confident. But he was clearly a dislikeable character, especially on first acquaintance. He could be domineering, impatient, arrogant and scornful. Berenson's wife Mary has been described as 'having to live in the shadow of an unfaithful, vain and self-obsessed man everywhere revered for his brilliance and expertise'. Berenson himself expressed bewilderment in his self-portrait of 1949 as to why so many people disliked him: perhaps they resented 'the intrusion of my egoism'.[1]

Wharton found out the best in Berenson, though, and he came to repent his first judgement of her. Their first meeting became an affectionate joke between them. Bernard told Mary in 1918: 'I made her scream with laughter as I gave her a truthful account of our first impressions of her. She gave her account of how . . . overcome and shy she was.'[2] But for some years they disliked the idea of Mrs Wharton (they pooh-poohed her attempt at 'attribution' in 'A Tuscan Shrine', republished in *Italian Backgrounds* in 1905), and it took a long time for the friendship to ignite. The alliance between the distinguished, wealthy, high-class 'Old New York' writer, and the Lithuanian Jew whose immigrant father was a pedlar and who made his money selling paintings to rich Americans, was an unlikely one – but their paths did converge at many points.

Berenson's prodigious career at Harvard in the 1880s (where his passion for Arnold, George Eliot, Ruskin and Pater fuelled his lifelong aesthetic investment in the 'intensified pleasure', the 'increase of consciousness' to be had from art), had brought him in contact with many of the figures in Wharton's life. He had a good friendship with Barrett Wendell. He worked on a respected literary magazine, the *Harvard Monthly*, alongside one W.M. Fullerton. He bore a lasting resentment against Charles Eliot Norton for denying him a Harvard Travelling Fellowship and for denigrating his work. Berenson rightly thought Norton prejudiced against what he called 'marginals like myself, on the ragged edge of the social body'. Like Wharton, Berenson fell in love early with Italy, and chose Europe. Like her, he put his childhood environment behind him, though in his case this meant poverty and Jewishness (he became a Catholic). Like her, he turned his back on America and was ferociously critical of it, but strongly identified himself as an American. He was aghast at a threat to revoke his citizenship in 1907, as 'an alien-born American who had absented himself from the country for more than five years'. His response was to call himself 'an American of Americans'; though he also described himself as having 'roots nowhere and associations everywhere'. They had similarly conflictual relations to their country.[3]

They had been criss-crossing each other's paths in Italy, England, America and France for years. Wharton's Italian journeys in the 1890s and early 1900s brought her in touch with Berenson's world, Anglo-Tuscans and American expatriates and art-historical rivals like Vernon Lee. The year of their first, unsatisfactory meeting was also the year in which Wharton went to the opening of Isabella Gardner's Fenway Court (filled with the pictures Berenson had been obtaining for his patroness) and notably did *not* make friends with 'Mrs Jack'. Berenson was close friends with another stylish hostess who was not to Wharton's taste, but who connected to her world at many points, the brilliant Elsie de Wolfe. (J.P. Morgan's biographer, Jean Strouse, notes that Mrs Astor, jealous of the New York social success of Elsie de Wolfe in the 1890s, decided to hold her own rival 'bohemian' party, and 'provoked hilarity' in the de Wolfe set by saying that she planned to invite, as leading bohemians, 'J.P. Morgan and Edith Wharton'.) Some of these networks of international, expatriate Americans never overlapped. James hardly mentioned Berenson to Wharton, for instance. But Wharton and Berenson had mutual friends in the Ralph Curtises, Bayard and Sybil Cutting, the Bourgets, Rosa de Fitzjames, and Daisy Chanler. (When she died in 1952, Berenson described Daisy Chanler as the last of his generation and a great reader in three languages, 'like Edith Wharton, with whom one could discuss any book of European interest – but never on the sociopolitical plane'.) The Walter Gays, too, were shared acquaintances. Matilda Gay found Berenson amusing, she liked Mary, and admired I Tatti. She was critical, however, of an 'oily' quality in Berenson – again, the standard upper-class euphemism for 'Jewish' – his 'tendency to pontificate' and his viciousness about his friends: 'when he talks of people his tongue is dipped in venom.'[4]

When Wharton and Berenson did at last meet properly, in Paris, in September 1909, it was through Wharton's coterie of distinguished Franco-Americans. Ambassador Henry White's wife, Margaret Rutherfurd, told Berenson that 'no higher-bred woman existed in America' than Edith, and that she was 'above all littleness'. Henry Adams and his close friend

Elizabeth Cameron introduced them, though the details of their encounter became blurred in Berenson's retelling of it. He wrote to Mary that he had been at Adams's apartment when Edith Wharton came in with Elizabeth Cameron, looking very different from how he remembered her six or seven years before. Then Mrs Wharton wrote to Mr Berenson saying that Mr Fullerton was trying to find a date to fit in with Mr Adams's idea of a 'happy combination'. These formal preliminaries resulted in a dinner in an upstairs room at Voisin's, a smart restaurant near the Ritz (Berenson's preferred Paris hotel), with Adams, Elizabeth Cameron and her daughter, Wharton and Fullerton, and Berenson. He told Mary that it had been 'very nice' and 'merely human', 'chatting, gossiping, exchanging limericks' (Edith Wharton's limericks, alas, were not recorded). Mrs Wharton had been 'affable to the last degree' and Fullerton was 'simple & likeable'. Berenson seems to have had no idea of any liaison between them. In Berenson's memoirs, many decades later, a more romanticised version is given, like a scene in a novel, in which, in a dusky dining room, he spends some time at the dinner-party in delightful talk with a pleasant-voiced woman whose face is hidden behind a black lace veil, who clearly knows all about Paris life, and who agrees with him about everything – people, 'loves and hates in the realm of art' – and whom he only discovers to be Edith Wharton after the lights have been switched on.[5]

At the point when Wharton met Berenson, his life was as stressful and complicated as hers. Since the 1890s he had made a great name for himself as a critic and connoisseur; the fourth volume (*North Italian Painters*) of his much-praised series of books on Italian Renaissance painting came out in 1907. Like Wharton in her novels, Berenson always broadened out his close analysis of detail into a discussion of cultural evolution. 'Art' (he wrote in his 1895 essay on Lorenzo Lotto) 'so faithfully registers the struggles and aspirations of humanity that to understand in what way it expresses a certain epoch it may be needful to venture beyond its narrow limits into the region of general history.'[6] He was interested in evolution, innovation, imitation and decline. Intellectually, they approached their materials in similar ways.

But inspiration seemed to be drying up for Berenson, just at the time when she met him. Instead of writing art-criticism, he absorbed himself in making 'Lists' of all the Italian paintings he knew – eventually published in 1932 as *Italian Pictures of the Renaissance*. He preferred to think of himself as a 'quiet scholar' and as 'very little of a businessman'. But his energies and talents were being swept up into his lucrative career as a connoisseur, much in demand for his expertise in attributions and as a purchaser of expensive works of art for immensely wealthy collectors. He bitterly resented the claims of the art-trade at this time, and particularly the increasingly 'burdensome obligations' of his business connections to the Duveens, Henry and his nephew Joseph, the aggressive 'supersalesman' of the international art-dealing world. He would feel that he was 'led astray into picture-fancying and expertising'; he regretted his 'equivocal business conduct', his loss of confidence in himself as a writer (friendship with Wharton made him even more conscious that he lacked the 'gift of tongues'), and the 'spiritual loss' all this entailed. The year before he met Wharton, he revised some earlier essays on Sassetta, the painter of the Franciscan legend, and his biographer thinks there may have been a symbolic 'act of contrition' involved in his publishing, now, a book on the unworldly St Francis.[7]

The conflict which Berenson described in himself between a life of creative integrity, and a career made out of selling his soul for profit, is uncannily like the many stories of artistic corruption which Wharton wrote both before and during their friendship. The narrator of 'The Rembrandt', published in 1900, is a museum curator who is forever visiting 'some distressed gentlewoman whose future hangs on my valuation of her old Saxe or of her grandfather's Marc Antonios'. He has a more hard-headed colleague, Crozier, who talks of acquisitions entirely in terms of 'strokes of business'. The art expert is soft-hearted enough to misattribute a bad painting as a Rembrandt for the sake of an old lady's peace of mind. In 'The Daunt Diana' (first published in 1909, just before she got to know Berenson), the struggling collector, whose 'taste was too fine for his means', and who despises the rich philistines who have the money to buy up treasures ('to think of that lumpy fool having those things to handle!'), inherits a fortune and buys his most desired objects, but because he has not struggled for them, they leave him cold; he has to sell them, and then laboriously buy them back, ruining himself in the process, in order to get any real pleasure out of his acquisitions. Most of her stories of artists or collectors are about corruption and disillusion, just as her stories about writers often set the true creative gift against the perils and temptations of the market-place. These art-world stories include 'In Trust', the 1907 story of the wasted inheritance; 'The Verdict', the Ralph Curtis story of the failed painter turned wealthy collector; 'The Pot-Boiler', of the painter who prostitutes his talent – pointlessly, as it turns out – for the sake of the woman he loves; and, later, 'False Dawn', the story of a visionary collector of Italian primitives, far ahead of his time. 'The Temperate Zone' (1924) bitterly contrasts the obscure true talent of a dead artist with a fashionable society portrait-painter, and with the artist's widow, who affirmed 'her husband's genius in terms of the auction room and the stock exchange'.[8]

It is unlikely that Wharton knew much about the shadier side of Berenson's career. Since 1894, he had been getting 5 per cent of what 'Mrs Jack' paid for a picture. Later accounts of his dealings with Fenway Court, which continued into the 1910s, have suggested that he exerted his formidable salesmanship, in his own interests, by selling her some false attributions (as well as some great paintings), using her as 'a depository for embarrassing pictures' and playing on the 'good-natured self-indulgence and credulity' of a rich and eager patroness (with whom he may also have had an affair). By the time he came to know Wharton, Berenson was in the thick of his lucrative, pressurised involvement with the Duveens, which began in 1906. In 1908 they were offering him 10 per cent of the profits of any pictures they sold endorsed by him. ('A future of affluence lies before us!' Mary Berenson wrote in her diary.) In 1912 they formally contracted him as their adviser, for 25 per cent of all the pictures which they sold on, at his recommendation, to the millionaire clients he so despised. (Berenson was extremely scornful of the kind of rich American collectors who competed for an artwork as a 'trophy' – and from whom he made his money.) The Duveens' practices were making headlines in the autumn of 1910 (they were accused of evading US customs duties by undervaluing the art objects they were selling), just when Berenson was meeting Wharton. It was well known that Berenson was a compromised figure. One art editor noted in 1903 that he had managed to find 'an honest dealer, though an art critic ... No Berenson business about him'. The Walter Gays, in later years, would be told by the director of Fenway Court, Morris Carter, 'several stories of Berenson's strategical performances in his life as an art dealer'. Retrospective attacks on Berenson for misattributions, picture-smuggling and crooked dealing may have been exaggerated, but as Jean Strouse puts it, 'the lines between aesthetic judgement and commerce were not always clear'. It is ironic that the friend who, to an extent, replaced Morton Fullerton in Wharton's life with a new, sympathetic intimacy, was just as much of a tricky character.[9]

Berenson kept his business dealings and his domestic and social life as separate as he could; the queue of dealers bringing their paintings for attribution came in a different door from the guests at I Tatti. This celebrated and enchanting house on a hill just outside Florence, just above the village of Settignano and the River Mensola, with a view of hills, vineyards, olive trees and cypresses, scattered stone houses and a little church, which might have come straight out of a Gozzoli painting, became one of Wharton's favourite places in the world. The Berensons first rented and then bought it, in 1907. When she first got to know it, the house was in the process of extensive developments, inside and out. It was, in essence, a simple country house, looking more like 'an overgrown farmhouse' than a grand Florentine villa. Nicky Mariano (who became, from the 1920s, its chatelaine, Berenson's life's companion, and the third member of the marriage) called it 'an unassuming well-proportioned Tuscan house'. Inside, she said, it was 'furnished quietly, almost severely, with antiques ... comfortable chairs, Italian Renaissance paintings and sculpture mixed with Oriental sculpture and *objets d'art*'. Harold Acton, whose father lived nearby at Villa La Pietra, said it had little to distract the eye 'from the magnificent collection of four-teenth- and fifteenth-century Italian paintings, except the view'. As soon as the Berensons bought it, they began to develop it, with the proceeds from his art-dealings. Electricity and bathrooms were put in, and a team of two young Englishmen, the talented designer Cecil Pinsent and his colleague, Geoffrey Scott, a gifted and neurotic architectural historian fresh from New College in Oxford, were redesigning the house and turning the grounds into an impressive Anglo-Florentine garden. I Tatti's famous features – the terrace of flowers, the *limonaria* sunk below it, the great stone staircase, inset with little ponds and fountains, plunging down the hillside in front of the house into the view, the long green side-alley of cypresses, the secret side-avenue towards the stone pond and its statues – were all beginning to take shape when Wharton first went there with Walter in October 1911. Inside, two libraries, a small one and a very grand one, were being built to house Berenson's splendid, and growing, collection of books. He would call I Tatti 'a library with rooms attached'. For Wharton, I Tatti was a dream of pleasure. Visiting New York in the winter of 1914, she wrote to him longingly: 'Is it possible that there is a place called Tatti, where you & I have walked together, & talked of the immortal things?'[10]

By 1911, I Tatti had already become a 'court' (as its *habitués* liked to call it) with troops of visitors and callers, disciples, art-lovers, and gossipy 'enemy-friends'. They came for the beauty of the place and the quality of the talk. Lance Cherry, another gay young man from New College, employed as a secretary at I Tatti, was horror-struck by the 'troops of self-assertive middle-aged females who surge through the house' – including Mrs Wharton. Though much romanticised by its devotees, it was not an entirely happy household. There were often too many visitors (those who could only speak one language, or who challenged their host's views on art, were regarded as a particular nuisance). The Berensons' marriage, though strong and lasting, was also a poisoned one. The startling contrast in their looks – Berenson dapper, elegant, small, fastidious, Mary large, slow-moving, bohemian-looking – reflected their conflicts. Even before Mary had left her first husband, Frank Costelloe, for Berenson, there were bitter arguments between them over his writing, which she fiercely criticised, and over money, about which they were both anxious. They quarrelled too about her family – her feminist Quaker-American mother, her depressive father, her clever literary brother, Logan Pearsall Smith, much liked by Wharton, and the daughters of her first marriage, whose claims Berenson resented. (One of them married Virginia Woolf's brother, but Berenson, like Wharton, had no interest in Bloomsbury.) Both the Berensons were deep in emotional imbroglios, which they told each other about, endlessly. When Edith first met Berenson, he was passionately in love with J.P. Morgan's beautiful, exotic librarian, Belle da Costa Greene. Mary had been confusedly in love since 1907 with Geoffrey Scott, twenty years her junior, as well as acting as his sexual confidante (which would include trying to encourage him to marry Nicky Mariano). When, much to Wharton's horror, Scott married Sybil Cutting (with whom Berenson was also involved) in 1918, Mary tried to kill herself. In 1910, long before that crisis, the marriage was under strain. Berenson would fly into terrifying rages, Mary would fall into dark depression; they were both jealous and critical, and complained about each other bitterly.[11]

As often with her new friendships, Wharton and Berenson were rapidly in sympathy, and she soon began to hear about his private life – probably more than he heard about hers. He was evidently never told about Morton, and, like most of her Paris acquaintances, he assumed that she and Walter Berry were lovers. It was Walter she depended on through the break-up of the marriage. At the time she was getting to know Berenson, and for years to come, Walter was her neighbour, travelling companion, reader, and closest friend. Meanwhile he had affairs, boasted to his male friends about his sex life and pursued married ladies, such as Elsie Goelet, with whom he was said to be involved around the time of Wharton's divorce.[12] Since no letters between them survive from this period, and since Wharton was so discreet about Walter in her letters to others, we do not know whether they were lovers at any point after her divorce and the end of her affair with Fullerton. The more likely story, given his taste for younger, glamorous women and the length of time the two friends had known each other, is that they were not. But that does not mean she did not love him.

Within weeks of the dinner at Voisin's, Berenson was 'loafing' away the afternoons in Paris with the two of them, and feeling that Wharton was becoming one of his 'real'-est friends, though 'her heart is Berry's', he told Mary, perhaps to reassure her. At times Berenson found Walter Berry an irritant, and he came to feel that Walter disliked him. Wharton (he said) told him that this 'was on her account, that he could not bear for her to have friends and resources apart from himself'. But the two men had phases of getting on well together; though very unlike in character, they were both hedonistic about women, books and other collectibles. Berry's brief notes to Berenson provide a little window on how he referred to Wharton, sounding more like one of her admiring friends than a lover: 'Edith, I suppose, has started off again, circling a new orbit'; 'She is in fine form . . .'; 'Edith is blooming . . .'; Edith is returning to France 'after a triumphant tour in England'.

Berenson quickly found evenings with Wharton 'perfect': 'exchanging views over our favourite writers, discussing prose and poetry'. By November she was 'human, cordial, even devoted' with him, and was encouraging him in his writing and urging him on to do more (as she had Fullerton). By 1912 he was her 'dear friend', or 'friendissimo', and she was 'Dearest Edith', urged to 'love me as I love you'; he had become, as to all his close friends, 'B.B.'.[13]

Though she visited I Tatti in 1911, she did not meet Mary until the following year. Mary was surprised to find herself liking her, though she found her 'heavy-handed'; Wharton was 'really very nice, so easy to get on with . . . more *our* sort than most people'. They all shared, Mary thought, 'a tempered New Englandism'. Mary reported on a revealing and touching conversation between the two women about 'Growing Old': 'She said she wasted her youth trying to be beautiful, but now that she has given up all hope she feels freer.' 'I think', Mary concluded perceptively, 'she is a very good friend to her friends.' As Mary's depressions became more severe and the rifts between her and Berenson deepened, she would sometimes resent Berenson's intimacy with Wharton, which left Mary to her own 'encumbering, unenjoying & unenjoyed existence'. Later visits to the house in Hyères made Mary feel inadequate: 'Her beautifully run household, so full of all human comforts & luxuries, & permeated by her courageous and life-enjoying spirit, has utterly destroyed me, it is all so desirable – so unattainable by me.' Wharton usually took Berenson's side in the dramas of his marriage; it was Nicky Mariano she would make friends with, not the more difficult and tormented Mary. She became impatient with Mary's crippling depressive illnesses. (Of the agonising cystitis which plagued Mary, she said, 'I don't know how serious that is', suggesting that she had never experienced this herself.) She compared Mary to Teddy, and told Berenson that she was 'frightened at the way' that his future with her was 'developing exactly in accordance with my own experience'. Still, at the height of Berenson's obsession with Belle Greene, she told Geoffrey Scott – who passed this on to Mary – that she thought Mary should take a stand against Berenson, and this would make him 'come back cured, and very happy to regain you, and realising where his real interests and real life lay'. After the war, she gave a suicidally depressed Mary some advice – with a touch of condescension – from her own experience:

> One may be strengthened & fed without the aid of Joy, & no one knows it better than I do; & I believe I know the only cure, which is to make one's centre of life inside of one's self, not selfishly or excludingly, but with a kind of unassailable serenity – to decorate one's inner house so richly that one is content there, glad to welcome any one who wants to come & stay, but happy all the same in the hours when one is inevitably alone.[14]

Wharton was one of the few women, Mary thought, with whom Berenson's friendship was not based on any kind of sexual attraction or flirtation, one of those rare women who was genuinely excited by '*Talk, Thought, Philosophizing, Chatting on Literary Subjects* etc etc'. Berenson said he preferred women as friends because he found such friendships less competitive than with men. He particularly liked 'society women' because they were so 'receptive' and 'appreciative', and therefore 'stimulating'. He told Ralph Curtis in 1912 that though he had a low opinion of women generally as intellectual equals, they could be delightful '1) as playthings, 2) as playmates, 3) as stimulants, 4) as inspiration'. Perhaps Wharton was the exceptional woman-as-equal in his life, just as he was the exceptional Jew in hers. In his early letters to her there are a few touches of gallantry. She is his 'fairy godmother' in Paris; he is disappointed when she leaves because he has 'got attached to what is you in particular', but won't say more: 'At 45 I am still shy.' But there is no erotic content to this correspondence (unlike his exchanges with Walter Berry, who tells Berenson about the attractions of 'ces Dames saying Yes to Life' in Paris in 1916, and agrees on the need for sexual variety: 'Look at me, *years* older, and still in the ring.'). Wharton was mostly kept outside this male banter. Berenson provided a telling detail, many years later, in 1931, of a walk alone at Hyères with Robert Norton, who recited (presumably out of earshot of their hostess) a rhyme which used to be sung in the British officers' messes during the war: 'Here's to the French / The noblest of races / Who talk with their hands / And f . . . with their faces.' 'The dots', Berenson noted for Mary's benefit, 'replace a word occurring frequently, you told me, in *Lady Chatterley's Lover.*' Still, the author of 'Beatrice Palmato' was not entirely demure in her conversation. Berenson learnt from her, for instance, as he wrote in 1913, that Walter Berry 'had a horror of fat women,

& *consequently* as I am sure Sigmund Freud would say, he collects pictures & caricatures of them'. (His caricaturing allusion to Freud suggests their shared attitudes: Wharton, in a letter to Berenson of 1922, equated 'Freudianism' with 'sewerage'.) Bored with Bourget's notorious love of obscene anecdotes, his endless stories of 'actresses & noctambules & restaurants de nuit', whispered in his soft voice, she told Berenson that she had said to him: '*Oh, taisez vous. C'est le cloaque de chez Maxim!*' and was rather proud of her Parisian joke.[15]

But sex was not their main subject. Wharton's attraction for Berenson was her social class and her fame. He liked her intelligence, her culture, her sympathetic attention, and her energy – he would sometimes call her 'O Vigorosa'. And he understood her reticence, too. All her life Wharton had been shy, bad at large gatherings, more at ease in a small circle of friends, surprised when people liked her, and faithful and responsive when they did. She told Mary Berenson (in 1918, with reference to Geoffrey, one of many young gay men who felt drawn to Wharton): 'Even when I was young I never suspected that people could "care" for me till they threw themselves into my arms – & old age has not increased my faith in my charms.' She confided in Berenson, after a few years of knowing him, the story of 'her cheerless, loveless youth, with parents & relations who meant nothing to her, in standards of heartless correctness'. He made an accurate assessment to Mary in 1917:

> With regard to friends ... she really expects nothing whatever from them except to see her and to love her. I am now convinced that she does not expect them to entertain and be brilliant although she enjoys that so much. But she is quite satisfied to be in the same room with a real friend ... I told her ... of my horrible outburst against you. She cried 'If only I had somebody who would scold me and quarrel with me.' Poor dear she suffers tortures from loneliness.[16]

From the time of the divorce onwards, Wharton's double manner – which kept private confessions and simple intimacy only for a few, and turned a defensive, even chilling, face to the social world and to strangers – became more pronounced. It was often remarked on in later years, particularly in the Berenson circle. Nicky Mariano, meeting her first in the early 1920s, described how difficult it was to get to know her, until, asking after Wharton's maid Elise, she was rewarded with 'a warmth, a tone of intimacy that I had never heard before. A gesture ... had let down the drawbridge leading into the fortress of her small intimate circle.' Kenneth Clark, who met Wharton a decade later through Berenson, commented on this (many years after Wharton's death) as a perceptive account of a 'maddening and lovable' woman who was 'a Janus figure, a boundary goddess staring icily at those outside, smiling at those within', who 'concealed herself from the outside world, a rich, warm hearted, vulnerable human being'. This became the standard description of Wharton; she used it herself, here to Mary Berenson: 'Those I'm *not* fond of have not, as a rule, considered "warmth" my distinguishing quality. I never could serve myself up in the same sauce to friends & to acquaintances.' Berenson, too, was said to be more sympathetic in a small group than when holding forth to a large circle.[17]

The tone of their letters (which survived) is, from the first, confiding and sympathetic, mixed on his side with a clear desire to impress and even to compete. In the letters between the Berensons, impatient affectionate criticism *about* Wharton often contrasted with the devoted tone of his letters *to* her. Berenson does not tell her much about his work, but he is open with her about his feelings. A long letter of 23 March 1912, for instance, shows the close and confiding terms they are on. He tells her that her story 'The Long Run' (of the renunciation of youthful ardour and passion) has come very close to the bone, and he is amazed by how good she is at getting inside her male character: 'To a hazardous degree you are bone of our bone, & flesh of our flesh.' He invites her warmly to Italy, as he so often did, and he asks fondly after Walter, as he always made a point of doing. Then he describes in great detail an accident he has just had, falling from a wall and injuring his back. He did not want to spend the rest of his life like the heroine of *Ethan Frome*, he says nicely. But the accident, he says, has brought on the most extraordinary and mysterious 'euphoria'.[18]

He knows that she will understand exactly what he means. And she confides in him, too, though (like him) not about everything. She tells him, very soon, about the tortures of Teddy and how worried and exhausted she is. She tells him some of her personal history, and how she has dealt with it: 'I begin to thank whatever Gods they be for breaking my spirit so long ago by a series of resounding whacks that I never expect to be well, happy, or out of misery, & am always ready to make irreverent gestures at them because I *am*, in their despite, all the same!' If she talks to him about love, it is in the most general – and to him, unconvincing – terms: 'She gave some totally false generalisations about man and woman. When I protested she confessed that she was speaking from personal experience and that hers had been both limited and unfortunate.' She tells him how her mind works – describing in one letter how she has imagined a whole journey to Egypt (which she never got to): 'I've made that same kind of mental excursion so often. It's the habit which has made it almost impossible for me to go to the theatre. I see the whole play, acting & all, when I read the *compte rendu*.' In the dark days of the war, she reached out to him with particular warmth and affection:

> I believe part of the *néant* with which I'm affected is an insidious force of missing you – missing our long & wide & many-dimensioned talks. With every one else I have the sense of having to fit into a space that cramps me – hitting my head or my funny-bone, or having to sit with my knees drawn up to my chin. You're the only person who has given me, for a long time past, what I used to call 'a good swim' – & what, after all, if I honestly survey my past, I find I've really cared for more than anything else, & have always found the necessary ingredient in other joys.[19]

She talks to him about her work-habits, telling him about her short-lived pleasure in receiving proofs ('I am in that state of fatuous satisfaction which evaporates as soon as the thing appears in *real* print'), or how *Ethan Frome* is dragging at her like a baby or a growing child, an image she often uses for her work ('I have to let its frocks down every day, and soon it will be in trousers!'), or – as the serialisation of *Custom* starts to come out – that she is up against a tight deadline: 'The time limit is inexorable ... The devil of it is that the book has outgrown my original scheme, and there are two more short chapters to be written. I *must* get them done this week, & though I think it can be done in the week I can't, of course, be absolutely sure.' And she is quick to defend her 'children' to him. He doesn't believe in the Midwestern names she's invented for *Custom*, like 'Indiana Frusk'? He should see some of the real ones! '. . . how about Lurline Spreckels ... & Floriday Yulee, two "actualities" who occur to me instantly?' He understands that *The Age of Innocence* is not a 'costume piece'? Good, that was what she intended, and a few readers like him have seen that it is a 'simple & grave' story of 'two people trying to live up to something that was still "felt in the blood" at that time'.[20] Berenson always had high praise for her novels: *The Age of Innocence*, in his view, had more of 'solid psychology and deeper humanity' than her earlier work; in 1929 he was reading *Hudson River Bracketed* with 'breathless interest', tremendously enjoying – perhaps with some solipsism – 'the study of raw genius and how his gifts develop, and culture comes to him'. On their visits to each other after the war, reading aloud became a habitual pleasure – of other authors (where Berenson was always analytic and attentive) and of Wharton's own work in progress. These were critical sessions. Berenson told her that *In*

Morocco was 'pedantic and vague' and that she should stick to fiction. One letter of 1921, to Mary, suggests how she responded to her readers: 'By the way, I've "fattened" "The Old Maid" at the point at which you & BB & Robert [Norton] thought her tissues needed reinforcing.' Her inscription in the Berensons' copy of *A Son at the Front*, kept at I Tatti, reads: 'For Mary and B.B., in remembrance of trial readings at St Brice, Edith, September 1923'. She dedicated her 1933 volume of stories, *Human Nature*, one of her darkest and most cynical books, to him.

Their literary conversation is informed, impassioned, and energetic. It is an exchange of precious objects – cherished quotations and allusions well known to them both. They test each other a little for their skill in attributions, but mainly draw on the same cultural fund. They cite Tennyson's *Ulysses*, Browning, Goethe and Dante to each other, exchange opinions on Petrarch, or Renan, or the *Oxford Book of German Verse*, or the relative merits of Dostoevsky and Tolstoy, or discuss her view that Melville's early travel-books are better (because 'simpler') than *Moby-Dick*. For light relief, they swap allusions to 'The Hunting of the Snark', or he tells her to read Daisy Ashford's *The Young Visiters*. They cultivate little verbal gags, like calling a particularly outrageous or unbelievable quotation or anecdote (usually American) 'textual' or 'textuel', or referring to the next generation as 'the youngs'.[21]

These literary exchanges were at the heart of their intimacy. At a bad time with Teddy, when she was trying to write, she told Berenson:

> When I'm trying to do anything I can't see people any more, but only read, read, read. I used to be passionately interested in anthropology and all the prehistoric kitchen-midden, but this last year I've had such a tired distracted head that I can't fasten my mind on anything but poetry and 'letters' (I mean *belles*, not missives). I think reading Keats gives me the completest joy I know.[22]

In wartime, she was rereading a childhood favourite, the Old Icelandic 'Edda', tales of gods and heroes (which underlay the story of Wagner's *Ring*, which she and Berenson heard together in Berlin in 1913). No one in Paris, she complained, understood this reference. 'Oh, dear!' she wrote to Berenson, 'isn't it queer that *we* can understand Racine, & that *they* can't hear the rustle of the Urwald [the Nordic forest].' He replied enthusiastically: 'You dear, we truly were if not made at least brought up for each other. Think of you as a small girl & I as a small boy living within a couple of hundred miles of each other, probably the only human beings in America of any age who wallowed in those northern incantations.' And he went on

into a long chat – what she would call an 'orge' – about William Morris
and Santayana.[23]

She did not deal in his currency as much as he in hers, though she made
occasional knowledgeable remarks about *putti* or baroque churches. But, at
the start of the relationship, she had an interesting exchange with him
about form. When Berenson congratulated her on 'The Pretext' (the story
of the New England wife misled into her moment of love by a visiting
young Englishman), he started an argument about whether short stories
were less valuable than novels. 'Do you do the same with pictures?' she
challenged him:

> Rembrandt's 'Philosophe devant le Livre Ouvert' is a short story in form,
> & so is the 'Descent from the Cross' of Veronese in the Louvre – & they
> are both, to me, very big things . . . this is not to say that 'The Pretext'
> has not the value of a novel, but only that its form is not, in my eyes,
> any excuse for its not having it! . . . Today there is a spring sky, & I'm
> off for Beauvais – which is *not* a short story!

When he asked if he could see *Ethan* in proof, she teased him: 'It's not
"your size" . . . only an anecdote in 45,000 words!' She was at work, though,
'on a real magnum opus [*Custom*], whose bulk alone ought to recommend
it to you: a vast novel that is piling up the words as if publishers paid by
the syllables'. She returned to the question of form in literature and painting,
in the National Gallery in December 1911, looking at Turner, 'who is still
to me the great magic-maker, the inciter to dreams, the opener of case-
ments on the faery foam – not in his big "machines", though, but in the
small quiet ones: the Frosty Morning, Chichester Canal, and countless little
water colours'.[24]

They also played to each other's haughtiness and snobbery. Wharton
told him how she had been 'wading in dirt' through the filthy 'kitchen-
middens' the French 'upper-middles' take their country holidays in, or
reported with horror from New York in 1914: 'It seems to me like Berlin
without the brains (& by brains, of course, I mean merely the things *I* care
about!).' In later years they went in for golden-age nostalgia: 'Oh, BB, when
we remember the people *we* have known!'[25] After the war, Wharton's right-
wing politics hardened more than his, and she would attack his 'hateful
Manchester Guardian ideas about the poor flapping scarecrow of French
militarism'. In the mid-1920s, she seems to have shown some admiration
for the Italian Fascist Party, though this may have been more of a running
joke between them than a firm position on her part. In April 1921 she told
Mary Berenson how good the post was now between France and Italy: 'If

this is the work of the Fascisti, please change your politics! They have evidently repaired all the roads between Ventimiglia & Settignano.' Mary – not an entirely reliable witness – occasionally reported on pro-Fascist sentiments at the Pavillon Colombe. On one occasion (in 1925) she said that Wharton had advised Berenson he would be wise to keep off politics as after all he was 'a stranger in Italy' – meaning a Jew? – and on another (in 1927) that she had agreed with Bourget on the merits of Mussolini, 'the first man who has the courage to assert the bankruptcy of universal suffrage'.[26]

She was at her best with Berenson in her travel-letters. She loved to make him visualise her journeys, and she knew that his own experiences made him a good audience. On journeys to Spain, Italy, Algeria, she wrote him fine enthusiastic letters, and she responded with feeling to *his* traveller's tales: 'I almost cried when you described your emotions at the descent from the Passo d'Aprica to the Valtellina. It is the most beautiful scene in Italy to me – perhaps partly because I was so happy when I saw it [in 1899]. I know every foot of that Edolo route, & before the Val Camonica was spoilt by the steam tram there was no more *riante* valley south of the Alps.'[27]

As travelling companions, however, these two discriminating and somewhat competitive cognoscenti were not good partners. She knew that her own travelling-habits could be demanding, and she told him so: 'Being myself of a barometrical instability . . . I *do* like to shilly-shally & deviate, & cover the map with "pentimenti".' He should have been forearmed. But the most difficult passage of their friendship was the journey they took to Germany in the summer of 1913. Wharton was determined to be away from Paris at the time of, and just after, her divorce. First, in April, she went to Italy with Walter, setting off from I Tatti through central Italy (Montepulciano, the cloister at Monte Oliveto Maggiore, Orvieto) down to Rome, Naples and Sicily. Ravished letters went to Berenson from Sicily in springtime: 'Segesta . . . the most inspired solitude on earth . . . those wonderful mountains behind Monreale . . . that strange little dream-town of S. Giuliano, with its beautiful patterned pavements, & silent little mouldering palaces & churches . . . almost like a mountain-Bruges in its cloistral silence & order . . .'[28]

After a brief return to Paris, she went back to Salso, and started from there on another journey through northern Italy with young Geoffrey Scott as her travelling-companion, who wrote enthusiastic, if rather overwhelmed, letters to Mary about what it felt like to travel with Mrs Wharton. The Berensons had warned him that she might be difficult, but 'far from fulfilling our fears and prophecies, [she] has been most awfully nice in choosing all the places which she thinks I would like most to see, and those which are new to me'. He liked the fact that she travelled spontaneously: 'Our future is quite dark and hypothetical. Mrs W. likes to make her plans from hour to hour, which suits me admirably.' They shared pleasure in a Palm Sunday service at Modena ('with fine old music and *such* ecclesiastics. We have neither of us ever felt such an anthropological "thrill"'), in the treasure house of the Palazzo del Te at Mantua, and in an exciting adventure at Sabbioneta 'where we were almost driven wild by a hundred howling little boys and were forced to go and get the guarda who came out with a sword, a guide book to Sabbioneta and a pair of pince-nez'. As they bowled along to Turin 'we have great fun together and die of laughter'. Once across the Alps and in France, they had a 'romantic experience' at Sens, seeing the stained glass in a thunderstorm: 'As the occasional flashes of lightning came the smouldering colours of the windows seemed to catch fire suddenly.' In Paris, the fastidious Scott accepted with gratitude 'Mrs W's' generosity and 'hospitableness', even if he was not over-impressed with the Rue de Varenne, which, though comfortable and spacious, did not have, he thought, 'any distinction of taste, and a good deal that is depressingly bad'. He preferred Walter Berry's apartment, which, he told Mary Berenson, 'is really charming, though it suggests a man who cares more for bindings than insides! All the same it is as cheerful and inviting a setting for a *bachelor* life as I can well imagine . . .' He added, fuelling the I Tatti gossip about this relationship: 'I feel almost *sure* from several things that Mrs W. has said, not specifically about the situation, that they do not intend to marry.'[29]

That was what a journey with 'Mrs W' was like when she was pleased and happy, secure in the role of patroness, and confident of being liked. Her travels a few months later with Berenson did not go so well. He wanted to look at as many Italian paintings as possible in North German galleries with an appreciative companion. She wanted a rest, and a few memorable high points, and not to be bullied through an arduous and rigid itinerary. He liked to travel light, she needed her entourage of Cook and White and Gross and the motor-car and the little dog Nicette. They were both used to setting their own agenda on their travels, and few things are more challenging to a friendship than when those kinds of determination collide. It began badly, at the start of August 1913, by her putting him off for a few days, on the grounds of exhaustion, and asking for some time 'in some green woody *walky* place where I can recover my nerves before we attack big towns'. She follows this plea with a revealing account of how she felt, in this painful year, about managing her own life: 'Remember that every-thing the all-beneficent Mary does for you falls on me alone – household, cheque book, publishers, servant questions, business letters, proofs – *and my book!*'

In short, she needed a good wife. But Berenson was not responsive. 'It promises far from well', he wrote to Mary. 'I am amusedly curious to see what particular specimen of womanliness she is going to treat me to.' Wharton wrote again a few days later, saying she would meet him in Luxembourg, but that if she found the trip too tiring after three weeks, she would tell him so frankly: 'I can't imagine how a friendship like ours can embarrass itself with pretenses of any sort.' Berenson interpreted this as being all about Walter, who was taking a rest-cure (he was often ill) which was due to end in – three weeks. He thought she was 'planning to chuck me to join him'. Perhaps, Mary replied, a 'habit of deceit where WB is concerned [has] become so instinctive that it seems quite simple & natural'.[30]

Once they were together, Berenson found her 'excellent company', loving to tell and listen to stories. He was particularly struck, in the hotel dining room at Cologne, by her looking across at a young man at the next table and saying: 'When I see such a type my first thought is how to put him into my next novel.' But, as she had warned him, she was 'tuckered out & no mistake', and this made her nervous, jumpy, and 'irritable'. At Cologne she did collapse, and offered him Cook and the car to go on his journey alone. He thought she might be shamming 'so as to have her way' about a rural detour. But after a forty-eight-hour rest (during which Berenson offered to look up a good 'alienist', or nerve-doctor) and the promise of green woods at Nauheim, they continued their cultural journey. It took them through Oberhof, Würzburg, Fulda (near Frankfurt), Altenburg, Dresden, and Berlin. Berenson (who after all was benefiting from the car and the chauffeur) complained about his companion's restiveness ('no sooner has she decided to do any one thing than every other passionately appeals to her as preferable') and her fussiness about hotels. If there were no private baths they had to go elsewhere; if the bed 'was so placed that she would not be able to read in the morning' it 'nearly drove her into hysterics' and meant that the hotel 'was the most impossible she ever put foot in'; at almost every meal 'she returned every dish'; 'Not once since we have been in Germany has the salad been to her taste.' He caricatured her to a receptive Mary (who may have needed to have her jealousy appeased) as impossibly spoilt and fussy: 'the most thoroughly luxurious party I've ever travelled with'. She hated approaching towns through 'ordinary suburbs', she had no notion of 'what it is to wander about', she only cared about finding a patch of grass where Nicette could get out of her basket. This sounds unfair to the resourceful and energetic traveller who (unlike Berenson) hated the luxury of the Ritz, loved spontaneous picnics, and was game for any journey, on any form of transport, to find the church or the cloister or the view she wanted.

Berenson did not think much, either, of her capacity for looking at paintings. She got impatient too quickly and she only liked the pictures which 'illustrated an anecdote within the range of her interests'. Mary agreed with him: 'I could have told thee [she always used the Quaker form of address] ... that Edith abhorred art ... What is rather extraordinary for a keen, clever woman is that she doesn't take advantage of this singular opportunity to try to learn a little of what it all means. But I suppose she despises it too much, or thinks she knows it all already.'

But when she was good she was 'a simply enchanting companion'. In Berlin, they went to the opera, to Strauss's *Rosenkavalier* and to a complete Ring cycle. For hours on end she was enraptured – though he noted that she preferred *Rheingold* to the *Walküre* because of its 'treatment of human society and situation'. After all, he concluded, 'she is infinitely preferable to most women, for she can talk & think, & listen to a million things that most people have no sense for'. Still, when he later read a letter Wharton had written to Mary, describing the trip as a 'golden journey', he put a scathing jagged line around the phrase. Berenson would caricature his dear friend in his memoirs as an impossible travelling-companion, and though they travelled together again it was never *à deux*. He preferred her as a guest (where she worked quietly in the mornings and was no bother) or as a hostess: 'Mrs Wharton is at her best in her own house', he wrote to a friend in 1930. But he did her justice too: 'She never fussed about her work, never made you feel that it obsessed her. Quite the contrary, even her familiars might have frequented her for years without discovering that she was a prolific and distinguished author.'[31]

Wharton's version of events was equally mixed. In a long and rather forced comic letter to Mary, she described Berenson as if he were her travelling-pupil, who needed to learn how to close a car window, or ask the way, or let the dog sit on his lap, or go 'through galleries with a quick firm step instead of gaping & dawdling'. She joked about her incompetence in the museums, putting it down to exhaustion: 'I thought Claude & Poussin were all one painter (because their pictures were all in the same room!).' After they parted, she went on to Baden Baden so that Gross could visit her family there, and wrote a sharper account, to John Hugh Smith, of what it was like to look at pictures with Berenson: 'much too technical, & reminds me often of the hero of a story I have never written, who killed himself, because, as the result of too continuous chemical research, he could see people & things only as aggregated atoms'. She was kinder about him to Morton, telling him that the trip had left her 'with an increased sense of [Berenson's] genuinely affectionate "niceness" & of his amazingly comprehensive brain'. He was 'an interesting & delightful travelling companion'. She added, with sad emphasis: 'Good it is – but not the best.'

But she knew she had been in a bad state, and was anxious that it should not spoil this new friendship. 'I wish I had been in better trim for your delectable company & our good trip – you must give me another chance', she wrote to him wistfully. She was worried that she had not heard from him after their parting: 'I thought it somehow reflected the depressing effect of my companionship during our giro. I pictured you as saying "Ouf!" when I whizzed away from Berlin, & couldn't wonder . . .' And she made an eloquent, poignant remark about looking at pictures when your heart is not in it: 'This time, everything I looked at hurt, as if there were too many things in the world – & I used to think there could never be enough for my avidity!'[32]

Berenson had underestimated the professional as well as the personal pressure she was under that year. As often happens in a writer's life, all the break-ups were happening at once: when her novel about infidelity and betrayal came out, in the year of her own divorce, Wharton was also being unfaithful to her old publishers. All through 1913, there were letters going back and forth between Wharton and her 'team' at Scribner's at 595–7 Fifth Avenue – Charles, the son of the founder, now in his late fifties; her courteous, pernickety editor William Brownell; and the magazine editor Edward Burlingame. They were corresponding over the James birthday fiasco, over the plot to smuggle her royalties into his account, over Morton's book, *The Problems of Power*, and above all over the progress of *The Custom of the Country*. There is a close attention to detail, on both sides, in these letters. She was going to hold back some chapters of *Custom*, she told Burlingame in February, so that she could get a legal expert to look at the conversation between Ralph and his lawyer. In September, as the novel's serialisation reached its end, Scribner wrote that he was 'profoundly interested' and relieved by the ending, as like many other male readers he had found Undine 'so convincing, such a *type*' that 'they had come to read of her with set teeth and a general desire of vengeance'. Scribner's were eager to know what serial she had next in mind for the magazine, and suggested that 'some American scenes' and characters would be 'desirable'. But in spite of this friendly attention, all was not well with relations at the House of Scribner.[33]

As she pointed out to Berenson, she had to do all her business herself, and even with considerable help from Anna Bahlmann (and from those friends and intimates she used for help with contracts or proof-reading, like Walter, Morton and Minnie), she was for years her own agent, manager, administrator, and negotiator. She kept a beady eye on sales and advertising, layout and design, illustrations (which she increasingly hated), jacket copy and author photos, typos, punctuation and spelling (especially lapses into American spelling, as in this robust example: 'Travel*e*r, cent*e*r, cle*w*! . . . It is all well enough if one is writing newspaper American; but if one still tries to write English, as I was taught to do – oh please, good, kind, editor, give me back my *l*s and my *ue*!').[34] She had always been exacting with the staff of Scribner's, though relations with them were affable. Since the publication of *Ethan Frome* in 1911, however, she had been discontented with them. In 1912 and 1913, at the period of greatest uncertainty in her life, this discontent came to a head. But she was a slow divorcer, and it would take another seven years, and several more phases of misunderstanding and mutual reproach, to make the break from Scribner's.

There were three overlapping problems, each with arguments to be made on both sides. The first was her increasing dissatisfaction with the appearance, promotion and sales of her books. She objected to some of the punctuation in *Ethan Frome* and she complained about 'flagrant misprints' in *Custom* – though she had corrected the proofs late and hurriedly. Her bitterest complaint was that although *Ethan* had been well reviewed, it was not (according to her friends) obtainable in bookstores and it was not being well advertised. 'Nothing is more difficult to meet', Scribner replied, as he must often have done, 'than the statements of an author's friends who report that a book . . . cannot be had at the best bookstores.' She asked for an additional advance of $1,000 for *Ethan* and was given it (the original advance was $2,500 for the magazine publication and $2,000 for book publication). But its sales were disappointing (4,200 in six weeks, 6,700 by the end of five months – as compared to *The House of Mirth*'s 100,000 in the first three months).[35] She began to feel she could do better elsewhere.

The second problem was that, after *Ethan*, she was working on three books at once, which made her publishers anxious: first *Custom*, which she started, and promised for the magazine, in the summer of 1908, but then put off for several years; then *The Reef*, which rushed up at her, replacing *Custom* in her mind, in the summer of 1911; and then 'Literature', her big novel about the disillusionments of the literary market-place, which was never finished, and was eventually turned into *Hudson River Bracketed*. (And she was writing short stories at the same time.) The third problem was the relationship between serial publication in the magazine and book publication, that vestige of nineteenth-century publishing practice which was central to Wharton's professional life. If the publishing house had a magazine attached to it, the editors usually wanted to make sure that they could publish their author's book both in their house magazine, as a serial, and then in book form. Failing that, if the magazine could not run the serial (either because the author wanted to place it elsewhere for more money, or because the magazine editor did not want to run it), the publishing house still wanted to keep the book. 'Our magazine is sometimes as much a source of trouble as a benefit to our book publications', Scribner wrote to Wharton in February 1917. It was as much on the tension between serialisation and book publication, as on sales, that the Wharton–Scribner relationship foundered. Scribner summed up his position to her in May 1918: 'When we have had to decline a serial of yours ourselves, it does not seem to me that we should lose the book.'[36]

From early in 1908, Scribner kept asking hopefully about *Custom*. Was it coming on? Could they have it for the magazine? Would it be ready by 1909 and if so – by spring? – or autumn? Privately they thought *Custom* might help what seemed to them at this point a flagging reputation. Burlingame told Scribner that serialising the new novel would 'do much to revive interest' as it is 'distinctively and aggressively in the earlier field' (i.e. it would remind people of *The House of Mirth*). But she ground to a halt with *Custom*, though Scribner's had the consolation of a volume of stories, *Tales of Men and Ghosts*, in 1910. And she withdrew *Custom* from its promised magazine serialisation. By the end of 1910 she was telling them about *The Reef*, which they did not like the sound of as much. Burlingame thought they had better run it, 'though not really wanted', 'rather than let it go to some rival firm'. In 1911, while *Ethan* was being serialised, and, in her view, under-promoted, and she was writing *The Reef*, Scribner's was still asking hopefully if she could let them have *Custom* in March 1912 (four years after she had originally promised it to them). But by the end of 1911, when her dissatisfaction over *Ethan* was at its height, she was telling them (unfairly, they felt) that it was because Burlingame had not found space for *Custom* in the magazine that she had switched to writing *The Reef*.[37] These misunderstandings and complaints, when she feared that her falling sales would make it hard to ask them for a big advance (like the $10,000 she had had for the not very successful *Fruit of the Tree*), coincided with a large and tempting offer from the rival firm of Appleton.

This was not a switch to a more 'popular' publisher. Though it was known for more enterprising business methods and aggressive advertising campaigns than Scribner's, Appleton was a solid and reputable concern, and William Appleton would be described as 'the last of the old-time publishers'. (Wharton would deal mainly with Joseph Sears in the firm and, after his retirement, with Rutger Jewett.) Appleton had a strong stable, which included Conrad, Kipling, Stephen Crane, Harold Frederic, Conan Doyle, George Moore, and David Phillips, an American novelist whose *Susan Lenox* (1917) Wharton greatly admired. Wharton was a catch for them (even if her recent sales had fallen off), and they offered her $15,000 for *The Reef* – with the understanding of the bigger novel, 'Literature', to come later. She asked Fullerton to help her negotiate the contract (he would do the same with *Summer*) and she held out for 20 per cent royalties: 'Scribner has been giving me 20% for years, & I know that some novelists receive 25%.'[38]

The contract for *The Reef* with Appleton was signed on 16 April 1912: the advance was $15,000 and 'English spelling' was specified. 'Anything you write should have the highest royalty', Sears would write to her in 1918, 'and 20% of the retail price is the highest royalty we have paid to anyone.' She would not give them *Custom*, though; it had been so long promised to Scribner's, and she told Morton that she 'didn't see her way to deserting' them again with that book. Only then, in May 1912, did she write to Charles Scribner to tell him she had received a 'very advantageous' offer from Appleton; and added, rather unconvincingly: 'I believe this will be to your advantage as well as mine, as it will perhaps be the means of reaching a somewhat different public, and – if the story is a success – will in some sort act as a preparation for *The Custom of the Country*.' (She gave the same explanation to her English publisher, Frederick Macmillan, whom she imagined would 'probably be surprised by this change of publisher'.) Scribner replied, with dignity, in June:

> It has taken me a month to recover from the shock caused by your announcement that you had arranged with Appleton for the publication of your next book, though indirectly a report to that effect had reached me. Of course I am very sorry to lose the honor of exclusive publication for you and it will be a little difficult for me to explain to others why you made the change. But I try to be broad minded about it and to be contented with *The Custom of the Country*, now assured for the magazine.[39]

Edith told her ex-lover, whose unreliability had partly inspired the novel which she had just sold to a rival: 'Scribner is mortally hurt by my infidelity.'[40]

In May 1913, while *Custom* was coming out in serial form, she told them she was hovering between two subjects, both 'chiefly laid in America': she seemed to be offering Scribner's both these fictions. In November 1913 (while *Custom* was having a big initial success, though sales then dropped off disappointingly), she used Appleton's big advance for *The Reef* as leverage to demand a bigger advance from Scribner's 'in the event of your taking my next novel'. They told her they could not give a bigger advance, and did not understand what she meant by 'in the event': she had surely promised them a serial? By February 1914 she was describing this new novel, 'Literature', as 'a full & leisurely chronicle of a young man's life from his childhood to his end . . . I want it to be my best & most comprehensive piece of work, & it must move slowly.' Perhaps it would be better not to serialise it, since it was going to be so long and slow. No, they replied, they wanted it for serial as well as book publication, and they wanted it by the summer of 1915. But then the war intervened. 'Literature' was derailed (the subject became impossible to treat, 'with the world crashing around one', she told them) and it would be the source of persistent misunderstanding. She offered them her 'Fighting France' articles instead of the novel; Scribner's took them, though they were still hoping for 'Literature'. But 'Literature' disappeared from her plans, and they concentrated instead on publishing *Fighting France*, *The Book of the Homeless* and their last collection of her stories, *Xingu*. In 1916, Wharton gave her new short novel, *Summer*, to Appleton, much to Scribner's hurt surprise. Her excuse was that Scribner's had told her they wanted to wait for 'Literature' for the magazine, and could not meanwhile place *Summer*, and she had been offered $7,000 by *McClure's* magazine for the serial and $7,000 by Appleton for the book. At the same time, she contracted with Appleton for $15,000 for 'a novel of the general type of her "House of Mirth"' – which became *The Age of Innocence*.[41]

Her claim that Scribner's had refused to place *Summer* in the magazine because they wanted to wait for 'Literature' and that this meant they could not have *Summer* as a book, hardened into a retrospective certainty. 'I should always prefer to have my novels appear in Scribner's, & I refused all other offers for these two ['Literature' and *Summer*] till you had declined them', she wrote to Charles Scribner in April 1918. Scribner argued, at first mildly ('We should have been very glad to have bought the serial rights of *Summer* for use elsewhere & then secured the book') and then in more injured tones, that she had broken faith with them:

I have not the heart to reread the old letters but you certainly interpreted them to mean something never intended by me . . . You now write that you will be glad to give us a serial for the magazine but make no mention of book publication. Is this not treating us with less consideration than our previous relations entitle us to expect?

She replied, implacably, that in spite of her 'old affection' for Scribner's, she could not afford to turn down bigger offers from other firms.[42]

Scribner's did not lose Wharton entirely. They published a ten-volume, low-price collected edition of her works in 1914. They captured one more post-war novel, *A Son at the Front*, in 1918, because Appleton did not want to publish any more war-fiction. And they published two more of her non-fiction books, *In Morocco* (1919) and *The Writing of Fiction* (1925). But, apart from that, they never published any more of her novels and story-collections. Charles Scribner never quite got over the divorce, and in 1921, still hoping to capture 'future novels', he wrote sadly: 'The loss of your books was the greatest blow ever given to my pride as publisher.' 'I am always glad to have my name associated with that of my first publishers', she returned in kind, later that year, giving them *A Son at the Front*. She continued to have a friendly, business-like relationship with him and his son, and the editor who succeeded Burlingame at the magazine, Robert Bridges, over matters such as the essays on fiction, a new introduction for a Modern Library edition of *Ethan*, or an unauthorised translation of *Ethan*, showing no let-up in the vigour they had come to expect from her, as here: 'I quite agree with you that a law-suit would be a very wasteful amusement, and should be perfectly satisfied if you could terrify the publisher sufficiently to extract $100 from him.' Charles Scribner's son, discussing plans for an 'omnibus' edition of her stories with her in 1936, told her that 'my father felt very keenly the unfortunate differences which led to your going to another publisher and often spoke to me about it'. Wharton, remorselessly divorcing her gentlemanly publisher, does seem to have behaved a little like Undine Spragg. (There would be more such changes made later in her life. She stayed loyal to Macmillan's until, in the 1920s, Appleton set up a London office for distribution, whereupon she finally left her old English publishing-house. And she would eventually become dissatisfied with Appleton, after decades of good professional relations with Rutger Jewett.) It seems ironically fitting that Appleton's advertising campaign for *The Age of Innocence* used, in bold letters at the top of their flyer, the tag: **'Was She Justified In Seeking A Divorce?'**[43]

*

Nothing tender, fragile, or wistful came out of this difficult period of Wharton's life. Quite the opposite: with many stops and starts, and a final rush of amazing energy, between 1907 and 1913 she wrote her most ruthless, harsh and ebullient novel, *The Custom of the Country*. It is utterly unautobiographical, though traces of her life are in it everywhere. It acts out an exploitative selfishness she did not have, but also her own determination and forcefulness.[44] It is a great imaginative performance and a triumph of authorial control.

Custom draws on her own time, place and situation: it is about Americans in New York and France, a story of unhappy marriage and divorce, set over a period of about twelve years at the turn of the century. But its main character looks nothing like Edith Wharton. The splendidly named Undine Spragg is an extremely beautiful young woman from a Midwestern city called Apex, the daughter of a wealthy self-made businessman, Abner Spragg. As a very young girl, Undine has been briefly involved with a coarse young man from God-knows-where, Elmer Moffatt, an alliance her parents put a stop to, before Moffatt went on to make his way east and carve out an immense fortune. Equally ambitious, Undine wants to put her provincial lower-class origins behind her and to pioneer her way into 'swell' society. Like a barbarian invader, she makes a successful assault on 'Old New York', in the person of the sensitive Ralph Marvell, son of a genteel family. She marries him and has a son. But Undine finds that her ambition to reign in New York is thwarted by her husband's quiet tastes and lack of commercial drive. She has cast her lot with a 'fallen cause',[45] when she wanted to be in the world of high-spending fashion and new money. Undine climbs over the people she has made use of, abandons her little boy, Paul, and moves on to an international social life in pursuit of a millionaire playboy, Peter Van Degen, whom she takes as a lover. But she makes the tactical mistake of divorcing Ralph before she has secured Van Degen as her next husband. Ralph, broken, disillusioned and ineffectual, does not contest the divorce or gain legal custody of his son, though he is looking after him.

After a phase of dissatisfied obscurity, Undine, languishing on the Riviera, becomes an object of desire to Raymond de Chelles, a French count from an old Catholic family. She sets out to have her marriage to Ralph annulled, and barters with him for the return of her son. (She wants him to pay her off, so that she can afford the annulment.) Ralph tries to raise money to keep Paul, by investing in a scheme proposed to him by Elmer Moffatt, now a figure to be reckoned with. But the scheme does not succeed; and at the same time he discovers (as the reader may have guessed) that Elmer Moffatt and Undine were once married. In a state of near-delirium and emotional exhaustion, Ralph shoots himself. His suicide helps Undine to marry the count, since a widow is not so appalling to the de Chelles family as a divorcee. After his death, Ralph's investment delivers a fortune for Undine's little boy, who is returned to his mother.

But Undine's marriage to the Comte de Chelles goes badly. She is baffled by his family's customs, and finds that her husband does not intend to gratify her social ambitions. What money he has goes into the upkeep of his estate in Burgundy. Raymond becomes bored with his beautiful but uncultured American wife, and begins to amuse himself elsewhere, in the French fashion. She finds herself shut up in the countryside with his disapproving family. Her attempt to sell the family tapestries for some ready cash sparks off a crisis between them. She flees the marriage and goes back to Moffatt, who acquires her out of old Apex sympathies, but also out of a canny collector's instinct for a perfect trophy wife. The rapid marriage and lavish international life-style of the Moffatts is seen, finally, through the eyes of Paul, Undine's neglected and sensitive little boy. But Undine Moffatt is still not satisfied: as a divorcee, she learns on the last page of the novel, she can never be an ambassador's wife.

Custom is not only about acquisition and ambition. It is what Undine destroys, as much as what she acquires, that interests us. Victory and defeat, triumph and failure, are bound together throughout. We can read her as a victim of the system as well as a successful product of it.[46] Her French rebuff is a brilliant coda: it clinches the devastating cultural analysis that Wharton is making of Undine as a national product, 'an American woman'.[47] Henry James (who was wickedly quick to note the resemblances between Edith and Undine) wished that Undine's experience of '*la Vieille France*' hadn't been so '*sommaire*', so packed into the last section.[48] But James was wrong: the heart of this heartless novel is Undine's destruction of Ralph, and what that story implies about American culture and society.

Custom looks expansive, like a nineteenth-century novel. Balzac, Thackeray, Trollope, even Dickens, come to mind. (It is as often compared to *Vanity Fair* as to Dreiser's *Sister Carrie*: both novels she admired.) It has huge amounts of dialogue and lavish amounts of decoration and social texture. Wharton gives a rather rapid account of Undine's pre-New York settings, like the hotel in Apex, the Mealey House, with its 'tessellated floors, plush parlours and organ-like radiators'. But no detail is missing of Undine's New York; the florid interiors of the monumental West Side hotels ranged up Central Park West (the Spraggs' is called the 'Stentorian'), from where Undine looks longingly across the Park towards fashionable Fifth Avenue and the East Side; the shimmer and glitter of the opera in high season (not the old Academy of Music which will feature in *The Age of Innocence* but the new Metropolitan on Broadway, Seventh Avenue and 40th Street); the faded gentility of Ralph's sister's little house on 38th Street 'down below Park Avenue', or his grandfather Dagonet's Dutch brownstone on Washington Square; Central Park in March, where the Ramble is a good place for a secret assignation; the harsh new landscape of Wall Street, reached via subway or elevated railway, where the towering office-blocks with their marble vestibules and 'express elevators' contain thousands of tiny, dingy offices like Mr Spragg's, looking onto 'a sooty perspective barred with chimneys'.[49] Looming offstage is the phenomenal expansion of Apex City (a Kansas City or a Chicago) from rural backwater to industrial and political power-house.

In Europe, the landscapes are painted both as Undine sees them and as they might look to others. So her grumpy dissatisfaction with Ralph's choice of honeymoon in Italy in hot summer (Undine leaning against a tree-trunk in an ilex grove in the hills near Siena 'with the slightly constrained air of a person unused to sylvan abandonments' is a wonderfully incongruous figure) is set against Ralph's pleasure in the magical sights of Tuscany. Undine's delight in the 'glare and movement' of the Paris of the Nouveau Luxe is undermined by Charles Bowen (the novel's essential spectator-philosopher) and his severe view of the 'promiscuity and incoherence' of its 'phantom "society"'. Once Undine gets into 'real' France, she is at a loss. The select Riviera health-spa she tries out depresses her by being so small, colourless and quiet. Her induction into the distinguished private life of the Faubourg, in the 'high-walled houses beyond the Seine which she had once thought so dull and dingy', pits her appetite for expenditure and show against the age-old economies that govern arrangements in the Hôtel de Chelles, that 'fine old mouldering house' with its sitting tenants and shared family quarters. Undine in the de Chelles family home in Burgundy, the Château de Saint-Désert – a great set-piece – feels incarcerated inside the park, the moat, the long corridors, the endless unchanging routines: 'Everything in the great empty house smelt of dampness: the stuffing of the chairs, the threadbare folds of the faded curtains, the splendid tapestries, that were fading too . . .' Nothing could be in sharper contrast than the garish grandeur of the Moffatts' newly acquired Parisian *hôtel*, as fabulously opulent as the house they have built on '5009 Fifth Avenue' (fantastically far uptown!) 'an exact copy of the Pitti Palace, Florence'. Architecture and the decoration of houses stand in throughout (as always in Wharton) for morality and personal values, from Ralph Marvell's meditation on the style of the old house in Washington Square as a representation of the 'inner consciousness' of its inhabitants, to the metaphor used for Raymond de Chelles's habits of mind: 'There was no more hope of shaking his resolve or altering his point of view than there would have been of transporting the deep-rooted masonry of Saint-Désert by means of the wheeled supports on which Apex architecture performed its easy transits.'[50]

As befits the story of a material girl, this novel is packed with goods and spoils, furniture and decor, clothes and jewellery. But for all Undine's prag-matic greed, it is not things in themselves she wants, but what they can do for her or show her to be. She is always altering things or casting things off: the 'old family ring' of sapphires Ralph gave her on their engagement, which she has reset, entirely unconscious of the 'wound she inflicted' in so doing; the pearls she gets from her lover, which her father (puritanical in private though not in business matters) tells her to give back, but which she sells for profit; the tapestries she finally acquires through Moffatt's stupendous wealth, but which, on the walls of the ballroom of their hastily purchased Parisian *hôtel*, somehow look 'smaller'. All through the novel there are mirrors in which Undine likes to catch sight of herself, and bunches of clippings from gossip columns and scandal sheets, carried about in the bag of the masseuse and manicurist Mrs Heeny (a benign social para-site and Dickensian comic turn), reflecting the public notoriety of Undine's private life.[51]

But this lavish display of paraphernalia is misleading. There is nothing excessive or sprawling about *Custom*: it is a tightly themed, highly controlled book. This is all the more striking, given that she was still writing it while it was being serialised in *Scribner's Magazine* (alongside material which now looks much more dated than *Custom*: a novel by Galsworthy, *The Dark Flower*, stories and poems by lady writers including Katherine Fullerton Gerould, and essays on such topics as the survivors of the *Titanic* and Charles Eliot Norton's English friendships, co-authored by Sara Norton). Wharton's revisions between publication as a serial and as a book – minute, but continual – are all in the interests of toning-down any romantic magazine-touches and making the whole thing drier. So, in the seduction scene between Undine and Van Degen, she cuts lines like 'He laughed and took her in his arms', or 'What the devil do you suppose I'm made of?' In the scene where Ralph, for the first time, resists Undine's physical charms, the magazine version is more emphatic, so a line like 'he was not conscious of resentment or revolt, but only of a kind of blank absence of feeling', is cut in the book. *Custom* betrays its origins as a serial with some suspenseful chapter-endings, like Ralph's suicide, or Undine's gamble to keep Peter Van

Degen: 'I'll do anything in God's world to keep you . . . !' (*To be continued* . . .). But, for all those dramatic underlinings, the plot is subtly managed. Since, as the narrator tells us, 'the turnings of life seldom show a sign-post; or rather, though the sign is always there, it is usually placed some distance back', many of the crisis-points are shown through retrospects. Some key scenes are cunningly saved up right to the end, like Undine's memoirs of her first involvement with Elmer in Apex City, or little Paul's desolating view of his mother's life. Wharton's working notes for *Custom* show her carefully planning each stage of the story, as here: 'Important [*in red*]: In chap.38 introduce change in Raymond's mentality after he inherits estate. Incomprehensible to Undine. His influence on Undine developed. The talk diverges to indirect narrative – a gradual irresistible outpouring like Mrs Spragg's to Ralph. Undine's whole mental atmosphere completely transformed by his mere presence.'[52]

This powerful narrative has a relentless theme. The words wanting, getting, having, are repeated over and over. 'She was going to know the right people at last – she was going to get what she wanted.' (But her father notes: 'You only want most things once, Undine.') Engaged to Ralph, 'now at last she was having what she wanted – she was in conscious possession of the real thing'. Married to de Chelles, 'at last she had what she wanted'. The phrase gets tangled up in her reaction to Ralph's death, which had 'given her what she wanted; yet she could honestly say to herself that she had not wanted him to die – at least not to die like that . . . she continued to wish that she could have got what she wanted without having had to pay that particular price for it'. In her reunions with Elmer Moffatt, the phrase repeats like the pounding of a hammer. He says to her: 'I hope you've got what you wanted.' She has always valued him, because 'Undine's estimate of people had always been based on their apparent power of getting what they wanted – provided it came under the category of things she understood wanting'. Her French training, however frustrating, has, she believes, improved her powers of wanting: 'She knew her wants so much better now, and was so much more worthy of the things she wanted!' But she can never be satisfied: 'She had everything she wanted, but she still felt, at times, that there were other things she might want if she knew about them.'[53]

Undine puts out her hand to get what she wants, from the first page of the novel, when she 'possesses herself' of her invitation to dinner with 'a turn of her quick young fingers'. Her hand is always referred to in the singular. Ralph notes that though it is smooth, small, dimpled, soft and rosy, her fingers 'were inelastic and did not spring back far', the 'pink palm' will not open. He comes to think of it as a 'miserly hand'. When he realises she is 'a creature of only skin-deep reactions', it is her hand that he rereads: 'Its surface-language had been sweet enough, but under the rosy lines he had seen the warning letters.'[54]

Undine says things like 'I want the best', or 'I want what the others want'. Her idea of 'the best' is entirely social. It involves 'going round' with the most 'swell' and 'stylish' people. In her 'baffled social yearnings' she is always trying to work out who the most 'stylish' people *are*. She keeps having to readjust her sights. She is embarrassed by the social blunders she makes on the way up (like going out in a Virginia resort with a dental assistant from Deposit), and tries to put them behind her. She is a fast learner, supremely 'imitative' and 'attentive', who quickly realises that '*It is better to watch than to ask questions*'. She has a talent for becoming 'the person she thought her interlocutors expected her to be'. But she is also 'fiercely independent', at once malleable and inflexible, attentive and obtuse, quick to acquire other people's standards but convinced of her own rights. Her social strategies are always envious and competitive. Even in disgrace she wants to 'make herself seen', and in triumph she wants admiration – hence all the mirrors. She recognises (as one critic has observed) that 'to be an object of envy drives up one's value as an object of desire'.[55]

Like Lily Bart, Undine Spragg is moved by an idea of 'beyond'. But their concepts of 'beyond' are opposites. Lily's is a visionary somewhere, finer than the world that contains her. (All readers of Edith Wharton know that there is, really, no such place.) Undine's 'beyond' is a material something: 'more luxurious, more exciting, more worthy of her!' But there are many things she does not know what to do with once she has got them. She does not want culture, though she wants to show that she has taste (quickly learning, for instance, that it is better to use plain white notepaper than the pigeon-blood-coloured, monogrammed stuff she first favours). She has no education. We never find out what she learned at her Midwestern boarding-school, and we wonder whether her French ever gets much beyond her reference to Sarah Bernhardt's appearance in 'what she pronounced "Fade"'. She only reads romance novels, 'society fiction', gossip columns and self-improvement tips (and, when she is depressed or ill, advertisements for patent medicines, diets and horoscopes). Wharton comes down as hard on Undine's fiction-reading as any eighteenth-century moralist inveighing against the corrupting effects of light novels on young girls. The (unspecified) bad novels Undine devours as a girl in Apex, or is lent in New York, or passes the time with, waiting for her divorce in Dakota, are seen to bolster her vulgarity and self-interest: she is always justifying her own behaviour as if she were the heroine of one of *those* novels, not this one. Her idea of Ralph's writing as a career, is limited to the possibility that literature could be 'fashionable': 'She already saw herself as the wife of a celebrated author, wearing "artistic" dresses and doing the drawing-room over with Gothic tapestries and dim lights in altar candle-sticks.'[56]

Undine's lack of culture shows up at its worst, of course, in Paris. After admiring her beauty, everyone finds her boring. 'Her entrances were always triumphs, but they had no sequels.' As Madame de Trézac (once Nettie Wincher from Virginia), her more successfully assimilated American confidante, tells her: 'You're as handsome as ever; but people here don't go on looking at each other forever as they do in London.'[57] Unlike us, Undine does not find this funny: she lacks a sense of humour. She never laughs, and she does not do irony.

She does not want love, either. She has a very limited capacity for warm feeling, and it is made clear that she does not love any of her partners – though she thinks Ralph is 'sweet' and is fond of de Chelles to begin with. They are all acquisitions. That is why she loses them: even the besotted Peter Van Degen is scared off by her heartlessness, when he finds out that she ruthlessly ignored the news of Ralph's illness in order to have a good time. Her women-friends are all to be made use of, and she is chilly with her little boy – in one compelling scene she forgets his birthday because she is having her portrait painted and going for a drive with Van Degen. And she has no love at all – their dark, angry scenes together are superbly done – for her cowed and feeble mother. Though Undine has four marriages, three divorces, a child and an affair, and though she knows how to use the slant of her lips and eyelids, her little pink hands, the curve of her neck and the glory of her hair to make herself seductive, she remains curiously virginal. (That partly explains why Ralph is taken in by her.) One of the novel's main themes is that American women of this kind are childish and infantile, always expecting to be looked after, as by their fathers. This childishness goes with a kind of innocence. Undine frequently blushes, and does not like sexual innuendo. Her 'Apex puritanism' and the legacy of a preacher-grandfather are always coming to the surface. What she wants is not scandal and adventure, but 'amusement and respectability'. So do her Midwestern counterparts, like Indiana Rolliver (née Frusk), who complains bitterly about 'those nasty French plays': 'I've told Mr Rolliver I won't go to the theatre with him again in Paris – it's too utterly low. And the swell society's just as bad: it's simply rotten. Thank goodness I was brought up in a place where there's some sense of decency left!'

Undine, similarly, prefers to ignore 'disgusting scandals' about women in high society. Her affair with Van Degen is a strategic gamble on her part, not a sexual adventure, and she dislikes the shady society she has to keep, after that, as a divorcee and adulteress. She bitterly resents being made use of in the clandestine affair of Raymond de Chelles's bohemian aristocratic cousin, Lili Estradina, the novel's most enticing minor character (a Madame de Treymes, kept in the margins here), who in one sentence is seen to be infinitely more passionate and sexy than Undine: 'She confessed to Undine that she was drawn to Nice by the presence there of the person without whom, for the moment, she found life intolerable.' By contrast, it is strongly implied that Undine is sexually frigid. Ralph finds in her, in response to his embraces, 'the coolness of the element from which she took her name'. Her hottest moments are her childish rages and bursts of hatred (the words 'violent' and 'primitive' are often used of her) and her 'throbbing' excitement at being at the centre of a glittering social display. Her sexiest relationship is with her father, whom she presses up close to and lavishes with flirtatious kisses when she wants something from him. It is suggested, as strongly as Wharton could put it in 1913, that Undine kills desire in all her sexual partners, and that both Ralph Marvell and Raymond de Chelles stop sleeping with her when they find out what she is like.[58]

Custom can be read as a dark fairy-tale, with Undine as a Cinderella who takes the ball by storm, or a Fisherman's Wife who is never contented with what she has. She is a kind of Galatea, turning on her Pygmalion. Her name comes from a nineteenth-century German novella (which became a popular opera and ballet), about a water-nymph who becomes a human but lacks a soul, who dooms the human she marries, and turns back into a nymph. Undine, though, is unaware of this association – she was named, Mrs Spragg explains to Ralph, after a hair-waver marketed by Mr Spragg. Ralph at first thinks Undine as enchanting as her name, but he ought to have taken it as a warning, especially as it evokes for him Montaigne's phrase about human nature being '*divers et ondoyant*', as unstable as the waves of the sea. He thinks of Undine as Andromeda, though she turns out to be more like Medusa. Unfortunately for him, the legendary figure he fails to associate with Undine is Lamia, the snake-turned-woman in Keats's poem, who is clearly in Wharton's mind (as Keats was for *Ethan Frome*). She marked the poem in one of her editions of Keats, and she quoted it in a late essay for its 'stealing sense of flesh-and-blood reality in a dream-world'. Undine has a serpentine shape, glittering eyes, a long neck, and is always 'doubling and twisting on herself'. Her hair catches in the 'spangles of the wrap' behind her when she is casting her enchantment on

Ralph, and he has to free 'the captive mesh'; so Lamia, with her starry tiara and spangled colours, tangles Lycius in her 'mesh'. When Undine is having her portrait painted, the 'dead white' of the 'long curve of her neck' and the 'hard glitter' of her look is like the 'deadly white' of Lamia's face when stared at by the cold philosopher. The 'sinister change' that comes over Undine when her will is crossed, and her eyes become 'like those of an enemy' is like Lamia's blinded and blinding stare as she is turning back into a snake: 'There was no recognition in those orbs.' *Custom* has its own cold philosopher in the clever, dry, observant personality of Charles Bowen, and its own doomed, dreamy Lycius-figure, Ralph, who dies from his entanglement with the snake-woman, and who, Wharton said, was meant to be seen as her predestined victim.[59]

Custom's dark fairy-tale strand shadows a harshly realistic novel about finance and business. Wharton cunningly combines both modes. Part of Undine's infantilism (in Wharton's punitive diagnosis) is that she wants what money can buy, but refuses to understand how it is made. The novel analyses the apparent separation, but actual parallels, between 'Fifth Avenue and Wall Street': the world of women's show and expenditure, and the world of male money-making. As in *The House of Mirth*, Wharton's thesis is closely based on Veblen's social anthropology of the American leisure classes. In a long, rather too explicit commentary, Charles Bowen gives Ralph's sister his own 'theory of the leisure-classes'. The American woman is kept separate from her husband's business-affairs because, in his heart, he 'looks down on his wife'; his real passion is for making money. That is the difference between American marriages and European ones where the wife is an equal and business-partner. (The same analysis is found in *French Ways and their Meaning*.) In America, Bowen argues, women take revenge on their 'preoccupied males' by lavish expenditure – and frequent divorces. That is 'the custom of the country', and Undine is the 'monstrously perfect result of the system'. Her marriage to de Chelles goes wrong because of her utter lack of understanding of, and interest in, his financial affairs, which makes him sideline her and treat her like a child even before he begins to despise her.[60]

Undine may be ignorant of business matters, but she also embodies the forces of capitalism. She works on the basis of expediency, not sentiment. Her dominant characteristic is seen as a 'business-like intentness on gaining her end'. Personal life is expressed in terms of the fluctuations of the stock market: characters have their exchange-value and their market-price. The divorced Undine is described as having 'diminished trading capacity'. Everyone – even characters with some moral integrity, like Abner Spragg and Ralph Marvell – has their price and can be bought. Repeated analogies are made between Undine's personal gambles and Wall Street 'strokes' or business ventures. Every so often Wharton pushes the financial exploits which underpin Undine's story into the foreground, in a series of masterly dialogues between men in their Wall Street offices. This could have been a different kind of novel – Theodore Dreiser, Frank Norris or William Dean Howells might have written it – about the rise and fall of tycoons, the increase in dubious practice in American business life, the connection between Midwestern urban development, the take-over of East Coast society by new money, and the political dominance of business interests in Washington.[61]

If that version were foregrounded, it would start with Abner Spragg as a working-class boy, marrying into a poor family in Apex, and trying out several careers – undertaker, religious minister, drugstore owner, land speculator – on his way to a fortune. Two of Spragg's three children die in a typhoid epidemic, and so he becomes involved in a move to bring 'Pure Water' to his city. He accepts some worthless land from his father-in-law in payment for a bad debt, and sells it at a big profit to the Apex Water Company, for building a reservoir. In these 'epic days', he joins forces with a local politician, James Rolliver. Abner moves to New York to advance his daughter Undine's social ambitions and to get her away from Elmer Moffatt. But Elmer's fortunes outpace Abner Spragg's. First he 'edges his way into the power-house of the Apex Water-Works', then (like the Nietzschean young man in Wharton's 1910 story, 'The Blond Beast') he is hired as private secretary to another Apex businessman, Hiram B. Driscoll, to whom he has given 'an inside tip on the Eubaw mine deal'. Driscoll wants to buy up all the 'commodities' in Apex City, and will stop at nothing: 'Now they've got all the street railroads in their pockets they want the water-supply too.' All these rival members of the Apex consortium have moved to New York and have their headquarters in the 'Ararat' Trust Building. (The name invokes Noah's flood, wiping out a corrupt civilisation.) Driscoll is competing with Rolliver, whose dubious business practices are well known to Abner Spragg. (Driscoll and Rolliver, two big beasts of the novel's business world, are both kept offstage.) Elmer blackmails Abner to 'shop' Rolliver to Driscoll, in return for Elmer's silence about having been married to Undine. (The portrait of Daniel Webster in Abner's office, and the Masonic emblem on his watch-chain, point at a vanished probity in American public life.) The way is cleared for Undine's marriage to Ralph, a deal brokered on Wall Street.

Shady dealings inside the Ararat Trust Building come to light, prompting a national inquiry. Moffatt, seeing an opportunity for another step up, turns on his old patron Driscoll and exposes him. But Driscoll wins this round, and Moffatt drops temporarily out of circulation (exactly like Undine in between marriages). Still, he gains a considerable reputation for having defied Driscoll in 'the great Ararat Trust fight', and New York society starts paying attention to him. Ralph, who is trying to earn his living in a real-estate office, is overawed by 'the dim underworld of affairs where men of the Moffatt and Driscoll type move like shadowy destructive monsters beneath the darting small fry of the surface'.

Driscoll is again threatened with indictment, and bribes Elmer Moffatt (just as Elmer has bribed Abner Spragg) not to testify against him. Elmer uses the bribe to build, rapidly, a vast fortune based on stock-market speculations, and makes a new alliance with Rolliver. (Rolliver, meanwhile, has divorced his wife at huge expense to marry Undine's old Apex companion, Indiana Frusk. The parallel between business alliances and divorce transactions is emphatic.) The Midwestern politician and tycoon plan to 'buy up all the works of public utility at Apex' and to get 'the Apex charter'. Ralph's attempt to buy off Undine's claim to her son is swept up into this deal. The Rolliver/Moffatt bid is thwarted by 'reformers' (acting against these huge corrupt monopolies), and Ralph fails to get his investment back in time. The story of Undine and Ralph again turns out to be dependent on a Wall Street deal.

Ralph kills himself, but 'The Apex consolidation' gets its charter, Moffatt and Rolliver triumph over Driscoll, and Elmer bounces back as one of the millionaire moguls and collectors of his time, a 'robber baron' like J.P. Morgan or John D. Rockefeller or Andrew Carnegie. 'I own pretty near the whole of Apex', he tells Undine. In one of the tight coincidences Wharton enjoys in this novel, Moffatt turns up at Saint-Désert (brought there by a swarthy Jewish businessman, Mr Fleischhauer, an unpleasant characterisation), looking to buy the family tapestries for his 'private car'. He gets his politician Rolliver into Congress ('I've got to have somebody up in Washington') – and the son of his old rival Driscoll ends up as American ambassador to London. Elmer's and Undine's business and marital careers run parallel, though Moffatt (like Simon Rosedale in *The House of Mirth*) is more sympathetic than the reader expects. Like Undine he is a vulgarian, a social climber and an opportunist, and like her he is out to get what he wants. But he is never a childish fantasist: he deals in 'facts', and his mind is like a 'great steel strong-box'. And he has a discriminating pleasure in fine things and beautiful places, and a capacity for warm feeling, shown in his tenderness for Paul Marvell.[62]

Wharton binds her plot in so tight to make the reader feel that there is no escape. There is no place in American society and politics uncorrupted by the exploitation and expansionism of American corporate culture – truly this is a tale for our times – and Undine's life-story shows how those business standards have infiltrated all aspects of American life. Wharton puts all her mixed feelings about the country she has left into this novel. (Not for nothing are the heroine's initials 'U.S.'.) It mounts a vigorous satire on American language. The novel is full of parodies of commercial writing – romance novels, gossip-columns, divorce announcements, adverts for private detective firms, all swamping Ralph's attempts to write something imaginatively truthful.[63] Undine, who only reads that kind of literature, has her own raw eloquence, which Wharton does in bursts of violent free indirect speech:

> She had always, when it came to that, done what her father and mother wanted, but she'd given up trying to make out what they were after, unless it was to make her miserable; and if that was it, hadn't they enough of it by this time? She had, anyhow. But after this she meant to lead her own life; and they needn't ask her where she was going, or what she meant to do, because this time she'd die before she told them – and they'd made life so hateful to her that she only wished she was dead already.

Though she is incapable of writing letters, Undine is 'never at a loss for the spoken word' (Ralph wonders if she has inherited a trace of a 'preaching grandfather's oratory'). Her raw speech is set against the civilised talk of the startled Dagonets and Marvells, listening in 'pained astonishment' as Undine (rather like Eliza Doolittle) holds forth about divorce: 'He isn't in the right set, and I think Mabel realizes she'll never really get anywhere till she gets rid of him.' The clash between Ralph's fine aspirations and Undine's pragmatism is done through perfectly contrasted dialogue ('I haven't shown you Lecceto yet; and the drive back by moonlight would be glorious' . . . 'It might be nice – but where could we get anything to eat?'). Even when Undine's rough edges have been smoothed, her singular tone persists: blithe, flat, banal, and unconsciously funny: 'It was dreadful that her little boy should be growing up far away from her, perhaps dressed in clothes she would have hated.'[64]

The book is full of loudly distinctive voices: Van Degen's masculine slang ('You ought to be painted yourself – no, I mean it, you know you ought to get old Popple to do you. He'd do your hair rippingly'), Popple's phoney romantic clichés with the ladies ('The memory of her words would thereafter hallow his life'), Mrs Spragg's 'dialect' ('He was always a beautiful speaker, and after a while he sorter drifted into the ministry'), the Dagonets' genteel 'vocabulary of evasion' ('All I ask is that you won't mention the subject to your grandfather . . .'), Elmer's forceful plain speech ('Look here, Undine, if I'm to have you again I don't want to have you that way'), and de Chelles's stylish French-in-translation, which to Undine is 'a strange language'. No wonder that Wharton's transatlantic passengers in this novel sail on the *Semantic*.[65]

Speech is the most vivid way of getting at class, and *Custom* is all about class and snobbery.[66] Wharton draws precise distinctions between the different social groups – the old New York family descended from 'signers' (of the Declaration of Independence), the getters and spenders of the new fortunes made on the stock market, the working businessmen, the continental drifters, the French aristocracy – even as she describes the merging of social demarcations. The plumber's daughter from the Midwestern town becomes a Congressman's wife; the society the Dagonets wish to control cares nothing about them, and their prejudices are like 'sign-posts warning off trespassers who have long since ceased to intrude'.

Undine is herself a tremendous snob, expressing great resentment at de Chelles's brother marrying an American girl called Looty Arlington he met at a skating-rink ('She must be horribly common'), aware that 'in the Marvell set Elmer Moffatt would have been stamped as "not a gentleman"', and, after her stupendous remarriage to him, coming to criticise 'his loudness and redness, his misplaced joviality, his familiarity with the servants' and 'his habit of leaving old newspapers about the drawing room'.[67] Undine is like her author, in feeling that there are such things as social gradations, but she is mocked for needing to learn them and for minding so much about 'social superiority'. So her snobbishness is the target of Wharton's own snobbery. Wharton speaks aggressively of her heroine's 'voracious ambitions' and 'impatient greed', her 'violent desires and cold tenacity'. But it is too simple to say that *Custom* snobbishly caricatures the new mixture of classes in twentieth-century America, given Wharton's treatment of her own class, the Dagonet/Marvell 'tribe'. She is scornful of the older, ineffectual members of that tribe – Ralph's grandfather and mother (a milder version than usual of Lucretia Jones), and the conventional girl he was supposed to marry. Ralph Marvell is Undine's easy prey because he is 'a survival, and destined, as such, to go down in any conflict with the rising forces'. Though Ralph starts the novel by thinking, of his old-fashioned tribe, that 'They're right – after all, in some ways they're right', he ends by feeling that their 'aboriginal customs' ('doomed to rapid extinction with the advance of the invading race') have also doomed him. He wanted to be 'modern', but he is held back by his inherited customs, and sees himself, by the end, 'stumbling about in his inherited prejudices like a modern man in medieval armour'.[68]

On the novel's big issue of divorce, the Dagonet/Marvell clan are hopelessly out-of-date. Bowen's cynical commentary treats the high rate of divorce in America as the inevitable outcome of the immaturity of American marriage. (The ladies of the Faubourg concur: "'She's an American – she's divorced", the Duchess replied, as if she were merely stating the same fact in two different ways.') Ralph's family's horror at divorce as a stain on their honour, to be concealed, is seen to be just as inadequate as the Midwestern girls' matter-of-fact acceptance of it ('Well – now you've got your divorce: anybody else it would come in handy for?'). Clare Van Degen's attitude to divorce as 'a vulgar and unnecessary way of taking the public into one's confidence' has some authorial support, and matches the novel's disgusted treatment of detective agencies, newspaper headlines about marital scandals, and 'quickie' divorces and remarriages in the new states. Wharton disapproves of divorce as a 'custom of the country'. But, unlike her own 'aboriginal' New Yorkers, she is unshockable and realistic about it.[69]

And she does not identify at all with the old family's attitude to the new democracy. There is admiration for Elmer Moffatt, the man from nowhere who carves a ruling place for himself out of what he has got for himself and not out of inherited privilege or wealth, and for the drive to win which is built into the democratic system. Elmer and Undine can break through in ways which old-style Anglophile New York, or hierarchical France, would prefer to resist. Democracy allows for social change, and also produces snobbery and social envy because everyone feels entitled to rise above their neighbours, and then look down on them. Wharton appreciates these impulses, pouring her fictional energy into the characters of Elmer and Undine, but she also scorns them, as in de Chelles's ferocious attack on American social mobility: 'You come from hotels as big as towns, and from towns as flimsy as paper, where the streets haven't had time to be named, and the buildings are demolished before they're dry, and the people are as proud of changing as we are of holding to what we have.' Though Wharton is writing about social flux, she is unable to abandon a concept of 'society' as some kind of recognisable stable entity. The word keeps coming up: in Ralph's critique of the hollow society of continental drifters, in Charles Bowen's view, watching the Americans in the Nouveau Luxe, of a 'phantom' society 'with all the rules, smirks, gestures of its model, but evoked out of promiscuity and incoherence while the other had been the product of continuity and choice'. There *is* such a thing as 'society', it is suggested, even while we watch it implode.[70]

The 'phantom' society of high-spending Americans in France looks very thin and brash when set against the novel's slice of French life. Wharton savagely indicts American cultural imperialism through its relationship with France. Undine is an American girl who believes ardently in her individual and personal 'rights', as opposed to the French family she marries into, who believe in traditional and communal obligations. She feels she is in Europe to take what she wants, not to learn: 'I don't believe an American woman needs to know such a lot about their old rules.' In her view it is almost a duty for 'an American woman' *not* to familiarise herself with 'the custom of the country', especially when it might be a threat to her native innocence.

Wharton's satire on Undine and her nouveau riche compatriots as glittering predators buying up Paris plays as dazzling social comedy. But when 'poor Undine' (as she is referred to once) is set down in Saint-Désert, the tone changes. Her despairing boredom almost makes us like her. The satire is certainly not all one way. As the ladies sit on the terrace with their needlework, and 'the curé or one of the visiting uncles read aloud the *Journal des Débats* and prognosticated dark things of the Republic', and 'the long succession of uneventful days' unrolls with 'benumbing sameness', we feel for Undine's horror at the thought that nothing will ever change here, sympathise with her childish attempts to provoke her mother-in-law the marquise, and share her alarmed sensation that 'people she had never seen and whose names she couldn't even remember seemed to be plotting and contriving against her under the escutcheoned grave-stones of Saint Désert'. Wharton understands her isolated 'American woman' in France. (She even gives Undine her own youthful nickname, 'Puss'.) She too might not want to live her whole life at Saint-Désert, even though she suggests that Undine (like George Sand going back to Nohant) is enriched, if unconsciously, by the 'spell' emanating from 'the old house which had so long been the custodian of an unbroken tradition'.[71] But the moment of enrichment passes, and (to our relief as well as Undine's), she goes back to her American partner.

It seems clear where Wharton stands in this novel. She believed in an old-fashioned idea of society as an entity with distinction and some moral function, and was appalled by its decomposition. But this view of Wharton as a snobbish critic of what she has invented does not allow for the relish, energy and appetite with which she plunges into the invention of Undine, or the feeling of sympathy we are allowed to have for Undine in her French marriage. And it does not do justice to Wharton's passionate interest in the idea of getting what you want, or the formidable bleakness of her whole enterprise. Underneath all the comic spectacle of *The Custom of the Country*, there is a grim sense of the forces that grind down human aspirations, whatever class or society they belong to. Wharton does not call these forces 'the Furies' or 'the Eumenides' here, as she does elsewhere, but they certainly have nothing to do with religion. (*Custom* is an irreligious book: Undine puts on Catholicism like a new frock, and her native Protestantism is a social, not a spiritual, attribute. Ralph's form of worship is aesthetic, Raymond's is formalist and traditional.) The forces in play here are relentless, destructive and impersonal. What kind of fiction can best deal with them? Ralph Marvell starts off his literary aspirations as a lyric or tragic romanticist; he ends up as a turn-of-the-century American determinist or 'naturalist', writing ironic fiction in which 'men look no bigger than the insects they were'. (He does acquire, though, the conviction that Wharton so much admired in Goethe and George Eliot, that 'his individual task was a necessary part of the world's machinery'.) Her vision of this 'machinery' is a remorseless one. Occasionally the dressed-up surface of the world is peeled away, and we see the inner workings. Ralph, recovering from his illness, observes the machine at work in the clouds: 'All his past life seemed to be symbolized by the building-up and breaking-down of those fluctuating shapes, which incalculable wind-currents perpetually shifted and remodelled or swept from the zenith like a pinch of dust.' Undine is only aware of it when, dispirited, she finds that the seductive murmur of Paris suddenly rings hollow: 'The immense murmur still sounded on, deafening and implacable as some elemental force; and the discord in her fate no more disturbed it than the motor wheels rolling by under the windows were disturbed by the particles of dust that they ground to finer powder as they passed.' The grinding of the machine sounds at its loudest when Ralph, in despair, and at the end of his life, makes his commuter's journey through the Waste Land of New York, from the heat of Wall Street, where he notices 'the swirls of dust in the cracks of the pavement, the rubbish in the gutters, the ceaseless stream of perspiring faces', onto the modern subway, with 'the nasal yelp of the stations ringing through the car like some repeated ritual wail'.[72] At last he has become a truly modern man, alienated in a mechanical world. And the world around him comes down to, and ends up as, nothing but dust.

14

Fighting France

Towards the end of 1913, Edith Wharton recorded a nightmare. She was in England, staying at Howard Sturgis's house, negotiating to buy Coopersale. *Custom* was just out; her friends were remarking on how difficult and restless and lonely she seemed; Walter Berry was involved with one of his married ladies, Elsie Goelet; Henry James was finding her troubling and alarming. This was her dream:

> My dream. Queens Acre, October 1913. *This was a real dream.*
>
> A pale demon with black hair came in, followed by four black gnome-like creatures carrying a great black trunk. They set it down and opened it, and the Demon crying out: 'Here's your year – here are all the horrors that have happened to you, and that are still going to happen!' dragged out a succession of limp black squirming things and threw them on the floor before me. They were not rags or creatures, not living or dead – they were Black Horrors, shapeless, and that seemed to writhe about as they fell at my feet, and yet were as inanimate as bits of stuff . . . I *knew* what they were: the hideous, the incredible things that had happened to me in this dreadful year, or were to happen to me before its close; and I stared, horror-struck, as the Demon dragged them out, more and more, till finally, flinging down a blacker, hatefuller one, he said laughing, 'There – that's the last of them!'
>
> The gnomes laughed too; but I, as I stared at the great black pile and at the empty trunk, I said to the Demon, '*Are you sure it hasn't a false bottom?*'[1]

It is a startling revelation of how much distress and humiliation underlay her proud determined outer self. And it is alarmingly prophetic. More Black Horrors were indeed on their way, and not for Edith Wharton alone: they would cover the world. But, like many others, she had no idea of what was to come. She carried on with the life she had made for herself, of writing ('Literature', never to be finished), of reading (Conrad's *The Secret Sharer*, the first volume of Proust's À *la Recherche*), and of what James called her 'great globe-rushes & vast gyrations'.[2]

In December she went for a rushed and stressful two weeks to America, her first visit for two years, her first New York season for eight, and her last transatlantic voyage until 1923. The occasion was Trix's marriage to her Yale professor of constitutional history, Max Farrand. She had planned to sail with Walter, but, still suffering from bouts of exhaustion, she came down with influenza just before she was due to leave, so Walter went on without her. She arrived too late for the wedding, but in time for the reception, hosted by Egerton Winthrop – the last time she would see this very old friend. (Minnie was ill too, so Beatrix had a decimated family attendance for her marriage. Ogden Codman came away with the impression that what was left of the Jones family was divided and forlorn.) Wharton settled into the Ritz-Carlton for a great deal of telephoning, telegraphing, hasty visits and reunions with people to whom she still signed herself 'Pussy' – the second week, she told Daisy, was 'cracking and bursting with obligations of every kind – family, friends, lame ducks, people ill, etc'. She took an aghast look at New York, and sent James a 'rich flash-out' of her 'buccaneering' raid. She told Berenson that New York was 'a great show', but 'ugly, patchy, scrappy', self-conscious – and stupid. All in all she found it 'a soul-destroying experience', and decided to leave early, taking back a reluctant Walter: 'We're off', he told Berenson on 7 January 1914, 'leaving banquets uneaten and sirens singing songs. Another fortnight would have rounded it out perfectly.' Mary Berenson, who witnessed this departure, thought that Edith was jealous of Walter's 'sirens', and was behaving badly: 'She spoiled several evenings especially arranged for her by evidently hating everything and has left some bitter enemies behind.' She was relieved to be back in Paris (in time for her fifty-second birthday – not that she paid much attention to her birthdays) but at once started planning more world-travels. Percy Lubbock and Gaillard Lapsley, two of her closest companions at this time, exchanged Jamesian views on her volatility: 'Edith actually *dares*, bless her heart, to lecture me about the moral danger of changing plans one has made – This from *her* – I ask you!' She warned Berenson that 'for the next few years' she planned 'to eat the world leaf by leaf, & I have *projets de voyage* to unfold that will, I hope, make you follow me as if I were the Pied Piper'. It is as if she had a reputation to keep up.[3]

She had long wanted to go to Egypt, and Walter's time there would have whetted her appetite. He went off on a jaunt to India and Ceylon, so, perhaps competitively, she planned a trip to Algeria and Tunisia. The 'magic land' of North Africa fired her imagination with a sense of culture and history beyond her range. She wrote to Morton from Biskra, in Algeria, that 'beyond the *so* narrow thread of civilization along the coast, Europe has made no mark . . . things are much as they must have been 5000 years ago'. She shared the interest of many other writers and artists of her time (including Conrad, whom she was reading with interest, and Stravinsky, whose *Rite of Spring* she so much admired) in the 'primitive' and the 'exotic'. (Undine Spragg was a good example of primitive forces within the civilised world.) This fascination with what lay beyond and before white civilisation was also bound up with her patriotic commitment to France. Algeria had been under French rule since it was invaded in 1830, and was sharply divided between the *pieds noirs*, the Europeans born in Algeria, and the Muslim population. Tunisia, with its amazing mixture of Roman, Phoenician, Arab, Berber, Turkish and French ingredients, was under an increasingly repressive French protectorate, set up after the French invasion of 1881. France's imperial conquest of Morocco, Wharton's next North African destination, was one of the key issues of conflict between France and Germany in the lead-up to the war.

This was the most adventurous trip she had made since the cruise of the *Vanadis* in 1888. This time she had no privately chartered steam-launch, and no husband. But as usual she wanted to travel in style, with companions. She tried the Bourgets without success, and then enlisted Percy and Gaillard. Anna Bahlmann and Cook were needed too. Domestic matters were in the hands of a new maid, Elise Devinck, a young woman who had just joined her household and who, though at first rather nervous (as who would not be with this particular employer?), fast became an essential presence in Edith's life. She stayed in her employment for twenty years, until her death in 1934. Elise's life-story has been obliterated by that of her mistress: her surname tends to be omitted or misspelt in Wharton biographies. She seems to have been pious, dog-loving (an essential), efficient at servicing her mistress's travels (taking the luggage by train, getting her houses ready for habitation), devoted and loyal.[4]

The party sailed on the SS *Timgad*, a sturdy French packet-boat, from Marseilles to Algiers, Edith armed with her 1911 Baedeker guide to Tunis and Algeria. Lapsley proved to be a broken reed – he arrived late and went home early with an attack of dysentery; perhaps travelling with Edith was too much for him. Even if Percy on his own was not the person she most wanted to be with – he had made an anxious fuss before setting out about not being able to pay his own way – he was an eager companion, and they went everywhere they could, by hired car, with the imperturbable Cook at the wheel. Excited travelogues went off to James, to Berenson, to Lapsley, to Sally Norton, and to Morton. She placed herself in a tradition of French romantic Sahara-lovers like Eugène Froment and intrepid lady travellers (*'How* I understand Lady Hester Stanhope!'). The scenery of the oasis villages on the edge of the desert, the colours of the mountains, the eloquent Roman ruins at Timgad and Carthage, the 'extraordinarily picturesque Berbers' of Kabylia, the Tunis souks, which she thought straight out of the Arabian Nights, the very sound of the names – 'the Red Village of the Oasis of El Kantara', 'Kairouan the fabulous', with its mosques, Djerba, supposed to be the island of the Lotus Eaters (which she never reached), 'mysterious Médenine', beyond which, at that time, even with French improvements to the infrastructure, no road travel was possible: the un-Europeanness of it all entranced her. Get here fast, she warned Berenson, before it is overrun by 'hordes of Teutons'.

Like most first-time travellers to Africa, she drew on her existing range of Eurocentric analogies to make sense of what she saw, as in this note-book account of 'the native quarter at Biskra: Looking down at it, under a full moon, from the roof-terrace of the hotel, the scene is like a Bellini or a Carpaccio, one expects to see St Stephen preaching to a circle of squatting infidels . . .' She described the people either as parts of the landscape ('the wonderful white figures in the silent sun-baked streets, the brilliant violet-&-rose-&-orange women washing in the "oued"'), or as exotic species. She told Berenson with glee about the 'effeminacy, obesity, obscenity or black savageness' of the 'native types' of Tunis. In her travel-notebook, she recorded the fluttering brown hands of the dancing girls, the air of 'youth, adventure, vivacity' in the moving crowds at Biskra, the 'Jewish women washing their clothes [who] wore the most gorgeous colours, the most fantastic jewelry'. She made cool notes on sex for sale: 'The professional prostitutes of this desert tribe [are] as different as possible from the subtle wistful faces of the other prostitutes of the bazaar. Some of the old courtesans were superb, with delicate aquiline faces, firm, noble and sad, under their high black turbans . . . They might have been Clytemnestra and Jocasta.' She joked with Gaillard about having bargained for a love-potion for him in a Tunis bazaar, and about buying a necklace from a 'coloured prostitute' at Sfax. She reported on Percy's giggling while she told an uncomprehending Anna that such necklaces are said 'to make the negresses irresistible to the Arabs'. Perhaps she did not see the homoerotic postcard Percy sent Gaillard (these were easily available for certain kinds of tourists in North Africa) showing three naked Arabian flute-playing boys, on which Percy wrote: 'The disconsolate are beginning to enjoy the distractions of travel.'[5]

She had an upsetting shock in this erotic land, which would have made her acutely conscious of being a woman alone. Staying at a remote inn at Timgad, after looking at the beautiful ruins by moonlight (she told Percy it must have been like this for her parents, seeing the Roman forum for the first time in the 1840s) she was woken in the middle of the night by some noises. Alone in the pitch darkness, she put out her hand for the matches, and touched a man bending over her. There was a brief struggle – he was, she said, rather a small man – and she got out of the room into the corridor, screaming loudly. Lights and people came; the hotel staff were very defensive, and accused her of having dreamed it. She took Elise into her room with her and spent a bad night. The next day, apart from having lost her voice, she got on with the trip with (as Percy told Gaillard) 'the sort of clear strong intelligence' one would expect. She behaved with courage, level-headedness and stoicism, qualities which would be displayed in force over the next few years. She told Morton, to whom she still, very occasionally, bared her soul: 'I should be very glad to die, but it's no fun struggling with you don't know what in the dark.'[6]

She did not write up her Tunisian travels, though James encouraged her to do a travel book called 'From the Duvet to the Desert'. But she immediately started a work called 'Peter Elsom', which she told Edward Burlingame could be 'a sort of pendant to Ethan Frome, at least in length! It's a wild embroidery, made out of the adventures of a young Englishman who goes to Tunisia soon after the French Occupation to work in some phosphate mines in the interior, and disappears.' (Phosphate mines were a growing industry in Tunisia under the French.) The drafts of the novella begin with someone chancing on a diary in Sfax, Tunisia, dated 1889. The writer of the diary is the Englishman who has disappeared. He follows a boy down an alley in a bazaar and is invited into an old man's house. Perhaps, he thinks, it is all 'too cheaply operatic', perhaps they are 'getting up Oriental effects for foreigners' (so Wharton knew how susceptible she was to 'wallowing in local colour'). The old man turns out to be the distant descendant of an Englishman; he offers the young man a woman, and asks him: 'At what age did your father buy you your first negress?' There follow elaborate descriptions of the Tunisian town at night, of a Bedouin camp, of a caravan of traders going into the desert. 'Well', he thinks, 'things are getting less and less like what they would be in Camberwell.' And the unfinished narrative breaks off. It is a story which acts out a longing to drop off the edge of the world, disappear into the desert, leave one's own life behind: 'I should be very glad to die . . .'[7]

They came back via Sicily and then Naples, on a terrible Italian boat where their sea-chairs were stolen, the stokers quarrelled, and the passengers were 'a jabbering rabble'. And how horrid to have to look at Europeans again! At home, there was disturbing news of Teddy's having another serious breakdown. Almost at once Wharton was off on another 'giro' to I Tatti, and then for three weeks in July, with Walter, to Spain, a country she had liked since her childhood travels and enjoyed returning to. She took her usual kind of mighty journey, going first to the great Benedictine monastery at Montserrat, in Catalonia ('By far the most romantically & improbably beautiful thing I know'), where they stayed in the monastery and had to ask for two cells instead of one (a clue dropped sideways into *A Backward Glance* about her 'unromantically' companionable travelling-relationship with Walter, even though James was calling them another George Sand and Chopin). Then they swept up to the Pyrenees, crossed to the coast, and went down from Bayonne to Santander (going to her first film in Bilbao, appropriately called '*Comment on visite une ville au galop*'). Then to Burgos and Pamplona and the prehistoric cave-drawings at Altamira, which they were shown by a peasant with 'a smoking candle', and from which Walter (one of whose intellectual hobbies was the study of cave-paintings) emerged with red chalk from the 'famous snorting bison' all over his immaculate white hat. It was the last of such leisurely travels for a long time.[8] With 'the international news looking fairly black' in all the papers, they began to hurry home. On their way back to Paris, at the very end of July 1914, travelling up through the 'sober disciplined landscape' around Poitiers, where they heard the crowds singing the 'Marseillaise' all night in the square outside the hotel, they stopped at Chartres. This was the place where Wharton would stage the beginning of the account she wrote a year later of 'Fighting France'. She described Chartres as symbolic of our life on earth, 'with its shadows . . . and its little islands of illusion'. 'All the tranquillizing power [a great cathedral] can breathe upon the soul, all the richness of detail it can fuse into a large utterance of strength and beauty, the cathedral of Chartres gave us in that perfect hour.'[9]

The legend of Wharton in wartime is that she sacrificed her writing almost entirely to working for France. In fact, the war produced all kinds of writing: essays, stories, novels, poems, appeals, reports, a vast mass of correspondence and an edited anthology poured out of her, but not in the tone her readers were used to. At the time, these writings were praised: *The Marne*, her war-novella of 1918, was thought moving by many reviewers, in contrast with the complaints about unsympathetic characters and sordid stories which had greeted *The Reef* and *The Custom of the Country*.[10] Later, her war-writing was felt to be embarrassing and sentimental, an aberration from the sharp satire and bitter social dramas she was known for. But the mixture of deep feeling and sharp observation continued – only the subject changed.

It is one of the staggering facts of twentieth-century history that the Great War came to so many people as 'a bolt from the blue' or 'out of a cloudless sky'. In France, war was thought by many to be avoidable or unlikely, right up to the moment of mobilisation. The French army and the French people were unprepared. In the few days which changed the world, at the end of July and the beginning of August, Austria-Hungary and Germany declared war on Serbia; Russia at once began to mobilise in Serbia's support; Germany issued ultimatums to Russia and France; France (under the political leadership of President Poincaré, a conservative nationalist, and the military leadership of the weighty General Joseph Joffre) ordered a general mobilisation on 2 August. Germany declared war on Russia and invaded Luxembourg, and on 3 August, declared war against France and began military operations in Belgium. The German Schlieffen Plan which called for an immediate invasion of France through Belgium drew France and then Britain into a general European war. On 4 August (after much diplomatic pressure from France) Britain declared war on Germany and Austria-Hungary, and Germany invaded Belgium, violating its neutrality. The historical consensus on France's position is that it had not started the war and was responding to German aggression, and that – for reasons both defensive and offensive – it had no choice: 'It could accept war, or the undoing of the whole great enterprise since 1871 of rehabilitating France as a Great Power'.[11]

Edith Wharton and Walter Berry, privileged, wealthy and well-informed members of the international community in Paris, may seem to us extraordinarily blithe, making luxurious journeys around North Africa and Europe, right up to the eve of war, and unwilling to believe what was about to happen: 'What nonsense! It can't be war,' they said to each other at the end of July, listening to the singing of the 'Marseillaise' outside their hotel windows in Poitiers. To Troy Belknap, the young Francophile American hero of The Marne (1918), 'this unfathomable thing called War . . . seemed suddenly to have escaped out of the history books like a dangerous lunatic escaping from the asylum in which he was supposed to be securely confined'. In A Son at the Front (written in 1919) she gave this ostrich-tendency to her most self-deceiving character, the painter John Campton: when he sees the announcement of war posted, 'He knew now that he had never for an instant believed it possible'. But many contemporaneous accounts gave the same impression of unpreparedness: 'When Germany declared war on

France', wrote one observer in 1914, 'Paris was indulging in dusty summer slackness and the tourists shared with the concierges the delights of the holiday season.' The American writer Julien Green, who was a schoolboy in Paris at the start of the war (and fighting for France by the end of it), said that 'A Franco-German war seemed of all things in the world the most improbable'. Paris was much more absorbed, in the summer of 1914, with a local sensation, the assassination in March of the journalist Gaston Calmette, the anti-German, conservative editor of the *Figaro*, by Mme Caillaux, the wife of the pro-detente, anti-militaristic Minister of Finance, whose sexual history Calmette had been threatening to expose in order to overthrow him, and the subsequent trial of Mme Caillaux. Wharton was particularly gripped by the case because Paul Bourget had been with Calmette in his office just before he was killed, heard the shots and rushed back in. The case was only swept from the front pages of the Paris newspapers after 28 July, the day that Mme Caillaux was (surprisingly) acquitted, the same day that Austria-Hungary declared war on Serbia. On 31 July, another assassination, and a much more significant one, took place in Paris: the Socialist anti-war leader Jean Jaurès was shot. The order for mobilisation followed the next day, and the French nation went to war. André Gide (whom the war would bring into close working contact with Wharton) wrote in his journal on 31 July: 'We are getting ready to enter a long tunnel full of blood and darkness.'[12]

All Frenchmen between the ages of twenty and forty-eight were called up. In Paris, as in the capital cities of Russia, England and Germany, wildly enthusiastic patriotic scenes greeted the announcement of war. The departure of the regiments from the Gare d'Est and the Gare du Nord was accompanied by vast cheering crowds singing the 'Marseillaise' and shouting '*Vive la France!*' Wharton watched the scenes and reported on them: the floods of people – conscripts, wives and families – going to the stations, the restaurants pouring out patriotic music (and most of the waiters gone to the war), the singing in the streets, the 'cheerful steadiness of spirit' and 'sense of exaltation'. And then the emptiness and paralysis of a city without traffic (or Metro) or boats on the Seine or gardeners in the park. And then everyone starting to get organised and get on with their lives, moved by 'an instinctive community of emotion', what she calls a kind of 'smiling fatalism'. And then the tangles of bureaucracy, the panicky rush of many foreigners trying to get money or get out, the closing of shops – all with signs reading 'Gone to the Front', and the turning of hotels into hospitals. All this, in a beautiful warm Paris August, the streets quiet and empty on dark moonlit nights. And, after the first excitement, no military music, no 'show of war', but a 'unanimity of self-restraint', a sense of 'foreseeing the cost and accepting it'. By early 1915, shops and restaurants, theatres and concert-halls reopened, and Paris was full of refugees and young wounded men with something 'strong and finely-tempered' in their faces. She described the Parisians' initial shock and paralysis quickly turning into a businesslike, stoical reorganisation: 'Paris was not to be shaken out of her self-imposed serenity' and 'steadiness of spirit'. This was her account of 'The Look of Paris', published in May 1915, collected in *Fighting France* later that year. She at once adopted the patriotic tone that would take her through the war – dedicated, moved, admiring, appalled, and in love with the spirit of France.[13]

Many other descriptions of Paris at the start of the war bear her out; everyone remarked on the cheerfulness and stoicism of the city, though some accounts were less idealised than Wharton's, and noted, also, the food queues and the severity of martial law, the weeping women, the smashing-up of German and Austrian shops and the defensive signs on boarded-up shops reading '*Maison Ultra-Française*'. All commentators agreed that the French response to the war was not 'mindless, aggressive patriotism' (in the words of one historian), even though there was a strong element of '*la revanche*', revenge on Germany for the loss of Alsace-Lorraine. But most agreed that the idea of the '*Union Sacrée*', the term coined by Poincaré, was not something imposed from above by government edict. It was a coming-together, post-Dreyfus, of civilian and military, civic and religious, in a state of 'shock, sadness and consternation', of indignation against German aggression, and with a strong resolve to defend the country. Even secular and Socialist thinkers became involved in a quasi-religious dedication, a spirit of '*foi patriotique*', at the start of the war. Julien Green described it as 'patriotism of a sombre quality and mixed with barely concealed anguish'. An anti-war movement was slow to develop in France. Those who were dubious about the French war-spirit were in a minority; one of them was Wharton's friend the Abbé Mugnier, who wrote in his diary for 18 August 1915: 'We have taken completely the wrong road.' The prevailing mood in 1914 was voiced by an American onlooker in Paris: 'We did not want this war, but as Germany has begun we will fight, and Germany will find that the heart of France is in a war for freedom.' This was Wharton's diagnosis, which she would give to one of the characters in *A Son at the Front*: 'He knew that the thought of Alsace-Lorraine still stirred in French hearts; but all Dastrey's eloquence could not convince him that these people wanted war, or would have sought it had it not been thrust on them.' For the rest of her life she would be 'dumb with indignation' if she heard it suggested that 'the world went gaily to war . . . or that France and England actually wanted war, and forced it on the peace-loving and reluctant Central Empires'.[14]

Everyone – including the soldiers and many of the politicians (and not just in France) – believed the war would be short. Walter Berry told Berenson on 14 August that 'Things can't last very long'. Wharton gave this blithe August optimism to her characters in her war novel ('It's a matter of weeks') and she looked back bitterly, to Berenson in February 1915, on 'the old optimistic sugar plums of last August. As I look back on those deluded days I realize that Robert Norton is the one & only person, in my group at least, who foresaw exactly what was coming – a long long struggle, with the all-too-great probability of a stalemate at the end.'[15] But how were civilian onlookers supposed to get it right, when the people in charge of planning the war were getting it so wrong? The German Schlieffen plan did not anticipate the extent of Belgian resistance; the French 'Plan XVII' of an offensive into Alsace and Lorraine did not anticipate the German onslaught from the north. The Germans tore through Belgium and into north-east France. By 28 August, to the horror and amazement of the French, the Germans had reached the Somme. Whole towns and villages in Belgium and the occupied territories were burnt and razed: huge numbers of refugees poured into Paris from these regions. Terrible atrocities took place (and even more were rumoured: there were innumerable stories of crucified prisoners, rapes, mutilated children). Wild stories that the Russian Army was coming to France via England were believed for a while both by Wharton and James. The burning of the library at Louvain on 25 August, with its priceless medieval treasures, was seen by the Belgians and the French as symbolic of the barbarism of the Germans and their ambition to destroy the civilised world. Between August and September, the French offensives failed, the British retreated from Mons, and the Germans made a rapid advance towards Paris. Half a million Parisians left the capital, and the government relocated to Bordeaux. In early September, there was a turning-point. Joffre rallied the army for the battle – or rather the battles – of the Marne. (Famously, a few thousand soldiers were rushed in taxis to the battle from Paris – and the taxi-drivers charged fares.) The German advance was halted, but there was no victory.

In the autumn, as both sides fought their way north in the 'race to the sea', particular horrors – the treatment of the civilians at Senlis, the bombing of Reims Cathedral, the death of the nationalist Catholic poet Charles Péguy – took their place in a series of appalling and inconclusive battles – the Aisne, Arras, Flanders, Yser, Ypres, Dixmunde. By the start of 1914, trenches were being dug along the front lines, a stalemate had developed that would hold for three years, and France – Occupied and Unoccupied alike – was in a condition of 'total war'. The French army remained 'firm in spirit', but all hopes of a quick victory had disappeared. In Paris, the sense of immediate threat receded. The casualty rate suffered by Parisians was extremely high in the first six weeks of the war, and the capital was braced for invasion. By the end of 1914 – until spring 1918, when the capital was again under imminent threat – Paris adapted to what one observer in 1916 called 'a condition of stolidity almost British: her citizens were difficult to rouse, impossible to depress'.

The French casualty figures in the first four months of the Great War are difficult to write down as cold facts. Over 50 per cent of the 1.3 million Frenchmen killed during the war died between August 1914 and December 1915. The rate was especially high in the first month of the war: there were 200,000 French losses in September. By the end of the year, there were 900,000 French casualties, which included 300,000 deaths. Two thousand young Frenchmen were killed in battle each day. The experiences of the men fighting at the Front, the inhabitants of the occupied territories, the refugees, the widows and orphans, the war-wounded and the shell-shocked, the victims of tuberculosis and, later, Spanish flu, encompassed every conceivable kind of human suffering.[16]

Edith Wharton dedicated herself to France and turned into a heroic worker on behalf of her adopted country. She focused her extraordinary energies in a formidable array of activities, and became, in the words of Henry James (who changed his attitude to her in this last terrible year of his life), 'the great generalissima'. In 1915, she wrote to Berenson (using a new American slang-word): 'The war has "vacuumed" everything else, as the housemaid said to me last winter at the New York Ritz.' In 1918 she said to an American friend: 'We all belong to the war now.' A scrap of an unfinished poem in her notebooks read: 'France! To give thee, o my more than country / Give thee of my blood's abundance all.' Cliché'd though the lines sound now, that is what she felt. The French would recognise her dedication. In 1918, one newspaper wrote of her: 'Mrs Warthon est un des meilleurs écrivains de l'Amérique contemporaine . . . son infatigable dévouement au cours de ces quatre années de guerre . . . lui avait acquis . . . parmi nous une sorte de grande naturalisation.'[17]

That adopted patriotism involved a cluster of strong emotions. A letter to Robert Grant on 31 August 1914, urging him to believe everything he heard about German atrocities, told him: 'For heaven's sake, when you get home, proclaim everywhere, and as publicly as possible, and with the authority of your name, what it will mean to all that we Americans cherish if England and France go under, and Prussianism becomes the law of life.' She would repeat this again and again; her letters to her American friends became a form of propaganda. To Sally Norton: 'The "atrocities" one hears of are *true* . . . Spread it abroad as much as you can. It should be known that it is to America's interest to help stem this hideous flood of savagery by opinion if it may not be by action. No civilized race can remain neutral in feeling now.' For all her love of Goethe and Nietzsche and Schopenhauer, these wartime Germans were always the Teutons or the Huns, the Boche or the Beast, or, in her fiction, the 'brutes' and the 'devils'. Those who argued – as in *The Marne* – that one 'couldn't believe all that was said of the Germans' get short shrift. She exchanged belligerent anti-German views with James and with Berenson (who dropped the 'h' from his first name early in 1915 to make it less German). 'It makes me ache to think of all the beauty lying open to the Beast beyond the Alps', she wrote to him in 1915; in 1918 she told him she refused to have her sense of life crushed out of her 'by the Boche or the Beast'.[18] She had no time for pacifists or critics of the war. Her tone for them is summed up by a phrase in *The Marne*: after the sinking of the *Lusitania*, the American pacifists 'crept back into their holes'.

She thought it the duty of young men to join up, and in her work, both fiction and non-fiction, she celebrated the sacrifices of the young. Both her war-novels centre on the passionate eagerness of young Americans to get involved and if necessary to die in the cause of France. 'This war will be the making of him', says a woman in *A Son at the Front* who wants the American boy to fight for France. When 'Bo', son of her cousin Thomas Newbold Rhinelander, joined the American Ambulance Corps in 1916 (and the US Army Corps in 1918), she wrote to his father: 'He is a dear, and I am so glad you have given him this opportunity of seeing this great moment of history, and lending a hand in the cause. I agree with you that such an experience ought to last throughout life, and I am sure Newbold is the kind to make the most of it.' 'Bo' was duly shot down, and Wharton sent his grieving father a copy of Laurence Binyon's poems *The New World*, expressing, she thought, 'exactly the spirit in which Newbold lived and died'. The poems included 'The English Youth' ('Who gave must give himself entire and whole'). Binyon's most famous poem is 'For the Fallen': 'They shall grow not old, as we that are left grow old: / Age shall not weary them, nor the years condemn. / At the going down of the sun and in the morning / We will remember them.'[19]

Wharton became very fierce about publishing her work in any organ that might be in the least anti-war or pro-German, and kept up this position long after the war was over. In 1916, using Fullerton once more as an intermediary, she withdrew the serialisation rights of *Summer* from William Randoph Hearst's magazine *Cosmopolitan*, because he published a defence of Roger Casement, who was executed in August 1916 for trying to get support from Germany for Irish Independence. She called Hearst a 'filthy Boche-Irish publisher' and a 'pro-Boche propagandist'. In 1917 she wrote to Minnie objecting to her son-in-law Max Farrand's writing for the *New Republic*, which published anti-war articles: 'Much as I love him, it is painful to have to read him in that vile sheet ... I do not like to see a good French name like his associated with such "boche" neutrality.' In 1918, she wrote to a Dutch publisher who wanted to translate *Summer*, agreeing 'if you will give me a written assurance that the political sentiments of the *Nieuwe Rotterdamsche Courant* are in sympathy with the cause of the Allies for whom my country is fighting'. As late as 1924 she was still wedded to this position. She wrote to Wilbur Cross, the editor of *The Yale Review*, apologising for the lateness of her article on Proust. But since he had now published that German Jew Max Beerbohm's 'abominable caricature against the Allies', she no longer wanted to have anything to do with his publication.[20]

She was aghast at the American position of neutrality under the Democrat President Woodrow Wilson, whose election she had not welcomed in 1912, and whose re-election in 1916 appalled her. Apart from her admiration for Theodore Roosevelt, she had not been engaged with American politics. But now she became vociferous in her critique of US foreign policy. A letter to Gaillard Lapsley at the end of 1914 voiced the almost unmentionable thought (which she shared with other conservative modernists such as Yeats, Lawrence and Ezra Pound) that the war was somehow an inevitability, a product of a decaying civilisation: 'The only consoling thought is that the beastly horror *had* to be gone through, for some mysterious cosmic reason of ripening and rotting, and the heads on whom that rotten German civilization are falling are bound to get cracked.' But the USA did not seem 'morally ready'. She was ashamed of her country, especially after the sinking of the *Lusitania* in May 1915. One of her war-poems, 'The Hymn of the Lusitania', written, with emphatic irony, as if it were a translation from the German, called neutral Uncle Sam's unused war-ships her 'shirkers' – adopting the lethal French insult, '*Embusqués*'. Like this poem, all Wharton's war-writings up to 1917 were designed to rouse up America. Her letters were full of phrases like 'sick with shame' or 'unable to hold up one's head'. She put smug Senators ('This isn't our war, young man') and Americans in France ashamed of their 'national dishonour', into her war novels.[21]

In both novels, a young American hero commits himself to the cause of France against the wishes of his family, who represent American 'self-satisfaction' and resistance to intervention. In *The Marne*, written between July and November 1918, the focus is on the young, ardent Troy Belknap, who (like many of Wharton's sensitive young male heroes) is inspired, from childhood, by a civilisation he prefers to his own: 'France was his holiday world, the world of his fancy and imagination, a great traceried window opening on the universe.' This emotion has been nourished by his French tutor, whose family village in the Argonne – which will be utterly destroyed by the Germans – he once visited. The tutor is killed at the first battle of the Marne, and Troy sees his grave on the battlefield. A fifteen-year-old boy when the war broke out, he is determined to 'participate in the struggle'. His dedication is contrasted with the cowardice of his socialite mother who fled Paris at the outbreak of war, and with the isolationist Senators, American lady relief-workers bent on carrying 'America right into the heart of France', and American soldiers with 'definite and unfavourable opinions about "this blasted place"' they have come to fight for. In the end, in a muddled sort of way (rather like the hero of Stephen Crane's *The Red Badge of Courage*) Troy finds himself, as a Red Cross ambulance driver, in the thick of the second battle of the Marne, where he is rescued – the emotional tone of the whole book leads up to this – by the ghost of his dead tutor. *The Marne* wholly endorses war-heroism and war-sacrifice, even quoting Henry V's Agincourt speech ('And gentlemen in England now abed / Shall think themselves accursed they were not here') in support of its ideology. Wharton had some trouble getting started with it. She told Berenson she was having 'the hateful sensation of rattling at the locked doors of memory, imagination, creative sensitivity . . . & perpetually getting the same answer: "No one there!" When it came out in December 1918 it was, at first, a great success. But there were poor sales and diminishing interest.[22]

Her second and much longer war-novel, *A Son at the Front*, which she promised in her outline would 'describe French and American life in Paris during the first two years of the war, somewhat on the scale of the social studies of *The House of Mirth*', did much worse. Unfortunately for her, though it was planned in 1918, at the same time as the writing of *The Marne*, it was held off by her new publisher Appleton because nobody wanted to read war-fiction just after the war: 'War Books Dead in America', they cabled her in July 1919. (She offered to change the title to the less warlike *Paris*.) When it finally came out with Scribner's in 1923, it was received as a 'belated essay in war propaganda'. Wharton thought it fulfilled a 'lest-we-forget' function, and always insisted on it as one of her favourite books.[23]

A *Son at the Front*'s focus is not the war itself but the civilian response to it in Franco-American Paris. George Campton, the young American, born in France, who wants to fight for his adoptive country, is less vivid to us than his father John, a cynical American painter long settled in Paris, who is united with his silly ex-wife and her wealthy second husband only in their protective love for George and their desire for him not to go into danger. (John Campton's jealousy of George's stepfather, a decent man, is well done.) George goes to the front without their knowing, is wounded and finally killed in battle. Campton's isolationism, which gradually changes to commitment, is set in the context of a detailed (but rather melancholy and under-energised) account of civilian types: the quarrelling relief-workers, the society ladies with their charity concerts, the heroic French parents, the foolish pacifists and 'subversive' modern Bohemians, and the ordinary French working people, sending their sons to war. Campton's change of heart is encouraged by the novel's key character, the practical, bashful, plump, shy young American Boylston. Like all the worthwhile characters in the book, Boylston is committed to an 'Idea' of French civilisation, which by 1923 read over-heroically:

> An Idea: they must cling to that ... An Idea: that was what France, ever since she had existed, had always been in the story of civilization; a luminous point about which striving visions and purposes could rally ... to thinkers, artists, to all creators, she had always been a second country. If France went, western civilization went with her.[24]

Edith Wharton shared these emotions with Walter Berry, who used his prominent position as the president of the American Chamber of Commerce to urge America to come into the war. (Proust dedicated *Pastiches et Mélanges* to him in 1919 in glowing political terms: 'To M. Walter Berry, lawyer and man of letters, who from the first day of the war, confronting an indecisive America, argued France's case with an incomparable energy and talent, and won'. Walter thanked him ironically for his elevation: 'I expect I'll end up in the Pantheon!'[25]) She agreed, too, with her two most distinguished American friends, Theodore Roosevelt and Henry James. Roosevelt (who had broken with the Republicans and formed his own party in 1912) wrote an ill-received book in 1915, *America and the World War*, which robustly opposed the 'peace prattlers' and accused Wilson's government of having failed in its international responsibilities: 'If, instead of observing a timid and spiritless neutrality, we had lived up to our obligations by taking action . . . we would have followed the only course that would both have told for world righteousness and have served our own self-respect.' The copy he gave to his old friend Edith Wharton bore the dedication: 'From an American – American!' They had identical feelings about pacifists, neutrals, and what she called, writing to Roosevelt, 'Wilson apologists'. 'If Wilson had done his duty' (Roosevelt wrote to Wharton after the sinking of the *Lusitania*),

> I and my four boys would now be training for positions in the trenches. I think Wilson the very worst President we have had since Buchanan. The dreadful part of it is that the educated people have backed him up . . . Until this nation realizes that no man is fit to be called a man unless he is ready to fight for what is right . . . we shall cut but a poor figure in the world.

He wrote a preface to this effect (against Charles Scribner's advice) for Wharton's *Book of the Homeless*.

James was similarly belligerent, outraged and ashamed. He was disgusted that the Americans 'mind the war so much less', and told Edith that he hoped the American ambassador to France would be blown up by a bomb, if it speeded up America's entry into the war. He enthused to Wharton about J. William White, the author of *A Primer of the War For Americans*, which argued in 1914 that 'for the sake of humanity and of civilization we cannot afford to permit Germany to win'. The bombing of Reims Cathedral, he wrote to her, was 'the most unspeakable & immeasurable terror & infamy'. Wharton passed on his letter of outrage to be read at a session of the Académie française, and to be published in *Le Journal des débats*. James spent the last year of his life, in spite of ill-health, doing what he could: giving up his studio at Lamb House for Belgian refugees, sending newspapers to the Red Cross, contributing to books for war-charities (including *The Book of the Homeless*, for which he helped her find contributors), visiting wounded soldiers in hospital, and carrying on with his work. Wharton agreed with one of his obituarists, Barrett Wendell, that James's taking British citizenship was in part a response to America's neutrality.[26]

Her own feeling about her nationality was expressed in one of her propagandist war-poems, 'The Great Blue Tent' (1915). This was one of the most effective of the ten or so war-poems she wrote between 1915 and 1919, which included a Whitmanesque elegy, 'With the Tide', for Theodore Roosevelt, imagining a great fleet of American warships, 'returning from their sacred quest / With the thrice-sacred burden of their dead' coming to take him away on his last journey. (She told his sister, Corinne Roosevelt Robinson, with whom she had some correspondence about poetry, that it was 'written out of a heart wrung with sorrow, sorrow for the lost friend & for the great leader gone when he was most needed'.) Like the Roosevelt elegy, and 'The Hymn of the *Lusitania*', most of her war-poems were printed in American newspapers or magazines, some in war-charity books like her *Book of the Homeless* or *King Albert's Book*; a few were reprinted in her small-press publication, *Twelve Poems*, in 1926. They were laments for Belgium, for the war-dead ('Ah, how I pity the young dead who gave / All that they were and might become . . .'), for the sorrowing wives and mothers, written out of, and intended to evoke, heartfelt emotion. (One of the most personal, an elegy for her friend Jean du Breuil, was unpublished.) The longest, 'You and You', a drumbeat celebration of 'The American Private Soldiers in the Great War', was a stentorian roll-call of honour: 'All the land loud with you / All our hearts proud with you / All our souls bowed with the awe of your coming!'[27]

In 'The Great Blue Tent', a four-line-stanza, Kiplingesque ballad, the flag of America speaks to those who have suffered in war, summoning them to a peaceful refuge, offering rest and bread and a warm fire, but is urged by 'the winds of war' to turn itself back into the tattered, 'shot-riddled' flag of freedom it once was in the War of Independence. The American flag, roused up to action once more, replies: 'Give back my stars to the skies / My stripes to the storm-striped seas! / Or else, if you bid me yield / Then down with my crimson bars / And o'er all my azure field / Sow poppies instead of stars.' Congratulated on this poem by the art critic Royal Cortissoz she wrote: 'Do you know, you are the only person who has written me about it except one lady who wrote that she "feared from my beautiful lines that I didn't realize how much America had given the refugees!" But I can't talk about my country – it hurts too much . . .' 'My country' reads more than ever ambivalently in 1915. She was upset when Henry James became an Englishman. But a change of citizenship had occurred to her too, as she told Beatrix in December 1915, speaking of the disgrace of 'a great nation like ours': 'The whole thing makes me so sick with shame that if I had time – & if it mattered – I'd run round to the Prefecture de Police and get myself naturalised . . . But it's much more important to try to make one's self useful.' She had never felt so ashamed of America or so admiring of France.[28]

She delighted in that untranslatable French attitude, '*le panache*' (a term derived from the plumed hats of French officers, fatal anachronisms now in an increasingly mechanised war). 'Panache', she said, was the flowering on 'so many battlefields' of French honour, and it fired the 'great flame of

self-dedication' of the entire French people. She respected their devotion
to the 'sacred soil', their defence of family life, the 'dignity and grace' with
which the civilians, especially the women, suffered privations and bereavements, and their intelligence, courage and ardour. It was not just for their
lives that the French were fighting, but for the preservation of those qualities, and in fear of the 'death by extinction of their national ideal'. The
armies along the long line of the front were guarding 'the civilised world'.[29]

Wharton's impassioned wartime rhetoric was part of an outpouring of
ideological narratives about France. '*Mon Dieu*', wrote Charles Du Bos in
his diary for 27 October 1914, '*Protégez la France, tous ceux que nous aimons,
tous ceux qui souffrent.*' That devotional tone was general. For the French,
the 'sacralisation' of the national territory was a reality. The defence of the
home was a profound emotion for the French at war (most of all at the
battle of Verdun in 1916). Not all were as gung-ho as the former pacifist
and art-historian Louis Gillet (later Wharton's friend) who wrote in 1914:
'We'll give a good shaking to this cloud of Germanism.' But most felt that
the war was a battle for civilisation. A French wartime anthology called
The Book of France (on which Wharton's *The Book of the Homeless* was
modelled), intended as a contribution to 'the greatest combat fought for
light and liberty against darkness and oppression', was full of references
(including Henry James's) to France as the zenith of civilisation. Anna de
Noailles called the German '*barbares*' the 'senile hordes'. Maurice Barrès,
who inherited the mantle of Charles Péguy, contributed an essay (which
James translated) called 'The Saints of France', in which he spoke of France
as '*la nation chevaleresque*', fighting against 'German barbarism'. Wharton
sent James some 1915 articles by Charles Le Goffic, calling them 'the one
good bit of literature (except our letters!) that the war has produced'. It
luridly described the advance of the German armies preceded by 'an aroma
of alcohol, ether and murder . . . the breath of the blood-stained machine'.[30]

The job of the writer in this struggle was to bear witness, and all
Wharton's contributors to her *Book of the Homeless* (with the notable exception of Yeats) subscribed to this doctrine. In France, the right wing especially
– Barrès, Léon Daudet, Charles Maurras, Bourget – thought that writers
should dedicate themselves to the cause of militant patriotism. Wharton's
thoughts on France sounded very like her old friend Bourget's, who used
the same words as she did for the French character – 'self-sacrifice', 'intelligence', 'ardour' – and who considered it the writer's task 'to foster support
for war in the country'. She decided from the start that her writing (poetry
and fiction included) should become part of her war-work. Wherever she
travelled, she asked for commissions; whenever the opportunity arose she

was an interpreter of France to America and an advocate of American intervention.[31]

After the Americans came into the war, she spoke in public, twice (very unusual for her: 'I consider it a man's job and not a woman's', she said). The first talk, on 8 February 1918, was in French, to explain the Americans to the French, to 'an audience of 400 intellectuals' at the Société des Conférences. She traced the converging strains in the American character of English Presbyterians and Dutch businessmen, and told some amusing anecdotes of everyday American life. 'It is a masterpiece', Berenson noted, 'and in French too. So clear & crisp & brief, and yet containing it all.' Matilda Gay called it 'a lady-like lecture' and noted that 'Edith's voice is weak, her English accent very strong'. The second, in April 1918, was to an audience of American soldiers, and became the basis for the first chapter of *French Ways and their Meaning*, written, she said, by 'an outsider familiar with both races', and intended 'for American soldiers and sailors, to help them understand the people and customs of France'. The book was ordered to be placed in all ships' libraries by the US Department of the Navy. The lecture, even more than the book, was couched in the terms she thought suitable for ignorant young American soldiers:

> I'm sure you agree with me that the best way of profiting by the study of a strange people is to see what we can learn from them ... We'd better ... apply ourselves to finding out what France can teach us ... Tastes are bound to differ in different countries – and ... liking corn-beef hash for breakfast instead of a roll and butter is not a necessary proof of superiority ... We all learn in time that we must put something into our lives besides business and hustle; and France learned it a little sooner because she's seven or eight centuries older than we are.

How this kind of thing went down with the army is not recorded. But Wharton would do anything that she thought would be 'good propper-gander'. 'I believe if I were dead', she told this audience, 'and anybody asked me to come back and witness for France, I should get out of my grave to do it.'[32]

At the outbreak of war, Wharton was scathing about the panic of many foreigners in Paris, especially Americans. Embassies were bombarded with crowds of applicants who found themselves suddenly stranded without access to their funds, wanting visas, money, and travel permits. This 'stampede' was quite a sight, and much remarked on. In 'The Look of Paris', Wharton described it as a phase of 'wild rushing to the station', 'bribing of concierges', 'vain quests for invisible cabs, haggard hours of waiting in the queue at Cook's'. (She used these scenes, vividly, in *The Marne*.) Walter Berry was very much in demand now, helping out – as Edith put it drily – innumerable 'stranded beauties' with funds he could access through his position at the Chamber of Commerce. He became an essential figure not just for Edith Wharton but in the lives of many Americans in France.

She wanted to 'make herself useful', too, like many other wealthy American and upper-class French women. One American observer wrote of 1914: 'In an amazingly short space of time after the war broke out, Paris bristled with hospitals and *ouvroirs*. Almost all the hotels and schools flew the [French] Red Cross flag and a great many luxurious private houses were put at the disposition of the Government.' Wharton was asked by one of her grandest Parisian friends, the Comtesse d'Haussonville (wife of the grandson of Mme de Staël, and one of Proust's models for his Duchesse de Guermantes), to set up an '*ouvroir*' (a 'work-room', or, more specifically, a 'needlework school for indigent young women') under the auspices of the French Red Cross. Wharton found an empty apartment just round the corner, in the Rue Vaneau. One observer of the Paris charities said that Wharton's was one of several 'sewing circles' meant 'to supply work to unmarried French women and widows'. In fact it was more ambitious than that. The point, as Wharton scathingly explained to Berenson, was that a lot of rich ladies had immediately rushed to 'turn their drawing rooms into hospitals' and to 'make shirts for the wounded', and the Red Cross was opening big sewing-rooms with large numbers of volunteers; as a result, the ordinary Parisian seamstresses (who had been dependent on the couture houses, now closing down for the war) suddenly found themselves out of work. It was typical of her, now and throughout the war, to dissociate herself from the other benevolent ladies and their organisations. Her war-work was always somewhat competitive.[33]

Wharton's *ouvroir* was initially small-scale, but it was eminently practical and sensible, and paid attention precisely to the 'useful activities' of ordinary working people which she was so horrified to see destroyed by the German advance. The unemployed women who had been working for the *salons de couture* were given 1 franc (later 1.50) and a hot meal a day; they worked for six hours, and were kept on for two (later three) months at a time. They made bandages, socks, sweaters and other war-supplies; later, they sewed fashionable lingerie as well. At first the garments were given away, then sold for low prices. There were about twenty women working there at a time, rising to sixty. Secretaries and other professional women were allowed in as well as seamstresses. The condition of employment was that they had no relations at the front and therefore received no 'military assistance'.[34]

Wharton at once began pressurising her friends and acquaintances for money and help. In the first two weeks alone, orders came pouring in for clothes, and she managed to raise $2,000. There were familiar names – Walter Berry, Morton Fullerton, the Abbé Mugnier, the Walter Gays – among her donors. International high society transformed itself now into a web of useful contacts, and Wharton's networking energies – once so thwarted in her attempts to give Henry James a birthday present – were now being put to greater use. For the next four years she milked her contacts untiringly for funds for her charities. It is an irony of Edith's war that the social world she had left behind in New York, and which she held up to such severe inspection in her novels, was now the main source of support for her work in France. By 1915, she was not only chairing a committee for her charities which had many of the great and good of the Franco-American world on its board (including Walter; Mildred Bliss, wife of the secretary of the American Embassy in Paris, Robert Bliss, art-collector, future owner of Dumbarton Oaks, and a rival Lady Bountiful; Walter's friend Alice Garrett, wife of the American ambassador's special assistant; Matilda Gay; Charles Du Bos; the Baron de Marmul; Edith's lawyer André Boccon-Gibod; and Mrs Blair Fairchild) but she had set up a network of 'American Auxiliary Committees' to raise funds for her char-ities. These were based in New York, Boston, Washington, Baltimore, Bar Harbor, and Montclair, New Jersey, and were stuffed with Lodges and Chandlers, Adamses and Roosevelts, Cuttings and Whitneys, Tuckermans and Griswolds. The list of the contributors to Mrs Wharton's charities reads like the New York Social Register. At the head of her team were two high-powered, well-connected divorced women, the inexhaustible Minnie Jones, now in her sixties, in New York, and, in Paris, a new friend, Elisina Tyler, whom the war was going to turn into Edith's indispensable companion.[35]

Though she was happy to have started work and was scathing about those who left Paris ('most of the fluffy fuzzy people have gone, & the ones left are working hard', she wrote to Berenson later in the year) her war got off to a curious false start. Once she had set up the *ouvroir* with a manageress, she too, like the panicky Americans she despised, was trying hard to get out of Paris: not because of fear, but because of a previous commitment. She had made arrangements to rent Mrs Humphry Ward's house, Stocks, and was in the process of moving herself there – some of the servants had already gone – when war broke out. Leaving France involved, for her as for anyone else, long days of queuing and much red tape, but like others of her class she was not averse to using her influence. (Walter told Berenson he was arranging for the Wharton vehicle to be shipped across the Channel to 'car-less Edith'.) Her war-story is one of hard work and dedication, but it is also one of special treatment, connections in high places, and servants to run errands. The tone is audible in a letter to the very wealthy Mrs Eleanor Belmont, inviting her to visit one of the convalescent homes at Groslay: 'It is only thirty minutes from Paris if one's chauffeur knows the way.'[36] A much-repeated story of Edith's trying to charter a battleship to get her across to England is no doubt apocryphal, but she certainly expected good treatment.

Wharton encountered the same obstacles as everyone else, however, when she tried to get out of Paris that summer. She wrote to her fellow novelist, Mrs Ward, with whom she was on courteous but not intimate terms, on 15 August 1914, describing the difficulties:

> I still hope to get to Stocks in the next few days, but the process is not as simple as it seems, no doubt, to you. There has never been any interruption in the boat service; the difficulties have been here, & they are many. First, & until the day before yesterday, there were no regular trains, & no assurance that civilians would not be put off any train that was running if their places were wanted. Secondly, it was impossible to take *any* luggage. – My French cook, who came back last week to join his regiment, was 48 hours between London & Paris ... The first regular train started the day before yesterday, & my sister-in-law left yesterday. It left at 7 a.m. & to get a seat she had to be at the station at 4.30 a.m., & then there was a large crowd ahead of her! – Moreover, no one can land in England without a passport visé [authorised] by the British Consulate, & as it is open only for 5 or 6 hours a day, the crowds are so dense that each time I have gone there I have been told to come back the next day – with the same result! Lastly, no French subject can leave France without permission, & as my maid's papers are at Boulogne, & she has now been trying for 8 days to have them sent here, I don't know when she will be able to leave! – You see a country under martial law in the Continental sense is different from anything we can picture in English-speaking lands. I forgot to add that the British government has just notified the Consulate here that 'aliens' (even friendly) are not wanted – & at Cook's they tell me that only travellers who can show steamer tickets for America are admitted. Still, I believe I can land if I say I have a house in England.[37]

This is Wharton in full spate, intelligent, emphatic, busy, strong-willed, impatient, wanting her own way, slightly condescending to anyone not in the know, and quick to pass judgement: all qualities that she would soon be using on behalf of others, not for herself. But at this moment she could not anticipate the course of the war, and she thought she should keep to her plans for going to England. She managed to get over to Folkestone, and was met there by Henry James.

It was the last phase of her long dream of having an English house. After the failure to 'Cooperbuy' in 1913, she was thinking in terms of short-term rentals rather than purchases. Mary Hunter had offered her Hill Hall for the summer of 1914, and she also toyed with the idea of a house in Oxfordshire, but the house she chose was Stocks. Wharton had mixed feelings about Mrs Humphry Ward. She and James used to satirise her love of fame and adulation, and her name came to stand for Wharton as an emblem of everything old-fashioned and passé in literature; she dreaded being compared to her. Nevertheless, her house was very desirable. It lay on the border of Hertfordshire and Buckinghamshire, 'on a high upland, under one of the last easterly spurs of the Chilterns', as its owner described it, a place of 'rural quiet beneath wooded hills'. Stocks was just up the road from the ancient village of Aldbury, and very near the Rothschilds' gigantic mansion at Tring Park. Mrs Ward, though certainly no Rothschild, had moved up the social ladder as a result of her immense popularity as a novelist to comfortable landowning status; Stocks, a substantial late-eighteenth-century house, reflected the rise in her fortunes and her social ambitions. The Wards had found the house in 1892, rented it for a few years, bought it in 1896 (for £18,000) and remodelled it extensively in 1908. It had 'old-walled and yew-hedged gardens, a small bit of beautiful park, an avenue of limes like a cathedral aisle'. They had shooting parties and balls there, put on theatricals for the village, and built a nine-hole golf-course. (Stocks has gone through some peculiar metamorphoses since Mrs Ward's day, from girls' school to a training centre for *Playboy*'s bunny girls and croupiers, and is now a golfers' hotel.) By 1914 the Wards' finances were in much poorer shape. Tax bills were crippling, Stocks had become too expensive for them, and they wanted to rent to their rich American friend in order to economise. Wharton's tenancy, which also involved her renting the Wards' London house at 25 Grosvenor Place, was a strictly business arrangement. Mrs Ward drove a hard bargain, failing to warn Wharton that there was no telephone, and charging her extra for the garden vegetables.[38]

James thought it perfect for her. 'It was much modernized & bathroomed some few years back – not, doubtless, on the American scale, but very workably & conveniently. And it's civilized & big-treed & gardened & library'd & pictured & garaged in a very sympathetic way ... I kind of see you *at rest there* under fine old English umbrage.'[39] Stocks has been so altered and modernised that it is hard to imagine it as James saw it. What does rouse the imagination, though, is the picture-postcard village of Aldbury, with its village pond, its ancient stocks (giving the house its name), its Tudor houses with their little gardens, its grey flint church, and its tiny post office, where Wharton walked down every day all through August and early September, to get the news from France. This settled, feudal English village, clustered below the big house, looks little changed. But there is no record of Edith Wharton here; unlike the Ward family, she did not settle in to play Lady Bountiful to the village, or be laid to rest in the yew-shaded English churchyard. The place knows nothing of her; she left no trace.

Wharton thought of England as a 'great rich garden'[40] protected from world-events. But there is something troubling and haunted about this protected place, too. These old English houses are perfect settings for ghosts, of course, and Wharton had a weakness for ghosts. Gaillard Lapsley told Percy Lubbock that when Mary Hunter put Wharton in the room at Hill Hall that was supposed to be haunted, she insisted on being moved. After all, she had read her *Turn of the Screw* and her Wilkie Collins, her *Jane Eyre* and her Kipling. The beautiful inherited old English house in the story 'Mr Jones' turns into a place of haunted horror. In 'Afterward', the old Dorsetshire house of Lyng, filled for its American purchasers with 'the charm of having been for centuries a deep dim reservoir of life', holds back its secrets until long 'afterward'. In the end it proves a baleful resting-place, and it ends with an American woman, Mary Boyne, sitting alone and terrified in the beautiful, peaceful old house.

Nothing terrifying happened at Stocks – nothing happened at all, and that was the trouble. In the deep seclusion of that English country retreat, she felt as alien, ghostly and alone as Mary Boyne in her story. James had imagined Stocks as a peaceable refuge, 'balm' for the soul of this restless wanderer. But this was not a time of rest for Wharton or anyone else. As the Germans got closer to Paris and the stories of their invasion filtered through, she passionately wished she had not come:

Now that the last grim news has come, I reproach myself for not having stuck to my job, for it looks now as if Paris might be invaded, & in that case I ought to have remained. But even when I left last Thursday such a possibility was unthinkable, & not till we got to Boulogne did we know that the coast towns were evacuated.

Alone at Stocks during the imminent invasion of Paris and the Battle of the Marne, she was wretched. 'She was much distressed at having appeared to flee', Percy told Gaillard, after visiting her and finding her 'all alone, very restless & lost in this great charming blooming place'. Woman's domestic wartime work was not for her (Percy described her 'knitting & knotting & unravelling & re-knitting what is understood to be a comforter for a wounded soldier'). She wanted to do something – she asked the Wards if she could open their house to convalescents – and she particularly wanted to rouse up the English, whose protected hedonism disgusted her:

> It is rather shocking to me here to see able-bodied young men about everywhere, at games, & philandering with young ladies, & I rather wish the Huns would drop a bomb – just a little one – in the midst of this English peace – lest you all forget how close they are! When one has seen the look in the French faces, men's & women's, it is a little painful to see England so calm.

(It was unfair of her: many of those young men would soon be dead.) She wondered whether she could 'give a small present to any of the Stocks men who are volunteering'. The 'beautiful soothing arms' of this 'dear domestic Paradise' were not for her: she was increasingly anxious to get back to her 'work in Paris'. She contacted the embassy, but they could not guarantee her return. She moved from Stocks to Grosvenor Place. Then she received the startling news that the manageress of her *ouvroir* had run away with all the money, in the general stampede out of Paris, and laid off the fifty work-women.

'I am going back to Paris!' she told Mrs Ward, in a tone of relief, even of triumph. Much detail followed about how to close up the London house and tidy things up at Stocks, when the servants would leave, whether she might come back, and how of course she could not stand in the way 'of your offering the house to others'. 'I only wish . . . that I could have enjoyed it more; but how can one *think* the word, even, in such days as these?' The whole episode must have been extremely irritating for Mrs Ward, who cannot have been pleased to lose her wealthy tenant so suddenly. But for Edith Wharton it was the end of her false start to the war, her phoney peace. She wrote to Bélugou from Stocks on 8 September: *'Jamais je n'ai senti comme en ce moment-ci combien j'aime la France et mes amis français. Cela me déchire le coeur de ne pas pouvoir le prouver en accourant à Paris. Il y a des "bouches inutiles", je le sais bien, mais des "coeurs inutiles"? Pas quand ils sentent vos tristesses comme je les sens!'* On 21 September, James – whom she would only see once more before he died – wrote in farewell to her: 'All my blessings on all your splendid resolution, your courage & charity!'[41] On 24 September 1914, with one of her surges of decisive energy, she made her choice, and went back to France. She never thought of living in England again, any more than she did of living in America. Seven years after her first move to Paris, at the age of fifty-two, her *'grande naturalisation'* was confirmed.

15

Une Seconde Patrie

The first thing Wharton did when she returned to Paris was to get the money back from the absconding manageress, via the Red Cross, and to relocate the *ouvroir* to a new address: '*Ouvroir de Mme Wharton, Au Petit St Thomas, 25 Rue de l'Université*'. It was on the corner of the Rue du Bac, very near her apartment. It stayed there until the building was taken over by the government at the end of 1915, and the whole operation had to be moved again to the Boulevard St Germain. She had help from two French sisters, the Landormys, nieces of a music-critic. The numbers expanded, and the *ouvroir* linked in to other initiatives, giving supplies to Mildred Bliss's 'Children of the Frontier', selling clothes to raise money for the 'Fund for the Serbian Wounded' and for the *Book of the Homeless*, providing boxes of lingerie and fine sewing (shipped c/o Walter at the Chamber of Commerce) for a New York charity bazaar. Wharton was very hands-on in her management, as a letter to Minnie in January 1916 shows: 'The small lingerie orders are very worrying. I think hereafter it wd be better to refuse any of less than $20, on the ground that the price of materials is going up so much. We certainly can't make chemises for less than 15–20 fcs, & night-gowns for less than 20–25 fcs.' It is hard to read a sentence like this and not think about the sort of sentences she might have been writing instead. But as she said to Sally: 'All this keeps me busy & interested, so that I feel the oppression of the war much less than I did in England.' This note is struck again in a condolence letter to a French friend whose son had been killed, written in 1917: '*Même pour ceux qui n'ont pas souffert personnellement dans leur affection de cette terrible guerre, le travail est le seul refuge.*' This was a time of opportunity and satisfaction for her, as well as anguish and stoic endurance.[1]

Wharton's managerial skills, which up to now she had mainly exercised on house-building, intelligent travel, and her own professional career, were considerable. If she had not been a novelist one can imagine her running a big house-design or landscaping business, like her niece; if she had married a Theodore Roosevelt or a Harry White instead of a Teddy Wharton she could have been an impressive president's or ambassador's wife (and an even better ambassador). High-powered managers are not always tolerant, though, and she was quick to match her own standards of administration against those of the many other bodies involved in civilian war-work. Her criticisms were levelled equally at incompetent French bureaucrats, overbearing American interventionists and silly rich ladies. 'It is profoundly discouraging to think of American money being raised by Mrs Belmont's entertainment and given to the Secours National, which is the laughing stock of Paris for its muddling niggling *fonctionnarisme*, when there is a big active American charity here [her own] which has been working hard for two months . . .' How stupid, she added, of people to send blankets from the States without finding out first whether they are still needed. A month later: 'The incompetence and callousness of the French charitable organisations is notorious among French people . . . these funds are administered by the "gros bonnets", social and political, who are so hide-bound, timid and unpractical that they spend most of their time inventing ways how *not* to give.' She was just as scathing about sentimental Americans back home 'sending toys and sugar-plums to the Belgian war-orphans, with little notes from "Happy American children", requesting to have their gifts acknowledged'.[2] Her war-novels and stories make the most of the foolish, competitive and self-serving aspects of philanthropic behaviour.

There were a thousand and one organisations in Paris by the end of 1914 ('The American Fund for French Wounded', 'The Women's War Relief Corps', 'The French Heroes' Fund', 'The American Committee for Training in Suitable Trades the Maimed Soldiers of France'), many of them run by American ladies – Astors, Vanderbilts, Payne Whitneys, Belmonts, Roosevelts. Wharton's name was often listed. She was on the women's executive committee of the American Ambulance Hospital of Paris (to raise funds for extra nurses and doctors); she served, with Walter, on an American Chamber of Commerce Charity for Wounded Soldiers; she led an initiative for a coal fund for refugees; she was on the board of directors of the Women's War Relief Corps. With Mrs Belmont, she raised funds for the Belgians under German occupation, her appeal couched in typically detailed, pragmatic terms: 'The Germans have taken all their blankets, warm quilts, bed-linen, shoes, metal door-knobs and window-handles, and even the stuffing of mattresses, and the women and children . . . are literally perishing of cold.' But her main work was for the Belgian refugees, especially women and children, and for the victims of TB: the unhoused and the dispossessed, the orphaned and the sick. Unlike the ladies she

caricatured in *A Son at the Front*, who 'flitted about, tragic and ineffectual', or a grand benefactress like Mrs William K. Vanderbilt, seen visiting
the American Ambulance Hospital at Neuilly wearing 'a double string of
pearls' half-concealed under her Red Cross uniform, she got to work
without airs and graces.[3]

It is a mark of Wharton's inwardness with French social networks that
her first large-scale wartime charity grew out of an affiliation with a
Parisian organisation, rather than being one of the many American-led
initiatives. Wharton's American Hostels for Refugees, for which she would
be very well known by the end of the war, began as a collaboration with
the Foyer Franco-Belge, set up by a remarkable small group of French and
Belgian Parisians, among them Charlie Du Bos, André Gide and his intimate friend Maria Van Rysselberghe, and the composer Darius Milhaud.
The 'Foyer' (the word means 'home', usually for soldiers or widows,
refugees or the sick) began when Gide and others helped out with the
streams of desperate refugees from Belgium and northern France gathered
at the Cirque de Paris in a makeshift refugee centre, and in need of everything: food, shelter, bedding, money, employment, solace. Gide and his
friends worked long hours to meet these needs, but the Foyer was rapidly
overwhelmed by demands. This was where Wharton came in. With the
help of some wealthy associates, she provided hostels for the refugees, and
arranged for them to be sent there from the Foyer. The administrative
headquarters were established at first in the Rue Royale and later in bigger
offices at 63 Avenue des Champs-Élysées, in a house provided by the
Comtesse de Béarn. The hostels were three big houses in the Rue Taitbout,
the Rue Pierre Nicole and the Rue du Colisée. 'We begged right and left
for beds and blankets, we hired linen and cutlery, and within a fortnight
we had opened two houses with beds for a hundred, and a third with a
restaurant for 550 and a free clinic and dispensary . . . for the poor creatures we sheltered were almost all ill from hunger, fatigue, and the horrors
they had undergone.' The hostels also provided a reading-room, sewing-
rooms for the women, a Montessori nursery school, an English class for
adults, and an employment agency. The idea was to find work and a home
for the refugees, not to keep them dependent. When they could, they
paid rent for their accommodation.

Wharton also opened a grocery depot in the Rue Pierre-Charron (run
by Lizzie Cameron, who started to help Wharton full-time in the autumn
of 1915) and a clothing depot in the Rue la Boétie (Gide often worked
there), later expanded and moved to the Rue Boissy-d'Anglas, and vividly
described in *A Son at the Front*. She set up her fund-raising committees in

America; she made numerous appeals, describing the hostels, to the American papers; she hosted a Christmas party for hundreds of refugees every year of the war, from 1914 onwards; and, though she delegated the running of the various depots and foyers, and the physical labour, to her many volunteers, she master-minded the fund-raising for and the expansion of the hostels. (Elisina Tyler described their partnership thus in a retrospective account of the charities: '*Mrs Wharton me dit un jour en riant: "Je suis le gagne-pain, vous êtes la ménagère, et nous pouvons nous vanter d'avoir eu une nombreuse progéniture."*') By April 1915, the hostels had provided for '5,113 refugees', with '142,480 free meals served; permanent employment found for 1,372 refugees; 51,918 garments distributed ... Total expenditure to date, 161,755 francs'. Lizzie Cameron, in 1916, described the refugees from Reims as 'very superior – patient and cheerful but with an intense longing to go home'. Robert Grant, visiting the hostels in 1916, gave a clear picture of their sensible, if paternalistic, arrangements:

23 bis rue de l'Université ~~63, RUE DE VARENNE~~

AMERICAN HOSTELS FOR REFUGEES

(WITH THE FOYER FRANCO-BELGE)

Since the founding of the American Hostels, Nov. 1914, they have provided (up to July 1st 1915) for

7,500 Refugees.

Found work for over 2000.

Clothed over 6000.

Served over 180,000 meals.

[The refugees occupy] sometimes one room, sometimes two, for which they pay eight to fifteen francs per month, including gas, electric light and clean bed-linen twice a month, with the use of the kitchen on the étage in common – decent, nice-mannered folk who seemed very contented and very grateful . . . The inmates who had been rescued from privation and filth beamed at us from their wash tubs, ironing-boards and kitchen stoves. One family of thirteen was neatly housed in two rooms . . . I was told that these people were in a pitiable plight before they were taken in.[4]

This Franco-American collaboration brought together two of the great writers of their day. Gide, who was forty-three in 1914, enjoyed getting to know Wharton; he found the idea of travelling with her 'amusing'; she would try to persuade him, unsuccessfully, to translate *Summer*. She took him, with Bélugou, to the South of France for a few days in the autumn of 1915 to meet Bourget, and Bourget and Gide had their conversation about pederasty in *L'Immoraliste*, which they broke off when Wharton came into the room. She felt that Gide got to know her a little better on this trip, describing to Elisina a lunch they had together in Toulon:

You should have seen his amazement and delight when he found that I *loved* buying eatables in bags out of queer little stalls full of anchovies and things in oil! We loaded ourselves with melons (lovely little green ones), 'noix de Grenoble', dried figs (no epithets good enough for *them*) and squashy dates; and therewith betook ourselves to a queer little restaurant overlooking the port, where, in an upper salle delightfully frescoed with steamers and tropical vegetations and 'scenes de chasse', we lunched on our spoils and a bottle of asti . . . And Gide has thought better of me ever since. I wonder why I'm so generally misunderstood?

When James died, Gide wrote Wharton a grave and affectionate letter. And at first he enjoyed the work at the Foyer, which he and Charlie (who would later quarrel) looked back on as '*les temps héroiques*'. But he did not have her staying-power or her appetite for charity work. He disliked the sort of wartime sensationalism that meant getting hold of a mutilated child war-victim for a potential American donor, and he got increasingly fed up with the bureaucracy and quarrels and the abuses of the charity. Gide noted the 'atmosphere of affection and bewilderment that pervades [the Foyer] and the dangerous intoxication that self-sacrifice brings'. Wharton too would become familiar with the obnoxious side of charity work, the 'exasperation of the would-be philanthropist when he first discovers that nothing complicates life as much as doing good', the pettiness and rivalry of which philanthropists are capable, the 'speculation' in war-charities, the 'Paris drawing rooms' echoing 'with the usual rumours of committee wrangles'. One of the problems at the Foyer was that Charlie Du Bos was a hopeless organiser, and very touchy about his role. To his lasting chagrin, he was ousted in 1916, and Edith was the person who had to do it, though she kept assuring him that it would not affect their friendship. (She was more forthright with Minnie: 'Charlie Du Bos resigned from the Hostels and the Foyer about two months ago. Though he was devoted to the refugees, it was very difficult for us all to work with him, as he had no method, and would not collaborate with anyone; so his departure was not an unmixed sorrow.') Du Bos always minded the fact that she refused to 'have this out' with him: '*Je persiste à regretter qu'Edith ait toujours refusé toute explication entre nous.*' Gide also left, and in October 1916, in a *coup d'état* which foreshadowed the takeover by the American Red Cross of numerous Paris charities at the end of 1917, the Foyer was merged into Wharton's better-run and more successful American Hostels.[5]

One of the emotions likely to assail volunteer workers in wartime was exasperation with the very people they were helping, and Wharton would, retrospectively, be drily humorous about 'the insoluble refugee question . . . how to stop their squabbling and being ill and getting double rations, and slandering and beating each other, and wanting to go home when they had no homes and to stay in Paris when rescued and refurnished homes awaited them'. Another was the conflict between the value of helping and the immensity of the need: a feeling that all the busyness made only a tiny bubble in the ocean of suffering. Wharton's way of dealing with any such uncertainties was to do more. She was especially exercised by the plight of the orphans of western Flanders, victims of the German attacks on Ypres, Poperinghe, Furnes, places she would see in June 1915. She made a heartfelt appeal in the spring of 1915 for American funds for the Flemish children, with good results, and was asked by the Belgian government to rescue and house a large consignment of children and nuns, whose convent had been taken over as a military hospital. Wharton said there were sixty children in her report on 'The Children of Flanders Rescue Committee', but she told Lily Norton there were two hundred, and by the end of June 1915, when she was writing to Charles Scribner to explain why she couldn't get on with 'Literature', she counted nearly seven hundred. This was Elisina Tyler's fiefdom, and she and Wharton set about raising funds, organising premises (two empty houses just outside Paris, in Sèvres and St Ouen, another at Montsoult in Seine-et-Oise and two at Arromanches in Normandy), and superintending the reception, cleaning, clothing, and looking after of large numbers of small children 'ill from privation, filth and fatigue'. Wharton was aware that this was 'her most appealing charity', and she spared no rhetoric in wringing potential donors' heartstrings with stories of the 'pitiful little creatures'. She told Elisina that this style of writing was 'the contrary of what I approve', but 'I always get money by the "tremolo" note'. In retrospect she was more grimly ironic about the 'cannibal greed' that came over these deprived orphans, who turned into a 'raging mob' when a Christmas party with toys and gifts was organised for them in 1916.[6]

Like the hostels, the Children of Flanders charity expanded, and got a regular subsidy from the Belgian government. Wharton had the inventive idea of incorporating a lace-making school, run by an expert and taught 'according to the methods of the celebrated École Normale of Bruges'. By 1917 the charity was caring for 270 children and 210 adults and needed 10,000 francs a month to keep going. The houses were stable centres of refuge until the bombardment of Paris in the spring of 1918, when the orphans of St Ouen had to be moved. Right up to the end of the war, Wharton was still fund-raising for the children – an appeal for shoes went out on Armistice Day – and it was not until August 1919 that she could record that 'all the children of Flanders went back to Belgium last week'. Photographs of the children show well-scrubbed, tidy, sturdy-looking rows of girls in neat pinafores and stout boots. She took Robert Grant to the house at St Ouen in 1916 to see two hundred little Belgian girls being confirmed by the Cardinal Archbishop of Paris. The children, he wrote, were demure, perfectly behaved and noiseless, until Wharton and Grant were leaving, when they were 'let loose out of doors' and 'waved their handkerchiefs at their benefactress and . . . cried enthusiastically: "Vive La Belgique!"'.[7]

From 1915 to 1918 the main effects of the war on Paris were the mass numbers of bereavements, the return of the wounded, unemployment, the commitment to war-work, and the huge influx of refugees, often resented. (Also blackouts, food and coal shortages, especially in the bitterly cold winter of 1917, and high prices of meat and sugar, milk and butter. Much hoarding and black-marketeering went on, and Parisians particularly resented restrictions on their meat-eating, as in a Hermann-Paul cartoon of a widow crying: 'They've killed my husband and taken my son prisoner, but they won't make me do without meat!') By 1915 it became possible to resume a 'normal' life in the capital. Those who managed to get to the city

from the horrors of the *'villes martyres'* in the occupied north had (as Richard
Cobb wrote)

> a sense almost of moral outrage. They had tried to convey to the Parisians
> what life had been like in the dark, beleaguered, frozen towns on the
> Belgian frontier, during the terrible winters of the occupation. Oh yes,
> replied the Parisians, they too had suffered, they too had been bombed,
> Paris had been in the front line, but it had *held*. Some Lillois came away
> with the impressions that the Parisians actually believed that they were
> in the process of winning the war.

Sections of Paris society – as caricatured in A *Son at the Front* – decided
to try and 'forget the war'. The city's 'panache' turned into what could be
seen as frivolity, though the young American war-hero of *The Marne* recognises this as a symptom of Paris's 'irrepressible' spirit: 'It was as if she wanted,
by a livelier renewal of activities, to proclaim her unshakeable faith in her
defenders.'[8] But what could not be ignored was illness.

Long before the impact of the Spanish flu epidemic, tuberculosis was on
the increase in France during the war, for all kinds of reasons: transmission
of the disease by refugees, women worn out by war-factory work, bad housing
conditions, malnutrition, and the takeover of many sanatoriums and hospitals for wounded soldiers. Numerous foundations were set up to try and deal
with the epidemic, including the French Tuberculosis War Victims' Fund,
started in October 1916. Wharton's work for TB victims came directly out
of her hostels. She launched an appeal at the end of 1914 for a small
hospital of about forty beds for soldiers with TB. In the summer of 1916,
she opened two sanatoriums for refugees with TB: but at the start of the
war there was a law against using the word 'tuberculosis', in case, presumably, of a panic-struck reaction against the refugees. The patients were said
to be suffering from *'bronchite chronique'*, and the houses were called
'Maisons Américaines de Convalescence'. One was at Groslay, a little village
with a beautiful church, set in orchards near the forest of Montmorency
and just north of St Denis: the very area where she used to go on some of
her 'happy days' with Morton, and where, after these war years, she would
find her next home. Two houses were rented, next to each other in the
park-grounds of the Château de Groslay, with kitchen-gardens. One house
was for the mothers, the other for the children: they could hear their little
ones playing on the other side of the wall, but were kept apart for fear of
further contamination. The other hospital was, like one of the orphan
homes, by the sea at Arromanches. Wharton described them as 'Fresh-air
sanatoriums . . . organized according to the most modern American methods

for the treatment of tuberculosis'. They led to the founding of a large-scale charity called Tuberculeux de la Guerre, for which joint French and American funding was sought. Like her hostels, the hospitals expanded during the war, with two more opening near Paris, another for children with bone diseases at Arromanches, and two sanatoriums in Burgundy. These created the most demanding call on Wharton's fund-raising efforts. They cost 40,000 francs a month to operate, and by 1917 cared for 135 refugee women and children from the hostels, and fifty children with TB of the bone, sent to the sanatoriums and paid for by the city of Paris. A letter to Berenson on headed notepaper urging him to come and help them, in February 1917, shows the status of the organisation:

> Les Tuberculeux De La Guerre [French Tuberculous War Victims], Maisons de Repos Franco-Américains, 61 Rue de Varenne, Paris VIIe. Président: Mme Edward Tuck. Vice Présidents: Mlle Chaptal, Mme Wharton. Administrateur: M. Le Comte Etienne de Beaumont, M. Rodier. Trésorier: Walter Berry. Secrétaire: Mme Barthez. Secrétaire 'Adjoint': M. Ronald Simmons. Présidents d'honneur: William Sharp, Ambassador; Leon Bourgeois, Ministre d'état. Comité: Comtesse de Béarn, Comtesse de Beaumont, Blair Fairchild, Mme la Marquise de Ganay, Mme Pierre Goujon, Mme la Princesse Soutzo, Mme Royall Tyler, Bertram Winthrop.

Three of these names were dear to Wharton's heart: Walter, as always; Elisina Tyler, from now on; and, for a very brief time, Ronald Simmons.[9]

This large, ambitious network of charities required an enormous level of commitment and expenditure of energy. Elisina (no mean administrator herself) looked back on Wharton's work as 'un travail de Titan': you had to have been working shoulder to shoulder with her, she said, and to have witnessed 'avec quel inlassable dévouement elle s'est prodiguée' ['with what tireless devotion she expended her energies'], to understand 'la grandeur de son sacrifice'. It comes as no surprise to find Wharton telling Charlie Du Bos's wife Zézette that she normally required only five hours' sleep a night.[10]

There seemed no end to what she would take on. One strenuous offshoot from the charities was a series of concerts she hosted at the Rue de Varenne in aid of the hostels, the first with the composer Vincent d'Indy. What with programming, dealing with quarrelling musicians and guest-lists, it was almost as taxing as the rest of her activities put together: 'Oh my!' (she told Mary Berenson) 'I'd rather write a three volume novel than do it again!' She would get a satirical scene out of it in A Son at the Front, in which the musicians play Stravinsky to a 'bored and restless' society crowd, and a much later story, 'A Glimpse', about the passions of rivalrous musicians. This was not her first try at a musical salon. Charlie Du Bos had been to a concert at her apartment in March 1914, in which the Spanish pianist Ricardo Viñes played a remarkable programme of Franck, Fauré, Debussy, Ravel, Bach, Granados and Albéniz. He remembered another concert on behalf of the hostels at which the César Franck quintet was played, by Darius Milhaud among others. And in 1918, Wharton organised a musical benefit concert at the Théâtre Femina, with a military band. These were not just useful ways of raising money: they also provided opportunities to hear some good music in wartime, and Wharton took a profound pleasure in music, from Bach and Beethoven to contemporaries like Ravel, Debussy, Hahn and Stravinsky. An even more ambitious scheme in December 1916, which she asked Minnie to mastermind in New York, with the help of Elsie de Wolfe and Elizabeth Marbury (much as Wharton felt 'degraded' by having anything to do with these two ladies), was to hold a charity performance of Diaghilev's Russian Ballet, with Nijinsky, at the Met. It came to nothing, and the attempt to arrange it was nearly the death of Minnie.[11]

Though not everything she took on was as difficult as hosting a society concert or trying to hire the Metropolitan Opera House long-distance, the complications of running, and fund-raising for, a number of proliferating and overlapping charities, were enormous. Though the different branches were put under the official footing of 'Mrs Wharton's War Charities' in October 1915, it was all too easy for muddles to arise in the directing of cheques or gifts from America to the different charities. It was often more effective to appeal for specific cases, and, though she mocked the sentimental American appetite for 'individual pathetic stories', Wharton got involved with several such cases, writing letters on behalf of particular orphans, widows, vagrants or amputees. Towards the end of the war she took a special interest – almost a maternal one – in four little Belgian brothers, the Herrewynns, whose mother had abandoned them and whose father had been gassed. She expended a great deal of time and thought on keeping them together and ensuring their welfare, spent her own money (300 francs a month) on their expenses, and made herself formally responsible for their education and upkeep after the war. One of them died in 1921; the adult life of the others is unknown.[12]

If there was a touch of Lady Bountiful in some of this, there was also a profound commitment, at every level of detail. She took on too much, with resulting short temper, exhaustion, and stress all round. One unfortunate circumstance was the illness in wartime of her lifelong secretary, Anna Bahlmann, who developed cancer. Faithful, long-serving Anna's increasing ill-health began as an inconvenience and ended as a tragedy; she died in 1916. It was one of several painful bereavements and breaks with the past at this time; and Anna's English replacement, Dolly Herbert, was incompetent and unsatisfactory. Wharton required high standards of her co-workers, and some people found this extremely difficult. The wealthy Mildred Bliss (whose husband was high up at the American embassy and who would have friendlier relations with Wharton after the war, in part since the Blisses hired Beatrix Farrand to landscape their great estate, Dumbarton Oaks) found her almost intolerable. She told Elisina that 'Edith was ruthless and autocratic, never worked with her committees and only let people slave away for her'. For her part (as Elisina reported to her husband Royall) 'Edith . . . is again most awfully cross with Mildred about something which it would be too long to explain. She [said] "I seem to poison her after I've been with her half an hour and she gets perfectly horrid."' Perhaps they were too much alike. Wharton, for her part, thought that Mildred Bliss was deliberately undermining her. In the autumn of 1916 there was an unpleasant episode to do with the Rockefeller Foundation. Wharton asked the foundation for money for the sanatoriums, but the foundation (whose medical officer at this time, coincidentally, was Max Farrand's brother, Livingston Farrand) was warned against her because 'Mrs Wharton [had] bitterly assailed and antagonized the [American] government and the best of the medical profession'. Wharton thought that Mildred might be behind this rumour. And she did not think much of the foundation herself:

> The great Dr Biggs of New York has arrived from the Rockefeller Commission to elaborate plans for exterminating tuberculosis. He came the other day to one of our committee meetings, with the Rockefeller lawyer who accompanies him. Neither one of them speaks a word of French, or has, apparently, the least glimmer of a notion of French conditions, French atavism, French history, or any of the million things that go to make up the 'problem'.[13]

It was an advance warning of what would happen when the American army and the Red Cross came in, and would provoke the writing of *French Ways and their Meaning*.

Even the women who admired and loved Wharton found her hard to work with at times; the same mixed feelings that coloured her social relations with James and his circle are re-enacted in the wartime context of her working relations with the other volunteers. Minnie Jones, labouring away on her sister-in-law's behalf in New York, became accustomed to receiving immense, itemised lists of commands and updates, as in this letter of May 1916 (written soon after Anna's death):

I cabled a few days ago to ask you to delay the printing of the report [on the hostels] till you receive this letter. I wrote the report at Costebelle and sent it to Paris to be printed, and owing to a misunderstanding, the dispensary report was not included. There are also one or two slight mistakes to be corrected, and our plans for a hospital and lodging houses have developed so much in the last few weeks, that it seems better to risk another delay and send a fuller report ... I am delighted with the good news of our earnings at the flower-show tea. I think $575.57 a very good figure ... Meanwhile, we have about 30,000 dollars in our general fund at present, and though our expenses are naturally increased by the opening of our three lodging houses, I hope we can hold out till the autumn with such stray help as the report may bring in during the summer ... I enclose a letter just received from the Virginia War Relief, as I think it would be better for you to write a line to Miss Cameron. I wonder why her letters never reached you? Will you please send her several copies of the report, for distribution? With regard to the question of Miss Robinson-Smith and M. de Beaumont: It is perfectly incomprehensible to him and to me that she should not have received his three cables and his letter about the radioscopic machines ... I have cabled to you proposing that her [Anna's] pupils should raise a fund to support a bed in our refugee hospital ... Thank you so much also for sending the wreath, and be sure to charge this to my account ... And now to speak of a different matter: my friend Recouly is writing for Scribner an article on the battle of Verdun ... and I have suggested to him to send you the manuscript ... as soon as it is finished and to ask you to translate it ...

And so on and on, unrelentingly. It seems unfair of her to nag Minnie, at one point, about organising *her* letters better: 'Your letters are so full of detail that I am always afraid, in the mad haste of my life here, that I may overlook some of your questions. Would you mind, in future, writing on a separate sheet of paper all the business questions and numbering them as I have done?'[14] A fine example of this masterful attention to detail is found in a heated communication dictated in December 1917 – when Wharton had plenty of more important things to concern her – to the owner of an umbrella shop.

Mrs Wharton begs to inform Mr Brigg that about a month ago she took to his shop to be repaired an umbrella which she had bought from him and of which the spring was broken . . . After waiting eight days . . . the woman in the shop said it had come back from the workroom but that she had mislaid it. After another delay . . . it was returned to Mrs Wharton . . . [but] on opening it in the rain she found that the repair had not been made, and that the umbrella would not stay open. As it was raining hard and Mrs Wharton was on foot, she went at once to Mr Brigg's shop and . . . asked for the loan of an umbrella for an hour. The woman replied that she was very sorry but she could not lend an umbrella to Mrs Wharton as there were none in the shop. Mrs Wharton mentioned that she had been a client of your house for at least twenty years, and as she saw about 100 umbrellas before her eyes, she could not understand the answer. The reply was that it was impossible to lend her a new umbrella for an hour as she might damage it . . . Mrs Wharton left the shop taking her broken umbrella away and she now writes to Mr Brigg in the firm belief that he would not wish to have a client treated by his representatives with such discourtesy. He is probably aware that there is not a dressmaker or a milliner who would not lend a cloak or a hat for an hour to a well-known customer in a similar case . . .[15]

This was what Elisina Tyler – less forbearing than Minnie – would call 'Edith at her Edithest'. She often complained to her husband about it: 'Edith . . . has again altered the committee meeting from next Monday till next Thursday at a very inconvenient hour . . . Anyhow we are suffering from the heat and spoke to each other in a rather emphatic manner.' 'The enclosed from Edith. It is harum scarum, isn't it? And why does she insist on having the Finance Committee so early in the month? I am quite indignant at her slave-driving ways . . . It is only fair to treat people decently if one expects to get their best out of them.' There was one particularly disastrous occasion in the last year of the war:

Edith . . . had two medicines to take, scolded Bertha [the maid] for not removing her medicine glasses, scolded her for giving her mineral water, complained about the bread, broke a water glass (with stem) by flinging it off the table, exclaimed with rapturous surprise at the pudding as if light had dawned at last. When we withdrew to the withdrawing room, she looked at her chair before sitting in it and changed its position in a marked manner.

All the same, Elisina had to admit that she was worth making allowances for: 'She is [really] a perfectly splendid person. One must give her rope because she is a full rigged vessel and can't manoeuvre in a toilet basin.'[16]

Though Wharton could be difficult and demanding in these exhausting times, there were ample excuses for her. Plenty of other people could be difficult too, from the manageress who ran off with the money from the *ouvrier*, to the hopeless Charlie Du Bos, to an alcoholic French volunteer at the sanatorium at Groslay, where 'the whole atmosphere' (Wharton told Elisina early in 1916) 'is seething with factions, and getting very poisonous'.[17] No wonder that many of her wartime letters took the form of complaints about overwork and irritations, and the need for 'a Refuge from the Refugees'.

She did not spend the whole of the war in Paris. The journeys she made between 1915 and 1918, though not the ones she had envisaged on her return from Tunisia, were adventures which excited as well as appalled her. She was anxious, though, not to be thought of as a war-tourist. After a visit in January 1915 to the military hospital in Chartres (more 'magically beautiful' than ever), where the Whartons' old doctor, Isch Wall, was working, she told Berenson that she could not think of anything 'ghastlier and more idiotic than "doing" hospitals en touriste, like museums'. She had nothing but scorn for the high-society French ladies who behaved foolishly at the front and made it more difficult for 'the dull & venerable' to 'penetrate to the military zone'. Her own reasons for going to the most ravaged areas of France and to the front line were twofold. She was asked by the French Red Cross to take supplies to, and 'report on the needs of', ambulances and hospitals near the front, at Châlons-sur-Marne. This justified the use of the Wharton car, now a Mercedes – which Henry James was still referring to, in awe, as 'Her' – and which, loaded up with 'shirts & boxes of fresh eggs & bags of oranges', medicaments, cigarettes and chocolate, was being put to use in 'motor-flights' which bitterly contrasted with their long-ago jaunts. (She was always scrupulous about using 'Her' and her petrol for war-work only, turning down invitations to dinner because 'I don't want to use my few remaining cans of essence for pleasure when they may be needed shortly to take coal to our infants'.)

Wharton volunteered to observe and write up the conditions in the war-zone. Her way was made smooth, by orders from on high, partly because of her evident usefulness as a well-connected American writer, already deeply involved in war-work, who could propagandise for American funds for France and for America's entry into the war; and also because Walter

Berry went with her, expediting the necessary 'laissez-passer' and making sure of access. She complained to James that Walter was too unemotional for her liking on these trips, contrasting with her own 'ardent old bones'. She found Walter in wartime bad at describing what he had seen, and a little too keen on hanging out with 'Ces Dames': 'pretending, by means of one professional beauty, a restaurant table, & a new cigarette-case, that he is Seeing Life in the good old Ritzian style.' 'I can't stand that scene of khaki & champagne', she told James, and turned down all invitations to lunch at the Ritz herself. Actually, as she well knew, Walter was working as hard as she was – he told Berenson: 'I am "organising" like a Boche!' – but his style had always been cool and detached.[18] She used Walter and other contacts (her 'magic passwords or open-Sesames' as James put it) – the diplomat Jules Cambon at the Ministry of Foreign Affairs, the writer Raymond Recouly, the novelist Jean-Louis Vaudoyer – in whatever way she could. She was determined to get some 'really rather exceptional chances' of 'sight-seeing in the zone'. She was sometimes helped, on her travels, by Frenchmen in the army who had read her books – one of whom, at Verdun, was Henry de Jouvenel, Colette's husband.

She was not the only writer at the front. Wartime 'sightseers' – journalists or well-connected civilians – were frequent during the long, static war of the trenches. There were regular procedures for making sure they were protected from real danger and for passing them down the chain of command. Clearly the officers she and Berry encountered at the front were quite used to showing visitors round the battle-zones on quiet days: '"And now", said our Captain of Chasseurs, "that you've seen the second-line trenches, what do you say to taking a look at the first?"' Robert Grant also gained access to the front, using Wharton as his contact, in the summer of 1915, and, looking into no man's land under escort, 'had to assure myself that I was a guest of the French War Office and not a tourist'. Rudyard Kipling gave an emotional account in *France at War* (1916) of seeing, at the front, under the kind and patient guidance of a staff officer, French soldiers holding the line against the 'evil' 'barbarian' Boche. He described himself as the visiting civilian who 'scuttled through their life for a few emotional minutes in order to make words out of their blood'.

On Wharton and Berry's third journey, they travelled with the war-cartoonist Abel Faivre, who did a brilliant and unkind caricature, titled 'Dans Les Ruines', of a large, well-covered and be-hatted Wharton standing in the back of her car and gazing through a lorgnette at the scene, while Walter, with hat and white moustache, sits glowering next to her, and the impassive back of the chauffeur's head is set against the distant outline of

'CE N'EST QUE ÇA!'

bombed and ruined houses. The caption is: '*Ce n'est que ça!*' ['Is that all?']
The cartoon appeared on the front of *Le Rire Rouge*, a humorous magazine
(before the war just called *Le Rire*), popular for its coloured cover-pages
and its cartoons in which the '*poilu*', the ordinary French soldier, was always
the hero. Wharton's response was mild and amused – 'such a good sketch
of us . . . Walter's expression whenever I suggested visiting a hospital or
doing anything good was caught to a line.'[19] She did not mind the satire
(which suggests how well-known she and Walter were in France) because
she felt she had a useful job to do. She made the most of her 'unexpected
opportunities', at once telling Charles Scribner that she would turn them
into articles with unique materials: 'We were given opportunities *no one
else* has had of seeing things at the front. I was in the first line trenches,

in 2 bombarded towns ...' Exhilarated telegrams arrived at the Scribner office: 'JUST RETURNED FROM FIGHTING LINE IN ARGONNE MAILING ARTICLE NEXT WEEK'. She was very keen to let her publishers and her friends know that she was being given special, unrivalled access. (Scribner was not entirely convinced: in reply to her asking whether he would not prefer her war-articles to the fiction she had promised them, he cabled back: 'PREFER SHORT STORY'.)

For all the horror of war, there is no doubt from her tone that her journeys elated her. Her letters are full of the excitement of getting close to the action; she uses phrases like 'an exquisite moment' or 'every moment of the trip was thrilling', even remarking on 'the picturesqueness' of the war-scene. (James responded in kind, referring to her opportunities at the front as 'great bonheurs & romantically happy chances'.) Her passion for cultured tourism was being translated into the ambitious curiosity of that dauntless and idiosyncratic twentieth-century breed, the woman 'special correspondent' at war. And her publishers were, in the end, duly impressed. Scribner wrote to Wharton in July 1915: 'What tremendous experiences you have been through! And I did not realise until your last letter that you were attended with real danger – that you had actually been under fire.'[20] Wharton made five journeys with Walter Berry into the war-zone between February and August 1915, which were condensed into four articles published in *Scribner's Magazine*, and then in *Fighting France* in November. (She also made use of her travels in fiction, particularly in a story called 'Coming Home', published in December 1915, set in the Vosges, which she made a point of telling Scribner's was drawn from 'direct personal impressions', and later in *The Marne*.)

The year 1915 was a grim period for France in the war, with no significant victories and appalling loss of life. The front line of trenches was dug in, for 700 kilometres all the way from the North Sea to Switzerland. In April, with renewed bombardments in western Belgium, the Germans used poison gas at the second battle of Ypres. All through the year the Germans repelled the Allies' repeated attempts to break through their lines, in the Artois region (in battles at Vimy Ridge, at Neuve Chapelle, at Loos) and in the Champagne region, with huge losses and little change in what was now called 'the stabilised front'. The sinking by a German U-boat of the British liner, the *Lusitania*, in May, with many British and American casualties, still did not bring America into the war. ('The Lusitania business has done for me', Berenson wrote to Wharton, 'it is so much beyond the worst I conceived possible in the conduct of any organised society ...'[21])

Like many observers, Wharton was acutely aware of what the war-historian John Keegan calls the abrupt 'transition from normality to the place of death'. Describing the relation between the French war-zones and the rest of France from 1915 onwards, Keegan writes of successive bands of impact: 'defoliation for a mile or two on each side of no man's land, heavy destruction of buildings for a mile or two more, scattered demolition beyond that. At Verdun, on the Somme and in the Ypres salient whole villages had disappeared . . . sizeable small towns were in ruins . . . Beyond the range of the heavy artillery, 10,000 yards at most, town and country-side lay untouched.' It was quite possible for Wharton to escape completely from the war by going, as she did periodically, for restful holidays to Brittany, to Fontainebleau, or to the South of France. The exhilaration of the war-journeys for her was the crossing from the civilian into the military world; she talks about 'beginning to feel the change' or being 'already in another world' or starting to have 'the positive feeling: *This is war!*'[22]

On their first journey, made in cold February weather, Wharton and Berry (travelling with Mildred Bliss and Victor Bérard) drove east out of Paris through Meaux and Épernay (just south of Reims) towards the Argonne and Verdun. They went through empty villages and once rich country, now a 'desert', to Châlons-en-Champagne, a busy hub of mili-tary activity, which would have been invigorating had they been able to 'think away' the long lines of shell-shocked soldiers, the '*éclopés*'. They visited an under-equipped typhoid hospital, then drove on into the hills of the Argonne, through ruined villages left after the attacks of September 1914, passing a convoy of German prisoners, and into the devastated town of Clermont-en-Argonne. Here they met heroic nuns (and ate 'filet and fried potatoes' with them) who had stayed on to look after their hospice. They were now within sight and sound of the battle of Vauquois, in which the French gained back, at huge cost, an important railway link. This, she told Mary Berenson proudly, 'is just the *one* spectacle that no one is supposed to see in this subterranean war'. Even Walter was excited by this, reporting to Berenson on a 'thrilling' journey. They visited a good makeshift hospital in the village of Blercourt, and witnessed a moving service in the church-turned-hospital. It made a profound impres-sion on her, and her accounts of it mark the strong shift in her feelings in wartime towards the Catholic Church and the Catholic faith, so deeply bound up, as she felt, with French resistance and heroism. She wrote the scene up several times, first in a letter to James on 28 February, then to Mary Berenson on 13 March, describing it as 'an exquisite moment': '. . . when, at a little place called Blercourt-en-Argonne, the médecin-chef took us to see his wounded, laid out in four rows of cots down the

length of the village church. It was Sunday, & when we went in the curé
was ringing the bell in the porch. Then he went & put on his chasuble &
said vespers, with a little white acolyte swinging incense that blew out in
soft clouds over the rows of brown beds, & a few peasants & convalescent
soldiers standing between the beds & wailing out the 1870 Cantique du
Sacré Coeur – "Sauvez, sauvez la France, ne l'abandonnez pas" – against
the continuous boom of cannon across the valley.'

In her letter to James, she added: 'It was poignant.' And James wrote
back with ardour: 'Do it, *do* it, my blest Edith, for all you're worth: rather,
rather – "sauvez la France"!' When she wrote up the scene again for publication, she certainly did 'do it for all she was worth', turning it into a
full-scale set-piece. It is a good example of her wartime writing: writing
from life, from the heart, and, also, for strategic effect:

> It was about three o'clock, and in the low porch the curé was ringing
> the bell for vespers. We pushed open the inner doors and went in. The
> church was without aisles, and down the nave stood four rows of wooden
> cots with brown blankets. In almost every one lay a soldier – the doctor's
> 'worst cases' – few of them wounded, the greater number stricken with
> fever, bronchitis, frost-bite, pleurisy, or some other form of trench-
> sickness ... A handful of women ... and some of the soldiers we had
> seen about the village, had entered the church and stood together
> between the rows of cots; and the service began. It was a sunless after-
> noon, and the picture was all in monastic shades of black and white and
> ashen grey: the sick under their earth-coloured blankets, their livid faces
> against the pillows, the black dresses of the women (they seemed all to
> be in mourning) and the silver haze floating out from the little acolyte's
> censer. The only light [*sic*] in the scene – the candle-gleams on the altar,
> and their reflection in the embroideries of the curé's chasuble – were
> like a faint streak of sunset on the winter dusk.
>
> For a while the Latin cadences sounded on through the church; but
> presently the curé took up in French the Canticle of the Sacred Heart,
> composed during the war of 1870, and the little congregation joined
> their trembling voices in the refrain:
>
> > 'Sauvez, sauvez la France,
> > Ne l'abandonnez pas!'
>
> The reiterated appeal rose in a sob above the rows of bodies in the nave:
> 'Sauvez, sauvez la France,' the women wailed it near the altar, the soldiers
> took it up from the door in stronger tones; but the bodies in the cots

never stirred, and more and more, as the day faded, the church looked like a quiet grave-yard in a battle-field.[23]

After Blercourt, they drove on to the desolate fortress of Verdun – which the following year would be the scene of months of carnage – where they stayed the night. Their journey back took (by order) a more southerly route, via Bar-le-Duc, where suddenly they were back in 'a busy unconscious' civilian community. Then they crossed the path of the August 1914 invasion, going through villages 'wiped out as if a cyclone had beheaded' them, and getting lost, only 60 or so kilometres outside Paris, because all the signposts had been defaced or removed to confuse the Germans. By chance they drove into a whole encampment on the march: she thought they were lucky not to be taken for spies. A few weeks later, in March, she and Walter went back to Verdun and visited more hospitals, in worse condition, further down the Meuse river. 'I shall never forget', she wrote, making pictures for Henry James, 'the 15 mile run from Verdun . . . across a snow-covered rolling country sweeping up to the white sky, with no one in sight but now & then a cavalry patrol with a blown cloak struggling along against the wind.' They tried to get down as far as Nancy, but were sent back via Châlons, where there was intense activity and nowhere to stay. By good luck, they encountered her friend Vaudoyer, who gave them a password which got them into lodgings for the night. Standing in the cold, pitch-black street, repeating the secret word which had been whispered to her by someone she used to talk books with in the Rue de Varenne, she felt an intense sense of unreality. In the morning they saw long convoys of men and artillery going off to fight for 'the bloody strip of ground gained between Perthes and Beauséjour', just south of Reims.[24]

Their next journey was made in May, while the second battle of Ypres was being fought, and this time they got further south from Verdun, down to Nancy and Pont-à-Mousson, only eighteen miles from Metz, in Lorraine, held by the Germans. Their route out of Paris (beyond Provins, where once she had gone romancing with Morton) followed – as she put it emotively in her essay 'In Lorraine and the Vosges' – 'one of the huge tiger-scratches that the Beast flung over the land last September, between Vitry-le-François and Bar-le-Duc'. A succession of small towns and villages, destroyed in 1914, were showing signs of rejuvenation. While they had their picnic in the forest of Commercy, they could hear the cannon at the front. Gerbéviller, on the River Meurthe, was completely destroyed, and they were told horrific stories of German atrocities by the survivors, including – as at Clermont-en-Argonne – a brave nun. They went to the beautiful town of Nancy, even

more striking in the blackout, and had lunch with General Humbert at his
village headquarters, with, outside, 'the untroubled continuance of a placid
and orderly bourgeois life'. They drove through the landscape of the previous
year's battles to the 'edge of war' at Pont-à-Mousson, where they visited a
much-shelled monastery hospital. They climbed a hill to look out at the
trenches, about a mile away, and the distant city of Metz, 'the Promised
City'. From Nancy they drove through Crévic, a village where the Germans
had singled out General Lyautey's house for destruction, and to Ménil-sur-
Belvitte, on the edge of the Vosges, site of some 'awful fighting' in August
1914, where they found a curé who had turned his house into a war-museum-
cum-chapel, and was meticulously tending the war-graves. It is telling that
Wharton picks out this man, of all the people she met on her war-travels,
as 'the happiest being on earth: a man who has found his job'.

At the front, on the edge of 'lost Lorraine', they were given tea by the
commanding officer just 'out of range of the guns', visited the well-
organised trenches ('everywhere we saw the same neatness and order, the
same amused pride in the look of things'), sighted a German war-plane, a
Taube, and were driven through the ravaged war-zone up into the beautiful hills to a camp of reservists, a sort of 'forest colony' with its domestic
routines and professional methods, much admired by Wharton, where the
soldiers wrote 'Vive l'Amérique!' on her car. Guided into the range of a
German sharpshooter, they were kept well under control by the officer in
charge: '"Not beyond, please," said the officer, holding me back . . .' She
had a vivid sense of 'actually and literally' being in the front line, 'of almost
feeling their breath on our faces'. Through the lookout's peephole, they
saw a dead German lying in no man's land. What impressed Wharton the
most was the dedication to the 'Defence of France' which she read in the
faces of all the 'poilus'.[25]

Going north from Paris, in June, they were even nearer the scenes of
battle. ('If I have anything like the good luck I had on my last expedition
I can promise you an interesting article', she told Burlingame at Scribner's.)
They drove through a 'river of troops' into peaceful country around
Montreuil, and into the English-looking landscape towards St Omer and
the little town of Cassel, 'a romantic stage-setting full of the flash of arms',
with its long views on the northern plain, looking towards western Flanders:
Dunkerque, Ypres, Dixmude, Poperinge, and Nieuwpoort. They made their
way in the middle of war-traffic – horses, artillery, gun-carriages, supply-
wagons, ambulances, tents by the side of the road. They saw what was left
of Ypres, 'bombarded to death', in a silence broken by a burst of cannon
fire and a German plane under attack. In deserted Poperinge, Wharton

went searching for a convent where she had heard that they made the lace-cushions which could be used as models for the lace-school in her hostels. She found them, laid out in rows, in an abandoned classroom in the empty convent. It was one of the key moments of her war:

> On each a bit of lace had been begun – and there they had been dropped when nuns and pupils fled. They had not been left in disorder: the rows had been laid out evenly, a handkerchief thrown over each cushion. And that orderly arrest of life seemed sadder than any scene of disarray. It symbolized the senseless paralysis of a whole nation's activities. Here were a houseful of women and children, yesterday engaged in a useful task and now aimlessly astray over the earth.

They went on to Dunkerque, for the moment quiet after the bombardments of the previous month; but the next day, back in Cassel, they heard the roar, sounding very close, of the guns at Dixmude firing on Dunkerque. They drove north to the sand dunes, through evacuated villages, and saw Admiral Ronarch inspecting the brigade of Fusiliers Marins who had fought with him at Dixmude the previous autumn (and, with the British 7th Infantry Division, had halted the Germans in the battle for Calais). Cleared by officers to go on, they went to the 'victim town' of Nieuwpoort, a grotesque wreckage, and yet, quite close to it, a gay little seaside town (Ostend), one of the 'rest-cures' of the front, with a band playing, and, at La Panne, hotels full of Belgian soldiers. Here, they witnessed the impressive spectacle of military exercises on the shore, and had an audience – they were VIPs – with the king and queen of Belgium, who were directing the Belgian resistance from a modest villa at La Panne, glowingly if discreetly written up in *Fighting France*. (The royal couple wanted to hear about the work Wharton was doing for their refugees. She had contributed a poem, 'Belgium', to *King Albert's Book: A Tribute to the Belgian King and People from Representative Men and Women Throughout the World* (1915), one of the models for *The Book of the Homeless*. Wharton's poem – 'Wherever men are staunch and free / There shall she keep her fearless state' – had as its epigram *'La Belgique ne regrette rien'*, a favourite quotation of hers, used after the fall of Liège by the Belgian Foreign Minister.)

Back in Dunkerque, they saw the effects of the attack they had heard from Cassel; where her car had been parked two days before was a large crater, and everywhere broken glass and ruined houses. It was her first sight of 'the raw wounds of a bombardment'. But already a market was being set up in the streets. As usual, Wharton was alert to the survival of women's 'useful activities' in war: 'In a few minutes the signs of German havoc would be hidden behind stacks of crockery and household utensils, and some of the pale women we had left in mournful contemplation of the ruins would be bargaining as sharply as ever for a sauce-pan or a butter-tub.' Driving back from St Omer, they encountered a large regiment of British and Indian cavalry. She felt they had passed 'through a great flashing gateway in the long wall of armies guarding the civilized world from the North Sea to the Vosges'.[26]

Her last, longest war-journey of 1915 was in August, all the way into the mountains of the heavily fought front in Alsace, down towards Switzerland, and back up again to the Vosges. They went first to the front line near Reims, and took a horror-struck look at Reims's bombed cathedral. Then they drove on to 'reconquered Alsace' ('hitherto inaccessible', she wrote with excitement). The journey through the Vosges in summertime was, in fact, a kind of holiday: they picnicked in the beautiful countryside in Wharton's old way, until the 'war-sadness' fell on them again. They were cheered up, though, by a rather bizarre interlude, a fully staged 'war-tournament' put on by a company of French dragoons just outside the town of Thann, with dashing lancers watched by the local Alsatian worthies. After this they went up a mountain, abandoning 'Her' half-way for a long ride on mules, past busy colonies of soldiers (some, she noted, producing their own newspapers on foolscap, such as the 'Journal des Poilus'), up to the big guns on the old borderline 'between the Republic and Empire'. Told to step back from the front lines, they went for a picnic on the mountainside, and thought about the irony of sitting in this beautiful landscape surrounded by 'the encircling line of death'. After their lunch, they did witness an exchange of fire, and then went down in the rain. Back in the valley, they were given a civic tour of one of the little Alsace towns, Dannemarie, recently taken back by the French from the Germans, where Wharton noticed approvingly that German as well as French was being spoken and that there was no 'lyrical patriotism' on show, only workmanlike realism. This is the only place in her reports where she strikes a tolerant, pragmatic tone about Germany. On their return journey to the front lines in the Vosges, the commanding officer led them through the trenches to 'the extreme verge of the defences', and there were the men, sitting around and smoking and talking in whispers, whose job it was 'to hold out to the death'.

Very large numbers of such Frenchmen – and Englishmen, and Germans – died in the long-drawn-out battles of 1916. The wars of '*grignotage*' [attrition] on the Western Front killed millions of people and hardly changed the balance of power. The five-month German offensive against Verdun, intended to 'bleed' the French army 'white' and to make France reach 'breaking-point' – with its heroic phrases of resistance, '*Courage, on les aura!*' and '*Ils ne passeront pas!*' – cost 460,000 French lives (and 300,000 Germans) and became the 'supreme symbol' of French resistance. The Allied offensive on the Somme from July to November, with 60,000 British casualties on the first day alone, ended with 340,000 Frenchmen dead as well as thousands of British and Germans, but with Allied gains of only a few miles. The Germans withdrew to their new Hindenburg line leaving a zone of catastrophic devastation behind them.[27]

Wharton's final visits to the war-zones were made in 1917, the first in April with Walter and the second in October with Berenson. The first journey was written up for the *New York Sun*, and she again repeated in her piece what she said in her letters (though now there was no Henry to write to). The area around the River Oise and the River Somme, north-east of Compiègne, which had been systematically wrecked by the Germans in their 'strategic retreat', was a frightful scene of devastation, 'just one long senseless slaughter of the country'. 'The horrors are unimaginable', she told Berenson, who, revisiting the scenes with her in the autumn, had the same sense of numb horror. All the towns and villages in the area had been completely destroyed. The list of names was like a list of the dead: Noyon, Chauny, Ham, Lassigny, Roye, Cuts, Carlepont, Appilly, Villequier, Nesle, Guiscard, Château Goyencourt. She wrote in a letter:

> I got back late last night after a journey that I shall never forget. The country we went through is so ravaged that one cannot even get a piece of bread at Noyon or any of the other towns . . . the Germans have taken literally everything. As many refugees from the ruined villages have taken refuge at Ham I asked the 'Maire' to distribute the 1,000 francs you so kindly sent me; but he handed me back the money and said: 'Money has no value here, there is nothing to buy. Please take this back to Paris and ask the lady who was kind enough to give it to you to send us clothes as quickly as possible.'[28]

Her piece for the *Sun* was intensely rhetorical:

> In that small fragment of ravaged France I saw woe enough to cover a kingdom with mourning . . . This latest retreat is a deliberately planned attempt to murder the land as well as the people, to drain its life blood . . . and this insidious deviltry has been slowly and systematically applied to a helpless people . . . It is impossible for any Christian nation not to be at war with Germany.

This language was intended to fire up Americans, but it points, also, to the problems of emotive war-writing. Wharton was as aware of the problems as James had been ('The war has used up words') or as Hemingway would be ('Abstract words such as glory, honor, courage or hallow were obscene beside the concrete names of villages, the numbers of roads, the names of rivers, the numbers of regiments and the dates'). She wrote about this in *A Son at the Front*, which, for all its emotional rhetoric, has a discussion between two characters about language: 'I was considering how the meaning had evaporated out of lots of our old words, as if the general smash-up had broken their stoppers . . . A good many of my own words have lost their meaning, and I'm not prepared to say where honour lies . . .' Boylston, the most heroic character in the novel, is also the most tongue-tied: his most fervent utterance is the word 'Preparedness'.

In a story self-referentially called 'Writing a War Story', which she published in a magazine in 1919 but did not reprint, a lady called Ivy Spang, from Cornwall-on-Hudson, the author of a little-noticed pre-war volume of poems, 'Vibrations', working as a tea-pourer in an Anglo-American hospital in Paris, is asked to write a war-story by a British magazine editor who wants 'a tragedy with a happy ending'. 'Give us a good stirring trench story, with a Coming-Home scene to close with.' (Wharton's own 'Coming Home' war-story, published in 1915, was a savage tale of a French soldier who takes his revenge on a barbaric German officer to whom the Frenchman's proud fiancée has given herself, so that he would spare the family and the house.) Miss Spang starts writing on her reams of mauve paper but (like Wharton at the start of *The Marne*) gets stuck. All the war-story openings ('A shot rang out –') seem so clichéd. So she gathers material from her French governess, based on a real French soldier's story, and between them they dress up the cold facts with 'heart interest'. Miss Spang is mocked for this by a professional male novelist, who nevertheless (like the other soldiers in the ward) likes the pretty photograph of her that goes with the story. Women cannot write about the war and be taken seriously unless they turn themselves into men, Wharton suggests. This unkind satire is harsh about the emotive language which she herself sometimes used in wartime.[29]

But she tried out many ways of writing about war. She wrote to rouse emotions. She wrote informatively, giving as vivid accounts as she could of war-scenes, war-work, and 'French ways'. She wrote harshly, in some of her war-fiction, about brutality, cowardice, and bereavement. She wrote ironically, satirising the very activities she was involved in. She wrote sentimentally (especially in her poems) about France, Belgium, fallen heroes, and the glory of sacrifice. Though she told Scribner at the start of the war (abandoning an idea for a light comic story, 'Count Underlinden') that 'there was too much to do for the unfortunate creatures all about me' to write for her own pleasure, she did, as the war ground on, write to escape it, in *Summer* and *In Morocco*. And she also produced, in one of her most strenuous and selfless war-efforts, a new kind of book for her, in which the relation between war and art was revealingly illustrated.[30] In *A Son at the Front*, the wartime dilemma of the writer – to give his services or to escape into 'beauty and art and the eternal things' – nags at the painter, Campton, without ever being resolved. He cannot 'forget' the war and go back to his art without guilt, but he cannot dedicate himself to war-work (which he does reluctantly) without feeling that he is abandoning his real gift. Wharton's decision in 1915 to ask artists and writers to contribute to a 'war' book raised all these tensions acutely.

The *Book of the Homeless* had international predecessors in earlier wartime anthologies, *The Book of France* and *King Albert's Book*. The formula was the same: a glossy production of poetry, pictures, prose and musical scores, contributed for no fee, and sold in aid of war-charities. The contributors overlapped. Edmond Rostand, Émile Verhaeren, Mrs Humphry Ward, Charles Dana Gibson, Monet, Barrès, Sarah Bernhardt, Bourget, Galsworthy, Gosse, Hardy, Paul Hervieu, William Dean Howells, James, Alice Meynell, and Wharton herself, appeared in more than one of these publications. The Belgian writer Maeterlinck appeared in all three, although in September 1914 he had said that 'none should be allowed to speak who cannot shoulder a rifle – for the written word seems so monstrously useless, so overwhelmingly trivial, in front of this mighty drama'.

Given what else Wharton was doing in 1915, her efforts for this book are astounding. She roused up contributors, ordered Scribner's about, ran an advertising campaign, and translated almost all the French pieces. The correspondence over *The Book of the Homeless* is enormous. She had a great deal of help from friends who negotiated with potential contributors on her behalf. James called in Hardy, Sargent, Howells, Yeats, Edward Marsh (Rupert Brooke's executor), and Conrad (though as Conrad 'produces by the sweat of his brow and tosses off, in considerable anguish, at the rate of about a word a month', he was not hopeful). 'Yours all bustlingly', James signed off a busy letter to her about the book. But he had his stroke on 2 December, and never saw it come out. The Berensons got hold of Herbert Trench, Santayana, Laurence Binyon, and Eleanora Duse. Alice Garrett, well connected in the art world, persuaded Bakst and Renoir.[31]

Some who were approached refused: the 'grim Rudyard', as James called him, Pierre Loti and Maxfield Parrish all said no (though Kipling had contributed to the other two charity books), much to Wharton's disgust. Some pieces, like John Masefield's, never came through, and some would not do: she had to ask Robert Grant to replace a light essay on life in Newport with a heartfelt poem, and she cut André Suarès's description of women left alone in wartime because she thought it was 'too Lesbian for publication'. Scribner was worried that the book would be too French for American readers, and that Roosevelt's gung-ho, anti-Wilson introduction would put people off – but she stood by it. Some contributions were late, of course, and the making of the book, to which she gave as much scrupulous attention as to her own, and which was being designed by her old friend Daniel Updike, took longer than expected. Wharton blamed Scribner, and Scribner blamed Wharton ('It seems to me that Mrs Wharton has not allowed enough time') for the fact that *The Book of the Homeless* missed its Christmas deadline and came out in January 1916, losing a lot of potential sales. (It was one more black mark against Scribner's, who would lose her fiction at the end of the war, apart from *A Son at the Front*.)[32]

Wharton introduced *The Book of the Homeless* (*Le Livre des Sans-Foyers*) as if it were a house. She prefaced it with a description of the refuge which the hostels had provided for the children, and she called the book itself a kind of 'foyer': 'What a gallant piece of architecture it is, what delightful pictures hang on its walls' and with what 'readiness' and 'kindliness' the collaborators 'have lent a hand to the building'. 'So I efface myself from the threshold, and ask you to walk in.' The poem she contributed, 'The Tryst', is about the ruined house of a Belgian woman whose husband and child have been killed but who refuses to leave: 'I shall crouch by the door till the bolt is down / And then go in to my dead.' The poem's narrator, who tries to offer the woman the very refuge which this book is in aid of, falls silent.

Most of the contributors were direct in their dealings with the war; she found that the book was getting more and more 'homogenous'. But in amongst the cries of outrage (like Gosse's 'The Arrogance and Servility of Germany'), battle-hymns, vows of fidelity, and descriptions of war-work (like James's meditation on visiting wounded British soldiers in the hospitals, 'The Long Wards'), there were some less warlike pieces, and some items of great beauty, such as Renoir's charcoal-sketch of his wounded son, or Rodin's faint water-colour of two women. Conrad did contribute, a long autobiographical account of getting out of Germany at the outbreak of war, which chimed in with Wharton's feelings about the inevitability of the crisis: 'For when a fruit ripens on a branch, it must fall. There is nothing

on earth that can prevent it.' There were some touches of humour –
Stravinsky's 'Souvenir d'une Marche Boche', and a Beerbohm cartoon of
Anglo-French relations. There were a number of fine portraits: of Cocteau
by Bakst, of Hardy, Stravinsky and George Moore by Jacques-Émile Blanche,
of Gide by Van Rysselberghe, and a reproduction of the Sargent portrait
of James which Wharton had commissioned. Walter Gay's delicate water-
colour sketch of a corner of the Gays' house at Le Bréau offered another
kind of 'foyer' as a retreat from war. The only writer who refused the conventions of war-writing was Yeats, who, apologising to Wharton for the
shortness of his contribution, sent her a powerfully evasive short rhyme
which he called 'A Reason for Keeping Silent' (and which in 1919 he
revised and renamed 'On Being Asked for a War Poem').[33]

> I think it better that at times like these
> We poets keep our mouths shut, for in truth
> We have no gift to set a statesman right;
> He's had enough of meddling, who can please
> A young girl in the indolence of her youth
> Or an old man upon a winter's night.

This was not Wharton's view.

In spite of the book's lateness, she busied herself with publicity, and had
Minnie stage a reading and an auction for the book in New York, both
written up by the *New York Times*. Wharton had the canny idea that
the auction could be in a wealthy patron's house ('It seems to me that the
auction might take place in a private house, if anyone would lend a big
room; this will give it a "society" flavour which might help') but in the
end Minnie organised it in the American Art Galleries at 6 West 23rd
Street, Wharton's old neighbourhood. A group of 'socially prominent' ladies
(including several of Wharton's old New York acquaintances) listened to
extracts being read the day before the auction, which raised $6,950. (The
prices paid make interesting reading: $500 for the James typescript, $100
paid by Charles Scribner for the Charles Dana Gibson drawing and $400
for a Monet pastel, $350 for the manuscript of Wharton's poem.) After all
the effort, and after the production costs had been paid, the sales of the
book and the auction brought in about $9,500 for the hostels.[34]

The Book of the Homeless is an extraordinary coming-together of her social
and literary worlds. Wharton milked her old New York contacts for money
and her literary contacts for contributions, for all they were worth. (Even
Walter was put to work translating a Rostand poem.) But few of the many

names in the book were close friends. Fullerton was conspicuously missing. At the end of 1916, he sent her a copy of his book, *Hesitations*, an attack on Woodrow Wilson's neutrality, inscribed 'To E.W. from W.M.F. Xmas 1916'. She replied: 'I admire your book, & smile at your inscription . . . we'll meet in a better world some day.' Wharton's personal life was shifting in these years, when she was at her most public and socially committed, but also rather isolated. She was becoming disenchanted with some of her old French friends, telling Berenson that in the procession of the 'usual figures', she was finding Bourget too 'whimsical', the Abbé Mugnier rather 'inadequate', Blanche 'lucid but depressing' and Bélugou taken up with a silly mid-life affair. Berenson, though, was a consolation to her. She and Berry set him up with a surprising job as an intelligence officer reporting on Italian and German affairs to the United States embassy in Paris, and she saw him often. But she was impatient with friends who allowed their personal tragedies to overcome them at this time. Elizabeth Cameron's understandable breakdown after the deaths, close together, of Henry Adams, her daughter, and her husband, was unsympathetically treated by Wharton, who described her as 'behaving like a mad-woman – sometimes I feel like saying simply, "like a woman!"'. She had little tolerance, either, for Mary Berenson, who was distraught, even suicidal, because of illness, Berenson's continuing affairs and Geoffrey Scott's engagement to Sybil Cutting. She was scornful of Mary's attempts to find refuge in Buddhism (perhaps she was reminded of Teddy's extremes of behaviour): 'It throws a new light on the weakness of the mind fed on the belief in short cuts & providential improvisations – & *how* it explains the success of Mrs Eddy, & mind-healing . . .' Adult behaviour meant self-control and not relying on support systems: 'Oh, BB, *nothing* matters in times like these but the sense of being the captain of one's soul!'[35]

Like everyone else, she was losing people. Some of these losses, inevitably, were war-casualties. Jean Du Breuil, the poet and sociologist and, latterly, dashing cavalry-officer, engaged to her friend Bessy Lodge, widow of Bay Lodge, was killed in action in February 1915; she wrote a solemn tribute to him in the *Revue Hebdomadaire*. Robert d'Humières was half-way through translating *Custom* when he was killed in the summer of 1915. One of her servants – a young footman, Henri – was killed. Others died, from age or sickness: her brother Frederic (not much lamented) in June 1918; and several old friends, all at once: Anna Bahlmann, Egerton Winthrop (at seventy-seven, in New York), and, most desolatingly of all, on 28 February 1916, Henry James. She had known Anna and Egerton since she was a child; she had grown even closer to James since the war broke out. These were profound losses, which merged in her emotions, as she told Sally Norton, still her faithful long-distance friend, with all the other war-deaths: 'My heart is heavy with the sorrow of all my friends who are in mourning, or trembling for the lives of sons & husbands.' 'The world is getting to be such a lonely place', she told Daisy.[36]

Yet there were some invigorating new connections. An interesting addition to her life now was the English art-curator Eric Maclagan, then in his thirties, a worldly, witty cosmopolitan gourmet who liked scurrilous stories and knew all about Byzantine art. He was a friend of Berenson's and the three of them often lunched together: he amused her. If the war shone a fierce light through some old friends, making them seem transparent (notably Morton, who was still helping her deal with some contractual matters, but who proved otherwise quite useless to her in these years), it also put her in touch with people she might not otherwise have known, like Gide, and consolidated some older friendships, as with Walter and Berenson.[37]

Her life was enriched, too, in spite of administrative clashes, by her new working friendship with Elisina Tyler. Wharton liked the style of this elegant, Florence-born, convent-educated Catholic descendant of the Bonapartes, trilingual (her French was as good as her Italian), with a rather prim, old-fashioned manner and a little 'sing-song' voice, but with great energy and dynamism. (Others, notably Berenson, found her bossy, irritating, and 'headstrong'.) Her history was somewhat scandalous: 'Elisina's "past" is what mine is, and yours, & that of any other woman whose marriage has been a calamity', she told Minnie, defending Elisina against gossip. She was married, young, to the English publisher Grant Richards, and after much unhappiness left him (their three children were in boarding-school) when she was thirty-four, in 1909, for Royall Tyler, a specialist in Spanish and Byzantine art and an American diplomat. Elisina and Royall (sometimes known as Peter) had a child, William, in 1910, but did not marry until 1914. William Tyler became a favourite of Wharton's, and from the age of six he would receive sweet birthday greetings from her ('I hope you will soon come to lunch with me. If your mother is very good perhaps you might bring her too'). The Tylers lived in style, with a castle in Burgundy (Antigny-le-Château at Arnay-le-Duc) and a Paris apartment. But Elisina kept up the TB sanatoriums long after the war was over, and would be something of a heroine in the Second World War, too, staying on in the castle under German occupation and helping the local people. She weathered a catastrophe, the accidental death of her fifteen-year-old son by her first marriage, while embroiled in war-work in 1916. Wharton admired her resilience: she called her, to Berenson, 'the indestructible Elisina'. And she envied Elisina her happy second marriage. She liked to flirt a little with Royall, and to write teasing letters to Elisina about this: 'How shall I tear myself away from Royall on Sat? *He's* been giving me another kind of cardiac crisis – but that one has been chronic since I first laid eyes on him.' Royall, who like his wife sometimes found Wharton daunting ('I dreamt last night that I was a child going to a school kept by Edith and terribly afraid of her', he told Elisina in 1916), also understood her loneliness and her envy of companionable, stable marriages. He told Elisina that on a visit to the Walter Gays with Wharton, she said 'when she saw two old people happy together as they are, it makes her feel so chilly. It struck me as infinitely pathetic.' These were friends who recognised her loneliness as well as her imperiousness, and they stuck by her till her death – and after it.[38]

Wharton went into deep mourning, in the last year of the war, for a relatively new friend. Throughout her life she liked to act as patron and confidante to artistic or intellectual young men, who were often gay or bisexual, clever, sensitive and artistic. The characters were different – Ogden Codman, John Hugh Smith, Percy Lubbock, Gaillard Lapsley, Geoffrey Scott (and, later, Kenneth Clark, William Gerhardi and Steven Runciman) – but the type repeated. Ronald Simmons fitted the pattern. He was thirty-one and she was fifty-four when they met at the end of 1916. He was something of a misfit, a Yale graduate who had left an American business family background (his father was president of a coal company in Providence, Rhode Island) to train as an architect and then as a painter in Paris. He was physically awkward, overweight (she would remember him as 'a teddy bear in uniform'), short-sighted, with a weak heart which kept him out of the military. She described him to a French acquaintance as '*un garçon extrêmement distingué*'. When war broke out he worked for the Comité des Étudiants Américains de L'École des Beaux-Arts, with fund-raising branches all over America, which helped the former students of the school who were at the front, and ran an *ouvroir* to send clothes and gas-masks to the army. He met Wharton through the American composer Blair Fairchild, who, with his wife (Howard Sturgis's cousin, also called Edith) was an old friend, and part of the network of artists and musicians now doing war-work in Paris. At the end of 1916 Simmons left the Beaux-Arts committee to help run Wharton's TB sanatoriums. In her fictional version of him as Boylston in *A Son at the Front* (unusually, she told people that the character was based on him, and at first wanted 'In Memory of Boylston' on the title-page), she presented him as ideal for this kind of work: energetic, resourceful, tactful, bilingual, a good listener who knew everyone and could negotiate Parisian bureaucracy.[39]

When the Americans came into the war in the spring of 1917, these qualities brought him to the notice of the US war department. Obituaries noted that 'Mr Simmons was asked to become one of its civilian members, because of his extensive knowledge of the French people, of their language and customs, and his instinctive ability to create an atmosphere of cordial intimacy between the French and the Americans'. He worked in the Inter-Allied Intelligence Division of the US Army, and in July 1918 was made a lieutenant. He was moved to the 'Service of Supply' agency, working to provision American forces in Europe, in Bordeaux, from where he wrote Wharton some happy, enthusiastic letters. But in August, at the age of thirty-three, he fell victim to the Spanish flu epidemic, developed pneumonia, and – due to his weak heart – was dead, in Marseilles, within three days.[40]

Wharton was grief-struck. 'She is dreadfully cut up about Simmons', Royall told Elisina. In the days after his death, she sent a rush of heartfelt letters to Berenson (who also liked 'Sim'), to Minnie, to Daisy, and to Elisina. She repeatedly said what a terrible shock it was, how dearly she had loved him, how he had been like a younger brother to her, what a bright future he had, how well they understood each other, and how lonely his death made her feel. 'It is so difficult for me to care really for anyone – especially in the last years – that when I do, the parting is agony.' To Minnie:

> You can't imagine the blow it is to me – not only because I loved him dearly, like a much younger brother, and because he returned my affection with such a tender & pathetic friendship – not only for that, but because he was such a frustrated, unappreciated, *undiscovered* being. Till our little group found him out ... he had never known people really capable of discovering all there was under his extreme modesty and shyness – and to the end he did not know (honestly did not) *why* we loved and appreciated him as we did. We are all heart-broken, and I perhaps most of all because I am lonelier than all the others.[41]

Berenson told Mary that they had 'wept together' over Simmons; and Wharton was not known for weeping. She pulled herself together quickly: a busy, difficult letter to Elisina about administrative problems, written a week after Simmons's death, makes no mention of him. But she committed herself to elegising him as a war-hero. She wrote a letter to the Paris edition of the *New York Herald* two days after his death, commemorating his virtues, above all 'his exceptional understanding of French character and the French point of view'. She published a sad little poem dedicated to him, called 'On Active Service'. After the war, when she found that he had been buried in a dismal grave in Marseilles, she undertook, on behalf of his mother (whose role she seemed to be appropriating), to have him moved under a fine new tombstone, which she would often visit. She dedicated both her war-novels to him and made such an idealised fictional version of him that at one point Boylston is even seen with a halo behind his head. (But she drew the line, in the early 1920s, at lending her name to a poorly edited collection of his letters, a project which came to nothing.)[42]

Much has been made of all this. Gaillard Lapsley suggested that it was an 'Indian-summer romance', and her biographers have used phrases like 'she took him into her deepest affections', she saw 'her younger self' in him, he filled 'a deep, unmet need in her busy life'. It is a story that can easily be sentimentalised and which falls invitingly into the cliché of lonely older woman consoling herself for past failures in love with one last *tendresse*. Her letters to Simmons have not survived, but the two he wrote to her do not suggest any kind of romantic intimacy. Addressed to 'Mrs Wharton' and signed 'devotedly', from 'your friend', they are written with the kind of eager, confiding respect she brought out in her younger male friends, speaking touchingly of his ugly body, his love of France, his dedication to his work, his hatred of institutional quarrels, and his hopes for the future. They are affectionately anxious about her health: 'We all worry about the effect of the nervous strain on your body, tired by these years of work under such pressure.' The most interesting part is his report of a conversation with Otto Kahn, the German-American banker and arts patron, who worked hard in the war years on behalf of the Allies, and whom Wharton wrote to congratulate, in 1917, on a speech about the 'public usefulness' of the arts: in return he sent her 1,700 francs for her charities. Kahn told Simmons that there was such a thing as a 'governing class' (from whatever actual social sphere) in Anglo-American life which had grown out of the 'best traditions of centuries of civilization' in those countries and which needed to be in charge if there was to be 'any future worthy of the past'.[43]

This idea, as much as personal bereavement, may have been at the heart of her deep grief at Simmons's death. She had lost someone she was fond of, but who also represented everything she minded about. She and her American friends in Paris – Royall Tyler, Walter Berry, Bernard Berenson – were all in the business of 'intelligence' in its broadest sense. That is, they were all trying to persuade America to help France, to further a cultural and political exchange between the two countries, to make it possible for them to understand each other. All her wartime activities and writings pointed towards what her novels had long been dealing with in darkly emotional and ironical terms, the possibilities of – and the obstacles to – cultural cross-fertilisation. (It was the opposite, in her view, of the aggressively Prussian concept of '*Kultur*'.) One of the things she praised Simmons for, long after his death, was the purity of his American language: 'He never used a word that wasn't real English.'[44] This was what she wanted the next generation, the 'governing class' of the western civilisation of the future, to be: artists with a sense of responsibility who could also do practical good, Americans who spoke good English, internationalists sympathetic to other cultures.

Wharton was recognised and honoured for her work, in France, in Belgium and in America. In March 1916, the French government made her a '*Chevalier de l'Ordre National de la Légion d'honneur*'. (The Orders are, ascending in distinction, *Chevaliers*, *Officiers*, *Commandeurs*, *Grands Officiers*, and *Grands-Croix*. In 1923 she was promoted from *Chevalier* to *Officier*, which required evidence of continuing 'distinguished services'.) The red ribbon and the star-shaped, six-pointed cross was awarded for '*actions d'éclat*' during the war. The number of women awarded the honour went up sharply during the early twentieth century, from 110 in 1914 to 3,000 in 1939. They included Anna de Noailles, Colette, an American painter, Cécile de Wentworth, and the artist Rosa Bonheur. It was a particular honour in 1916, as Wharton told Scribner, because the government had decided not to give out honours to civilians or foreigners during the war. For Edith Wharton, '*qui a toujours eu pour la France le sentiment qu'on donne à une seconde patrie*' (as the newspapers put it) they made an exception. Letters of congratulation to '*Madame la Chevalière*' flooded in from French, English and American friends, including a touching hand-made scroll from the seamstresses at the *ouvroir*. (It was just after James had died, and she must have felt the loss very acutely at this moment: how he would have praised her!) She did not go to the ceremony, where the honours were awarded by Poincaré. Wharton said she would not wear her cross: 'for the women never do wear it do they?' (The cross is only worn on the most formal occasions, but the ribbon, which varies in width and colour depending on the level of the Order, may be worn in the button-hole of an ordinary suit or coat. Nicky Mariano would tell a story of wearing Wharton's coat to the opening session of the Italian Academy at the Farnesina in the early 1930s, to find herself greeted with a 'certain commotion' and moved to the front row. She realised it was because 'the "*cocarde*" of the Legion of Honour' was on her lapel.)

Other honours followed: in June 1917, a gold medal for '*Dévouement*' was awarded to both Wharton and Tyler; and, after the war, she was given the Prix de Vertu from the Académie française, awarded by Poincaré in November 1920. This prize, founded in the early nineteenth century by a M. de Montyon, was given annually by the academy (with a sum of money, fluctuating according to how many prizes were awarded) for individuals noted for their 'virtuous actions', who could range from fire-fighters to nuns. The founder's reasoning was characteristically French in its analytical solemnity: 'M. de Montyon believed that only the intelligence is fully capable of understanding virtue, which is itself but an aspect of intelligence achieved through our duties and our destiny. As the poet said, it is in our sensibility that our genius lies, and virtue is genius in all its glory, applied to the moral life.' Poincaré, in his speech, said that in her writings on France, '*jamais la France n'a été mieux comprise ni mieux aimée*'. But Mrs Wharton was not only a writer, he added, she was also '*une femme d'action et une femme de bien*'. And he pointed to the contrast between her beautiful book *Chez les Heureux du Monde* (the French title of *The House of Mirth*) and her wartime commitment to helping '*les malheureux*'.

She was less gratified by the Medaille Reine Elisabeth from Belgium in July 1918, because she felt it came too late; the Belgians made amends in 1919 with the honour of 'Chevalier of the Order of Leopold', awarded by King Albert. Recognition came from her own country too: a solemn letter from General Pershing, commander of the American Expeditionary Forces, when America entered the war, paid tribute to her work which 'stands out pre-eminently in the long list of devoted efforts that our people have voluntarily given to France'. She made good use of this in her fund-raising. Surveys of Americans working in France made much of her achievements, though they were not always accurate: one newspaper report, under a photograph of Teddy Wharton, and dated 1917, described 'an American and his wife' doing 'splendid things over in France': 'She is Edith Wharton, author, among other books, of "The House of Mirth" – and this is her guide, counselor, and husband, Edward Wharton.'[45]

But in spite of the recognition and the honours, Wharton was sick of the war and of war-work even before the death of Simmons. Literally sick: the endless output of energy, the constant strain of the work, was making her ill, as Simmons and other friends noted anxiously. Wharton's health had always been vulnerable, from the asthma, nausea and lassitude of her youth to the persistent problems with vertigo, blood-pressure and bronchial symptoms which sent her repeatedly to Salso – though she had a sceptical distrust of 'cures'. (She told Charlie Du Bos's wife Zézette, soon after the war, that in her youth she had been *'presque tuée par une succession de régimes'*.) In July 1916, the doctors told her she had anaemia and an irregular heartbeat. She planned to visit Lizzie Cameron in the mountains at Chamonix, but her maid fell ill too, so instead she went to stay with the Comtesse de Béarn at her castle in Fleury and to a hotel in Fontainebleau for a few days. On 9 November, Gross found her in a faint on the floor in the Rue de Varenne – apparently an attack of ptomaine poisoning. A few days in bed followed. All through 1917 she complained of exhaustion, with bouts of 'flu, and in November 1917, just after her trip to Morocco, her doctor, Isch Wall, told her she was suffering from 'brain & nerve fatigue'. These accumulative health problems came to a head in May 1918, when she had the first of three 'cardiac crises' – minor heart attacks linked to anaemia, which occurred between May and July – and was told by Dr Wall to go to bed for three weeks: no letters, no telephones, no talking. Anxious letters went between the Berensons: 'Does she know that pernicious anaemia is *fatal?*' Mary wrote to Bernard. 'We *can't* lose her, the best of friends!' He responded that perhaps 'she would rather die active than live a quiet life', but noted a 'rusty & dull' look in her eyes. Instead of taking a long rest cure in the Auvergne, as her doctor recommended, she took a few days off at Fleury, and went back to work. Her heart was never strong after this. In more than a manner of speaking, she gave her life to France.[46]

In 1917 and 1918 she increasingly delegated – and complained of – her labours. Wharton's low morale in 1917 was symptomatic of the mood of the whole country. The winter of 1916–17 was horribly cold. 'I've adopted as my motto a variant of Wilson's "Too proud to fight" – which runs "Too cold to sleep"', she told Berenson. In the spring, a disastrous offensive by the French commander Nivelle, against the Hindenburg line, along the Chemin des Dames, led to enormous casualties (130,000 in five days, 220,000 within one month) and no breakthrough. There was a great crisis of morale in the traumatised and decimated French army and among civilians. Army mutinies and civilian strikes broke out, and spread. The anti-war movement – linked to socialism, as in Barbusse's novel *Le Feu* – grew in strength. In Paris, the clothing and construction industry, car factories and public transport were involved in strikes, and calls of 'Down with War' and 'Long Live Peace' were more often heard. (Wharton made no reference to the mutinies, but her anti-socialism and anti-bolshevism, forcefully aired from this time on, had their roots in her support for the war.) Nivelle was replaced by Pétain, and on 6 April 1917 the Americans at last entered the war. But the terrible battles of Flanders, of Ypres, of Passchendaele (a sea of mud and corpses) in the spring and summer of 1917, mass slaughters of 'awful futility', created little change by the end of 1917, even with the British use of tanks at the battle of Cambrai in November. It took a year for the French army to recover its morale, with new conscripts coming into the army, and Clemenceau, as the new premier, harshly suppressing defeatism.

In March 1918 the Germans began one of their last major offensives, and Paris again came under siege, for the first time since the war started, from the 'Big Berthas', the German long-range guns. Wharton showed her sangfroid: 'My household is in the cellar . . . all except dear old Gross, & my maid & I, who prefer bombs to pneumonia, & are all too busy to bother, anyhow.' The second battles of the Somme (mustard gas, hand-to-hand fighting, shrapnel, bayonets, revolvers, bombs) and the Marne caused mass casualties. But with American troops now making a great difference to the Allied armies, General Foch as the new Allied commander-in-chief, and the Axis army under-provisioned and weakened, the Germans began to fall back. The Allied offensive at Champagne was the beginning of the end; the slaughter (306,000 Frenchmen killed, wounded or taken prisoner between March and November 1918) finished on 11 November 1918. No other nation involved in the war had suffered such high losses as the French. Eleven per cent of the French population had been killed or injured. Of the eight million men mobilised, five million were killed or wounded.[47]

Wharton's demoralisation was, ironically enough, partly the result of the American presence in France. She wrote the essays in French Ways and their Meaning to help America understand the French, but this could be an uphill struggle. Once the USA entered the war, the American Red Cross got to work, taking over the many individual charities already in existence and bringing them under its own central organisation. This caused tremendous problems for Wharton, as for others who had been running their own charities. By 1917, her sewing ouvroir was self-supporting, but the other, bigger enterprises – the Children of Flanders charity, the American hostels for refugees, the TB sanatoriums and the convalescent homes for women and children at Groslay and Arromanches – all needed large amounts of funding. She agreed that the Red Cross should take over the hostels and the sanatoriums for the military, but she did not want to turn over the Children of Flanders (which was directly linked to the Belgian government) or her civilian convalescent homes. She was unimpressed by the Red Cross's aggressive and insensitive bureaucracy and its lack of understanding of French customs: 'To hand over these houses to the Red Cross would be to absorb in one gigantic organisation a small formation of a special kind, which owed its success in great measure to the fact that Mrs Royall Tyler and I are both exceptionally familiar with French ideas and social conditions . . . these qualifications are exactly those which the Red Cross workers lack.'

The struggle led to dissent between herself and Elisina, who was made responsible for the hand-over of the hostels, and was at the receiving end of all the complaints from the staff about the behaviour of the Red Cross officials. Wharton herself complained furiously about their inefficiency and high-handedness, and refused to let them name a newly converted chateau 'the Edith Wharton Sanatorium'. She did manage to keep the houses at Groslay and Arromanches, and went to the lengths of getting her biggest donors to transfer their funds from the hostels which the Red Cross had taken over, to her privately run convalescent homes. These would be kept going, by dint of continuing fund-raising efforts (mainly by Elisina) long after the war was over. But it was a bitter irony that the American involvement she had so longed for, and so welcomed ('the stars and stripes are shining', she told Berenson in June 1917), led to such disillusionment. She felt like Raymond de Chelles faced with Undine Spragg.[48]

She was beginning to hate Paris, too. She was tired of it, and she wanted a retreat. By the end of the war she had started to look elsewhere for a home, and she wrote to Berenson in 1920: 'Paris is simply awful – a kind of continuous earth-quake of motor-busses, trams, lorries, taxis & other howling & swooping & colliding engines, with hundreds & thousands of US citizens rushing about in them & tumbling out of them at one's door – &, through it all, the same people placidly telephoning one to come to tea.'[49]

A great deal of her discontent towards the end of the war had to do with the tension between being a war-worker and being a writer. Though she wrote all through the war years, she felt increasingly frustrated about what was happening to Edith Wharton the novelist. 'Will it *ever* be over??' she wrote to Berenson in the spring of 1917. 'Shall we ever be *we* (or us) again???' She tried to start a novel around this time, which she told Scribner's 'has nothing to do with the war!', but this (*The Glimpses of the Moon*) took five more years before it was published. Tormentedly, she told Elisina in January 1919, during a discussion of how much fund-raising they should do after the war: 'Personally, I feel quite utterly unable to go on . . . so many deferred and broken engagements with my publishers and editors weigh on me so heavily that if I should try to struggle on with more letter-writing for charity I should simply collapse. It will take me the rest of my waning existence to get over the strain of the last year.' She did, however, have two writerly escapades during the war, which took her away in her imagination from her responsibilities. One was her short novel, *Summer*, written in the summer of 1916 and published in 1917; the other was her travel book, *In Morocco*, the product of her visit there in September 1917, published in 1919. Yet even these apparent deviations carried the burden of her wartime concerns. They are both high-coloured, full-blooded, sensual narratives with an intense appetite for life. But both are shadowed by violence and death, and both contain implicit arguments about imperialism, nationalism and patriotism.[50]

Summer was a short novel (she did not have time for anything else), written at 'a high pitch of creative joy', as much of an antidote as possible to 'refugees and hospitals'. The idea for it had suddenly come into focus, but she had had it in mind for several years, probably since *Ethan Frome*, which she repeatedly paired with it, famously calling *Summer* the 'Hot Ethan'. Like *Ethan*, *Summer* is a novella set in the poorest and remotest part of New England, in which an inarticulate, provincial character, with an obscure sense that there might be some preferable life elsewhere, has a brief idyll of romance which seems to open a window onto freedom, but is pulled back by the harsh realities of the place she lives in. *Summer*'s romance is a fulfilled, not a thwarted one, as in *Ethan*. It is one of the few Wharton fictions in which a love-affair is acted out rather than being denied or deferred. But, as with those few other sexual involvements in her fiction, pain, loss and grief rush up behind it.[51]

The novel is brimful of, and best known for, an intense and sensual evocation of the New England countryside in heat, rendered through the perceptions of a young woman close to nature: uneducated, speechless, throbbing with awakening eroticism. She feels and thinks through her blood, she lies on the ground like an animal, 'her face pressed to the earth and the warm currents of the grass running through her'. She feels earth and water, heat and light, sun and the colour of skies (*Summer* is full of fine sunsets) and the 'long wheeling fires' of stars on her pulses. She is all sap, growth and passive sun-warmed earth-life, and Wharton piles this on with a Whitmanish feel for minute, creaturely animalism. Heroine and author seem far apart, but Wharton gives her her own passionate feeling for nature and her nostalgia for the lost New England countryside, so remote from the war-bound Rue de Varenne.[52]

That pagan sensuality is at the heart of the novel's escapism. But the heroine is not a joyous figure, and the summery outdoors is not the novel's only landscape. 'Charity Royall' is a discontented creature, more like a small-town Undine than like Mattie. (Conrad, who enjoyed *Summer*, praised her 'bewildered wilfulness'.) She is trapped in an intensely parochial, gossipy, puritanical and philistine New England town, which is almost all she has ever known. Partly she confines herself, choosing not to go away to boarding-school. But her life seems to her, even given nothing to compare it with, 'too desolate, too ugly and intolerable', and she lets out hot bursts of inarticulate resentment: 'How I hate everything!' 'Things don't change at North Dormer: people just get used to them.' The name of the town puns on the French for sleep, implying 'dormant' and 'dormitory'. North Dormer defines its level of civilisation not against Boston or New York or the wider world, but against 'the Mountain', a 'bad place' that looms over the town from fifteen miles away, where a squalid and promiscuous community – 'a little colony of squatters' – lives beyond the pale of the law or the church or any genteel 'household order'. (They are said to be descendants of the men who built the local railways fifty years before, who took to drink and 'disappeared into the woods'. Wharton derived them, she tells us in *A Backward Glance*, from a real colony of 'drunken mountain outlaws' on Bear Mountain, near Lenox.) As a little girl 'Charity Royall' was rescued by 'Lawyer Royall' from this colony and brought up first by him and his wife, and then, after Mrs Royall's death, by him alone. Her name marks her out as a recipient of philanthropy, and a possession. She is made to feel 'poor and ignorant' and ashamed of her origins, protected only by the distinction and dominance of her guardian.[53]

Mr Royall, though banked down for a great deal of *Summer* (because we mainly see him through Charity's eyes), is its most powerful and problematic character: Wharton always insisted that '*he's* the book'. A disappointed man who could have had a better career somewhere else, vigorous, intelligent, impressive, even grand, he is also gloomy, bitter, given to drink, and in need of sex and female company. (If Charity has something of Tess of the D'Urbervilles about her, then Royall is a kind of American Michael Henchard.) He once tries to break his way into Charity's room when she is seventeen; she holds him at bay by force of will, and never forgives him. When, after this, he asks to marry her, he seems to become 'a hideous parody of the fatherly old man she had always known'. She continues to live in his house, but on her own terms, which include taking a pointless job at the moribund local library, where she sits furiously all day surrounded by books she has no idea how to read.

This is where she is at the start of the novel, which immediately introduces the blithe, handsome, cultured young visitor, Lucius Harney, an architect interested in old New England houses, and an entirely insubstantial figure throughout (an intentionally, but irritatingly, lightweight characterisation) with whom Charity falls in love. Her love-affair makes her even more conscious of her ignorance and provincialism, but liberates her into 'a wondrous unfolding of her new self'. (The writing in *Summer*, perhaps because of the pressures that surrounded it, is not always first-rate.) It is carried on in secret, but falls under a constant dark pressure of small-town surveillance. And for all its romantic ardour, it is increasingly felt to be a risky illusion, shadowed by a sense of menace and fear.

Large-scale realistic local set-pieces interrupt, which combine, as much of Wharton's writing about America will from now on, nostalgia and distaste. There is a 4 July celebration in Nettleton (based, to her own amusement, on Pittsfield), complete with omnibuses, shop-displays of confectionery and fancy goods, a firemen's band and a picture-show, trolley-rides to the lake and fireworks displaying 'Washington Crossing the Delaware'. A romantic adventure for Charity, it ends in a humiliating encounter with a drunken, abusive Royall, in the company of the town prostitutes, accusing Charity of the same behaviour. And there is North Dormer's marking of Old Home Week, with a banquet and a dance, a procession to the church and speeches, and the local girls dressed (highly ironically in Charity's case) in vestal – or sacrificial – white. Wharton enjoys herself with these provincial American rituals, viewed through Charity's impressionable eyes. T.S. Eliot, reviewing this novel (alone among Wharton's works) thought the whole thing was a satire on the New England novel, done by 'suppressing all evidence of European culture'. But this is not quite true, as French culture is slipped into the Nettleton outing: Lucius takes a baffled Charity to a little French restaurant. And 'Old Home Week' provides a display of the very American insularity and isolationism that Wharton was so busy complaining about before the USA came into the war. She calls it, in one of her driest authorial moments, a form of 'senti-mental decentralization', and makes fun of the genteel spinster who insists on the town's 'Associations' and on the importance of 'reverting to the old ideals, the family and the homestead, and so on'.

But there is more to this idea of home than a critique of a blinkered dedication to the 'homeland'. Lawyer Royall makes a speech at the ceremony, which shows him at his best, about the idea of home as a site of potential, not of confinement. Those who have gone away from their old home may return 'for good': to make it a 'larger place' and 'to make the best of it'. Wharton may have been imagining, as she often did in her fiction, an alternative possibility for herself; but she was also implying that small-town America needed to look outward, and could be improved by sending its sons off to war.[54]

Summer, like *Ethan Frome* and 'Bunner Sisters' (finally published in 1916), looks like an exception in Wharton's fiction, but is as much about the idea of home as many of her more upper-class narratives. Lucius comes to investigate the fine old buildings of New England for which their occupants (at that time) have no historical respect. The secret trysting-place is a deserted, ghostly little house in an abandoned orchard, a fragile, pathetic, makeshift home for the lovers. Beyond the pale, the home Charity comes from is a derelict shed on the mountain, filled with a rabble of degenerate, even bestial types, described with as much savagery as Wharton can muster. This is where Charity goes when her lover leaves her for a girl of his own class and she becomes pregnant, and this is where she tells herself she 'belongs'. There is no romance or gentility or decorum here to cover over the life of the body, displayed with shocking ruthlessness in the figure of Charity's dead mother:

> A woman lay on it [a mattress on the floor] but she did not look like a dead woman; she seemed to have fallen across her squalid bed in a drunken sleep, and to have been left lying where she fell, in her ragged disordered clothes. One arm was flung above her head, one leg drawn up under a torn skirt that left the other bare to the knee; a swollen glistening leg with a ragged stocking rolled down about the ankle ... She looked at her mother's face, thin yet swollen, with lips parted in a frozen gasp above the broken teeth. There was no sign in it of anything human: she lay there like a dead dog in a ditch.

Charity's only consolation for this sight is the burial service, administered by the priest who is going to help her return to her guardian and her town, where she also 'belongs' – and does not belong. The powerful burial scene on the mountain takes us back to the world of war which *Summer* was meant to escape. The slaughtered corpses, the wretched women and children, the refugees with their homes destroyed, the balm of religious ritual (increasingly appreciated by Wharton in wartime), the efforts, however partial and difficult, of charity, cluster behind this scene. And Charity, like so many of the war-survivors Wharton was dealing with, is a victim. The choices she has to make as a woman are few and grim. This is one of Wharton's most outspoken and lacerating books about the limitations of women's lives. She is not easily described as a feminist writer, but *Summer* is particularly bitter about female oppression. Charity is at the mercy of a male double standard. Royall, himself prone to 'debauchery', is violently abusive about Charity's 'half human' mother and Charity's bad blood, and the person he tells this to is the two-timing Lucius, as though both men are conspiring to judge and define the speechless and exploited girl. Charity's choices are to return to the 'animal' life of her mother, or to have an abortion, or to become a prostitute. These options are very clearly spelt out, much more openly than in any previous novel of Wharton's. There is even a visit to the abortionist (the sign reads 'Private Consultations . . . Lady Attendants'; the lady doctor seems to be Jewish) and several uses of the word 'whore'. (As a result, *Summer* was banned in Pittsfield and much disapproved of by Wharton's old Boston readers, like Sally Norton.) Charity reads no books herself, but to literary readers she is recognisably in the tradition of 'the woman who pays': pregnant Hetty Sorel in *Adam Bede*, Tess abandoned by her lover in Hardy's novel (Wharton even has Charity encountering a preacher on the road, in a 'gospel tent', like Tess's encounter with a surprising evangelist), and most of all Hester Prynne in *The Scarlet Letter*, cast out by the puritan community for adultery, more in tune with the wilderness than the town, and listening, as Charity listens, to the patriarchal rhetoric of the preacher giving his great Election Day sermon on the values of America. Wharton plants the clue herself, comparing *Summer's* realism with Hawthorne's in *A Backward Glance*. And there is a strong echo of Hawthorne's dark, obsessional old husband Chillingworth in Royall.[55]

This makes the ending of *Summer* extremely difficult, and to some readers as harrowing as the ending of *Ethan Frome*. The window onto joy and romance closes down for ever, and Charity, in a state of passive horror and exhaustion, allows herself to be led off the mountain, and married, by her much-hated father-figure. (This is not the first or the last time that Wharton does a marriage ceremony going by in a blur of disbelief and unreality.) The ending can be read as a depressing and sinister immolation of youth and hope in a hypocritical (and quasi-incestuous) social compromise. Or it can be seen as a realist adjustment on both sides, where Royall becomes grave and kindly and forbearing (not approaching Charity on their wedding-night, not asking her what she does with money he gives her) and Charity feels reassured and secure, as in a refuge. Royall's acceptance of Charity and her baby could be read not as exploitative, but bravely introducing into self-protective small-town America a necessary new influx of strange 'blood'. Wharton's readers cannot agree about the ending, because the book pulls against itself. The loss of midsummer love is felt as unbearable, but inevitable. Growing up (for countries as for people) is a process of 'tragic initiation', and it means moving from romance to 'ineluctable reality', adopting the stoicism that is the only virtue left in the face of great catastrophe, and 'making the best of it'.[56]

*

There were complicated negotiations over *Summer* with Scribner's. At the same time they were being told of her plans, in the late summer of 1917, to go to Morocco for a month. She sold her old publisher the idea of a series of illustrated articles for the magazine, and then a book, pitching it to Scribner as a combination of exotic travel guide ('there will probably be a good deal in the way of picturesque native ceremonies'), unique exposé ('the opportunity is an unequalled one . . . for one brief moment to see the interior of the country as it was before civilization invaded it') and Francophile propaganda. She and Walter Berry would be travelling 'with the official party who are being sent by the French government to see the Fair at Rabat' at the invitation of, and with the full support of, General Lyautey, 'whom I know'. Again, she was particularly pleased to be getting special access and VIP treatment, and made much of this in her letters: 'We have simply floated about in Résidence motors.' She boasted to Blanche that they were being welcomed everywhere *'par les ordres du général Lyautey'*.[57]

The journey took place between 15 September and 25 October 1917; the pieces (set aside for war-work and for the writing of *French Ways* and *The Marne*) were written up in the winter of 1918–19; the book was serialised in the summer of 1919 and published in the autumn of 1920, a month before *The Age of Innocence*. So *In Morocco* appeared as part of her 1920s work, but (like *A Son at the Front*, held back till 1923) it was very much a part of her war-years. And though it was a joyous and adventurous escapade from work in Paris ('Oh, the relief of a real holiday!' she wrote to Minnie from Rabat), the experience was deeply connected to her feelings about France in the war.[58]

Control of Morocco had been one of the key issues between France and Germany leading up to 1914. Germany instigated two diplomatic crises in the 1900s and 1910s over the French occupation of Morocco, and though France ceded some of its territory in the Congo in exchange, the Germans continued to use military intelligence in the Spanish zones of Morocco to destabilise the French. (Wharton made repeated derogatory remarks about the Germans and the Spanish in *In Morocco*.) In 1912, her friend André Tardieu described the Moroccan crisis as a crucial moment in French policy towards the Germans; it was now, he said, that France *'échappe à la reverie pacifiste'*. That year, the French government appointed Louis-Hubert Lyautey to be the first 'Resident-General' of Morocco, a position he held until 1925 (with a brief and unsatisfactory interlude in 1917 as Minister of War, just before Wharton visited Morocco).[59]

Lyautey was a cultured, highly intelligent, aristocratic soldier, by all accounts charming, forceful, manipulative, short-tempered, and probably homosexual (though Mme Lyautey played a good public role). Opinions differ on whether he was ruthlessly Napoleonic or a romantic idealist. He had a strong vision of colonialism, believing that the only moral justification for it was that it should contribute to mankind's well-being and that it should be flexible, sympathetic and respectful. He had a powerful attachment to Morocco, combined with a patriarchal belief in its infantilism: 'Like all children, we must let her grow up.' (Wharton similarly talks of the Moroccans as 'a people in the making'.) He respected the natives, but did not put Moroccans in his government. His mission was pacification (by military means), civilisation, 'association' and progress, and he insisted that the French protectorate in Morocco was not direct rule. But the role of this protectorate was ambiguous. 'L'action combinée de la politique et de la force' was his by-word, and his tactics mixed expediency with ideology. In the end Lyautey failed in Morocco and was replaced by the much more heavy-handed Pétain; and Morocco finally won its independence in 1956. Like Odo Valsecca in The Valley of Decision, and like her other great political hero, Theodore Roosevelt, Lyautey became a lost leader.[60]

Wharton particularly admired his cultural work. He was at pains to support the sultan he had put in place, Moulai Yousseff, and to bolster his prestige with ceremony. So the ritual of the 'Sacrifice of the Sheep', which Wharton set out with great excitement to witness from the Governor's Residence in Rabat, had been reinvigorated with Lyautey's encouragement; the ruins of Chella, outside Rabat, which enormously impressed her, and the repaired tombs of the sixteenth-century sultans at Marrakesh, which she boasted that no European travellers had been able to see before (since they only came to light in 1917), were all evidence of Lyautey's programme to preserve the holy places and historical sites of Morocco. He greatly improved the infrastructure (Wharton never misses a chance of praising the good French roads, as opposed to the terrible Spanish ones), and kept the European 'new' towns at a tactful distance from the old cities of Fez, Rabat, Salé, Marrakesh and Meknèz. (She noted this 'respect for native habits, native beliefs and native architecture'.) As part of the war-effort, Lyautey set up trade fairs, like the one she had been invited to at Rabat, promoting Moroccan and French (not German) products. He made a speech at the opening of the Rabat fair she attended, which summed up his colonial policy. 'The grandeur and beauty of the colonial war', he said, was that as soon as the fighting stopped, 'it begins to create life' [elle est créatrice de vie].

Lyautey was a brilliant propagandist. Many of the high-class French writers and politicians he and Wharton both knew – Tardieu, Chevrillon, the Marquis de Segonzac, the Vicomte de Vogüé – were spokesmen in France (where he was detested by the socialists) for his policies in Morocco. The diplomat Paul Morand noted in his journal in September 1917 that it was all the rage to go to Morocco: 'Tout le monde est à la foire de Rabat. C'est la mode d'automne.' (He added in a gossipy aside that Mrs Wharton and Walter Berry were going, Mrs Wharton having '*remis la main*' on Berry after his pining over Mrs Garrett.) So when Wharton reported on the sultan's mother saying to her that 'All is well in Morocco as long as all is well with France', or spoke of 'the political stability which France is helping them to acquire', she was acting as Lyautey's mouthpiece. It was part of her willing contribution to the war-effort.[61]

Wharton did her homework, as she always did before travelling, and her reading underlined her nationalistic, Francophile attitude to North Africa. She wrote to the expert, André Chevrillon (whose *Un Crépuscule d'Islam: Maroc* she read) asking him for advice, and she discussed her journey with Gide, who sent her a copy of *L'Immoraliste*: she said that his evocations of the desert were whetting her appetite. She told Chevrillon that she was reading Pierre Loti (*Au Maroc*), Augustin Bernard's *Le Maroc*, and the Marquis de Segonzac's 'ponderous octavo', *Voyages Au Maroc*, which she thought was dull and too heavy to carry. Her reading of Morocco was indistinguishable from the dominant French approach. This is seen in many details in the book. When she described the Sultan Moulay-Ismaël's negotiations with Louis XIV, she copied out their exchange of gifts from Bernard's history; when she told the story of Moulay-el-Hassan, who 'was indignant as Canute' to find a rough sea interfering with his military plans, she lifted it straight from Bernard's version, except his comparison is with Xerxes. When she praised Lyautey, she sounded as if she were writing in translation: 'The policy of France in Morocco had been weak and spasmodic; in his hands it became firm and consecutive. A sympathetic understanding of the native prejudices, and a real affection for the native character, made him try to build up an administration which should be, not an application of French ideas to African conditions, but a development of the best native aspirations.' She entirely accepted the French imperialist version of Moroccan history as a recurrent cycle of 'instability and despotism'. The Hachette guide to Morocco, which she praised, and which came out soon after she went there, mirrored her views:

Morocco, so long aloof from Western civilisation, has been striding along rapidly on the road to progress since 1912 . . . In the French zone, under the eminent management of Marshal Lyautey, a masterly work has been realised, which the war of 1914–1918 did not put a stop to ... improvement by careful and wise administration ... care taken not to interfere with agelong customs ...

The point of these books, and of *In Morocco*, was that this was a better form of imperialism than that which the Germans were attempting to force upon the world.[62]

Wharton's account of the scenes and people of Morocco is (like her views of Tunisia) at once fascinated by their exoticism, and based on hierarchical assumptions about gradations of civilisation. She has a sharp eye for the 'types' she sees (a letter to Minnie takes pleasure in the opportunity that the trade fair gave her to 'watch the faces' of the sultan's entourage), and describes them like specimens of fascinating alien species. Whether she is encountering a group of beturbanned pilgrims winding their way through the desert under parti-coloured banners, breaking off their procession to help pull the official car back on to the track and turning into a screaming, rapacious mob the minute payment is thrown to them; or coming across a village of blacks, 'big, friendly creatures' with 'countless jolly children'; or noting the filth and poverty of the Jews in the 'Mellah' (the ghettoes), the women 'waddling', 'huge lumps of tallowy flesh', the 'greasy round-bellied' fathers 'bumping along like black balloons'; or visiting a salon of fat, well-fed, reclining merchants, passing their feast day in 'a prolonged state of obese ecstasy': her view is always anthropological and often satirical. In her letters, her terms are blunter: 'It was most awfully queer' (she told Minnie, staying in what had once been the Grand Vizier's favourite's apartment, in the resident-general's palace of Bahia at Marrakesh, where from her 'divan' she could see the palace lamplighters walking past) 'to look out of my painted niche and see two tall Ballet-Russe niggers with bare feet marching slowly across the blue and white tiles of my private patio!'

She observed Moroccan women closely, and thought about their lives. Her stay in the 'favourite's' apartment, this 'lovely prison', was one of many moments when the attraction of erotic luxury was combined with a puritanical distaste for the conditions of women's lives. Her attention (as in all her foreign trips) always goes to them: the women in their finery for a feast in the white town of Moulay Idriss, looking like the 'ladies-in-waiting of the Queen of Sheba', the women down from the hills, haggling at the market at Sefrou, an oasis near Fez, 'with brilliant hennaed eyes and smiles that lifted their short upper lips maliciously', the fluttering girls at the sultan's court, the impressive figure of the sultan's mother, a manager and a politician in her own right. She is laconic about the well-known sexual exploitation of boys and the 'hermaphrodite fry' in the Moroccan harems, but her 'open-air Occidental mind' is appalled by the enslavement of women, the 'vacuity' of their minds, and 'a sexual and domestic life based on slave-service and incessant espionage'. Wharton's attraction to the sensual intensity of Morocco, combined with her horror at what she saw of women's lives there, overlaps with the dark eroticism and female passivity of *Summer*. And perhaps Morocco in part inspired her lush exercise in erotic writing, 'Beatrice Palmato', with the daughter's surrender to the oriental father's penetration in a heated mixture of abjection and appetite, a cruel plot of female enslavement and suicide. At a time when Wharton had started to think of herself as old (one of her conversations in the harem, carefully transcribed, is about the pitiableness of a childless woman), she was thinking about cruelty to women and about female exploitation and oppression.[63]

Ultimately, though, the women in Morocco are obscure to her, and it is partly that mystery she likes. The French romanticising of Africa and the Orient, with which she was so imbued, made much of the ancient mystery of the desert and its people. Wharton is always describing the 'mystery and menace' emanating from 'hundreds of unknown and unknowable people', the difficulty of getting into places, or the sense of 'looking down into the heart of forbidden things'. She turns Morocco into a dream world (wrily punctuated, occasionally, with telephones and acetylene lamps), a fairy-tale out of the Arabian Nights with djinns and magic carpets. She is fascinated by the sense of an unbroken line stretching back from this 'rich and stagnant civilization' to the times of the Romans. And, like all the French writers on Morocco, she finds there a sense of fatalism, apathy, and sombre melancholy.[64]

This French view has a built-in contradiction. She loves the country's remoteness from Europe and the spell of 'unknown Africa' that grows as she travels further towards the Atlas mountains. She wants the bazaars of Fez to be more 'Oriental', 'if "Oriental" means colour and gaiety'. But all her analogies (as in Tunisia) are with European art. She compares the figures outside the walls of Fez to a picture by Carpaccio or Bellini, or the black lamplighters at the palaces to 'a fragment from a Delacroix'. She wants the country to keep its ancient mystery and resents the prospect of imminent tourism that will change it for ever; but she welcomes the French civilising process and may have been aware that, as in her motor-travels in France, she herself is part of what will change it.[65]

In this escape from war, there is plenty of blood and death. Wharton is fascinated by the country's 'ancient traffic in flesh and blood' and the 'dark magic' of its sacrificial rituals, and by its ruins. The city of Chella, across from Rabat, 'fallen like a Babylonian city', in a 'red powdery waste' makes her think of 'death and the desert for ever creeping up to overwhelm the puny works of man'. The Roman fragments of Volubilis, facing across the valley the vast remains of Moulay-Ismael's seventeenth-century citadel at Meknèz, built by slave labour, the remains of a 'barbarous empire', is now a scene of 'catastrophic desolation'.[66] Wharton has Shelley's 'Ozymandias' in mind ('Look on my works, ye mighty, and despair'). And she has in mind too, at this time, the rise and fall of civilisations, the ending of all empires in ruins.

For Wharton, as for millions of others, the war left her haunted by the dead. The legendary French story of wounded soldiers in the trenches rising to their feet with the cry *'Debout les Morts!'* came to have the mythic status of a ghost story, with the dead coming back to help the living. Julien Green called it the expression of a kind of 'mass hallucination', and Edith Wharton drew on it for her heroic ghost-story, *The Marne*. The struggle to find a meaning for the sacrifices of the dead took over France. The creation of the *'lieux de mémoire'*, the public outbreaks of grief on All Saints' Day, 1 November (so huge that the processions had to be banned in 1916), the monuments and memorialising, the rituals of 11 November, coloured life for many years in her 'second country'. Of course there were celebrations when the war ended. Wharton wrote a piece (for an issue of *Reveille* edited by John Galsworthy in aid of disabled soldiers and sailors) called 'How Paris Welcomed the King'. It described King George's arrival in Paris on a rainy day, and spoke again, for what she must have hoped would be the last time, about good Franco-American relations. But for many the burden of loss outweighed the joy of victory. And Wharton too was changed by the war. She became more dedicated to the memory of her dead, more moved by the religious ceremonies which had provided consolation for so many in wartime, even more attuned to the ghostliness of the modern world. Paris especially, in post-war novels like *The Glimpses of the Moon* or *The Children*, became for her a spectral and melancholy city.[67]

The strangest piece of fiction to come out of her war-years was a story called 'Kerfol', published in 1916 and included in *Xingu*. The narrator (nationality and gender unspecified, but presumably American and male) is looking for a house to buy – just as Wharton was at the end of the war – and is sent by his French friends to a lonely house in Brittany called

Kerfol. It is a dark autumn day: All Saints' Day, as it turns out. He finds Kerfol to be a romantically beautiful, sad and abandoned old house, with a long avenue of trees, an overgrown moat, and a chapel with some ancient tombs. But there is nobody there except a pack of silent, wary dogs. Back with his hosts, he is told that the dogs were ghosts, and, in the best tradition of ghost-stories, is given a book to read which contains the gruesome story of what happened in the seventeenth century at Kerfol, a story of a cruel marriage, a lonely wife, a thwarted love-affair and the husband's horrible murder by a pack of – ghostly – dogs. The ghost-story itself is much less frightening and suggestive than the narrator's opening visit to the haunting, haunted French house, which like so many of Wharton's houses seems to stand in for a whole civilisation, and feels to the narrator as if it exudes 'the sheer weight of many associated lives and deaths which gives a majesty to all old houses'. But it suggests 'something more', too: 'a perspective of stern and cruel memories stretching away, like its own grey avenues, into a blur of darkness'. The house 'might have been its own funeral monument. "Tombs in the chapel? The whole place is a tomb!"'[68]

PART III

16

Pavillon/Château

Edith Wharton was fifty-seven when she acquired two new homes. Though she sometimes described herself, now, as an old woman, and though she was worn out from her war-efforts, her appetite and her determination were unchecked. The double property acquisition, and the new pattern of life it involved, are typical. She was a woman of dynamic organisational energies, busy and managerial, who also had a profound need for peace and rest. She liked her solitude, and did not enjoy 'society', but she could also feel very lonely and wanted her friends around her. She had grown up and lived in big cities, but she preferred the country. She was committed to a life in France, but not to Paris, which was now tainted for her by a taxing ten-year history of love and loss, marital horrors, and war-strain. She was wealthy, but she wanted to use her money for quiet, sensible pleasures and luxuries, not for flash and show. Her income depended to a great extent on her work, and she needed a way of life that could both feed and benefit from her earnings.

Above all, she was a writer desperate to get back to a settled routine. She saw her way to it in the two places which were going to become her second skins. These settings would frame her image from now on: one can imagine her in the 1920s and 1930s sitting on a flowery terrace, with a peke under her arm, looking down towards the distant Mediterranean, or walking in the blue garden of an eighteenth-century villa, with water playing in a fountain. Or, equally well, she might be sitting at her desk paying her electricity bills, or arguing with the local authorities about the upkeep of her access road. Buying and renovating houses is not a romantic business, however much vision and emotion are invested in it. The story of Wharton's French houses has a great deal to do with business and practicalities. And the first purchase came directly out of her wartime work. She knew she would want to leave Paris when the war ended, and she started looking for properties in and around Fontainebleau in the autumn of 1917. It was Elisina who noticed a likely house in a quiet side-street in St-Brice, a

still-rural village half an hour's drive from Paris, which she passed regularly
on her journeys to and from 'Bon Acceuil', the sanatorium at nearby Groslay.
During the war, especially as the German advance neared Paris, many of
the houses in the villages to the north and east of the city were 'deserted
by their owners'. As Wharton said in *A Backward Glance*, when Elisina
asked the concierge if it was for sale, 'the answer was a foregone conclusion . . . Every house in the Northern Suburbs of Paris was to be bought at
that darkest moment of the spring of 1918.'

'Jean-Marie', as it was then called, was a dilapidated-looking empty
building behind a forbidding street-façade, which turned out on closer
inspection to be a charming eighteenth-century 'Pavillon' (country retreat
or *'maison de plaisance'*) with extensive grounds. She went to see it, 'fell in
love with it in spite of its dirt and squalor', started negotiations for it early
in 1918, and bought it in March, for the modest sum of 90,000 francs.
Work started at once on the house and its neglected grounds. She hired
an architect, Charles Knight, and she took advice from her old collaborator Ogden Codman (who acquired his own fine French house, the
seventeenth-century Château de Grégy-sur-Yerres, eighteen miles from
Paris). He had once envisaged buying 'Jean-Marie' and 'thought its possibilities endless'. A stable was converted into a guest house, the interior of
the house was completely renovated and redecorated, and the seven acres
of tall trees and wilderness began to be turned into a garden. While these
renovations were going on in the winter of 1918, Wharton went to stay in
the South of France, where she found her second house. So both her new
properties were acquired and made over, in an impressive burst of energy
and resolution, within the same two-year period. The end of the war was
also, for her, the end of her life in Paris.[1]

In July 1919, some of the furniture was moved from the Rue de Varenne
(the rest was kept in storage) and she started to invite friends out to see
the Pavillon. The Walter Gays came over from Le Bréau, and though
Matilda thought 'the approach through St Denis [the northern suburb of
Paris surrounding the great church] deplorably bad – there is an undesir-
able populace there', she was charmed by the 'little 18th-century country
house' which 'has a *cachet* of its own with its simple *boiseries*, its stone
baskets of fruit on the corner, and its railing on the roof . . . It will be a
healthy toy for Edith, and an accessible spot where she can rest her tired
brain.'

All through that year Paris was crowded with people working on the
Peace Treaty – especially 'yanks', as Wharton noted resentfully. She had
little to say about the bitter and ominous decisions made at the Treaty of

Versailles: she was in retreat from the war, and wanted to resume a private life. But the symbolic moment of the Victory Parade on 14 July 1919 was important to her. She told Berenson that she would not move her household to St-Brice until after the '*rentrée*' of the troops, as 'no Frenchman or woman ought to miss it'. She watched it from a sixth-floor window on the Champs-Élysées, and her account of it was stirring: 'We seemed really to be looking at a poet's Vision of Victory, so simple, so solemn, so really august . . . was the whole proceeding . . . our hearts were choking & bursting with the too-muchness of what it all meant!' In *A Backward Glance* she termed it 'a golden blur of emotion'. But onto the vision of shining arms and helmets and glossy chargers she superimposed the 'dusty, dirty, mud-encrusted, blood-stained' memory of the troops she had seen at the front: 'the two visions merge into one, and my heart is broken with them.' She starts the last chapter of her memoir with that sight, in a chapter called 'And After', even though fifteen vigorous and productive years came between the end of the war and the writing of the memoir. Everything that happened to her afterwards would be tinged with that sense of living on after a great catastrophe.[2]

In August, she had a house-warming party, but she had still not quite moved in: she was dividing her time in the autumn of 1919 between St-Brice and Paris, hating the crowds and the building-works and finding the Rue de Varenne depressing and cold. She thought at this point that she would need a Paris base (she was still renting a garage there), and made enquiries about another flat, near Les Invalides. In the end, Walter took over the lease at number 53, and she gave up the idea of a Paris pied-à-terre. By May 1920, she was settled into 'Jean-Marie' – 'looking, oh, so sweet this spring!' – and telling Berenson how much she liked the 'banlieue' and her 'humble potager', now 'gushing with nightingales': 'The heaps of rubble & various kitchen-midden have been cleared away, & the little place looks really welcoming.'[3]

These new arrangements in Wharton's life bring dramatically into focus the two essential underpinnings of her life, money and servants. At the end of the war she was anxious about money: it was a risky moment for her to invest in new houses, however keen she was to stop paying rent on her 'large & expensive apartment'. The trust income and the properties in New York which (going back to the terms of her father's will) she co-owned with her brother Harry, were not doing well at the end of the war. (Minnie was in bad financial straits because of this depression in real-estate, and Wharton was paying a regular annual sum to her and to Beatrix.) Her literary earnings had plummeted during the war and she told Beatrix in

October 1920 that her combined income (from literary earnings, property and trust fund) had dropped in the last three years from about $50,000 to between $18,000 and $20,000. Out of that, the 'dreadful double income tax' had to be paid, which came to 40,000 francs in 1919. The war had meant, too, 'the doubling of wages, & tripling of all living expenses'. And there was a poor market for the war-writing she was publishing between 1919 and 1923. Still, by 1920, things were looking better. She transferred her trust funds to new management, the Lincoln Trust Company. Real estate in New York began to pick up, and she told her financial adviser, her cousin Herman Edgar, to sell 'that incubus of a building' the family had owned for many years at 737 Broadway. The dollar quadrupled in value against the franc. She felt more secure about the future, since, as she told Beatrix, 'luckily you and I and Max are all good breadwinners, and have a good many precious possessions that we could dispose of if our incomes shrank'. But her main wealth in the 1920s would come from her writing. She had her new literary editor at Appleton's, Rutger Jewett, who would also act as her agent and who, over the next fifteen years, would negotiate some extremely profitable deals for her. From the moment she moved into the new houses, she set to work on the novels and stories which would bring in a huge literary income until the end of the decade. (Another unexpected source of profit was the $1,000 Pulitzer Prize for *The Age of Innocence* in 1921, which 'tainted money', she told Berenson gleefully, 'will come in particularly handy to polish off the gardens at Ste-Claire'.) The mid- and late 1920s were her highest-earning, and most extravagant years.[4]

When Wharton is thought of as a rich lady rather than as a writer, it is her travelling arrangements (the expensive cars, the servants sent on ahead to the hotels, the Mediterranean cruises of 1888 and 1926) which most often come to mind, since she did not go in for extravagant parties, diamond tiaras, racehorses or yachts. Perhaps of all her domestic luxuries, the seasonal weeks she spent at the Hôtel Crillon, from 1920 onwards, while her servants closed down one house and opened up the other, are the most eloquent marks of a life-style which she took for granted but which to most of us now seems opulent. This is not only because the Crillon, an eighteenth-century palace of Louis XV's on the Place de la Concorde, was – and is – one of the most luxurious hotels in Paris. It is also because of the dependency it assumes on live-in servants: a dependency common even to middle-class households, let alone to rich Americans living in beautiful European houses, up to the start of the Second World War.

Wharton's relations with her servants had been crucial to her all through her childhood (when her nurse Doyley was closer to her than her mother),

her upbringing, her marriage and her divorce. Now that she was setting up as the mistress of two houses, they were more important to her than ever. It is a mark of her good character as an employer that she kept a small group of people with her for life. Catherine Gross would be the mainstay of life at St-Brice and Hyères, though in her seventies, until she fell ill in 1933. Alfred White, her butler since 1888, who had transferred to her service from Teddy's, suffered increasingly from rheumatism, and was promoted to the more honorary position of 'general manager' in 1920, with a French butler, Favre, placed under him. (She had always admired White for keeping 'a firm hand over his footmen'.) After Wharton's death, White issued a devoted statement: 'For forty-nine years it was my privilege to save her and protect her from household cares, [so] that she could carry on her work in peace.' Charles Cook, who had been her chauffeur since 1904, and who had coped stoically with the transition from New England roads to Paris streets, Italian alpine bends and the war-zones of France, had to stop work in 1921 – he had a slight stroke and was no longer allowed to drive. It was painful for her to part with him (she gave him a life-pension and he went back to America in 1923 with his Swedish wife). She acquired a successor, Franklin, but motor-flights were never quite the same without Cook, and, ten years on, 'that idiot Franklin and his odious wife' would be in her bad books. Elise Devinck was her maid from 1914 until she fell ill in 1933. A second maid, an Englishwoman, Louisa Butler, also became a long-term fixture. Anna Bahlmann had been hard to replace; Wharton's wartime secretary, Dolly Herbert, turned out to be incompetent and tiresome (though long after getting rid of her, Wharton continued to pay funds to her and her mother). The much more efficient Jeanne Duprat, later Fridérich, took over, working mainly at St-Brice (she disliked going too far from Paris). She married in 1927, but her husband died less than a year later; and she worked on for Wharton, taking dictation, dealing with all comers, and typing manuscripts, until her employer died.[5]

This was the key team, of housekeeper, butler, staff-manager, chauffeur, secretary, and two maids, and she made no bones about how essential they were to her. Elisina, who ran an even bigger household herself, noted, in 1928, Wharton's need for 'a butler, a maid, a chef, a housemaid and a housekeeper ... She isn't foolishly attached to such things, but she needs the freedom which perfect servants bestow on one'. There were also, for each house, a head-gardener with four or five gardeners below him, a kitchen-staff, a footman to replace poor Henri, killed in 1915, and a second housemaid. Wharton treated her servants like servants; a letter about travel-plans, to an imminent guest, gives the tone: 'White will meet you at Toulon *with a motor* and will put the maid and luggage into the train, and the hotel bus will meet her at Hyères. The Hyères train leaves from the adjoining platform, and a child couldn't miss it, as it is the only object in sight. And I insist on the motor because, if the train is late, it is depressing to hang about Toulon for two hours!' Her idea of an ideal employee was sketched out in an advertisement sent to a Bond Street Social Bureau in 1921:

> Mrs Wharton requires a thoroughly competent lady's maid, accustomed to travel and to the care of a lady's wardrobe, and to hair-dressing . . . a French maid, if she could find one who is thoroughly reliable and has been well-trained in England . . . or . . . English if speaks a little French . . . ready to give the highest wages now given provided she can find a thoroughly respectable, good-tempered and competent maid.

This request came out of an unfortunate episode with a French maid called Alice, who decided to leave Wharton's employment, without warning, just at the moment she was setting up her household in the South of France for the winter of 1919–20. An ex-employer would normally provide a servant with a reference; Wharton disliked doing this for such an inconsiderate servant, and asked Elisina her advice about the 'minimum' that could be said. She was going to pay her 'not a penny more' than her due. 'If I ever completely lose my faith in human nature it will be owing to my dealings with French servants!' To another friend, Dorothy Allhusen, she wrote: 'It depressed me so much to be treated rudely, especially by someone to whom I have done my best to be kind and considerate.' There would be many later remarks about the difficulty of getting good maids after the war; Wharton was not alone in complaining that 'the old type of quiet lady's maid, who is "in" it for anything but the wardrobe, & high jinks at Palace Hotels, has vanished from the post-war world, and one had best cling to the survivors with hooks of steel'. Socialism, she thought, had a lot to answer for.[6]

The Pavillon was a house used to servants. It was built in 1769, in the reign of Louis XV, and had its origins in a pre-Revolutionary, aristocratic way of life, a history which was part of its appeal. And its story is wonderfully worldly, like something out of an eighteenth-century novel. (Percy reported nudgingly to Gaillard that Wharton had bought a house which was 'the scene apparently in the past of lawless & historic amours'.) In 1761, a colourful Venetian family, the Rocomboli-Riggieris, the father a singer who also played the mandolin and exhibited wild animals, the mother a dancer, and three beautiful young daughters, came to Paris. The oldest, Marie-Madeleine, a blonde beauty, was hired to play at the king's theatre, the Comédie Italienne, at the age of fifteen, and took the stage-name Mademoiselle Colombe. One version of her story says that she was sold by her mother for 100 *louis d'or* to an Irish nobleman called Masserene, by whom she had a son, and who was later imprisoned for shady dealings. She found herself another protector, the Comte Jean-André Vassal, keeper of the king's finances. Vassal bought a house in St-Brice for her, demolished it, and built in its place, from 1770 onwards, on the Rue de Gournay (now the Rue Edith Wharton) an elegant folly, a setting for his mistress which he wanted to be '*riant, aimable, et gracieux*'. Indoors, it had sumptuous carved wood panelling (with dove motifs and intertwined 'MC's everywhere), Venetian mirrors, Brussels tapestries, lace curtains, Chinese porcelain, and wall-panels by Fragonard, who painted Mlle Colombe frequently, often as the goddess of Love, and is said to have had an affair with her. Outside, there was an elaborate garden, renowned for its trellises and statuary, stables, a farm, a coach-house, a pond and fine trees. But in the end Vassal married and left Mlle Colombe alone in St-Brice. Her place in the theatre had been taken over by one of her younger sisters (who may also have lived with her in the Pavillon) and she pursued a career as a courtesan. In 1794, Vassal took back the house, and Mlle Colombe went to live in Paris, where she died at the age of eighty in 1830. After her time, the Pavillon had several owners, including a great Russian singer known for her Wagner, Félia Litvinne (1860–1936). The last owners before Wharton had been a doctor, Jean-Marie Bineau, and his wife; he had killed himself, and she had named the house after him. Delighting in its eighteenth-century history (and perhaps wanting to avoid the gloomy associations of the previous owner), Wharton renamed the house the Pavillon Colombe.[7]

The Pavillon is a long white house hiding behind the north wall of its courtyard, with a massive carriage-door set into the wall facing the street. Its look says 'private, no entry'; but once inside it has charm, light, and classical elegance. The interior cobbled courtyard leads to the main door. On the ground floor the rooms (as at The Mount) open sideways into each other through communicating doors, and, on the south side, onto the terrace overlooking the garden. From east to west one passed from the dining room (black-and-white marble floor, marble tables, grey-painted panelling edged in black, a niche for a marble urn) to the long high salon or drawing room (wooden parquet floor, Italianate wall decorations, large built-in mirrors, marble fireplace, arcaded wooden panelling, high French windows), the sitting room, the library, and Mlle Colombe's little boudoir, with her doves in the plaster-work, and her bathroom, with its wooden bath and brass taps, still intact. At right angles on the courtyard side is a wing with three French windows. On the garden side, the tall French windows and the windows of the second-floor bedrooms all have shutters; on the third floor (the servants' rooms) there are port-hole windows set into the tiled roof, and on the top of the roof a little square balustraded cupola. Edith's bedroom and dressing-room were at the west end of the second-floor bedrooms, with windows looking south and west over the gardens.[8]

Photographs of the interiors of the Pavillon in her time show a formal dining room with cane-backed chairs and vases, a drawing room carefully furnished with elegant French eighteenth-century (or imitation) pieces, with flower-patterned fabric on the sofas and armchairs; a cosier sitting room with Chinese wallpaper and pots and all manner of screens, side-tables, shaded table-lamps, clocks and flower-vases, and a dark library with built-in bookcases, comfortable chairs, and a desk by the window. Most visitors found the effects pleasing. The English garden-designer Russell Page spoke of the affinity between the garden and the 'spirit of the house', its 'panelled rooms filled with books and eighteenth-century furniture'. One French friend would write indulgently about the 'soft-coloured library, with the low tables covered with new books, the flower-paintings on the walls, the door wide open to the garden and its scents, the bowls of great poppies or blue larkspurs, shedding their petals, or a tall white lily, alone in a crystal jar, in noiseless attendance'. Not all her friends were as impressed. Ogden Codman, of course, thought the salon very bad: 'of a cold hard Louis Philippe gray, with *bois naturel* furniture covered with quite the ugliest *cretonne* I ever saw, chinese but much europeanised flowers and hideous colour'. Their mutual friends the Gays were as critical: 'Had the little place fallen into other hands, it could have been made a gem', Matilda wrote sniffily in her diary. Codman noticed that when Walter Gay painted the Pavillon's interiors, he 'improved it': 'Walter ... painted the room a lovely soft yellowish gray, and ... put in a sofa of painted wood ... covered with a charming material. [The Gays] do not think she has much taste, no eye for colour. Alas I must quite agree to both.' Yet Walter Gay frequently painted the Pavillon, always showing the rooms light and full of flowers, with the green of the garden shining through the open windows, catching the sense of a secluded French country house.[9]

Towards the end of her life, Wharton described her domain as 'a quiet garden in the banlieue, where I have five or six acres of trees and quiet'.[10] Her 'acres', in summer at St-Brice and in winter at Ste-Claire, now became one of the main interests of her life, as they had been at The Mount between 1902 and 1910, but then more interrupted by European travels, and in a less propitious climate and landscape. This expensive, pleasurable, and profound obsession should not be thought of by non-gardeners as a form of quietism or as a mere hobby. Though she had gardeners to do the digging and the planting, the staking and the weeding, the same mighty energies, appetite for planning, eye for detail, and cogent vision went into her gardening as into the writing of fiction, and as they had into her war-activities and her travels. Apart from travelling, writing, reading and seeing her friends, this, for the rest of her life, was what she did. She did not 'do' politics, or journalism, or sports, or public appearances, or large-scale socialising, or (any longer) extensive charity work. She was a writer and a gardener, and her gardens became, for those who saw them and heard about them, as admired as her books.

Over seventeen years, she turned the wilderness at St-Brice, which had once been a magical eighteenth-century pleasure-ground for Mlle Colombe, back into a perfect, orderly, and interesting French garden. She brought to bear on this Île-de-France landscape her deep knowledge of Italian villa-gardens and her experience at The Mount, though now with the confidence produced by a milder climate. She described this 'horticultural heaven', in an unpublished piece on 'Gardening in France', in humorous terms which are revealing, too, about her sense of her own new life:

> The mere fact that box, ivy, jasmine and climbing hybrid tea-roses belong to the fundamental make-up of the least favoured garden; that roses begin to bloom in June and go on till December; that nearly everything is 'remontant' and has plenty of time to flower twice over; this blessed sense of the leisureliness and dependableness of the seasons in France, of the way the picture stays in its frame instead of dissolving like a fidgetty tableau-vivant, creates a sense of serenity in the mind inured to transiency and failure.

Her design was arranged in stages, leading away from the French windows and their three shallow stone-steps, flanked by urns, going down to a long terrace stretching along the garden side of the house, dressed with comfortable wooden garden furniture, urns of flowers and orange trees in boxes. Below that, and a long bed of lavender, she reconstructed a formal, green French garden of geometrical 'parterres' edged with little pointed box hedges, with a lawn to the side. (A 'humpy' old lawn dotted with ornamental trees had to be got rid of first, and some of the St-Brice neighbours were shocked by her ruthless removal of a large monkey-puzzle tree.) A straight alley bordered with box led away through a little wood, which she called her 'grove', to a big oval stone pond, with fish and water-lilies, where she had a central fountain playing out of a stone cherub blowing his own trumpet on the back of a dolphin. Behind it, through an iron gate overhung with climbers set into a high, clipped box hedge, was her '*potager*', a kitchen garden, and her '*jardin fleuriste*' intercut with alleys, one an avenue of limes, one of rhododendrons. Beyond that were an orchard, with many espaliered fruit trees, a rose-garden, a blue garden, an avenue of lilies, and the high stone walls with many magnificent climbers which bordered what she called her 'little world', or *hortus inclusus*. She cultivated her fruit trees like a Frenchwoman: 'In all well-regulated gardens in this part of France the east wall belongs to peaches and nectarines, the south to winter pears and apples, and to early ripening grapes, and the west to earlier varieties of pears, apples and cherries.' She sold her surplus vegetables to her neighbours, and fed her guests on them; Royall Tyler noted a 'salad of raw vegetables' from the kitchen garden in June 1923. She protected her space, buying up land around her so that no one could build near the gardens, and extending the *potager* across the road.

Wharton's early plans for her French head-gardener at St-Brice show a gardener passionate about groupings of strong, vivid colours and extremely knowledgeable about how to contrive her effects. She asks for groupings of '*oranges, jaunes, et jaunes pâles*', or of '*les bleus, violets et mauve*', with white and pink beyond them, then more yellows, then blues: '*L'essentiel*' (she says, characteristically spelling it out) '*c'est que les groupes jaunes soient séparés des groupes roses par les groupes bleus ou violets.*' Long lists of recommended plantings follow, with notes and queries ('*les Godetias ne durent pas très longtemps, mais l'effet est si brilliant que je ne veux pas m'en passer*' . . . '*Les Pyrèthres vont-ils fleurir cette année si vous les semez immédiatement?*'), and always with the relation between detail and broad effects in mind: '*Je voudrais que cette bordure, comme celle de droite, soit tout à fait en couleurs qui s'harmonisent.*' She made an inventive list of plants for the 'blue' garden she designed. The 'parterres' directly in front of the house were plain and green, relieved by her stone urns full of geraniums, begonias or petunias, but the flower gardens would have been intensely, theatrically, continuously colourful.

Like all serious gardeners, she always saw failings:

I should be delighted to have your [Codman's] gardeners come and see the Pavillon Colombe, but this is a very bad moment, as the roses, which have been beautiful, are nearly over and will not be on again for another fortnight, and the Madonna lilies are also over, and the big herbaceous border, which is very backward this year, will not be 'en beauté' for another two weeks. I don't know how other people manage to avoid this period at the beginning of July when there is an interruption between the roses and lilies and the later things, but I have always struggled against it in vain.

But there were times when even she had no complaints, when she simply enjoyed the singing of the birds (she invited one friend to 'a concert given by the private symphony orchestra of the Pavillon Colombe consisting of 2 golden orioles, 2 stock doves, supported by a countless number of blackbirds, thrushes, warblers, robins, finches & other songsters'), or when her garden's rich dazzle of colour and scents was a sensual delight and a comfort to her. Just back from a (last) journey to America in 1923, she sat, as her annual custom had become, thinking about the friends she had lost, on All Souls' Day, the second of November, and was consoled by her blazing autumn garden: 'I sat alone in evening with all my dead. Flowers in bloom: Dahlias, Chrysanthemums, Roses, Mignonette, Snapdragons, Gilia, Aconite, Blue lupin, Marigolds, Coreopsis, Helenium, Salpiglossis, Verbena, Michaelmas daisies, Begonias, Penstemmons, Japanese anemones, Salvia, Heliotrope, Zinnias, Cosmos, Nasturtiums.'[11]

Wharton was helped at St-Brice (as she would be in the South of France) by a gardener of genius, the reclusive expatriate American Major Lawrence Johnston, whom she described to Berenson in October 1924 as 'a new and very nice gardening friend'. 'Johnnie', as his friends called him, had started his magical design of exuberant green outdoor rooms ('a wild garden in a formal setting', he called it) at Hidcote, in the Cotswolds, in the 1900s. Russell Page, who knew Hidcote well from his youth in the 1920s, and was greatly influenced by it (as many other fine gardeners were, including Vita Sackville-West at Sissinghurst), saw the gardens at the Pavillon Colombe when Wharton was there, and redeveloped them in the 1950s for the Duchesse de Talleyrand. He viewed Wharton's design as a 'Hidcote-type plan of a connecting series of garden compartments', in which 'one narrow path traversing half a dozen openings through hedge or wall will lead into as many different gardens, each retaining a domestic scale'. The style was perfectly illustrated at the Pavillon Colombe, where, said Page, 'with Major Johnston's help, she made a garden setting exactly in the spirit of the house'. He described with a gardener's eye the sequences of sun and shade, open spaces and high hedges, grass plots and woodland, flower garden, avenues, and grassy orchards: 'Each section of this long garden is seen from the house as a succession of narrow glimpses of sunshine and shade, the full shape and treatment of each part only being evident as you pass in turn through them.' Page says that Wharton created her 'blue garden' with the help of

Lawrence Johnston, though he may have overstated Johnston's initial influence, since she did not visit Hidcote until several years after she had started gardening at St-Brice (it was Johnston's second garden in the Riviera which she saw first). Still, in the 1920s and 1930s Wharton would be a frequent, delighted, and often envious visitor to Hidcote, telling Elisina in 1929, for example, that she had just been to see it and some other beautiful English gardens, and hoped that 'some modest results will appear next year at Colombe! The things they do with flowers under these mild grey skies are magical!'[12]

Wharton had her own influence as a gardener, on Ogden Codman, whom she advised on his planting plans at Château de Grégy, and on another expatriate American, the novelist Louis Bromfield, who, according to Russell Page, 'had learnt much of his gardening from Edith Wharton at St-Brice'. Bromfield, who came originally from Ohio, and became a popular novelist in the 1930s and 1940s, went to France as an ambulance driver in the war, and came back with his wife to create an enchanting garden, famous for its hybrid musk roses and lilies, at the Presbytère de St-Etienne, on the banks of the River Nonette at Senlis, not far from St-Brice. He and Wharton became amicably competitive gardening-friends. (He was also the friend of another expatriate American woman writer-gardener, Gertrude Stein, but did not succeed in bringing these two together.) Wharton and Bromfield exchanged recommendations and cuttings, boasted about their successes and sympathised with failures. 'We seldom discussed our writing', Bromfield recalled, 'but we talked frequently and at great length of our dahlias and petunias, our green peas and our lettuces.' So she would end a letter to him: 'I want to swank about the roses . . . for they've got their second wind now.' Or: 'Please note that gazanias & dahlias *Athies* are at your disposal whenever you want them'. Bromfield told a touching story of taking Edith, in old age, to visit a local dahlia-grower who was also a fervent communist (he had named his favourite species after Henri Barbusse). In spite of their differences, and her ill-health, she had spent the afternoon eagerly talking to him: 'For a time they became brother and sister. They talked of flowers, of soil, of fertilizers, of experiments, of climates, and she ordered from him dahlia after dahlia which she never lived to see in flower.'[13]

Senlis and St-Brice were in a part of the world which she already knew well, in love and war. Guide-books of the time show how raw the wounds of war were and how strange the transition to peaceful tourism must have felt. The 1921 Guide Bleu to *Les Environs de Paris* gives as much space to the appalling story of the occupation of Senlis by the Germans in September 1914 – the executions, the burning of buildings, the cruel treatment of the mayor (*'objet des plus odieuses brutalités'*) – as it does to the beauties of its cathedral, churches and castle. But it also notes that the Syndicat d'Initiative, in abeyance during the war, has now been reorganised. Holidays and leisure-pastimes were gaining ground in the early 1920s. Of Wharton's nearest town, Montmorency, the Guide Bleu observes that *'les Parisiens viennent en foule le dimanche'* to this charming *'villégiature'* [holiday-spot], for its forest of chestnuts, its associations with Rousseau, its cherry trees, its church with the memorials to the Montmorency family, its delightful country houses and its closeness to the lake of Enghien. Of St-Brice itself, a tiny village on the eastern edge of the Montmorency forest, the Guide notes briefly: '*1,229 habs., au pied du massif de Montmorency, a un clocher de la fin du XII^s; dans le cour de la mairie, monument aux morts de 1914–1918'*. But it lavishes praise on the beautiful and tranquil scenery of the Valley of the Oise and on the wealth of fine sights in this part of the Île de France. This countryside of poplars, rivers, forests and gentle hills, much loved of painters, had been royal hunting-country, and was bristling with abbeys, castles and grey-steepled churches. After the war it returned to its profitable agricultural way of life. Groslay was a fruit-growing centre, and in the 1930s Wharton nostalgically remembered her route to St-Brice, 'through pleasant market-gardens, and acres of pear and apple orchard'. By the 1930s it had been 'disfigured by the growth of Paris'.

There were plenty of things to show her visitors: churches at Montfort l'Amaury (with such strong associations for her), at Chars near Pontoise, and at l'Isle-Adam, the village in the forest which had been the Prince of Conti's court; castles, like the eighteenth-century Champlatreux, or Écouen, built by the Montmorency family in the sixteenth century; the Abbey of Royaumont, ruins of St Louis's medieval monastery; or the romantic gardens of Ermenonville, with Rousseau's tomb on an island in the middle of a lake. Further afield, there were the famous sights of Versailles, Rambouillet, Fontainebleau and Vaux-le-Vicomte. Wharton developed a particularly close connection, not only with Bromfield at Senlis, but also with the Abbaye de Châalis, next door to Ermenonville, an eighteenth-century monastery built on the ruins of a Cistercian abbey surrounded by forests, with a beautiful rose-garden, which had been bought by the collector and financier's widow Nélie Jacquemart-André in 1902 and turned into a luxurious setting for her eclectic and opulent collection. She died in 1902, and the Institut de France appointed Louis Gillet as the museum's curator, who came to live in the castle with his wife and six children. He was a learned art-historian, a friend of the Bromfields ('a kindly and learned man', they said of him), of the Gays (who thought him 'modest and erudite'), of Charlie

Du Bos and of Berenson, some of whose work he translated. Gillet had a wide range of interests: Charles Péguy had been his hero, he had a passion for Italian art and English literature, but he also got to grips with modern art, loved Cézanne and Matisse and struggled with what he saw as the dangerous new art of Picasso and Cubism, its combination of egotism and impersonality. He liked to think of art as universal, and of a 'secret unity' between works of every age (*'une page de Corot, une scène de Poussin, une scène de Cézanne'*). Such discussions must often have taken place between Gillet, Berenson and Wharton, as the dedication to his 1938 essays on French art suggests: '*À Bernard Berenson, en souvenir de . . . Florence, d'Hyères et de Saint-Brice*'. Wharton came to like Gillet very much, and he translated two of her best 1920s novels, *The Mother's Recompense* and *The Children*. She often visited Châalis, and enjoyed the mixture there of artistic distinction and domestic life, as in this description (to Berenson) of Gillet's daughter's wedding, in 1933:

> A charming example of a simple, rustic French family gathering, the guests seated on kitchen chairs, the knives & forks brought back unwashed on each plate, &c. – & all gay, friendly, full of discours & accolades. Valéry & H[enri] de Régnier were Louisette's witnesses, & Valéry read aloud a singularly artless poem by Mme H. de Régnier, which M. de Monzie took for an effusion of Valéry's, no doubt to the latter's unbounded surprise![14]

There are no such accounts of her dropping in on neighbouring houses at St-Brice. Wharton made no contact with the town's other writer, the poet Paul Eluard, then in his twenties, who was enjoying the *'bon air suburbain de St-Brice'* between 1921 and 1923, with his wife Gala and his young daughter, while involved in turbulent relations with the Dadaists and Surrealists. If Wharton had gone to visit the Eluards, just down the road, she might have encountered Tristan Tzara, Louis Aragon, Man Ray, Duchamp, André Breton, or Max Ernst, with whom Gala was having a passionate affair. But Wharton confined her social life to her old friends from America, Paris and England, rather than making a life in the town. She was the lady of the manor, keeping her eye on the convalescent homes at Groslay, giving a donation to the curé of St-Brice and paying out sums to local schools and charities. She regularly opened her gardens to the public, in a patriotic American gesture, on the Sundays nearest to Independence Day. On every Feast of the Assumption (15 August) she would play host to a religious ritual: young girls going to their first communion, dressed in white, with hats and veils ('*Les Enfants de la Marie*'), would process behind the nuns of the convent, through the gardens, past a statue of the Virgin Mary in the wall of the Pavillon, to sing hymns in front of its owner. St-Brice was a quiet, rural suburb then, with few contacts with the outside world or with Parisian celebrities; the townsfolk used to refer to Wharton as '*l'Américaine*'. But it was noted that '*des rapports plein de respect s'étaient établis entre elle et les saintbriciens*'. At her death, the municipal council sent a representative carrying the flag of the region to follow her funeral procession; and years later, a plaque would be placed on her house and her street renamed after her.[15]

She had plenty of visitors, some of them acquaintances from the old Paris days, some her closest friends, some – as time went on – Americans passing through, just wanting to see the garden and pay their respects. She liked seeing the Berensons, the Gays, the Du Boses, the Tylers, the Maynards, the Bromfields, Boccon-Gibod, Bélugou, Lawrence Johnston, Gillet, Mme Taillandier, the Abbé Mugnier, Gaillard, John Hugh, Walter, Robert or Percy (up to a point). It was more pleasant seeing people at St-Brice than in Paris, and it was easy to get to, with trains via Groslay or Montmorency to the Sarcelles St-Brice station taking only half an hour from the Gare du Nord – almost quicker, at first, than telephoning: '*Pour téléphoner d'ici*' (she joked to Bélugou in 1920) '*il faut commencer à 8 hres du matin et n'avoir pas d'autre occupation pendant toute la journée*'. All the same, this was her place of work as well as her place of refuge, as she told Berenson in the summer of 1924:

> As for me, I'm trying, as usual to *finish* – finish my novel, finish 3 articles for Scribner, & another (on Proust) for the *Yale Rev.*; finish thanking people for the books they keep sending me; finish my garden here; finish my ditto at Hyères; finish answering urgent letters; finish arranging my books; finish looking up motor-roads for my trip to England; finish settling business matters with publishers, trustees & what not; finish the book I'm actually reading (*Fraser's Old Testament Folklore* – great fun) & this letter – & so on. And so it will be till the great Finis stamps itself at the end of my page. And it's a jolly sight better than stagnation.

Once she had settled at St-Brice, she often complained that these activities were disrupted all summer long by streams of guests. She was a sitting target for passing 'yanks' and others dropping in from Paris. Sometimes she even resented her friends' visits, and she particularly 'cursed', as the years went by, 'the casual désoeuvrée tourist, who merely wants *to have been here*, & wastes my time & temper'. 'Too many visitors' was a constant cry at

St-Brice; she came to feel that her real refuge was elsewhere. 'Oh for my fortress in the South!'[16]

The usual story of Wharton's affair with the South of France is that she fell in love with it in the autumn of 1915, on an escapade from war-work with Gide, Bélugou and Robert Norton, visiting the Bourgets at their villa at Costebelle, a few miles from Hyères. From 1894, until Bourget's death in 1935, he and Minnie spent all their winters there, in a fine, nineteenth-century, Palladian-style villa called Le Plantier, with a park full of rare palm-trees. But this was not Wharton's first discovery of what had been known, since the phrase was coined in 1887, as the Côte d'Azur. She had not liked it much in her youth, probably because her father died in Cannes in 1880. Though she reacted more enthusiastically to the beauty of the Provençal coast when she and Teddy went for the first time to Hyères to see the Bourgets in January 1904, she did not enjoy Grasse, Cannes and Monte Carlo. But in March 1907, her motor-flight with Henry and Teddy included Hyères, and she poured her pleasure into the travel-book: 'Looking out . . . from the pine-woods of Costebelle, above Hyères, one is beset by classic allusions, analogies of the golden age – so divinely does the green plain open to the sea, between mountain lines of such Attic purity . . . This surrender to the spell of the landscape tempts one to indefinite idling . . . It is all a tranquil backwater.' That sense of Hyères as a magical refuge came rushing back in 1915. She spent nearly a month there, 'placidly stagnating in divine sunshine'. The South of France was relatively untouched by the war, though it had its share of wounded and invalid soldiers and bereaved families, and at the end of the war, she told Charles Scribner, was still 'swarming with American troops'.

In December 1918, recovering from the 'flu, and exhausted, she went back there with Robert Norton, who was unwell with pleurisy, and was happy to join the convalescents pouring down to the South of France, and to do some painting. He was to be her most steadfast and regular companion in this post-war refuge, much more so than Walter. While the renovations were going on at St-Brice, she stayed at the Hôtel du Parc for about four months, recuperating and exploring. She talked to 'Norts' with passion about her sense of the antiquity and beauty of 'the true Provence', quite separate and hidden away from the fashionable Riviera; and to Berenson she wrote with ecstatic relief about the golden light, the 'Odyssean' land-scape, the 'healing silence', the sun, the flowers, the smells, and the long days of rest: 'Seven hours of blue-&-gold & thyme & rosemary & hyacinth & roses every day that the Lord makes; & in the evenings, dozing over a good book!' She described their days to John Hugh Smith: 'I work all the morning, and he goes off sketching. About 12 we meet, and start off with a lunch basket for the sea shore or the hills. After lunch we walk for 2 hours or more, then we come back deliciously air and sun drunk, and after dinner we talk books – and *not* peace or war!'

While she and Norts were exploring together, they found a remarkable and alluring house called 'Ste-Claire-du-Vieux-Château', on the site of a seventeenth-century convent, built into the ruined walls of the town's medieval castle, standing empty, high above the old town, much in need of renovation and with grounds of great potential. By April 1919, she had arranged to rent it on a long lease, and work started on the house at the beginning of 1920. She rented a temporary home in Hyères from January to April 1920 (a grand English-owned villa, Le Bocage, with a vast lawn surrounded by palm-trees, mimosas, pines and olives) while she supervised the reconstruction of her property and the plans for its garden. She moved in, for Christmas 1920, to the house she renamed – as she renamed 'Jean-Marie' – 'Ste-Claire-du-Château'. There was a fanciful touch to this androgynous name, since the house was not quite a convent or quite a castle, yet the name combined the sense of both.[17]

Wharton chose Hyères not so much for the proximity of the Bourgets, whom by the end of the war she had begun to find depressing, but because she saw it as the perfect writer's refuge and winter complement to St-Brice.[18] Eighteen kilometres east of Toulon, Hyères is the most southerly town of the Var, with a wonderful climate – hot dry air all through the winter, sheltered from the mistral and the cold. The very occasional bitter frosts could be a great shock to its inhabitants, as Wharton would discover to her cost, since Hyères felt so protected, at the bottom of the Rhône valley, surrounded by wooded hills. Below the hills, a vast agricultural plain stretched away to miles of sandy beaches, to the long '*presqu'île*' or promontory of Giens, with its salt-marshes and wild birds, leading to the ancient garrison of La Tour-Fondue, and, just offshore, the complex archipelago of the 'Îles d'Or', the golden islands of Porquerolles, Port Cros and Le Levant, scattered with old fortifications (built first against pirates, then bolstered by Napoleon) and rich in wild fauna and flora. Hyères was known for its trees, native and exotic: cedars, chestnuts, pines, olives, an astounding variety of palms, mimosas, yuccas, eucalyptus. It had a thriving range of local industries: salt-works, vineyards, fishing, the culture of figs and artichokes and fruit trees, cut flowers. Anemones, roses, carnations and – for perfumes and eau de Cologne – jasmine, tuberose, and the famous Hyères Parma violets, were picked by peasants who made their living from these products, and sent off to the cities of France.

To choose a house in old Hyères in 1919 was to invest in that particular idea of French life – tradition, beauty, taste, exclusiveness – which had always inspired Wharton's writing on France and her commitment to her 'seconde patrie'. Hyères had its 'new' parts, but what she chose to live in was an old Provençal town set well away from the seaside, which had kept its customs, its rural and provincial atmosphere and its regional dialect. It was typical of her to settle in a quiet backwater with a strong sense of history, not in any of the rapidly developing Riviera towns. As the Rue de Varenne was to the Right Bank and the Ritz, so Hyères was to Nice, Cannes, Antibes or Monte Carlo. It had a completely different feeling from those tourist Meccas, the glittering destinations of the 'monde and the demi-monde'. Wharton's South of France was a separate world from the Riviera – what Somerset Maugham called 'a sunny place for shady people' – with its vast landscaped mansions, casinos and spas, elegant restaurants and grand hotels, brothels and decadent house-parties, fast cars, jazz, yachts, cocktails and drugs, sunbathing and swimming-pools, beach pajamas and high fashion. The gregarious joie de vivre of rich bohemian Americans like the talented painter Gerald Murphy and his wife Sarah at the Cap d'Antibes, thriving on the exchange rate between the high dollar and low franc – the models for the Divers in Scott Fitzgerald's Tender is the Night – was not at all Whartonian. A glossy French picture-book called La Côte d'Azur au temps d'Edith Wharton, full of pictures of flappers, models, casinos, and grand hotels in Cannes, gets it exactly wrong.[19]

She would make jokes about how well known Hyères was for its 'dissipated night-life'. Still, she was not entirely without her connections to the 'other' French Riviera. Walter had to have his dose of casinos and fashionable ladies at Nice or Monte Carlo when he came to visit her, or – as she ruefully noted to the Berensons – he would be bored. (On at least one occasion he left Hyères early because it was not amusing enough.) Her remarks are revealing about the tone of their relationship in their sixties: 'I shall try to import fairies from Cannes & Beaulieu, & one or the other of them will carry him off there before he can have discovered the extreme other-worldiness of Hyères!' On Walter's first visit to Ste-Claire in March 1922, it was cold and grey, and he went off in despair to 'Fairyland' (Cannes and Cap Ferrat) where he 'saw all the wonder-gardens' and 'the wonder-ladies'; but when the sun came out he began to like the Var: 'There must be some magic in this landscape, for I never saw him so moved &

fascinated by mere unmixed scenery.' One of the Berensons wrote on this letter: 'This is what she still *really* cares about.'[20]

Berry's nephew, Harry Crosby, who would play an unpleasant part in Wharton's life when Walter died, was one of the notable oddities among the sun-worshippers. Walter's old flame, Mrs Robert Goelet, now Marie Clews, remarried to an American painter, Henry Clews, was establishing her gigantic castle and landscaped grounds at La Napoule, near Cannes, at the same time that Wharton was doing up Ste-Claire. Wharton's old acquaintance Cocteau, whom she had so much liked at first, was creating his own very different way of life at the yellow Welcome Hotel at Villefranche, looking down on a port full of sailors, with companions such as Stravinsky and Picasso, Isadora Duncan and Glenway Westcott. Wharton stayed clear of such groups, and had wary relations with her most *avant-garde* neighbours. Just along the road from her was the Château or Clos Saint-Bernard, the amazing household of the Vicomte Charles de Noailles (a distant relation of Anna de Noailles) and his much younger wife, Marie Laure (née de Bischoffsheim, granddaughter of Laure de Sade, Comtesse de Chevigné, the main model for Proust's Duchesse de Guermantes). Marie Laure was as passionate about modernism as her husband was about gardening. (Charles de Noailles had another fine garden at Grasse, and though Wharton did not warm to Marie Laure, Wharton and the vicomte became fast gardening-friends.) Saint-Bernard, started in 1923 by the architect Robert Mallet-Stevens, was a startling invention, with its geometric shapes in the latest materials, its uncompromisingly experimental colour-schemes, its interior design and furnishings by the latest decorators, its electric wall-clocks and plastic trimmings. There was a gymnasium, a covered swimming-pool, a squash court, and extensive grounds, including a triangular 'Cubist' garden cut into geometric coloured squares, with a statue by Jacques Lipschitz. (Mallet-Stevens's show-garden at the 1925 'Exposition des Arts Décoratifs' was much mocked for its cement trees.) The de Noailles hung Picasso, Ernst, Braque, Gris, Chagall, and Miró on their walls; they financed Artaud's *La Révolte du Boucher* and Cocteau's *Le Sang d'un poète*; Buñuel wrote the screenplay for *L'Âge d'or* there, and they screened showings of his *Un Chien Andalou*, and of Man Ray's *Les Mystères du Château du Dé*. The short distance between Ste-Claire and Saint-Bernard has been described as being the distance between the nineteenth century and the twentieth, and the contrast is most obvious in an incident involving Cocteau and Berenson. When Berenson was staying with her for Christmas 1929, Wharton took him for lunch to Saint-Bernard, and Cocteau, who was visiting the de Noailles, teased him by showing him a 'Picasso collage' of newspaper, nails and sacking (which Cocteau had made himself), to expose Berenson's blindness about modern art. Cocteau harangued Berenson, insisting 'that this was as complete and satisfactory a work of art as any Raphael'. Wharton and Berenson withdrew to Ste-Claire, dignified and put out. Though Robert Norton tried to tell them it had been a hoax, they were never undeceived, and were always very satirical to each other about what Wharton, in her letters to Berenson, called 'Noaillism': 'They have just inaugurated a new salon where the furniture is painted with the new rain-resisting motor paint, and the armchairs are covered with the thin rubber sheeting put under leaking patients in hospital wards.' This is '*textuel*', she added, using the French for 'word-for-word quotation', their favourite short-hand for 'not *true*!'.[21]

Like many of her more fashion-conscious Riviera neighbours, Edith Wharton took the Train Bleu, the luxurious express train launched in 1922, which by 1929 ran every day from Calais via Paris to the Mediterranean, and was so iconic that it became the title of a 1924 ballet which was, as much as the de Noailles' villa, a high point of French modernism. *Le Train Bleu* had music by Diaghilev, with a story by Cocteau, music by Darius Milhaud, choreography by Nijinska, costumes by Chanel, and a front curtain by Picasso of two gigantic half-naked women running along the beach. The ballet, with its 'flappers and aesthetes, sun-worshipping tarts and gigolos', Suzanne Lenglen-style tennis-star, golfer, bathing-belle and acrobats, displayed everything about the Riviera which Wharton, once she had alighted from the Train Bleu, did her best to avoid.[22]

Hyères stood apart from the Côte d'Azur; and old Hyères stood apart from the new. The old town rose steeply uphill, clustered on the side of the sharp peak of the rock of the 'Castéou', the site of ancient Greek and Roman settlements. It had – has – a market-place with a round medieval tower, the Tour Saint Blaise, two ancient churches, St Paul and St Louis, a sixteenth-century row of houses arched over the road, steep narrow streets with steps or cobbles. At the very top are the castle-ruins and, raying out from them, a triple row of medieval ramparts, the walls of the old city, much of it still remaining. This medieval town had been a centre for religious communities from the thirteenth century to the eighteenth: Cistercian monks at the monastery of St Pierre, Augustinian nuns, and the Sisters of Ste Claire – an order of Franciscan nuns known as the Clairines or Clarisses, dedicated to the education of young women – in the seventeenth century. After the Revolution, the old town sank into silence and decay, and Hyères lived off agriculture and fishing. But in the nineteenth century, the exceptionally balmy climate and the seclusion and beauty of Hyères began to attract the new breed of winter-tourists, as the '*villégiature*' of two or three months became the fashion. Long-term visitors, especially the English, began to build substantial, ornate villas, some on a scale of grandiosity to match Newport. In 1859 the railway reached Hyères from Toulon, cutting the journey to Paris from four and a half days to twenty-six hours. It became a fashionable place for the winter season, and a sanatorium for convalescent – and terminally ill – TB patients. (Tolstoy, who went there with his dying brother in 1860, thought he had never seen anywhere so sad.) Giant hotels, electric trams, 'omnibus hippomobiles', newly laid-out avenues, a landscaped park outside the town with rare plants, golf-courses, eventually a casino and a cinema, followed. Queen Victoria graced Costebelle with her presence in 1892; no guide-book failed to mention it. But at the turn of the century (and this was probably part of its appeal for Wharton), Hyères began to fall out of favour with the winter-tourists. Even though the guide-book for 1914 advertised it as '*la station hivernale par excellence*', it was too far from the sea; the hotels were getting old, and it had no bathing station. In the war years, it was in the doldrums. Winter-tourists moved off to other more exciting spots on the Riviera, and by 1929 had stopped coming. After 1920, summer tourism began, but this was modest in scale. The craze for aviation, the port, the beach-resort, the hippodrome, the cycling, sailing and water-sports which would attract tourists to the seaside below Hyères-les-Palmiers (as it came to be called) were later twentieth-century inventions.

Wharton was not the only writer to take advantage of Hyères' climate, beauty, and quiet. In 1878, the mayor and promoter of Hyères, Alphonse Denis, listed the large number of famous and titled people who had graced the town, including Chateaubriand, Thierry, Lamartine, Dumas père, and Michelet. Turgenev (who complained that it rained all the time he was there), Rudyard Kipling, a visitor in the early 1920s, and the novelist Roger Martin du Gard, who had a house in Porquerolles, all came here. In 1884, Robert Louis Stevenson rented a cottage called La Solitude, just down the hill from Ste-Claire (to be incorporated into its outbuildings), for his health; he said at the end of his life: 'I was only happy once . . . that was at Hyères.' Apart from Bourget (who over the years was visited at Le Plantier by many writers, including James, Barrès and Melchior de Voguë), the most notable literary devotee of Hyères was Joseph Conrad, who had gone there when he first arrived in France in the 1870s, and drew on its scenery for the coast-town in *Nostromo*. In 1921, as an old man, he revisited the town, and called on Wharton, who took him out with Paul Bourget for a day's excursion to the *presqu'île* of Giens. A photograph shows all three, with their hats and sticks, leaning against a fishing-boat. Conrad used the setting vividly in his next novel, *The Rover*, prefaced by a quotation from Spenser which might have pleased Wharton: 'Sleep after toyle, port after stormie seas / Ease after war, death after life, does greatly please.' *The Rover* is eloquent about the enchanting light and calm of the landscape, which to the old hero, who has come home here after years of wanderings, seems 'so remote from all thoughts of strife and death . . . Yes, this was the place for him . . . his instinct of rest had found its home at last.' The words are strangely close to Wharton's feelings: 'It is good to grow old – as well as to die – "in beauty"; & the beauty of this little place is inexhaustible.'[23]

There were plenty of holidaying writers passing through – Wharton told Charles Du Bos in 1924 that you could find a whole colony of the *Nouvelle Revue Française* in the South of France.[24] But she was, of course, selective in her friendships. Later, she would make contact with a few of the writers in her neighbourhood, such as Huxley and William Gerhardi. Living nearby with her aged mother was Philomène de Lévis-Mirepoix, who had been an acquaintance in the Rue de Varenne but would now become a much closer friend. As well as literary visitors, there were also a few upper-class villa residents, including some of Wharton's English country-house acquaintances, and the immensely wealthy art-loving Comtesse de Béarn (known after her divorce as Martine de Béhague) who in 1924 had a stupendous villa, La Polynésie, designed and built for her on the *presqu'île* of Giens, with a magnificent landscaped garden, a rival to the de Noailles in Mediterannean modernism and to Wharton in horticulture. Gerhardi called her 'a sort of combined Mrs Guinness–Lady Cunard'.

Neither of Wharton's houses was anything like as grand as Martine de Béhague's or as experimental as the de Noailles'. Unlike her aristocratic and adventurous French neighbours, she did not design from scratch, but adapted two substantial houses to her needs, carefully preserving their best features while making some comfortable and elegant additions. Ste-Claire and the Pavillon Colombe were the first houses that she had made for herself since 1902 (53 Rue de Varenne, though a long-term rental, which she furnished, was never reworked or redesigned). She did not have to imitate or invent an architectural style here as she had at The Mount: her French houses had their own well-defined styles, which she wanted to improve on, rather than alter. Unlike The Mount, neither house was a massive show-place, with huge neighbouring mansions to live up to. By comparison with the European homes she visited – I Tatti, or the Gays' house Le Bréau, or Martine de Béhague's mansions – her French houses were not imposing residences. Coopersale would have been on a much larger scale. She insisted on calling these new acquisitions, to her friends (with what might seem rather over-modest bashfulness, given the number of bedrooms and the amount of land in both places) her *little* houses, and her extensive gardens her 'humble *potagers*'. The Pavillon was always her 'tiny bungalow', her 'little shanty'. Planning the renovations and the moves in February 1920, she told Berenson jokingly that she knew she was talking 'as if I were moving into Caprarola, & putting, at the same time, the finishing touches to Chatsworth' instead of moving into her '*two bicoques*' (shacks). Ste-Claire was a 'toy-citadel', she told him; to the Du Boses she described it as '*une minuscule propriété*', to Sally Norton (whose death in 1922 would bring to a close that old, kind, long-distance friendship) as an adorable 'little eyrie'.[25] The history of her two 'little' houses, so remote from her American past, delighted her. She was now going to divide her life between a pleasure-house for an actress/courtesan, and a refurbished convent for nuns with an educational mission: a split which nicely mirrors two sides of her character. Life at Ste-Claire-du-Château was to be a mixture of luxurious and monastic, restful and hard-working. Tantalisingly, guarding her privacy as usual, Wharton does not describe Ste-Claire in *A Backward Glance* – she says it would require another book to do so. But there are plenty of other descriptions of the house and its curious history. Robert Norton remembered how romantic she first thought it, with its 'pure Albrecht Dürer background' and its 'tangled wilderness' which might have daunted a less determined person. Berenson called it 'a romantic monastery on a rocky hill'.

The old road of St-Pierre led up from the high town towards the castle walls. In a zig-zag of the walls stood Ste-Claire, a Romanesque-style house built in 1849 on the site of the seventeenth-century convent, with the rough '*maquis*' running up behind the house to the castle ruins. Alphonse Denis said it was like '*une forteresse gothique*'. It had been built by a colourful character called Olivier Voutier, a naval officer and archaeologist and hero of the Greek war of independence, whose main claim to fame was to have discovered the Venus de Milo when travelling in the Cyclades. He died in 1877, and was buried in the grounds of Ste-Claire, which passed into the hands of a chemicals manufacturer; but the house had been empty for many years when Wharton found it. It had a touch of whimsical fantasy about it, a long two-storey brown building with two crenellated stone towers at either end and a triple arcade of stone pillars leading onto a long stone-flagged terrace. By the time Wharton had restored it, with the help (as at St-Brice) of the architect Charles Knight, it had a new brown-tiled roof, and had been refurbished and extended.

The front of the house, looking onto the terrace, had a row of French windows surmounted by curved arches filled in with decorated tympanums, and above them a row of curved windows, subdivided by little ornamental pillars – the design picking up the arcade onto the terrace.

As at St-Brice, the terrace was furnished with comfortable wicker and wooden furniture, a stone table, and many pots. There were two pollarded plane trees for shade, and an astounding view over the red roofs of old Hyères down to the plain, the distant sea, and the islands beyond. The 'endless beauty' of the view was equally overwhelming, she told Minnie, by day or night, 'for we look south, east & west, "miles & miles," & our quiet-coloured end of evening presents us with a full moon standing over the tower of the great Romanesque church just below the house, & a sunset silhouetting the "Iles d'Or" in black on a sea of silver'. As she had, once, on the terrace at The Mount, she felt in touch with the elements, in 'communion with sun & moon risings & settings, & the wheeling of the great winter constellations'. (Even with a main road, heavy building all the way to the coast, and an airport, the view is still spectacular.) An old stable was converted into a guest house, drains and electricity and running water were installed, a road was made for cars to come up to the house, a garage for five cars and a house for the chauffeur and the gardener were built, and large amounts of earth were trundled up to make the terraced gardens. Total cost, in addition to the rent, was around 1 million old francs. Wharton rented Ste-Claire (and the land around it, including the castle ruins) for seven years, while she continued to develop it and to work on the garden. In 1927, another, smaller, neo-Romanesque house just along the hill from Ste-Claire, 'Pierre-Lisse', which was built in the early 1920s by a neighbouring vicomtesse, fell vacant at her death, and Wharton snapped it up smartly (as a house for Alfred White) before her neighbours the de Noailles could get it. At the same time, she bought Ste-Claire outright for 1,250,000 francs.[26]

Indoors, the moderate-sized ground-floor rooms opened out from each other in the *enfilade* style of The Mount and the Pavillon. Though the entrance hall had black-and-white marble flooring and Chinese wallpaper and a few antique pieces, the rooms it led to – dining room, drawing room, study/reading room, morning room – were not so formal. The walls were light, the curtains hung simply on rods, there were pleasantly shaded sidelights, comfortable sofas, Turkish carpets, vases of fresh flowers, mixed with grander pieces – Louis XVI chairs, chaises longues, an Empire table, ornate mirrors over the hearths, the flower-paintings from The Mount, an attractive scattering of eighteenth-century French furniture. The general effect was welcoming, comfortable and orderly, and a little more rural and relaxed than at St-Brice. There were seven bedrooms (and six bathrooms) upstairs, all with wonderful views. And kitchen, scullery, pantry, linen-room, sewing-room, and butler's 'brushing room' were all (as the sale catalogue for the house would put it) 'conveniently installed on modern lines'. The last improvement was a smaller version of the I Tatti library. In 1924, getting ready to divide up her books, she asked Updike to design two bookplates for her with an olive-plant design, one edged in brown, for the Pavillon Colombe, and one in grey for Ste-Claire. In 1928, she moved about two thousand of her books to Ste-Claire, with the help of Robert Norton and Gaillard Lapsley – not always an easy task, Norton recalled: 'When after two hours of exhausting . . . labour the hostess coming to review our efforts condemned one shelf after another and ruthlessly ordered all the volumes back upon the floor, we retired . . . in some dudgeon.' Once completed, the library, with elegant floor-to-ceiling wooden shelves, matting, and dark wood side-tables, had a cooler, more minimalist look than the living-rooms, which had a distinctly nineteenth-century air. With the warm tones of Wharton's well-bound books in it, shaded from the dazzling blue outdoor air, it would have been a lovely sight.

Over and over again, and not just when she first moved in, Wharton exclaimed at the 'heavenly beauty & the heavenly quiet' of Ste-Claire. It was (as she put it to Berenson in 1922, finishing a novel), 'A Holiday for Edith'. She took it on with the feelings of a lover. 'I feel as if I were going to get married – to the right man at last', she told Royall Tyler, with whom she liked to flirt. She made a point of describing it to Morton Fullerton – to whom she hardly ever wrote in these terms now – as the very paradise of tranquillity they had read about 'together' in Dante. 'I've found the Great Good Place', she added, clearly implying that it was a satisfaction to have found it alone. A later letter to Elisina, describing her arrival off the train to Marseilles in 'a glitter of blue & gold', said that she felt 'like the people in M[atthew] Arnold's poem, who wake in their tomb at Brou, & looking at the stained glass, say, "Is this the court of heaven?" I certainly care for sunlight & trees & the sea more than I do for anything but a few beloved friends . . .' 'Sometimes I ask myself', she confided in Berenson, 'why I have two houses & gardens & a motor, with all their attendant cares – & then I realise that it's not paying too dear for the greedy joy I get out of it all – the order, the loveliness, & the blessed *privacy* . . . No; I'm that kind of a person, a rooted possessive person, & I always shall be.' 'It's only at Hyères that I own myself.'[27] Matilda Gay's description of a visit to Ste-Claire in February 1924 bore witness to this contentment:

At Toulon Edith's motor met us, and we drove through a lovely winding road landing at Edith's sunny terrace of Ste-Claire, and were immediately folded in her hospitable embrace . . . A wide and lovely view spreads before you. Every possible and conceivable comfort is provided for the body and Edith's brilliant conversation is rich nourishment for the mind . . . Beautifully kept terraced gardens lead up to the top of the hill. Edith seems happier here than at St-Brice; it is indeed a lovely place.[28]

As soon as the house was habitable, the patterns she had established at The Mount for country-house life – but without the disruptions from Teddy – were resumed, as at St-Brice. The morning was for work, letter-writing, and planning the day's arrangements. 'We begin to be sociable after eleven', Berenson noted. There would be lunch on the terrace, or an afternoon walk or excursion with a well-planned picnic – or, if no visitors, the garden to supervise. The excursions allowed her to share her passion for the history and the landscape of her new home. Visitors would have had pointed out to them the gigantic, ancient 'roche à cupules' on the road just below the house, carved all over with tiny and mysterious marks – relics of prehistoric astronomic signs, or funerary rites, or water-cults? They would have climbed up the terraced gardens to the wilderness of herbs and shrubs behind, where the castle-ruins were; and they would have been shown the town's two churches and its old streets. The car would take them down to the *presqu'île* or to go by boat to one of the islands, as she described going to Port Cros with Robert Norton: 'A real Epipsychidion isle – a tiny cliff-locked harbour with a perfect toy village is hidden, as one approaches, by a great rocky height with an old fort . . . We lunched . . . literally stretched out on sheets of rosy-red mesembryanthemum, silver cineraria, yellow coronilla, with pillows of myrtle to "incense" us, & a peacock-coloured sea just under us . . .' On longer trips, she might take friends to a beauty-spot like Grasse, or through Provence, as described here, 'to Pont du Gard, Uzès, Les Baux, St-Rémy . . . Yesterday we spent the whole afternoon lizarding on top of the Fort St André, at Villeneuve-les-Avignon, with the Rhône in flood under us, dividing the meadows & willow-groves with streaks of sky, & just opposite the Mont Ventoux covered with sun.'[29]

In the evenings, there would be a good dinner. Berenson, who had digestive problems, spoke wistfully on Christmas Day 1930 of 'plum pudding, *soupe à l'oignon* and other dishes the mere sight of which affected my digestion' and of 'Edith and her three cavaliers singing the praise of good food and of the restaurants all over France'. The Tylers noted the substantial menus that Edith went in for. As her guest at the Hôtel Crillon in 1928,

Royall Tyler had 'Petite Marmite, Truite Meunière, and Poularde au Riz; a sort of soufflé ice; wines perfectly delicious and some very good "fine" after the coffee'. At one lunch at St-Brice in June, Edith's cook produced 'rice and chicken's liver, then a roast chicken of the tenderest, peas, and strawberries and cream'; at another, described as 'heavy', there was 'lobster à l'Américaine combined with fillets of sole, and a very creamy and delicious strawberry dish at the other end of the meal, with chicken in between'. One excellent St-Brice dinner consisted of 'a very good potage, grilled turbot, salsifis sauté, and apple charlotte'. The recipes she wrote down, a few of which survive, are all rich and creamy: Pumpkin Pie, Potage à la Crème, Moussaka. She served good wines, which she ordered from Douat Frères in Bordeaux for both St-Brice and Ste-Claire (at prices ranging between five and thirteen francs a bottle). In 1922 she ordered Cheval Blanc 1912, Ch. Brane Cantenac 1908 and Ch. Pichon Longueville 1908, and an excellent Sauternes, Ch. Caillou Haut Barsac 1914. In 1923, she ordered for Ste-Claire two dozen Ch. Haut Brion 1910, three dozen Haut Sauternes 1916, six dozen Ch. Margaux 1917 and six dozen Brane Cantenac 1909. For St-Brice, the same, with ten dozen Ch. Haut Milon (Pauillac) 1911. In 1927 she ordered six cases of Corton-Charlemagne 1923, and in 1928, Ch. Rayne Vigneau Sauternes 1922, Ch. Lagrange St Julien 1928, and an excellent medium dry white Bordeaux (with, as one wine expert describes it, 'a whiff of old tom-cats'), Pavillon Blanc du Ch. Margaux 1926. This was a classy mixture of well-reputed clarets, quality white burgundies, fine sauternes and good white bordeaux that showed good, classic taste. But they were for her guests, not for her; she did not drink wine herself and lamented, late in life, that it had taken her far too long to find out why her 'good Burgundian vintages had such a diminished taste' – they were being kept in a cellar at Ste-Claire 'in which the temperature changed about 365 times a year! . . . *Why* did no one ever tell me before . . . ?' Some of her regular guests complained that her wines 'though good, are desperately monotonous . . . as if I gave my visitors the same menus for every meal'. She put in a plea, via Elisina, to the Comte de Vogüé, to let her have some of his red Musigny.[30]

If there were too many visitors, she complained – though less than at St-Brice – that she felt 'like a Palace Hotel!' But she wanted them too. She berated her close friends if they let her down, and called them in affectionately or imperiously: 'The months and years pass, and I see less and less of you'; 'And you? How are you? What are your summer plans? You *must* write soon!' She was not entirely averse to the less intimate callers: Berenson noted that 'when visitors join or interrupt we rather resent it, & Edith chimes in, though I suspect she does not mind half so much'. But what she most enjoyed, in both houses, was a gentle flow of old friends she could rely on to fit in with her plans. She had a regular Christmas gathering at Ste-Claire. For Berenson, the annual visit to 'an exquisitely furnished house whose luxury and strict daily ritual met his fastidious standards' was a lasting pleasure, and he described in letters home what it was like to spend Christmas with Wharton and her old friends, Norton, Lapsley, and John Hugh Smith: 'We tell stories, we discuss books and politics or people, we walk a good deal and in the evening we read aloud together. There is no such company as three men with one woman whom they all love without having been or wanting to be her lovers.' This remark is made in 1931, after the death of the other regular, Walter Berry. By that time Berenson could get a little restive with this group, finding Gaillard sometimes a bore, in 'the atmosphere he exhales of being the only repository of decency, gentility, scholarship and correct thinking'. Wharton, however, loved the companionable evenings of reading to a small circle of like-minded friends. Before the war, she seems only to have shown her work to Walter, or Morton, but now she was reading out her own work to them, as well as Dickens or Trollope, Jane Austen or George Eliot. Trying out her books on the group, at St-Brice and at Ste-Claire, came to be an essential part of her writing process – as the inscriptions in presentation copies of her books at I Tatti suggest. A *Son at the Front*'s reads: 'For Mary & B.B., in remembrance of trial readings at St Brice, Edith, September 1923'. *Human Nature* (1933) is dedicated 'To Bernard Berenson', and she has inscribed underneath the dedication: 'because he liked some of these stories, & to Mary, in the hope that she will too, From their affectionate Edith'. *The Children* is dedicated 'To My Patient Listeners at Sainte-Claire'. The word 'patient' there was somewhat ironic. She told Mary that 'no one before has ever cursed me for the ending of any of my books as my little group of Patient Listeners have over *The Children*. The only solution would be to write a sequel . . .' It sounds from this as if she resisted whatever advice she got, quite as much as she took it.[31]

Mary Berenson was excluded from the group of Patient Listeners: Berenson spent his Christmasses at Ste-Claire in part to get away from his increasingly depressed, and depressing, invalid wife, and she was naturally jealous: 'Tell Edith her beautifully run household, so full of all human comforts & luxuries, & permeated by her courageous and life-enjoying spirit, has utterly destroyed me, it is all so desirable – so unattainable by me.'[32] Mary's lament strikes a note which is often found in hostile versions of Wharton: that she was too organised, too perfectionist. Lubbock took pleasure in quoting Madeleine St-René Taillandier (Chevrillon's sister and the translator of *The Age of Innocence*) saying that she found something 'chilling' in 'the perfection of her taste, extending to . . . the smallest details of her establishment'. She had heard before she met Wharton that the tiled paths of Ste-Claire 'were bordered with hyacinths, alternately blue and pink, all of which had to bud and blossom in harmony together'. Lubbock pursues with gusto this version of the chilly, controlling chatelaine, which can make Edith Wharton sound like the character played by Margaret Dumont in the Marx Brothers films. He describes her at Ste-Claire ruthlessly disciplining, rather than enjoying, her plants ('she would have no shirking or sulking, and it was a stupid little plant that ever dreamed of dodging her eye'), brow-beating her books by gutting them at speed ('sometimes it was thought that the book had a scared look as she carried it off, as though it knew what it was in for'), and bullying her guests with her fanatic quest for the perfect picnic ('there could be no disagreeing where Edith led'). Since, after one long and gloomy visit to Ste-Claire in the winter of 1921, which Wharton complained was very depressing, Percy was not a regular guest there, and since their friendship ended badly after his marriage to Sybil Cutting in 1927, there is exaggeration and vindictiveness in these accounts.[33] A warmer sense of Edith's busy domestic management comes through in a Christmas verse she sent in 1928 (joking about her Montyon Prize for Virtue, awarded in 1920) to one of Daisy Chanler's daughters, Mrs White, who had a large young family:

> Goldfinch, four Pekes, a Poodle, and a flock
> Of fan-tail Pigeons roosting in the rock –
> For mothering these no Montyon prize is given;
> Yet, enviable parents of the Seven,
> Some merit to this humble task ascribe,
> And from Ste Claire's furred, finned and feathered tribe
> Receive a greeting sent across the sea
> To how so ever many Whites there be.[34]

She could be exacting and importunate, in every area of her life: with publishers, with her wartime colleagues, with servants, and with friends. And such traits tend to intensify with age. Yet she was flexible, warmhearted and open enough to continue to make friendships in her late fifties and sixties, though these could also bring out her demanding, bossy qualities. There is a good example of this in her relationship with Philomène, who was twenty-five years younger than Edith and whom she only came to know well after she had settled at Ste-Claire. Philomène was a romantic aristocratic character, a French lady out of a novel. She is always referred to as 'shyly charming' or 'glowingly lovely' or 'exquisite', though a photograph of her at I Tatti shows a sharper, more humorous face than those adjectives imply. Berenson, who was enchanted by her (she travelled to Egypt with the Berensons in 1922) found her 'subtle, unreasonable, fanciful, affectionate'. Her maiden name was, in full, Charlotte Felicité Ghislaine Ganderique Marie Philomène de Lévis-Mirepoix, daughter of the duchesse, whose high-handedness, conservatism and religiosity were legendary. Philomène had a small literary success with her first book, *La Cité des Lampes*, and a youthful affair with a married man of equally ancient pedigree, Count Jean de Lubersac, by whom she had an illegitimate daughter, Florence. She moved to Hyères after the war with her mother and daughter and lived there quietly, getting to know some of Edith's friends and running her own salon (modest compared to Martine de Béhague's). William Gerhardi gave a characteristically succinct summary of her: 'At the foot of Mrs Wharton's hill, the gifted and charming Comtesse de Lévis-Mirepoix, authoress, gave small literary parties.' In June 1927, she married, in Hyères, and became the Comtesse Jules de la Forest-Divonne. (She and her husband would both live long lives, into the mid-1970s.) And she pursued her career as 'authoress' under the pseudonym 'Claude Silve', writing small-scale, evocative, fanciful novels, one of which, *Bénédiction*, won the Prix Femina in 1935 and was translated into English by Robert Norton (whom Berenson thought should have married her) with an introduction by Wharton. A 'charming and ghostlike' tale of two children in an ancient French castle in the Ile-de-France, full of old stories, vibrating nerves, and haunting magical dreams, *Bénédiction* is written in a breathlessly precious style, rather well-captured in Norton's translation: 'Does our earth, as it goes spinning under the constellations' golden eyes, draw down upon the heads of certain mortals here the tenuous fringes of distant happier worlds?' The same tone is to be heard in her admiring, intense, illegible letters to Berenson, whom she thought of as her guru (she liked gurus) and in her tender, spiritual recollections of Wharton.

Nothing could be less like Wharton's own cool ironies and strong passions, so it was both easy, and generous of her, to lavish Philomène's book with praise. Her work fell into the same category for Wharton as Anna de Noailles's romantic poetry. She used her favourite lines of poetic escapism to describe its atmosphere ('Kilmeny had been she knew not where – / And Kilmeny had seen what she could not declare') and in her Foreword poured out words like 'elfin', 'faery', 'delicate', 'haunting', 'charm', 'spell' and 'dream'. There was also some condescension in this. Philomène would speak of her as modest, motherly, simple, gracious, and generous. Edith was sympathetic – as with Bessy Lodge, or Elisina – to a woman with a troubled past, but she also thought Philomène should be more decisive about her life: 'Everyone likes her, & is prepared to sympathize with her, & she will dream away one opportunity after another, perpetually making & unmaking plans . . .' She was scornful of what she saw as the younger woman's naive idealism and her search for uplift, whether through spiritualism, or Buddhism, or 'Coué-ism'. Philomène's spiritual fads – her attraction to 'The Land of Tosh' – would find their way into a number of Wharton's novels of the 1920s. She was critical of Philomène's intellectual weaknesses, especially to Berenson, in terms which point to her post-war attitudes: 'Her charming eager helpless intelligence has not been left empty, but filled with third-rate flashy rubbish, of the kind that most enervates the mental muscles – "occultism", the Sar Peladan [the French leader of the Catholic Rosicrucian Salon], mediums . . . vital fluids . . . There is hardly a vicious sentimentalism, or a specious pretext for mental laziness, that doesn't run off her tongue . . .' The worst thing would be for Mary to introduce her to Freudianism, which Philomène would take to 'like a duck to – sewerage. And what she wants is to develop the *conscious*, & not grub after the subconscious.' While the Berensons were with her in Egypt, Wharton had high hopes for Philomène's intellectual improvement. But, as she said to Berenson, with admirable candour, perhaps, at the age of sixty, she was not the best judge: 'I often wonder whether a frumpy old woman can ever be quite fair in her estimate of a young & lovely one. What is really fine & interesting in her is her *nature*, which is large, generous, incapable of pettiness or unkindness. The brain, as you perceived, struck work ten or fifteen years ago. If anyone can start it going again *you* can . . .' But she did not think all that highly of the brain: 'We are trying to get her to read, in the hope that we may thus guide her toward writing.' 'Philomène is *really* at work on a book, with the sort of all-overish activity which the amateur believes to be the only way to do it: hours & hours a day. But I'm so glad for her – & persuaded that something charming will come of it.'[35]

Wharton's mixed feelings about Philomène, and the tone she could take with her intimate friends, is vividly illustrated in a complicated and energetic letter, written from Ste-Claire to Daisy Chanler in 1924. The letter begins with some forceful advice about Daisy's travel-plans:

If you *do* get to Avignon, you will find the Hotel d'Europe (and all the others there) so filthy and disgusting that you won't be able to stand it long. Why *didn't* you ask me for an *itinéraire*? I know Provence even better than Royall! There is a first-class new hotel, Hotel Sextius, at Aix, and from there you could have motored to Avignon in an hour! . . . If you go to Nîmes, you can go from there to Les Saintes-Maries-de-la-Mer and Aigues-Mortes in one day, I should think – you must see Les Baux if possible, and certainly St-Rémy, its Roman tomb and beautiful Romanesque cloister. From there you can motor over a lovely little pass to Les Baux. I'm told there is a decent little hotel at St-Rémy. Avoid a night at Arles *at all costs*! Don't fail to see Uzès and the Pont du Gard (from Nîmes, where the hotel is fairly good). At Montpellier . . . the Metropole is good.

The letter then turns to a conversation which Robert Norton had reported from the Comtesse de Béarn's recent house-party:

Robert told me that the conversation turned on Philomène's future . . . and that you said that Lubersac wanted to marry her, but that she had not decided. I was terribly upset, for I was sure I had asked you to consider what I told you as absolutely confidential, and the people before whom you mentioned it are the very ones to carry it all back to her old milieu and her family in Paris! The situation is so complicated that I never speak of it to *anyone*, and she is naturally anxious not to attract notice, or to involve anyone in her future plans . . . she is very reticent, and I ought to have explained that even the little I said to you was rather conjectural on my part. My object in writing this is to beg you to say *nothing more* to anyone on the subject . . . Between Faubourg, Church and State, it is all a labyrinth of inhibitions in which she is trying to walk 'advisedly and soberly' if she can! I reproach myself very much for not having said this to you more emphatically, but I was sure I had at least asked you not to repeat what I said. Above all, if you see the good B.B.s later in Florence, say nothing of all this, please. They are devoted to Philomène, and she to them, but I know she wants silence about herself and her affairs, and I broke through the prohibition with you (with her consent) only because she has a great admiration for you, and was touched by your sympathy.[36]

It is a characteristic performance, partly because it speaks frankly about the need for reticence and secrecy; partly because she seems to be turning Philomène into a character in a novel (a kind of Madame de Treymes); partly because of its inwardness with the complexities of French ways; and partly because of its mixture of affection and insistence, which could make Edith Wharton, as a friend, both lovable and formidable.

The tone is often heard in letters from Ste-Claire, whether she is having her secretary tell her new literary editor at Appleton how to manage the train journey ('Mrs Wharton advises you to take provisions with you and not try to get to the dining car on the train, as you would certainly lose your place, or at least be unable to get back to it through the crowded corridors') or asking Elisina, as a favour, to buy her a bed-quilt for Gross from Paris, which had to be 'anything with pinks and mauves, on a cream ground, or pinks and greens, fresh looking & "spriggy"' – but which when it arrived turned out not to be *quite* right: 'Don't think me a monster of ingratitude for returning the bed-quilt unopened. I know from your description that it is *just* what I want, but, alas, blue is about the only colour that won't do! Vieux rose & gold, green & gold, mauve, heliotrope, would all be right – so I judged it best to send back the parcel as soon as it comes.'[37]

When she is asserting herself in a purely formal or business correspondence, haughtiness is added to perfectionism, as in a French correspondence with the mayor of Hyères, starting in 1923. Attached as she is to his beautiful town, she takes a lively interest in its upkeep. (So the correspondence starts, somewhat ominously, and proceeds with daunting persistence.) There is a very sharp angle on the main road, at the level of the toll-gate, just at the point where the steep road goes up to her house, which greatly impedes the circulation of traffic. No doubt when the road up to the castle was first built, no one imagined the cars of today. But the junction of the two roads is often blocked up with trams and parked cars waiting to get through the toll-gate. In her view it would be a great help to anyone coming up or down the Boulevard Marie-Louise if this sharp junction could be eliminated, as in the rough sketch she encloses, and she would be happy to carry the costs of this improvement. Also, before the war (suggesting more frequent early visits to Hyères than we know of) she used to admire the wall of the toll-gate, rough-cast and surrounded with pretty plants. Would he authorise her to restore the building and to renew those long-lost flowers (*'les fleurs d'antan'*) at her own expense? It would please her greatly to think that she had contributed to the beautifying (*'l'embellissement'*) of this picturesque corner. And she would just have one small request to make in return, that no advertisements be pasted onto the restored walls of the toll-gate. Also, at the same time, she would like to bring to his attention the deplorable condition of the Boulevard Marie-Louise, and if he would let her pay for the works she has mentioned, then she is sure that the town of Hyères would at last take on the complete repair of this road-surface. In 1926, the mayor received another letter about the road leading up to her property. She has already had the road repaired at her own cost; now, if the Commune of Hyères would undertake to do the repairs at once, she would place at their disposal the sum of 15,000 francs. But she must insist that the work would be finished by the end of January 1927, since this was the only road giving access to her house.

The mayor accepted this generous offer, but he was not to be left in peace. In December 1934, Wharton was still complaining about the lamentable state of the road, particularly since the pavements were covered with rubbish blown by the wind from the disgusting dustbins, without lids, which stood all day on the side of the road. Some years ago she had offered to pay for a lean-to for these dustbins, but no notice had ever been taken of her offer. Meanwhile walkers had to go down the middle of the road to avoid them, and it was needless to add that because the dustbins had no lids, they were surrounded by all the cats and dogs of the neighbourhood, who dragged their contents out into the road. She has also pointed out that the inhabitants of the first house on the right as you go up the road dried all their linen on the wall by the side of the pavement, and she had been told that this was against the law and action would be taken; but since the linen was still there she presumed that her request had been forgotten. She was particularly grieved ('navrée') by the state of the road because she had English and American friends staying with her, some of whom might have been interested in living in Hyères, if the town kept itself in a cleaner and more hygienic manner. 'Je vous remercie d'avance, Monsieur le Maire, de la suite que vous voudrez certaine-ment donner à ma demande, et je vous prie de trouver ici l'expression de mes sentiments distingués.'[38]

This is probably the only occasion on which Edith Wharton is on record talking about dustbins, and it gives a strong picture of her in her role as property-owner and civic watch-dog – her sense of entitlement, her relent-lessness, her attention to detail, her eager involvement with the place. That she wanted to replant 'the flowers of yesteryear' on the old wall, as well as have the road repaired and the dustbins tidied away, points to her main passion at Hyères. From the moment she saw the house, the potential of its terraces on the steep slopes up to the castle was clear to her: here she was going to be able to combine her rapturous pleasure in the natural scents and colours and vegetation of the Mediterranean with her keen organisa-tional talents as a landscape-gardener. Much of the preparation-time before she moved into Ste-Claire was spent setting up the terracing and the first planting of the gardens, which loomed large in almost all her letters about her new property. This was especially so, of course, in her letters to Minnie and Beatrix, for whom she evokes the pleasures (and the pains) of gardening with sensual immediacy – boasting, for instance, about the warm weather one New Year's Day at Ste-Claire: 'Here we're still closing our mosquito-nets about our virgin pillows, & the bees are growling in the heliotrope & jasmine on the terrace; & yesterday the first almond-tree came into blossom on the hill.'[39]

That gardening, here and in the Île de France, was a consolation to her, is clear in a 1920 letter to Berenson, written in Hyères: 'I have always been more deeply sylvan, & horti & agri & all the rest of it, than anything else, & now the flowers & birds & woods literally "fill the room up" of oh, so many absent friends.' But, as with everything else in her life, what was pleasurable was also strenuous. The gardens at Ste-Claire were neither trouble-free nor conventional. The Pavillon gardens were an amalgamation of French, English and Italian traditions. At Ste-Claire she was more adventurous. As at The Mount, where she had been among the pioneers bringing French and Italian principles to bear on American landscaping, so on the Riviera she was one of a group of enterprising landscapers now moving away from the accepted nineteenth-century fashion of villa gardening, with their planting out of massive blocks of brightly coloured bedding plants and their English-style lawns. (A comic example of this style is provided in *The Mother's Recompense*, where an American Riviera hostess shows off her vast slabs of bedded-out plants, interspersed with giant blue china frogs, 'which made the garden look "more natural"'.) What a fellow-gardener and friend, Alice Martineau, called 'a rising-up against the tyranny of the potted plant' involved using native as well as imported, tropical or sub-tropical species, replacing the old bedding-out effects with 'great masses of rock plants, flowering shrubs, mimosa (or acacia), and climbing plants', and thinking more imaginatively about the relationship between the gardens, the landscape, and the wild '*maquis*'. Mrs Martineau left a detailed description of Wharton's imaginative and colourful garden at Ste-Claire in *Gardening in Sunny Lands*, for which Wharton wrote an introduction.

But Wharton's Riviera garden was not an experiment like the Cubist garden at Saint-Bernard. She would have had the same reaction to Mallet-Stevens's concrete trees as the French garden-critic who compared the 'puerilities' and sensationalism of the 'modern' garden to vogues like nudism, jazz and Cubism. That kind of garden-criticism filled the luxurious French garden-journal, *La Gazette Illustrée des Amateurs de Jardins* (whose subscribers included many of Wharton's French friends, such as Jacques-Émile Blanche, the Comtesse de Béhague, Rosa de Fitzjames, the de Noailles, the Comtesse de Cossé-Brissac and Robert de Montesquiou), which in the 1920s lamented the passing of the old-style, formal, grand-house French garden, and called the traditional gardens of France *'les jardins d'intelligence'*.[40]

That would have been a good phrase for Wharton's gardens. At Hyères, she wanted to make the most intelligent use possible of the romantic landscape she had discovered. She embarked on the making of what she called her *'folles terrasses de Ste-Claire'* with palpable excitement. She wrote excitedly of how 'to a gardener accustomed to the rigours of New England, it is like a dream to be planting out camellias, cypresses, and every known rose'. She was ambitious and experimental in the range of plants she wanted to use; and she wanted a dramatic, various and surprising garden which would provide continuing interest and beauty and colour, all through the months she spent in the South of France – which would usually be from late November to April (May and September would often be for travelling, and the summers were spent at St-Brice).

As in her book on Italian gardens, she was interested in the relation between the house, the garden and the landscape. She liked to mix the artificial with the wild, and she liked a firm structural design mixed with Jekyll-style drifts of colour. She had her own ideas, but she also learnt all the time from other gardeners such as Charles de Noailles. A letter to Beatrix Farrand in March 1922 described a visit to a group of 'the best gardens on the Riviera', at Cap Ferrat, belonging to the Arthur Wilsons, Adele Essex, the Ralph Curtises at the Villa Sylvia, and Jean Ward at the Villa Rosemary. 'I never saw anything in England even remotely approaching them as pure *flower gardening*.' In 1923, with Alice Martineau, she visited the fine garden of her friends Alan and Nettie Johnstone at La Napoule, near Cannes, with its magnificent camellias. Her book-requests to her London book-dealer in 1923 included Gertrude Jekyll's and Lawrence Weaver's *Gardens for Small Country Houses* and books on the care of fan-tailed pigeons. As at St-Brice, she had practical help from Lawrence Johnston, and here it was his spectacular Riviera garden at 'La Serre de la Madone', near Menton, created, like hers, in the 1920s, which enthralled and influenced her. Like Ste-Claire, Johnston's Menton garden was built on a steep hill, and required similar work of terracing and irrigation. (La Serre had an elaborate construction of pools – and an amazing population of tropical birds.) Like Ste-Claire, it was a carefully structured garden which had an organic relationship with the *maquis* that surrounded it, full of theatrical contrasts and bold colour effects. Johnston, who was an outstanding collector of rare plants from China, Mexico and Africa, gave Wharton as much advice here as he did at St-Brice: 'The angelic Lawrence Johnston came from Menton to spend two days with me and helped me incalculably in all my planting plans', she told Minnie in October 1924; and in her papers there are lists of plants sent from Hidcote to both her French gardens.[41]

Like La Serre, the garden at Ste-Claire was a major operation, expensive, complex, and labour-intensive. A great deal of forward planning and close supervision was required. The climate was dry and liable to droughts; the soil on the rocky terraces was 'poor and shallow', as she described it (though the 'light warm soil makes happy many moisture-dreading plants'). Over the six acres of terraced gardens she had built (within a twenty-five-acre spread of land), irrigation was essential; so was drainage, since there could also be heavy and damaging rain-storms in the autumn. Shade and shelter (even though Hyères was much more protected from the mistral than other parts of the Riviera) were vital. And these would not necessarily protect the garden against the sudden extreme frosts or 'scorching rainless summers' for which the South of France was famous. Some plants would not take, and there were unexpected pests and diseases. As one gardening expert put it, the best-trained gardener had to 'learn his art all over again to succeed on the Riviera'. Wharton's first head-gardener, Bérard, had problems: he was good at building the stone walls for the terraces, but 'he kills flowers much more successfully & effectually than he does their enemies, such as caterpillars & green-fly'. By 1923 poor Bérard has been replaced, since the gardens had got 'beyond him': 'I was throwing away a great deal of money quite uselessly.'

A great deal of money was indeed spent on this garden. The initial expenses of transporting soil, building terraces, hiring gardeners, constructing pergolas and paths, and doing the first plantings, were compounded by large, seasonal plant orders. Wharton acquired her plants in a variety of ways, partly by getting seeds or plants from fellow-gardeners (including Beatrix Farrand and Lawrence Johnston), partly (as she described it in her Foreword to Alice Martineau's book on gardening in the South of France) by discovering 'treasures' in the catalogues of the local nurserymen and wandering through their nurseries. She sent off long lists of plant-orders to firms like the French family business of Vilmorin, or to Gerald Telkamp, the Dutch tulip and iris growers (ordering bulbs in their thousands for both St-Brice and Ste-Claire). She met specialists such as the famous rose-grower Nabormand, who visited Ste-Claire in 1920, when the terraces were in the making, and (she told Beatrix) 'was in raptures at the opportunity for growing camellias & gardenias, besides all the roses that ever *were*'. She never stopped looking out for new plants and new ideas: in the last year of her life she was still eagerly noting a 'wonderful new rose . . . a climbing hybrid tea called H.V. Machin' which she had seen at Hyères 'covering a house in glaring sun & howling wind which did not seem to affect it in the least. The flower is very large & dark crimson, & the rose was covered with hundreds & hundreds of buds.'[42]

There are many records of Wharton's dramatic and enchanting garden at Ste-Claire. There are photographs of her standing beaming, with peke and stick in hand, on paths edged with mighty succulents and shaded by olives and cypresses, or sitting on the terrace backed by climbers and surrounded by pots of annuals. Snapshots of the garden give glimpses of its variety: neat terraces of lawns with pergolas or pavilions, bordered by 'packed drifts' of coloured flowers on the slopes; exotic and native plants setting each other off; and at every point interconnections made between the gardens, the view, and the castle ruins. There are the garden-notes she made to herself in her diary of 1921 ('Feb 6: Wistaria in bloom on terrace! February 26: Judas tree and arums budding. Anemones in full bloom. April 20: Nightingales at last at Ste-Claire'). There are the typed orders for the French gardener, showing her unremitting attention, her typical balancing of the parts against the whole, and her confidence in pulling things up and replacing them. '*Transplanter les brachysema latifolia de chaque côté de la petite fontaine et les remplacer par capucines doubles*'; '*Arracher les pyrus Japonica de la bordure de la grande terrasse en haut et les mettre à mis-ombre sur la nouvelle terrasse ouest*'. There are two lyrical unpublished essays on 'A French Riviera Garden', in which she describes the moment of transition between winter and spring, or the wonderful colours of the garden in December (making special mention of her flowering shrubs from China and Central America, like her great fifteen-foot-high daisy tree, her spectacular *Montanoa Grandiflora*, with its broad leaves and white flowers, the 'fantastic Dahlia Arborea' with its burst of mauve flowers at the top of bamboo-like stalks, or her 'great sheets of Bougainvillea Sanderina, so resplendent in its bold magenta bloom if it is given a green background'). This is one corner of her southern garden in spring:

> The last almond blossoms wave a goodbye to winter toward the middle of February, just as the reddening of the peach-buds begins to announce the new season. By that time, too, Prunus Blieriani [a variety of almond] is a great rosy cloud, Kennedya trifoliata is hanging out its violet fringes, buds are thick on the Deutzias, Exorchorda Grandiflora, Prunus Moseriana, Paeonia arborea [tree paeony], the hybrid Pyrus Japonicas, and the early-blooming lilacs, and in the hot sheltered rock garden Aloe Cilaria is covering itself with scarlet spikes and Aloe Salm-Dyckiana [a

striking aloe with scarlet flowers in the form of candelabra] and its hybrids are throwing up their fiery rockets.[43]

Even on paper the sense of colour is almost overwhelming: these were gardens to make one gasp. The terraces were opulent, theatrical and intense. But, said one visitor in 1928, 'although massed colour effects are aimed at to a great extent, yet the colour is never allowed to overwhelm the natural beauty'.

Gardens are changing and ephemeral things, but there were enough descriptions and photographs from the time to allow one garden-expert to deduce that

> in making her garden [Wharton] displayed all the energy and forthright-
> ness that had made her novels so popular. She blasted the hillside and
> built up retaining walls for the terraces; she made a splendid pergola and
> covered it in climbing roses; she planted a walk of orange trees and
> trained her cypresses into Moorish arches. Olives and agaves were kept
> as a natural background to her bold schemes. Edith Wharton lined a
> long straight narrow walk entirely with orange freesias and she made an
> extensive collection of cacti and succulents.

The 1928 visitor, a journalist for *Country Life*, noted that this collection was 'said to be even more complete than the famous collection at the Prince of Monaco's on the borders of Monte Carlo'. Fellow gardeners admired her (the Vicomte de Noailles called her 'a great gardener . . . and very serious technically'), and the reputation of her gardens spread: when the house was sold after her death, they were described as 'among the most celebrated in France'.

The most affectionate and intimate description of Ste-Claire was by Daisy Chanler:

> A succession of rock gardens skilfully planted look as if they had nestled
> there of themselves, whereas they are full of exotic rarities collected from
> all parts of the world. There is no end to the flowers and the flowering
> trees and shrubs . . . There are few paths; the beauties of the garden are
> reached by a maze of stone steps. A flock of dazzling white pouter pigeons
> . . . group themselves about the drinking fountain . . . they strut and
> make love with tender monotonous cooings.

Breaking off her description, she adds, revealingly:

> I seem to feel Edith's searching eye upon me as I write. 'What are you
> saying about my garden?' she seems to ask, and I hardly dare to say more.
> She could do it so much better herself, but I doubt if she would try to

describe it. It would be telling something too intimate, for her garden is somehow an image of her spirit, of her inmost self. It shows her love of beauty, her imagination, her varied knowledge and masterly attention to detail; like her, it is somewhat inaccessible. Her garden is a symbol of the real Edith.[44]

This magnificent achievement was also a vulnerable one. As the garden was evolving, there were some painful setbacks. In 1920, a cold mistral and a hard frost wiped out a great swathe of the 'stock-in-trade of a Riviera garden' (her heliotropes, tradescantia, plumbago, arums and geraniums), froze her orange trees, shrivelled up her eucalyptus and pepper trees, and stripped the plumes of her best climbing buddleia. In 1924, a sudden rainstorm completely washed away some terraces she had just had made. But neither of these crises was as severe as the catastrophic frost of the winter of 1928–29, one of the worst in the Riviera's history, which killed most of her garden, and was profoundly distressing to her. She tried to make the best of it, joking to Ogden Codman that she was 'going to replace the wreckage with Norway spruces and the flora of New England'. But she also told her friends how hard hit she was by 'the utter destruction', and how she was having to struggle against 'the profound depression' it was causing: 'Oh, Gaillard, that my old fibres should have been so closely intertwined with all those roots and tendrils! . . . *Everything* is killed. Though I say to others: "Allons, donc! It might have been an earthquake", I must weep a moment on your shoulder, and confess that to *me* it is one. Those Furies!' Elisina reported that 'all the rare and precious plants are being carted away, dead, in cartloads.' One French friend said that it looked as if the garden had been gassed by a raid of enemy aircraft; and this disaster did, indeed, bring back to her, in the very place where she had built a consolatory refuge for herself, some of the worst feelings of wartime. Her line-a-day diary for January and February 1929 makes heartbreaking reading:

> January 4. The snow has broken down my two glorious caroubiers [carob trees], the pride of the garden. How dangerous to care too much even for a garden! Trees and shrubs smashed and rooted up everywhere . . .
> February 15: Everything in garden destroyed . . . February 21: It is torture to me to think of my dead garden wh. grows worse every day. February 23: Terrible drought. Destroying last hope of saving any plants.

Within days, she became very ill herself. Wharton would stoically replant and remake the garden, and in the early 1930s she would often say, as to Louis Bromfield in 1934, that it was 'a great joy' to her. But the catastrophe was a kind of death, and she never quite recovered her full energies and spirits again.[45]

Wharton did not write a novel about a gardener, but it might not be too fanciful to think that gardening and novel-writing have something in common. The mixture of disciplined structure and imaginative freedom, the reworking of traditions into a new idea, the ruthless elimination of dull, incongruous or surplus materials, and the creation of a dramatic narrative, all come to mind – not to mention patience, stamina, and attentiveness. John Hugh Smith reported to Lubbock, in 1938, that 'she told me that she thought her gardens were better than her books'. In her seventeen years of writing at St-Brice and Ste-Claire, she made no extensive fictional use of her experiences there as home-owner and gardener. These were alternatives to, not material for, the writing. The unfashionable end of the Riviera provides material for *The Mother's Recompense*, and for a couple of comic stories ('Her Son', partly set in a small resort between Marseilles and Toulon, in which the main character 'seemed to have forgotten that there had ever been a war', and 'Velvet Ear-Pads', which caricatures her own desire for quiet seclusion, as against the turmoil of the casinos in Monte Carlo and Cannes). Her last full-length novel of the 1930s, *The Gods Arrive*, has a long section in 'Oubli-sur-Mer', a small, unfashionable English seaside colony, which has some lyrical descriptions of the Mediterranean countryside. In Wharton's unfinished manuscripts, there are two interesting traces of Hyères, though none of St-Brice. The unfinished fragment 'The Great Miss Netherby', set in a house very like Ste-Claire, is about an ironical old expatriate New Yorker, a woman horticulturalist who has created a fabulous garden of irises for herself. Wharton also planned, some time in the 1920s, to write (as Conrad did in *The Rover*) a historical novel set in eighteenth-century Hyères, *The Happy Isles*. The young American hero, Mark, travels to Toulon on business, and is inspired by books of the time on 'The Natural History of Provence'. He learns to eat bouillabaisse and falls in love with the countryside. He meets an old French lady ('She seemed like a nymph that some wicked spell had changed into a crone') who introduces him to the beautiful daughter of the Count of Hyères, Douce de Mauvanne, who sounds like Philomène. Wharton wrote thirty pages of this novel before she abandoned it, including an eloquent description of Mark's arrival at Hyères, in which, all his senses alert, he flings himself down on a bed of rue, absorbs the sight of 'bare thymy slopes above plunging forests', the distant islands, the olives, the vines, and the 'ancient fortress towering against the flaming background of the sea', and hears the 'peals of the noonday angelus' from behind the convent wall, while 'the homely smell of olive oil and garlic mixed its welcome with the scent of the orange blossoms'. It looks as if she was going to imagine herself back into the old convent of Ste-Claire; but the plan, along with so many other unfinished Wharton projects, came to nothing. Perhaps her houses and gardens played so little part in her later books because the Pavillon Colombe and Ste-Claire-du-Château were works of art in themselves and did not need to be written about. They were her private refuges. In a fragmentary diary she was keeping in 1926, she marked a return to Ste-Claire with the words: 'Back again after eight months away. Oh the joy of being alone – alone; of walking about in the garden of my soul!'[46]

The Age of Innocence

Newland Archer, taking tea by the fire with Ellen Olenska in her curious little house far down West 23rd Street, on their second meeting in private, feels that in the 'intimate', 'foreign' atmosphere of her room, 'New York seemed much further off than Samarkand.' He realises that she is making him 'look at his native city objectively. Viewed thus, as though through the wrong end of a telescope, it looked disconcertingly small and distant; but then from Samarkand it would.' The reference is to a poem much loved by Wharton's generation, James Elroy Flecker's romantic fantasy of the exotic Orient, 'The Golden Journey to Samarkand'. It suggests a bold, sensual quest for knowledge and adventure – exactly what Newland Archer fails in.

> For lust of knowing what should not be known
> We make the Golden Journey to Samarkand.

Flecker's poem dates from 1913, long after the time of *The Age of Innocence*, which is set in the early 1870s. By this and many other distancing devices, Wharton makes us look back on him 'objectively', as a little figure in the past. But she also draws us close. The title of her most famous novel tells us she is going to look back. It is what she is best known for: providing a retrospect on a vanished 'age', a retrospect that, as the word 'innocence' suggests, is going to be at once ironical and tender. The figures, which seem 'disconcertingly small and distant' to start with, come closer and closer. We see through their 'old-fashioned' clothes and habits, their rituals and customs, right into their hearts.

Wharton wrote *The Age of Innocence* at speed, just after the end of the war, between September 1919 and the end of March 1920, because (she said retrospectively) she wanted a 'momentary escape', and 'had to get away from the present altogether'.[1] Retrospect was natural, and widespread, at this time. The pre-war world already looked strange and 'distant'; what would it feel like, now, to go back to 1870s New York, the world of her childhood? This was an exercise in consolatory remembering, a nostalgic refuge from the bitter experiences of the last few years. The gap between when she is writing (1919–20) and the time she is writing about (1871–3, with a coda at the turn of the century) is at its widest here and in the companion volume to *The Age of Innocence*, the four novellas of *Old New York*, which move between the 1840s and the 1920s. (*The House of Mirth* was set at the time of its writing, *The Custom of the Country* looked back from the early 1910s to the 1900s.) Only her early historical novel, *The Valley of Decision* (with a similarly compromised hero), and her last, unfinished novel, *The Buccaneers*, have a longer span of time between their setting and their writing. The fictions in between *The Age of Innocence* and *The Buccaneers* would be bitingly contemporaneous.

But escapism is not the whole motive behind *The Age of Innocence*. The writing of this novel was a strategic professional move, reviving her reputation as the author of *The House of Mirth* after seven years without a big novel on 'old New York' themes, and at a time of high expenditure on her new houses, when she needed another best-seller. More profoundly, *The Age of Innocence* carries the weight of many of her own feelings. Like *Summer*, it may feel worlds away from wartime France, but it is also a novel of cruelty, loss and grief. It replays, in historical guise, her current feelings about America and Europe. Like other American writers thinking about the post-war world – Scott Fitzgerald's Dick Diver on the battlefields lamenting the breaking of the golden bowl, or Willa Cather imagining the world broken in half and calling her 1920s essays *Not Under Forty*, to warn off readers with no memories before the 1880s – Wharton's title implies a lost pre-war world. It also suggests a connection between the America of fifty years ago and the America of the present, which she so often complains about for its infantilism, naive optimism, and parochialism. When 'innocence' is used most pejoratively in the novel, it is called 'invincible innocence'. That adjective is more usually coupled with 'ignorance' (after Aquinas's '*ignorantia invincibilis*'), and Wharton's diagnosis of American innocence does, often, make it look like ignorance. So a novel which markets itself as a historical escape into a vanished era is deeply bound up with her current feelings about her native country.

And with her current feelings about herself. *The Age of Innocence* makes a kind of autobiography, though, as usual, personal emotions are carefully distanced and dressed up. The novel is told entirely from the point of view of a young man of good family, in his mid-twenties, who gets suitably engaged to the adoring and beautiful May Welland at exactly the moment that her cousin, Ellen Olenska, returns to New York. The cousins, both grandchildren of the wilful and unconventional Mrs Manson Mingott, are contrasted throughout. May is blonde, statuesque, innocent, philistine, and entirely conventional, a good American girl. Ellen is quick, elegant, 'brown', stylish, experienced and thoroughly Europeanised (her mother married an Italian, and she grew up mainly abroad under the guardianship of an eccentric and much-married aunt, Medora Manson). She is separated from her husband, a Polish count with an (unspecified) decadent and brutal lifestyle. She is rumoured to have run away with the count's secretary, and has returned to her childhood scene of New York in the hopes of finding a safe refuge and of making a home for herself. Newland, who has always had a passion for European art and literature, prides himself on taking an objective view of his own society but is fundamentally conventional and unassertive. He is involved, both as a family member and through his law firm, with the delicate question of Ellen Olenska's future. Should she divorce the count, with a possible ensuing scandal which might affect May's family, should she put up forever, in a kind of limbo, with being the Countess Olenska, or should she go back to Europe and her horrible husband? Newland falls deeply in love with her, and, it becomes apparent, she with him, even as the inevitable processes of his New York engagement, wedding, honeymoon and married life go forward. His attempt to oppose the family's opinion that Ellen is a difficult misfit who should be sent back to Europe, his inarticulate but increasingly urgent attempt to find a life with her, is thwarted at every point by the coded strategies of the self-preserving New York network – in which May, for all her innocence, is also complicit and active. Newland and Ellen are silently separated by the tribe's watchful manoeuvres, without ever becoming lovers. In a poignant and startling coda, we find that Newland, now widowed, has lived a decent life as a husband, father and good citizen, while knowing that he has missed 'the flower of life'. Times do change, and the next generation have freed themselves of many of the codes of the last. Newland, however (like a number of Wharton's characters, fixed in a time that has gone), is still a creature of his 'age'. Given an opportunity, almost thirty years after he last saw her, of meeting Ellen Olenska again in Paris, he chooses not to do so, and turns away, 'alone'.

The novel invokes Wharton's own loneliness: 'lonely' and 'alone' are key words. The hollow mockery of Newland's marriage recalls her own past; the conflict between an upbringing in America and a life in Europe is hers. Ellen's critical reception by her American relations as a woman with a failed marriage living alone in Europe has Wharton's own history in it. The picture of New York is 'drawn from the life' (as *The House of Mirth* was more notoriously thought to have been, fifteen years before). There are recognisable portraits: Newland's mother's views are Lucretia Jones's; the social commentator Ward McAllister (crossed with Egerton Winthrop) appears (here and in *Old New York*) as Sillerton Jackson, arbiter of 'form' and 'taste' and the repository of scandalous family histories. Wharton's pioneering great-aunt, Mrs Mason Jones, is robustly and brilliantly 'done' as Mrs Manson Mingott; the shady financier August Belmont and his scandalous mistress are drawn on for Julius Beaufort and Fanny Ring; the parvenu Mrs Paran Stevens inspires the Shoe-Polish millionairess, Mrs Lemuel Struthers. Nothing is lost or wasted from the past: Wharton uses her own street, her own work on the decoration of houses (from the 'sincere' furniture in Newland's study to the decor of May Archer's drawing room), her memories of Newport, her entire family network, and every vase, net curtain and picture-frame in the Jones household, in the most ruthless and lavish way. Her details of the upper-class New York way of life in *The Age of Innocence* are corroborated in *Old New York* and in Wharton's autobiographies, 'Life & I', 'A Little Girl's New York', and *A Backward Glance*. (That the novel was received, in part, as a form of autobiographical reminiscence, is suggested by the fact that a month after it came out, Charles Scribner sent her a copy of a book he thought would appeal to her, Maitland Armstrong's *Day Before Yesterday: Reminiscences of a Varied Life*, a rambling memoir of New York from the 1840s to the 1880s. 'Personally it has interested me very much', she replied, 'as I am an old New Yorker.')

Newland is in his twenties at the time when Pussy Jones was a child; but this is her world, complete, and she was anxious to get the details right, asking Minnie (Newland Archer's contemporary) in New York to check the dates of operas and plays for her. (It is like Joyce, self-exiled in Trieste and Zurich in the 1910s, writing home for exact details of Dublin in 1904, for *Ulysses*.) A rush of information came back from Minnie, 'gleaned from the back files of the *New York Tribune*', noting that Christine Nilsson was not singing in *Faust* at the old Academy of Music in 1875, that Ward McAllister started the Patriarchs Balls in 1872, that Boucicault's play *The Shaughraun* (which Wharton wanted to use for its touching, silent farewell scene between the lovers) was running at Wallack's Theatre from 1874, and that Archer could not have read *Middlemarch* until 1873. Minnie wondered how many people would 'recognise old Aunt Mary, and August Belmont'. Her sister-in-law's memories were rousing her own: 'I remember your mother's saying that when she was a girl one knew all the carriages in town.' She was amazed and impressed by Wharton's eloquent recall. Walter, who was reading the novel chapter by chapter, was less encouraging: he thought that no one would remember or be interested in 'New York and Newport as they were then'.

Wharton replied to Minnie, slightly irritably, that she had decided to place the novel at an 'uncertain' date in 'the early seventies', so that absolute accuracy would not be necessary. 'What I especially want is to give the atmosphere of old New York in my youth', she added (with the emphasis on 'atmosphere'), and for a time 'Old New York' was the working title of the novel. Still, she was keen to make an authentic picture, and when there was talk of a theatrical adaptation by Zoë Akins in 1921, she told Minnie that she was 'very anxious' about accuracy. 'I could do every stick of furniture & every rag of clothing myself, for every detail of that far-off scene was indelibly stamped on my infant brain.' And she goes on to issue detailed instructions: the actors must have the right kind of moustaches, they must wear 'buttonhole-violets by day, a gardenia in evening dress', pumps with evening clothes, and so on: and above all they must speak good English. 'A drawing room of my childhood was far more like a London one – a du Maurier one of old-fashioned gentlefolk.' This dramatisation did not materialise, but when the book was adapted for the stage, very successfully, in 1928, by Margaret Ayer Barnes, with advice and help from the playwright Edward Sheldon, Wharton was equally concerned about accuracy. Altering Archer's political career (as the adaptors wanted to do) to make him a more Rooseveltian hero, an active reformer with a history of fighting Indians, 'would take away all meaning from his history'. And she was equally worried about their plan to take out her gentleman-hero's experience of Europe; as one of the adaptors wrote exasperatedly to the other: 'It nearly killed Mrs Wharton to have us say that Archer had never been abroad.'[2]

A form of revenge as well as resuscitation is taking place. The hypocrisy, philistinism and resentful narrow-mindedness of her parents' generation are cruelly on display. But there is also, increasingly towards the end of the book, a sense of mourning for a lost world. It is as if she could not stop asking herself, at this time (as she made her new homes and confirmed her complete alienation from America): What did this upbringing do to her? Why was it so oppressive? Why did it make her want to leave? Why was it such an adverse environment for a writer? And yet, was there anything valuable about it? What would it have been like *not* to leave, or to go back and live there permanently? She was asking these questions now (with as much reticence and self-concealment as her characters) partly because, like Newland Archer at the end of the novel, she was very conscious of age and mortality. She was the same age as her hero. 'He found himself saying: "But I'm only fifty-seven –" and then he turned away.'[3]

The Age of Innocence is about age, too, in that it reminds Wharton – and her readers – of her own past as a writer. Partly for strategic marketing reasons, but also because these are her obsessions, she is reusing what all her readers thought (and think) of as the essentially Whartonian materials: money, status, marriage and divorce in late nineteenth-century New York; determinist stories of confined lives in that particular world; harsh diagnoses of American manners; double standards, sexual betrayals, failures in love and renunciations; culture clashes between America and Europe. But *The Age of Innocence* was a new kind of post-war writing. It is more muted and equivocal in its tone, less harshly and brilliantly satirical than *The House of Mirth* or *The Custom of the Country*. Though there are as many fixtures and fittings as in the earlier New York novels, and as insistent an emphasis on location, all the stuff of the book keeps coming undone. The effect, for all the set-dressing, is more elegiac and unreal than before (though she has always been interested in the unreality of the material world). And though past novels had also generalised from particular cases, there will be more attention now on group behaviour, less involvement in the psychology of isolated individuals. (As a result, her later work, post-*Age of Innocence*, is much less popular; there are no more Lily Barts to identify with.)

Her survey of the age uses, and describes, surveillance. Like *The House of Mirth*, this novel is all about being watched. It describes a society of spies and observers, and attempts at secrecy and concealment. It is a drama with spectators (in a society dedicated to inaction and leisure) which starts in an opera-house with an audience watching itself more than it is watching the stage, and ends with the figure of a solitary watcher, unable to act. Men who pride themselves on their taste, and their judgement of 'form', stare at women through their opera-glasses, looking for departures from 'conformity'. In the very small theatre of activities that is 1870s New York, privacy is a figment. The prototypical scene is the one in which Newland Archer, strolling after dinner up the little slice of Fifth Avenue that is the stage of his world, can read all the signs at a glance: 'Thus, as Archer crossed Washington Square, he remarked that old Mr du Lac was calling on his cousins the Dagonets, and turning down the corner of West Tenth Street he saw Mr Skipworth, of his own firm, obviously bound on a visit to the Miss Lannings' – and so on. The thwarted lovers are under observation from their first conversation to their last; 'somewhere where we can be alone' is almost impossible to find. Ellen Olenska sums this up, as Wharton herself had done long before, as a matter of house-design: 'One can't be alone for a minute . . . Is there nowhere in an American house where one may be by one's self? You're so shy, and yet you're so public.' In their horrible last public scene together, when Newland understands that they have been silently observed – and misread – at all points, he feels 'like a prisoner in the centre of an armed camp'.[4]

Wharton is like one of the watchers in the novel who applies to the affairs of his friends 'the patience of a collector and the science of a naturalist'. On the first page of the novel, the world of fashion, assembling in 'the early seventies' at the 'old' Academy of Music to hear its favourite soprano singing in *Faust*, is brought to life so rapidly and effectively as to make the method almost imperceptible. The page is thick with knowing allusions to details of the time, swiftly footnoted so as at once to familiarise us with vanished customs, and to make fun of them: like the opera-goers being transported by the 'Brown *coupé*', the shared horse-drawn carriages which could drop you off and take you home without your having to wait for your own coachman (allowing for playful allusions to 'democratic principles'), the brainwave of the influential sexton of Grace Church, Isaac Brown, who also had a livery-business. That one detail makes a snapshot of 'the age', and invokes the attitudes of the society she is going to describe. Ironical inverted commas are scattered about, as in her references to the beginnings of newspaper reporting on social events ('what the daily press had already learned to describe as "an exceptionally brilliant audience"'), or to the influx of 'new people' whom 'New York was beginning to dread and yet be drawn to'. We are presented with a long-past society which seems to itself secure, but which is already changing as we look at it. The narrating voice is knowingly, even affectionately, close to what it describes ('the shabby red and gold boxes of the sociable old Academy') yet has a historian's remoteness and a taste for (still applicable) ironic generalisations: 'Americans want to get away from amusement even more quickly than they want to get to it.'[5]

Wharton does this double act repeatedly. At moments of closest, heartfelt intimacy, she jumps forward and away. So when Newland sets off on his wedding-journey, an excruciating moment of unreality for him, we are reminded coolly of the habitual rituals of an 1870s honeymoon ('It was thought "very English" to have a country-house lent to one'); when he has an intimate, tender meeting with Ellen Olenska in Boston, he shows her how to use one of the 'new stylographic pens'. Set-piece scenes, like a Grace Church wedding, a Newport archery contest, or the menu for a young couple's first dinner-party, are pinpointed in every detail; at the same time they are made to look remote and quaint. The characters talk with resistance, wonder and disbelief about 'trends', 'minute signs of disintegration' in their society. They joke about 'fantastic possibilities': the invention of 'talking along a wire', of 'flying machines' or high-speed transatlantic ships, 'lighting by electricity' and 'other Arabian Night marvels'.[6]

This tactic of making 'the age' feel both fixed in its ways, and ephemeral, is especially noticeable when she mentions forms of transport. In one scene, Newland has to get as fast as he can from his Wall Street lawyer's office to Mrs Mingott's house, in the East Fifties on Fifth Avenue – an address considered, then, to be recklessly far uptown. To do so, he has to take a crowded 'horse-car' to 14th Street, and then change onto 'one of the high staggering omnibuses of the Fifth Avenue line'. A whole history of New York public transport is invoked: the choice in the 1870s between slow, dilapidated, horse-drawn omnibuses running on fixed routes and holding twelve passengers, and the faster street-cars, or street-railways, which ran on iron rails and were pulled by horses, giving way from the 1880s to electric street-cars and then, by the 1920s, to cars and motor-buses. Again, when Newland goes to fetch Ellen Olenska, who is arriving in New York from Washington, he takes his wife's brougham on the ferry to the Pennsylvania terminus in New Jersey, finds Ellen on the train, walks her along the ferry-wharf back to the carriage, and rides back with her inside the carriage, which throws them together in their intense, despairing love-scene, as it negotiates the gang-plank back onto the ferry and then bumps against the ferry-landing on the Manhattan side. Newland thinks, as he sets out, of the visionaries who say there will one day be a tunnel under the Hudson river. 'I don't care which of their visions comes true,' Archer mused, 'as long as the tunnel isn't built yet.' The reader feels a queasy rocking movement, as on a horse-drawn omnibus or a ferry-crossing, between being confined in the past with the characters, and watching them from the distant future.[7]

The sense of queasiness is compounded by the vision of a peculiarly unstable watcher. Newland Archer is a critical spectator who is also a help-less participant. Like Ralph Marvell in *Custom*, and the narrator of *The House of Mirth*, he makes anthropological readings of his own society, imagining it as a primitive tribe whose taboos or rites of passage are re-enacted in modern dress, ironically relating its customs to their underlying primitive motives – sexual appetite, reproductive drive, survival of the fittest, exclusion of the alien. He compares the rituals of engagement visits with the showing-off of 'a wild animal cunningly trapped'; or compares May with the 'much-cited instances' from his 'new' scientific books of the Kentucky cave-fish which 'had ceased to develop eyes because they had no use for them'; or sees that the final dinner at which he and Ellen are to be separated with every appearance of good behaviour and perfect manners is 'the tribal rally around a kinswoman about to be eliminated from the tribe'. Wharton is well known for doing this sort of thing – it is her own way of distancing herself from her parents' world – but here she is careful to show that Newland's ethnographic readings, derived from his new books (Darwin and Spencer), are as much part of their time – and of her own past – as the social habits they are applied to. The fact that Newland reads his culture as an anthropologist or ethnologist might does not make him any less a member of the tribe.[8]

Newland sees that every form of group action is a code: 'they all lived in a kind of hieroglyphic world, where the real thing was never said or done or even thought, but only represented by a set of arbitrary signs.' And the codes have to be sustained through the utmost watchfulness, so that any threatening departures from the norm can be kept at bay. But he also sees, as we do, that this 'small and slippery pyramid' of society, of which people like his mother, or Sillerton Jackson, are the self-appointed monitors, is subject to change and always shifting. He enjoys noting how New York 'managed its transitions'. This is a society which wants at all costs to preserve itself, but which is in a continuous process of evolutionary slippage. His alienation from this process makes his own life seem farcically unreal: he is always breaking out in a kind of dissociated, demonic hollow laughter at the performance he is engaged in, like a spectator at the play of his own life.

But though Newland laughs, he also blushes, hesitates, and gives in. His readings are not as objective as he would like. And he is as much a target of the novel's irony as he is its agent. He thinks he is a New Man and a feminist ('Women ought to be free – as free as we are') and he criticises his society's 'purity' for being really a means of 'barricading itself against the unpleasant'. But he has just as much of a double standard as the other men in this puritanical, hypocritical environment, where there are euphemisms for prostitution and adultery, young women are not supposed to hear about family scandals, and pregnancy is only spoken of with 'blushing circumlocution'. Newland has had an affair before his engagement and thinks of the married woman in the case with derision; he condescends to his wife, as well as revering her, for her sexual 'innocence'; he is shocked by Ellen's use of the word 'mistress', and he even begins to despise her at the point when she offers to 'give herself' to him. Though he plans to educate May into a more liberated state of mind, he 'reverts to all his old inherited ideas' very soon after their wedding, and settles into standard nineteenth-century American marital relations: 'There was no use in trying to emancipate a wife who had not the dimmest notion that she was not free.' He is extremely confused in his attitude to Ellen's marriage and divorce, making generalisations about 'woman's rights to her liberty' which are not borne out by his dread of scandal or his being shocked by what he imag- ines of her past. He finds it as difficult to speak out about any of this as any other conventional member of his tribe: 'Better keep on the surface, in the prudent old New York way.'[9]

How *does* a society of 'precise and inflexible rituals' ever shift? Its conven- tions are systematised because they function as self-preserving rules: they 'tied things together and bound people down to the old pattern'. As Newland himself says, and it will turn out to be horribly true in his case, 'the individual is nearly always sacrificed to what is supposed to be the collective interest'. But exceptions to the rules do, eventually, succeed in changing them. What Newland's story shows, though he cannot quite see it himself, is the process whereby individual variations from the norm gradu- ally alter the behaviour of the group. As we are drawn into the picture of 1870s New York, we see that there are a number of individualists, half-in and half-out of the community, whose actions and attitudes create 'transi- tions'. An independent woman like Mrs Mingott started the move to build uptown, which was thought shocking in its day, but is accepted by the 1870s. The Shoe-Polish queen, once thought scandalously vulgar by the arbiters of society, is beginning to be visitable. The financier Julius Beaufort has succeeded through immense entrepreneurial power in having his dubious antecedents discounted. No one quite knows where he is from: 'The ques- tion was: who *was* Beaufort?' Quite possibly he is Jewish, like Simon Rosedale in *The House of Mirth*. His scandalous liaison with New York's well-known courtesan, Fanny Ring, and the dishonourable crash of his bank, would seem to ensure his ejection from the tribe, just as Ellen's uncon- ventional (though scrupulously honourable) behaviour ensures hers. (Beaufort and Ellen, in a subtle balancing-act, are kept in parallel throughout the novel; Fanny Ring's offstage career is a reminder of the society's double standards and of the fate that Ellen needs to avoid.) But Beaufort's energies do feed back into the next generation. The unthink- able prospect, that (as one particularly hypocritical New Yorker prophesies) 'Beaufort's bastards' will end up marrying 'our' children, does come to pass. Beaufort makes an honest woman of Fanny Ring after his wife dies, and their daughter Fanny Beaufort (born out of wedlock), a second-generation Ellen Olenska, who, instead of being ostracised, will be at the centre of the next 'age' of New York life, marries Newland's and May's son, Dallas. Fanny Archer, like her mother, is an offstage character; Wharton thought of writing a sequel about her marriage to Dallas, called 'Homo Sapiens' or

'The Age of Wisdom', in which she would show 'the omniscient youth of the present date, who has settled in advance all social, religious and moral problems, and yet comes to grief over the same old human difficulties'. Characters like Mrs Mingott and Julius Beaufort and Ellen Olenska change the society even as it judges them; 'new blood' courses in, for good or ill, and what looks fixed is gradually, and perpetually, coming undone.

Newland Archer's own partial, unsuccessful unconventionality is itself a pointer towards the coming of the new, as his symbolic, New World name suggests: he changes in the course of the novel, and, without knowing it, he changes what surrounds him. His unstable identity is connected to a tension, which is at the heart of this book, between America and Europe. It is made clear that Newland's 'new' ideas, his critique of his society and his susceptibility to Ellen are all linked to his attraction to European society and culture. He has often visited Europe and prides himself on keeping up with all the latest art-shows and cultural events when he is there. He is capable of snobbish worldly-wise French references (such as calling the bare dining-room of a country inn outside Boston an innocent version of a *cabinet particulier*). He has a vision of a society where the idea of meeting people in order to enjoy 'good conversation' would not be thought of as a joke, where there is free play of mind, and where 'painters and poets and novelists and men of science, and even great actors, were as sought after as Dukes'. That place, of course, is Paris. The curious reappearance in the plot – its weakest strand – of the French secretary with whom Ellen Olenska may or (more probably) may not have had an affair, keeps up the contrast between Parisian intellectual liberty and New York philistinism and parochialism.[10]

Newland's emotions are very literary. His tastes are partly satirised – he is a would-be free-thinking 'dilettante' whose reading is advanced but whose behaviour is ultimately conventional. But everything he reads was read with equal passion by Edith Wharton in the 1870s: Darwin and Spencer, Swinburne and Rossetti (his passionate series of love-poems, 'The House of Life'), *Middlemarch* and William Morris, and, above all, the great nineteenth-century French writers. Newland's heroes are Maupassant, Mérimée, Alphonse Daudet and Balzac, and such 'new names' as Paul Bourget, Huysmans and the Goncourts. (Of course these are all influences on Wharton, too: when Plon-Nourrit published *Au Temps de l'innocence*, the blurb compared her to *'notre grand Balzac'*.) When he switches from reading poetry after dinner to reading prose (to prevent May's asking him to read out loud and his having to listen to her comments on the poems), he chooses a volume of Michelet's history of France. This is in Wharton's library, much annotated; in Michelet's Preface, she underlined the sentence: 'Ma vie fut en ce livre, elle a passé en lui. Il a été mon seul événement.' A culture in which a man could write: 'My life has been in this book, it has passed into it, it has been the sole event of my life', is quite remote from the one in which Newland – and Wharton – grew up. Newland's European cultural preferences are close to Wharton's lifelong argument with herself about America and Europe.[11]

The Age of Innocence is obviously a novel about America. But it is just as much a novel about America's relationship to Europe. A letter to Barrett Wendell, written just as French Ways and their Meaning came out and while she was working on the novel, annotates her mixed feelings about America. Gaillard Lapsley had edited a book of lectures called The America of Today, which included an account of contemporary American literature by a Yale professor, Henry Canby, which classed Wharton (and James) as 'aristocratic' literature, set against a more American tradition of 'democratic' literature (Whitman, of course). Irritated by this, to her, 'tiresome' distinction, she burst out to Wendell: 'How much longer are we going to think it necessary to be "American" before (or in contradistinction to) being cultivated, being enlightened, being humane, and having the same intellectual discipline as other civilized countries? "Our" shortcomings should not be dressed up as "a form of patriotism".'[12] This quarrel with her country underlies The Age of Innocence. But the novel is more complex than that letter, since it presents an America which defines itself against Europe, but is also in thrall to it.

For Wharton to write a novel set in 1870s America which placed its upper-class characters between ideas of home and exile, native and foreign, American and European, inevitably meant having Henry James in mind. She was thinking about him while she was writing the novel, because Percy Lubbock's selection of his letters (which had involved her, after James's death in 1916, in an argument with the family over who should edit them, and which included many of his letters to her) was published in 1920. This was the first full-length novel she had written for a very long time which would not be read by him. The Age of Innocence gestures towards him, in mixed tribute and parody. Newland Archer (whose name is a composite of Christopher Newman in The American and Isabel Archer in The Portrait of a Lady) is accused by his writer-friend Ned Winsett, because he will have nothing to do with politics, of being like 'the pictures on the walls of a deserted house: "The Portrait of a Gentleman"'. Like the character in the James story 'The Beast in the Jungle', Newland sees himself as 'a man to whom nothing was ever to happen'; and like Catherine Sloper in the last chapter of *Washington Square*, he substitutes for love a life of civic virtue. Ellen Olenska's return to America invokes the Baroness's unsuccessful attempt to make a life for herself in New England in James's 1878 novel *The Europeans*, and her offer to 'come' to Newland once before she leaves is like Kate Croy's offer to Merton Densher in *The Wings of the Dove*. There are tiny echoes of James scattered about, like Ellen coming into a room fastening a bracelet on her wrist, one of the tricks James used to bring a character to life.[13] It is as though Wharton is respectfully and lovingly acknowledging an influence she has always resisted, but is also asking what more there is to say about those nineteenth-century relations between America and Europe. She is rewriting his plot. Where James punished his Europeanised Americans – Mme Merle or Charlotte Stant – by sending them back home, Wharton sends her Europeanisèd heroine back to Paris, and asks what it would mean to stay on in America. Newland Archer feels like a foreigner in his own country, 'a traveller from distant lands'. But his wild idea of running away with Ellen Olenska to Japan remains a fantasy. He stays at home, and at the end of the novel the shutters of the house in Paris are closed to him.[14]

It is not only Newland who lives with a consciousness of cultural altern-atives. So does everyone in the novel. From the opening scenes, New York measures itself against Europe, at the same time that it distrusts it. At the opera, conventions dictate that 'the German text of French operas sung by Swedish artists should be translated into Italian for the clearer under-standing of English-speaking audiences', and the new Opera House is intended to compete with 'those of the great European capitals'. At the Beaufort ball, the house that New Yorkers liked to 'show off to foreigners' is full of Spanish furniture and French paintings, and every fashion detail (*coiffure*, *glacé* gloves, *bouton d'or* drawing room) is French.

Ellen Olenska, back from a life in Europe, shows up the cultural cringe in nineteenth-century New York. 'It seems stupid to have discovered America only to make it into a copy of another country', she says. To Newman's shocked delight, she is constantly deflating the society's pride in its rituals and seeing them as childish and imitative. But Ellen is wrong about New York too: she thinks it is a good, 'safe' place, and does not see what a 'labyrinth' its 'straight up and down' streets can be, what a 'powerful engine' its surveillance system is. By the end of the novel the word 'inno-cence' takes on an ominous ring. Reading America against Europe is complicated. At times the novel does make simple, condescending contrasts: for instance, when a hot summer day in Boston is said to produce a level of shirt-sleeved abandon and untidiness 'to which no excess of heat ever degrades the European cities'. But more often the contrasts feed into the novel's disquieting uncertainty.[15]

Ellen tells Newland more than once that she wants 'to do what you all do', 'to become just like everybody else here'. But whenever she identifies herself with Americans, she pronounces 'we' with 'a faint emphasis that gave it an ironic sound'. It is impossible for her to turn into a 'complete American'. (The only really 'complete American' in the novel is a comic grotesque, Medora's *protégé* Dr Agathon Carver of the Valley of Love Community, a passing satire on the utopian movements of the time, awkwardly dropped in to show the ridiculousness, to Wharton, of an idealised, 'pure' American community.) Ellen is too foreign for a New York which is caught between its self-protective parochialism, and its consciousness of European models. Even Newland, who comes to know and understand her much better than anyone else, identifies her story with what he rather vaguely thinks of as 'complicated old European communities', and feels that the 'tragic possibilities' she suggests to him may be 'a projection of her mysterious and outlandish background'.[16]

The novel analyses American provincialism, mainly through the Archer and Welland families. Their life-styles are sustained against a caricatured version of the 'foreign': outrage at the idea that on a Sunday in New York Ellen might visit a house where there is dancing, smoking and champagne ('I don't suppose, dear, you're really defending the French Sunday?'), derision at the thought that one might go somewhere for the sake of good conversation ('Oh, Newland, how funny! Isn't that *French*?'). At the final dinner where Newland realises that Ellen is being expelled from the tribe, the word 'foreign' rings through the scene: the fact of her 'foreignness' is emphasised by her place at the dinner-table, they are suspected of being lovers 'in the extreme sense peculiar to "foreign" vocabularies', the desperate dinner-party conversation is all about foreign travel, and his parting word to her – his last word ever to her, as it turns out – is 'Paris'.

The New Yorkers' main associations with 'foreign' are writing, sex and Bohemianism (a word which in the 1870s carried connotations of Gypsy life, sexual goings-on in French attics and cafés, revolutionary, free-thinking artists and writers, and unrespectable clothes). Ellen is remembered, as a brilliantly pretty child in New York, dressed by Medora in high colours 'like a gypsy foundling'. It does not help her adult reputation that when she returns, she lives in a 'Bohemian' quarter given over to 'people who wrote', that she chooses whom she talks to and goes around with, that she decorates her house in a strange, exotic foreign manner, wears sexy and unconventional clothes, and wants to find in New York the same kind of 'society of dramatic artists, singers, actors, musicians' that she was used to in Europe. The worst that can be said about her, in the end, is that 'she had become simply "Bohemian"'.[17]

Wharton represents exactly the same attitudes towards writers and artists here (and in *Old New York*) as she attributes to her parents' generation in her memoir. She puts in a writer, Ned Winsett, who has the misfortune to have been 'born into a world that had no need of letters', and so has to be a magazine hack instead of a real writer, and she turns Ellen herself into something of an artist – decorating her house and herself in an original style – doomed to be driven out by this philistine society. Ellen's initial desire to get divorced, and the family's resistance to it, is at the heart of the muddled conflict between American and European conventions (though *The Age of Innocence* is not as much 'about' divorce as the novel set thirty years later, *The Custom of the Country*). Newland warns Ellen that though 'our legislation favours divorce – our social customs don't'. Divorce, in 1870s New York, was thought scandalous – especially for the woman. Yet Europeans viewed divorce as an American habit, as Newland points out to May's mother: 'Countess Olenska thought she would be conforming to American ideas in asking for her freedom.' That, responds Mrs Welland, is 'just like the extraordinary things that foreigners invent about us'.[18]

So an unforgiving account seems to be given of the morality of old New York. It is snobbish, excluding, and punitive. It is sexually hypocritical. It brings its women up as little girls, victims of a 'factitious' 'innocence that seals the mind against imagination and the heart against experience'. It dislikes tragedy, pessimism and savage irony, preferring nice, well-mannered optimism. ('I have to keep my mind bright and happy', says May's mother.) It avoids truth-telling and plain speech at all costs, communicating by 'faint implications and pale delicacies', barricading itself against 'the unpleasant' by means of coded indirection – in what Dallas Archer, a generation on, rudely calls 'a deaf-and-dumb asylum'. Newland and May never discuss his feelings for Ellen, though he tries to, and he never knows, until long after May's death, what she knew – though it is apparent all through to the reader that May, too, is struggling with the situation, and her unspoken story presses on the narrative (like Zenobia's version in *Ethan Frome*). One of the most powerful moments in the novel is when May's 'mute message' about Newland and Ellen, expressed entirely in code, is spelt out as if she has spoken aloud. But it never is spoken.[19]

Better by far, it would seem, for someone like Ellen Olenska (and someone like Edith Wharton) to leave this stifling environment, and make a life for herself alone in Paris. All the same, there is something wrong with Europe, and it has to do with decency. New York's 'old-fashioned Episcopalian' rituals seem stuffy and prim, but set against the hedonism and worldliness of an old European Catholic aristocracy, New World puritanism comes into its own. Everything dark and unpleasant about Europe is embodied in the powerful offstage figure of Count Olenski, and the shocking, if short, letter he writes to his wife, which Newland reads in the lawyer's office. With as much reticence as her old New Yorkers, Wharton never gives us the contents of the count's letter, or any details about Ellen's horrible life with him, but it is referred to several times, and it makes both Newland and Ellen blush even to think about it. It stands for everything that she should not have to go back to. It is the secretary, once an employee of the count's, who spells this out to Newland, explaining that the count's behaviour made Ellen feel like – an American: 'And if you're an American of *her* kind – of your kind – things that are accepted in certain other societies, or at least put up with as part of general convenient give-and-take – become unthinkable, simply unthinkable.' Newland listens to this speech in his office, standing under a calendar-portrait of the President of the United States (probably the Civil War hero Ulysses Grant, re-elected in 1872). The collision of the virtual president and the virtual count seems extremely strange to Newland, as it does to us. And it points towards the novel's equally surprising political coda, where Newland, having renounced the 'flower of life', is consoled by a mid-life friendship with Theodore Roosevelt (when he was governor of New York) and a brief foray into political life.[20]

Though Wharton does not give specific dates, Roosevelt's tenure as governor was from 1899 to 1900, and his irruption into the novel ('banging his clenched fist on the table and gnashing his eye-glasses') shows us how she thinks the ruling classes in America have changed since the 1870s. Newland is a 'decent' man: Ellen Olenska falls in love with him because of his decency, his integrity and sensitivity. But he was brought up to think that gentlemen should play no part in politics; as Ned Winsett tells him, he won't 'roll up his sleeves and get down in the muck'. Roosevelt encourages his sort – decent, intelligent members of the upper class – to get involved, and though Newland's career does not amount to much – a stint in the State Assembly, a commitment to municipal work, respect as a 'good citizen' – it represents what Wharton saw as a shift from the inertia of her parents' generation, who practised their professions, if at all, in 'a leisurely manner', and who always took 'the line of least resistance'.[21] An admiring emulation of Theodore Roosevelt seems a poor consolation prize for having missed 'the flower of life' with Ellen Olenska. But Newland's political career makes sense if *The Age of Innocence* is read as a post-war novel about the dangers of American isolationism. Roosevelt's post-presidential wartime position, passionately and publicly endorsed by Wharton, was fiercely anti-isolationist. The whole novel has exposed the damaging limitations of an inward-looking, defensive and parochial American history, which Newland's love for Ellen made him struggle to reach beyond.

Yet the decency of Newland's life, summed up in the last chapter, is meant to make us feel that there was something good in the 'old-fashioned' ways, after all. The new generation, embodied in Dallas Archer and Fanny Beaufort, is thoroughly international, thinking nothing of 'nipping across' the Atlantic on a fast liner to check out some Italian villa-gardens (as models for a young millionaire's Chicago palace) or pick up the scores of 'the last Debussy songs'. They don't have time for guilt, reticence, or delicate strategies of exclusion; they are too busy with their own passing 'fads and fetishes'. At the end, Newland's renunciation is seen to have been what conserved his decency. The shift is marked in her use of the word 'dignity'. What was thought 'dignified' or 'undignified' – as with the etiquette for honeymooning abroad in the 1870s – has been in ironical quote-marks until the end of the novel, when 'the dignity of a duty' sums up, without irony, the value of Newland's marriage.[22]

Wharton told Berenson that she wanted the novel to be read not as a 'costume piece' 'but as a "simple & grave" story of two people trying to live up to something that was still "felt in the blood" at that time'. All the same, it is extremely hard – as hard as it is with *Summer* – to read *The Age of Innocence* as a novel with a happy ending. This is a highly theatrical work, poised between comedy and tragedy. In addition to the scenes set at the opera or the theatre, it is full of public spectacles (the ball, the wedding, the archery contest) and stagy moments, like Ellen's outburst of temper ('She flung her velvet opera cloak over the maid's shoulders and turned back into the drawing room, shutting the door sharply. Her bosom was rising high under its lace, and for a moment Archer thought she was about to cry; but she burst into a laugh instead . . .') or the culminating scene of renunciation between the lovers: '"Don't – don't be unhappy," she said, with a break in her voice, as she drew her hands away; and he answered: "You won't go back – you won't go back?"' Ellen is a tragic heroine inside a comedy of manners. But what dominates the novel, increasingly, is a feeling of profound desolation. The succession of scenes in which Ellen and Newland fall in love, realise it to be impossible, choose renunciation, find they cannot bear to be apart, but understand that they must be divided, are some of the most poignant dialogues Wharton ever wrote. Even in their first private conversation, Ellen weeps, and Newland tries to console her;

by the end of their relationship, he feels his own tears frozen on his cheeks. The repression of emotion produces a terrible sense of unreality; Newland's 'real' life passes before him (as at his wedding) like a hallucination. The domestic becomes unfamiliar to him, the 'homelike' becomes fearful and 'uncanny'. And the uncanny is closely related to the ghostly and the haunted.[23]

The characters in *The Age of Innocence*, whose story took place so long ago, are the living dead. The old forms – and the old ladies – of the leading families, like the Van der Luydens, seem 'gruesomely preserved', like bodies in glaciers keeping a 'rosy life-in-death'. The 'innocent' New Yorkers, busy with their sports and pastimes, seem like 'children playing in a graveyard'. Ellen and Newland haunt each other like figures in 'a line of ghosts'. 'Her life is finished', Mrs Mingott says of her, coldly, as though 'throwing earth into the grave of young hopes', and Newland's heart grows 'chill'. The truths that have to be spoken between them turn them to stone, like victims of the Gorgon. In their love-scene in the carriage in the snow, they pass 'an empty hearse', and Newland kisses the palm of her hand as if it is 'a relic'. He returns to the 'real' world as if 'from the other side of the grave'.[24]

This spectral quality – at its most violent (and psychologically acute) when Newland, with May, thinks of himself as dead and wishes her dead – reaches its climax in a haunting scene set in the 'new' museum. Though so careful, on the whole, with her historical authenticity, Wharton allows a destabilising anomaly in here. She has her thwarted lovers finding a secluded place to meet in the 'queer wilderness' of the newly built, unfinished Metropolitan Museum of Art 'in the Park' – though it was not opened until 1880. They choose the 'unvisited' and 'melancholy' rooms of the Cesnola Collection, a hoard of classical antiquities in which Wharton includes some 'recovered fragments of Ilium'. Cesnola's great collection of tomb objects from Cyprus, in what is now the medieval sculpture hall of the Met, was in fact a great draw when the museum opened. But it provides a fine example for Wharton of civilisations passing and succeeding each other, since the collection goes from the late Bronze Age through the successive arrivals in Cyprus of a great many 'foreigners': Phoenicians, Assyrians, Egyptians, Persians and Greeks, even, legend has it, the heroes from the Trojan war, passing through on their way home. And the artefacts, many very tiny, like her details of New York in the 1870s, illuminate every detail of these long-ago lives: things like coins, amphorae, spindle whorls, flasks, pestles, lids and tripods, little boxes for needles or other small objects. As they contemplate these relics of vanished civilisations, they think both forward and backward in time. Newland imagines, wistfully, that 'some day' this will be a great museum; Ellen sadly contemplates the 'small broken objects' from the past:

> 'It seems cruel,' she said, 'that after a while nothing matters . . . any more than these little things, that used to be necessary and important to forgotten people, and now have to be guessed at under a magnifying glass and labelled "Use unknown."'[25]

'Use unknown' is the key phrase for Newland Archer and his world. Long, long after, returning to the Metropolitan at its height of fashionable popularity, he will remember this scene in 'the old Cesnola rooms', and see in his mind's eye 'a slight figure' moving away from him 'down the meagrely-fitted vista of the old Museum'. The scene is at the heart of the melancholy of *The Age of Innocence*, which is different in tone from the vivid, full-blooded, high-powered dramas of *The House of Mirth* or *The Custom of the Country*. Now the weight of the war pushes down on Wharton's writing; the wiping-out of an entire civilisation is all too possible, and the whole world seems full of ghosts.

The most troubling subject in *The Age of Innocence* is sex. It is talked round, and unconsummated. (Archer's and May's conception of three children takes place safely and uninterestingly offstage.) But the novel is charged with sexual feeling. Ellen is an erotic creature, even though she sublimates her love for Newland into a self-sacrificial renunciation ('I can't love you unless I give you up'). Her sexual history is mysterious, but her looks spell sexual experience – unlike May's, which are repeatedly described, especially when she wins the archery tournament, as virginal or boyish, like the chaste huntress Diana. By contrast, Ellen's low-cut 'Josephine'-style dress at the opera, exposing her bosom, her fur-lined red velvet sheath with her bare arms, make Newland blush: he finds her style 'perverse and provocative'. And Ellen is seductive with him (though Wharton plays this down) whenever they meet, setting a tone of intimacy. Newland's physical contacts with her express a painful, stifled desire, almost fetishistic in its intensity. He kneels down and kisses her satin shoe, he unbuttons her glove and kisses her palm, he is fixated on her thin hands with their three rings. In a brilliantly disconcerting moment, the sensual, knowing old Mrs Mingott, whose fat little hands 'nestled in a hollow of her huge lap like pet animals', laughs at him when he kisses one of them with fervour, after she has promised to support Ellen: 'Eh – eh – eh! Whose hand did you think you were kissing, young man – your wife's, I hope?'[26]

Mrs Mingott, with her Parisian experiences and her cynical hedonism, is one of the few outspoken characters in this society of sexual hypocrisy.

Newland fantasises an escape with Ellen to some far country where there would be no such 'categories' as 'mistress', but Ellen knows that there is no alternative world. She spells this out for him in her most bitter and eloquent speech: 'Oh, my dear – where is that country? Have you ever been there? . . . I know so many who've tried to find it; and, believe me, they all got out by mistake at wayside stations: at places like Boulogne, or Pisa, or Monte Carlo – and it wasn't at all different from the old world they'd left, but only rather smaller and dingier and more promiscuous.'[27]

Wharton is preoccupied by the idea that there is no escape, in place or time, for the person (especially the woman) who has been stigmatised. She has written before, in stories such as 'Souls Belated' or 'Autres Temps . . .', about adulterous lovers in Europe who find the social conventions of America catching up with them, or about the disgraced woman who finds, returning to New York a generation on, that she is still the target of disapproving ostracism. She will return to this theme again in the *Old New York* story 'New Year's Day' and in *The Mother's Recompense*. Her alternative plans for *The Age of Innocence* show her trying out different versions of this obsessive story. In one draft-plan, Archer falls in love with Ellen, breaks off his engagement to May, but is deeply shocked when Ellen suggests they try out living together before they are married and thinks that she is tainted by 'European corruption'. (This theme of the 'trial marriage' would be used instead in *Glimpses of the Moon*.) So they marry, but she realises she is going to be bored: 'for the next 30 or 40 years they are going to live in Madison Ave in winter & on the Hudson in the spring and autumn, with a few weeks of Europe or Newport every summer', and 'her whole soul recoils'. She has eaten 'the pomegranate seed' of another kind of life in Europe, and goes back there. 'She is very poor, & very lonely, but she has a real life.' May marries someone else, and Archer, who has agreed to a separation from Ellen, occasionally calls on her, becomes more and more involved in business, 'and nothing ever happens to him again'. In another draft-plan, the return of 'Clementina' Olenska to New York, escaping from her husband who is a 'charming gambler, drug-taker and debauché', the marriage of 'Newland Langdon' and May, and Newland's falling in love, proceed as in the novel, but in this version, after Newland has got married and May is pregnant, the lovers have an affair (in Florida). Wharton notes: 'Contrast between bridal night with May & *this* one . . .' But they find that she cannot live without 'Europe & emotion', nor he without 'New York & respectability'. She returns to Europe after a farewell dinner given by May at which 'all of Old New York is present'. A third and even fuller version, which Wharton heads 'the scene is laid in 1875', adds a few more details:

the lovers' 'few mad weeks' together, Ellen's inability to divorce because she and her husband are Catholics, her growing exasperation with Newland's 'scruples'.[28]

In the end, Wharton chose unfulfilment for her lovers. That is what life is like, she tells us. Perhaps we are even meant to feel that there is some value for the soul in not getting what you want. Perhaps, too, in the intensity of 'old-fashioned' thwarted love, as compared with the relative freedom of modern sexuality, there may be more passion and depth. By 'current valuation', a love-scene in which 'he had not so much touched [her] hand with his lips' would be judged a failure; but Newland will come to wonder, looking at the next generation's emotional arrangements, whether 'the thing one's so certain of in advance' can 'ever make one's heart beat as wildly'. But this faint argument in favour of frustration and renunciation is outweighed by the novel's haunting atmosphere of loss and grief.[29]

Wharton was thinking a great deal about sexuality and how to write about it in these years, when she was feeling her age and setting up a permanent way of life on her own. *Summer*, published three years before *The Age of Innocence*, was one of her most erotic books, and one of her most troubling treatments of a sexual mismatch. *In Morocco*, reworked while *The Age of Innocence* was being serialised, and published in the same month as the novel, showed her fascination and horror at the sexual submission of the women in the harem. 'Beatrice Palmato' is an unfinished exercise in writing about the most prohibited and shameful of sexual acts – a father making love to his willing daughter – in the most graphic and shame-free terms that Wharton was capable of. (The moral of which might be that reticence has its stylistic advantages.) It seems fairly certain (as Cynthia Griffin Wolff argued when she found the fragment in Wharton's papers at Yale, in time for Lewis to include it as an appendix to his biography in 1975) that Wharton drafted her plan for the story and wrote the short section of it between 1918 and 1919, though the evidence is arguable. Lewis maintains, not so convincingly, that 'Beatrice Palmato' dates from the mid-1930s. His evidence is Wharton's reference, in a letter to Berenson of 1935, in an exchange about Moravia, Faulkner and Céline's respective 'nastiness', to having 'an incest *donnée* up my sleeve that wd make them all look like nursery-rhymes – but business is too bad to sell such Berquinades nowadays' (the term, after an eighteenth-century writer called Berquin, means a 'puerile or insipid piece of literature'). But 'Beatrice Palmato' could have been written long before this letter – and Wharton might also have been thinking of another, later, fragment in a notebook of 1924–8, called 'Cold

Green-House', in which two old maids whisper about their dead stepmother's sexual relationship with their brother. As an exercise in erotic
writing, 'Beatrice Palmato' seems more likely to have come from Wharton's
late fifties, when she was writing so much about sexuality, than her early
seventies.

The fragments and the plan of the story in Wharton's papers are undated.
But a notebook which has the title 'Subjects & Notes 1918–1923' has, at
the back, a 'Table of Contents', which lists 'Beatrice Palmato' with *A Son
at the Front*, *The Age of Innocence*, and some of the *Old New York* stories.
Earlier in the notebook is a page with three lines, two of them scored out.
They are, one under the other:

~~Begun 1919~~

~~The Age of Innocence~~

Beatrice Palmato

A separate notebook contains a 'Plot Summary' for 'Beatrice Palmato',
under the heading 'Powers of Darkness: Vol. Of Short Stories. I.: Beatrice
Palmato', and a couple of pages of the story, under the wry title
'Unpublishable Fragment'.

The name Beatrice invokes Beatrice Cenci, the heroine of Shelley's
verse-drama *The Cenci*, much admired by Wharton, which was inspired by
Guido Reni's portrait of Beatrice and by the true story of the Renaissance
Cenci family. Beatrice was executed for conspiring to murder her father,
the tyrannical Count Cenci, who had raped her and her sister, but whose
crimes she will not speak of openly at her trial. Wharton's own plot is of
an exotically Oriental 'rich half-Levantine, half-Portuguese banker', Mr
Palmato, with an English wife, whose eldest daughter mysteriously commits
suicide at seventeen. The mother has a breakdown, and the younger
daughter, Beatrice, is left alone, at twelve, with her father. There is also a
sensible son, away at school. The mother tries to kill herself and dies in
an 'insane asylum', the father marries the governess, and Beatrice continues
to live with them till she marries a dull young man, at eighteen. She sees
her father occasionally after her marriage, and when she does her moods
fluctuate from depressed to 'febrile and restless'. But she settles into married
life and has two children, a boy and a girl. Her father dies. Beatrice's husband
is very fond of the little girl, and Beatrice becomes irrationally and 'morbidly'
jealous of their relationship. Coming upon her husband giving the little
girl a kiss, she screams at him to put the child down, and then realises she
has given herself away. 'As the husband looks at her, many mysterious things
in their married life – the sense of some hidden power controlling her, and

perpetually coming between them, and of some strange initiation, some profound moral perversion of which he had always been afraid to face the thought – all these things become suddenly clear to him, lit up in a glare of horror.' Beatrice rushes upstairs and shoots herself; the brother comes to see the widowed husband 'and they have a long talk – about Mr Palmato'.

The 'Unpublishable Fragment', heavily corrected in pencil, describes Mr Palmato making love to his highly aroused daughter. It is made clear that they have already had a prolonged sexual relationship, consisting of fellatio and cunnilingus, always in the dark, but that he has patiently waited until she has been married (a 'dull misery' to her) and lost her virginity, so that they can make love completely, and in the light. All Wharton's pencil corrections in the manuscript, adding 'as of old' and 'again' to the proceedings, emphasise how long they have been almost-lovers. A contrast is drawn between Beatrice's wedding-night with her husband, 'last week', and the joys to come: 'That experience is a cruel one – but it has to come once in all women's lives', her father tells her. 'Now we shall reap its fruit.' In a luxurious, exotic setting (bearskin rug, velvet cushions, pink-shaded lamps), Mr Palmato plunges his tongue through her 'burning lips' 'into the depths of her mouth', licking and sucking and fondling her breasts in his 'warm palms', undresses her, rubs 'the secret bud of her body' in a circular touch with his 'subtle forefinger' ('subtle' was an afterthought) so that she feels 'the old swooning sweetness creeping over her', tongues her 'quivering invisible bud' so that she cries out and 'flings her legs apart', pushes his 'strong fiery muscle that they used, in their old joke, to call his third hand' into her hand, calls her 'my little girl', encourages her to 'caress it with her tongue', even more exciting to her now that she can see it, so that she sucks on it more and more deeply, 'till at length the member, thrusting her lips open, held her gasping, as if at its mercy', and finally 'plunges' it 'into the deepest depths of her thirsting body'. In the last line of the fragment, he whispers: 'Was it . . . like this . . . last week?' Her reply, crossed out in the manuscript, is: 'Oh . . .'[30]

When this fragment was published in 1975 in Lewis's biography, along with 'Terminus', but well before the publication of the letters to Fullerton in 1988, it caused a great stir. It seemed to be startlingly out of character with what had been thought of, up to then, as the ladylike, grande-dame Wharton style, and with the indirections and euphemisms about sex which magazine editors and respectable publishers like Appleton and Macmillan's required of their authors well into the 1930s. Wharton's biographers avoided, for lack of evidence, making any direct link to childhood abuse. Lewis, dating 'Beatrice Palmato' late, suggested that in old age Wharton could confront and 'give fantasy form' to 'the strong physical attraction she had once felt for her own father'. He described it as a literary exercise in 'elegant pornography', and said that its eroticism drew on Wharton's 'vividly remembered personal experience' with Fullerton. Cynthia Griffin Wolff, putting Wharton on the analyst's couch, diagnosed 'Beatrice Palmato' as her expression of a 'flaming, consuming love for her father', long repressed. Benstock argued carefully that the 'passionate eroticism' of the fragment 'seemed to undercut the likelihood that it was composed by an incest survivor', but agreed with Lewis that Wharton must have, as she put it, 'experienced her own body in similar ways'. Other critics (especially in the early 1990s, when childhood sexual abuse and recovered memory were much under discussion) took 'Beatrice Palmato' as the 'clue to the traumatic experience that wrecked her life'. 'Beatrice Palmato' was linked to *Summer* as 'autobiographical'; both works, it was argued, pointed to her childhood experience of 'incestuous stimulation', which had led to lifelong guilt, and to an 'astonishing repression of all sexual knowledge'. Wharton, it was asserted, was 'probably an incest-victim in early childhood'. A link was noted between Mr Palmato's third hand and Wharton's early memory of holding her father's hand. The real story of Wharton's sexual life, it was suggested, was that Teddy was a closet homosexual who had an affair with one of her brothers; she may have been abused by the brothers as well as by her father. The incest theme was noted again – rightly – in *The Mother's Recompense*, where Beatrice Cenci makes another ominous appearance; Wharton herself commented (to John Hugh Smith) on her interest in 'the incest-element' in that novel. That incest-element between mother and daughter has been attributed to Wharton's lifelong unresolved attachment to her father and her need for affection, stemming from her hostile relationship with her mother and her deprivation as a childless woman. Some critics have politicised the theme of incest in Wharton's work, reading it as part of her critique of 'the condition of American sex' or of her indictment of patriarchal oppression. 'Beatrice Palmato' has also been seen as evidence of Wharton's racism, in its fantasy of a 'degrading sexual assault' coming from 'a race different from Wharton's own'.[31]

Certainly 'Beatrice Palmato', a lush and dated piece of writing, is an experiment in taboo-breaking, an exercise in writing sexual fantasy, like writing 'Terminus' as a modern free-verse erotic love-poem. She was, partly, trying to be more French – after all, Gide, Cocteau, and Colette (whom she was reading with enthusiasm in the early 1920s) were much more sexually candid and exhibitionist than she ever allowed herself to be in print. Why not try it, too? The fragment, with its sensational surrounding plot, is no more directly autobiographical than Lily Bart's story, or Charity's, or Undine's. But it is loaded with what obsessed her: double lives, repression, sexual hypocrisy, hidden longings. Sexual pleasure – so rarely felt by Wharton's characters – is set about here, as always, with prohibitions, shame and secrecy.

And, though more explicit, 'Beatrice Palmato' fits with much else that she was writing at the time. It even overlaps with the draft plan of *The Age of Innocence* which, like 'Beatrice Palmato', planned to compare a dutiful wedding night with a wild night of desire. Among the other draft plans in the notebook containing the 'Table of Contents' which lists 'Beatrice Palmato' are a story called 'The Family' about suicide, adultery and divorce all going on in one household (which she notes to herself she cannot use because people would say that such 'unpleasant' things could never happen in one family); and a story set in an upmarket brothel in the Philippines, in which the man discovers from the prostitute that his wife is having an affair with a friend whose name he has used as an alibi in the brothel. In *Old New York*, set in the 'age of innocence', there is one story ('New Year's Day') about a woman who prostitutes herself for the sake of the money she needed for her husband's medical care, whose lover thinks it 'indecent' of her to speak the words 'mistress' and 'prostitute' even though she has roused his 'primitive instincts', and who is never forgiven for her sins. Another, 'The Old Maid', set in the 1850s, is about an unmarried woman, Charlotte Lovell, whose secret illegitimate child is being brought up by her married cousin, and the bitter rivalry which grows up over the child between the two women. The polite world seems to the married woman, Delia Ralston, like 'a prison she must break out of'; there is great anxiety about 'disease' being implanted in the race and 'blood' being stained by illegitimacy; and there is a grimly suggestive account of the wedding-night of the average young woman of the time ('the startled puzzled surrender' as in 'a fiery pit scorching the brow of innocence', followed by 'a week or a month of flushed distress, confusion, embarrassed pleasure' and gradually 'the growth of habit'). The 'years of silence and evasiveness' between the cousins rear up to the surface 'like a corpse too hastily buried', and the effect of secrets and sexual hypocrisy is seen to poison their relationship. Other stories of the 1920s hint at half-revealed taboos. 'A Bottle of Perrier' (1926) is a North African desert story of a 'queer' Englishman who has been living alone with his cockney servant and whose fate is shrouded in 'guilty darkness'. In 'Bewitched', a darkly suggestive return to the grim, snowy New England of *Ethan Frome*, a dead girl has been (supposedly) haunting the village and tempting one of the married villagers. Her forbidding father (named Brand, out of Hawthorne) is bringing up her sister on his own. He and the other villagers, a gloomy, small-minded bunch, set out to track the 'ghost', and Brand shoots at it. A few days later, the living sister dies. If the true, hidden story here is of repeated incest, with the two sisters as Brand's victims, Brand is not telling: 'Brand's face was the closed door of a vault, barred with wrinkles like bands of iron.' Clearly Wharton is extremely preoccupied, at this time – in 'Beatrice Palmato' and other works – with how to write about the truths of female sexuality, the cruelty that is in marriage, and taboo subjects like incest, homosexuality, prostitution, adultery, the horrors of repression, and the baleful effects of silencing.[32]

All the more ironic, then (she thought), that in 1921 *The Age of Innocence* should be awarded the $1,000 Pulitzer Prize for Fiction, given by Columbia University, which since 1917 had gone annually to the novel of the year 'which shall best present the wholesome atmosphere of American life and the highest standard of American manners and manhood'. She was the first woman to win it for fiction. The other awards had the same high tone. The best play was supposed to show how the stage could 'raise the standard of good morals, good taste and good manners'. This year it went to Zona Gale for *Miss Lulu Bett*, a sharp, idiosyncratic realist drama set in a small south-western town about the escape of an oppressed unmarried sister from her unpleasantly tyrannical family. The author would become a friendly and admiring correspondent of Wharton's in the 1920s. (It was a double win for Appleton; this cannot have been a happy day for Scribner's.) The best American biography was supposed to teach 'patriotic and unselfish services to the people', and the best journalism prize had to be for 'the accomplishment of some public good commanding public attention and respect'. The prize was funded by Joseph Pulitzer at the same time as the founding of the Columbia School of Journalism; in the terms of the prize he had required that the winning novel should give 'the whole atmosphere of American life'. The redoubtable and reactionary President of Columbia, Nicholas Murray Butler, changed the wording from 'whole' to 'wholesome'. (In 1927, after Sinclair Lewis turned down the prize, it reverted to 'whole', and the terms were later abolished altogether.) A jury of three, chosen from the American Academy of Arts and Letters and the National Institute of Arts and Letters, made their recommendation to an anonymous advisory board of eminent (male) journalists, under the supervision of President Butler. These high-minded proceedings were attended by the usual squabbles that accompany literary prizes. The literary jury, the novelist Hamlin Garland, and academics and journalists Stuart Pratt Sherman and Robert Morss Lovett, recommended Sinclair Lewis's controversial and forcefully satirical *Main Street* to the advisory board, who turned it down (apparently because of pressure from the conservative Butler) in favour of *The Age of Innocence*. Sherman and Lovett wrote in outrage to the *New Republic*, not dispraising Wharton but protesting at what had happened.

There was some publicity, to which Wharton reacted with shrugging despair: 'What a country!' she wrote to Minnie, as she often would write from now on: all this, she thought, had nothing to do with 'literary merit'. Lewis, though furious with the prize-givers (he would call it the '*Main Street* burglary'), wrote a generous letter to Wharton, who replied with friendly and equally generous words, saying that she was in despair when she found out that the prize should have gone to him. She told him how much she admired his book, one of the few things to have come out of America recently 'that have made me cease to despair of the republic – of letters', and said how comforting it was to find that she was not regarded entirely by 'les jeunes' as 'the Mrs Humphry Ward of the Western Hemisphere'. It was a theme she would frequently return to in the 1920s. A tentative friendship grew up between them, and he dedicated *Babbitt* to her in 1923 (which was also beaten to the prize by a great woman writer, Willa Cather, though not for her best book: it was her war-novel, *One of Ours*). Wharton would win the prize by proxy, again, in 1935, when Zoë Akins's adaptation of *The Old Maid* (though disliked by the critics, who preferred Lillian Hellman's *The Children's Hour*) won the drama prize. By that time, Wharton had made mock of the Pulitzer as the 'Pulsifer Prize', 'with its half-confessed background of wire-pulling and influencing', part of her satire on the whole state of the contemporary American literary market-place in *Hudson River Bracketed*.[33]

The prize had a paradoxical effect on her literary standing at the start of the 1920s. The move to Appleton in 1919 meant that she was now with a firm which, though a solid conservative establishment, would market her more aggressively than Scribner's had. The advertisement Appleton ran for *The Age of Innocence*, with its titillating (if not exactly appropriate) headline, 'WAS SHE JUSTIFIED IN SEEKING A DIVORCE?', and its lurid plot-summary ('Why was this American girl forced to leave her brutal Polish husband? . . . shall she create a scandal just because she is unhappy?') marketed the book both for scandalous subject-matter and as an escapist wallow in a vanished era: 'All the glamor of the society life of the original Four Hundred is the background for this story . . . the intimate amusements of the society leaders of the day.' Wharton's status as 'America's Greatest Woman Novelist', capable of presenting 'living human beings against the

keen pictures of society', and her authorship of *The House of Mirth*, were loudly flagged. She made no objection any more (as she had in 1905 to Scribner's presenting *The House of Mirth* as an exposé of New York society) to this kind of advertising – after all, her reasons for changing publishers were to ensure big advances, competitive marketing and high sales.

She established a new kind of professional relationship with Rutger Bleecker Jewett, the vice-president and editor-in-chief at Appleton from 1911 to 1935. For the next fifteen years, he would negotiate and fix prices for her magazine serialisations (the kind of thing she had asked Fullerton or Berry to help her with in past years) as well as dealing with the advances on and the promotion of her books. Wharton and Jewett did not develop a close friendship, but he came from the same kind of upper-class New York background as she did, and they got on well, mainly by letter. He was a gentleman-publisher, like William Brownell or Edward Burlingame, who appreciated her kind of work, and who was liked by his authors for 'idealizing and serving with enthusiastic devotion those with whom he came in contact'. (Eventually, when she was suffering badly from the recession of the mid-1930s, she came to think of him as not nearly forceful enough, and at long last acquired an independent agent.) But he had good contacts with the magazine world and was able, at least in the 1920s, to get her some very lucrative contracts, while maintaining in his letters to her a suitably ironic attitude to the absurdities of the literary market-place. Jewett's tone – which did not always endear him to the hard-headed popular magazine editors he dealt with on Wharton's behalf – can be heard in a letter of 1921 to the theatrical agent Elizabeth Marbury about casting *The Age of Innocence*:

> I am so used to seeing dramatic productions in which the descendant of a thousand earls is played by some hopeless little Jewess from the lower East Side, or where people of education and traditions are portrayed by a group of bounders who have hired dress suits to wear them for the first time in their lives.[34]

Wharton had started to command large sums for serialisations and magazine publication during the war – a fee of $7,000 from McClure's, for instance, for the serialisation of *Summer* in 1917. *The Age of Innocence* placed her firmly back at the best-selling level of *The House of Mirth*. It was serialised in the *Pictorial Review*, starting in July 1920, for a payment of $18,000, and was published as a book on 10 October 1920, quickly earning back its advance of $15,000, selling 66,000 copies by April 1921 and 115,000 copies in its first year, and earning Wharton $50,000 within two years of publication.

That sum included a contract for a silent movie of the novel, with Warner Brothers, for $9,000: at which point Wharton became aware that 'fillums' of her books could become a good source of income. She did not want to be in any way involved with them, and was not an enthusiast for the new cinema, but she could see that her novels were promising material for the movies: 'I have always thought "The Age" would make a splendid film if done by someone with brains – & education!' she wrote to Minnie in 1926, when Edward Sheldon, whom she liked and admired, was expressing an interest in writing a screenplay. (After the Warner Brothers' silent film of *The Age of Innocence* in 1924 there was talk in 1933 of another film version, possibly starring, Wharton was told, someone called Katharine Hepburn, whom she had heard was 'a Hartford lady and a fine actress'. But this came to nothing, and *The Age of Innocence* had to wait until 1993 for Martin Scorsese.) So that she would not have to be involved in the business of adaptations in America, she appointed Minnie, in February 1921, her representative in 'theatrical and cinematographic matters', with legal power to sign contracts and deal with all such matters. (This document was signed at Hyères and witnessed by 'Robert D Norton'.) *The House of Mirth* had been filmed by Metro in 1918; there was talk of a film of *Ethan Frome* in 1920 with Lionel Barrymore; the silent film rights of *The Glimpses of the Moon* were sold for $15,000 to Paramount in 1922, with uncredited titles written by the young Scott Fitzgerald (mostly unused, but he was paid $500). The Warner Brothers silent film of *The Age of Innocence* was followed by a talking film of *The Children*, called *The Marriage Playground*, sold for $25,000, with Fredric March in the lead. There were later screen adaptations, in and just after her lifetime, of her comic story 'Bread Upon the Waters' (as *Strange Wives*, in 1935, made by Universal) and of *The Old Maid*, in 1939, in a Warner Brothers movie with Bette Davis as Charlotte Lovell, the woman who gives up her illegitimate child to her cousin and becomes embittered and jealous. That film was based on the Pulitzer Prize-winning 1935 Zoë Akins theatrical adaptation of *The Old Maid* ('too delicate for our barbarous press', Edith noted, after bad reviews). She was more involved in her theatrical adaptations than in the films of her books, following with interest (as she had the doomed Clyde Fitch adaptation of *The House of Mirth* in 1906, which she felt failed because of the tragic ending) the much more successful 1928 dramatisation by Margaret Ayer Barnes and Sheldon of *The Age of Innocence*, and the stage-play of *Ethan Frome* in 1936, with Raymond Massey as Ethan and Ruth Gordon as Mattie.

Royalties on these dramatisations (half of 15 per cent from Scribner's on the play of *Ethan Frome*) and box-office returns (5 per cent going up to 10 per cent on *The Old Maid*) were a matter of concern to her in the 1930s.[35]

In the early 1920s there were no such financial anxieties. Jumping at the opportunity to publish one more of her novels, *A Son at the Front*, Charles Scribner offered $15,000 for the serialisation and a $15,000 advance for the book in 1921. But he warned her in 1923 that, although they were printing 80,000 copies, 'it will probably not prove to be what is known as a best seller. What we feared . . . at the outset applies now. Readers who wish something merely entertaining are a little afraid that the book may be too serious or too sad.' Sales were poor, and did not pick up: in the last six months of 1925, for instance, *A Son at the Front* sold 15 copies, as compared with *Ethan Frome* (1,151) or *The House of Mirth* (264); in the first six months of 1926 *A Son at the Front* sold 19 copies while *Ethan Frome* sold 888. But with the other novels of the 1920s, published by Appleton, there were no problems with sales: *The Glimpses of the Moon*, a light, 'modern' romance, published in 1922, a year after *The Age of Innocence* had won the Pulitzer Prize, had a serialisation contract for $18,000, and sold 60,000 copies in three weeks. This level of income kept up till almost the end of the decade: looking ahead to her fortunes in 1928, the year in which she earned the most money in her life, *The Children* (now little-read), earned her over $95,000 in Book-of-the-Month Club sales, serial and film rights; the stage-play of *The Age of Innocence* made her $15,000 from box-office receipts by the end of its New York run, and she was offered $25,000 for her memoir.[36]

The disadvantage of such a high profile and such big sales was that she was expected to provide a certain sort of book. (The editor of *Cosmopolitan* magazine had written to the head of Appleton, Joseph Sears, in December 1916: 'Considering the hint of increasing output . . . in the present activities of Edith Wharton, what would you think of a joint proposal to her for book and serial rights on the *next* full length novel . . . provided that she is agreeable again to an American setting and to world-wise characters?') At the same time, after the Pulitzer, she was having increasing difficulties with the concept of 'wholesomeness'. If she was going to be offered very large sums by magazine editors, she was going to have to submit, at least to some extent, to their demands. And these demands often seemed to her both timid and simplistic. Jewett had difficulty placing 'The Old Maid', and Wharton told the Berensons that the story (which she had read aloud to them as work-in-progress) was being turned down by a leading magazine, just as she was awarded the Pulitzer, because 'its readers can't be told about illegitimate children'. ('*Textual*', she added, in their code for eyebrow-raising realities.) Jewett told her that the *Ladies' Home Journal* thought it 'a bit too vigorous for us', 'powerful but unpleasant'. She responded scornfully: 'I despair of ever understanding the point of view of the American public.' Hadn't they read *The Scarlet Letter*, she added, or *Adam Bede*, or her own *Summer*? In 1922 Jewett sent her a list of the magazines where she might hope to place 'New Year's Day', the prostitution story. The *Ladies' Home Journal*, as she already knew, would never take anything 'that deals too frankly with the sex problem'; the *Delineator* was almost 'as restricted'; by contrast the *Woman's Home Companion* was 'not afraid of sex when handled in a serious way, especially if some moral lesson is included'. The editor of the *Red Book Magazine*, Karl Harriman, who had taken 'The Old Maid', was very much hoping that the next story would be 'less strong'. 'He made a contract with his readers that they could place the *Red Book* . . . on the round center table under the library lamp, to be enjoyed by the whole family . . . If a story is too frank, it means letters of protest and loss of subscribers.' A 1929 letter sent to 'Miss Wharton' from *The People's Popular Monthly* in Des Moines, Iowa, offering her $10,000 for a serial, stated as its 'only requirement' 'that the story must be clean, wholesome, and happy and must have a great deal of human interest. It must be a story that will appeal to real home folks and the love theme should be quite prominent . . . We will not print any story that is morbid in any way.' This insistence on wholesomeness played into her treatment of America in the 1920s, and in *Hudson River Bracketed* she satirised the whole publishing ethos, as when the young writer Vance is urged by a celebrated Western authoress to 'come straight back West, where he belonged, and write pure manly stories about young fellows prospecting in the Yukon, or that sort of thing, because the big reading public was fed up with descriptions of corrupt society people'.[37]

Vance's name, in her novel about the corrupting American literary industry, may have been a sarcastic private allusion to the editor of the *Pictorial Review*, Arthur Vance, who felt that his big expenditure on Mrs Wharton entitled him to some control over what she gave them next. (The magazine would serialise her next three novels, *The Mother's Recompense*, *Twilight Sleep* and *The Children*, as well as publishing four of her 1920s stories, 'The Temperate Zone', 'Bewitched', 'Miss Mary Pask' and 'The Young Gentlemen'.) Serialising *The Age of Innocence* in the *Pictorial Review* was one of Wharton's first forays into popular mass-market magazine publishing (as opposed to the more highbrow *Scribner's* or *Century* magazines). The novel was promoted in its pages, where it ran from July to

November 1920, in a cunningly double-edged way. It was trailed as another 'classic' of 'New York society of forty years ago by a world-famous writer', 'the author of *The House of Mirth*', with 'characters typical of the times in which they lived'. The illustrations (by W.B. King) were stately, romantic drawings of stuffy-looking figures in the period costumes of the 1870s, with emotional captions from the novel like: 'I Have Never Made Love to You, And I Never Shall. But You Are the Woman I Would Have Married if it Had Been Possible for Either of Us'. These were in marked contrast to the advertisements surrounding the serial, for up-to-the-minute Eureka Vacuum Cleaners, Rust-Resistant Corsets, Manicures ('You Can Never Know When People Are Looking At Your Finger-Nails'), Complexion Powder, Brassieres, and Odorono ('She Had Overlooked One Weakness: Perspiration'). But at the same time as promoting *The Age of Innocence* as an escapist classic, the magazine also wanted it to look exciting and relevant. Arousing plot-summaries accompanied each issue ('On the day of his marriage, he cared no more for his wife than he did for his own sister. Every drop of blood in him cried out for another woman!'). A competition ran ahead of the first issue headed 'Tell Us What You Really Think About Marriage' ('Out with it! Tell us the truth ... If you are happily married, tell us why. If you are not, tell us what is the matter. Here is a real chance to make marriage pay, as for every letter [printed] we will pay $25.'). A box alongside read: 'Does Your Husband Really Love You? Honestly now, does he? Or does he just tolerate you? You may be in young Mrs Archer's position without knowing it ...'

Even with these incitements, Arthur Vance felt that *The Age of Innocence* was a little too highbrow for his readers, who were more used to the best-selling authors Booth Tarkington and Kathleen Norris. (Norris's new novel, *The Beloved Woman*, also set in wealthy New York, about a spirited young girl temporarily infatuated with an older married man, started serialisation just as Wharton's ended, and the contrast in styles shows what Vance was after. Norris's happy ending reads: 'But when he saw her, the familiar, lovely face that he had loved for so many years, when he felt the little gloved hand on his arm, and realized that somehow, out of the utter desolation and loneliness of the big city, she had come to him again, that she was here, mistily smiling at him, and he could touch her and hear her voice, everything else vanished, as if it had never been, and he put his big arm about her hungrily, and kissed her, and they were both in tears.') For Wharton's next serialisation, Vance wrote to Jewett, since 'we are paying her a great sum of money', 'we would most certainly appreciate it if she could divide her story in four parts, so that each part leads up to a climax or interesting situation that will leave the reader in suspense and eager to get to the next issue of the magazine ... I do not expect Mrs Wharton to do a dime novel or family-story-paper break, but it can be done in a dignified, artistic way.'[38]

The reception of *The Age of Innocence* showed the contradictions in Wharton's status and reputation at the start of the 1920s, the height of her fame. As at the start of her career and at the time of *The House of Mirth*, she was much concerned with the relationship between good writing and high sales, literary independence and popularity. Though she had abandoned 'Literature' more than once, these preoccupations kept on surfacing in the 1920s novels, and would come pouring out in the 'Vance Weston' novels, transposed from the late nineteenth-century setting she had envisaged for 'Literature' into a post-war context.

The paradox in her position, which she would make use of in the 'Literature' novels, was that she was beginning to be seen as a 'classic' author, but also as too shocking and grim for optimistic American post-war readers. *The Age of Innocence* was praised for its 'uncanny' accuracy and its brilliantly ironical treatment of the period setting (as by Percy Lubbock, writing anonymously in the *Times Literary Supplement*). But she was attacked, now, for being cold, well-mannered and exclusive. Katherine Mansfield, in the *Athenaeum*, complained that the temperature was too 'sparklingly cool' and longed for 'a little wildness, a dark place or two in the soul'. Vernon Parrington wrote a critique in the *Pacific Review* which would be extremely influential, headed 'Our Literary Aristocrat', in which he accused her of being inextricably part of 'an earlier age', belonging 'in spite of herself to the caste which she satirizes'. 'She has paid a great price in aloofness from her own America', he concluded, citing Ned Winslett's advice to Newland Archer to roll up his sleeves and get down into the muck: 'That she should ever roll up her sleeves and get down into the muck is unthinkable'. This line of attack on her as out-of-touch with democratic America, snobbish, ladylike, and indistinguishable from her subject-matter – 'unconsciously shut in behind plate glass, where butlers serve formal dinners, and white shoulders go up at the mere suggestion of everyday gingham' – settled in from now on, and still influences her reputation. One of the Pulitzer judges who had wanted to give the prize to *Main Street*, Lovett, wrote a book-length study of Wharton in 1925 which summed her up as a snob and a relic of the Victorian age ('The notion of a democratic or proletarian culture which shall absorb the upper class is not within the range of her vision') and this would become a standard anti-Wharton formulation in the 1930s. Other readers were finding her too gloomy and foreign: one critic attacked

The Age of Innocence for being 'Parisian' and 'Zolaesque'. As one commentator on book-publishing said in 1920: 'Most books published today have no relation to literature. They should be sold for what they are – entertainment and a few pleasant evenings, a good story, a good cry or two and a good laugh or two . . . There is a large number of people who would buy this kind of book who don't want to buy George Moore or Edith Wharton.'[39]

Though to an extent Wharton did not care what people said about her, and wrote what interested and excited her, she also wanted to keep her readership. The money she made came mainly from her sales in America, not from France or England, and she had to sell to that audience, even if she felt distanced from it. The pressures of the war-years, the expensive house-purchases and house-moves, and the change of publishers, complicated her literary plans in the immediate post-war years. But there was also some inner turbulence, it seems, about what to write next. As often, she had more than one thing going on at a time, telling Jewett in 1921 that 'I have never been able to write one novel without having another going at the same time, or at least writing 2 or 3 short stories, and I always return to my chief work stimulated by the change'. But the period between 1919 and 1922 was more of a juggling act than usual. The order of her publications (*The Age of Innocence* and *In Morocco* in 1920, *The Glimpses of the Moon* in 1922, *A Son at the Front* in 1923, *Old New York* in 1924) did not exactly reflect the order of composition. She had planned, and started to write, her second war-novel, *A Son at the Front*, in the summer of 1918. Early in 1919, while reworking the essays on Morocco, she started work on her story of modern marriage, *The Glimpses of the Moon* (for which she had a contract with the *Pictorial Review* going back to 1916). She told Scribner's that she felt she was 'gradually approaching the time when it will again be possible to write a novel that is not concerned with the war'. But she could not get on with it, and instead, in the summer and autumn of 1919 (alongside the serialisation of *In Morocco* and the publication of *French Ways and their Meaning*), she worked hard on *A Son at the Front*. She tried again to write 'Literature', but gave it up and wrote *The Age of Innocence*, quickly, instead.[40]

A Son at the Front was contracted for serialisation (as a substitute for *Glimpses*, which had run aground) with the *Pictorial Review* for $18,000. In June 1919, Arthur Vance was told he had to put off the serialisation, and that summer Appleton also said that they would have to withdraw their advance of $15,000 if it was to be for the war-novel. There was no market for war-books at all; in fact it is 'almost grotesque', Sears told her, to see the 'aversion' of the public, since the Armistice, for such books. Jewett advised that it would be much better to offer *The Age of Innocence* to the

Pictorial Review as a substitute for *A Son at the Front*, finish *The Age of Innocence* and *Glimpses*, and wait to publish the war-book 'until the magazine market is ready for it'. Wharton was extremely upset about this. (The American public's post-war dislike of war-writing – 'a drug in the market' – would be bitterly noted in *Hudson River Bracketed*.) But she needed the $18,000, and agreed to publish *The Age of Innocence* first. A year later, just as *The Age of Innocence* and *In Morocco* were appearing in book form in October 1920, Vance again said he could not use *A Son at the Front*, and asked for *Glimpses* instead. Scribner's jumped in to get the magazine serialisation (and the book) of *A Son at the Front*, which was finally, and unsuccessfully, published in 1923. Meanwhile, Wharton went back to writing *Glimpses* and finished it in September 1921. In November she had the idea for a group of 'Old New York stories', including 'The Old Maid'. And she was planning a sequel to *The Age of Innocence*, which she did not write. She turned down a publisher's suggestion for another 'spin-off' from the novel, a series of articles on her 'recollections of New York Society, at $2,500 an article'. But it did feed an idea she had had for some time of writing her 'own early memories', 'to avoid having it inaccurately done by someone else after my death'.[41]

In all these post-war works, one subject keeps creeping in. It is that of the displaced person, one who does not feel at home in their time or place. The four stories in *Old New York*, which look like lightweight spin-offs from the success of *The Age of Innocence*, but which are painful treatments of individuals crushed by their 'age', are full of such characters, like Lizzie Hazeldean, the woman in 'New Year's Day' who is never forgiven for her sin. Spied on by the conventional New York families and condemned for ever, like Hawthorne's Hester Prynne, as a Scarlet Woman, she turns a bold face to her condemners: 'If all New York wants to ostracize me, let it! I've had my day ... no woman has more than one. Why shouldn't I have to pay for it? I'm ready.' But she spends her whole life in isolation, never able to free herself: 'A perpetual longing to relive the past, a perpetual need to explain and justify herself ... became the luxury of her empty life.'

'False Dawn', the story set earliest of the four, in the 1840s, the time of her parents' courtship and youth (gently retold here), is a comic and pathetic story of a young man from a good New York family who, sent to Europe by his bullying father to buy up Italian paintings for the family walls, falls under the influence of an exciting person called John Ruskin, and comes back, not with the requisite Raphaels and Carlo Dolcis, but with a collection of baffling early Italians ('Carpatcher, you say this fellow's called? ... And Angelico you say did this kind of Noah's Ark soldier in pink armour on gold-leaf? . . . And you say the thing was a *bargain?*'). The son inherits nothing but the pictures, and with his devoted wife he exhibits them to an uncomprehending public as a 'Gallery of Christian Art' (as the Italian Primitives used to be referred to). But the attempt fails and the paintings are stashed away in a relative's attic for decades, until they are spotted and sold for a fortune. The story is based on the life of James Jackson Jarves, whose priceless and pioneering collection of Italian Primitives, assembled in the 1850s, went unregarded for years before it was bought by Yale, and would have been a private joke with Berenson, who was an expert on one of Jarves's favourite painters, Sassetta. 'False Dawn' is an ironic comedy about a man whose perceptions are far ahead of his 'age': and a sad one too.

A less good story, 'The Spark', pursues the idea of the person embedded in the conventions of their time, but who can still be half lifted out of it. It uses the same device of a real writer in an imaginary landscape, in this case not Ruskin but Whitman, who ignites a 'spark' in an otherwise dull and decent New Yorker, Hayley Delane. Delane seems to the younger narrator like 'a finished monument', another 'venerable institution' of his time, like 'Trinity Church, the Reservoir, or the Knickerbocker Club'. But he seems also to have a touch of something 'greater' than 'the dead-level of old New York's respectability', and turns out to have acquired this in his Civil War days (unlike many of his 'indolent' generation, who 'stood aside' from the fight). He met a 'queer gentleman', he tells the narrator, when he was wounded at Bull Run, in a Washington hospital for soldiers, and this fellow's ideas – about charity, and courage, and being true to one's self – have never left his mind. But when the younger man tries to read him a Whitman poem about the war, he backs off, baffled by the 'new verse forms'.

'The Old Maid', the most powerful story of the four, set in the 1850s, seems to contrast the conventional Delia, married into one of those deeply conservative New York families, the Ralstons (which gives Wharton the opportunity to 'do', yet again, the furniture and clothes and habits of the Joneses and their type), and her cousin Charlotte, mother of the illegitimate daughter. But as the bitter and brilliantly controlled story of female conspiracy and rivalry develops, it becomes apparent that both women are equally victims of their 'age', in which 'social tolerance was not dealt in the same measure to men and to women, and neither Delia nor Charlotte had ever wondered why: like all the young women of their class they simply bowed to the ineluctable'.[42]

*

Newland Archer and the protagonists of *Old New York* all stay in New York, though they are deeply ill-at-ease in their place and time. Later characters like Kate Clephane in *The Mother's Recompense* and Martin Boyne in *The Children*, will be exiles, or alienated, dismayed, returning visitors. Edith Wharton returned to America herself, for the last time, in 1923, when she was sixty-one. She was offered an honorary degree of Doctor of Letters from Yale University in May. She had been ill that spring, suffering from a series of 'flu attacks and an 'aortic murmur', and spending a few weeks at Salso with Philomène, and she did not much want to go. At first she refused; but Yale impressed on her that this was the first time they had offered a D. Litt to a woman. Letters to friends hovered between what was perhaps mock-reluctance and proud gratification. To Elisina: 'I can't very well refuse'; to Gaillard, 'I badly need [to have a look at the USA] if I'm to go on writing about it'; to Charles Du Bos, 'C'est la première fois qu'il est donné à une femme.'[43]

She sailed in the *Mauretania* in June and after the six-day ocean-voyage spent twelve busy and sociable days in a heatwave in America, coming back in the *Berengaria* on 2 July and plunging straightaway into her European life: going to a literary conference at Pontigny with Walter and talking there with Du Bos, Gide (who dedicated his book on Dostoevsky to her that summer), Maurois and Lytton Strachey (whom she admired); mourning the death of Rosa de Fitzjames, the last of her pre-war Paris salon hostesses; complaining about the French translation of *The Reef*; reading and disliking Valéry; writing on Proust; visiting Hill Hall and Rye (where Norton now lived at Lamb House), and making an autumn visit to I Tatti, where she first came to know Nicky Mariano. She took up again her well-regulated expatriate life, and the visit to America came to feel like a strange diversion.

It had its interest and enjoyment for her, even though the crossing was dull ('Same old Atlantic', she wrote in her diary). She was met by Minnie, and went to stay at Westbrook, on Long Island, the stately home of her old friends the Cuttings, with a visit, also, to the Maynards at their Mount-like house, Hautbois. (Bayard and Olivia Cutting were old New York acquaintances; their late son Bayard, Edith's friend, had married Sybil, now unhappily married to Geoffrey Scott.) Old Olivia Cutting was still living in state at Westbrook, and Edith's visit coincided with one from Sybil's daughter Iris, a beautiful and intelligent twenty-one-year-old who had just announced her engagement, to maternal disapproval, to the much older Count Antonio Origo. Iris Cutting became the mistress of the great Origo family house in Tuscany, La Foce, a wartime heroine, and an extremely good writer. Edith liked her very much, and told her encouragingly what good things Olivia Cutting had said about Iris's fiancé – remarks, Edith noted to Iris, which when 'communicated to a third person, carry added conviction'. Iris Origo gave a sympathetic but misguided description of Wharton at Westbrook (a house, Iris thought, which could have come straight out of *The Age of Innocence*), dwelling insistently on old times:

> The W's house on 11th Street, had it really been pulled down? Did her hostess remember the night they had dined there before the Colony Club ball? The X's daughter, the fair one, had she married her young Bostonian? Had Z indeed lost all his money? For the whole evening this mood continued. At one moment only – as the last guest had gone, she turned half-way up the stairs to wave goodnight – I caught a glimpse of the other Edith, elegant, formidable, as hard and dry as porcelain. Then, as she looked down on her old friends, the face *softened*, even the erectness of her spine relaxed a little. She was no longer the trim, hard European hostess, but a nice old American lady. Edith had come home.

In New York after the Yale ceremony, staying at the St Regis, seeing Minnie Jones, her cousin Thomas Newbold, her old and her new publishers, and talking business with Jewett, she had two interesting encounters with younger writers. One was with Edward Sheldon, a close friend of Minnie's and an intelligent and witty playwright, paralysed with arthritis from his late twenties (he was thirty-seven in 1923, and died at sixty), but gallantly stoic about his condition. They immediately took a liking to each other: she told him that when they met, she had thought: 'Why this is a live human being at last.' A warm correspondence followed, mostly on their mutual passion for crime novels, his close involvement with the dramatisations of her plays, and Minnie's state of health. Another, possibly apocryphal, brief encounter was with Scott Fitzgerald, who, hearing she was in Charles Scribner's office while he was in the building, is said to have burst in and knelt at her feet (described by his biographer as an act of 'high-spirited charm').[44]

But it was the ceremony at Yale which most gripped her attention; the detail with which she entered the day into her otherwise laconic diary for 1923 shows how much it meant to her: 'June 20. Max [Farrand] called at 8.30. Took me to Corporation Room where Hon Degrees assembled. We walked in procession to Wolsey Hall. Received D Litt.Degree. We left at 3.' The Yale dignitaries were pleased that (as her presenter, the affable English professor William Lyon Phelps said) she had 'left her pleasant home in France and a half-written novel to come to New Haven and receive the degree, even as Mark Twain travelled to Oxford'. And they were impressed with her for putting up with the weather as she processed across the campus in her heavy, colourful robes and sat for hours on the stage of the great hall. Phelps joked: 'Had she known in advance what was to be the terrific heat of that commencement day, would she have come? On the commencement stage that morning, I lost three pounds.' He praised her as 'a master in the creation of original and living characters' whose 'powers of ironical description are exerted to salutary ends . . . a realist in the best sense of the word' who has 'elevated the level of American literature'. To Berenson, who had poured scorn on the event before she had left (she called it 'the doctorate you despise'), she described her pleasure in the 'medieval pageant' and the 'really impressive' ceremony. And, in a caustic note which showed off, at its worst, her feelings about her native land: 'It remains a mystery that the straw-hatted pot-bellied "homme moyen" of the modern US should demand such a show, & know how to create it.' What she did not mention in her account of the event was that the Italian ambassador, Prince Caetani, was also receiving an honorary degree on that day, and the New Haven police were having to take elaborate precautions against 'anti-Fascisti protests'. At his speech at the dinner for the graduates (which Wharton may not have attended, judging from that diary note, 'We left at 3'), Caetani praised the Fascist movement, which he said was 'working out the salvation of Italy on ideals of the loftiest patriotism and self-sacrifice'. Mussolini, he said, was 'the personification of a great spiritual movement . . . supported by Italy's youth'. It struck an ominous warning note for the Europe that Wharton returned to after her brief, final visit home. But 'home' was not the right word for America, now. Wharton told Berenson: 'Coming back here after ten years is to me like coming to a cemetery. All the people I loved best in America have died since 1914.'

18

Jazz

Edith Wharton was thinking a great deal, in her early sixties, about her reputation and her position in relation to younger American writers. She wrote some letters to Charles Scribner in 1922 and 1923, when they were corresponding about A Son at the Front, which kept reverting to the subject. Scribner sent her Scott Fitzgerald's second novel (The Beautiful and the Damned) in 1922, with the comment that 'he should do well if he will exercise some restraint'; she replied that she was interested 'in all that the new generation of novelists is doing at home'. Faintly praising some younger, now forgotten, women writers, Grace Flandrau and Thyra Winslow, she criticised their works' lack of 'plan and curve' ('like most novels of the new school') and their poor knowledge of 'the riches of the English language': 'but ... I imagine they read only each other.' Responding to the muted reception of A Son at the Front, she wrote:

> I do not write 'jazz-books' and never expected to be a best-seller. The success of The Age of Innocence was, I believe, due to the accident of my having resuscitated old New York at a time when the contrast was great enough to amuse the curiosity of a new generation. I believe my books have a certain staying power which ... I would far rather think they possess than the qualities requisite at present for a sensational sale.[1]

'Jazz-books' versus 'staying power' sums up Wharton's critical approach to the post-war years, but it was a position which should not be simplified just as a hardening of the arteries. There was much that she disapproved of, but there was also a great deal that fascinated her. In her fiction of this decade she was not entirely setting her face against 'modernism'. Topical and shocking subjects, techniques that created a sense of surface glitter and of speeding time and dislocation, urban chatter and alienated characters, would jostle in her work of the 1920s with more familiar Whartonian features: stories of personal losses and regrets, memories of the past, characters locked in their social world, studies of transition, perfectly ordered sentences. The results are discomforting and uneven, and disturbing for readers of Wharton who want her to go on writing novels like *The House of Mirth*; but they are certainly not as staid and old-fashioned as she has often been accused of being.

Still, Wharton did use the word 'jazz' as a term of abuse. She had nothing to do with the expatriate American writers in the Paris cafés after the war, like Hemingway or Dos Passos or Cummings, or with gay Parisian life in the 1920s: Toulouse-Lautrec's Montparnasse, the Moulin Rouge and the Folies Bergères, Mistinguett and Josephine Baker, La Revue Nègre, Léger and Picasso, cocaine and the Charleston, Chaplin at the cinema, Cole Porter and Gershwin. She told Berenson at the end of 1922 that she was 'gloating' at the 'general blessedness of being so far from Jazzery' at Hyères. The word epitomised for her the unpleasantness of modernity: trends, instant gratification, 'pseudo-culture', slang, noise, impermanence, fast living, and standardisation. She uses it as a verb as well as a noun ('I suppose in your set a young man who doesn't jazz all day and drink all night . . . is a back number', someone says in *Twilight Sleep*). She uses it as an all-purpose term for the life-style of the international jet-set, referring to the Prince of Wales, for instance, in 1935, as a curious mixture of 'jazz & the resolute fulfilment of royal duties'. The international pleasure-seeking crowd (the modern version of her Americans abroad in *The House of Mirth* or *Custom of the Country*) is often her subject, now, as in *The Children*: 'cosmopolitan people, who, in countries not their own, lived in houses as big as hotels, or in hotels where the guests were as international as the waiters, had inter-married, inter-loved and inter-divorced each other over the whole face of Europe'. She sees this society as artificial and lacking in distinctiveness (and distinction):

> Every one of the women in the vast crowded restaurant seemed to be of the same age, dressed by the same dress-maker, loved by the same lovers . . . and massaged and manipulated by the same Beauty doctors . . . A double jazz-band drowned their conversation, but from the movement of their lips, and the accompanying gestures, Boyne surmised that they were all saying exactly the same things . . .

At the centre of this crowd is the blithe, bobbed-haired, made-up, mani-cured 'flapper', summed up by Lita Wyant in *Twilight Sleep*, 'perpetually craving for new "thrills"', 'half-dancing, half-drifting', her life made up of 'jazz and night-clubs' and her world populated by 'a pseudo-artistic rabble of house-decorators, cinema stars and theatrical riff-raff'. 'Lita is – jazz', Wharton noted in her plan for the novel. The young women who gain our sympathy in Wharton's post-war novels – Susie in *The Glimpses of the Moon*, Nona in *Twilight Sleep*, Judith in *The Children* – are all exposed to 'jazz', but have something old-fashioned about them which puts them at odds with their modern world.[2]

Wharton had always disliked the kind of American optimism which makes Mrs Welland, in *The Age of Innocence*, say that she needs to keep her mind 'bright and happy', and which meant, she thought, that tragic subjects like *The House of Mirth* could not succeed in the American theatre, since, as William Dean Howells famously told her after the play failed in 1906: 'What the American public wants is a tragedy with a happy ending'. That infantile refusal of dark realities was the main subject of *Twilight Sleep*. Wharton's persistent reading of American culture as unrealistically 'bright and happy' found rich pickings (especially in that novel) in the post-war emphasis on cures and regimes. Emile Coué's *Self-Mastery Through Conscious Auto-Suggestion*, one of the best-sellers of 1923, containing the famous advice to repeat to yourself in front of the mirror, 'Every day, in every way, I am getting better and better', summed up for Wharton what was stupid about post-war America. She referred scathingly to Philomène's being taken up, in 1922, with 'Coué-ism & spiritualism'; joking to Elisina in 1929 about her son's visit, she said that 'Bill, like a Coué patient, gets "better & better" – I mean as a guest & companion!' Belief in the possibility of endless self-improvement went with a childish desire for total happiness and for the avoidance of pain. Wharton often referred to drink and drugs when she talked about 'jazz'. The fashion in the 1920s for the drug (scopolamine, mixed with morphine as an analgesic-amnesic) which made childbirth a completely pain-free experience gave her the title and the theme of *Twilight Sleep*.[3]

In the 1920s and '30s, Wharton saved up clippings from America which particularly amused or amazed her. Some of them reflected what she saw as democracy run amok, like the 'enclosed jewels' she retailed to Lapsley in 1927 from the *New York Herald*: 'Woman Swindled by Fake Egg Message. Bobbed Hair Fad Makes Cows Happy. Mrs Mabel Latham Gump announces the engagement of her daughter, Miss Marcella Louise Gump.' Among her clippings are two 1928 advertisements for 'Elbert Hubbard's Scrap Book Selections for 500 Great Writers'. Hubbard was a soap-salesman, and an arts-and-crafts ideologue, founder of the Roycroft printing and bookbinding works; his 'Scrap Books' were collections of 'inspired and inspiring selections' of literature, short-cuts to cultural self-improvement. (She drew on this for the purveyor of cultural commodities, Bunty Hayes, in *Hudson River Bracketed*.) In the illustrated advertisements, a wife reproaches her husband for having nothing to say at a dinner party, and a hostess tells a friend how she has made herself more interesting. Both recommend Hubbard's 'whole library condensed into one fascinating scrap-book . . . the greatest thoughts of the greatest men of all ages . . . in one wonderful volume'. Hubbard 'did all the reading for you! You don't need to go through long, tiresome volumes – you can get at a glance what Hubbard has to read days and days to find.' Hubbard's ads were like others surrounding the magazine serialisations of Wharton's novels, for brand-new products providing the quick relief of pain, labour-saving devices like canned food, and endless life-enhancing formulas: hip-reducing perfolastic girdles, freckle-removing creams, anti-perspirants, energy-giving breakfasts, brighter light-bulbs. In a sketch for an unwritten 1920s story called 'The First Born of Egypt', Wharton imagines the bored daughter of a German Jew called Krebs, who has patented a drug which has made his fortune, looking out of the window at a huge billboard advertising his product: 'Baby Fretful? Brain Forgetful? *Try Mend-All.* Business Slumpy? Heart Jumpy? *Try Mend-All.* Bones Achy? Nerves Shaky? *Try Mend-All.*' The daughter thinks of adding 'Day Empty?' to the list.[4]

Hubbard's Scrap Books have indexes with topics like 'Ambition, attainment of', 'Goodness, power of', 'Life, sacredness of', 'Success, secret of', 'Woman, uplift of'. A culture of self-improvement and pain-avoidance seemed to require a literature to match it. The biggest-selling American woman-writer of the early twentieth century was the backwoods Indiana novelist, Gene Stratton Porter. Her heart-warming stories of rural children, like *Freckles* (1904) and *A Girl of the Limberlost* (1909), and her story of her brother's childhood, *Laddie* (1913), sold about eight million copies. Stratton Porter was once accused of writing 'molasses fiction', and retaliated: 'What a wonderful compliment! All the world loves sweets . . . I shall keep straight on writing of the love and joy of life.' In Wharton's draft of 'Literature', she clipped a Doubleday advertisement extolling the amazing sales of *Laddie*, and underlined this passage in red: '*Laddie* goes to the heart of a vast reading public because it is true to life, a picture of genuine American people – people who love their homes, who figure neither in newspaper nor divorce court; who are the source of the real vitality of the nation.'[5]

One side of Wharton's critique of modern America, then, was that it was childish and self-deceiving, refusing to admit to primitive, tragic emotions or to let in the realities of death and pain. But she was also harshly critical of a great deal of modernist art for what she saw as its squalor and its deliberate sensationalism. American post-war optimism and the shock of international modernism might seem like two different things, but

Wharton linked them through their emphasis on self-expression and their negation of history. Psychoanalysis and therapy – she very much disliked the idea of 'Freudianism' – stream-of-consciousness, jazz and Cubism, seemed to her to come out of the same post-war break with the past and the same cult of the self. But her attitude to modernity is not simple.[6]

She disliked modernism because she thought it was formulaic and over-theorised, and so linked it to the 'standardisation' of modern American life. She and Berenson had an intermittent, anxious discussion about this all through the 1920s, especially about Joyce, whom she never met. (She left Paris just as he arrived; though, curiously, they shared an ophthamologist, Dr Borsch, who recommended bi-focals for her 'new tortoise-shell' lorgnettes.) Berenson thought A *Portrait of the Artist* had 'elements of great-ness', but she found Joyce impossible, especially *Ulysses*. She burst out about it to Berenson early in 1923, sounding both prim and defensive:

> a turgid welter of schoolboy pornography (the rudest schoolboy kind) & unformed & unimportant drivel; & until the raw ingredients of a pudding *make* a pudding, I shall never believe that the raw material of sensation & thought can make a work of art without the cook's intervening. The same applies to Eliot. I *know* it's not because I'm getting old that I'm unresponsive. The trouble with all this new stuff is that it's à thèse: the theory comes first, & dominates it.

This was not an unusual line on *Ulysses* at the time: their mutual friend, the curator Louis Gillet, reviewed the French translation in the *Revue des Deux Mondes* in 1925 as a farrago of 'consciousness, sub-consciousness, psychoanalysis, Freudianism, the self, the non-self, opening of "the gates of the future", what a to-do!'. Her attack closely resembled the opinions of Virginia Woolf and D.H. Lawrence on *Ulysses*, though she had no time for them, either.[7]

Wharton did not like the sound of Bloomsbury. She was not looking forward to meeting Arthur Waley, whose translations from the Chinese she liked, because she 'had been told he was the incarnation of Bloomsbury, but found him rather the contrary – expansive, amiable, and, of course, supremely intelligent'. Waley's much-admired translation of *The Tale of Genji*, the long Japanese court-novel from AD 1000, was a great discovery for her; she told Berenson in 1928 that she had just finished 'Blue Trousers' (the sad section on the death of Murasaki and Genji's mourning for her), and compared it with Proust, and with trivial modern works by David Garnett and Thornton Wilder: 'The solemn symphonic close reminds me of the end of *Le Temps Retrouvé*. Think of these two great books having been given to us within the space of less than twenty years, & all the plentiful mannikins running up & down & making a fuss about *Lady Into Fox* & *The Bridge of San Luis Rey*! How the populace *hates* anything big.'

Bloomsbury liked Waley and *The Tale of Genji* too, but Wharton did not know that. Mary Berenson tried to persuade her to read *Orlando*; she was reluctant: 'I haven't read *Orlando* yet but the photos [the novel was illustrated with alluring pictures of Vita Sackville-West] made me quite ill. I can't believe that where there is exhibitionism of that order there can be any real creative gift – But I'll read it, since you think one ought to.' She did not enjoy having *The Mother's Recompense* described as 'an old-fashioned novel', as opposed to *Mrs Dalloway*'s 'brilliant experimentalism', when they both came out in 1925. Yes, it is, she told John Hugh Smith: 'I was not trying to follow the new methods . . . & my heroine belongs to the day when scruples existed.' That year, Woolf (twenty years her junior) wrote a sweeping and somewhat condescending essay on 'American Fiction' in *The Saturday Review*, lumping Wharton together with Henry James and with the popular novelist Joseph Hergesheimer (whose first name she gets wrong) as American writers who are too like English writers ('they do not give us anything that we have not got already'). They are too taken up with 'English good manners' and 'obsessed with surface distinction', in comparison to Sinclair Lewis, Ring Lardner, and Willa Cather. Wharton was extremely irritated: 'Mrs Virginia Woolf writes a long article . . . to say that no interesting American fiction is, or should be, written in English; and that Henry Hergesheimer [*sic*] and I are negligible because we have nothing new to give – not even a language! Well – such discipline is salutary.'[8]

She identified Bloomsbury with a number of things she disliked: lesbianism (Gertrude Stein, Natalie Barney and Elsie de Wolfe were also written off for this), feminism, bad manners, socialism and 'Bolshevism', obscenity, exhibitionism, and experimental art. Mary Berenson (more sympathetic to modernism than her husband, and linked to Bloomsbury through her daughters) encouraged Wharton to read her daughter Ray Strachey's feminist polemic *The Cause*. The reply came: 'To read a book called "The Cause" (& *that* cause!) will require all my affection for you.' She did glance at it: 'I, who think that women were made for pleasure & procreation, note with satisfaction that the leaders of the movement, judging from their photos, all look unfitted for the first, & many for both functions!' Stella Benson's novel *The Poor Man* (1922), a satire on weak, modish English people in California and China talking about 'Art and Sex', saying things like 'we are all somehow metallically unsimple in these days', and having nervous breakdowns, which Wharton had heard was admired by all the 'youngs', she thought a fatiguing 'jazz book'. It made her want to 'crawl away & die'. When Mary tried *The Well of Loneliness* on her, she noted with satisfaction that 'the dull twaddle of Miss Radclyffe Hall has to be boosted by the censors! It's a good world after all.'[9]

These responses clearly go beyond matters of style. Wharton's critique of modernism was tangled up with her attitudes to class, race, and democracy. She did not distinguish much between an elite modernist art, intended for a highbrow audience, and a democratic American art in which 'only the man with the dinner pail shall be deemed worthy of attention', and the story has to be 'situated among the least developed classes'. Though these kinds of literature, the modernist and the democratic (Woolf's *Orlando* and Upton Sinclair's *The Jungle*, say) were often the opposite of each other, they could sometimes overlap (as in Faulkner's *Sanctuary*, a target of Wharton's distaste). And she saw in both – the new American realism and the new international experimentation – evidence of 'the amorphous and the agglutinative'.[10]

Wharton's snobbery, racism, anti-Semitism and anti-feminism are much more crudely voiced (as is almost always the case with the bigotry of intelligent people) in her private letters than in her fiction. Accounts of American literary anti-Semitism which use Simon Rosedale in *The House of Mirth* as an example of an upper-class writer expressing her fear of social disintegration through the figure of the Jew, have nothing to say about the complexity, even attractiveness, of that Jewish character, but Wharton's private statements about 'yids' have none of that complexity. Her remarks are not as offensive as those of some of her contemporaries (including some of her own close friends, notably John Hugh Smith, a rancid anti-Semite who, when summing up Wharton's life-story, described her as part of a wave of American émigrés who could not continue to live in a world where 'the American working class was smothered by the peasants of Eastern Europe and the middle class poisoned by a plague of Jews'). Her own attitudes were commonplace among upper-class Anglo-Americans, and the French, in pre-Holocaust times. But comparisons, historical tolerance, and recognition of the licence we all take in private correspondence do not make good excuses here; the casual remarks and jokes have survived on paper, they must form part of our sense of her, and it was a polite misrepresentation to leave most of them out of the selected *Letters*. These remarks are made mainly to Minnie Jones or to Gaillard Lapsley. (With the Berensons, or William Gerhardi, or Sinclair Lewis, she tried harder to adapt to the new.) In 1921, reporting on one of the criminal trials she and Lapsley liked to follow, she noted: 'Of course you've seen the Daily Mail that they've caught Mrs Rachel Gobsweib, and sent *her* up. Her name alone makes the nature of her offence sufficiently clear.' Recommending Charles Merz's *The Great American Bandwagon* (itself a horrified portrayal of democracy and modernity run amok in modern America) she says she supposes he is 'a German Yid'; meeting Rebecca West ('the "amie", I believe, of Wells'), she describes her to Minnie as 'a handsome and penetrating little Jewess, who despises my work in her reviews, but who rather took a shine to me'. André Maurois, she tells Lapsley, is 'a very bright little Jew . . . about as well fitted for lecturing on English poetry to the English as one of my Pekes'. In 1933 she sends Lapsley a joke-rhyme which Desmond MacCarthy got from Hilaire Belloc: '"Rupert de Vere is sad today / His wife's run away / And he grieves for the Kid – Poor little Yid!" Don't you admire that?' When she read, and liked, *The Great Gatsby*, in 1925, she congratulated Fitzgerald on the invention of a 'perfect Jew' in the character of Wolfsheim (called Hildesheim in the first version). In 1923 she wrote a particularly unpleasant letter to Minnie Jones (in response to an unidentified request), which airs more than one prejudice in one go: 'I'm not much interested in travelling scholarships for women – or in fact in scholarships, tout court! – they'd much better stay at home and mind the baby. Still less am I interested in scholarships for female Yids, and young ladies who address a total stranger as "Chère Madame" and sign "meilleurs sentiments" . . .' The name of Vance's publishing firm in *Hudson River Bracketed* is Dreck & Saltzer. As she became more drawn, in old age, to Catholicism, her anti-Semitic feelings solidified; Elisina noted that one of Wharton's last remarks, when she was dying, was that she 'hated the Jews' because of the Crucifixion.[11]

Her attitudes to black culture and racial assimilation are similarly unappealing, though standard for her class and time. Wharton's fictional black characters are servants, cleaners and cooks, notably in *A Backward Glance* and *Old New York*, where the opulent family meals are served up by black women from Virginia, and in *A Mother's Recompense*, where a 'negress' servant has a crucial role in the plot. In *The Buccaneers*, English racism and xenophobia will be played as broad comedy, and 'blackness' becomes a more outspoken topic of discussion than ever before.[12] Like everyone else of her type, she used the verb 'niggering', without self-consciousness, to mean slaving away at a job. She was alarmed at the idea of black art developing its own status and becoming part of American cultural life. Writing to Lapsley in 1925, she enclosed a letter she had received from a black artist in America, with a request to paint her portrait 'in an effort to gain for the Negro a place of recognition in the art world', and an advertisement for a Christian 'anti-Marxian' and 'anti-Jewish' society': 'It is an amazing commentary on the chaos là-bas, and makes one long for Holy Church and the long arm of the Inquisition.' Asking him if he had read the (white) novelist Carl Van Vechten's 1927 celebration of the Harlem Renaissance, she burst out: 'Have you read *Nigger Heaven*? It is so nauseating (& such rubbish too) that I despair of the Republic.' She had thought it was 'all made up', but some French friends had told her they had seen the première of the play of the novel in New York, '& had been taken by the "Jeunes" into nigger society in Harlem, "et que c'était comme dans le livre". And now I must *stop & be sick*.'[13]

She was more temperate about the white Anglo-American younger generation. She had been pleased, in 1918, to be sent a copy of *Prufrock* (with a little book of surrealist verse called *Spectra*, written by Witter Bynner and Arthur Ficke, under pseudonyms). Her praise was faint ('amusing, but I don't think they mean much') and she thought them too much influenced by Whitman ('rather a big meal for such small digestions'). But: 'I am glad to know what the new American songsters are doing.' Her preferences in modern poetry were for Housman (whom she saw on visits to England) and Yeats, several of whose first editions, much ticked, were in her library, whose *Oxford Book of English Verse* was a present to her from Robert Norton for their last Christmas together at Hyères, and whose 'When you are old' was the final poem in Wharton's and Norton's selection of English poetry.

Among the younger critics, she liked Desmond MacCarthy, whom she met at the Berensons'. She offered to write him an essay for his *Life and Letters* (bearding the enemy in a Bloomsbury-linked publication) 'called "Deep Sea Soundings", on this tiresome stream-of-consciousness theory which is deflecting so much real narrative talent out of its proper course'. MacCarthy knew the Berensons through Mary's quirky brother Logan Pearsall Smith, a fastidious, depressive Anglicised American essayist, best-known for his collections of belletrist pieces, *Trivia* and *More Trivia*, who shared Wharton's views on the younger generation and delighted to call himself 'an old fogey'. Pearsall Smith was one of her companions on her Mediterranean cruise in 1926, but was spiteful about 'the lady's' inferiority to James behind her back: 'Good God, her style, or rather her appalling lack of that quality ... But still, she has a marvellous cook.'

She took little notice of E.M. Forster, though she found his Alexandrian essays, *Pharos and Pharillon*, 'a charming little book, full of whimsical grace', even if its themes had been 'cruelly over-worked': 'the trouble is that so few of "ces Jeunes" ... have heard of their precursors.' (Mocking herself, she added: 'Here is the Empress's edict, & with that *no* fault can be found.') She was rude about D.H. Lawrence and associated him with 'megaphones'

– as did Virginia Woolf. (Edward Marsh was met with withering scorn when he recommended *Sons and Lovers*: 'How could I have recommended such a botched and bungled piece of work?') But she was curious about him, reading with interest the memoir by the model for Miriam in *Sons and Lovers* while referring to 'that fraud of a great man', or commenting to Lapsley about the editing of his letters: 'Isn't it perfect that Aldous Huxley should be editing D.H. Lawrence's letters? The new Percy editing the new Henry!' William Gerhardi told her to read *Lady Chatterley's Lover*, 'a very good book', but her response to this suggestion, unfortunately, does not survive.[14]

The Bloomsbury writer she did admire, at least for a time, was Lytton Strachey, whom she met at Pontigny in 1923. She and her friends all read his *Queen Victoria*, in 1921, with pleasure, telling Mary Berenson: 'With sobs & tears we last night finished *Victoria*. The whole of literature seems insipid after it. Your brother [Pearsall Smith] in his excellent article is quite right in saying that Mr Strachey has discovered a new procédé.' She liked the way, for instance, he had represented 'Disraeli's mind, full of melancholy & sparkles'. She ordered all his books from her regular book-supplier. Later she would come to think him a bad influence on other biographers. She told Lapsley in 1930: 'I've just read two of the worst books ever written, on two of the best subjects: Leigh Hunt & Trelawney, by Blunden and Massingham. The latter's cheap Socialism is intruded on every page – so fittingly on such a theme! It's a pity that Maurois and Strachey have broken down so completely the fine old tradition of the British biography . . .' But she was sorry when Strachey died in 1932, calling him, with Aldous Huxley, 'the only light left in that particular quarter of the heavens'.[15]

Wharton's late work satirises what she and Berenson used to call 'Noaillism'. But her anxious resistance to the new – something that almost all great writers in their sixties and older are liable to feel, particularly if they are living in isolation or away from their native culture – was full of exceptions. She had well-attested passions not only for Yeats and Stravinsky, but for Isadora Duncan, Cézanne, Gauguin (though not Matisse), Gide, Huxley and Rilke. She relished lighter modern works like Gerhardi's *Futility* and Anita Loos's *Gentlemen Prefer Blondes*. She often let slip surprising preferences: for instance, in a late letter to her friend Alice Garrett (who had an interest in modern painters) saying that she would have given 'her boots' to see Vuillard's portrait of the couturière Mme Lanvin, and praising Stravinsky's 'a capella' chants. Her book orders from the London bookseller James Bain show her looking out for new interests, listing, for instance, May Sinclair's *Harriett Frean*, Elizabeth Bowen's *The Hotel*, Mansfield's stories, Margaret Kennedy's *The Constant Nymph*, Somerset Maugham's *The Moon and Sixpence*, Bertrand Russell's *Sceptical Essays* and Evelyn Waugh's *Decline and Fall*. (She met Waugh in England in 1929, and liked *Vile Bodies*.) Her friendships with younger figures like Huxley and Gerhardi contradict the version of her which increasingly held sway as stuffy, remote, and grandly old-fashioned.[16]

Some of her involvements with her contemporaries took the form of ongoing arguments. She kept copies of three books by Colette in her library, *La Vagabonde*, *Mitsou*, and *Chéri*, and when Berenson wrote to her in 1932 warily recommending *Ces Plaisirs* ('I seem to remember you don't enjoy Colette'), she replied:

No, it must have been some other lady who told you she didn't like Colette, for I not only marvel at her but delight in her. But this last book seems to me just pornography *pour la vente*, except those wonderful last pages on jealousy where she comes into her own again, with her unrivalled gift for the expressing of the tears in sensual things. The rest, I own, bored & depressed me ... all the *à clef* side of the book seems to me a pitiful performance for a woman of Colette's exquisite genius.

Ces Plaisirs explored sado-masochistic sexual relations, starting with an orgy in an opium den, and detailed Colette's 'own sensual torments'. It was the self-advertisement and exhibitionism Wharton disliked, more than the sex.[17]

The same kind of problems undermined her admiration for Proust. She went on writing and thinking about him, in old age still exchanging examples of favourite minor characters with Gaillard, and going back to reconsider vitality and realism in an essay of 1934. But, though she was not shocked by the treatment of homosexuality in the *Cities of the Plain* volumes, she found them perverse, as she explained to Berenson: 'I think he has fourvoyé himself [led himself astray] into a subject that can't lead anywhere in art, & belongs only to pathology. What a pity he didn't devote himself to the abnormalities of the normal, which offer a wide enough & untilled enough field, heaven knows.' It amused her to receive, by the same post as Proust's *Sodom et Gomorrhe II* (on which her final comment was 'Alas! Alas!'), a letter from an admiring American lady who wanted to 'kiss my eyes into smiles, & draw some of the sadness from my mouth'. Comparing this 'frank expression of good will' with the 'new gomorrhas', she concluded that America, as usual, 'is unsurpassed in efficiency'. So even in the area of sexual 'perversity' (as she called it), the American style of lesbianism struck her as ludicrously bright and cheery, compared with subtle French decadence.[18]

An endearing exception to her suspicion of 'les jeunes' was her enthusiasm for William Gerhardi (or Gerhardie), whose childhood had been spent in St Petersburg, and who published an original and funny novel, *Futility*, in 1922, at the age of twenty-seven. It was written, while he was a student at Oxford, out of his experiences of witnessing the 'Bolshevik' Revolution in what was then Petrograd, spending two years in Vladivostok, in Siberia, attached to the British Military Mission from 1918 to 1920, and falling in love with a Chekhovian family of 'three sisters'. *Futility* is a novel about 'intervention', personal and political, and it treats the shambles of the Allied intervention in Russia as a bizarre comedy of love, incompetence and bureaucracy, an 'adventure in futility'. Wharton was given it to read by Lapsley on a trip to England in September 1922, as she was getting on a train from Cambridge, and she fell in love with it. Gerhardi was steeped in Russian literature – she thought *Futility* was like *Oblomov* – and she particularly liked its lightness and melancholy and its insight into the two nationalities. She wrote to him generously, telling him: 'You not only make your people live, but move & grow – & that's the very devil to achieve.' Gerhardi knew nothing about her, and thought she might be 'a lovely flapper polishing off her French at a Paris finishing school', until a visit to a bookshop showed him his mistake.

A comical attachment grew out of this first letter, in which Gerhardi played the sensitive, eccentric, wide-eyed disciple, and she the benign grande dame. He wrote effusively to thank her, addressing her as 'Miss Wharton', for which he was duly reproached. 'Do please forgive me for the "Miss" in my last letter. After all, it was a tentative "Miss", and I remember I took great care to make it look something between "Miss" and "Mrs".' He immediately asked her if he could use her letter in an advertisement for his next book, *The Polyglots* ('Is it a very shameless request? Are you very angry?'), and, amazingly, she said yes. Furthermore, she offered to help him with a French translation, she asked Canby at the *Saturday Review of Literature* if she could review it, and she wrote a preface for the American publication of *Futility*, in which she praised its insight into the double culture of the Russians and the English and for being 'extremely modern'. Gerhardi thanked her in his own particular way: 'The only adequate thing would be for me to transfer from the Anglican Church to the Orthodox, and put up candles for the salvation of your soul, in the Russian manner! (This might look as if I was a clergyman. Oh, no!)' They began to exchange literary views, on Constance Garnett's translations from the Russian (which she did not like), or on Katherine Mansfield (he had dedicated *Futility* to her, but Wharton found her stories too 'sliced off'). He asked her what it felt like to be a successful author ('Is it really, *really* nice to be famous?') and sympathised with her having too many house-guests ('Why not drown them in the Mediterranean?'). He praised her new novels in great detail, especially *The Children*, which made him cry.

Wharton seems to have enjoyed all this, since she invited him to stay at Ste-Claire in January 1924, a meeting which at first did not go tremendously well. Gerhardi gave his own version of it, some years later, in his *Memoirs of a Polyglot*. He had travelled on the train from Innsbruck with a large packet of sandwiches, and had some bread left over when he arrived, late in the evening, driven by the chauffeur from Toulon to Hyères, and greeted by Wharton, in the dark, from her bedroom window. Worried by what the butler would think of the bread and butter in his bag, he flushed the remains of the sandwiches down the lavatory, and went to bed. In the morning there was a great to-do about a blocked pipe. 'Edith Wharton, I heard afterwards, told people that I, coming from Siberia, had brought bread with me thinking there might be a shortage of food in her house.' Gerhardi spent the afternoon with Wharton in the garden, her face shaded by a hat. (He noticed several signposts in the grounds reading PRIVATE PROPERTY NO TRESPASSERS and POSITIVELY NO ADMITTANCE.)

> When I came down in the evening there was a woman in the drawing-room with yellowish hair whom I thought I had not seen before.
>
> We sat there waiting, as I thought, for our hostess. Presently we went in to dinner and I found myself sitting by the side of the woman to whom I had not been introduced, because of the absence of our hostess, I supposed. It seemed odd to me ... and after the soup I said to the woman at my side: 'But where is Mrs Wharton?'
>
> She looked at me with sad, inquiring thoughtfulness and said – very pertinently, as it seems to me now: 'I am Mrs Wharton.'
>
> 'Oh,' I said, 'are you Mrs Wharton?'
>
> She looked at me as if she thought I couldn't be all there. 'Of course I am,' she said.
>
> 'Oh ... good evening,' I said.

Wharton's version, to Berenson, was that this 'wistful Russianized English boy' was 'so shy that when I came down to dinner the first night he didn't recognize me, & thought I was "another lady" in evening dress, & wondered why we went in to dinner without our hostess!!!'

She was not in the least offended, and found 'poor little Gerhardi's' 'elfin' shyness and eccentricity charming, in spite of his over-eager literariness: 'He prefaced every remark with "Chekhov says" "Arnold Bennett says" or "Middleton Murry says".' She told Lapsley that he '*far surpassed* our united expectations in queerness'. The extent of his 'queerness' was a matter of frank discussion between her and John Hugh Smith: 'I never thought the poor creature was a homo, though he has many of the external signs; but he is certainly swamped in sex.' (She was right on all counts.) They discussed Proust and Chekhov and her habit of writing in bed in the mornings ('Of course, the great advantage you enjoy over me,' I said, while Mrs Wharton looked suspiciously at me, 'is that you needn't shave in the morning.'). He told her how difficult it was writing a novel: 'And let me tell you at once,' she said eagerly, 'that it doesn't get any easier as time goes on.' Gerhardi rented a tumbledown cottage near Toulon for a while, and became a regular visitor. He bought a horse and trap, but Wharton tried to persuade him to buy a Citroën. 'I don't at all want to seem inhospitable,' she told him, 'but I admit one would scarcely enjoy seeing your horse nibbling one's favourite pear tree.' He met her friends, Philomène, Robert Norton, the Comtesse de Béarn. Misunderstandings could still occur, as when Gerhardi told her that he thought she called her butler (whose name was Favre) 'Father', and it took them some time to work out what he was talking about. And she did not particularly want to be introduced to his millionaire friends, Lord Beaverbrook and Lord Rothermere: 'I don't mind if they come here to lunch', she told Gerhardi. 'But that does not mean I want to *go on* seeing them *always*.' On the whole, though, they were in sympathy. On one of his visits, Valéry was describing an 'extravagant' welcome he had had from D'Annunzio, and Wharton 'shook her head' and said: 'Yes, but think of the simplicity, the modesty of someone like Bach. No, great souls aren't made of such stuff.' Gerhardi continued grateful and affectionate towards Wharton (though she did not like his later work as much), inscribing his books to her: 'Soliciting an indulgent reception', or 'To Edith Wharton. With trepidation. William Gerhardi. Don't read it!'[19]

Wharton's pleasure in this brilliant oddity was like her relationship with Geoffrey Scott – they were the admiring, gifted young men, she was the generous, famous older novelist. The role did not work so well with the young American literary lions. She thought Faulkner's work deliberately unpleasant (*Sanctuary* made her want to write an article called 'Wuthering Depths'), but she liked Frank Norris's grimly realistic story of a tragic dentist, *McTeague*, and David Phillips's naturalist treatment of a prostitute's struggle for respectability, *Susan Lenox: Her Fall and Rise*, which was censored by the New York Society for the Suppression of Vice, and of which she possessed an unexpurgated copy. She admired Dreiser's *An American Tragedy*, and she thought Eugene O'Neill was 'our only real playwright'. She was tremendously taken by *Gentlemen Prefer Blondes* ('The Illuminating Diary of a Professional Lady'), a dazzling pastiche of American vulgarity and materialism which pretends to be much dumber than it is. The narrative of blonde bombshell Lorelei Lee from Little Rock, Arkansas, who tells the stories of her ruthless self-advancement and quest for cultural self-improvement in a blithe, racy, illiterate slang, hits all the targets Wharton was fond of attacking herself, like 'Bolshevicks', the Ritz, motion pictures, Jewish sugar-daddies, Dr Froyd (who tells Lorelei she 'needs to cultivate a few inhibitions') and Americans abroad ('I mean London is really nothing at all', but 'Paris is devine', says Lorelei). It seemed to her like a latter-day *Custom of the Country* ('Undine at last is vindicated!'). The readers at Ste-Claire decided it was '*the* greatest novel since *Manon Lescaut*'. Exceptionally, Wharton allowed the publisher Frank Crowninshield to use her praise for a blurb, and he arranged a meeting between Anita Loos and Wharton in Paris, which seemed to go well. She was always praising it and passing it around, testing her friends by whether they found it funny or not. She ordered the sequel, *But Gentlemen Marry Brunettes*, from her bookseller. And on her Mediterranean cruise, the evening readings alternated between the *Odyssey* and *Blondes*.

Wharton had less enthusiasm for a much more serious novel on contemporary social themes. She told Upton Sinclair in 1927 that she was impressed by the literary achievement of *Oil!*, his hard-hitting exposure of capitalist corruption and celebration of the Bolshevik revolution, which he had sent her, respectfully, and that she would defend it against charges of obscenity (it was banned in Boston for its outspokenness about birth-control). But it suffered from being a political pamphlet. 'The views which you teach . . . are detestable to me', she told him, adding grimly: 'I believe that a wider experience would have shown you that the evils you rightly satirize will be replaced by others more harmful to any sort of civilized living when your hero and his friends have had their way.' (The same note is struck in a letter of 1920 to Alice Garrett, about a revolutionary relation of hers: 'She seems to think the necessary regeneration of the world, for which the whole creation groans, could be rapidly accomplished by exterminating the Vanderbilts . . . I had no idea it was as easy as that – & yet tremble to think of the effect of one well-directed bomb – for what would the world be without Beauty? *Has she asked herself that?*') Wharton was unconvinced by the merits of the Sacco and Vanzetti cause. The trial and execution of the two radical working-class Italian Bostonians was the *cause célèbre* of the

American Left in the 1920s which was passionately supported by writers such as Upton Sinclair and Dos Passos. (Her friend Robert Grant was one of the judges who confirmed their sentence in 1927.) She wrote to Gerhardi: 'Have you noticed . . . that while the humanitarian world (or its *soi-disant* spokesmen) have – whether rightly or wrongly – raised a world outcry over the supposed mis-trial of Sacco and Vanzetti, not one protest has been made public as to the murder without trial at present going on in Russia?'[20]

Her mixed feelings were most evident over Scott Fitzgerald: but the difficulties were mutual. He sent her a copy of *Gatsby*, and she wrote to tell him that she liked it – except that he should have filled out Gatsby's early career, instead of giving 'a short résumé' of it. 'That would have *situated* him.' But 'you'll tell me that's the old way, & consequently not *your* way'. Despite the legend that he had gone down on his knees to her in their publishers' office, Fitzgerald did identify her with 'the old way'. In a 1920 sketch called 'This Is A Magazine', Fitzgerald has all the standard 'characters' to be found in the pages of any American magazine quarrelling and competing with each other. They include 'The Baseball Yarn', 'The British Serial', 'The Robert Chambers Story' (author of hugely popular romances and horror stories), and 'The Edith Wharton Story'. The 'Edith Wharton Story' is standoffish and snooty, responding to the crudity of 'The Baseball Story' with 'a frigid and Jamesian silence', dubious about the status of a new little story ('My Dear Man, she's nobody. Seems to have no family – nothing but a past') and tangling with 'The Robert Chambers Story', who tells her: 'My dear lady, your climax is on crooked.' The Edith Wharton Story replies huffily: 'At least I have one. They tell me you drag horribly.' In 1924 Fitzgerald dismissed her as 'having fought the good fight with stone-age weapons'; the motto of the younger generation of American writers was 'Down with Henry James! Down with Edith Wharton! Down with the sterility of *The Waste Land*!'

None of this boded well for Fitzgerald's visit to the Pavillon Colombe, which took place on Sunday, 5 July 1925. Fitzgerald came to tea with the composer-son of Daisy Chanler, Teddy (a depressive character whom Fitzgerald knew quite well and would use as the model for Francis Melarky, an early version of Dick Diver in *Tender is the Night*). There are, of course, different versions of what took place. Wharton's version is the most succinct: 'To tea, Teddy Chanler & Scott Fitzgerald, the novelist (horrible)'. The story retailed in the 1951 biography of Fitzgerald by Arthur Mizener is that Zelda Fitzgerald refused to go because she did not want to be patronised, Fitzgerald had several drinks on the way out of Paris, arrived drunk, and immediately tried to shock Wharton (and the other guest,

Lapsley) by telling her that he and Zelda had been living for three weeks in a brothel. Wharton 'squelched' him, and he 'fled' back to Paris and burst out to Zelda: 'They beat me! They beat me! They *beat* me!' Meanwhile Wharton told Lapsley that there seemed to be something peculiar about that young man, and Lapsley said Fitzgerald was drunk. Teddy Chanler corrected this story in the late 1950s, saying that Fitzgerald was not drunk, but 'overawed by Mrs Wharton's formal manner'. He tried her with compliments, but 'she would not play along with him'. Then, to jolly the party along, he asked permission to tell a story 'about an American couple he knew who had mistakenly spent their first days in Paris in a brothel'. Wharton asked 'what they did there'. Chanler thought that Fitzgerald had been driven to his 'desperate conversational measure' by 'Mrs Wharton's unyielding formality and stiffness'. Another Fitzgerald biographer, Matthew Bruccoli, commented that Wharton 'apparently missed the point of the story'. But her response was perhaps more ironic than anyone observed. (She is also supposed to have told him that his brothel story 'lacked data'.) They never met again.[21]

Wharton was at her stiffest with Fitzgerald because she would have known that he thought her old-fashioned, as others of 'les jeunes' did. After *The Glimpses of the Moon* came out, Jewett told her that 'we are preparing a broadside in answer . . . to the Young Intellectuals who, like young terriers worrying a muff, have lashed themselves into an idle rage over your novel'. ('Empty', 'cold', 'trivial', 'not worth doing', were the phrases used; Rebecca West accused it of 'deadly sterility'. Only Katherine Fullerton Gerould, her long-ago secret rival in love, whom she was amused to hear was reviewing it, praised it warmly.) A typical caricature of her was made by Somerset Maugham, who met her only once, in London, in 1908 (though they were Riviera neighbours). His memory of her, written down many years after the event, is a perfect example of how she was regarded by many younger, male writers, and of her formal manner with strangers when she felt ill-at-ease. (It also, interestingly, presents her as an expert on all things French, rather than as an American.)

> She was seated in the middle of a small French sofa in such a way as to give it the appearance of a throne, and since she gave no indication that she wished to share it with me I took a chair and sat down in front of her. She was a smallish woman, with fine eyes, regular features and a pale clear skin drawn rather tightly over the bones of her face. She was dressed with the sober magnificence suitable to women of birth, of wealth and of letters . . . She talked and I listened. She talked very well. She

talked for twenty minutes. In that time, with a light touch and well-chosen words, she traversed the fields of painting, music and literature. Nothing she said was commonplace, everything she said was just. She said exactly the right things about Maurice Barrès, André Gide and Paul Valéry; it was impossible not to concur with her admirable remarks upon Debussy and Stravinsky; and of course what she had to say about Rodin and Maillol, about Cézanne, Degas and Renoir, was just what one would have wished her to say. . . . But Mrs Wharton got me down . . . She was devoid of frailty. Her taste was faultless . . . but in the end I began to grow a trifle restive. It would have been a comfort to me if I could have found a chink in the shining armour of her impeccable refinement, if she had unaccountably expressed a sneaking tenderness for something that was downright vulgar . . . But no. She said nothing but the right thing about the right person . . . At last I said to her: 'And what do you think of Edgar Wallace?'

'Who is Edgar Wallace?' she replied.

'Do you never read thrillers?'

'No.'

Never has a monosyllable contained more frigid displeasure, more shocked disapproval nor more wounded surprise . . . Her manner was that of a woman to whom a man has made proposals offensive to her modesty, but which her good breeding tells her it will be more dignified to ignore than to make a scene about.

'I'm afraid it's getting very late,' said Mrs Wharton.

I knew my audience was at an end. I never saw her again. She was an admirable creature, but not my cup of tea.[22]

Wharton had much warmer relations with two younger American writers, one a big name in his time (though not much read now), the other an almost forgotten woman writer. She wrote some of her most generous professional letters to Sinclair Lewis and Zona Gale; but she did not form close personal friendships with either of them. Lewis, twenty-seven years her junior, had been an Edith Wharton addict in his early years, and when he learnt that *The Age of Innocence* had replaced *Main Street* for the Pulitzer Prize, he wrote her a friendly and admiring letter and received a warm reply. He and his wife Grace went to the Pavillon Colombe in October 1921, to have lunch with her and with John Hugh Smith and Gaillard Lapsley. Grace Lewis remembered 'an atmosphere of good taste and liveried servants', 'much delicate dissecting of the technique of writing', and Mrs Wharton wearing white gloves as they went round the garden. A few weeks later, Lewis wrote to ask if he could dedicate *Babbitt* to her, and she replied sweetly: 'I am a little dizzy! No one has ever wanted to dedicate a book to me before.' As it turned out, though she enjoyed its 'vitality & vivacity', she liked *Babbitt* less than *Main Street*, for very Whartonian reasons. She thought that Carol Kennicott's critical detachment from her small-town environment made *Main Street* a better novel than *Babbitt*, because Babbitt was 'in & of Zenith up to his chin & over', and the author had to keep intervening. She was not sure whether 'the American public' would be able to understand the irony, and she thought it had too much 'slang'. 'Slang' was very much on her mind. A letter to Daisy Chanler, thanking her for her praise of *A Son at the Front*, summed up her sense of linguistic estrangement:

> No, I'm afraid my young Americans don't talk the language as spoken by the Scott Fitzgerald & Sinclair Lewis jeunesse; but I saw dozens of young Americans from all parts of America during the war, & none of them talked it . . . I believe it's a colossal literary convention, invented by the delightful Sinclair Lewis, & adopted by the throng of lesser ones.

Her correspondence with Lewis continued, but each of them became less enthusiastic about the other. In March 1925, in Hyères, she got out of bed with a cold to have tea with the Lewises, but it was a mutually unsatisfactory meeting. Wharton wrote to Lapsley that Lewis was 'utterly unperceiving, & frankly interested only in the sale of *Arrowsmith*! What a queer product – for he really *is* an artist, though he seems so unaware of it.' And Lewis wrote, in an unfinished piece for H.L. Mencken: 'These damned Americans who live in So. France or Italy – they are so thin-blooded, so introverted, so refined, so Literary. But how the hell could one find 'em in any save a Henry James book . . . ?' Of his next novel, *Elmer Gantry*, she said scathingly: '[It] is a pitiful production. America *is* like that, no doubt, but not all and only like that – As I said to Walter the other day, the trouble with them all is that they don't know what a gentleman is, & after all it was a useful standard to get one's perspective by.' In 1928, when Lewis was planning a novel, *Dodsworth*, in part about Americans in Europe, she warned him, tellingly:

> I hope your Americans in Europe . . . will really be in Europe and not in little continental Americas like the café du Dôme and kindred haunts. Do let them forget America for a while and become aware of Europe, for current fiction has had too many of the other kind lately, and it would be an exciting change to have young American [*sic*] in Paris become even faintly aware that he was not in Broadway.

Her target was the generation described in Malcolm Cowley's *Exile's Return*, including Hemingway, Fitzgerald, Dos Passos and Cummings.

Yet Lewis made a profound impression on her. Vance Weston in *Hudson River Bracketed* and *The Gods Arrive*, though partly autobiographical, is also inspired by Sinclair Lewis's raw upbringing in 1890s Minnesota, his passionate youthful self-education and religious fervour, his struggle to make it in New York as a freelance journalist, his false starts and poverty, his tentative early novels and his destruction of the first draft of *Main Street* before its huge success, his problems with publishers, and his unhappy marriage. When Wharton praised *Main Street* in 1927 as an 'epoch-making' work which 'with a swing of the pen hacked away the sentimental vegetation from the American small town', she was thinking about her own story of an American writer from the Midwest who wanted to be true to the realities of America. He is also a graceless and aggressive young man, who embodies her sense that being a genius, in early twentieth-century America, was thought to be man's work. She felt out of sympathy with the *machismo* of the 'lost generation'. When the Lewises were divorced she wrote kindly to Grace Lewis (pointedly saying that 'for his case, especially, I wish it had been otherwise'). When Grace Lewis wrote *Half a Loaf*, a transparent *roman à clef* about her marriage, Lewis's infidelity and alcoholism, and sent it to Wharton with an effusive dedication, she welcomed it. And her other literary friendship at this time was with a woman writing, like Wharton, about the restrictions of American women's lives.[23]

Zona Gale, a talented Wisconsin writer about ten years younger than Wharton, who had won the Pulitzer for her stage adaptation of *Miss Lulu Bett* in the same year that *The Age of Innocence* won, and who was also an Appleton author, wrote enthusiastically to Rutger Jewett about *The Glimpses of the Moon*. He passed the letter on, and used it in an ad for the book. Wharton wrote gratefully, putting *Miss Lulu Bett* alongside *Main Street* as one of the few American novels which 'extracted significance & beauty out of plain things As They Are' and praising the 'unerring economy' with which Gale had built up her 'hard little picture'. But she gave her a long lecture on her deliberate use of an impoverished American language: 'It's as if you had nothing but pennies in your pocket ... To me this endless succession of chopped up, click-click sentences, each with its own little adroit "pop" of a surprise ... suggests the *tempo* of hurried, racing, breathless lives ... And there is that mighty inheritance of English speech ... that great river of innumerable tributaries ... all to your hand.' Gale replied emotionally: 'It is like being knighted & as if I might now at last begin the long quest.' A mutually attentive correspondence started up, in which (as always now) Wharton was the grand master and Gale was the disciple. But she wrote more candidly to Gale than to her male correspondents about her fear of being regarded as a back number:

> I'm always, watchfully and patiently, on the look-out for what you young people are doing, and exulting and triumphing when a Lulu or a Babbitt emerges – the real surprise is that any of you should care about my work and my point of view. I thought you all regarded me as the Mrs – well, fill in a respectable deceased Victorian name [she means Mrs Ward] – of America, for, having all through my early career been condemned by the reviewers of my native land for 'not knowing how to construct' a novel, I am now far more utterly banned by their descendants for 'constructing'.

She was less enthusiastic about Gale's next novel, *Faint Perfume*, writing to say (just as James used to say to her) that she thought Gale had slighted her best subject, the mother's retrospective jealousy – that ought to have been, she told her, her 'front centre'. Gale stood up to this criticism and said she had learned a great deal from it. 'This look of yours towards me', she wrote 'is very dear to me, the wise word, the friendly hand.' Wharton wrote more warmly about the next book, *Preface to a Life*, saying it had 'the deep undertone of emotion which the hollow and tinny fiction of today so signally fails to give forth'. However, her essays and her short book on fiction did not mention Gale, and Gale's review of *The Writing of Fiction* wished it had included some 'modern writers'. Still, Wharton was grateful for the review: 'Why, you've actually read my book! You've thought about it! You've re-thought it, actually, in your own mind!' The correspondence turned into a polite exchange of apologies, criss-crossing between Wisconsin and France, for their never managing to meet; but clearly this exceptional connection to a younger American woman writer was important, even comforting, to Wharton.[24]

She wanted to put her mixed feelings towards the next generation of writers on record. *The Writing of Fiction*, suggested to her by Charles Scribner for his magazine, came out between autumn 1924 and early 1925, and was dedicated to Lapsley. It is a short collection of essays on topics like how to construct a novel, or 'character and situation', with an enthusiastic coda on Proust. Under the surface of this dogmatic meditation on the art of fiction (in the genre of Robert Norton's book on painting, Percy Lubbock's *The Craft of Fiction* or James's essays) there are some interesting self-revelations. She distrusts representations of the unconscious and the 'stream-of-consciousness' method because 'in the world of normal men life

is conducted . . . on fairly coherent and selective lines'. She says the imagination needs to work through a mixture of immersion and detachment.
She believes in ordering and objectivity. Personal confession always needs
to be 'transposed'. 'Self-confession' does not make a good novel. Selection
is all: make the main character 'typical' and you can have fewer minor
characters; shift the point of view as seldom as possible. To get across the
passage of time, go 'very quietly', and 'keep down the tone of the narrative'. Emotions should be kept under control (here she sounds like Flaubert):
'The business of the artist is to make weep, and not to weep, to make laugh,
and not to laugh.' Occasionally she mentions something which by implication has influenced her, like Balzac's construction of witnesses to a tragic
provincial story in 'La Grande Bretèche' (see *Ethan Frome*), or Proust's brilliant realisation of 'the hopeless incurable passion of a sensitive man for a
stupid uncomprehending woman' (see *Custom*). She keeps coming back to
the same nineteenth-century novelists – Balzac, Tolstoy, Thackeray, George
Eliot, Flaubert, Stendhal, Trollope, James – and she insists on the qualities
of objectivity, ordering, 'working over', economy, patience and quietness.
The comparisons with modern writing are mostly by inference, though there
are some pointed passages on a 'pathological' writing which becomes
'an idiot's tale, signifying nothing' (see Faulkner) or on 'dirt-for-dirt's sake'
(see Joyce). She resents the contemporary insistence on speed and sensation and the public's demand for popular authors to keep on repeating
themselves.

All this is firm, opinionated and clear-cut. But at the end of the book
there is suddenly a strange passage in which she says that 'fear' is Proust's
main motive: 'Fear ruled his moral world: fear of death, fear of responsibility, fear of draughts, fear of fear. It formed the inexorable horizon of his
universe and the hard delimitation of his artist's temperament.' Everything
he did, she says, was done 'in conflict with these disabilities'. And she
concludes with one of her favourite sayings from Nietzsche (which is also
in her Commonplace Book): 'Everything worth while is accomplished
notwithstanding'. For her to end this authoritative rubric on the novel with
a passage on fear and disabilities makes for a touching, even anxious,
moment.[25]

A series of essays in the late 1920s and early 1930s continued the argument. Wharton suggested these pieces herself to magazine editors (Henry
Canby at the *Saturday Review of Literature*, Wilbur Cross at the *Yale Review*),
concerned not to be thought 'a novelist of the old school incapable of
understanding the new generation'. 'The Great American Novel' (1927)
complained about the democratisation of American fiction. Why should

all of it now have to deal with 'local life' on Main Street, and with 'persons so limited in education and opportunity that they live cut off from all the varied sources of culture which used to be considered the common heritage of English-speaking people'? The narrowing of subject had coincided with an impoverished use of the English language. The new American novel should range more widely, and deal with the 'wandering' or 'expatriate' American. But she did not think the modern world should be ignored or shuddered at by the novelist: he must 'use his opportunity by plunging both hands into the motley welter'. In 'A Cycle of Reviewing' (1928) she reflected ironically on how her critics accuse her of writing only about the rich. Even if that were true (which she rightly denies), then – why not? Proust wrote only about 'the fashionable', and consider his range! Reviewers now seemed only to want 'a certain line of goods'. In 'Visibility in Fiction' (1929) and 'Tendencies in Modern Fiction' (1934) she compared the short-cuts and 'kodak' methods deriving from Zola and naturalism with the depth and patience of Balzac, Jane Austen, Thackeray and the great Russians. She complained again about modern writers' arbitrary slices of life (citing Mansfield) and characters who are 'helpless puppets on a sluggish stream of fatality'. In 'Permanent Values in Fiction', she castigated Joyce, Woolf and Lawrence for using their characters as 'megaphones' for a 'message', and compared them adversely with the more 'lasting stuff' of Lewis and Dreiser and with the deep characterisations of Anna Karenina, Becky Sharp, or Père Goriot. She blamed the 'passing notoriety' of modern fiction on 'a long course of cinema obviousnesses and tabloid culture'.[26]

A part of her wanted to shut herself away and cultivate her garden: indeed her gardens became almost symbolic of her retreat from the modern. She was finished with public works, and the politics of France was becoming almost as alienating to her as American culture. She had a horror of what she saw happening to her adoptive country. The tragic mass mourning of a decimated nation, terribly afraid for its security, was entangled with a bitter debate over what the war had been for, and what France could gain from its victory. The attempt to create a 'national triumph' out of the horror of the war involved an (understandably) vindictive attitude to Germany. The bitter, and unworkable, Treaty of Versailles with its insistence on 'reparations', led to a poisoned and increasingly divided post-war attitude between the international powers, a chronically unstable and polarised Third Republic, and, as one historian sums it up, 'a vengeful but unvanquished Germany'. The French trade unions, looking to the Bolshevik republic as their example and guide, were flexing their muscles against the bourgeoisie: there were strikes, mutinies, and a great increase in worker militarism, all repulsive to Wharton. There was also a violent split on the left between the socialists and the communists. The franc toppled in value. Seven ministers of finance in the early 1920s failed to bring stability. After Poincaré's retirement in 1929, there were five successive governments, and a battle between the divided left and the right-of-centre 'Bloc National'. The terror of renewed German aggression led to the building of the expensive and misconceived 'Maginot Line' in the 1930s. Coinciding with the rise of Hitler in Germany, there was what amounted in France to a civil war between the revolutionary left-wing and the extreme right-wing nationalists. The 'Front Populaire' under Léon Blum, anxiously opposing fascism within France, was blind to the threat of Hitler until too late, and would disintegrate in June 1937 – as it happened, a few weeks before the death of Edith Wharton. Lucky for her that she did not live to see the defeat and invasion of France in 1940. Like Henry James in 1916, she would have died in horror.[27]

In 1919 she had written to Alice Garrett: 'I shall pop into my little châteaulet at St Brice . . . and all my winters to come, please the Lord, I shall spend in the sun. There's my political programme.'[28] But although she invested so much in privacy, and seemed to cut herself off from the contemporary politics and popular culture of her adopted and her native country, she was drawn to the 'welter' which also repelled her. Though living so far away from it, she took American culture as her subject in all her later novels, even if she transferred her American characters to Europe (the Riviera, Paris, Venice or Switzerland). It was a shrewd commercial strategy to write this run of novels, The Glimpses of the Moon (1922), The Mother's Recompense (1925), Twilight Sleep (1927), The Children (1928), Hudson River Bracketed (1929) and The Gods Arrive (1932). Though they are much less read now than her earlier work, they were big successes at the time and made her a great deal of money. And they emerged out of an abiding fascination with the stuff of modern America. They are filled with detail about the very culture from which she felt herself so alienated. Her position in the novels is much more complex than it is in the letters or the essays.

The translation of emotional values into a false currency is at the heart of The Glimpses of the Moon. The story is light and slight, but has a sombre moralistic undertow. A bargain is struck between a young couple, Susy Branch and a would-be writer, Nick Lansing, charming but impecunious members of the drifting, international set. The two are so mutually charmed, but so clearly unable to afford each other, that they decide to try out a short-term marriage, living off the wedding presents and in whatever honey-mooning houses they are offered by their rich friends, for as long as they can – perhaps for a year, perhaps a little more. If either of them sees a chance to do better, or gets bored, the 'transferable' experiment can be discontinued, with no 'sneaking' or 'fibbing'. (All the characters speak in facile slang.) The bargain is made possible by the ease of divorce and the indifference to scandal in their transient social world. It will be a 'free-masonry', a good companionship, and an adventure. Their sexual attraction to each other is made clear, but kept light. Wharton is turning her tragic themes into comedy. Susy and Nick are in the same predicament as Lily Bart and Lawrence Selden in *The House of Mirth*, but they find a different solution, a very up-to-date one, since 'companionate', or 'trial', marriage (childless by means of birth-control) was becoming a hot topic in the 1920s.[29]

As their light, parasitic, rootless story develops, Nick feels increasing revulsion at the situations they land themselves in (involving bribes, lies, and other people's adulteries), and Susy's primitive – and maternal – instincts begin to assert themselves. They split up, and only reunite, at the last, when 'deep-seated instinctive needs' have overridden the modern experiment. Wharton sums up the subject to Berenson as an attempt 'to picture the adventures of a young couple who believe themselves to be completely *affranchis* & up-to-date, but are continually tripped up by obsolete sensibilities & discarded ideals. – A difficult subject, which of course seemed the easiest in the world when I began it.' To the editor of the *Revue de France*, which published it in translation, she explained: '*La lune en question est la lune de miel qui re-apparait entre les épais nuages d'un mariage très agité et très "modern style".*'[30]

She enjoys herself with her 'denationalized' jet-set, invoking one of her favourite poems, Browning's elegy for hedonism, 'A Toccata of Galuppi's', as their signature-tune: 'What of soul was left, I wonder, when the kissing had to stop?' These are the kind of people who regard Venice 'simply as affording exceptional opportunities for bathing and adultery'. (The Appleton proof-reader took fright at this, she told Mary Berenson: 'Could not this be replaced by a less Biblical word?' Wharton commented: 'Quel pays!!'[31]) The problem with the novel is that Susy and Nick have to be part of that world, but also capable of moral recoil from it. The deliberate echoes of Lily Bart (Susy turns down an advantageous marriage, looks at a Reynolds portrait, thinks about working as a milliner) point up the lack of social pressures here. Because there is no ruling standard of behaviour or fear of scandal, because divorce is easy and reputation is not an issue (unlike in *The House of Mirth, Old New York* or *The Age of Innocence*), correctives to behaviour have to come from some inner instinct. This makes for unconvincing gestures towards integrity and remorse, in characters whose whole *raison d'être* is lightness and superficiality.[32]

Wharton generates some flashes of her power in this uneven book. She has a strong minor character, Coral Hicks, a Midwestern heiress from Undine Spragg's old town, a female Morgan or Rockefeller, who tells Nick that she 'wants to promote culture, like those Renaissance women you're always talking about. I want to do it for Apex City.' And she treats with pathos the couple's confused misery while they are separated, Nick's truce with 'that bright enemy called happiness', Susy's inability to escape her memories ('waiting quietly, patiently, obstinately, like poor people in a doctor's office') and the unreality that comes over solitaries in the great city: 'The eyes of the metropolis seemed fixed on him in an immense unblinking stare.' The reunion scenes, in the sad, grey little Paris suburban street, are tender and delicate. There is a peculiar ambiguity about the novel's historical moment. Because Wharton had begun it in 1916, set it aside, then finished it in 1921, it reads at first like a pre-war novel, but it was marketed in 1922 as contemporaneous, 'a novel of society today'. Yet almost all the way through there is a disconcerting gap, as though all these blithe characters had agreed not to mention the war. Only towards the end of the novel it presses in. Susy, alone at night near the Arc de Triomphe, feels she is looking at the city 'from the other side of the grave; and as she got up and wandered down the Champs-Élysées, half empty in the evening lull between dusk and dinner, she felt as if the glittering avenue were really changed into the Field of Shadows from which it takes its name, and as if she were a ghost among ghosts'. Nick, also pacing alone through the Paris crowds, watches 'people bargain, argue, philander, work-girls stroll past in linked bands, beggars whine on the bridges, derelicts doze in the pale winter sun, mothers in mourning hasten by taking children to school, and street-walkers beat their weary rounds before the cafés'. At last the terrible, silent historical fact underlying this light romance is glimpsed.[33]

Badly reviewed though it was, *Glimpses* fitted the 1922 market very well, as Jewett had anticipated. Aggressively advertised, it was a huge best-seller, as big as *The House of Mirth*, selling 60,000 copies in three weeks and 100,000 within a few months. The film-rights were sold to Paramount for $15,000 and the film was made within a year. There was a bidding war between two magazines, *McCall's* and *The Pictorial Review*, for the next novel, *The Mother's Recompense*, for which she was paid an advance of $27,000. Her stories were commanding magazine prices like $6,000 (for

'New Year's Day'). She made about $60,000 in a year from *Glimpses*. And although *A Son at the Front* (1923), as expected, did not do well, and *Old New York* (1924) took her readers back in time, there was an eager appetite for more contemporaneous stuff from Edith Wharton. *The Mother's Recompense* (1925) had it both ways: it was a story of modern New York, but it was about a character who could have come out of, and feels that she belongs to, a pre-war novel.[34]

The Mother's Recompense was written in 1923, serialised in 1924 (starting its run before the last chapters were finished) and published in April 1925. Wharton gave her modern book the air of a nineteenth-century novel by 'appropriating' (as she said) her title from an immensely popular, decorous English lady novelist. Grace Aguilar's *The Mother's Recompense* (1851), like her other works, *Home Influence* and *Woman's Friendship*, was a pious, sentimental celebration of feminine virtues: 'There are many sorrows and many cares inseparable from maternal love', says the mother of the title, 'but they are forgotten, utterly forgotten, or only remembered to enhance the sweetness of the recompense that ever follows.' Though it made the novel look old-fashioned, this was an ironic borrowing. In a prefatory note, Wharton said that she had completely changed the emphasis of Aguilar's work, 'loved of our grandmothers'. She stole the title to subvert the standards of the past and to cast a dark light on mother–daughter relations.[35] Though it has a bland surface, this is a disconcerting and troubling book. It is shaken up by the violent split between the pre-war and post-war world – what Wharton calls the 'universal eclipse'. It is full of ghosts and memories crowding ominously into the present. It ties its heroine inside a net of social pressures. And (written by a daughterless woman) it imagines a difficult relationship between mother and daughter. In all these respects it resembles *Mrs Dalloway* more than Wharton might have thought herself.[36]

Dates matter in this novel, though they are hardly ever mentioned. It is set in 1919, and describes a post-war return from France to America. In 'flashback', we learn that Kate Clephane, an American woman born in 1874 in the Midwest ('Meridia', this time, not Apex) made a dull, oppressive New York marriage in 1895; had one daughter, Anne, two years later; and ran away from the marriage in 1900 with a worldly dilettante whom she left after two years. She is forbidden by her formidable mother-in-law, Mrs Clephane, ever to see her daughter again, though in 1907 she tries, like Anna Karenina, to visit her. She lives a dim, purposeless Continental life, like other women in her position, for many 'lonely humdrum' years. In 1913, aged thirty-nine, she meets the great love of her life, a young American, Chris Fenno, and they have a passionate affair. They move into the Riviera world of 'jazz-bands and baccarat tables'. But, like a modern Vronsky, he becomes restless in wartime, and leaves her, in spite of her pleas, to fight for France. Kate Clephane is not much like Edith Wharton, but her obtuse, self-important husband, her choice of a life in France, and her failed love-affair, echo her author's past. The war gives Kate and her set a kind of spurious respectability: 'for those uprooted drifting women [it] was chiefly a healing and amalgamating influence'. Like her author, she is awarded a French medal for her war-work. But after the war she settles back into bridge parties at the rectory, visits to the casinos, the milliners and the hairdressers.

In 1919, when the novel begins, she is summoned to America by her forgiving daughter, who is about to marry. But in a savage – and forced – twist of the plot, Anne's fiancé turns out to be Kate's ex-lover. The fragile reunion between mother and daughter comes undone, as Kate tries to prevent the marriage while keeping her secret. The woman who pays, who must be childless or lose her child, the woman alone and jealous, the thwarted or inadequate mother – some of Wharton's most obsessive themes – are painfully insistent here. The novel echoes 'Autres Temps . . .', 'The Old Maid', and 'New Year's Day'. In all these stories, secrets come out, what has been repressed returns to haunt the characters, and the past never loses its power.

As soon as Kate wakes up at the beginning of the novel, she starts to think about time (like the Marschallin in *Der Rosenkavalier*, who also loses her much younger lover to a young girl, and who wants to stop all the clocks in her house. Wharton watched this opera 'ecstatic & spellbound' with Berenson in 1913, just after her divorce). In the first few pages, Kate counts back the days to her affair, lies to herself about her age, recalls the years since her marriage, tries to work out how old her lover and her daughter must be now, counts time on her fingers, hears her heart beat, sees the grey in her hair. After this urgent, nervy first chapter, time rules the book, and there are always clocks within earshot. When Kate goes to confront Chris, 'a clock she had not noticed began to tick insistently. It seemed to be measuring out the last seconds before some nightmare crash that she felt herself powerless to arrest.'[37]

In the Clephane Fifth Avenue house, heavy with its old furnishings, which she ran away from eighteen years before, her past surrounds her. She increasingly feels that nothing has changed for her. Yet she is 'morbidly receptive of details' of the rapidly changing city. The old house still has its Aubusson carpets, but it also has a lift and a telephone. The city has its 'Undergrounds and its Elevateds', its skyscrapers and motors and huge shops. The lives of the young are made up of 'sudden comings and goings, and violent changes of plan'. One of Anne's friends, a typical flapper, Lilla, seems to Kate a hateful 'symptom' of the times, 'tawny and staring, in white furs and big pendulous earrings . . . as she stood there, circling the room with her sulky contemptuous gaze'. Lilla says she 'only likes noises that don't mean anything'.

Kate's image of the city is of mechanical flow, like that of a 'moving staircase', a 'flood of material ease, the torrent of facilities on which they were all embarked'. Everyone is beginning to look the same, to have the 'collective American Face', as if it had been 'made by the manufacturer of sporting-goods'. Everyone is on the same level: so Chris, former war-hero, gets a job 'interviewing film-stars and baseball fans and female prohibitionists'. Language is being standardised. Anne, who is trying to be a painter, can barely write a letter, and her way of telling her mother she loves her is to say that they have agreed to be 'the two most perfect pals that ever were'.[38] To Kate, this flow of the new seems to be surreally passing her by: 'her tired bewildered eyes seemed to see the buildings move with the vehicles, as a stationary train appears to move to travellers on another line'. But some features of the new world have their beauty. When she goes into Anne's barely furnished studio at dusk, she is struck by the glamour of the modern city:

> Kate, coming out of the winter twilight, found herself in a great half-lit room with a single wide window overlooking the reaches of the Sound all jewelled and netted with lights, the fairy span of the Brooklyn Bridge, and the dark roof-forest of the intervening city. It all seemed strangely significant and mysterious in that disguising dusk – full of shadows, distances, invitations. Kate leaned in the window, surprised at this brush of the wings of poetry.[39]

For a moment, Wharton (not the only writer to be moved by the Brooklyn Bridge) acknowledges the romantic possibilities of the twentieth-century American urban landscape. But this is a rare moment of pleasure. For most of the novel Kate Clephane feels like a 'tenuous and spectral' guest, or ghost, at the feast. She creeps up on Anne and Chris embracing in front of Anne's wedding-dress like a spooky voyeur; and she fears the time when mother and daughter would be left 'facing each other like two ghosts in a gray world of disenchantment'.[40] Her self-engrossed narrative is full of strange gaps and evasions. Even when she is at last telling the truth, she still fabricates and hedges:

'It was – long ago?'

'Yes. Six years – eight years. I don't know . . .' She heard herself pushing the date back farther and farther, but she could not help it.

That feeling of helplessness invades all her emotional life. She can hardly control or understand her own feelings. Her emotions for her daughter are as powerful as those she had for her lover; she is sometimes frightened by the similarity between these two 'isolated and devouring' desires. 'She thirsted to have the girl to herself, where she could touch her hair, stroke her face, draw the gloves from her hands, kiss her over and over again, and little by little, from that tall black-swathed figure, disengage the round child's body she had so long continued to feel against her own, like a warmth and an ache, as the amputated feel the life in a lost limb.' But we are never sure how much Kate understands any of this: 'Was she physically jealous? . . . Was that why she had felt from the first as if some incestuous horror hung between them?' A portrait of Beatrice Cenci hangs above the guest-room double-bed (like a planted clue about incestuous desire), and Kate is grimly amused by its incongruity. Wharton told John Hugh Smith that 'the incest-element' was important 'in justifying her anguish', but that it 'wd hardly be visible in its exact sense to *her*'. But it is not clear whether the 'incest-element' is the mother's desire for her daughter, or her horror at the spectacle of her daughter with her own lover.[41]

The key to the novel, Wharton said, was its title-page quotation from Shelley's *Prometheus*, 'Desolation is a delicate thing'. That phrase leads on to an image of sleepers who dream 'visions of aëreal joy, and call the monster, Love, / And wake, and find the shadow Pain'. Kate's greatest horror is the idea of 'sterile pain'. She sacrifices herself so that her daughter will not experience such pain; and this seems to be her only ·'recompense'. But to read recompense as 'reward', in Grace Aguilar's sense, is misleading. The original sense of recompense is 'atonement', and this fits better. Wharton did not like Louis Gillet's French title for his translation of the novel, *Le Bilan*, with its sense of 'reckoning' or 'balance-sheet', which she thought had a Bourget-like over-emphasis. (She suggested 'Vendanges', wine-harvests, 'Le Retour', or 'Demeter'. But she was pleased with his translation, and amused that their mutual friend Schlumberger had said: '*Comme Madame Wharton écrit merveilleusement le français!*') She wanted the title to have a religious undertone. Kate Clephane half confides in an Episcopalian bishop, and is tempted to step inside a Catholic church on the Upper West Side and go to confession. These moments in the novel point to Wharton's growing interest in Catholicism after the war. But in this novel there is no forgiveness and no reward. The woman has to atone, not for having left her husband, or for being divorced, or for having had an affair, but for having abandoned her child.[42]

Like *The Glimpses of the Moon, The Mother's Recompense* had extremely mixed reviews and huge sales, competing with *The Great Gatsby* on the best-seller lists. She made $55,000 from it within a few months. (Her tax bills were correspondingly enormous: she had already told Jewett in 1923 that the American tax on her earnings was 'of such magnitude that it is a distinct discouragement to further work'. Her double taxes became an increasing source of anxiety.) She was also winning prizes and honours. In 1924 she declined her election to the post of honorary vice-president of the Authors' League of America. At the start of 1925 she was the first woman to be awarded the gold medal of the National Institute of Arts and Letters for 'distinguished achievement in Fiction'. In 1929 she took the gold medal of the American Academy of Arts and Letters for 'special distinction in literature', and was elected, in Britain, to the Royal Society of Literature (though she later resigned because she did not want to go on paying the four-guinea subscription when she never attended meetings). In 1930, and again in 1931, Columbia University offered her a second D.Litt., but she turned it down on grounds of health, unwilling to make the journey, in spite of some forcefully persuasive letters from President Butler. Her reply, which gave away her feelings, hoped that in future years she might be well enough 'to support such honours unflinchingly'. In 1930 she was made a member of the American Academy. One nomination came to nothing: in 1927, Mildred and Robert Bliss (he was then American ambassador to Sweden), with support from Bourget and some eminent Yale professors, proposed her for the Nobel Prize. She did not expect to get it; it went in 1926 to a Sardinian writer, Grazia Deledda, in 1927 to Henri Bergson, and in 1928 to Sigrid Undset. (Kenneth Clark would say that *The Custom of the Country* was too cynical for the Swedish jury.)[43]

As soon as *The Mother's Recompense* was out, she proposed to Jewett 'another novel of ultra-modern New York life'. This was her 'jazz' novel, *Twilight Sleep*, the first full-length novel set entirely in America she had written since *The Fruit of the Tree*, twenty years before. The difference between them shows how much her interests and style had changed. *The Fruit of the Tree* was slow, realist, influenced by George Eliot, and absorbed in the agonised dilemmas of its two central characters. *Twilight Sleep* is rapid, chattery, farcical, thinly spread, and deliberately superficial – more like *Gatsby* than *Middlemarch*. Yet the two very different novels ask some similar questions. The most 'old-fashioned' character in *Twilight Sleep*, Nona, wants to know what her 'obligations and responsibilities' are, or if such things any longer exist, and is always puzzling over the relationship between her individual life and the social fabric: 'Where did one's own personality end, and that of people, landscape, chairs, or spectacle-cases, begin?'[44] Philosophical statements in this novel, however, mostly come with a health warning. *Twilight Sleep* is a vortex of fatuously competing, fashionable belief-systems. It is the only one of these 1920s experiments which tries to be relentlessly modern and American, without allowing in depths of character, backward glances of memory or nostalgia, or enriching European influences. (Europe is referred to only as the site of 'obsolete superstition unworthy of enlightened Americans' or of the wicked Catholic oppression of women who cannot get divorced.) It is a family story of 'dark and lurid' unpleasant-ness acted out as bright farce. The effect is peculiar, at once enjoyable and repellent.

The central figure in the family (there are no heroes or heroines) is dedi-cated to optimism and to the idea of life without pain. Pauline Manford is extremely like the New York lady in Ruth Draper's famous 1925 mono-logue, 'The Italian Lesson' (first called 'The Busy Mother'). Wharton had heard Draper in England, and called her 'a clever little American'. While studying Dante's *Inferno* for its uplifting beauty, Draper's character is also planning her dinner menu, organising her badly behaved children, their new puppy and their governess, arranging riding and gym lessons, dental appointments, dancing classes, concert-tickets, and the dropping-off of her husband's golf-clubs, talking to her lover on the 'phone, running through her schedule with her secretary, ordering a lampshade cover, having a mani-cure, and telling a school teacher that her son's psychoanalyst says he is traumatised by arithmetic. Pauline, whose stream of thoughts and talk rushes past us just like a Draper monologue, is similarly juggling a timetable of strenuous and aspirational activities. '7.30. Mental uplift. 7.45. Breakfast. 8. Psycho-analysis. 8.15. See cook. 8.30. Silent meditation. 8.45. Facial massage.' This Ford production line or efficient 'Taylorised' programme of improving activities has every moment accounted for. (Even 'relaxation' is a scheduled task.) Her daughter has to make an appointment to see her, and often cannot be fitted into 'the close mosaic of Mrs Manford's engage-ment-list'. Intimacy for her means 'the tireless discussion of facts', anything from 'Birth Control to neo-impressionism'. There must be a panacea for everything. Childbirth with the 'twilight sleep' drug is a beautiful and bright experience; divorce is just a form of house-cleaning. Direct contact with physical suffering is to be avoided: 'We ought to refuse ourselves to pain.' Not to believe in evil is 'to prevent its coming into being'. Her bathroom is like 'a biological laboratory, with its white tiles, polished pipes, weighing machines, mysterious appliances for douches, gymnastics and "physical culture"'. Plumbing, gymnastics, hygiene and mental uplift are run together in this relentless satire on American optimism: 'She wanted to de-microbe life.' On her enormous country estate, Cedarledge, the same organisational mania is applied to nature, which is being improved on a grand scale – seventy-five thousand bulbs planted, an up-to-date ventilating system in the cow-stables, rows of dwarf topiary, miles of glossy lawn. 'Pauline was persuaded that she was fond of the country – but what she was really fond of was doing things to the country.' It is as if Wharton is caricaturing the extremes of her own 'house-keeping' behaviour.[45]

Pauline's highest commitment is to her causes and her quest for the perfect guru. There is the Mahatma (that 'nigger chap', her ex-husband calls him) whose exercises dispel wrinkles and achieve hip-reduction, but whose 'wonderful mystical teachings' have also led to a spot of trouble, with photographs in the scandal-press of upper-class young girls cavorting naked at his School of Oriental Thought. There is Alvah Loft, the Busy Man's Christ, whose rapid system of 'spiritual vacuum-cleaning' ($25 a session) relieves you of your 'frustrations' in five minutes, 'as if they'd been adenoids'. There is Sacha Gobine, 'the new Russian initiate', who does 'rejuvenation', very calmly. Pauline's highest social ambition is to give a dinner for the Bishop of New York, the Chief Rabbi, and the Roman cardinal, to 'bring together the representatives of the conflicting creeds' in one transcendent unity. This spiritual eclecticism applies to her women's causes, which encompass 'Birth Control and unlimited maternity, free love or the return to the traditions of the American home'. In a laboured comic scene, she gets her speech to the Motherhood Meeting muddled up with the one to the Birth Control Association, but easily corrects herself. After all, both causes involve the universal American right to self-expression and personal freedom.[46]

Wharton is often accused of being out of touch with modern America, but she was keeping an eagle eye on it from a distance, and all the ingredients of *Twilight Sleep* have a basis in fact. Pauline is (by inference) an advocate of eugenics: she celebrates the American treatment of the 'mentally deficient' and is a believer in the production of exceptional offspring bred of 'superbly sound progenitors'. (No wonder Aldous Huxley drew on *Twilight Sleep* for *Brave New World* – which Wharton greatly admired – and praised Mrs Manford as 'an example of the contemporary tendency for superstition to be magical rather than religious – to aim at specific acts of power, such as hip-slimming, rather than at a theory of the cosmos.' He thought the novel 'beautifully and ruthlessly exemplified' that tendency.) Pauline is a combination of Margaret Sanger, organiser of the American Birth Control League and advocate of woman's 'self-expression', and Grace Abbott, the head of the Children's Bureau, who worked for the Sheppard-Turner Maternity and Infancy Protection Act. Her confusion between her birth-control and motherhood speeches is not so ridiculous, since both groups were concerned with the rights and fulfilment of women, and often overlapped.

The gurus in *Twilight Sleep* are also startlingly true to life. Alvah Loft draws on the sayings of Ella Wheeler Wilcox, just as the American Rosicrucians did, because her 'mission of optimism' 'gave no quarter to negativity'. The scandalous Mahatma combines two figures. Paramahansa Yogananda was a Hindu yogi whose Self-Realisation Fellowship was extremely popular in America in the mid-1920s, and who gave lectures at Carnegie Hall on topics like 'Everlasting Youth: Psycho-Physiological Rejuvenation of Cells by Recharging the Body Battery'. His book, *The Science of Religion* (1920), preached the unity of all religions and 'the avoidance of pain' as the 'ultimate end'. A more dubious character was 'Oom the Omnipotent' (alias Pierre Bernard), who with his wife, Blanche de Vries, instructed wealthy New York ladies from the Vanderbilt/ Rutherfurd/Ogden Mills clan in exercises for breathing and 'the body beautiful'. His 'Mystic Order of the Tantriks of India', at Clarkstown Country Club, New York State, was the subject, like Pauline's Mahatma, of a series of scandals: 'Omnipotent Oom Held as Kidnapper ... Girls kept like Prisoners ... Country Club Specializes in Sex Worship'.[47]

In her busy search for a spiritual guide who will negate pain (unlike Christ, as her daughter points out), Pauline Manford is, in fact, a pitiful figure, unable to cope with empty time, to enjoy nature or to recognise happiness, terrified of 'indifference' (the most-repeated word in the book, and the worst fate of all) and in denial about what is really going on in her family. She thinks she has efficiently tidied away her first husband, Arthur Wyant, a weak and degenerate specimen – 'Exhibit A' – of old New York blood, and ignores the troubling fact that he is a broken man, an alcoholic on the edge of a nervous breakdown. She refuses to admit that her second husband, Dexter Manford, a lawyer of energetic Midwestern stock, is bored with her and their life, and looking for satisfaction elsewhere. She consoles herself rationally for their lack of sex ('She had no patience with the silly old women who expected "that sort of nonsense" to last') and sublimates her libido in managerial activities: 'She enjoys it as much as other women do love-making', her husband thinks. She fails to notice her daughter Nona's unhappiness, and averts her eyes from Nona's worries about her half-brother Jim, the son of Mrs Manford's first marriage, whose own marriage to the feckless Lita, in spite of their painlessly born baby, is going badly wrong. This 'bewildered' and 'disenchanted' younger, post-war generation have reacted against their parents and are afloat on a sea of 'thrills'. Lita's only resemblance to Pauline is her belief in a woman's right to self-expression. She is the iconic figure of the Age of Jazz, which Wharton 'does' in this novel with fascination and repulsion. The 'Cubist Cabaret' and the Harlem clubs, complete with black dancers, falsetto-voiced male interior decorator, 'octoroon' woman pianist with 'sausage arms and bolster legs' and thick-lipped, buttery-voiced Jewish Hollywood producer (who wants to cast Lita as Salome or Lucrezia Borgia), are all meant to seem horribly 'sham'. Wharton does her own interior decorating, amusing herself with Lita's all-black boudoir and her minimalist Japanese drawing room, its insomniac goldfish kept awake all night by electric bulbs.

As in *The Glimpses of the Moon*, primitive passions come to the surface. Lita and her stepfather-in-law Dexter have a semi-incestuous affair right under Pauline's nose. A near-deranged Wyant bursts into the country house, tries to shoot one of the lovers, but wounds Nona instead. (American news-papers in the mid-1920s were dominated by some sensational crime-stories and murder trials, much enjoyed by Wharton.) She tries to give the story mythic status, suggesting that Nona is an 'Iphigenia', sacrificed to the demons which her mother's generation have been holding at bay. (In her summary of the novel for her publishers she wrote: 'It is an Aeschylean tragedy with no Aeschylean moral ideals.') But the superficial texture of the novel will not carry this weighty sense of doom. *Twilight Sleep* is so busy with topical satire, so determined to be speedy and grotesque, that it wears itself and the reader out, and reads thin and harsh.[48]

Yet this try at a new style can have a disturbing surreal effect. In one scene, Pauline is trying to leave town, the butler, the maid and the secretary are all pursuing her with last-minute questions, and the whole sequence is done on the run, in rapid, interrupted dialogue: 'Mrs Manford, wait! Here are two more telegrams, and a special –' 'Take care, Maisie; you'll slip and break your leg . . .' 'Yes, but Mrs Manford! The special is from Mrs Swoffer. She says the committee have just discovered a new genius . . . and couldn't you possibly –' 'No, no, Maisie – I can't! Say I've *left* –' In another, Nona is telling a funny story: 'Nona was still in the whirlpool of her laugh. She struggled to its edge only to be caught back, with retrospective sobs and gasps, into its central coil. "It was too screamingly funny," she flung at them out of the vortex.' And the others all start to laugh, in a kind of contagion.

This screaming laughter over a void is a frightening new note in Wharton; we do not hear it again.[49]

Wharton also wrote a large number of stories in her sixties and seventies – five volumes between 1926 and 1937 – which kept up her profile in the American magazines. *Here and Beyond*, her collection of the mid-1920s, is a curious mixture. There is an awkward story of a 'nervous' narrator who encounters what he thinks is the ghost of a spinster lady, 'Miss Mary Pask', in a lonely house fog-bound in Brittany. The ghost, who is embarrassingly coy (and who turns out to be Miss Pask in a 'cataleptic trance'), complains bitterly of her aloneness: 'Lonely, lonely! If you *knew* how lonely!' In 'The Young Gentlemen', an old bachelor in a New England seaside town, of mixed American and Spanish blood, has been secretly bringing up two dwarves in his old house, his sons, and when they are discovered, he kills himself. He, and the loyal old woman who tells the story, are, like Miss Mary Pask, condemned to a life of utter loneliness. Both stories have an intrusive narrator from the outside world.

A more colourful story, 'The Seed of the Faith', is left over from the Moroccan journey (it was originally published in 1919). It is full of the same kind of Orientalist details as *In Morocco* (verminous crowds, exotic bazaars, magical starlit nights in the desert), the setting for a satire on the fanaticism of an old American Baptist missionary, who has spent his life trying to convert the Arabs, the 'poor ignorant heathen', to Christianity. His young companion is devoted to him (unusually for Wharton, this is a touching story of homoerotic friendship), but sees their work as futile: 'What did they know of these people, of their antecedents, the origin of their beliefs and superstitions, the meaning of their habits and passions and precautions?'

Two other stories are set among the cosmopolitan Americans of the 1920s novels. Gerhardi's influence is felt in 'Velvet Ear-Pads', her light Riviera comedy of a professor looking for peace and quiet who is distracted by an effusive Russian princess. 'The Temperate Zone' takes up the old subject of *The Touchstone* or 'The Muse's Tragedy'. A painter of genius who has only become famous since his death, and a fine, obscure woman poet (named 'Emily'), who may have been lovers, are being rediscovered by the dead painter's ardent young disciple. The young disciple finds the artists' legacies being betrayed by the widow of the painter and the ex-lover of the poet, now a rich married couple only interested in the market-value of what they have inherited. The dead are left behind, lonely and misunderstood.[50]

*

Wharton complained to Jewett in her early sixties that she was working 'less rapidly than she used to': 'If only I were 20 years younger, and had two brains and four hands!' She often expressed anxiety about overwork (she had 'made herself ill' finishing *The Mother's Recompense*, she said, and could not 'risk that kind of fatigue again') or relief at having managed to clear the decks: 'I finished *Twilight Sleep*, [and] said: "Oof", as Napoleon said that Europe wd when he died.' She protested at deadlines, engineered delays and created difficulties for her editors more frequently from now on – often with good cause: 'When my work is delayed' (she told Jewett in 1927) 'it is almost always . . . because I feel the need of a few weeks' interruption in order to get my story into perspective again.' But she was still capable of Napoleonic energies. Jewett was amazed at her, and nicely told her so: 'You are a wonder. In the busy rush of the day's work I doubt if I have ever taken the opportunity to tell you of my inability to grasp how you find time, in a life complicated by multiplied demands, to write so surely and steadily. Your powerful work, your fertility and ingenuity, fill me with envy.'[51]

As usual, she had a number of projects running alongside the novels, stories and essays. One pleasurable indulgence was the publication of *Twelve Poems*, in a beautiful slim grey-blue limited edition of 130 copies (thirty for her private distribution), printed in October 1926 by the Riccardi Press for the English Medici Society (whose editor, Harry Lawrence, was her guest that year on her Aegean cruise, which inspired some of these poems). It was a mixture of verses from the war (including the Roosevelt elegy) and celebrations of nature, in France ('Nightingales in Provence', 'Mistral in the Maquis'), in a castle in Cyprus (which was also the setting of a laboured historical romance, 'Dieu d'Amour'), and at the unroofed Greek temple of Segesta in Sicily. The tone of these was ecstatic and spiritual. 'Les Salettes', set on a secret beach, imagines the 'lost years' coming out of the sea to tell her 'All is not pain': 'Rejoice, because such skies are blue, / Each dawn, above a world so fair, / Because such glories still renew, / To transient eyes the morning's hue.' At the end come three interesting experiments. One is a ghoulish fantasy (in debt to Tennyson and Hardy) of a dead woman on All Souls' Day returning to her old home and seeing herself replaced, which has a strong edgy tone ('Was it always so queer and inexplicable? / Yes, but the fresh smell of things . . .'). Another is 'La Folle du Logis' (meaning the imagination, or the wild, untamed secret self), a revealing meditation on double identity. The speaker has been yoked, all her life, to a 'wild wingèd' creature who is imprisoned inside her, but who has led her to love and stormy seas, nature's secrets and 'the heart of wonder in familiar things'. The last is a pair of 'Alternative Epitaphs' for one who died 'of heart failure', farewells to love: 'Love came, and gave me wind and sun, / Love went, and left me light and air. / Nor gave he anything more fair / Than what I found when love was gone.' She had published some haiku-like 'Lyrical Epigrams' a few years before in the *Yale Review* (trying them out first on the end-pages of her volume of *Sages et Poètes d'Asie*), one on her Pekinese ('My little old dog: / A heart-beat / At my feet'), one on friendship /('The silence of midnight / A dying fire, / And the best unsaid . . .'. As often, she is using poems, in contrast to the novels, to sum up her life to herself.[52]

Not all her literary plans came to completion. She thought of, but abandoned, a sequel to *The Glimpses of the Moon*, to be called *Love Among the Ruins*, in which Nick and Susy would be living in a studio flat in Harlem while he wrote and she took up house-decoration, and they gradually 'become a humdrum married couple'. Another was to write her eighteenth-century novel set in Hyères, *The Happy Isles*, or perhaps *The Sapphire Way*. Another, less clearly formulated as yet, was to write her autobiography. In Salso, in 1924, she bought an Italian notebook called *Quaderno dello studente*, and started keeping a sporadic diary, which amounted only to a few stray thoughts and reflections, but was clearly meant as a first pre-emptive move against future biographers.

> Perhaps at last I shall be able to write down some disconnected thoughts, old and new – gather together the floating scraps of experience that have lurked for years in corners of my mind. And gradually, when the student has had more practice, I may even be able to jot down a sketch of myself – my own growth and history. When I get glimpses, in books and reviews, of the things people are going to assert about me after I am dead, I feel I must have the courage and perseverance, some day, to forestall them.

There follow a few melancholy notes, made over several years, on her feelings about animals, solitude, the death of friends, being reviewed, beauty, loss, and happiness. ('The secret of happiness is to have forgotten what it is to be happy'.)[53]

One persistent idea for a plot in the 1920s was the story of a woman accused of a notorious crime, who makes a new anonymous life for herself. Though it connected to the crime-story element in *Twilight Sleep*, the idea had been nudging her for some years. It went through several formulations, but in the end produced only one late short story, whose change of title, from 'Unconfessed Crime' to 'Confession', suggested the ambiguity which attracted her to this plot. She first thought of it as a novel called *The Keys of Heaven*, which was promised by Jewett, in a lucrative deal, to the editor of the *Delineator* magazine in 1926. It was based on the famous 1847 French murder-case which she and James had offered to each other as a subject as far back as 1909. A French governess, Henriette Deluzy, was implicated in the brutal murder of the Duchesse de Choiseul by her husband (whom she had suspected of having an affair with the governess) in the Hôtel Praslin in the Faubourg Saint-Germain. The murder was a political sensation because the duc, who later killed himself, was closely attached to the king, Louis-Philippe. The governess made a new life for herself in Gramercy Park and Stockbridge, Massachusetts, as an American minister's wife and a New York hostess, Mrs Deluzy-Field. (James remembered the 'closed & blighted' Hôtel Praslin from his childhood in Paris and had met Mrs Deluzy-Field in New York.) In the outlines of *The Keys of Heaven*, the French governess, 'Laure de Lassy', walking through 'Sloebridge', contemplates the 'little white wooden houses behind their palings' as if they are toys, and thinks this is 'a world like a children's Noah's ark', with 'no misery, no splendour, no vices, no passions'. She sounds very like Ellen Olenska.

The Keys of Heaven, much to the irritation of the editor of the *Delineator*, came to nothing. But Wharton's fixation on the woman who takes on a new identity to get away from her (supposedly) criminal past resurfaced years later in a plan to rework the notorious Lizzie Borden story, a favourite American murder-trial. (In 1892, this young woman was accused of the grisly murders of her father and stepmother in the town of Fall River; she was found not guilty, and lived on for many years in the shadow of her past.) Wharton first thought of turning the story into a play called *Kate Spain*, but – interestingly – without the murdered father: 'My young woman could quite as well have murdered an intolerable husband.' She sent a sketch of it to Ned Sheldon, who gave her a detailed critique, and, uncannily, since he did not know of her pre-existing interest in it, suggested that she should adapt the Praslin case, instead, into a play. (Rachel Field, a descendant of Henriette Deluzy-Field, had by now fictionalised the case, and her novel became a popular movie, *All This, And Heaven Too*, in 1940). Wharton used the idea as a story, 'Confession', in which the narrator (called 'Severance') finds to his horror that the mysterious American woman he has fallen in love with in a hotel in the French Alps is Kate Spain, recently acquitted of her father's notorious murder, and attended by her vulgar companion a blackmailing maid. The story's real interest is in the oppressive relationship between the two women, not in the devoted narrator, who refuses to read his future wife's 'confession' and marries her never knowing whether she was guilty or not. What haunts Wharton about this theme is the woman's attempt at 'severance' between past and present, America and Europe.[54]

A great deal of money was changing hands on these titles – what Arthur Vance of *The Pictorial Review* called 'top-notch figures'. Wharton was keeping Jewett very busy on her behalf. In 1926 *The Delineator* offered $35,000 for *The Sapphire Way*. In 1927, while *Twilight Sleep*, to her amusement, was described by Appleton as 'knocking *Elmer Gantry* off the top rung', there was a complicated bidding war between two magazines for her next titles. This resulted in an offer of $40,000 from Vance for *The Children*, and a two-book offer from *The Delineator*, of $42,000 for *The Keys of Heaven* and $50,000 for the next one, which would be *Hudson River Bracketed*. (Before *The Keys of Heaven* faded from the picture, that order of submission would be switched around; and in July 1930, the editor of *The Delineator* was still complaining about the non-appearance of *The Keys of Heaven*, which by then had turned into a continuation of Vance Weston's life-story, *The Gods Arrive*.) Magazines were eager for whatever they could get. The *Saturday Evening Post* told Jewett in 1928 that they 'appreciate your promise to shoot us the next story that comes through from Mrs Wharton'. They would be prepared to pay $3,000, which they thought was 'an increase over the prices that have been paid for her short stories in the past'. In 1928, a 'banner year', her total earnings from serialisations, book advances, royalties and film rights were $95,387.08. Jewett said, in his courtly way, that her popularity reminded him of the tasselled dance-cards of the balls of their youth. She was 'the belle of the ball', and he was attempting to chaperone her under 'hectic circumstances'. (This sort of treatment did not stop her complaining vociferously to him about the level of proof-reading at Appleton.)

There were problems in being so sought after. Quite apart from the enormous taxes she had to pay ($28,500 in 1926), there was a danger in being treated by the magazine editors as a cash-cow. The exchanges between Jewett and the magazine editors, which Wharton did not see, take an aggressive tone about their rights in their hot property. Arthur Vance was very annoyed about the bidding war, since he felt the *Pictorial Review* ought to have prior claim. 'This editing a magazine is certainly a hell of a fine job ... We want Mrs Wharton and we think we ought to have first call ... But I do wish ... that we could get some assurance from her that she won't tie herself up with any other magazines.' Wharton was frightened – justifiably – at 'the idea of planning so far in advance'. These anxieties were written into *Hudson River Bracketed*.[55]

*

The money went into the upkeep of the two houses, the gardens, new cars, some luxury purchases (a new silver service, reset pearls), the maintenance of her staff, the purchase of Ste-Claire, with more land and another property (for which she took out a loan from her bank), and on travel. In the autumn of 1924 she made one of her regular English visits. It was her last visit to Hill Hall (sadly, the widowed Mary Hunter would have to sell it in 1925), and her first to Lawrence Johnston at Hidcote. She rented a Daimler and spent some days 'radiating about', visiting Oxford (tea at the Mitre), Cambridge, 'Malmesbury, Northampton (amazingly rich), Southwell (splendid), Peterborough & Lincoln', and making her usual complicated arrangements with Robert and Gaillard: '(1) If you prefer to come by train, say to Malvern, I could join you there, on the 7th, in the Daimler for lunch, & we cd proceed into the unknown ... or (2) (which I naturally prefer) you join me at Hidcote by motor for lunch ... & we proceed together in the p.m. .... wire me to Hidcote Manor, "stating alternatives preferred, & reasons for your choice".' In May of 1925 she took a ten-day motor-flight with Robert to the Pyrenees, with a one-day dash across to Spain to look at 'strange ancient villages' in the Val d'Aran, relishing the springtime beauty of the 'narcissus & gentian & golden poplars & flowering fruit-trees & cold rushing rivulets'.

In September she went back to Spain with Walter, their first return there since 1914. Her brief diary for this trip was retrospectively headed: 'Last Spanish Journey with W.'. They stayed in the northern half of Spain, but their itinerary, as usual, was ambitious, spurred on by their appetite for Romanesque and pre-Romanesque churches, monasteries and cathedrals. With undiminished energy, the two old friends put up with mule-rides, hotels' flea-ridden attic rooms, and long mountain drives, and were rewarded, in 'divine' weather, with the 'ineffable beauty' of sights like the cathedrals at Pamplona, León and Salamanca and the palace of the dukes at Guadalajara, picnics in ilex woods, and climbs through vine-clad groves up to wonderful mountain heights above the clouds: 'just like the aeroplane photos'. She returned to Spain twice with Daisy Chanler, in 1928 following the pilgrim trail to Santiago de Compostela (and seeing a magnificent Goya exhibition), and in 1930 travelling south from Barcelona through 'Moorish' Spain. She planned to do a 'Motor Flight through Spain' to match her book on France, but wrote only a few pages, on the remoteness and beauty of Compostela, on the mysterious impenetrability of the landscape, and on the smell of incense in all the Spanish churches. She put a vivid description of life in Córdoba and Granada into *The Gods Arrive*. Spain was not a country she took possession of as she did Italy or France, but it made a profound, romantic impression on her, and she associated it most of all with her travels with Walter.[56]

But Walter did not come on the great travelling adventure of her mid-sixties, her ten-week Mediterranean and Aegean cruise in the spring and early summer of 1926, a reprise of the cruise of the *Vanadis* nearly forty years before. She wanted, she told Daisy Chanler, to make it 'a sort of sunset-party that I am hoping to offer to a few chosen friends ... I did the same thing in my sunrise-days, and never forgot it, or found anything to equal it – and I want the last light to shine again on the same wonders'. Her ideal companions on this trip might well have included Walter, the Berensons, the Tylers, or Gaillard Lapsley. But none of them could – or would – come, though the Berensons met up with her party in Naples (and Minnie Jones coincided with their Athens stop). Of her oldest friends, only Robert Norton and Daisy Chanler were able to join her. The Berensons recommended Mary's brother Logan, and an even slighter acquaintance, Harry Lawrence of the Medici Society, was the fifth passenger.

She hurled herself into the planning of the cruise with as much energy as if she had been organising one of her refugee centres. She sent Norton and John Hugh Smith looking for suitable vessels in England (the *Osprey* was an extremely comfortable, large, white, 360-ton steam yacht). She gathered together a large library of relevant books (from Gilbert Murray on Greek religions to Butcher and Lang's *Iliad* and *Odyssey*, for Robert to read out loud, with Keats, Shelley, Browning, and *The Oxford Book of English Verse* as staples). She sorted out the finances, which drew mainly on the income from *The Mother's Recompense* (about £4,000 for the cruise, plus £5 per ton for the fuel-oil), and ordered in the supplies, which included 168 bottles of vin rosé, champagne, port, brandy, benedictine, kirsch, cooking oil, coffee, cane sugar, peppermint drops, 'Captain's Thin' biscuits, Petites Tartines, piccalilli and chutney, orange jam, honey, bottled cherries, cigarettes and cigars, candles and paper napkins. She set Daisy, in Paris, searching for 'portable mosquito nets and silk sleeping bags' (in the event only to be found at Harrods). She arranged visas for her party for France, Italy, Greece, and Turkey. She told Captain Liddell to have the *Osprey* at the Vieux Port of Hyères on the afternoon of 31 March, 'in order to start at daylight on the 1st of April'. She made advance hotel bookings; for example, for five good rooms, three baths, and a room for the maid, at the Hotel Grand Bretagne in Athens, which Berenson had recommended. And she plotted an itinerary which overlapped a little with the *Vanadis* cruise (the changes she saw, for instance in Rhodes, would be very interesting to her) but which also took her to parts of the Peloponnese and to Greek islands she had never seen.[57]

They started in Sicily, with a glimpse of the great church at Cefalu, retraced her old voyage via Cephalonia and Zanthe, landed at Athens, and 'did' the great sights of southern Greece: the Parthenon by moonlight, the Hermes of Praxiteles at Olympia ('the last wind of a dying great art, lost in sweetness', she noted in her short cruise diary), Delphi, Nauplion, the theatre at Epidaurus, the fearful tombs of the House of Atreus at Mycenae, Marathon, Sparta, and the cliff-edge temple at Sounium. (Here they co-incided with the pianist Cortot – whose recording of the Archduke Trio with Thibaud and Casals she greatly admired – having his photograph taken in front of the ruins.) She was ecstatic about Delphi, which she saw now for the first and last time: 'the great sanctuary there before us lifted high on the bare hillside . . . all was beauty, serenity, and awe!' Robert, however, was put off by a large party of his countrywomen from the British Hellenic Association, and she found the Delphic charioteer 'too stupid-looking for my liking'. Their island stops were Aegina, Delos, Rhodes, Cyprus (where she made a new English friend, the Colonial Home Secretary Rex Nicholson) and Santorini. On Crete, the travellers drove in two cars, for two hours, across to Hagia Triada, where the summer palace of the Minoan kings had recently been excavated. They had lunch by a brook smothered in pink oleanders, in an olive grove, with nightingales singing, 'snow-covered Ida soaring in the blue above'. She recalled this ten years later in her last letter to Berenson, written a few months before her death: 'Oh, how clearly I remember saying to myself that day by the stream, as I looked up at the snow through the pink oleanders: "Old girl, this is one of the pinnacles –" as I did the last time I was at Compostela. (A . . . feeling of inalienable ownership of beauty!)'.

The yacht made a quick stop at Alexandria, but she stayed on board, not wanting to mix Egyptian and Greek impressions. But her appetite was undiminished by the time they got back to Sicily at the end of May, their last stop before joining the Berensons at Naples (where the church of Santa Chiara, with its decorated columns, entranced her). Daisy Chanler gives a good example, in Palermo, of what it was like to travel with Wharton:

We had not made any plans for the day, excepting to sail for Naples as soon as the oil was on board. Presently the resourceful Edith came on deck and told us she had just found out that if we lunched immediately and did not stop to change our clothes we should have time to go ashore and see Segesta before night. A couple of hours by motor followed by a long donkey ride would take us there ... We were glad to do as we were told.

Logan Pearsall Smith was not quite such an obliging companion as Daisy Chanler. At one point he and his hostess had a fierce argument over whether peonies were indigenous to the East or grew native in Europe; the other members of the party 'gazed at the view and wisely said nothing'. And though he found Mrs Wharton generally 'amusing', 'her rage for picture postcards' and 'her passion for buying spoons and paperweights in every city', while 'everything has to pause until it is satisfied', was in his view excessive. He was gleeful, too, about her battles of will with the stern and pious Scottish captain, who refused to let his crew of eighteen go ashore on Sundays and avoided sailing on the Sabbath. But Wharton had no complaints: this was all pleasure for her, and she told Daisy Chanler, wistfully, after their return, that 'the Kilmeny feeling' was 'growing in her daily instead of diminishing'.[58]

One of the subjects of conversation on the *Osprey* was Percy Lubbock, who would very likely have been among the passengers a few years earlier. Just before leaving on the cruise, Wharton had been appalled to hear that Geoffrey and Sybil Scott were divorcing, and that Percy – surprisingly, given his earlier membership of the homosocial circle around Henry James – had fallen in love with Sybil. Logan Pearsall Smith wrote in his cruise diary: 'Mrs W is convinced that Lady Sybil will marry Percy if she gets her divorce. She says he is thoroughly caught, and seems quite disgusted with him. She only hopes that she won't marry Norton next!' That was her line on Sybil, who seemed to be taking possession, one by one, of all her male friends. She told Gaillard, only half-joking: 'This is the third of my friends she has annexed, & I see you & Robert going next, & then BB, & finally even Walter – kicking & screaming!!!' (To Daisy, she said that Robert, Walter and Gaillard had all promised her, 'with solemn oaths, not to marry Sybil for at least a year'.) She had not seen very much of Percy since his gloomy visit to Ste-Claire in 1921, but she still thought of him as one of her inner circle – what Nicky Mariano called her male wives. This quarrel was unusual for her. Though she broke off with her own close family and with Teddy's family, and had offended a few old New York acquaintances because of her divorce, or her use of recognisable characters in her writing, she was usually a loyal friend, who liked to keep hold of all her people. There was something about this marriage, though, which she could not bear. It was a small irritant, not a major event in her life. But the breach with Percy would have a baleful effect on her posthumous reputation.

For a mixture of reasons, Wharton found Sybil detestable. She seems to have been an acquired taste: intense, self-absorbed, hypochondriacal, demanding, with a high-pitched voice which could launch (as Mary Berenson said) into 'torrents of chatter', an elegant, exotically dressed, blue-eyed blonde, given to tantrums, fainting, and quarrels. The child of a wealthy and prominent Anglo-Irish family (her father was the lawyer Lord Desart, her mother a Lascelles from Harewood House in Yorkshire), she had married Wharton's New York friend Bayard Cutting very young, and after his early death in 1910, rented the Villa Medici in Fiesole, with its long terraces and wonderful views. Sybil and her remarkable daughter Iris were intimately bound in with the tangled Anglo-Florentine and I Tatti set. During the war she was Berenson's mistress (at first to Mary's relief, as an antidote to Belle Greene), and after it, to Mary's intense distress, she married Geoffrey Scott. Though it was Scott who was almost immediately unfaithful to Sybil, first falling unreciprocatedly in love with Nicky Mariano, then with Vita Sackville-West, Wharton blamed Sybil entirely for the failure of that marriage and for the unfair 'spin' she gave it: 'As Sybil is spreading abroad (to justify herself) stories of his [Geoffrey's] misdemeanours, & of her having been forced to divorce him, etc . . . I think it ought to be said that not once . . . has a single unkind or even ironic comment on the subject escaped him.' When Scott died young, in 1929, two years after the divorce, she hardened her heart still more: 'Sybil's crocodile tears revolt me', she told Mary.[59]

It was not just that she found Sybil silly and affected, or that she (rightly) detected some hostility from her. (Sybil's own jaundiced memoirs, transcribed by Percy, emphasised Wharton's formality, her greedy shopping for antiques, and her cutting ways with people she did not approve of.) Like Pauline in *Twilight Sleep*, Wharton was critical, perhaps resentful and jealous, of middle-aged seductresses: 'Oh, these lubie [lubricious] grandmothers! They make me sick.' She saw her as a rival in the I Tatti network. (Her own allegiance there was shifting, at this time, from Mary, always unwell and depressed, to the benign and sympathetic Nicky Mariano, who by the early 1920s had become Berenson's virtual wife and the manager of I Tatti.) In some ways Sybil was like a caricature of Wharton. She was a chatelaine, good at interior design and garden-making. She was an ambitious traveller, going off adventurously to Syria, Lebanon and Egypt. And she was a talented, effusive amateur writer, publishing a handful of books on her childhood, anthologies and travel-writing.

Wharton never tired of telling Gaillard what she had heard about Sybil and Percy. 'What indeed has become of *our* Percy . . . ? *Englouti* in the quicksands of his beloved's torrential ego! Do you know that she is "medi-umistic", and that Bayard (how much against his will, I can imagine!) is still being consulted about family affairs ... ?' 'Philomène, who lunched here last Sunday, told me that Nicky had told her that Sybil gave Geoffrey, as a reason for divorcing him, & marrying P, that "mawwiage is constwuc-tive".' The estrangement solidified. Sybil, to Berenson's horror, became an ardent fascist supporter. In 1933, Wharton was at the Salzburg music festival, when she ran into Percy at the Grand Hôtel de l'Europe. Her version of this encounter (to Berenson, and to Gaillard) was that she tried to be civil, but Percy made it insultingly clear that Sybil was not available for 'an audi-ence'. Percy expressed mortification (also in letters to Gaillard, who was caught in the middle) that the break was so irreparable, but said that there could be no reconciliation 'unless she apologizes freely & frankly to Sybil for the way she has treated her'. There was another failed attempt at a *rapprochement*, when Wharton was staying at I Tatti in November 1933: 'O Edith – you see *I* felt ... that *you* might have thought you owed it to our old friendship ... to make sure you rightly & fairly understood what had happened ... And you wouldn't even try ...' She was tired, she told Gaillard, 'of all this backing & filling'. That was the end of it, until after Wharton died, at which point Gaillard Lapsley, as her literary executor, took the curious decision to appoint Percy Lubbock to write her memoir.[60]

Percy had been part of the family she had made for herself, all the more important because her own family, and her childless marriage, had been so disastrously unsatisfactory. Apart from the ageing but still impressively ener-getic Minnie, and the very successful Beatrix (less of a friend, because Wharton never warmed to Max Farrand), there was no family left. The 1913 quarrel with her brother Harry had never been resolved. She told Berenson when he died in August 1922 that she had not seen him for nearly ten years. She may have been wiping from the record one dismal visit to Harry's house outside Paris in 1920 or 1921, which she told Minnie had been 'utterly useless'. A story has trickled down that at this visit she was told about the long-circulating rumour that she was not her father's child, but the product of her mother's affair with the English tutor or with an English aristocrat. (Benstock cites, as proof of this, an undated letter to Fullerton which talks of being 'heart-sick' from a meeting with her brother, during which she '*drank mud*'.) These stories – of her illegitimacy, and of her learning of it from her brother after the war – sound hypothetical. What is certain, though, is her lasting bitterness at Harry's having cast off his family for Anna Tekla, whom he married in 1920. At Harry's funeral in

Paris in October 1922, where she sat with Walter Berry on the other side of the church from the 'Bereaved One', she noted with equal disdain the carnations on the coffin and the sobbing widow being led from the scene, and made a deliberately conspicuous exit so that the 'few Americans' who were there would note that she had attended. She found that her brother had left his wife everything, disinheriting her and Beatrix, and when Anna Tekla died in 1929, Wharton had to go to law to recover some family heirlooms and portraits. The mismanagement of her inheritance, the product of long-ago family divisions, would haunt her into old age. In 1931, when she remade her will, she found, to her distress, that what she thought she was entitled to from the residue of her mother's trust fund was much less than she had imagined.[61]

As everyone does in their sixties, she was losing old friends and connections. Rosa de Fitzjames and Sally Norton both died in the early 1920s. Sally left her a Turner mezzotint, and she was delighted to get this 'last affectionate message out of the great silence, like a hand-clasp on the threshold'. Her old friend Walter Maynard died in 1925, Daisy's husband Winthrop Chanler in 1926. Minnie Bourget was sinking into senile dementia. There was a happier parting with Philomène, who was married in May 1927 and saw less of Edith thereafter. Teddy Wharton died, a sad, broken seventy-seven-year-old, in 1928, in New York, and had his funeral in Grace Church, where Edith was baptised. For years, he had sat in his room, with a shawl over his knees, in the family home at Lenox, looked after by Nannie and two nurses. When Nannie died in 1922, she left directions in her will that he be cared for by their brother William's children. He left most of his money and possessions to his day-nurse, including his victrola, his editions of Bret Harte, and his Sloane vacuum cleaner.[62]

No other loss came close, in its desolating effect on her, to the death of Walter Berry in October 1927. The event played as tragedy and as farce. It is the first and last time that their relationship comes into close focus, with all its ambiguities, irritants and intimacy. It is a public as well as a private story, a reminder of what a respected part these two well-known, distinguished American citizens played in France. It shows her at her most impressive, vulnerable, and difficult. Wharton's own death, ten years later, would be a quiet fading-away; but this was her big death-bed scene, and for her it was a kind of inner death.

Walter and Edith had a holiday in northern Italy in September 1926, a round trip from Bergamo to Venice and back (via Cortina and other towns in the Dolomites, and Lake Garda). It was not a great success: there was too much 'jazzery' in Venice, too much dust and heat in the Lombard plains, and heavy rain on the mountain pass from Italy to Annecy. They had a last 'good day' with Berenson and Nicky Mariano in Aosta, in the Italian Alps. Two months later, while Edith was staying at the Crillon during the change-over from St-Brice to Ste-Claire, Walter was diagnosed with appendicitis, and rushed into hospital from 53 Rue de Varenne (his home since she had transferred the lease to him in 1920). The operation was performed by 'the great surgeon' Dr de Martel with a local anaesthetic; there were no complications and it was declared a complete success. Since Walter's married sister, Nathalie Alden, could not get to Paris in time, Edith felt herself to be in charge, and (she told Gaillard) 'had a good deal of anxiety, & of rushing about'. Walter was not an easy patient. Edith told Berenson that she had to get him a 'good English nurse' because he found the 'chocolate-box beauty of eighteen' incompetent; she never thought she would hear Walter say, 'Oh, for God's sake get me one who's old & ugly.' He was convinced the operation had been unnecessary, and though she persuaded him to come to Ste-Claire for a restful Christmas with Robert and Gaillard, he was back in Paris by 1 January. He had retired as president of the American Chamber of Commerce four years before, but he was still extremely involved in Franco–American relations and the Parisian diplomatic, legal and literary worlds, and he plunged back, as Edith described it, into 'all his usual very active life – business, charities, legal affairs, & society'. On 11 January he played – as he did regularly – a game of tennis, and on 12 January he had a stroke, which left him, not paralysed, but unable to speak, or, at first, to read or write. Edith rushed to Paris to 'guard the door', and was appalled to witness his frustration: 'He is like a great powerful bird caught in a net.' He became extremely exasperated and depressed, and very irritated with her. He wrote a note to Berenson, which said grimly: 'Can't go anywhere . . . Stale-mate!' Edith was afraid that her 'hanging around' and 'hovering over him' would make him think he was dangerously ill. She told Walter's intimate friend Alice Garrett (whose husband was soon to become the American ambassador to Italy) that he was 'very hard to manage'. She asked John Hugh Smith if he could come and help her: 'It will be a great comfort, dear, if you chance to be in Paris these next few days, for I'm singularly alone.'[63]

Two weeks later, Edith left for Ste-Claire, 'not wishing' (she said to Alice) 'to give the impression that I was mounting guard over him'. He was 'very sensitive about his illness', she told Mildred Bliss. After she left, there was a disaster. Edith had secretly cabled Walter's sister, Nathalie Alden, not to come over from the States. (She was, as Edith cruelly described her to Gaillard, a 'crippled' woman of sixty who had made what Walter considered a 'foolish' late marriage to a much younger man, and he had just disinherited her in favour of his cousin, Harry Crosby.) But Nathalie arrived with the husband, telling Walter that she was only there in response to Edith's stream of anxious cables. Walter was 'perfectly furious', and wrote Edith a reproachful letter. 'I could wring her neck!' Edith told Alice. To Berenson: 'Preserve us from fools, from family, & most of all from family fools!' It was like other battles for control that she had had, with Teddy's sister and mother over his illness, with the James family when Henry died, or with Ronald Simmons's mother over arrangements for his tombstone.[64]

A week later, on 18 February, Walter turned up alone at Ste-Claire. An extremely difficult convalescence followed, witnessed by Daisy Chanler, who was visiting, and saw Edith continuously putting herself out for Walter and Walter continuously complaining. His 'sadness is so profound', Edith told Gaillard, 'that I was benumbed by it.' After five weeks of this, he left for a sanatorium in Berne, sending Edith a morose apology for having forced her to look after a 'stuttering paralytic'. Over the next few months some normality resumed. *Twilight Sleep* was published, and she began to write *The Children* (sending an outline of it to Appleton in February). She saw other friends that summer – Louis Metman, Eric Maclagen, Louis Gillet, Berenson and Nicky, the young Kenneth Clarks. But none of these would replace Walter.[65]

In September, there was an influx of American Legion War Veterans to Paris for the tenth anniversary of America's entry into the war. Walter was much involved and very busy. He and Edith went out together on the evening of 23 September. On 2 October, he had a second, much more severe stroke, which left him paralysed and speechless. He had told his manservant that if this happened, he wanted no one told, and that included Edith. She knew why this was, she told Mildred Bliss later: 'He thought I wd get the Drs to prolong his life in the dreadful new ways they have.' The servant disobeyed him and sent her the news; she waited at the Hôtel Crillon to be summoned to number 53. In the brief diary she was keeping, she wrote some notes to herself about religion. 'October 4: I don't believe in God, but I believe in his saints. Then – ?' 'October 5 (in the night): Lying awake in my despair over W, it came to me that whatever God is, he is not an anaesthetic. Bringing one's human sorrow to Him wd never make me suffer less, but only differently.' On 9 October, Walter communicated to his servant – by blinking in response to her name – that he wanted to see her. She went back to the Rue de Varenne, where so many of the dramas of her life had taken place: the romance with Fullerton, the writing of great books like *Ethan Frome* and *The Custom of the Country*, the last struggles of her marriage, the wartime labours. As she entered the bedroom, she said to him: 'I will never let any one do anything to prolong your life.' He could not speak but (she told Alice Garrett) 'he knew me perfectly, & we talked by his pressing my hand for "yes", & pushing it away for "no"'. She sent her bulletins to her closest friends, Gaillard, John Hugh, Berenson (none of whom had liked Walter Berry so very much). 'I held him in my arms & talked to him of old times, & he pressed my hand & remembered.' She kept naming people he might want to see, but he kept gesturing 'no'. She felt that now, as in the last phase of his life, 'He liked to have me with him, because he knew I wouldn't fuss or sentimentalize . . . He hated humbug – so do I.' She stayed with him for three days, hoping that 'the end may come quickly'. On 11 October, she recorded in her diary: 'Went twice to Rue de V. Failing fast, but understood everything. Held me fast & kissed me. Said "Dear" once.' He died early the next morning; she was not with him, but on her way back there from the hotel. At once, she started writing, turning her grief into a fine dramatic sentence in her diary ('The Love of all my life died today, & I with him') and writing a tender, formal poem, which she called 'Garden Valedictory' when she published it the following January.[66]

> I will not say that you are dead, but only
> Scattered like seed upon the autumn breeze,
> Renewing life where all seemed locked and lonely,
> Stored in shut buds and inarticulate trees,
> So that this earth, this meaningless earth, may yet
> Regain some sense for me, because a word
> You spoke in passing trembles in the jet
> Of the frail fountain in my garden-close,
> Because you stopped one day before this rose,
> Or I can hear you in the migrant bird
> Throating good-bye along the lime-tree aisle,
> And feel your hand in mind, and breathe awhile.

Friends rallied round: Robert and Elisina came at once, to be with her for the funeral. Elisina was 'more than a sister to me during those dreadful days', and she never forgot it. From this moment of loss onwards, her dependency on Elisina solidified. Berenson came too, and was with her in Paris and at Ste-Claire that autumn. Even Fullerton was enlisted, at a distance (by her secretary) to collect together all Berry's obituaries. Consolatory letters flooded in, desolate letters went back: she told Berenson that 'for the first time in my life I feel utterly rudderless' and was undergoing 'a passion of loneliness'. Her letters reaffirmed Berry's central place in her life, as if to herself as well as to others. To Louis Gillet (who did not know Berry) she said: '*Je perds l'ami unique, l'ami de toujours, le soutien, le guide le plus sûr et le plus clairvoyant.*' The most revealing letter went not to a close friend but to a great admirer of Berry's, the art critic Royall Cortissoz, to whom she gave an elitist account of Berry as a member of a vanishing species:

> Apart from all his brilliant qualities, he had that of being almost the last of the type of old New York men of my youth – the cultivated man of action & also of leisure, linguist, traveller, man of the world, who is no longer represented in the modern America of Babbitt & Main St . . . He was a *great influence*, in the most stimulating sense, wherever he went; & of how many Americans nowadays can that be said, outside of plumbing, dentistry, & money-making?[67]

The modern world was encroaching on her private grief. Walter's will had made his artistic and eccentric young cousin Harry Crosby his legatee and executor (mischievously choosing him instead of the sister he disliked – or Edith). He had left a large number of individual legacies which had to be sorted out, and had directed that after his funeral 'my so-called "ashes" be not taken to America for burial, but shall be chucked out anywhere'. Harry Crosby, nephew of J.P. Morgan, a Bostonian of Van Rensselaer ancestry, poet, editor of the *Black Sun Press* (where he published Lawrence and Joyce), sun-worshipper and drug-addict, was one of the most bohemian of the 'jazz-age' Americans in Paris whom Edith usually did her best to avoid. He was married to the equally flamboyant 'Caresse' (an invented name), and was the cousin of Nina, wife of the Marquis de Polignac. Walter had found him stimulating, and had been urging him to write a life of Rimbaud. The quarrels between Edith, Harry Crosby, Caresse, and Nina de Polignac, began over the arrangements for the funeral on 17 October, which was an enormous display of Parisian respect for one of its most admired American public figures. Harry insisted on a horse-drawn carriage, with gold and silver ornamentation, loaded with flowers; Edith would have preferred cars. Among the eight hundred mourners – including the Minister of Justice, General Pershing, war veterans and *mutilés de guerre*, many members of the American Chamber of Commerce, 'Cabinet members, diplomats, and prominent figures in society, literature and public life', who walked in procession from the Rue de Varenne to the American Cathedral Church of the Holy Trinity – was 'Mrs Edith Wharton, the novelist, who had been a close friend of the deceased. She wore a heavy black veil.' The body was cremated at the Père Lachaise cemetery, where Crosby read Baudelaire, drank a toast to his cousin from his brandy-flask, and ordered that the wreath be placed on Oscar Wilde's grave. (Berry had admired Wilde, and had given Edith a copy of Wilde's *Poems* in 1903.) He then took the ashes to the Pavillon Colombe, where Edith (according to Caresse) had set up a kind of altar: 'The soft notes of a requiem seeped from under the stairs and a distinct odour of incense permeated the villa. In the parlour a small altar had been arranged with enormous silver candlesticks alight.' Edith planned to scatter the ashes in the garden at the Pavillon, but Crosby's arrival with the urn was followed by two gendarmes in black, who had tailed the Crosbys from the cemetery. They banged loudly on the door and asked what was going on. Caresse Crosby told the story, twenty-five years later, with unconvincing vividness:

> Mrs Wharton, in her perfect French, tried to explain that we were gathered together for a very simple ceremony, merely a Mass for the dead. 'And what's going to happen after that?' they asked. 'I am placing the ashes of my friend in the bottom of my garden,' she replied. 'Oh, you are! . . . Don't you know, lady, that it's against French law to bury anyone in unconsecrated ground?'

Crosby signed papers taking responsibility for the ashes; 'Mrs Wharton' was 'fighting her tears'.

For twelve days, the urn stayed at the Pavillon, while everyone involved – now including Walter's sister and her husband – argued over where it should be placed and how the legacies should be distributed. Harry told his mother that 'Edith Wharton worries only about what people will say'. Edith told Gaillard: 'The youth is inexperienced and unmanageable . . . and I am called on to advise and arbitrate and pacify when, every time I think of that apartment, and what I have lived through there of joy and sorrow, my soul recoils from the idea of ever crossing its threshold again.' She wrote to Alice Garrett that she was longing to 'get out of all these matters, & go back quietly to the thought of the incomparable being he was – At present, seeing all the little people crawling over him nearly kills me.' With Berry's sister, however, she managed to go into the apartment, find, and burn almost all the letters she had ever written to Walter Berry. On 29 October, the urn was placed in a tomb at the Cimetière des Gonards, at Versailles. She noted in her diary: 'The stone closed over all my life.'

But the indignities were not over. The codicil to Walter's will left all his books to Harry Crosby, 'except those books which Edith Wharton may desire to take . . . and as many of them as she may desire to take'. It was a clause guaranteed to produce tension. Crosby said he thought Mrs Wharton was going to make off with all the books and 'she should damned well be ashamed of herself'; Edith thought Crosby was 'a sort of half-crazy cad'. In the end, when the will was finally probated in May 1928, she took fewer than a hundred of Walter's books. They included his collected Maurice Barrès, his Conrads, his Lucretius and his Rimbaud, his copy of George Sand's *Elle et Lui*, his poems of Victor Hugo, Whitman's *Drum Taps*, which Alice Garrett had given him before she was married, and his first edition of Joyce's *Ulysses*. She also took back copies of her own work which she had given him – *The Greater Inclination, Crucial Instances, Artemis to Actaeon, The Reef, Summer, The Glimpses of the Moon, Twilight Sleep* – many of them inscribed 'W from E'. Thousands more books went to the Crosbys, some of them first editions of great value, which Harry Crosby started to carry out of the apartment in bags, giving them away to passers-by, or infiltrating them onto second-hand bookstalls along the Seine. Two years later, he shot his new mistress, Josephine Bigelow, and himself, in New York. Edith would refer to him thereafter as 'the murderer'.[68]

The distressing fallout from Walter's will, and the feelings involved in burning her letters to him, made her very anxious about after-lives. In November 1927, she put together a packet of documents and labelled them 'For my biographer'. (This packet was dispersed when her archive was catalogued at Yale, but it consisted of forty-two letters including 'a full account of Teddy's illness, E.W's arrangements with his family & the divorce', press cuttings, letters from Ronald Simmons and from Gross, and an envelope of reviews. 'The bulk of the material concerned Teddy & his illness', and presumably included the letters to Teddy she had copied, leading up to the divorce.) Also, at this time, she wrote on the inside cover of the notebook called *Quaderno dello studente*, where she had been jotting personal thoughts since 1924: 'If ever I have a biographer, it is in these notes that he will find the gist of me.' She remade her own will in the autumn of 1927 and again in the spring of 1928, choosing for her epitaph: '*Tranquillus Deus tranquillat omnia*' (from St Bernard's sermons on 'The Song of Solomon': 'A God at peace with us spreads peace throughout', or 'When God is at peace, he makes all so'). She bought herself a plot near Walter's in the Cimetière des Gonards, and complained to Nathalie that his tomb was not being well kept up ('I am going to send my gardener out to manure the ivy and put it in proper order'). She gave some money towards a 'Walter Berry Room' in a new charitable hospital in Paris, the Fondation Foch. Approached in 1931 by the young Leon Edel, 'a shy little Jew', then writing a thesis on Henry James at the Sorbonne, who seemed to want to write something on Walter, she anxiously asked Berenson's advice (explaining, not quite candidly, that she had kept hardly any of Walter's letters except some early ones and that her 'impression' was that Walter had 'destroyed all his private correspondence'): 'I am perfectly willing, in order to try to block Mr Edel, to say that I *may* write a life of Walter myself. Of course there is no material for a Life, but a vulgar gossipy book could be manufactured by Edel and Mrs Crosby, and this, naturally, I want to prevent at all costs.' She even suggested to Nathalie that Morton Fullerton should be approached to write a life of Berry, but nothing came of this intriguing idea. Berenson replied: 'Christ what a bore, & how I sympathise with you [for] the time you will waste over this impudent imposition. We can't help passing up occasionally from being the public or semi-public creatures that we are . . . Walter will certainly live . . . in your autobiography, and that is what he would have liked – trusting his memory to your skilful hands.' As James had tried to do, they were setting up their defences against future biographers, 'publishing scoundrels'.[69]

Gaillard remembered her being obsessed by Walter's death: 'her grief was in complete possession of her'. But she was resolute and stoic, too. Her diary records her taking up work on *The Children* again, impressively, two days after the ceremony at Versailles, and she finished it in January: 'I feel exhausted but happy!' She told Mary Berenson (partly wanting to give her an example): 'At my age, & with a will-to-live (& to work) as strong as mine, one comes soon, I find, to accept sorrows & renunciations, & to *build* with them, instead of letting them tear one down.' She had over forty years of memories of Walter, and she had some relics. There were the early letters, and there was the letter of loving regret about their past which he had written to her, and asked her to keep, in 1923. There was an ornate paper-knife decorated with two naked classical male figures doing battle, above a shield, with the letters WB engraved on it. Still in existence, unknown to her, were four letters she had written to Walter long ago, from 884 Park Avenue, from The Mount, and from Qu'Acre, dating from 1905, 1906 and 1908, which had somehow ended up in Alice Garrett's papers. (Berry must have lent them to her or left them with her.) Their whole life together of shared interests and people comes rushing back in these affectionate, gossipy, lively letters. They are about his planned visit to Lenox ('It is *dear* of you to take that long journey to come & celebrate with your rustic friends'), her desire to keep him entertained with female company ('If I could find a fairy who would suit you I should secure her at once'), their reading of Dante together ('It is too bad that we should have struggled together through the desert to part on the verge of the *divina foresta*'), the plans for the play of *The House of Mirth*, the fact that a racehorse owner has named one of his fillies 'Lily Bart', Bourget's reaction when Teddy had 'cheerfully remarked that Dreyfus was "all right"' ('Non, Dreyfus n'est pas *all right*'), her call on Meredith with Henry James, and her ill-health, in motor-car metaphors ('When I was with you & Henry I had a sort of illusion that the machine was running again – but it was only the crank whizzing around. I'm still en panne . . .'). Though one is addressed to 'Caro mio', they are not the letters of a lover, but a dear and intimate friend.

Two other mementoes sum up the values of these early twentieth-century Francophile Americans. Walter had also left her a painting: Kenneth Clark would call it one of her few fine pictures. It was Cézanne's enchanting small landscape, *L'Allée du Jas de Bouffan* (now in the Tate Gallery), a view of the grounds of his home painted around 1871. The painting speaks of their mutual passion for French art and French landscapes. In her library, another legacy invokes the American cultural background which was also so important to them both. In Washington in 1898, when she was ill and depressed, Walter had given her a copy of their favourite poet's *Leaves of Grass*, inscribed with a quotation from Whitman:

> Who can stray from me?
> I follow you whoever you are from the present hour.[70]

In the year of Walter Berry's illness and death, Wharton published *Twilight Sleep*, and a fine, grim story, 'Atrophy', in which a married New York lady, imprisoned, like so many of Wharton's heroines, by old conventions, in spite of the 1920s freedoms all around her, tries to visit her long-time secret lover on his death-bed, but is kept at bay by his spinster sister. In a scene of horrifying good manners, in which no truth is spoken but everything is known, she is defeated and turned away. The novel Wharton wrote that year is also about defeat. *The Children* is a daring and profoundly sad book, which carried the weight of all her own feelings, as usual at once intensely close and carefully distanced. At first sight it looks like the other novels of the 1920s, an experiment with modern issues and settings. Appleton's blurb, which she called 'uncomprehending drivel' ('What of the children in a world of nonchalant divorce?'), encouraged reviewers to misread it as yet another Wharton novel on that topic. Though it was met with critical condescension ('Unfortunately, Mrs Wharton has already told us everything she knows . . . she is becoming an old-fashioned writer'), it was a huge popular success. One of her more scathing critics, Janet Flanner, noted that it had 'been sold for a cinema, was the Book of the Month Club's selection, and reached two hundred thousand copies within a month of publication'. The sums for *The Children*, Wharton told Jewett – over $95,000 from serialisation and royalties, $25,000 from Paramount – would enable her to pay off the loan she had taken out for the purchase of Ste-Claire. This combination of instant popular sales and critical disdain made *The Children*, later, one of her most underrated books. But, though it has its flaws, it is the most remarkable and surprising of the novels that came after *The Age of Innocence*.[71]

Her summary, sent to Jewett in February 1927, describes a group of 'rich frivolous friends, all divorced, all remarried, all rushing about in the breath-less pursuit of new thrills, with their children tossed from pillar to post as the result of all these marital changes – children supplied with "all that money can give", but lacking all else'. This does make it sound like another treatment of the jazz-age world, with her now familiar fast-living charac-ters, who have produced a gang of nomadic, uneducated, neglected children, promiscuously thrown together, and washing up in all the fashionable European destinations. But there is more going on than topical satire.

Martin Boyne, a forty-six-year-old New Yorker who has spent most of his life working abroad as a civil engineer, is on his way back to Europe for a reunion with an old attachment, a discreet, charming, recently widowed American lady, Rose Sellars, whom he has not seen for five years and with whom he thinks he may be in love. He is accidentally thrown into contact, on a ship going from Algiers via Sicily to Venice, with the itinerant group of children. (The long-deferred suitor, unexpectedly distracted on his way to his beloved, goes back to the plot of *The Reef*.) He sees from the start that they are held together by the affection and force of personality of the oldest of them, a fifteen-year-old girl, Judith Wheater, and by their loyal, old-fashioned English governess, Miss Scope, who travels with them everywhere. Martin spends the first two chapters trying confusedly, like us, to work out the children's relationships, to which he is coincidentally connected. In his distant past, he had a flir-tation with a chic young girl called Joyce Mervin, who married his old Harvard 'chum', Cliffe Wheater, now a millionaire. The Wheaters have divorced, married other people, and remarried, collecting, en route, four children of their own – Judith, the twins Terry and Blanca, and the baby Chipstone – and three 'steps'. These are Zinnie, the red-headed American daughter of Cliffe Wheater's brief marriage to a film-star, Zinnia Lacrosse (now with a dubious English aristocrat, Lord Wrench), and two Italian children, Beechy and Bun (short for Beatrice and Astorre), whom Joyce Wheater took over during her equally brief (and, on his side, bigamous) marriage to a Prince Buondelmonte. Their 'real' mother was a circus artiste. (In further permutations, Joyce will run off with a young tutor and then a rich old lawyer, and Cliffe with a notorious seducer of million-aires, a woman 'who sticks at nothing' called Sybil – the name a wicked in-joke for Wharton's Ste-Claire listeners.) When Martin tries to make the parents discuss the fate of their children, he has to do so in a large Moroccan tent, pitched on the Venice Lido; and 'Scopy' describes these marriages as 'just like tents – folded up and thrown away when you've done with them'.

Each child has its character trait, vividly, if repetitively, acted out. Terry is frail, well-mannered, intelligent, and longing for a proper education (like a less sinister Miles from *The Turn of the Screw*). Blanca is ingratiating, worldly and stylish, like her mother. Chip is a jolly, solid, lovable baby, done (Wharton said much later), because she was always being told that 'I didn't know anything about children, [so] I wrote *The Children*, & created, in Chipstone, the baby I had dreamed of, & never met'. Zinnie is greedy, sly and materialistic, a baby-Undine. The Italians (or as Zinnie calls them, 'the wops') are emotional and exhibitionist. As a group, the children are meant to be exhaustingly delightful and funny. This does not come off: their scenes are coy and laboured, and not as entrancing as she thought they were. She told friends that she was 'passionately attached' to her seven children, and that proved to be the novel's weakness. But Judith is another matter, an ardent chameleon-like creature, half-girl and half-woman – she is 'between fifteen and seventeen', an energetic young heroine who loves racing up forest-clad mountains, calling 'Up, up, up!' She has dedicated her short life to keeping these seven together, in reaction to the sabotaging of family life by the previous generation. The question of what Judith 'knows', and the extent to which she has a 'moral sense', connect her to Henry James's Maisie. But Wharton had also read, with pleasure, the English novelist Margaret Kennedy's enchanting novel, *The Constant Nymph*, when it came out in 1925, and Judith with her travelling family owes something (as the reviews observed) to the young, tragic Tessa, one of the musical bohemian tribe of Sangers, in childish, uncompromising love with the narcissistic composer Lewis Dodd.[72]

Like many of Wharton's earlier novels, *The Children* is partly about educa-tion. The upbringing of the American girl had always been one of her concerns. Now, given that the old philistine conservatism and sexual hypocrisy she used to criticise have been replaced, in her view, with a morally feckless, rootless cosmopolitanism, the question of how the next generation of her class is to be brought up is even more puzzling. The older characters – Martin, Rose, Miss Scope – are baffled by the question and

shocked (in Rose's case, disgusted) by the circumstances. (As if to prove
the shocking aspect of these lives, an extreme offstage case is provided of
the 'modern hotel child', Doll Westway, Sybil's daughter, a 'wretched drug-
soaked girl' who killed herself at Deauville.) But Judith has a Utopian vision
– these are always doomed to failure in Wharton – of how the children
can all be brought up together. It is a system of upbringing based on warmth,
play, trust, spontaneity, rough-and-ready discipline, and, above all, love. A
lot of shrieking, shouting, tumbling about and 'cuffing' goes on. Their health
is taken care of by fresh air, spontaneous games, and treatments from Miss
Scope's ancient 'Cyclopaedia of Nursery Remedies', on which they swear
an oath of fidelity to each other, and on which 'Scopy's' robust Lancashire
family of fourteen children was once brought up – like the tough old pioneer
mothers nostalgically invoked in Twilight Sleep. In spite of the unnatural
'wilderness' of their circumstances, they make an artificial, grafted kind of
natural family. This haphazard nurturing is felt to be preferable to the care-
less neglect of the rich parents (Joyce Wheater is seen 'clasping the children
. . . to her pearls'), or to Rose Sellars's well-mannered idea of turning the
children into 'happy useful members of society', or to more advanced systems
of educational psychology. These are satirised, in the Twilight Sleep manner,
towards the end of the novel, when the latest American wife of Prince
Boundelmonte arrives, fresh from her degree in 'Eugenics and Infant
Psychology' at the Vocational Department of Juvenile Psychology at
Lohengrin College, Texas. (Wagner is invoked for his idea of developing a
master-race.) She believes in scientific gymnastics, birth-control on the
basis of heredity, improvement of the fittest, and elimination of all the old
savage instincts. But her vocabulary (The Children has many clashes of
different languages) does not cover 'the instinctive motions of the heart'.
Wharton is once more attacking the unrealistic American meliorism which
imagines that pain, evil, and primitive urges can be done away with. The
children are frequently referred to as savages by the adults, and Judith is
amoral, passionate, and illiterate ('it would be ridiculous to marry till I can
learn to spell'). Wharton is obviously not recommending a childhood of
uneducated wandering, but she knows that savagery cannot be whitewashed
out of human beings.[73]

Though the novel's hero is a nomadic American, there is also a French
inspiration for his character. The close friend of her Fullerton days, Léon
Bélugou, a much-travelled civil engineer who had been a teacher (and who
married a very young wife) was a vociferous critic of the new educational
methods of Alfred Binet. Binet's psychological testing of children, derived
from his teacher Charcot, was adopted in America by the racist eugenicist

H.H. Goddard and by Lewis Terman, who devised the original 'IQ' test. In the early 1900s Bélugou wrote a number of scathing pieces about Binet, much admired by Fullerton, where he says, of the psychological testing of children: '*Les instruments de précision ne remplacent pas l'esprit de finesse* [shrewd common sense], *et il y a plus de véritable psychologie chez un montreur d'ours ou de chiens savants que dans tous les coqs a l'âne* [cock and bull stories] *des néopsychologues.*' These arguments filter into *The Children*, and Wharton had Bélugou in mind for Martin Boyne.[74]

Martin is one of Wharton's most painfully self-deceiving male characters. He is the person to whom adventures have never happened (unlike his Bostonian Uncle Edward, whom he always measures himself against). He is awkward, confused and tactless, always (as Wharton suggestively puts it) 'taking the wrong parcel out of his pocket'. *The Children* is full of jaundiced, and unusually aggressive, comments about male inadequacy: the male desire to have it both ways, the busy man's way of 'liquidating hopeless situations' by walking away from them, the standard male procedure of 'endowing the woman of the moment with every quality which made life interesting to himself'. But in spite of these acid remarks, and Martin's frequent bursts of muddled self-justification, his quandary is profoundly distressing. Everything rational in him directs him towards marrying Rose Sellars (even though, 'manlike', he would 'have repudiated . . . indignantly . . . the idea that she was less desirable because she was to be had'). But he slowly realises that he has fallen obsessionally in love with Judith, who appears to be completely unaware of his sexual interest in her. He comes to see that he must never let her know it, and must internally renounce her.

This is very delicately and interestingly done. Judith's mixture of sexual innocence, adult knowingness (derived from watching her parents) and physical expressiveness (she is always kissing and hugging him and calling him 'darling') is finely balanced. Like Tess Sanger in *The Constant Nymph* (or a similarly ambiguous young heroine, ten years later, Elizabeth Bowen's Portia in *The Death of the Heart*) she vacillates continually between being a child and an adult. (The illustrations by R.F. James to the serialisation in *The Pictorial Review* make her a sexy, high-heeled adult, entirely missing the point.) Judith is no Lolita (though Martin's desire for her intriguingly anticipates Humbert Humbert's mournful nympholepsy). The playful, trusting relationship between Martin and Judith is not an erotic exchange, unlike the affair between Dexter and Lita in *Twilight Sleep*, or Royall's feeling for Charity in *Summer*, or the sex between Mr Palmato and his daughter. There is an acute scene in which Martin's own erotic longing is displaced onto the much less attractive figure of Mr Dobree, a middle-aged lawyer, whom Martin jealously thinks is eyeing Judith at a picnic: 'I never could stand your elderly men who look at little girls', he tells Rose angrily. Clearly – to us, though not to him – this is his way of denying 'the tumult in his own veins'. In a revealing letter to Royal Cortissoz, Wharton explains her sympathetic understanding for that kind of inadmissible desire. 'I was by many years the youngest in our family, & much thrown, at Judy's age, with men who were my brothers' friends, men 15 or 20 years older than I was, who were the most delightful of comrades & play-fellows. Looking back now, I see there were Boynes among them, but I was all unconscious then . . .' In her plan for the novel, she allows an ending of 'quiet' yet 'hopeful' emotion, in which Boyne is to marry Judith, 'but as if he were taking a little sister home'.[75]

We might expect our sympathy to go to the Whartonian character, the discreet, old-fashioned woman (like Anna Leath or Kate Clephane) who tries to fight the alarming threat to her happiness with the only weapons she has, tact, diplomacy and a talent for 'arrangements'. All the culture and good taste in the novel come from Rose Sellars. Her lifelong devotion to Martin ('she had trained herself to go on waiting for happiness . . .'), her grief at her own childlessness (which makes Martin's obsession with these random children all the more painful to her), her desolation at losing him, and the covering over of that 'great emptiness' with good form and habitual routines, are all eloquently done. She acts out, perhaps, something of Edith Wharton's feelings about Walter Berry. But, after all, she is no match in the novel for the slangy, noisy, impetuous 'modern' children. All the energy and desire in this surprising work are directed towards the characters Wharton might have been expected to hold at arm's length.[76]

There is hardly any mention of the war in *The Children*, though Martin at one point alludes to Armistice Day. (In her plan for the novel, she described his war-work as 'on a destroyer escorting troops to England'; this was not used.) But, for all the jolly scenes with the children, a profound sense of desolation hangs over the book, as though the whole world is in mourning. There are no onstage deaths, but a death-bed is invoked: 'Boyne turned over these things with the nervous minuteness with which one makes plans for someone who is dying, and will never survive to see them carried out.' The end of the season in Cortina, the town in the Italian mountains where most of the novel takes place, is charged with elegiac feeling: 'Summer was waning in the high valleys of the Dolomites . . .' The rain falls, the season ends, just as on her visit there with Walter in September

1926. Her 'patient listeners' at Ste-Claire (to whom she dedicated the book), and friends who read it, like Gerhardi, were in tears at the end of the novel. Martin has failed in his attempt to keep the children together, has left Judith without telling her what he feels, and has gone away for three years (to South America, where Wharton's male characters go when life gets too complicated). Returning, he meets one of the children again, in a hotel in Biarritz, learns the sad story of what has happened to them, and stands outside in the dark and the rain looking in on the hotel dance, in a deep, quiet scene of longing, sorrow, and recognition. 'A faint wind from the sea drove the wet air against his face; he might almost have fancied he was crying. The pain of not seeing her was unendurable. It seemed to empty his world.' As he stands there, Judith comes into view, on the other side of the glass, grown up, beautiful, and unaware of him: 'And there she was . . . He knew now that if she had appeared to him as a bent old woman he would have known her . . . He watched her with a passionate attentiveness.' Then he turns and goes away, 'a lonely man'.[77]

Three years before that last scene, on his steamer to Rio de Janeiro, Martin Boyne falls asleep and dreams that he and the children are on a picnic together at Versailles. In this dream-scene, set in the ancient, formal, eighteenth-century royal pleasure-grounds (close to where Wharton had just buried Walter's ashes, and where Wharton herself would be buried in 1937), he seems a ghost in a world of shadows. There are French influences and parallels for this vision of homeless Americans: the contemporaneous photographs of an empty, misty, coldly formal Saint-Cloud by Eugène Atget; Verlaine's poem 'Colloque Sentimentale', where the old estranged lovers wander together in the frozen park; the scene (marked up and greatly admired by Wharton) at the end of Flaubert's *L'Éducation Sentimentale*, where Frédéric meets his once-beloved Mme Arnoux again and they walk together in Paris 'as if they were walking in the country on a bed of dead leaves'; or the end of Proust's *À la Recherche* (also much marked by Wharton) where all the characters appear to the narrator again as ghosts of their former selves.

At Versailles too it was mild; there were yellow leaves still on the beeches of the long walks; they formed golden tunnels, with hazy blueish vistas where the park melted into the blur of the forest. But the gardens were almost deserted; it was too late in the season for the children chasing their hoops and balls down the alleys, the groups of nurses knitting and gossiping on wooden chairs under the great stone Dianas and Apollos.

Funny – he and the little Wheaters seemed to have the lordly pleasure-grounds to themselves . . .

Boyne and Judith were alone. They had wandered away into one of the *bosquets*: solitary even in summer, with vacant-faced divinities niched in green, broken arcades, toy temples deserted of their gods. On this November day, when mist was everywhere, mist trailing through the half-bare trees, lying in a faint bloom on the lichened statues, oozing up from the layers of leaves underfoot, the place seemed the ghostly setting of dead days. Boyne looked down at Judith, and even her face was ghostly . . . 'Come', he said with a shiver, 'let's get back into the sun –'[78]

19

A Private Library

The raw young writer-hero of *Hudson River Bracketed* (1929) has his first encounter with books in an old house, The Willows (built in the 1840s, it seems old to him) which feels benignly haunted by the presence of the solitary, book-loving woman who lived there all her life. 'Vance stood alone in Miss Lorburn's library. He had never been in a private library before; he hardly knew that collections of books existed as personal possessions, outside of colleges and other public institutions. And all these books had been a woman's, had been this Miss Lorburn's, and she had sat among them, lived among them, died reading them . . .'[1]

Vance Weston, a natural writer, comes to the Hudson River from one of Wharton's caricatured Midwest towns, Euphoria in Illinois (all 'pep' and real estate and homespun religions), discovers other worlds of literature and culture, and becomes a novelist. The catalyst for his imagination is this dead woman's private library, to which he is introduced by the girl he is going to fall in love with, the romantically named Halo Spear. To the naive uncultured Vance, Miss Lorburn's library is a place of wonder; to Halo it is a quaint vestige of the past.

> 'I've never before been in a house with a library – a real library like this.'
>
> She gave a little shrug. 'Oh, it's a funny library, antiquated, like the house. But Cousin Elinor does seem to have cared for good poetry. When other ladies were reading "Friendship's Garland" she chose Coleridge.'
>
> His gaze returned perplexed to her face. 'Why do you call it a funny library?'
>
> 'Well, it's not exactly up-to-date. I suppose it's a fairly good specimen of what used to be called a "gentleman's library" in my great-grandfather's time. With additions, naturally, from each generation. Cousin Elinor must have bought a good many books herself.'

Vance is falsely accused of stealing some of Miss Lorburn's books, and, cast out of The Willows as out of a Garden of Eden, he goes to New York, and starts to educate himself more thoroughly in the reading room of the New York Public Library, that democratic sanctuary where he finds, to his amazement, that he is allowed 'to go in and read . . . and without paying a cent, for many hours of the day'. This fills him with excitement, but does not have the magic of Miss Lorburn's library, where he could 'move at will from shelf to shelf, subject to the mysterious, the almost physical appeal of books actually visible and accessible'. Later, he returns to it – it will be the setting of some of the key events of his life – and eventually the story of the solitary woman who was 'kept warm' by her books, standing for a richer literary culture than the one he is trying to enter in present-day New York, becomes the subject of his own first successful novel, *Instead*.[2]

The image of the lonely woman in her private library, an inspiration to the young aspiring American writer, shows again how complex Wharton's use of her own life and feelings was in her fiction. The old lady and her house returns her to her distant past. She had used the big country houses on the Hudson River before as a fictional setting in *The House of Mirth* (the Gus Trenors' house, Bellomont, near Rhinebeck, where the first act of Lily's drama is acted out, is closely based on the Ogden Mills mansion overlooking the east bank of the Hudson at Staatsburg). Though she does not describe late nineteenth-century social life on the Hudson in her memoirs as she does her own territories of Newport and Lenox, she would have been familiar with the network of big houses – Clermont, Montgomery Place, the Vanderbilt mansion at Hyde Park – built for grand weekend parties, two hours away from New York by train. Sloanes and Vanderbilts overlapped at Lenox and on the Hudson; Ogden Codman did interior designs for the Vanderbilt mansion a year after *The Decoration of Houses*. In the novel, Halo Spear's family home, Eaglewood, an old house from the 1680s, is shabby and bohemian, standing aloof from the millionaires' country mansions. High above the river, with spectacular views immortalised – Mr Spear boasts – by Bryant, Washington Irving and Whitman, it takes Wharton back to one of the most beautiful of American landscapes, which she had not set eyes on for about fifty years. Old Miss Lorburn, too, goes back to that long-ago figure of Wharton's childhood, her wealthy aunt Elizabeth Schemerhorn Jones, who lived alone in the ugly 'Hudson River Gothic' house of Rhinecliff. In the novel, she turns the lonely old woman's house into the much prettier, more endearing architectural style of the region – all pointed shingled roofs, curly pillars, and fanciful, delicate balconies – that gives its name to the novel and was defined by the great American landscape artist Andrew Jackson Downing (quoted by Halo) as 'Hudson River Bracketed'.[3]

So she 'improves' her memory of the old lady, and splits herself in the novel between the figure of the cultured woman alone with her books and the raw, ambitious American writer. The woman of a vanished age who has left her reading-spectacles on the open page of 'Kubla Khan', and the young American genius who is going to be wrung through the mill of modern commercial publishing, both return her to one of her main pre-occupations: what is the native American writer to do? Where should he or she live, what read and write, what should her or his subject be? Vance Weston and Miss Lorburn provide two models for a literary American: a reclusive, cultured, antiquated privacy; and an energetic involvement with the modern world and the market-place. Wharton acted out both roles. In her late years, the dominant image was that of the private recluse; but right to the end of her life she was also engaged, like Vance, with literary deals, arguments, compromises and successes.

One of Wharton's legendary habits was her writing in bed in the morn-ings, and tossing the completed pages over the side of the bed for the secretary to collect and type up. There can be no more private and privil-eged image of a writing life. Her bedroom, for many years no longer a sexual arena, was her secret space as a writer – and reader.[4] But though this 'private' Wharton dominates our posthumous image of her, in fact she moved easily between her private writing space and the sharing of her work. She quite often received visitors in bed. Gaillard Lapsley left a vivid description of her in her bed at the beginning of her working day, with its rose-coloured blankets and thin linen sheets, 'flanked by night tables charged with telephone, travelling clock, reading light . . .'. She would be wearing

> a thin silk sacque with short loose sleeves, open at the neck and trimmed with lace and on her head a cap of the same material also trimmed with lace which fell about her brow and ears like the edging of a lamp shade . . . Edith's mask stood out sculpturally beneath it. She would have her writing-board perilously furnished with an inkpot on her knee, the dog of the moment under her left elbow and the bed strewn with correspon-dence, newspapers and books.

Downstairs, her evening readings of work-in-progress (and of favourite authors) to her group of 'patient listeners' in the French houses had become as much part of the underpinning of her writing life as her morning sessions composing in bed.

As with writing, so with reading. Her private libraries in her French houses, such important places for her in her solitude, were also where her friendships were rooted. Her relationships had always been based on inter-changes of books: the painful story of the posthumous quarrel over Walter's library shows the symbolic importance of his books to her. Her conversa-tions – in letters, in meetings, in long-term friendships – were based on literary sympathies. All her friends remarked on her passionate way of talking about books. Even Lubbock was generous about this:

> Edith sat in her *bergère*, not as upright as usual; for when she was freely interested, her shoulders sank, her eyes warmed, her face relaxed, and she seemed to shake off and push aside everything that didn't matter as she reached forward to the subject of her talk. It was thus that she talked of books – of books from the inside, books as they are brought into being . . .[5]

By extraordinary good luck, some of Wharton's 'private library' survived her, rather like Miss Lorburn's library in *Hudson River Bracketed*, and gives a vivid insight into her reading life. By her late sixties, Wharton had accumu-lated about four thousand books, divided between her two houses and stamped with the elegant bookplates that Daniel Updike had designed for her in 1924. When she came to dispose of her property (in a last will made in 1937 which was to be bitterly contested), she divided her library in half. About fifteen hundred books were left to Elisina and Royall's son William, who became, in her old age, one of her favourites. When Wharton died, Bill Tyler was living with his wife and child in London, and the books she had bequeathed him were shipped there, and then left in store while they went back to the States. In November 1940, the entire collection was blown up in the Blitz. Those lost books were mostly on art, archaeology and history, which would have been redundant gifts to Wharton's other legatee, her infant godson Colin Clark. He presumably did not need art-books, since he was the younger son of the art-historian and museum director Kenneth Clark, who, with his wife Jane, became close friends of Wharton's in the 1930s. After her death, the books Wharton had left to Colin Clark were moved to the Clarks' London house and then to the medieval Archbishop's Hall at Saltwood Castle, in Kent, under the guardianship of Kenneth Clark's older son, the politician Alan Clark. There they remained for many years, surviving fire and damp, until in 1983 they were bought by the London bookdealer Jack Maggs, and sold on to the York bookseller George Ramsden, who made the upkeep and cataloguing of the collection into his life's work. In 2006, Wharton's books were sold to The Mount, and went back to the first library she had designed for herself just over a hundred years before.

The sizeable surviving remnant of Wharton's private library gives a good sense of what the libraries at St-Brice and Ste-Claire must have been like. Many of the books are beautifully bound sets, in dark, gleaming, black, red, blue and brown bindings, what Wharton in *The Decoration of Houses* called 'warm-toned' books. George Ramsden describes her method of distinguishing her books by their bindings: 'French books are bound in half dark-blue (occasionally red) morocco gilt with the original wrappers bound-in, otherwise in half cloth or marbled paper boards, always with a morocco label gilt-lettered on the spine; German literature is usually in half-red and Italian literature in half-brown morocco gilt.'[6] She had always had strong feelings about the look of books, from her childhood days in her father's library. *The Decoration of Houses* was full of firm statements about this: 'Plain shelves filled with good editions in good bindings are more truly decorative than ornate bookcases lined with tawdry books . . . The general decoration of the library should be of such a character as to form a background or setting to the books, rather than to distract attention from them. The richly adorned room in which books are but a minor incident is, in fact, no library at all.' In her fiction, her characters' books and their choice of reading play a key part in their life-stories.

She always insisted that books must be *used*. Nothing is sadder, as in *Hudson River Bracketed*, than an unused library. In her copy of Barbellion's *Journal of a Disappointed Man* (once a well-known autobiography of depression, published in 1919), she marks a passage which describes the porter in a library who 'spends his days keeping strict vigil over this catacomb of books, passing along between the shelves and yet never paying heed to the almost audible susurrus of desire – the desire every book has to be taken down and read, to live, to come into being in somebody's mind . . . A Book is a Person and not a Thing.' Wharton certainly used her own books. Many of them show the trace of her reading, in bold, confident, pencil underlinings, exclamation marks, queries, and occasional trenchant remarks. What remains of her library reflects her impressive cultural range and her life-long passion for self-education. Her range of reading is immense. It is of course very rich in international, especially French, fiction. Some of her most marked-up books are Flaubert's *L'Éducation Sentimentale*, and the early, and last, volumes of Proust. Tolstoy and Dostoevsky are here in French translations. Of English novelists, Stevenson, Fielding, Eliot, Conrad, Hardy and Trollope appear in bulk. The large American section has plenty of Henry Adams, Emerson, Charles Eliot Norton (Sally's edition of his letters), Santayana and Whitman, all marked up. She kept two sets of James's work, his 'Prefaces' heavily marked. There is a great deal of Greek and Latin in translation (Homer, Marcus Aurelius, Gilbert Murray on the Greeks, Plato, Seneca, Aeschylus, Epictetus), Italian and German prose and poetry in the originals (Petrarch, Dante, Schopenhauer, Goethe, Nietzsche, Hofmannsthal), and French philosophers, essayists, historians and letter-writers (the Daudets, Joubert, the Goncourts, Jusserand, Lamartine, La Rochefoucauld, Le Dantec, Lyautey, Michelet, Montaigne, Pascal, Renan, Sainte-Beuve, Taine, de Vigny). The evidence of her travels comes from her heavily annotated, battered Baedekers and Blue Guides. There are many books on evolution, astronomy, popular science, French history, and land-scape gardening, including a fine copy of the book Halo cites to Vance, Andrew Jackson Downing's *Treatise on the Theory and Practice of Landscape Gardening.*

The developments in her thinking are indexed by her copies of Ostwald, Haeckel, Thomas Huxley, Kellogg on Darwinism, and Lock (the book on evolution in which Teddy was so uninterested). Historians, philosophers and essayists such as Brownell, Burke, Samuel Butler, Arnold, Hazlitt, Coleridge, Pater, Joshua Reynolds, and Lewes are intensively marked. And she also had many lives of saints and histories of religion. Her library contained, for instance, lives of St François Xavier, Ste Jeanne de Chantal, St John of the Cross, St Francis of Assisi, St Thomas Aquinas, St Bridget and St Bernard; *The Golden Legend,* and a book of saints compiled by Benedictine monks. She had books on the psychology of saints, the dogmas of ancient Christianity, the symbolism of churches, Catholic doctrine, the Jesuits, and the Church in France – and also on oriental religions and on Persian and Chinese mystics. She kept her childhood *Book of Common Prayer,* dated 1855, and her Bible, much marked, and inscribed to her by Lucretia on 29 August 1878, no doubt the day of her confirmation.

Her rich collection of poetry books (some in beautiful, carefully cher-ished early editions) is much marked up: especially passages of deep emotion, romantic descriptions, sad, tender expressions of love, feelings of solitude and longings for death. She paid close attention to Shakespeare's *Sonnets,* Meredith's *Modern Love,* the poems and letters of the Brownings, including Elizabeth Barrett Browning's 'Sonnets from the Portuguese' ('When our two souls stand up erect and strong . . .'), Keats's letters, Donne's 'A Valediction: Forbidding Mourning', Christina and Dante Gabriel Rossetti's poems (among them her 'When I am Dead' and 'Up-Hill', and his 'Silent Noon', with its celebration of 'this close-companioned inartic-ulate hour / When two-fold silence was the song of love'), Matthew Arnold's 'Resignation', Meredith's 'Lucifer in Starlight', Anna de Noailles's *Éblouisse-ments,* Crashaw, Baudelaire, the *Rubáiyát of Omar Khayyám,* Emerson's

'Threnody' ('Heaven . . . Built of furtherance and pursuing / Not of spent deeds but of doing'), Dante's *Vita Nuova*, William Morris's 'The Defence of Guenevere' and Hardy. Above all, she treasured and marked the poetry of Whitman. Many of the poems marked in her library or quoted in her Commonplace Book show up again in the anthology of love-poetry which she coedited with Robert Norton – one of her last literary treats – posthumously published in 1939 with the indulgent title, *Eternal Passion in English Poetry*. 'These are poems read aloud again and again by the winter fireside, and again and again found enchanting and satisfying', she wrote in her introduction, one of her last pieces of writing. Here are her favourites: Browning's 'Two in the Campagna', Hardy's 'The Going', Emily Brontë's 'Remembrance', Donne's 'A Valediction: Forbidding Mourning', Michael Drayton's 'Since there's no help', Marvell's 'To His Coy Mistress', Keats's 'Bright Star', Patmore's 'A Farewell', Christina Rossetti's 'Remember', some of Dante Gabriel Rossetti's sonnets from *The House of Life*, many Shakespeare sonnets, Yeats's 'When You are Old', Meredith's Sonnet XLVII from *Modern Love* ('Love, that had robbed us of immortal things / This little moment mercifully gave . . .') and Tennyson's 'O that 'twere possible / After long grief and pain / To find the arms of my true love / Round me once again'.

In her prose books, by contrast, she tended to mark ironical epigrams and disillusioned philosophies. Her own marginal comments are few and dry. An exclamation mark accompanies Samuel Butler's aphorism: 'The only absolute morality is absolute stagnation, but this is unpractical.' There are some outraged end-notes to George Saintsbury's *History of English Prose Rhythm* (given to her by Minnie): 'Why omit Tyndall? Why omit the Prologue to Romola? And "who has not felt the beauty of a woman's arm", etc, from the M. on the Floss? Above all, *why* [omit] Keats's Letters?' Santayana, whom she greatly admired, gets one annotation in *The Life of Reason*. Next to this remark – 'In some nations everybody is by nature so astute, versatile, and sympathetic that education hardly makes any difference in manners or mind' – she writes 'France'.

Sometimes she has paused over a line which has been useful to her, or has marked something that speaks to her own circumstances (like her annotations to Shaw's Preface to *Getting Married* in 1911). 'People wish to be settled; only as far as they are unsettled is there any hope for them' (Emerson). 'To be wise indeed and happy and self-possessed, we must often be alone' (Landor, on Epicurus). 'Do you see how necessary a world of pains and troubles is to school an Intelligence and make it a Soul? (Keats). 'You could neither have everything nor be everything – you had to choose; you could not at once sit firm at your job and wander through space inviting invitations' (James, on Zola). 'Art to be progressive must also be conservative' (Butcher's *Lectures on Greek Subjects*). Her marked examples often get into *The Writing of Fiction*, like Proust on the writer Bergotte's dedication to his task, or the reunion scene between Frédéric and Mme Arnoux in *L'Éducation sentimentale*. One example of this cross-fertilisation comes in her markings of Shakespeare. She marks, in *Cymbeline*, Imogen's question to Pisanio, the man she thinks is taking her to her husband but who has been told to take her to her death: 'How far to Milford Haven? / Why one that rode to's execution, man, could never go so slow.' In the margin Wharton writes: '*What a stroke!*' She quoted the lines in a 1902 essay as 'a lightning flash of significance', and again in *The Writing of Fiction*, as an example of 'the swift touch of genius darting its rays on the path to come'.[7]

These marginal marks make a form of autobiography. There are love-gifts from Fullerton and copies of his work; affectionate dedications from James; copies of Berry's books; books she could not discuss with Teddy, or that were left over from his own minimal collection; books that once belonged to her father, her mother, or her brothers; early gifts from Emelyn Washburn or Sally Norton, effusive inscriptions from a great variety of French writers, presentation copies from Theodore Roosevelt. There are old book-plates from Land's End, and the ownership signatures of 'Edith Jones'. There are corrections she made in her copies of her own works. Her books do not just provide evidence for her life-story, they were also protagonists in it, and the equivalent of old friends. So she underlines, in Hazlitt's essay 'On Reading Old Books':

> ... I shake hands with, and look an old, tried, and valued friend in the face, – compare notes, and chat the hours away ... [These] are landmarks and guides in our journey through life. They are pegs and loops on which we can hang up, or from which we can take down, at pleasure, the wardrobe of a moral imagination, the relics of our best affections, the tokens and records of our happiest hours.

> ... Whether those observations will survive me, I neither know nor do I much care: but to the works themselves ... and to the feelings they have always excited in me since I could distinguish a meaning in language, nothing shall ever prevent me from looking back with gratitude and triumph. To have lived in the cultivation of an intimacy with such works, and to have familiarly relished such names, is not to have lived quite in vain.

Her literary loyalties can be tracked in the cross-over between her library and the Commonplace Book of favourite quotations which she kept, inter-mittently, through her life. This handwritten collection of extracts was a legacy of the century she grew up in, when, for Pussy Jones, as for her mother, copying out favourite quotations was a habitual female pursuit. But Edith Wharton's anthology was a far cry from the average American woman's of her time – though it does favour some authors who were strong influences then and who are now almost forgotten, like Samuel Butler and Meredith. Started in 1896 at Land's End, kept most intensively between 1901 and 1910 (especially in the Fullerton years), and with a few entries between 1911 and 1933, it is a fascinating record of her thinking and her tastes, overlapping with the markings in her books, her quotations in letters and essays, and her late selection of poetry. Like her library, it is strong on philosophy and poetry, with many passages on evolution, scientific curiosity, the search for knowledge and the development of ideas. There is much copying-out of Schopenhauer, Goethe, Pascal, Dante, Emerson, Meredith, Plato, Pater, Tyndall and Nietzsche. Stoic realism dominates, in quotations from Marcus Aurelius, Epictetus and Seneca – the latter on the danger of following other people's ideas, on the need for calm in the face of death, and: 'How late it is to begin life just when we have to be leaving it.' There are many passages on love (Pascal's '*le coeur a ses raisons*' is found more than once), friendship, discontent, resignation, art and originality – espe-cially from Flaubert ('*Plus une idée est belle, plus la phrase est sonore*'). Plato's 'Phaedrus' on beauty interests her: 'Beloved Pan, & all ye other gods . . . give me beauty in the inward soul; & may the outward & the inward be one.' (The same passage is quoted in Robert Norton's book on art.) Many of her favourite quotations are lessons on life, sceptical but encouraging. Nietzsche's line from the Preface to *Zarathustra*, '*Entscheidende entsteht trotzdem . . .*' 'Everything worth while is accomplished notwithstanding', is copied here, marked in her copy of Elisabeth Forster-Nietzsche's *Das Leben Friedrich Nietzsche*, and used (as a 'great saying') in her conclusion to *The Writing of Fiction*. A verse she copies out from Chesterton in 1911 – 'The old world glows with colours clear, / And if, as saith the Saint, / This world is but a painted show, / O let us lick the paint!' – is quoted in a letter of 1928 to Elisina, as 'my favourite philosophic axiom'. In the few late entries, there is a noticeable shift to religious quotations (from the Gnostic 'Hymn to Jesus', or from St Augustine), evidence of her shift from scepticism to belief. On the last page, dated 1933, she has pasted in the words of Schubert's transcendent song of resignation and joy, '*Im Abendrot*' ("In the Evening Glow"), as though it sums up her religious beliefs: 'Could I ever complain?

Could I be fearful? / Be unsure of Thee and myself? / No, for in my breast I will carry / Thy heaven here with me / And this heart, before it breaks / May still drink brightness, still quaff light.'[8]

Wharton's quotations from Whitman in the Commonplace Book, mostly copied in 1898, which closely overlap with her markings of his poems and the notes she made for an unwritten essay on him in 1907, are some of the most revealing of these entries. In the notes she made, and kept, for the essay, she wrote: 'He sees through the layers of the conventional point of view and of the conventional adjective, straight to the thing itself and . . . to the endless thread connecting it with the universe.' She particularly liked his phrase 'the inherences of things'. In the Commonplace Book, and in her edition of *Leaves of Grass*, she marked the same three words (italicised here) in his poem 'Life':

> Ever the undiscouraged, resolute, struggling soul of man;
> (Have former armies failed? then we send fresh armies – & fresh again);
> Ever the grappled mysteries of all earth's ages, old or new;
> Ever the eager eyes, hurrahs, the welcome-clapping hands, the loud applause;
> Ever the soul dissatisfied, curious, *unconvinced at last*;
> Struggling today the same – battling the same.

In 1898, she also copied a long passage from his autobiographical essay, 'A Backward Glance O'er Travel'd Roads', on his refusal to believe that poetry will cease to be read because of the 'tendency to science'. It seems to be a message to herself about what her own work might do, and a much less elitist one than might be expected: 'The true use for the imaginative faculty of modern times is to give ultimate vivification to facts, to science, and to common lives, endowing them with glows and glories and final illustriousness which belong to every real thing, and to real things only. Without that ultimate vivification – which the poet or other artist alone can give – reality would seem incomplete, and science, democracy, and life itself, finally in vain.' Thirty-six years later, she borrowed the title of this essay for her own autobiography.

Apart from Whitman, Goethe – first read with Emelyn Washburn when she was thirteen – was her most enduring literary companion. Berenson gave her a fine copy of *Faust* in 1925 from his own library, with an inscription, under his book-plate ('Ex Libris Bernardi Et Mariae Berenson'): 'Nunc Edithae Wharton B.B.'. Her last big novels were full of her rereading and rethinking of Goethe; Kenneth Clark, who met her while she was writing them, noted in his reminiscences of her that 'to the end of her life she revered Goethe more than any other author'. Her copies of *Faust*, *Italienische Reise* [The Italian Journey], *Wilhelm Meister's Lehrjahre* [Apprenticeship] and *Wanderjahre* [Travels], *Die Wahlverwandtschaften* [Elective Affinities], *Gedichte* [two volumes of poems] and *Autobiographische Schriften* [autobiographical writings] are some of the most heavily marked of all her books; her Commonplace Book is full of him, and his influence stretches from *The Valley of Decision* to *The Gods Arrive*. One epigraph for *A Backward Glance* was the line from *Wilhelm Meister* which she often quoted to her friends: '*Kein Genuss ist vorübergehend*' ['No pleasure is transitory']. She often quotes from *Faust*, for example, the lines 'Two souls, dwell, alas, within my breast' ['*Zwei Seelen Wohnen, ach, in meiner Brust!*'] which she applies to herself (as in the poem 'La Folle au Logis') and to her most autobiographical characters. She is moved by the passage about the bareness of the room we live in, its lack of furniture: 'It was lent for a moment only.' And she is haunted by the moment when (as she puts it in an essay of 1902), 'Mephistopheles tells Faust that, to evoke the phantom of Helen, he must descend to the *Mothers*, the hero shudders at the mysterious word, and the reader feels the recoil of the shudder.' This passage sounds all through the story of Vance.[9]

So does the line of the 'Merry Person' in the Prologue to *Faust*: 'Wherever you seize it, there it is interesting.' Vance's literary mentor, one of Wharton's cynical, wise observers, George Frenside, cites this passage in *Hudson River Bracketed*: 'Well, now take hold of life as it lies around you; you remember Goethe: "Wherever you take hold of it, it's interesting." So it is – but only in proportion as you are.' Vance has to learn this lesson, to plunge into the welter, to take hold of the 'it' that is all around him. Private communication with books is only one side of the writer's life; she or he must also be involved with contemporary life and with the market-place. That is the other side of Vance's story. The struggle of the literary spirit to make its way through, and keep its integrity in spite of the demands of the world, is the theme (as originally planned for 'Literature') of *Hudson River Bracketed* and *The Gods Arrive*. As a result, these books are uncharacteristically polemical, sprawling, and emotional. The English novelist V.S. Pritchett, reviewing *Hudson River Bracketed* in *The Spectator*, described it as 'a good old-fashioned novel of huge proportions'. Wharton had tried her hand at being 'modern', and instead decided, relaxing her usual disciplines – structure, comedy, sharpness – to write exactly what she felt, in full, about the predicament of the writer in the contemporary world. The outline of *Hudson River Bracketed* for Appleton's describes Vance's discoveries thus:

[At The Willows] he touches The Past with his actual bodily hands, and its magic pours into his blood ... I want to try and draw the experiences of an unusually intelligent modern American youth, of average education and situation, on whom the great revelation of the Past, which everything in modern American training tends to exclude, or at least to minimize, rushes in through the million channels of art, of history, of human beings of another civilisation ... Vance Weston becomes a writer ... and dies young, full of the awe of the world's wonder and beauty.

She told Elisina that *Hudson River Bracketed* came out of a long-ago promise to Walter (the ghostly dedicatee of *The Gods Arrive*), and had been transposed from a pre- to a post-war setting. To Eleanor Carroll from *The Delineator*, the magazine which serialised the novels, who managed to interview Wharton at the Pavillon (with the pekes in attendance) in the summer of 1931, she gave a solemn account of the subject of *The Gods Arrive*. Emerson's lines from 'Give All to Love' had inspired the title: 'When half-gods go / The gods arrive' (she had copied these lines into the Commonplace Book as long ago as 1896). 'It is my ambition to portray the half-gods that are worshipped by all people – but especially by the creative artist – the mistakes, the sufferings, the glimpses of glory, that go into the painful perfecting of a human spirit.' (In answer to Carroll's question about how she could possibly write about Americans so far from America, she replied, more drily: 'I stay four weeks every year at the Hôtel Crillon in Paris ... And I always listen to everything my American fellow-passengers say when I go up and down in the lift!') Her tone about the Vance novels suggests that she thought of them as a sort of sacred task. More than any of her other novels, they are philosophical attempts to examine how creativity works, how the 'indestructible inmost self' is made and what integrity it can sustain.[10]

The 'self' is what the author has to draw on; if he sells it, there may be nothing left. Vance Weston has an acute sense of his 'irreducible core of selfness' – he finds it in nature, by the sea, in the heat of creation – but everything he encounters threatens it. He needs 'time to let his mind ripen', but the pressures of the market force him to speed up. He makes his name as a very young man with a raw, passionate story written at heat, out of the experience of losing his first love (Turgenev-like) to his lecherous, crafty grandfather. He follows 'One Day' with a quiet, arresting tale, 'Unclaimed', about a soldier's body being returned from the war (cue for some bitter remarks about the lack of post-war readership for war-stories). His success and his naivety put him in the power of his magazine editor (who, unfor-

tunately for him, is also Halo's vain and jealous husband) and an exploitative publishing firm. He is courted by literary fixers like the ludicrous society
lady Jet 'Pulsifer', funder of a famous short-story prize, but loses all chance
of winning it when he asks her for a loan instead of making love to her. He
is exposed to all the latest literary fashions. (The theme of a group of young,
competitive writers promoting various kinds of artificial products is like
Gide's *Les Faux-Monnayeurs* [*The Counterfeiters*], published in 1926.) Vance
encounters all the little New York cliques (like the 'Tomorrowists') who
hang out in 'The Loafers' Club' and 'The Cocoanut Tree', talking about
obscure volumes of poetry called *Voodoo*, or 'discontinuous' new novels like
Jerks and Jazzes. One author has a success with a big realist novel of small-
town American life, *The Corner Grocery* (clearly a version of *Main Street*);
but this is superseded by Gratz Blemer's *This Globe* – more like an American
Ulysses – which 'takes three hundred thousand words to tell the story of a
streetwalker and a bootblack'. Wise old Frenside, speaking for Wharton,
sums up the problem: 'Yes – it's a bad time for a creator of any sort to be
born, in this after-war welter, with its new recipe for immortality every
morning.'

In *The Gods Arrive*, artistic bohemia is transported (with decreasing vividness) to the cafés of Montparnasse and the salons of London. A succession
of minor characters exposes the fatuousness of the literary environment and
the rareness of real talent. (The exception to this is a keen-minded young
Parisian intellectual, Savignac, tantalisingly undeveloped.) There is Alders,
a magpie for intellectual titbits, with what Halo snootily calls 'a thin glaze
of culture over an unlettered origin'. There is Halo's crook brother, Lorry
Spear, described in the notes for the novel as 'an artistic rotter', always at
the modish artists' studios and the Left Bank bookshop, run by two dubious
girls, which deals in censored books. (Clearly Wharton disapproved of
'Shakespeare & Co'.) There is the eager, unstable Chris Churley, fanta-
sising about a literary career but unable to write a word, who kills himself;
and there is the wondrous English aesthete, Octavius, whose 'reign extends
from Bloomsbury to Chelsea', and whose permanently unfinished work in
progress is treated as a living masterpiece. There are ridiculous fans and
interviewers, asking the famous American novelist 'Did you take a course?'
or: 'Of course she knew novelists always pretended they invented their
characters – but wouldn't he be a darling, and just whisper to her some of
the real names of the people in his books?'[11]

Vance is a 'success', but his only really good novel is his first, the quiet,
unfashionable book inspired by Miss Lorburn. After *Instead*, he tries to write
a massive social analysis of 'the tumult of life and wealth and energy' that

is New York, to be called *Loot* – but in a quarrel with Lewis Tarrant over his contract, tears up his only copy. His next idea, *Magic*, about a group of people with 'starved' 'spiritual lives', does not develop. But he does have a popular hit with a colourful, facile historical novel written out of time spent abroad, *The Puritan in Spain*. After a long struggle, he then produces a critical flop, a modernist epic called *Colossus*, 'an attempt to deal microscopically, with the infinitely little of human experience, incalculably magnified'.[12]

The marketing of literature is thoroughly, and grimly, satirised. (Some flashes of Wharton's old lightness come through: 'When people break appointments it's never because they're dead.') The promotion of the author as product – a phenomenon which kept pace with Wharton's own career – sets the rhetoric of commercialism against the creative self. The publishers 'Dreck and Saltzer' and the 'glib young Jew' who is the assistant editor of Tarrant's magazine, *The New Hour*, imprison Vance in a disadvantageous contract while agreeing to put him 'in the limelight'. (Wharton's anti-Semitism is also evident in the fat-fingered, cigar-smoking German-Jewish novelist, Gratz Blemer, only interested in counting 'the shekels', who speaks in a voice 'oiled by Jewish gutturals' and makes Vance wonder 'why American novels were so seldom written by Americans'.) The best-selling novel of the moment is called *Price of Meat*. Vance quickly discovers that his contract with the magazine entails 'booming' his fellow writers in its pages. Halo complains that literature 'has to be shoved down people's throats like Beauty Products and patent collar buttons'. When *Instead* is a success, Dreck & Saltzer halve his percentage on the grounds that it is short-measure: 'When readers have paid their money they like to sit down to a square meal. An oyster cocktail won't satisfy 'em. They want their money's worth; and that's at least a hundred thousand.' In a laboured parallel side-plot, Vance's inspirational grandmother, Mrs Scrimser, comes to New York from Euphoria to preach her optimistic brand of spiritualism, and she too becomes a product, managed by publicists, 'selling her hazy rhetoric to audiences more ignorant than herself'. Vance calls it 'another form of bootlegging'.[13]

Vance's opposite in the novel is the dynamic entrepreneur Bunty Hayes, who starts a firm called 'Storecraft', providing all the latest products, arte-facts, and cultural experiences for consumers – including religion and literature. Hayes is not a bad sort – he is generously devoted to Vance's wife Laura Lou – but he is commerce incarnate. One of his many jobs on his way up is as a 'barker' on tourist cars going round New York. His patter sums up Wharton's vision of what has happened to her city: 'This vacant lot on your right ... was formerly the site of Selfridge B. Merry's five-million-dollar marble mansion, lately sold to the Amalgamated Searchlight Company, who are about to erect on it a twenty-five-million-dollar skyscraper of fifty stories, with roof gymnasium, cabaret terraces, New Thought church and airplane landing ...' Vance writes copy for Hayes, advertisements for silk stockings or face cream, circulars for the lecture tours managed by Storecraft's Arts and Letters Department. 'Writing a good advertisement', Hayes tells him, 'was just as much of an art as turning out *Paradise Lost* or *Gentlemen Prefer Blondes.*' Vance's belief that salesmanship and creativity should be separate is clearly meant to move us, but we can see that he is hopelessly unrealistic:

> The use of the business vocabulary was what he recoiled from. That there should be 'deals', transactions, compromises in business was a matter of course to him ... But Vance had never taken any interest in business, or heard applied to it the standards of loyalty which are supposed to regulate men's private lives, and which he had always thought of as prevailing in the republic of letters. To him an artist's work was essentially a part of the private life, something closer than the marrow to the bone. Any thing that touched the sanctity, the incorruptibility, of the creative art was too contemptible to be seriously considered.[14]

The difficulty Wharton sets herself in the figure of Vance is that he has to carry so much. He has to voice many of her own feelings and views, while also being a Dostoevskian holy fool, straight out of a Russian novel (he reads the Russians avidly, and there is even a scene when he beats the owner of an ill-treated horse in the street). He is also an inarticulate, uneducated Westerner who would fit into a novel by Dreiser or Lewis, given to saying things like 'I guess I don't know how to talk'. Like the novels he inhabits, he seems a misfit in his own time (traces of Hardy's Jude, Gissing, Zola, and Balzac hang about him, while Halo is compared to an Ibsen heroine). He is a creature of passion and impulse, a kind of natural genius, obsessed with the need for the artist to descend for inspiration to some subterranean place: 'that mysterious Sea of Being of which the dark reaches swayed and rumoured in his soul'. This is Goethe's ambiguous, fearsome place of 'the Mothers', who seem here to be sources of inspiration, primal experiences, spirits of the dead, the writer's true audience, or the voice of the sea – as in another of Wharton's favourite texts, Whitman's 'Out of the Cradle Endlessly Rocking', in which the sea, 'the savage old mother incessantly crying', whispers to the writer 'the low and delicious word death'.

In the real world, Vance is a bad judge of character and a hopeless husband and lover, childish, egotistical and unfaithful. In *Hudson River Bracketed*, he marries, blindly, a dim, pretty, uneducated young girl, Laura Lou, whom he meets when he first goes East. She is adoringly dependent on him, baffled by his genius, and jealous of his New York world. Their struggle to make ends meet, living in one room in a dismal West Side boarding-house and in a tumbledown rural retreat in the North Bronx, while the pathetic Laura Lou gets more like her complaining mother (as Mattie turned into Zenobia in *Ethan Frome*) and tries to hide from him her rapidly developing TB, makes a touching novel inside the novel. It is an interesting return (informed by her wartime observation of TB victims) to the social realism of her earliest work, 'Bunner Sisters' or 'Mrs Manstey's View': Vance cries out against 'the cruelty of social conditions'. Set against Laura Lou, Halo (who has married the wealthy literary dilettante Lewis Tarrant because he can keep her incompetent parents in style) with her 'aloof and reticent grace', seems to Vance at first a vision of high-minded intelligent sympathy, and only gradually – and then not for long – an object of desire.[15]

In *The Gods Arrive*, Halo leaves with Vance for Europe as his mistress, without waiting for a divorce from Lewis (whose injured pride and obstructiveness make him the most subtle character in the novel, Wharton's Karenin). The lovers go on bohemian wanderings in Spain, Paris and the South of France (with evocative accounts of Wharton's favourite Spanish cities, Córdoba and Granada, of lovers' trips to Senlis and Chartres, and of the unfashionable Mediterranean resort of Oubli-sur-Mer). Halo, who is not at all bohemian at heart, is always trying to create a home where Vance can write, and Vance is always wandering off. Their relationship goes through 'harrowing extremes' dismaying to them both. Vance goes to England, while Halo waits sadly in the South of France, consoling herself with gardening. He is seduced, as he had been in his youth, by the heartless Floss Delaney, now making a meteoric ascent, Undine-like, through the shoddy side of European society. After a cruel disillusionment Vance returns to America, where he undergoes purgation through illness and suffering. In a strange scene, which invokes Wharton's deepening religious feelings, he recovers by reading St Augustine, in midwinter, in a remote Midwestern lakeside forest, his only companions a 'half-educated naturalist' and some lumbermen. He reads the words which Wharton was currently copying into her Commonplace Book: 'I was shaken with a gust of indignation because I could not enter into Thy Will, yet all my bones were crying out that this was the way, and no ship is needed for that way, nor chariot, no, nor feet; for it is not as far from me as from the house to the spot where we are seated.' Vance appropriates as a definition of 'experience' St Augustine's description of Faith as 'food of the full grown'; and by experience he means suffering. Pain provides the lesson; the grandmother, on her death-bed, renounces the childish American optimism Wharton so much complains of, and murmurs to Vance: 'Maybe we haven't made enough of pain – been too afraid of it. Don't be afraid of it.'[16]

Halo (more in focus in *The Gods Arrive*) is also made wiser through suffering. At first she seems culturally superior to Vance, a spirited and independent New Woman. But Wharton puts her intelligent heroine through a series of mortifications. She has no 'creative talent' and no money, so, even in late 1920s America, she sees no way to freedom except through marriage. As Tarrant's wife she has to be demeaningly diplomatic; and even when 'she had at last emerged into the bald light of day from the mist of illusion she had tried to create about her marriage', and risked all for love of Vance, she finds herself no less servile and needy. She still has to manage and pretend, and is terrified of losing him. She is 'reduced to the same abject level by the big primitive passions' as all other women. This is a bleak lesson in relationships, which could apply to any of Wharton's heroines: 'Don't we all make each other unhappy, sooner or later – often without knowing it?' As Ellen Olenska once warned Newland Archer, and as the runaway couple found in 'Souls Belated', 'free union' is a disappointment. As elsewhere, Wharton argues, in *The Gods Arrive*, for the institution of marriage, not for reasons of social conformity, nor because it guarantees happiness (the reverse in most of Wharton) but because it provides continuity and structure for the emotions. Vance perceives this confusedly: 'How did two people who had once filled each other's universe manage to hold together as the tide receded? Why, by the world-old compulsion of marriage, he supposed.' Frenside understands it more clearly, and tells Halo: 'We most of us need a frame-work, a support – the maddest lovers do. Marriage may be too tight a fit – may dislocate and deform. But it shapes life too; prevents growing lopsided, or drifting.'[17]

It is not until Halo is pregnant, at the end of *The Gods Arrive*, that Wharton gives her some control over her life. She is allowed, momentarily, a strong feminist voice – 'Can't you understand that a woman should want to be free, and alone with her child?' – but, more conventionally, she is turned into a calm maternal figure of acceptance, a sort of nurse-goddess, one of the Mothers. Halo and Vance are reconciled in a mood of quiet, mystic transcendence, and she takes him back as if he is a child. Whatever their future is going to be, it will take place, of course, at The Willows. The American writer comes home, the implication being that he will now turn his back on the distractions of contemporary life, and plunge down below the surface for his true materials. But by this time the novels' literary concerns have fallen away, and The Gods Arrive has become much more a philosophical and religious meditation on how the true self can be found and what it should live by.[18]

In these long, prolix late novels Wharton splits herself between the male artist and the woman of feeling, and, less smoothly than of old, injects her own emotions and experiences into her social analysis. The two books were poorly received and are not much read now: their weaknesses are obvious. But they are also curiously absorbing and touching. There is a great deal of her own writing life in Vance's. At one point, when Halo is wanting to continue as his literary muse and confidante, and Vance is holding her at bay, his work is described as 'a secret garden in which he needs to shut himself away'. The most revealing section of A Backward Glance, which overlapped with the writing of The Gods Arrive, is about Wharton's writing practices (many of which resemble Vance's) and is called 'The Secret Garden'.[19]

The year after Walter's death, Wharton made valiant efforts to get back to normal. She responded calmly and regretfully to the news of Teddy Wharton's death in February, writing to the friends (such as Sally's sister Lily Norton and Robert Grant), who could 'remember him as a charming companion, & the kindest & most sympathetic of beings'. She knew that 'the real Teddy went years ago'; she knew 'for how many years I struggled to carry on some sort of life with him'. Some bitterness did remain: 'When I remember what the Drs assured his family before our marriage, that his father's insanity was not hereditary, I wonder at the blindness that exists on that subject – still exists, probably.'[20]

In May 1928, she took a trip with Daisy Chanler to Spain. These two lifelong friends still got on very well, though Wharton could have her moments of impatience with her: 'I cannot see' (she wrote a year or two later) 'why she cannot let her grown-up and thoroughly competent children look after themselves, and arrange her own life as she pleases.'[21] Wharton travelled and socialised in England in the summer (meeting Evelyn Waugh and Arthur Waley, seeing Robert at Lamb House and Eric Maclagen, and visiting Tintagel in Cornwall for the first time). She had her new library built at Ste-Claire, benefiting from the big sales of The Children. As well as writing Hudson River Bracketed she published a couple of stories (including the coldly brilliant 'After Holbein'). She contracted to write her memoirs, and followed with interest the success of the Broadway adaptation of The Age of Innocence.

She made a new will, which involved bequeathing the Pavillon to be used as another of her TB sanatoriums (still going strong under Elisina's super-vision) – a plan which came to nothing. She collected her usual friends around her for Christmas at Ste-Claire. But at the end of the year she had some very serious blows, beginning with the destruction of her garden in the sudden and terrible frosts which hit her part of the Var. Very soon afterwards, while she was still grieving bitterly, and the weather was still icy, her health collapsed. In January she had influenza and a high fever. 'Wretchedly tired and shaky', she wrote in her line-a-day diary in February. On 3 March – still keeping her diary, remarkably – she noted 'an attack of heart failure'. In the weeks following, Jeanne Fridérich wrote on her behalf to friends, describing '*une crise cardiaque*' followed by a bad throat infection. She was being treated with an anti-diphtheria serum (a precursor of the vaccine) and with digitalis for a tired heart, and was going to need a long convalescence. Elisina noted that the doctor had diagnosed, not a coronary thrombosis, but 'acute myocarditis' (inflammation of the heart muscle) produced by 'a stoppage in the natural processes of the assimilation of food', the result of 'great distress and fatigue, complicated by a chill'. The use of digitalis suggests an irregular heartbeat (atrial fibrillation), which would make her more liable to a later stroke. She would have been uncomfortably conscious of these 'palpitations'. She was also given, Elisina said, 'drastic treatment with a stomach-pump'. She was extremely weakened by the illness and by the treatment; she could not walk, and had to be carried every day from her bed to a day-bed. As after Walter's death, she felt intensely grateful to Elisina for coming to look after her, and increasingly dependent on her: 'I can never forget what you did', she wrote later. Not until the end of April 1929 did her diary resume: 'Crawling back to life after two months' illness' – and in May she had another relapse. All her travel plans – Syria with the Berensons, Egypt with Daisy, New York for the Columbia D.Litt – were cancelled, though she did manage to get to England in the summer. While she was there, the news of Geoffrey Scott's sudden death at forty-six, was another blow. She was as stoical as she could be, writing self-critically to Daisy in June: 'This is a real invalid's letter, with "I – I – I" all over the first page.' But, as she often put it, the Furies were awake, and had her in their grip.[22]

She had a professional disaster too, stressful enough to have exacerbated her illness. Towards the end of 1928, an editor on the *Delineator*, Oscar Graeve, who had been sent the early chapters of *Hudson River Bracketed* by Jewett, started the serialisation of the novel without warning her. Wharton was extremely upset about this, and felt it placed her under impos-sible pressure. Even before her illness, she wrote complaining to Graeve:

I have been very much disturbed by the fact that you began the publication of *Hudson River Bracketed* before the novel was finished ... I cannot be bound by a fixed date, because I am a slow worker, and also because it is impossible to see what interruptions I may be subjected to by illness or other accidents ... It was entirely at your own risk that you started to bring out the opening chapters ... without notifying me.

During her illness, she wrote to Jewett: 'I cannot tell you the harm that Mr Graeve's inexcusable action has done to me and, I fear, to my novel. Though I knew that I was not in the least to blame, the sense of failing to keep an obligation (which was not one, really) made me so nervous that the work has gone much more slowly than it would have otherwise.' Graeve, for his part, was dissatisfied. Not without reason, he had never liked the title ('I believe any title to be unfortunate that requires explanation') and he felt he was not getting his money's worth: 'Mrs Wharton has fallen so far behind in her delivery of this novel that we have been forced to publish absurdly inadequate instalments ... The finished *mss* should have been here by December 1st 1928.' All through her illness this was preying on her mind, and while she was still convalescing she was racing to keep up with the serialisation. The novel suffered from all this; and the irony would not have escaped her that these pressures made her feel like Vance, trapped and exploited by his publishers.[23]

By July 1929, the *Delineator*'s editors were discussing whether she should cut the novel short, and Jewett unwisely forwarded to her one of their letters, which argued that 'with so much that is already unsatisfactory, a special ending to top it off would indeed be the last straw'. She was all the more outraged because she was convinced (at this moment) that *Hudson River Bracketed* was her best book: 'When I consider what the *Delineator* is, and what the poorest of my work is in comparison, I confess that I feel indignant at such a tone ...' The novel was published by Appleton in November (the ending so long delayed by her illness, she told Mildred Bliss, that 'the last chapter must almost have been shoved into the book as it went to the binders!'). Graeve was incensed that the book had come out before the 'interminable' serialisation had finished its run, and wrote rude letters to Jewett. Difficult negotiations ensued over the sequel: Jewett, this time, was not allowed to send Graeve the early chapters; he was trying to protect his author:

Mrs Wharton is not very strong and is not able to work steadily. There is no telling when she will finish *The Gods Arrive*, but it will be a fine novel ... of the Wharton standard. This time no date for serialisation can be established until we are certain when the work is finished. There will be no harassing delays and the necessary pressure in order to keep the story running serially, which is devastating for you and bad for the author's best work.[24]

By now this was not just a local difficulty between a distinguished author in her late sixties, an old-style gentlemanly publisher doubling as agent, and a businesslike magazine editor with a big market to satisfy. American publishers, magazine editors, writers, and their target audiences, were all suffering from the effects of the Stock Market crash at the end of 1929 and the subsequent economic depression. These factors would profoundly affect Wharton's personal and professional life from now on.

The fall in the value of the dollar meant that life in France rapidly ceased to be as cheap for expatriates as it had been in the 1920s, and many Americans went home. 'The last drop of the dollar has curtailed my balance a good deal', Wharton told her publisher in 1934. She was not bankrupted and she never became poor; she did not have to sell her houses or cut down on her staff, and she did not noticeably curtail her travels: in the 1930s she went regularly to England and Italy, and also to Spain, Salzburg and Holland. Not being able, for instance, to buy a beautiful inkstand, because 'with all the heavy loads I have on my budget . . . I can't indulge in anything so expensive' seems a trivial hardship. But she did have to worry about money in a new way (much more than in 1919) at a time when her health and energies were failing, and in the last years of her life these anxieties became acute. There were financial losses on the New York properties which she co-owned and rented out (with Minnie and Beatrix). These rentals were no longer a main source of income, but they still mattered to her. Another anxiety was the discovery in 1931 that the income from the old disputed trust fund was much smaller than she had thought. Minnie, who depended on her for regular support, was, like Beatrix, in financial difficulties because of the crash: Trix and her aunt exchanged anxious letters about possible economies (though the Farrands' were not exactly punitive: 'We are careful to watch the heat and light, and I expect to sell our big old motor and leave the chauffeur here and drive myself in the little Chevrolet'). Wharton did not want Minnie to be worried by her own financial problems. She told Trix: 'My income has been so much reduced in the last few years that, in the years when I don't publish a novel, I have very little superfluous cash . . . volumes of short stories bring in very little! *I beg of you*, don't on any account tell your mother that I am a little less well off than usual.'

Other claimants on her income were the TB sanatoriums, her difficult ex-secretary Dolly Herbert and her mother, and a left-over protégé from her war-work, Gabrielle Landormy. She wrote to Elisina in 1931, complaining about the impossible Dolly: 'My own income is much reduced, I have to help Minnie out to the tune of $5000 a year, & moreover I have on my shoulders so many poor protégés who are far more to be pitied, that I feel I can no longer devote thousands annually to the Herberts.' 'I must say', Elisina noted, 'Edoo [the Tylers' pet-name for Wharton] often collects strange characters for pets . . . she has a weakness for a kind of picturesque help-lessness.' Gabrielle was the subject of much exasperated correspondence between Wharton and Lily Norton (who also knew her) in the 1930s. Wharton told Lily in 1932: 'I am beset with obligations towards old & help-less people.' And she warned Gabrielle at the same time: 'Comme tout le monde, je souffre pécuniairement de la crise.' Other wealthy friends were in trouble too: the Berensons told her in 1932 that they might have to sell I Tatti. All Americans living permanently in France were additionally hit by the French government's new tax laws in 1934, which now taxed not only properties and incomes in France but also properties held in other countries. The double tax became a source of great anxiety and stress for Wharton in her old age; she put off paying her French taxes, and Elisina (on whom she depended much more, in the 1930s, for practical and finan-cial advice, now that Walter was dead) had to help her sort it out. In 1935 Elisina consulted Benjamin Conner, who had been a colleague of Walter's at the American Chamber of Commerce, who worked out that although Wharton's income in 1934 had sunk to a quarter of what it was in 1932, it was 'still large enough to justify a considerable increase in the assessment of her income tax' and that if Wharton had to pay French taxes, retrospec-tively, on her earnings from 1932 to 1935, it would come to 'about 476,000 [old] Francs'. He suggested that 'Mrs Wharton should try to establish that . . . she is not domiciled in France' but that 'she is an American citizen [who] already pays heavy taxes on her literary income in America.' 'You have to pay punctually in future', Elisina told her, bossily: 'You need to estab-lish a fixed budget. By judicious retrenchment there is no reason why you should give up either of your properties.' But Wharton went on putting off her payments, hoping that 'the Dark Divinities, the tax-assessors' would be 'humanely disposed' to her, and that 'someone in power . . . might point out to them that I am ill & ancient (though even yet I don't feel so!), & that a great part of the superfluous wealth they are now trying to recoup, has been spent for a quarter of a century on French charities'.[25]

Servants, too, were becoming much harder to find, and Wharton had very definite views about that: 'How I sympathise with your cookless condition' (she wrote to Dorothy Allhusen, the daughter of her old friend Lady St Helier, in 1932). 'My French under-housemaid had to leave suddenly, and after a vain hunt for another here (for they don't exist) I engaged one in London, only to learn that she can't come to France unless I go to fetch her! Isn't it too grotesque? And there are still people who don't yet realise that the whole world is living under a socialist regime.' The sight of dear old Gross, welcoming her back after a journey, prompted the same thought, to Lily Norton: 'They don't make Grosses any more. Democracy wouldn't tolerate them. When I saw that rosy face, & the *best dress*, & the two sleek little Pekes trotting ahead, I felt the real warmth of homecoming.' Travel, beautiful and well-run homes and gardens, generosity and hospitality to her friends, were her life's pleasures, outside of her writing: she wanted to continue to take them for granted. She wrote to Daisy in 1933: 'I can't pretend that I shall ever like "living simply" in the sense of economizing, but there's nothing to be done about it . . . (Think what stupid things the people must have done with their money who say they're "happier without"!).'[26]

The Depression created a crisis in the American publishing industry. The magazine trade was especially hard hit, all complaining of having to publish much smaller issues, 'with a consequent reduction in the length of stories and serial instalments'. Jewett told Wharton in 1932 that all magazines were suffering from 'drastic reduction' in advertisements: 'Corporations which in the past have spent fortunes advertising food products, cosmetics, automobiles, etc, have cut . . . to the bone.' As for booksellers: 'Today [they] would not purchase even a copy of a book unless it is on some timely popular subject and promises a quick turnover. You cannot blame them. They are bankrupt, banks will not extend credit, they have more clerks on the payroll than customers in the store.' Wharton's royalties plummeted from $95,000 in 1929 to $5,000 in 1930. An itemised list from Appleton in 1934 noted royalties from *The Children* as $28,908.43 and for *The Gods Arrive* as $8,265.05. She told John Hugh Smith in 1932 that 'the price of serial fiction (my main support) has dropped *three fourths*'. By 1934 her literary income was 70 per cent less than it had been at the end of the 1920s. She wrote to the managing director of Appleton, identifying herself completely with the American economic crisis: 'Like everyone in America, I find my income diminishing from day to day.'[27]

'Times are hard', she kept saying. But this was not only a result of the Depression; it also had to do with her diminishing popularity. All her professional contacts were starting to give her the same message. Since about 1927, the London firm of Curtis Brown ('International Publicity Bureau') were dealing with her European translations and her English serialisations. (The Henrietta Street office received a regular trickle of demands from Wharton: why was the Hungarian translation fee for *Twilight Sleep* so low, how dare the Dutch version of *Ethan Frome* put 'translated from the American' on the title-page, how could there be a difficulty getting *Hudson River Bracketed* translated into Swedish 'when she has so many offers for the translation of all her books into the principal northern languages'?) By the mid-1930s the Curtis Brown office was telling her that her stories 'did not fit in' with the magazines they were trying to sell them to, or 'had been declined by the better paying markets'.[28]

Meanwhile, though Appleton was completely committed to publishing her books, Jewett was having difficulties placing some of her stories and serialisations in American magazines. Edith Wharton's stocks were falling for a number of reasons. She was still a big name, with a dedicated following. But she was beginning to be thought of as stuffy, remote and old-fashioned. Those sorts of criticisms, in the 1930s, began to outweigh respectful admiration; and when she was celebrated, it was usually with the killing word 'distinguished'. Fiction readers during the Depression either wanted gritty political realism (in which case she was thought of, rather like Scott Fitzgerald, as trivial and irrelevant) or romantic escapism (in which case she was too bleak and darkly ironic). And she was still coming up against the squeamishness and puritanism of the 'family' magazine editors.

In 1930, Jewett tried about twelve magazines, unsuccessfully, with a bitter story called 'Diagnosis', in which an egotistical man is tricked into marriage by the woman he only half-loves, because he thinks he has terminal cancer, and that she will look after him till his death; only to find that in fact he is well, and has to live with her, and learns after *her* death that she always knew the 'diagnosis' was false. 'Duration', a grotesque comedy of the hundredth birthday of a vain and revengeful spinster of a good old Boston family – Boston which 'forgot nothing, altered nothing' – was accepted by the *Woman's Home Companion* in 1933, but they asked her for a new ending. Though she was usually haughty about making alterations on demand ('I should consider that I was rendering a poor service to younger writers if I went against my literary conscience, in modifying any detail of my work, however trifling'), she did change it, only to have it turned down brusquely by the editor, Gertrude Lane. 'We ordered it, we have bought it and paid for it, but we cannot publish it.' Wharton was furious: 'I am really staggered by the insolence of this letter ... I cannot write down to the present standard of the American picture magazines.' ('Duration' was published for the first time in her 1936 collection, *The World Over*.) Since the war she had been adamant about not being published by 'that old black-guard' William Randolph Hearst, whom she considered a 'pro-Boche' 'hound'. But she weakened when Hearst's *Cosmopolitan* offered $5,000 for a story, having been assured that he had nothing to do with the editorial policy. This was good money: Appleton told her in 1934 that $3,000 (for her marvellous late story 'Roman Fever') was 'a very good price for these times'. And 'I am in as much need of money as everybody else at this moment', she told Jewett. She allowed him to sell *Cosmopolitan* a strag-gling Gerhardiesque comedy (successively called 'Kouradjine Limited', 'Bread upon the Waters', and 'Charm Incorporated', and made into a now-lost film by Universal called *Strange Wives*). It dealt with an opportunist, demanding Eastern European family, driven out of 'Daghestan' by Bolshevism and climbing up in pre-Depression New York. Given current circumstances, she took ironic relish in its satire, for instance, of the portraitist who paints his millionaire clients 'literally surrounded' by the sources of their wealth, posed in front of a motor-works or an oil well instead of a 'Gothic library or . . . Quattrocento *salon*'.[29]

Jewett had trouble, too, in 1931, with a fine ghost-story, 'Pomegranate Seed', in which the dead wife of a remarried widower sends letters back to him from the underworld – much to his second wife's and his mother's horror – to haunt and destroy his happy new marriage. The editor of the *Ladies' Home Journal*, Loring Schuler, wanted to accept it, but thought the plot too obscure: 'the great mass of journal readers would be lost and indignant because there is no explanation of the situation.' Rather than writing a new ending, Wharton withdrew it in some impatience, and it was published in the *Saturday Evening Post* instead. But there were more prob-lems with the *Ladies' Home Journal* over her memoirs. Schuler bought them in 1928 for $25,000. When the first chapters of what was then called 'Retrospect' eventually arrived, he was disappointed, and his disappoint-ment summed up the prevailing attitude to Wharton in the 1930s: 'The writing, of course, is beautiful; one expects that from Mrs Wharton . . . But a [large] part is so "snooty" and consciously intellectual that it would be over the heads of a tremendous portion of a popular audience. It deals in great measure with people who are either dead and gone or else entirely out of the present picture, and certainly of no particular interest to people outside the old select group of New York society.' He tried to wriggle out of the now five-year-old contract, and said he would pay her $5,000 less if she would cut it. The response was firm: 'I will neither take back the manu-script nor accept a lower price for it . . . No doubt the *Ladies' Home Journal* is hard up, but so am I.' She threatened to sue, and won the battle. But when *A Backward Glance* was duly serialised in the magazine, between October 1933 and March 1934, much hacked up (she told her friends to wait and read the book instead of these 'choppy fragments'), and trailed as 'telling of the New York Age of Innocence', it did look fusty and anachronistic. Its anecdotes of Henry James and Theodore Roosevelt, illustrated with pictures of ladies and gentlemen in 1890s evening dress at the opera, were squashed in between advertisements for 'Glo-Coat' ('Watch me make this floor beautiful with only 10 minutes work!'), 'Smart-Shoes that cry "Let's Go!" to eager active feet', household tips ('How fast can a good secretary become a good wife?'), Belle-Sharmeer Stockings and Canned Pineapple. Wharton's 'Retrospect' belonged to another world.[30]

At the same time, paradoxically, she was often thought to be too hot to handle. Prudery in the Depression era was increasing rather than decreasing. Graeve, of the *Delineator*, wrote to Jewett in 1931 about *The Gods Arrive* that its situation, 'of a man and woman unmarried and living together is a little startling for magazine publication . . . We will, of course, get some protests.' 'The Day of the Funeral', a harsh and masterful story of adultery, suicide, guilt, bad faith and inadequate passion set in a small New England academic town, had one of Wharton's most implacable openings: 'His wife had said: "If you don't give her up, I'll throw myself from the roof." He had not given her up, and his wife had thrown herself from the roof.' The story was thought 'too strong' for the *Ladies' Home Journal* in 1931: could she not leave the reader 'guessing as to the exact relationship' between the man and the girl? She agreed, scornfully, to modify the text: 'If American readers prefer to be shown the awful consequences of misconduct without having the dreaded word mentioned, it is usually easy for the novelist to comply.' Even in less censorious Paris, *Revue de France*, which was to publish it in translation, objected to the title, which the editor thought might trouble '*la masse des lecteurs superstitieux qui n'aiment pas à envisager les choses de la mort*'. Jewett also had difficulty placing 'Joy in the House' in 1932, a story of a married woman whose dull, generous husband has allowed her to run away to Paris with her painter-lover, who returns home to son and husband forgiven, after realising that (like Halo) she has made a 'terrible mistake', but who feels horribly tricked and imprisoned. She kills her lover by leaving him, and he warns her that 'You'll die of losing me'. And so she does, stifled by the 'atmosphere of tolerance and benevolence, of smoothing over and ignoring and dissembling' in her provincial America home. This was a hard one to sell, because the public wanted 'bright optimistic tales which will distract the mind from world affairs'. Just as when she won the Pulitzer Prize, requests for wholesome fiction were still coming in.

Told that she might have to censor the elopement she planned at the end of *The Buccaneers* because the 'conservative readers' of the *Woman's Home Companion* might be shocked by it, she burst out to Minnie in 1934: 'What a country! With Faulkner & Hemingway acclaimed as the greatest American novelists, & magazine editors still taking the view they did when I began to write! Brains & culture seem non-existent from one end of the social scale to the other, & half the morons yell for filth, & the other half continue to put pants on the piano-legs.'[31]

She kept a collection of what she considered her most absurd fan-letters and editors' requests from America, sometimes marking them 'funny', like the letter to 'Miss Wharton' from the *Globe* in Minnesota, offering her one cent a word for an article with a 'light touch' and 'local colour', which 'should not shrink at portraying the little quirks of human nature', and should be 'true (authentic, authoritative, believable, etc.)'. 'We hope you will go in to bat for us,' the letter concluded. 'The deadline was yesterday.' She was ever more alienated from the readership on which she depended for a living. The double act she had sustained all through her writing life, since *The House of Mirth*, appealing to a big best-seller market while writing at the highest level of aesthetic distinction, was in peril. She noted grimly in a letter to Ned Sheldon:

> The question is not only what people like to read, but what they can understand if you offer it to them. The mental level has gone down with such a rush that even people of merely honourable general culture seem to be pushed aloft on the top of a high mountain surrounded by an uninhabited desert. As for book-reviewing, even in England, it appears to be written by cinema-fans in their teens.[32]

Inevitably, she blamed her publishers for some of her difficulties, particularly in England, where she felt they were not advertising her well enough. Macmillan had continued to publish her in England until the early 1920s, when she left Scribner's. Macmillan and Scribner published *A Son at the Front* in 1923; but her other titles, from *The Glimpses of the Moon* onwards, were published in England through Appleton's London office, which they had opened in 1921. (They simply reissued the American first editions in new covers.) 'It seemed to me only fair to give them the English rights of the novels which they publish for me', she explained to Macmillan, breaking the news of her divorce from them after twenty years. 'I am sure you will understand this, and believe that it does not in any way affect my pleasant associations with the house of Macmillan.' In 1928, her back-list, at Macmillan's suggestion, was transferred to Appleton: 'I will not say goodbye to Macmillan & Co, as I hope to survive in the memories of the firm as an appreciative and grateful author.' The transfer did not increase her gratitude to Appleton, though. She felt they were not doing well by her, either. The difference in her sales between America and England continued to be very marked: *The Children* sold 50,231 copies in its first three months in America, 4,445 copies in its first three months in England; *Hudson River Bracketed* sold 14,998 copies between November 1929 and March 1930 in America, and 4,175 copies between January and March 1930 in England; *The Gods Arrive* sold 4,638 (a huge drop) in its first three months in America, 2,327 in England. She was particularly anxious about prospective English sales when the contract for *The Buccaneers* was drawn up in 1934: it was to be a historical novel set mainly in England which she hoped would have a lucrative appeal there. After transferring from Macmillan to Appleton for English publication, she complained vociferously to Jewett about Appleton's failure to advertise her in the English papers. Her writer-friend Louis Bromfield was encouraging her to get herself 'a first-rate agent'. 'I suspect Mr Jewett does not much impress the type of editor & picture-people now in power', he told her. As Henry James had, long ago, he recommended the house of Pinker. She wrote to Jewett in May 1934 that she wanted to 'try putting *The Buccaneers* in the hands of a professional literary agent'. Jewett tried to dissuade her, but was, at this time, very ill, suffering from exhaustion and a 'severe nervous breakdown'. For all their long working relationship, she was relentless. She sent his substitute a long list of grievances, and said she wanted to 'try her luck elsewhere'. The chairman of Appleton responded strongly in the firm's defence, accusing her letter of being 'manifestly unfair and unjust', reminding her that Macmillan's had allowed her titles to go out of print, and noting that she had unearned advances amounting to $10,689 on the first three titles she had published with Appleton. She backed down, noting in her diary in July, 'quarrel with Appleton', and a few weeks later, 'an endless chain of worries & preoccupations. Better luck next year!' Not for Jewett: he died in January 1935, and Wharton did go to the house of Pinker, which had now passed from the famous father, James Pinker, to his second son, J. Ralph Pinker (who also dealt, among others, with Arnold Bennett and Richard Aldington). So, in almost the last year of her writing life, she acquired a literary agent. Trouble started at once, and would no doubt have continued: 'I note that you cannot place [*The Buccaneers*] until it is finished. This is the first time that I have been told that a novel of mine could not be sold before its completion'.[33]

While she was demanding more advertising for her books, she was doing everything in her power to protect her seclusion. Like many famous, ageing writers, she wanted to keep her literary name prominent and her private life secluded. An enormous amount of her professional correspondence in the 1930s has to do with self-protection. She makes sure that organisations like the American Library in Paris do not give out her address: 'I have great difficulty as it is in safeguarding my privacy'. Letter after letter – mostly typed by Jeanne Fridérich, but some in her own hand – consists of refusals (some not entirely truthful). No, she will not give lectures: 'She never speaks in public'. No, she will not write 'puffs' for other authors. No, she will not allow personal letters to be used on book-jackets: 'I entirely disapprove of the use of private correspondence for such a purpose, and have never allowed any personal appreciation of my work to be published.' No, she will not send autographs. And 'she wishes me to add that she is not in the habit of having her letters addressed to "Edith Wharton", and thinks that it would be well if you adopted a more courteous form of address to those from whom you are asking favours'. No, she will not be the guest of honour at the ladies' evening ('when the wives of the members attend') of the Mile High Club of Denver: 'I regret that the long distance between Hyères and Denver makes it impossible, for the present, that I should accept your kind suggestion.' No, she will not give a bio. for the French publication of *The Children*, because, as Mme Fridérich reiterated, '*comme je vous l'ai dit, elle n'aime pas qu'on parle d'elle*'. Strangers looking for intimacy were always rebuffed; Elisina reported on an unfortunate encounter at the Du Bos' in 1929: 'One lady went up to Edoo and told her that it was a turning point in her life when she read the translation of *The House of Mirth*. Poor Edoo looked at her in a pained frozen way, and when we left, the enthusiast gave her a tart little nod, having evidently been disappointed of a flow from the heart.' Nicky Mariano said that 'the change in her if anybody from the outside world showed up was almost unbelievable. From being simply gay, ready to tease her friends and to let herself be teased by them, she became stiff, conventional, almost frozen up and created an atmosphere of *gêne* all around her.' In a firm, but not unkind, letter to a young French admirer, studying English at a college in Toulon, who wanted to come and visit her, she said that she only saw '*quelques amis intimes*'. It would be in reading her books, not in talking to her, that the young woman would be able to form an idea of the value of her work. '*La seule manière de juger l'artiste, est par ses oeuvres.*'[34]

The '*amis intimes*', the gentlemen friends, most of them now in their late sixties, who had been devoted to her for much of their lives – 'Norts',

'Dearest B.B.', 'Dearest Gaillard', 'My dear John' – could find her taxing too. Even before her illness, the word was that she was 'getting very fussy & peculiar as she grows older'. Berenson often found her exasperating in her seventies, as when, setting out for a picnic in January 1932: 'Edith got cross because she had forgotten to tell Norts and so had to wait for him. He was cross because he was painting and so did not like to break off . . . Then she went on to spit on my nasty habit of napping after lunch. Why could I not in these brief hours of sunshine take advantage of them, and put off my nap till after tea, etc, etc. As she was not my wife I let her snarl and spit, and it seemed to relieve her, for later she was angelic.' Gaillard observed an 'increase in restlessness, dislike of sustained conversation and outbreaks of petulance'. Nicky Mariano noted the 'possessive and jealous' side of her friendships, the 'thorny moments' that arose when travelling with her, and the mixture at Ste-Claire of 'ritual' and 'incalculable whims'. Difficult she may have been, but she was also admirably determined to stay in control of her own life. She once told Lily Norton (speaking of the dependent old age of Daniel Updike) that she could never bear that: 'How I should probably hate any life that my friends undertook to arrange for me!' She continued to tease, boss, and rouse up her old friends, as in this affectionate letter to John Hugh Smith, berating him for not seeing her in Paris on his way to America:

Well, my dear, this is all very well, but I've just been offered $25,000 for the serial rights of my autobiography, & I'm going to accept, & show you up, & publish photos of myself before & after your Heartless Treatment – & if British public opinion is what it used to be, you'll lose your job . . . so there! . . . I hope you're having a beastly time in America, & I won't dedicate my next book to you, as I meant to – & I hope you'll have an Awful Crossing coming back. And now you know what I think of you! Your fond but broken hearted Edith.

Her 'patient readers' continued to be on call, and she took their responses to heart, as when Robert was given the end of *The Gods Arrive* to read. He told Berenson: 'The last page seems to me a masterpiece. But then I am sentimental and like happy endings, and I was terribly afraid she was going to be perverse enough to condemn her couple to irrevocable separation and unhappiness.' She wrote triumphantly to Gaillard:

After a long wrestle with chapters 40 and 41 *I forced them*, much against their will, to be the last, and after countless revisions handed them to Robert for inspection. When I returned to get them I found him, (liter-

ally) choking with emotion, and unable to ejaculate more than: 'Ah –
parbleu!' But whether this was due to admiration, or relief at the thought
that there wd be no more chapters to read, history knoweth not.

Faithful friends like the Tylers were as much in demand as ever for errands
and services. In one letter, Edith remembered eating some 'delicious little
long – oblong – objects' tasting of peppermint and lemon, when she last
dined with Elisina, and asked Elisina to arrange for 'a pound of these delec-
tables' to be sent her from Paris: 'Merci d'avance for this, as for other
kindnesses.' Elisina, who took such requests in her stride, was always struck
by the standards Edith kept up. She noted in 1930: 'I see why Edith makes
such a fetish of dressing. She considers it an absolute sign of civilisation to
dress in the evening.'[35]

Sometimes it feels as if her small, loyal circle was fixed in aspic. But it
was a mark of her energy and appetite for life that she made some close –
and impressive – new friends in the 1930s. Aldous Huxley was in his early
forties when they became neighbours in the South of France, in the period
when he was writing *Brave New World*, editing Lawrence's letters, painting
and writing plays, and working on *Eyeless in Gaza*. The group who lived or
stayed at the Villa Huley in Sanary – Aldous and Maria, Sybille Bedford,
Raymond Mortimer, Eddie Sackville-West, Gerard Heard, Bronislaw
Malinowski – mixed with all the intellectuals, writers and artists who came
to the South of France, especially the German-Jewish refugees like the
Manns, Arnold Zweig, Brecht, Stephan Zweig and the palm-reading psychoanalyst Charlotte Wolff (who read Edith Wharton's palm, as she did Virginia
Woolf's). They also mixed with the Franco-American 'gratin' like the
Comtesse de Béhague, the de Noailles, and the Ste-Claire group. Like almost
everyone who came in contact with him, Wharton found Aldous Huxley
compellingly interesting and attractive. She told John Hugh that he was
'human, conversible, full of fun and eminently social'. Perhaps they discussed
his current preoccupations – mass production, eugenics, pacifism, fascism,
social inequality. She was quick to appreciate *Brave New World*, calling it
'a masterpiece of tragic indictment of our ghastly age of Fordian culture'.
She told the Du Boses it was '*un chef-d'oeuvre digne de Swift*'. In the 'social
desert' she increasingly felt Hyères to be, 'an Ultima Thule of the most ultimate sort', Aldous and Maria were 'a great joy', and when they decided to
leave the South of France in 1937 she wrote lamenting to Berenson: 'They
will be a great loss to me, as they supply the only real talk I get, except for
my guests.' For their part, the Huxleys thought her, at first, 'rather a formidable lady who lives in a mist of footmen, *bibelots*, bad good-taste and rich

food in a castle overlooking Hyères' (this in a letter to Ottoline Morrell, a much more lavish hostess than Wharton). A vivid, satirical account was given by Cyril Connolly, Huxley's competitive friend, of a visit he and his wife Jean made with Aldous and Maria to what Connolly called 'Castle Wharton', where they were received by Wharton and Robert Norton, described by Connolly as 'Mrs Wharton's companion'. Logan Pearsall Smith (whose private secretary Connolly had been for a time) had given him grave warnings: 'the meeting had to be carefully prepared with many letters telling us how to behave and what to talk about.' Connolly was jealous of his hostess's evident preference for the Huxleys: the two couples were like 'two opposing tennis teams before an already biassed umpire'.

> The food was delicious. What eggs! But the conversation, except for some rallies from Aldous, hung fire. Unfortunately, it turned on differences between Americans and Europeans – and Jean [Connolly] mentioned that Americans had a different way of holding the fork, shifting it to the right hand. This was received by her hostess with blank incomprehension . . . Jean went on to say that many Americans addressed each other as 'Mr' on envelopes, not as 'Esq', like the English. 'None that I know,' exclaimed Mrs Wharton, and awarded game to the Huxleys.

Nicky Mariano reported to Mary Berenson that Wharton thought 'Cyril's wife an awful lump, but her descriptions of people are not to be trusted especially if they are young and conceivably intimidated by her not always reassuring manner'. Logan told Cyril: 'It is plain that she was *terrified* of you all – thought you regarded her as an old has-been and Mrs Humphry Ward, and that she put on, as she does to protect herself, her masque [sic] of wealth and worldliness.' The Connollys were invited back once, and were 'grilled about Joyce and the modern movement'.

The Huxleys' young, beautiful and keenly observant companion, the future writer and biographer Sybille Bedford, had no better a time with Wharton than Jean Connolly. Bedford would say, unfairly, that Wharton was 'frightening because she only liked men, she hated women. And young women who wanted to become writers were the worst news in the world.' In her biography of Huxley, Bedford did allow her a nicer side; she recalled Huxley's once patting 'Mrs Wharton's behind' as he shepherded her down the Villa Huley's steep stairs to lunch: 'The entourage froze; Mrs Wharton turned her head, not abruptly . . . and gave him a sweet smile.' And Bedford described a picnic on the beach at the bottom of a very steep cliff, accessible only by 'a precipitous goat track', which Wharton and some other elderly friends climbed down with great difficulty, though behaving throughout ('by the force of the iron discipline bred into their class and generation') as if they had just strolled into the garden from the dining-room. But when, in a conversation with Sybille Bedford, I enthused about my excitement at her having known Edith, quoting Browning at her – "And did you once see Shelley plain?" – she replied briskly: 'Well, in this case, my dear, *fat* and plain.'[36]

Wharton's congenial acquaintance with Huxley was one of her few friendships with other notable writers. Henry James, Vernon Lee, Bourget, Gide, Cocteau, Sinclair Lewis, Gerhardi and Huxley: it was not a long list, and few of those relationships went deep. Berenson was an immensely influential art-historian, collector and connoisseur, but writing itself was not his greatest skill. The women writers she respected – Zona Gale, Anna de Noailles, Anita Loos – she did not get close to; the writer friends she was involved with were all minor talents: Howard Sturgis, Percy Lubbock, 'Claude Silve', Geoffrey Scott. Her friendship with the Berensons put her in touch with a few Italian writers, the novelist Carlo Placci, the critic Ugo Ojetti, and the liberal, anti-fascist Count Umberto Morra, who translated Virginia Woolf. Morra was a brave and charming man with a beautiful villa in Cortona. He was a great friend of Kenneth Clark, Nicky Mariano and Iris Origo, and a welcome guest at Wharton's houses, even if he and Nicky occasionally needed to go off in a corner 'and have a good laugh by ourselves'. Wharton also met Alberto Moravia through Berenson. He sent her his first youthful novel, *Gli Indifferenti*, a cruel, realistic account of middle-class corruption in Rome, which caused a scandal, and which she admired for its portrayal of 'a desert of moral corruption'. But when she met him in Rome she found him, personally, too 'self-engrossed', and when Morra read out a particularly graphic bit of Moravia to the seventy-three-year-old Wharton at the Pavillon in 1935, she was 'unconverted' and unshocked: Faulkner and Céline had already done it 'nastier', and her own incest story, she told Berenson ('Beatrice Palmato' still biding its time among her old manuscripts), would make them all look like 'nursery-rhymes'. But 'business is too bad' now, she added ruefully, to try and sell anything like *that*.[37]

In her late years she preferred the company of museum curators and art-historians, and had some of her most pleasurable moments visiting galleries and exhibitions. (Till the end of her life, she always used a code of sensual pleasure with her friends for aesthetic experiences: talking about a new book was 'orging', to look at pictures was '*se prélasser*', to bask.) She was ravished by Dutch art on her trip to Holland in 1933 and delighted that Ojetti got her in, outside public hours, to a big Italian exhibition in Paris in 1935, where she singled out paintings by Leonardo, Caravaggio, Lotto and Tintoretto. She took a keen interest in her friends' shows and collections, like the Byzantine exhibition Royall ('Peter') Tyler was organising in 1931 (he had collected the Byzantine treasures for the Blisses at Dumbarton Oaks), or the big French show that Louis Metman, the head of the Musée des Arts Décoratifs in Paris, curated in 1932; she knew that the sudden death of his collaborator, Raymond Koechlin, also an acquaintance of hers, would be a blow to him. She kept up her friendship with Eric Maclagen, who was made the director of the Victoria and Albert Museum in 1924 and gave the Charles Eliot Norton lectures at Harvard in 1927. In the 1930s, he was working on a monumental catalogue of Italian sculpture, making the V&A more accessible and curating exhibitions on English medieval art and William Morris. He also had a passion for Blake, translated Rimbaud and Valéry, wrote poetry and designed book-jackets and bookplates (including one for Berenson). He described himself to her in 1931 as (like T.S. Eliot) 'traditionalist in literature, royalist in politics, and Anglo-Catholic in religion'; Kenneth Clark called him 'one of the most civilized men in London'. She still corresponded with the art-critic Royal Cortissoz, and her friendship deepened with Louis Gillet, the curator at the Abbaye de Châalis. Three of her pall-bearers, Metman, Gillet and Clark, would be museum directors. The most influential of these, and the closest of her new friends in the last six years of her life, was the wealthy, clever, highly cultured Kenneth Clark, whose name came to stand, in the 1960s, for a particular concept of 'Civilization' which Wharton – had she ever watched television – would have endorsed.[38]

Clark was twenty-nine to her seventy in 1932, but they had a good deal in common. From an early age, he had had a passion for poetry, Italy, and Renaissance art. By the time they met, he had catalogued the Windsor Castle da Vincis, worked with Berenson at I Tatti on the revision of his *Florentine Drawings* (where he found B.B. arrogant and spoilt, Nicky Mariano lovable, and Mary Berenson recklessly emotional), married and had a son, and been appointed Keeper of the Department of Fine Art at the Ashmolean Museum in Oxford. Clark met Wharton first at I Tatti in 1927, where she gave him 'the frozen mitt for which she was famous'. But in the summer of 1931 she was telling Mildred Bliss that the Kenneth Clarks were 'among the most charming new friends that I have made in the last year'. She liked Jane Clark, a dark-eyed beauty, described by her younger son Colin as an emotional, generous and passionate woman. The fractures in the Clark marriage which Colin Clark documented – his mother's alcoholism and his father's infidelities – were still to come, or at any rate not apparent to their new friend. Wharton stayed with them several times in their successive houses on Richmond Green, on Shotover Hill near Oxford, and in Portland Place, and greatly enjoyed being shown round the Ashmolean (and New College) by Clark, noting especially 'the incomparable Guardis, the Canaletto of the Brenta, the dazzling Uccello ['The Hunt in the Forest'], the rosy St Vincent Ferrer, one or two lovely little Wilsons' and 'the quiet green spaces of . . . the Claude landscape'.

Clark would say that he liked looking at paintings with her, not because she was good on the 'purely pictorial qualities of paintings' but because of her 'highly civilised non-specialist point of view'. When they went to stay with her in France, as they did regularly through the 1930s, he admired her few good paintings: the Cézanne left to her by Walter, a Renoir still life and her 'two ravishing Odilon Redons'. On their trips together, she learnt from him: for instance, when she took them to Beauvais and was inspired by his enthusiasm for the Renaissance stained glass at St-Étienne, or when they went to see a Renoir show together in Paris in 1933 and 'I who am a confirmed anti-Renoiriste, had to own that before the fatal period of the Michelin women bathed in currant jelly he did some wonderful things'. Clark told her mischievous stories about people he knew, and found her completely unshockable: she would 'laugh like a girl'. He sent her cultured letters from his travels in Greece, or asked if the garden at the Pavillon was at its 'most Fragonardish'. He admired her cultural range and was struck by her growing interest in religion. On the journey to Beauvais from St-Brice, she told him that she had long thought of writing a novel about 'the conflict of two impulses, the Protestant and the Catholic'. He became one of her 'listeners', and particularly admired her reading of Whitman in the style she told him she had learnt from James. They talked about writing, and he noted that 'she enjoyed speculating on the future of her characters'.[39]

When Jane Clark had twins, in 1932, they asked Edith to be godmother to the boy, Colin (Nicky Mariano was godmother to Colette). She gave him the christening mug which had belonged to Lucretia, and eventually left him half her library and the 1870 portrait of her as a little girl, by Edward Harrison May. Colin Clark has said that he was not told about his legacy until he was eighteen. (He would store the books in his brother's house, give the christening mug to The Mount, and the portrait to the National Portrait Gallery.) In his view, the friendship, of which his father was very proud, was a link to the nineteenth century: Wharton was a rare collector's piece. Her letter describing the provenance of the christening cup certainly played up to that sort of valuation: 'My mother was born in

1824, & her name was Lucretia Stevens Rhinelander – nothing like as good as *her* mother, who was Mary Lucille Lucy Anne Stevens, & the daughter of Genl Stevens, who was on Washington's staff, commanded the artillery in the Revolutionary army, & figures twice in the big Trumbull paintings in the Capitol at Washington.' On her side, Wharton took pleasure in hearing about the Clarks' grand English life: 'I laughed for an hour at the idea of you spending one weekend at St. Brice, & the next at Chatsworth. What a jolly antithesis!'⁴⁰

When Clark was asked to be the director of the National Gallery at the astoundingly young age of thirty, she was one of the people whose advice he sought. He wrote: 'B.B. is my conscience in such matters, and I know that he will be furious . . . he will say that in [five years] I will be wholly corrupted, and will never be able to drink the pure water of scholarship again . . .' She wrote back saying that she disagreed with Berenson. 'I'm sure you're right to have accepted . . . anything is better than to dangle an uncertain foot & not jump in . . . It was dear of you to write to me as soon as the matter was settled, & I am much touched by your finding the time.' As her health failed, the Clarks were loyal and kind to her, treating her as they might 'an elderly relative'; one of her last treats, in the summer of 1936, was an outing to Glyndebourne with them to hear *Don Giovanni*. Like all her visitors to her houses, he could find the entourage of 'old pussies' tiresome and Wharton's fidgeteness as a hostess exasperating: 'She couldn't bear anyone to sit down without a little table beside him, and I used to say that "little tables" should be her telegraphic address.' 'Every few minutes she rang the bell in order that her servants, whom she treated angelically, should find her glasses or her bag, or let in her beloved dog.' Clark was not fond of the dogs: 'She had the usual following of asthmatic pekes – one very old and blind, which she really loved.' But these visits were also a refuge for him. By 1937 he was not only running the National Gallery but had also become Surveyor of the King's Pictures for George VI. (He told Wharton in 1937, on the back of three National Gallery postcards – of Uccello's *The Rout of San Romano*, Van Eyck's *Arnolfini and His Wife* and Bellini's *The Madonna of the Meadow* – that he had found 'the new King and Queen very pleasant – she just above the average country house type, he just below it'.) One of the only places he had time to write his book on Leonardo Da Vinci was on his visits to 'Edith Wharton at her dotty, comfortable, converted convent in Hyères'. Clark was appalled by the portrayal in Lubbock's memoir of an 'unsympathetic character, efficient, domineering, *mondaine*, restless and stuck up to the last degree . . . It is really impossible to imagine that the polished American duchess of Mr

Lubbock's biography could have written *Summer*; and she didn't.' Like others, he noted the 'exaggerated distinction' she made between those who were 'of the family' and those outside; 'within the family she laughed, told scandalous stories, read poetry and talked about the art of writing. She felt safe.' For a few years, he and Jane were very much part of that 'family'.[41]

Since Walter's death she had looked to people she could count on and who would interest her. She became particularly fond of Rex and Molly Nicholson, an English couple in their fifties who were devoted to her. Rex (full name Reginald Popham) Nicholson had been in charge at the British consulate in Cyprus when she went there on the *Osprey* cruise. He and Molly were friends of the Berensons; Nicky recalled that Edith had met Rex before he got married, and 'feared the worst', but was won over by Molly, who was attractive and witty – rather like the heroine of an Edith Wharton novel, Nicky thought. They lived in a house called Tallboys in Abinger Hammer and knew E.M. Forster, whom they introduced to her (she thought he looked 'spectrally ill'). They stayed with her often in the 1930s, and in the summer of 1934 she took them to Chartres, Senlis, Provins and Troyes: 'They are so intensely appreciative that it is a joy to take them about.' They were always, whenever she referred to them, her 'dear Nicholsons'. When Edith died, Berenson told Rex Nicholson that he would miss her as 'a term of reference, as the focus for so many wishes and the object of so many thoughts', and said how good the Nicholsons had been to her.[42]

When new visitors came who were attentive or fired her attention, she always gave generous praise – for instance, of that 'thoroughly delightful person' Walter Lippmann, the political commentator, who had met Berenson in Paris during the Peace Conference, and whom Edith met in the 1930s and read avidly. (Berenson told her he had only one fault, his Pittsburgh accent.) His anti-isolationist recommendations for American democracy, belief in the need of an 'aristocracy' of informed and know-ledgeable leaders, intellectuals and educators, and philosophical commitment to scepticism and disinterestedness in public affairs, would have been very sympathetic to her.[43] Another less intellectually strenuous late enthusiasm was for the travel-writer and naturalist Vivienne Goschen (who wrote as Vivienne De Watteville). When De Watteville was working in her mid-thirties on *Speak to the Earth*, her 'wanderings and reflections' on Kenya and how its wild-life should be treated, Wharton helped her with the manuscript, wrote a kind introduction in 1935, and plugged it to her friends, telling Royal Cortissoz, for instance, that Vivienne was 'one of the most charming and interesting young women I know, and greatly gifted as a writer ... with a touch of mysticism, of Pantheism'. She liked best De Watteville's feeling for animals: 'I too, have lived that life and stammered that language, though my mountain tent was only the library lamp-shade, my wilderness a garden, my wildebeest stealing down to drink two astute and arrogant Pekingese ...' Vivienne wrote her an effusive dedication ('Herewith your godchild at last fully fledged and ever boundlessly grateful that you first set his feathers straight & equipped him for his flight with your bright Talisman') and left a tender account of the atmosphere of the Pavillon and of Wharton's 'generous help to young writers'.[44]

Of all the friendships she made in her seventies, one of the most exhilarating was with the young Byzantine scholar Steven Runciman. He was the same age as Kenneth Clark (both born in 1903) and had already, by the time Edith met him in 1929, travelled widely in China, Turkey, Serbia and Greece, become a don at Trinity College, Cambridge, and published several books on Byzantine civilisation. He would become the greatest Byzantinist of the twentieth century, and would live to nearly a hundred. His family, wealthy aristocratic Scottish MPs and shipping magnates, lived in Scotland and Northumberland, where Edith paid a visit in 1934, while Steven was in the Balkans. She found them all very kind, though Steven's mother, Hilda Runciman, was not so happy with the visit. She took Edith, with some other friends, on a visit to Holy Island (Lindisfarne) in two cars. The tide was unusually high, and Hilda sent Edith and another guest on ahead in the first car, while she and the others had to wait to cross from the coast to Lindisfarne. She wrote crossly to her son:

> She [Edith] barged on to the castle instead of waiting, as I had arranged, at the abbey till we could cross ... To my horror I found they had stormed the castle where poor Edward de Stein [the owner of Lindisfarne Castle] was NOT expecting them ... I was a little annoyed at Mrs W doing this but I fancy she is accustomed to taking charge. Do you love her dearly Steven? I found her rather the hard type of American, certainly interesting but we felt all her sympathy and humanity had gone into her novels and she had not much interest in real alive actual beings!

Meanwhile Steven was amusing Edith with his description of an astounding bedroom in the Balkans: 'I don't wonder', she replied, 'that the combination of Byzantine-Baroque & Ruritarian bedroom set for a movie scene detained you far from the simple severities of Lindisfarne.' (A more chilling version of the Runcimans as a family would be given by Rosamond Lehmann, who temporarily married into them. Lehmann never met Wharton, but they had a connection through Berenson, who enjoyed a friendship with Lehmann in his late years, and used to say that she replaced Wharton in his life – and that she never stopped quizzing him about her.)

Though the brilliant young man remained 'Mr Runciman' in her letters to him, Wharton's tone was friendly, responding eagerly to his praise of *The Children* and particularly pleased that he liked 'the St Bridget story': 'I have a passion for romantic writing, & would give way to it continuously & entirely with any encouragement.' (This was her highly coloured story 'Dieu d'Amour', set in Byzantine Cyprus – which would naturally have interested him – in which St Bridget of Sweden converts a young princess from the sensual worship of Venus to a life of holiness.) Runciman was known in his youth for Wildean aestheticism, and they shared a passion for antique shops. She recommended 'antiquairesses' in Hyères to him, deriding one who had 'opened a huge new shop, so full of shams & rubbish & general hideousness that I hope it will perish, as it deserves to'. In later years, he would say that their friendship foundered over 'his refusal to carry her evil-tempered Pekinese dog'. But he was a favourite for a while, and she was charming about their age-gap: 'I was so incorrigibly juvenile myself, & your bright young things were so grave & reserved, that I didn't notice any difference in our ages that day at lunch, & enjoyed it all immensely.'[45]

Such glimpses suggest that though Wharton could be a demanding guest, she was not always so difficult to get to know as her older friends maintained. There were also exceptions to her supposed dislike of children, even though a number of reminiscences make much of this. A story came down from Justine Cutting Ward (Bayard Cutting's sister, who became a teacher of Gregorian chant), via her niece Iris Origo to Louis Auchincloss, that when Justine Cutting was a young girl, Edith and Teddy Wharton came to visit while she was playing the piano, and that as they left, Edith turned to Teddy and said: 'Well, Teddy, it may be just as well that we never had any children. Just think, one of them might have been musical!' Auchincloss told me, too, that as a young girl his friend Audrey Maynard felt ignored and uncomfortable on visits to the Pavillon with her mother, Wharton's very old friend Eunice Maynard. Lubbock maintained that Edith was 'terrified of very young children', and Daisy Chanler said that she did not like them. A young friend of Louis Bromfield, the son of a New York beauty of Wharton's generation, Josephine Griswold, was taken by Bromfield to the Pavillon to meet Edith Wharton, and recollected, fifty years later, that 'it was impossible to get a word in edgeways'; Wharton commented afterwards to Bromfield: 'Josephine's son is a very silent boy, isn't he?'[46]

Yet Audrey's father, Walter Maynard, told Lubbock that 'Edith had the rare gift of treating children like adults', and all the evidence of the Tyler

family points that way. Bill Tyler, son of Elisina and 'Peter', Wharton's
godson and, after Elisina's and Lapsley's deaths, her executor, had nothing
but fond memories of her behaviour towards him. He knew that he had an
exceptional relationship with 'Edoo'; he was the only 'boy in whose earliest
consciousness she was present, who stayed with her many times, and who
told her more about himself than he ever did to his own family'. William
Tyler's daughter, Eve Thompson, was once reported as saying that Elisina
(who had left the children of her first marriage) was not a good mother,
and that 'Edoo' was William Tyler's 'surrogate mother'. One letter corrob-
orates this; Bill, at school at Harrow, wrote to tell Wharton (but not his
mother) that he had been having some bad headaches; she wrote anxiously
to Elisina: 'I feel worried lest he may not have told you . . . I hope you
won't mind my "butting in" – but I know the inferiority of English oculists
– & doctors – & bad headaches are symptoms of so many bad things, &
so unnatural in a boy of that age.' (Elisina, for her part, left a sentimental
recollection that 'Edith's childlessness had been a great grief to her'.) In
his sixties, Bill Tyler wrote an account of Wharton's attentiveness to him
when he was growing up, which suggests sensitivity and tact towards a
teenage boy. 'She used to ask me casually what I had read, what I liked,
and why. Thus I came to think of her as someone with whom literature
could be discussed in an entirely unacademic and unintellectual manner
. . . I found myself making notes of the things I wanted to keep for her,
and for her only . . . She never crushed an opinion, however immature or
uncongenial to her, by a show of learning or authority.' When he was ten,
in 1917, she gave him a 'sumptuous folio edition' of the *Contes de Perrault*,
with the inscription: 'His old friend and admirer sends to William Tyler
the stories she used to read half-a-hundred years ago'. As he grew up, he
'confided in her naturally on personal matters in which my emotions were
deeply involved . . . I never remember her shying away from me on those
occasions'. They shared musical tastes, especially for Mozart, Bach and
Haydn; he bought her a phonograph and chose records for her. He remembered one visit when they played 'The Clock Symphony' three times in
two evenings; on another occasion, Wharton told Elisina that Bill had
'caught me in a guilty honeymoon with a gramophone, and we listened to
Mozart, Weber and the Rosenkavalier till 9.30'. When Bill married Bettina
Fisher-Rowe in 1933, and he and 'Betsy' brought their baby to the Pavillon,
she went to a great deal of trouble preparing for Royall Jr's comfort and his
cohabitation with the Pekes, and was greatly taken with the 'Infant
Hercules', as she called him. She described him vividly to Berenson as 'an
enchanting "Yes" boy of 3 months, always smiling, agreeing with people,

& laughing with a round mouth when his father boxes with him – the nicest child I ever met'. She compared him to, and makes him sound like, Chip Wheater, the baby in *The Children*.

One other anecdote pays tribute to her kindness to children. A Jewish boy whose father, Dr Léon Smolizanski, was the medical director of one of her TB sanatoriums at the Château de la Tuyolle at Taverny just outside Paris, which continued to function after the war, used to see Wharton when she visited; his English mother got on well with Elisina.

> On what must have been one of her last visits, in 1936, Edith Wharton turned to me, aged 5, and asked what I would most like in the world. Much to my mother's annoyance I answered 'an electric train'. The train arrived from the *Magasin du Printemps* soon after. It became my most prized possession. It was lost with everything else when, being Jews, we were arrested by the Milice [the Vichy secret police] in 1943.[47]

She needed the young, because so many of the old were dying. She kept up her sad habit of sitting alone with the increasing numbers of her dead on All Souls' Night, 2 November, writing in her diary: 'Eternal light shine upon them!' In America, apart from the indomitable Minnie, she had few friends left: Olivia Cutting, Florence La Farge, Eunice Maynard, Josephine and Frank Griswold, Edward Sheldon, Bessie Lodge. Mary Berenson was in and out of nursing homes; Wharton's sympathy was limited: 'I can't help feeling' (she told Elisina) 'that there is a strong element of hysteria or neurasthenia in this incessant preoccupation with her health, & I so often feel tempted to hand over to that type of chronic invalid the wise axiom which Teddy taught me soon after we were married: – "Fish, cut bait – *or get out of the boat*." It applies to nearly every situation in life.' In France, the Abbé Mugnier went blind, and was being helped by his friends; he wrote sad letters reminiscing about '*le temps perdu*'. Jacques-Émile Blanche was unwell, and thinking of giving up the house at Offranville; she wrote advising him against it: 'too many good memories are attached to it, and you would feel "trop dépaysés" [too disoriented]'. She told him she was writing her memoirs, but did not like to send them to all her friends: it would be like issuing one's full-length portrait, and obliging everyone to say: '*Quelle merveille! Et comme vous êtes belle!*' Charlie Du Bos had to have an operation in 1935 and she asked after him anxiously, sending Biedermann's 'Conversations de Goethe' for light convalescent reading. The Bourgets' story was grim. Wharton told Minnie Jones in 1931 that 'the news was too tragic to be believable'. Minnie Bourget, suffering from senile dementia, had a succession of strokes and died in a sanatorium, at sixty-seven, in 1933; Bourget, who had cut himself off from his old friends, died two years later. Léon Bélugou's melancholy funeral was held in Paris in October 1934 – he died at sixty-nine, leaving his young widow and daughter – attended by 'all the old group of long ago Paris' including St André and Valéry. Morton Fullerton, once Bélugou's closest friend, was, as so often, conspicuous by his absence.

But Fullerton did turn up again. A few humorous, affectionate letters were exchanged in the early 1930s, and she welcomed this: 'I have had so many losses in the last few years that I cling as never before to the friends who are left.' She sent sympathy on the death of his mother; he wrote praising *Hudson River Bracketed*, and she teased him in return: 'It is a shock to find that your avoidance of my presence has for so many years extended to my books!' She urged him to visit her ('Of course I want to see you – always!') and to send her his news of Paris: 'I wish you'd send me your impressions. This is where they will be read.' He helped her with a newspaper appeal for a local priest, and sent her, for interest (of all things), a family paper which a French friend of his had inherited, a letter from a woman writing to an 'unrequited suitor' who was asking for 'total' commitment. At first Wharton took it for a literary pastiche, 'an exercise in style', and then, touchingly, commented: 'I have had many dear friends – & only two in whose case I wanted the friendship to be total.' He came to see her at St-Brice in June 1931, and once more in September, in order to discuss the (unlikely) possibility of his writing a life of Walter. After the first of these visits, she told him that Gross had said: '*J'ai été contente de voir Mr Fullerton. Il est toujours le même.*' Edith signed off, in their old tone: '*L'est-il?*'[48]

Catherine Gross's fond recognition of Fullerton was one of the old lady's last pleasures. Wharton had all kinds of dramatic troubles with her household staff now, when she most depended on them. While she was unwell again with a 'heart relapse' in the spring of 1930, her cook Roger Vapperau, who had been with her since he was seventeen, was killed, at the age of thirty-three, in a motor-cycle accident. She used robust language about this to John Hugh ('My fool of a cook was picked up on the road near here in a horrible motor cycle accident, with the base of his skull fractured . . . He had an accident last year, and I gave him a talking-to then, for he was apparently very imprudent. And he only bought a bigger machine!') but she was 'a good deal shattered'. In August, the replacement cook was found 'lying in the kitchen covered in blood'; he had haemorrhaged, nearly died, and had to be replaced. 'These two tragedies . . . have really been too much for me.' The next cook, though good at his job, could not get on with the chauffeur; in 1934 she told Elisina that he and 'that idiot Franklin, no doubt instigated by his odious wife, had a real fisticuff fight in the house the other day, and I had to sack them both'. She could see why old ladies went to live in hotels.[49]

By far the worst of these troubles was the painful and rapid deterioration of Gross's faculties. From being Wharton's rock of strength, her devoted companion, efficient house-manager and dog-guardian, as she had been for nearly fifty years – far more essential to her mistress than any mother, husband or lover – she turned, almost overnight, aged eighty, into an angry, confused and suicidal old woman suffering from senile dementia. Edith sent aghast reports to Elisina: 'Gross's softening of the brain ... produces a complete change of character, so that she now seems to hate us all, which is far worse than not knowing us.' 'Gross is mostly a wild, frightened and obstinate stranger.' She had to be taken away to be looked after by the nuns at the convent of Ésperance in Hyères. At exactly the same time, Elise Devinck, Wharton's maid, who had been with her for twenty years, developed pernicious anaemia. There had been an earlier history of problems with Elise, who was given to fits of 'nervous excitement', and in the early stages of her illness Wharton thought it was a 'temporary physiological disturbance' and childish behaviour. She wrote to Daisy, in her haughtiest tone: 'The servant class can never grasp anything like that ... If they *could* (as dear Egerton used to tell me) they wouldn't be servants, but Presidents and Prime Ministers.' But Elise was, in fact, seriously ill, and she died in May 1933. A few months later Gross, peaceful, but not knowing where she was or who Edith Wharton was, also died, and was buried beside Elise on 4 October 1933. Edith's wording for their monument was:

Catherine Gross de Brumath	Elise Devinck de Boulogne-sur-Mer
1852–1933	1880–1933
Pendant quarante-huit ans sa	Pendant vingt ans sa femme de
fidèle ami et sa gouvernante	chambre dévouée

'Oh, how I miss the old faces!' Edith wrote in her diary. These were catastrophic bereavements for a seventy-one-year-old woman in poor health who had been dependent on, used to, and fond of, the same women in her household, for most of her adult life. She was shocked and disrupted. She hired new staff – Marie Anettaz, Madeleine Vigna, Mrs Ward. (By the end of her life, counting all the staff at both houses, she had twenty-two employees.) But she could not get used to new people in the house, and she felt 'incurably lonely'. Even keeping her line-a-day diary was painful, as she wrote on 17 June 1933: 'I can't write yet in this book. Elise used to say: "Est-ce-que Madame a fait son diary?" No one will ever care again!' 'It is a bitter blow to me', she told Elisina, 'for those two women had mothered me, first one, then the other, for 49 years – & I am in a trackless desert now, with all my past buried.'[50]

But she had indomitable inner resources, and she always did her work. She was proud of this, as she had told Mary Berenson (by way of bucking her up, too) in 1928: 'At my age, & with a will-to-live (& to work) as strong as mine, one comes soon, I find, to accept sorrows & renunciations, & to *build* with them, instead of letting them tear one down'. She often said to Berenson that work kept her going. In the summer of 1931, tired after travelling, she thought it might have been a mistake to start work so soon. 'And yet I wonder if it is not as unrestful to turn in the void, waiting to be rested?' Even in the last weeks of her life, when she was terminally ill, she wrote to him: 'In spite of everything I stick to my work, & so do you, I know.' Writing, as always, continued to be her addiction, her greatest pleasure and her toughest challenge. Over 150 pages into *The Buccaneers* by the end of 1934, she wrote ruefully in her diary:

> What is writing a novel like?
> 1. The beginning: A ride through a spring wood.
> 2. The middle: The Gobi desert.
> 3. The end: A night with a lover.
> I am now in the Gobi desert.

There was no slacking off, though, in her production rate. Between 1930 and 1934, as well as writing *The Buccaneers*, she finished *The Gods Arrive*, which was serialised and published in 1932, wrote *A Backward Glance*, placed a number of stories in magazines and published two collections (with contents mostly dating from between 1926 and 1932), *Certain People* (1930) and *Human Nature* (1933). She encouraged herself, drove herself on, and congratulated herself on her unwaning energies and enthusiasms: 'Another year. The tired heart still beats as vehemently as ever. Ah, well – in summing it all up, let me say: Love and Beauty have poured such glowing cups for me that when the last drop of the last is drained, I shall go away grateful – if not satisfied. Satisfied! What a beggarly state! – Who would be satisfied with being satisfied?' 'I never cease to miss the one comrade of my soul and my two dear maids, and life without them is a hollow business. But here I am again in a sunny garden, and among my books, and still to wake in the mornings is an adventure for me! Oh, incorrigible lover that I am . . .'[51] Her gardens – the terraces at Ste-Claire now renewed – were a great consolation to her. Writing a sympathy-for-illness letter to Lady John Leslie (née Leonie Jerome, sister of Jennie Jerome, who married Randolph Churchill – aristocratic Anglo-Americans much in her mind for *The Buccaneers*), she told her: 'I have never enjoyed my garden so much!' Another intense pleasure was music. She heard the great Polish harpsichordist Wanda Landowska playing in Marseilles in 1932, and made friends with her, fascinated by her stories of playing seventeenth-century music to Tolstoy. She and Robert enjoyed a Mozart festival in Nice that summer, and in 1933 she heard some magnificent things at Salzburg – a Mozart Mass, Bruno Walter conducting the Sinfonia Concertante, Lotte Lehmann singing lieder, performances of *Faust* and *Oberon* – which more than made up for the awkward encounter with an embarrassed Percy Lubbock, fussily shielding Sybil from view. She was as competent and determined as ever about travelling – noting insouciantly to Lily Norton, for instance, that she and Daisy were setting off to Spain in the spring of 1930, unless 'there is a Spanish revolution, or any other contretemps to change our plans'. I Tatti and Salso were still regular ports of call. It moved and excited her to go back to Rome, after many years, with Nicky Mariano (rescuing her from Mary's sick-bed at I Tatti) in 1931, and again in the spring of 1932. (Another return there in May 1934 was less successful, as she was very unwell on that journey.)[52]

Her most frequent destination in her seventies was England, where she went every year from 1931 to 1936. Moving from one grand house to another, with an undiminished appetite for new exploring (for instance, of Wales, with Gaillard, in the summer of 1933), her travel arrangements were complicated and demanding. Her hosts and friends had to fall in with her itinerary, and she often cut her plans rather fine, as here, writing from Hidcote Manor in Gloucestershire to Dorothy Allhusen, in July 1933:

> I am so glad it will suit you to have me on Thursday. I rashly said that I wd turn up for tea, but I had forgotten that my host had asked my old friends from Oxford, the Wm Bucklers, to lunch with me here that day, and as my chauffeur says the run is about 85 miles, and I may not be able to get away till 3.30 or after, I may even turn up a little late for dinner – though I hope not! But I know you will be indulgent. I am obliged to leave on Friday afternoon, as I am due at Stanway for the weekend ... If you want to make any change in this programme, you have only to call me up here.

She was late going to visit the Kiplings at Batemans, too, on 25 July 1931, where the Visitors' Book, kept by Carrie Kipling, had her down for lunch (as 'Mrs Warton') with Mr John Hugh Smith:

Left Tusmore Park ('a beautiful derelict Adam house') at 9.40 yesterday, assured by all and sundry that we shd reach Batemans before 1.30. Owing to wet roads and intensive traffic we arrived at 2.30! I stopped on the way to telephone – and they *have no telephone!* The lovely glades between Dorking and Sevenoaks rang with my curses. They hadn't waited to lunch, luckily – and, less luckily, had apparently eaten nearly all there was in the house. However, it was very pleasant, and I punished them by staying to tea (to get more food!).

She particularly liked going back to Stanway, though she had the same kind of problems with her timing: 'I staggered in, dog-tired, at 7.30, to learn that we were to dine in 15 minutes, on account of a village feast, so I participated in tweeds, surrounded by lovely visions in cloth of gold & rosy chiffon!' Stanway's remote, golden beauty never diminished, and she enjoyed seeing her very old friend Lady Wemyss and her glittering tribe (the daughter, Lady Cynthia Asquith, the son, Hugo Charteris), and the guests they collected – 'that agreeable ruffian Wells', Beerbohm, Eddie Marsh, David Cecil, Sybil Colefax. As ever, she noted the level of conversation and the home entertainments of the English upper classes: 'I'm always so amused by the inexhaustible English devices for avoiding rational intercourse.' She struck the same note in a letter to Ned Sheldon: 'about thirty amiable people with beautiful voices endeavoured by every known means to avoid any sort of consecutive conversation, but in the brief snatches of talk between bridge and boating and walking, they were all as agreeable as possible'. And she repeated to him an anecdote which Housman had told her: 'The Duke of Devonshire heard someone speaking of napkin-rings. On asking what a napkin-ring was he was told that people of small means, who are not able to spend much on their washing bills, sometimes used a napkin more than once, and consequently kept them in rings in order to tell them apart. "Good God!" was his only comment.' All this poured immediately into *The Buccaneers*. She never stopped collecting copy.[53]

Back home, she invited many guests and visitors, felt lonely if no one came, and complained frequently, especially at St-Brice, of feeling 'like a palace hotel', or of all her guests arriving at once: 'The neat little Furies love to telescope visits in this way.' But she relied on old friends. A page of names and addresses in her papers lists most of the key figures who were left to her in the 1930s, and gives the flavour of her social world:

Lady Aberconway, Comtesse de Béhague, Berensons, J.-E. Blanche, Mildred and Robert Bliss, André Boccon-Gibod, Louis Bromfield, William Buckler, Countess Buxton, Mrs Winthrop Chanler, Sir Kenneth Clark, Ogden Codman, Comtesse Jules de Divonne, Charles Du Bos, Mr and Mrs Max Farrand, Morton Fullerton, Mrs John Garrett, Mrs Walter Gay, Louis Gillet, Mrs Gerard Goschen, Robert Grant, Major Lawrence Johnston, Frederic King, Le Roy King, Mrs Grant La Farge, Gaillard Lapsley, Mrs George Cabot Lodge, Sir Eric Maclagan, Mrs Walter Maynard, Miss Mariano, R.P. Nicholson, Miss Elizabeth Norton, R.D. Norton, Carlo Placci, Alfred de St André, Mme St René Taillandier, John Hugh Smith, Mr and Mrs Royall Tyler, Daniel Berkeley Updike, Arnold and Janetta Whitridge.

Many of the pages of A *Backward Glance* read rather like this address-book: it is, to a great extent, a grand old lady's decorous list of distinguished acquaintances, fondly remembered.[54]

Wharton's 'retrospect', a beautifully produced and illustrated book, is an impressively evasive exercise in good manners and self-screening. Pre-empting unwanted biographical intrusion, it selects out mildly satirised scenes from her childhood and New York world, recalls her American

homes, her Italian travels, French and English society, the 'slow stammering beginnings' of her literary career, and her war-work, and draws affectionate portraits of old friends, notably Vernon Lee, Egerton Winthrop, Paul Bourget, Mary Hunter, Howard Sturgis, Bay Lodge, Bayard Cutting, Theodore Roosevelt, Geoffrey Scott, and, above all, Henry James.

There is plenty of humour, affection, and lively remembering: though loosely organised, it is a carefully managed narrative, and she makes a fine hostess into the past. Many events, people, and concerns in her life are silently obliterated or glancingly passed over: money, sex, family feuds, rows with publishers, servants, the reasons for the breakdown of her marriage, her close friendships with women like Sally Norton, Minnie Jones or Daisy Chanler, most of her life-story after 1919. Fullerton is not mentioned. Very occasionally she does expose her deep feelings, if indirectly, as in a curious and revealing sentence about the start of her marriage ('At the end of my second winter in New York I was married; and thenceforth my thirst for travel was to be gratified'), or in the tidy drama she constructs of her escape from the constrictions of her upbringing into her life as a writer: 'The publishing of *The Greater Inclination* broke the chains which had held me so long in a kind of torpor.' There are two moments where she speaks out as she might to a close friend. One is her idealising but none the less touching lament for Walter Berry:

> I suppose there is one friend in the life of each of us who seems not a separate person, however dear and beloved, but an expansion, an inter-pretation, of one's self, the very meaning of one's soul. Such a friend I found in Walter Berry . . . That understanding lasted as long as my friend lived; and no words can say, because such things are unsayable, how the influence of his thought, his character, his deepest personality, were interwoven with mine.

The other is the short section on the 'secret garden' of her writing processes, in which she tried to explain the obscure relationship between what is controlled and what is involuntary in the making of a novel: 'I do not think I can get any nearer than this to the sources of my story-telling; I can only say that the process, though it takes place in some secret region on the sheer edge of consciousness, is always illuminated by the full light of my critical attention.' *A Backward Glance* was politely received, on the whole. Virginia Woolf liked 'the way she places colour in her sentences', but added, loftily, 'There's the shell of a distinguished mind.' The book ends with some gloomy remarks about the chaos and darkness of the world, but with consolations stoically provided: 'Though the years are sad, the days have a way of being jubilant.' Jubilation is derived from nature and travel and above all from the private library of her mind, where she expects, still, to find 'new books to read (and, I hope, to write)'.[55]

20

All Souls'

Charles Du Bos had a letter from Wharton's secretary in May 1935 (she was too unwell to write herself) thanking him for having sent her a book about the rituals of the Catholic Mass. '*Vous savez l'intérêt passionné que Mme Wharton prend à la Liturgie*', Jeanne Fridérich wrote. 'She thinks that she might find in this book the extraordinary prayer of the Saturday Saint at the moment when the candles are re-lit, and which was, she thinks, an "exultet" of the primitive church . . . and she hopes to find something interesting on the mysterious "Ange du Canon de la Messe".' Wharton was thinking of the Angel of the Mass, who mediates between man and God, in the Eucharistic prayer (the '*Canon de la Messe*') which commemorates the Last Supper. And she wanted to find the Latin hymn of Holy Saturday, sung at the Easter Vigil. This was the kind of ancient, dramatic ritual that most appealed to her in the Roman Catholic Church. All the lights are extinguished in the church except for the single paschal candle, carried in by the white-robed deacon as he sings '*Lumen Christi*'. All the congregation respond, gradually lighting their candles as they do so, so that by the time the candle reaches the altar and the deacon chants the mighty '*Exultet!*' ('Christ has conquered! Glory fills you! Darkness vanishes for ever!'), the church is full of light. It was to the Catholic Du Boses, too, that Wharton wrote one of her most enthusiastic letters about her return to Rome. These visits – with Nicky Mariano in November and December 1931, and the following spring on her own, then joined by Nicky and Berenson – were her first sight of Rome since 1914. She was very moved. She told Daisy Chanler – with whom, as a child, she had played on the Monte Pincio for days on end, memories that went into *A Backward Glance* – that Rome had never seemed to her 'so beautiful, so matchless'. To John Hugh Smith, from her hotel at the top of the Spanish Steps, in the spring, with views over the gardens of the Villa Medici from one terrace and to the Trinità dei Monti and 'all s.western Rome' from the other, she quoted Mignon's lines of longing for Italy from 'Kennst du das Land' which had haunted her all her life: '*Dahin, dahin, möcht Ich mit Dir, O mein Geliebter, gehn!*'

Since she was a five-year-old child watching the processions of cardinals and the incense-laden ceremonials in St Peter's, she had always loved Italian religious spectacle. Now, in her old age, she sought out church services and described them fervently, especially to her Catholic friends – Daisy Chanler, Elisina, Charlie, Matilda Gay. 'We were fortunate enough to be here', she told Du Bos, 'at the time of the feast of the Dedication of the Basilicas of St Peter and St Paul without-the-walls [S. Paolo fuori le Mura], and we assisted at the most beautiful pontifical Masses and vespers, and also at a very fine requiem Mass sung by the Benedictines at Santa Maria-sopra-Minerva.' At the Pontifical High Mass at S. Anselmo, she told Berenson ecstatically, 'the Benedictines, candles in hand, [walked] in procession around the cloister, singing the Corpus Christi anthems, and treading on box leaves and rose-petals'. Travelling on from Rome in the spring of 1932 to Spoleto, Assisi, Loreto, Recanati (Leopardi's birthplace), Rimini, Ravenna and Ferrara, ending up at Salso, she was constantly on the lookout for more Masses. At the 'Albergo dei Pellegrini' in Loreto (where the House of Mary, in the Santuario della Santa Casa, is a pilgrimage shrine), she wrote to Nicky, wishing she were there: 'This being the last day of the mois de Marie, the high altar of the Basilica flamed with lights, & canons in glorious reds & purples intoned without ceasing, while in the Casa Santa two nuns remained in adoration, & a young Franciscan knelt on the doorstep in pallid ecstasy.' The tone of this suggests that she was not praying herself, exactly, but delighting in the spectacle of prayer.[1]

At home at St-Brice, she opened the Pavillon every 15 August to the procession of '*Les Enfants de la Marie*', and was well known in the village for her support of the curé and the local church. One of her late bursts of organisational energy was in support of a French priest, the Abbé Comptour, who converted Gross in her last years from Protestantism to Catholicism and who was working in the '*lotissement*' of Lutèce, quite near St-Brice. She described him as a 'heroic curé waging a successful war against the communism of the Zone Rouge', and set up an appeal for him, publicised in the Paris *Herald* (calling on Fullerton, yet once more, for help with publicising this campaign). The 'settlement' of Lutèce was, she said in her fund-raising letter, one of the 'sad communities' set up after the war 'without school, church, doctors, light, water or drainage', and Comptour was one of the priests who was trying to consolidate the Church's presence in the area. He was playing a part in the factional conflicts in France in the years leading up to the Second World War, as between the Soviet-dominated

Communists, dedicated to working-class unity, and particularly active in the 'zone rouge' of the workers' suburbs around Paris, and Catholic movements ranging from 'Catholic Action' to the Péguy-inspired 'Catholicisme de gauche', which believed that Catholicism could be reconciled with socialism and republicanism. Elisina, Walter and Matilda Gay, and Ogden Codman all contributed to funding a bell for the church; Wharton attended the ceremony of the christening of the bell (the 'Edith-Matilda' bell) on 23 August 1931 with great satisfaction, noting in her diary: 'We all went to Lutèce for christening of bell. Church full of lights and flowers. W. Gay and I were godparents. Over 200 people present. Great occasion.'[2]

Many of Wharton's friends supposed that she might be thinking of converting, as Gross did (and as Matilda Gay's husband Walter did on his death-bed in 1937). Nicky Mariano said that she spoke of Catholic ritual giving a 'sublime frame' to the three great events in human life, birth, marriage and death; Berenson, observing her in Rome in 1932, thought that she was moving 'towards the Church'. So did Kenneth Clark, who noticed that she 'saw a great deal of the Curé at St-Brice and the nuns at Hyères', but thought that might have been 'partly because they told her what was going on in the locality'. Bill Tyler concluded his reminiscence of Wharton by saying that she was 'a devout Christian and felt strongly drawn toward the Church of Rome'. Her annual ritual of sitting alone and thinking of her dead on 'All Souls' Night' (A Backward Glance is dedicated to these dead friends) included reading 'L'Office des Morts'. But her attraction to Catholicism was aesthetic as much as devotional.[3]

Her late work, then, might be expected to be mystical and pious, as when Vance draws lessons from his reading of St Augustine at the end of The Gods Arrive. But this was not generally the case. Wharton's late stories are cool, secular, implacable and disillusioned. If they have an other-worldly flavour, it is in a pagan rather than an orthodox spirit. She is more than ever interested in the return of the past, in the un-dead, in being half in and half out of the living world. She is engrossed by the idea of the 'Memento Mori', the death's-head. These stories of old age, returnings and atrophy, and of long-brewed revenges, have tremendous power: all her energy and experience go into them.

The most grotesque of these fine late stories is 'After Holbein' (published in magazine form in 1928 and in the collection Certain People in 1930). It is a ghost-story, a murder-story, and a story of living death. The old New York socialite Anson Warley has murdered his better self, who used to want to read books and discuss ideas instead of going out into society all the time; but the 'social' Anson Warley asphyxiated him long ago. The idea of the double self – the one who goes out and the one who stays in – bows to Henry James and his story 'The Private Life'. But 'After Holbein' brilliantly mixes that idea with the story of an ancient New York hostess who has had a stroke and is reduced to second childhood, but who still insists on dining in state, dressed in her diamonds and silks and a purple wig, surrounded by imaginary guests. The spectral performance is observed by a contemptuous, matter-of-fact young night-nurse, and a devoted old servant, the story's real heroine, almost as tottery as her mistress but with 'watchful grey eyes in which intelligence and comprehension burned like two fixed stars'. On the night of the story, old Anson Warley forgets where he is supposed to be dining, and turns up at Mrs Jaspar's mansion, where all the lights are burning. Dining on bottled water, mashed potatoes and spinach, with kitchen plates on the table and crumpled newspapers in the priceless flower bowls, the two aged, senile socialites, hardly able to sit upright, exchange small talk and courtesies with the 'imaginary presences' across the table, and comment on the oysters and the Perrier-Jouet '95, watched with a mixture of compassion and derision by the servants: it is a macabre illusory 'dance of death' on the edge of the abyss. Wharton based the story on the pathetic old age of her distant relation Caroline Astor, once the queen of Old New York, and wrote it as she was thinking about the remote days of her own New York childhood for her memoir. What if that world of social niceties, snobbery and malice, which she had so often written about, were to have lingered on long after its time? The idea of an atrophied remnant, a life withering away inside its fixed conventions, haunts her terribly.

'After Holbein' slightly resembles a 'donnée' she noted in 1925, but sadly did not make use of, about a 'little group of clever agreeable worldly people who have so arranged their lives as to see a great deal of each other, in New York in winter, and in a smart "artists' colony" somewhere on the Sound or in the Adirondacks in summer. All full of taste, animation, interest in things.' She planned to

> set the stage, bring them on, let them come and go, talk, discuss all the up to date things; and then suddenly reveal that they are all nearly 70 years old, but marvellously well preserved, careful of diet, exercise etc and really unconscious of their age. And then, suddenly, one of the men, the most youthful minded and active of them all, dies – and all the others become shivering old people, frightened of a draught, of fatigue, of excitement, of a sleepless night, of a telegram, of late hours, of motoring – and sit at home watching for their turn to come.

Another 'donnée' told to her at St-Brice in 1925, was about a couple who live together before they are married, and have a son. The birth is hushed up, the son is taken care of, and they never see him. 'Then they marry. They have another, adored son. The husband dies. The son dies of fever in an American training camp. The widow is searching Europe for the repudiated son.' 'What a subject', she noted. This was saved up for several years and became a long, cruel story, ironically called 'Her Son', published in Scribner's in 1932 and collected in Human Nature (1933). A dignified New York lady, searching for the illegitimate son she secretly gave up for adoption, is exploited by a seedy, fraudulent 'trio of society adventurers' on the Riviera, who fasten onto the mother's desperate longing. It is a dark example of how these late stories return to Wharton's obsessive subjects: the lost child, the false or inadequate parents, the women competing for control, the hidden secret from the past taking its revenge.

All stories of mothers questing for a lost child have something in them of Demeter looking for Persephone, the myth that Wharton kept returning to. (She summarised it to Jewett, cross that her magazine editors and readers did not know their classical tales: 'When Persephone left the under-world to revisit her mother, Demeter, her husband, Hades, lord of the infernal regions, gave her a pomegranate seed to eat, because he knew that if he did so she would never be able to remain among the living, but would be drawn back to the company of the dead.') Wharton used the title 'Pomegranate Seed' several times. It is the title of the woman writer's novel in The Touchstone (1900) – her power returns from the grave – and again is a novel-title in 'Copy' (1901). In 1912, she published a long, solemn verse-play in Scribner's on the story of Demeter and Persephone, in which Persephone, because she has 'eaten of the seed of death', turns her back on her mother's world of earth and light ('Hide me, O mother, hide me from the day!') and is called back to the underworld where she has seen 'ghosts of dead babes and ghosts of tired men'.

In 'Life and I', Wharton used the story as an image for her early fascination with words, that 'lured me from the wholesome noonday air of childhood into the strange supernatural region where the normal pleasures of my age seemed as insipid as the fruits of the earth to Persephone after she had eaten of the Pomegranate seed'.[4] And in 1931, she gave a sinister twist to the myth in the alarming story 'Pomegranate Seed' (collected in 1936 in The World Over). This time the revenant from the underworld is not the daughter. As in Daphne du Maurier's Rebecca, or Elizabeth Bowen's 'The Demon Lover' – both written a few years later – it is a first wife so powerful, demanding and possessive that she will not let the husband go after her death. Like 'After Holbein', this is about a life hanging on too long, after its natural end. As the nine mysterious grey envelopes arrive, throwing the husband (and his mother) into horrified distress and the new wife, Charlotte Ashby, into a torment of suspicion, the suspense builds up beautifully. The letters that call him back to the underworld are never explained (cause for much bafflement from Wharton's magazine editors) and the one she opens ('the tearing of the paper as she slit the envelope sounded like a human cry') can hardly be read: 'I can make out something like "mine" – oh, and "come". It might be "come".' Their strangeness is felt all the more strongly because it is in such peculiar contrast to the modern world. Charlotte Ashby thinks: 'Outside there ... skyscrapers, advertisements, telephones, wireless, airplanes, movies, motors, and all the rest of the twentieth century; and on the other side of the door something I can't explain, can't relate to them. Something as old as the world, as mysterious as life.' The husband – who apart from being haunted is quite uninteresting – tries to change the subject from the letters by 'rambling on about municipal politics, aviation, an exhibition of modern French painting ... and the installing of the automatic telephone'. This is the opposite tactic from a story like 'Afterward' or 'Mr Jones', where the ancient other-worldliness of the house gets the reader ready for a ghost. What Wharton wanted to do now, as she said in her preface to her last, posthumously published collection, *Ghosts* (1937), was to show how ghosts did not require 'battlemented castles' or 'hidden doors behind tapestries'. To argue that 'ghosts went out when electricity came in' was 'to misapprehend the nature of the ghostly'. Something very old from the past, lingering on into the modern world – that is what frightens her, and, she hopes, her readers.[5]

The hand of the dead wife reaches out from the grave, too, in 'The Day of the Funeral', the story of adultery and suicide written in 1931, published, after difficulties, in magazine form as 'In a Day' (so as not to sound too morbid) and collected in 1933 in *Human Nature*. With cool, savage irony, the main character's hedonism and emotional laziness are minutely unpicked. His crime, it becomes clear, is not so much that he deceived his wife and drove her to suicide, or that he is too cowardly to tell his girl-friend that his wife killed herself because of their affair, but that he has been so 'niggardly' in his dealings with both women. He prefers his home comforts, and the description of his eating a late lunch after having buried his wife and deciding to get rid of his mistress is immaculate: 'Had he ever before known the complex exquisiteness of a slice of pressed beef? He filled his glass again, leaned luxuriously, waited without hurry for the cheese and biscuits, the black coffee, and a slice of apple pie apologetically added from the maids' dinner – and then – oh, resurrection! – felt for his cigar case, and calmly, carelessly almost ... cut his Corona and lit it.'[6]

Of all these quiet, dark, masterful late tales, the most perfectly controlled and profound is 'Roman Fever', published in *Liberty* in 1934 and in *The World Over* in 1936. Apart from *Ethan Frome*, it is Wharton's best-known and most influential story (it is frequently anthologised, has been adapted as a one-act opera, a radio play and a screenplay, and has inspired a fine tribute-story by Julian Barnes, 'The Things You Know'). But familiarity does not lessen its effect. Because it is a story with a startling twist in its last sentence, it changes after the first reading; but every reading confirms its depth and its subtlety. It has a complicated appeal, partly elegiac (it is a late story by an ageing woman writer about two elderly women looking back on their lives, and on the lives of their mothers and grandmothers), partly evocative (it draws a wonderfully still, eloquent picture of Rome, past and present), and partly shocking, as the split develops between its well-mannered surface and its violent emotional depths. It is as deceptive as one of its characters. What appears to be a story about long friendship turns out to be about long enmity; resignation turns out to be resentment; one character's apparent dominance is completely overturned. This impeccable, ruthless masterpiece is how Wharton transformed her religious sentiments and nostalgia on her return to Rome. It is one of the best examples of the indirect, rich and surprising ways in which she makes use of her own experiences.

The story begins with two affable, conventional, elderly American ladies deciding to spend the afternoon on the terrace of a restaurant overlooking Rome. The location is unnamed, but it is clearly on the Janiculum, with its magnificent view down over the Palatine Hill towards the Forum and the Colosseum. Their independent daughters are going off on a jaunt – we hear them disappearing as the story begins – with two Italian aviators, one a marchese, who are going to fly them to Tarquinia before tea. (So, in a quick aside, Wharton touches in the high society of Mussolini's Italy, the speed and freedom of life for contemporary girls, and the famous burial-chambers of the Etruscans, where the secrets of a vanished civilisation were hidden away for centuries on the cave-walls of Tarquinia.) The two ladies have lived opposite each other in the same Upper East Side, New York street, they have known each other for most of their lives, and they are both widowed. But they do not know each other well enough to feel comfortable being 'silent' together; they are going to talk. The apparent balance of power between them is carefully and quickly set up, mostly from the point of view of the more forceful and worldly of the ladies,

Alida, Mrs Delphin Slade, who was married to a glamorous lawyer. She looks down on her companion, Grace, Mrs Horace Ansley, for having had a dull marriage and for being so docile and conventional: it is hard to remember (Alida thinks) that she was once very beautiful. She notes Grace's habit of slightly emphasising her words, 'like the random under-lining of old letter-writers': but she misses the implications of her emphases. Grace's taking out her knitting, in front of the astounding view of Rome, seems to Alida typically prim: she does not see that the knitting-needles might be weapons of defence. Alida Slade, who has lost a son as well as a husband, and finds her own daughter a little disappointing – too nice and well behaved – envies Grace Ansley her brilliant and spirited daughter Babs. All we know about Mrs Ansley is that she feels rather sorry for Mrs Slade. 'So these two ladies visualised each other, each through the wrong end of her little telescope.'

As the bells of Rome ring out for five o'clock and the glow of the Roman afternoon begins to dim, Alida Slade begins to talk, and the second half of the story consists entirely of a dialogue between the two women, rising in speed, intensity and urgency as the sun sets and night falls over the city. Mrs Slade begins by thinking about the differences in the risks and dangers for four generations of American women in Rome. (Wharton's own seventy-year experience of Rome, from the 1860s to the 1930s, takes in these generations.) Their grandmothers had less trouble chaperoning their daughters, because of the malaria – the 'Roman fever' – that meant everyone had to go indoors at dusk. (James's Daisy Miller, who is in Wharton's mind, catches her death from 'Roman fever' after a night-time assignation in the Colosseum in the 1870s.) Their own mothers had more difficulty keeping their daughters out of mischief at night. And now they are not required as chaperones at all. The subject – of mothers wanting to keep their daughters virginal for the marriage-market – leads Alida unstoppably towards her jealousy of Grace's daughter, whom she thinks will outclass her own daughter in any sexual competition – and so on into her own long-ago rivalry with her companion. Grace does not take the bait: she will not meet Mrs Slade's eye, but looks 'straight out at the great accumulated wreckage of passion and splendour at her feet'.

In that one phrase, Wharton brings in a mighty sense of all the conquests, triumphs and betrayals that make a great civilisation, and of their passing: the two women's lives, set in this context, seem tiny and ephemeral; but the 'wreckage of passion' may be just as great. This is the hinge on which the story turns; after this Alida Slade rushes into her real, primitive feelings of envy and hatred towards the other woman. She tells a story of a great-aunt of Grace's who was said to have sent her sister to the Forum at night because they were rivals in love, and the sister died of the Roman fever. And, unable to hold back any longer her twenty-five-year-old secret, she tells the same story of herself (so, though malaria is a thing of the past and the mothers' roles have changed, the same old passions continue to prevail). When the two women were young girls in Rome together, and Alida was engaged to Delphin Slade, she saw that Grace was in love with him, and forged a love-letter from her fiancé to her friend, telling her to meet him in the Colosseum at night. 'Of course I never thought you'd die', she tells her now, brutally: she had just wanted her to catch a chill, and be 'out of the way'. Grace Ansley has never known that the love-letter was written by Alida, and we see her, all at once, bitterly mourning the loss of that memory. But Alida now finds out what *she* never knew – that the letter was replied to, the assignation kept – and what came of it. The quieter and less impassioned of the two women turns out to have had the deeper passion, the lifelong secret, and the means of revenge. The shift in power is measured in the last phrase: as they leave the story to take up their altered lives and move towards their deaths, Grace Ansley 'began to move ahead of Mrs Slade towards the stairway'.

The intense drama of revelation is interrupted only once, as the waiters begin to get the terrace ready for the evening, and 'a stout lady in a dust coat suddenly appeared, asking in broken Italian if anyone had seen the elastic band which held together her tattered Baedeker'. Though Edith Wharton's Italian was better than that, and it was many years since she had been a tourist in Rome, it is tempting to read this as a fleeting Hitchcockian appearance by the author, stepping, for once, in and out of her last European story.[7]

'Roman Fever' reworks, with austerity and concentration, subjects which had preoccupied Wharton since she started to write: lifelong hidden love, maternal rivalry and deception, the constrictions of women's lives, the imprisonment of secrecy, social conventions which continue to bind indi-viduals even as they pass away, the persistence of primitive passions. Alongside the writing of this great story, she was constructing a comic version of some of the same themes, which begins, like 'Roman Fever', with rival mothers on the side-lines, discussing their daughters' marital prospects. *The Buccaneers*, Wharton's last, and unfinished novel, is a high-spirited, socially acute, lavish historical comedy. Like other great artists' terminal works – Verdi's last opera *Falstaff*, Jane Austen's *Sanditon*, Flaubert's *Bouvard et Pécuchet* – it prefers robustness and vigour to an elegiac or melancholy spirit. But it has a bitter theme: once more, Wharton's women discover that their freedoms have been taken away from them and their desires curbed, and that they are living like ghosts in their own lives.

There has been a biographical tendency to describe *The Buccaneers* as a benign, consolatory last work. Lewis says that 'an air of fairy-tale enchantment breathes through its pages', Benstock calls it 'arguably the most charming novel Edith Wharton ever wrote'. Its young Americans (the 'buccaneers') are indeed a group of charmers, and the English stately homes they marry into have their enchantments. But under its frothy surface is a harsh exposure of society marriage as a form of prostitution and gambling, mothers trading their daughters, sex as a threat and a bargain, marital sadism and neglect, and several kinds of prejudice and racism.

Wharton planned the novel to appeal to readers who still liked *The House of Mirth* or *The Age of Innocence*, and Jewett thought this a very good idea. She hoped it would be a lucrative project, and that was why she took on Pinker as an agent now, anxious to get better sales in England. She was offended to be offered only $1,000 for the serialisation in *Cosmopolitan*, and to be asked to submit the first half of the novel in advance: 'I have never before been treated like a beginner, and I do not like it', she told Jewett. When the next magazine it was tried out on, the *Woman's Home Companion*, also asked for 'a more detailed outline' before agreeing to serialise it, she responded: 'I never know more than the main lines of any novel that I am writing. The subsidiary incidents develop as I write.' The idea for the novel first surfaced in a notebook dated 1924–8, with notes to herself like: 'The first to marry marries off all the others'. It was set aside, and then started again with encouragement from Ned Sheldon, to whom she worried that it might be 'too like *The Age of Innocence*'? Once launched on it again, she was pleased (and surprised) when – as Kenneth Clark noted – the abdication crisis at the end of 1936, and the ex-King Edward VIII's marriage to an American divorcee, made her historical subject, the period in the 1870s when wealthy, beautiful American girls were picking off the English aristocracy, suddenly seem topical again. 'You will be amused to hear' (she told Elisina early in 1937) 'that Mrs Simpson has made my tale "de l'actualité", & that publishers & editors in England & the US are prodding me to finish it!!'

When *The Buccaneers* did come out, posthumously and unfinished, edited from her final typescripts by Gaillard Lapsley (with her synopsis of the whole novel appended), many American readers disliked it. As Lily Norton said to Elisina in 1938: 'Of course, it's not a story that commends itself to Americans; they never can bear to see themselves as others possibly have seen them.' It sealed her reputation, then and for many years, as a representative of a vanished way of life, always cited in books on the Gilded Age and *Mrs Astor's New York*. For those who dismissed her as a writer who kept doing the same kind of book, or who saw – and see – her as entirely identified with the society, wealth and class she wrote about, *The Buccaneers* looked like a final confirmation. (It has not been well served by a later 'completion' and screen adaptation, which sentimentalised its characters, added in some banal emotional emphases, and gave it a thunderously romantic conclusion.) But its attitude to its subject is far from indulgent. These fashionable Anglo-American marriages had been a strong subject for late nineteenth-century novels (Lord Warburton's proposal to Isabel Archer in James's *Portrait of a Lady*, Lord Silverbridge's marriage to Isabel Boncassen in Trollope's *The Duke's Children*, which Wharton was rereading in February 1935), but *The Buccaneers* was an undoing, not a rewriting, of a nineteenth-century genre, brutally exposing the morality on both sides of these marriage bargains. Like much of her work in her seventies, it was a returning. But, like 'Roman Fever', it was a self-concealing dramatisation of a lifelong preoccupation, how the social regulations of her parents' generation doomed the next generation of American women to traps which they either struggled out of or succumbed to – and how painfully and slowly any radical change begins to alter a social organism. Under the ironic, worldly surface of the novel is a dark retrospect on the spoiling of her own young life through a 'good' marriage.[8]

As she had often done before – once upon a time to shocking effect – she drew on case-histories that were well known to her. The novel centres on four attractive young girls from the Americas – Virginia and Nan St George, Conchita Closson and Lizzie Emsworth – guided by a remarkable Anglo-Italian governess, Laura Testvalley, into making spectacular English marriages, three of them, more or less unhappily, into the aristocracy, one, much more satisfactorily, to a wealthy, rising young Conservative MP. Wharton knew several of the American women who had made such matches, and their stories took her back to the time of her entry into society and her early married life. We do not know whether Pussy Jones went to Alva and William K. Vanderbilt's famously extravagant fancy-dress ball in 1883 (the year she 'came out' at the Patriarchs' Ball), where a Virginia reel was danced and Mrs Paran Stevens, who had recently passed up the chance of being Edith's mother-in-law, appeared as Queen Elizabeth. (Wharton never mentions this famous occasion in any reminiscence; but she would certainly have heard all about it, even if she was not present.) She was all too familiar with the assembly balls, the equivalent of a 'court' in New

York, so exclusive in the 1870s that her fictional 'buccaneers' have to cheat their way in disguised as English aristocrats.

She was ten years into her own marriage, unwell and depressed, in 1895, when Alva Vanderbilt's beautiful daughter Consuelo was forced by her mother into an enormously publicised New York marriage with the 9th Duke of Marlborough. Wharton made use of such society marriages in *The House of Mirth* and *The Custom of the Country*. She knew the man whom Consuelo was really in love with, Winthrop Rutherfurd: he and his sisters had been Wharton's neighbours at Newport, and she had a childhood crush on him. Anna Bahlmann – whose figure stands shadowily behind Laura Testvalley in the novel – had been his sisters' governess. Consuelo described her marriage to 'Sunny' (who got $2.5 million in railroad stock for the deal) as a heartless business arrangement. His proposal, in the Gothic Room of the Marble House at Newport, took place, she said, in 'an atmosphere propitious to sacrifice. There was no need for sentiment.' The world knew 'every incident' of her engagement, and made up the rest: 'I read to my stupefaction that my garters had gold clasps studded with diamonds.' Their life at Blenheim Palace – which Consuelo found chilling and comfortless – lasted until 1920, when Consuelo obtained a divorce. The duke then married an ex-mistress of Berenson's, a Bostonian dazzler, Gladys Deacon (whom Wharton met at I Tatti) and Consuelo married a French aviator, Jacques Balsan. Wharton had known Consuelo slightly in youth, and met her again, as Mme Balsan, at Jacques-Émile Blanche's house, in 1928. In *The Buccaneers*, Nan St George's unhappy marriage to the 'Duke of Tintagel' in the enormous stately house of Longlands evokes Consuelo's life at Blenheim. (A passing reference in the novel to 'the Marlborough set' clinches the allusion.)[9]

There was an even closer parallel between another glamorous Consuelo, and Wharton's Conchita Closson, whose mother is a Brazilian divorcee and shocks the American mothers in the novel by smoking Cuban cigars in bed, and who marries a younger son of a great house, Lord Richard Marable, a gambler and a wastrel. Conchita's historical model was Consuelo Yznaga, a striking Louisianan heiress whose father was a wealthy Cuban immigrant. She married Lord Mandeville, the future Duke of Manchester, in 1876, a feckless philanderer who squandered her money; she stayed with him, but pleased herself, entertained on a huge scale, and went her own way. She was notorious for strumming the banjo in London drawing rooms, and for being the mistress of the Prince of Wales (and possibly also of William K. Vanderbilt, Consuelo Marlborough's father). These were two of the most famous and disastrous examples of many such alliances, in which the English landowning classes exchanged dollars and heirs for titles and grand houses. Between 1870 and 1914, about a hundred Americans married into the British peerage, several of them connected to Wharton. Mrs Paran Stevens's daughter Minnie Stevens (who could have been Wharton's sister-in-law) married Lord Arthur Paget, and became an unofficial marriage-broker for her compatriots. The Jerome sisters, Jennie and Leonie, whom Wharton knew in New York and Newport, married Lord Randolph Churchill and, more happily, Sir John Leslie. Adèle Grant from New York, whom Wharton used to meet at Lady St Helier's in the 1900s, married the 7th Earl of Essex. One of the most conspicuous Grace Church weddings of the 1890s was between Cornelia Bradley-Martin and Lord Craven; *Town Topics* said of it that the crowds 'would have led a stranger to believe that some great national event was taking place'. Wharton told Ned Sheldon that she used to see some of these women 'as a little girl when they were in their twenties'; later, she saw them metamorphosed into the wives of marquesses, dukes and earls in Edwardian London, and, sometimes, turning up again in Paris or the South of France, divorced and remarried. Their marriages were an excellent subject for her, flamboyant examples of her cross-cultural clashes and rich fodder for her inexhaustible study of American women's lives. She told Sheldon: 'I suppose I am the only person alive who could tell that story, & knows how to do it.'[10]

For the first part of the novel she jumped back to the 1870s, the period of *Old New York* and *The Age of Innocence* – and of *A Backward Glance* – and had fun with the bouncy, ambitious, pretty outsiders from the South and the West (more sympathetically done than in *Custom*), visiting the Fifth Avenue Hotel, realising that an address in Madison Avenue meant 'decent mediocrity', and taking the assembly balls by storm. She did her homework into what she called 'the vulgar milieu from which my young ladies are to be drawn', fact-checking with her old American friends, Gaillard, Sheldon, and – of course – Minnie. Were there races at Saratoga in the 1870s or was it still only a 'cure' (i.e. a spa) then? Would the 'same set of people have done a bathing session [at Long Beach] and then at Saratoga'? 'Please pick up as many points for me as you can on this subject', she told Minnie. Her first lively letter to Sheldon about *The Buccaneers* was written on the day of Gross's death, suggesting how much of a consolatory escapade this novel was to be for her.[11]

The anxious, competitive mothers, trying at once to protect and sell off their daughters (familiar from *The House of Mirth* and *The Custom of the Country*) make a funny start to the novel, but the setting of the Saratoga races makes it cruelly obvious that the girls' 'points' are being compared, and their marital potential assessed, exactly like horseflesh. Because the novel was unfinished, some of the characters are only sketched in: Wharton told Berenson that she was in the process of 'fattening' the scenes, as she always did. There is a promising but undeveloped marriage between Nan St George's pathetic mother and her bullying, unfaithful father, the wealthy 'Colonel', always bribing his wife into submission: 'Mrs St George did not own many jewels, but ... each one marked the date of a similar episode. Either a woman, or a business deal – something she had to be indulgent about. She liked trinkets as well as any woman, but at that moment she wished that all of hers were at the bottom of the sea.' Laura Testvalley, the independent governess with the romantic Italianate name, the 'splendid eyes' and the diplomatic manner, who comes to look after Nan, is our observation post, and through her eyes we see the weaknesses of the mothers and the inadequate education of the daughters.

Wharton also paints the charm of the American scene. When the young girls and their friends, and Conchita's poodle, and a guitar-player, all tumble out of the hotel carriage at the railway station at Saratoga to meet Miss Testvalley, in an undifferentiated 'spring torrent of muslins, sash ends and bright cheeks under swaying hat-brims', and make her guess which one is her pupil, we feel the innocent energy of these 'new' Americans. Wharton is drawing on Proust (as Lapsley observes in his pernickety afterword to the novel). In her first edition of À L'Ombre des jeunes filles en fleurs (1919), she marked two passages about the group of lovely young girls whom Marcel sees at Balbec. One is about the group as a conglomerate image of Beauty: 'Although each was of a type absolutely different from the others, they all had beauty [but] ... I had not yet individualised any of them ... The want, in my vision, of the demarcations which I should presently establish between them permeated the group with a sort of shimmering harmony ...' The other develops his idea of the undifferentiated group: 'Like those primitive organisms in which the individual barely exists by itself, is constituted by the polypary rather than by each of the polyps that compose it, they were still pressed one against another.' Like Proust, she gives a pictorial sense of the 'shimmering harmony' of the group; and she is interested in how a social organism develops. And she wants to evoke the national identity of these girls, whom marriage will split apart but who always retain a sense of community. As usual, her American subject is treated with a good deal of French style.[12]

Wharton gets her American girls quickly to England, by having Conchita marry into the Brightlingsea family. The girls make headway in English high society more easily than in old New York, but the room for cultural misunderstandings is huge. The English section of the book, by far the largest part of what was completed, expressed Wharton's long affection for the country. But, with the energy and high spirits of a much younger writer, it also makes a full-blooded satire on its ruling classes. Apart from her juvenile novel *Fast and Loose* and her war-story 'The Refugees', this was the first time she had sunk her teeth into English country-house life, which she had first experienced over thirty years before, and had come so close to choosing for herself before the war.

Nan St George, who unlike the other American girls has a poetic interest in the history of England (the only convincing explanation for her marriage to the unappealing duke), expresses Wharton's Anglophile enthusiasms. She is enchanted by the ruins of the castle at Tintagel, legendary setting for King Arthur's court, rising out of the mist, or by an idyllic Thames-side cottage at Runnymede (where Magna Carta was sealed), which seems to Nan 'a fairy galleon making, all sails set, for the river'. Nan's feelings for England are most aroused by 'Honourslove', ancestral Cotswold seat of Guy Thwarte (with whom she will fall in love), closely based on Stanway, where Wharton's visits in the 1930s were so charged with nostalgic memories.

> The irregular silver-grey building, when approached from the village by a drive winding under ancient beech-trees, seemed, like so many old dwellings in England, to lie almost in a hollow, screened to the north by hanging woods, and surveying from its many windows only its own lawns and trees; but the terrace on the other front overlooked an immensity of hill and vale, with huddled village roofs and floating spires ... to the two men strolling up and down before the house long familiarity made every fold of the landscape visible.[13]

Even the more forbidding stately home of 'Longlands' (a mixture of Longleat, Castle Howard and Blenheim) has its attractions. Like Undine grudgingly recognising the virtue of traditions in the French chateau she hates, the more susceptible Nan, once transformed into Lady Annabel Tintagel, is struck by the advantages of having house-rules: 'In spite of her desperate sense of being trapped, Annabel felt in a confused way that the business of living was conducted more wisely at Longlands.' But though Wharton, like her character, has a passion for the houses which nurtured the privileged classes, she is scathing about the limitations of that class. Her critique of Englishness was nothing new, as in this letter to Berenson of 1918 about Samuel Butler's notebooks: 'The love of rather trivial paradox so ingrained in the British mind is very like a genteel survival of the horse-play & the dodging in at windows & under furniture of the old farce &

pantomime ... It isn't *grown up*, any of it.'[14] The tone is echoed in her impatient remarks in the 1930s about the unintellectual pastimes at Stanway, and about Lady Wemyss's intellectual limitations in old age: 'If anything were ever needed to teach me to value the precious gift of *la vie intérieure*', she wrote harshly of her in 1936, 'it is the old age of some of my English great lady friends, with minds unfurnished by anything less concrete than the Grand National!'[15] (Even so, Lady Wemyss's death in 1937 was a great blow to her.) For all her romantic feelings for English traditions, and her many personal friendships in the country (all politely recalled in A *Backward Glance*) she cast a cold eye here, as if breaking out from the good manners of her memoir, on the English upper classes' bigotry, dullness, immorality, and breathtaking insularity.[16]

The Marquess of Brightlingsea (pronounced Brittlesey, as the snobbish Americans anxiously inform each other) exists in a universe which was 'a brilliantly illuminated circle extending from himself at its centre to the exact limit of his occupations and interests'. He cannot remember most of his own life, let alone show an interest in anyone else's. (A nice comic sub-plot concerns the Anglicised American woman Jacky Marsh, who failed to catch Lord Brightlingsea years ago, but has stayed on in England and made herself a useful companion and mentor to the next generation of American 'buccaneers'. Lord Brightlingsea, however, can never remember who she is.) His wife 'could not imagine why any one should ever want to leave England, and her idea of the continent was one enormous fog from which two places called Paris and Rome indistinctly emerged; while the whole western hemisphere was little more clear to her than to the fore-runners of Columbus'. Her first entry into the novel is the telegram she sends on hearing of her son's engagement to Conchita Closson. It reads: 'Is she black his anguished mother Selina Brightlingsea.' There are plenty of these kinds of jokes about the English aristocracy's xenophobia, meant to amuse Wharton's American readers. To Lady Brightlingsea all Americans are indistinguishable: 'I can never remember any of their names. I don't see how they can tell each other apart, all herded together, without any titles or distinctions.' She and her kind are shocked at the Spanish dances and 'Negro songs' brought in by the high-spirited young Americans, and they think the Virginia reel danced at the Christmas ball at Longlands is a 'wild Indian war-dance'. Against that New World vigour is set the horrible sexual repression of the old English families: Ushant, the Duke of Tintagel, would rather mend clocks than deal with women, and his idea of marital relations, inherited from his forebears, is to force himself on an unwilling young spouse in order to propagate the ancestral line.

American 'savagery' is seen by the narrator as a healthy mixture of innocence and openness. The native loyalties of the American girls are set
against the decadent wiles of their English rivals: there is a strong scene
at Runnymede where Virginia St George, backed by the other girls, does
battle over Lord Seadown with his corrupt, venomous English mistress,
Lady Churt. The mixed blood – Spanish, Brazilian, possibly Negro – of
the newcomers is preferred to that of the inbred English upper classes. The
best of these have foreign links and interests. Guy Thwarte (like Martin
Boyne) has spent years in Brazil, and was briefly married to a Brazilian
girl, who died. He finds it very difficult to 'fit himself into his place in
the old scheme of things'. The only admirable aristocratic family is the
easy-going, active household of Lady Glenloe (with a touch of Mary
Hunter), where Annabel takes refuge, and where they are all intrepid
world-travellers, interested in everything new. In these characterisations
of a nation's ruling classes, Wharton, by implication, justified her own life
of cultural travels and comparisons. She was fond of a famous line of
Kipling's (who had his own quarrels with the English establishment), from
'The English Flag' (1891): 'And what should they know of England who
only England know?' Wharton quoted it in her 1936 tribute to Bourget,
and in *The Writing of Fiction*, where she said that it could be 'the symbolic
watchword of the creative artist'.

The Buccaneers has rightly been called 'a comedy of assimilation'. We
want success for what Jacky Churt calls the 'new kind of marauders, social
aliens though they were'. (The book Wharton stole her title from, and
which was in her library at Ste-Claire, John Esquemeling's *The Buccaneers
of America*, a seventeenth-century Dutch account of English and French
pirates marauding the coast of the West Indies, had an introduction by
Andrew Lang who said that these romantic Robin Hoods of the waters
were in reality 'hideously ruthless miscreants'. But Wharton likes the idea
of a later generation of female American pirates raiding the English.) There
is no desire, though, for England to become a republic. The conflict is
summed up in a letter written by Guy's rakish, cynical father, Sir Helmsley
Thwarte, who is violently anti-American but sees the attractions of the
'strange beings' from the New World. He thinks that 'having been afflicted
with Dukes, we'd better keep 'em'. Wharton agrees: but the dukes need to
be roused up and to mix their blood. Her idea of the value of raw American
vigour for the old world has shifted since Undine's grotesque failure in
France. *The Buccaneers* is like *The Children* in its sympathies for adventurous youthful energy, up against traditional elitism.[17]

Annabel Tintagel and Laura Testvalley carry most of these ideas, and they jostle for our attention. The plan for the novel was that Sir Helmsley would fall in love with Laura but that she would sacrifice this opportunity in order to help Nan run off with Guy Thwarte. Laura's fiery Italian ancestry, her '*risorgimento*' spirit and her romantic links to Dante Gabriel Rossetti, make for a promising heroine. Perhaps Wharton's halting progress with the book and her remarks to herself about being in the middle of the Gobi desert while writing it, were due to authorial indecision about which heroine should dominate, as well as to failing health. The last chapters Wharton wrote set Laura aside and give more attention to Nan's predicament: her democratic revolt against Tintagel's hierarchical assumptions, her self-alienation, her puritan horror of old-world corruption. Nan's last appearance, and almost the novel's last scene, after a tender encounter with Guy, brings in a note of sad longing, and makes a haunting end to Wharton's novel-writing:

> In this great lonely desert of life stretching out before her she had a friend – a friend who understood not only all she said, but everything she could not say. At the end of the long road on which the regular rap of the horses' feet was beating out the hours, she saw him standing, waiting for her, watching for her through the night.[18]

The Buccaneers is a typically theatrical novel, full of dramatic scenes – the arrival of the governess, the ball at the great house, the gamble between the rivals at Runnymede. That Wharton was writing to Ned Sheldon about the novel and getting encouragement from him ('I want to see Nan settle happily at Honourslove', he wrote) suggests that she was thinking about the possibility of a theatrical adaptation. Sheldon was her link to the theatre; she wrote to him about the need for accuracy in the stage-play of *The Age of Innocence* in 1928, or about her ideas for future dramas, like the Lizzie Borden case. (Their shared passion for crime-novels fitted in with their interest in drama: he told her in 1935 that he was looking forward to 'Confession' 'both as a Wharton & a murder fan'. In the end her version of the Lizzie Borden case did not make a play, but what *Cosmopolitan* magazine, in 1935, called 'a novelette'.) He forwarded to her the news of how her plays were doing in America – the run of *The Old Maid* in 1935, the adaptation of *Ethan Frome* by Owen and Donald Davis in 1936. (As she had with *The Age of Innocence*, Wharton complained about the 'modern slang' – like 'crush' and 'whatever' – they had introduced.) Sheldon had Ruth Draper read aloud to him an early version of the play, to check the dialogue ('the way she did Zeena [Zenobia] was marvellous', he told Edith) and he persuaded Ruth Gordon to play Mattie, which she did brilliantly.

They both enjoyed Ruth Gordon's telegram about the dress-rehearsal: 'FIRST REHEARSAL WITH SCENERY VERY VERY GOOD . . . PICKLE DISH BROKE ON RAYMOND [MASSEY]S FOOT AND FOR A WHILE THERE I THOUGHT WED HAVE TO PLAY IT LIKE RAYS FOOT WAS BROKEN INSTEAD OF THE DISH THE SLED GOES DOWN A 25 FOOT DROP AND IS THE MOST FUN OF ANY RIDE I EVER TOOK.' Wharton had been anxious that the play would not do well in New York, 'where people are still afraid of tragedy'. (That was certainly true of Hollywood, where discussions about making a film of *Ethan Frome* always foundered on its 'tragic ending and bitter quality'.) But the reviews of *Ethan Frome* at the New York National Theatre in 1936 (with Pauline Lord as Zeena) confirmed Gordon's enthusiasm: they praised the adaptation, the acting and the set, and were moved by the tragedy. There was an excited account of how the backstage machinery worked to move from the Frome kitchen out to the village, and how the sled-ride was managed: 'The sled actually goes downhill at a speed that would carry it straight into the wall of the playhouse; that catastrophe is prevented by a couple of husky stagehands waiting to catch it at the bottom.' The original was referred to with deferential respect, as though speaking of a monument: 'Mrs Wharton would be grateful for the splendid gifts the theatre has laid at the feet of her masterpiece.' Mrs Wharton, for her part, was touched that the play had given *Ethan Frome* a new lease of life.[19]

Zoë Akins's adaptation of *The Old Maid*, meanwhile, was doing well on the road in America, touring under Howard Moss's management in 1936, far away from its original author, through 'Salt Lake City, Sacramento, Los Angeles, San Diego, Phoenix, Tucson, Austin, Waco, Denton, Fort Worth, Dallas, Oklahoma, Tulsa, Little Rock, Memphis', with a 'Holy Week Layoff', and ending up in Washington. She took a keen interest in these dramatisations, since their 'fruitful rounds' sent a 'regular click of coins into my savings-box'. Minnie was still acting as her representative in all 'theatrical and cinematographic matters', and she took 50 per cent of Wharton's slice of *The Old Maid*'s box-office returns (over $700 dollars in May and June of 1935). But, though it had a motion picture contract with Paramount in 1935 (the film would star Bette Davis), the play was a disaster in London in 1936, under Hugh ['Binkie'] Beaumont's management, with Lilian Gish as Charlotte Lovell. The American theatre agent, Alice Krauser, who dealt with Wharton's dramatisations, forwarded her a telegram from London in April 1936: 'CAST IN GENERAL BAD PRODUCTION HOPELESS GISH INTER-ESTING WITH EXCITING MOMENTS PLAY CLOSED INDEFINITELY POSTPONED.' Wharton thanked her for her frankness: 'I have reached a philosophic age, & prefer to know exactly what is happening.' She was not entirely surprised: 'perhaps', she thought, it was 'owing to the unfamiliarity of the atmosphere'.²⁰

The Depression-era drop in her earnings in the Depression years (which were beginning to pick up again in 1935) and the shift in her reputation, had made her all too aware of the remoteness of her subjects and 'atmosphere' from contemporary audiences. Inevitably, she was being asked now for introductions and forewords to reissues of her work. She wrote several times about *Ethan Frome*, once in 1922 for the third American edition, once for *Colophon* in 1932 (an essay reprinted in 1937 in a collection called *Breaking into Print*), once in *A Backward Glance* and finally in her 1936 preface to the play-text. In most of these accounts she recalled starting it in the Rue de Varenne as an exercise in writing French, firmly repudiated accusations that she knew nothing about its setting, spoke about the structure of the novel and said that she had been concerned to bring more realism to bear on fiction about New England.

The other work she often returned to was *The House of Mirth*. Oxford University Press asked to reissue it in 1936 as a World's Classic (she wished they had chosen *Ethan Frome* instead, or *The Custom of the Country* which she told them was 'a much better book'). In her preface to this edition, she said that to go back to the New York of this novel 'seems like going back to the Pharaohs'. It was as hard now as it would be for a 'French novelist of manners' whose work spanned the period from the execution of Louis XVI to the Battle of Waterloo, to make an audience imagine the world before those cataclysms. She was amused to think of how the novel shocked its first readers. But, though 'everything dates in a work of art, and should do so', what survives is 'whatever of unchanging human nature the novelist has contrived to bring to life beneath the passing fripperies of clothes and custom'. In a rare interview given in November 1936 (in the Hôtel Crillon) to the Paris edition of the *New York Herald Tribune*, in which the interviewer was struck by 'her vigour and sharp concision of speech', she was wry about the shifts in her reputation, speaking dismissively about 'this violets and old lace affair'. 'It is startling to find that phrase creeping into a review of my latest book of short stories . . . since most of them deal with grim subjects, including suicide and murder. I was once called, you know, a "revolutionary writer". Critics then talked about my "audacious treatment of unpleasant themes".' In a preface written in 1937 for Appleton's collection of her ghost-stories (all but one of which were reprints), published soon after her death, she dwelt on the differences between her earlier audiences, who still seemed to have 'the ghost-instinct', and her modern readers, who were having their imaginations 'atrophied' by 'the wireless and the cinema'. She paid tribute to her competitors in the field – Henry James, Stevenson, Le Fanu, Walter de la Mare – and disclosed the secret of the writing of ghost-stories, that the teller of the tale should be 'well frightened in the telling'.[21]

Haunting her own past, she wrote unpublished pieces on returns to Italy ('Italy Again', written in October 1934), with a note on 'how circumscribed our lives would be if the accumulated past were not there to feed upon', and Spain ('Back to Compostella'), remembering the time when tourist guides had not yet told us how to get to places that had 'almost vanished from the map'. A long tribute to Bourget (written in 1936 for René Doumic's *Revue des Deux Mondes*, but published instead in the *Revue Hebdomadaire* after Doumic dared to suggest some unwelcome cuts) dwelt on their travels in Italy. She praised his internationalism, lamented his increasing rigidity of habits, confessed that she had never much liked his novels, even though 'we both saw the irony and sadness of the human lot in the same way', and cited him as an example of how best to know one's own country (much in her mind during the writing of *A Backward Glance* and *The Buccaneers*): 'It is only in seeing other countries, in studying their customs, reading their books, associating with their inhabitants, that one can situate one's own country in the history of civilization.'

She was fond, at this stage of her life, of making such generalisations, well-earned through long years of experience. In her conversations with Steven Runciman, she more than once told him that 'novels are about development of character, short stories are about incident'. A letter of 1936 to Mme Clara Chambron (a Parisianised American from an old Cincinnati family, whose husband commanded the French artillery forces at Rabat in 1917) provides a good example of this late tone. Mme Chambron dabbled in letters, and had written a romantic fictional life of Shakespeare called 'My Shakespeare, Rise!' (1934), full of sentences like: 'As a writer Will was not much given to biting his pen.' Wharton politely turned the gift of this book into an opportunity to talk about the challenge of historical fiction – as usual, without explicitly mentioning her own work. She advised her friend 'not to let a bit of the historic skeleton peep through the live flesh-and-blood of the story', adding: 'It requires a great hold on one's characters to keep them alive and active.'[22]

In these late returns to her past and to her literary experience, Wharton reprised her memories of childhood and youth ever more nostalgically. The last of these writings, a pendant to *A Backward Glance*, was 'A Little Girl's New York', written early in 1937 but not published till a year after her death. Her motive for writing this last, vivid account of old New York, which lingers over every detail of the rooms, furnishings, customs and past-times of her childhood, was that the 'convulsions, social and political' since she wrote her memoir in 1934 had made the period of her childhood seem even more remote. All the 'little incidents, habits, traditions, which when I began to record my past seemed too insignificant to set down, have acquired the historical importance of fragments of dress and furniture dug up in a Babylonian tomb'. The phrase recalls, from very long ago, Ellen Olenska gazing sadly at the relics of a vanished civilisation in the Metropolitan Museum, and thinking how sad that things which used to be 'important to forgotten people' are now labelled 'Use unknown'. The word 'important' echoes into 'A Little Girl's New York', as though Wharton is claiming for herself her own importance for posterity, if for nothing else, as archaeologist and analyst of a vanished society. She ended the memoir with a poignant quotation from one of her old favourites, Robert Louis Stevenson, a rhyme from *A Child's Garden of Verses*: 'Yet as I saw it, I see it again, / The kirk and the palace, the ships and the men, / And as long as I live, and where'er I may be, / I'll always remember my town by the sea.' The ships in her own childhood town, she says at the end of the essay, were her books, 'ready to spread their dream-sails to all the winds of my imagination'.[23]

The social and political 'convulsions' between the publication of *A Backward Glance* in 1934 and the writing of 'A Little Girl's New York' four years later, pressed in on the protected spaces of Wharton's French homes. Sitting alone in Ste-Claire in February 1934, she was appalled to hear on her wireless shocking news coming through (in censored form) about the violent riots in Paris. She wrote in her diary: 'It is depressing alone here with these sombre events going on ... My solitude weighs on me.' She turned down, yet again, Columbia's invitation to honour her, because, she told Minnie, she didn't want to leave her properties – 'I feel about my houses as a crab must about its carapace' – and there might be a civil war. 'In the circumstances ... I would rather be in France.' She was not over-reacting. One of the Third Republic's many shortlived inter-war governments fell in January 1934. The general loathing of politicians and the long-running hostilities between France's extreme right-wingers, with links to Nazism and fascism, and the communists and socialists, came to a crisis with the revel-ation of links between the government and the criminal Serge Stavisky, who was assassinated (or committed suicide). On 6 February 1934, fascistic *Croix de Feu* supporters and other right-wing groups marched on the French Assembly, while the communists grouped in the Champs-Élysées. The police fired on the crowd in the Place de la Concorde, and many were killed or wounded. Daladier, the new Prime Minister, resigned, a right-wing *coup d'état* was feared, there were mass marches against fascism by left-wingers, a general strike, and the formation of the Popular Front, which would come to power under the socialist Léon Blum after a bitterly fought election early in 1936. The economy was in a disastrous state, there were frequent strikes and sit-ins, rearmament was lagging, the army was under-budgeted and ill-prepared, and the threat of Hitler (who occupied the Rhineland in March 1936 and was building up his munitions and his air force) was not being adequately recognised or met. The riots of 1934 presaged France's disunity and weakness in the face of the Nazi–Soviet pact in 1939.[24]

Her sympathies were with the right and against the 'Bolsheviks': at the start of the Spanish revolution she wrote to Gaillard: 'I see Spain has gone red! What a world!' To Mildred Bliss, in November 1936, she said that she was reading and admiring André Tardieu's *Souverain Captif*, a conservative analysis of France's 'internal maladies'. Tardieu prophesied the end of the world as he knew it within two or three years. 'At the rate at which events are moving', Wharton commented, 'the whole of Western Europe may be Sovietized' before that. 'It's a pity.' Of the Paris riots, she exclaimed to Minnie that 'the Commune was upon us again'. But the days were gone when she joked to the passionately anti-fascist Berenson (who called Italy 'Mussolinia') about Mussolini making the trains run on time. While she was in Rome in 1934, she turned her favourite image for adverse circumstances, the Furies, into fascist blackshirts. 'There must be a new head to the Furies' Bureau, for the little things, always so active and milling, now seem to me much more prompt and consecutive in their action; as though black shirts encased their meagre but lively frames, and "Giovinezza" echoed through their infernal assemblages.' Though she had been appalled in 1932 to hear about the kidnapping of the Lindbergh baby, her hopes for American politics were higher than they had been for a long time, with the inauguration of Franklin D. Roosevelt and the start of the New Deal. She wrote to Minnie in March 1933, showing a surprising interest in Prohibition: 'It really looks from this distance as if Franklin Roosevelt were the man we needed. At any rate the bank clean-up is all to the good! May he get beer licensed at once, & then I shall feel we are on the upgrade again . . . How does it feel to have a *man* at the helm at last?' But in Europe all was ominous; unlike in 1914, they all saw what was coming. After the Night of the Long Knives at the end of June 1934, when Hitler had all his rivals in the Nazi Party assassinated, Berenson wrote to her about the 'Machiavellian' actions of the 'Hitler gang'. Louis Gillet sent her a report of the Nuremberg Rally in 1934, 'like a vision of Antichrist, a scene from the Apocalypse'. Elisina gave her 'Hitler' (presumably *Mein Kampf*) to read, that summer; she told her she wouldn't spoil the trips she was making from the Pavillon with the Nicholsons by reading it and would save it until her guests had left: 'Hitler would seem a blasphemy against all this beauty.' Even England seemed unsettled. In January 1936, she wrote to Lady Wemyss that they were all very 'sad at the death of your King [George V]', and were wondering 'what his successor is going to be . . . What a terrible ordeal to find oneself in twenty-four hours transformed from a gay prince to a grave monarch at such a momentous hour of history! . . . I wish his father could have lived a few years longer, until the world had got into less troubled waters.'[25]

'I don't think this world gloom agrees with me', she told Elisina in March 1936, as though politics were a poison. At home, there was her own ill-health to do battle with. After 1929, she had regular bouts of 'flu (or 'grippe'), high blood pressure, dizziness, weakness and exhaustion. Her heart palpitations greatly increased her risk of a stroke. In May 1934 she had a serious attack of 'flu while in Rome. On 24 January 1935 she recorded a dismal seventy-third birthday, 'in bed with 'flu'. On 11 April 1935 she had a mild stroke ('Taken suddenly ill – "troubles de la circulation"', she noted) involving some loss of sight. Elisina came to look after her, and she made a slow recovery through May and June, telling Kenneth Clark that her eyes were getting slowly better but that 'no fatigue' was the *'mot d'ordre'*. Jeanne Fridérich sent reports to all friends. She explained that Mme Wharton had had *'une brusque crise d'hypertension artérielle* [a sudden crisis of high blood pressure] *provoquée, d'après son docteur, par un excés d'activité dans son jardin et trops d'escalades de rochers'*. And, added the doctor, as well as too much clambering over rocks, there had been too many visits from friends, too much literary work, and too many attacks of 'flu. But the secretary assured one and all that *'Mme Wharton est très raisonnable, et fait tout ce que le docteur lui ordonne'*. Elisina told Berenson that Edith was being treated with 'hypodermic injections' and a 'vegetarian diet (a grievance)' – red meat was thought to raise blood pressure. She would note, just over a year later, that according to the oculist and the doctor, Edith's *'spasme artérielle'* had 'restricted the field of vision of the left eye [and that] each time she suffers a recurrence the field of vision grows less'.[26]

Amazingly, though, Edith rallied her energies a few months later for a family crisis, and responded to one last call on her managerial skills. The inexhaustible Minnie Jones was now eighty-four, and right up till that year had continued to act as agent for her sister-in-law's American film and theatre contracts, to fact-check and research for her and to keep her up-to-date with all their old American contacts. Edith used to call her 'my valued assistant-in-law'. Their allegiance, which had begun in 1871, was sturdy, practical, and unwavering. They exchanged views on old age; Edith told her: 'As long as I love books & flowers & travel – & my friends – *and* good food, as much as I do now, I want no allowances made for me!' On Minnie's eightieth birthday in 1930, Edith told her that she had only ever had one criticism of her:

> When I was 7 years old, & you, I conjecture, 19 (& newly married), I one day . . . entrusted you with the care of my pet rabbit – & you forgot him in the park, & went home to lunch without him! This incident . . . is the only blot that, after a microscopic scrutiny of the ensuing sixty years, I am able to discover in your perfect record as sister-in-law, friend & comrade.

But Minnie was in poor health, with heart problems and emphysema, and could be exhausting company; Edith told John Hugh that she was rather dreading her visit to the Pavillon in 1935. The two splendid old ladies spent a quiet fortnight together, and Minnie went on to England, where she developed pneumonia, and died, in a hotel in London, on 22 September. Beatrix and Max were in America; it was quicker for Edith to get there. She rushed over, too quickly to get a travel-visa, on the day of Minnie's death; a note from the American Embassy to the 'Landing Authorities at Dover' expedited her way: 'The celebrated American authoress, Mrs Edith Wharton, has suddenly been called to England by the serious illness of her sister which it is feared may be mortal. Her visa has expired and it being Sunday she is unable to get it renewed. Mrs Wharton is well known to the Embassy who will be grateful if the authorities will facilitate her landing in England.' Once in London, she organised everything, with help from Lily Norton, Eric MacLagen, and Mrs Humphry Ward's daughter Dorothy, including the disinfecting of the hotel room, the securing of Minnie's trunks, the paying-off of Minnie's faithful old maid, Murkett, and the arrangements for her funeral. Full reports were dashed off to Trix, who was on her way over. Edith told Trix that 'I should not grieve at her dying now if only it had happened in my house, and not alone in a Hotel. It was far better for her to go before her faculties were dimmed.' They agreed that Minnie should not be transported back to America – 'like me' (Edith told Berenson) 'she had a horror of dead bodies carried from one end of the world to the other'. She was buried in the churchyard at Aldbury, near the grave of their mutual friend Mrs Ward, in the village where Edith had spent her lonely weeks at the beginning of the war. After doing all this, Edith retired to St-Brice, completely exhausted. The memorial service for Minnie took place in New York on 12 December 1935, which would have been her eighty-fifth birthday. In his address, Royal Cortissoz imagined Minnie saying to him, with her usual smile, 'Don't moralise, my friend. Don't tell them how good I was. Tell them of my common sense and my humour, and tell them how I liked life.' The family published her unfinished memoirs, *Lantern Slides*, which Edith agreed to introduce; but when it came to publication, in 1937, she was too ill to write, and all that was found was a pencilled note about Minnie's prose style, nicely turning her slow speed of writing into a virtue: 'She has such a love of our English speech, such a sense of its rhythmic beauty, that she is forever trying to keep step with it as she goes on; and the attempt is not a labour, but an enchantment.' This pencilled note was her last gift to Minnie, and she had told Trix that she wanted nothing in return, 'except the memory of all she did for me'.[27]

She continued to travel, to garden, to host visitors, and to write. Not for nothing did Berenson lovingly address her as 'O Vigorosa!' 'I'm an incorrigible life-lover', she told the very depressed Mary Berenson in October 1936. She saw her income begin to rise again ($130,000 in 1936), mainly from the plays. All the while, she was plagued by illness. Through 1936 and early 1937 she reported to her diary on dizzy spells, or on being 'in bed, much bored' in March 1937. She told Berenson in April 1937 that she was having repeated attacks of 'flu. The disposition of her affairs preyed on her mind. She listed the arrangements she wanted for her funeral and burial in a document addressed to Elisina and dated 23 May 1936. In December 1936, she revised the American will she had made in 1929, had it ratified by the US Consulate in Nice in March 1937, and sent the papers to her American bank, the Chase National in New York. (For the purposes of avoiding French taxes, she told Beatrix in 1929 that 'it is advisable not to mention this will in winding up my affairs in France'.) She kept another will, 'disposing of my property in France', always with her, either in the 'chiffonnier' of her bedroom at Ste-Claire or at St-Brice, and altered it, under Elisina's supervision, in June 1937. These wills would lead to a great deal of trouble after her death.[28]

In these months of declining health, while she was continuing to work on *The Buccaneers*, Wharton wrote a remarkable story. She noted in her diary on 20 January 1937 that she had finished 'Weekend', and told Elisina that it was a 'preliminary canter' before getting back to *The Buccaneers*. It was sent off to Pinker, with the title 'All Souls'', in February, and was published, posthumously, in her last collection, *Ghosts*. The title was a private reference to her long annual habit of sitting alone, remembering her dead, as in Yeats's poem, 'All Souls' Night': 'And it is All Souls' Night ... A ghost may come / For it is a ghost's right.' But whereas in Wharton's own life these vigils were consolatory, the story is one of pain, loneliness, and terror. Her long-vanished life at The Mount, the loss of her dear old servants, her dread of helplessness in old age, her experiences of solitude and illness, her horror at what was happening in the world, and, deepest down, what she never spoke of, her fear of death, are all felt in this last story. But, as ever, it works not as personal confession, but as a tightly constructed, perfectly controlled tale.[29]

'All Souls" is not exactly a ghost-story but has a traditional ghost-story structure. A narrator (ungendered, but evidently a woman, since she keeps a maid not a manservant) pieces together the story from the accounts given by her older cousin Sara Clayburn, who must (it is implied) by now be dead, since the narrator has been left with her story. She wants to give as clear a version as possible of what happened to her cousin, since so many 'ridiculously inaccurate' accounts of it have got into circulation – like a biographer trying to do justice to a subject who can no longer speak for herself. As the story gets underway, the cousin 'effaces' herself (like all the best ghost-story 'frame' narrators), to return at the end as witness, audience, and recorder.

In a return to the landscape of America Wharton had known so well, and used so powerfully in *Ethan Frome*, and other stories, she places her character in an isolated house in Connecticut. Unlike The Mount, 'Whitegates' is an eighteenth-century house with modern additions, a model of sensible, restrained good taste. Its owner, the widowed Mrs Clayburn, acts out the managerial, housekeeperish, bossy side of Wharton. She is practical, assertive, energetic, impatient, used to giving orders and having her way. She is unimaginative (she never reads poetry) and non-religious (her cousin knows the Church dates better than she does), the last person likely to believe in any supernatural happenings.

Whitegates is unusual, in the modern days in which the story is very explicitly and deliberately set, in having retained the services of its old staff, whom Mrs Clayburn inherited from her mother-in-law: a butler, Agnes the old Scottish housekeeper, a housemaid and a junior maid, a chauffeur and a gardener. The story begins on a snowy evening on the last day of October, when Mrs Clayburn meets a strange woman with a pale face and a 'foreign' accent coming up to the house, and immediately afterwards slips on the ice and breaks her ankle. Confined to her room, and told by her doctor not to put weight on her foot, settled down (with unusually tender care) by her trusty Scottish servant, she spends a painful and restless night.

In the morning, she gradually realises that the house, sealed in by the snow, is completely empty, and growing terribly cold. In a residence 'admirably equipped ... with every practical appliance', the electricity, the central heating and the telephone have all shut off. The radiators are icy. The servants are nowhere to be found and their beds have not been slept in. Something strange and terrifying – she has no idea what – has happened. 'Who was at work downstairs, isolating her thus from the world?' As she crawls her way down through the house, helpless, injured, and terrified, she feels that the empty house and its 'cold unanswering silence' have become sentient and hostile, that the house 'was watching her as she was watching it', and that the silence is stalking her: 'She seemed to feel its steps just behind her, softly keeping time with hers.' Finally, after an interminable journey through the empty house, she gets to the kitchen, where the silence is broken, out of sight, by 'a man's voice, low and emphatic ... passion-ately earnest, almost threatening ... speaking in a foreign language, a language unknown to her'. It is a voice coming from that most ordinary and modern of appliances, a 'portable wireless'.

A gap of unconsciousness, like a dotted line, follows, and we cut to the Monday morning, with the arrival of a new doctor (her own, who could be a witness to the timing of the events, has been called away) and the 'X-ray' machine. The servants are there, pretending that nothing has happened. The house is as warm and comfortable as usual. The cousin (who seems to have no life of her own) comes to keep her company while the ankle slowly mends, and gradually the 'lost weekend' recedes. But exactly a year later, the narrator finds an ashen Mrs Clayburn on her New York doorstep. She had fled (by hired car) from her house, having encountered the same strange woman going towards it. This time she has challenged her, and the woman laughed at her – and disappeared. And Mrs Clayburn never goes home again.

The narrator advances various theories about what has happened, all less interesting and alarming than the unexplained events themselves. Everyone knows that the dead walk on All Souls' Eve, and the strange woman was a ghost, or 'fetch', or perhaps a witch, come to lure the house-keeper (who after all comes from the Hebrides, where ghosts are plentiful) and the other servants to a witches' 'coven'. These spooky readings put the story in company with Wharton's other tales of haunted houses or returns from the dead, like 'Afterward' or 'Mr Jones' or 'Pomegranate Seed', or with her sinister, Hawthorne-influenced New England tales like 'Bewitched'. But the ghostly conclusion to the story is not where its impact lies.

It would be easy, especially for readers in 1938, to find the subject trivial.

A wealthy American house-owner, used to relying on a large, old-fashioned staff of servants, hurts her ankle and has to fend for herself for two nights: not much of a horror-story! What overrides that reaction is the powerful sense of rising panic in the story. Its old-fashioned social assumptions are X-rayed by a white light of alienating disruption. (It could almost have been written by Elizabeth Bowen.) The house takes on its own inimical life, the silence is actively confining: the woman, as her surname implies, is buried alive in her own tomb. And the only sound that comes through is the 'foreign', threatening voice of the man on the radio. It is a story about the terror of death. But it also suggests that, even in the isolated, insulated American house, the voice of Hitler is making itself heard, more frightening than any ghost. It was a voice which Edith Wharton (just like Virginia Woolf in England) had been listening to, aghast: 'all angry screams of accusation of cowardice against anyone who loves peace & beauty better than a general massacre'.[30]

Mrs Clayburn repeatedly says that she is not brave, but the story is about stoic resolution and courage, as well as fear. Edith Wharton continued to show those qualities in the last months of her life. In April, at Ste-Claire, while planning a trip to I Tatti, her aged Pekingese dog, Linky, who had been her pet for over eleven years, suddenly sickened. She wrote in her diary for 11 April: 'Dear little Linky suddenly taken ill. I feel ill too.' In her own state of weakness, her reaction to the dog's death was severe. 'Now, for the first time, literally, I am faced with real loneliness', she told Trix. 'There goes my last link with my dear past . . . Oh, what a train of ghosts will follow her burial today!' She imagined 'her little ghost wailing for me tonight beside my bed'. About a week later she received the news of Lady Wemyss's death in England. The combination of these two events, both uprooting her sense of the past, was at this moment too much for her. 'It would seem odd to most people that I would group them together', she told Bill Tyler, another dog-lover, 'but you will know & understand.' To his mother she signed herself 'Edith Agonistes'. Her line-a-day diary became uncharacteristically pathetic, and tailed off: 'Can't remember . . . Very shaky & tired . . . Gave up record for May, too tired & depressed.'[31]

A strange, almost mystical passage in her letter to Bill Tyler mused on her closeness to her dogs, like the legendary Roman boy *who understood what the birds said*. It echoed things she had said in the past about her feelings for her pets, like a note on her 'Ruling Passions' ('Justice – Order – Dogs – Books – Flowers – Architecture – Travel – a good joke – & perhaps that should have come first') and a diary entry in the mid-1920s:

I am secretly afraid of animals – of *all* animals except dogs, and even of some dogs. I think it is because of the Usness in their eyes, with the underlying *Not-Usness* which belies it, and is so tragic a reminder of the lost age when we human beings branched off and left them; left them to eternal inarticulateness and slavery. *Why?* their eyes seem to ask us.

She cancelled her trip to Italy, and wrote to Berenson, envying him a journey to Crete and remembering with thanks the beautiful things she had seen in her life. But she continued to make plans. In May, while St-Brice was being got ready for occupation, she was invited to visit Ogden Codman, her old friend, critic and collaborator, who since 1926 had been restoring and landscaping (with her advice) an exquisite seventeenth-century chateau eighteen miles south-east of Paris, Grégy-sur-Yerres. (In the war, he would have to share it with sixty German soldiers.) A new edition of their book, *The Decoration of Houses* – Wharton's first profes-sional publication – was under discussion (though it did not materialise until long after Codman's death in 1951), and they wanted to revise the introduction. So this visit was planned as a working trip, as well as a pleas-urable stop-off on the way to St-Brice. Edith and her servants arrived on Friday 28 May. She was very weak and unwell, and on Tuesday 1 June she had a heart attack, and had to be taken home to St-Brice in an ambulance with a doctor and nurses in attendance, and with her staff following behind in the car. Codman, with all his old vigour and spite, gave an appalled account of the visit to his brother:

> I feel as if a great responsibility has been removed from my shoulders. It has been no joke putting up all her people. She had her own maid, then added her secretary, then a house-maid, then a nurse, and her chauf-feur was here . . . Everyone was on the jump all the time. It was all very complicated and upsetting. Her almost last words as she left in the ambu-lance were, 'This will teach you not to ask decrepit old ladies to stay.' *I think it will!*

Edith summoned Elisina on 3 June with a telegram announcing a '*crise cardiaque*'. Elisina rushed to St-Brice and sent her reports on 6 June to Berenson and to Kenneth Clark. 'Edith had a serious heart attack . . . I found her shockingly changed in appearance, with hardly any strength left. She [has] had three fainting fits . . . It was decided to resort to artificial feeding by a new method of '*piqûres goutte à goutte*', as she was unable to retain any food. [These were subcutaneous injections of a sugar solution, the precursors of a gluco-saline drip.] Her mind is clear, though she can only utter occasional words.' To Clark she described the fits as 'very painful & frightening'.[32]

Elisina took control of the sick-room, answering letters, restricting visitors, consulting with the doctors, watching devotedly over her friend and keeping notes. The appointments Edith had noted in advance in her line-a-day diary for July and August could not be kept: 'July 29: Robert Norton to tea; July 30: Mme René [Taillandier] to lunch, Bill and Betsy arrive in evening; August 11: To lunch, Codman . . .' The Clarks came on 28 July, but Elisina would not let them see Edith. Louis Gillet also lunched there, but did not see her. A trickle of visitors – Walter Berry's sister (whom Edith disliked), Ogden Codman, Robert Norton, Gaillard Lapsley, Bessie Lodge, John Hugh Smith, Royall Tyler – went up to the bedroom, the last of these two going out weeping into the garden, as in a Victorian death-bed scene. Beatrix arrived on 21 June, but Elisina did not want her there, and thought that her visit made Edith more anxious. (She left on 3 July.) On 23 June, the doctors told Elisina that 'the heart was worn out' and that Edith had arterio-sclerosis. On 9 July they told Elisina there was no hope, and she noted 'twitching in left side, sudden drooping of the eyelid, weakness in walking a few steps' – suggesting that a stroke may have followed on from the heart attack. Through July, Edith's sight began to fail and her concentration became intermittent. She slept a great deal, could walk a few steps, and was taken out daily in her bath-chair into the garden to look at the flowers and to feed the fish in her pond, which gave her pleasure. The weather was very fine all that summer. By 26 July, she was almost blind. On 29 July, 'Peter' (Royall) Tyler reported to Robert Bliss that she was having 'trouble with vision, mind wandering, utterance thick, softening of the brain'. On 31 July, Elisina told Berenson that she had read Edith a letter from him, as Edith herself could not read; she described her to him as 'serene' but 'at times confused'. On 4 August, in trembling, barely legible handwriting, but not sounding at all confused, Edith wrote a note to Matilda Gay (Walter Gay had died on 13 July) apologising for not going to visit her. 'Elisina & my maid behaved so awfully about it that I had no alternative.' She sent her 'best love' and 'deepest sympathy', and told her she was lying under the 'mauve poppies' which Walter had given her eighteen years ago – his 1919 painting of *Poppies at the Pavillon Colombe*. It was her last letter. On 7 August, the doctors decided to bleed her (a traditional, and outdated, last resort) while Elisina sat with her. She had a stroke which left her paralysed and unconscious, and she died four days later, in her bedroom at the Pavillon Colombe, at about 5.30 p.m. on Wednesday, 11 August, 1937.[33]

From 6 June to 11 August, Elisina had kept a diary, which she wrote up and 'improved' in a typed version, which gave a tender account of her ten-week vigil with her old friend. To what extent this record of Edith in her last days was touched up, partly out of emotional involvement, partly to emphasise Edith's dependency on and gratitude to Elisina, is hard to judge. According to these notes, Edith quoted Shakespeare's lines ('I am dying, Egypt, dying'), and said 'I don't think I shall ever be well again.' She talked about her love of Balzac, her strong feelings for the Catholic Church and her dislike of Jews. She said that she and Elisina had 'hooked at once' as friends, spoke of her shyness, and described her mind as a 'steam-engine'. She dwelt on her pleasure in her garden and her sense of good fortune: 'I might just be an old woman taking the air on a bench in a public garden, with the children knocking their hoops into my skirts – and why was so much beauty given to me instead?' She reminisced about Anna Bahlmann and Doyley and her guilt about her 'naughtinesses as a child'. She said that her father, not her mother, had encouraged her 'making up' as a child and had printed her first volume of poems. She spoke more than once of Walter, of how much he helped her and how much she missed him. Without naming him, she told Elisina of a love-letter she had had from him when she was young, and of how glad she was that 'I dealt with it as I did. I should never have had his precious friendship all my life, if it had been otherwise.' She talked about Teddy and her marriage, what a 'hopeless case' it was, how Teddy thought of her writing as 'a kind of witchcraft'. She asked Elisina to go downstairs and burn Teddy's letters (which presumably she did). She talked about Henry James, remembering (or misremembering) his last cogent words: 'He is coming at last, the Distinguished Visitor.' She mentioned, with unusual endearments, a number of her friends. Her last words, on 7 August, according to Elisina, were 'I want to go home', and then a call for 'Mrs Tyler'.[34]

The mood of resignation and tranquillity which Elisina emphasised concurs with several late reports, some written long after the event, from friends who visited Edith in her last year. Berenson, who saw her last in the spring of 1936, fondly remembered walking up and down with her along the terraces of violets, and listening to her reading *The Buccaneers*. Philomène recalled visiting Edith alone, one autumn day at the Pavillon, and going through old photographs 'in the gracious orderly room, with the rain beating and the leaves falling outside' and feeling that she was 'in the presence of a power at rest, controlled by a lonely and generous spirit'. Vivienne de Watteville gave an idyllic account of staying at the Pavillon in the summer of 1936, where Edith gardened, read aloud, and fed the fishes, calling out, *'Poisse! Poisse!'*[35]

But Elisina's letters just after Edith's death are less tranquil; on 13 August she noted that Edith died 'after a long & very painful agony', and later that year, to Berenson, that it was painful to have had 'to note the loosening up of that splendid instrument, Edith's mind'. A more robust, less pitiful last view of Edith Wharton was given by her friend Louis Gillet (in a letter to Berenson of 25 August) who saw her on 13 August, when she was lying in her open coffin in her bedroom.[36]

Cher ami,

Je pensais à votre chagrin, je n'en séparais pas le mien ... On était telle-ment sûr d'elle, tellement confiant dans sa puissante vitalité. Elle se defendait si splendidement, depuis huit ans! Même ce dernier samedi, où j'avais déjeuné chez elle, on ne désesperait pas encore: la veille elle était si brillante! ... On ne voulait pas s'avouer qu'elle était terrassée ... Elle comptait gagner l'au-tomne. Alors, on mettrait la malade dans une ambulance, et elle passerait l'hiver doucement en veilleuse entre son lit et sa terrasse. Cette perspective ne paraissait alors nullement impossible. Elle était étonnante à voir, sur son lit de mort. Je ne l'avais pas revue depuis une soirée à Ste Claire, au mois de mars, où elle s'était montrée toujours la même, charmante d'abandon et de jeunesse. Je la revois, étendue, son ouvrage à la main, sous son portrait d'en-fant, qui la représente en petite fille, sortie d'un conte de fées, sérieuse, avec ses boucles d'or. Morte, vous n'imaginez pas ce visage. Elle avait sur le front un bonnet de dentelles, c'était la première fois que je ne voyais plus ses cheveux, cette foison ardente qui ne voulait pas grisonner. C'était surprenant de voir éteint ce visage, jadis merveilleux d'energie, de rayonnement et de l'anima-tion, jusque sous ses rides de l'âge. Ces rides étaient éffacés, mais les joues extrêmement creuses. Le masque avait un caractère tout nouveau de sévérité. Elle avait son air de vieille reine, nullement l'aspect détendu, refusé qu'ont souvent les morts, ni non plus un aspect de bataille et de lutte, mais un prodigieux accent d'indifférence et de mépris, comme si elle disait: 'Et après? Que m'importe? Crois-tu que je m'en vais me rendre et m'humilier, parce que tu es la plus forte?' Voilà ce qu'on lisait sur ses traits, et son silence semblait une expression de fierté. Ce n'etait pas très Chrétien, mais c'était magnifique.

[Dear friend,

I was thinking about your grief, which is inseparable from my own ... We were so sure of her, we had such confidence in her powerful vitality. She fought so splendidly, these last eight years. Even last Saturday, when I lunched at her house, people had not given up hope. The night before she had been so brilliant! No one wanted to admit that she was struck down. She thought she would get through the autumn, then we would put her in an ambulance [to Ste-Claire] and she would spend the winter quietly, resting up between her bed and the terrace. This prospect seemed in no way implausible. She was astonishing to see, on her death-bed. I had not seen her myself since March, at an evening at Ste-Claire, when she had been just exactly the same as ever, charmingly relaxed and youthful. I can still see her, lying down, her work in her hand, beneath the portrait of herself as a little girl who had just stepped out of a fairy-story, solemn-faced, with golden ringlets. You can't imagine what this face looked like in death. She had a lace bonnet covering her forehead, and it was the first time I hadn't been able to see her hair – that fiery abundance which refused to turn grey. It was shocking to see that face, formerly so marvellously full of energy, radiance and animation, despite the wrinkles of age – to see that face dead. Those wrinkles were now ironed out, but her cheeks were deeply hollowed. Her mask-like features gave her a completely new severity, and she had her familiar regal air. Not the slack, unwilling look which the dead often have, nor the appearance of struggle and fight, but rather a prodigious air of indifference and scorn, as if she were saying: 'So? What does it matter to me? Do you think I'm going to give in and abase myself just because you are the stronger?' That's what her expression seemed to say, and her silence appeared to be an expression of pride. It was not very Christian, but it was magnificent.]

The news of her death reached the American and French papers on 12 August; one French paper announced '*la mort d'Edith Wharton, le dernier écrivain Victorien*'. The *New York Times* reported that she had had 'an apoplectic stroke' on the day of her death. After her 'lying-in-state' on the 13th, her oak coffin (which had to be lowered out of the window of her bedroom) left the house. It bore a silver cross and wreaths, and the Catholic, Latin inscription she had asked for, O CRUX AVE SPES UNICA, from the Vesper Hymn to the Cross for Passiontide, 'Vexilla Regis', in the Roman Office. 'O Cross, our only hope / In this time of suffering / Grant justice to the faithful / And mercy to those awaiting judgement.' A guard of honour of local firemen and war-veterans (who followed the coffin in procession) stood to attention in the courtyard of the Pavillon, and sounded the Last Post on a bugle as she left. The funeral took place at 11 a.m. on Saturday 14 August at the Protestant Cemetery at Versailles. All but one of the pall-bearers she had asked for carried her coffin to the grave, which was as near as possible to Walter Berry's: Royall Tyler, Kenneth Clark, Gaillard Lapsley, Robert Norton, André Boccon-Gibbod, Louis Metman and Louis Gillet.

(John Hugh Smith was the only one missing.) Dean Frederick Beekman, of the American Cathedral in Paris, read the prayers; there was no music and no address. The gardener, Emile Gaillet, brought flowers from the garden. The pall-bearers threw earth onto the coffin. Norton told Berenson that about thirty people were there, the *New York Herald* reported a hundred, listing one 'Hugh Fullerton' among the mourners. At the memorial service, at 11 a.m. on 23 August, in the American Cathedral in Paris on the Avenue George V, which was organised by Elisina, the Anglican hymns Edith had asked for were sung: 'Lead, Kindly Light', 'Art Thou Weary', and 'O Paradise'.[37]

The American obituaries spoke of her upbringing in, and treatment of, New York and Newport society, her debts to James, her war-work, her Pulitzer Prize, and the theatrical adaptations of her work, and singled out *The House of Mirth, Ethan Frome*, and *The Age of Innocence*. The *New World Telegraph* pronounced her 'a bit dated'. A respectful summing-up of her work in the *New York Times* in September, when *Ghosts* was published, regretted that she had confined herself to 'the drawing room'. The French obituaries emphasised her friendship with Bourget and her love of France. Gillet, writing in *L'Époque*, spoke of her as *'une amie de la France, un grand esprit et un grand coeur'*. André Chaumieux, in *L'Écho de Paris*, said that 'Mrs Warthon' died *'parmi les fleurs de France qu'elle aimait'*, and Philomène, writing in *Le Figaro* as Claude Silve, tenderly remembered her in her rose-garden.[38]

The immediate aftermath of Wharton's death was not, however, so tranquil. The uneasy relationship between Beatrix and Elisina, apparent during Beatrix's visit to her dying aunt, broke down within a year. Both in their sixties, the two women were both generously treated in Wharton's two wills; nevertheless, there was a bitter legal wrangle between them. The issue arose from the American will, and had its source in the old quarrels in the Jones family and in Wharton's relationship with her mother and her brothers. A résumé of the long story helps to clarify the dispute.

In her lifetime, Wharton had received three inheritances. Until 1905, when she became a high-earning literary success, these were what she had lived on; after that, her literary income exceeded her inheritances. The first was from her father's will in 1882, which left her about $600,000 in real-estate holdings, in a trust fund controlled by her brothers. She was entitled to live off the interest (which greatly diminished during her life-time) and to dispose of the principal after her death, to a relative by blood. On her death, this principal amounted to about $610,000 (about one-third of Wharton's residual estate), and this was left, in her American will, entirely to Beatrix. Wharton's second inheritance, in 1888, was the windfall of $120,000 from her relation Joshua Jones. And her third inheritance, the one which had always caused all the trouble, was from her mother's will, made in 1896. Lucretia Jones divided her estate into three parts, one for each brother, and one, amounting to about $92,000, held in trust for Wharton by her two brothers. The will stipulated that if Lucretia's daughter died without issue, her share was to be transferred 'to my lawful heirs'. Wharton felt that this was a punitive will, made to punish her for having sided with Minnie after the breakup of her marriage to Frederic, whom Lucretia favoured, and for having refused to acknowledge Frederic's mistress. In 1901, after Lucretia Jones's death, she, Teddy, and Harry Jones (who supported her), persuaded Frederic to agree to 'break' the will: to waive his rights over Wharton's third, so that, if she died without issue, she would be entitled to leave it to whomever she chose. Frederic's daughter Beatrix, then in her twenties, was, however, not consulted about this by Wharton's lawyers, and never agreed to the 'breaking' of her grandmother's will. In 1931, Wharton discovered that the trust was not going to yield as much as she had expected.[39]

Wharton's French will was revised and signed on 11 June 1937, and her American one finalised in December 1936. Elisina was the executrix and residuary legatee of both. The co-executors of the American will were Wharton's cousins, Le Roy and Frederic Rhinelander King. The co-executors of the French will were John Hugh Smith and André Boccon-Gibbod. Elisina wanted to get the French will sorted out as quickly as possible without alerting the French tax authorities to the American legacy, for fear they would claim back-taxes on it. Wharton's French will left Ste-Claire-du-Château to Elisina, and ordered that the Pavillon Colombe be sold for an endowment for the TB sanatoriums (not turned into a sanatorium itself, as Wharton had once hoped). It was sold to Arthur Sachs (brother of Paul Sachs, the director of the Fogg Museum at Harvard) for 1,200,000 old francs, the money going to the endowment. He took on all the staff at St-Brice except for Jeanne Fridérich. (Sachs sold it on in 1948 to the Duc de Talleyrand.) Elisina found the punitive French inheritance taxes and the high cost of the upkeep of Ste-Claire too much. She moved Alfred White into Pierre Lisse, the smaller house on the Ste-Claire estate, but sold Ste-Claire-du-Château during the war.

Under the French will, there were many specific bequests, all of which Elisina took charge of, sorting out all the objects left to individuals, paying the customs bills on things like 'Dog collar in pearls with a star-sapphire surrounded with diamonds' (to Mrs Winthrop Chanler), or 'Cartier chain with diamonds and pearls' (to Mrs George Cabot Lodge), shipping all the household objects from St-Brice left to Beatrix at Bar Harbor in Maine (lace caps and sheets, organdy bed-cover, pink silk bed-coverlets, Chinese scarf, box of tortoiseshell combs, family photos, French and Belgian medals, Walter Gay's painting of poppies, family portraits, jade vases, writing board . . .), sending the books from both houses to her son and to the Clarks, and so on. There were also a large number of outstanding servants' wages and unpaid bills (mainly for gas, coal, garden manure, architects, cleaners, doctors, and funeral expenses) amounting to about 340,000 old francs, which she paid.

The list of individual bequests in Wharton's French will summed up a whole way of life. There were the portraits: of herself as an eight-year-old (the one so admired by Gillet), by Edward May, and of her great-grandparents and grandparents (all for Beatrix). There were her pictures: a landscape of her great-grandparents' house at Hell Gate, a view of Pencraig, two Brabazon water-colours (for Robert Norton, who was also left her *Dictionary of National Biography*), a Norwich School painting, Manet's 'Raven', an Allan Ramsay portrait from Wemyss Castle of a young man (left to Gaillard, to be bequeathed to the Louvre), an eighteenth-century painting of a French nobleman, two flower-paintings by Jacques-Émile Blanche, Norton's water-colours of the Pavillon (to go to Philomène) and of Ste-Claire (for her head-gardener at Ste-Claire, Joseph Cherrer). There were her ancestral treasures: a plated silver kettle which had belonged to General Ebenezer Stevens, and his Hepplewhite chairs, her eighteenth-century silver sugar-bowl and milk-pots. There were her most valuable house-furnishings, such as a large Persian rug (for Royall Tyler), a Second Empire silver tray bought by her mother in Paris (for Louis Metman), and a Louis XVI clock. (All the furniture and fittings of Pierre Lisse went to Alfred White, though not the house itself, which Elisina gave him.) There were her best clothes and jewellery: a sapphire and diamond brooch, her chinchilla and sable wraps, her bejewelled dog-collars, an eighteenth-century watch 'set into a crystal triangle, surrounded with brilliants' (for Jane Clark), a sapphire ring (for Nicky Mariano), a moleskin coat and coral necklace (for Gabrielle Landormy), a pearl-and-enamel Cartier watch (for Jeanne Fridérich). And, apart from the main division of the books between Bill Tyler and Colin Clark, there were a few specific, carefully planned book-bequests: Charlie Du Bos was to have her first edition of Proust and her association copy of Barbey d'Aurevilly's *Une Vieille Maîtresse*, 'The Old Mistress', dedicated to Bourget, who had given it to her; Boccon-Gibbod was left the *Memoirs* of Saint-Simon and Mme de Sévigné's *Letters*. Gaillard, whom she made her literary executor, was left 'all my manuscripts, literary correspondence and documents, with the request that he shall take care of the publication, sale, preservation or destruction of all such documents and manuscripts', calling if necessary on Kenneth Clark for help.[40]

The quarrel arose over the American will and Lucretia's trust fund. Elisina said that Wharton had intended to leave her a large sum of money out of the trust fund, to help with settling the outstanding expenses and for a gift to Bill Tyler. A letter from Wharton written in December 1936, telling Elisina where her wills were, did say: 'I have left you (in my American will) a sum of money part of which I will ask you to dispose of according to written instructions.' But this was a sum of $5,000 to be distributed to 'charitable institutions' and 'certain poor persons'. Elisina wrote to Beatrix in December 1937, saying that she could 'take her oath with a clear conscience' that Edith intended to leave her a 'lump sum' and that she had told her last June that it 'should be about 140,000 dollars'. 'It would be quite dreadful', she went on, 'if an open conflict took place between us.' Beatrix said that the trust fund should be hers entirely as she was the last of Lucretia's 'lawful heirs'. The dispute went to law at the end of 1937, Elisina's lawyers arguing that by 'lawful heirs' Lucretia had meant her three children only, not their descendants. The sum of money in contestation was referred to, legally, as the 'Ambiguous Remainder'. In 1938 the lawyers settled for Beatrix; but, after the decision, the two agreed on a compromise, and split the disputed sum in half. Until her death at eighty-six, in 1959, Beatrix continued to complain about Elisina. When approached by would-be Wharton biographers or editors, she referrred to Mrs Tyler as an Italian with an uncertain social position, who exerted undue influence when Wharton fell ill; during her 'final years of domination' she 'attached herself like a limpet to my aunt'. Elisina, for her part, criticised Beatrix bitterly for her greed and her neglectfulness: 'Edith's niece has shown no interest whatever in giving proper care to Edith's grave', she told John Hugh Smith in 1939. 'And . . . I confess that the ink freezes on my pen at the thought of making any request on the subject to her.' As a result of the litigation, the gravestone, with the same inscription that had been on the coffin, was not carved and set in place until two years after Wharton's death.[41]

The after-life of Edith Wharton has gone through great changes since her death in 1937. Writing to Daisy Chanler in 1925, Wharton said she felt discouraged by the 'densities of incomprehension' in her recent reviews, and asked herself what the value of her work might be. 'I never have minded before; but as my work reaches its close, I feel so sure that it is either nothing, or far more than they know . . . And I wonder, a little desolately, which?' The question seemed to hang fire during her early posthumous life in the late 1930s and 1940s. A small group of posthumous publications – *Ghosts* in 1937 (with 'All Souls" the only new story), the unfinished *Buccaneers* in 1938, and her collaboration with Robert Norton, *Eternal Passion in English Poetry*, in 1939 – did not attract great attention. Lapsley, who had been left (as Jeanne Fridérich put it) 'four hundred kilos' of paper, sold the letters and manuscripts to Yale University in 1938, embargoing the publication of 'anything of a biographical sort' for thirty years. After anxious consultations with Kenneth Clark (who thought Lapsley a 'pompous prig'), Robert Norton and John Hugh Smith, Lapsley, surprisingly, asked Percy Lubbock to write a memoir. Lubbock agreed, on condition he could structure it out of a medley of different voices, reminiscences which would fill in his own gaps, and set about collecting memories from many of Wharton's friends. Lapsley embarked on a collection of Wharton's critical essays, to be called *The Service of Letters*. But after his death in 1949 there was no enthusiasm at Appleton for the project, and the idea languished for about forty years, until Frederick Wegener's fine edition of Wharton's *Uncollected Critical Writings* in 1996. Lubbock's memoir came out in 1947, embalming Wharton as a grand, fussy, imperious Jamesian. It was much disliked by some who had known her, like Kenneth Clark and Elisina. Elisina was in possession of a large stash of Wharton papers (and had an intriguing correspondence with Fullerton in 1946, about the 'Love Diary' in her possession and the copy of 'Terminus' in his). She thought of writing her own memoir in retaliation, though this project came to nothing, and was going to call it (quoting something Matilda Gay had once said to her about Edith) *The Story of a Soul in Pain*. As the copyright holder and executrix of Wharton's wills, the literary executorship passed to her when Lapsley died. She placed the management of the literary estate in the hands of Armitage and Ann Watkins's agency (which later became the Watkins/Loomis agency) but all requests for adaptations and editions of, or books about, Wharton, were vetted by her. When Elisina died in 1957, Bill Tyler (who had a distinguished public career, including a stint as American ambassador to the Netherlands) took it over. In his old age, in 1992, he passed it on to his daughter.[42]

At first there was not a great deal for the agency to do. Wharton's repu-tation was at a low ebb in the 1940s and 1950s (apart from a spirited defence by Edmund Wilson, 'Justice to Edith Wharton', in 1947). Her name was almost always linked, to her disadvantage, with Henry James, and her work was largely felt to be stuffy, minor, and dated. Those who did admire her often had their own kind of reasons, as in an anecdote told by Clifton Fadiman in an introduction to a 1939 edition of *Ethan Frome*:

> A delightful *ancien régime* lady of Beacon Hill once asked me, in a tone marvellously combining dignity, irritation and bewilderment, why nobody read Edith Wharton any more. Why, she asked, did they prefer the vulgar sensationalism of Mr Cain and Mr O'Hara, for example, to the well-bred perceptions of Edith Wharton? 'Do you still read Edith Wharton?' I asked. It developed she did not, and in fact had not read her for years. Her allegiance to Edith Wharton was a social tribute, not a literary one. It was not a question of literary judgment but of class fidelity.

When an *Edith Wharton Treasury* came out in 1950, it was trailed as a publication by 'a great lady of American letters'.

Sales were flagging – in 1952, for instance, Scribner's told Ann Watkins that there were no current sales of *The Custom of the Country*, and that there had been between seven and fifteen copies sold per year for the last four years. In response to the publication of the *Edith Wharton Treasury*, the editor of *New Directions*, James Laughlin, wrote to Appleton: 'I hope the whole Wharton revival is a big thing, because she is such a wonderful writer.' These kinds of remarks about a Wharton revival were frequent well into the 1960s. In the early 1960s, the agency was trying to re-establish Wharton's reputation in Britain. In 1963, a Wharton devotee, Grace Shaw Smith (later Kellogg), who was writing a thesis on Wharton, and was asking Kenneth Clark for information (as all writers on Wharton did, to his increasing irritation) maintained that 'She is highly valued (again – after some years of obscurity)'.[43]

Grace Kellogg was one of the few women at this time who were working on Wharton. Another was Millicent Bell, who published an interesting book on James and Wharton, also in 1965, but ran into trouble with the Wharton estate for trying to quote from the embargoed papers. Wharton's posthumous life at this time was very much a male preserve, as it had been since Lubbock and Lapsley, Clark, Norton and Hugh Smith, consulted over her literary remains. Bill Tyler, his lawyer Herb Fierst, and Donald Gallup, the curator of American archives at Yale, decided who should write the biography. A number of eminent male American literary names were canvassed – Arthur Mizener, Andrew Turnbull, Edmund Wilson, Leon Edel, Mark Schorer, Alfred Kazin – and one woman, the extraordinary writer

Jean Stafford. R. W. B. Lewis, English professor at Yale, was appointed in 1966.

The choosing of a biographer and the lifting of the embargo on the Yale papers in 1968 coincided with a shift in interest in Wharton's work. The complicated trail of her life was slowly beginning to become public, and at the same time the first wave of feminist academic criticism was reconsidering women writers of the past, and new editions, such as Scribner's two-volume collection of her stories in 1968, were re-establishing her reputation. In 1971, Louis Auchincloss wrote an elegantly illustrated, much livelier and more gossipy 'portrait' than Lubbock's. Lewis's prize-winning, authorised biography came out in 1975. It drew on a wide range of archives and personal testimonies, told the story of the love-affair, with long extracts from 'The Life Apart: L'Âme Close', the secret diary of 1907–8 (then in Tyler's possession), printed the 'Beatrice Palmato' fragment as an Appendix, and quoted 'Terminus' in full. The following year, Bill Tyler sold the Wharton papers he had been left by Elisina (and to which Lewis had had access) to the Lilly Library at the University of Indiana.[44]

Lewis's biography was followed in 1977, by a psychoanalytical, feminist version of her life by Cynthia Griffin Wolff. The editing and reissuing began to get underway, slowly, of Wharton's minor, non-canonical texts, starting with her juvenile novel, *Fast and Loose*, in 1977. Paperback reissues and new editions of her work, in France, England and America, began to appear in the 1970s, and have continued to do so ever since. The letters from Wharton to Fullerton, which Lewis did not have access to, were suddenly offered for sale to the Harry Ransom Humanities Center at the University of Texas in 1980, and were partially published in 1985. In England, Virago Press reissued many of Wharton's novels in the 1980s. R.W.B. Lewis and his wife published a large selection of Wharton's letters in 1988, which was followed in 1990 by an edition of the letters from James to Wharton (and of the few surviving ones from her to him). That year, Stephen Garrison published an invaluable Wharton bibliography, and the Library of America began its series of Wharton volumes – the seal of a 'classic' reputation – printing the unpublished version of her memoir, 'Life and I', in the first volume. (The *Poems* were published in 2005.) 'The Life Apart' diary was published in 1994. By then, an enormous academic Wharton industry – essays, monographs, new editions, companions, anthologies – was flourishing. An Edith Wharton society, with a newsletter (which became a review), and regular conferences, was founded in 1984. Two new lives of Wharton in 1994, Shari Benstock's thorough, revisionist biography, and Eleanor Dwight's lavishly illustrated life-in-pictures, both used a great deal of new material. Sarah Bird Wright's *Edith Wharton A-Z* provided a working encyclopaedia of her life and writings in 1998. George Ramsden, the owner of Wharton's library, published his catalogue in 1999. An experimental life of Morton Fullerton by Lewis's one-time research assistant, Marion Mainwaring, correcting the chronology and details of the affair, and exposing Lewis's errors, came out in 2001. Some glamorous books on Wharton's houses and gardens (Theresa Craig, 1996) and Italian villas (Vivien Russell, 1997), and a new edition of *The Cruise of the Vanadis*, with contemporary photographs, played to the 'coffee-table', luxury market for Whartoniana, in which she is seamlessly identified with the social world and class she grew up in and wrote about.[45]

For all this massive interest among general readers and academics, much still remains to be done with the posthumous life of Edith Wharton. Unlike James, Wharton is not (yet) benefiting from a large-scale, multi-volume, annotated edition of her complete letters. My own work, which makes use of the recent publication of her letters to Léon Bélugou and Louis Bromfield, draws on a large scatter of unpublished letters (for instance, to Charles and Zézette Du Bos, Jacques-Émile Blanche, William Gerhardi, Ogden Codman, Mrs Humphry Ward, Lily Norton, Steven Runciman and Walter Berry), and follows her trail more closely in France, Italy and England, has made me acutely aware of the gaps in her published record. As I write, in 2006, most of her surviving manuscripts have not been edited and published. The original collections of her short stories have not been separately reprinted. Her non-fiction work could benefit from new, annotated editions. For all the efforts of editors and publishers, the 'Wharton boom' is centred on a few works: far more readers know *Ethan Frome*, *The House of Mirth*, *Summer*, *The Age of Innocence* or 'Roman Fever' than 'Bunner Sisters', or *Madame de Treymes*, or *A Motor-Flight Through France*.

The 'Wharton boom', as it began to be described in the early 1990s, and which invested in her as a figure of grandeur, high style, and social elitism, had a great deal to do with the movies. The files of the Watkins/Loomis agency are full of references to film options on Wharton titles, but some of these foundered on the darkness of her plots (Undine, for instance, was felt in 1961 to be 'too evil' to command 'public support'). Ideas floated for musicals of *The Children* (or *The House of Mirth*!) not surprisingly came to nothing. 'Roman Fever', though, was much-adapted, and there were TV films in the early 1980s of *Summer* and *The House of Mirth*. But it was not until 1993 that Wharton came sensationally to the big screen. A worthy film of *Ethan Frome* (with Liam Neeson) and a film of *The Children* (with Ben Kingsley) were followed by Martin Scorsese's dazzling, lavish, high-profile film of *The Age of Innocence*, with Daniel Day-Lewis, Michelle Pfeiffer, and Winona Ryder. A rash of articles followed about the rediscovery of Edith Wharton. John Updike, in a long reconsideration of Wharton in the *New Yorker*, observed that she was 'having a lively time of it'. An article in the *Observer* said that 'only a few years ago [she was] mouldering on the shelves of public libraries, a half-forgotten, mostly out-of-print lady novelist'. An interview with Bill Tyler's daughter Eve Thompson described her inheritance of the Wharton copyrights as suddenly turning into gold: 'the writings of Edith Wharton have become the hottest literary property in Hollywood'. A BBC TV film of the 'completed' *Buccaneers* followed in 1995 (and a beautifully curated exhibition of 'Edith Wharton's World' at the Smithsonian Institution in Washington at the end of 1997). There was an opera of *Summer* (by Stephen Paulus) in 1999, staged performances of her work by the actress Gayle Hunnicutt and by Tina Packer's theatre company at The Mount, and a sensitive and interesting film of *The House of Mirth* by the English director Terence Davies in 2000.[46]

Wharton is no longer always mentioned in the same breath as Henry James; in fact she is mentioned (at least in America) more often than he is, now, as an indicator for certain subjects: wealth, social status, old New York. In 2004–5, for instance, her name came up in New York papers in discussions of the city's history, of celebrity and fame, of new money, of the American public's reaction to the election campaign (Frank Rich, citing Howells's famous remark to Wharton that 'what the American public wants is a tragedy with a happy ending') and in an advertisement in *In Style* magazine for an 18-carat gold-and-diamond watch (price $5,950), as worn by Angelina Jolie, called 'The Wharton.'[47]

Wharton's places reflect the fall and rise of her posthumous reputation. The Mount changed hands several times after its sale in 1911, and was a girls' boarding school, the Foxhollow School, between 1942 and 1976. After that it fell into disrepair, from which it began to be rescued by Tina Packer, the director of the theatre group Shakespeare & Company, in 1978. In the 1980s and 1990s there was a battle for control of The Mount (worthy of a Wharton short story) between the theatre company, which eventually left, and the 'Edith Wharton Restoration' company. The restoration of the house was devotedly watched over by the late Scott Marshall (who wrote a vivid account of The Mount's history) and by the current president and executive director of 'Edith Wharton Restoration, Inc.', Stephanie Copeland. It is now lavishly preserved, re-landscaped, and fitted up, and houses Wharton's books.

Wharton's childhood homes in New York at 14 West 23rd and 28 West 25th Street, and her Park Avenue house, have been demolished or altered out of recognition; Trinity Church on 25th Street, where she was married, is now a Serbian church. Pencraig Cottage and Land's End in Newport still stand and are privately owned. In Paris, her apartment-buildings in the forbidding Rue de Varenne, armed police at every corner guarding the President's palace, are remarkably unchanged. Number 58 has its gigantic doors closed to the street, not even a street-number to give it away. On number 53, an undated plaque put up by the 'Association de la Mémoire des Lieux' commemorates *'Edith Wharton, Romancière Américaine'* (*'le premier écrivain des Etats-Unis à s'expatrier en France, par amour pour ce pays et sa littérature'*) and says that she lived there from 1910 to 1920. It does not refer to her war-work, but quotes, in French and English, the line from *A Backward Glance* about spending 'rich, crowded and happy years' in Paris in the Rue de Varenne, and adds: *'Proche de Henry James, l'oeuvre d'Edith Wharton met en scène d'un trait à la fois délicat et mordant, la bonne société dont elle est issué.'* A lover of France, a Jamesian, a delicate and caustic satirist of her own high society: that is the French view of Edith Wharton. At Hyères, the house fell into disrepair in the 1970s (it was described in 1979 as 'empty and decaying', with the gardens 'overgrown and unkempt'). But, renamed Castel St-Claire, it is now the offices of the Parc National; and the garden, advertised in the guide-book as the Jardin Exotique Sainte-Claire, is efficiently maintained. There is an 'Avenue Edith Warthon' in the town.[48]

After the Duc and Duchesse de Talleyrand bought the Pavillon Colombe in 1948, they refurbished it extensively (employing the English landscape-artist Russell Page to do the gardens). Then it stood empty for a time, until it was bought by the Prince and Princess of Liechtenstein, who like to make Wharton scholars welcome. I paid my visit on a summer day in 2002, after battling through the Paris suburbs to the now rather dingy St-Brice. The butler, complete with gloves and uniform, led me into the central reception room, done up in chinoiserie style. The princess, though upset that day by the death of her borzoi, was extremely hospitable. She told me that the house was largely redesigned and refurnished by the Duchesse de Talleyrand, and by herself: she does not think much of Wharton's taste in furniture. But the garden was being lovingly kept up, and from the bedroom where Wharton died, I looked out at the pond where she used to feed the fish, with the scents and sounds of the garden coming up through the windows. Some things have had to go: the princess told me that unlike Wharton, she hates white dahlias, but, in tribute to her great predecessor, has obtained satisfactory replacements. Sure enough, out on the terrace, there were two rather shame-faced looking white peacocks, pretending to be dahlias.

After my visit to the Pavillon, I travelled the short journey south through the Île-de-France from St-Brice to the haunted pleasure-grounds of Versailles, the setting of Martin Boyne's sad dream of reunion in *The Children*, and then to visit Edith Wharton's grave. Appropriately enough, it was raining when I found the Cimetière des Gonards on a road leading out of Versailles past the railway station, heavy with traffic. The cemetery is mixed: the guardian at the gate, who spoke no English, told me there were Protestants and Catholics and even 'some Israelites' buried there. He looked Wharton up for me in his filing cabinet of old index cards, her entry hand-written in the same copperplate italic handwriting as the card written, ten years before hers, for Walter Berry. Mme Wharton's details – married, divorced, 'perpetuelle' resident in the graveyard, depth of body 1 m 50 cm – are given on the card, as well as her location. She is up the hill in a plain, rather ugly grave, with its carved motto, 'O CRUX AVE SPES UNICA', her two names, Edith Wharton and Edith Newbold Jones, her dates (in French) and no other detail. Another grave has been fitted in between hers and Walter Berry's. A cotoneaster had been planted in the earth frame around the stone, but the tomb was covered with weeds, old bottles and a very ancient pot of dead flowers. Clearly no one had been there for a long time. It struck me as an unvisited and lonely tomb, of a person who died without close relatives nearby to look after it, the casualty of a disputed will. There is no 'Society for the Preservation of the Grave of Edith Wharton', as there undoubtedly would have been if she had been buried, like Teddy Wharton, in Lenox. It said something to me, in parting, about Edith Wharton's relationship to France: part 'perpetuelle' inhabitant, part stranger in exile. She herself was a dedicated visitor and keeper-up of the graves of her loved ones, and, as she said of herself, a very housekeeperish person. So this neglect seemed sad. In the rain, I weeded Edith, and planted a single white silk azalea, bought from the flower-shop at the cemetery gate. She would probably have been scornful about the artificial flower, but would, I felt, have been glad to have her grave tidied up.

Acknowledgements

I have incurred many debts during my years of work on this biography. I am enormously grateful to the Beinecke Library for appointing me as the visiting Donald C. Gallup Visiting Fellow in 1999, to the Lilly Library for appointing me as an Everett Helm Visiting Fellow in 2001, and to Princeton University for appointing me as a Whitney J. Oates Short-Term Fellow of the Council of the Humanities in 2001. These fellowships allowed me to make use of the magnificent archives in those institutions, essential to my research. I had the great privilege of spending the academic year 2004–5 as the Mel and Lois Tukman Fellow at the Cullman Center for Scholars and Writers at the New York Public Library, without which I could not have finished this book, and where I was the happy recipient of Jean Strouse's intellectual example and warm friendship, the companionship of a fine fellowship of writers, and the unparalleled resources of that great library. I am grateful to the English Faculty at the University of Oxford for allowing me to take unpaid leave in that academic year 2004-5, and to my students at Oxford for much talking and thinking about biography. I am grateful to the Edith Wharton Society for inviting me to give the keynote speech at its 2003 Conference at Roehampton, and to the Chicago Humanities Festival for inviting me to speak about Wharton in November 2005. I thank Patricia Willis at the Beinecke Library for all her helpfulness and scholarship. I am grateful to George Ramsden for allowing me to work with Edith Wharton's library. My parents, Benjamin Lee and the late Josephine Lee, followed the progress of this book with interest, and my father helped with medical information. My sister, Bridget Patterson, provided most of the translations. I thank Julian Barnes for his affectionate advice and encouragement, and his invaluable and stringent reading of the typescript. I thank my agent and friend, Pat Kavanagh. I am deeply grateful, as always and ever, to my editor, fellow-biographer and dear friend Jenny Uglow. I thank my husband John Barnard, here and in the dedication, for his love, his help, his advice and his patience.

*

Acknowledgements

I am indebted to the following individuals for advice, information, inspiration, hospitality, editorial guidance, and encouragement of many kinds: George Andreou; Louis Auchincloss; Clio Barnard; Josie Barnard; the late Sybille Bedford; Janet Beer; Dinah Birch; Gaynor Blandford; Nicholas Boyle; Helen Brann and Faith Stewart-Gordon; Daniel Bratton; Michael Burden; Carmen Callil; Susan Campbell; the late Colin Clark; Stephanie Copeland and the staff of the Edith Wharton Restoration at The Mount, especially Anne Miller and the late Scott Marshall; Fiona Cowell; Camilla Dinkel; the late Barbara Epstein; Annick Fennet; Kate Flint; Roy Foster; Lucy Gent; Cornelia Gilder; Victoria Glendinning; Vanessa Guignery; Lu Harper; Ruth Harris; Selina Hastings; Hugh Haughton; Chris Hoare; Howard Hodgkin; Ernest Hofer; Philip Horne; Maisie Houghton; Maureen Howard; Michael Janeway; Ann Jefferson; Steve Jobe; Robin Lane Fox; Mark Lefanu at the Society of Authors; Prince Philippe and Princess Isabelle of Liechtenstein; Amanda Lillie; Rosemary and Paul Lloyd; Annalena McAfee; Jean McGarry; Deborah McVea; Maren Michel; Caroline Moorehead; Nicholas Murray; Elsa Nettels; Lucy Newlyn; Lord Niedpath; Adriana Nova; Anne Padfield; Lisandro Perez; John and William Pym; in the Rue de Varenne, Lou-Ann Alsip, Ghislaine Barissat, Patrick Lindsay Bowles, Carole Butor, Anne-Marie and Christian Casper and Françoise de Valence; Jane Ramsden; Robyn Read; Michèle Roberts; Isabel Rushmore; Desmond Seward; Fiona Shaw; Ann Shukman; Janna Malamud Smith; Gabriel Smol; the late Nikos Stangos; T.J.Stiles; Michael Suarez; Shaf Toweed; Marina Warner; Fred Wegener; David Wheeler; Edmund White; Gertrude Wilmers; Margaretta Wood; Julian Wright; Sarah Bird Wright.

I am extremely grateful to the librarians, archivists and staff at the following institutions: all those who helped me at the Beinecke Library; Steve Crook and his colleagues at the Berg Collection and, elsewhere in the New York Public Library, Rebecca Federman, Paul Holdengraber, Declan Kiely Paul LeClerc, Pamela Leo, David Smith and William Stingone; Carrie McDade at the Environmental Design Archives, Berkeley; Chris Sheppard at the Brotherton Library, Leeds; Jocelyn Wilks at Columbia University Library; Margaret Burri and Jacqueline O'Regan at Evergreen House and the Johns Hopkins University Library, Baltimore; Susan Halpert at the Houghton Library; Saundra Taylor at the Lilly Library at Indiana University; Margaret Sherry Rich and the staff at the Firestone Library at Princeton University; Leslie Fields and Robert Parks at the Pierpont Morgan Library; The Rev Barry A. Orford at Pusey House; Cathy Henderson and Richard Workman at the Harry Ransom Humanities Research Center; Karen Kukil at the William Allan Nielson Library, Smith College; Pauline Adams at

Somerville College; Lorna Condon at the SPNEA; Michael Roche and Fiorella Superbi at I Tatti; Gloria Loomis and all who helped me at the Watkins/Loomis Agency.

I would like to thank the following individuals, agencies and institutions for permission to quote materials in their possession, details of which appear in the endnotes: Alice Warder Garrett Archive, Evergreen House Foundation, Johns Hopkins University, Baltimore; Overbury Collection, Barnard College, New York; The Edith Wharton Collection, Yale Collection of American Literature, Beinecke Rare Book and Manuscript Library, Yale University; Fototeca Berenson, Villa I Tatti, Harvard University; The Berg Collection of English and American Literature, the Rare Books Division and the Richard Watson Gilder Papers, Manuscripts and Archives Division, The New York Public Library, Astor, Lenox and Tilden Foundations; Bradley Family Papers, Radcliffe Institute for Advanced Study, Schlesinger Library, Harvard University; The British Library for the Macmillan Archive; The Brotherton Collection, Leeds University Library; The Butler Library and Rare Books and Manuscripts Library, Columbia University, New York; The Camphill Village Trust, 19 South Road, Sturbridge, West Midlands, DY8 3YA, for the estate of Mary Berenson; The Curtis Brown Group Ltd, London, on behalf of the Estate of William Gerhardie; The Beatrix Jones Farrand Collection, Environmental Design Archives, University of California, Berkeley; The John Work Garrett Papers, Special Collections, Milton S. Eisenhower Library, The Johns Hopkins University, Baltimore; Houghton Library, Harvard University; Bay James for the estate of Henry James; Wharton mss, The Lilly Library, and Appleton-Century mss, The Lilly Library, Indiana University, Bloomington, Indiana; Leon Edel Papers at McGill University, Rare Books and Special Collections, McLennan Library, McGill University; Edith Wharton Restoration Archives at The Mount; Manuscripts and Archives Division, Humanities & Social Sciences Library, New York Public Library; Pierpont Morgan Library, New York; The Principal and Chapter of Pusey House, Oxford; The Reece Halsey Agency for the estate of Aldous Huxley; Charles Scribner's Sons Archive, Scribner Room, Department of Rare Books and Special Collections, Firestone Library, Princeton University; Grace Kellogg Smith Papers, Sophia Smith Collection, Smith College; The Principal and Fellows of Somerville College, Oxford; The Society for the Preservation of New England Antiquities, Boston; Kenneth Clark papers, Hyman Kreitman Research Centre, Tate Gallery Archives, and the Estate of Kenneth Clark, c/o Margaret Hanbury, 27 Walcot Square, London SE11 4UB; The Harry Ransom Humanities Research Center, University of Texas at Austin; The

Acknowledgements

Master and Fellows of Trinity College, Cambridge; The Watkins/Loomis Agency Archives at the Watkins/Loomis office and Watkins/Loomis Agency Records, Columbia University Rare Book and Manuscript Library, New York; A.P. Watt Ltd on behalf of Michael B.Yeats for the estate of W.B.Yeats.

The authors and publishers are grateful to the following institutions and individuals for kind permission to reproduce illustrative material:
The American Academy of Arts and Letters, New York 8; AP/ World Wide Photos 80; Ashfield Historical Society, Ashfield, Massachusetts 23; reproduced in Louis Auchincloss, *Edith Wharton; a Woman in Her Time* (Michael Joseph, 1971) 4, 74; Author photograph 42; The Beinecke Rare Book and Manuscript Library, Yale University Library 14, 15, 17, 18, 24, 29, 30, 31, 32, 33, 36, 45, 47, 55, 57, 64, 66, 67, 68, 78; The Berenson Archive, Villa I Tatti, Florence 71; Bibliothèque Historique de la Ville de Paris 56; reproduced in *Berkshire: The First 300 Years*, (Eagle Publishing, Mass., 1976) 34; *Country Life* 43, 44; reproduced in P.V. Desplaces, *C'etait Hier: Le VIIeme Arrondissement*, (Editions LM-Le Point, 1993) 48; Dumbarton Oaks Research Library, Washington 81, 82; reproduced in Eleanor Dwight, *Edith Wharton: An Extraordinary Life* (Harry N. Abrams, 1994) 6, 49, 50, 54; reproduced in Anne Heurgon-Desjardins, *Paul Desjardins et les Décades de Pontigny* (Presses Universitaires de France, 1964) 75; The Houghton Library, Harvard University 35; Hulton Deutsch/ Getty Images 70; From *L'Illustration*, 1913, Vol. 2, 53; Knickerbocker Club, New York 20; reproduced in R.W.B. Lewis, *Edith Wharton: A Biography* (Harper and Row, 1975) 71; courtesy, The Lilly Library, Indiana University, Bloomington, Indiana 2, 3, 16, 25, 26, 28, 30, 38, 46, 58, 59, 60, 63, 68, 72, 76, 77, 84; Newport Historical Society, Newport, Rhode Island 13; The New York Public Library, Astor, Lenox and Tilden Foundations 5, 10, 11, 12, 21, 27, 39, 40, 41, 61, 62, 69; The Origo Archive, La Foce, Italy 73; reproduced in *Paul Bourget et l'Italie*, ed. M-G. Martin-Gistucci, (Editions Slatkine, Geneva, 1985) 51, 52; reproduced in William Rieder, *A Charmed Couple: The Art and Life of Walter and Mathilda Gay* (Harry N. Abrams, 2000) 85; Society for the Preservation of New England Antiquities, Historic New England, Boston 22; Smith College Library 37; Watkins/Loomis Agency, Inc. 1, 7, 9; Ann Shukman 83, William Royall Tyler Collection, Vermont Historical Society 19; reproduced in Sarah Bird Wright, *Edith Wharton A-Z* (Checkmark Books, 1998) 65, 79. Every effort has been made to trace and contact all copyright holders. If there are any inadvertent omissions or errors, the publishers will be pleased to correct these at the earliest opportunity.

Notes

CHAPTER 1: AN AMERICAN IN
PARIS

1 Diary of George Frederic Jones,
    1847–8, Lilly.
2 BG, ch. 3, i.
3 BG, ch. 1, iii.
4 BG, ch. 1, iii. Gordon Wright, *France
    in Modern Times*, Norton, 1987,
    126–32.
5 'The Look of Paris', ii, FF. See EW
    to BB, 30 September 1914, Letters
    341.
6 EW to BB, 12 February 1934, Letters
    574.
7 L&I, 1077. See EW, Introduction to
    Claude Silve's *Benediction*, Wegener,
    252.
8 L&I, 1081.
9 BG, ch. 3, iii. EW and her father
    were both avid Ruskinians – his
    library had *Modern Painters* and
    Seven Lamps and he gave her *Stones
    of Venice* and *Mornings in Florence*.
    She calls the latter *Walks in Florence*
    in BG.
10 L&I, 1096.
11 *Exelsior*, 8 April 1916; obituaries,
    Andre Chaumeix, *L'Écho de Paris*, 14
    August 1937 and Louis Gillet,
    L'Époque, 16 August 1937.
12 LGNY, Wegener, 274–5. The MSS
    of LGNY, 2–3, Beinecke, reads:
    'Everything that used to form the
    woof of our daily life has been torn
    up, trampled on, destroyed; and
    hundreds of little incidents, habits,
    traditions, which, when I began my
    Backward Glance, seemed too utterly
    insignificant to set down, have since

taken on the historical importance
of details of dress and furniture in an
18th century conversation piece.'

CHAPTER 2: MAKING UP

1 FT, ch.18.
2 'Logic', MSS, Beinecke.
3 BG, ch. 1, i.
4 BG, ch. 1, iii, ch. 3, i.
5 L&I, 1079.
6 Montgomery Schuyler, 'The Churches
    of New York', *New York World*, 22
    October 1871, 2, quoted in Robert
    Stern, *New York 1880*, Monacelli
    Press, 1999, 568. For Gramercy Park
    as a new district in the 1850s, see
    'The Old Maid', Part I, 1, ONY.
    BG, ch. 1, iii. G.A. Sala, *America
    Revisited*, 1879, quoted in Stern, 43.
    AI, ch. 9.
7 BG, ch. 1, i.
8 BG, ch. 1, iii; LGNY, 275.
9 See EW to KC, 25 November 1932,
    Letters 556–7.
10 BG, ch. 1, iii.
11 BG, ch. 2, iv; 'Literature', MSS, 20.
12 BG, ch. 1, iii; 'The Old Maid', Part
    I, ch. 1, ONY; BG, ch. 1, iii.
13 'The Old Maid', Part II, ch. 11,
    ONY; BG, ch. 1, iii.
14 Morris, 141.
15 'False Dawn', Part I, ch. 1, ONY.
16 Stern, 334.
17 Stern, 577; Morris, 141; Arnold
    Lewis, James Turner and Steve
    McQuillin, eds, *The Opulent Interiors
    of the Gilded Age*, Dover, 1986;
    Dwight, 22, 35.
18 BG, ch. 2, i.

19　Preston, 22, 196–7; Nancy Bentley, 'Edith Wharton and the Science of Manners', CCEW, 48.

20　BG, ch. 1, ii.

21　Homberger, 8, 212.

22　Allan Nevins, ed., *The Diary of Philip Hone, 1828–1851*, Dodd, Mead, 1927, 2 vols, II, 757, 781, 796. Terminology cited from Lewis, Benstock, and Dwight; Lewis *et al.*, *op. cit.*, 8. Auchincloss, 12.

23　H.D. Eberlein, *Manors and Historic Houses of the Hudson Valley*, Lippincott, 1924. BG, ch. 3, ii.

24　L&I, 1073; 'The Old Maid', Part I, ch. 1, ONY.

25　Benstock, 16, 11, 4.

26　LGNY, 282–3; L&I, 1071, BG, ch. 3, i.

27　Stern, 10; Strouse, 150.

28　AI, ch. 3; BG, ch. 3, ii; LGNY, 280, 282.

29　'The Old Maid', Part I, ch. 4, ONY.

30　AI, ch. 33.

31　LGNY, 277.

32　DH, ch. 2.

33　BG, ch. 3, i; AI, ch. 21. On the 'exact economy' of calls and card-leaving, see Preston, 3.

34　BG, ch. 3, ii; see Elizabeth Ammons, 'Edith Wharton and Race', in CCEW, 74–6.

35　Benstock, 11.

36　Benstock, 7–8; BG, ch. 2, iii, LGNY, 276; 'Disintegration', MSS, Beinecke; BG, ch. 1, iii; L&I, 1087; BG, ch. 3, iii; L&I, 1075.

37　BG, ch. 3, i; L&I, 1089.

38　BG, ch. 2, iv; L&I, 1074.

39　BG, ch. 3, iii, L&I, 1083.

40　BG, ch. 3, iii. Re 'weird', letter to Hermione Lee, 1 October 2001, from Christopher Morris, whose grandfather was EW's first cousin. Thomas Bender, *New York Intellect: A History of Intellectual Life in New York City*, Knopf, 1987, 214; John Tomsich, *A Genteel Endeavour: American Culture and Politics in the Gilded Age*, Stanford, 1971, 5 (quoting Malcolm Cowley, *After the Genteel Tradition*, 1936, Southern Illinois University Press, 1965, 15). LGNY, 282. Homberger, 185, accuses EW of exaggeration, and lists a number of upper-class post-Civil War writers.

41　AI, chs. 11, 2. For rumours re EW's paternity, Benstock, 7–11, 375–7; Lewis, 535–9, who considers the rumours and thinks them 'on balance false', as most Whartonians, apart from Mainwaring, do. Derived from anecdotes told by MG (MG to PL, Beinecke; Lewis, 536), ET (Frederick Rhinelander King to ET, 21 August, 10 September 1949, Lilly), MC (MC to PL, Beinecke), OC (Benstock, 377). Edmund Wilson (to ET, 21 September 1949, Lilly) said he heard the rumour from Robert Morss Lovett who had been told it by one of EW's friends. Wilson checked it with MC who said EW had some reason to believe that she was the daughter of a young English tutor engaged to teach her brothers. 'She was born years later than they and displayed intellectual tastes and gifts which are said never to have appeared in the family before.' ET replies to Wilson that she had also heard the rumour from MG. 'Old Style', MSS, Beinecke.

42　AI, ch. 7; 'The Spark', ch. 3, ONY; BG, ch. 1, iii. Louis Auchincloss, *The Vanderbilt Era*, Scribner's, 1989, 192.

43　BG, ch. 2, iv.

44　Lucretia Jones, Commonplace Book, Lilly.

45　Emelyn Washburn to ET, September 3 [1938], Lilly.

46　BG, ch. 3, ii.

47　BG, ch. 3, iii,

48　EW to WCB, 31 March 1904, Scribner Archive, Princeton. L&I, 1073–4; EW to MJ, 1 March 1921, Beinecke. On EW's Calvinism, Singley, 1998, ch. 3. Benstock, 24. ET, Diary, June–August 1937, Lilly.

49　Margaret Chanler, *Autumn in the Valley*, Little, Brown, 1936, 109–11; *Roman Spring*, Little, Brown, 1934, 122–3, 128; 'Mrs W.A. Chanler', Obituary, *New York Times*, 20 December 1952.

50　'Memoirs of Margaret Cadwalader Jones' by Jane Maulsby Pindell,

Florence LaFarge, Arnold Whitridge, and Royal Cortissoz, Memorial Service, 12 December 1935, B.J. Farrand Collection, Environmental Design Archives, University of California.

51 MJ, *Lantern Slides*, Merrymount, 1937.

52 EW to MJ, 13 January 1924, Beinecke.

53 L&I, 1085. Emelyn Washburn to ET, 26 September 1938, Lilly.

54 EW to SN, 11 May 1905, Beinecke; BG, ch. 3, i; L&I, 1087; MC, *Autumn in the Valley*, 110.

55 BG, ch. 2, i; L&I, 1079.

56 Emelyn Washburn to ET, 26 September 1938; L&I, 1077, 1084, 1091. Wolff, 22–8, gives a Freudian interpretation of 'oral deprivation', 'rage against the mother', and a transferral of thwarted affection into an insatiable hunger for 'visual and aural beauty'.

57 Morris, 102–3.

58 MJ to EW, 22 November 1919, Beinecke.

59 BG, ch. 3, iii; L&I, 1090.

60 Benstock, 360. Emelyn Washburn to ET, 26 September 1938.

61 Copy in Beinecke. *Verses*, P, 1–25.

62 Millicent Bell, '"Eagdyth" Wharton in the *New York World*, 1879', *Yale University Library Gazette*, Vol. 30, no. 2, October 1955, 64–9.

63 *Fast and Loose*, 107, 111.

64 *Fast and Loose*, 117.

CHAPTER 3: PUSSY JONES

1 Elizabeth Bowen, Preface to *The Last September*, 1929.

2 See Strouse for the definitive account of this period of 'turbulent growth'.

3 Henry James, *The American Scene*, Chapman & Hall, Harper & Brothers, 1907, ch. 2, 'New York Revisited', section iii; Rieder, 88.

4 The art critic Earl Shinn, writing as Edward Strahan, introduction, *Mr Vanderbilt's House and Collection*, 1883–4, quoted in Strouse, 225, and in Arnold Lewis, James Turner and

Steve McQuillin, eds, *The Opulent Interiors of the Gilded Age*, Dover, 1986, 17.

5 Strouse, 110, on the millionaires who profited from the war: Alexander T. Stewart's income in 1863 was over $1.8 million; William B. Astor's $838,525, and Cornelius Vanderbilt's $680,728. On Morgan, Strouse, 236. HJ/EW, 8 February 1905, 48.

6 EW to William Roscoe Taylor, 11 November 1905, Letters 96. Louis Auchincloss, *The Vanderbilt Era*, Scribner's, 1989, 7. Stern, 23. Lewis *et al.*, *op. cit.*, 29.

7 HM, Book I, ch. 14.

8 Auchincloss, *op. cit.*, 31, 38. Lewis *et al.*, *op. cit.*, 27.

9 Two hundred million dollars = about ninety-seven billion in the 2000s. Richard Cheek, *Newport Mansions*, Fort Church Publishers, 1996. *Newport History: Bulletin of the Newport Historical Society*, Summer 1989, Vol. 62, Part 3, no. 215.

10 James, *op. cit.*, 1907, ch. 6, 'The Sense of Newport'. J.K. Van Rensselaer, *The Social Ladder*, Nash & Grayson, 1925, 238. AI, ch. 21, 'The Introducers', CS I, 551, 553.

11 Montgomery, 27, for the rival resorts.

12 HM, Book II, ch. 8.

13 Homberger, 27, 185. Auchincloss, *op. cit.*, 62.

14 Montgomery, 20.

15 Rhea Dulles Foster, *Americans Abroad*, Urlich, 1964, 134. Montgomery, 19, 27, 30, 32; Preston, 3–4, on the protocol of 'calling'.

16 Elaine Showalter, 'Spragg: The Art of the Deal', in CCEW, 87–8. Stern, 571; Morris, 148. Foster, *op. cit.*, 129. LGNY, 278; B, ch. 6. Van Rensselaer, *op. cit.*, 55.

17 Auchincloss, *op. cit.*, 187. Ward McAllister, *Society As I Have Found It*, Cassell, 1890, 136, 214, 239, 244.

18 Homberger, 8; Lewis *et al.*, *op. cit.*, 8. *New York Social Register* in Yale University Library.

19 Stern, 592; Morris, 154; Homberger, 272, points out that Alva Vanderbilt was by no means a social *arriviste*,

and that the ball 'did not introduce the Vanderbilts to society, but set them on a pinnacle of lavish expenditure'. Foster, *Americans Abroad*, 135; Lewis *et al.*, *op. cit.*, 16; Morris, 240; Van Rensselaer, *op. cit.*, 229.

20 Auchincloss, *op. cit.*, 192, 187. Van Rensselaer, *op. cit*; 230. Morris, 253.

21 Stern, 678–88, and Homberger, 227–35, give the fullest account of the battle over the opera houses.

22 See Thomas Bender, *New York Intellect: A History of Intellectual Life in New York City*, Knopf, 1987, 216.

23 Homberger, 32, 166. See Montgomery for a full account of the 'privacy' debate.

24 B, ch. 6.

25 For the Mortons, see Strouse, 184. For EW's coming-out, see LGNY, 278–9, BG, ch. 4, i; for 'checked', L&I, 1093, Benstock, 42, Montgomery, 23, 46–52.

26 EW to Royal Cortissoz, 11 October 1928, Letters 518. Rieder, 19. BG, ch. 4, i.

27 See Jane Brown, *Beatrix: The Gardening Life of Beatrix Jones Farrand, 1872–1959*, Viking, 1995, 24–6. John Wilmerding, *The Artist's Mount Desert: American Painters on the Maine Coast*, Princeton University Press, 1994. 'Bar Harbor Guide' in Clive Aslet, *The American Country House*, Yale University Press, 1990, 245. Francis Marion Crawford, *Love in Idleness: A Bar Harbor Tale*, Macmillan, 1894, 8–10.

28 Lewis, 38–42; Benstock, 43–5; Emelyn Washburn to ET, 16 October 1938, Lilly. Stern, 716; Morris, 142, 154; Lewis, 40–2. Emelyn Washburn, quoted Benstock, 45.

29 Emelyn Washburn to ET, 16 October 1938, Lilly.

30 Benstock, 48.

31 Benstock, 45–7; Lewis, 44–5; L&I, 1093.

32 EW to Anna Robinson, 2 November 1905, Beinecke; SN to PL, November 1906?, Beinecke.

33 BG, ch. 5, iii.

34 WB to EW, 23 February 1923, Lilly. Letters from EW to WB, 2 February

[1906], 15 November [1905], August [1906], nd [1908?], in Alice Garrett Archives, Evergreen House, Baltimore: see ch. 18, note 70.

35 WB to EW, 25 February 1923, Beinecke; in Benstock, 52, missing the 'all' in 'would all have been good'. Benstock has 'you' where I read 'yours', in the last line of the letter.

36 R, ch. 9.

37 OC to Sarah Codman, 27 October 1913, SPNEA. Edmund Wilson, typescript of review of Lubbock, 1947, Lilly. HJ/EW, 17 November 1906, 68. Royal Cortissoz to EW, 12 May 1936, Lilly. BG, ch. 6, i; Geoffrey Wolff, *Black Sun: The Brief Transit and Violent Eclipse of Harry Crosby*, Random House, 1976, 123, 125. Ramsden, 73.

38 HJ/EW, 3 February 1913, 245; Lewis, 476. WB to EW, 9 November 1898, Beinecke. WB to EW, 26 December 1900, Beinecke. Geoffrey Wolff, *op. cit.*, 129.

39 WB to EW, 15 February 1900, Beinecke.

40 WB to EW, 28 August 1900, 15 February 1901, 5 March 1901, Beinecke.

41 VD, Book I, 9.

42 EW refers to his many letters, to MC, 8 March 1903, Letters 79.

43 EW to MJ, 1 March 1921, Beinecke; Benstock, 376. WB to EW, January 1902, Beinecke.

44 Benstock, 179. BG, ch. 5, i. EW to MC, 18 July 1903, Beinecke.

45 BG, ch. 5, i; EW to SN, 14 June 1916, Letters 379; EW to BB, 16 May 1911, Letters 240; Auchincloss, 62; HM, Book I, ch. 14, Book II, ch. 4; Price, 90; paraphrased in Benstock, 483.

46 EW, markings, Huxley, *Discourses*, 1897; Haeckel, *The History of Creation*, 1893. Ramsden, 55, 60.

47 Lewis, 54, 149; Benstock, 59. BB to MB, 24 December 1931, I Tatti.

48 GL, notes to PL, Beinecke.

49 BG, ch. 3, ii; ch. 5, ii; ch. 6, i. MR, Book I, ch. 3. R, Book 2, ch. 9.

50 Benstock, 73.

51 William Wharton to Grace Kellogg, 2 November 1958, Smith; Emelyn Washburn to ET, 3 September 1938, Beinecke; EW to Robert Grant, 10 February 1928, Beinecke. Benstock, 54; Ramsden, i.

52 Morgan Dix to EW, 1 December 1905, Beinecke.

53 Wedding invitation, Benstock, 56. 'The Old Maid', Part I, i, ONY.

54 Lewis, 547–8.

55 L&I, 1087–8.

56 'Unnamed story', Beinecke.

57 Wolff, 51, Lewis, 53. Benstock, 60.

CHAPTER 4: ITALIAN BACKGROUNDS

1 BG, ch. 8, i, ch. 6, i. Auchincloss, 51–2.

2 WF, ch. 5, iv. Wolff, 51.

3 EW to SN, 12 April 1908, Letters 140; EW to BB, June 1912, I Tatti.

4 Benstock, 60. EW to WCB, 18 October 1898, Scribner Archive, Princeton; EW to Barrett Wendell, 15 May 1899, Letters 39.

5 Wolff, 51–2. See Hermione Lee, Virginia Woolf, Chatto & Windus, 1996, 183. Benstock, 95. Chronology, CS, II, 827.

6 See, for example, Edmund Wilson, 'Justice to Edith Wharton', The Wound and the Bow, W.H. Allen & Co Ltd, 1941; Claudia Roth Pierpont, 'Cries and Whispers', New Yorker, 2 April 2001, 68; collected in her Passionate Minds, Random House, 2001; Tom Lutz, American Nervousness, Cornell University Press, 1991, 14–15, 232.

7 BG, ch. 6, i, ii.

8 EW to WCB, 11 June 1903, Scribner Archive, Princeton; EW to SN, 24 January 1902, Letters 55; 9 March 1902, Beinecke.

9 Benstock, 68, 74.

10 EW to OC, 28 November 1896, SPNEA; Margaret Chanler, Autumn in the Valley, Little Brown, 1936, 12.

11 EW to BB, 6 January 1925, I Tatti; BG, ch. 5, ii; EW to MC, 2 October 1925, Beinecke.

12 Lewis, 59; EW to BB, 6 January 1925, I Tatti. All quotations, pp. 81–85, from Vanadis.

13 Thought to be the first ever account by an American of Mount Athos; see SBW, 18.

14 EW to MC, 20 February 1926; EW to GL, 22 April 1926, in Benstock, 64.

15 Also quoted in her Diary, 26 October 1931, Beinecke, and in EW to GL, 2 April 1936, Letters 593.

16 IB, 'March in Italy', ii.

17 EW to JHS, 23 May 1932, Letters 549. Translation, William Mann, 1965.

18 Goethe, Italian Journey, trans. W.H. Auden and Elizabeth Mayer, Penguin, 1970, 165. EW to SN, 1 July 1901, 8 August 1901, 13 November 1900, Beinecke.

19 Goethe, op. cit., 309, 125, 167, 282, 376, 133.

20 BG, ch. 5, i.

21 'The Blashfields' Italian Cities', Wegener, 63; IB, 'A Tuscan Shrine'.

22 Goethe, op. cit., 93. MF would note the connection between Goethe's Roman Elegies and EW's most passionate love-poem, 'Terminus'. Beinecke.

23 EW to OC, 5 May 1895, SPNEA. See Beer 1990, 9, and SBW, 9, on how Italy helped to make her a writer. 'The House of the Dead Hand', CS, I, 528. MF quotes it in his essay on HJ, 1910, which she helped him to write. Wegener, 317.

24 BG, ch. 6, iii; ch. 5, ii; EW to MC, March 8 1903, Letters 78; BG, ch. 5, ii.

25 Mary Cadwalader Jones, European Travel for Women, Macmillan, 1900.

26 BG, ch. 6, iii.

27 BG, ch. 5, i; IB, 'March in Italy', v; 'A Midsummer Week's Dream', iii; Benstock, 81. EW to OC, 17 June 1896, SPNEA.

28 EW to SN, 17 March 1903, Letters 80; 23 March 1903, Beinecke.

29 For first meeting with Berensons: Bernard Berenson: Sketch for a Self-Portrait, Pantheon, 1949, 24; Mary Berenson, A Self-Portrait from Her Letters and Diaries, eds Barbara

30 Strachey and Jayne Samuels, Gollancz, 1983, 109; cited Lewis, 269, Dwight, 74. See ch. 12.

30 Janet Ross, *The Florentine Villas*, Dent, 1901, 115; BG, ch. 6, iii; *A Passionate Apprentice: the Early Journals of Virginia Woolf*, ed. Mitchell Leaska, Hogarth Press, 1990, 397. EW refers in BG to Maria Pasolini as Angelica Rasponi's sister, but must mean sister-in-law, since she married Angelica's brother, Piero Pasolini.

31 EW to BB, 16 May 1911, Letters 239, in Benstock, 253; EW to WCB, 29 April 1903, Scribner Archive, Princeton.

32 EW to MF, 12 May 1911, Letters 237; EW to ET, 21 May 1924, Lilly; *Gazzettino Balneare*, Salsomaggiore, 30 September 1911, 1 June 1912, 22 June 1912; *Il Gazzettino di Salso-maggiore*, 29 May 1912, 12 June 1912; Pietro Delfanti, *Salsomaggiore Therme*, edizioni Pontegobbo, 1995, 39–56; R. Bossaglia and M.B. Bucchini, *Tra Liberty é Déco: Salsomaggiore*, Casa di Risparmio di Parma, 1986, 112–20. EW recorded visits to Salso in 1905, 1911, 1912, 1923, 1924, 1930 and 1932.

33 EW to WCB, 16 August 1903, Letters 86. For the 'age of mass tourism' of Americans in Italy, see T.E. Stebbins, *The Lure of Italy: American Artists and the Italian Experience 1760–1914*, Harry Abrams, 1982, 94. WCB to EW, 24 August 1903, EW to Edward Burlinghame, 31 September 1903, Scribner Archive, Princeton.

34 IB, 'An Alpine Posting Inn', 'A Midsummer Week's Dream, i, 'Sanctuaries of the Alps', 'Picturesque Milan', v; 'Italian Backgrounds', i, ii. 'Mona Lisa', P, 60.

35 IB, 'Sanctuaries of the Alps', 'Picturesque Milan', ii, 56, 168, 'Italian Backgrounds', v, 'A Tuscan Shrine'.

36 IB, 'Sanctuaries of the Alps', 'A Tuscan Shrine'.

37 IB, 'Picturesque Milan', iii.

38 EW to MC, 8 March 1903, Letters 77–8.

39 EW to CEN, 19 November 1901, 26 November 1901, Houghton; CEN to Samuel Ward, 10 March 1902. SN included this in her edition of his *Collected Letters*, Constable, 1913, Vol. 2, 319, and EW marked it in her copy. Ramsden, 93. CEN, *Collected Letters*, 2, 195. CEN to Howells, 26 March 1902, quoted in John Tomsich, *A Genteel Endeavour*, Stanford, 1971, 83.

40 EW to SN, 5 June 1903, Letters 84.

41 For Norton's relation to EW see also Van Wyck Brooks, *The Dream of Arcadia: American Writers and Artists in Italy, 1760–1915*, Dent, 1958, 122, 244.

42 'Memories of Bourget Overseas', 1936, Wegener, 211–25.

43 For Minnie Bourget, Elisabeth Sylvain-David in M.G. Martin-Gistucci, ed., *Paul Bourget et l'Italie*, Editions Slatkine, Geneva, 1985, 61. BG, ch. 7, iii; 'Italy Again', October 1934, Beinecke. See SBW, 9, on EW's distinction from 'amateur' tourism. Wegener, 217. IB, 'March in Italy', v. EW to SN, 18 August 1901, Beinecke; EW to MC, 8 March 1903, Letters 77. *Sensations* was translated in 1923 as 'The Glamour of Italy', but really means 'impressions'.

44 PB, *Sensations d'Italie*, translated by Lauretta Maitland as *The Glamour of Italy*, Elkin Mathews, 1923, 218, 209–10.

45 Benstock, 77.

46 EW to 'Miss Paget', 31 December, nd, Somerville. BG, ch. 6, iii. Bell, 61. Wegener, 118.

47 Peter Gunn, *Vernon Lee/Violet Paget, 1853–1935*, Oxford University Press, 1964, 66, 104, 3. Caroline Moorehead, *Iris Origo*, John Murray, 2000, 28.

48 EW notes, Beinecke.

49 Vernon Lee, 'Old Italian Gardens', *Limbo and Other Essays*, Grant Richards, 1897, 130. Verlaine, 'Clair de Lune', *Fêtes Galantes*, slightly misquoted by VL in 'Old Italian Gardens' in *Ariadne in Mantua and Limbo*, 1930, 131.

50 IVG, I. IB, 'A Midsummer Week's Dream', v. BG, ch. 5, i.

51 VL, review of VD, *La Cultura*, 21, no. 20 (1903), 305–7, translated Marcella Barzetti for CCEW, 199–202. EW to VL, 4 December 1932, Somerville: 'One of the dearest [memories] was my first meeting with you & your brother, & I did so enjoy setting down all I could remember of those good old days, & my visits to the Palmerino, & the Italian translation of *The Valley of Decision* which so mysteriously vanished in the oubliettes of the *Nuova Antologia*; & your beautiful introduction to it, which I still cherish.'

52 Richard M. Dunn, *Geoffrey Scott and the Berenson Circle*, Edwin Mellon Press, 1998, 110.

53 EW to WCB, 7 January 1904, Letters 34. Gunn, *Vernon Lee/Violet Paget*, 179. VL to EW, 6 February 1926; EW to GL, 10 July 1930, Beinecke. VL to EW, 8 December 1928, Lilly. EW to VL, 1 November 1928, 17 May 1932, Somerville.

54 BG, ch. 5, i.

55 Ramsden lists L. G. Blanc, *Vocabolario Dantesco* (1896), 13; Edmund Gardner, *Dante's Ten Heavens* (1898), 45; A.F. Ozanam, *Dante et La Philosophie Catholique au 13e Siècle* (1840), 95; G.A. Scartazzini, *Prolegomeni Della Divina Commedia* (1890), 110; Paget Toynbee, *Dante Studies and Researches* (1902), 130. BG, ch. 5, i, ch. 6, iii;' J.A. Symonds, *Sketches in Italy and Greece*, Smith Elder, 1879, p. 155. Jacob Burckhardt, *The Civilization of the Renaissance*, trans. S. G. Middlemore, Macmillan, New York, 1904, 56, 460, 471, 185, 320. J.A. Symonds, *The Renaissance in Italy*, Scribners, 1875–6, 9, 460.

56 EW to NM, 31 May 1932, Letters 552; PB also visited Leopardi's home, and wrote it up in 'Ancona', in *The Glamour of Italy*, trans. Lauretta Maitland, Elkin Mathews, 1923, 96–107.

57 BG, ch. 6, ii. Charles de Brosses, *Lettres familières écrites d'Italie, 1739–1740*, Didier, Paris, 3rd edition, 1861, Vol. II, 352.

58 IB, 'Italian Backgrounds', viii.

59 IB, 'Italian Backgrounds', vii. EW to MC, 17 May 1902, Letters 63, for VD and Longhi. J.A. Symonds, introduction and translation, *The Memoirs of Count Carlo Gozzi*, 2 vols, 1889, LI 341. EW copies a paragraph into her notes for VD on how we can learn from the eighteenth-century Venetians: what we want in our art, in this scientific age, are 'transcripts from life' like theirs.

60 De Brosses, *op. cit.*, II, 352, on immorality and improvisations of the *commedia dell'arte*, and its amazing influence on Molière. Symonds, *op. cit.*, Vol. I, 26–73; EW, Notes and plan for VD, Beinecke.

61 BG, II, ii. VD, Book II, ch. 7. IB, 'Sub Umbra Liliorum', 'A Midsummer Week's Dream', i.

62 IB, 'Italian Backgrounds', ix.

63 Lewis, 192; Ramsden, 22. VD, Book II, ch. 8.

64 'The Last Giustiniani', *Scribner's Magazine*, October 1889; see EW to EB, 23 November 1905, Letters 98. James Morris tells the Giustiniani story in *Venice*, Faber, 1960, 47. EW to WCB, 6 November 1902, Letters 75. *Artemis to Actaeon*, 1906, 23. See also 'The Tomb of Ilaria Giunigi at Lucca' (1891), 'Margaret of Cortona' (1901), and 'Vesalius in Zante' (1902). P, 116, 27–83.

65 Notebook, Lilly.

66 CS I, 238.

67 CS I, 538.

68 Nathaniel Hawthorne, *The Marble Faun*, Everyman, 1995, 327, 350, 354, 272.

69 Henry James, *Roderick Hudson*, World's Classics, 1980, 127, 204, 247, 26.

70 WF, ch. 3, vi. EW to WCB, 4 February 1902, Letters 58.

71 IB, 'Italian Backgrounds', viii. J.H.

Stonehouse, *John Inglesant*, Macmillan, 1894, 284, 350. VD, Book III, ch. 3.

72 Notes to VD, Beinecke.

73 Wegener, 112.

74 VD, Book IV, ch. 2.

75 VD, Book II, chs 10, 9, 1; Book IV, chs 3, 7, 10, 8.

76 'The New Day', MSS, Beinecke. WB to EW, 16 April 1902, Beinecke. HJ/EW, 17 August 1902, 34.

77 WB to EW, 1 May 1900, 7 November 1901, 27 February 1902, Beinecke. EW to WCB, 4 March 1902, Scribner Archive, Princeton, notes that many of the reviews of VD were looking for 'what a friend of mine calls When-Valley-Was-in-Flower, & are proportionally disappointed'.

78 Benstock, 126. Margaret Wagner, *Maxfield Parrish & The Illustrators of the American Golden Age*, San Francisco, Pomegranate, 2000, 111.

79 Sales of VD, Benstock, 125–6. BG, ch. 6, iii. Henry Hope Reed, Introduction to IVG, Da Capo Press, 1988, vii. EW to Richard Gilder, 3 August 1903, Beinecke. EW to 'Miss Paget', 31 December, nd, Somerville.

80 EW to Gilder, 10 October 1902, 4 August 1908, Beinecke. EW to Gilder, 18 March 1903, Letters 83; BG, ch. 6, iii.

81 IVG, 'Introduction'; ch. 5.

82 Charles Quest-Ritson, *The English Garden Abroad*, Penguin, 1992, 124.

83 Harold Acton, *Tuscan Villas*, Thames & Hudson, 1973, 253. Quest-Ritson, *op. cit.*, 122. Robin Lane Fox, 'Come into the Garden, Edith', *Financial Times*, 16 August 1998. Van Wyck Brooks, *op. cit.*, 243.

84 Moorehead, *op. cit.*, 26–8. Keith Morgan, Introduction, Charles Platt, *Italian Gardens*, 1894, Saga Press edition, 1993, 113–15. Charles Platt, *op. cit.*, 15, 83, 32, 35, 60; IVG, 26, 109, 93, 155.

85 Charles Latham and Evelyn March Phillips, *The Gardens of Italy*, Country Life, 1905, I, 82; IVG, ch. 3. In a 1919 revision, with plans and architectural commentary added by Arthur Botton, Latham and Phillips incorporated echoes of EW, who is cited in the bibliography.

86 Inigo Triggs, *The Art of Garden Design in Italy*, Longman's, 1906, Preface.

87 IVG, chs 3, 6, 1, 4.

88 IVG, ch. 6.

89 IVG, ch. 4.

90 For similar remarks see Latham and Phillips, *op. cit.*, II, 72; Triggs, *op. cit.*, 39; H.D. Eberlein, *Manors and Historic Houses of the Hudson Valley*, Lippincott, 1924, 67. But recent garden historians disagree about there being no flowers in old Italian gardens. See Henry Hope Reed, Introduction to IVG, viii, citing Georgina Masson, *Italian Gardens*, Abrams, 1962. IVG, chs 2, 3, 'Introduction', ch. 5.

91 Stebbins, *op. cit.*, 361.

92 IVG, ch. 6.

93 IVG, chs 4, 7, 1, 5.

94 IVG, chs 3, 2, 7, 6.

95 IVG, chs 7, 4.

96 Acton, *op. cit.*, 144, 276; Triggs, *op. cit.*, 83; BB, *Sunset and Twilight: Diaries 1947–1958*, 1964, all describe its perfection. Quest-Ritson, *op. cit.*, 121. Judith Kinnard, 'The Villa Gamberaia in Settignano: the street in the garden', *Journal of Garden History*, 1986, Vol. 6, Part I, 14. IVG, 47.

CHAPTER 5: THE DECORATION OF HOUSES

1 Beatrix Jones, Diary, 1895, Environmental Design Archives, University of California.

2 DH, ch. 3.

3 Clive Aslet, *The American Country House*, Yale University Press, 1990, 27; Charles Beveridge and Paul Rocheleau, *Frederick Law Olmsted: Designing the American Landscape*, Universe, 1998, 28.

4 EW to SN, 21 February 1906, Letters 101. Beveridge and Rocheleau, *op. cit.*, 40, 115, 118.

5 Jane Brown, *Beatrix: The Gardening Life of Beatrix Jones Farrand, 1872–1959*, Viking, 1995, 28. Charles Platt, *Italian Gardens*, 1894, Saga Press edition, 1993, with 'Overview' by Keith Morgan, 113–15; Alan Emmet, 'Faulkner Farm: An Italian Garden in Massachusetts', *Journal of Garden History*, Vol. 6, No. 2, 1986, 162–78; Richard Kennedy, 'Italianate Gardens in America', *Journal of Garden History*, Vol. 10, no. 1, 1990, 10–70.

6 Brown, *op. cit.*, 47.

7 Brown, *op. cit.*, 53; BG, ch. 10, vi.

8 Ramsden, 13.

9 Eleanor Dwight, review of Brown, *op. cit.*, in *New York Times Book Review*, 26 March 1995, 26.

10 Beatrix Jones, 'The Garden as a Picture', *Scribner's Magazine*, Vol. 42, July 1907, 2–8.

11 'The Valley of Childish Things', 1896, CS I, 46–7. Aslet, *op. cit.*, 26. Antoinette Downing and Vincent Scully, *The Architectural Heritage of Newport, Rhode Island, 1640–1915*, Harvard University Press, 1952, 141, 158–9. EW to OC, 2 May 1897, in Dwight, 52. Aslet, *op. cit.*, 63.

12 Lewis, 115, Benstock, 135; story derived from Louise Hall Thorp, *Mrs Jack: A Biography of Isabella Stewart Gardner*, Little, Brown, 1965.

13 Brown, *op. cit.*, 26; David Gebhard, ed., *Accents as Well as Broad Effects: Mariana Griswold Van Rensselaer, Writings on Architecture, Landscape and the Environment*, University of California, 1996, 17, 18, 245, 346, 257, 206.

14 BG, ch. 7, i. Lewis, 77; Benstock, 84, 86; Metcalf, 34. EW to BB, 27 October 1909, I Tatti. OC to Sarah Codman, 2 October 1913, SPNEA; Metcalf, 42, 25; Aslet, *op. cit.*, 56.

15 Metcalf, 9, 68, 42.

16 OC to Sarah Codman, Summer 1896, SPNEA. Metcalf, 85; Dwight, 38; Benstock, 59; Mount, 27.

17 *Atlas of the City of Newport*, 1883, 1893; Mount, 28; Dwight, 42–3; Lewis, 68.

18 Benstock notes that she took out the mortgage at the same time as buying 882 Park Avenue, 483, note 37. Lewis, 68.

19 For Land's End, Dwight, 48, 59; Metcalf, 85, 140, 142, 146; Mount, 29–30.

20 EW to OC, 4 May 1896, 7 June 1896, SPNEA; OC to Sarah Codman, 5 January 1897, in Dwight, 62.

21 Elsie de Wolfe, *After All*, Heinemann, 1935, 35, in Mount, 32. For 882, BG, ch. 7, i; Mount, 31–2; Lewis, 67. HJ to HS, in Leon Edel, *Henry James: A Life*, Collins, 1987, 601.

22 Lubbock, 38–9; retold, Lewis, 118.

23 Metcalf, 148; BG, ch. 5, iii. BG, ch. 5, iii. Metcalf, 153, 150. OC to Sarah Codman, January 1897, Dwight, 58.

24 'Newport's Old Houses', 8 January 1896, *Newport Daily News*, Wegener, 55. Benstock, 84; Wegener, 60–1.

25 Metcalf, 133; William A. Coles, 'The Genesis of a Classic', DH, The Classical America Series, 1993, 263. BG, ch. 5, iii. AI, ch. 33.

26 DH, chs 1, 4, 5, 7, 6.

27 DH, chs 1, 3. EW to WCB, 9 July 1897, Scribner archive, Princeton.

28 DH, chs 1, 2.

29 DH, 'Introduction', chs 2, 3. 'Introduction', IVG.

30 By Ruby Ross Goodnow, 1914, in Aslet, *op. cit.*, 29.

31 DH, ch. 3.

32 DH, chs 7, 10. 'Bewitched', CS II, 349.

33 DH, ch. 12. By the mid-eighteenth century, the library of the large English house was 'a focal living and entertaining room . . . the communal centre of the house' (as in Hogarth's 1738 painting of the Cholmondeley family). James Raven in *The Practice and Representation of Reading in England*, eds James Raven, Helen Small and Naomi Tadmore, Cambridge University Press, 1996, 176, 188.

34 *The Touchstone*, EWCS I, 179.

35 DH, ch. 10. 'New Year's Day', ch. 7, ONY. See Vanessa Chase, 'Edith Wharton, The Decoration of Houses, and Gender in Turn-of-the-Century America', in *Architecture and Feminism*,

Yale University Press, 1996, 132, on EW's agenda re house-decoration as that of 'a woman who is truly in control'.

36 DH, chs. 2, 14, 8.

37 Metcalf, 42–3. EW to WCB, 18 September 1898, Scribner archive, Princeton. DH, 'Introduction', chs 16, 2, 8, 6, 10, 16, 7, 3, 16.

38 DH, ch. 15.

39 Mount, 64; Metcalf, 160, 133. EW suggested a sequel called *Garden Architecture* or *The Garden in Relation to the House* (which became her own IVG). Forty years later, she wanted to do a new, cheap, popular edition of *The Decoration of Houses*, but her illness prevented it. EW to Gilder, 10 June 1903, Beinecke. Batsford, circular for DH, 1899, SPNEA. John B. Bayley, 'The Decoration of Houses as a Practical Handbook', *The Decoration of Houses* 1993 edition, 255. Elsie de Wolfe, *The House in Good Taste*, Pitman, 1914, 21.

40 EW to OC, 18 April 1898, 20 February 1899, SPNEA. WB to EW, 2 November 1899, Beinecke. TW to OC, 8 December 1897, SPNEA. Brown, *op. cit.*, 78.

41 EW to OC, 1 August 1900, Dwight, 67. WB to EW, 8 August 1900, Beinecke.

42 EW to SN, 3 June 1901, Beinecke.

43 ET, document relating to EW's Will, 1939, Lilly, and EWRA. On LJ's will, Benstock 82–3, 120; Lewis, 101; Wolff, 79.

44 EW to SN, 18 August 1901, Beinecke.

45 Lewis, 101.

46 Benstock, 116, 131, 138, 271; Lewis, 100, 122; Metcalf, 182, note 87; Mount, 51; Carole Owens, *The Berkshire Cottages*, Cottage Press, 1984, 140ff.

47 Dwight, 60–1, Metcalf, 146. EW to OC, 10 November 1899, SPNEA. Mount, 48.

48 OC to Sarah Codman, 20 August 1896, SPNEA. TW to OC, 4 September 1895, 24 May 1895, 11 May 1902, 12 September 1897, 11 November 1897, SPNEA. OC to

Sarah Codman, 1 March 1901, 17 February 1901, 23 February 1901, 25 February 1901, 11 March 1901, 7 February 1901; Mount, 40–1.

49 EW to OC, 25 March 1901, SPNEA. OC to Sarah Codman, 16 April 1901, 5 January 1914, SPNEA.

50 OC to Sarah Codman, 19 December 1902, SPNEA.

51 Mount, 42–3.

52 WB to EW, 5 March 1901, 27 March 1901, Beinecke.

53 OC to Sarah Codman, 8 October 1902, SPNEA. Cornelia Gilder, 'Pine Acre', March 2001, unpublished; Scott Marshall, 'Notes on Pine Acre', nd, unpublished.

54 *The Berkshire Hills: A WPA Guide*, Northeastern University Press, Boston, 1939, 1987, 161. EW to MF, 12 May [1911], Letters 238; Ramsden, 85. Rev. R. DeWitt Mallary, *Lenox and the Berkshire Highlands*, Putnam, 1902, 62, 24, 83.

55 In *The Berkshire Hills*, 133.

56 HJ to EW, 5 October 1904, HJ/EW, 39; EW to SN, 27 September 1904, Beinecke; EW to SN, 5 July 1905, Beinecke, and EW to CEN, 1 July 1905, Letters 93. Herman Melville, 'The Piazza', 1856, *Piazza Tales*.

57 William Tague and Robert Kimball, eds, revised Tyler Resch, *Berkshire: The First Three Hundred Years*, Eagle Publishing Co, Pittsfield, 1961, 1976, 20–1, 40.

58 Owens, *op. cit.*, 18, 88. *The Berkshire Hills*, 125, 126–31; DeWitt Mallary, *op. cit.*, 170, 204.

59 *The Berkshire Hills*, 125; Owens, *op. cit.*, 119, 163; DeWitt Mallary, *op. cit.*, 193; on Mrs Sloane, OC to Sarah Codman, 19 March 1901, in Dwight, 101, Metcalf, 162.

60 Henry James, *The American Scene*, 1907, ch. 6, 'The Sense of Newport', in Aslet, *op. cit.*, 155; Aslet, *op. cit.*, 157–8; *The Berkshire Hills*, 125; Owens, *op. cit.*, 19, 117; *Lenox Life* in Mount, 52. 'American Country Dwellings', *Century*, 32, 10, June 1886, 200–20, in Gebhard, *op. cit.*, 245; Aslet, *op. cit.*, 78.

61 Metcalf, 164; Mount, 63; Dwight, 95; DeWitt Mallary, *op. cit.*, 201.

62 EW to BB, 6 August 1911, Letters 251–2, in Mount, 67.

63 HJ to HS, 17 October 1904, in HJL, 4, 325–6, frequently quoted, e.g. in Benstock, 130; Charles Quest-Ritson, *The English Garden Abroad*, Penguin, 1992, 122.

64 Mount, 53, 68; Metcalf, 164, 166.

65 Mount, 148, 151; Lewis, 136, 160.

66 Benstock, 131; Metcalf, 98, 166; Dwight, 93, describing 'a series of barriers to protect Edith at her work and yet allow the house to function with visitors and guests'.

67 HJ, *The American Scene*, 1907, 'New York', ch. 4, pt ii.

68 Metcalf, 169; Mount, 78, 99, 81–6; Ramsden, xx.

69 EW to OC, 31 December 1901, SPNEA.

70 Mount, 110.

71 Mount, 110, 107, 106; Scott Marshall, 'Staff at The Mount', *Vista*, Edith Wharton Restoration, 1994; 'Employee – E.R. Wharton', *Vista*, Summer 87, 4; Owens, *op. cit.*, 92.

72 BG, ch. 6, ii, ch. 7, i. Aslet, *op. cit.*, 90; Dwight, 112; EW to George Dorr, 3 September 1904, Beinecke, in Dwight, 116.

73 Metcalf, 171; EW to SN, 23 July 1905, Beinecke; Dwight, 114, 116; Owens, *op. cit.*, 72; *The Royal Horticultural Society Gardeners' Encyclopaedia*, 1989.

74 Hildegarde Hawthorne, *The Lure of the Garden*, Century, 1911, 135–6. In Metcalf, 171; Dwight, 112.

75 Brown, *op. cit.*, 80, quoting Lubbock, 29. Choate's remark, however, could also be (and has been) taken as a compliment.

76 Dogs: Lewis, 105, 160, 168, 495; Benstock, 152; Dwight, 5, 35, 40, 101, 182 (notes Paris dogs); Bauer, 188. EW to SN, 29 August 1902, Letters 67; EW to WT, 16 May 1937.

77 EW to MC, 8 June 1908, Beinecke; EW to SN, 30 December 1904, Beinecke. EW to 'Miss Phelps', Smith; Lewis, 136; Helen and Mary

MacDonald, *A History of the Lenox Library*, Lenox, 1956, 12; 'Lenox Library Annual Reports', 1901–2. *Newport Daily News*, 4 November 1907.

78 Katherine Sargent Osborn (née Haven), 'Highwood to 1914', unpublished; property of Cornelia Gilder.

79 OC to Sarah Codman, 1 July 1901, 25 February 1901, SPNEA; EW to SN, 1 September 1902, Beinecke, speaks of gathering information about America at the Vanderbilts. Lewis, 148–9. HS to EW, 3 December 1905, Beinecke. Helen Aldis Lathrop to 'Anny', Bradley Family Papers, MC 424 #279, Schlesinger Library, Radcliffe Institute, Harvard University.

80 Diary, 1905–6, Beinecke.

81 BG, ch. 7, ii.

82 EW to SN, 24 June 1906, 7 July 1906, Diary, 28 June 1906, Beinecke; Wegener, 196.

83 J.B. Bishop, *Theodore Roosevelt and his Time*, Hodder & Stoughton, 1920, Vol. I, 61. *Letters of Theodore Roosevelt and Henry Cabot Lodge* (4 March 1910), Scribner's, 1925.

84 EW to SN, 29 August, 1 September, 2 September 1902, Beinecke; Letters 67; Lewis, 112–13; Bishop, *op. cit.*, I, 196; Benstock, 90, 129; *Leslie's Weekly*, August 1902, in Tague and Kimball, rev. Resch, *op. cit.*, 71.

85 Diary, 22 June 1905, Beinecke; John Morton Blum, *The Republican Roosevelt*, Harvard University Press, 1997, 30; Theodore Roosevelt, *An Autobiography*, Scribner's, 1913, 1926 edition, 322; Lewis, 145; TR to EW, 15 August 1918, in Bishop, *op. cit.*, II, 455.

86 Lewis, 144; Blum, *op. cit.*, 32; *Henry James: A Life in Letters*, ed. Philip Horne, Allen Lane, 1999, 163; HJ/EW, 16 January 1906, 44–5.

87 EW to SN, 5 June 1903, Letters 84; 5 May 1904, Letters 90; 19 July 1906, 23 June 1907, Beinecke; 18 December 1907, Letters 125.

88 BG, ch. 7, i.

CHAPTER 6: THE REPUBLIC OF LETTERS

1 Helen Killoran, *The Critical Reception of Edith Wharton*, Camden House, 2001, 27; Linda Wagner-Martin, *The House of Mirth: A Novel of Admonition*, Twayne, 1990, 5; BG, ch. 6, i; ch. 7, ii.

2 BG, ch. 5, iii; EW to WCB, 29 September 1897, 31 October 1897, Scribner Archive, Princeton.

3 Roger Burlingame, *Of Making Many Books*, Penn State University, 1946, 1996, 53.

4 Benstock, 84; BG, ch. 5, iii.

5 Lewis, 71, 77; Benstock, 70. CS to EW, 26 July 1916, Scribner Archive, Princeton.

6 'The Fulness of Life', CS, I, 14.

7 Benstock, 72; Lewis, 65. EW to EB, 19 July 1898, Letters 36.

8 EW to EB, 26 March 1894, Letters 32–3. EW to EB, 16 February 1898, Scribner Archive, Princeton. EW to Barrett Wendell, 15 May 1899, Letters 39.

9 WB to EW, 28 November 1899, 2 April 1901, Beinecke. EW to WCB, 14 December 1900, 22 February 1903; WCB to EW, 7 April 1903; EW to EB, 7 December 1906, Scribner Archive, Princeton.

10 'Finis', MS, Beinecke.

11 Scribner legal records, Scribner Archive, Princeton; Benstock, 99; Killoran, *op. cit.*, 12; EW to Barrett Wendell, 15 May 1899, Letters 39; BG, ch. 6, i.

12 EW to WCB, 3 October 1897, Scribner Archive, Princeton. EW to OC, 9 May 1897, SPNEA, Metcalf, 150; EW to WCB, 3 September 1897, 31 October 1897; Benstock, 86–7.

13 Burlingame, *op. cit.*, 117; EW to CS, 20 March 1899, EW to WCB, 25 April 1899, Scribner Archive, Princeton; Letters 37.

14 Ramsden, 137. EW to Gilder, 3 August 1903, Beinecke; EW to R.U. Johnson, 4 August 1903, Beinecke; EW to WCB, 5 August 1905, Letters 94; EW to WCB, 5 October 1900,

Scribner Archive, Princeton.

15 EW to Robert Grant, 5 December [1904], Houghton.

16 EW to WCB, 27 February 1901, Scribner Archive, Princeton; EW to WCB, 10 July 1898, Letters 36. EW to EB, 18 September 1898, Scribner Archive, Princeton; EW to Richard Gilder, 10 October 1902, Letters 73–4; WCB to EW, 19 November 1900, 30 October 1901, Scribner Archive, Princeton.

17 Ellen Dupree, 'Usually the Reward of Tosh: Edith Wharton's Business Education', EWR, XVII, 2, Fall 2001, 3.

18 Burlingame, *op. cit.*, 8, 80, 86; BG, ch. 7, i.

19 Frederick Macmillan to EW, 11 March 1907, Beinecke.

20 EW to Frederick Macmillan, 19 September 1908, 19 September 1912, Macmillan Archive, British Library ADD MSS 54965–54957.

21 EW to MC, 28 September 1928, Beinecke; Wegener, 209. WCB, 'George Eliot', *Scribner's Magazine*, December 1900, 726.

22 BG, ch. 7, i; WCB to EW, 15 January 1900; 5 July 1897; 22 September 1899; EW to WCB, 14 November 1901, Scribner Archive, Princeton; Burlingame, *op. cit.*, 134.

23 WCB to EW, 27 May 1903, Scribner Archive, Princeton. The plan for the monthly article came to nothing. WCB to EW, 6 July 1904.

24 BG, ch. 7, i, ch. 9, ii; EW to WCB, 31 October 1902, Scribner Archive, Princeton.

25 *The Letters of Richard Watson Gilder*, ed. Rosamond Gilder, Constable, 1916, 114, 389, 294, 401. 'Certain Tendencies in Current Literature', 1887, in Rosamond Gilder, 151.

26 Lewis, 147; Benstock, 87; EW to Annie Fields, Summer 1902, Letters 65; Metcalf, 12. OC to Sarah Codman, 1 July 1901, DBU to OC, 27 February 1901, SPNEA.

27 Martin Hutner, *The Merrymount Press*, The Houghton Library, 1993, xi; Daniel Berkeley Updike, *In the Day's Work*, Harvard, 1924, 49 [in

EW's library]; *Printing Types*, Merrymount Press, 1922, 1937, xiii.

28 G.P. Winship, *Daniel Updike*, Hart, 1947, 43; DBU to EW, 31 May 1937, 26 May 1913, Beinecke; EW to SN, 7 June 1902, Letters 66.

29 *Scribner's Magazine*, Vol. 14, 1893, Vol. 27, 1900, Vol. 34, 1903.

30 James D. Hart, *The Popular Book*, Oxford University Press, 1950, 1976, 184; John Tebbel, *A History of Book Publishing in the US*, Booker, 1975, Vol. I, 148, Vol. III, 39; Michael Anesko, *Friction with the Market: Henry James and the Profession of Authorship*, Oxford University Press, 1986, 308, note 23.

31 The same mixed feelings are found in May Sinclair's novel *The Divine Fire* (1904), which EW admired. EW to SN, 13 February 1904, Beinecke.

32 EW to Bliss Perry, 8 August [1905], Houghton.

33 EW to SN, 2 August 1906, 4 July 1907, 23 June 1907, Beinecke.

34 WB to EW, 27 December 1899, Beinecke; EW to WCB, 31 March 1902, Scribner Archive, Princeton. EW to SN, 2 April 1902, Letters 60. EW to WCB, 25 July 1902, Scribner Archive, Princeton, 12 September 1902, Letters 70. EW to SN, 21 May 1902, Beinecke.

35 WB to EW, 11 November 1898, Beinecke. EW to WCB, 14 February 1902, Letters 58; EW to CS, 11 November 1905, Scribner Archive, Princeton. The Kipling limerick was published in *The Cantab*, 13 October 1898. With thanks to the Kipling Society.

36 For 'Literature' and autobiography, see Beer 1990, ch. 6.

37 'A Glimpse', CS II, 622. EW to SN, 23 January 1908; Letters 140.

38 EW to CS, 22 November 1905, Scribner Archive, Princeton. EW to WCB, 6 November 1902, Letters 75.

39 BG, ch. 9, I; Jeanne Fridérich to PL, 13 October 1951, Beinecke. AI, ch. 29; HM, Book II, ch. 13. R, ch. 23. All MSS, Beinecke.

40 'The Great Miss Netherby', MS, Beinecke.

41 Lewis, 107; Benstock, 125; Wolff, 99, 422; EW to SN, 10 May 1902, Beinecke; WB to EW, 16 April 1902, Beinecke.

42 'Disintegration', Beinecke.

43 'Donnée Book, 1900', Beinecke.

44 EWCS I, 130, 134. CS I, 179.

45 WB to EW, 31 January 1900, 15 February 1900, 'Sat 17' 1900, 27 March 1901, Beinecke; Lewis, 109. 'The Man of Genius', MS, Beinecke.

46 *Lenox Life*, 27 July 1901. Benstock, 110, has the 'two little plays' taking place in 1901 in Lenox, but the paper reports that they were given 'two summers ago' in Lakewood, the home of George Gould in New Jersey. Benstock (113, 117, 121) gives Elsie de Wolfe the cold water story, though WB's letter clearly applies it to Marlowe, and says that EW called the production off herself. WB to EW, 30 July 1900, 22 May 1900, 25 February 1901, 30 March 1901, Beinecke; BG, ch. 7, iii.

47 Wegener, 80.

48 Benstock, 486.

49 EW to SN, 24 January 1902, Letters 56; Benstock, 133, BG, ch. 6, iii; 'Translator's Note', 1902, Benstock, 235.

50 *The Joy of Living*, Scribner's, 1902, Duckworth, 1903, 152, 135, 120.

51 For EW as critic, see Wegener, 'Introduction'. BG, ch. 6, i. EW to WCB, 5 August 1905, Letters 94, cited Wegener, 22. Wegener, 20, 112, 25; BG, ch. 9, ii; EW to Robert Grant, 25 July 1900, Letters 40; 'The Criticism of Fiction', 1914, Wegener, 125.

52 Wegener, 30, 77; EW to Morgan Dix, 5 December 1905, Letters 99. 'The Criticism of Fiction', 1914, Wegener, 127.

53 'Friends', CS I, 214; 'A Cup of Cold Water', CS, I 160.

54 'Bunner Sisters' (written 1892 or 1893, published 1916), CS II, 177, 198, 237.

55 EW to EB, 10 July 1898, Letters 36.

56 'The Quicksand', CS I, 403.

57 'The Reckoning', CS I, 462.

58 EW to WCB, 22 September 1905, Scribner Archive, Princeton.

59 'Souls Belated', CS I, 97, 118.
60 *Sanctuary*, CS I, 339, 386.
61 'The Quicksand', CS I, 409. 'Copy: A Dialogue', CS I, 278. See Mark A. Eaton, 'Publicity and Authorship in *The Touchstone*, or A Portrait of the Artist as a Dead Woman', EWR, XIV, 1, Spring 1997, 7.
62 EW to WCB, 2 February 1904, Scribner Archive, Princeton. 'The Pelican', CS I, 80.
63 'The Muse's Tragedy' was EW's first French publication, translated for the *Revue Hebdomadaire* in July 1900.
64 'The Muse's Tragedy', CS I, 53, 60, 63. See Bridget Bennett, 'Precious Allusions': Female Muses and Authorised Writing', in *Romanticism & Gender*, ed. A. Janowitz, English Association, 1998, 140–59.
65 For the theme of 'Pomegranate Seed' and Persephone's return from the underworld in Wharton, see Waid, 1991.
66 *The Touchstone*, CS I, 193, 172, 164.

CHAPTER 7: OBLIGATIONS

1 EW to SN, August 1903, Beinecke; Lewis, 122, Benstock, 134, 140.
2 EW to SN, 5 May 1904, Beinecke.
3 EW to SN, 19 August 1904, Letters 93.
4 HM, Book I, ch. 15. The story of Tarpeia occurs in Livy, Propertius' Elegies, Book IV (where she is a Vestal Virgin), Ovid, and Plutarch's 'Life of Romulus', where EW would have read it. Thanks to Robin Lane Fox.
5 HM, Book I, ch. 5.
6 HM, Book I, ch. 6, Book II, ch. 2.
7 HM, Book II, ch. 11.
8 HM, Book II, ch. 9.
9 HM, Book II, ch. 3; Book I, ch. 6, 5.
10 HM, Book I, ch. 12.
11 HM, Book I, chs 12, 14.
12 HM, Book 2, ch. 10.
13 BG, ch. 9, ii; EW to Dr Morgan Dix, 5 December 1905, Letters 99.
14 HM, Book 2, chs 8, 2, 10, 7; Book I, chs 13, 15.
15 HM, Book I, ch. 4; Book 2, ch. 11.

16 HM, Book I, chs 6, 15.
17 HM, Book 2, ch. 5.
18 HM, Book II, ch. 1.
19 HM, Book II, chs 6, 3.
20 HM, Book I, ch. 4; Book, II, ch. 4; Book I, chs 11, 12; Book II, ch. 1.
21 HM, Book I, chs 5, 6; Book II, ch. 2. For social Darwinism in HM, see Maureen Howard, 'The Bachelor and the Baby: *The House of Mirth*', CCEW, 153, and Preston, 56–7. Veblen's *The Theory of the Leisure Class* came out in 1899, and applied an anthropological approach to the study of American wealth.
22 HM, Book I, ch. 9.
23 HM, Book II, ch. 7, Book I, ch. 15.
24 HM, Book II, ch. 9.
25 HM Book I, ch. 7; Book II, ch. 10.
26 HM, Book II, ch. 12.
27 WCB to EW, 16 October 1905, Scribner Archive, Princeton.
28 EW to W. R. Thayer, 11 November 1905, Letters 96–7; Benstock, 151.
29 John Tebbel, *A History of Book Publishing in the US*, Booker, 1975, Vol. II, 161.
30 Wegener, 268.
31 HM, Book II, ch. 5; Book I, chs 12, 4.
32 HM, Book II, ch. 2.
33 HM, Book I, ch. 1; Book II, chs 8, 13.
34 HM, Book II, ch. 3.
35 Winthrop Chanler wrote to MC: 'I think Walter Berry is the hero.' Lewis, 153.
36 HM, Book II, ch. 12.
37 HM, Book I, chs 10, 14; Book II, chs 8, 12.
38 Lewis, 151; Dwight, 111.
39 CS I, 630. Diary, 30 November 1905, Beinecke.
40 1905 Diary, Beinecke.
41 EW to SN, 14 June 1906, Beinecke.
42 Diary, 17 September 1905, 22 October 1905, Beinecke.
43 HJ/EW, 8 November 1905, 53.
44 EW to CS, 22 November 1905, Scribner Archive, Princeton.
45 EW to EB, 7 December 1906, Scribner Archive, Princeton.
46 EW to CS, 29 June 1907, Scribner Archive, Princeton.

47 EW to W. R. Thayer, 11 December 1905, Houghton.
48 Lewis, 181.
49 Diary, 25 December 1905, Beinecke.
50 EW to Robert Grant, 26 February 1906, Letters 103; Benstock, 152, 159.
51 See ch. 5 for the Cram accident. Benstock, 148; Diary, 13 July 1905; EW to SN, 15 September 1905; Dwight, 124–5. For EW's interest in euthanasia, see Donna Campbell, Introduction, *The Fruit of the Tree*, Northeastern University Press, 2000, xl.
52 EW to SN, 7 August 1906, Beinecke; Letters 105.
53 EW to SN, [14] March 1906, Beinecke.
54 FT, ch. 2.
55 HJ/EW, 24 November 1907, 78.
56 EW to Robert Grant, 19 November 1907, Letters 124.
57 FT, ch. 43.
58 FT, ch. 29.
59 FT, ch. 36.
60 FT, ch. 4.

CHAPTER 8: THE LEGEND

1 'The Legend', CS I, 790–909.
2 HJ to George Harvey, 21 October 1904, HJL IV, 326. HJ/EW, 2 March 1910, 150.
3 EW to MF, 19 March 1910, Letters 202.
4 'Henry James in his Letters', *Quarterly Review*, July 1920, Wegener, 143; BG, ch. 8, iii.
5 'The Velvet Glove', CTHJ, Vol. 12, 250, 263.
6 HJ/EW, 9 May 1909, 112. HJ/EW, 30 August 1907, 74; 4 October 1907, 74; 24 November 1907, 78; Tintner, 30. EW to SN, 10 May 1909, Beinecke; EW to JHS, 16 May 1909, Beinecke; BG, ch. 12, iii.
7 Lubbock, 70.
8 BG, ch. 10, v.
9 Leon Edel, *Henry James*, Vol. 5, *The Master: 1910–1916*, Lippincott, 1972, 364. HJ, 'Crapy Cornelia', CTHJ, Vol. 12, 201, 212.
10 Henry James, *The Ivory Tower*,

Collins, 1917, 45, 108, 344. Book I, iii, Book II, ii, 'Notes for The Ivory Tower'. HJ, 'A Round of Visits', CTHJ, Vol. 12, 439–40. Henry James, *The Sense of the Past*, Collins, 1917, 4, 11.
11 EW to WCB, 25 June 1904, Letters 91; WCB to EW, 6 July 1904, Scribner Archive, Princeton.
12 HJ/EW, 7 January 1908, 87–8; Bell, 262; 'The Pretext', CS I, 600.
13 HJ/EW, 25 July 1909, 115.
14 Bell, 240.
15 WB to EW, 28 February 1900, Beinecke.
16 FT, ch. 42.
17 Henry James, *The Wings of the Dove*, Scribner, 1902, ch. 38.
18 EW to SN, 1 September 1902, Beinecke; EW to WCB, 12 September 1902, Letters 71; EW to CS, 5 September 1902, Scribner Archive, Princeton; Bell, 77, 202; EW to SN, 12 March 1901, Letters 45; EW to SN, 3 January 1905; EW to SN, 26 November 1905, Beinecke; EW to WCB, 7 January 1904, Letters 88; EW to JHS, 21 January 1911, Beinecke. EW to GL, 4 September 1911, Beinecke.
19 HJ, 'The Younger Generation', TLS, 18 March 1914, 2 April 1914, as 'The New Novel', in *Notes on Novelists, Literary Criticism of Henry James*, Library of America, Vol. I. EW, 'Criticism of Fiction', 14 May 1914, Wegener, 120–8. EW to JHS, 6 August 1911, Letters 253.
20 'Henry James in his Letters', *Quarterly Review*, July 1920, Wegener, 137–49.
21 BG, ch. 8, i. HJ to Edmund Gosse, 27 October 1904, HJL IV, 373. Fred Kaplan, *Henry James*, Hodder & Stoughton, 1992, 453.
22 HJ to Minnie Bourget, 8 April 1899, HJL IV, 104. HJ/EW, 26 October 1900, as in Horne, 347–8; WB to EW, 16 November 1900, Beinecke. HJ to Florence La Farge, Edel, *op. cit.*, 214. HJ/EW, 4 September 1904, 36.
23 HJ to HS, 17 October 1904, HJL IV, 325. HJ to Jessie Allan, 22 October

1904, HJL IV, 329. HJ to Edmund Gosse, 27 October 1904, HJL IV, 331. W.M. Rossetti told Desmond MacCarthy that there was a style of reading poetry aloud which went back to Swinburne, 'who would read with ever-increasing emphasis and lilt'. James and Gosse were both known for this. Evan Charteris, *Life and Letters of Edmund Gosse*, Heinemann, 1931, 59.

24 R.C. Holliday, quoted Edel, *op. cit.*, 315.

25 EW, Diary, Wednesday 4 January 1905, Beinecke; HJ to MJ, 13 January 1905, HJL IV, 338; HJ to HS, Edel, *op. cit.*, 272, 884; BG, ch. 8, v. BG, ch. 7, ii; 'The Whartons' first motor-car', Scott Marshall, EWRA 1990.

26 HJ to William James, 2 July 1905, in Percy Lubbock, *Letters of Henry James*, Macmillan & Scribner's, 1920, Vol. II, 36. EW to CN, 1 July 1905, Letters 93; EW to SN, 1 July 1905, Beinecke.

27 HJ/EW, 8 November 1905, 18 December 1905, 55–7.

28 HJ/EW, 29 March 1906, 61. EW, Diary, 3–4 May 1906, Beinecke. EW to Eunice Maynard, 24 May 1906, Beinecke. 'Swift Camilla' is from Pope's *Essay on Criticism*.

29 HJ/EW, 2 July 1906, 66. HJ to MJ, 8 June 1906, Houghton.

30 HJ to MJ, 18 November 1906, Houghton; HJ to PB 19 December 1906, HJL IV, 433. HJ to Margaret White, 29 December 1908, PL, *op. cit.*, 'Scribner's', Vol. II, 121. HJ/EW, 17 November 1906, 67.

31 SBW, 170.

32 HJ/EW, 4 October 1907, 75.

33 HJ to Jessie Allen, 28 March 1907, HJL IV, 441.

34 HJ/EW, 13 March 1912, 215; EW to SN, 22 March 1907, Beinecke; BG, ch. 12, iii; MFF, Part 2, ch. 1.

35 Dwight, 138; MFF, Part 2, ch. 1. BG, ch. 8, i.

36 MFF, Part 2, chs 2, 3; Bell, 135; EW to SN, 28 March 1907, Beinecke; EW to CEN, 15 May 1907, Letters 115.

37 EW to CEN, 15 May 1907, Letters 115; EW to SN, 28 March 1907, Beinecke. HJ to HS, 15 April 1907, PL, *op. cit.*, Vol. II, 75.

38 For MFF, see SBW, and Bell, 122, 126, 134, 136.

39 MFF, Part 2, chs 3, 4; Henry James, *A Little Tour in France*, Heinemann, 1900, ch. 26; Julian Barnes, 'Introduction', MFF, Picador, 1995. HJ, *A Little Tour in France*, ch. 17; MFF, Part 2, ch. 1. HJ, *A Little Tour in France*, ch. 40; MFF, Part 2, ch. 4. Hermione Lee and Julian Barnes made a two-part radio programme on EW and HJ in France, 'The Proper Vehicle of Passion', aired BBC Radio 4 29 April and 6 May 2004.

40 HJ/EW, 4 October, 24 November, 13 December, 16 December 1907, 2 January 1908, 75–81; HJ to William Norris, 23 December 1907, HJL IV, 481.

CHAPTER 9: FRIENDS IN ENGLAND

1 Lewis, 239; HJ to WB, 12 December 1908, HJL IV, 506; EW to SN, 20 May 1908, Letters 146.

2 EW to OC, 11 July 1899, SPNEA.

3 BG, ch. 4, ii; EW to OC, 1896, SPNEA; EW to SN, 5 June 1903, Letters 84.

4 EW to ET, 27 October 1928, Lilly.

5 BG, ch. 10, vii, EW to SN, 18 November 1908, Letters 165.

6 Percy Lubbock, *Letters of Henry James*, Scribner's, 1920, Vol. II, 75.

7 For Consuelo Yznaga, see Marian Fowler, *In a Gilded Cage*, Random House, 1993, and Amanda Mackenzie Stuart, *Consuelo & Alva: Love and Power in the Gilded Age*, HarperCollins, 2005.

8 Lewis, 243; Adrian Frazier, *George Moore*, Yale University Press, 2000, 248; EW to GL, 19 August 1912, Letters 276; Leon Edel, *Henry James*, Vol. 5, *The Master: 1910–1916*, Lippincott, 1972, 466; Lewis, 242; EW to SN, 3 December 1908, Letters 167.

9 JHS to PL quoting HS, 17 February 1938, Beinecke.

10 Letters 169 n. 10; BG, ch. 10, ii; Benstock, 195.

11 HJ/EW, 13 March 1912, 217; BG, ch. 10, ii; EW to MF, 22 September [1911], Letters, 257.

12 Lady Jeune, *Memories of Fifty Years*, Edward Arnold, 1909, 186–92.

13 BG, ch. 10, ii.

14 HJ to William James, 20 February 1888, Horne, 199.

15 Lewis, 244; Mrs Humphry Ward, *A Writer's Recollections*, Collins, 1918, 310–11. For Stanway see B, ch. 20.

16 EW to Lady Wemyss, 29 October 1915, 28 December 1934, Stanway House. By kind permission of Lord Neidpath and with thanks to Daniel Bratton. Lady Cynthia Asquith, *Diaries 1915–1918*, Hutchinson, 1968, xiv–xv, 91. Colin Clifford, *The Asquiths*, John Murray, 2002, 173, 169. Nicola Beauman, *Cynthia Asquith*, Hamish Hamilton, 1987, 16. Mark Bonham-Carter and Mark Pottle, eds, *Lantern Slides: The Diaries and Letters of Violet Bonham-Carter, 1904–1914*, Weidenfeld & Nicolson, 1996: Diary, November 1905, 93.

17 HJ to Isabella Gardner, 3 September 1911, PL *op. cit.*, Vol. II, 203; Ethel Smyth, *As Time Went On . . .* , Longmans, 1936, 177–8; Horne, 492; John Bird, *Percy Grainger*, Faber, 1982, 139; HJ/EW, 20 October 1914, 313. On the ambiguous relation of Mary Hunter and Sargent, see Stanley Olson, *John Singer Sargent*, St Martin's Press, 1986, 210–15.

18 HJ to Isabella Gardner, 3 September 1911, Lubbock, 203.

19 BG, ch. 12, ii. Philip Tilden, *True Remembrance: The Memoirs of an Architect*, Country Life, 1954, 95; Rachel Padfield, 'Hill Hall: A People's Landscape', unpublished University of Exeter dissertation, April 2001.

20 Jacques-Émile Blanche, *Portraits of a Lifetime*, Dent, 1937, 239.

21 'Hill Hall', English Heritage pamphlet, 1998.

22 *Country Life*, 12 May 1917, 476; Tilden, *op. cit.*, 95.

23 Tilden, *op. cit.*, 95.

24 EW to BF, 2 October 1923, Letters 473.

25 C.M. Mount, *John Singer Sargent*, Cresset Press, 1937, 177–8.

26 In the 1950s, Hill Hall was an overflow open prison for Holloway; its women prisoners included the notorious Christine Keeler. In the 1960s it was gutted by fire. It has now been restored by English Heritage, and is lived in by tenants.

27 HJ to Henry James Jr ('Harry'), 26 November 1911, Horne, 504.

28 Bird, *op. cit.*, 139; HJ to Mary Hunter, 12 May 1910, McGill.

29 HJ/EW, 15 October 1908, 102.

30 HJ to Mary Hunter, 21 February 1909, McGill.

31 HJ/EW, 30 November 1911, 200.

32 HJ/EW, 19 November 1911, 197.

33 HJ/EW, 7 June 1913, 254.

34 HJ/EW, 11 June 1913, 256.

35 HJ to Mary Hunter, 3 July 1912, McGill.

36 BG, ch. 12, ii.

37 EW to Edmund Gosse, 21 July —, Brotherton Library, University of Leeds.

38 EW to JHS, 2 February 1909, Letters 173; BG, ch. 12, ii.

39 HJ/EW, 29 March 1912, 220; 13 March 1912, 216.

40 EW to SN, 18 November, 3 December 1908, Letters 165, 168.

41 BG, ch. 10, i; CC, ch. 42.

42 'The Refugees', CS II, 586.

43 BG, ch. 10, vi.

44 GL MSS, Trinity College Cambridge; Clark, review of Lubbock, 1947, Smith.

45 Percy Lubbock, *Mary Cholmondeley*, Cape, 1928, 58–9.

46 Fred Kaplan, *Henry James*, Hodder & Stoughton, 1992, 518; Lewis, 141; BG, ch. 10; Noel Annan, introduction to Howard Sturgis, *Belchamber*, Oxford University Press, 1986.

47 Ramsden, 120; Sturgis, *op. cit.*, 158, 320, 86, 212; Wegener, 109.

48 BG, ch. 8, ii; Miranda Seymour, *A Ring of Conspirators*, Hodder & Stoughton, 1988, 232.

49 HJ/EW, 29 October 1909, 126.

50 HJ to HS, 2 August 1910, HJL IV, 558.

51 HS to GL, 8 September 1912, Beinecke.
52 HJ/EW, 8 October 1909, 124; HJ to GL, 17 March 1908, PL, *Letters of Henry James*, Vol. II, 95.
53 GL, reminiscence, to PL, Beinecke.
54 EW to GL, 14 February 1925, 28 January 1927, 13 August 1925, Beinecke.
55 PL, *Mary Cholmondeley*, 15, 45.
56 Bell, 111; Seymour, *op. cit.*, 188; HJ/EW, 9 October 1913, 269; HJ to Arthur Benson, 9 May 1912, Horne, 512; Kaplan, *op. cit.*, 453; HJ to PL, 21 April 1913, PL, *Letters of Henry James*, Vol. II, 321; HJ to HS, 11 July 1909, HJL IV, 525; Edel, *op. cit.*, 195.
57 PL to GL, 19 March 1906, Beinecke; PL to GL, 9 July 1914, Beinecke.
58 PL to EW, 7 January 1913, Beinecke.
59 PL to EW, 23 March 1918, Beinecke.
60 JHS to EW, 19 December 1908, Beinecke; EW to JHS, 16 December 1908, Letters 170; 6 February 1909, Beinecke.
61 JHS to PL, 17 February 1938, Beinecke.
62 For Robert Norton: Vicomte de Noailles in 1951, Markow-Totevy, Beinecke; Maurice Paléologue, 'Preface', exhibition, Le Goupy, Paris, 26 April 1922, *Le Maroc: Aquarelles de Robert Douglas Norton*. Walter Gay, 'Preface', exhibition, Galeries Georges Petit, Paris, 2–15 June 1919, *Exposition R.D. Norton: Aquarelles. Exhibition of Water Colours by Robert Douglas Norton, 'In the South of France'*, nd, Brown Robertson Gallery, Madison Avenue, NYC. *Exhibition of Modern American Watercolours*, February–March 1926 [included three Norton paintings of Rome], and *June Exhibition of . . . Water Colours by Robert D Norton*, June 1927 [including Norton paintings of Greece, Normandy, Aix-en-Provence, St Tropez, and the Presqu'Île de Giens, Hyères], Memorial Art Gallery, Rochester, reviewed in *Rochester Democrat & Chronicle*, 26 June 1927, 8. All referenced in *Exhibition Catalogues, Frick Art Reference Library*.

Thanks to Gertrude Wilmers and to Lu Harper, director of library services, Memorial Art Gallery, Rochester. Robert Norton, *Painting in East and West*, Edward Arnold, 1913, 123, 156, 168, 193, 299. WF, I, i; Ramsden, 109, 53, 99. EW, 'Commonplace Book', 1905, 109. Lewis, 382, Letters 363, Benstock, 312, all describe Robert Norton as working in the war at 'the British Admiralty'; but Paléologue's preface to his exhibition describes him as Secretary to the British Ambassador in Paris.
63 HJ to HS, 16 July 1909, HJL IV, 527; HS to HJ, undated [1909], Beinecke; HS to EW, 16 July 1909, Beinecke.
64 Wegener, 299–304; HJ/EW, 25 September 1910, 170.
65 HJ/EW, 21 June 1910, 164; 8 February 1910, 147.
66 HJ/EW, 30 July 1913, 262.
67 Lewis, 348; HJ/EW, 30 July 1913, 6 September 1913, 262–3; Fiona Cowell, 'The Archer Family and Coopersale House' (unpublished) and 'Adam Holt, Gardener: His Work at Coopersale House, Essex', *Garden History*, Winter 1998, Vol. 26, no. 2, 214–17. Fred Brown, 'Coopersale House Circa 17th Century' in *The Scribe, Coopersale Institute*; Coopersale House description in *Register of Parks and Gardens of Special Historic Interest*; *Victoria History of Essex*, Vol. IV, 268–9; I am grateful for information about Coopersale from Chris Hoare, Isabel Rushmore, Fiona Cowell and Susan Campbell.
68 EW to MB, 24 August 1913, Letters 308; HJ/EW, 10 September 1913, 265; HJ/EW, 16 September 1913, 268. HJ to MJ, 31 October 1913, Houghton; HJ to Mary Hunter, 25 July 1913, McGill.
69 HJ/EW, 28 June 1913, 259; HJ to Mary Hunter, 15 August 1913, McGill.
70 HJ/EW, 19 December 1909, 11 April 1910, 2 March 1914, 128, 156, 281.
71 Edel, *op. cit.*, 480; EW to MJ, 23 September 1911, Letters 259; EW to Edmund Gosse, 17 November 1911, 18 February 1911, Brotherton.

72 For Blanche portrait (now in the Smithsonian), see HJL IV, 493, 501–3, Bell, 143–4, HJ to Ellen Emmet Rand, 2 November 1908, HJL IV, 500. For Sargent drawing (in the Queen's Collection at Windsor), HJ/EW, 5 February 1912, 29 March 1912, 212, 219.

73 CS to HJ, 1 September, 27 September 1912, HJL IV, 789–90; HJ to CS, 31 January 1913, HJL IV, 649; HJ to James Pinker, 8 October 1912, HJL IV, 626; Horne, 518.

74 EW to CS, 29 April 1913, Letters 300; CS to EW, 3 April 1913, in HJL IV, 789, and Letters 300.

75 For birthday gift: Horne, 518, 539; Edel, *op. cit.*, 487, 492; Kaplan, *op. cit.*, 547; EW to Barrett Wendell, 13 March 1913, Letters 287; EW to SN, 12 April 1913, Letters 294; HJ to William James II, 29 March 1913, HJL IV, 653; HJ to Alice James, 1–16 April 1913, HJL IV, 661; HJ to Henry James III, 24 April 1913, Horne, 519; EW to GL, 2 April 1913, Letters 290; EW to Barrett Wendell, 12 April 1913, Letters 293; Bell, 192; PL to GL, 16 April 1913, Beinecke.

76 EW to MF, 22 April 1913, Letters 298; HJ, 21 April 1913, HJL IV.

77 HJ/EW, 2 May 1913, 253; HJ/EW, 11 June 1913, 257.

78 HJ/EW, 6 August 1913, 289; 23 May 1915, 342; 19 August 1914, 293; 21 September 1914, 303; 1 December 1914, 319.

79 EW to GL, 8 November 1914, Letters 342; HJ/EW, 16/17 January 1915, 321, 3 September 1914, 299; HJ to Henry James III, 16 January 1915, HJL IV 735; HJ to MJ, 4 September 1915, Houghton; HJ/EW, 17 October 1914, 310, 21 August 1915, 352, 23 May 1915, 341.

80 HJ/EW, 22 September 1915, 355; HJ to MJ, 2 October 1915, Houghton; Lewis, 381; EW to GL, 10 January 1916, Letters 369; Bosanquet to EW, 11 December 1915, Beinecke; Edel, *op. cit.*, 545; HJ, HJL IV, 810.

81 HJ/EW, EW to Bosanquet, 16 February 1913, 364.

82 EW to Bosanquet, 17 January 1916, Letters 390; Edel, *op. cit.*, 561; EW to GL, 1 March 1916, Letters 370.

83 HJ to Sargent, 30 July 1915, HJL IV 774; Bell, 209; HJ/EW, 26 July 1915, 347; EW to Barrett Wendell, 17 April 1916, Letters 373; BG, ch. 14, i.

84 Horne, 163 [quoting Roosevelt in 1884]; HJ/EW, 4 December 1912, 9 December 1912, 240; 17 November 1906, 67.

85 HJ/EW, 18 November 1912, 235; 12 May 1912, 222.

CHAPTER 10: MME WARTHON

1 EW to HJ, 3–4 September 1912, Letters 278–9; HJ/EW, 6 September 1912, 233.

2 Frederic Jones lived in Paris with his second wife (she died there in 1905 and he in 1922, long estranged from EW). Harry Jones lived in Paris for many years and then fifty miles outside, in Compiègne. Benstock, 81, 375; Lewis, 447.

3 'The Lamp of Psyche', *Scribner's Magazine*, 1895, republished posthumously in CS I, 53.

4 GA, ch. 8.

5 CC, ch. 20.

6 M, ch. 7. SF, ch. 20.

7 Edmond Jaloux, *Figures Étrangères*, Plon-Nourrit, 1925, 252.

8 Jaloux, *op. cit.*, 17.

9 MFF, Part 3.

10 Jean Pavans, ed., *Les Moeurs Françaises et comment les comprendre*, Petite Bibliothèque Payot, 1999.

11 Wegener, 120–1. WF, ch. 2, v.

12 For Franco-American links in the 1900s, see Theodore Zeldin, *France 1848–1945*, Vol. II, *Intellect, Taste and Anxiety*, Oxford University Press, 1977, 131–6.

13 Wegener, 214–17. Paul Bourget, *Outre-Mer*, Lemerre, 1895, 129–30, 327; Lubbock, 96; Benstock, 76.

14 André Chevrillon, *Nouvelles Études Anglaises*, Hachette, 1914, 137. Georges Duhamel, *Scènes de la Vie Future*, Mercure de France, 1930, 246. EW to GL, 13 August 1925,

Beinecke. André Tardieu, *France and America*, Allen & Unwin, 1927, 58–9.

15 BG, ch. 7, i; Thomas Bender, *New York Intellect*, Knopf, 1987, ch. 6. EW to SN, 16 March 1908, Letters 137; Wegener, 210, 206.

16 Benstock, 374. FWTM, 30, 34. Barrett Wendell, *The France of Today*, Constable, 1908, 82, 141.

17 Sisley Huddleston, *France and the French*, Methuen, 1925, 111, 79; Sisley Huddleston, *In and About Paris*, Methuen, 1927; Sisley Huddleston, *Bohemian Literary and Social Life in Paris*, Harrap, 1928, 189. Anon., *A Woman's Paris*, Small, Maynard & Co, Boston, 1900.

18 E.g. of 'Mme Warthon': André Gide, *Journal*, Pleiade, 1939, 16 January 1916, 527; street-name in Hyères. BG, ch. 2, v; Lewis, 187.

19 Benstock, 103; Wegener, 219. Eugen Weber, *France: Fin de Siècle*, Belknap Press, 1986, 120–5; Gordon Wright, *France in Modern Times*, Norton, 1960, 4th edition, 1987, 249–52. EW to Bayard Cutting, 15 July [1906], I Tatti.

20 Lewis, 197; Benstock, 114. EW to WCB, 31 May 1900, Scribner Archive, Princeton. WB to EW, 16 September 1904, Beinecke. For exhibition: Jan Romein, *The Watershed of Two Eras: Europe in 1900*, trans. A. Pomerans, Wesleyan University Press, 1978, 75–9; Jean Roman, *Paris: Fin de siècle*, Prentice Hall, 1963, 297.

21 EW to SN, 1 March 1906, Letters 104. Lewis, 258.

22 HJ/EW, 20 October 1914, 313; Lewis, 225–6; Viola Hopkins Winner, 'The Paris Circle of Edith Wharton and Henry Adams', EWN, IX, i, Spring 92, 3, quoting from Henry Adams's *Letters*, VI, 394. For Henry White, see EW to MF, 5 June [1908], Letters 149, note 1. EW to SN, 12 April 1913, Letters 295, note 1.

23 Rieder, 124, 38, 146, 38, 126, 69, 126–7, 219, 106.

24 MT, ch. 5.

25 For the Faubourg buildings: Jacques Hillairet, *Connaissance Du Vieux Paris*, Rivages, 1951, 1993; Philippe Viguié Desplaces, *C'Était Hier: Le VIIeme Arrondissement*, Editions L.M.-Le Point, 1995; J. Vacquier, *Les Vieux Hôtels de Paris*, Vols 1–6, Contet, 1926; Georges Pillement, *Les Hôtels du Faubourg Saint-Germain*, Bellenand, 1950.

26 For the interior of 53 Rue de Varenne: EW to JHS, 30 April 1909, Letters 188; Lewis, 258, 279, Dwight, 141, Benstock, 157, 219. I am grateful to the inhabitants (Lou-Ann Alsip, Ghislaine Barissat, Carole Butor and Anne-Marie and Christian Casper) for allowing me to visit their apartments, and to the Caspers for the loan of the 'Reglement De Co-Propriété, Immeuble à Paris, 53 Rue de Varenne, 1951'. Also to Françoise de Valence at Number 41 and to Patrick Lindsay Bowles at Number 60.

27 R, ch. 4. Paul Bourget, *Un Divorce*, Phoenix Library, 1904, trans. E.L. Charlwood; Tintner, 106–10. MT, chs 1, 3, 5.

28 'The Associates', Beinecke.

29 Vacquier, *op. cit.*, Vol. I, 2. Marcel Proust, *À la recherche du temps perdu*, trans. T. Kilmartin and D.J. Enright as *In Search of Lost Time*, Vintage Classics, 2002 [Proust]; VI, *Time Regained*, 331. BG, ch. 11, i. J.K. McMillan, *Housewife or Harlot: The Place of Women in French Society*, St Martin's Press, 1981, 92.

30 Gordon Wright, *France in Modern Times*, Norton, 1987, 275. René Remond, *The Right Wing in France*, trans. J.M. Laux, University of Pennsylvania Press, 1954, 112–16. Jean Roman, *Paris: Fin de Siècle*, Prentice Hall, 1963, 99. Roger Shattuck, *The Banquet Years*, Faber, 1959, 8; Zeldin, *op. cit.*, Vol. I, *Ambition, Love, Politics*, Oxford University Press, 1973, 402–3; Weber, *op. cit.*, 107–8.

31 Michael Sprinker, *History and Ideology in Proust*, Verso, 1998, 30, 55, 49, 64. Gordon Wright, *op. cit.*,

275. J.K. McMillan, *Dreyfus to De Gaulle: Twentieth Century France*, E. Arnold, 1985, 50. Zeldin, *op. cit.*, I, 17; Zeldin, *op. cit.*, II, 402; Romein, *op. cit.*, 233, 237.

32 For the politics of the Faubourg, thanks to Julian Wright. Eugen Weber, *The Hollow Years: France in the 1930s*, Sinclair-Stevenson, 1995, 102. Robert Gildea, *The Past in French History*, Yale University Press, 1994, 305–11. Remond, *op. cit.*, 237; McMillan, *op. cit.*, 30; E de Gramont, *Years of Plenty*, Cape, 1932, 70. Proust, *op. cit.*, VI, 337. Lewis, 403, suggests that Proust was referring to EW in VI, 205 as 'an American hostess in whom I took not the slightest interest', who had taken over the Prince de Guermantes' house after the prince moved to the Avenue du Bois. Lewis's version of the passage is inaccurate.

33 Proust, III, *Guermantes Way*, 622. EW to GL, 2 June 1930, Beinecke. Lewis, 442; WF, 'Marcel Proust', V, iii; EW to BB, 7 June 1921, Letters 441; EW to JHS, 14 January 1926, Beinecke.

34 Proust, *Pastiches et mélanges*, marks in EW's 1921 copy, Ramsden, 101.

35 Edmund White, *Proust*, Weidenfeld & Nicolson, 1999, 136; Proust, IV, *Sodom & Gomorrah*, 231.

36 Proust, II, *In the Shadow of Young Girls in Flower*, 84; VI, 237; II, 562; III, 633; VI, 206; VI, 235, 247. II, 217. VI, 222. II 143. II, 418. II, 418; III, 258; III, 565–74. III, 41.

37 First published in the *Yale Review* in January 1925, reprinted in WF, V. Wegener, 182.

38 Benstock, 316, Lewis, 196, EW to Gide, 5 March 1916, Letters 372. EW to MB, 4 May 1930, I Tatti, in Benstock, 421, Lewis, 494.

39 BG, ch. 12, vii. 'To be *labelled* a homosexual in print (as opposed to living a homosexual life in private or discreetly among friends) was social anathema, even in Paris, until the very recent past.' Edmund White, *op. cit.*, 70.

40 Mainwaring, 181. BG, ch. 11, iii.

Charles Du Bos, *Approximations*, 1924, Edition Des Syrles, 2000, with epilogue by Maurois, 903; Janet Flanner, *An American in Paris*, Hamish Hamilton, 1940, 190, 'New York Letter', *New Yorker*, 2 March 1929, 26–8; quoted Kristin Olson Lauer, 'Can France Survive this Defender?' in Joslin and Price, 89.

41 EW to GL, 3 May 1923, 29 November 1924, Beinecke, 3 April 1931, Letters 537; Funeral notice for the *duchesse*, Beinecke.

42 For Cairo: BG, ch. 12, v; Gordon Wright, *op. cit.*, 200–1; Gildea, *op. cit.*, 121; Zeldin, *op. cit.*, I, 104.

43 Benstock, 172, 400, Lewis, 213, 324, 401. Caresse Crosby, *The Passionate Years*, Alvin Redman, 1955, 116; Paul Morand, *Journal d'un Attaché d'Ambassade, 1916–1917*, Gallimard, 1949, 172. Geoffrey Wolff, *Black Sun: The Brief Transit and Violent Eclipse of Harry Crosby*, Random House, 1976, 121, 81. (Mainwaring, 18, attributes the first remark to the Vicomte de Noailles.) William C. Carter, *Marcel Proust: A Life*, Yale University Press, 2000, 639; Francis Steegmuller, *Cocteau*, Macmillan, 1970, 234. Gustave Schlumberger, *Mes Souvenirs*, II, Plon, 1934, 274. *Journal de l'Abbé Mugnier, 1879–1939*, Mercure de France, 1985, 13 August 1915, my translation; BB to MB, 3 July 1913, I Tatti. GS to MB, nd [1913], I Tatti.

44 Morand, *op. cit.*, 14 September 1917, 352; Crosby, *op. cit.*, 119.

45 HJ/EW, 3 February 1913, 244.

46 Philip Whitcomb, *Seventy-Five Years in the Franco-American Economy: A Short History of the First American Chamber of Commerce*, American Chamber of Commerce, 1970; Schlumberger, *op. cit.*, 274.

47 Zeldin, *op. cit.*, II, 809; Wegener, 212; Ramsden, 17; Tintner, 'The Portrait of Edith in Bourget's "L'Indicatrice"', 99–103. De Gramont, *op. cit.*, 261; Ernest Dimnet, *Paul Bourget*, Constable, 1913; Armand Singer, *Paul Bourget*, Twayne, 1976; *Essais de Psychologie Contemporaine*,

Gallimard, 1993; Jean-Marie Mayeur, *The Third Republic 1871–1944*, trans. J.R. Foster, Cambridge University Press, 1987, 288.

48 BG, ch. 11, ii; EW to MF, 17 April [1912], Texas; Jean-Yves Tadié, *Marcel Proust*, trans. Euan Cameron, Viking, 1996, 676; Reider, 158; Schlumberger, *op. cit.*, 177; HJ/EW, 4 October 1907, 76. For Rosa de Fitz-James as one of several Jewish hostesses in pre-war Paris, see Emily Biski and Emily Braun, eds, *Jewish Women and their Salons*, the Jewish Museum, Yale University Press, 2005, 64–5.

49 BG, ch. 11, i; EW to JHS, 26 December 1908, Letters 171; Schlumberger, *op. cit.*, 395; EW to SN, 17 March 1908, Letters 171.

50 BG, ch. 11, iii; Tadié, *op. cit.*, 169, 139, 287; Jules Jusserand, *What Me Befell*, Constable, 1933, 156.

51 For Anna de Noailles: BG, ch. 11, iii; Abel Hermant, *La Vie à Paris*, Flammarion, 1919, 227; Jean Cocteau, *My Contemporaries*, trans. M. Crosland, Peter Owen, 1968, 726; Jean Cocteau, *La Comtesse de Noailles, Oui et Non*, Librairie Académique Perrin, 1963; André Gide, *Journals, 1889–1949*, ed. Justin O'Brien, Penguin, 1967, 20 January 1910, 150; EW, Diary, 8 April 1906, Lilly; Ramsden, 91; EW to WCB, in Wolff, 144; Wegener, 50; de Noailles to EW, 8 April 1916, Beinecke; Vincent Cronin, *Paris on the Eve, 1900–1914*, Collins, 1989, 301; Huddleston, *Bohemian Paris*, 189, 437; Edmée de la Rochefoucauld, *Anna de Noailles*, Editions Universitaires, 1956, 115; Claude Mignon-Ogliastri, *Anna de Noailles: Une Amie de La Princesse Edmond de Polignac*, Meridiens Klincksieck, 1986.

52 For the Abbé Mugnier; BG, ch. 11, iii; Tadié, *op. cit.*, 229, 230, 574; Cronin, *op. cit.*, 452; de Gramont, *op. cit.*, 61–3; Benstock, 404; Marthe Bibesco, *La Vie d'une Amitié*, Plon, 1951, I, 74; Morand, *op. cit.*, 306; *Journal de l'Abbé Mugnier*, *op. cit.*, 150; Weber, *The Hollow Years*, *op. cit.*, 25.

53 BG, ch. 11, iii; Tadié, *op. cit.*, 229, 230.

54 BG, ch. 11, iii, v; Henry James, 'Matilde Serao', 1902, *Notes on Novelists*, Dent, 1914, 239; Ramsden, 111; Wegener, 47; EW to CEN, 2 March 1908, Letters 131; Lubbock, ch. 11; EW to BB, 12 December 1920, Letters 434; Lewis, 408.

55 EW to BB, 31 March 1936, I Tatti.

56 BG, ch. 11, iii; Wegener, 204.

57 For du Breuil: BG, ch. 14, ii; EW to MC, 11 April 1914, Beinecke; Wegener, 197–204. Lewis mistakenly has TW on the trip to Spain, 318.

58 For d'Humières: BG, ch. 11, v [EW gives his death inaccurately as 1916]; EW to MF, 22 September 1911, Letters 258; HJ/EW, 11/12 August 1907, 69; Tadié, *op. cit.*, 854.

59 For Bremond: BG, ch. 11, v; Ramsden, 112, 18; de Gramont, *op. cit.*, 59; EW to MC, 3 July 1924, Letters 477, 478; Huddleston, *Bohemian Paris*, 392; Schlumberger, *op. cit.*, 23 November 1922; BB to MB, July 1914, I Tatti.

60 EW to MF, 27 June 1912, Texas. Maurice Barrès, *Scènes et Doctrines de Nationalisme*, Juven, 1910. Gordon Wright, *op. cit.*, 264, 350; *Journal de l'Abbé Mugnier*, *op. cit.*, 20 January 1911, 204; Wegener, 202–4; EW to BB, 27 January 1915, I Tatti; Robert Soucy, *French Fascism: The First Wave*, Yale University Press, 1986, 89, 105, xvii, 19; EW to SN, 16 March [1908], Letters 137; Ramsden, 122; Weber, *France*, *op. cit.*, 23; Zeldin, II, 604–6; EW to MC, 3 July 1924, Letters 477; McMillan, *op. cit.*, 22; Tadié, *op. cit.*, 703. For Bonnard, see Carmen Callil, *Bad Faith: A Forgotten History of Family & Fatherland*, Jonathan Cape, 2006, 316, 551.

61 Ramsden 95; EW to MC, 3 July 1924, Letters 477; BG, ch. 11, v; EW to BB, 7 June [1921], Letters 441; EW to BB, 30 September [1914], Letters 341.

62 Lesage: EW to LB, 15 August 1910; LB to EW, 13 November 1909; EW to LB, 9 June 1912; EW to LB, 30 April 1912; EW to LB, 28 March

63 For Blanche: BG, ch. 11, iv; HJ to Ellen Rand, 2 November 1908, HJL IV, 501; Steegmuller, *op. cit.*, 90; Schlumberger, *op. cit.*, 160; Gide, *Journals*, 256; Rieder, 141; Tadié, *op. cit.*, 140; de Gramont, *op. cit.*, 179; HJ/EW, 29 June 1912, 225, 21 July 1911, 184; Jacques-Émile Blanche, *Portraits of a Lifetime, 1870–1914*, trans. W. Clement, Dent, 1937, 237; Adrian Frazier, *George Moore*, Yale University Press, 2000, 387.

1914; EW to LB, 5 September 1913; translations by Bridget Patterson. EW to MF, 22 September 1911, Letters 257; EW to BB, 10 February 1915, I Tatti; Lewis, 335; Benstock, 250.

64 EW to AG, 10 August 1917, Letters 395. *Journal de l'Abbé Mugnier, op. cit.*, 9 February 1918; EW to AG, 23 July 1923, Letters 469; Wegener, 50; EW to GL, 18 October 1918, Letters 410.

65 BG, ch. 11, iv; Steegmuller, *op. cit.*, 419. EW to MC, 5 August 1923, Letters 470; Ramsden, 132. My translation, with help from J. Barnes.

66 For Charles Du Bos: Lubbock, 95–8; Rieder, 125; Jean Pavans, Introduction to *Le moeurs Françaises et comment les comprendres*, Payot, 1997, 7; EW to WCB, 29 December 1907, 16 August 1908, Scribner Archive, Princeton; EW to BB, 7 January 1912, Letters 266; Wegener, 260; BG, ch. 12, i. Mario Praz, *The House of Life*, trans. Angus Davidson, Methuen, 1958, 1964 edition, 207; Cronin, *op. cit.*, 416; Gide, *Journals*, 1929, 428; Lewis, 163; Jacques Bossière, *Perception Critique et Sentiment de Vivre chez Charles Du Bos*, Nicet, 1969; Angelo Philip Bertocci, *Charles Du Bos and English Literature*, Cumberledge, 1949; *Lettres du Charles Du Bos et Réponses de André Gide*, Correa, 1950. Charles Du Bos, *La Comtesse de Noailles et le Climat du Génie*, La Table Ronde, 1949; Du Bos, *Approximations*; and various editions of CDB's journals containing entries on EW: *Cahiers Charles Du Bos*, Société des Amis

Charles Du Bos, 1969–1974; *Journals, 1921–1933*, Correa, 1946; *Journals, 1930–1931*, Vieux Colombier, 1955; *Journals, 1934–1939*, La Colombe, 1961 [NB: entries for 19 August 1921, 10 January 1913, 24 March 1913, 25 March 1913, 23 May 1913, 22 May 1913, 23 December 1916, 27 December 1917, 9 December 1927, 9 May 1928, 26 May 1931.] For Plon-Nourrit: Roger Chartier, *Histoire de l'Edition Française, 1900–1950*, Promodis, 1986; for Pontigny: Anne Heurgon, *Paul Desjardins et les Décades de Pontigny*, Presses Universitaires de France, 1964. The Pontigny seminars continued after the second war at Cérisy-la-Salle in Normandy.

67 Jules Bertaut, *Paris 1870–1935*, Eyre & Spottiswoode, 1926, 191; de Gramont, *op. cit.*, 358; *Diaries and Letters of Marie Belloc Lowndes, 1911–1947*, ed. Susan Lowndes, Chatto & Windus, 1971, 43, with thanks to Roy Foster; EW [secretary] to Mme Denise, 12 May 1923, Beinecke.

68 Steegmuller, *op. cit.*, 151; Gide, *Journals*, 232–3; Schlumberger, *op. cit.*, 16 November 1922; *Journal de l'Abbé Mugnier, op. cit.*, 285, 328; Morand, *op. cit.*, 174.

69 Heurgon, *op. cit.*, 193, 330; *Journal de l'Abbé Mugnier, op. cit.*, 11 October 1923.

70 French version: Jeanne Fridérich to J. Bois, 25 February 1925, my translation; Benstock, 420. Dwight, 158; BG, ch. 12, i; 'The Verdict', CS I 662; Roger Asselinau, 'Edith Wharton: She Thought in French and Wrote in English', in Joslin and Price, 356–62. On Plon-Nourrit's publishing of *Les Metteurs en Scène* in May 1909, see Garrison, AA2, 399. 'Atrophy', CS, II, 437; 'Atrophie', *Revue des Deux Mondes*, 15 July 1929, 376.

71 Benstock, 282; EW, Diary, 19 February 1908, 7 February 1908, Lilly; B. Knapp and M. Chipman, *That Was Yvette*, Muller, 194, 188; Du Bos, *Journals*, 12 March 1914; BG, ch. 12, vii.

CHAPTER 11: L'ÂME CLOSE

1 Dwight, 146. MT, ch. 1.
2 For MF: Mainwaring, Benstock, Lewis, Dwight; Fred Kaplan, *Henry James*, Hodder & Stoughton, 1992, 406. For MF and LB, see Lesage. For MF's journalism, see Mainwaring, 284.
3 EW to MF [late February 1908], Letters 129. All EW to MF letters are at Texas; some are also published in Letters, as noted here, with any misdatings in Letters noted.
4 EW to SN, 21 April 1907, Letters 113. MF to his mother, 22 April 1907, quoted Mainwaring, 159. EW to MF, 15 October [1907], Letters 116; HJ/EW, 4 October 1907, 76.
5 EW to SN, 26 October, 27 October, 1 November, 4 November, 11 November 1907, Beinecke; EW to CEN, 23 October 1907, Houghton. HJ/EW, 24 November 1907, 78.
6 LA, 29 October 1907, 27 November 1907, Lilly.
7 EW to SN, 18 December 1907, Letters 125; 23 January, 6 February 1908, Beinecke. EW to MF, 'Mardi soir' [December 1908]; EW to MF, 13 January 1908, Letters 127 [Benstock, 499, dates it as 5 January 1908]. Engagement Diary, 9 January, 13 January 1908, Lilly. André Aubine, *Le Théâtre*, Paris, 1932, on the year 1908.
8 LA, 21 February, 22 February 1908, Lilly. Engagement Diary, 15 February, 20 February 1908, Lilly. EW to SN, 6 February 1908, Beinecke. HJ/EW, 7 March 1908, 92; 11 March 1908, 94. André Billy, *Hortense et ses Amants*, Flammarin, 1961; Léon Séché, *Hortense Allart de Méritens*, *Lettres Inédites à Sainte-Beuve*, Société du Mercure de France, 1908.
9 EW to SN, 25 March 1908, Beinecke. Benstock, 181; Wolff, 221.
10 R, chs 5, 7. Engagement diary for February–May 1908; LA, 3 March, 19 May 1908, Lilly; EW to MF, 1 July [1908], Letters 157; Aubine, *op.*

cit., for 1908; Jules Bertaut, *Paris, 1830–1935*, Eyre & Spottiswoode, 1936, 191–208.

11 Engagement Diary, 18 February, 1 March, 12 March, 23 March, 24 March, 8 April, 12 April 1908; LA, 3 March, 25 April, 19 May 1908, Lilly; EW to MF, 'Wednesday Eve' [early March 1908], Letters 134.
12 EW to MF [29 April 1908], Letters 142; LA, 7 May 1908, Lilly; EW to MF [late April 1908], Letters 141; EW to MF, 'Friday' [March 1908]; Engagement Diary, 28 March 1908, Lilly; EW to MF, 'Friday evening' [Spring 1908].
13 Engagement Diary, 17 March 1908, Lilly; EW to MF, 'Wednesday' [late April 1908], Letters 141; LA, 13 May 1908, Lilly; EW to MF, 'Friday 2.30'; EW to MF, 'Wednesday eve' [early March 1908], Letters 134.
14 LA, 27 April, Lilly; EW to MF, 'Friday' [1908]; EW to MF, '10 o'clock Monday Night' [22 April 1908].
15 EW to MF, 'Monday morning' [May 1908]. EW to MF, 'Friday'; LA, 19 May 1908, Lilly. EW to MF, 'Sunday' [May 1908].
16 Engagement Diary, 11 April 1908, Lilly. Ian Dunlop, *The Companion Guide to the Île de France*, Collins, 1979, 86ff., 'Montfort l'Amaury: Les Verrières de L'Église Paroissiale Saint-Pierre', 1994; EW to MF, 'Monday evening'.
17 Engagement Diary, 18 April 1908, Lilly; Dunlop, *op. cit.*, 164 ff.; 'Provins: Guide Du Visiteur', 2001.
18 EW to MF, '5 pm'; EW to MF, 'Wednesday' [29 April 1908]; EW to MF, 'Wednesday', Letters 141; EW to MF, 'Thursday morning' [early May 1908].
19 HJ to Henry Adams, 8 May 1908, HJL IV, 490; HJ to MJ, 8 May 1908, Houghton.
20 EW to MF, 'Friday morning', 1 May [1908]. LA, 3 May 1908, Lilly; Letters 143. Opinions vary about the start of the affair: 'Physical union began to take place (with some regularity, one gathers . . .) at the Place

des États-Unis [in May 1908]' (Lewis, 222); 'Edith's rhetoric of passion outdistances her action . . . Torn between loyalty to her husband and love for Fullerton, afraid of losing the respect of her staff, of being subjected to blackmail threats . . . and possibly losing her public reputation, she hesitated in spring 1908. When she finally decided . . . it was too late. Presented with a second chance for intimacy a year later, she took it' (Benstock, 474 and 184); 'Sometime in February or March 1908, Edith Wharton and Morton Fullerton became lovers' (Dwight, 145); 'They went to Montmorency, where they made love for the first time' (Mainwaring, 162).

21 EW to MF, 5 June [1908], Letters 147; LA, 9 May, Lilly; Mainwaring, 162; Dunlop, *op. cit.*, 281.

22 Engagement Diary, LA, 16 May, 19 May, Lilly; 'Senlis', [17 May 1908?, P, 157; EW to MF, misdated 'Late summer 1909' (Benstock dates October 1909, 224), Letters 189; EW to MF, 8 June [1908], Letters 150.

23 Engagement diary, 20 May 1908, Lilly; Mainwaring, 16.

24 EW to SN, 29 May 1908, Letters 146.

25 LA, 19 May, 3 March 1908, Lilly.

26 LA, 25 April 1908, Lilly.

27 EW to MF, 'Friday evening' [April 1908]; '2.30 p.m.' [April 1908]; 'Friday morning, May 1' [1908]; 'Wed evening' [early March 1908], Letters 134; 'Friday night' [March 1908]; 'Friday' [1908]; 'Friday evening' [early March 1908], Letters 133.

28 EW to MF, 'Thursday night' [9 April 1908]; 'Friday' [spring 1908], 'Monday 20th' [April 1908]; [early March 1908], Letters 135.

29 EW to MF, 'Sunday evening' [1910?]; 'Jeudi Matin'; 'Thursday' [March 1908]; 'Wednesday evening'; 'Wednesday'; 'Samedi'; 'Cher'.

30 EW to MF, 26 August [1908], Letters 160–1; 'Thursday' [October 1909], Letters 189, misdated 'Late Summer 1909'; LA, 20 April 1908, Lilly.

31 Julia Fullerton to MF, 25 May 1904,

Beinecke. For Santayana, Mainwaring, 268; for Carman, Mainwaring, 242; Brooke to MF, nd, Beinecke, and Mainwaring, 44; For Roosevelt visit, Mainwaring, 96–7; Aidé to MF, nd, Beinecke; HJ to MF, 22 March 1900, HJL IV, 137; HJ to MF, 21 September 1900, quoted Kaplan, *op. cit.*, 409; 14 November 1907, quoted Kaplan, *op. cit.*, 511; HJ/EW, 13 August 1915, 350.

32 Morton Fullerton, *Problems of Power*, Constable, 1913, 131; Morton Fullerton, *Hesitations: The American Crisis and the War*, Doubleday, Page, 1916, 146, 160, Ramsden, 45; MF's career: Mainwaring, 189–90, 125–6, 81–2, 172, 305–6.

33 I have followed Mainwaring's account of MF's affairs and noted her bitter corrections of Lewis's version. After Camille's death, the papers, strewn round her rooms, were salvaged by a neighbour and eventually tracked down in the 1970s by Mainwaring, forming the basis of the Beinecke's collection of MF papers; EW's love-letters to MF came to light later and were bought by the University of Texas. Mainwaring, 298.

34 HJ to MF, 14, 19, 26, 29 November 1907, HJL IV, 473–80; Mainwaring, 29, 32.

35 EW to Katherine Fullerton, 3 February 1909, Texas. EW to MF, 'Sunday' [February 1909]; 'Tuesday morning'.

36 EW to MF, '5 July' [1910]. Benstock, 200, 211–12; Mainwaring, 52, 55–6, 166–7, 193; Katherine Fullerton to MF, 21 August 1899, 9 November 1907, 5? January 1910, Beinecke; *Scribner's Magazine*, July, August 1911, Vol. 50; EW to MF, 3 July [1911], Letters 242.

37 EW markings in Vernon L. Kellogg, *Darwinism Today*, Holt, 1907, 53, 57, Ramsden, 69. EW to SN, 29 May 1908, Letters 145–6; EW to MF, Friday 5 June [1908], Letters 147; LA, 22, 24, 25, 26, 31 May 1908; Engagement Diary, 23, 27, 28 May, Lilly.

38 EW to MF, 5 June [1908], Letters 149. EW to MF, 1 July 1908, Letters 156; EW to SN, 7 July 1908, Letters 149.

39 EW to MF, 19 June 1908, 1 July [1908], 26 August [1908], Letters 154–62.

40 HJ/EW, 13 October 1908, 101.

41 EW to SN, 17 October 1908, Letters 162.

42 EW to MF, 'December 31, Friday evening' [1909].

43 EW to SN, 5 May 1909, Houghton; EW to MF [February 1909], Letters 176; EW to MF, 10 May 1909, EW to MF [February 1909], Letters 179 [with underlining inaccurately transcribed]. EW to MF, 19 June [1912], Letters 270.

44 EW to LB, 30 March 1909, LB to EW, 30 March 1909; EW to LB, 5 April 1909, LB to EW, 28 May 1909, EW to LB, 6 September 1910, LB to EW, 15 November 1911, Claudine Lesage, *Lettres à l'ami français*, Houdiard, Paris, 2001, 32–5, 61, 71; translations by Bridget Patterson.

45 EW to MF, 'Oh, I am too disappointed'; 'Tuesday'; 'Sunday'; 'March 31st' [1908]; 'Sunday morning' [March 1909?], Letters 138, misdated 'early April 1908' (Mainwaring, 310).

46 EW to MF, 'Sunday'; 'Thursday'; 'Tuesday eve'g'; 'Vendredi matin'; 'Tuesday morning'.

47 EW to MF [February/March 1909?], Letters 138, misdated 'early April 1908' (Mainwaring, 168–9, 300). EW to JHS, 30 April [1909], Letters 177.

48 Benstock, 213.

49 EW to Macmillan, 29 May 1909, BL 54956, f 107–9, Letters 181. HJ/EW, 26 July, 3 August, 15 August, 23 August, 8 October 1909, 115–17; EW to MF, 'Thursday evening' [October 1909?], Letters 182, misdated 'May 1909' (Mainwaring, 302–3). The details of the blackmail case are hard to untangle and provide one of Mainwaring's main areas of attack on Lewis and the Letters for inaccuracy: for variant versions, see Mainwaring, 178, 188; Benstock, 216; Lewis, 263–4; Letters 183.

50 EW to MF, 'Monday 24 March' [in fact 21] 1910, Letters 206; Benstock, 213; MF to ET, 30 March 1950, Lilly; Mainwaring, 174, 301, note 144; Lewis, 259.

51 EW to MF, '34 Brook Street, Thursday July 8 [1909]'; Mainwaring, 175; EW to LB, 15 June 1909, Lesage, *op. cit.*, 36; EW to MF, 12 August [1909], Letters 189; EW to JHS, 21 July [1909], Letters 188; EW to MF, 'Thursday, 1.0'c'.

52 EW to MF, 27 November 1909, Letters 193; 'Monday' [1910]; 'Monday afternoon'. HJ's first bonfire was in November 1909 (HJ/EW, 26), just when she started trying to get her letters back from MF. (EW to MF, 27 November 1909, Letters 193).

53 EW to MF, 'Sunday' [autumn 1909?], Letters 144, misdated 'May 1908'; 'Saturday night' [December 1909?], Letters 189–90, misdated 'Late Summer 1909' (Benstock, 224); 'Tuesday' [February 1910?], 'Sunday night' [28 November 1909?], Letters 197, misdated 'Winter 1910' (Mainwaring, 304).

54 EW to MF, 'Wednesday' [8 December 1909]; Benstock, 228.

55 HJ/EW, Christmas Eve 1909, 133; 'Friday December 3rd' [1909]; EW to MF, 'Friday 9 pm' [31 December 1909?], Letters 195, misdated 'Early January 1910']; 'Saturday' [8 January 1910]; 'Thursday 24th' [March 1910]; 'Tuesday 22' [March 1910]; 'March 19' [1910], Letters 201.

56 EW to MF, 'Tuesday 17th May' [1910].

57 EW to MF, 'Thursday' [31 March 1910?], Letters 206, misdated 'Mid-April 1910' (Mainwaring, 314); 'Thursday eve'g' [May 1910], Letters 215; 'Wednesday evening' [summer 1910], Letters 219. 14 April [1910], Benstock, 236; 'Sunday' [17 April 1910]; 'Feb 16' [1910]; 'Tuesday' [17 May 1910?], Letters 145, misdated '17 May 1908' (Mainwaring, 304); 'Wednesday' [1910]; 'Wednesday evening' [1910].

58 EW to MF, 24 October [1910], Letters 224; Benstock, 242, Mainwaring, 188 on the loan.

59 EW to MF, 'Sunday' [17 April 1910]; 27 April [1910], Letters 212; 'Friday 29' [April 1910], Letters 213. MF, notes, 28 April and 26 May 1910, cited Mainwaring, 186, 305, note 216. On Roosevelt visit, Benstock, 236–7, Mainwaring, 190, 314.

60 EW to MF, 'Tuesday'; 'July 5' [1910]; 'Monday evening' [March 1910]. MF, Introduction to *Gil Blas*, Routledge, 1912, xiv, xxii, Ramsden, 77.

61 HJ/EW, 19 November 1911, 198. EW to MF, 'Saturday' [4 March 1911]; 'Wed. evening' [1912]; '27 June' [1912?]; 'Saturday' [January 1913]; 'Sunday' [October 1912], Letters 281. Morton Fullerton, *Problems of Power*, Constable, 1913, 210, Ramsden, 45.

62 EW to MF, 25 June [1910], Letters 218.

63 EW to MF, 'Tuesday morning' [spring 1910]. EW to MF, 'Friday morning' [late June 1910], Letters 220; 'Thursday evening' [May 1910], Letters 215.

64 Appleton wrote to MF re Macmillan's English contract for *The Reef*, 28 March 1912: 'We ought to have the mss. in our hands at least two months before the day of publication. We ought not to publish later than the 15th October on account of the holiday season.' Beinecke.

65 On professional matters, EW to MF, 17 April [1911], 3 July [1911], Letters 242; 30 July [1911]; 6 June [1911]; 17 June [1912]; 17 August [1912]; 27 June [1912]; 14 July [1912]. On her reading, EW to MF, 12 May [1911], Letters 238. On her work: 24 May [1911]; undated [February–April 1912?]; 3 May [1913], Letters 300. On letters and books: 22 September [1911], Letters 255; 17 October [1911]; on Mitou, [December 1911]; on her brother, November [1912?]; Benstock dates this 1920 (375, note 48, 522) but with no firm grounds, and there is another reference to seeing her brother in EW to JHS, 25

November [1912], Letters 284. On WB and BB: 15 May [1911]; 22 September [1911], Letters 255. On MF's little friend, undated [early 1911?]. On travelling and hotel: undated [spring 1912]; 13 August [1913]; undated [1911]; 9 April [1914].

66 EW to MF, 3 July [1911], Letters, 242; 8 June [1908], Letters 152; 5 July [1911]; 'Saturday morning'.

67 EW to MF, 'Wednesday Eve' [1912]; 10 June [1912]; 12 August [1912], Letters 275; 27 June [1912]; 28 May [1912]. Mainwaring, 304.

68 Mainwaring, 212, for an explanation of MF's Légion d'honneur, his work on a city-planning exhibition in 1913 and his lobbying 'on behalf of French official interests backing the Panama canal'; EW to MF, 13 August [1913]; 30 October [1913]; 11 May [1914], Letters 323. HJ to EW, 23–4 March 1915, HJ/EW, 334. EW to HJ, 11 August 1915, Letters 359; EW to MF, 5 September 1915, Letters 360.

69 EW to MF, 26 August [1908], Letters 161.

70 In Meredith's *Modern Love*, Sonnet VIII, the unhappy husband and wife are imagined as 'two reed-pipes' whom 'The God once filled . . . with his mellow breath'. P, 82, 74, 34–6, 30–4

71 P, 133 'Ogrin the Hermit', *Atlantic Monthly*, 104, December 1909, 844–8, P, 125–131; Letters 179–80, EW to MF, 'Tuesday evening' [April 1910?]; Benstock, 208, argues that 'Ogrin' was EW's way of telling MF that she would not leave her marriage for him.

72 Benstock, 191, notes Yeats's influence on 'When I am gone'. EW to MF, 'April 14' [1910]; [17 April 1910]. P, 156, 163.

73 Poems, MSS, Beinecke. P, 166

74 Poems, MSS, Beinecke. P, 167

75 P, 160, 162. For MF's annotations of 'Terminus', made in 1950 for ET when he sent her a copy of the poem (having returned the original to EW), and for Yale's purchase of a copy of the poem in 1972, via Hugh

Fullerton and Marian Mainwaring, see Beinecke, Box 21, 682; Mainwaring, 173; Benstock, 226. For Commonplace Book, see Benstock, 168, 171, 208; Wolff, 90, and my ch. 19, 'A Private Library'.

76 'Colophon to the Mortal Lease', dated in Beinecke 23 April 1909. P, 158–9. See Lewis, 255–6, and Benstock, 208, 225, note 20, 503. Mainwaring, 275.

77 For 'Xingu', EWCS II, 1–25. EW to MF, 'Sat morning' [October 1910]. 'The Last Asset', EWCS I, 602, 632.

78 'The Choice', CS II, 354. EW to Richard Gilder, 9 July 1908, Beinecke: 'I suggest the November number because my story has what it is agreed to call a "sad ending" – though a highly moral one – and therefore would probably not be thought Christmassy.'

79 'The Pretext', CS I, 632–54.

80 'The Letters', CS II, 188–190.

81 EW to MF, June [1910]; 'I am working on "your" story', EW to MF, 1 September [1910].

82 'Autres Temps . . .', CS II, 257–81.

83 'The Long Run', CS II, 301–23.

84 EW to MF, 16 October [1911].

85 Letters 261. Benstock, 272; EW to MJ, 17 February 1921, Letters 439. R, ch. 38.

86 R, chs 9, 14. HJ/EW, 4/9 December 1912, 240.

87 R, chs 11, 12, 3.

88 R, chs 35, 37, 32.

89 As Beer 1990 notes, 32.

90 R, ch. 9.

91 R, chs 5, 26.

92 R, chs 4, 20, 26.

93 Bauer, 18–24, compares American imperialist expansionism in South America with Darrow's annexation of his women. R, chs 8, 22, 33, 7, 32.

94 R, chs 10, 19, 23, 29, 6.

95 R, chs 11, 29, 36.

96 R, chs 36, 32.

97 EW to MF, 14 October [1911], Portofino: 'I am staying in this unimaginably beautiful place to rest & to steep my soul in light & air. This high promontory . . . with deep

blue siren-haunted inlets far below, is – *is like being happy*.'

CHAPTER 12: LA DEMANDERESSE

1 Scott Marshall, 'Whatever Happened to Teddy Wharton?', *Vista: EWRA Newsletter*, Winter 1987–8. Ramsden, 113. Benstock, 482, note 9.

2 TW to Sarah Perkins Cleveland, 20 May 1884, Berg. TW to Mr Post, 19 June 1905, EWRA.

3 TW to SN, 26 February 1907, Beinecke.

4 See Tintner, 194–5.

5 OC to Sarah Codman, 20 September 1910, SPNEA.

6 Lewis, 333–4; Auchincloss, 95. EW to Richard Gilder, 23 April 1902, Gilder collection, NYPL MSS; Richard Gilder, 'Topics of the Time', *Century Magazine*, May 1902, 320; 'The Reckoning', CS I, 427–8.

7 EW to JHS, 12 February 1909, Beinecke.

8 Ramsden, 115.

9 Frank Bergmann, *Robert Grant*, Twayne, 1982, 89; Debra MacComb, *Tales of Liberation, Strategies of Containment*, Garland, 2000, 122–3, 159, note 9. *New York Times*, 15 January 1913, 3 September 1912, 22 September 1912, 29 October 1912.

10 'Disintegration' Beinecke; AI, ch. 12; 'Irreparable', Notes 1910–1914, Beinecke.

11 On American divorce, see Roderick Phillips, *Putting Asunder: A History of Divorce in Western Society*, Cambridge University Press, 1988, 455–75; *Town Topics*, 8 September 1910, 6; 11 August 1910, 15; 13 March 1913, 5; 27 March 1913, 5.

12 EW to MF, 3 May 1913, Letters 300.

13 Obituary, Francis Parker Kinnicutt, *Boston Medical and Surgical Journal*, 22 May 1913, with thanks to Maisie Houghton.

14 EW to Eunice Maynard, 3 March [1907, but has been dated 1909], Beinecke. EW to WCB, 24 February 1908, Letters 129; EW to SN, 23 January, 6 February 1908, Beinecke.

15 EW to CEN, 2 March 1908, Letters 130; EW to SN, 21 March 1908, Letters 136; EW to EB, 27 March 1908, Scribner Archive, Princeton. EW to SN, 12 April 1908, Letters 140; EW to WCB, 27 July 1918, Scribner Archive, Princeton, quoted Benstock, 96.

16 See A. Proust and G. Ballet, *The Treatment of Neurasthenia*, 1902; Henry Upton, *Insomnia and Nerve Strain*, 1908; Roger Vittoz, *The Treatment of Neurasthenia by Means of Brain Control*, trans. H.B. Brooke, Longmans, 1911; Hermione Lee, *Virginia Woolf*, Chatto & Windus, 1996, ch. 10, 'Madness'.

17 EW to SN, [13th?] February 1909, Houghton.

18 EW to SN, February 1909, 5 May [1909], Houghton.

19 Dr Kinnicutt to EW, 14 June 1909, Beinecke; Benstock, 219–20, Nannie Wharton to EW, Lewis, 267.

20 HJ/EW, 20 August 1909, 120. Mainwaring, 182, Benstock, 224.

21 Dr Kinnicutt to EW, 13 December 1909, Beinecke [but events suggest earlier as Benstock supposes, 220]. EW to SN, 2 December 1909, Letters 193. EW to MF, 8 December 1909, Texas.

22 See chs 3 and 20 for the details of EW's inheritance. Benstock, 48, 54, 227–8, 231; Lewis, 275–6, 330 (on TW's annual income) and 333.

23 EW to MF, 8 December 1909, Texas.

24 Nancy Wharton to EW, 13 December 1909, Beinecke. Lewis, 275–6; Benstock, 228. HJ/EW, Christmas Eve, 1909, 133. HJ to HS, early 1910, in Lewis, 276; HJ to GL, 1 January 1910, Leon Edel, *Henry James*, Vol. 5, *The Master: 1910–1916*, Lippincott, 1972, 454; HJ/EW, 30 December 1909, 136.

25 EW to TW, 30 May 1911, Beinecke.

26 Dr Kinnicutt to EW, 9 February 1910, Beinecke. EW to WCB, 31 January 1910, Scribner Archive, Princeton. EW to SN, February 1910, Beinecke.

27 OC to Sarah Codman, nd, SPNEA. EW to MF, nd, Texas; EW to JHS, 2 March 1910, Beinecke; EW to MF, March 1910, Texas; EW to MF, 29 April 1910, Texas.

28 Sturgis Bigelow to EW [March 1910], quoted Lewis, 282.

29 EW to WCB, 9 April 1910, Scribner Archive, in Benstock, 232. EW to Robert Grant, 4 April [1910], Beinecke.

30 EW to MF, 27 April 1910, Letters 212. EW to MF, nd, Texas; EW to MF, May 1910, Letters 215.

31 EW to MF, 17 May [1910], Texas. This letter is misunderstood by Benstock, 237, who says that Vittoz *confirmed* TW as neurasthenic. Roger Vittoz's best-known book, *The Treatment of Neurasthenia by Means of Brain Control*, (10, 74), firmly distinguishes neurasthenia, which he claims can be cured through 'the strength' of the patient's 'will', from 'all cases of insanity and purely mental illnesses'.

32 EW to BB, 21 May 1910, I Tatti. EW to Nancy Wharton [November 1910], Beinecke.

33 HJ/EW, 25 October 1911, 195.

34 EF published in *La Revue de Paris* in February 1912. EF, chs 1, 4, 9, 2, 9.

35 EF, chs 8, 4.

36 In the dramatised version of EF, in 1936, Zeena came across as the strongest character.

37 EF, chs 4, 5, 2, 7, 9.

38 EW to CS, 19 August 1911, Scribner Archive, Princeton: The dots were 'not a sufficient indication of the pause, & interval in time, which must be shown here'.

39 EW, Introduction to 1922 edition of EF, Wegener, 259–61; EW and Hawthorne, Judith Fryer, *Felicitous Space: The Imaginative Structures of Edith Wharton and Willa Cather*, University of North Carolina Press, 1986, 180–93; EW to SN, 7 July [1908], Letters 160, on reading Nietzsche. The narrator of EF has aroused mixed critical feelings, some finding him redundant or condescending, some [e.g. Wolff, Fryer] arguing that the story is really his fantasy or nightmare. See EF, Norton

Critical Edition, ed. Kristin Lauer and Cynthia Griffin Wolff, 1995, 99–183, for differing critical views; for EW's response to critics of EW, see Wegener, 259–61 and BG, 293–296. For sledding accident, Scott Marshall on EW and Kate Spencer, and Ethel Cram, see EF, Norton Critical Edition, 86–93. EF, chs 8, 4.

40 HJ/EW, 25 October 1911, 195, HJL, Benstock, 247. EW, chs 1, 2, 4, 5. 'When I have fears that I may cease to be' and 'The Eve of St Agnes', *John Keats: The Complete Poems*, ed. John Barnard, Penguin, Second Edition, 1977, 221, 312–24.

41 EW to BB, 4 January [1911], Letters 232. BG, Ch 12, i 293. EF was serialised in *Scribner's* August–October 1911 and published in September 1911. EF, ch. 8.

42 EW to Bessie Lodge, 20 June 1910, Letters 217; Dr Binswanger to EW, 11 June 1910, Beinecke. Dr Isch Wall to TW, nd, Beinecke.

43 EW to TW, 6 July 1910, Beinecke. EW to TW, 28 July 1910, Beinecke. 'For my biographer', November 1927, listed in original headings of MSS sale of EW papers to Beinecke. See also my ch. 18, pp. 653–4 and ch. 18, n. 69.

44 BG, Ch 12, i 296. Bigelow to EW, 16 August 1910, Beinecke, quoted in Benstock, 240. HJ/EW, 9 September 1910, 168. EW to MF, 7 September 1910, Texas.

45 EW to Dorothy Allhusen (Lady St Helier's daughter), 18 November 1922, with thanks to Camille Dinkel, DA's great-granddaughter. EW to MF, October 1910, Texas. OC to Sarah Codman, 20 September 1910, SPNEA.

46 BG, ch. 10, vii; EW to MF, 25 October [1910], Letters 225; HJ/EW, 2 November 1910, 174; Fred Kaplan, *Henry James*, Hodder & Stoughton, 1992, 533; HJ to HS, 18 October 1910, HJL IV, 563–4; Edel, *op. cit.*, 454.

47 HJ to Sally Darwin, 15 March 1910, HJL IV, 549.

48 EW to SN, 19 November 1910, Beinecke. BB to MB, 26 October 1910, I Tatti. Barrett Wendell to MF, 22 February 1911, Beinecke. EW to Barrett Wendell, 5 March 1911, Letters 234. EW to BB, 17 February 1911, I Tatti.

49 EW to BB, 10 March 1911, I Tatti; PL to GL, 13 April 1911, Beinecke. Benstock, 252–3, on health problems. TW to Herman Edgar, 8 May 1911, typed copy, Beinecke; EW to MF, 24 May 1911, Texas; EW to TW, 30 May 1911, Beinecke.

50 EW to BB, 6 August 1911, Letters 252–3.

51 EW to MF, 3 July [1911], Texas 87, Letters 242–3. EW to SN, 3 July 1911, Houghton. EW to JHS, 6 August 1911, Letters 253; EW to BB, 6 August 1911, Letters 252.

52 HJ/EW, 19 July 1911, 181. EW to MF, 2 July 1911, Letters 242–3; 5 July 1911, Texas. EW to GL, 6 July 1911, Beinecke; EW to TW, 24 July 1911, Letters 251; HJ to GL, 17? August 1911, quoted Lewis, 304; HJ to EW, 19 July 1911, 7 September 1911, HJ/EW, 181, 187. HJ to MJ, 17 August 1911, Houghton.

53 EW to MF, 19 July 1911, Texas. EW to Billy Wharton, 22 July 1911, Letters 245; EW to TW, 24 July 1911, Letters 250. EW to GL, 23 July 1911, Beinecke. EW to Billy Wharton, 23 July 1911, Letters 248; EW to TW, 24 July 1911, Beinecke.

54 EW to MF, 30 July 1911, Texas. EW to MJ, 23 September 1911, Letters 259. EW to Billy Wharton, quoted Letters 249. HJ to MJ, 10 August, 17 August 1911, Houghton.

55 HJ/EW, 27 September 1911, 193; HJ to WB, 27 September 1911, HJL IV, 581, EW/WB to HJ, Florence, 17 October 1911, Letters 359.

56 EW to SN, 26 August 1911, Letters 254; EW to GL, 30 August 1911, Beinecke. Benstock, 257, and note 8, 507, citing Scott Marshall on sale of The Mount. EW to MF, 22 September 1911, Letters 256; HJ/EW, 19 September 1911, 191;

57 *Town Topics*, NYPL, 3 August, 10 August, 31 August 1911.

58 EW to LB, 12 December 1911, Lesage, 73. Dr George Kahlo to Dr Kinnicut, 17 November 1911; Dr Kinnicutt to EW, 1 December 1911, Beinecke; EW to BB, 26 January 1912, I Tatti; EW to SN, 26 January 1912, 12 July 1912. HJ/EW, 2 December 1911, 201. EW to BB, 26 January 1912, I Tatti. HJ/EW, 2 February 1912, 211; 5 February 1912, 212; 24 February 1912, 213; HJ to HS, 22 February 1911. *Town Topics*, 23 November 1911, NYPL.

59 EW to MF, nd [February 1912], Texas; EW to BB, 14 March 1912, Letters 268.

60 HJ/EW, 19 April 1909, 110; 29 October 1909, 125; 13 December 1909, 129; HJ to WB, 23 September 1911, HJL IV, 581.

61 HJ to MJ, 4 January 1912, Houghton; HJ/EW, 27 September 1911, 193, 2 May 1913, 251, 1 and 2 June 1914, 283, 6 September 1913, 263; HJ to MJ, 1 October 1913, Houghton; HJ to Mary Hunter, 14 May 1912, McGill.

62 EW to JHS, 12 July 1910; EW to GL, 8 July 1914, Beinecke.

63 HJ to HS, 20 July 1912, HJL IV, 620.

64 Edel, *op. cit.*, 467; HJ to HS, 9 August 1912, HJL IV, 622; HJ to MJ, 29 July 1914, Houghton; HJ to Mary Hunter, 27 July 1912, McGill; HJ/EW, 6 August 1912, 229.

65 EW to LB, 30 April 1912, Lesage, 78, translation by Bridget Patterson; HJ to EW, HJ/EW, 12 May 1912, 221; EW to BB, 27 May 1912, Letters 269; EW to BB, 28 June 1912, Letters 273; EW to HJ, 3 September 1912, Letters 278.

66 EW to SN, 12 July 1912, Beinecke. EW to GL, 19 August 1912, Letters 276. EW to SN, 18 September 1912, 1 November 1912, Beinecke; EW to BB, 7 November 1912, I Tatti; Lewis, 330, on EW paying TW an annual sum of about $6,000; EW to GL, 11 November 1912, Beinecke; HJ/EW, 10 December 1912, 294. Matilda Gay, Diary, 4 December, 6 December 1912, in Rieder, 127. HJ to MJ, 31 January 1913, Houghton.

67 EW to GL, 11 December 1912, Beinecke; EW to MB, 15 January 1913, I Tatti. MB to BB, 21 August 1913, I Tatti. OC to Sarah Codman, 20 February 1913, SPNEA.

68 OC to Sarah Codman, 7 December 1913, SPNEA; EW to GL, 8 February 1913, Letters 285; Lewis, 332. On the Jones family and their money, Benstock, 275–6, 376. On Frederic's stroke, EW to MF, 26 October 1911, 30 November 1911, Texas, cited Benstock, 259, correcting Lewis, 332. OC to Sarah Codman, 13 December 1913, SPNEA.

69 MB to BB, 21 August 1913, I Tatti. EW to MF, nd, Texas, quoted Benstock, 275. EW to MB, 7 February 1913, I Tatti. EW to GL, 12 April 1913, Beinecke. Auchincloss, 94.

70 EW to MJ, 2 February [1913], Beinecke.

71 EW to Barrett Wendell, 14 April 1913, Beinecke.

72 EW to GL, 23 March 1913, 2 April 1913, Letters 289, 290.

73 In Lewis, 336.

74 EW to Tom Newbold, 9 April 1913, Beinecke; OC to Sarah Codman, 19 October 1913, SPNEA; EW to MF, 3 May 1913, Letters 301. *Town Topics*, 24 April 1913, NYPL.

75 On divorce in France, Anthony Copley, *Sexual Moralities in France 1780–1980*, Routledge, 1989, 121–31; J.K. McMillan, *Housewife or Harlot*, St Martin's Press, 1984, 27; Theodore Zeldin, *France, 1848–1916*, Vol. I, *Ambition, Love, Politics*, Oxford University Press, 1973, 358; Roderick Phillips, *Putting Asunder: A History of Divorce in Western Society*, Cambridge University State, 1988, 462.

76 HJ to HS, 12/13 May 1913, HJL, IV, 671; OC to Sarah Codman, 5 May 1913, SPNEA; EW to MB, 18 May 1914, I Tatti; EW to Robert Grant, 29 April 1914, Beinecke. On the use

The first column also begins with:

EW to MJ, 19 September 1911, Houghton; EW to MF, 16 October 1911, Letters 260.

of her name, Lewis, 362, Benstock, 279. EW to SN, 12 August 1913, Beinecke. EW to BF, 18 January [1914], Beinecke.

CHAPTER 13: GETTING WHAT YOU WANT

1 For first meeting, Bernard Berenson, *Sketch for a Self-Portrait*, Pantheon, 1949, 24; Mary Berenson, *A Self-Portrait from Her Letters and Diaries*, eds Barbara Strachey and Jayne Samuels, Gollancz, 1983, 109; cited Lewis, 269, Dwight, 74. For BB's character, Ernest Samuels, *Bernard Berenson: The Making of a Legend*, Belknap, 1987, 89; Ronald Gower, *Records & Reminiscences*, Murray, 1903, 534; BB, *op. cit.*, 78; Caroline Moorehead, *Iris Origo*, John Murray, 2000, 53.
2 BB to MB, 2 January 1918, I Tatti.
3 On BB and art: *The Bernard Berenson Treasury*, ed. H. Kiel, Simon & Schuster, 1962; BB to MB, 3 August, 5 August 1895, 84. BB and CEN: BB, *self-portrait*, 52. BB and America: Samuels, *op. cit.*, 44, 59.
4 Strouse, 523. Bernard Berenson, *Sunset and Twilight*, Hamish Hamilton, 1964, 290; Rieder, 170.
5 Dwight, 74; Lewis, 270; Benstock, 222; Samuels, *op. cit.*, 85; BB to MB, 30 September, 2 October 1909, I Tatti; BB, *Self-Portrait*, 24. EW to BB, late September 1909, Letters 191.
6 BB, *Treasury*, 88.
7 Samuels, *op. cit.*, 54, 87, 39, 99; BB, *Treasury*, BB to MB, 5 September 1929, 163; BB, *Sunset*, xxii; BB, *Self-Portrait*, 47. BB to EW, 6 February 1917, I Tatti.
8 'The Rembrandt', CS I, 287–300. 'The Daunt Diana', CS II, 50–60; 'The Temperate Zone', CS II, 462. 'False Dawn', ch. 9, ONY. Sylvia Sprigge, *Berenson*, Allen & Unwin, 1960, 97.
9 Colin Simpson, *Artful Partners*, Macmillan, 1986, 71, 75; Samuels, *op. cit.*, 62, 143, 148; Sprigge, *op. cit.*, 207; Strouse, 504; Rieder, 170.
10 Moorehead, *op. cit.*, 129; Mariano, 7.

Harold Acton, *The Villas of Tuscany*, Thames & Hudson, 1973, 170; EW to BB, 1 January 1914, I Tatti.
11 Moorehead, *op. cit.*, 29–30; Samuels, *op. cit.*, 130–1, 96; Richard Dunn, *Geoffrey Scott and the Berenson Circle*, Edwin Mellon Press, 1998, 97, 49ff.; Mariano, 7. On Belle Green's amazing story, see Strouse, 511–20.
12 On WB and Mrs Robert Goelet, see Benstock, 288, citing OC.
13 WB to BB, 27 October 1912, 23 December 1913, 13 October 1919, 23 September 1924, I Tatti; BB to MB, 29 October 1910, 31 October 1910, 5 November 1910, 23 March 1912, 31 March 1919, I Tatti.
14 MB to her family, 11 October 1912; to BB, 6 July 1912, Mary Berenson, *op. cit.*, 180, 183–4. MB to BB, 2 April 1919, I Tatti. EW to BB, 12 July 1918, 28 July 1918. EW to MB, 6 July 1918, I Tatti.
15 BB, *Self-Portrait*, 12; Samuels, *op. cit.*, 140; BB to EW, 15 July, 31 July 1910; WB to BB, 16 July, 23 September 1916; BB to MB, 9 August 1913, 24 December 1931, I Tatti; EW to BB, 22 February 1914, I Tatti. EW to BB, 21 February 1922, Letters 451. WB reported to the Abbé Mugnier BB's anxieties about lack of success with women, and his own inability to understand that copulation could be a sin; WB found it as natural as eating.
16 BB to MB, 10 November 1917, I Tatti.
17 BB to EW, 2 February 1933, Lilly: 'I am working a bit, but how little compared with what you do, O *Vigorosa!*' EW to MB, 18 February 1918, I Tatti; BB to MB, 2 November 1917, I Tatti; EW to MB, 17 October 1920, I Tatti; Mariano, 161. Kenneth Clark, Introduction, 1966, to Mariano, x.
18 BB to EW, 23 March 1912, I Tatti.
19 EW to BB, 10 March 1911, 28 July 1918, 19 June 1910, end 1912, 1 July 1918, I Tatti.
20 EW to BB, 12 April 1911, I Tatti; 4 January 1911, Letters 232; 28 July 1913, 18 November 1913, 12 December 1920, I Tatti.

21 Samuels, *op. cit.*, 262–3; EW to MB, 21 April 1021; BB to MB, 28 December 1929, I Tatti. BB to Judge Learned Hand, 26 December 1927, *Selected Letters of Bernard Berenson*, ed. A.K. McComb, Houghton Mifflin, 1964.

22 EW to BB, 26 January 1912, I Tatti.

23 EW to BB, 17 February 1917, Letters 393. BB to EW, 19 February 1917, I Tatti.

24 EW to BB, 19 March 1911, I Tatti. EW to BB, 16 May 1911, Letters 240. EW to BB, 16 December 1911, I Tatti.

25 EW to BB, 15 July 1912, 1 January 1914, 27 June 1928, I Tatti.

26 EW to BB, 5 July 1922, 28 April 1921, I Tatti. Samuels, *op. cit.*, 334, 358.

27 EW to BB, 29 June 1912, Letters 273–4.

28 EW to BB, 6 October 1911, I Tatti; 19 April 1913, Letters 296.

29 Geoffrey Scott, letters to MB, May 1913, I Tatti.

30 EW to BB, 2 August 1913, Letters 303; BB to MB, 3 August 1913, I Tatti; EW to BB, 5 August 1913, Letters 305; BB to MB, 4 August 1913, I Tatti; MB to BB, 7 August 1913, I Tatti.

31 BB to MB, 9 August, 10 August, 15 August, 21 August, 25 August, 26 August, 30 August 1913, I Tatti. MB to BB, 24 August 1913, I Tatti. EW to MB, 24 August 1913, Letters 309. BB, *Self-Portrait*, 125; BB, *Sunset & Twilight*, 473; *Selected Letters*, 110.

32 EW to MB, 14 August 1913, Letters 306; EW to JHS, 4 September 1913, Letters 310; EW to MF, 13 August, 10 September 1913, Texas; EW to BB, 5 September, 8 November 1913, I Tatti.

33 EW to EB, 3 February 1913, 6 June 1913, Scribner Archive, Princeton. CS to EW, 12 September 1913, 6 May 1913, Scribner Archive, Princeton.

34 EW to James Barnes, 8 December 1907, in James Barnes, *From Then Till Now*, Appleton-Century, 1934, 221.

35 EW to CS, 18 August 1911, 2 November 1913; CS to EW, 13 December 1911, Scribner Archive, Princeton.

36 CS to EW, 16 February 1917, 6 May 1918, Scribner Archive, Princeton.

37 EB to CS, 4 August 1908; EB to CS, 26 July 1910; EW to CS, 7 November 1911, Scribner Archive, Princeton.

38 Benstock, 99, 326; Grant Overton *Portrait of a Publisher*, Appleton, 1925, 2. EW to MF, 17 June 1912, Texas. Contracts, EW, Professional Correspondence, Beinecke.

39 Sears to EW, 5 April 1918, Beinecke; EW to MF, 14 July 1912, Texas. EW to CS, 3 May 1912. CS to EW, 13 June 1912, Scribner Archive, Princeton. She also told Macmillan that she thought she would 'reach a different public' through switching to Appleton. EW to Frederick Macmillan, 17 July 1912, Macmillan Archive, 54956, f.135–7, BL. For EW's earnings at this time see Benstock, 261: between 1905 and 1912 she earned about $125,000 in book royalties and serial contracts; an EW story cost $1,000, a poem $200, and the advance for R for $15,000 set the 'baseline' for future contracts.

40 EW to MF, 27 June 1912, Texas.

41 EW to CS, 19 May 1913, 2 November 1913, 23 February 1914, 13 April 1918, 15 January 1914, Scribner Archive, Princeton. Contracts, Appleton, 19 July 1916, 31 October 1916, Beinecke.

42 EW to CS, 13 April 1918; CS to EW, 16 February 1917, 6 May 1918; EW to CS, 23 May 1918, Scribner Archive, Princeton.

43 CS to EW, 20 February 8 December 1914, Scribner Archive, Princeton. Benstock, 356, 329, 355. CS to EW, 9 February 1921, EW to CS, 17 September 1921, Scribner Archive, Princeton; EW to Robert Bridges, 30 June 1931, Beinecke; Charles Scribner [III] to EW, 25 February 1936, Beinecke.

44 Ammons, 90, cites Lewis and Wolff

on EW's partial resemblance to Undine, and notes that 'Wharton cast Undine as her opposite . . . yet also as her twin'.

45 CC, ch. 14.

46 Critics read Undine both ways: Edmund Wilson as the prototype of 'the international cocktail-bitch' (*The Wound and the Bow*, 1941, 202), Janet Malcolm as the invention of a misogynist (*New York Times Books Review*, 16 November 1986, 11), numerous readers as a 'monster'. But she is also read as a victim of the patriarchal system (these readings summed up by Debra MacComb, *Tales of Liberation, Strategies of Containment*, Garland, 2000, 158–9), or as a means for EW to 'reveal her criticism of . . . leisure-class marriage' (Ammons, 102), or as a product of our own misogyny as readers (Beth Kowaleski-Wallace, 'The Reader as Misogynist in *The Custom of the Country*', *Modern Language Studies*, 21:2, Winter 1991, 45–53); or, conversely, as giving off 'an exhilarating power and glamour' (Nancy Bentley, in CCEW, 1995, 63).

47 CC, ch. 12.

48 HJ/EW, 9 October 1913, 270.

49 CC, chs 4, 10, 21.

50 CC, chs 11, 19, 25, 20, 5.

51 CC, chs 12, 15, 26. For 'the complicity between society, journalism and the nouveaux riches', and the coverage of society women in the press, see Montgomery, ch. 6.

52 CC, *Scribner's Magazine*, April 1913, May 1913. CC, chs 10, 16. EW, Writings, Beinecke.

53 CC, chs 2, 4, 8, 37, 41, 44, 46.

54 CC, chs 1, 11, 13, 16, 44.

55 CC, chs 2, 8, 5, 26, 27. MacComb, *op. cit.*, 145.

56 CC, chs 4, 2, 20, 3, 16, 40, 36.

57 CC, chs 4, 20, 42.

58 CC, chs 11, 28, 24, 43.

59 Richard H. Lawson, *Edith Wharton and German Literature*, Grundmann, 1974, 109–19, and Waid, 136, 140–8; note on Montaigne, 225, note 22. For myths and literary allusions in CC see also Maureen Honey, in

Colquitt *et al.*, 76–99. Ramsden, 68; Wegener, 250. CC, ch 1, ch. 4; 'Lamia', Part I, 59, 295; Part II, 277, 260, in *John Keats: The Complete Poems*, ed. John Barnard, Penguin, Second Edition, 1977, 414–33; see 665–6 on the Lamia story.

60 FWTM, ch. 6. CC, chs 15, 38.

61 CC, chs 12, 25, 41. For W.D. Howells's influence on CC, see Ammons, 109.

62 CC, chs 35, 44.

63 CC, chs 10, 17, 42, 9, 18, 35, 41, 46. On CC as a novel about the failure to write, in which the language of consumption devours the language of the imagination, see Waid, 131–55.

64 CC, chs 10, 21, 7, 11, 29.

65 CC, chs 5, 14, 6, 32, 10, 45, 38.

66 Stephen Orgel, Introduction, CC, Oxford University Press, 1995, notes how often EW uses inverted commas when she is citing her Westerners, as if to emphasise the decorum of her own language in contrast to their raw slang.

67 CC, chs 38, 21, 9, 46.

68 CC, chs 5, 21, 19, 26, 35. On CC as a Darwinian novel about evolution and the survival of the fittest, see Cecelia Tichi, 'Emerson, Darwin, and *The Custom of the Country*', in Singley, 2003, 89–114. On Undine as the force of primitivism in civilisation, see Bauer, 15.

69 CC, chs 22, 27, 24, 21. On CC containing a commentary on 'problem novels', see Robert Caserio, 'EW and the Fiction of Public Commentary', *Western Humanities Review*, XXXX, 3, Autumn 1986, 208. On divorce as the social theme of CC, see MacComb, *op. cit.*, 158–69, and Ammons, 97–109.

70 Jason Epstein, *Snobbery: The American Version*, Houghton Mifflin, 2002, 29. CC, chs 42, 12, 14, 19.

71 Undine is once addressed as 'Puss' by Elmer (noted by MacComb, *op. cit.*, 155). CC, chs 37, 12, 29, 39, 43, 40.

72 CC, chs 31, 23, 24, 36.

CHAPTER 14: FIGHTING FRANCE

1 'My dream', Beinecke, quoted Wolff, 430, and [with some mistranscriptions] Lewis, 355.

2 Conrad, see Wolff, 269; HJ/EW, 6 September 1913, 261.

3 Arrived late, and signed 'Pussy', EW to Ella Douglas, 18 January [1914], Barnard College, Overbury Collection; Benstock, 290; HJ/EW, 16 January 1914, 274; EW to BB, 30 January 1914, Letters 313; EW to BB, 1 January 1914, I Tatti; EW to MC, 31 December [1913], Beinecke; EW to MJ, 20 January 1914, Benstock, 292; WB to BB, 14 January 1914, I Tatti; MB to GS, January 1914, in Benstock, 291; PL to GL, 9 July 1914, Beinecke; EW to BB, 19 February 1914, I Tatti.

4 EW to MF, 9 April 1914, Letters 315. Wolff on EW and the 'primitive', 270. Elise Devinck: Benstock notes misspelt 'Duvlenck' throughout Lewis and Letters; Dwight indexes her as 'Elise'.

5 Baedeker, *The Mediterranean*, Ramsden, 6. PL to GL, 25 February 1914, Beinecke: 'If I accept her offer, I should be accepting a good deal, and accepting *constantly*, day by day.' EW to MF, 9 April 1914, Letters 316. EW to BB, 16 April 1914, Letters 117; Donnée Book, Beinecke, quoted Wolff, 270; PL to GL, 13 April 1914, Beinecke. Tunisian travels: Benstock, 293–4; BG, ch. 12, vii; Lewis, 360. EW, Notebook, April 1914, Lilly. PL's postcard was in the style of the Baron Wilhelm von Gloeden's famous homoerotic 'classical' Sicilian photographs.

6 PL to GL, 20 April 1914, Beinecke. EW to BB, 16 April 1918, Letters 318; EW to MF, 11 May 1914, Letters 324.

7 HJ/EW, 2 March 1914, 281. EW to EB, 10 May 1914, Scribner Archive, Princeton. Anthony Sylvester, *Tunisia*, Bodley Head, 1969, 42. 'Peter Elsom', MSS, Beinecke; EW to MJ, 21 April 1914, Beinecke.

8 EW to BB, 1 May 1914, Letters 322; 'EW and Spain' in Joslin and Price, 204; EW to BB, 26 July 1914, Letters 326; BG, ch. 12, vii; 'George Sand and Chopin': HJ to HS, 4/5 August 1914, in Benstock, 296. For WB's expertise in cave-painting see William C. Carter, *Marcel Proust: A Life*, Yale University Press, 2000, 639. EW to LB, 25 July 1914, Lesage, 114.

9 BG, ch. 12, vii; 'The Look of Paris', FF.

10 For very full accounts of EW's wartime publications and war-work, see Olin-Ammentorp and Price. For reviews see Tuttleton.

11 On the causes of the Great War, see Keegan, 59; Smith, 25; Ernest Samuels, *Bernard Berenson: The Making of a Legend*, Belknap, 1987, 185; Becker, 3.

12 On 'It can't be war': BG, ch. 13, i; Julian [sic] Green, *Memories of Happy Days*, Dent, 1944, 82. On Caillaux, Samuels, *op. cit.*, 176; Vincent Cronin, *Paris on the Eve, 1900–1914*, Collins, 1989, 430. M, ch. 2; SF, ch. 5; on Paris in August 1914, Moma Clarke, *Paris Waits, 1914*, Smith, Elder, 1915, 1; H. Pearl Adam, *Paris Sees It Through*, Hodder & Stoughton, 1919, 10.

13 Keegan, 82. 'The Look of Paris', FF.

14 Adam, *op. cit.*, 19–20; Green, *op. cit.*, 92. Mugnier quoted in Cronin, *op. cit.*, 452. Michel Corday, *The Paris Front*, Dutton, 1934, 13, 15, 19. Charles Inman Barnard, *Paris War Days*, Little Brown, 1914, 14, 20–40. Smith, 27–30; Becker, 77; SF, ch. 7; BG, ch. 13, i.

15 WB to BB, 14 August 1914; EW to BB, 10 February 1915, I Tatti; SF, 77.

16 Smith, 37, 42–3, 69. Jay Winter and Jean-Louis Robert, *Capital Cities at War*, Cambridge University Press, 1997, 88, 151; Keegan, 148, 343; Adam, *op. cit.*, 72; Becker, 3.

17 HJ/EW, 16/17 January 1915, 320; EW to BB, 24 February 1915, I Tatti; poem, MSS, Beinecke; report on EW's talk to the Société des Conférences, February 1918, Beinecke;

EW to Elizabeth Hoyt, 12 June 1918, Beinecke, quoted Price, 154.

18 EW to Robert Grant, 31 August 1914, Beinecke; EW to SN, 2 September 1914, Letters 335; EW to Robert Grant, 13 February 1915, Houghton, in Price, 44. EW to BB, 11 June 1915, 28 July 1918, I Tatti. M, ch. 4, ch. 8.

19 M, ch. 5; SF, ch. 8; EW to Thomas Newbold Rhinelander, 6 October 1916, October 1918, Beinecke. Binyon poems, see Ramsden, 13, and Olin-Ammentorp, 151. *The New World* was in EW's library.

20 EW to MJ, 3 January 1917, Beinecke; EW on Hearst, Benstock, 326, EW to MF, 12 August 1916, Letters 381–2; EW to *Nieuwe Rot-terdamsche Courant*, 10 February 1918, Beinecke; EW to Wilbur Cross, 7 May 1924, Beinecke. Beerbohm's cartoons on 'England, France and Germany' in *Yale Review*, 24 January 1924, go from Napoleon to World War I. His caricatures of Germany get bigger and more martial; of England, fatter, at a tradesman's desk; of France, smaller, more anxious and more militarised.

21 EW to GL, 23 December 1914, Beinecke, in Price, 35; EW to MJ, 9 February 1917, Beinecke, in Price, 110; EW to SN, 5 May 1917, Beinecke, in Price, 117. M, ch. 3; SF, ch. 23.

22 Olin-Ammentorp, 65, 89; M, chs 2, 7, 8; Benstock, 346; Tuttleton, 268. EW to BB, 1 July 1918, I Tatti.

23 Summary of SF, Beinecke; RJ to EW, 3 July 1919, EW to RJ, 23 July 1919, Beinecke; Tuttleton, 344; EW to MC, 1 October 1923, Letters 471.

24 SF, ch. 32.

25 Carter, *op. cit.*, 686.

26 HJ/EW, 6 August 1913, 289; 23 May 1915, 342; 19 August 1914, 293; 21 September 1914, 303; 1 December 1914, 319.

27 EW to Corinne Robinson, 11 June 1919, Letters 422. 'With The Tide' in *Saturday Evening Post*, 29 May 1919; in Olin-Ammentorp, 244; 'Elegy', in Olin-Ammentorp, 240; 'You and You' in *Scribner's Magazine*, February 1919; short version in Olin-Ammentorp, 241–2. 'The Hymm of the Lusitania', *New York Herald*, 7 May 1915, 1. P, 134–5, 96–8, 139–42.

28 EW to Theodore Roosevelt, Price 69. Roosevelt to EW, 23 June 1915, Beinecke. Theodore Roosevelt, *America and the World War*, Scribner's, 1915, p. 248, and Ramsden, 105–6. EW to GL, 8 November 1914, Letters 342. HL/EW, 2 October 1914, 305; 25 June 1915, 344; J. William White, *A Primer of the War for Americans*, John. C. Whinston, 1914, 98. EW to Barrett Wendell, 27 April 1916, Letters 373. 'The Great Blue Tent', 25 August 1915, *New York Times*. P, 135, 7 EW to Royal Cortissoz, 27 October 1915, Beinecke, 16 January 1926, Letters 488. EW to BF, 28 December 1915, Beinecke.

29 'The Tone of France', 'In Argonne', 'In the North', FF; 'Conclusion', Part 4, FWTM.

30 *Cahiers Charles Du Bos*, 1969–1974, Société des Amis de Charles Du Bos, 46. Sacralisation: Smith, 108–9. Gillet quoted in Cronin, *op. cit.*, 438. *The Book of France*, ed. Winifred Stephens, Macmillan, 1915, 159, 71, 173, 180. EW to HJ, 26 March 1915, HJ/EW, 335. Charles Le Goffic, articles in *Revue des Deux Mondes*, March 1915, collected as *Dixmunde*, trans. Florence Simmonds, Heinemann, 1916, 74.

31 PB cited in Clarke, *op. cit.*, 272; see also Robert Grant, *Their Spirit: Some Impressions of the English and the French during the summer of 1916*, Houghton Mifflin, 1916, 100. Becker, 162.

32 'L'Amérique en Guerre', *Revue Hebdomadaire*, 27, 2 March 1918; reviewed in *Journal des Debats*, February 1918. Price, 150. EW, 'Talk to American Soldiers', April 1918, TS, Beinecke, and in Olin-Ammentorp, 261–72. BB to MB, 24 January 1918, I Tatti; Price, 143–4; Rieder, 125; Diane de Margerie, Introduction to Edith Wharton, *French Ways and their Meaning*, Berkshire House Publishers, 1997,

xiii; SWB, 29. 'proppergander', quoted Price, 148; 'if I were dead', Price, 150, from 'Talk to American Soldiers', 1918.

33 Clarke, *op. cit.*, 51, 213; Barnard, *op. cit.*, 67, 113; M, ch. 1; 'The Look of Paris', FF. EW to BB, 22 August 1914, Letters 334.

34 BG, ch. 11, iii; Price, 17–18; Dwight, 84; EW, 'My Work Among the Women Workers of Paris', *New York Times*, 28 November 1915.

35 'American Hostels for Refugees', Lists and Description, 15 May 1915, Beinecke.

36 EW to BB, 30 September 1914, Letters 341; WB to BB, 5 September 1914, I Tatti. EW to Mrs Eleanor Belmont, 16 November [1915], Butler Library, Columbia University, Spec. MS. Coll. Belmont.

37 EW to Mrs Humphry Ward, 15 August 1914, Ward Papers, Pusey House, Oxford.

38 Bell, 190. Benstock, 305. The Wards' next two sets of tenants, in 1915 paid £1,100 a year for Stocks, and £300 a year for Grosvenor Place. Mrs Humphry Ward, *A Writer's Recollections*, 1918, 207. John Sutherland, *Mrs Humphry Ward*, Oxford University Press, 1991, 187, 342.

39 HJ/EW, 5 June 1914, 287.

40 'The Refugees', CS II, 583.

41 HJ/EW, 30 August 1914, 295. PL to GL, 8 September 1914, Beinecke. EW to Mrs Humphry Ward, 'Thursday 30th' [August 1914]; 'Thursday' [August 1914]; EW to Mrs Humphry Ward, 'Monday' [September 1914], Ward Papers, Pusey House; EW to LB, 8 Sept-ember 1914, Lesage, 116 ['Never have I felt so much as at this moment how much I love France and my French friends. It tears at my heart not to be able to prove it by rushing to Paris. There are "useless mouths", I know it well, but "useless hearts"? Not when they feel your sufferings as I feel them.']; HJ/EW, 21 September 1914, 302.

CHAPTER 15: UNE SECONDE PATRIE

1 EW to MB, 12 January 1915, Letters 345; Price, 26, 46, 124; EW to MJ, 7 January 1916, Letters 367; EW to SN, 27 September 1914, Letters 339; EW to Mme de Marthille, 13 June 1917, Beinecke.

2 EW to MJ, 28 December 1914, 3 January 1915, Beinecke. Toys, M, ch. 4.

3 Price, 72, 145; Ida Clarke, *American Women and the World War*, Appleton, 1918, 460, 454; Appeal for Belgians, draft for *New York Times*, with Mrs Belmont, Butler Library, Columbia University, Spec. MS Coll., Belmont. Charles Inman Barnard, *Paris War Days*, Little Brown, 1914, 48; for Mrs W. Vanderbilt, 220; SF, ch. 17.

4 Price, 34, 47, 49, 72; ET to Mme Scheikievick, 31 January 1931, Lilly. EW, Report on the American Hostels for Refugees, *New York Herald*, 27 April 1915, Olin-Ammentorp, 248–51. Arline Boucher Tehan, *Henry Adams in Love*, Universe Books, 1983, 257; Robert Grant, *Their Spirit*, Houghton Mifflin, 1916, 90–1.

5 Gide, Journal, 28 September, 1 October, 15 October, 26 November 1915, in *The Journals of André Gide*, ed. Justin O'Brian, Knopf, 1948, 99–110; Alan Sheridan, *André Gide: A Life in the Present*, Hamish Hamilton, 1998, 285; Lesage, 119–21; CdB to Gide, 8 May 1927, *Letters de Charles Du Bos et Réponses de André Gide*, Corréa, 1950, 124; EW to CdB, nd, Bibliothèque Doucet, MS 27567. EW to ET, 30 November 1915, Lilly; EW to MJ: 20 December 1916, Beinecke. *Cahiers Charles Du Bos*, 23 December 1916, Société des Amis Charles Du Bos, 1971, 45; Charles Du Bos, *Approximations*, Edition Des Syrles, 2000, 1485. For satire on charities, see SF, esp. chs 14, 29.

6 EW, 'Christmas Tinsel', December 1923, Olin-Ammentorp, 276; 'Dire Need of Poor Children of Ypres', 24 March 1915, Price, 48–51, 197; 'The

Children of Flanders Rescue Committee', 28 November 1915, Olin-Ammentorp, 251–2; EW to CS, 28 June 1915, Letters 358; EW to ET, 19 April 1916, quoted Price, 91.

7   Price, 164, 221, note 6. Grant, *op. cit.*, 89. Lace-making: 'Mrs Wharton's War Charities', TS, August 1916, Beinecke.

8   Jay Winter and Jean-Louis Robert, *Capital Cities at War*, Cambridge University Press, 1997, 318; food restrictions: Pearl Adam, *Paris Sees It Through*, Hodder & Stoughton, 1919, 109; Richard Cobb, *French and Germans, Germans and French*, University Press of New England, 1983, 30; M, ch. 8.

9   TB epidemic: Winter and Robert, 468; Clarke, *op. cit.*, 485. EW's appeal, 18 January 1915; details of TB homes, ET, letter, 31 January 1931, Lilly; Price, 35, 94, 111, 123, 132; EW to MJ, 14 November 1917. EW to BB, 13 February 1917, I Tatti.

10 ET to Mme Scheikievick, 31 January 1931, Lilly; EW to Z. Du Bos, 21 February [1918?]: '*Mois qui me contente généralement de cinq heures du sommeil.*' Bibliothèque Doucet, Paris, MS 275638–3/4.

11 EW to MB, 12 January 1915, Letters 346. CdB, Cahier 14, 33, 12 March 1914, Cahier 16, 31, 18 October 1917 [remembering a concert in May 1915]; EW to MJ, 15 April 1916, Beinecke, and Price, 81.

12 Benstock, 343; EW to MJ, 21 December 1917, Beinecke; Price, 138, 169.

13 ET to RT, 31 July 1917; ET to RT, 22 July 1916, Lilly. On the Rockefeller Foundation, Price, 97, quoting from the Rockefeller Archives, 16 November 1916; Benstock, 335; Price, 109. EW to BB, 28 January 1917, I Tatti.

14 EW to MJ, 11 May 1916, 23 January 1916, Beinecke.

15 EW to Mr Brigg, 3 December 1917, TS, unsigned, Beinecke.

16 ET to RT, 16 August 1916, 22 July 1916, 18 August 1916, 27 October 1916, 24 March 1917, 29 March 1917, 7 May 1918, 26 July 1917, Lilly.

17 EW to ET, 2 March 1916, Lilly.

18 EW to BB, 12 January, 27 January 1915; EW to MB, 24 February 1915, EW to BB, 15 July 1915, I Tatti. BG, ch. 13, iv. HJ/EW, 23 May 1915, 342; EW to HJ, 28 February 1915, 11 March 1915, 25 March 1915, 14–15 May 1915, HJ/EW, 323, 327, 335, 339. Re Isch Wall, EW to Joseph Reinach, 16 April 1915, Bibliothèque Nationale, NAF 13566, pièce 179–80. Re 'Her', EW to Mrs Belmont, 'Fri 7th' [nd]; re Ritz, EW to Mrs Belmont, 4 January [nd], Butler Library, Columbia University, Spec. MS Coll., Belmont. WB to BB, 16 July 1916, I Tatti.

19 'In Lorraine', FF. Grant, *op. cit.*, 74; Rudyard Kipling, *France At War*, Doubleday, 1915, 11, 69, 98, 100. On being passed down the chain of command, see Dwight, 192–202, very good on EW's war-journeys. Faivre cartoon reproduced in Dwight, 195, and Olin-Ammentorp, 17. *Le Rire Rouge*, 'Dans Les Ruines', 22 May 1915. E.g. of '*poilu*' cartoon: a *poilu* coming back from leave to a scene of devastation in the trenches is asked: '*Qu'est-ce qu'ils disent à Pantruche? Que l'hiver sera dur: le sucre va manquer. Ah! les pauv'gars!*' ['What are they saying at home?' 'That the winter will be hard – there are going to be sugar shortages.' 'Oh, the poor little things!'], 'Retour de Permission', Ricardo Flores, *Le Rire Rouge*, 16 November 1917. EW to Alice Garrett, May 1915, Evergreen House, Johns Hopkins, quoted Dwight, 195.

20 EW to CS, 28 June 1915, Letter 357. EW to CS, telegram, 3 March 1915, Scribner Archive, Princeton; CS to EW, telegram, 14 April 1915, Scribner Archive, Princeton; EW to Robert Bridges, 27 May 1915, Scribner Archive, Princeton. EW to CS, May 1915, in Price, 56; EW to MB, 13 March 1915, I Tatti. CS to EW, 15 July 1915, Scribner Archive, Princeton. Benstock, 314;

HJ/EW, EW to HJ, 324; 'In Argonne', FF.

21 BB to EW, 12 May 1915, I Tatti; Keegan, 212, 275.

22 Keegan, 335. 'In Argonne', FF.

23 EW to HJ, 324; HJ/EW, 5 March 1915, 326. EW to MB, 13 March 1915, I Tatti; 'In Argonne', FF.

24 EW to HJ, 28 February 1915, 11 March 1915, HJ/EW, 323–4; 'In Argonne', FF; EW to MB, 13 March 1915, I Tatti. WB to BB, 5 March 1915, I Tatti. Dwight, 197.

25 EW to HJ, HJ/EW, 14–15 May 1915, 340; 'In Lorraine and the Vosges', FF.

26 Price, 56; 'Belgium', in King Albert's Book, Hearst, 1915, 165, and in Olin-Ammentorp, 42. Albert at La Panne: The War Diaries of King Albert I, William Kimber, 1954, xvii; 'In the North', FF.

27 Smith, 83; Keegan, 300–36.

28 Olin-Ammentorp, 12; Ernest Samuels, Bernard Berenson: The Making of a Legend, Belknap, 1987, 226; EW to Miss Reubell, 4 April 1917, Beinecke; EW to BB, 17 April 1917, I Tatti.

29 James, interview, 21 March 1915; Hemingway, A Farewell to Arms, 1929, cited in this context in Olin-Ammentorp, 12, and Price, xiii. SF, ch. 16. 'Writing a War Story', September 1919, in CS II, 359–70.

30 EW to CS, 14 November 1914, 29 December 1914, Scribner Archive, Princeton.

31 Maeterlinck, Daily Mail, 14 September 1914, with thanks to Roy Foster. HJ/EW, 19 July 1915, 345. Price, 60.

32 HJ/EW, 26 July 1915, 346; EW to MJ, 26 October 1915, Beinecke; Price, 63–4; CS to EW, 8 October 1915, Scribner Archive, Princeton; CS to Robert Grant, 26 December 1915, quoted Price, 70.

33 P, 94. BH, xxiv–xxv, 41. EW to CS, 19 September 1915, Scribner Archive, Princeton. BH, 76, 104; Olin-Ammentorp, 122. William Butler Yeats to EW, Price, 63, and see R.F. Foster, William Butler Yeats, Vol. II, The Arch-Poet, ch. I, Oxford University Press, 2003, 5–6. The full list of contributors to BH is: Barrès, Bernhardt, Binyon, Bourget, Brooke, Claudel, Cocteau, Conrad, D'Indy, Duse, Galsworthy, Gosse, Grant, Hardy, Hervieu, Howells, Général Humbert, James, Jammes, Joffre, Maeterlinck, Edward Sandford Martin, Meynell, Paul Elmer More, De Noailles, Josephine Preston Peabody, Lilla Cabot Perry, Agnes Repplier, De Régnier, Roosevelt, Rostand, Santayana, Stravinsky, Suarès, Edith Thomas, Trench, Verhaeren, Ward, Wendell, Wharton, Margaret L. Woods, Yeats, and [illustrations]: Bakst, Beerbohm, Blanche, Blashfield, Bonnat, Dagnan-Bouveret, Gay, Gérôme, Gibson, Ménard, Monet, Renoir, Rodin, Van Rysselberghe, and Sargent.

34 New York Times, 25 and 26 January 1916, Benstock, 319, Price, 79. EW to Walter Maynard, 12 October 1915, Beinecke.

35 Fullerton: Ramsden, 219; EW to MF, 21 December [1916], Houghton. For Elizabeth Cameron, Lewis, 413; EW to Elizabeth Cameron, 22 June 1918, Letters 405; Elizabeth Cameron to MB, 7 March 1919, I Tatti ('the sense of isolation & helplessness is reducing me to pulp . . . why make an effort when there is no one to make it for?'). EW to BB, 19 February 1918, I Tatti. Samuels, op. cit., 226–7. EW to MJ, 7 July 1918, Letters 408. EW to BB, 15 February 1918, Letters 403. EW to BB, 20 July 1918, I Tatti. On MB and Geoffrey Scott, see Richard M. Dunn, Geoffrey Scott and the Berenson Circle, Edwin Mellon Press, 1998, ch. 11, and Samuels, op. cit., 235–6. EW to BB, 26 June 1918, I Tatti.

36 Revue Hebdomadaire, 15 May 1915, Wegener, 195–204. EW to AG, 5 March 1916, Letters 372; EW to BB, 15 October 1915, Letters 361. EW to Elizabeth Cameron, 22 June 1918, Letters 405; EW to SN, 14 June 1916, Letters 379; EW to MC, 10 May 1915, Beinecke.

37 Lubbock, 133; Lewis, 409; BB to MB, 16 November 1917, Letters 391.

38 Benstock, 309; Lewis, 372, 385 ('headstrong'); EW to MJ, 25 January 1919, 8 May 1919, EW to MC, 12 April 1928, Beinecke; EW to WT, 11 November 1916, Letters 383; EW to BB, 15 May 1916, 17 December 1925, I Tatti. RT to ET, 23 January 1916, Lilly. EW to ET, 30 July 1918, Lilly; RT to ET, 12 October 1916, Lilly; RT to ET, 23 January 1916, Lilly.

39 For RS, see Lewis, 384, 411–12, 531; Benstock, 342; Price, 159–60; Dwight, 228; Olin-Ammentorp, 57; and especially Frederick Wegener, 'Edith Wharton and Ronald Simmons: Documenting A Pivotal War-Time Friendship', *Yale University Library Gazette*, Vol. 77 (2002), 51–85. 'Garçon', TS re Comité des Étudiants Américains de L'Ecole des Beaux-Arts, 16 February 1917, Beinecke; 'teddy-bear', ET on EW's last days, Lilly; on the Committee of the Beaux-Arts, Clarke, *op. cit.*, 471. Title-page: EW to Robert Bridges, 7 February 1923, Scribner Archive, Princeton.

40 Obituary, 15 September 1918, *Providence Daily Journal*, in Wegener in *Yale University Library Gazette*, 54, 58, 61; BG, ch. 14, ii; Olin-Ammentorp, 57.

41 RT to ET, 14 August 1918, Lilly. EW to BB, 13 August, 15 August, 11 September 1918, I Tatti and Letters 409; EW to ET, 16 August 1918, Lilly; EW to MJ, 13 August 1918, Beinecke; quoted Benstock, 342, and Wegener in *Yale University Library Gazette*, 66–7.

42 BB to MB, Lewis, 412, 428; EW to ET, 19 August 1918, Lilly. 'Captain Ronald Simmons Dies On Active Service', 14 August 1918, *New York Herald*; 'On Active Service', Wegener in *Yale University Library Gazette*, 84–5, 66, 81; Olin-Ammentorp, 240.

43 Lewis, 411; Benstock, 342; Price, 181; RS to EW, 7 July 1918, Beinecke. For Kahn's philanthropic activism on behalf of the Allies, see John Kobler, *Otto the Magnificent*,

Scribner's, 1988, ch. 12. Like EW, he was made a chevalier (later a commander) of the French Légion d'honneur.

44 EW to MC, 1 October 1923, Letters 472.

45 F. Lavenir, *La Légion d'honneur*, Charles-Lavauselle, 1936, 43–4; Haryett Fontanges, *La Légion d'honneur et les Femmes Décorées*, Paris, 1905; Jean Damiel, *La Légion d'honneur*, Editions André Brume, 1946, 172. Price, 87–99, 122, 205; EW to CS, 30 March 1916, 7 May 1916, Scribner Archive, Princeton; clipping from *Exelsior*, 8 April 1916, Beinecke; Mariano, 168, paraphrased Price. For details on the Order, thanks to Julian Barnes, Commandeur de l'Ordre des Arts et des Lettres. *Rapport sur Les Prix de Vertu par M. Raymond Poincaré*, Paris, 1920, 13–16. Montyon: 'M. de Montyon pensait qu'il n'appartient qu'à l'intelligence d'apprécier convenablement la vertu, qui n'est elle-même qu'une intelligence accomplie de nos devoirs et de notre destinée. La sensibilité, dit un poëte, c'est tout notre génie; et la vertu, c'est le génie dans toute sa puissance, appliqué à la vie morale.' Translation by Bridget Patterson. Prix de Vertu, Discours de M. Nodier, 11 August 1836, *www.bmlisieux.com/archives/privertu.htm* (with thanks to Vanessa Guignery). Belgian honours, Benstock, 344; EW to MC, 5 June 1917, 2 August 1918, Beinecke. Pershing to EW, 19 July 1917, in Price, 122, Dwight, 206, EW to Pershing, 22 July 1917, Letters 395. Clarke, *op. cit.*, 462, gave a detailed account of 'Edith Wharton's war charities in France'. Newspaper clipping re TW, 1917, Beinecke, and quoted Benstock, 319.

46 EW to BB, 4 February 1917; EW to Zézette Du Bos, nd, Bibliothèque Doucet, MS 27568–8/9. Price, 93, 102; EW to MJ, 15 November 1917, Beinecke; EW to BB, 12 May 1918, MB to BB, 23 May 1918, BB to MB, 21 May, 28 May 1918, I Tatti; EW

to Alice Garrett, 22 June 1918, quoted Price, 155; EW to MJ, 7 July 1918, Beinecke; Benstock, 345.

47 EW to Alice Garrett, 23 March 1918, quoted Price, 149. Keegan, 348, 356, 390, 436, 438; Gordon Wright, *France in Modern Times*, Norton, 1987, 309, 313; Smith, 137, 154; Becker, 205.

48 EW to Louis Ledyard, 20 August 1917, Beinecke, quoted Price, 128. Price, 124, 126, 128, 130, 135, 172. EW to BB, 28 June 1917, I Tatti. On the Red Cross in France, Ruth Gaines, *Helping France*, Dutton, 1919, 51: 'Co-ordination and co-operation with all existing agencies [was] a policy by no means easy to attain.'

49 EW to BB, 23 May 1920, I Tatti.

50 EW to BB, 24 May 1917, I Tatti; EW to CS, 30 March 1917, Scribner Archive, Princeton; EW to ET, 25 January 1919, Lilly.

51 BG, ch. 13, iv; EW to Robert Grant, 17 September 1916, in Price, 95; EW to CS, 16 August 1916; EW to Robert Bridges, 2 August 1916, Scribner Archive, Princeton; EW to CS, 16 August 1916, Scribner Archive, Princeton; EW to GL, 21 December 1916, Letters 385.

52 S, chs 1, 5, 15. For Whitman and S, see Singley, 148–52, 154–61.

53 Conrad to EW, 1 October 1917, Beinecke; S, chs 3, 1, 8, 6. BG, Ch 12, i.

54 EW to GL, 21 December 1916, Letters 385; T.S. Eliot, *Egoist*, January 1919, in Tuttleton, 363; EW to BB, 4 September 1917, Letters 398. S, chs 2, 12, 13.

55 S, chs 16, 12. Price, 139; BG, ch. 12, i; EW to SN, 5 October 1913, Beinecke.

56 S, chs 18, 17. For contradictory readings of S, see Ammons, 131–9; Bauer, ch. 1; Beer 2002, 48–9; Jean Frantz Blackall in Bendixen, 115–26; Blake Nevius, *Edith Wharton: A Study of her Fiction*, University of California Press, 1953, 169; Singley, 147–54; Rhonda Skillern in CCEW, 117–36; Waid, 79–114; Wolff, 292–5.

57 Negotiations over S, see ch. 12. EW to CS, 28 August, 6 October 1917, Scribner Archive, Princeton. EW to MJ, 26 September 1917, Letters 400; EW to JEB, Fez, 3 October [1917], Bibliothèque De l'Institut, 318.

58 EW to MJ, 26 September 1917, Letters 410.

59 For Morocco, see André Tardieu, *Le Mystère d'Agadir*, Calmann-Lévy, 1912; C.R. Pennell, *Morocco since 1930: A History*, Hurst, 2000; Walter Harris, *Morocco That Was*, Blackwood, 1921. For Lyautey, see Robin Bidwell, *Morocco Under Colonial Rule*, Frank Cass, 1973; William Hoisington, *Lyautey and the French Conquest of Morocco*, St Martin's Press, 1995; Douglas Porch, *The Conquest of Morocco*, Knopf, 1982; Alan Scham, *Lyautey in Morocco*, University of California Press, 1970.

60 Children: Scham, *op. cit.*, 40–1, 48. Protectorate: Bidwell, *op. cit.*, 68, 156, 23; Pennell, *op. cit*, 163.

61 Bidwell, *op. cit.*, 13, 65, 23; Pennell, *op. cit.*, 160, 172; Scham, *op. cit.*, 28, 34, Porch, *op. cit.*, 294, 296. Paul Morand, *Journal d'un Attaché d'Ambassade*, Gallimard, 1996, 14 September 1917, 352. IM, chs 4, 5.

62 EW to Chevrillon, 21 August [1917], 27 August [1917], Bibliothèque Doucet, 23520–2, 23520–3. EW to Gide, 10 August 1917, Letters 395. André Bernard, *Le Maroc*, Felix Alcan, 1918, 125, 294–5, 359 ff. IM, ch. 6. 'Instability', Pennell, xvi. Preface to *Mysterious Islam: Morocco*, Hachette, 1924.

63 EW to MJ, 26 September 1917, Letters 399; IM, chs 2, 3, 4, 5. EW to MJ, 5 October 1917, Beinecke.

64 IM, chs 4, 3.

65 IM, chs 3, 4.

66 IM, chs 4, 5, 1, 2. For attitudes in IM, see Nancy Bentley in Singley, 2003, 147–80; Mary Suzanne Schriber in Joslin and Price, 147–64; Judith L. Sensibar and Stephanie Batcos in Colquitt *et al.*, 149–71, 172–87.

67 Smith, 55–6; Julian [sic] Green, *Memories of Happy Days*, Dent, 1944, 105; Jay Winter and Jean-Louis

Robert, *Capital Cities at War*, Cambridge University Press, 1997, 90; EW, 'How Paris Welcomed the King', *Reveille*, 3 November 1919, 367–9; Olin-Ammentorp, 93–5.

68 'Kerfol', EWCS II, 90.

CHAPTER 16: PAVILLON/CHÂTEAU

1 BG, ch. 14, ii; RT to ET, 19 March 1917, Lilly; Price, 137 on EW's telling estate agents to look out houses for her at Fontainebleau, in November 1917. RT to ET, 23 July 1923, Lilly. PL to GL, 11 March 1918, Beinecke; EW to MJ, 7 July 1918, Letters 407. Metcalf, 30.

2 EW to BB, 5 July 1919, I Tatti. EW to Barrett Wendell, 19 July 1919, Letters 423–4; BG, ch. 14, i.

3 Rieder, 129–30; EW to BB, 5 July 1919; EW to Barrett Wendell, 19 July 1919, Letters, 424. EW to BB, 22 November 1919. Price, 165, 170. Lewis, 437; EW to BB, 23 May 1920, Letters 431.

4 EW to BF, December 1919, quoted Dwight, 209. Benstock, 355; EW to BF, 6 October 1920, 25 March, 30 June 1920; Benstock, 48, 352, 355. EW to BB, 7 June 1921, Letters 441.

5 Lewis, 427, 494; Benstock, 372–3; on Cook, EW to GL, 29 November 1921, Letters 449; on Herberts, EW to MJ, 7 January 1916, Letters, 367; on Duprat/Fridérich, Benstock, 373, 413; on White, EW to MB, 20 May 1913, I Tatti; White on EW, quoted Dwight, 230; on Louisa, EW to ET, 14 September 1921, Letters 447–8; on Franklin, EW to ET, 13 March 1934, Lilly.

6 ET to RT, 4 July 1928, Lilly; EW to Henrietta Haven, 8 December 1926, Beinecke; EW, 16 July 1921, to Secretary of Social Bureau, Bond Street, Beinecke; EW to ET, 25 January 1920, Lilly. EW to ET, 27 January 1920; EW to Dorothy Allhusen, 15 January 1920, Beinecke; EW to BF, quoted Dwight, 231.

7 PL to GL, 11 March 1918, Beinecke. History of Pavillon Colombe: Cyril Connolly, *Les Pavillons*, Hamish Hamilton, 1962, 62–7; Jacques Fosse, 'Marie Catherine Colombe et La Construction Du Pavillon Colombe', *Les Amis du Vieux Saint-Brice*, 1987; Jean Stern, *Mesdemoiselles Colombe de la Comédie-Italienne*, Calmann-Levy, 1923; www.saint-brice.com/ville/histoire/demeures; Dwight, 212–13; Craig, 156.

8 Descriptions of Pavillon Colombe: Vivienne de Watteville to PL, February 1938, quoted Dwight, 212; Matilda Gay and Ogden Codman in Rieder, 132–5; Craig, 164–6; Lewis, 419, 453–5; Lubbock, 137–9. 161; Russell Page, *The Education of a Gardener*, Collins, 1962, 19; BG, ch. 14, ii.

9 Page, *op. cit.*, 19; Lubbock, quoting Mme de Taillandier, 161; OC, the Gays, in Rieder, 132.

10 EW to Countess Senni, 19 July 1935, Beinecke.

11 'Gardening in France', Beinecke; RT to ET, July 1923, Lilly; EW to LB, 16 February 1927, Lesage, 136; BG, ch. 14, ii; 'Projet pour les bordures du Potager', Beinecke (quoted extensively in translation in Dwight, 216–33); EW to OC, 12 July 1935, Beinecke; EW to Alice Garrett, 2 August 1930, quoted Daniel Bratton, ed., *The Correspondence of Edith Wharton and Louis Bromfield*, Michigan State University Press, 2000, 25; 'Flowers in Bloom in garden Oct 30 1923', Beinecke; Diary, 1 November 1923, Lilly; information from Princesse Isabelle de Liechtenstein, St-Brice, 2002.

12 Page, *op. cit.*, 19, 131–2; Gabrielle Van Zuylen, *The Gardens of Russell Page*, Stewart, Tabori & Chang, 1991, 111–12. EW to BB, 23 October 1924, I Tatti; EW to ET, August 1929, Lilly; ET to RT, 14 June 1929, Lilly.

13 Page, *op. cit.*, 23. Metcalf, 30. EW to Bromfield, 30 July 1932, EW to Bromfield, 14 September 1932, EW to Bromfield, 11 December 1935, Bromfield to PL, 1938: Bratton, *op. cit.*, xlv, 29, 31, 75, 110, 113.

14 For the Île de France: Guide Bleu, *Les Environs de Paris*, Hachette, 1921; George Pillement, *Les Environs de Paris Inconnus*, 2 vols, Grasset, 1961; R. Biais, *Connaître et aimer Montmorency*, Valhermeil, 1993; Ian Dunlop, *The Companion Guide to the Île de France*, Collins, 1979; BG, Ch 14, ii; *Montmorency en cartes postales anciennes*, 1974. For Gillet, Rieder, 184–5; EW to BB, 25 July 1933, Letters 564; Louis Gillet, *Essais sur l'Art Français*, Flammarion, 1938.

15 Price, 171; EW to OC, 27 June 1932, Beinecke; Dwight, 234; Jacques Fosse, Introduction, 'Edith Wharton: Colloque du Cinquantenaire', St-Brice, 6 September 1987; Jean-Charles Gateau, *Paul Eluard*, Laffont, 1988, 89.

16 EW, 17 June 1931, Beinecke: EW to LB, 31 July 1920, Lesage, 126; EW to BB, 8 August 1924, EW to BB, 19 June 1921, 21 June 1924, I Tatti; EW to MJ, 10 April 1921, Beinecke.

17 Lewis, 399, 129, 421; Benstock, 321, 141; François Fray *et al.*, *Hyères, Images du Patrimoine*, 2000, 42; Mary Blume, *Côte d'Azur: Inventing the French Riviera*, Thames & Hudson, 1992, 42–3; MFF, ch. 3; EW to CS, 11 February 1919, Scribner Archive, Princeton; EW to GL, 17 December 1915, Letters 364; Norton, quoted Dwight, 235; EW to BB, 27 January 1919, 21 February 1920, Letters 421, 429; EW to JHS, 2 February 1919, Beinecke.

18 For Hyères, the Riviera, and Ste-Claire: Charles Amic and Jacques Olivo, *À la découverte de Hyères Les Palmiers*, Editions Aris, 1993; Christian Arthaud and Eric Paul, *La Côte d'Azur des écrivains*, Édisud, 1999; Blume, *op. cit.*; Vincent Borel, *Autour des Salins à Hyères, Vers 1900*, La Rosalba, 1996; Dwight, 25–3, particularly good on the garden at Ste-Claire; Craig, 178–93, with lavish illustrations of Ste-Claire; Philippe Collas, *Edith Wharton's French Riviera*, Flammarion, 2000; M.A. Denis, *Hyères Ancien & Moderne*, Souchon, 1878; Fray *et al.*,

op. cit., 42; *Guide Touristique: Hyères Les Palmiers*, 1997; Marie Ingram, 'Beyond the Plan', on EW's gardening, in *Hortus*, Vol. 21, Spring 1992, 77–91; Odile Jacquemin and Catherine Berro, *Territoires Littéraires des îles à la ville Hyères Les Palmiers*, Hyères, 1998; Raymond Lassarat, *Hyères-les-Palmiers en cartes postales anciennes*, Bibliothèque Européenne, 1978; John Pemble, *The Mediterranean Passion: Victorians and Edwardians in the South*, Clarendon Press, 1987.

19 Philippe Colas's *La Côte d'Azur au temps d'Edith Wharton*, Flammarion, 2002, also refers to EW's attraction to the sea, 'irrational and terrible', 'like a sister soul', 64, and to her grief at the death of 'her cousin, Wallace Berry', 94.

20 EW to ET, 20 March 1924, Lilly; EW to MB, 21 February 1922; EW to BB, 20 March 1922, I Tatti; GS on WB in Richard M. Dunn, *Geoffrey Scott and the Berenson Circle*, Edwin Mellon Press, 283.

21 EW to BB, 3 February 1928, I Tatti; Francis Steegmuller, *Cocteau*, Constable, 1986, 403–4. Lewis, 494; Fray *et al.*, *op. cit.*, 62; Blume, *op. cit.*, 77, 86; Arthaud and Paul, *op. cit.*, 97 ('*la distance qui séparait les deux propriétés séparait aussi deux siècles*'); Ernest Samuels, *Bernard Berenson: The Making of a Legend*, Belknap, 1987, 378.

22 Lynn Garafola, *Diaghilev's Ballets Russes*, Oxford University Press, 1989, 108–9. Lewis, 480.

23 Robert Louis Stevenson at Hyères, quoted in PL's account of EW at Ste-Claire, Lubbock, ch. 12. Joseph Conrad, *The Rover*, Doubleday, 1923, ch. 3. EW to MJ, 26 December 1920, Letters 436. On the day out with JC, see Lesage, 128, recorded in Maurice Ravel, *Ravel Au Miroir De Ses Lettres*, Robert Laffont, 1956.

24 EW to CdB, 8 March 1924, Bibliothèque Doucet, MS 27567.

25 William Gerhardi, *Memoirs of a Polyglot*, Duckworth, 1931, 291; EW to BB, 21 February 1920, Letters 429; EW to GL, 27 May 1918, Beinecke;

EW to Elizabeth Cameron, 27 June 1919, in Price, 168; EW to MJ, 26 December 1920, Letters 436; EW to Zézette Du Bos, nd, Bibliothèque Doucet, MS 27568; EW to SN, 4 January 1912, Beinecke.

26 EW to BB, 3 January 1921, I Tatti; EW to MJ, 26 December 1920, Letters 436; Benstock, 352, who estimates this at $60,000 in 1998 (sum in old francs is 12,500 nf or £1,250). For descriptions and costings of Ste-C: Robert Norton, quoted Dwight, 239; Samuels, *op. cit.*, 291; Benstock, 352; Dwight, 235–53; Craig, 185–90.

27 Bookplates reproduced in Ramsden, xxxi. EW to BB, 12 December 1920, Letters 434, 5 July 1922, I Tatti, 23 August 1922, Letters 453; EW to ET, 2 December 1928, Lilly, citing Arnold's poem 'The Church of Brou' on the tomb of Margaret of Austria ('then unclose / Your eyelids on the stone where ye repose, / And from your broider'd pillows lift your heads, / And rise upon your cold white marble beds; / And, looking down on the warm rosy tints, / Which chequer, at your feet, the illumined flints, / Say: – *"What is this? we are in bliss – forgiven – Behold the pavement of the courts of Heaven! –"*) which she also quotes, critically, in MFF; EW to MF, 12 June 1921, Letters 443.

28 MG in Rieder, 133.

29 BB to MB, New Year's Day, 1930; EW to BB, nd, I Tatti.

30 Samuels, *op. cit.*, 385. RT to ET, 27 November 1928; ET, 22 June 1929, 21 June 1930, 8 October 1931, Lilly; EW recipes, Lilly; Michael Broadbent, *The Great Vintage Wine Book*, 2nd edition, Knopf, 1991; EW wine orders, Beinecke; EW to ET, 19 February 1929, 19 September 1936, Lilly; all wine advice from J. Barnes.

31 EW to JHS, 21 March 1925, Beinecke; EW to GL, 13 May 1922, Letters 452. Samuels, *op. cit.*, 359, 391, 397. EW to MJ, 2 December 1929, Beinecke. Inscriptions, Wharton copies, I Tatti library. EW to MB, 26 March 1928, I Tatti.

32 MB to BB, 25 December, 28 December 1927, I Tatti.

33 Lubbock, 161, 158, 182, 185, 180.

34 EW to the Lawrence Whites, Christmas 1928, Lichtenberg Materials, Beinecke.

35 Letters 435, Lewis, 438; Samuels, *op. cit.*, 397. Gerhardi, *op. cit.*, 291. EW to BB, 12 December 1922, I Tatti. For Coué, see James Hart, *The Popular Book*, Oxford University Press, (1950) 1976, 240; Claude Silve, *Benediction*, trans. Robert Norton, Appleton, 1936, 236, 1; EW's Foreword also in Wegener, 250–2. EW to BB, 23 August 1922, 454; Lewis, 438; EW to BB, 19 December 1921, I Tatti; EW to BB, 21 February 1922, Letters, 451; 20 March 1922, 17 December 1925, I Tatti; 15 January 1924, Letters 475.

36 EW to MC, 22 February 1924, Beinecke.

37 EW to RJ, 6 February 1919, Beinecke; EW to ES, 3 December, 10 December 1923, Lilly.

38 EW to the Mayor of Hyères, 15 January 1923, 27 November 1926, 30 December 1934, Jacquemin and Berro, *op. cit.*, 150–3. My translations/paraphrase.

39 EW to MJ, 1 January 1923, Beinecke.

40 MR, ch. 30. Lucien Corpechot and Raymond de Passillé, in *La Gazette Illustrée des Amateurs de Jardins*, 1922, 13, 1923, 16, 1925, 24. Achille Duchêne, *Les Jardins de L'Avenir*, Vincent, Fréal, 1935, 15.

41 EW to BF, 22 March 1922, Beinecke. Mrs Philip Martineau, *Gardening in Sunny Lands*, Cobden-Sandersen, 1924, 177; Dwight, 222 on Lawrence Johnston and St-Brice, and on EW's garden visits in the Riviera, 250. EW to MJ, 19 October 1924, Beinecke; plants from Hidcote, Lilly; information on Lawrence Johnston, Charles Quest-Ritson, *The English Garden Abroad*, Penguin, 1992, 50; *www.serredelamadone.com*. Thanks to Robin Lane Fox.

42 EW to BB, 3 March 1920, I Tatti. Martineau, *op. cit.*, 164. On Riviera gardening, Quest-Ritson, *op. cit.*, 23.

EW to BF, 12 December 1922, Letters 460; EW to MJ, 15 November 1923, Beinecke; Martineau, *op. cit.*, 17; Diary, 1920, Beinecke, 16 March 1920; book orders to Bain, 31 January 1923, 15 May 1925, Beinecke. EW to Norah —, 23 April 1937, Beinecke. EW to BF, March 1920, quoted Dwight, 243. Plant orders: EW, Diary, 17 April 1920, Beinecke, 'get dahlias from Vilmorin'; EW to Gerard Telkamp, Holland, 21 September 1933, Beinecke: 'Send to head gardener at Ste-Claire, Joseph Cherrier, 1000 tulips Darwin arc-en-ciel at 185 f, 200 Iris Hispanica at 12.50. And to the gardener at St Brice, Émile Gaillet, 200 Iris Anglica, mélange de toutes couleurs, 25 frs for 100.'

43 EW to CdB and Zézette Du Bos, 24 August [nd], MS 27567–30, Bibliothèque Doucet; EW to Mildred Bliss[?], nd, first page missing, Beinecke; EW, 'December in a French Riviera Garden', 'Spring in a French Riviera Garden', Beinecke. Dwight, 241–9.

44 E.C., 'A Riviera Garden: Sainte-Claire le Château, Hyères', *Country Life*, 30 November 1928, 610–12, quoted and commented on in Quest-Ritson, *op. cit.*, 23; Lewis, 448; sale notice for Ste-Claire; Martineau, *op. cit.*, 175–6; Mrs Winthrop [Margaret] Chanler, *Autumn in the Valley*, Little Brown, 1936, 115.

45 EW to GL, 14 February 1929, Beinecke. ET, 16 March 1929, Lilly. EW to MJ, 26 December 1920, Letters 436–7; in Dwight, 249; EW to MJ, 19 October 1924, Beinecke; EW to OC, 13 February 1929, Beinecke; EW to GL, 25 February 1929, Letters 519; EW to ET, 14 February 1928, 19 February 1929, 2 March 1929, Lilly. 1929 Diary, Lilly.

46 JHS to PL, 17 February 1938, Beinecke; CS II, 630; Diary, 22 November 1926, Beinecke.

CHAPTER 17: THE AGE OF INNOCENCE

1 AI, ch. 9; BG, ch. 14, iv; Diary, 1920, Beinecke.

2 EW to CS, 4 November 1920, Scribner Archive, Princeton; MJ to EW, 5 November, 22 November, 19 December 1919, Beinecke; Benstock, 360, Dwight, 224–5; EW to MJ, 14 January 1920; RJ to EW, 3 July 1919, Beinecke; BG, ch. 14, iv; EW to MJ, 21 September 1927; E.W. Barnes, *The Man Who Lived Twice: The Biography of Edward Sheldon*, Scribner's, 1956, 154–5.

3 Benstock, 358.

4 AI, chs 12, 31, 15, 33.

5 AI, ch. 5, ch. 1.

6 AI, chs 19, 23, 26, 15, 29.

7 AI, chs 27, 29.

8 AI, chs 9, 6, 10, 25, 33; and see chs 2, 16. For useful readings of AI, see Ammons, 142–50; Bauer, 131, 167, 171–8; Beer 2002, 32–35; Pamela Knights, 'Forms of Disembodiment', and Nancy Bentley 'Hunting for the Real', in CCEW, 220–65; Anne MacMaster, 'Wharton, Race, and *The Age of Innocence*' in Colquitt *et al.*, 188–205; Kristin Olson Lauer, 'Can France Survive This Defender?' in Joslin and Price, 87; Montgomery, 68–75; Alan Price, 'The Composition of *The Age of Innocence*', *Yale University Library Gazette*, 55, 1981, 23–8; Martha Banta, 'Wharton's Women', in Singley, 2003, 51–88; Singley, 163–83, 229; Tintner, 58–73 (on links to James); Waid, 12–13; Wolff, 310–34.

9 AI, chs 10, 26, 5, 20, 16, 12.

10 AI, chs 23, 20, 12. On sequel, EW to RJ, 9 November 1921, Beinecke; list of titles, 'Subjects and Notes, 1918–1923', Beinecke.

11 AI, chs 10, 15, 30; Plon-Nourrit blurb for AI, Beinecke; Ramsden, 86.

12 EW to Barrett Wendell, 19 July 1919, Letters 424; re Henry Canby, 'Literature in Contemporary America', in *The America of Today*, ed. Gaillard Lapsley, Cambridge University Press, 1919.

13 For PL's editing of HJ letters, see Lewis, 425–6; Letters 375–81; HJL, xvii, on Mrs William James and her daughter Peggy's disapproval of EW: Peggy James told Alice James that she had heard 'things about Mrs Wharton of which I had not dreamed. Her morals are scarcely such as to fit her to be the companion of the young and innocent.' Beerbohm wanted either Gosse or EW to edit the letters. Bosanquet and Pinker persuaded the family to accept PL as editor, but both agreed it was 'a pity that Mrs Wharton had not been left in charge'; Peggy James thought there was 'too much' EW in PL's selection. Edel, *op. cit.*, xvii–xxi. AI, chs 14, 23; Tintner, 'Jamesian Structures in *The Age of Innocence*', 58–74, and Wolff, 312–13, find more echoes of HJ in AI.

14 AI, ch. 23.

15 AI, chs 9, 23.

16 AI, chs 8, 9, 12, 18, 17, 11, 14.

17 AI, chs 10, 20, 31, 12, 26, 33. Bauer, 173, writes on America, Europe, and Bohemianism.

18 AI, chs 14, 16.

19 AI, chs 2, 3, 11, 16, 34, 26.

20 AI, chs 11, 18, 23, 25.

21 AI, chs 34, 18, 24.

22 AI, chs 20, 34.

23 EW to BB, 12 December 1920, Letters 433. AI, chs 18, 25, 32. EW did not read Freud, but Archer's alienation fits perfectly with Freud's theory of the '*unheimlich*', in his much-cited essay published in 1919, the same year AI was being written.

24 AI, chs 7, 17, 21, 29, 30, 31.

25 AI, chs 31, 34.

26 AI, chs 1, 2, 12, 18, 19, 20, 21, 29, 30. See Bauer, 175, on sado-masochism. This repressed eroticism was one of the best things in Scorsese's lavish film version of AI.

27 AI, chs 34, 29.

28 Draft MSS plans of AI, Beinecke. See Bauer, 131, Waid, 12–13, and Alan Price, 'The Composition of *The Age of Innocence*', *Yale University Library Gazette*, 55, 1981, 23–8.

29 AI, chs 25, 34.

30 EW to BB, 14 August 1925, Letters

589. BP: Wolff, 300–6, 407–15; Lewis, 524, 544–8; Benstock, 379–80. 'Subjects and Notes, 1918–1923', 'Shorter Works', Beinecke. On Shelley, EW to MC, 9 June 1925, Letters 483.

31 Lewis, 525. Wolff, 304–8. Benstock, 380. Opinions of BP: 'clue', David Holbrook, *Edith Wharton and the Unsatisfactory Man*, Vision Press, 1991, 18; 'autobiographical', Gloria C. Erlich, *The Sexual Education of Edith Wharton*, University of California Press, 1992, 38–9; 'incest-victim', Barbara White, *EWR*, Fall 1991, 3, and Barbara White, *Edith Wharton: A Study of the Shorter Fiction*, Hall, 1991, 62–70; Teddy; Helen Killoran, *Edith Wharton: Art and Allusion*, University of Alabama Press, 1996, 188–9. EW to JHS, 25 May 1925, Letters 480. 'Mother-daughter incest', Tintner, 124–8, 132; 'American sex', Bauer in Singley, 2003, 135; 'patriarchal oppression', Ammons, 41; 'racism', Stuart Hutchinson, 'Sex, Race and Class in Edith Wharton', *Texas Studies in Literature*, Vol. 42, no. 4., 2000, 433.

32 'Subjects and Notes, 1918–1923', Beinecke. 'The Old Maid', ch. 6, ONY. 'A Bottle of Perrier', CS II, 511–532. 'Bewitched', CS II, 419. CS II, 367. See Richard Kaye, *The Flirt's Tragedy*, University Press of Virginia, 1997, on homosexuality in EW; Cristina Giorcelli, 'Plays of White and Black in EW's "A Bottle of Perrier"', *Letteratura d'America*, 1996, 65–131, on homosexuality in 'Perrier'.

33 RJ/EW correspondence, April 1921, Beinecke; 'Columbia Arranges for Pulitzer Prizes', *New York Times*, 27 November 1921; John Hohenberg, *The Pulitzer Prizes*, Columbia University Press, 1974; Carlos Baker, 'Forty Years of Pulitzer Prizes', Grolier Club Address, 1956; Robert Morss Lovett, *All Our Years*, Stratford Press, 1948, 199; Mark Schorer, *Sinclair Lewis: An American Life*, McGraw Hill, 1961, 299; Lewis, 433; Benstock, 362–5. EW to BB, 7 June,

19 June 1921, I Tatti; EW to MJ, 4 July 1921, Beinecke. EW to Sinclair Lewis, 6 August 1921, Letters 445; HRB, ch. 29. For the friendship of EW and Zona Gale, see D.L. Williams, *Not in Sisterhood: Edith Wharton, Willa Cather, Zona Gale, and the Politics of Female Authorship*, Palgrave, 2001, 15–38.

34 EW/RJ correspondence; Appleton ad for AI, Beinecke. On RJ, Gerard Wolfe, *The House of Appleton*, Scarecrow Press, 1981, 367; John Tebbel, *A History of Book Publishing in the US*, Vol. II, Barker, 1975, 212; Grant Overton, *Portrait of a Publisher*, Appleton, 1925, 87–8; RJ to Elizabeth Marbury, 12 March 1921, Lilly.

35 EW, legal document re MJ, 27 February 1921, Watkins-Loomis Agency Records, Columbia University Rare Book and Manuscript Library. EW films. EW to MJ, 14 November 1926, 28 January 1934, MJ to EW, 8 October 1920, Beinecke. Scott Marshall, 'Media Adaptations of Edith Wharton's Works', Appendix II, SBW, 287–93; Benstock, 361, 372. Matthew J. Broccoli, *Some Sort of Grandeur: The Life of F. Scott Fitzgerald*, Harcourt Brace, 1981, 179; Mary Jo Tate, *F Scott Fitzgerald A–Z*, Facts on File, 1998, 271. Details on film adaptations and EW copyright in the Watkins/Loomis Agency Records, Watkins-Loomis office and Columbia University Rare Book and Manuscript Library.

36 Benstock, 361, 407, 435; Lewis, 484. CS to EW, 19 November 1923; Royalty Report for Mrs Edith Wharton, February and August 1926, Scribner Archive, Princeton. EW/RJ correspondence, 1920–1923, Beinecke, Lilly.

37 *Cosmopolitan* to Sears, 11 December 1916, Lilly. *Popular Monthly* to EW, February 1929, Beinecke. 'Old Maid', EW to BB, 7 June 1921, 19 June 1921, I Tatti; RJ to EW, May 1921; EW to RJ, 23 May 1921, RJ to EW, 1 June 1922, Beinecke. HRB, ch. 23.

38 *Pictorial Review*, July–November 1920; Kathleen Norris, *The Beloved Woman*, Doubleday, 1921, 352; RJ to EW, 14 October 1920, Beinecke.

39 EW to CS, 22 September 1919, Beinecke; EW to ET, 1 January 1930, Letters 525. Reviews of AI in *Times Literary Supplement* [PL], Mansfield and Parrington in Tuttleton, 289–95. Joslin and Price, 78–9; Helen Woodward, speech to the Women's National Book Association in January 1920, in Tebbel, *op. cit.*, Vol. III, 316. Robert Morss Lovett, *Edith Wharton*, McBride, 1925, 80.

40 EW to RJ, 1 February 1921, Beinecke; EW to CS, 16 March 1919, Scribner Archive, Princeton; Benstock, 356; EW to Sears, 13 June 1919, Beinecke.

41 RJ to EW, 3 July 1919; EW to RJ, 4 September 1919; EW to RJ, 23 July 1919; Beinecke. Sears to EW, 11 April 1919, Beinecke; Benstock, 357, 361, 378; RJ to EW, 14 October 1920, EW to RJ, 9 November 1921, Beinecke; EW to CS, 16 March 1919, 17 September 1921, Scribner Archive, Princeton. EW to RJ, 21 February 1923, Letters 464–6. HRB, ch. 20.

42 'New Year's Day', chs 6, 7. 'The False Dawn', ch. 6. 'The Spark', ch. 1. 'The Old Maid', ch. 4, ONY.

43 EW to BB, 19 May 1923, Letters 466; EW to ET, 4 May 1923, Lilly; EW to GL, April 1923, in Lewis, 451; EW to CdB, 4 May 1923, Bibliothèque Doucet, MS27567/59/60.

44 Maynards at Hautbois, Metcalf, 137; Bruccoli, *op. cit.*, 135. Benstock, 382.

CHAPTER 18: JAZZ

1 CS to EW, 30 January 1922; EW to CS, 15 February 1922; EW to CS, 25 May 1923, 10 December 1923, Scribner Archive, Princeton.

2 EW to BB, 9 December 1922, I Tatti; on Cole Porter, EW to GL, 28 September 1926, Letters 493. GM, ch. 5. EW summary of TS, Beinecke; TS, ch. 3; C, ch. 15; Bauer, chs 2 and 3, on EW and modern life.

3   AI, ch. 16; Lewis, 172; James Hart, *The Popular Book*, Oxford University Press, 1950, 1976, 240; EW to BB, 23 August 1922, Letters 454; EW to ET, 30 October 1929, Lilly; Bauer, 92–8, on 'Twilight Sleep'.

4   EW to GL, 28 January 1927, Beinecke; Hubbard advertisements, Beinecke. *Elbert Hubbard's Scrap Book*, Roycroft, 1923; on Hubbard, T.J. Jackson Lears, *No Place of Grace: AntiModernism and the Transformation of American Culture*, Pantheon, 1981, 61. 'The First Born of Egypt', Beinecke.

5   Hart, *op. cit.*, 210, 212; *Laddie* clipping, Beinecke.

6   'The Land of Tosh', EW to BB, 21 February 1922, I Tatti; 'writing against modernism', Bauer, 144; 'Freudianism', EW to BB, 21 February 1922, Letters 451.

7   BB to EW, 18 April 1932, Lilly; EW to BB, 6 January 1923, Letters 461. Glasses, Benstock, 419; EW to Mr Lambrecht, 20 March 1925, Beinecke.

8   Wegener, 183. EW to GL, 26 June 1928, Beinecke. EW to MB, 20 November 1928, I Tatti, and Lewis, 483. EW to JHS, 25 May 1925, Letters 480; EW to GL, 17 August 1925, Beinecke. Virginia Woolf, 'American Fiction', *Collected Essays*, II, Hogarth Press, 1966, 111–21. EW to BB, 15 June 1928, I Tatti. MR review, *The Saturday Review*, 30 May 1925, in Hermione Lee, Introduction, MR, Virago, 1995, v.

9   EW to MB, 20 October, 26 October 1928, I Tatti; Lewis, 486. EW to MB, 12 November 1928, I Tatti; EW to MC, 1 October 1923, Letters 471.

10 BG, 206. Wegener, 'Form, "Selection" and Ideology in EW's Antimodernist Aesthetic', in Colquitt *et al.*, 33, compares this with 'The Great American Novel', 1927, and 'Tendencies', 1934, both in Wegener.

11 On EW and literary anti-Semitism, see Sol Liptzin, *The Jew in American Literature*, Bloch, 1966, 164; Jonathan Freedman, *The Temple of Culture*, Oxford University Press, 2000, 16,

118; Michael Dobkowski, *The Tarnished Dream*, Greenwood, 1979, 115, 133; Bauer, 150–2, 164–6; Annette Zilversmit, 'EW, Jews, and Capitalism', paper read at the *Modern Languages Association* meeting, 1985. JHS to PL, 17 February 1938, Beinecke, part-quoted in Goodman, 131, note 33. EW to GL, 21 September 1921, quoted Price, 147. EW to GL, 13 August 1928, Letters 517; EW to MJ, 21 October 1923, EW to GL, 15 April 1933, EW to GL, 1 April 1927, Beinecke; EW to MJ, 25 April 1923, Beinecke. EW to Scott Fitzgerald, 8 June 1925, Letters 482; Benstock, 388.

12 On EW and race, see Bauer, especially 166–7 and 178–86; Anne MacMaster, 'Wharton, Race and *The Age of Innocence*', in Colquitt *et al.*

13 EW to GL, 13 August 1925, EW to GL, 1 April 1927, Beinecke. Bauer, 59–61, 119–20. HRB, ch. 34.

14 EW to Eleanor Robson Belmont, 24 December 1918, Special MSS Collection, Belmont, Columbia University Library; Lewis, 442, 485–6. Diary, 1924, Lilly. Logan Pearsall Smith, *Unforgotten Years*, Little, Brown, 1939, 296; Robert Gathorne-Hardy, *Recollections of Logan Pearsall Smith*, Macmillan, 1950, 63; for Logan Pearsall Smith on the *Osprey* cruise, see Edwin Tribble, *A Chime of Words: The Letters of Logan Pearsall Smith*, Ticknor & Fields, 1984, 93–7. EW to D. MacCarthy, 17 October 1928, Beinecke, in Wegener, 174, and Wegener, 'Form . . . in EW', in Colquitt *et al.*, 122 (see note for *Life and Letters*). EW to Frederick William Felkin, 16 October 1928, MSS Collection, Columbia University Library; EW on D.H. Lawrence: Edward Marsh, *A Number of People*, Harper & Bros, 1939, in Wegener, 'Form . . . in EW', in Colquitt *et al.*, 117–18. EW to GL, 10 July 1930, Beinecke; WG to EW, 25 December 1928, Lilly.

15 EW to MB, 28 April 1921, I Tatti; EW to GL, 10 July 1930, Beinecke.

EW to BB, 23 January 1925, *Letters* 545.

16 EW to Alice Garrett, 10 May 1934, Evergreen House, Baltimore. For EW's attitudes to modernism and post-war American culture, see Bauer; Benstock, 'Landscapes of Desire: EW and Europe', in Joslin and Price, Wegener, and Wegener, 'Form . . . in EW', in Colquitt *et al.* EW and Rilke, BG, ch. 12, vii. On painters, EW to Royal Cortissoz, 15 January 1926, *Letters* 488: 'The work of . . . Cézanne & Gauguin seems to me finer than you seem willing to admit.' On Yeats, Ramsden, 94, 145. On EW's lack of appreciation for Matisse, Royall Tyler to ET, 11 August 1915, Lilly. Booklists to Bain, Beinecke. On Waugh, Benstock, 413.

17 BB to EW, 24 April 1932, Lilly; EW to BB, 29 April 1932, I Tatti; Ramsden, 26. Judith Thurman, *Secrets of the Flesh: A Life of Colette*, Knopf, 1999, 391–2.

18 EW to BB, 7 June 1921, *Letters* 441; EW to GL, 13 May 1922, *Letters* 450–1; EW to GL, 28 February 1926, Beinecke.

19 EW to WG, 3 October 1922, *Letters* 456. WG to EW, 10 October, 14 October 1922, Lilly. Reproduced with permission of Curtis Brown Group, Ltd, London, on behalf of the Estate of William Gerhardie. © William Gerhardie 1932. EW to Henry Canby, 7 October 1922, Beinecke; WG to EW, 14 November 1922, 5 December 1922, Lilly. 'Permanent Values', Wegener, 172; WG to EW, 13 January 1923, Lilly; William Gerhardie, *Memoirs of a Polyglot*, Duckworth, 1932, 200–1; EW to BB, 15 January 1924, *Letters* 475; EW to MB, 20 January 1924, I Tatti; EW to GL, 25 January 1924, EW to JHS, 20 March 1926, 21 September 27, Beinecke. William Gerhardie, *Futility*, with an introduction by EW, Duffield, 1922; Dido Davies, *William Gerhardie: A Biography*, Oxford University Press, 1990, 132–3; Ramsden, 47.

20 'Great American Novel', Wegener in 152; 'Wuthering Depths', EW to Ned Sheldon, 8 July 1931, in Wegener in Colquitt *et al.*, 1999, 119, note 17. On Loos: EW to JHS, 26 January 1926; EW to GL, 11 April 1926, *Letters* 491; book-orders to Bain, 1928, Beinecke; Bauer, 63 ff.; Anita Loos, *Gentlemen Prefer Blondes*, Brentano's, 1926. EW to Upton Sinclair, 19 August 1927, *Letters* 500–1; EW to Alice Garrett, 5 May 1920, Evergreen House, Baltimore; Davies, *op. cit.*, 180.

21 Kay Boyle, 'Afterword', in Robert McAlman, *Being Geniuses Together*, North Point Press, 1984, quoted in K.O. Lauer, 'Can France Survive This Defender?' in Joslin and Price, 89. F. Scott Fitzgerald, 'This Is A Magazine', *Vanity Fair*, XV, December 1920, 71, in *F. Scott Fitzgerald: In His Own Time*, ed. Matthew Bruccoli and Jackson Bryer, Kent State University Press, 1971, 227–30; EW to FSF, 8 June 1925, *Letters* 481–2. FSF's meeting with EW: Benstock, 382–3; Lewis, 467; EW, Diary, 5 July 1925, Lilly (misquoted in *Letters* 482.) Matthew Bruccoli, *Some Sort of Epic Grandeur: The Life of F Scott Fitzgerald*, University of South Carolina Press, 2002, 229. 'What Really Happened at the Pavillon Colombe', *Fitzgerald Newsletter*, ed. Matthew Bruccoli, no. 7, Fall 1959, 1–2. Entries on Chanler and EW, Mary Jo Tate, *The Scott Fitzgerald A–Z*, Checkmark Books, 1998.

22 RJ to EW, 7 September 1922, EW to RJ, 2 August 1922 Beinecke; Somerset Maugham, 'Some Novelists I have Known', *The Vagrant Mood*, Heinemann, 1952, 239–41. The encounter was commented on by A.S. Frere of Heinemann (whose wife was Edgar Wallace's daughter) in a letter to Ted Morgan, Maugham's first biographer, on 11 March 1978: 'As for Willie's question to Edith Wharton in 1908 about Edgar Wallace, Pat, my wife, assures me that this is viable because her father

had by then written *The Four Just Men* which became a spectacular best-seller ... As neither Willie nor Mrs Wharton could have been considered "popular" in those days no wonder she considered the question frivolous.' Thanks to Selina Hastings.

23 EW to GL, 21 March 1925, 13 April 1927, Beinecke. EW to Sinclair Lewis, 28 November 1921, 27 August 1922, Letters 448, 455; 12 April 1928, Beinecke; Mark Schorer, *Sinclair Lewis*, McGraw Hill, 1961, 421; EW to Grace Lewis, 20 August 1929, Letters 524; Grace Lewis, *Half a Loaf*, Ramsden, 78; Grace Lewis, *With Love From Gracie: Sinclair Lewis, 1912–1925*, Harcourt Brace, 1955, 185. Wegener, 153.

24 EW to ZG, 1 September 1922, 22 October 1922, 26 September 1922, 29 November 1926, 5 March 1926; ZG to EW, 7 May 1923; quoted in Deborah Williams, *Not in Sisterhood*, Palgrave, 2001, 17, 18, 23, 28, and in Elsa Nettels, 'EW's Correspondence with ZG: "An Elder's Warm Admiration and Interest"', *Resources for American Literary Study*, 1998, 24 (2), 207–34; ZG, review of WF, *NY Herald Tribune*, 31 January 1926. Williams and Nettels make much of the relationship.

25 All quotations from WF, Scribner's, 1925.

26 Wegener, 174, note 1. EW to Wilbur Cross, 4 November 1926; EW to Henry Canby, 15 March 1934, Beinecke; 'The Great American Novel', *Yale Review*, July 1927, Wegener, 151–9; 'A Cycle of Reviewing', *Spectator*, 3 November 1928, Wegener, 159–62; 'Visibility in Fiction', *Yale Review*, March 1929 [reprinted in *Life and Letters*, Vol 2, no. II, April 1929], Wegener, 163–9; 'Tendencies in Modern Fiction', *Saturday Review of Literature*, 27 January 1934, Wegener, 169–74; 'Permanent Values in Fiction', *ibid*, 7 April 1934, Wegener, 175–9.

27 On France between the wars, Smith 146–90; Alistair Horne, *To Lose a Battle: France 1940*, Little, Brown, 1969, 3–77; René de Chambrun, *I Saw France Fall*, Morrow, 1940, 11–15; D.W. Brogan, *The Development of Modern France*, Hamish Hamilton, 1943, 556, 581–6.

28 EW to Alice Garrett, 27 May 1919, Evergreen House, Baltimore.

29 See Bauer, 132–6, on companionate marriage in GM and GA.

30 EW to BB, 20 August 1921, Letters 446; EW to Marcel Prevost, 25 November 1919, Beinecke.

31 GM, chs 5, 7, 13, 17; EW to MB, 30 August 1922, I Tatti; for Browning, cf. IB, ch. 4, and see EW to GL, 28 September 1926, Letters 493.

32 GM, chs 17, 12, 20.

33 GM, chs 10, 24, 23, 26. Some critics (Wolff, Tintner) read it as a pre-war novel, e.g. Tintner, 170–80, noting that Nick looks at the Tiepolo fresco in the Scalzi church in Venice (mentioned in IB) which was bombed and destroyed in 1915. But EW's use of the Cesnola collection in AI shows that she could allow anomalies.

34 Sales: Benstock, 371, 394–5; RJ/EW correspondence, 1922, Lilly; Joslin and Price, 103; Garrison, 246.

35 Grace Aguilar, *The Mother's Recompense*, Harper & Brothers, 1851, 193. EW, note, MR.

36 MR, ch. 3.

37 MR, chs 1, 13.

38 MR, chs 3, 4, 20, 8.

39 MR, ch. 7.

40 MR, chs 20, 14.

41 MR, chs 24, 3, 7; EW to JHS, 25 May 1925, Letters 480. Critical opinions vary on incest in MR. Tintner, 125–33, and Holbrook, *Edith Wharton and the Unsatisfactory Man*, Vision Press, 1991, 171, read it as an Oedipal story; Katherine Joslin, *Women Writers: Edith Wharton*, Macmillan, 1991, 124–5, as Oedipal from Jocasta's viewpoint, horrified by the prospect of 'her lover becoming her son'; Gloria C. Erlich, *The Sexual Education of Edith Wharton*, University of California Press, 1992, 147, as about the mother's own infantile need for

nurturing; Bauer, 78, thinks that Chris is 'oedipalized' and becomes a patriarchal authority. Ammons, 163, sees EW as obsessed with 'mothers who refuse to mother'. Beer 2002, 74, notes that 'incest as a motif, as a sign of the kind of secret that might lie at the heart of a series of otherwise inexplicable events' recurs in the late work.

42 Shelley, *Prometheus Bound*, 1820, Act I, l.777. EW to Louis Gillet, 15 September 1927, 11 October 1927, 13 December 1927, 9 April 1928, Beinecke. Benstock, 419. 'Le Bilan' was LB's title for his translation of 'The Letters' in the *Revue des Deux Mondes* in September 1910.

43 Prizes: Benstock, 385–6, Lewis, 481–2. 'The National Institute of Arts and Letters', NIAL leaflet, 1958. Nicholas Murray Butler to EW, 8 May 1931, EW to Butler, 26 April 1931, University Archives, WA 1930–1931, Box 298, folder 23, Columbiana Library, Columbia University, with thanks to Jocelyn K. Wilde. Taxes: EW to RJ, 5 April 23, Beinecke. EW to Authors' League, November 1924, Beinecke. Kenneth Clark, *Another Part of the Wood*, Hodder & Stoughton, 1974, 181.

44 EW to RJ, 1 May 1925, Lilly; TS, ch. 19.

45 TS, chs 1, 2, 16, 5, 8, 26, 27, 29, 20.

46 TS, chs 14, 4, 11, 27, 1, 9.

47 Aldous Huxley to EW, 19 March 1932, Berg, NYPL. Margaret Sanger, *Pivot of Civilization*, Humanity Books, 2003, 27; TS, chs 18, 26; Paramahansa Yogananda, *The Science of Religion*, Self-Realization Fellowship, Los Angeles, 1982, 4, 7; *New York Times*, 10 April 1926, 4 May 1910; *San Francisco Chronicle*, 1 October 1922. Dr John Palo, *The Sayings of Ella Wheeler Wilcox*, 1996. For TS's influence on Huxley, EW to MC, 25 March 1932, Letters 547. For eugenics, motherhood and feminism in TS, see Bauer, 96–105. On Taylorism, see Bauer, and Martha Banta, *Taylored Lives: Narrative Production in the Age of Taylor, Veblen and Ford*, University of Chicago Press, 1993.

48 TS, chs 7, 23, 25, 20, 18. EW summary of TS, Beinecke. For the gap between surface and reality in TS, see Beer 2002, 73–7. For criminal trials (the 1926 trial of the Rev. Edward Hall and Mrs Mills's murderers in 1922, the murder of Albert Snyder by his wife and her lover in 1926) see F.L. Allen, *Only Yesterday*, Harper, 1931, 212–15.

49 TS, ch. 13, ch. 20.

50 CS II, 380, 419, 441.

51 EW to GL, 29 November 1924, Beinecke; EW to GL, 28 November 1926, Letters 495; EW to RJ, 21 February 1924, RJ to EW, 26 January 1923, Beinecke; EW to RJ, 8 July 1926, EW to RJ, 28 June 1927, 26 September 1927, Beinecke.

52 *Twelve Poems*, Printed at the Riccardi Press Fount at the Chiswick Press for the Medici Society, October 1926, copy in NYPL Rare Books Room; 'Lyrical Epigrams', *Yale Review*, Vol. 9, January 1920. Paul-Louis Couchoud, *Sages et Poètes d'Asie*, EW's copy, Ramsden, 28. P, 90, 103, 98–9, 107, 142.

53 Plan for *Love Among the Ruins*, Beinecke; Lewis, 446. Diary, 1920–1927, Beinecke.

54 Ned Sheldon to EW, 14 March 1935, Lilly; EW to MJ, 9 March 1935, Letters 584–5; 'Confession', CS II, 801–32.

55 RJ to EW, 14 October 1928, Beinecke; EW to RJ, 16 February 1927, Beinecke; EW to MB, 15 August 1927, I Tatti; *Delineator* (Loren Palmer) to RJ, 12 May 1927, Lilly; RJ to EW, 23 July 1930, Lilly. Benstock, 394–5; *Saturday Evening Post* to RJ, 22 November 1928, Lilly; RJ to EW, 14 June 1927, Beinecke; quoted Benstock, 395; RJ to EW, 2 November 1928, Beinecke; Arthur Vance to RJ, 20 May 1927, Beinecke; RJ to Arthur Vance, 19 July 1927, Lilly.

56 EW to BB, 8 October 1924, I Tatti; EW to GL, 8 September 1924, Beinecke; EW to JHS, 25 May 1925,

Letters 480; EW to MC, 9 June 1925, Letters 483; EW, Spain Diary, 1925, Lilly; EW to MJ, 9 September, 21 September 1925, Beinecke; EW to BB, 24 May 1928, I Tatti. For EW and Spain, see Teresa Gómez Reus, in Joslin and Price, 201–15.

57 Benstock, 390–1, 394; Dwight, 261–5; BG, 372–3; EW to MC, 2 October 1925, Beinecke; EW to MB and BB, 2 January, 31 January, 12 March, 6 June 1926, I Tatti; EW to GL, 11 April 1926, Letters 490–1; Mrs Winthrop Chanler, *Autumn in the Valley*, Little, Brown, 1936, ch. 18; EW to J.A. Smith, 6 February 1926, J.A. Smith to EW, 17 May 1926, Beinecke; *Osprey* accounts, Beinecke.

58 EW to BB, 9 April 1937, Letters 605; EW to MB, 6 June 1926, Beinecke; EW to WT, 8 December 1929, Lilly; Logan Pearsall Smith, 12 April 1926, Lilly. Logan Pearsall Smith, *Unforgotten Years*, Little, Brown, 1939, ch. 10. EW to MC, 17 July 1926, Beinecke.

59 Logan Pearsall Smith, *Osprey* cruise diary, 15 April 1926, Lilly. EW to GL, 30 October 1925, Letters 487; EW to MC, 2 January 1927, Beinecke. Goodman, quoting Nicky Mariano, *Forty Years with Berenson*, Hamish Hamilton, 1966, 164; Caroline Moorehead, *Iris Origo*, John Murray, 2000, 150, 233, 97, 110–12; EW to BB, 4 February 1917, Letters 390; EW to GL, 1 April 1927, Beinecke; EW to MB, 20 August 1929, I Tatti.

60 EW to MC, 11 August 1926, Letters 492. Sybil Cutting/Scott/Lubbock, *On Ancient Ways: A Winter Journey*, Jonathan Cape, 1928; *A Page from the Past: Memories of The Earl of Desart*, Jonathan Cape, 1936; *A Book of the Sea*, Clarendon Press, 1919. EW to GL, 18 April 1927, 13 August 1928, Beinecke; Ernest Samuels, *Bernard Berenson: The Making of a Legend*, Belknap, 1987, 330. EW to GL, 28 August 1933, Letters 566; PL to GL, 19 March 1933, Beinecke; PL to EW, 28 November 1933, Lilly;

EW to GL, 21 November 1933, Beinecke. Lewis, 515.

61 EW to BB, 23 August 1922, Letters 453, EW to MJ, 19 June 1921, 9 October 1922, Beinecke; EW to BF, 1 December 1922, Beinecke; EW to P. Beckley (lawyers), 29 January, 4 February 1929, Beinecke. On visit to Harry in 1920/1921, Benstock, 375–7 and 522, notes 48–50, citing a story passed from Frederic Rhinelander King to Louis Auchincloss, and dating the EW/MF letter as 1920, which seems improbably late. On recovering heirlooms, EW to P. Beckley, 4 February 1929, Beinecke: 'All I can hope for is to try to get back a few of the family heirlooms from the late Mrs Harry Jones's heiress.' She lists: 'A large portrait of Mrs Wharton as a young girl in a red velvet dress by an American painter, George [*sic*: in fact Edward Harrison] May. A small oval portrait of the late Georges [*sic*] Frederic Jones as a young man. Two or three 18th century family miniatures. A small landscape taken from the lawn of a family property near NY, overlooking the East River. A portrait of my eldest brother, Frederic Jones, as a boy.' On mother's trust fund, EW to Herman Edgar, 5 August 1931, Beinecke, outlining the history of her mother's having 'cut off' her third of the inheritance because of their argument over Frederick's 'disreputable second wife', and her brother and Teddy's persuading Fred to waive his claim to the property. She had now discovered that she was not entitled to bequeath the income from those properties. Benstock, in Joslin and Price, 40: 'Edith learned of the true circumstances of her inheritance only six years before she died.'

62 SN: EW to Lily Norton, 16 January 1923, Houghton. Death of TW: Scott Marshall, 'Whatever happened to TW?', EWRA, Winter 87–8.

63 EW to GL, 28 September 1926, Beinecke, Letters 493; WB to BB, 30 October 1926, I Tatti; EW to BB, 13

October 1927, I Tatti; EW to MJ, 14 November 1926, Beinecke; EW to GL, 28 November 1926, Letters 495; EW to BB, 30 November 1926, I Tatti. EW to MJ, 25 January 1927, Letters 498; EW to JHS, 22 January 1927, Beinecke; WB to BB, 25 January 1927, I Tatti; EW to JHS, 22 January 1927, Beinecke; EW to BB, 26 January 1927, I Tatti; EW to Alice Garrett, 15 February 1927, Evergreen House, Baltimore; EW to JHS, 13 January 1927, Beinecke.

64 EW to Alice Garrett, 15 February 1927, Evergreen House, Baltimore; EW to Mildred Bliss, 18 January 1927, Beinecke. EW to BB, 5 February 1927, I Tatti.

65 Lewis, 472; EW to GL, 1 April 1927, Beinecke; EW to MJ, 22 March 1927, Beinecke; Benstock, 399, quoting WB to EW, 31 March 1927.

66 EW to Mildred Bliss, 19 October 1927, Beinecke. EW, Diary, 1927, Beinecke; EW to Alice Garrett, 28 October 1927, Evergreen House, Baltimore; EW to JHS, 12 October and 15 October 1927, Letters 503–5; EW to BB, 11 October 1927, I Tatti; EW to GL, 12 October 1927, Letters 504. Benstock, 401; 'Garden Valedictory', Diary, 12 October 1927, Beinecke, and Scribner's, January 1928, P, 143. Diary, 1927, Lilly.

67 EW to Mildred Bliss, 19 October 1927, Beinecke; EW to ET, 14 October, 31 October 1927, Lilly; EW to MF, 14 October 1927, Beinecke. EW to BB, 22 October 1927, I Tatti; EW to Louis Gillet: 18 October 1927, Beinecke; EW to Royal Cortissoz, 3 November 1927, Beinecke.

68 Geoffrey Wolff, *Black Sun: The Brief Transit and Violent Eclipse of Harry Crosby*, Random House, 1976, 124–32; Edward Germain, ed., *Shadows of the Sun: The Diaries of Henry Crosby*, Black Sparrow Press, 1977, 158–87; Caresse Crosby, *The Passionate Years*, The Dial, 1953, 212–20. Reports on WB's funeral, *New York Herald Tribune*, 8 October 1927, *New York Times*, 18 October 1927; EW to GL, 28 October 1927,

Beinecke; EW to Alice Garrett, 28 October 1927, Evergreen House, Baltimore. Ramsden, for WB copies in EW's library.

69 Benstock, 411–12, 405; Diary, 1927, Lilly. EW to Nathalie Alden, 13 October 1931, Beinecke. Diary, 28 January 1928, Beinecke. Diary, 25 June 1931, Lilly. EW to BB, 18 February 1931, Letters 534–5; BB to EW, 19 February 1931, I Tatti. 'Inventory of Mrs Wharton's Mss & Literary Papers: Three Packing Cases sent from St-Brice', Beinecke.

70 GL, notes for PL, Beinecke; Diary, 31 October 1927, Lilly, EW to MB, 19 January 1928, 11 January 1928, I Tatti. Paper-knife, Beinecke. Letters from EW to WB, 2 February [1906], 15 November [1905], [August 1906], [1908], in the Alice Garrett Archives, Evergreen House, Baltimore. KC to Grace Kellogg Smith, 1959. Denys Sutton, ed., *Fads and Fancies*, Wittenborn, 1979, 123, notes her ownership of the painting; thanks to Lucy Askew at the Tate. Ramsden, 141. EW loaned it in 1936 to the Cézanne Exhibition at the Musée de l'Orangerie; the catalogue read: '*Elle s'enfonce dans l'ombre profonde des marronniers . . . Dans le fond, le bassin du parc du Jas de Bouffan.*'

71 EW to RJ, nd [1927], Lilly; Janet Flanner, 'Dearest Edith', *New Yorker*, 2 March 1929, 26–8, in Tuttleton, 464; Francis Birrell, 'New Novels', *Nation & Athenaeum*, 6 October 1928, in Tuttleton, 457; Benstock, 407.

72 TS 'Summary' of C, Beinecke; EW to Royal Cortissoz, 11 October 1928, Letters 518; Reviews of C, in Tuttleton, 447–64. EW to ET, 19 April 1937, Lilly. C, ch. 18. EW to GL, 14 February 1924, re Kennedy, Beinecke.

73 C, chs 15, 22, 6, 24, 26, 27.

74 Léon Bélugou, 'Les néopsychologues', *La Revue des Idées*, 15 August 1904, 618. Bauer, 106–10.

75 C, chs 14, 17, 31, 9, 21. EW to Royal Cortissoz, 11 October 1928, Letters

518. TS 'Summary' of C, Beinecke.

76   C, chs 22, 10, 30, 32.

77   C, ch. 28; WG to EW, 29 January 1929, Lilly ('The reader who has been on the verge of tears . . . at that sentence bursts into tears and reads the beautiful, tender, agonising description with wet eyes'); EW to MB, 26 March 1928, I Tatti.

78   C, ch. 31.

CHAPTER 19: A PRIVATE LIBRARY

1   HRB, ch. 6.

2   HRB, chs 14, 28.

3   HRB, ch. 14; BG, ch. 2, i.

4   For EW's private pleasure in reading and writing in bed, see Alberto Manguel, A History of Reading, Flamingo, 1997, 153; Cynthia Ozick, Art and Ardor, Knopf, 1983, quoted Manguel, 160, and Hermione Lee, 'Reading in Bed', Body Parts, Chatto & Windus, 2005, 57–9.

5   GL to PL, PL materials, Beinecke; PL, 81.

6   Ramsden, xx.

7   WF, ch. 5, pt 2. Wegener, 94.

8   For all library citations, see Ramsden. The passage from The Mill on the Floss is also cited in WF, ch. 3, pt 7. For Commonplace Book, see Benstock, 168, 171, 208; Wolff, 90; my copy seen with thanks to Maureen Howard and the Watkins/ Loomis Agency. For Tyndall, Ramsden, 131; WF, ch. 5, pt 2. For Nietzsche, WF, ch. 5, pt 4. For Chesterton, EW to ET, 14 April 1928, Lilly. 'Im Abendrot', Karl Lappe, set by Schubert, 1824/5, trans. William Mann. 'Sketch of an Essay on Walt Whitman' [1907], Beinecke. See Beer 2002, 81, 84, on EW's Whitman essay and markings.

9   KC, Times Literary Supplement, 19 December 1975, quoted Ramsden, 51; 'No pleasure', BG title page and EW to GL, 2 April 1936, Letters 593; 'Two souls', e.g. EW to SN, 30 September 1902, Wegener, 73, 178, note 7. 'The Mothers', Wegener, 69, 70, note 5; Waid, note 21, 228–9.

10   'Take hold of it': Wegener, 157, 159,

note 13; 178–9. HRB, ch. 32. V.S. Pritchett in Tuttleton, 474. Summary of HRB, nd, Beinecke. EW to ET, 1 January 1930, Letters 525; Eleanor Carroll, 'Edith Wharton', The Delineator, January 1932, Vol. 120, 4. On change of period for GA, EW to Royal Cortissoz, 8 December 1932, Beinecke: 'The tale planned before the war had become as remote as an historical novel, & I had to re-think & re-situate it altogether.' HRB, ch. 26.

11   HRB, chs 23, 22, 35, 32, 24, 34. GA, ch. 5. Notes to GA, Beinecke. GA, chs 27, 23, 26.

12   HRB, chs 14, 28, 42; GA, ch. 10.

13   HRB, chs 19, 22; GA, ch. 27. HRB, chs 26, 29, 34, 32, 43. For religion in HRB and contemporary evangelical campaigns, see Bauer, ch. 4.

14   HRB, chs 17, 44, 22.

15   HRB, chs 30, 37, 33. For differing interpretations of 'The Mothers' in HRB and GA, see Waid, 3, 198, 229, note 21; Ammons, ch. 7.

16   GA, chs 34, 39, 38. Belair, Wisconsin: Bauer, 143.

17   HRB, chs 10, 29. GA, chs 15, 34, 12, 30. On marriage in HRB and GA, see Beer 1990, 128, and Goodman, 130–1.

18   GA, ch. 34.

19   GA, ch. 32; BG, ch. 9.

20   EW to Lily Norton, 22 February 1928, Houghton, EW to GL, 11 February 1928, Letters 514; EW to Robert Grant, 10 February 1928, Beinecke.

21   EW to MJ, 19 December 1931, Beinecke.

22   ET, 19 March 1929, 29 March 1929, Lilly. EW to Mildred Bliss, 10 February 1928, Letters 512; EW to GL, 25 February 1929, Letters 520. EW to ET, 1 January 1930, Letters 526. Jeanne Fridérich to MB, Vernon Lee, B.H. Conner, 11 March to 12 April 1929, Beinecke. Diary, January-April 1929, Lilly. EW to GL, 15 August 1929, Letters 522. EW to MC, 11 June 1929, Beinecke. Benstock, 412–14. Thanks to Benjamin Lee for medical details.

23 EW to Oscar Graeve, 29 December 1928, 31 January 1929, EW to RJ, 25 February 1929, Beinecke; Loren Palmer to RJ, 29 August 1927, Lilly, 16 January 1929, Beinecke.

24 EW to RJ, 15 July 1929, Letters 521. EW to Mildred Bliss, 27 November 1929, Beinecke. Oscar Graeve to RJ, 12 November 1929; RJ to Eleanor Carroll, 6 September 1930, Lilly.

25 EW to RJ, 26 April 1934, Beinecke. ET to EW, 29 July 1935, 31 August 1935, Lilly; EW to ET, 2 September 1935. ET, 3 March 1931, Lilly.

26 Benstock in Joslin and Price, 41, note 5; EW to ET, 2 April 1931, Lilly; BF to EW, 10 July 1932, Lilly. Benstock in Joslin and Price, 40; EW to Herman Edgar, 5 August 1931, Beinecke. For trust fund see ch. 14, 4. EW to Lily Norton, 3 January 1932, Houghton; EW to BF, 7 January 1931, Beinecke; EW to ET, 9 March 1931, Letters 536; EW to Gabrielle Landormy, 20 June 1932, Beinecke; BB to EW, 3 September 1932, I Tatti. EW to Dorothy Allhusen, 6 October 1932, Beinecke. EW to Lily Norton, 2 October 1925, Houghton. EW to MC, 20 October 1933, Letters 571.

27 *Ladies' Home Journal* to RJ, 1933, cited Dwight, 274. RJ to EW, 5 March 1932, Beinecke; RJ to EW, 1933, cited Dwight. Benstock, 422, 441. EW to JHS, 23 May 1932, Letters 549. EW to D. Hiltman, 13 August 1934, Beinecke.

28 EW to Curtis Brown, 17 January 1928, 8 March 1930, Curtis Brown to EW, 27 February 1930, 18 June, 5 July 1935, Beinecke.

29 EW to RJ, 23 September 1927, Beinecke; RJ to EW, 29 September 1933; EW to RJ, 26 October 1933, Letters 572–3; On 'Duration': Jessica Levine, *EW Review*, 13, 1, Fall 1996, 4–12. EW to MF, 10 August, 12 August 1916, Texas; EW to RJ, 25 July 1922, Beinecke. EW to Louis Bromfield, 20 April 1934, Lilly; EW to RJ, 26 October 1933, Letters 571–3. J.B. Williams to EW, 14 August 1934, Beinecke. CS II, 736;

Daniel Bratton, ed., *The Correspondence of Edith Wharton and Louis Bromfield*, Michigan State University Press, 2000, 61.

30 Loring Schuler to RJ, 16 January 1931, Beinecke, 15 November 1932, Lilly. EW to RJ, 29 April, 2 May 1933, Letters 558–60. BG in *Ladies' Home Journal*, October 1933–March 1934. EW to MC, 20 October 1933, Letters 571.

31 EW to RJ, 23 September 1931, 24 June 1932, Beinecke; CS II, 710, 715, 721. *Delineator* to RJ, 1931, RJ to EW, 12 September 1931, Beinecke; CS II, 669; RJ to EW, 12 September 1931, *La Revue de France* to EW, 26 April 1932; RJ to EW, 24 June 1932, *People's Popular Monthly* to EW, 5 February 1929, Beinecke. EW to MJ, 2 November 1934, Beinecke.

32 *Globe* to EW, 6 August 1936, Lilly. EW to Ned Sheldon, 17 September 1936, Beinecke.

33 Garrison, 328, 331, 340, 387. Louis Bromfield to EW, April 1934, Beinecke. See Bratton, *op. cit.*, 68–71. EW to Frederick Macmillan, 18 September 1921, 24 January 1928, 3 February 1928, British Library. EW to RJ, 9 May 1934, Beinecke. EW to J.B. Williams, 11 July 1934, Letters 580. D. Hiltman to EW, 25 July 1934, cited Letters 581. EW, Diary, July–August 1934, Lilly. EW to J.R. Pinker, 1 July 1935, Beinecke.

34 EW to American Library of Paris, 8 September 1932; EW to Smith College, 8 July 1925; EW to Doubleday, 1 June 1931; EW to James Monahan, *The Century Co*, 8 October 1928; EW to —, 14 October 1931; EW to Denver Club, 13 April 1921; J. Fridérich to George Poupet, 14 August 1931, Beinecke. ET, 27 May 1929, Lilly. Mariano, 174.

35 Frank Crowninshield to Anita Loos, 12 February 1926, Pierpont Morgan Library. BB to MB, 10 January 1932, I Tatti. GL to PL, notes, Beinecke. EW to Lily Norton, 2 November 1924, Houghton. EW to JHS, 9 April

1928, Beinecke. Robert Norton to BB, 19 January [1932], I Tatti. EW to GL, 24 January 1932, Beinecke. EW to ET, 4 December 1928, Lilly. ET, 5 February 1930, Lilly.

36   Huxleys: EW to MC, 25 March 1932, Letters 547; EW to BB, 1 February 1937, I Tatti. EW to JHS, 13 December 1930, Beinecke. EW to Zézette Du Bos, 29 April 1932, Bibliothèque Doucet, MS 27568–24. Sybille Bedford, *Aldous Huxley: A Biography*, Vol. I, Chatto & Windus, 1973, Part 5, ch. I, 'Villa Huley', 230–1, 258, 283, 327; Nicholas Murray, *Aldous Huxley: An English Intellectual*, Little, Brown, 2002, 236–7, 242, 257, 261; Huxley to Ottoline Morrell, 18 December 1930, Texas, quoted Murray, *op. cit.*, 242; Jeremy Lewis, *Cyril Connolly*, Cape, 1997, 236–7, citing Connolly, *The Rock Pool*. Mary Blume, *Cote d'Azur: Inventing the French Riviera*, Thames & Hudson, 1992, 86; Sybille Bedford to the author, 1999. NM to MB, 19 December 1930, in Mariano, 164.

37   Mariano, 172. EW to BB, 6 September 1930, Letters 530. EW to MB, 15 November 1931, I Tatti, in Dwight, 271; Lewis, 496–7. EW to BB, 14 August 1935, Letters 589.

38   Eric Maclagen to EW, August 1921, quoted Benstock, 449; Kenneth Clark, *Another Part of the Wood*, Hodder & Stoughton, 1974, 205. EW to MC, 20 October 1933, Letters 570; EW to JHS, 25 July 1935, Letters 587; to Mildred Bliss, 8 August 1931, Letters 540. EW to MC, 18 November 1931, Letters 542.

39   KC, *op. cit.*, 180. EW to Mildred Bliss, 8 August 1931, Letters 539. EW to Jane Clark, 19 July 1932, Letters 555. Diary, 30 June 1933, Lilly. KC to PL, 22 November 1938, Beinecke. Lubbock, 215; Benstock, 430. KC to Grace Kellogg Smith, 24 February 1959, Smith. EW to Jane Clark, 21 October 1934, Letters 582; EW to BB, 25 July 1933, I Tatti. KC to EW, nd, Beinecke.

40   Colin Clark to the author, 2000;

Colin Clark, *Younger Brother, Younger Son*, HarperCollins, 1998, 167. EW to KC, 12 October 1932, 25 November 1932, Letters 555, 556–7. EW to Jane Clark, 21 October 1934, Letters 582.

41   KC to EW, 22 August 1933, Lilly. EW to KC, 28 August 1933, Letters 567. KC to Grace Kellogg Smith, 24 February 1959, Smith. KC, *op. cit.*, 181. KC to EW, April 1937, Beinecke. KC, *op. cit.*, 227. KC, unsigned review of PL, 1947, in Smith, copied with KC to Grace Kellogg Smith, 24 February 1959.

42   EW to Jane Clark, July 1936, Letters 596; EW to GL, 3 April 1931, Letters 538; EW to ET, 19 August 1934, Lilly. BB to Rex Nicholson, 28 August 1937, in *Selected Letters of Bernard Berenson*, ed. A.K. McComb, Houghton Mifflin, 1964, 140.

43   EW to MJ, 17 November 1934, Letters 583. EW to ET, 31 September 1932, Lilly. Arthur Schlesinger, 'Walter Lippmann: The Intellectual v. Politics', in Marquis Childs and James Reston, eds, *Walter Lippmann and His Times*, Harcourt Brace, 1959, 189–225. BB to EW, 12 June 1931, I Tatti.

44   De Watteville: EW to GL, 2 April 1936; Wegener, 248–9; Ramsden, 135; Dwight, 212–13; Lubbock, 186–8; EW to Royal Cortissoz, 27 October 1935, Beinecke.

45   Hilda Runciman to Steven Runciman, 3 October 1934, quoted by permission of Ann Shukman. EW to Steven Runciman, 15 February 1929, 'April 4', nd, 21 October 1934, 13 August 1932, with thanks to the late Nikos Stangos and to Ann Shukman. Steven Runciman, obituaries, *Guardian*, 3 November 2000, 24, and Desmond Seward, *The Art Newspaper*, December 2000, 6, with thanks to J. Barnes. Selina Hastings, *Rosamond Lehmann: A Life*, Chatto & Windus, 2002.

46   Auchincloss, 44, 55; Auchincloss to the author, 2005; MC to PL, Beinecke; Cass Canfield, quoted Bratton, *op. cit.*, 79.

47 William Tyler, *Personal Memories of Edith Wharton*, Massachusetts Historical Society Proceedings, Vol. 85, 1973, 91–104; EW to ET, 20 October 1924, 25 October 1929, Good Friday 1937, Lilly. (The *Perrault* escaped the Blitz.) EW to BB, 9 April 1937, Letters 604. Gabriel Smol, retired Senior Lecturer, Open University, letter to the author, 8 January 1999.

48 EW to MJ, 30 November 1931, Beinecke; EW to ET, 24 September 1932, Lilly. EW to MF, 16 November 1930, Letters 530, 18 November 1930, Letters 531, 10 December 1930, Houghton, 11 January 1931, Letters 531, EW to MF, 10 June, 16 June 1931, EW to MF, 6 January 1932, Houghton; Diary, 23 September 1931, Lilly.

49 EW to JHS, 1 July 1930, 5 August 1930, Beinecke. EW to GL, 8 August 1930, Letters 528. EW to ET, 6 July 1930, 21 August 1930, Lilly. EW to ET, 13 March 1934, Lilly.

50 EW to ET, April–May 1933, Lilly; Diary, 17 June 1933, Lilly; EW to MB, 26 May 1933, Letters 561; Diary, 4 October, 24 October 1933, Lilly; wording for monument, 1934, Beinecke; EW to Dorothy Allhusen, 29 May 1933, Beinecke. EW to MC on servants, 6 March, 4 April 1933, quoted Dwight, 229. New servants' names in 'Notice of EW's unpaid bills at her death', 17 August 1937, Lilly. Staff numbers in ET, 'Statement re Mrs Wharton's Last Will and Testament', 1939, Lilly.

51 EW to MB, 11 January 1928, EW to BB, 15 August 1931, 9 April 1937, I Tatti. Diary, 12 May 1933, 10 December 1934, 8 December 1934, Beinecke.

52 EW to Lady John Leslie, 5 February 1932, Pierpont Morgan Library. EW to BB, 17 January 1932, Letters 543. EW to GL, 28 August 1933, Letters 566. EW to Lily Norton, 18 February 1930, Houghton.

53 EW to Ned Sheldon, 3 August 1931, Beinecke. EW to MJ, 10 April 1934, Letters 577. EW to BB, 10 July 1933,

Letters 562. EW to Dorothy Allhusen, 7 July 1933, EW to GL, 26 July 1931, Beinecke. Bateman's Visitors Book, 25 July 1931. EW to Jane Clark, July 1936, Letters 596.

54 EW to MJ, 2 December 1929, Beinecke; EW to GL, 19 February 1936, Letters 590; EW to CdB, Bibliothèque Doucet, Paris, MS 27567–99, 11 August 1930. Addresses, Lubbock papers, Beinecke.

55 BG, chs 5, i; 6, ii; 6, i; ch. 9, i; ch. 14, vii. Virginia Woolf to Ethel Smyth, *Letters*, V, 1932–1935, 305, quoted in K. Joslin, 'Embattled Tendencies: Wharton, Woolf, and the Nature of Modernism', in *Special Relationships: Anglo-American Affinities and Antagonisms 1854–1936*, eds. Janet Beer and Bridget Bennett, Manchester University Press, 2002, 202–20.

CHAPTER 20: ALL SOULS'

1 EW to CdB, 3 May 1935, MS 27567–111, Bibliothèque Doucet, Paris. 'Exultet': *Catholic Encyclopedia*, Appleton, 1909, Vol. V; Missale Romanum, 1970, on *http://en.wikipedia.org/wiki/Exultet*: grateful thanks to Michael Suarez. EW to MC, 18 November 1931, Letters 541. EW to JHS, 23 May 1932, Letters 550. EW to CdB, 8 December 1931, MS 27567–100, Bibliothèque Doucet, Paris. EW to BB, 27 May 1932, I Tatti. EW to NM, 31 May 1932, Letters 551.

2 Benstock, 427–8. EW to MF, 28 December 1929, Houghton. EW to Editor, Paris *Herald*, 10 December 1930, Letters 531–2. Gordon Wright, *France in Modern Times*, Norton, 1987, 333; Robert Gildea, *The Past in French History*, Yale University Press, 1994, ch. 5.

3 Benstock, 427; Diary, 2 November 1930, Lilly. BB to MB, 28 May 1932, I Tatti. KC to Grace Kellogg Smith, 13 February 1959, Smith. Bernard Berenson, *Sunset and Twilight*, ed. Nicky Mariano, Hamish Hamilton,

1964, 533. William Tyler, 'Personal Memories of Edith Wharton', 1973. All Souls' Eve is 31 October; All Souls' Day, when EW would sit at night and think of her dead, is 2 November.

4 CS II, 539. Notebook, 1925, Lilly. CS II, 632, 655. EW to RJ, 31 January 1931, Letters 531–2. See Goodman, 145–8, Waid, 195–6, and Gloria C. Erlich, *The Sexual Education of Edith Wharton*, University of California Press, 1992, ch. 1, on EW's use of this theme. 'Life and I', Beinecke, and L&I. 'Pomegranate Seed', *Scribner's Magazine*, 51, March 1912, 284–91.

5 CS II, 775, 767, 786. 'Preface' to *Ghosts*, Appleton, 1937, CS II, 875.

6 CS II, 672.

7 CS II, 838, 843, 842.

8 Lewis, 524; Benstock, 460; RJ to EW, 22 March, 26 April 1934, cited Benstock, 439; EW to RJ, 26 May 1934, Lilly; EW to Appleton, 20 July 1934, Lilly; EW to Pinker, 1 July 1935, Lilly, also complained about having to finish B before he could sell it. EW to Ned Sheldon, 6 September 1933, Beinecke; EW to ET, 3 February 1937, Lilly. Lily Norton to ET, 10 December 1938, Lilly. Versions of EW as Gilded Age representative: Auchincloss; Morris; Homberger. *The Buccaneers: A Novel by Edith Wharton*, completed by Marion Mainwaring, Fourth Estate, 1993, scathingly reviewed by Andrew Del Banco, in 'Missed Manners', *The New Republic*, 25 October 1993, 34–5, as a 'bad fit' and a 'pastiche . . . by a writer whose ear is uncertain and who cannot leave the original work alone'. Diary, February 1935, Lilly.

9 Benstock, 45–7; Lewis, 44–5, 213; L&I, 1093; Auchincloss, 42, Dwight, 250; Homberger, 9–10, 251; Tintner, 146; BG, ch. 3. Consuelo Balsan, *Gold and Glitter*, Heinemann, 1953, cited in Montgomery, 59–60.

10 Benstock, 198, Montgomery, 180, note 88. Lewis, 41. For these marriages see Marian Fowler, *In a*

Gilded Cage: From Heiress to Duchess, Random House, 1993, Ruth Brandon, *The Dollar Princesses*, Weidenfeld & Nicolson, 1980, and Amanda Mackenzie Stuart's lively *Consuelo & Alva: Love and Power in the Gilded Age*, HarperCollins, 2005, esp. 109–11. EW to Ned Sheldon, 14 August 1933, Beinecke.

11 EW to Ned Sheldon, 3 October 1933, Beinecke. EW to MJ, 10 October 1933, Beinecke.

12 EW to BB, 17 December 1934, I Tatti. B, ch. 3, ch. 4. Proust, trans. T. Kilmartin and D.J. Enright, *In Search of Lost Time: Within a Budding Grove*, Vintage, 2002, II, 427–8, 466.

13 B, chs 13, 50.

14 B, ch. 23. EW to BB, 28 July 1918, I Tatti.

15 EW to GL, 2 April 1936, Letters 593.

16 BG, ch. 10, i.

17 B, chs 25, 8, 7, 21. WF, I, 3; Wegener, 218, 226. Beer, 1990, 150; Bauer, 181–2, 186. B, ch. 18. Esquemeling: Ramsden, 40, Tintner, 151–2.

18 B, ch. 28.

19 Ned Sheldon to EW, 14 March 1935, Lilly. EW to Ned Sheldon, 13 January 1936, Beinecke. Ruth Gordon to Edward Sheldon, telegram, 3 January 1936, Lilly. EW to BF, 17 April 1936, Beinecke. Appleton to EW, 17 January 1934, Beinecke. Brooks Atkinson, 'Under Winter Skies', *New York Times*, 2 February 1936. 'The Frome Residence', *New York Times*, 1 March 1936. EW, 1936: Wegener, 263.

20 Howard Moss, *The Old Maid* schedule, 1936, Beinecke. EW to GL, 19 February 1936, Letters 591; 2 April 1936, Letters 592. EW to MJ, 11 June 1935, Beinecke. Alice Krauser agency to EW, 9 August 1935, 17 January 1936, 23 April 1936, EW to Alice Krauser, 27 April, 1 May 1936, Beinecke.

21 EW to ET, 7 September 1935, Lilly. Garrison, 147; Wegener, 261–3, 269, 267, 271; EW to Milford, 18 May 1935, Beinecke. 'The Writing of Ethan Frome' in Wegener, 261–3, also reprinted in Elmer Adler,

Breaking into Print, Simon & Schuster, 1937. Loren Carroll, 'Edith Wharton in Profile', *New York Herald Tribune*, Paris edition, 16 November 1936.

22 'Italy Again', 1934, 'Back to Compostella', Beinecke. Wegener, 218. Runciman: Desmond Seward to the author, August 2005. EW to Clara Chambron, 27 October [1936], Berg Collection, NYPL.

23 AI, ch. 31. Wegener, 274, 287.

24 Diary, February 1934, Lilly. EW to BB, 12 February 1934, Letters 574; EW to MJ, 10 April 1934, Letters 576. Wright, *op. cit.*, 360–84; Alastair Horne, *To Lose a Battle*, Little, Brown, 1969, 59–77.

25 Ernest Samuels, *Bernard Berenson: The Making of a Legend*, Belknap, 1987, 422–3. EW to Mildred Bliss, November 1936, Beinecke. EW to GL, 29 May 1934, Beinecke. EW to MJ, 14 March, 17 March 1933, 10 February 1934, Beinecke. BB to EW, 1 July 1934, Lilly. LG to EW, 20 September 1934, Lilly. EW to ET, 19 August 1934, Lilly. EW, Diary, 15 May 1932, cited Lewis, 504. EW to Lady Wemyss, 23 January 1936, Stanway House.

26 Diary, 24 January 1935, 11 April 1935, Lilly. EW to KC, 28 May 1935, Letters 586. Fridérich to CdB, BB, Lawrence Johnston, ET, Jane Clark, 14 April, 15 April, 25 April 1935, Lilly. ET to BB, 24 June 1935, I Tatti. ET, Diary, 13 June 1937, Lilly.

27 Royal Cortissoz, Address, Memorial Service for Mary Cadwalader Jones, 12 December 1935, Environmental Design Archives, University of California. EW to MJ, 24 January 1932, Beinecke; 12 December 1930, Lilly. EW to JHS, 25 July 1935, Letters 588. Note from Sir Charles Mendl to Dover Authorities, 22 September 1935, Lilly. EW to BB, 30 September 1935, I Tatti; cut version in Letters 590. EW to BF, 25 September, 11 November 1935, Beinecke; Benstock, 446. Introduction to Mary Cadwalader Jones, *Lantern Slides*, printed by DBU,

Merrymount Press, 1937; NYPL copy given by Max and Beatrix Farrand, 22 January 1938.

28 EW to BF, 29 September 1929, Lilly. BB to EW, 2 February 1933, Lilly. EW, Diary, 12 January, 9 February, 11 February, 8–9 March 1937, Lilly. EW to MB, 11 October 1936, Letters 598. Lewis, 529, Letters 592. Diary, 8–9 March 1937, Lilly. EW to BB, 9 April 1937, Letters 603. Wills: EW to ET, 23 May 1936, Letters 595. EW to ET, 4 December 1936; EW, Diary, 20 March 1937, Lilly. Benstock, 452. ET, Diary, 11 June 1937, Lilly.

29 Diary, 20 January 1937, EW to ET, 3 February 1937, Lilly. There are intriguing readings of 'All Souls''; e.g. by Annette Zilversmit in Bendixen, 315–29, and by Barbara A. White, 'Introduction', *Wharton's New England*, University of New Hampshire Press, 1995, xxv–xxvi, who reads it as a tale about child abuse. Tintner, 139–42, compares it to a Hugh Walpole story in his 1933 collection *All Souls' Night*; Waid, 175, suggests it is Hitler's voice on the wireless; Judith Fryer, *Felicitous Space: The Imaginative Structures of Edith Wharton and Willa Cather*, University of North Carolina Press, 1986, 158, reads it as about a fear of '*something that is not there*', and suggests that writing was for EW 'like being haunted'.

30 CS II, 879–97. EW to BB, 30 November 1933, quoted Benstock, 448, Lewis, 505.

31 EW, Diary, April 1937, Lilly. EW to BF, April 1937. EW to William Tyler, 16 May 1937, Letters 605–6. EW to ET, 25 May 1937, Lilly. EW, Diary, April–May 1937, Lilly.

32 List, quoted Lewis, 160, Dwight, 282. Notebook, 1924, Beinecke. EW to BB, 9 April 1937, Letters 605. Metcalf, 32–4. Ogden Codman to his brother, 5 June 1937, in Dwight, 288, note 282. EW to ET, telegram, 3 June 1937, Lilly. ET to BB, 5 June 1937, I Tatti. ET to KC, 6 June 1837, Tate, KC papers, 8812/1/3/3405. Biographical opinion varies about

whether EW had a heart-attack or a stroke on 1 June. Lewis, 530, Letters 624, and Dwight, 282, call it a stroke; Benstock, 452, calls it a heart-attack. The telegram from EW to ET and ET's letters confirm the latter.

33 ET to BB, 31 July 1937, I Tatti. KC to Lewis, 6 December 1972, Tate, KC papers, 8812/1/3/3426. Reproduced by permission of the Estate of Kenneth Clark, c/o Margaret Hanbury, 27 Walcot Square, London SE11 4UB. Benstock, 455. ET, 23 June 1937, Lilly. ET to BF, 8 July 1937, Beinecke. RT to Robert Bliss, 29 July 1937, Lilly. ET to BB, 31 July 1937, I Tatti. EW to MG, 4 August 1937, Lilly. 'Poppies': Rieder, Fig. 76, opp. 130. Lewis, 531.

34 ET, Diary, June-August 1937, Lilly. ET to BB, 3 November 1937, I Tatti. BG, ch. 14.

35 Samuels, *op. cit.*, 422–3. Benstock, 453–4, Lubbock, 222.

36 ET, 13 August 1937, Lilly. ET to BB, 3 November 1937, I Tatti. ET, Diary, June–August 1937, Lilly. Louis Gillet to BB, 25 August 1937, I Tatti. Translation assisted by Julian Barnes and Bridget Patterson.

37 William Tyler, 'Personal Memories of Edith Wharton', *Massachusetts Historical Society Proceedings*, Vol. 85, 1973, 104, cites the line as 'the first line of the sixth stanza of the vesper hymn'. For the vesper hymn translation, thanks to Michael Suarez. *New York Times*, 12 August 1937, *New York Herald*, 15 August 1937. MF had a cousin called Hugh in Paris; or it may have been the reporter's mistake. Dwight, 282. EW, Memorandum for ET, 23 May 1937, Beinecke.

38 *New York Times*, 13 August 1937, 5 September 1937; *New York World Telegraph*, nd Louis Gillet, *L'Époque*, 16 August 1937; André Chaumieux, *L'Echo de Paris*, 14 August 1937; Claude Silve, *Le Figaro*, 13 August 1937.

39 The quarrel over the wills is ignored by Lewis, and outlined with great clarity by Benstock, 456–9. Benstock, 48, 120; Dwight, 288, n. 282.

40 GL to BB, 7 October 1937, I Tatti, outlining the two wills. ET to Frederic King, 5 September 1937, Lilly, to JHS, 6 January 1948, Lilly, on the properties. ET, list of 'Unpaid Bills', 17 August 1937, Lilly. Customs Statement, 8 September 1937, Lilly. Copy, French will (translated), 17 September 1937, EWR.

41 EW to ET, 4 December 1936, ET to BF, 15 December 1937, Lilly. ET, 'Statement concerning the circumstances of Mrs Wharton's last illness and of the execution of her last Will and Testament', Lilly. Copy of EW's American will, 3 December 1936, Watkins/Loomis Agency Archives. BF to Wayne Andrews, 3 December 1958, Beinecke; BF to Grace Kellogg Smith, 24 November 1958, Smith. ET to JHS, 14 January 1939, Lilly.

42 EW to MC, 9 June 1925, Letters 483, quoted Singley, 2003, 4. Jeanne Fridérich, notes for PL, Beinecke. GL to the president of Yale, 7 May 1938, Watkins/Loomis Agency Archives. GL to KC, 10 October 1937, Tate, KC papers, 8812/1/3/1586. KC to Lewis, 9 October 1975, Tate, KC papers, 8812/1/4/465. GL to PL, 14 November 1937, Beinecke. GL notes on EW's essays, Trinity College Cambridge, GL papers. MF to ET, 18 November 1946, Lilly. ET to Frederic King, 9 June 1949, Lilly.

43 Clifton Fadiman, introduction, *Ethan Frome*, Limited Editions Club, 1939, in Smith. Advert for *EW Treasury*, *New York Times*, 8 October 1950. Whitney Darrow to Ann Watkins, 7 October 1952, Watkins/Loomis Agency Archives. James Laughlin to Archibald Ogden at Appleton, *New Directions* file, 31 May 1950, Houghton Library, Harvard. LP Ltd to Watkins Agency, 9 April 1962, Watkins/Loomis Agency Archives. Grace Shaw Smith to KC, 28 June 1963, Tate, KC papers, 8812/1/3/3416.

44 Correspondence over EW biography, 1964–6, Watkins/Loomis Agency Archives.

45 Mainwaring, 298, 313, gives detailed accounts of how the EW/MF letters must have come to Texas, and also of the criticisms by herself, Mary Pitlick and others, of the Lewises' edition of EW's letters. Notable academic work has been done on EW in the last twenty years, especially by women critics such as Elizabeth Ammons, Dale Bauer, Janet Beer, Clare Colquitt, Marilyn French, Judith Fryer, Susan Goodman, Katherine Joslin, Maureen E. Montgomery, Elsa Nettels, Carol J. Singley, Adeline R. Tintner, Candace Waid, Sarah Bird Wright and Annette Zilversmit.

46 *Publishers Weekly*, 30 August 1993, on the 'Wharton boom'. John Updike, 'Reworking Wharton', *New Yorker*, 4 October 1993. Kate Muir, *Observer*, 29 August 1993. Parker Ladd to Armitage Watkins, 2 January 1961, Watkins/Loomis Agency Archives. Sharon Churcher, 'Legacy from a Lost Life', *The Mail on Sunday*, 12 September 1933. *Edith Wharton's World: Portraits of People and Places*, the National Portrait Gallery, Smithsonian Institution, Washington, 26 September 1997 to 25 January 1998.

47 *New York Times*, 12 September 2004, 1 October 2004, 31 October 2004. *Style*, December 2004.

48 Roger Betteridge to KC, 24 October 1979, Tate, KC papers, 8812/1/3/3437.

Select Bibliography and Abbreviations

EW's novels and non-fiction have appeared in many different editions, and readers may not be able to refer back to page-numbers in first editions: so first publication dates are given here, and note references are to chapters, not to page numbers. All abbreviations used in the notes are noted here. Secondary sources cited and not included in the select bibliography are found in full in the notes.

ABBREVIATIONS OF NAMES IN NOTES

AG: André Gide
BB: Bernard Berenson
BF: Beatrix Farrand
CEN: Charles Eliot Norton
CdB: Charles Du Bos
CS: Charles Scribner (1854–1930)
DBU: Daniel Berkeley Updike
EB: Edward Burlingame
ET: Elisina Tyler
FSF: F. Scott Fitzgerald
GL: Gaillard Lapsley
GS: Geoffrey Scott
HJ: Henry James
HS: Howard Sturgis
JEB: Jacques-Émile Blanche
JHS: John Hugh Smith
KC: Kenneth Clark
LB: Léon Bélugou
MB: Mary Berenson
MC: Margaret ('Daisy') Chanler
MF: Morton Fullerton
MG: Matilda Gay
MJ: Mary Cadwalader ('Minnie') Jones
NM: Nicky Mariano
OC: Ogden Codman
PB: Paul Bourget
PL: Percy Lubbock
RJ: Rutger Jewett
RS: Ronald Simmons
RT: Royall Tyler
SN: Sara ('Sally') Norton
TW: Edward ('Teddy') Wharton
VL: Vernon Lee (Violet Paget)

WB: Walter Berry
WCB: William Crary Brownell
WG: William Gerhardi
ZG: Zona Gale

ARCHIVES

Alice Warder Garrett Archives, Evergreen House Foundation, at Evergreen House, Johns Hopkins University, Baltimore
Barnard College, Overbury Collection, New York
Beinecke: Edith Wharton Collection, Yale Collection of American Literature, Beinecke Rare Book and Manuscript Library, Yale University
Berg: The Henry and Albert Berg Collection of English and American Literature, New York Public Library and Astor, Lenox, and Tilden Foundation
Bibliothèque de l'Institut, Paris
Bibliothèque Doucet, Paris
Bibliothèque Nationale, Paris
Beatrix Jones Farrand Collection, Environmental Design Archives, University of California, Berkeley
Bradley Family Papers, Radcliffe Institute for Advanced Study, Schlesinger Library, Harvard University
BL: The British Library
Brotherton: The Brotherton Collection, Leeds University Library
Butler Library and Rare Books and Manuscripts Library, Columbia University, New York
EWRA: Edith Wharton Restoration Archives, The Mount
Houghton: The Houghton Library, Harvard University
I Tatti: Fototeca Berenson, Villa I Tatti, Harvard University
John Work Garrett Papers, Special Collections, Milton S. Eisenhower Library, Johns Hopkins University, Baltimore
Lilly: Wharton MSS and Appleton-Century MSS, the Lilly Library, Indiana University, Bloomington, Indiana
McGill: Leon Edel Papers at McGill University, Rare Books and Special Collections, McLennan Library, McGill University
The Mortimer Rare Book Room, Smith College
NYPL MSS: Manuscripts and Archives Division, Humanities & Social Sciences Library, New York Public Library
The Pierpont Morgan Library, New York
Pusey House, Oxford: Mrs Humphry Ward Papers, The Principal and Chapter of Pusey House, Oxford
Scribner Archive, Princeton: Charles Scribner's Sons Archive, Scribner Room, Department of Rare Books and Special Collections, Firestone Library, Princeton University
Smith: Grace Kellogg Smith Papers, Sophia Smith Collection, Smith College
Somerville: Somerville College, Oxford: Vernon Lee Papers, The Principal and Fellows of Somerville College, Oxford
SPNEA: Society for the Preservation of New England Antiquities, Boston
Tate: Hyman Kreitman Research Centre, Tate Gallery Archives, Kenneth Clark papers
Texas: The Harry Ransom Humanities Research Center, University of Texas at Austin
Trinity College Cambridge: Gaillard Lapsley papers, The Master and Fellows of Trinity College, Cambridge
Watkins/Loomis Agency Archives: Watkins/Loomis office and Watkins-Loomis agency records, Columbia University Rare Book and Manuscript Library, New York

UNPUBLISHED OR UNCOLLECTED MSS

CB: EW's Commonplace Book: with thanks to Watkins/Loomis Agency and Maureen Howard.

Colquitt, Clare, 'Unpacking her Treasures: Edith Wharton's "Mysterious Correspondence" with Morton Fullerton', *The Library Chronicle of the University of Texas at Austin*, ns 31 (1985).

Gribben, Alan, '"The Heart is Insatiable": A Selection from Edith Wharton's Letters to Morton Fullerton, 1907–1915', *The Library Chronicle of the University of Texas at Austin*, ns. 31 (1985).

PRIMARY SOURCES

EW's stories are cited in the footnotes in CS and EWCS, not as they appeared in individual volumes, which are currently out of print: *The Greater Inclination* (1899), *Crucial Instances* (1901), *The Descent of Man* (1904), *The Hermit and the Wild Woman* (1908), *Tales of Men and Ghosts* (1910), *Xingu* (1916), *Here and Beyond* (1926), *Certain People* (1930), *Human Nature* (1933), *The World Over* (1936), *Ghosts* (1937). CS contains all the uncollected stories as well as almost all the contents of the original volumes; EWCS is not a complete collection, but does contain the novellas *The Touchstone* (1900), *Sanctuary* (1903) and *Bunner Sisters* (1916). Poems are mainly cited from the Library of America Selection (2005), not by individual volumes (*Verses* [1878], *Artemis to Actaeon and Other Verse* [1909], *Twelve Poems* [1926]).

AI: *The Age of Innocence*, 1920
B: *The Buccaneers*, 1937
BG: *A Backward Glance*, 1934
BH: *The Book of the Homeless*, ed. Edith Wharton, 1916
BP: 'Beatrice Palmato', undated
C: *The Children*, 1928
CC: *The Custom of the Country*, 1913
CS I and CS II: *Edith Wharton: The Collected Short Stories*, ed. R.W.B. Lewis, Scribner's, 1968
CTHJ: *The Complete Tales of Henry James*, ed. Leon Edel, Rupert Hart-Davis, 1964
DH: *The Decoration of Houses*, with Ogden Codman, 1897
EF: *Ethan Frome*, 1911
EWCS I and EWCS II: *Edith Wharton: Collected Stories 1891–1910*, *Collected Stories 1911–1937*, Library of America, 2001
Fast and Loose, ed. Viola Hopkins Winner, University Press of Virginia, 1993
FF: *Fighting France*, 1915
FT: *The Fruit of the Tree*, 1907
FWTM: *French Ways and their Meaning*, 1919
GA: *The Gods Arrive*, 1932
GM: *The Glimpses of the Moon*, 1922
HJ/EW: *Henry James and Edith Wharton, Letters 1900–1915*, ed. Lyall H. Powers, Weidenfeld & Nicolson, 1990
HJL: *Henry James: Letters*, ed. Leon Edel, Belknap Press at Harvard University Press, 1984
HM: *The House of Mirth*, 1905
HRB: *Hudson River Bracketed*, 1929
IB: *Italian Backgrounds*, 1905
IM: *In Morocco*, 1920
IVG: *Italian Villas and Their Gardens*, 1904
LA: Kenneth Price and Phyllis McBride, eds, '"The Life Apart": Texts and Contexts of Edith Wharton's Love Diary', *American Literature*, Vol. 66, No. 4 (December 1994),

663–8. Also in Paul Lauter, ed., *The Heath Anthology of American Literature*, 4th edn, Houghton Mifflin, 2002, 1044–55.

L&I: 'Life and I', *Novellas and Other Writings*, Library of America, 1990

Letters: *The Letters of Edith Wharton*, eds R.W.B. Lewis and Nancy Lewis, Simon & Schuster, 1988

LGNY: 'A Little Girl's New York', Wegener, 1996, 274–88

M: *The Marne*, 1918

MFF: *A Motor-Flight Through France*, 1908

MR: *The Mother's Recompense*, 1925

MT: *Madame de Treymes*, 1907

ONY: *Old New York*, 1924

P: *Edith Wharton: Selected Poems*, Library of America, 2005

R: *The Reef*, 1912

ed. Louis Auchincloss Ramsden: *Edith Wharton's Library*, a catalogue compiled by George Ramsden, introduction by Hermione Lee, Stone Trough Books, Settrington, N. Yorkshire, 1999

S: *Summer*, 1917

SF: *A Son at the Front*, 1923

TS: *Twilight Sleep*, 1927

Vanadis: *The Cruise of the Vanadis*, ed. Claudine Lesage, Sterne, Presses de l'UFR Clerc Université Picardie, 1991. Reissued as *The Cruise of the Vanadis*, illustrated by Jonas Dovydenas, Rizzoli International Publications, 2004

VD: *The Valley of Decision*, 1902

Wegener: Frederick Wegener, ed., *The Uncollected Critical Writings of Edith Wharton*, Princeton University Press, 1996

WF: *The Writing of Fiction*, 1925

SECONDARY SOURCES

Ammons: Ammons, Elizabeth, *Edith Wharton's Argument with America*, University of Georgia Press, 1980

Auchincloss: Auchincloss, Louis, *Edith Wharton: A Woman in Her Time*, Michael Joseph, 1971

Auchincloss, Louis, *The Vanderbilt Era*, Scribner's, 1989

Barnes, E.W., *The Man Who Lived Twice: The Biography of Edward Sheldon*, Scribner's, 1956

Barnes, James, *From Then Till Now*, Appleton-Century, 1934

Bauer: Bauer, Dale, *Edith Wharton's Brave New Politics*, University of Wisconsin Press, 1994

Bedford, Sybille, *Aldous Huxley: A Biography*, Vol. I, Chatto & Windus, 1973

Becker: Becker J.J., *The Great War and the French People*, Berg, 1985

Beer 1990: Beer, Janet, *Edith Wharton: Traveller in the Land of Letters*, Macmillan, 1990

Beer 2002: Beer, Janet, *Edith Wharton*, Writers and their Work, Northcote House Publishers, 2002

Bell: Bell, Millicent, *Edith Wharton and Henry James*, Peter Owen, 1966

Bendixen: Bendixen, Alfred and Zilversmit, Annette, *Edith Wharton: New Critical Essays*, Garland, 1992

Benstock: Benstock, Shari, *No Gifts From Chance: A Biography of Edith Wharton*, Scribner's and Hamish Hamilton, 1994, Penguin Books, 1995; references in the Notes are to the Penguin edn.

Berenson, Bernard, *Sunset and Twilight: Diaries 1947–1958*, Hamish Hamilton, 1964

Berenson, Bernard, *Sketch for a Self-Portrait*, Pantheon, 1949

Berenson, Mary, *A Self-Portrait from Her Letters and Diaries*, eds Barbara Strachey and Jayne Samuels, Gollancz, 1983

Blanche, Jacques-Émile, *Portraits of a Lifetime, 1870–1914*, trans. W. Clement, Dent, 1937

Bourget, Paul, *Outre-Mer*, Lemerre, 1895

Bratton, Daniel, ed., *The Correspondence of Edith Wharton and Louis Bromfield*, Michigan State University Press, 2000

Brown, Jane, *Beatrix: The Gardening Life of Beatrix Jones Farrand, 1872–1959*, Viking, 1995

Burlingame, Roger, *Of Making Many Books* (1946) Pennsylvania State University, 1996

CCEW: *The Cambridge Companion to Edith Wharton*, ed. Millicent Bell, Cambridge University Press, 1995

Chanler, Margaret, *Autumn in the Valley*, Little, Brown, 1936

Clark, Kenneth, *Another Part of the Wood*, Hodder & Stoughton, 1974

Clarke, Ida, *American Women and the World War*, Appleton, 1918

Colquitt *et al.*: Colquitt, Clare, Goodman, Susan and Waid, Candace, eds, *A Forward Glance: New Essays on Edith Wharton*, University of Delaware Press, 1999

Craig: Craig, Theresa, *Edith Wharton: A House Full of Rooms*, Monacelli Press, 1996

Cronin, Vincent, *Paris on the Eve, 1900–1914*, Collins, 1989

Dwight: Dwight, Eleanor, *Edith Wharton: An Extraordinary Life*, Harry N. Abrams, 1994

Dunn, Richard M., *Geoffrey Scott and the Berenson Circle*, Edwin Mellon Press, 1998

Edel, Leon, *Henry James*, Vol. 5, *The Master: 1910–1916*, Lippincott, 1972

Erlich, Gloria C., *The Sexual Education of Edith Wharton*, University of California Press, 1992

EWN: *Edith Wharton Newsletter.*

EWR: *Edith Wharton Review*, Edith Wharton Society, Kean University, New Jersey

Fryer, Judith, *Felicitous Space: The Imaginative Structures of Edith Wharton and Willa Cather*, University of North Carolina Press, 1986

Garrison: Garrison, Stephen, *Edith Wharton: A Descriptive Bibliography*, University of Pittsburgh Press, 1990

Gerhardi, William, *Memoirs of a Polyglot*, Duckworth, 1931

Gide, André, *The Journals of André Gide*, ed. Justin O'Brian, Knopf, 1948; Penguin, 1967

Gildea, Robert, *The Past in French History*, Yale University Press, 1994

Goodman: Goodman, Susan, *Edith Wharton's Inner Circle*, University of Texas Press, 1994

Homberger: Homberger, Eric, *Mrs Astor's New York*, Yale University Press, 2002

Horne: Horne, Philip, *Henry James: A Life in Letters*, Allen Lane, 1999

Jacquemin, Odile and Berro, Catherine, *Territoires Littéraires des îles à la ville Hyères Les Palmiers*, Hyères, 1998

James, Henry, *The American Scene*, Chapman & Hall, 1907.

Jones, Mary Cadwalader, *Lantern Slides*, Merrymount Press, 1937

Joslin and Price: Joslin, K. and Price, A., eds, *Wretched Exotic: Essays on Edith Wharton in Europe*, Peter Lang, 1993

Kaplan, Amy, *The Social Construction of American Realism*, Chicago University Press, 1988

Kaplan, Fred, *Henry James*, Hodder & Stoughton, 1992

Keegan: Keegan, John, *The First World War*, Random House, 1998

Lesage: Lesage, Claudine, *Lettres à l'ami français*, Houdiard, 2001

Lewis, Arnold, Turner, James and McQuillin, Steve, *The Opulent Interiors of the Gilded Age*, Dover, 1986

Lewis: Lewis, R. W. B., *Edith Wharton: A Biography*, Harper & Row, 1975, Harper Colophon Books, 1977; references in the Notes are to the Harper Colophon edn

Lubbock: Lubbock, Percy, *Portrait of Edith Wharton*, Jonathan Cape, 1947

McAllister, Ward, *Society As I Have Found It*, Cassell, 1890

Mainwaring: Mainwaring, Marion, *Mysteries of Paris: The Quest for Morton Fullerton*, University Press of New England, 2000

Mariano: Mariano, Nicky, *Forty Years with Berenson*, Hamish Hamilton, 1966

Martineau, Mrs Philip, *Gardening in Sunny Lands*, Cobden-Sandersen, 1924

Metcalf: Metcalf, Pauline C, ed., *Ogden Codman and the Decoration of Houses*, Boston Athenaeum, 1988

Montgomery: Montgomery, Maureen E., *Displaying Women: Spectacles of Leisure in Edith Wharton's New York*, Routledge, 1998

Moorehead, Caroline, *Iris Origo*, John Murray, 2000

Morand, Paul, *Journal d'un Attaché d'Ambassade*, Gallimard, 1996

Morris: Morris, Lloyd, *Incredible New York*, Syracuse, 1951

Mount: *The Mount, Home of Edith Wharton*, Edith Wharton Restoration, Lenox Mass, 1997

Mugnier, Abbé, *Journal 1879–1939*, Mercure de France, 1985

Nevins, Allan, ed., *The Diary of Philip Hone, 1828–1851*, Dodd, Mead, 1927

Olin-Ammentorp: Olin-Ammentorp, Julie, *Edith Wharton's Writings from the Great War*, Florida University Press, 2004

Pearsall Smith, Logan, *Unforgotten Years*, Little, Brown, 1939

Preston: Preston, Claire, *Edith Wharton's Social Register*, Macmillan, 2000

Price: Price, Alan, *The End of the Age of Innocence: Edith Wharton and the First World War*, Robert Hale, 1996

Proust, Marcel, *À la recherche du temps perdu*, trans. T. Kilmartin and D.J. Enright as *In Search of Lost Time*, Vintage Classics, 2002

Quest-Ritson, Charles, *The English Garden Abroad*, Penguin, 1992

Rieder: Rieder, William, *A Charmed Couple: The Art and Life of Walter & Matilda Gay*, Harry N. Abrams, 2000

Samuels, Ernest, *Bernard Berenson: The Making of a Legend*, Belknap, 1987

SBW: see Wright, Sarah Bird

Schorer, Mark, *Sinclair Lewis*, McGraw Hill, 1961

Singley: Singley, Carol J., *Edith Wharton: Matters of Mind and Spirit*, Houghton Mifflin, 2000

Singley 2003: Singley, Carol J., ed., *A Historical Guide to Edith Wharton*, Oxford University Press, 2003

Smith: Smith, Leonard V., Audoin-Rouzeau, Stephane and Becker, Annette, *France and the Great War, 1914–1918*, Cambridge University Press, 2003

Stern: Stern, Robert, *New York 1880*, Monacelli Press, 1999

Strouse: Strouse, Jean, *Morgan: American Financier*, Random House and Harvill Press, 1999

Stuart, Amanda Mackenzie, *Consuelo & Alva: Love and Power in the Gilded Age*, HarperCollins, 2005

Tadié, Jean-Yves, *Marcel Proust*, trans. Euan Cameron, Viking, 1996

Tintner: Tintner, Adeline R., *Edith Wharton in Context*, University of Alabama Press, 1999

Tuttleton: Tuttleton, James W., Lauer, Kristin O., and Murray, Margaret P., eds, *Edith Wharton: The Contemporary Reviews*, Cambridge University Press, 1992

Tyler, William, 'Personal Memories of Edith Wharton', *Massachusetts Historical Society Proceedings*, Vol. 85, 1973

Van Rensselaer, J.K., *The Social Ladder*, Nash & Grayson, 1925

Waid: Waid, Candace, *Edith Wharton's Letters from the Underworld: Fictions of Women and Writing*, University of North Carolina Press, 1991

Weber, Eugen, *France: Fin de Siècle*, Belknap Press, 1986

Weber, Eugen, *The Hollow Years: France in the 1930s*, Sinclair-Stevenson, 1995

Wegener, Frederick, 'Form, "Selection" and Ideology in EW's Antimodernist Aesthetic', in Colquitt *et al.*, 1999

Whitcomb, Philip, *Seventy-Five Years in the Franco-American Economy: A Short History of the First American Chamber of Commerce*, Paris, 1970

Williams, Deborah, *Not in Sisterhood: Edith Wharton, Willa Cather, Zona Gale, and the Politics of Female Authorship*, Palgrave, 2001

Wolff: Wolff, Cynthia Griffin, A *Feast of Words: The Triumph of Edith Wharton*, Oxford University Press, 1977

Wolff, Geoffrey, *Black Sun: The Brief Transit and Violent Eclipse of Harry Crosby*, Random House, 1976

Wright, Gordon, *France in Modern Times*, 4th edn, (1960), Norton, 1987

SBW: Wright, Sarah Bird, *Edith Wharton Abroad*, St Martin's, Griffin, 1995

Zeldin, Theodore, *France 1848–1945*, Vol. II, *Intellect, Taste and Anxiety*, Oxford University Press, 1977

Edith Wharton's Family Tree

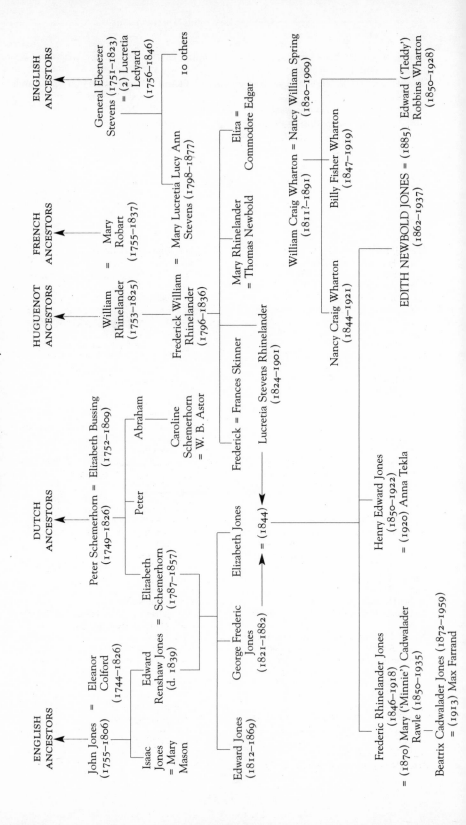

Index

protected by Harry Jones 394; ill for
daughter's wedding 441; supports EW's
wartime charities 460, 475, 476–7; arranges
auction of *Book of the Homeless* 493;
receives regular payments from EW 521;
and *Age of Innocence* 564, 565; EW's
representative in 'theatrical and cinematographic matters' 590, 730, 735; sees EW on
trip to America 598, 599; meets EW on
Aegean cruise 642; financial losses on New
York rentals 683; fact-checks for EW 724,
735–6; last visit to Pavillon 736; death and
funeral in England 736; memorial service
in New York 737
  EW's letters to 253, 395, 452, 466, 471, 47
  7, 497, 512, 542, 552–3, 555, 565, 587,
  607, 608
Jones, Mary Mason 22, 59–60
Joubert, Joseph 304
Le Journal des Débats 324, 455
Jouvenal, Henry de 480
Joyce, James 296, 564, 605, 622, 623, 651
  Dubliners 300
  A Portrait of the Artist as a Young Man 605
  Ulysses 564, 605, 653
Jusserand, Jules 263, 293, 668

Kahn, Otto 498
Kaplan, Fred 257
Karénine, Wladimir: *George Sand* 223
Kazin, Alfred 751
Keats, John 41, 299, 379, 668, 669; 'The Eve
  of St Agnes' 379–80; 'Lamia' 431–2
Keegan, John 483
Kellogg, Grace 751
Kellogg, Vernon: *Darwinism Today* 327–8, 668
Kemble, Fanny 141
Kennedy, Margaret: *The Constant Nymph* 611,
  657, 659
King, Caroline 16
King, Frederic Rhinelander 16, 747
King, Le Roy 16, 327, 747
King, W.B. 593
King Albert's Book 456, 487, 491
Kinnicutt, Dr Francis Parker 140, 366, 368,
  369, 370, 371, 372, 389, 393
Kipling, Carrie 707
Kipling, Rudyard 169, 421 491–2, 539, 707;
  limerick 173
  'The English Flag' 728
  France at War 480
  'Wireless' 169
Knight, Charles 520, 541
Koechlin, Raymond 696
Krauser, Alice 730

Laborde, Alexandre de 292
Ladies' Home Journal 592, 687–8
La Farge, Florence 58, 221, 703
La Farge, John 58
La Forest-Divonne, Comtesse Jules de *see*

Lévis-Mirepoix, Philomène
Lamb House, Rye 222, 242, 244, 249, 329,
  382, 455, 598
Landormy, Gabrielle 466, 684, 748
Landowska, Wanda 707
Land's End, Newport, RI 80, 126–7, 129, 137,
  148, 755; garden 121
Lane, Gertrude 686
Lane, John (publisher) 162
Lang, Andrew 728; (trs.) *Odyssey* 84
Lapsley, Gaillard 246: and Henry James 243,
  246–7, 259; first meeting and friendship
  with EW 247, 308; friendship with
  Lubbock 246, 247; and EW's plot to help
  James 256, 257; abandons EW's North
  African trip 442; on EW and ghosts 463;
  on EW and Simmons 498; edits *The
  America of Today* 246, 572; at the Pavillon
  533; at the Lewises lunch with EW 618;
  witnesses Fitzgerald's visit to EW 616–17;
  on EW's grief at Berry's death 654; helps
  EW move books to Ste-Claire 543;
  Christmases with EW 546, 648; and EW's
  break with Lubbock 646; explores Wales
  with EW 707; and EW's last illness 742; as
  EW's pall-bearer 745; EW's bequests 748,
  749; on EW's writing in bed 665; on EW
  in later life 692; as EW's literary executor
  246, 749; asks Lubbock to write EW's
  memoir 646, 750; edits *The Buccaneers*
  721, 725; plans collection of EW's critical
  essays 750
  Lubbock's letters to 248, 257, 384, 441, 44
  4, 464, 524
  EW's letters to 256–7, 259, 281, 284, 385,
  386, 391, 392, 393, 395, 396, 443, 452,
  558, 603, 607, 608–9, 610, 619, 650,
  652, 692–3
Latham, Charles 113
Lathrop, Helen Aldis 152–3
Laugel, Auguste 288–9
Laughlin, James 751
Lawrence, D.H. 452, 605, 609–10, 623, 651
  Lady Chatterley's Lover 408, 610
  Sons and Lovers 610
Lawrence, Harry 637, 642
'Lee, Vernon' (Violet Paget) 95, 97–100, 102,
  112, 115, 221, 695, 710; EW to 97, 100,
  110–11
  Ariadne in Mantua 100
  Belcaro 97
  Miss Brown 98
  'Old Italian Gardens' 99
  Ottilie 98
  Studies of the Eighteenth Century in Italy
  97, 98
Lee-Hamilton, Eugene 97–8
Le Goffic, Charles 457
Lehmann, Rosamond 700–1
Lehr, Harry 55
Lenox, New York 51, 78, 135, 136, 139–43,